Exceptional Children

An Introduction to Special Education

Twelfth Edition

William L. Heward, Sheila R. Alber-Morgan, and Moira Konrad
The Ohio State University

Content Management: Rebecca Fox-Gieg
Content Production: Janelle Rogers
Product Management: Drew Bennett
Rights and Permissions: Jenell Forschler

Please contact https://support.pearson.com/getsupport/s with any queries on this content.

Cover Image: Many Hats Media

Acknowledgments of third-party content appear on the appropriate page within the text.

Library of Congress Cataloging-in-Publication Data

Names: Heward, William L., author. | Alber, Sheila René, author. | Konrad, Moira, author.
Title: Exceptional children : an introduction to special education / William L. Heward with Sheila R. Alber-Morgan & Moira Konrad, The Ohio State University.
Description: Twelfth edition. | Hoboken : Pearson, [2022] | Includes bibliographical references and index.
Identifiers: LCCN 2020044172 (print) | LCCN 2020044173 (ebook) | ISBN 9780135756621 (paperback) | ISBN 9780135756096 (ebook)
Subjects: LCSH: Special education—United States. | Exceptional children—United States.
Classification: LCC LC3981 .H49 2022 (print) | LCC LC3981 (ebook) | DDC 371.9—dc23
LC record available at https://lccn.loc.gov/2020044172
LC ebook record available at https://lccn.loc.gov/2020044173

12 2024

ISBN 10: 0-13-575662-6
ISBN 13: 978-0-13-575662-1

FOR SIEGFRIED ENGELMANN

Countless children and adults owe their literacy to Engelmann. He dedicated his life to developing and refining Direct Instruction (DI), a powerful teaching approach that combines logical analysis and sequencing of skills, clear communication, high rates of student engagement, and mastery learning.

Photo courtesy National Institute for Direct Instruction.

Siegfried "Zig" Engelmann (1931–2019)

"If the student hasn't learned, the teacher hasn't taught—that's not a slogan, it's an operating principle."

About the Authors

William L. Heward, Ed.D., BCBA-D, is Professor Emeritus in the College of Education and Human Ecology at The Ohio State University, where he helped train special education teachers for 30 years. Dr. Heward has been a Fulbright Scholar in Portugal and a Visiting Professor of Psychology at Keio University in Tokyo and at the University of São Paulo, and he has lectured and given workshops for teachers in 23 other countries. Among the honors Bill has received are The Ohio State University's Distinguished Teaching Award and the American Psychological Association's Division 25 Fred S. Keller Behavioral Education Award for lifetime achievements in education. His publications include co-authoring the books *Applied Behavior Analysis* and *Sign Here: Behavioral Contracting for Families*, each of which has been translated into numerous languages. Bill's research interests include "low-tech" methods for increasing the effectiveness of group instruction in inclusive classrooms.

Sheila R. Alber-Morgan, Ph.D., BCBA-D, is Professor of Special Education in the College of Education and Human Ecology at The Ohio State University. Dr. Alber-Morgan taught for seven years in inclusive K–8 classrooms in urban and rural South Carolina and for more than 20 years in higher education. She has authored more than 80 peer-reviewed research and practitioner articles, book chapters, textbook ancillaries, and the book *Using RTI to Teach Literacy to Diverse Learners, K–8: Strategies for the Inclusive Classroom* (Corwin Press, 2010). Sheila's research, most of which has been designed and implemented in collaboration with classroom teachers, has focused on behavioral interventions and strategies for promoting the generalization and maintenance of academic, functional, and social skills.

Moira Konrad, Ph.D., is Associate Professor of Special Education in the College of Education and Human Ecology at The Ohio State University. Dr. Konrad has nine years of public school experience teaching students with a range of disabilities and has been involved in teacher preparation for more than 20 years. Moira's publications include more than 50 peer-reviewed publications on instructional efficiency, self-determination, and written expression. She currently serves as Associate Editor for *Intervention in School and Clinic* and on the Editorial Boards for *Remedial and Special Education* and the *Journal of Vocational Rehabilitation*.

Preface

About This Book

Special education is an ongoing story of people. It is the story of a preschool child with multiple disabilities who benefits from early intervention services. It is the story of a child with intellectual disabilities whose parents and teachers work together to ensure she participates in classroom and extracurricular activities with her peers. It is the story of a middle school student with learning disabilities who helps his parents and teachers plan an instructional program that builds on his strengths and addresses his weaknesses. It is the story of the gifted and talented child who brings new insights to old problems, the high school student with cerebral palsy who is learning English as his second language, and the young woman with visual impairments who has recently moved into her own apartment and rides a city bus to work. Special education is also the story of the parents and families of exceptional children and of the teachers and other professionals who work with them.

The most important of these professionals is the teacher. And so, special education is the story of the preschool teacher who embeds culturally relevant learning opportunities into his art and music lessons. It is the story of the fourth-grade resource room teacher who carefully designs reading instruction for her students with learning disabilities. It is the story of the middle school teacher who breaks down complex independent living skills into their smallest steps so he can teach them to his students with intellectual disabilities. It is the teacher who coaches young adult students with autism as they complete their high school experiences at a local college.

We hope you will find the Twelfth Edition of *Exceptional Children* an informative, accessible, and interesting introduction to the ongoing story of special education. Whether you are an undergraduate in a preservice teacher training program, a student enrolled in a related human services program, or a general education teacher with years of experience, we encourage you to continue your study and involvement with children and adults with exceptionalities.

New to This Edition

Our primary goals for this edition remain the same as for previous editions: to present an informative and responsible introduction to the professional practices, trends, and research that define contemporary special education—an exciting, ever-evolving field. Significant among the many changes we made to the Twelfth Edition are these additions:

- Successful transition into adulthood is the ultimate goal of special education. Every student with disabilities deserves a transition-focused education, and it must begin early. As such, we have added a **"Transition: Next Year Is Now"** feature to every chapter.
- **Videos filmed expressly for this edition** highlight special education teachers and their colleagues providing evidence-based instruction and related services to students with disabilities in various settings.
- Special education's leading professional organization, the Council for Exceptional Children (CEC), and the Collaboration for Effective Educator Development, Accountability, and Reform (CEEDAR) Center identified 22 **High-Leverage Practices (HLPs)**. Research shows these practices and priorities have significant potential for improving academic or behavior outcomes for students with disabilities. To help readers learn about these HLPs we highlight them throughout the text.
- Five fantastic teachers join a returning all-star cast of **Featured Teachers** (one of whom is about to become CEC president!). Aspiring teachers will find no better models than these 15 special educators.

Key Content Updates by Chapter

- **Chapter 1:** Updated sections on special education legislation and recent court cases; discussion of 2017 U.S. Supreme Court's decision on *Endrew F. v. Douglas*, which set new standards for FAPE; introduction of Tyler Lewis, a young man with autism whose retrospective video clips illustrate how special education contributed to his success.
- **Chapter 2:** Updated discussion of IEPs to reflect the recent *Endrew* Supreme Court case; improved examples of IEP content (e.g., goals, objectives, services); updated section on response to intervention (RTI) and positive behavioral interventions and supports (PBIS) to situate these ideas within a multi-tiered system of support (MTSS) framework.
- **Chapter 3:** Greater emphasis on collaborating with families from culturally and linguistically diverse backgrounds, including a section on culturally responsive transition planning; greater focus on technology (e.g., high-tech tools for family engagement); discussion of supporting families engaged in virtual learning activities (specifically in the context of a global pandemic).
- **Chapter 4:** New Featured Teacher (Madonna Wilburn, Buffalo, New York); new *Teaching & Learning* box on cooperative learning; specific mention of teaching personal hygiene and safety skills during a global pandemic (e.g., handwashing, mask wearing, social distancing); greater emphasis on teaching "soft skills."

- **Chapter 5:** New Featured Teacher (Amaris Johnson, New York, New York); new *Teaching & Learning* box on Direct Instruction for reading; addition of multi-tiered system of supports (MTSS); increased emphasis on learning strategies.
- **Chapter 6:** New video of an inspiring young woman with a behavior disorder; increased emphasis on self-advocacy and self-determination; greater emphasis on dropout prevention.
- **Chapter 7:** New Featured Teacher (Katelyn Johnson, Salt Lake City, Utah); new feature on behavioral skills training for job/employment skills; enhanced discussion of the importance of distinguishing evidence-based practices for children with autism from fads and unproven treatments.
- **Chapter 8:** New Featured Teacher (Emily Pickard, Lewes, Delaware); new content on self-advocacy; increased emphasis on visual supports.
- **Chapter 9:** New *Teaching & Learning* box on supporting children with cochlear implants in inclusive classrooms; featured teacher recommendations for transitioning elementary students to middle school.
- **Chapter 10:** Greater emphasis on assistive technology, including new feature box for promoting students' independence with high-tech tools.
- **Chapter 11:** More emphasis on assistive technology, including high-tech tools for time, productivity, and medication self-management; reordered ADHD treatment section to focus on behavioral interventions before pharmacological interventions; added specific mention of children with health impairments (i.e., those with compromised immune systems) needing special attention in times of pandemic.
- **Chapter 12:** New video and content from Featured Teacher (Carey Creech-Galloway, Clark County, Kentucky); updated *Teaching & Learning* box on peer helpers with video and suggestions from Featured Teacher Carey; additional discussion of community-based instruction (featuring video and suggestions from Featured Teacher).
- **Chapter 13:** Expanded section on mentoring programs for gifted students; expanded discussion of the challenges gifted girls face; increased emphasis on differentiation outside the classroom.
- **Chapter 14:** Expanded section on peer-mediated interventions; discussion of the importance of classroom jobs for preschoolers and implementation suggestions from Featured Teacher Mark Fraley.
- **Chapter 15:** New Featured Teacher (Michael Craig, Detroit, Michigan); section on teaching reading at the secondary level; content on school-based enterprises (including suggestions from Featured Teacher Michael); removed sections on residential placements and supported employment models; increased emphasis on evidence-based predictors and practices for secondary transition.

Pedagogical Features

FEATURED TEACHER CONTRIBUTIONS The story of special education is written every day by teachers working in a variety of settings. Fifteen of these exceptional teachers share their stories in these pages. These highly skilled and dedicated educators use research-based instructional strategies to promote their students' achievement and successful transition to adulthood.

Featured Teacher Essays. Each chapter opens with a first-person essay describing the joys, challenges, and realities of teaching exceptional children. Drawn from urban, suburban, and rural school districts across the country, the 15 Featured Teachers share personal wisdom gathered from their experiences teaching exceptional children in a variety of school settings. For example, Keisha Whitfield (Gahanna, Ohio) describes how she and her colleagues collaborate to meet students' individual needs; Joshua Hoppe (Wai'anae, Hawaii) tells what he has learned about respecting the cultural and linguistic diversity of his students and their families; Amaris Johnson (New York City) explains how she uses schema-based instruction to teach strategies for solving math problems; Katelyn Johnson (Salt Lake City, Utah) details how to construct and use independent task materials for preschoolers with autism; Jennifer Sheffield (Bowling Green, Kentucky) discusses how open-ended learning opportunities motivate her gifted students; and Michael Craig (Detroit, Michigan) explains how a school-based enterprise provides a service to the community while building students' skills for successful transition to adult life.

412 Chapter 14 Early Childhood Special Education

Education, Teaching Credentials, and Experience

- *B.S., physical education, MidAmerica Nazarene University, 1999*
- *M.Ed., early childhood special education, University of Kansas, 2003*
- *Idaho State, professional teaching certificate, special education, pre K–3*
- *16 years as an early childhood special education teacher and 2 years of paraprofessional work in a self-contained special education preschool classroom*

Featured Teacher

Mark Fraley

Skyway Elementary School

Vallivue School District • Caldwell, ID

Source: Breanne Fraley

I teach 22 preschoolers who have been found eligible to receive special education services following a process that involves a child find screening, a consent to assess, an evaluation report, and eligibility determination. Each of my students falls into one of the disability categories, most often developmental delay or language impairment. I do have students who are on the autism spectrum and several who have multiple disabilities. I work alongside a terrific team composed of two educational assistants, a speech-language therapist, a school psychologist, an occupational therapist, a physical therapist, and supportive administrators. The way we work together as a team helps us keep student needs always at the forefront.

On a typical school day, we start off with reviewing our daily routine so students are aware of the activities and how the day will proceed. Having a structured routine is very beneficial for young children; predictability limits anxiety and brings a level of reassurance that helps them thrive in the classroom. For students who are on the autism spectrum, we provide a visual schedule that enables them to make successful transitions. In planning the day, I consider striking a balance between teacher-led and child-led activities, high energy versus quiet listening, and highly motivating work versus a less preferred type of work. I look for my students to participate fully and implement accommodations as needed.

Collaborating with families is critical for student success. I make my classroom a welcoming place from day one by inviting the families to participate in volunteer opportunities and visits. Upon arrival at school, we talk with families and see how their children's day has started. Did they sleep well? Did they eat a good breakfast? Are they in a good mood? Significant communication delays prevent many of my students from providing a satisfactory answer when their parents ask, "What did you do in school today?" To help with that, I create take-home sheets by importing the day's photos from my digital camera to my classroom computer, pasting a few of the most telling shots on a PowerPoint, and making copies on a printer in the school work office.

I take countless pictures during the school year. These photos are a powerful, effective form of communication that lets parents and families see what their children do in school. I get so excited when seeing families celebrate their children's progress, when they begin seeing new possibilities that were originally crushed with a diagnosis or a traumatic event.

Content Extension 14.1

Example of Featured Teacher Mark's take-home sheets.

Content Extensions. The special educators featured in this text provide examples of actual materials used in their classrooms. These artifacts are practical tools for planning instruction, arranging learning environments, collecting data, engaging learners, and collaborating with families. Additional Content Extensions include essays and other supplemental resources that enable readers to deepen their understanding of various topics.

Sustainability Problem-Solving | Sustainable Food Production

Seven Billion People...and Rising

How can students conceptualize the magnitude of Earth's human population of over 7 billion people, and rising?

These lesson suggestions are designed as introductory activities for the topic of sustainability. Individual and group activities can be used as informal pre- and formative assessments; providing students engaging and creative ways to demonstrate existing knowledge of connected math and science principles.

Math & Science Connections

Common Core Standards

Understand the place value system.

CCSS.Math.Content.5.NBT.A.1
Recognize that in a multi-digit number, a digit in one place represents 10 times as much as it represents in the place to its right and 1/10 of what it represents in the place to its left.

Convert like measurement units within a given measurement system.

CCSS.Math.Content.5.MD.A.1
Convert among different-sized standard measurement units within a given measurement system (e.g., convert 5 cm to 0.05 m), and use these conversions in solving multi-step, real world problems.

NGSS Science Content Standard MS-ESS3-4

Construct an argument supported by evidence for how increases in human population and per-capita consumption of natural resources impact Earth's systems.

Can students create scale representations of a rising human population that numbers in the billions and communicate the potential outcomes for our planet?

How can students conceptualize the idea of the population of our planet being over 7 billion people? That's a REALLY big number! Population estimates project that number to rise to over 9 billion people by 2050. How can students even begin to grasp the magnitude of such a large quantity? Can students find ways to creatively use their understanding of the Base Ten number system to visually represent large numbers? Can students design clear and accurate graphic representations the population growth curve to scale? This lesson can be a one-day activity or can span throughout the unit - it's up to you and your class to decide!

Sustainable Food Production unit was created by Jennifer Sheffield for Project GEMS, a research collaborative between Warren County Public Schools and The Center for Gifted Studies at Western Kentucky University. Project GEMS was funded through a federal Jacob K. Javits gifted and talented education grant.

Content Extension 13.3

Featured Teacher Jennifer Sheffield's PBL activity on sustainable food production.

Advice from the Featured Teacher. Each chapter ends with practical tips for enhancing student learning and avoiding common pitfalls in the classroom. Suggestions cover a wide range of topics, such as organizing your classroom; learning about and respecting students' cultures; successful co-teaching; collaborating with families; handling paperwork; minimizing stress; and celebrating each student's accomplishments, no matter how small.

Chapter 14 Early Childhood Special Education 435

ADVICE FROM THE FEATURED TEACHER by Mark Fraley

Use Child-Centered Teaching Tactics

Children learn by playing. If a child is on the floor playing with building blocks, I sit on the floor and simply join her. This shows I value her as a person and respect what she has to say or contribute. When I am at the student's level, I follow her lead. By allowing students to self-direct their learning to a certain degree, it is easy to find what they are interested in and plan activities that incorporate these things. The following tips can help increase student learning and enjoyment during child-centered activities.

Source: Breanne Fraley

- **Give students choices.** I use a choice board that contains photos of each learning center and Velcro-backed pictures of the students. Each child sticks his picture next to the center of his choice.
- **Don't ask too many questions during play.** Asking questions is not only intrusive to play but also changes my role from play partner to test giver. How much fun is it to play with a test giver? Not much! Instead, I'll make comments like a sports broadcaster: "I see you are building a green tower with long rectangle blocks. It is very tall!"
- **Let students make and learn from their mistakes.** I used to get upset when my students responded incorrectly or took too long to complete a task. I have to remember that young children, especially those with developmental disabilities, need many, many opportunities to master a skill. Allowing room for mistakes gives them a chance to try another strategy or method. It is fun as a teacher to make a mistake in front of students, such as trying to put the wrong lid on a bin during clean-up. Your students will see this and step in to help or guide you as you have taught them through problem solving. Making mistakes can also encourage more communication opportunities as they will need to request items or identify the problem.

Create an Organized and Predictable Environment

Preschool classrooms are busy places with many activities occurring simultaneously throughout the day. Posting your plans and intentions reduces the chance of conflicts with staff or parents over misunderstandings of who was supposed to be doing what, with whom, and when. When a conflict occurs or if there is breakdown in the way services are delivered, posted schedules can be a reference tool to review and troubleshoot.

- **Create a master activity schedule.** The master schedule shows what activities everyone in your classroom, professionals and children, should be doing during each time period of the day. One matrix hanging on my classroom wall indicates the roles that all members of the teaching team—my instructional assistants, the speech-language pathologist, physical therapists, and occupational therapists—are to assume throughout the day (e.g., lead teacher, collector of child performance data). Another matrix makes it easy for parents and classroom volunteers to quickly see what's going on and how they might help.

Transition: Next Year Is Now boxes address special education's ultimate goal—preparing students for successful transition to adulthood. These features present a range of strategies for effective transition-focused instruction for students across ages, skill levels, and abilities. Topics include teaching "soft skills" for employment (Chapter 4); teaching learning strategies for transitioning to college (Chapter 5); preventing school dropout (Chapter 6); teaching self-advocacy to students with communication challenges (Chapter 8); teaching students with visual impairments to use technology for independence (Chapter 10); and implementing classroom jobs for preschoolers (Chapter 14).

In Chapter 1's *Transition: Next Year Is Now* box, readers will meet Tyler Lewis, a young man with autism spectrum disorder. Tyler describes his experiences in videos of himself as a fourth grader, a ninth grader, and an adult with a full-time job. Tyler continues his story in a series of captivating videos presented in Chapters 3, 7, and 15. Tyler and his father discuss some of the challenges posed by autism and how school achievement and successful transition depend upon high expectations and the understanding that disability does not mean inability. Tyler's story is a powerful testament to what can be accomplished when students, teachers, and families work together.

Chapter 1 The Purpose and Promise of Special Education 29

Transition: Next Year Is Now

Every Teacher Is a Transition Teacher

Although increasing numbers of special education students are leaving high school for college or a job, a place to live on their own, and friends with whom to share recreation and leisure activities in the community, such positive outcomes elude far too many young adults with disabilities. Special education cannot be satisfied with improving students' achievement on classroom-based measures only. We must work equally hard to ensure that the education students receive during their school years prepares them to cope with and enjoy the multifaceted demands and opportunities of adulthood.

To achieve optimal outcomes for a student's independence and quality of life, transition planning and implementation must begin early and continue throughout elementary, middle, and high school. From preschool through the last year of high school, every teacher in a child's life can be a positive force for accomplishing ambitious long-term transition goals.

Meet Tyler Lewis: A Special Education Success Story

Let us introduce you to Tyler Lewis, a young man with autism who describes his experiences with school and work life in a series of videos. In elementary school, Tyler made friends, participated in extracurricular activities, and discovered his love for dancing and maps. In high school, Tyler was fully included in regular education classes, developed social skills and self-confidence singing in the choir, and began exploring vocational interests. Today, Tyler works full time at Kroger, a job he's held since graduating from high school. This retrospective of Tyler illustrates what effective transition looks like.

Tyler grew into a self-determined 24-year-old man who gets himself to work independently, leads the store safety team, and asks for help when he needs it. Tyler's father says he's an "utterly reliable, independent, and affectionate adult." The quality of life Tyler experiences today is the joint product of his own hard work and that of his teachers, specialists, and family members all striving for the same goals with skill, passion, and persistence throughout his school years.

Transition goals must emphasize self-advocacy and self-determination so that students are equipped to access what they need in all aspects of life, make responsible decisions, and reap the rewards of their accomplishments—now and in the future. Indeed, today's lessons are for the learner's benefit tomorrow; not only tomorrow, but next year's tomorrow and all the tomorrows in all of the years to come.

Each chapter in this text includes a "Transition: Next Year Is Now" box focusing on intervention strategies and supports that address a variety of transition needs across ages and exceptionalities. Topics include culturally responsive transition planning (Chapter 3), college success strategies (Chapter 5), dropout prevention (Chapter 6), self-advocacy (Chapter 8), friendship building (Chapter 9), self-management technology (Chapter 11), and even classroom jobs for preschoolers (Chapter 14).

As you continue reading this book, consider how you—and every teacher—can be a transition teacher.

Pearson eText
Video Example 1.8
Tyler in fourth grade.

Pearson eText
Video Example 1.9
Tyler as a high school freshman.

Pearson eText
Video Example 1.10
Tyler as a young adult.

Chapter 1 The Purpose and Promise of Special Education 25

TEACHING & LEARNING

It's Good to Go Fast! Fluency Building Promotes Student Achievement

What Is Fluency and Why Does It Matter? **Fluency** is the combination of accuracy and speed that characterizes highly skilled performance. Although accuracy, typically in the form of percent correct, is commonly used to assess student performance, fluency gives a more complete picture. Whereas two students might each complete a page of math problems with 100% accuracy, the one who finishes in 2 minutes is much more accomplished than the one who needs 7 minutes to solve the same problems. Fluent students perform skills automatically, without hesitations, as if by second nature.

Fluency has important functional implications. Many skills used every day must be performed at a certain rate or speed. A student who needs 5 minutes to read the directions on a worksheet that his classmates read in 1 minute may not be able to finish the task in the time allotted.

Students who are fluent with a particular skill are likely to exhibit (Stocker et al., 2019):

- *Better retention.* The ability to use the skill or knowledge at a later point in time.
- *Greater endurance.* The ability to stay engaged in the task for longer periods of time. Fluent performers are also less likely to be distracted by minor events in the environment.
- *Improved application and generalization.* The ability to apply new skills in novel situations. Students fluent with component skills (e.g., multiplication facts and subtraction) may learn composite skills (e.g., long division) more quickly.

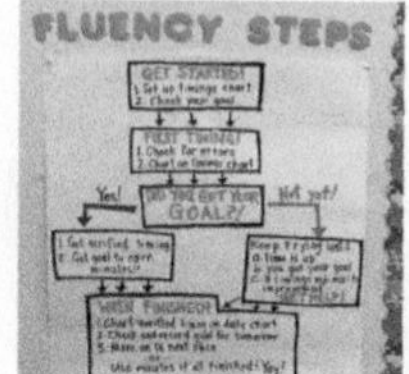

How Can I Promote Fluency? The three fluency-building techniques described next can be teacher-directed, peer-managed, or independent approaches.

Repeated Reading. With **repeated reading**, the student orally reads the same passage, usually three to five times per session and/or until a predetermined goal is met (e.g., 100 words per minute). With each successive reading, the student self-graphs and tries to increase the number of words read correctly per minute. When the student achieves the fluency criterion on a given passage, the teacher introduces a new, perhaps slightly more advanced, passage. Numerous studies show repeated reading improves oral reading fluency for elementary, middle, and secondary students with and without disabilities (Alber-Morgan et al., 2007; Kostewicz & Kubina, 2011; Lee & Yoon, 2017; Tam et al., 2006; Yurick et al., 2006).

Timed Practice Trials. Giving students the opportunity to perform a skill as many times as they can in a brief period is an excellent way to build fluency. Practice in the form of 1-minute timings helps students with and without disabilities achieve fluency with a wide range of academic (e.g., math facts), vocational (e.g., assembling tasks), and other skills (Fishley et al., 2012; Greene et al., 2018; Ramey et al., 2016).

SAFMEDS. Say All Fast a Minute Each Day Shuffled (**SAFMEDS**) consists of a deck of cards with a question, vocabulary term, or problem on one side of each card and the answer on the other. A student answers as many items in the deck as he can in 1 minute. The student looks at the question or problem, states the answer, flips the card over to reveal the correct answer, and

Pearson eText
Video Example 1.6
Use fluency practice to improve students' skills while building their confidence and a supportive classroom community.

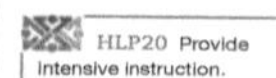 HLP20 Provide intensive instruction.

Emphasis on Research-Based Practices

Good instruction provided by skilled teachers is the foundation of special education. In every chapter, *Teaching & Learning* features and video examples illustrate a wide range of evidence-based teaching practices. Additionally, *High-Leverage Practices* recommended by the Council for Exceptional Children are highlighted throughout the text.

Teaching & Learning Boxes. Each strategy described in the *Teaching & Learning* features is classroom tested and supported by scientific research documenting its effectiveness. A complete list of all the *Teaching & Learning* features is found on page xviii. Here is a sampling of the topics covered:

- It's Good to Go Fast! Fluency-Building Promotes Student Achievement (Chapter 1)
- Guided Notes: Helping All Students Succeed in the General Education Curriculum (Chapter 5)
- Behavior Traps: Turning Obsessions to Motivational Gold (Chapter 7)
- Supporting Children with Cochlear Implants in Inclusive Classrooms (Chapter 9)
- Peer Helpers: Including Students with Severe Disabilities (Chapter 12)

High-Leverage Practices (HLPs). Throughout this text, margin notes with this symbol alert readers to *High-Leverage Practices* (HLPs) identified by the Council for Exceptional Children (CEC) and the Collaboration for Effective Educator Development, Accountability, and Reform (CEEDAR) Center. HLPs are 22 practices and priorities focusing on collaboration, assessment, instruction, and social/emotional behaviors. Examples include the following: HLP 3 *Collaborate with families to support student learning and secure needed services.* HLP 6 *Use student assessment data, analyze instructional practices, and make necessary adjustments that improve student outcomes.* HLP 7 *Provide a consistent, organized, respectful learning environment.* HLP 18 *Use strategies to promote active student engagement.*

Pearson eText, Learning Management System (LMS)-Compatible Assessment Bank, and Other Instructor Resources

The Pearson eText is a simple-to-use, mobile-optimized, personalized reading experience. It allows you to easily highlight, take notes, and review key vocabulary all in one place—even when offline. Seamlessly integrated videos and other rich media will engage you and give access to the help you need, when you need it. To gain access or to sign in to your Pearson eText, visit https://www.pearson.com/pearson-etext. Features include:

- **Video Examples** Each chapter includes *Video Examples* illustrating principles or concepts aligned pedagogically with the chapter. Here's a sampling of the 114 videos embedded within the Twelfth Edition:
    - Video Example 2.4—Featured Teacher Keisha creates vision boards to help students prepare for IEP meetings.
    - Video Example 5.6—Direct Instruction gives children a strong foundation in reading, which makes everything in class more enjoyable.
    - Video Example 6.5—Students of all ages and skill levels benefit from clear expectations and consistent daily routines.
    - Video Example 9.6—Deaf students describe how they want their teachers to act in the classroom.
    - Video Example 12.7—Featured Teacher Carey and a student explain and demonstrate classroom routines and motivation system.
- **IRIS Center Modules** IRIS Center modules, headquartered at Vanderbilt University, are interactive online learning modules that describe strategies shown to be effective in teaching students with disabilities. In Chapter 10, readers will have an opportunity to use an IRIS module to learn how to set up a classroom to support students with visual impairments.
- **Interactive Glossary** All key terms in the eText are bolded and provide instant access to full glossary definitions, allowing you to quickly build your professional vocabulary as you are reading.

LMS-Compatible Assessment Bank

With this new edition, all assessment types—quizzes, application exercises, and chapter tests—are included in LMS-compatible banks for the following learning management systems: Blackboard (**978-0-13-734675-2**), Canvas (**978-0-13-734681-3**), D2L (**978-0-13-734683-7**), and Moodle (**978-0-13-734679-0**). These packaged files allow maximum flexibility for instructors when it comes to importing, assigning, and grading. Assessment types include:

- **Learning Outcome Quizzes** Each chapter learning outcome is the focus of a *Learning Outcome Quiz* that is available for instructors to assign through their learning management system. Learning outcomes identify chapter content that is most important for learners and serve as the organizational framework for each chapter. The higher order, multiple choice questions in each quiz will measure your understanding of chapter content, guide the expectations for your learning, and inform the accountability and the applications of your new knowledge. When used in the LMS environment, these multiple choice questions are automatically graded and include feedback for the correct answer and for each distractor to help guide students' learning.
- **Application Exercises** Each chapter provides opportunities to apply what you have learned through *Application Exercises*. These exercises have a short-answer format based on Pearson eText Video Examples, written cases, and scenarios. They provide students with active learning experiences with text content through (1) *analysis*, examining the complexities of teaching and learning processes; (2) *application*, considering how concepts and strategies are put into practice; and (3) *reflection*, thinking critically about these classroom processes. When used in the LMS environment, a model response written by experts is provided after you submit the exercise. This feedback helps guide your learning and can assist your instructor in grading.

    Examples of the 45 Application Exercises developed for the Twelfth Edition are as follows:

    - **Application Exercise 1.1 Writing Measurable Learning Objectives**—Readers identify missing or poorly written components in learning objectives and rewrite the objectives to add or improve the missing or poorly written component.
    - **Application Exercise 3.1 Engaging Parents Effectively**—After reading a case about a parent–teacher conference, readers are asked to identify statements an "arguer" might say to parents and to provide what a skilled dialoguer might say instead.
    - **Application Exercise 6.1 Helping Kids Stay in School**—After watching a video of a secondary student with emotional or behavioral disorders, readers are asked to identify what supports were in place for the student and what additional supports they would recommend as a member of the student's IEP team.
    - **Application Exercise 12.2 Community-Based Instruction**—After reading a case about a high school student with a traumatic brain injury, readers are asked how they would plan community-based instruction to align with the student's IEP goals.
- **Chapter Tests** Suggested test items are provided for each chapter and include questions in various formats: true/false, multiple choice, and short answer/essay. When used in the LMS environment, true/false and multiple choice questions are automatically graded, and model responses are provided for short-answer and essay questions.

Instructor's Manual (978-0-13-575599-0)

The *Instructor's Manual* is provided as a Word document and includes resources to assist professors in planning their course. These resources consist of chapter overviews, learning outcomes, guidance for using available PowerPoint® slides to promote concept development, questions for discussion, supplemental teaching suggestions, and worksheets.

PowerPoint® Slides (978-0-13-575594-5)

PowerPoint® slides are provided for each chapter; they highlight key concepts and summarize the content of the text to make it more meaningful for students. Often, these slides also include questions and problems designed to stimulate discussion and to encourage students to elaborate and deepen their understanding of chapter topics.

Note: All instructor resources—the LMS-compatible assessment bank, the *Instructor's Manual*, and the PowerPoint slides—are available for download at www.pearsonhighered.com. Use one of the following methods:

- From the main page, use the search function to look up the lead author (i.e., Heward) or the title (i.e., Exceptional Children). Select the desired search result, then access the "Resources" tab to view and download all available resources.
- From the main page, use the search function to look up the ISBN (provided above) of the specific instructor resource you would like to download. When the product page loads, access the "Downloadable Resources" tab.

Acknowledgments

Many people contributed ideas, insights, and suggestions that greatly enhanced the substance and quality of each of the past editions of this text, and the Twelfth Edition of *Exceptional Children* is no exception. Fifteen amazing special educators graciously shared their knowledge and personal experience with essays, instructional materials, videos, and advice: Michael Craig, Carey Creech-Galloway, Mark Fraley, Joshua Hoppe, Amaris Johnson, Katelyn Johnson, Danielle Kovach, Dave Martinez, Emily Pickard, Michelle Nielson-Pugmire, Cecelia Peirano, Jennifer Sheffield, Jessica Stultz, Keisha Whitfield, and Madonna Wilburn. These special educators represent the very best of our field. We are inspired by their commitment to exceptional children and grateful for their substantial contributions to this book.

The currency and quality of this edition have been enhanced tremendously by original essays, videos, instructional examples, and artifacts contributed by the following: Amanda Aspen and Liza Stack (both, California Autism Professional Training and Information Network); Amy Aenchbacher (Cherokee County School District, Canton, GA); Andy Bondy and Lori Frost (Pyramid Educational Consultants); Cassidy Aughe, Christina Billman, Helen Cannella-Malone, Carrie Davenport, Timothy Heron, Terri Hessler, Diane Sainato (all, The Ohio State University); Jill Dardig (Ohio Dominican University); Eli Jimenez (Georgia State University); Rick Kubina (CentralReach); Catherine Maurice (Association for Science in Autism Treatment); Stacie McConnell (Reynoldsburg, OH, public schools); Rebecca Morrison (Oakstone Academy); Kimberly Rich (Davis Country School District, Farmington, UT); Mary Salmon (Columbus Public Schools); Lorraine Thomas (Fayette County Public Schools, Lexington, KY); and Sandy Trask-Tyler.

A special shout- out goes to Hamilton STEM Elementary School (Columbus, OH) principal Christopher Brady, assistant principal Mary Jane Pettigrew, kindergarten teacher Kim Calloway, and fourth-grade teacher Michael Mitchell; and to Conkwright Elementary School (Winchester, KY) principal Julie Bonfield, speech-language pathologist Payton Schmidt, physical therapist Lori Howard, occupational therapist Angie Thomas, vision specialist Jasamyn DeGrant, second-grade teacher Danielle Keeton, fourth-grade teacher Melissa Redman, and art teacher John Joseph. These educators welcomed us and our film crew into their schools and classrooms to get a glimpse into the everyday reality of professionals who serve children with exceptionalities.

A brilliant team of videographers at Many Hats Media worked with us to produce compelling and instructive videos exclusively for this edition. Thank you, Jon Theiss (director), Andy Eggert (camera), Alberto Viglietta (camera), and Eric Vucelich (sound).

The following special education teacher educators reviewed the previous edition and provided comments and suggestions that contributed to this edition: Joseph Boyle (Temple University), Brittany Hott (Texas A&M–Commerce), Amy M. Papacek (Arizona State University), Gretchen G. Robinson (University of North Carolina at Pembroke), and John Schaefer (Cleveland State University). Special thanks go to Adam Jordan (College of Charleston) for developing the application exercises and quizzes.

Special education is a team game and the same can be said for publishing. A talented team of professionals at Pearson Education helped bring this book to life. Senior Analyst Rebecca Fox-Gieg provided support and encouragement. Developmental Editor Jeff Johnston coached us through every stage: from revision planning to final draft. Copyeditor Joanne "Bonnie" Boehme improved the manuscript with a balance of technical skill and respect for our writing style, proofreader Sheila Joyce's eegle eye prevented countless typos, and Production Project Manager Gowthaman Sadhanandham waved us home as we rounded third. Content Producer Janelle Rogers (All-Star Problem Solver) worked closely and patiently with the entire team throughout.

Most of all, we continue to benefit from the support and love of our families—wife Jill Dardig, son Lee, and daughter Lynn; husband David Morgan; and husband Mark Engelhardt, daughters Charlotte and Zaya.

Brief Contents

Part I Foundations for Understanding Special Education

1 The Purpose and Promise of Special Education 4

2 Planning and Providing Special Education Services 34

3 Collaborating with Families 66

Part II Educational Needs of Exceptional Students

4 Intellectual Disabilities 97

5 Learning Disabilities 126

6 Emotional or Behavioral Disorders 160

7 Autism Spectrum Disorder 193

8 Communication Disorders 227

9 Deafness and Hearing Loss 259

10 Blindness and Low Vision 286

11 Attention-Deficit/Hyperactivity Disorder, Health Impairments, and Physical Disabilities 316

12 Low-Incidence Disabilities: Multiple Disabilities, Deaf-Blindness, and Traumatic Brain Injury 350

13 Gifted and Talented 382

Part III Special Education Across The Life Span

14 Early Childhood Special Education 411

15 Transition to Adulthood 438

Contents

About the Authors iv
Preface v
Acknowledgments xi

Prologue 1

Part I Foundations for Understanding Special Education

1 The Purpose and Promise of Special Education 4

Who Are Exceptional Children? 6
How Many Exceptional Children Are There? 7
Why Are Exceptional Children Labeled and Classified? 8
- Labeling and Eligibility for Special Education 8
- Possible Benefits of Labeling and Classification 8
- Possible Disadvantages of Labeling and Classification 9
- Alternatives to Labeling and Classification 9

Why Are Laws Governing the Education of Exceptional Children Necessary? 10
- An Exclusionary Past 10
- Separate Is Not Equal 11
- Equal Protection 12

The Individuals with Disabilities Education Act 12
- Major Principles of IDEA 13
- Other Provisions of IDEA 16
- Legal Challenges to IDEA 17
- Related Legislation 19

What Is Special Education? 23
- Special Education as Intervention 23
- Special Education as Instruction 24
- A Definition of Special Education 27

Current and Future Challenges 28
- Close the Research-to-Practice Gap 28

2 Planning and Providing Special Education Services 34

The Process of Special Education 36
- Prereferral 36
- Evaluation and Eligibility Determination 40
- Program Planning 41
- Placement 41
- Progress Monitoring, Annual Review, and Reevaluation 42

Disproportionate Representation of Students from Culturally and Linguistically Diverse Groups 42
- Recognizing and Combating Cultural and Racial Bias in Referral and Identification Procedures 44

Collaboration and Teaming 45
- Collaboration 45
- Teaming 45

Individualized Education Program 46
- IEP Team 46
- IEP Components 47
- IEP Functions and Formats 48
- IEP Problems and Potential Solutions 51

Least Restrictive Environment 53
- Continuum of Alternative Placements 53
- Determining LRE 54

Inclusive Education 55
- Promoting Inclusion with Co-teaching and Cooperative Learning 56
- Arguments For and Against Full Inclusion 57

Where Does Special Education Go from Here? 60

3 Collaborating with Families 66

Support for Family Involvement 68
- Parents: Advocating for Change 68
- Legislators: Mandating Parent and Family Involvement 68
- Educators and Parents: Seeking Greater Effectiveness 68

Understanding Families of Children with Disabilities 69
- Family Responses to Disability 70
- The Many Roles of the Exceptional Parent 70

Understanding and Respecting Cultural Differences 74
- Changing Needs as Children Grow 75

Developing and Maintaining Family–Professional Partnerships 76
- Culturally Responsive Services for Families 77
- Principles of Effective Communication 78
- Identifying and Breaking Down Barriers to Parent–Teacher Partnerships 81

Home–School Communication Methods 83
- Face-to-Face Communication 83
- Written Communication 85
- Telephone Communication 87

Other Forms of Parent Involvement 90
- Parents as Tutors 90
- Parent Education and Training Programs 91
- Parent Support Groups 91
- How Much Family Involvement? 93

Part II Educational Needs of Exceptional Students

4 Intellectual Disabilities 97

Definitions 98
IDEA Definition 99
AAIDD Definition 99
Classification of Intellectual Disabilities 100
Identification and Assessment 100
Assessing Intellectual Functioning 100
Assessing Adaptive Behavior 102
Characteristics 103
Positive Attributes 103
Cognitive Functioning and Learning 103
Adaptive Behavior 106
Behavioral Excesses and Challenging Behavior 106
Prevalence 108
Causes 109
Prevention 110
Educational Approaches 111
Curriculum Goals 111
Instructional Methods 114
Placement Options 119
Acceptance and Membership 122

5 Learning Disabilities 126

Definitions 129
Federal Definition 129
NJCLD Definition 131
American Psychiatric Association Definition 132
Characteristics 132
Reading Problems 132
Written Language Deficits 133
Math Underachievement 134
Poor Social Skills 134
Attention Deficits and Hyperactivity 134
Challenging Behavior 135
Low Self-Esteem or Self-Efficacy 135
The Signature Characteristic 135
Prevalence 136
Causes 137
Brain Damage or Dysfunction 137
Heredity 137
Experiential Factors 138
Identification and Assessment 138
Intelligence and Achievement Tests 138
Criterion-Referenced Tests 138
Curriculum-Based Measurement 139
Identifying Learning Disabilities with Response to Intervention 141
Educational Approaches 146
Reading 148
Writing 151
Math 152
Content Areas 152
Nonacademic Needs 154
Placement Options 155
Regular Classroom 155
Resource Room 156
Separate Classroom 156

6 Emotional or Behavioral Disorders 160

Definitions 162
Federal Definition 162
CCBD Definition 163
Characteristics 163
Externalizing Behaviors 163
Internalizing Behaviors 164
Academic Achievement 166
Intelligence 168
Social Skills and Interpersonal Relationships 169
Involvement with Juvenile Justice System 169
Prevalence 170
Gender 170
Causes 170
Biological Factors 170
Environmental Factors 171
A Complex Pathway of Risks 173
Identification and Assessment 174
Screening Tests 174
Direct Observation and Measurement of Behavior 175
Functional Behavior Assessment 176
Educational Approaches 177
Curriculum Goals 177
Research-Based Teaching Practices 179
Fostering Strong Teacher–Student Relationships 186
Focus on Alterable Variables 187
Placement Options 187
Challenges, Achievements, and Advocacy 189

7 Autism Spectrum Disorder 193

Definitions 195
IDEA Definition of Autism 196
The DSM Definition of Autism Spectrum Disorder 196
Characteristics 197
Impaired Social Interactions 197
Communication and Language Deficits 198
Repetitive, Ritualistic, and Unusual Behavior Patterns 198
Insistence on Sameness 198

Unusual Responsiveness to Sensory Stimuli 199
Cognitive Functioning 199
Challenging Behavior 202
Asperger Syndrome 202
Positive Attributes and Strengths of Students with Autism Spectrum Disorder 203
Prevalence 204
Causes 205
Neuropathology 205
Genetic Factors 205
Environmental Factors 206
Identification and Assessment 207
Screening 208
Diagnosis 209
Educational Approaches 210
Critical Importance of Early Intensive Behavioral Intervention 211
Applied Behavior Analysis 212
Behavior Skills Training 214
Building on Skills 214
Visual Supports: Helping Students with Autism Cope with Social Situations and Increase Their Independence in the Classroom 215
Distinguishing Unproven Treatments from Evidence-Based Practices 219
Placement Options 221
Regular Classroom 221
Resource and Special Classrooms 222

8 Communication Disorders 227

Definitions 229
Communication 229
Language 230
Speech 232
Typical Speech and Language Development 233
Communication Disorders Defined 235
Characteristics 237
Speech-Sound Errors 237
Fluency Disorders 238
Voice Disorders 240
Language Disorders 241
Prevalence 241
Causes 242
Causes of Speech Impairments 242
Causes of Language Disorders 242
Identification and Assessment 243
Screening and Teacher Observation 243
Evaluation Components 244
Assessment of Communication Disorders in Children Whose First Language Is Not English or Who Use Nonstandard English 245
Educational Approaches 247
Treating Speech-Sound Errors 247
Treating Fluency Disorders 248
Treating Voice Disorders 249
Treating Language Disorders 249
Augmentative and Alternative Communication 251
Placement Options 253
Monitoring 253
Pull-Out 253
Collaborative Consultation 253
Classroom or Curriculum Based 253
Separate Classroom 255
Community Based 255

9 Deafness and Hearing Loss 259

Definitions 261
How We Hear 262
The Nature of Sound 262
Characteristics 263
English Literacy 263
Speaking 264
Academic Achievement 264
Social Functioning 265
Prevalence 265
Types and Causes of Hearing Loss 265
Types and Age of Onset 265
Causes of Congenital Hearing Loss 266
Causes of Acquired Hearing Loss 267
Identification and Assessment 267
Assessment of Infants 267
Pure-Tone Audiometry 268
Speech Reception Test 269
Alternative Audiometric Techniques 269
Classification of Hearing Loss 269
Technologies and Supports 270
Technologies That Amplify or Provide Sound 270
Supports and Technologies That Supplement or Replace Sound 273
Educational Approaches 274
Oral/Aural Approaches 275
American Sign Language and the Bilingual-Bicultural Approach 278
Which Approach for Whom? 279
Placement Options 281
Postsecondary Education 282

10 Blindness and Low Vision 286

Definitions 288
Legal Definitions of Blindness 288
Educational Definitions of Visual Impairment 290
Age at Onset 290
Characteristics 291
Cognition and Language 291

Motor Development and Mobility 291
Social Adjustment and Interaction 292
Prevalence 293
Types and Causes of Visual Impairments 293
How We See 293
Causes of Visual Impairments 294
Educational Approaches 295
Specialized Instruction for Students Who Are Blind 295
Specialized Instruction for Students with Low Vision 300
Expanded Core Curriculum 304
Placement Options 309
Inclusive Classroom and Itinerant Teacher Model 310
Residential Schools 312
Equal Opportunity and the Right to Be Different 312

11 Attention-Deficit/Hyperactivity Disorder, Health Impairments, and Physical Disabilities 316

Attention-Deficit/Hyperactivity Disorder 318
Definition and Diagnosis 318
Eligibility for Special Education 319
Prevalence 319
Academic Achievement and Comorbidity with Other Disabilities 320
Causes 320
Treatment 320
Definitions of Health Impairments and Physical Disabilities 324
Prevalence 325
Types and Causes 325
Epilepsy 326
Diabetes 327
Asthma 328
Autosomal Recessive Disorders 328
HIV and AIDS 329
Cerebral Palsy 330
Spina Bifida 331
Muscular Dystrophy 332
Spinal Cord Injuries 333
Characteristics of Children with Health Impairments and Physical Disabilities 333
Variables Affecting the Impact of Health Impairments and Physical Disabilities on Educational Performance 334
Educational Approaches 336
Teaming and Related Services 338
Environmental Modifications 339
Assistive Technology 340
Animal Assistance 341
Special Health Care Routines 341
Independence and Self-Esteem 342
Placement Options 344
Related Services in the Classroom 344
Inclusive Attitudes 345

12 Low-Incidence Disabilities: Multiple Disabilities, Deaf-Blindness, and Traumatic Brain Injury 350

Definitions 352
Severe and Profound Disabilities 352
Multiple Disabilities 353
Deaf-Blindness 353
Traumatic Brain Injury 353
Characteristics of Students with Low-Incidence Disabilities 355
Multiple and Severe Disabilities 355
Deaf-Blindness 356
Traumatic Brain Injury 357
Prevalence of Low-Incidence Disabilities 358
Multiple Disabilities 358
Deaf-Blindness 359
Traumatic Brain Injury 359
Causes of Low-Incidence Disabilities 359
Multiple and Severe Disabilities 359
Traumatic Brain Injury 360
Deaf-Blindness 360
Educational Approaches 360
Curriculum: What Should Be Taught? 360
Instructional Methods: How Should Students with Severe and Multiple Disabilities Be Taught? 366
Special Considerations for Students with Deaf-Blindness 372
Special Educational Considerations for Students with Traumatic Brain Injuries 373
Placement Options 374
Where Are Students with Low-Incidence Disabilities Being Educated? 374
Benefits of Neighborhood Schools 374
How Much Time in the Regular Classroom? 376
The Challenge and Rewards of Teaching Students with Severe and Multiple Disabilities 377

13 Gifted and Talented 382

Definitions 384
Federal Definitions 384
National Association for Gifted Children 385
Other Contemporary Definitions 385
State-by-State Definitions 386
Characteristics 387
Creativity 388
Precociousness 388
Individual Differences Among Gifted and Talented Students 389

Prevalence 389
Identification and Assessment 390
Multicultural Assessment and Identification 391
Gifted and Talented Girls 393
Gifted and Talented Boys 393
Gifted and Talented Students with Disabilities 393
Educational Approaches 394
Curriculum Differentiation 395
Acceleration and Enrichment 395
Differentiating Instruction in the Classroom 397
Differentiation Outside the Classroom 400
Placement Options 403
Full-Time Grouping Options 404
Part-Time Grouping Options 404
Consulting Teacher Model 406

Part III Special Education Across The Life Span

14 Early Childhood Special Education 411

The Importance of Early Intervention 413
What Is Early Intervention? 413
Does Early Intervention Work? 413
The Individuals with Disabilities Education Act, Early Intervention, and Early Childhood Special Education 415
Early Intervention for Infants and Toddlers 416
Special Education for Preschoolers 417
Screening, Identification, and Assessment 420
Screening 420
Determining Eligibility for Services 422
Program Planning and Monitoring Progress 423
Individual Growth and Development Indicators 423
Direct Systematic Observation 423
Curriculum and Instruction in Early Childhood Special Education 423
Curriculum and Program Goals 423
Developmentally Appropriate Practice 424
Selecting IFSP and IEP Goals and Objectives 427
Instructional Adaptations and Modifications 428
Preschool Activity Schedules 430
A Supportive Physical Environment 431
Service Delivery Options for Early Intervention 432
Hospital-Based Programs 432
Home-Based Programs 433
Center-Based Programs 433
Combined Home-Center Programs 434
Families: Most Important of All 434

15 Transition to Adulthood 438

What Happens When Students with Disabilities Leave High School? 440
High School Completion 440
Postsecondary Education 440
Employment 441
Community Involvement 442
The Individuals with Disabilities Education Act and Transition Services 442
Transition Services 443
Transition Planning 443
Developing the Transition IEP 443
Evidence-Based Predictors and Practices 447
Postsecondary Education 448
Employment 451
Independent Living and Community Participation 457
Recreation, Leisure, and Social Engagement 460
The Ultimate Transition Goal: A Better Quality of Life 461
Misguided and Limiting Presumptions 462
Self-Advocacy and Self-Determination 462
Still a Long Way to Go 463

Postscript 466

Glossary 469
References 478
Name Index 525
Subject Index 550

Special Features

TITLE	STRATEGY	PAGE
First, Get a Goal	Writing measureable and meaningful learning objectives	14
It's Good to Go Fast! Fluency Building Promotes Student Achievement	Effective fluency building can be teacher-directed, peer-managed, or independent approaches	25
Every Teacher Is a Transition Teacher	Ensure that the students are prepared to cope with and enjoy the demands and opportunities of adulthood.	29
Choral Responding: Good Noise in the Classroom	Choral responding increases student participation during group lessons	39
Whose IEP Is This?	Involving students in the development and implementation of their IEPs result in more meaningful IEPs.	51
Classwide Peer Tutoring: Cooperative Learning for All Students in Inclusive Classrooms	Collaborative learning for all students in inclusive classrooms	58
Culturally Responsive Transition Planning	Understand the biases, listen, to and collaborate closely with families, to facilitate student engagement in their own planning.	79
Parent Appreciation Letters	Letting parents know their efforts and contributions toward their child's achievements are valued	88
Parents as Tutors	Supporting parents in tutoring their children at home	92
Teaching Soft Skills to Prepare Students for the Future	Use a systematic approach to implement the seven steps to teach a student to self-monitor and improve soft skills.	107
Task Analysis	Breaking skills down into smaller components for assessment and teaching	116
Cooperative Learning	Effective cooperative learning includes peer tutoring, reciprocal teaching, and Kagan structures	120
Guided Notes: Helping All Students Succeed in the General Education Curriculum	Teacher-prepared handouts that guide a student through a lecture with standard cues and specific space in which to write key facts, concepts, or relationships	143
Learning Strategies for Transitioning to College	Use self-regulated strategy development for teaching learning strategies to help students prepare for college.	147
Direct Instruction for Reading	Direct Instruction goal: include all necessary and sufficient components for the lesson's success, and nothing extraneous	150
It's Cool to Stay in School	Identify and implement effective interventions on the four categories of predictors to help students stay in school.	167
"Look, I'm All Finished!" Recruiting Teacher Attention	Recruiting reinforcement, positive teacher attention, and feedback enhance student's acceptance and success in the classroom	168
Response Cards: Everyone Participates	Increasing active engagement by encouraging whole class simultaneous responses teachers can see	181
Behavior Traps: Turning Obsessions to Motivational Gold	Using the special interests of children as bait to increase their academic, functional, and social skills	200
Behavioral Skills Training for Job/ Employment Skills	Use behavior skills training to teach a wide range of social and vocational skills to students and gradually fade your support during role play to push the student toward independent mastery of the skills.	214
Visual Activity Schedules: Promoting Independence for Students with Autism	Creating visual activity schedules promote independence for children with autism	215

TITLE	STRATEGY	PAGE
Helping Students Who Stutter	Tips for working with students who stutter	239
When Is a Difference a Disability?	Using culturally and linguistically appropriate assessments to distinguish communication differences from speech and language disorders	246
Teaching Self-Advocacy to Students with Communication Challenges	Plan for generalization to prepare students for a wide variety of situations over time and use various examples on how to self-advocate across situations.	254
Supporting Children with Cochlear Implants in Inclusive Classrooms	Support children by improving the listening and visual environment, facilitating social interactions, and encouraging self-advocacy	272
Making Friends in Middle School	Collaboration between elementary and middle school teachers and activities such as planning a field trip can help elementary students feel less anxious about the transition to middle school.	280
Help Me Succeed in Your Classroom: Tips from Deaf Students	Suggestions for working with students who are deaf from the student perspective	282
Setting Up a Classroom for Students with Visual Impairments	Tutorial on arrangement of a classroom environment for students with visual impairments	304
High-Tech Tools for Independence	Introduce new high-tech tool to students and help them navigate various aspects to assist them in daily living and getting around town.	307
"I Made It Myself, and It's Good!": Increasing Independence with Self-Operated Auditory Prompts	Self-operated audio prompting systems help students learn daily living skills	309
Self-Monitoring Helps Students Do More Than Just Stay on Task	Teaching students to achieve a form of self-determination by taking responsibility for their learning	321
Self-Management Tools for Adult Success	Provide instructions to middle and high school students to access high-tech self-management tools that help with time management, productivity, and their health and wellness.	337
P.E. Is for Everyone!	Adapting physical education for students with disabilities	339
Embedding Core Academic Content into Functional Skill Instruction	Planning instruction that balances academic skills and life skills for student with significant disabilities	365
It's Not Just a Field Trip: Community-Based Instruction	Keep improving your classroom instruction and assessment based on your learnings from community-based instruction outings.	369
Peer Helpers: Including Students with Severe Disabilities	Promoting interaction and friendships among secondary students with and without disabilities	376
The Two PBLs: Problem-Based Learning and Project-Based Learning	Two instructional approaches for challenging and engaging gifted students	401
Mentors for Gifted Students	Identify student interests, prepare students to be mentored, locate a good match, and evaluate the mentorship for an effective mentoring program that helps students with career certainty.	402
High-Ability Cooperative Learning Groups	Steps for implementing cooperative learning with gifted students	405
It's Never Too Early to Have a Job: Classroom Jobs for Preschoolers	Assign classroom jobs to help children contribute to the classroom community, shape positive social interactions, and acquire a sense of accomplishment.	425
Using Puppets in the Early Childhood Classroom	Putting puppets to instructional use in presenting activities in developmentally appropriate ways	426
Peer-Mediated Instruction in Inclusive Preschool Classrooms	Strategies for involving peer models to help pre-schoolers achieve their IEP goals	429

TITLE	STRATEGY	PAGE
When Secondary Students Can't Read	Improve a student's reading skill with appropriate intervention such as decoding and comprehension strategies, explicit instructions, providing frequent opportunities	450
Sowing Seeds for Successful Transition: The Gardens at Drew	Adequate time, careful planning, and teamwork, help from students and the community can help set up a successful school-based enterprise.	457
Self-Directed Video Prompting for Transition	Increasing independence using mobile devices and video prompting	459

Prologue

A Personal View of Special Education

OUR PRIMARY GOAL IN WRITING THIS BOOK is to provide tomorrow's educators with information and tools to improve the lives of individuals with exceptionalities. In pursuit of that goal, we have described the history, practices, advances, challenges, and opportunities that make up the complex and dynamic field of special education in as clear, current, and accurate a manner as possible. This is easier said than done: Authors' descriptions of anything they hold dear are influenced by personal views. Because our personal beliefs and assumptions about special education—which are by no means unique, but neither are they held by everyone in the field—affect both the substance and the tone of this book, we believe we owe you, the reader, an explicit summary of those views. So, here are 10 assumptions that underlie and guide our efforts to understand, contribute to, and convey the field of special education.

People with disabilities have a fundamental right to live and participate in the same settings and programs—in school, at home, in the workplace, and in the community—as do people without disabilities. That is, children and adults with disabilities should, to the greatest extent possible, learn, live, work, and play alongside people without disabilities. People with disabilities and those without have a great deal to contribute to one another and to society. We cannot do that without regular, meaningful interactions in shared environments.

People with disabilities have the right to self-determination. Special educators have no more important teaching task than that of helping students with disabilities learn how to increase autonomy over their own lives. Teaching students with disabilities self-determination and self-advocacy skills should be a primary goal for all special educators.

Special education must expand the effectiveness of its early identification and prevention efforts. When a disability or a condition that places a child at risk for a disability is detected early, the chance of lessening its impact (or preventing it altogether) is greater. Significant strides have been made in the early detection of physical disabilities, sensory impairments, and developmental delays in infants and preschoolers. An approach called *multi-tiered system of support (MTSS)*, which you will read about in this edition, is improving the field's ability to identify and prevent less visible disabilities, such as learning disabilities and emotional or behavioral disorders.

Special education must do a better job of helping students with disabilities transition from school to adult life. Although increasing numbers of students with disabilities are leaving high school for college or a job, a place to live on their own, and friends with whom to share recreation and leisure activities in the community, these positive outcomes still elude far too many young adults with disabilities. Special education cannot be satisfied with improving students' performance on classroom-based measures only. We must work equally hard to ensure the education students receive during their school years prepares them to cope with and enjoy the demands and opportunities of adulthood. We feel so strongly about special education's imperative to improve postschool outcomes that we have added a new feature to each chapter in this edition. Its title, *Transition: Next Year Is Now,* underscores the importance of transition-focused instruction for students with disabilities, no matter their age or disability.

Special education must continue to improve its cultural competence and promote social justice. As we write this prologue, our nation is grappling with many social issues—a pandemic, economic inequality, use of deadly force by the police, climate change—that disproportionately affect people with disabilities and people of color. We believe teachers—and special educators, in particular—are well positioned to help address these challenges. Educators should see themselves as global citizens, equipped with evidence-based tools to right wrongs. We should ask ourselves every day, what am I doing to fight racism, to celebrate each child's strengths and intersectional identities, to teach children of color effectively, to welcome all families, to disrupt the school-to-prison pipeline, to promote health and environmental sustainability, to make the world a more just place? Special educators, like the featured teachers you'll meet in this edition, are the world's best teachers. They know how to identify a problem, set an ambitious goal, and work systematically toward reaching that goal. Let's get to it!

School and family partnerships enhance the meaningfulness and the effectiveness of special education. Professionals have too long ignored the needs of parents and families of exceptional children, often treating them as patients, clients, or even adversaries instead of realizing they are partners with the same goals. Some special educators have given the impression (and, worse, believed it to be true) that parents are there to serve professionals, when in fact the opposite is more correct. Parents are a child's first—and, in many ways, best—teachers. Learning to work effectively with parents and families is one of the most important skills a special educator can acquire.

The work of special educators is most effective when supplemented by the knowledge and services of all the helping professions. It is foolish for special educators to argue over territorial rights when more can be accomplished for our students when we work together within an interdisciplinary team that includes our colleagues in medical and health services, behavior analysis, counseling, social services, and vocational rehabilitation.

All students have the right to an effective education. An educator's primary responsibility is designing and implementing instruction that helps students learn useful academic, social, vocational, and personal skills. These skills are the same ones that influence the quality of our own lives: working effectively and efficiently at our jobs, being productive members of our communities, maintaining a comfortable lifestyle in our homes, communicating with our friends and family, and using our leisure time meaningfully and enjoyably. Instruction is ultimately effective when it helps students acquire and maintain positive lifestyle changes. To put it another way, the proof of the process is in the product. Therefore,...

Teachers must demand effectiveness from the curriculum materials and instructional tools they use. For many years, conventional wisdom has fostered the belief, still held by some, that teaching children with disabilities requires unending patience. We believe this notion does a great disservice to students with exceptionalities and to the educators—both special and general education teachers—who teach them. A teacher should not wait patiently for an exceptional student to learn, attributing lack of progress to some inherent attribute or faulty process within the child, such as intellectual disability, learning disability, attention-deficit/hyperactivity disorder, or emotional disturbance. Instead, the teacher should implement evidence-based practices and use direct and frequent measures of the student's performance as the primary guide for modifying those methods as needed to improve their effectiveness. This, we believe, is the real work of the special educator. Numerous examples of instructional strategies and tactics demonstrated to be effective through rigorous scientific research are described and illustrated throughout this text. Although you will not know everything you need to know to teach exceptional children after reading this or any other introductory text, you will gain an appreciation for the importance of explicit, systematic instruction and an understanding of the kinds of teaching skills a competent special educator must have. And finally, we believe...

The future for people with disabilities holds great promise. Special education has only begun to discover the myriad ways to improve teaching, increase learning, prevent and minimize conditions that cause and exacerbate the effects of disabilities, encourage acceptance, and use technology to compensate for the effects of disabilities. Although we make no specific predictions for the future, we are certain that we have not come as far as we can in learning how to help exceptional children and adults build and enjoy fuller, more independent lives in the school, home, workplace, and community.

Chapter 1
The Purpose and Promise of Special Education

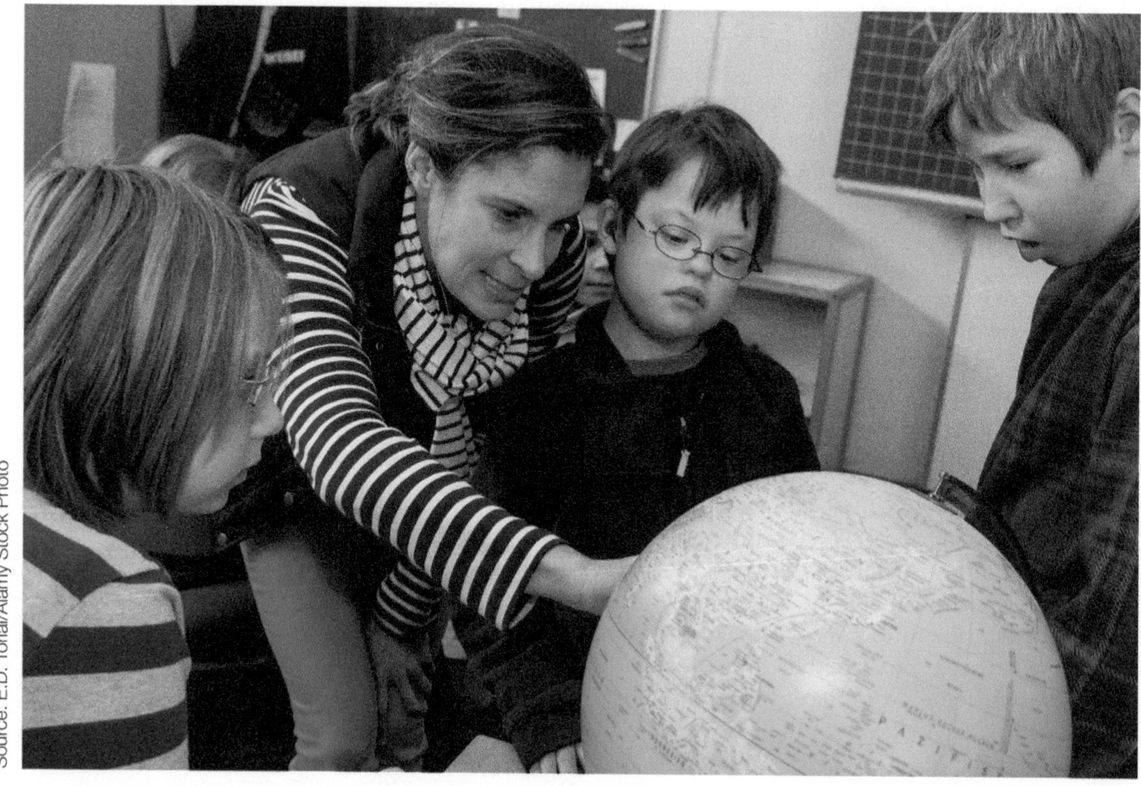

Source: E.D. Torial/Alamy Stock Photo

Learning Outcomes

After reading this chapter and completing the embedded activities, you should be able to

1.1 Distinguish among the following terms: *impairment, disability, handicap*, and *at risk*.

1.2 Identify the percentage of school-age children served in special education by disability category and explain the advantages and disadvantages of disability labels.

1.3 Explain why laws governing the education of exceptional children are needed and identify key court cases and federal legislation that have led to mandates for a free appropriate public education for children with disabilities.

1.4 Define and give an example of each of the three types of intervention—preventive, remedial, and compensatory.

1.5 Describe the defining dimensions of special education and identify several challenges facing the field of special education.

Featured Teacher

Danielle Kovach

Tulsa Trail Elementary School, Hopatcong Borough Schools, Hopatcong, NJ

Source: Danielle Kovach

Ever since I was a little girl, I knew in my heart I wanted to be a teacher. I would wear my mother's high-heel shoes and pretend to teach to my stuffed animals. In high school, I volunteered at a camp for children with exceptionalities. The experience left me humbled and inspired by the perseverance the children displayed despite their challenges. It was that summer I knew I wanted to make a difference in the lives of children with disabilities.

My classroom always bustles with activity! We sing, dance, and act. I find ways to get my students moving to enhance their learning. Interactive lessons help students retain information and help students who have difficulty sitting still for long periods of time. My students often work harder and retain more when instructional time is segmented into small, manageable pieces. I design "learning labs" as 10- to 15-minute blocks of time for students to focus on one curriculum or skill area. It keeps them moving around the room, and I can address individual needs.

Using research and evidence-based practices as a guide to what works best for students with special needs, I create lessons incorporating technology, creative thinking, and collaboration. This gives my students the ability to become critical thinkers, working together to achieve success. Every day I count and measure some aspect of each student's performance. These formative assessments enable me to track their progress and modify, differentiate, and accommodate as needed.

When I teach, I strive to find the avenue to success. When one way does not work, I look for another path until I find a method that works. My experience as a special education teacher has taught me never to underestimate what a child can do. I cherish and celebrate each success, no matter how great or small.

I do not expect perfection, but I promote success. I do not lower the standards for my students to achieve, but I strive to make each child's work equally as challenging as it would be for any other student without a disability. My focus is not on what they cannot do but what they can. We are the "Can Do" class and the outside of my classroom door says, "No challenge too big, no victory too small!"

Let's face it. Teaching is hard work. If I do not go home exhausted, I know I have not worked to the best of my ability. The old saying "Never let them see you sweat" doesn't apply in my classroom. I want my students to see just how hard I work in the classroom. If I show them I am giving 100%, then my hope is they will give 100% of themselves. Teaching is not always a glorious job, but at the end of the day, the rewards far outweigh the challenges.

Education, Teaching Credentials, and Experience

- *B.S.Ed., Elementary Education/Special Education, Kutztown University, 1997; M.Ed., Special Education, East Stroudsburg University, 2002; M.A., Educational Technology, New Jersey City University, 2007; Ed.D., Special Education, Walden University, 2014*
- *Elementary education and special education, New Jersey*
- *19 years of experience as a special education and general education teacher*
- *2011 New Jersey State Teacher of the Year; 2012 National Education Association (NEA) Award for Teaching Excellence; 2014 Council for Exceptional Children (CEC) Teacher of the Year*
- *CEC President-Elect (2021-2022); CEC President (2022-2023)*

Pearson eText
Video Example 1.1
Danielle and two of her students describe some of the features in her classroom.

Content Extension 1.1

Danielle's "Can Do" class poster.

EDUCATING EXCEPTIONAL CHILDREN IS A REWARDING PROFESSION. Special educators such as Danielle Kovach work in a dynamic and exciting field. To appreciate their work, as well as the persistent and emerging challenges and controversies that characterize special education, it is necessary to examine some concepts and perspectives that are basic to understanding exceptional children.

Who Are Exceptional Children?

Learning Outcome 1.1 Distinguish among the following terms: *impairment, disability, handicap*, and *at risk.*

All children exhibit differences from one another in terms of their physical attributes (e.g., some are shorter, some are stronger) and learning abilities (e.g., some pick up new skills easily, others need intensive instruction). The physical attributes and/or learning characteristics of **exceptional children** differ from the norm (below or above) to such an extent that they require an individualized program of special education and related services to fully benefit from education. The term *exceptional children* includes children who experience difficulties in learning as well as those whose performance is so advanced that modifications in curriculum and instruction are necessary to help them fulfill their potential. Thus, *exceptional children* is an inclusive term that refers to children with learning and/or behavior problems, children with physical disabilities or sensory impairments, and children with superior intellectual abilities and/or special talents. The term *children with disabilities* is more restrictive than *exceptional children* because it does not include gifted and talented children. Learning the definitions of several related terms will help you better understand the concept of exceptionality.

Although the terms *impairment, disability*, and *handicap* are sometimes used interchangeably, they are not synonymous. **Impairment** refers to the loss or reduced function of a particular body part or organ (e.g., missing limb). A **disability** exists when an impairment limits a person's ability to perform certain tasks (e.g., walk, see, read). A person with a disability is not *handicapped*, however, unless the disability leads to educational, personal, social, vocational, or other problems. For example, if a child who has lost a leg learns to use a prosthetic limb and functions in and out of school without problems, she is not handicapped, at least in terms of her functioning in the physical environment.

Handicap refers to a problem or a disadvantage a person with a disability or impairment encounters when interacting with the environment. A disability may pose a handicap in one environment but not in another. The child with a prosthetic limb may be handicapped (i.e., disadvantaged) when competing against peers without disabilities on the basketball court but experience no disadvantage in the classroom. Many people with disabilities experience handicaps that are the result of negative attitudes and inappropriate behavior of others who needlessly restrict their access and ability to participate fully in school, work, or community activities.

The term **at risk** refers to children who are considered to have a greater than usual chance of developing a disability. Educators often apply the term to infants and preschoolers who, because of biological conditions, events surrounding their births, or environmental deprivation, may be expected to experience developmental problems at a later time. The term is also used to refer to students who are experiencing significant learning or behavioral problems in the regular classroom and are therefore at risk of being diagnosed with a disability.

Source: Laura Bolesta/Millennium/Merrill Education

Although children with disabilities have special instructional needs, they are more similar to other children than they are different.

Although all children differ from one another in individual characteristics, exceptional children differ so markedly from the norm that an individually designed program of instruction—special education—is required if they are to benefit fully from school. Although exceptional children are more similar to other children than they are different, an exceptional child differs in important ways from his same-age peers without exceptionalities. Whether and how families and professionals recognize and respond to those differences will have a major impact on the child's success in school and beyond.

How Many Exceptional Children Are There?

Learning Outcome 1.2 Identify the percentage of school-age children served in special education by disability category and explain the advantages and disadvantages of disability labels.

Approximately 7.3 million children and youth with disabilities, age 3 through 21, received special education services during the 2018–2019 school year (U.S. Department of Education, 2020a). Table 1.1 shows the number of school-age children in each of the 13 disability categories used by the federal government. Here are some demographic facts about special education in the United States:

- Students with disabilities represent 9.5% of the school-age population.
- About twice as many males as females receive special education.
- In 2017, 388,694 infants and toddlers (birth through age 2) and 815,010 children age 3 to 5 received special education services.
- Although each child receiving special education is classified under a primary disability category, many children are affected by more than one disability. In a nationwide study of more than 11,000 elementary school students in special education, school staff reported that 40% of the students were affected by a secondary disability (Marder, 2009).
- There are 3 to 5 million academically gifted and talented students in grades K through 12 in the United States (National Association for the Gifted, 2020a).

TABLE 1.1 Number of students age 6 through 21 who received special education and related services by type of disability (2018–2019 school year)

DISABILITY CATEGORY	NUMBER (IN THOUSANDS)	PERCENT OF TOTAL
Specific learning disability	2,377,739	37.6
Speech or language impairment	1,036,790	16.4
Other health impairment	1,025,953	16.2
Autism	633,844	10.0
Intellectual disability	423,215	6.7
Emotional disturbance	344,473	5.5
Developmental delay*	167,704	6.2
Multiple disabilities	126,697	2.0
Hearing impairment	64,359	1.0
Orthopedic impairment	33,516	0.5
Traumatic brain injury	25,344	0.4
Visual impairment	24,169	0.4
Deaf-blindness	1,425	<0.1
All Disabilities	6,315,228	100.0

*Non-disability-specific category states may use to identify children age 3 through 9.

Source: U.S. Department of Education, IDEA Section 618 Data Products (2020a).

Why Are Exceptional Children Labeled and Classified?

Labeling people was of little consequence centuries ago; survival was the main concern. Those whose disabilities prevented full participation in the activities necessary for survival were left on their own to perish and, in some instances, were even killed (Berkson, 2004). In later years, people used derogatory words such as *dunce, imbecile,* and *fool* to refer to people with intellectual disabilities or challenging behavior, and other demeaning words were used for people with health impairments or physical disabilities. These terms shared a common function: to exclude people with disabilities from the activities and privileges of everyday life.

Labeling and Eligibility for Special Education

To receive special education and related services under the federal Individuals with Disabilities Education Act (IDEA), a child must be identified as having a disability (i.e., labeled) and, in most cases, further classified into categories, such as learning disabilities or orthopedic impairments. (Children age 3–9 years can be identified with *developmental delay* and receive special education services without a specific disability category label.) In practice, therefore, a student becomes eligible for special education and related services because of membership in a given disability category.

Some educators believe labels used to identify and classify exceptional children stigmatize them and serve to deny them opportunities (e.g., Karten, 2017; Lockwood & Coulter, 2017). Others argue that a workable system of classifying exceptional children is a prerequisite to providing needed special educational services and that using more "pleasant" terms minimizes and devalues the individual's situation and need for supports (e.g., Arishi & Boyle, 2017; Kauffman & Badar, 2013).

Labeling and classification are complex issues involving emotional, political, and ethical considerations in addition to scientific, fiscal, and educational interests (Florian et al., 2006; McLaughlin et al., 2006; Valle & O'Connor, 2019). As with most complex issues, valid perspectives and arguments exist on both sides of the labeling question. Reasons most often cited for and against the labeling and classification of exceptional children follow.

Possible Benefits of Labeling and Classification

- Labeling recognizes meaningful differences in learning or behavior and is a first and necessary step in responding responsibly to those differences.
- A disability label can provide access to accommodations and services not available to people without the label. For example, some parents of secondary students seek a learning disability label so their child will be eligible for accommodations such as additional time on college entrance exams.
- Labeling may lead to a protective response in which peers are more accepting of the atypical behavior of a child with disabilities.
- Classification helps practitioners and researchers communicate with one another and classify and evaluate research findings (e.g., National Autism Center, 2020).
- Funding and resources for research and other programs are often based on specific categories of exceptionality.
- Labels enable disability-specific advocacy groups to promote specific programs and spur legislative action (e.g., Autism Speaks, American Federation for the Blind).
- Labeling helps make exceptional children's special needs more visible to policymakers and the public.

Possible Disadvantages of Labeling and Classification

- Because the labels used in special education usually focus on disability, impairment, or performance deficits, they may lead some people to think only in terms of what the individual cannot do instead of what the individual can do or might be capable of doing.
- Labels may stigmatize the child and lead peers to reject or ridicule the labeled child.
- Teachers may hold low expectations for a labeled student and treat the student differentially as a result. Such differential treatment could impede the rate at which a child learns new skills and contribute to a level of performance consistent with the label's prediction.
- Labels may negatively affect the child's self-esteem.
- Disability labels are often misused as explanatory constructs (e.g., "Sherry acts that way *because* she is emotionally disturbed"). When labels suggest that learning problems are the result of something inherently wrong with the child, they reduce the systematic examination of and accountability for instructional variables as causes of performance deficits. This is an especially damaging outcome when a label provides a built-in excuse for ineffective instruction (e.g., "Jalen's learning disability prevents him from comprehending print text").
- Because all members in a disability category share a particular characteristic (e.g., deafness), there is a tendency to assume that all children in a category share other traits as well, thereby diminishing the detection and appreciation of each child's uniqueness (Smith & Mitchell, 2001a, 2001b).
- A disproportionate number of children from some racial or ethnic backgrounds have been assigned disability labels.
- Classifying exceptional children requires the expenditure of a great amount of money and professional and student time that might be better spent delivering and evaluating the effects of intervention for struggling students.

Although the pros and cons of using disability category labels have been debated for several decades (Hobbs, 1976a, 1976b), neither conceptual arguments nor research has produced a conclusive case for the total acceptance or absolute rejection of labeling practices. Most of the studies conducted to assess the effects of labeling have produced inconclusive, often contradictory evidence and have generally been marked by methodological weakness.

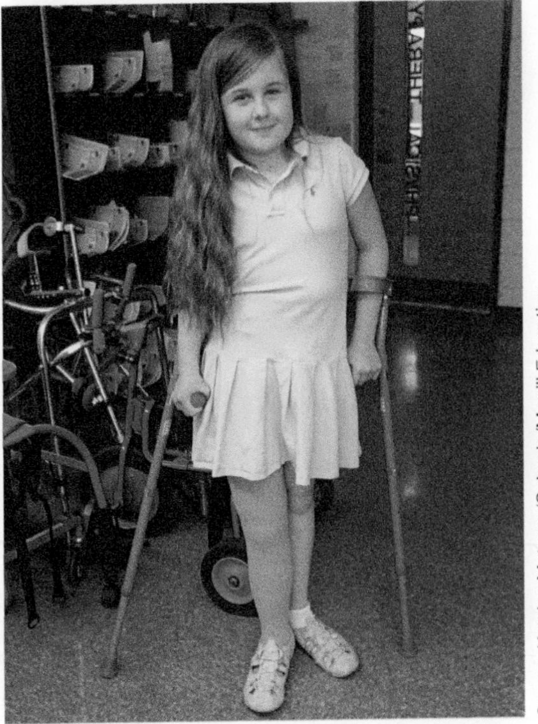

Source: Katelyn Metzger/Colerain/Merrill Education

Changing the label used to identify Charlotte's for special education won't lessen the impact of her disability. But referring to her as "Charlotte, a fifth grader who likes to read mysteries," helps us recognize her strengths and abilities—what she can do—instead of focusing on a disability label.

Alternatives to Labeling and Classification

Educators have proposed a number of alternative approaches for classifying exceptional children that focus on educationally relevant variables (e.g., Hardman et al., 1997; Sontag et al., 1977; Terzi, 2005). For example, Reynolds et al. (1996) proposed that the lowest achieving 20% and the highest achieving 20% of students be eligible for broad (noncategorical) approaches to improvement of learning outcomes.

Some special educators have suggested that exceptional children be classified according to the curriculum and skills they need to learn:

> If we shouldn't refer to these special children by using those old labels, then how should we refer to them? For openers, call them Rob, Amy, and Jose. Beyond that, refer to them on the basis of what you're trying to teach them.

> For example, if a teacher wants to teach Brandon to compute, read, and comprehend, he might call him a student of computation, reading, and comprehension. We do this all the time with older students. Sam, who attends Juilliard, is referred to as "the trumpet student"; Jane, who attends Harvard, is called "the law student" (T. C. Lovitt, personal communication, August 7, 2011).

Labels, in and of themselves, are not the problem. Most special educators agree that a common language for referring to children who share instructional and related service needs is necessary. The words that we use as labels do, however, influence the degree to which those words effectively and appropriately communicate variables relevant to the design and delivery of educational and other human services. For example, blanket labels such as *the handicapped* or *the blind* imply that everyone in the labeled group is alike; individuality has been lost. At the personal level, describing a child as a "physically handicapped boy" suggests that the disability is the most important thing to know about him.

How, then, should we refer to exceptional children? We can begin by following Tom Lovitt's advice and calling them by their names: Linda, Shawon, and Jackie. Referring to "Mitch, a fifth-grade student with learning disabilities" helps us focus on the individual child and his primary role as a student. Such a description does not ignore or gloss over Mitch's learning problems but acknowledges that there are other things we should know about him.

Professional and advocacy organizations have taken differing views on disability labels. On the one hand, the National Federation of the Blind adopted a resolution against the use of terms such as *visually challenged* and *people with blindness*, stating that such politically correct euphemisms are "totally unacceptable and deserving only ridicule because of their strained and ludicrous attempt to avoid such straightforward, respectable words as *blind, the blind, blind person*, or *blind persons*" (Jernigan, 1993, p. 867). The American Association on Mental Retardation (AAMR), on the other hand, changed its name to the American Association on Intellectual and Developmental Disabilities (AAIDD) because it considered *intellectual disabilities* to be less stigmatizing than *mental retardation* (Prabhala, 2007). In 2010, President Barack Obama signed into law Rosa's Law, which changed all references to *mental retardation* in federal statutes to *intellectual disabilities*.

Why Are Laws Governing the Education of Exceptional Children Necessary?

Learning Outcome 1.3 Explain why laws governing the education of exceptional children are needed and identify key court cases and federal legislation that have led to mandates for a free appropriate public education for children with disabilities.

An Exclusionary Past

It is said that a society can be judged by the way it treats those who are different. By this criterion, the U.S. educational system has a less than distinguished history. Children have often been denied full and fair access to educational opportunities because of race, culture, language, gender, socioeconomic status, or exceptionality (Banks & Banks, 2020).

In the not so distant past, many children with disabilities were entirely excluded from any publicly supported program of education. Before the 1970s, laws in many states permitted public schools to deny enrollment to children with disabilities. One state law, for example, allowed schools to refuse to serve "children physically or mentally incapacitated for school work"; another state had a law stipulating that children with "bodily or mental conditions rendering attendance inadvisable" could be turned away. When these laws were contested, the nation's courts generally supported exclusion. In a 1919 case, for example, a

13-year-old student with physical disabilities (but normal intellectual ability) was excluded from his local school because he "produces a depressing and nauseating effect upon the teachers and school children" (J. D. Smith, 2004, p. 4).

In 1913, the Commission for the Care of the Feeble-Minded determined that individuals with significant disabilities were considered "unfit for citizenship." They were given labels such as "imbecile," "insane," or "epileptic" and confined to large state-run institutions where education and treatment were an afterthought at best. In some cases, the conditions of neglect were cruel and dehumanizing.

When public schools began to accept a measure of responsibility for educating certain exceptional students, a philosophy and practice of segregation prevailed. Children with disabilities were confined to segregated classrooms, isolated from the students and teachers in the general education program. Children with mild learning and behavioral problems usually remained in regular classrooms but received no special help. Those who did not make satisfactory academic progress were termed "slow learners" or "failures." If they did not meet the teacher's behavioral expectations, they were labeled "disciplinary problems" and suspended from school. Children with more severe disabilities—including many with visual, hearing, and physical or health impairments—were placed in segregated schools or institutions or kept at home. Gifted and talented children seldom received special attention in schools. It was assumed they could make it on their own without help.

Society's response to exceptional children has come a long way. As our concepts of equality, freedom, and justice have expanded, children with disabilities and their families have moved from exclusion and isolation to inclusion and participation. Society no longer regards children with disabilities as beyond the responsibility of the local public schools. A child with disabilities cannot be excluded from school because someone believes the child is unable to benefit from education. Federal legislation and court rulings have made it clear that all children with disabilities have the right to a **free appropriate public education (FAPE)** in the **least restrictive environment (LRE)** (Yell, 2019a).

Pearson eText
Video Example 1.2
Consider how you would feel if one of your family members were institutionalized at a facility such as Pennhurst.
https://www.youtube.com/watch?v=kFOBVjJxAWA

Separate Is Not Equal

The history of special education is closely related to the civil rights movement. Special education was strongly influenced by social developments and court decisions in the 1950s and 1960s, especially the landmark case *Brown v. Board of Education of Topeka* (1954), which challenged the practice of segregating students according to race. In its ruling in the *Brown* case, the U.S. Supreme Court declared that education must be made available to all children on equal terms:

> Today, education is perhaps the most important function of state and local governments. Compulsory school attendance laws and the great expenditure for education both demonstrate our recognition of the importance of education to our democratic society. It is required in the performance of our most basic responsibilities.... In these days, it is doubtful that any child may reasonably be expected to succeed in life if he is denied the opportunity of an education (*Brown v. Board of Education*, 1954).

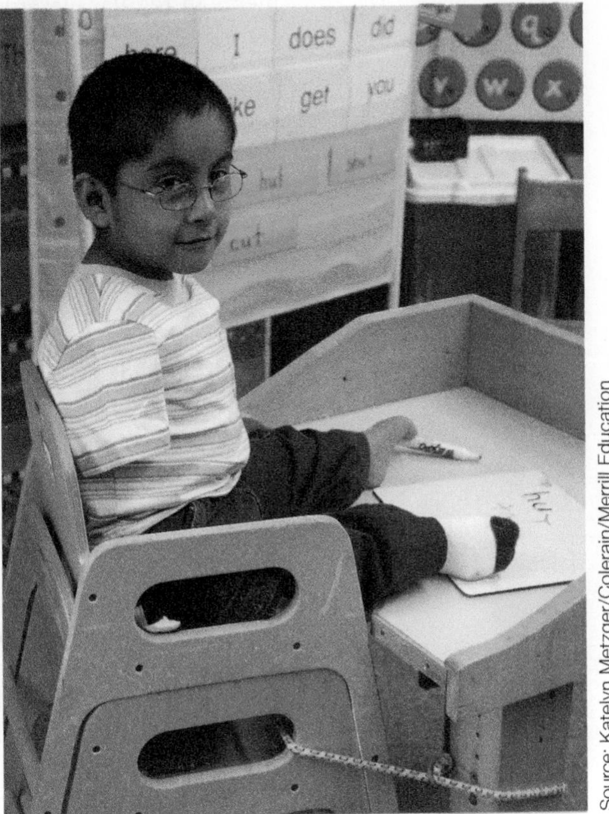

Source: Katelyn Metzger/Colerain/Merrill Education

In the past, children like Jose were denied access to public education.

The *Brown* decision began a period of intense questioning among parents of children with disabilities, who asked why the same principles of equal access to education should not apply to their children. Parents and other advocates dissatisfied with an educational system that denied equal access to children with disabilities initiated numerous court cases in the 1960s and early 1970s. Generally, the parents based their arguments on the 14th Amendment to the Constitution, which provides that no state shall deny any person within its jurisdiction the equal protection of the law and that no state shall deprive any person of life, liberty, or property without **due process**.

Equal Protection

In the past, children with disabilities were denied access to certain educational programs or received special education only in segregated settings. When asked to rule on the practice of denial or segregation, judges have examined whether such differential treatment is rational and necessary. One of the most historically significant cases to examine these questions was the class action suit *Pennsylvania Association for Retarded Children (PARC) v. Commonwealth of Pennsylvania* (1972). *PARC* challenged a state law that denied public school education to children considered "unable to profit from public school attendance."

The lawyers and parents supporting *PARC* argued that even though the children had intellectual disabilities, it was neither rational nor necessary to assume they were ineducable. Because the state was unable to prove that the children were, in fact, ineducable or to demonstrate a rational need for excluding them from public school programs, the court decided that the children were entitled to receive a free, public education. In addition, the court ruled that parents had the right to be notified before any change was made in their children's educational program.

The wording of the *PARC* decision proved particularly important because of its influence on subsequent federal legislation. Not only did the court rule that all children with intellectual disabilities were entitled to FAPE, but it also stipulated that placements in regular classrooms and regular public schools were preferable to segregated settings.

> It is the Commonwealth's obligation to place each mentally retarded child in a free, public program of education and training appropriate to the child's capacity. . . . Placement in a regular public school class is preferable to placement in a special public school class and placement in a special public school is preferable to placement in any other type of program of education and training (*PARC v. Commonwealth of Pennsylvania*, 1972).

The *Brown* and *PARC* cases had far-reaching effects on special education (Yell, 2019a). The rulings from these landmark cases were incorporated into subsequent federal legislation, most notably IDEA.

The Individuals with Disabilities Education Act

Congress passed Public Law 94-142, the Education for All Handicapped Children Act, in 1975. This legislation completely changed the face of education in this country. Congress has reauthorized and amended PL 94-142 five times. The 1990 amendments renamed the law the Individuals with Disabilities Education Act (IDEA). The most recent reauthorization of IDEA, PL 108-466, is titled The Individuals with Disabilities Education Improvement Act of 2004.

IDEA exerts profound influence on what takes place in every school building in the country and has changed the roles and responsibilities of general and special educators, school administrators, parents, and students with disabilities. The law reflects society's concern about treating people with disabilities as full citizens with the same rights and privileges all other citizens enjoy. The purposes of IDEA are as follows:

1. (A) to ensure that all children with disabilities have available to them a free appropriate public education that emphasizes special education and related services designed to meet their unique needs and prepare them for further education, employment, and independent living; (B) to ensure that the rights of children with disabilities and parents of such children are protected; and (C) to assist states, localities, educational service agencies, and Federal agencies to provide for the education of all children with disabilities;
2. to assist States in the implementation of a statewide, comprehensive, coordinated, multidisciplinary, interagency system of early intervention services for infants and toddlers with disabilities and their families;
3. to ensure that educators and parents have the necessary tools to improve educational results for children with disabilities by supporting system improvement activities; coordinated research and personnel preparation; coordinated technical assistance, dissemination, and support; and technology development and media services; and
4. to assess, and ensure the effectiveness of, efforts to educate children with disabilities. (PL 108-466, Sec. 601 [d])

Major Principles of IDEA

The majority of IDEA rules and regulations fall within six major principles, most of which have remained basically unchanged since 1975.

ZERO REJECT Schools must educate *all* children with disabilities. No child with disabilities may be excluded from a free public education, regardless of the nature or severity of the disability. The requirement to provide special education to all students with disabilities is absolute between the ages of 6 and 17 years. If a state provides educational services to children without disabilities who are 3 to 5 years old and 18 to 21 years old, it must also educate all children with disabilities in those age groups. Each state's education agency must locate, identify, and evaluate all children with disabilities or suspected of having disabilities, from birth to age 21 years. This component of IDEA is called the *child find system*.

NONDISCRIMINATORY EVALUATION Schools must use nonbiased, multifactored methods of evaluation to determine whether a child has a disability and, if so, whether the child needs specially designed instruction to benefit from education. Testing and evaluation procedures must not discriminate on the basis of race, culture, or native language. All tests must be administered in the child's native language, and identification and placement decisions cannot be made on the basis of a single test score.

HLP4 Use multiple sources of information to develop a comprehensive understanding of a student's strengths and needs.

FREE APPROPRIATE PUBLIC EDUCATION All children with disabilities, regardless of the type or severity of their disability, shall receive a FAPE. This education must be provided at public expense—that is, without cost to the child's family. An **individualized education program (IEP)** must be developed and implemented to meet the unique needs of each student with a disability. The IEP (described in detail in Chapter 2) specifies the child's present levels of performance, identifies measurable annual goals, and describes the specific special education and related services that will be provided to help the child attain those goals and benefit from education. See *Teaching & Learning*, "First, Get a Goal."

Children with disabilities have sometimes been prevented from attending their neighborhood schools or benefiting from educational activities by circumstances that impede their access or participation. A child who uses a wheelchair, for example, may require a specially equipped school bus. A child with special health needs may require medication several times a day. A child with an orthopedic impairment may need physical therapy to

HLP11 Identify and prioritize long- and short-term learning goals.

TEACHING & LEARNING

First, Get a Goal

Why Are Learning Objectives Important? Special education is goal-directed instruction. Effective teaching methods will do little good if not focused on clearly defined learning objectives. In a skit he called "How to Be a Millionaire," comedian Steve Martin said, "First, get a million dollars!" How to teach a goal-directed lesson? First, get a goal. Just as you cannot *be* a millionaire without a million bucks, you cannot *teach* a goal-directed lesson without a goal. Fortunately, setting a good learning goal is a lot easier than getting a million dollars.

How Do I Write a Measurable Learning Objective? Learning objectives specify skills or content knowledge students should be able to demonstrate as an outcome of instruction. Learning objectives include three parts: an observable and measurable behavior, the conditions under which the behavior will occur, and the performance criteria for mastery.

Behavior Learning objectives include specific statements about what the student will *do*—observable and measurable behaviors such as reading words aloud, writing a paragraph, and stating one's home address. Phrases such as *will know how, will understand*, and *will demonstrate knowledge of* should not be used in objectives because they do not identify specific actions.

NOT OBSERVABLE AND MEASURABLE	OBSERVABLE AND MEASURABLE
enjoying literature	reading orally
understanding history	constructing a timeline
becoming independent	dressing oneself
respecting authority	speaking to adults without vulgarities
improving, feeling, knowing	pointing, drawing, identifying, writing, etc.

Source: Adapted from Bateman and Herr (2019).

Conditions An objective must also state the specific conditions that must be present when the behavior occurs. When teachers have clarified these conditions, they have a vision for exactly how they will assess their students' mastery of the objective. Conditions might include the following: "When provided a 250-word reading passage at the fourth-grade level. . . ."; "When given a worksheet with 10 angles between 0° and 180° and a protractor. . ."; "When given a picture activity schedule and directions to begin the first activity. . ."

Mastery Criteria How well must the student perform the behavior for the objective to be considered "met"? When selecting mastery criteria, teachers should consider productivity, accuracy, rate or speed, duration, and endurance. Examples of mastery criteria statements include ". . . read 150 words correctly in 1 minute with no more than 5 errors"; ". . . write a paragraph containing a minimum of 5 complete, on-topic sentences, including a topic sentence, 3 supporting details, and a concluding sentence"; ". . . measure each angle to 100% accuracy."

Mastery criteria should be ambitious (but attainable) and consistent with the general education curriculum standards, IEP goals and objectives, and progress monitoring data. They should also make sense and be appropriate for the behavior. For example, although 90% accuracy might sound good, it would be completely unsatisfactory if the skill to be learned is crossing busy streets or using a chain saw!

maintain sufficient strength and flexibility in her arms and legs. IDEA requires that schools provide any related services and assistive technology that a child with a disability may need to access and benefit from special education.

Types of related services included in the IDEA regulations are shown in Table 1.2.

LEAST RESTRICTIVE ENVIRONMENT IDEA requires that (a) schools educate students with disabilities together with children without disabilities to the maximum extent appropriate and (b) students with disabilities be removed to separate settings only when the nature or severity of their disabilities is such that they cannot benefit from instruction in a regular classroom with supplementary aids and services. IDEA creates a presumption in favor of inclusion in the regular classroom by requiring that a student's IEP contain a justification for

TABLE 1.2 Types and definitions of related services that students with disabilities may need to benefit from special education

RELATED SERVICE	IDEA DEFINITION
Audiology	(1) Identification of children with hearing loss; (2) Determination of the range, nature, and degree of hearing loss, including referral for medical or other professional attention for the habilitation of hearing; (3) Provision of habilitative activities, such as auditory training, speech reading (lipreading), hearing evaluation, and speech conservation; (4) Creation and administration of programs for prevention of hearing loss; (5) Counseling and guidance of children, parents, and teachers, regarding hearing loss; and (6) Determining the child's need for group and individual amplification, selecting and fitting an appropriate hearing aid, and evaluating the effectiveness of amplification.
Counseling Services	Services provided by qualified social workers, psychologists, guidance counselors, or other qualified personnel.
Early Identification and Assessment	Implementation of a formal plan for identifying a disability as early as possible in a child's life.
Interpreting Services	(1) The following, when used with respect to children who are deaf or hard of hearing: Oral transliteration services, cued language transliteration services, sign language transliteration and interpreting services, and transcription services, such as communication access real time translation (CART), C-Print, and TypeWell; and (2) Special interpreting services for children who are deaf-blind.
Medical Services	Services provided by a licensed physician for diagnostic or evaluation purposes to determine a child's medically related disability that results in the child's need for special education and related services.
Occupational Therapy	(1) Services provided by a qualified occupational therapist; and (2) includes (A) Improving, developing, or restoring functions impaired or lost through illness, injury, or deprivation; (B) Improving ability to perform tasks for independent functioning if functions are impaired or lost; and (C) Preventing, through early intervention, initial or further impairment or loss of function.
Orientation and Mobility Services	Services provided to blind or visually impaired children by qualified personnel to enable those students to obtain systematic orientation to and safe movement within their environments in school, home, and community.
Parent Counseling and Training	(1) Assisting parents in understanding the special needs of their child; (2) Providing parents with information about child development; and (3) Helping parents to acquire the necessary skills that will allow them to support the implementation of their child's IEP or IFSP.
Physical Therapy	Services provided by a qualified physical therapist.
Psychological Services	(1) Administering psychological and educational tests, and other assessment procedures; (2) Interpreting assessment results; (3) Obtaining, integrating, and interpreting information about child behavior and conditions relating to learning; (4) Consulting with other staff members in planning school programs to meet the special needs of children as indicated by psychological tests, interviews, and behavioral evaluations; (5) Planning and managing a program of psychological services, including psychological counseling for children and parents; and (6) Assisting in developing positive behavioral intervention strategies.
Recreation	(1) Assessment of leisure function; (2) Therapeutic recreation services; (3) Recreation programs in schools and community agencies; and (4) Leisure education.
Rehabilitative Counseling Services	Services provided by qualified personnel in individual or group sessions that focus specifically on career development, employment preparation, achieving independence, and integration in the workplace and community.
School Health Services and School Nurse Services	Health services designed to enable a child with a disability to receive FAPE as described by the child's IEP. School nurse services are provided by a qualified school nurse or other qualified person. School health services are services provided by either a qualified school nurse or other qualified person.
Social Work Services in the Schools	(1) Preparing a social or developmental history on a child with a disability; (2) Group and individual counseling with the child and family; (3) Working in partnership with parents and others on those problems in a child's living situation (home, school, and community) that affect the child's adjustment in school; (4) Mobilizing school and community resources to enable the child to learn as effectively as possible; and (5) Assisting in developing positive behavioral intervention strategies.

(Continued)

TABLE 1.2 (Continued)

RELATED SERVICE	IDEA DEFINITION
Speech-Language Pathology Services	(1) Identification of children with speech or language impairments; (2) Diagnosis and appraisal of specific speech or language impairments; (3) Referral for medical or other professional attention necessary for the habilitation of speech or language impairments; (4) Provision of speech and language services for the habilitation and prevention of communicative problems; and (5) Counseling and guidance of parents, children, and teachers regarding speech and language impairments.
Transportation	(1) Travel to and from school and between schools. (2) Travel in and around school buildings. (3) Specialized equipment (such as special or adapted buses, lifts, and ramps), if required to provide special transportation for a child with a disability.
Exception	(1) Related services do not include a medical device that is surgically implanted, the optimization of that device's functioning (e.g., mapping), maintenance of that device, or the replacement of that device. (2) Nothing in paragraph (b)(1) of this section—(i) Limits the right of a child with a surgically implanted device (e.g., cochlear implant) to receive related services that are determined by the IEP Team to be necessary for the child to receive FAPE; (ii) Limits the responsibility of a public agency to appropriately monitor and maintain medical devices that are needed to maintain the health and safety of the child, including breathing, nutrition, or operation of other bodily functions, while the child is transported to and from school or is at school; or (iii) Prevents the routine checking of an external component of a surgically implanted device to make sure it is functioning properly.

Source: From IDEA Regulations, 34 Code of Federal Regulations (CFR) §300.34; Authority: 20 USC §1401 (26).

Pearson eText
Video Example 1.3
Physical therapists (PTs) and occupational therapists (OTs) provide related services for many students with disabilities.

why the student will not participate with peers without disabilities in regular classrooms, extracurricular activities, and other nonacademic activities (e.g., lunch, recess, transportation, dances). To ensure each student with disabilities is educated in the LRE appropriate for the student's needs, school districts must provide a continuum of alternative placements and service alternatives (e.g., regular classroom with consultation, resource room, special class, special schools). (Chapter 2 discusses LRE and the continuum of services in detail.)

PROCEDURAL SAFEGUARDS Schools must follow an extensive set of procedures to safeguard and protect the rights and interests of children with disabilities and their parents. Parental consent must be obtained for initial and all subsequent evaluations and placement decisions. Schools must maintain the confidentiality of all records pertaining to a child with disabilities and make those records available to the parents. When parents of a child with disabilities disagree with the results of an evaluation performed by the school, they can obtain an independent evaluation at public expense. When the school and parents disagree on the identification, evaluation, placement, or provision of a FAPE and related services for the child, the parents may request a *due process hearing*. States also must offer parents an opportunity to resolve the matter through mediation by a third party before holding a due process hearing.

HLP3 Collaborate with families to support student learning and secure needed services.

PARENT PARTICIPATION AND SHARED DECISION MAKING Schools must collaborate with parents and students with disabilities in the planning and implementation of special education and related services. The parents' (and, when appropriate, the student's) input and wishes must be considered in determining IEP goals, related-service needs, and placement decisions.

Other Provisions of IDEA

SPECIAL EDUCATION SERVICES FOR PRESCHOOLERS Noting that early intervention services for infants and toddlers with disabilities from birth through age 2 years were scarce or nonexistent in many states, Congress included provisions in the Education of the Handicapped Act Amendments in 1986 (PL 99-457) to expand services. Beginning with the 1990–1991 school year, PL 99-457 required each state to fully serve all preschool children with disabilities age 3 to 5 years—that is, to provide the same services and protections available to school-age children.

EARLY INTERVENTION FOR INFANTS AND TODDLERS PL 99-457 included an incentive grant program to encourage states to provide early intervention services to infants and toddlers with disabilities and their families. The children served are those from birth through age 2 years who need early intervention services because of developmental delays or diagnosed medical conditions likely to result in developmental delays. Rather than mandate special services for this age group, IDEA encourages each state to develop and implement a statewide, comprehensive, coordinated, multidisciplinary, interagency program of early intervention services for infants and toddlers with disabilities and their families. The encouragement is in the form of a gradually increasing amount of federal money awarded to states that identify and serve all infants and toddlers with disabilities. Various education and human services agencies within each state work together to provide services such as medical and educational assessment, physical therapy, speech and language intervention, and parent counseling and training. These early intervention services are prescribed and implemented according to an **individualized family service plan (IFSP)** written by a multidisciplinary team that includes the child's parents (see Chapter 14).

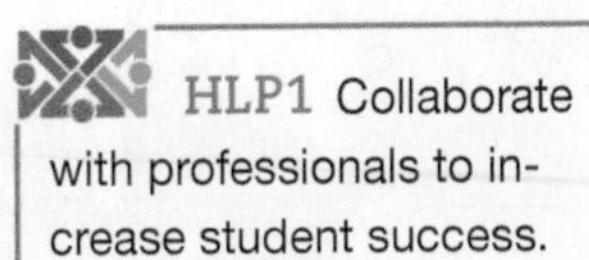
HLP1 Collaborate with professionals to increase student success.

ASSISTIVE TECHNOLOGY IDEA requires IEP teams to consider whether assistive technology is necessary for a child to receive a FAPE. The law defines **assistive technology** as "any item, piece of equipment, or product system, whether acquired commercially off the shelf, modified, or customized, that is used to increase, maintain, or improve functional capabilities of a child with a disability" (20 USC 1401, Sec. 602[1]). Assistive technology includes devices and services such as alternative and augmentative communication devices (Chapter 8), low-vision aids (Chapter 10), positioning and mobility devices (Chapter 11), and adaptive toys and games (Chapter 14).

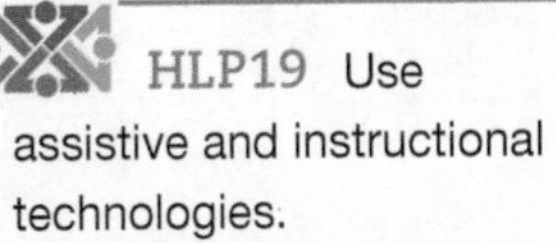
HLP19 Use assistive and instructional technologies.

UNIVERSAL DESIGN FOR LEARNING The concept of universal design originated in architecture, with the design and construction of barrier-free physical environments (e.g., installing ramps and curb cuts for wheelchair users). IDEA 2004 defines *universal design* consistent with the Assistive Technology Act as "a concept or philosophy for designing and delivering products and services that are usable by people with the widest possible range of functional capabilities, which include products and services that are directly accessible (without requiring assistive technologies) and products and services that are interoperable with assistive technologies" (Sec. 3[19]).

The basic idea of **universal design for learning (UDL)** is that curricular materials and learning technologies should be designed from the beginning to be flexible enough to accommodate the learning needs of a wide range of individuals, including children with disabilities. UDL applied to curriculum and instruction encompasses three principles: (a) *multiple means of representation* to give diverse learners options for acquiring information and knowledge (e.g., presenting material in different formats, such as print, print with audio pictures, accessible Web pages); (b) *multiple means of action and expression* to provide learners options for demonstrating what they know (e.g., speaking, writing, and using voice-operated switches); and (c) *multiple means of engagement* to tap into students' interests, offer appropriate challenges, and increase motivation (Center for Applied Special Technology, 2020).

Pearson eText
Video Example 1.4
How does assistive technology help you each day?
https://www.youtube.com/watch?v=DB9pKkZoJDc

Legal Challenges to IDEA

Although IDEA has resulted in dramatic increases in the number of students receiving special education services and greater recognition of the legal rights of children with disabilities and their families, it has also resulted in numerous disputes concerning the education of students with disabilities. Parents and other advocates have brought about thousands of due process hearings and hundreds of court cases. Due process hearings and court cases place parents and schools in confrontation and are expensive and time consuming.

It is difficult to generalize how courts have resolved the various legal challenges based on IDEA. The federal statutes and regulations use these terms repeatedly; but in the view of many parents, educators, judges, and attorneys, key pillars of law such as FAPE and LRE are not defined with sufficient clarity. Thus, the questions of what is appropriate and least restrictive for a particular child and whether a public school district should be compelled to provide a certain type of program or service must often be decided by courts based on the evidence presented. Some of the key issues that courts have ruled on are the extended school year (ESY), FAPE and related services, disciplinary procedures, and the fundamental right to education for students with the most severe disabilities.

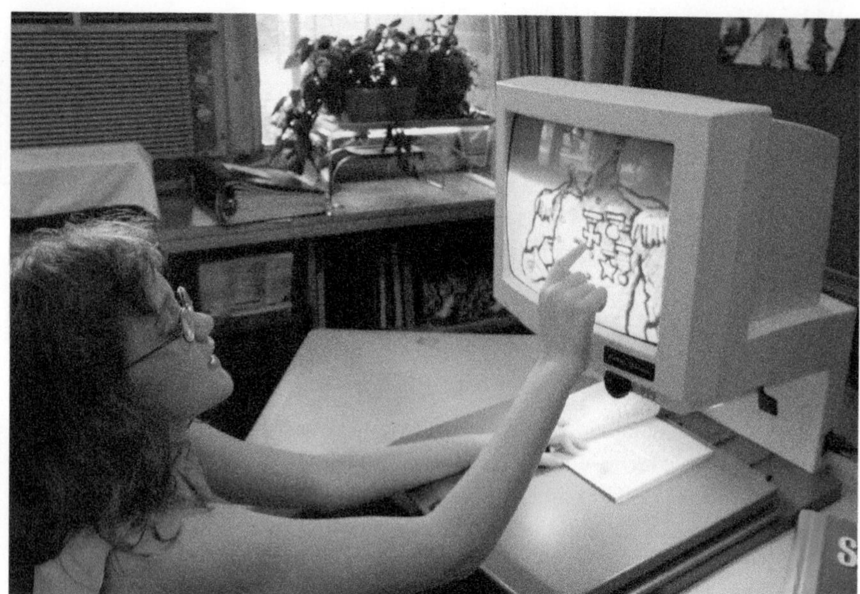

Source: Katelyn Metzger/Ohio State School for the Blind/Merrill Education

School districts must provide related services and assistive technology—such as this device that enlarges printed material—to students with disabilities so they can access and benefit from a public education.

EXTENDED SCHOOL YEAR Most public schools operate for approximately 180 days per year. Parents and advocates have argued that, for some children with disabilities, particularly those with severe and multiple disabilities, a 180-day school year is not sufficient to meet their needs. In *Armstrong v. Kline* (1979), the parents of five students with severe disabilities claimed that their children tended to regress during the usual breaks in the school year and called on the schools to provide instruction for more than 180 days. The court agreed and ordered the schools to extend the school year for these students. As a result of this and other related judicial rulings, the IDEA regulations require school districts to provide ESY services if an IEP team determines they are necessary for a student to receive a FAPE (34 *CFR* § 300.309).

FAPE AND RELATED SERVICES The related-services provision of IDEA has been highly controversial, creating much disagreement about what kinds of related services are necessary and reasonable for the schools to provide a FAPE and what services should be the responsibility of the child's parents. The first case based on IDEA to reach the U.S. Supreme Court was *Board of Education of the Hendrick Hudson Central School District v. Rowley* (1982). Amy Rowley was a fourth grader who needed special education and related services because of her hearing loss. The school district had originally provided Amy with a hearing aid, speech therapy, a tutor, and a sign language interpreter. The school withdrew the sign language services after the interpreter reported that Amy did not make use of her services. Amy reportedly looked at the teacher to read her lips and asked the teacher to repeat instructions rather than getting the information from the interpreter. Amy's parents contended that she was missing up to 50% of the ongoing instruction and was therefore being denied an appropriate public education. The school district's position was that Amy, with the help of the other special services she was still receiving, was passing from grade to grade without an interpreter. School personnel thought, in fact, that an interpreter might hinder Amy's interactions with her teachers and peers. It was also noted that this service would cost the school district as much as $25,000 per year. The Supreme Court ruled that Amy, who was making satisfactory progress in school without an interpreter, was receiving an adequate education and the school district could not be compelled to hire a full-time interpreter.

FAPE AND EDUCATIONAL BENEFIT The *Rowley* ruling sanctioning low standards of educational benefit needed to fulfill FAPE requirements was addressed in the U.S. Supreme Court's decision on the *Endrew F. v. Douglas County School District* case in 2017. Endrew F. was an elementary student with autism and attention/deficit hyperactivity disorder (ADHD) who had serious academic and behavior problems. When he was in fourth grade, Endrew's progress worsened, so his parents placed him in a private school, where he showed substantial improvement. When they attempted to place him back in public school, the school team's IEP development did not improve. So, his parents rejected the IEP, placed Endrew back in the private school, and requested a due process hearing to have his private school tuition reimbursed by the Douglas County School District. After this request was denied, the case went through a series of lower circuit and appeals courts that found in favor of the school district. Ultimately, this case was reviewed by the U.S. Supreme Court, who rejected the lower standard of educational benefit established in *Rowley* and ordered the school to pay the parents' tuition fees and court costs.

> The new standard, which may correctly be called the *Rowley/Endrew* test, still includes the procedural test from *Rowley;* that is, did the school district adhere to the procedural requirements? The second part of the test, however, is the new *Endrew* test: Was the IEP reasonably calculated to enable a student to make progress appropriate in light of his or her circumstances? (Yell, 2019b, p. 57).

DISCIPLINE Some court cases have resulted from parents' protesting the suspension or expulsion of children with disabilities. The case of *Stuart v. Nappi* (1978), for example, concerned a high school student who spent much of her time wandering the halls even though she was assigned to special classes. The school sought to have the student expelled on disciplinary grounds because her conduct was considered detrimental to order in the school. The court agreed with the student's mother that expulsion would deny her daughter a FAPE. In other cases, courts have upheld the expulsion of students with disabilities if the school could show that the grounds for expulsion did not relate to the student's disability. In 1988, however, the Supreme Court ruled in *Honig v. Doe* that schools could not recommend expulsion or suspend a student with disabilities for more than 10 days.

The IDEA amendments of 1997 (PL 105-17) contained provisions that enable school districts to discipline students with disabilities in the same manner as students without disabilities, with a few notable exceptions. If the school seeks a change of placement, suspension in excess of 10 days, or expulsion, the IEP team and other qualified personnel must review the relationship between the student's misconduct and her disability. This review is called a **manifestation determination** (Katsiyannis & Maag, 2001). If the team determines the student's misconduct is not related to the disability, the same disciplinary procedures used with other students may be imposed. However, the school must continue to provide educational services in the alternative placement.

IDEA 2004 revised the discipline provisions of the law such that under special circumstances (e.g., student possesses a weapon, uses illegal drugs, inflicts serious injury upon someone at school), school personnel have the authority to remove a student with disabilities to an interim alternative educational setting for up to 45 school days, whether or not the misconduct was related to the child's disability.

RIGHT TO EDUCATION The case of *Timothy W. v. Rochester School District* (1989) threatened the zero-reject philosophy of IDEA. In July 1988, Judge Loughlin of the district court in New Hampshire ruled that a 13-year-old boy with severe disabilities and quadriplegia was ineligible for education services because he could not benefit from special education. The judge ruled in favor of the Rochester School Board, which claimed that IDEA was not intended to provide educational services to "all handicapped students." In his decision, the judge determined that the federal law was not explicit regarding a "rare child" with severe disabilities and declared that special evaluations and examinations should be used to determine "qualifications for education under PL 94-142."

In May 1989, a court of appeals overturned the lower court's decision, ruling that public schools must educate all children with disabilities regardless of how little they might benefit or the nature or severity of their disabilities. The three-judge panel concluded "schools cannot avoid the provisions of the Education for All Handicapped Children Act (EHA) by returning to the practices that were widespread prior to the Act's passage ... of unilaterally excluding certain handicapped children from a public education on the grounds that they are uneducable" (U.S. Court of Appeals, 875 F.2d 954 [1st Cir.]).

Related Legislation

JAVITS AND GIFTED AND TALENTED STUDENTS EDUCATION ACT The Jacob K. Javits Gifted and Talented Student Education Act (PL 100-297), enacted in 1988, is the only federal program that addresses the needs of the nation's 3 million gifted and talented students. This act provides federal support for demonstration programs at a national research center on gifted and talented students, competitive grants to develop and expand models serving students who are underrepresented in gifted and talented programs, and competitive grants to enhance gifted education curricula and programs. Although the purpose of the Javits Act is laudable, it has been "chronically underfunded" (CEC, 2015).

SECTION 504 OF THE REHABILITATION ACT OF 1973 Another important law that extends civil rights to people with disabilities is Section 504 of the Rehabilitation Act of 1973, which states that "no otherwise qualified handicapped individual shall ... solely by reason of his handicap, be excluded from the participation in, be denied the benefits of, or be subject to discrimination under any program or activity receiving federal financial assistance" (Sec. 504, 29 USC § 794[a]). This law, worded almost identically to the Civil Rights Act of 1964 (which prohibits discrimination based on race, color, or national origin), expanded opportunities to children and adults with disabilities in education, employment, and various other settings. It requires provision of "auxiliary aids for students with impaired sensory, manual, or speaking skills"—for example, readers for students who are blind and people to assist students with physical disabilities in moving from place to place. This requirement does not mean that schools, colleges, and employers must have all such aids available at all times; it simply means that no person with disabilities may be excluded from a program because of the lack of an appropriate support.

Section 504 is not a federal grant program; unlike IDEA, it does not provide any federal money to assist people with disabilities. Rather, it "imposes a duty on every recipient of federal funds not to discriminate against handicapped persons" (Johnson, 1986, p. 8). "Recipient," of course, includes public school districts, virtually all of which receive federal support. Most colleges and universities have also been affected; many students in private institutions receive federal financial aid. The Office of Civil Rights conducts periodic compliance reviews and acts on complaints when parents, individuals with disabilities, or others contend that a school district is violating Section 504.

Architectural accessibility for students, teachers, and others with physical and sensory impairments is an important feature of Section 504; however, the law does not call for completely barrier-free environments. Emphasis is on accessibility to programs, not on physical modification of all existing structures. If a chemistry class is required for a pre-med program of study, for example, a college might make this program accessible to a student with physical disabilities by reassigning the class to an accessible location. Similar to IDEA, Section 504 calls for nondiscriminatory placement in the "most integrated setting appropriate" and has served as the basis for many court cases over alleged discrimination against individuals with disabilities, particularly in their right to employment. For a discussion of what teachers need to know about Section 504, see O'Connor et al. (2016).

AMERICANS WITH DISABILITIES ACT The Americans with Disabilities Act (ADA) was signed into law in 1990 and amended in 2008. Patterned after Section 504 of the Rehabilitation Act of 1973, ADA extends civil rights protection of people with disabilities to private sector employment, public services, transportation, and telecommunications. A person with a disability is defined in ADA as a person who (a) has a physical or mental impairment that substantially limits one or more major life activities (e.g., caring for oneself, communicating, working), (b) has a record of such an impairment (e.g., a person who no longer has heart disease but who is discriminated against because of that history), or (c) is regarded as having such an impairment (e.g., a person with significant facial disfiguration due to a burn who is not limited in any major life activity but is discriminated against). The major provisions of ADA fall under four areas:

- *Employment.* Employers with 15 or more workers may not discriminate against a qualified individual with a disability in the hiring process or in opportunities for advancement. Employers must make reasonable accommodations that will allow a person with a disability to perform essential job functions. The employer must make reasonable accommodations in job requirements or situations if they will not impose "undue hardship" or expense on the employer.
- *Public entities (including public transportation).* ADA regulations detail requirements for making public transportation accessible to people with disabilities. New vehicles purchased by public transit authorities must be accessible to people with disabilities. All intercity and commuter rail services must be accessible and usable.
- *Public accommodations and commercial facilities.* Businesses open to the public, such as hotels, restaurants, grocery stores, and parks and recreation facilities, must not discriminate against people with disabilities. New buildings must be made accessible, and existing facilities must

remove barriers if doing so is "readily achievable." The law recognizes that what might be readily achievable by a large company might not be so for a small, local business.

- *Telecommunications.* Companies offering telecommunications services to the general public must offer telecommunications relay services (TRS) to consumers with disabilities, notably those who are deaf or hard of hearing, 24 hours per day, 7 days per week. In TRS, communication assistants translate between the signed or typed words of a consumer and the spoken words of others.

EVERY STUDENT SUCCEEDS ACT (ESSA) Signed into law by President Obama in 2015, the Every Student Succeeds Act (PL 114-95) reauthorized the Elementary and Secondary Education Act first enacted in 1965 as part of President Lyndon Johnson's war on poverty. Key provisions of ESSA affecting special education include the following (National Council on Disability, 2018a).

Standards. ESSA requires schools to implement "challenging" content standards in reading, math, and science. States are allowed to develop alternative assessments for students with disabilities, but those assessments must align with rigorous academic content, enable access to the general education curriculum, and "reflect professional judgement of the highest possible standards achievable" (National Council on Disability, 2018a, p. 19). Additionally, state standards must prepare all students for entrance into higher education or competitive employment.

Disciplinary Practices. ESSA requires states to explain how they will improve their school environments by describing how they will (a) reduce bullying and harassment, (b) avoid removing students from the classroom as a form of discipline, and (c) refrain from the use of aversive behavioral consequences such as seclusion and restraint.

Professional Learning. ESSA requires special education teachers to possess at least a bachelor's degree and full state certification as a special education teacher. Schools may not waive special education licensure requirements on an emergency, temporary, or provisional basis.

Table 1.3 summarizes federal legislation regarding the education of exceptional children and rights of individuals with disabilities.

TABLE 1.3 Federal legislation concerning the education of exceptional children and rights of individuals with disabilities

DATE	LEGISLATION	EDUCATIONAL IMPLICATIONS
1958	National Defense Education Act (PL 85-926)	Provided funds for training professionals to train teachers of children with intellectual disabilities
1961	Special Education Act (PL 87-276)	Provided funds for training professionals to train teachers of deaf children
1963	Mental Retardation Facility and Community Center Construction Act (PL 88-164)	Extended support given in PL 85-926 to training teachers of children with other disabilities
1965	Elementary and Secondary -Education Act (PL 89-10)	Provided money to states and local districts for developing programs for children with disabilities and economic disadvantages
1966	Amendment to Title I of the Elementary and Secondary Education Act (PL 89-313)	Provided funding for state-supported programs in institutions and other settings for children with disabilities
1966	Amendments to the Elementary and Secondary Education Act (PL 89-750)	Created the federal Bureau of Education for the Handicapped (today's Office of Special Education)
1968	Handicapped Children's Early Assistance Act (PL 90-538)	Established the "first chance network" of experimental programs for preschool children with disabilities
1969	Elementary, Secondary, and Other Educational Amendments (PL 91-230)	Defined learning disabilities and provided funds for state-level programs for children with learning disabilities
1970	Education Amendments of 1970 (PL 92-318)	Mandated a study of the gifted that resulted in the *Marland Report* (1972), which many states used as a basis for building programs for gifted and talented students
1973	Section 504 of the Rehabilitation Act (PL 93-112)	Declared that a person cannot be excluded on the basis of disability alone from any program or activity receiving federal funds

(Continued)

TABLE 1.3 (Continued)

DATE	LEGISLATION	EDUCATIONAL IMPLICATIONS
1974	Education Amendments (PL 93-380)	Extended previous legislation; provided money to state and local districts for programs for gifted and talented students for the first time; protected the rights of children with disabilities and their parents in placement decisions
1975	Developmental Disabilities Assistance and Bill of Rights Act (PL 94-103)	Affirmed the rights of citizens with intellectual disabilities and cited areas in which services must be provided
1975	Education for All Handicapped Children Act (EAHCA) (PL 94-142)	Mandated free appropriate public education for all children with disabilities age 6 to 21 years; protected the rights of children with disabilities and their parents in educational decision making; required the development of an individualized education program (IEP) for each child with a disability; stated that students with disabilities must receive educational services in the least restrictive environment
1978	Gifted and Talented Children's Education Act of 1978 (PL 95-561)	Provided funds for in-service training programs, research, and other projects aimed at meeting the needs of gifted and talented students
1983	Amendments to the Education of the Handicapped Act (PL 98-199)	Required states to collect data on the number of youth with disabilities exiting their systems and to address the needs of secondary students making the transition to adulthood; gave incentives to states to provide services to infants and preschool children with disabilities
1984	Developmental Disabilities Assistance and Bill of Rights Acts (PL 98-527)	Mandated the development of employment-related training activities for adults with disabilities
1986	Handicapped Children's Protection Act (PL 99-372)	Provided authority for the reimbursement of attorney's fees to parents who prevail in a hearing or court case to secure an appropriate education for their child
1986	Education for the Handicapped Act Amendments of 1986 (PL 99-457)	Required states to provide free appropriate education to all 3- to 5-year-olds with disabilities who were eligible to apply for federal preschool funding; included incentive grants to encourage states to develop comprehensive interdisciplinary services for infants and toddlers (birth through age 2 years) and their families
1986	Rehabilitation Act Amendments (PL 99-506)	Set forth regulations for the development of supported employment programs for adults with disabilities
1988	Jacob K. Javits Gifted and Talented Students Education Act (PL 100-297)	Provided federal funds in support of research, teacher training, and program development for the education of gifted and talented students
1988	Technology-Related Assistance for Individuals with Disabilities Act of 1988 (PL 100-407)	Created statewide programs of technology assistance for people of all ages with disabilities
1990	Americans with Disabilities Act (PL 101-336)	Provided civil rights protection against discrimination to citizens with disabilities in private sector employment; provided access to all public services, public accommodations, transportation, and telecommunications
1990	Individuals with Disabilities Education Act (IDEA) Amendments of 1990 (PL 101-476)	Renamed the EAHCA; added autism and traumatic brain injury as new categories of disability; required all IEPs to include a statement of needed transition services no later than age 16 years; expanded the definition of related services to include rehabilitation counseling and social work services
1994	Goals 2000: Educate America Act (PL 103-227)	Provided federal funds for the development and implementation of educational reforms to help achieve eight national education goals by the year 2000
1997	Individuals with Disabilities Education Act (IDEA) of 1997 (PL 105-17)	Added several major provisions, including that a regular education teacher must be a member of the IEP team; students with disabilities must have access to the general curriculum; IEPs must address positive behavior support plans when appropriate; students with disabilities must be included in state or districtwide testing programs; if a school seeks to discipline a student with disabilities resulting in change of placement, suspension, or expulsion for more than 10 days, the IEP team must conduct a "manifestation determination"
2001	No Child Left Behind Act of 2001 (Reauthorization of the Elementary and Secondary Education Act [PL 107-110])	School districts are expected to make adequate yearly progress (AYP), ensure that all children are taught by "highly qualified" teachers, and use curriculum and instructional methods validated by rigorous scientific research; schools that do not make AYP are initially targeted for assistance and then subject to corrective action and ultimately restructuring
2004	Individuals with Disabilities Education Improvement Act of 2004 (PL 108-446)	Retained major components and principles of IDEA; key changes include benchmarks and short-term objectives required only in IEPs for students who take alternative assessments related to alternative achievement standards; pilot program for multiyear IEPs; "response-to-intervention" may be used to identify learning disabilities; "highly qualified" special education teacher defined; under special circumstances (e.g., brings a weapon to school) a student with disabilities may be removed from school to an interim setting for up to 45 school days whether or not the misconduct was related to the child's disability
2015	Every Student Succeeds Act (PL 114-95)	Mandated challenging academic standards for all students; appropriate accommodations for assessments, including assistive technology; improved school environments by reducing bullying and aversive discipline practices; and that special education teachers are licensed in special education

What Is Special Education?

Learning Outcome 1.4 Define and give an example of each of the three types of intervention—preventive, remedial, and compensatory.

Special education is a complex enterprise that can be defined and evaluated from many perspectives. One may, for example, view special education as a legislatively governed enterprise in which practitioners are concerned with issues such as due process procedures and developing IDEA-compliant IEPs. From a sociopolitical perspective, special education can be seen as an outgrowth of the civil rights movement and society's changing attitudes about people with disabilities. Each of these perspectives has some validity, and each has had and continues to play an important role in defining special education and its practice. Neither view, however, reveals the fundamental purpose of special education as *instructionally based intervention*.

Special Education as Intervention

Special education is, first of all, purposeful intervention designed to prevent, eliminate, and/or overcome the obstacles that might keep a child with disabilities from learning and from full and active participation in school and society. Special education provides three basic types of intervention: preventive, remedial, and compensatory.

PREVENTATIVE INTERVENTION Special educators design preventive intervention to keep a potential or minor problem from becoming a disability. Prevention can occur at three levels:

- **Primary prevention** is designed to reduce the number of new cases (**incidence**) of a disability; it consists of efforts to eliminate or counteract risk factors so that a child never acquires a disability. Educators use primary prevention efforts for all students who could be affected by the targeted problem. For example, in a schoolwide program to prevent behavior disorders, primary prevention would include building- and classroom-wide systems of positive behavior support for all students (Simonsen & Sugai, 2019).
- **Secondary prevention** is aimed at individuals who have been exposed to or are displaying specific risk factors and is intended to eliminate or counteract the effects of those risk factors. Secondary prevention in a schoolwide program to prevent behavior disorders would entail specialized interventions for those students exhibiting early signs of problem behavior.
- **Tertiary prevention** is aimed at individuals with a disability and intended to minimize the impact of a specific condition or disability. For example, intensive interventions would be provided for students identified with emotional or behavioral disorders.

Preventive efforts are most promising when begun as early as possible—even before birth, in many cases. Later chapters describe some of the promising methods for preventing and minimizing the effects of disabilities. Unfortunately, widespread primary and secondary prevention programs are rare, and it will be decades before a significant reduction in the incidence and prevalence of most disabilities is achieved.

REMEDIAL INTERVENTION Remediation attempts to eliminate specific effects of a disability. The word *remediation* is primarily an educational term; social service agencies more often use the word *rehabilitation*. Both terms convey a common purpose: to teach a person with disabilities skills for independent and successful functioning. In school, those skills may be academic (e.g., reading, writing, computing), social (e.g., initiating and maintaining a conversation), self-care (e.g., eating, dressing, toileting), or vocational (career and job skills to prepare students for the world of work). The underlying assumption of remedial intervention is that a person with disabilities needs special instruction to succeed in typical settings.

COMPENSATORY INTERVENTION Compensatory intervention teaches a substitute skill that enables a person to engage in an activity or perform a task despite a disability. Teaching students to use assistive devices or providing special training in orientation and mobility are examples of compensatory intervention. Although remedial instruction might help a child with cerebral palsy learn to use her hands for some tasks, a compensatory approach is necessary to help her learn to use a headstick and a template placed over a computer keyboard to compensate for her limited fine-motor control.

Special Education as Instruction

Learning Outcome 1.5 Describe the defining dimensions of special education and identify several challenges facing the field of special education.

Ultimately, *teaching* is what special education is about. But the same can be said of all of education. What, then, is *special* about special education? One way to answer that question is to examine special education in terms of the who, what, how, and where of its teaching.

WHO An interdisciplinary team of professionals, working together with parents and families, bears the primary responsibility for helping exceptional children learn. Teachers provide the instruction that is the heart of each child's IEP. These teachers include both general education and special education teachers—teachers "with a special certification who [are] specially trained to do special things with special students" (Zigmond, 2007, p. 151). Working with special educators and general education teachers are many other professionals (e.g., school psychologists, speech-language pathologists, physical therapists, counselors) and paraprofessionals (e.g., instructional assistants) who help provide the educational and related services that exceptional children need.

Pearson eText
Video Example 1.5
Featured Teacher Danielle Kovach and her colleague explain how their Café Kids program supports students' IEP goals in social skills, speech and language, and daily living skills.
http://youtu.be/fnRKp6ybSmg

WHAT Special education can sometimes be differentiated from general education by its curriculum—that is, by *what* is taught. Although all students with disabilities need access to and support in learning as much of the general education curriculum as they can, the IEP goals for some special education students will not be found in Common Core State Standards or the school district's curriculum guide. Some children need intensive, systematic instruction to learn skills that most children acquire without instruction.

Special educators often use the term **functional curriculum** to describe the knowledge and skills that some students with disabilities need in order to achieve as much success and independence as they can in school, home, community, and work settings. Skills such as dressing, toileting, making a purchase, and preparing a snack are critically important components of the special education received by many students with severe disabilities. Also, as discussed previously, some children are taught certain skills, such as reading Braille or using a voice-output device, to compensate for or reduce the effects of a disability.

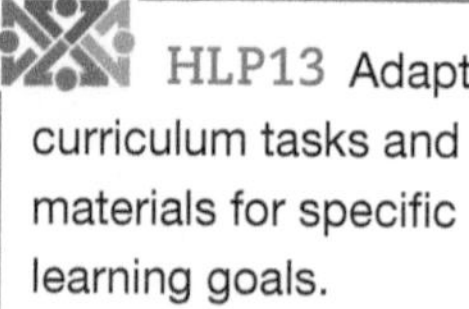

HLP13 Adapt curriculum tasks and materials for specific learning goals.

HOW Special education also differs from general education by its use of specialized or adapted materials and methods. This difference is obvious when you observe a special educator use sign language with students who are deaf. When watching a special educator gradually and systematically withdraw verbal and physical prompts while helping a student learn to perform the steps of a task, you may find the differentiated nature of special education instruction less obvious, but it is no less specialized.

Other features that often distinguish special education teaching from instruction in general education are its precision, focus, and intensity. For example, Mellard et al. (2011) identified 10 dimensions by which the intensity of instruction can be varied, including dosage (number of minutes, frequency, and duration of instruction), group size, number of response opportunities, and immediacy of feedback. See *Teaching & Learning*, "It's Good to Go Fast!"

TEACHING & LEARNING

It's Good to Go Fast! Fluency Building Promotes Student Achievement

What Is Fluency and Why Does It Matter? **Fluency** is the combination of accuracy and speed that characterizes highly skilled performance. Although accuracy, typically in the form of percent correct, is commonly used to assess student performance, fluency gives a more complete picture. Whereas two students might each complete a page of math problems with 100% accuracy, the one who finishes in 2 minutes is much more accomplished than the one who needs 7 minutes to solve the same problems. Fluent students perform skills automatically, without hesitations, as if by second nature.

Fluency has important functional implications. Many skills used every day must be performed at a certain rate or speed. A student who needs 5 minutes to read the directions on a worksheet that his classmates read in 1 minute may not be able to finish the task in the time allotted.

Students who are fluent with a particular skill are likely to exhibit (Stocker et al., 2019):

- *Better retention.* The ability to use the skill or knowledge at a later point in time.
- *Greater endurance.* The ability to stay engaged in the task for longer periods of time. Fluent performers are also less likely to be distracted by minor events in the environment.
- *Improved application and generalization.* The ability to apply new skills in novel situations. Students fluent with component skills (e.g., multiplication facts and subtraction) may learn composite skills (e.g., long division) more quickly.

Pearson eText
Video Example 1.6
Use fluency practice to improve students' skills while building their confidence and a supportive classroom community.

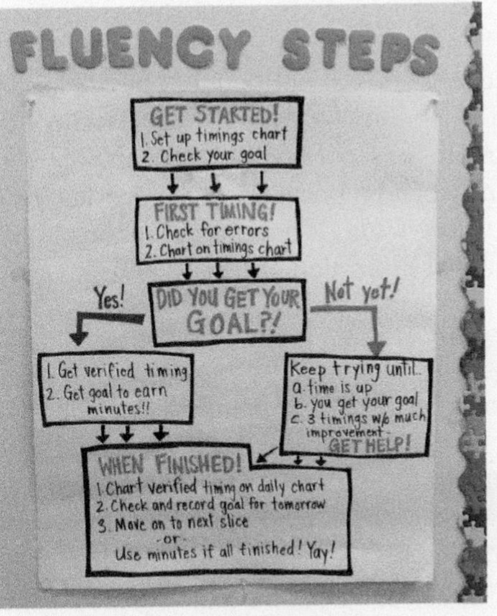

Source: William L. Heward

How Can I Promote Fluency? The three fluency-building techniques described next can be teacher-directed, peer-managed, or independent approaches.

HLP20 Provide intensive instruction.

Repeated Reading. With **repeated reading**, the student orally reads the same passage, usually three to five times per session and/or until a predetermined goal is met (e.g., 100 words per minute). With each successive reading, the student self-graphs and tries to increase the number of words read correctly per minute. When the student achieves the fluency criterion on a given passage, the teacher introduces a new, perhaps slightly more advanced, passage. Numerous studies show repeated reading improves oral reading fluency for elementary, middle, and secondary students with and without disabilities (Alber-Morgan et al., 2007; Kostewicz & Kubina, 2011; Lee & Yoon, 2017; Tam et al., 2006; Yurick et al., 2006).

Timed Practice Trials. Giving students the opportunity to perform a skill as many times as they can in a brief period is an excellent way to build fluency. Practice in the form of 1-minute timings helps students with and without disabilities achieve fluency with a wide range of academic (e.g., math facts), vocational (e.g., assembling tasks), and other skills (Fishley et al., 2012; Greene et al., 2018; Ramey et al., 2016).

SAFMEDS. Say All Fast a Minute Each Day Shuffled (**SAFMEDS**) consists of a deck of cards with a question, vocabulary term, or problem on one side of each card and the answer on the other. A student answers as many items in the deck as he can in 1 minute. The student looks at the question or problem, states the answer, flips the card over to reveal the correct answer, and

Pearson eText
Video Example 1.7
Skilled teachers make fluency building fun!

puts the card on either a "correct" or "incorrect" pile. Behaviorbabe (2020) provides examples and guidelines for making and using SAFMEDS.

Fluency-Building Tips and Guidelines

- **Build fluency during the practice stage of learning.** During the initial acquisition stage of learning, the student should focus on learning to perform the skill correctly. A student who tries to "go fast" before she can perform the skill correctly more often than incorrectly might end up "practicing errors" instead of building fluency. (Because they reveal the correct answer to each question, SAFMEDS can be used during the acquisition stage of learning.)
- **Keep the time for each fluency-building trial brief.** One minute is sufficient for most academic skills. Brief sprints of 10 seconds, then 15 seconds, 20 seconds, and so on, can help students gradually build their fluency (Kostewicz & Kubina, 2011).
- **Do fluency building daily.** For example, two or three 1-minute oral reading time trials could be conducted at the end of each day's lesson.
- **Make fluency building fun.** Time trials should not be presented as a test; they are a learning activity that can be approached like a game.
- **Feedback should emphasize proficiency** (number correct), not simply accuracy (percentage correct).
- **Encourage students to set personal goals and try to beat their best scores.**
- **Have students keep track of their progress** by self-graphing their best performance each day.

WHERE Special education can sometimes be identified (but not defined) by where it takes place. Although the majority of children with disabilities spend most of the school day in regular classrooms, others are in separate classrooms or separate residential and day schools. And many of the students in regular classrooms spend a portion of each day in a resource room, where they receive individualized instruction. Table 1.4 lists the definitions of six educational placements used by the U.S. Department of Education.

TABLE 1.4 Federal government's definitions of educational environments for students with disabilities

EDUCATIONAL SETTING	DEFINITION
Regular class	Student spends 80% or more of the school day inside regular class.
Resource room	Student spends between 40% and 79% of the school day inside regular class.
Separate class	Student spends less than 40% of the school day inside regular class.
Separate school	Student receives special education and related services at public expense for greater than 50% of the school day.
Residential facility	Student receives special education and related services in a public or privately operated residential facility in which children receive care or services 24 hours a day.
Homebound or hospital	Student receives special education and related services in a hospital or homebound program.

Source: Adapted from U.S. Department of Education. (2019a). *Forty-first annual report to Congress on the implementation of the Individuals with Disabilities Education Act*. Washington, DC: Office of Special Education and Rehabilitative Services.

Notes: The U.S. Office of Special Education Programs categorizes placements for students with disabilities based on the percentage of time spent in the regular class. Therefore, the federal government's definition of "regular classroom" placement enables a student to leave the classroom for supplemental instruction and related services for up to one full day per week. Conversely, a student with a "separate classroom" placement may receive some education within the regular classroom.

FIGURE 1.1 Percentage of School-Age Students with Disabilities Served in Different Educational Environments

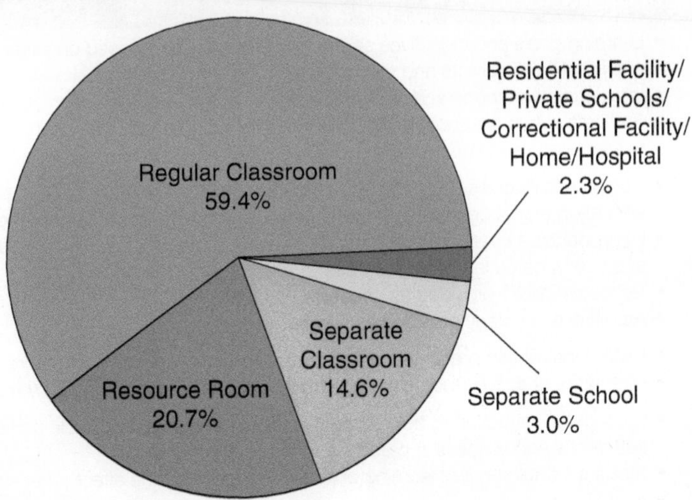

Source: From *U.S. Department of Education, IDEA Section* 618 Data Products (2020a).

Special educators also teach in settings not usually thought of as school. Early childhood special educators may spend much of their time teaching parents how to work with their infant or toddler at home. Special education teachers of students with severe disabilities often conduct community-based instruction, helping their students learn and practice functional daily living and job skills in the actual environments where these skills must be used.

Approximately four of five school-age children with disabilities received at least part of their education in regular classrooms during the 2018–2019 school year (see Figure 1.1). This includes 64% who were served in a regular classroom and about 18% who were served for part of each school day in a resource room, a special setting where a special educator provides individualized instruction. About one in seven children with disabilities is educated in separate classrooms within a regular public school and about 4% of school-age students with disabilities are educated in separate or private schools. Residential schools and non-school environments such as homebound or hospital programs combined serve less than 1% of all children with disabilities.

A Definition of Special Education

At one level, special education is a product of society's response to the needs of exceptional children and the rights of individuals with disabilities—a response brought about by parent advocacy, litigation, legislation, and self-advocacy by people with disabilities. At another level, special education is a profession with its own history, cultural practices, tools, and research base focused on the learning needs of exceptional children and adults. But at the level where exceptional children most meaningfully and frequently contact it, *special education is individually planned, specialized, intensive, goal-directed instruction.*

When practiced most effectively and ethically, special education is also characterized by research-based teaching methods guided by direct and frequent measures of student performance. Table 1.5 shows the fundamental dimensions and defining features of special education.

HLP6 Use student data, analyze instructional practices, and make necessary adjustments to improve student outcomes.

TABLE 1.5 Dimensions and defining features of special education instruction

DIMENSION	DEFINING FEATURES
Individually planned	• Learning goals and objectives selected for each student based on assessment results and input from parents and student • Instructional methods and materials selected and adapted for each student • Setting(s) where instruction will occur determined relative to opportunities for student to learn and use targeted skills
Specialized	• Sometimes involves unique or adapted teaching procedures seldom used in general education (e.g., constant time delay, token reinforcement, self-monitoring) • Incorporates a variety of instructional materials and supports to help student acquire and use targeted learning objectives • Related services provided as needed • Assistive technology provided as needed
Intensive	• Explicit instruction presented with attention to detail, precision, structure, and clarity • High rates of active student engagement, repeated practice, and systematic feedback
Goal directed	• Purposeful instruction to help student achieve the greatest possible personal self-sufficiency and success in present and future environments • Student's attainment of learning objectives determines the effectiveness of instruction
Research based	• Recognition that not all teaching practices are equally effective • Instructional programs and teaching procedures selected on basis of research support
Guided by student performance	• Systematic, ongoing monitoring of student progress • Results of direct and frequent measures of student learning inform modifications in instruction

Current and Future Challenges

Special educators have legitimate reason to feel good about the progress their field has made. Much has been accomplished in terms of making FAPE available to children with disabilities. Educators have learned much about how to effectively teach children with severe disabilities, whom many previously had assumed were incapable of learning. Special educators and families are working as partners on behalf of exceptional children. Technological advances have helped many students overcome challenges related to physical impairments and communication disabilities. The remaining chapters will introduce you to many of these advances.

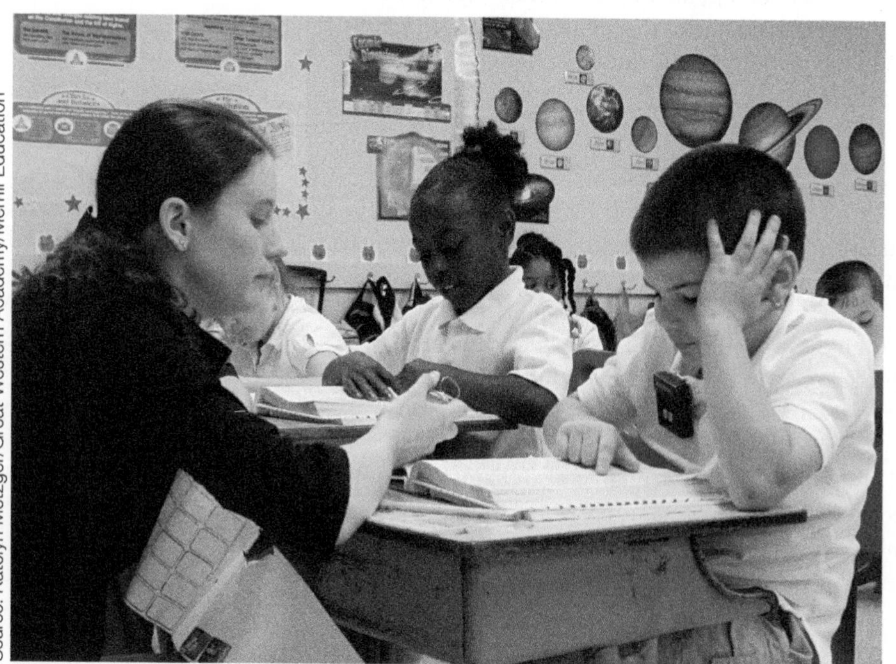

Source: Katelyn Metzger/Great Western Academy/Merrill Education

Special education is individually planned, specially designed, intensive instruction.

Of the many challenges special education faces, none is more critical than getting effective teaching practices more widely implemented so that students with disabilities can experience the greatest level of success and independence as they transition to adulthood. See *Transition: Next Year Is Now*, "Every Teacher Is a Transition Teacher."

Close the Research-to-Practice Gap

Researchers have discovered and continue to refine reliable, science-based knowledge about effective teaching practices for students with disabilities (Cook & Tankersley, 2013; Rumrill et al., 2020). For example, we know what features of early reading instruction will reduce the number of

Transition: Next Year Is Now

Every Teacher Is a Transition Teacher

Although increasing numbers of special education students are leaving high school for college or a job, a place to live on their own, and friends with whom to share recreation and leisure activities in the community, such positive outcomes elude far too many young adults with disabilities. Special education cannot be satisfied with improving students' achievement on classroom-based measures only. We must work equally hard to ensure that the education students receive during their school years prepares them to cope with and enjoy the multifaceted demands and opportunities of adulthood.

To achieve optimal outcomes for a student's independence and quality of life, transition planning and implementation must begin early and continue throughout elementary, middle, and high school. From preschool through the last year of high school, every teacher in a child's life can be a positive force for accomplishing ambitious long-term transition goals.

Meet Tyler Lewis: A Special Education Success Story

Let us introduce you to Tyler Lewis, a young man with autism who describes his experiences with school and work life in a series of videos. In elementary school, Tyler made friends, participated in extracurricular activities, and discovered his love for dancing and maps. In high school, Tyler was fully included in regular education classes, developed social skills and self-confidence singing in the choir, and began exploring vocational interests. Today, Tyler works full time at Kroger, a job he's held since graduating from high school. This retrospective of Tyler illustrates what effective transition looks like.

Tyler grew into a self-determined 24-year-old man who gets himself to work independently, leads the store safety team, and asks for help when he needs it. Tyler's father says he's an "utterly reliable, independent, and affectionate adult." The quality of life Tyler experiences today is the joint product of his own hard work and that of his teachers, specialists, and family members all striving for the same goals with skill, passion, and persistence throughout his school years.

Transition goals must emphasize self-advocacy and self-determination so that students are equipped to access what they need in all aspects of life, make responsible decisions, and reap the rewards of their accomplishments—now and in the future. Indeed, today's lessons are for the learner's benefit tomorrow; not only tomorrow, but next year's tomorrow and all the tomorrows in all of the years to come.

Each chapter in this text includes a "Transition: Next Year Is Now" box focusing on intervention strategies and supports that address a variety of transition needs across ages and exceptionalities. Topics include culturally responsive transition planning (Chapter 3), college success strategies (Chapter 5), dropout prevention (Chapter 6), self-advocacy (Chapter 8), friendship building (Chapter 9), self-management technology (Chapter 11), and even classroom jobs for preschoolers (Chapter 14).

As you continue reading this book, consider how you—and every teacher—can be a transition teacher.

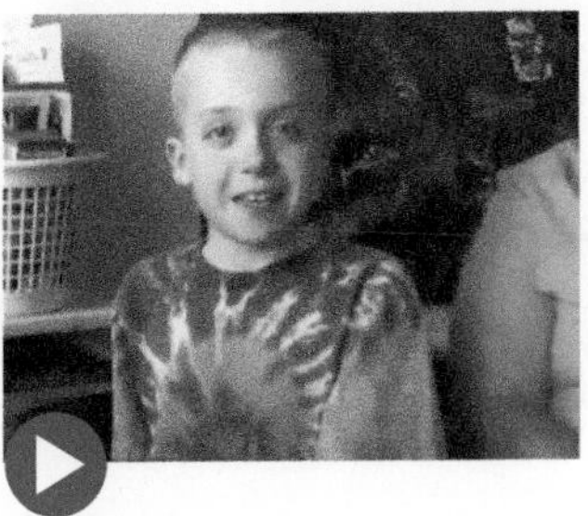

Pearson eText
Video Example 1.8
Tyler in fourth grade.

Pearson eText
Video Example 1.9
Tyler as a high school freshman.

Pearson eText
Video Example 1.10
Tyler as a young adult.

children who later develop reading problems (Simmons et al., 2011; Stahl et al., 2020), how to use a teaching tactic called **time delay** to help students with severe intellectual disabilities learn new skills (Horn et al., 2020; Seward et al., 2014), and the components of secondary special education programs that increase the success of youth with disabilities transitioning from school to adult life (Morgan & Riesen, 2016; Simmons & Flexer, 2013). Instructional practices supported by scientific research are described throughout this text and highlighted in the *Teaching & Learning* features.

Sadly, the instruction received by many students with disabilities not only fails to take advantage of that knowledge (e.g., Fuchs et al., 2015; McLeskey & Waldron, 2011; Zigmond & Kloo, 2011), but often embraces methods scientific studies have shown to be ineffective (Botts et al., 2008; Heward, 2003, 2005; Kauffman, 2011; Silvestri & Heward, 2016). Special educators must close the gap between their field's knowledge of evidence-based practices and the curriculum and instruction that most students with disabilities receive. Getting available knowledge to work in the classroom is by no means the only problem and challenge facing special education today. The field faces numerous other challenges, including the need to

- Improve the quality of pre- and in-service training programs to ensure that all special educators meet professional standards (CEC, 2020).
- Increase the availability and quality of special education programs for gifted and talented students.
- Help secondary students with disabilities transition to adult life.
- Apply advances in technologies that reduce or eliminate the disabling effects of physical and sensory impairments.
- Increase access to assistive technology that enhances the educational performance and personal independence of individuals with disabilities.
- Increase funding for special education. Teaching children with disabilities is expensive. Laws and regulations calling for special education and related services have limited value if the schools lack the financial resources to provide them. When Congress passed IDEA in 1975, it promised to provide federal funds for 40% of the "excess costs" of educating children with disabilities. Congress has never appropriated more than about 18% (National Council on Disability, 2018b). A bill being considered by the U.S. House of Representatives Education and Workforce Committee (H.R.551, IDEA Full Funding Act) would increase federal funding to the states from the 17.7% level of funding in fiscal year 2015 to 40% by 2025.
- Improve the behavior and attitudes of people without disabilities toward those with disabilities.
- Open more opportunities for individuals with disabilities to participate in the full range of residential, employment, and recreational options available to people without disabilities.

Only time will tell how successful special education will be in meeting these challenges. And, of course, special education does not face these challenges alone. General education, adult service agencies (e.g., vocational rehabilitation and social work), medical researchers and practitioners, government agencies, and society as a whole must all help find solutions.

ADVICE FROM THE FEATURED TEACHER by Danielle Kovach

Sail the Seven Cs of Special Education

Source: Danielle Kovach

A special educator's day is always an adventure. No matter how challenging things may get, these seven tips can help new teachers succeed in the classroom.

- ***Climate.*** Create an environment that emanates love, safety, happiness, and mutual respect to help address the social and emotional learning needs for all students. Don't just tell students you care for them; show them with your daily actions: greet each student every morning, make eye contact, use encouraging words, and keep a positive attitude.
- ***Collaboration.*** To collaborate effectively, you should be open to giving and receiving ideas. This collaboration encompasses all stakeholders in a child's education: teachers, administrators, parents, paraprofessionals, therapists, child study team members, and the student.
- ***Communication.*** Keep an open, ongoing dialogue with parents through phone calls, conferences, email, and communication journals. Consider using digital communication

tools such as websites or social media (but know and follow your school's policies on these platforms).

- ***Construction.*** Construct equitable and flexible lesson plans and assessments. Tasks should be challenging and engaging and build upon each student's current skills and preferences. My students know that everyone gets what is needed to be successful.
- ***Consistency.*** If you say something, do it. Don't waiver or deviate. Before you set an ultimatum, consider the consequences of your actions. Are you really going to take away recess for the entire year?
- ***Classroom management.*** Research strategies and methods that have been proven to provide effective classroom management. Give your students time to learn your system but be prepared with a backup plan if it does not work. Not all approaches work with every child. Consider individual behavior plans for students who need additional support. Use what motivates students and consider the age appropriateness of the plan.
- ***Constantly strive to improve.*** Learn to teach; teach to learn. These six words should embody who you are as a teacher. Be a lifelong learner. Constantly seek more effective ways to teach your students. Further your knowledge by completing graduate courses. Stay current by attending workshops, webinars, and conferences. Most important, continually learn from your students. They are the true educators.

Key Terms and Concepts

assistive technology
at risk
disability
due process
exceptional children
fluency
free appropriate public education (FAPE)
functional curriculum
handicap
impairment
incidence
individualized education program (IEP)
individualized family service plan (IFSP)
least restrictive environment (LRE)
manifestation determination
primary prevention
repeated reading
SAFMEDS
secondary prevention
tertiary prevention
time delay
universal design for learning (UDL)

Summary

Who Are Exceptional Children?

- Exceptional children are those whose physical attributes and/or learning abilities differ from the norm, either above or below, to such an extent that an individualized program of special education is necessary.
- *Impairment* refers to the reduced function or loss of a particular body part or organ.
- *A disability* exists when an impairment limits a person's ability to perform certain tasks in the same way that most people do.
- *Handicap* refers to the problems a person with a disability encounters when interacting with the environment.
- A child who is *at risk* is not currently identified as having a disability but is considered to have a greater than usual chance of developing one if intervention is not provided.

How Many Exceptional Children Are There?

- About 7.4 million children with disabilities, age 3 through 21 years, received special education services in 2018–2019.
- Children in special education represent approximately 9.5% of the school-age population.
- Children receiving special education under the two largest disability categories, learning disabilities and speech or language impairments, make up 54% of all school-age special education students.

Why Are Exceptional Children Labeled and Classified?

- Some educators believe that disability labels have negative effects on the child and on others' perceptions of the child and can lead to exclusion; others believe that labeling is a necessary first step to providing needed intervention and is important for comparing and communicating about research findings.

- Alternative approaches to classifying exceptional children that do not rely on disability labels have been proposed (e.g., classifying students by the curriculum and skill areas they are learning).

Why Are Laws Governing the Education of Exceptional Children Necessary?

- Before the 1970s, many states had laws permitting public schools to deny enrollment to children with disabilities. When local public schools began to accept a measure of responsibility for educating certain exceptional students, a philosophy of segregation prevailed.
- Special education was strongly influenced by the case of *Brown v. Board of Education* in 1954, in which the U.S. Supreme Court declared that education must be made available to all children on equal terms.
- In the class action lawsuit *PARC* (1972), the court ruled that all children with intellectual disabilities were entitled to FAPE and that placements in regular classrooms and regular public schools were preferable to segregated settings.
- All children with disabilities have the right to equal protection under the law, which has been interpreted to mean the right to a free appropriate public education in the least restrictive environment (LRE).
- All children with disabilities and their parents have the right to due process under the law, which includes the rights to be notified of any decision affecting the child's educational placement, to have a hearing and present a defense, to see a written decision, and to appeal any decision.

The Individuals with Disabilities Education Act

- IDEA, first enacted by Congress in 1975 and amended and reauthorized most recently in 2004, encompasses six major principles:
  - *Zero reject.* Schools must educate all children with disabilities. This principle applies regardless of the nature or severity of the disability.
  - *Nondiscriminatory identification and evaluation.* Schools must use nonbiased, multifactored methods of evaluation to determine whether a child has a disability and, if so, whether special education is needed.
  - *Free appropriate public education.* All children with disabilities shall receive FAPE at public expense. An IEP must be developed and implemented for each student with a disability that addresses the student's unique needs by providing specially designed instruction and related services based on peer-reviewed research to the extent practicable.
  - *Least restrictive environment.* Students with disabilities must be educated with children without disabilities to the maximum extent appropriate, and they should be removed to separate classes or schools only when the nature or severity of their disabilities is such that they cannot receive an appropriate education in a regular classroom.
  - *Procedural safeguards.* Schools must follow certain procedures to safeguard and protect the rights and interests of children with disabilities and their parents.
  - *Parent participation and shared decision making.* Schools must collaborate with parents and with students with disabilities in the design and implementation of special education services.
- IDEA requires states to provide special education services to all preschoolers with disabilities age 3 to 5 years. This law also makes federal money available to states that develop early intervention programs for disabled and at-risk infants and toddlers from birth through age 2 years. Early intervention services must be coordinated by an IFSP.
- IDEA requires that schools provide related services and assistive technology that a child with a disability needs to access and benefit from special education.
- IDEA encourages the use of UDL to ensure that new curricular materials and learning technologies accommodate the learning needs of the widest possible range of individuals, including children with disabilities.
- Court cases have challenged the way in which particular school districts implement specific provisions of IDEA. Rulings from the various cases have established the principle that each student with disabilities is entitled to a personalized program of instruction and related services that will enable the student to benefit from an education in as integrated a setting as possible.
- The Javits Gifted and Talented Children's Education Act provides financial incentives to states for developing programs for gifted and talented students.
- Section 504 of the Rehabilitation Act forbids discrimination in all federally funded programs, including educational and vocational programs, on the basis of disability.
- The ADA extends the civil rights protections for people with disabilities to private sector employment, all public services, public accommodations, transportation, and telecommunications.
- ESSA mandated challenging academic standards for all students; appropriate accommodations for assessments, including assistive technology; improved school environments by reducing bullying and aversive discipline practices; and that special education teachers are licensed in special education.

What Is Special Education?

- Special education consists of purposeful intervention efforts at three levels: preventive, remedial, and compensatory.
- Special education is individually planned, specialized, intensive, goal-directed instruction. When practiced most effectively and ethically, special education is also characterized by research-based teaching methods guided by direct and frequent measures of student performance.

Current and Future Challenges

- Special education faces many challenges, but none is more important than reducing the gap between what scientific research tells us about effective teaching practices and what exceptional children experience in the classroom.

Chapter 2
Planning and Providing Special Education Services

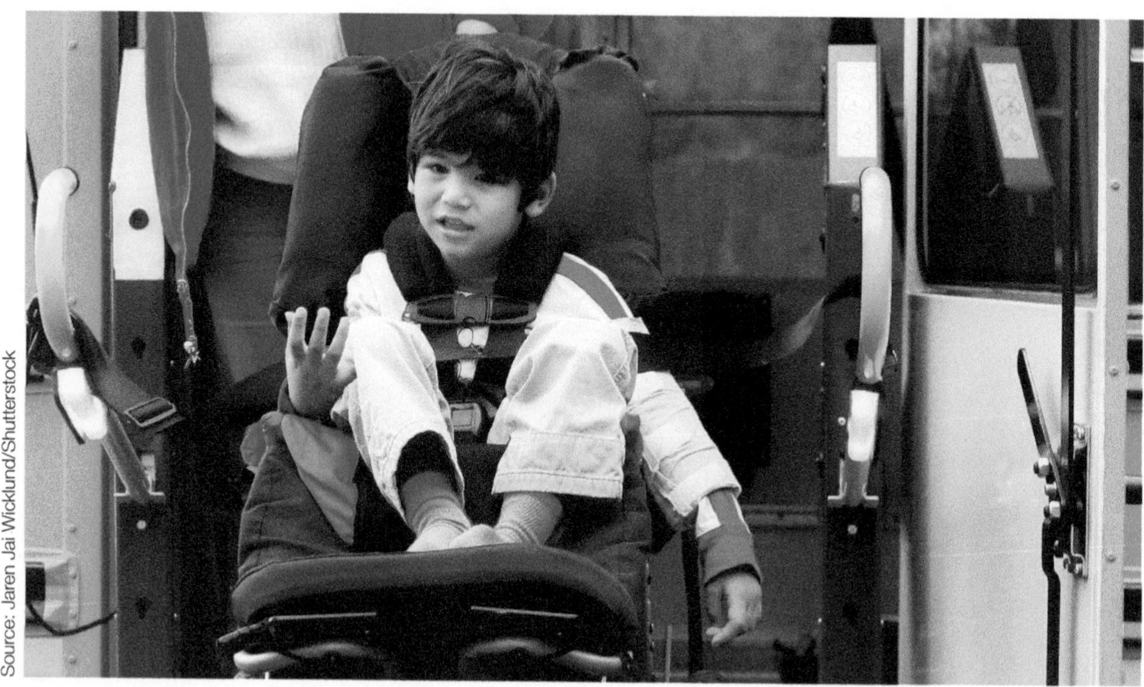
Source: Jaren Jai Wicklund/Shutterstock

Learning Outcomes

After reading this chapter and completing the embedded activities, you should be able to

- **2.1** Identify and describe the function of each step of the special education process.
- **2.2** Define *disproportionate representation*, identify groups that are over- and underrepresented in special education, and explain why this is problematic.
- **2.3** Compare and contrast three teaming models.
- **2.4** List the required components of an individualized education program.
- **2.5** Define *least restrictive environment*, and explain how the least restrictive environment for a given student is not necessarily the regular classroom.

Featured Teacher

Keisha Whitfield

Jefferson Elementary School, Gahanna-Jefferson Public Schools, Gahanna, OH

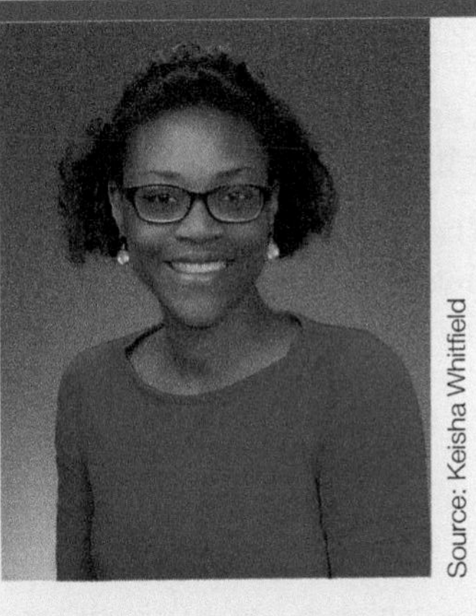
Source: Keisha Whitfield

I spend 80% of each day supporting my students in regular classrooms and the remaining time providing intensive individual and small-group instruction in a resource classroom. I enjoy co-teaching in regular classrooms because I have the opportunity to work with teachers to plan and implement lessons based on state standards and the needs of all the students in the classroom. The amount of planning and collaboration involved in effectively executing this model is immense, but the overall results are well worth the effort. I also like teaching my own small-group classes in which I can provide intensive intervention and really get to know and connect with each of my students.

Most of my students have deficits in academic skills; they are working below grade level in reading, writing, and/or math. I also have many students with communication challenges who receive speech-language services. In general, my students have good working relationships with their teachers and peers, but I do have a few students who struggle with making and keeping friends, participating in unstructured activities without altercations, and inviting peers to join in on games or activities during unstructured time.

Especially with the adoption of the Common Core State Standards, the rigorous academic demands today are a challenge for students with and without disabilities. It is my job, as a special educator, to help students persevere and find their strengths no matter what tasks are placed before them. I spend a great deal of time breaking large projects into smaller chunks, locating informational texts on different reading levels, scaffolding lessons, and helping students get organized. It's a huge task, one I continue to grapple with every day.

Fortunately, the rewards outweigh the challenges. A few years ago, I had a classroom of students with a 0% pass rate on our state-mandated achievement test. They were all reading below grade level and, not surprisingly, hated to read. That year we worked on developing comprehension, fluency, written expression, goal setting, and a growth mindset. By the end of the school year, all of my students made significant gains, and several passed the state reading test! It was an amazing school year, one that continues to serve as a motivating benchmark for me.

Education, Teaching Credentials, and Experience

- *B.S., political science and public administration, Central State University, 2001*
- *M.Ed., special education, The Ohio State University, 2007*
- *Certifications: Ohio, mild-moderate intervention specialist, K–12; Orton-Gillingham Specialist*
- *14 years of teaching experience*

Content Extension 2.1

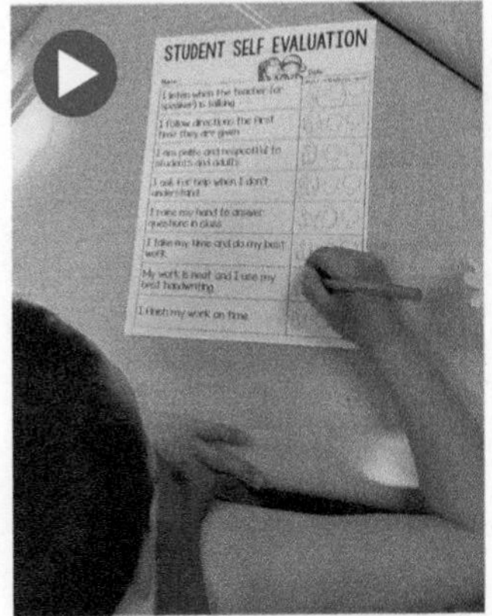

Featured Teacher Keisha's students prepare for IEP meetings by completing self-evaluation activities.

SPECIAL EDUCATION IS DEFINED IN CHAPTER 1 AS INDIVIDUALLY PLANNED, specialized, intensive, goal-directed instruction. But how do teachers know what adaptations to curriculum and instruction an individual child needs? And toward what goals should that specialized instruction be directed? In this chapter, we examine the process by which special education is planned, devoting particular attention to four critical aspects of educating students with disabilities: (a) teaming and collaboration among professionals, (b) the individualized education program (IEP), (c) least restrictive environment (LRE), and (d) inclusive education.

The Process of Special Education

Learning Outcome 2.1 Identify and describe the function of each step of the special education process.

The Individuals with Disabilities Education Act (IDEA) mandates a sequence of events schools must follow to identify and educate children with disabilities. Although the federal regulations that state and local education agencies must follow are lengthy and sometimes redundant, the process they proscribe is intended to answer the following common-sense questions:

- Which students might need special education?
- Is this student eligible for special education? In other words, does this particular child have a disability that adversely affects his educational performance?
- What specific educational needs result from the child's disability?
- What specialized methods of instruction, accommodations, modifications, related services, and/or supplementary supports are necessary to meet those needs so the student can achieve increased levels of academic achievement and functional performance to thrive in the school community?
- What educational setting is the LRE in which the student can receive an appropriate education?
- Is special education helping? If not, what changes should be made to the program?

Figure 2.1 identifies the major steps in the sequence of planning, implementing, and evaluating special education and highlights some of the key procedures, elements, and requirements of each step.

Prereferral

A child who may need special education usually comes to the school's attention because (a) a teacher or parent reports concern about differences in learning, behavior, or development, or (b) the results of a screening test suggest a possible disability. Screening tests are relatively quick, inexpensive, and easy-to-administer assessments given to large groups of children to find out who *might* have a disability and need further testing. For example, most schools administer vision screening tests to all elementary children.

Before referring the child for formal testing and evaluation for special education, most schools initiate a **prereferral intervention** process. Although IDEA does not require prereferral intervention, local educational agencies may use up to 15% of their IDEA funds "to develop and implement coordinated, early intervening services ... for students in kindergarten through grade 12 (with a particular emphasis on students in kindergarten through grade 3) who have not been identified as needing special education or related services but who need additional academic and behavioral support to succeed in a general education environment" (PL 108-466, Sec. 613[f][1]).

Prereferral intervention is most often conducted by a building-based **intervention assistance team** (also called *student support team, teacher assistance team*, or *problem-solving team*), which helps teachers devise and implement interventions for students who are experiencing academic or behavioral difficulties in the regular classroom. Intervention assistance teams typically consist of the building principal or designated administrator; school nurse; guidance counselor; several general education teachers with experience across grade levels; and one or more special education teachers, at least one of whom is skilled in designing behavior intervention plans. The classroom teacher describes for the team the academic and/or behavior challenges the student has been experiencing, and the group "brainstorms not only on the possible etiology of the problem, but more importantly, on possible solutions to it" (Spinelli, 2012, p. 6). The team develops an intervention strategy and assists the classroom teacher in implementing and evaluating it with student progress data.

FIGURE 2.1 Planning, Providing, and Evaluating Special Education: The Basic Steps

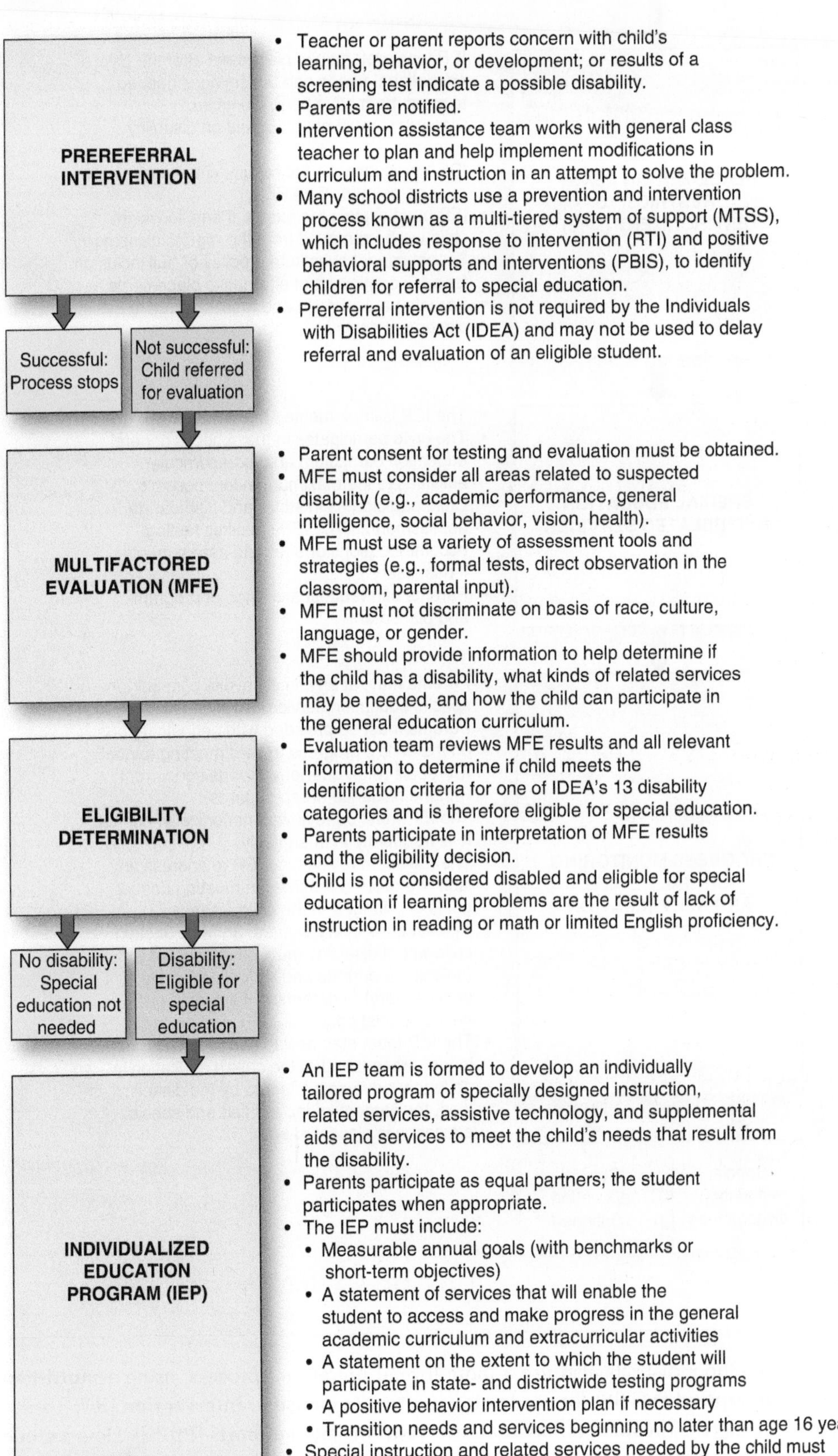

PREREFERRAL INTERVENTION
• Teacher or parent reports concern with child's learning, behavior, or development; or results of a screening test indicate a possible disability.
• Parents are notified.
• Intervention assistance team works with general class teacher to plan and help implement modifications in curriculum and instruction in an attempt to solve the problem.
• Many school districts use a prevention and intervention process known as a multi-tiered system of support (MTSS), which includes response to intervention (RTI) and positive behavioral supports and interventions (PBIS), to identify children for referral to special education.
• Prereferral intervention is not required by the Individuals with Disabilities Act (IDEA) and may not be used to delay referral and evaluation of an eligible student.
Successful: Process stops
Not successful: Child referred for evaluation
MULTIFACTORED EVALUATION (MFE)
• Parent consent for testing and evaluation must be obtained.
• MFE must consider all areas related to suspected disability (e.g., academic performance, general intelligence, social behavior, vision, health).
• MFE must use a variety of assessment tools and strategies (e.g., formal tests, direct observation in the classroom, parental input).
• MFE must not discriminate on basis of race, culture, language, or gender.
• MFE should provide information to help determine if the child has a disability, what kinds of related services may be needed, and how the child can participate in the general education curriculum.
ELIGIBILITY DETERMINATION
• Evaluation team reviews MFE results and all relevant information to determine if child meets the identification criteria for one of IDEA's 13 disability categories and is therefore eligible for special education.
• Parents participate in interpretation of MFE results and the eligibility decision.
• Child is not considered disabled and eligible for special education if learning problems are the result of lack of instruction in reading or math or limited English proficiency.
No disability: Special education not needed
Disability: Eligible for special education
INDIVIDUALIZED EDUCATION PROGRAM (IEP)
• An IEP team is formed to develop an individually tailored program of specially designed instruction, related services, assistive technology, and supplemental aids and services to meet the child's needs that result from the disability.
• Parents participate as equal partners; the student participates when appropriate.
• The IEP must include:
• Measurable annual goals (with benchmarks or short-term objectives)
• A statement of services that will enable the student to access and make progress in the general academic curriculum and extracurricular activities
• A statement on the extent to which the student will participate in state- and districtwide testing programs
• A positive behavior intervention plan if necessary
• Transition needs and services beginning no later than age 16 years
• Special instruction and related services needed by the child must be identified without regard to cost or availability in the district.

(Continued)

FIGURE 2.1 (Continued)

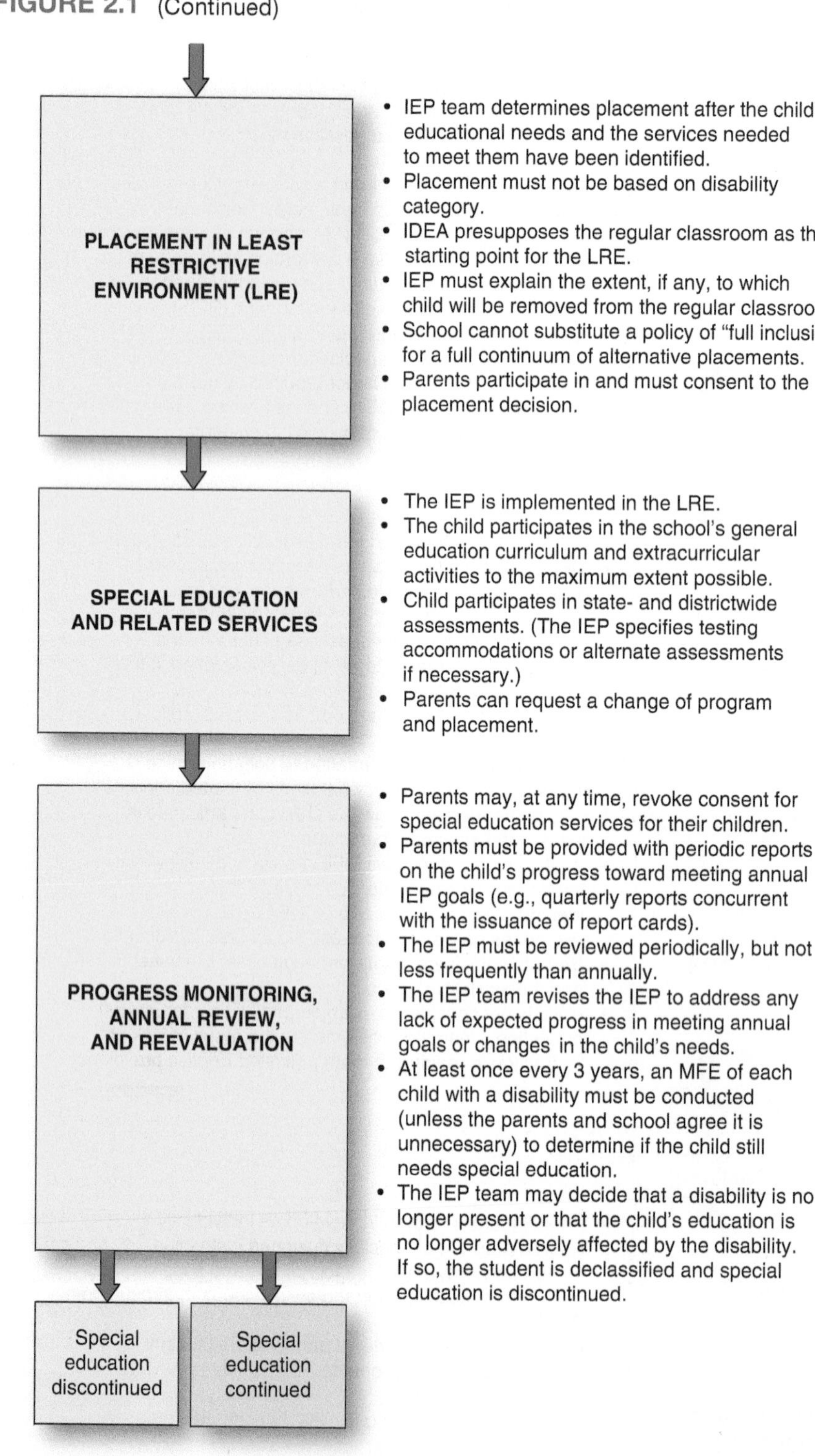

PLACEMENT IN LEAST RESTRICTIVE ENVIRONMENT (LRE)
• IEP team determines placement after the child's educational needs and the services needed to meet them have been identified.
• Placement must not be based on disability category.
• IDEA presupposes the regular classroom as the starting point for the LRE.
• IEP must explain the extent, if any, to which child will be removed from the regular classroom.
• School cannot substitute a policy of "full inclusion" for a full continuum of alternative placements.
• Parents participate in and must consent to the placement decision.
SPECIAL EDUCATION AND RELATED SERVICES
• The IEP is implemented in the LRE.
• The child participates in the school's general education curriculum and extracurricular activities to the maximum extent possible.
• Child participates in state- and districtwide assessments. (The IEP specifies testing accommodations or alternate assessments if necessary.)
• Parents can request a change of program and placement.
PROGRESS MONITORING, ANNUAL REVIEW, AND REEVALUATION
• Parents may, at any time, revoke consent for special education services for their children.
• Parents must be provided with periodic reports on the child's progress toward meeting annual IEP goals (e.g., quarterly reports concurrent with the issuance of report cards).
• The IEP must be reviewed periodically, but not less frequently than annually.
• The IEP team revises the IEP to address any lack of expected progress in meeting annual goals or changes in the child's needs.
• At least once every 3 years, an MFE of each child with a disability must be conducted (unless the parents and school agree it is unnecessary) to determine if the child still needs special education.
• The IEP team may decide that a disability is no longer present or that the child's education is no longer adversely affected by the disability. If so, the student is declassified and special education is discontinued.
Special education discontinued
Special education continued

Many school districts also use a more formal prereferral process, using a **multi-tiered system of support (MTSS)** for academic concerns (**response to intervention [RTI]**) and/or behavior concerns (**positive behavioral interventions and supports [PBIS]**). How a student responds to increasingly intensive, scientifically validated instruction and behavioral supports can help determine whether the child's struggles to learn and meet behavioral expectations are the result of insufficient instruction or a disability. "If the child responds poorly to validated instruction, the assessment eliminates instructional quality as a viable explanation for poor ... growth and instead provides evidence of a disability. For children who do respond nicely, RTI serves a critical prevention function" (L. S. Fuchs et al., 2007, p. 13).

MTSS requires that scientifically validated instruction and supports be present within each of the tiers. See *Teaching & Learning,* "Choral Responding: Good Noise in the Classroom," for an example of a validated instructional technique that encourages active student engagement and is particularly useful in Tier 1 instruction. MTSS also relies on effective teamwork (e.g., Avant & Swerdlik, 2016). Strategies for collaborating effectively within teams are discussed later in the chapter and in Chapter 3. RTI is discussed further in Chapter 5, and PBIS is discussed further in Chapter 6.

HLP18 Use strategies to promote active student engagement.

TEACHING & LEARNING

Choral Responding: Good Noise in the Classroom

What Is Choral Responding? **Choral responding (CR)**—students responding orally in unison to questions presented by the teacher—is the simplest, quickest way to increase student participation during group lessons.

In contrast to a rowdy class of off-task students, choral responding provides "good noise": the sound of students' voices engaged in active learning. Although teachers have used CR since the days of the one-room schoolhouse, research on its effects is a more recent phenomenon. Peer-reviewed studies reporting positive effects of CR on active student responding, learning, and on-task behavior have been published since the late 1970s (Heward & Wood, 2015; Twyman & Heward, 2018).

Teachers can use CR with any curriculum content that meets three criteria: (a) each question, problem, or item presented has only one correct answer; (b) each question is answered with a brief oral response; and (c) the material can be presented at a lively pace. CR has been used in lessons to teach basic academic skills, subject matter content, and a series or sequence of steps to solve higher level problems (e.g., math word problems).

Pearson eText
Video Example 2.1
Teachers use choral responding to review skills, set an enthusiastic tone for the day, and check students' understanding while learning new concepts.

How Do You Use Choral Responding?

- *Give clear directions and model the activity.* Tell students the type of questions you will ask and model one or two trials by acting out the roles of teacher and students.
- *Provide a brief thinking pause.* Let the complexity of the question or problem and students' relative level of mastery determine the duration of the pause. If a thinking pause longer than 4 or 5 seconds is required, break the content into smaller chunks.
- *Signal students to respond.* Use a clear, consistent auditory or visual cue for student response (e.g., "Class," a finger snap, or a hand or arm movement). Saying, "Get ready" immediately before signaling promotes unison responding.
- *Provide feedback.* When you hear only correct answers, confirm or praise and immediately present the next question. When you hear one or two errors, (a) confirm the majority response and restate the correct answer (e.g., "Yes. Lithium is an alkali metal") and (b) repeat the question a few trials later (e.g., "What type of element is lithium?"). When more than a few incorrect responses are heard, (a) state the correct answer with a *brief* explanation (e.g., "Remember lithium is the first of six alkali metals on the periodic table."), (b) immediately repeat the question for CR, and (c) repeat the question several trials later.
- *Intersperse individual turns.* Now and then, instead of signaling a CR, call on an individual student. To increase the likelihood all students are listening and ready to answer, present the question before calling the student's name.
- *Maintain a lively pace.* When teachers conduct CR at a fast pace, students make more responses, respond with higher accuracy, and are more on-task.
- *Have fun.* Students enjoy CR team games and matching the sound of their responses to the volume, tone, and rhythm of the teacher's voice. For example, when teaching skip counting by multiples of 3, the teacher might say a number and point to one half of the class, which then quickly chorally responds with the next multiple in the sequence. Each team chorally responds "back and forth" (e.g., left side, "3"; right side, "6"; left side, "9" ...) until one side makes a mistake.

Pearson eText
Video Example 2.2
Students have fun with choral responding!

Source: Lord and Leverett/Pearson Education

Students who respond well to scientifically validated instruction during prereferral intervention need not be evaluated for special education.

Regardless of its form, prereferral intervention is designed to achieve the following:

- Provide immediate instructional and/or behavior management assistance to the child and teacher.
- Reduce the frequency of special education placement for children whose learning or behavior problems are the result of inappropriate instruction.
- Prevent relatively minor problems from worsening to a degree that would eventually require special education.
- Strengthen teachers' capacity to intervene effectively on a diversity of problems, thereby reducing the number of future referrals for special education.
- Prevent the costly and time-consuming process of assessment for special education eligibility by solving the problems that originally caused teachers or parents to be concerned about the child.
- Provide IEP teams with valuable baseline data for planning and evaluating special education and related services for students who are referred and found eligible for special education.

A school district may not use MTSS or other prereferral intervention approaches to delay formal evaluation and assessment of a student who is eligible for special education. At any time during the prereferral process, parents have the right to request their child receive a comprehensive evaluation for identification and eligibility for special education services.

Evaluation and Eligibility Determination

> HLP4 Use multiple sources of information to develop a comprehensive understanding of a student's strengths and needs.

IDEA requires that all children suspected of having a disability receive a nondiscriminatory **multifactored evaluation (MFE)**.

The school or the parents can request an evaluation. Regardless of the source of the referral, the parents must be notified of the school's intent to test their child, and they must give their consent for the evaluation. Within 60 days of receiving parental consent, the school district must complete the evaluation to determine whether the child has a disability and identify the educational needs of the child (IDEA, Sec. 614[a][1][C]).

IDEA is explicit in describing some do's and don'ts that school districts must follow when evaluating a child for special education:

In conducting the evaluation, the local education agency shall—

A. use a variety of assessment tools and strategies to gather relevant functional, developmental, and academic information, including information provided by the parent, that may assist in determining—

i. whether the child is a child with a disability; and

ii. the content of the child's individualized education program, including information related to enabling the child to be involved in and progress in the general education curriculum, or, for preschool children, to participate in appropriate activities;

B. not use any single measure or assessment as the sole criterion for determining whether a child has a disability, or determining an appropriate educational program for the child; and

C. use technically sound instruments that may assess the relative contribution of cognitive and behavioral factors, in addition to physical or developmental factors.

Additional Requirements—Each local educational agency shall ensure that

A. assessments and other evaluation materials used to assess a child—

i. are selected and administered so as not to be discriminatory on a racial or cultural basis;

ii. are provided and administered in the language and form most likely to yield accurate information on what the child knows and can do academically, developmentally, and functionally, unless it is not feasible to so provide or administer;

iii. are used for purposes for which the assessments or measures are valid and reliable;

iv. are administered by trained and knowledgeable personnel; and

v. are administered in accordance with any instructions provided by the producer of such assessments

B. the child is assessed in all areas of suspected disability;

C. assessment tools and strategies that provide relevant information that directly assists persons in determining the educational needs of the child are provided; and

D. assessments of children with disabilities who transfer from one school district to another school district in the same academic year are coordinated with such children's prior and subsequent schools, as necessary and as expeditiously as possible, to ensure prompt completion of full evaluations. (PL 108-446, Sec. 614 [2])

The MFE is conducted by a school-based *multidisciplinary evaluation team*, sometimes called a *student study team*, which includes the child's parents. The team examines the test results and all other relevant information to determine if the child has a disability that adversely affects his or her educational performance and is therefore entitled to special education. IDEA stipulates that a child shall not be identified with a disability if his learning difficulties are the result of a "lack of appropriate instruction in reading . . .; lack of instruction in math; or limited English proficiency" (PL 108-446, Sec. 614[b][4]). An MFE must do more than provide information on the existence of a disability for determining eligibility for special education. IDEA requires that evaluation reports also provide information about the child's educational needs and how to meet them.

> **HLP5** Interpret and communicate assessment information with stakeholders to collaboratively design and implement educational programs.

Program Planning

If the evaluation team determines that a child has a disability that is adversely affecting his or her educational performance, an IEP is developed. The IEP team determines the what (learning goals and objectives), how (specialized instruction and related services), who (teachers and related-service providers), and when (frequency of specialized instruction and related services) of a child's special education program. The IEP is the centerpiece of the special education process. A detailed description of the IEP appears later in this chapter.

Placement

After the IEP team determines the child's educational needs and the special education and related services necessary to meet those needs, the team then determines an educational setting where the child can receive an appropriate education in the LRE. Where children with disabilities are taught is one of the most debated and often misunderstood aspects of special education and IDEA, and it is discussed in depth later in this chapter and throughout the text.

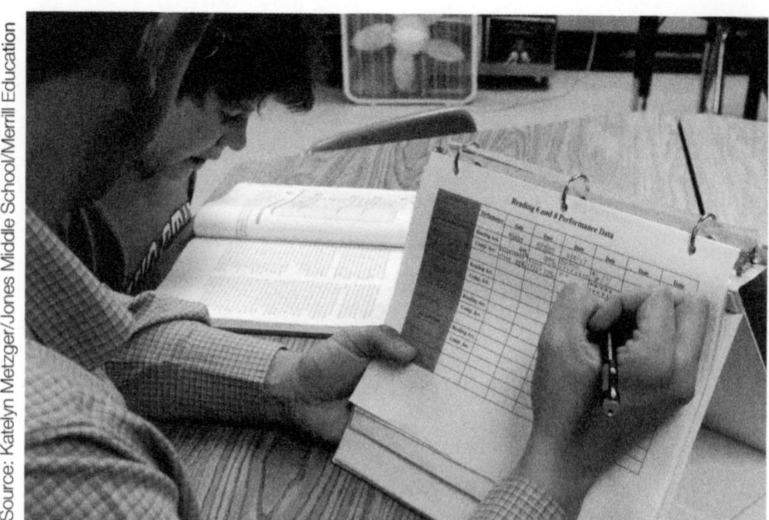
Source: Katelyn Metzger/Jones Middle School/Merrill Education

Direct and frequent measures of student performance provide the most meaningful information about student progress and the effectiveness of instruction.

Progress Monitoring, Annual Review, and Reevaluation

In addition to being specialized, intensive, and goal directed, special education is also continuously evaluated.

ONGOING MONITORING OF PROGRESS No matter how appropriate the IEP goals, the planned instruction, and the identified related services, the document's usefulness is limited without ongoing monitoring of student progress. Schools are accountable for providing a free appropriate public education (FAPE) to all children with disabilities, and accountability requires measurement. Direct and frequent measurement of student performance (see Chapter 4) provides the most meaningful information about student progress and the effectiveness of instruction (Berkeley & Riccomini, 2011; Tindal et al., 2016).

> HLP6 Use student assessment data, analyze instructional practices, and make necessary adjustments that improve student outcomes.

ANNUAL REVIEW A child's IEP is not intended to be a permanent document. All aspects of an IEP—the annual goals and outcomes, delivery of specially designed instruction and related services, appropriateness of placement—must be thoroughly reviewed at least annually. The team revises the IEP to address any lack of expected progress in meeting annual goals or changes in the child's needs.

REEVALUATION For some students, the specially designed instruction and related services they receive may ameliorate a problem (e.g., speech therapy for an articulation disorder) or accommodate an impairment (e.g., a prosthesis or mobility device) such that they are no longer eligible for special education. At least once every 3 years, the school must conduct an MFE of each child with a disability (unless the parents and school agree it is unnecessary) to determine if the child still needs special education. If the IEP team decides a disability is no longer present or the child's education is no longer adversely affected by the disability, special education discontinues.

Although special education is sometimes characterized as a "one-way street" down which "it's relatively easy to send children ... but they rarely return" (Finn et al., 2001, p. 339), a nationwide study of more than 11,000 students in special education age 6 to 12 years found 17% of the students had been declassified after 2 years and were no longer receiving special education services (SRI International, 2005). Another study based on a nationally representative sample of children found that 16% of preschoolers who had received special education services were declassified after 2 years (Daley & Carlson, 2009).

In 2008, IDEA regulations were amended to give parents the right to revoke their consent for special education for their child at any time. After receipt of parents' written request for revocation, the school must cease the provision of all special education and related services to the child.

Disproportionate Representation of Students from Culturally and Linguistically Diverse Groups

Learning Outcome 2.2 Define *disproportionate representation*, identify groups that are over- and underrepresented in special education, and explain why this is problematic.

Disproportionate representation exists when a particular group receives special education at a rate significantly higher or lower than would be expected based on the proportion of the general student population that group represents. Culturally and linguistically diverse students are both overrepresented and underrepresented in special education, depending on the group and disability category. Table 2.1 shows the special education risk ratios for students

TABLE 2.1 Risk ratios by race/ethnicity for children age 6 through 21 years served under IDEA in the 2017–2018 school year

RACE/ETHNICITY	PERCENTAGE OF RACIAL/ ETHNIC GROUP SERVED (%)	RISK RATIO
American Indian or Alaska Native	15.1	1.6
Asian	4.3	0.5
Black or African American	12.0	1.4
Hispanic/Latino	9.4	1.0
Native Hawaiian or Other Pacific Islander	13.8	1.5
White	8.5	0.9
Two or more races	8.6	1.0

Note: Percentages and ratios rounded to nearest one tenth.

Source: U.S. Department of Education. (2019a). *Forty-first annual report to Congress on the implementation of the Individuals with Disabilities Education Act* (Exhibit 26, p. 48). Washington, DC: Author.

from different racial/ethnic backgrounds. A *risk ratio* is the relative likelihood of a member of a given group to be, in this case, receiving special education, compared to members of the general population. A risk ratio of 1.0 means the number of students identified with a given disability matches the proportion of the overall student population represented. A risk ratio greater than 1.0 indicates overrepresentation; a risk ratio less than 1.0 indicates underrepresentation.

Native American students, Native Hawaiian or Other Pacific Islander students, and Black or African American students are overrepresented in the special education population. Asian students are underrepresented in the special education population. Hispanic, White, and multi-racial students are generally represented among the special education population at an overall rate close to their proportion of the resident school-age population.

Some disparities are especially evident when the data are examined by disability category. The risk ratios for African American students, for instance, are particularly high for the emotional disturbance (risk ratio = 2.0) and intellectual disability (risk ratio = 2.2) categories (U.S. Department of Education, 2019). For decades, reports and census studies have shown three groups of students—African American, Hispanic American, and Native American—have consistently been underrepresented in gifted education programs (Donovan & Cross, 2002; Ford, 1998; Peters et al., 2019).

Is this disproportionate representation appropriate? Identification and classification for special education should be based solely on the presence of a disability that adversely affects the child's educational performance. The fact that students are identified as having a disability is not, in itself, a problem. All students with disabilities that adversely affect their educational performance have the right to special education services, whatever their racial, ethnic, or linguistic backgrounds. Disproportionate representation is problematic if it means children have been wrongly placed in special education programs that deny them appropriate educational interventions that match their full learning capacities, stigmatize them, or segregate them (Cartledge et al., 2016). For example, African American students with disabilities are more likely to be placed in more restrictive educational settings than are White students with disabilities (National Council on Disability, 2018c).

Disproportionate representation is also a problem if it means students with disabilities are overlooked because of their membership in a racial or ethnic minority group, resulting in their being denied access to needed special education (De Valenzuela et al., 2006). Racial disparity has also been found in the autism category, in which African American and Hispanic children are underrepresented (Travers et al., 2014).

The causes of disproportionate representation have been difficult to pinpoint and often controversial (Cartledge & Dukes, 2009; Connor et al., 2019; Ford & Toldson, 2015; Harry & Klingner, 2006, 2007). Are students from some cultural and linguistic groups more likely to have a disability than are White children? For example, a much greater proportion of students from some cultural groups are born to mothers without access to maternal health care and live in poverty—factors that are associated with an increased incidence of disability. In 2016, 45% of the nation's

Black and Hispanic public school students attended high-poverty schools (based on federal eligibility criteria for free or reduced-price school lunch) (National Center for Education Statistics, 2019a). By comparison, only 8% of White students attended such high-poverty schools. Or, as some researchers have suggested, do inherent problems in the referral and placement process bias the identification of minority children (Harry & Klingner, 2006)? The answer to these controversial and complex questions is that probably both explanations are partly true.

Recognizing and Combating Cultural and Racial Bias in Referral and Identification Procedures

Understanding the reasons for the disproportionality phenomenon in special education is not simple. Numerous factors must be considered, and educators have identified three areas as integral to this problem: (a) cultural differences between teachers and students and families, which may lead to biased referrals; (b) inaccurate assessment of students from some cultural or linguistic backgrounds; and (c) lack of culturally responsive curriculum and instructional practices.

Today's teachers are mostly White (79%) and female (76%) (National Center for Education Statistics, 2019b) and are teaching an increasingly diverse student population. For example, with respect to the overrepresentation of African American students in the emotional and behavior disorders category, some researchers contend that an African American behavioral style conflicts with White teachers' expectations for classroom behavior (Hale, 2001; Kunesh & Noltemeyer, 2019). "When African American students 'behave' in modes affirmed and sanctioned by dimensions of African American culture (Boykin, 1983) and those modes are unfamiliar to or misinterpreted by teachers, most of whom are white, their behavior is often perceived as inappropriate" (Webb-Johnson, 2003, p. 5).

Bias in the assessment process may contribute to the problem of disproportionate representation in special education. The methods used to identify students for services are an inexact science, and many authors have argued the likelihood of obtaining valid and unbiased assessment results is lower when the student being assessed is from a traditionally marginalized cultural group (Ford, 2010; Newkirk-Turner & Johnson, 2018; Utley & Obiakor, 2001).

Inappropriate referral to special education can occur if educators and school psychologists confuse cultural differences with disabilities. Fiedler and colleagues (2008) have developed a checklist to help school personnel identify and consider relevant external factors (e.g., accountability demands, school district priorities) and internal factors (e.g., beliefs of teachers, school practices at the referral, assessment, and eligibility determination stages) that lead to disproportionate representation. See Chapter 8 and Klingner and Eppolito (2014) for further discussion of distinguishing differences from disabilities.

Understanding the complex issues related to diversity requires that educators understand the problems related to (a) cultural incongruity between teachers and students and families, (b) the assessment and referral process in special education, and (c) ineffective instructional and discipline practices (Kunesh & Noltemeyer, 2019; Salend & Garrick Duhaney, 2005; West et al., 2007). To better meet the needs of students with disabilities from diverse backgrounds, schools should address three issues. First, staff must become culturally responsive to students and families (Cartledge & Kourea, 2008; Harry, 2008). Second, staff must implement appropriate assessment strategies for determining the educational needs of culturally diverse students. Third, educators should implement culturally responsive practices that support a multicultural approach to curriculum and instruction (Banks & Banks, 2016; Lo et al., 2014; Yuan & Jiang, 2019).

Source: blue jean images/Getty Images

Teachers are most effective when curriculum and instruction are responsive to the cultural, ethnic, and linguistic diversity of their students.

Collaboration and Teaming

Learning Outcome 2.3 Compare and contrast three teaming models.

Special education is a team game. For instance, the team that plans, delivers, and evaluates the program of specially designed instruction and related services to meet the unique needs of 10-year-old "Jessica" might include the following: the third-grade teacher who works with Jessica in the regular classroom; the speech-language pathologist who meets with Jessica's teacher each week to co-plan language activities; the special education teacher who provides Jessica with intensive reading instruction each day in the resource room and collaborates with her general education teacher on instructional accommodations for Jessica in math and science; the adapted physical education teacher who works with Jessica in the gymnasium; and Jessica's parents, who help with homework and keep everyone informed of their daughter's progress at home. Without open, honest, and frequent communication and collaboration between and among the members of Jessica's team, the quality of her education is likely to suffer.

Collaboration

HLP1 Collaborate with professionals to increase student success.

Collaboration has become a common and necessary practice in special education. Teachers are better able to diagnose and solve learning and behavior problems in the classroom when they work together. Three ways in which team members can work collaboratively are through coordination, consultation, and teaming (Bigge et al., 1999).

Coordination is the simplest form of collaboration, requiring only ongoing communication and cooperation to ensure that services are provided in a timely and systematic fashion. Although an important and necessary element of special education, coordination does not require service providers to share information or specifics of their efforts with one another. Fortunately for Jessica, the four educators on her IEP team do much more than simply coordinate who is going to work with her when.

In *consultation*, team members provide information and expertise to one another. Consultation is traditionally considered unidirectional, with the expert providing assistance and advice to the novice. However, team members can, and often do, switch roles from consultant to consultee and back again. Jessica's third-grade teacher, for example, receives expert advice from the speech-language pathologist on strategies for extending Jessica's language expression during cooperative learning groups but takes the consultant's role when explaining details of the science curriculum to Jessica's resource room teacher.

Teaming

Each step of the special education process involves a group of people who must work together for the benefit of a child with special needs. For special education to be most effective, these groups must become functioning and effective teams (Correa et al., 2005; Janney et al., 2015). Teaming is the most difficult level of collaboration to achieve; it also pays the most dividends. Teaming "bridges the two previous modes of working together and builds on their strengths while adding the component of reciprocity and sharing of information among all team members through a more equal exchange" (Bigge et al., 1999, p. 13).

Source: Laura Bolesta/Millennium/Merrill Education

Teaming helps educators identify and solve problems.

Although the team approach has many variations, each member of a team

Pearson eText
Video Example 2.3
Effective related-service providers collaborate with teachers on interdisciplinary and transdisciplinary teams.

generally assumes certain clearly assigned responsibilities and recognizes the importance of learning from, contributing to, and interacting with the other members of the team. Many believe the consensus and group decisions arising from a team's involvement provide a form of insurance against erroneous or arbitrary conclusions in the complex issues that face educators of students with disabilities. In practice, three team models have emerged (McGonigel et al., 1994)—multidisciplinary, interdisciplinary, and transdisciplinary.

MULTIDISCIPLINARY TEAMS *Multidisciplinary teams* are composed of professionals from different disciplines who work independently of one another. Each team member conducts assessments, plans interventions, and delivers services. Teams that operate according to a multidisciplinary structure risk the danger of not providing services that recognize the child as an integrated whole; they must be careful not to "splinter" the child into segments along disciplinary lines. (An old saying described the child with disabilities as giving "his hands to the occupational therapist, his legs to the physical therapist, and his brain to the teacher" [Williamson, 1978].) Another concern is the lack of communication among team members.

INTERDISCIPLINARY TEAMS *Interdisciplinary teams* are characterized by formal channels of communication between members. Although each professional usually conducts discipline-specific assessments, the interdisciplinary team meets to share information and develop intervention plans. Each team member is generally responsible for implementing a portion of the service plan related to his or her discipline.

TRANSDISCIPLINARY TEAMS The highest level of team involvement, but also the most difficult to accomplish, is the *transdisciplinary team*. Members of transdisciplinary teams seek to provide services in a uniform and integrated fashion by conducting joint assessments, sharing information and expertise across discipline boundaries, and selecting goals and interventions that are discipline free (Delano et al., 2020; Friend & Cook, 2017). Members of transdisciplinary teams also share roles (often referred to as *role release*); in contrast, members of multidisciplinary and interdisciplinary teams generally operate in isolation and may not coordinate their services to achieve the integrated delivery of related services. Regardless of the team model, team members must learn to put aside professional rivalries and work collaboratively for the benefit of the student (Zigmond et al., 2011).

Individualized Education Program

Learning Outcome 2.4 List the required components of an individualized education program.

IEPs are "the heart and soul of IDEA and of a FAPE for children who have disabilities" (Bateman, 2017, p. 102). IDEA requires that educators develop and implement an IEP for each student with disabilities between the ages of 3 and 21 years. (Educators develop an *individualized family service plan* [IFSP] for each infant and toddler [from birth through age 2 years] with disabilities. See Chapter 14 for a description of the IFSP.) IDEA is specific about who is to develop the IEP and what it must include.

IEP Team

Each IEP must be the product of the collaborative efforts of the members of an **IEP team**, the membership of which is specified in IDEA as the following:

Pearson eText
Video Example 2.4
Winning IEP teams depend on input and expertise from multiple players. https://www.youtube.com/watch?v=wTQvd_bKTOo

The term "individualized education program team" or "IEP team" means a group of individuals composed of—

1. the parents of a child with a disability;
2. not less than 1 regular education teacher of the child (if the child is, or may be, participating in the regular education environment);
3. not less than 1 special education teacher, or where appropriate, at least 1 special education provider of the child;

4. a representative of the local education agency who—
   i. is qualified to provide, or supervise the provision of, specially designed instruction to meet the unique needs of children with disabilities;
   ii. is knowledgeable about the general curriculum; and
   iii. is knowledgeable about the availability of resources of the local education agency;
5. an individual who can interpret the instructional implications of evaluation results, who may be a member of the team described in clauses (2) through (6);
6. at the discretion of the parent or the agency, other individuals who have knowledge or special expertise regarding the child, including related service personnel as appropriate; and
7. whenever appropriate, the child with a disability. (PL 108-446, Sec. 614 [d][1][B])

IEP Components

Each IEP must include the following components:

1. A statement of the child's present levels of academic achievement and functional performance, including—
   a. how the child's disability affects the child's involvement and progress in the general education curriculum;
   b. for preschool children, as appropriate, how the disability affects the child's participation in appropriate activities; and
   c. for children with disabilities who take alternate assessments aligned to alternate achievement standards, a description of benchmarks or short-term objectives;
2. A statement of measurable annual goals, including academic and functional goals, designed to—
   a. meet the child's needs that result from the child's disability in order to enable the child to be involved in and make progress in the general education curriculum; and
   b. meet each of the child's other educational needs that result from the child's disability;
3. A description of how the child's progress toward meeting the annual goals described in subclause (2) will be measured and when periodic reports on the progress the child is making toward meeting the annual goals (such as through the use of quarterly or other periodic reports, concurrent with the issuance of report cards) will be provided;
4. A statement of the special education and related services and supplementary aids and services, based on peer-reviewed research to the extent practicable, to be provided to the child, or on behalf of the child, and a statement of the program modifications or supports for school personnel that will be provided for the child—
   a. to advance appropriately toward attaining the annual goals;
   b. to be involved in and make progress in the general education curriculum in accordance with subclause (1) and to participate in extracurricular and other nonacademic activities; and
   c. to be educated and participate with other children with disabilities and nondisabled children in the activities described in this subparagraph;
5. An explanation of the extent, if any, to which the child will not participate with nondisabled children in the regular class and in the activities described in subclause (4)(c);
6. (a) statement of any individual appropriate accommodations that are necessary to measure the academic achievement and functional performance of the child on State and districtwide assessments consistent with section 612(a)(16)(A); and (b) if the IEP team determines that the child shall take an alternate assessment on a particular State or districtwide assessment of student achievement, a statement of why—

   (aa) the child cannot participate in the regular assessment; and

   (bb) the particular alternate assessment selected is appropriate for the child;

7. The projected date for the beginning of the services and modifications described in subclause (4), and the anticipated frequency, location, and duration of those services and modifications. (PL 108-446, Sec. 614 [d][1][B]) IEPs for students age 16 years and older must include information on how the child's transition from school to adult life will be supported:
8. Beginning not later than the first IEP to be in effect when the child is 16, and updated annually thereafter—
   a. appropriate measurable postsecondary goals based upon age-appropriate transition assessments related to training, education, employment, and, where appropriate, independent living skills;
   b. the transition services (including courses of study) needed to assist the child in reaching those goals; and
   c. beginning not later than 1 year before the child reaches the age of majority under State law, a statement that the child has been informed of the child's rights under this title, if any, that will transfer to the child on reaching the age of majority under section 615(m). (PL 108-446, Sec. 614 [d][1][A][i])

When developing a child's IEP, the IEP team must consider the following factors:

1. *General.* The IEP team must consider (i) the strengths of the child; (ii) the concerns of the parents for enhancing the education of their child; (iii) the results of the initial or most recent evaluation of the child; and (iv) the academic, developmental, and functional needs of the child.
2. *Consideration of special factors.* The IEP team must—
   i. In the case of a child whose behavior impedes the child's learning or that of others, consider the use of positive behavioral interventions and supports, and other strategies, to address that behavior;
   ii. In the case of a child with limited English proficiency, consider the language needs of the child as those needs relate to the child's IEP;
   iii. In the case of a child who is blind or visually impaired, provide for instruction in Braille and the use of Braille unless the IEP team determines, after an evaluation of the child's reading and writing skills, that instruction in Braille or the use of Braille is not appropriate for the child;
   iv. Consider the communication needs of the child, and in the case of a child who is deaf or hard of hearing, consider the child's language and communication needs; and
   v. Consider whether the child needs assistive technology devices and services. (PL 108-446, Sec. 614 [d][3][A & B])

IEP Functions and Formats

An IEP spells out where the child is, where she should be going, how she will get there, how long it is expected to take, and how to tell if and when she has arrived. An IEP provides teachers and families with the opportunity—and the responsibility—to first be realistic about the child's needs and goals and then to be creative about how to meet them. Being realistic does not mean taking a pessimistic or limited view of the child's current capabilities or potential to reach improved levels of academic achievement or functional performance; rather, it means analyzing how specially designed instruction and related services can help the child get from her present levels of performance to future goals.

The IEP is also a measure of accountability for teachers and schools. Whether a particular school or educational program is effective will be judged, to some extent, by how well it is able to help children meet the goals and objectives set forth in their IEPs. Similar to other professionals, teachers are being called on to demonstrate effectiveness, and the IEP provides one way for them to do so. The school district is legally bound to provide the special education and related services identified in the IEP, and the school must "offer an IEP that shows reasonable calculation of progress for the child in light of their circumstances" (Couvillon et al., 2018, p. 292).

IEP formats vary widely across school districts, and schools may exceed the requirements of the law and include additional information. Bateman and Linden (2012) cautioned against overreliance on standardized forms and computers for creating

IEPs. "Forms by their nature interfere significantly with true individualization.... [A] proper form will contain all the required elements in the simplest way possible, allowing for the most flexibility and creativity" (p. 65). Figure 2.2 shows portions of an IEP for Lucas, a fourth grader with learning disabilities and ADHD.

One of the most difficult tasks for the IEP team is determining how inclusive the IEP document should be. It is important for educators and parents to recognize that an IEP is not the same as a curriculum. "IEP objectives are not comprehensive enough to cover the entire scope and sequence of what a student is to learn. The content taught by most special educators goes

FIGURE 2.2 Portions of an IEP for a Fourth Grader with Learning Disabilities and ADHD

PRESENT LEVELS OF ACADEMIC ACHIEVEMENT & FUNCTIONAL PERFORMANCE	ANNUAL GOALS AND OBJECTIVES/ BENCHMARKS	SPECIAL EDUCATION & RELATED SERVICES
Lucas has a strong vocabulary. He uses interesting and age-appropriate words when he speaks and writes, and he understands complex words and content, when text is read to him. He has mastered high-frequency sight words and decodes phonetically regular, single-syllable words. Lucas enjoys reading about baseball players and sea creatures (especially sharks). His standardized reading test scores show relative strength in comprehension and weakness in reading fluency. In third grade, Lucas earned passing grades in all classes, but his lowest grades were in reading. On the state test, he passed the math portion but failed reading (score was very close to passing). When given a 4th-grade reading passage, Lucas currently reads 55 words per minute (WPM) with 4 to 6 errors. His errors generally consist of skipping "little" words (e.g., *the, an*) and getting stuck on polysyllabic words (e.g., *recognize, appreciated*). He needs to work on reading fluency and decoding of longer words.	When given a 4th-grade reading passage, Lucas will read 90 words per minute with no more than 2 errors, across three consecutive passages. *Benchmarks* When given a 4th-grade reading passage, Lucas will read... 1a. 64 WPM with no more than 2 errors, across three passages 1b. 73 WPM with no more than 2 errors, across three passages 1c. 82 WPM with no more than 2 errors, across three passages 1d. 90 WPM with no more than 2 errors, across three passages	Small-group, individualized instruction for reading Explicit, systematic phonics instruction focused on polysyllabic words Explicit, systematic instruction in Greek & Latin roots Timed repeated readings of grade level passages with feedback and opportunities for self-graphing of fluency
Lucas is interested in baseball, sharks, and helping his grandfather in the garden. He has relative strength in math and is especially engaged when his teacher presents "the problem of the day" (a challenging math problem presented at the start of each math block). When interested in the task and/or when working with peers, Lucas is generally on task at rates comparable to his peers. His time on task in math, art, PE, and music are better than in other subjects. When given reading, language arts, science, and social studies tasks to complete independently and quietly, he often chats with peers, doodles on his paper, or fiddles with small toys from his pockets. When given an academic task to complete independently, Lucas is currently on task about 40% of the time. Observations of peers in his class indicate typical time on-task during similar activities ranges from 60% to 90%.	Given an academic assignment to complete independently in 20 min, Lucas will be on-task at least 75% of the time and complete at least 90% of the assignment across 8 out of 10 observations. *Objectives* Given instructions to complete an academic assignment in 20 minutes, Lucas will... 2a. restate the teacher's directions for 8/10 observations 2b. begin the task within 30 sec for 8/10 observations 2c. raise his hand to show the teacher his progress or ask for help 1–2 times for 8/10 observations	Explicit instruction in self-management techniques (e.g., using a timer, recruiting teacher assistance) Positive reinforcement system to reward Lucas when he is on task Preferential seating (near teacher & away from distractions, such as doors & high-traffic areas in the classroom) Use of a cue card (reminders to stay on task) taped to his desk and inside of his planner Monthly meetings with school counselor to practice self-management skills

Note: A complete IEP would also include results from the student's multi-factored evaluation, progress monitoring plan, participation in regular classroom, accommodations (including for state and district assessments), dates of services, and transition plan for students ages 16 and older. Goals may be broken down into benchmarks (as illustrated with Lucas' reading goal) or objectives (as illustrated with Lucas' behavior goal). For more examples of goals, see Chapter 1. For discussion of goals appropriate for students with more significant disabilities, see Chapter 12. For examples of transition-focused IEPs for older students, see Chapter 15.

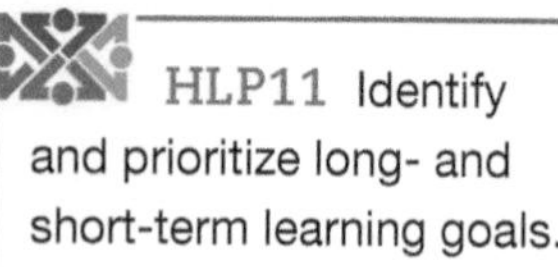
HLP11 Identify and prioritize long- and short-term learning goals.

far beyond what is written in the IEP. Sometimes special educators try to incorporate an entire curriculum into the IEP, resulting in an overly long, detailed IEP" (Browder, 2001, p. 35).

Remembering that special education is "specially designed instruction" will help IEP teams determine the content of a student's IEP (Strickland & Turnbull, 1993). Adaptations to curriculum and instruction that differ significantly from the range of adaptations normally made for general education students or that the IEP team deems necessary to remediate or compensate for the adverse affects on the child's educational performance should be considered "specially designed instruction" and be included as part of the student's IEP.

Each area of functioning that is adversely affected by the student's disability must be represented by an annual goal on the IEP. Annual goals are statements of what the IEP team believes the student can accomplish in 1 year if the special services provided are effective.

Too often, IEP teams' hard work and best intentions for a child's progress are muddled at best, or lost altogether, by IEP goals that are impossible to measure. Figure 2.3 presents

FIGURE 2.3 Turning Nonmeasurable IEP Goals into Measurable Goals

"Measurable" is the essential characteristic of an Individualized Education Program (IEP) goal or objective. When a goal isn't measurable, it cannot be measured. If it cannot be measured, it violates the Individuals with Disabilities Act and may result in denial of a free appropriate public education to the child. A measurable goal contains a given or condition, the learner's performance, and the desired level of performance or criteria. The learner's performance must be an observable, visible, or countable behavior.

Not Observable or Countable	Observable and Countable
enjoying literature	reading orally
understanding history	constructing a timeline
becoming independent	dressing oneself
respecting authority	speaking to adults without vulgarities
improving, feeling, knowing	pointing, drawing, identifying, writing, etc.

Not-Measurable Goals Made Measurable

Rebecca will increase her active listening skills. This goal has no criterion to indicate the level at which Rebecca must perform to reach the goal, nor does it specify the behavior of "active listening." We could not tell if Rebecca has "improved" without knowing the previous level of her skills. Thousands and thousands of goals have used this "student will improve X" format. It is not measurable, not acceptable, and not useful. To improve this goal, we must ask what the writer meant by "active listening." Perhaps "following oral directions" would be an acceptable visible learner performance. If so, this measurable version is probably closer to what was intended: "Given 5 simple, two-step oral directions such as 'Fold your paper and hand it in,' Rebecca will correctly complete 4 directions."

Sara will make wise choices in her use of leisure time. Sara may, indeed, "make wise choices," but we really can't see her doing this. This goal does not describe a visible learner performance and does not include a criterion. Perhaps the writer meant something like "Sara will attend a supervised, school-sponsored extracurricular activity at least once a week."

Beth will show an appropriate level of upper body strength. This goal is easily fixed. The goal writer may well have meant, "Beth will pass the XYZ test of upper body strength at her age level."

The following two objectives appeared under the totally nonmeasurable goal of "develop functional academics" on the IEP for Alex, a highly intelligent 16-year-old nonreader who has severe dyslexia and a high level of anger and confusion about why he can't read, write, or spell.

Given 10 words, Alex shall group letters and pronounce letter sounds in words with 80% accuracy. How do we determine whether Alex has met this progress marker? Clearly, we give 10 words to Alex (perhaps a list) and ask him to do something, but what? Is it possibly as simple as "Alex, would you read these aloud"? That's a good guess, but does the list look like "sit, bun, log, cat," or does it look like "exegesis, ophthalmology, entrepreneur"? What is 80% accuracy in reading the list? If the word "palace" were read as "place," "tentative" as "tantative," or "when" as "where," what percentage of accuracy do we assign to each effort? Or did the writer really mean that Alex should read 80% of the words accurately? How long a time frame is Alex to be allowed to read the words? Perhaps the objective writer meant something like this: "Given 10 unfamiliar, regular CVC words, Alex will decode 9 of 10 correctly in 20 seconds."

Alex will research the history and culture of the given country with 80% accuracy. Remembering that Alex reads at a mid-first-grade level and is presently working on letter sounds and decoding, what are we to make of this objective? If Alex comes to school tomorrow morning and says, "I researched the history and culture of China without any mistakes last night," are we to check off the objective as complete? Is that what the writer intended? What about something like this: "Given a 1-hour PBS video on the history and culture of China and a tape recorder, after viewing the tape, Alex will dictate and record 10 things he learned about China, with no more than one factual error."

Source: Adapted from Bateman, B. D., & Herr, C. M. (2006). *Writing measurable IEP goals and objectives* (pp. 153–155). Verona, WI: Attainment Company, Inc. Used by permission.

some examples of nonmeasurable IEP goals and how IEP teams might change them into measurable goals.

IEP Problems and Potential Solutions

Since its inception, the IEP process has been problematic. J. J. Gallagher (1984) wrote that the IEP is "probably the single most unpopular aspect of the law, not only because it requires a great deal of work, but also because the essence of the plan itself seems to have been lost in the mountains of paperwork" (p. 228). Nearly 30 years later, Bateman and Linden (2012) expressed a similar opinion:

> Sadly, many IEPs are horrendously burdensome to teachers and other professionals and nearly useless to parents and children. Far from being a creative, flexible, data-based, and individualized application of the best of educational interventions to a child with unique needs, the typical IEP is "empty," devoid of specific services to be provided (p. 71).

Studies of actual IEPs seem to support such harsh descriptions. For example, Grigal et al. (1997) examined IEPs for high school students and found that transition-related goals included vague outcomes (e.g., "will think about best place to live," "will explore jobs"), no evaluation procedures, and very few adaptations in activities or materials. Properly including all of the mandated components in an IEP is no guarantee that the document will guide the student's learning and teachers' teaching in the classroom, as intended by IDEA. Although most educators support the idealized concept of the IEP, inspection of IEPs often reveals inconsistencies between what is written on the document and the instruction that students experience in the classroom (S. W. Smith & Brownell, 1995).

Although IDEA requires parents to participate in IEP meetings and encourages student participation, research on parent and student involvement in the IEP process has produced mixed results (Test, 2004). In a study of 109 middle school and high school IEP meetings, Martin et al. (2006) concluded that students' "presence can at best be viewed as tokenism because of the very low levels of student engagement and low student [expression of] opinions of their IEP meetings" (p. 197).

HLP2 Organize and facilitate effective meetings with professionals and families.

On the bright side, numerous studies have shown that students with widely varying disabilities can learn to be actively involved in the IEP process, even to the point of leading the meeting (e.g., Arndt et al., 2006; Diegelmann & Test, 2018). Resources, curricula, and strategies for involving students and their families in their IEPs are available from Davis and Cumming (2019a); Giangreco et al. (2011); Konrad (2008); Turnbull et al. (2015); and Van Dycke et al. (2006). See *Transition: Next Year Is Now,* "Whose IEP Is This?"

General education teachers also benefit from instruction in the IEP process. In a study of 393 middle school and high school IEP meetings, general education teachers rated themselves lower than all other IEP meeting participants, including students, on the extent to which they helped make decisions and knew what to do next (Martin et al., 2004). General education teachers ranked second lowest (only to students) in knowing the reason for the meetings, talking at the meetings, feeling comfortable saying what they thought, understanding what was said, and feeling good about the meeting.

Transition: Next Year Is Now

Whose IEP Is This?

Why Should We Increase Student Involvement in the IEP Process?

There are at least three good reasons to involve students in the development and implementation of their IEPs. First, active participation in the IEP process gives students opportunities to practice a range of self-determination skills necessary for successful transition to postsecondary life, including self-awareness, goal setting, self-advocacy, and decision making. Second, when IEP teams listen to and seriously consider students' input, the teams are likely to develop more meaningful IEPs, ones in which the students are invested. Third, IDEA requires that students be present at their IEP meetings "whenever appropriate." In virtually all cases, it is "appropriate" to have students involved in at least a portion of the process.

How Can We Involve Students in the IEP Process?

Konrad (2008) suggests students may be involved in five stages: developing background knowledge, planning, drafting, meeting, and implementing. Developing background knowledge includes helping students learn about the IEP process, their disabilities, and their legal rights. During the planning stage, students can take an active role in the assessment process, learning more about their own strengths and needs. They may also practice their written communication skills by writing vision statements for themselves and inviting meeting participants. As teachers begin drafting the IEP, students may be involved by writing about their own present level of academic achievement and functional performance, perhaps even as a first-person narrative. Students may be in charge of taking their IEP drafts home to share with their families before the upcoming meeting. At the actual IEP meeting, students can participate in a variety of ways, ranging from making introductions to leading the entire meeting. Students need to prepare and practice in advance so their participation in the meeting is meaningful and productive. Many free and low-cost ready-to-use materials are available for preparing students to participate in their IEP meetings (see Mazzotti et al., 2018; Uphold et al., 2007).

During implementation, the final and most important stage of the IEP process, students can become their own data collectors and self-advocates. If they have been actively involved in the other stages, they know their needs, goals, and accommodations, so now they can reflect on their progress and ask for what they need. Their involvement in this stage then sets the stage for more active involvement in the planning stage of the next IEP and helps prepare students to advocate on their own behalf when they transition into postsecondary environments.

Here are 10 steps Featured Teacher Keisha Whitfield follows to prepare her elementary students to participate in the IEP process:

1. I provide my students with background knowledge. I teach them what an IEP is and why they have one.
2. We look at their current IEPs together. We review their current goals and objectives, discussing where they are currently and emphasizing how much growth they have made. I try to help them identify areas of strength and weakness. The easiest way to do this is to review with them their IEP progress reports.
3. Each of my students completes a behavior and academic self-evaluation.
4. I interview each of my students and create a "vision board." As the student provides responses, I write key words and draw pictures on chart paper to use at the IEP meeting.
5. Each student creates a "SMART" goal for himself and benchmark steps to reach that goal.
6. My older students create a PowerPoint show to present at the meeting. Younger students create a video reviewing their vision board.
7. We practice by role-playing how to participate in and/or lead the IEP meeting. I provide students with individualized checklists before the meeting to make sure they go through all the steps.
8. Older students lead their meetings by presenting their PowerPoint presentations. Younger students actively participate by referring to their vision boards or showing their video.
9. I encourage families to take students' vision boards when they leave the meeting so they can hang them up at home.
10. I build in ways for my students to continue to self-evaluate their performance throughout the year, so that when the next IEP is developed, they'll be prepared to have an even more active role. The best way I've found to do this is to involve them in the creation of their own progress reports. Holding periodic conferences with students is also a great way to ensure students are monitoring their own progress.

Pearson eText Education Video Example 2.5
Featured Teacher Keisha Whitfield creates vision boards to help students prepare for IEP meetings.

Regardless of the level of parent and student participation, appropriateness and measurability of the goals, and satisfaction with the IEP document, many children with disabilities will make little progress without instruction of the highest quality. This reality led to the requirement in IDEA 2004 that teachers must use evidence-based practices to ensure their students receive the highest quality instruction.

Least Restrictive Environment

Learning Outcome 2.5 Define *least restrictive environment*, and explain how the least restrictive environment for a given student is not necessarily the regular classroom.

IDEA requires that every student with disabilities be educated in the **least restrictive environment (LRE)**. Specifically, the law stipulates that to the maximum extent appropriate, children with disabilities, including children in public or private institutions or other care facilities, are educated with children who are not disabled, and special classes, separate schooling, or other removal of children with disabilities from the regular educational environment occurs only when the nature or severity of the disability of a child is such that education in regular classes with the use of supplementary aids and services cannot be achieved satisfactorily (PL 108-446, Sec. 612 [a][5][A]).

The LRE is the setting that is most similar to a regular classroom and that meets the child's special educational needs. LRE is a relative and wholly individualized concept; it is not to be determined by disability category. The LRE for one 10-year-old student who is blind might be inappropriate for another 10-year-old with the same type and degree of visual impairment. And the LRE for both students may change over time. Since the passage of IDEA, there have been many differences of opinion over which type of setting is least restrictive and most appropriate for students with disabilities. Some educators and parents consider any decision to place a student with disabilities outside the regular classroom to be overly restrictive; most, however, recognize that full-time placement in a regular classroom is restrictive and inappropriate if the child's educational needs cannot be met adequately in that environment.

Continuum of Alternative Placements

IDEA requires schools to provide a **continuum of alternative placements**—a range of placement and service options—to meet the individual needs of all students with disabilities.

> *Continuum of alternative placements.*
>
> (a) Each public agency must ensure that a continuum of alternative placements is available to meet the needs of children with disabilities for special education and related services. (b) The continuum required in paragraph (a) of this section must—(1) Include the alternative placements listed in the definition of special education under §300.38 (instruction in regular classes, special classes, special schools, home instruction, and instruction in hospitals and institutions); and (2) Make provision for supplementary services (such as resource room or itinerant instruction) to be provided in conjunction with regular class placement. (Authority: 20 USC 1412 §300.115 [a][5])

The continuum can be depicted symbolically as a pyramid, with placements ranging from the regular classroom at the bottom to special schools, residential facilities, and homebound or hospital placements at the top (Figure 2.4). The fact that the pyramid is widest at the bottom indicates that most children with disabilities are served in *regular classrooms* and that the number of children who require more intensive instruction and highly specialized services decreases as we move up the continuum.

Five of the eight placement options depicted in Figure 2.4 are available in regular public school buildings. Children at the first three levels on the continuum have full-time placements in regular classrooms and receive various degrees and types of support by special education teachers who consult or co-teach with the general education teachers. In a *resource room*, a special educator provides instruction to students with disabilities outside of the regular classroom for part of the school day. Children who require full-time placement in a *separate classroom* (also called a *self-contained classroom*) are with other children with disabilities for most of the school day and participate with children without disabilities only at certain times, such as during lunch, recess, or perhaps art and music. Although the separate classroom provides significantly fewer opportunities for interaction with children without disabilities than does the regular classroom, it provides more integration than does placement

FIGURE 2.4 Continuum of Placements for Students with Disabilities

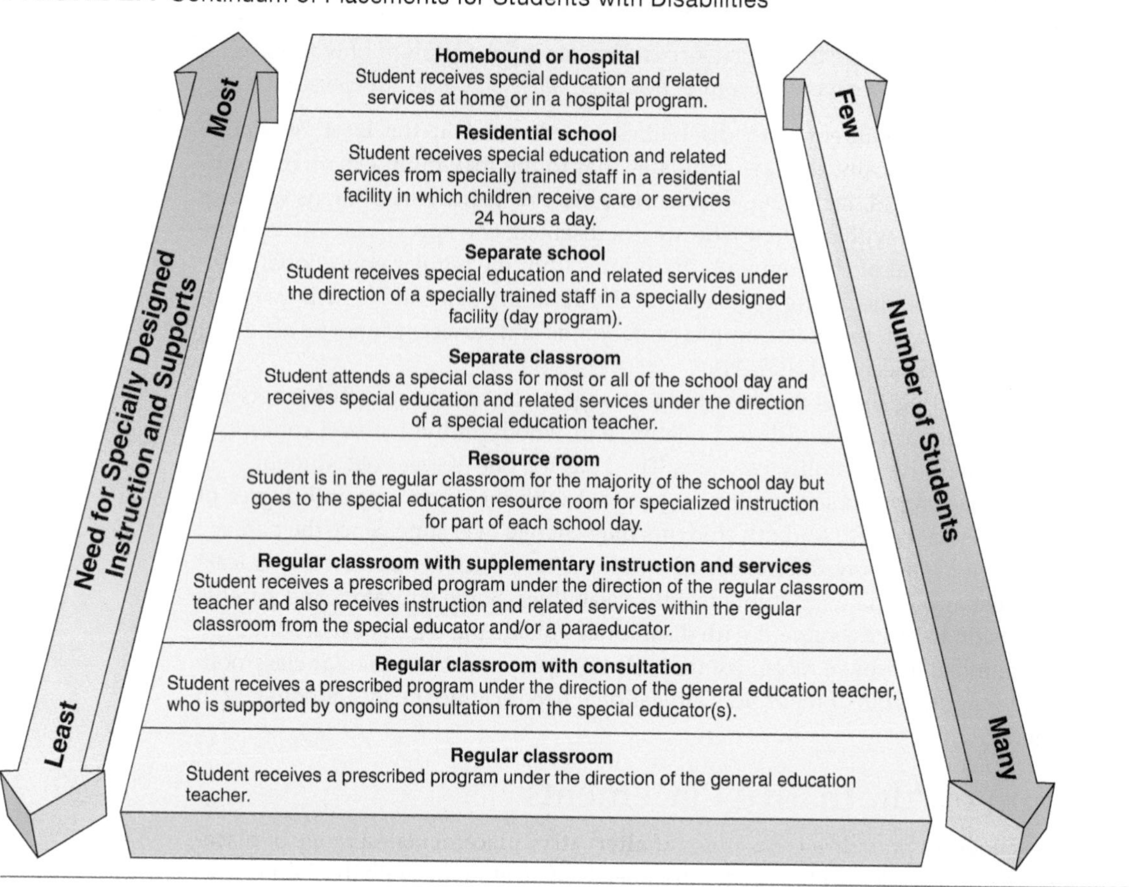

in *separate schools* or *residential schools*, which are attended only by children with disabilities. A child in a *homebound* or *hospital* setting receives special education and related services on an individual basis and may have few opportunities to interact with other children.

Determining LRE

HLP7 Provide a consistent, organized, and respectful learning environment.

The IEP team determines the proper placement after identifying the child's needs and the special education and related services necessary to meet those needs. The legally mandated and educationally sound sequence is as follows: (a) The school determines whether the child has a disability and is therefore eligible for special education, (b) the IEP team determines the child's individual needs and develops an IEP that specifies the special education and related services needed to meet those needs, and (c) the child is placed in the LRE in which educators can provide an appropriate program and the child can make satisfactory educational progress.

The regular classroom is the starting point for the IEP team's discussion of placement. Removing a student with disabilities from the regular classroom is justified only if the IEP team determines the specially designed instruction and related services necessary for the student to achieve her IEP goals cannot be provided in that setting. Mercer et al. (2011) suggest that IEP teams think of LRE as the *most enabling environment* for the child with disabilities.

Placement of a student with disabilities should not be viewed as all-or-nothing at any one level on the continuum. The IEP team should consider the extent to which the student can effectively be included into each of three dimensions of school life: the general curriculum, extracurricular activities (e.g., clubs), and other school activities (e.g., recess, mealtimes). IDEA allows IEP teams to determine if total integration is appropriate in one dimension and partial integration is appropriate in another dimension (H. R. Turnbull et al., 2009).

A student's placement must not be regarded as permanent. The continuum concept is intended to be flexible, with students moving from one placement to another as dictated by their individual educational needs. The IEP team should periodically review the specific goals and objectives for each child—they are required to do so at least annually—and make new placement decisions if warranted. The child's parents must be informed whenever the school considers any change in placement so that the parents can either consent or object to the change and present additional information if they wish.

Inclusive Education

Although often confused, the terms *inclusion* and *least restrictive environment* are not synonymous. **Inclusion** means educating students with disabilities in general education classrooms; the LRE principle requires that students with disabilities be educated in settings as close to the regular class as possible in which an appropriate program can be provided and the students can make satisfactory educational progress. For many students with disabilities, an inclusive classroom and the LRE are one and the same, but that is not always so.

Much discussion and controversy and many misconceptions have arisen regarding the inclusion of students with disabilities. Although many parents of children with disabilities strongly support inclusion, others have resisted it just as strongly, thinking that the regular classroom does not offer the intensive, individualized education their children need (Garrick Duhaney & Salend, 2000). For example, studies of parents of children with severe disabilities have found some parents in favor of and some against inclusion (Gallagher et al., 2000; Palmer et al., 2001). Havey (1999) reported that in 67% of the cases in which parents contested the schools' placement decision, the parents sought a more restrictive educational setting (e.g., parents wanted the child to attend a resource room for part of each day instead of full-time placement in a general education class).

As we have seen, IDEA calls for the education of each child with a disability in the LRE, removed no further than necessary from the general education public school program. The law does not require placement of all children with disabilities in general education classes or suggest that general education teachers should educate students with disabilities without the necessary support services, including help from special educators and other specialists. Although not all children with disabilities attend general education classes, general education teachers are expected to teach students with a much wider range of learning, behavioral, sensory, and physical differences than ever before. Thus, provision of in-service training for general educators is an important (and sometimes overlooked) requirement of IDEA. General education teachers are understandably wary of having students with disabilities placed in their classes if the school provides little or no training or support (DeSimone & Parmar, 2006; Waldron et al., 2011). The role of general education teachers is already a highly demanding one; they do not want their classes to become any larger, especially if they perceive children with special needs as unmanageable (Cook et al., 2007). General education teachers are entitled to be involved in decisions about children who are placed in their classes and to be offered continuous consultation and other support services from administrators and their special education colleagues (Kochhar-Bryant, 2008).

Although some educators have expressed concern that the presence of students with disabilities impairs the academic achievement of students without disabilities, no evidence supports this. In fact, Cole et al. (2004) reported that 334 students without disabilities in inclusive classrooms actually made greater gains in reading and math than did a comparison group of 272 students without disabilities who were educated in "traditional" classrooms. A longitudinal study of students with disabilities found that those who spent 80% or more time in inclusive classrooms from the fourth grade through the eighth grade did significantly better on state reading and math assessments than their peers who spent more time in special education classrooms (Cole et al., 2020). When considering the results of studies such as these, it is important to consider that the most critical factor affecting

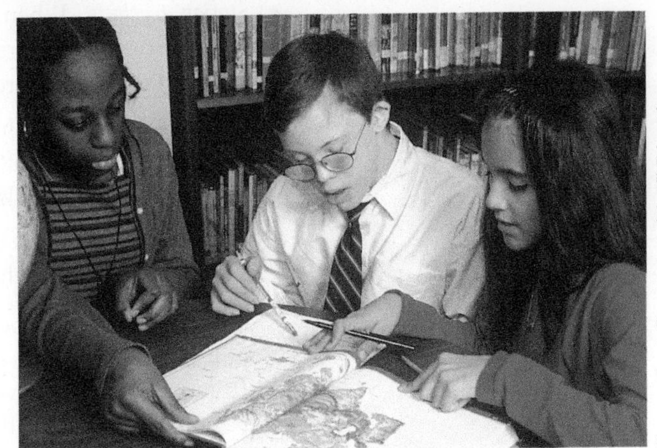

Source: Scott Cunningham/Merrill Education

Shared activities and cooperative learning contribute to a sense of belonging in inclusive classrooms.

student achievement is most likely to be quality of instruction and not the presence or absence of students with disabilities.

Placing a child with disabilities in a resource room or separate class is no guarantee that the child will receive the specialized instruction he needs (e.g., Lemons et al., 2018; McLeskey & Waldron, 2011). We also know that simply including a child with disabilities in a regular classroom does not mean that she will learn and behave appropriately or be socially accepted by the teacher or by children without disabilities (Cook, 2004; Siperstein et al., 2007). It is important for special educators to teach appropriate social skills and behavior to the child with disabilities and to educate children without disabilities about their classmates with special needs.

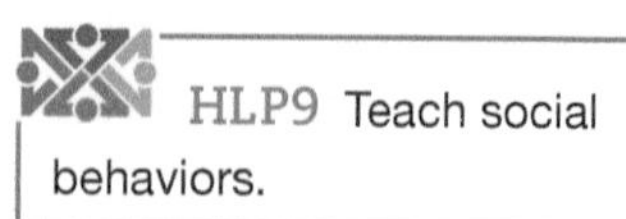
HLP9 Teach social behaviors.

Examples of effective inclusion programs can be found at age levels ranging from preschool (Lawrence et al., 2016; Sainato et al., 2015) to high school (Carter et al., 2016; Cobb Morocco et al., 2006), and they include children with high-incidence disabilities (Rojewski et al., 2015) and severe disabilities (Ryndak & Fisher, 2007). Strategies for including students with disabilities in the general education program can be found in publications by Friend and Bursuck (2019); Giangreco and Doyle (2007); Mastropieri and Scruggs (2018); McLeskey et al. (2018); Salend (2016); and Storey (2020).

Promoting Inclusion with Co-teaching and Cooperative Learning

CO-TEACHING *Co-teaching*—a general education teacher and special education teacher planning and delivering instruction together in an inclusive classroom—has become increasingly common. Indeed, many of the Featured Teachers in this book spend at least a portion of each day co-teaching in regular classrooms, and some, like Amaris Johnson (Chapter 5), spend almost all their teaching time in co-teaching arrangements. Co-teaching takes many different forms, depending on the purpose of the lesson, the individualized objectives and needed supports for students with disabilities, and the teachers' relative levels of expertise with the content (Potts & Howard, 2011; Scruggs & Mastropieri, 2017). As Featured Teacher Keisha Whitfield notes, "Not all general education teachers understand how co-teaching classes can work. I work to help general education teachers recognize various models of co-teaching and the role I can play in helping them with their teaching." Five co-teaching formats are commonly used:

- *One teaching/one helping.* One teacher instructs the whole class while the other circulates to collect information on student performance and to offer help. This arrangement takes advantage of the expertise of one teacher in a specific subject area. Featured Teacher Keisha Whitfield uses this format to collect formative assessment data to "more efficiently use the time I do have with students and help me and my collaborative partners retool and improve group instruction."
- *Parallel teaching.* When it is necessary to lower the student–teacher ratio, both teachers teach the same content to two equal-sized groups of students.
- *Station teaching.* When teaching material that is difficult but not sequential, both teachers present different content to different groups of students at the same time, and students rotate through each station.
- *Alternative teaching.* When teachers need to individualize instruction, remediate skills, promote mastery, or offer enrichment, one teacher works with a smaller group or individual students while the other teacher works with the rest of the class.
- *Team teaching.* When it is desirable to blend the talents and expertise of teachers, both teachers plan and teach a lesson together. (Adapted from Salend, 2016.)

Meticulous planning, open communication, and flexibility are keys to successful co-teaching. It is a mistake, however, to assume that two teachers in the classroom instead of one will automatically improve the effectiveness of a lesson. Although the rationale and suggested techniques for co-teaching are logical, much more outcome research on the effects of co-teaching is needed (Szumski et al., 2017; Zigmond, 2007).

COOPERATIVE LEARNING Cooperative learning activities provide a strategic approach for differentiating instruction and integrating students with disabilities into both the academic curriculum and the social fabric of the classroom. Cooperative learning can take many forms, but in most models, all students in the class are assigned to small heterogeneous groups and help one another achieve a shared academic goal (Johnson & Johnson, 2017). However, merely placing students in groups to "work together" does not necessarily lead to *cooperative* learning (Gillies, 2016). According to Slavin (1995), cooperative learning arrangements should include the following:

1. *Group goals.* All members of the group work together to earn grades, rewards, or other recognition of success for the group.
2. *Individual accountability.* Each student within the group must demonstrate his or her learning and contribute in a specific way for the group to obtain success. However, the manner in which group members contribute may differ to meet individualized needs and learning objectives.

Well-designed cooperative learning activities keep students actively engaged and motivated to succeed.

In addition to improved academic outcomes, cooperative learning can also promote positive social relationships, friendships, and mutual supports among students with and without disabilities in the classroom, which are vital to successful inclusion (Maheady et al., 2006; Moeyaert et al., 2019). See *Teaching & Learning,* "Classwide Peer Tutoring." For more on cooperative learning, see Chapter 4.

Classwide peer tutoring (CWPT) is a form of cooperative learning with more than three decades of research demonstrating its effectiveness for teaching reading, math, social studies, and a wide range of specialized subject areas to (and by) students with and without disabilities in inclusive classrooms (Gardner et al., 2007; Mackiewicz et al., 2011; Moeyaert et al., 2019). See *Teaching & Learning,* "Classwide Peer Tutoring."

Pearson eText
Video Example 2.6
A successful co-teaching "marriage" demands mutual respect and shared responsibility for all students' success. https://www.youtube.com/watch?v=_pnxst7dkLk

HLP18 Use strategies to promote active student engagement.

Arguments For and Against Full Inclusion

Some special educators believe the continuum of alternative placements should be dismantled and all students with disabilities placed in general education classes. For example, in a paper widely cited by advocates of full inclusion, S. J. Taylor (2005) contends the LRE model

- *Confuses segregation and integration with intensity of services.* The LRE assumes the intensive services needed by people with severe disabilities cannot be provided in integrated settings. Segregation and integration and intensity of services are separate dimensions.
- *Requires a readiness model.* LRE implies people with disabilities must earn the right to move to the LRE.
- *Sanctions infringements on students' rights.* LRE asks not whether people with disabilities should be restricted but to what extent.
- *Requires people to move as they develop and change.* LRE expects people with disabilities to move through a series of progressively less restrictive environments. Even if people move smoothly through a continuum, their lives would be a series of stops between transitional placements.
- *Directs attention to physical settings rather than to the services and supports people need.* LRE emphasizes facilities and environments designed specifically for people with disabilities. The field created "facilities," first large ones and now smaller ones, and "programs," rather than providing the services and supports to enable people with disabilities to participate in the same settings as other people. (Adapted from Taylor, 2005.)

Pearson eText
Video Example 2.7
These co-teachers engage students during a science lesson with "think, pair, share."

Some authors view full inclusion as a matter of social justice (e.g., Artiles et al., 2006; Beneke et al., 2019; Stainback et al., 1996). No clear consensus exists in the field about the meaning of inclusion. To some, *inclusion* means full-time placement of all students with disabilities in regular classrooms; to others, the term refers to any degree of integration into the

TEACHING & LEARNING

Classwide Peer Tutoring: Cooperative Learning for All Students in Inclusive Classrooms

What Is Classwide Peer Tutoring (CWPT)? Individualized curriculum content, high rates of responding, immediate feedback, daily assessment of progress, positive social interaction, and fun—each of these elements that enhance student learning is embodied in a well-designed CWPT program. The idea of students teaching one another is not new (Lancaster, 1806). With traditional approaches, the teacher identifies a high-achieving student to help a classmate who has not mastered a particular skill.

Contemporary CWPT programs include low achievers and students with disabilities as full participants in an ongoing, whole-class activity in which all students help one another learn new curriculum content. This makes CWPT an excellent vehicle for effective MTSS Tier 1 instruction. Four rigorously tested CWPT models have emerged from more than three decades of research in inclusive classrooms: Juniper Gardens Children's Project CWPT (Greenwood et al., 1997), Peer-Assisted Learning Strategies (McMaster et al., 2006), Classwide Student Tutoring Teams (Maheady et al., 2006), and The Ohio State University (OSU) CWPT model (Heward et al., 1982).

How Can I Use CWPT? To implement the basic elements of the OSU model, follow these steps:

Pretest and Make Task Cards—Select curriculum area and pretest the class to determine individual learning tasks (e.g., math problems, science definitions, history facts). Make an individualized set of task cards for each student, writing each problem or question on one side of an index card and the answer or solution on the other side.

Construct Tutoring Folders—Each student's tutoring folder includes a "GO" pocket for task cards to be to be taught to his tutee and a "STOP" pocket for learned cards, a chart for tracking the tutee's progress, markers to use for recording, and a Star Card for collecting stamps from the teacher for excellence in tutoring procedures. See Figure 2.5 for an example of a Peer Tutoring Folder. Students can help make task cards and folders.

FIGURE 2.5 Peer Tutoring Folder

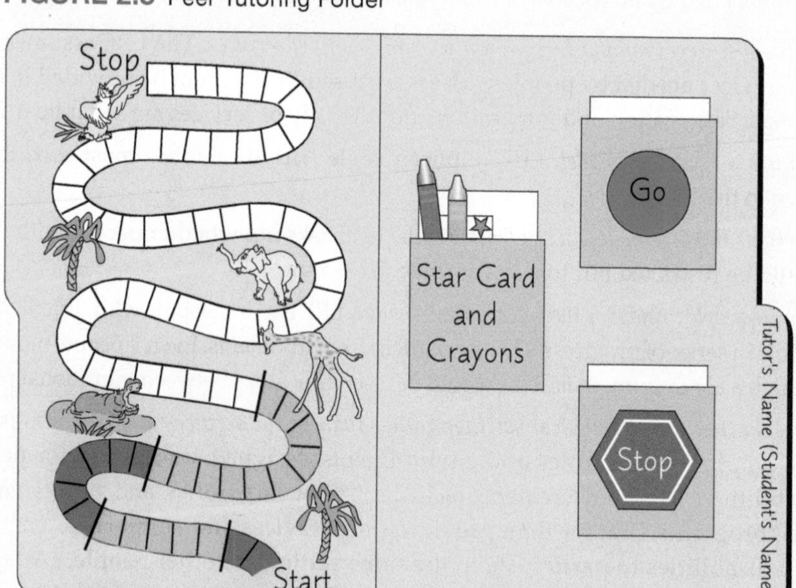

Source: Adapted from *Total tutoring for special and general educators [instructor's manual]* by T.E. Heron & W.L. Heward, 2000. Columbus, OH: The Ohio State University Special Education Program. Used by permission.

Teach CWPT Procedures—Explicitly describe and model the behaviors expected of tutors and tutees. Tutors should present the task cards as many times as possible during a session, shuffle the cards after each round, praise their partners' correct responses, and follow a consistent error correction procedure. For example, when a tutee makes an error, the tutor says, "Try again." If the tutee again responds incorrectly, the tutor says, for example, "This word is *tree*; say *tree*." Tutees are to look at the task cards, promptly respond to their tutor's questions, and accept feedback. Role-play the procedures with a few students, then create tutor–tutee pairs and have them practice.

Conduct Daily CWPT Sessions—Set a timer for 5 minutes and tell the students to begin. The student who is tutoring first presents the task cards as many times as possible during the practice period. When the timer signals the end of the practice period, the partners switch roles. While students are tutoring, walk around the room and prompt, praise, and occasionally stamp students' Star Cards for good tutoring behaviors; answer questions; and supervise the activity.

After both students have practiced, they reverse roles again; the first tutor tests her partner by presenting each task card with no prompts or cues. Allow about 5 minutes for each tutoring pair to test and record each other's progress.

- The tutor places correct cards in one pile and incorrect cards in another.
- The students switch roles again, and the first tutor is now tested.
- The tutors mark the back of each card to identify if it was "correct" or "incorrect" during the test and then record daily progress on the chart.
- When a child correctly responds to a task card on the test for three consecutive sessions, that item is considered learned, and the tutor moves it to the STOP pocket.
- When the students have learned all 10 cards, the teacher places a new set of words in the GO pocket.
- Each session ends with the partners praising and complimenting each other for their good work.

Make it a game. CWPT should be fun! Use game-like formats, individual and team goals, charting their progress, and reward systems to engage and motivate students.

Pearson eText
Video Example 2.8
The Ohio State University peer tutoring model features individualized learning tasks, high rates of student responding, and immediate feedback.

mainstream. Stainback and Stainback (1996), strong advocates and leaders of the inclusion movement, define an inclusive school as "a place where everyone belongs, is accepted, supports, and is supported by his or her peers and other members of the school community in the course of having his or her educational needs met" (p. 3). Giangreco et al. (2020) state that inclusive education exists only when each of the six characteristics shown in Figure 2.6 "occurs on an ongoing, daily basis" (p. 7).

Virtually all special educators support the responsible inclusion of students with disabilities in regular classrooms and the development and evaluation of new models for working more cooperatively with general educators to serve all students (e.g., D. Fuchs et al., 2010; Kauffman et al., 2018; McLeskey & Waldron, 2011; Smith & Hilton, 1997). Throughout this text, you will find descriptions of many research-based model programs and strategies for successfully and meaningfully including students with disabilities as full members of the academic and social life of regular classrooms.

Very few special educators support eliminating the continuum of alternative placements in favor of a policy of universal full inclusion. The Council for Exceptional Children (CEC) (2014), the major professional organization in special education, supports inclusion as a "meaningful goal" to be pursued by schools but believes the continuum of services and program options must be maintained and IEP planning teams must make placement decisions based on the student's individual educational needs. The discussion of inclusion continues throughout the text.

> CEC believes that a continuum of services must be available for all children, youth, and young adults. CEC also believes that the concept of inclusion is a meaningful goal to be pursued in our schools and communities. In addition, CEC believes

FIGURE 2.6 Elements of Inclusive Education

1. All students are welcomed in general education. The first placement options considered are the general education classes in the school that the students would attend if they did not have a disability.
2. Disability is recognized as a form of human diversity. Hence, students with disabilities are accepted as individuals and are not denied access because of their disabilities.
3. Appropriate supports, regardless of disability type or severity, are available. Supports are provided in typical environments instead of sending students to specialized settings to receive supports.
4. The composition of classrooms reflects the naturally occurring proportion of students with and without disabilities. The percentage of students without disabilities is substantially higher than the percentage of students with disabilities.
5. Students, irrespective of their developmental or performance levels, are educated with peers in the same age groupings available to those without disability labels instead of with younger students.
6. Students with and without disabilities participate in shared educational experiences while pursuing individually appropriate learning outcomes with necessary supports. Educational experiences are designed to enhance valued life outcomes that seek an individualized balance between both the academic-functional and the social-personal aspects of schooling.

Source: From Giangreco, M. F., Shogren, K. A., & Dymond, S. K. (2020). In F. Brown, J. McDonnell, & M. E. Snell (Eds.), *Instruction of students with severe disabilities* (9th ed., p. 7). Upper Saddle River, NJ: Pearson. Used by permission.

> children, youth, and young adults with disabilities should be served whenever possible in general education classrooms in inclusive neighborhood schools and community settings. Such settings should be strengthened and supported by an infusion of specially trained personnel and other appropriate supportive practices according to the individual needs of the child (CEC Policy Manual Sec. 3, Part 1, H-13).

Zigmond (2003) reminds us that asking what is the "best place" to educate students with disabilities misses the point of what special education is all about. The bedrock of special education is instruction focused on individual needs. The very concept of "one best place" contradicts this commitment to individualization.

> I can say with some certainty that place is not what makes special education "special" or effective. Effective teaching strategies and an individualized approach are the more critical ingredients in special education, and neither of these is associated solely with one particular environment (pp. 196, 198).

Thoughtful discussions of the full range of assumptions, perspectives, practices, potential benefits, and realities of inclusion can be found in D. Fuchs et al. (2010); Giangreco et al. (2018); Kauffman et al. (2018); McLeskey and Waldron (2011); Simpson (2004a); and Zigmond et al. (2009).

Where Does Special Education Go from Here?

The promise of FAPE for all children with disabilities is an ambitious one. The process of bringing about this goal has been described in such lofty terms as a "new Bill of Rights" and a "Magna Carta" for children with disabilities (Goodman, 1976). Weintraub and Abeson (1974) wrote in support of IDEA before the bill's passage: "At the minimum, it will make educational opportunities a reality for all handicapped children. At the maximum, it will make our schools healthier learning environments for all our children" (p. 529). Today, most observers acknowledge substantial progress has been made toward fulfillment of that promise.

IDEA has had far-reaching effects. In place of the once-prevalent practice of excluding children with disabilities, schools now seek the most appropriate ways of including them. The student is no longer required to meet the requirements of the school, but the school is required to fit the needs of the student. Today's schools provide far more than academic instruction.

Schools are expected to provide wide-ranging services to children from diverse backgrounds and with different learning needs. In effect, they have become diversified agencies offering services such as medical support, physical therapy, vocational training, parent counseling, recreation, special transportation, and in-service education for staff members.

Source: Laura Bolesta/Millennium/Merrill Education

Regardless of where services are delivered, the most crucial variable is the quality of instruction each student receives.

Most people—both within and outside the field of education—have welcomed the inclusion and participation of children with disabilities in their schools and communities. Despite ample evidence of progress toward providing equal educational opportunity, it is equally true that many people—again, inside and outside the field of education—have detected significant problems and concerns with the very nature of special education (e.g., D. Fuchs et al., 2010; D. Gallagher et al., 2004) or the implementation of IDEA (e.g., Arden et al., 2017; Finn et al., 2001). States and local school administrators maintain the federal government has never allocated sufficient funds to cover its promised share of the high costs of educating students with disabilities (Council for Exceptional Children, 2019). Special education teachers express dissatisfaction about excessive paperwork, unclear guidelines, and inappropriate grouping of students with disabilities. Too many students from culturally diverse groups are identified for special education and are disproportionately placed in more restrictive settings. General education teachers contend they receive little or no training or support when students with disabilities are placed in their classes. There are many other problems, real and perceived, and no quick fix or easy solution can be offered.

Special education is at a crossroads. Once, access to educational opportunity was the primary issue for children with disabilities. Would they receive an education at all? Could they be served in their local community and neighborhood schools? Although some access problems persist (e.g., particularly for children who live in poverty or in extremely isolated areas and for children of migrant and homeless families), as the *Endrew* case (see Chapter 1) reminds us, the primary concern today is about the appropriateness and effectiveness of special education.

Today, all children identified with disabilities receive special education and related services. Many of these children benefit from a truly special education that includes curricular elements and instructional technologies that were unavailable just a few years ago. Although special education can rightfully be proud of its accomplishments, the educational outcomes for the majority of students with disabilities are disappointing. As a group, students with disabilities fare poorly on virtually every measure of academic achievement and social adaptation. We believe the poor outcomes experienced by students with disabilities . . .

> . . . reflect not so much the field's lack of knowledge about how to teach these students, as they are testament to education's collective failure to systematically implement available knowledge. . . . As a result, many children with disabilities are receiving a special education that is not nearly as effective as it could be. In essence, the potential effectiveness of the special education received by many of the more than 6 million children who participate in special education today is neutralized by the presence of weak approaches that are selected on the basis of ideology instead of research results (Silvestri & Heward, 2016, p. 137).

Can special education fulfill the promise of FAPE for all students with disabilities? The answer depends in part on the ability of professionals to work together; assume new roles;

communicate with each other; and involve parents, families, and students with disabilities themselves. But above all, special educators must realize the most crucial variable in the effectiveness of special education is the quality of instruction that children receive. They must rediscover "special education's necessary and noble mission" of teaching the most difficult-to-teach children (D. Fuchs et al., 2010).

Special education is serious business. The learning and adjustment problems faced by students with disabilities are real, and their prevention, remediation, and compensation require intensive, systematic intervention. Regardless of who does it or where it takes place, good teaching must occur. Exceptional children deserve no less.

ADVICE FROM THE FEATURED TEACHER by Keisha Whitfield

Use Self-Management Strategies to Help You Prepare for IEP Meetings

Source: Keisha Whitfield

- ***Prepare a checklist of all the steps you need to complete before, during, and after the IEP meeting.*** Use your checklist as a self-audit to ensure each IEP has all the required information in each section and as a reminder of what needs to be done after the meeting. Check with your colleagues or district administrator to see if such a checklist already exists!
- ***Make sure all your IEP goals and objectives are "SMART."*** Use the SMART acronym (Wright & Wright, 2006) as a reminder to write goals that are Specific, Measurable, Actionable (use action verbs), Relevant and realistic, and Time limited. This acronym will help you self-evaluate each objective you write.
- ***Prepare well in advance.*** Don't wait until two weeks before the meeting to start gathering survey information and data. I keep a ½-inch binder for each of my students with survey information, data (behavior and academic), observations, parent and teacher communication, and work samples. Having this information readily available will increase your efficiency and will result in a more meaningful IEP.

Actively Involve Students and Families in the IEP Process

- ***Assume that every parent wants to be involved.*** Just because a parent doesn't show up for a meeting doesn't mean they don't have input. Try to schedule meetings when they're convenient for families, and if necessary, find other ways to get their input.
- ***Take advantage of multiple ways to conduct meetings.*** In-person, at-school meetings are not always the best fit for all parents. I've had meetings via Facetime, over the phone, and in families' homes because of conflicts of schedules.
- ***Send home an IEP draft before the meeting.*** By sending home the document several days before the meeting, you give parents the opportunity to review, formulate questions, and generate suggestions ahead of time. This will lead to greater input from the family and a more efficient meeting.
- ***Conduct student-led IEPs.*** Be sure to train students in advance so they know their role in the meeting.

Help General Education Teachers Be More Effective

- ***Provide general education teachers with "at-a-glance" IEPs.*** It is vital that all general education teachers who work with your students have a clear understanding of what each student's specially designed instruction includes. The IEP At-A-Glance summarizes the portions of the IEP that are most relevant to general educators:

goals, objectives, important dates, and specially designed instruction (including accommodations). General education teachers usually appreciate having this document, and it is well worth the time it takes to prepare it. Preparing this document at the start of the year will also help you get to know your students' academic and behavioral strengths and weaknesses.

- ***Train your colleagues.*** At the beginning of the year, I give each of my co-teachers a sheet explaining different co-teaching models. This helps them realize the range of possibilities for how we can work together to support students. You can provide training for general educators who are not your co-teachers as well. For instance, you might train them in teaching strategies or provide them with tips for adjusting assessments.
- ***Meet with your co-teachers on a regular basis.*** At these meetings, discuss what your role will be in the class and how this role needs to change based on the needs in the class. Your responsibilities may include any or all of the following: making accommodations within lessons, giving input on how to differentiate lessons, sharing different teaching strategies to reach all students, designing or adapting formative assessments, and instructing the whole class or small groups of students.
- ***Share what you know.*** Never be afraid to let your general education colleagues know when students are missing key parts of lessons or that they may need to present a topic in a different way to benefit all learners. If you have suggestions, speak up, or students may lose out.

Key Terms and Concepts

choral responding
continuum of alternative placements
disproportionate representation
IEP team
inclusion
intervention assistance team
least restrictive environment (LRE)
multifactored evaluation (MFE)
multi-tiered system of support (MTSS)
positive behavioral interventions and supports (PBIS)
prereferral intervention
response to intervention (RTI)

Summary

The Process of Special Education

- The Individuals with Disabilities Education Act (IDEA) mandates a particular sequence of events that schools must follow to identify and educate children with disabilities.
- Prereferral intervention is a problem-solving process used to (1) provide immediate instructional and/or behavior management assistance to the child and teacher, (2) reduce the chances of identifying a child for special education who may not be disabled, and (3) identify students for evaluation.
- A multi-tiered system of supports, including response to intervention (RTI) and positive behavioral interventions and supports (PBIS), is a form of prereferral intervention that measures a student's response to increasingly intensive, scientifically validated instruction to determine whether the child's struggles to learn are the result of poor or insufficient instruction or of a disability for which special education is needed.
- Any child suspected of having a disability must receive a nondiscriminatory multifactored evaluation (MFE) to determine eligibility for special education and to provide information about the child's educational needs and how to meet them.
- Culturally and linguistically diverse students are both underrepresented and overrepresented in special education, depending on the cultural/ethnic group and disability category.
- Inappropriate referral to special education and false identification of a disability can occur if educators and school psychologists cannot separate the presence of unrecognized diversity or deficits from disability.
- Schools must plan and provide an individualized education program (IEP) for each child with a disability.
- After identifying the child's educational needs and the services required to meet them, the IEP team determines the

least restrictive environment (LRE) in which the child can receive an appropriate education.

- The IEP team must review the IEP periodically but not less frequently than annually.
- At least once every 3 years, the IEP team conducts an evaluation to determine if the child still needs special education.
- Parents may at any time revoke their consent for special education services for their child.

Collaboration and Teaming

- Coordination, consultation, and teaming are three models of collaboration team members can use.
- Three models for teaming are multidisciplinary, interdisciplinary, and transdisciplinary.

Individualized Education Program

- An IEP planning team must include (1) the parents of the child with a disability; (2) at least one general education teacher of the child; (3) at least one special education teacher; (4) a representative of the local education agency; (5) an individual who can interpret the instructional implications of evaluation results; (6) at the discretion of the parent or school, other individuals who have knowledge or special expertise regarding the child; and (7) whenever appropriate, the child.
- Each IEP must include these seven components:
  - A description of the child's present levels of educational performance
  - Measurable annual goals, including benchmarks or short-term objectives for students who take alternative assessments aligned to alternate standards
  - How the child's progress toward the annual goals will be measured and when reports on the child's progress toward meeting the annual goals will be provided
  - The special education and related services and supplementary aids and services, based on peer-reviewed research to the extent practical, to be provided to the child
  - An explanation of the extent, if any, to which the child will not participate with nondisabled children in the regular class
  - Any individual accommodations that are necessary to measure the academic achievement and functional performance of the child on State and districtwide assessments (or alternate assessment selected if appropriate)
  - The projected date for the beginning of the services and modifications and the anticipated frequency, location, and duration of those services and modifications
- Beginning when the student reaches age 16 years, IEPs must also include information on how the educational program will support the child's transition from school to adult life.
- Without direct and ongoing monitoring of student progress toward IEP goals and objectives, the document's usefulness is limited.
- The IEP provides teachers and parents with the opportunity—and the responsibility—to first be realistic about the child's needs and goals and then to be creative about how to meet them.
- IEP formats vary widely across school districts, and schools may exceed the requirement of the law and include additional information.
- Each area of functioning that is adversely affected by the student's disability must be represented by an annual goal on the IEP.

Least Restrictive Environment

- The LRE is the setting closest to the regular classroom that also meets the child's special educational needs.
- The LRE is a relative concept; the LRE for one child might be inappropriate for another child with the same disability.
- The continuum of alternative placements is a range of placement and service options to meet the individual needs of students with disabilities.
- The IEP team must determine the LRE after it has designed a program of special education and related services to meet the child's unique needs.
- Removal of a child with disabilities from the regular classroom is to occur only if the IEP team determines the specially designed instruction and related services necessary for the student to achieve her IEP goals cannot be provided in that setting.

Inclusive Education

- Inclusion is the process of integrating children with disabilities into the academic and social activities of regular schools and general education classes.
- Well-planned, carefully conducted inclusion can generally be effective with students of all ages, types, and degrees of disability.
- Some special educators believe the LRE principle and continuum of alternative placements should be replaced with a policy of full inclusion, in which all students with disabilities are placed full time in regular classrooms.
- Co-teaching is two or more teachers planning and delivering instruction together. Co-teaching arrangements include one teaching/one helping, parallel teaching, station teaching, alternative teaching, and team teaching.
- Cooperative learning activities in which students work in small heterogeneous groups to help one another achieve a common academic goal or product can be an effective

strategy for integrating students with disabilities into the academic and social fabric of the classroom.

Where Does Special Education Go from Here?

- Special education has made substantial progress toward fulfilling the promise of a free appropriate public education (FAPE) for all children with disabilities.
- Implementation of IDEA has brought problems of funding, inadequate training and support for teachers, and opposition by some to including children with disabilities in general education classes.
- Regardless of where special education services are delivered, the most crucial variable is the quality of instruction that each child receives.

Chapter 3
Collaborating with Families

Source: SDI Productions/E+/Getty Images

Learning Outcomes

After reading this chapter and completing the embedded activities, you should be able to

3.1 Identify three factors that contribute to increased emphasis on parent and family involvement.

3.2 Describe challenges, characteristics, and roles of families of children with disabilities.

3.3 Examine cultural backgrounds, beliefs, and linguistic practices that can impede parent involvement and identify ways school personnel can help families feel welcome and appreciated.

3.4 Describe principles of effective communication between educators and families, and contrast several common modes of home–school communication.

3.5 Discuss a variety of strategies for engaging parents of children with disabilities.

Featured Teacher

Joshua Hoppe

Leeward District • Campbell, Kapolei, Wai'anae, HI

Source: Joshua Hoppe

Hawaii is often described as a melting pot of cultures. In addition to a large population of "Islanders," including Native Hawaiians and other Pacific Islanders, the dominant immigrant populations on the Wai'anae Coast are Filipino, Samoan, and Micronesian. We also have students from Japanese, Chinese, Korean, European, African American, and Hispanic families. The majority of families in our district are multiracial.

Currently, I provide support to teachers, school teams, and families across Oahu's Leeward District, primarily in the area of autism. My role includes providing general resource support to teachers and classroom staff (training, materials, coaching, etc.) and direct service for individual students, including conducting assessments, developing student plans, training staff, and providing teacher consultation and parent training. I draw on my classroom experience, what worked and what did not, to guide teams toward improved outcomes for our students.

Knowing how to communicate with students, teachers, and school-level teams is an important aspect of my job; communicating with parents, while respecting cultural differences, is another. I have had many students whose parents are learning English but who are not yet comfortable or fluent enough to use it when discussing educational programming for their child. In these situations, we provide the procedural safeguards notice in their native language and make sure a skilled interpreter attends IEP meetings. Aside from being required by IDEA, these steps show families that their involvement and input are valuable. I have found that as soon as you develop rapport with a parent of a child with special needs, regardless of his or her cultural backgrounds, life gets easier for everyone. I need to understand a family's values and priorities before I can provide them any kind of meaningful support. Once they are comfortable with the team and the process, real collaboration can begin.

A recent example of this that comes to mind is from a wonderful preschool teacher I am working with. She has a student of Chuukese descent and gave the parent the option of having the meeting "Western style" (sitting at a table) or "Chuukese style" (sitting in a circle on the floor). The parent appreciated the choice, and said she preferred "Chuukese style." Since then, there has been a boost in rapport and communication, and more follow-through with the behavior plan at home, which should greatly improve the student's long-term outcomes. Hawaii's incredibly diverse population presents wonderful opportunities for cross-cultural learning and challenges for teachers.

Education, Teaching Credentials, and Experience

- *B.A., psychology, 2005, University of Hawaii*
- *M.A., special education, 2007, University of Phoenix; M.Ed., curriculum studies, 2009, University of Hawaii*
- *Applied Behavior Analysis course sequence, University of West Florida, 2017*
- *Board Certified Behavior Analyst, Licensed Behavior Analyst in Hawaii*
- *Licensed Highly Qualified teacher in Hawaii—elementary, special education K–12, mild, moderate, and severe*
- *11 years of experience as a special education teacher; 3 years of experience as a district resource teacher for students with autism spectrum disorder in Nanakuli/Waianae Complex*

FAMILY IS THE MOST POWERFUL INFLUENCE in a young child's life. Long before a professional with the job title "teacher" arrives, a child has learned countless skills from parents and family members. With rare exceptions, no one ever knows or cares about a child as much as a parent.

Too often in the past, educators viewed parents as either troublesome (if they asked too many questions or, worse, offered suggestions about their child's education) or uncaring (if they did not jump to attention whenever the professional determined the parent needed something—usually advice from the professional). Today, parent involvement and family support are understood as essential elements of special education.

Support for Family Involvement

Learning Outcome 3.1 Identify three factors that contribute to increased emphasis on parent and family involvement.

Although many factors have contributed to increased emphasis on collaboration between parents and teachers in the education of exceptional children, three influences are clear: (a) parents want to be involved, (b) federal law requires collaboration between schools and parents, and (c) educational outcomes are enhanced when parents are involved.

Parents: Advocating for Change

Parents of exceptional children have long advocated for equal access to educational opportunities for their children, and they have done so with impressive effectiveness. As you learned in Chapters 1 and 2, parents were instrumental in the litigation and legislation that established the right to a free and appropriate public education (FAPE) for all children with disabilities.

The first parent group for the benefit of children with disabilities was the National Society for Crippled Children, organized in 1921. The United Cerebral Palsy Association, founded in 1948, and the National Association for Retarded Citizens (now called The Arc), organized in 1950, are two national parent organizations largely responsible for making the public aware of the special needs of children with disabilities. The Learning Disabilities Association of America, formed in 1963, also organized by and consisting mostly of parents, has been instrumental in bringing about educational reform. Parent members of The Association for Persons with Severe Handicaps (now called TASH), founded in 1975, have been effective advocates for family-focused educational services and the inclusion of students with severe disabilities in neighborhood schools and general education classrooms. The mission of the Association for Science in Autism Treatment (ASAT), founded in 1998 by parents and professionals, is to disseminate accurate, scientifically sound information about autism and its treatment. Many other parent-led organizations continue today to advocate for effective education, community acceptance, needed services, and the rights of individuals with disabilities.

Legislators: Mandating Parent and Family Involvement

As a result of parent advocacy, Congress included parent involvement as a key component of the Education of All Handicapped Children Act (PL 94–142), the original federal special education law. Each reauthorization of the law has strengthened and extended parent and family participation in the education of children with disabilities. Congress reaffirmed its belief in the importance of parent and family involvement in the introduction to the Individuals with Disabilities Education Act (IDEA) of 2004: "Over 30 years of research and experience has demonstrated that the education of children with disabilities can be made more effective by ... strengthening the role and responsibility of parents and ensuring that families of such children have meaningful opportunities to participate in the education of their children at school and at home" (20 USC 601[c][5][B]).

Parent participation in the form of shared decision making is one of the basic principles of IDEA, which stipulates procedures to ensure parents have input with regard to referral, testing, program planning, placement, and evaluation. The law also mandates due process procedures if parents believe their child's needs are not being met.

Educators and Parents: Seeking Greater Effectiveness

So, parents want to be involved, and the law requires it, but the most important reasons for collaborative partnerships between educators and families are the benefits to children with disabilities:

- increased likelihood of targeting meaningful IEP goals;
- greater consistency and support in their two most important environments—home and school;
- increased opportunities for learning and development; and
- access to expanded resources and services.

Indeed, research shows a strong correlation between parent involvement and improvements in a variety of measures of academic achievement and school performance, such as better attendance, higher grades, better scores on standardized tests, higher graduation rates, improved social skills, and better postschool outcomes (Fan & Chen, 2001; McConnell & Kubina, 2014; O'Donnell & Kirkner, 2014; Park & Holloway, 2017; Test et al., 2009). The effectiveness of educational programs for children with disabilities is increased when parents and families are actively involved (e.g., Newman, 2004; Resetar et al., 2006; Test et al., 2009).

To meet the needs of children with disabilities, educators must extend their focus beyond academic skills in the classroom. Effective special educators design and implement instructional programs that enable students with disabilities to use and maintain academic, language, social, self-help, recreation, and vocational skills in school, home, and community settings. In their home and community lives, children may participate in some 150 different kinds of social and physical settings (Dunst, 2001). The large number of nonschool settings where children live, play, and learn presents both challenges and opportunities. First, the many different settings and situations exemplify the extent of the challenge teachers face in helping children use newly learned skills throughout their daily lives. Second, the many different settings and situations children experience in their homes and communities provide extended opportunities for learning and practicing important skills. To be maximally effective, teachers must look beyond the classroom for assistance and support; parents and families are natural and necessary allies.

At the very least, teachers and students benefit when parents provide information about their children's use of specific skills outside the classroom. Families know certain aspects of their children better than anyone else does (Meadan et al., 2010). It is helpful for teachers to remind themselves that they spend roughly half the days of the year with their students, seeing them for less than a third of each of those days. Parental reports on what their children do (and do not do) during nonschool time and information, such as their children's interests, motivations, habits, fears, routines, pressures, needs, and health status, have tremendous educational implications.

HLP4 Use multiple sources of information to develop a comprehensive understanding of a student's strengths and needs.

The following organizations provide educators and families with parent involvement resources: the National Parent Teacher Association, the National Parental Information and Resource Coordination Center, and the PACER Center. But parents can do much more than report on their children's activities and interests. They can also teach their children new skills and provide extra skill practice in the home and community (Harte, 2009; McConnell & Kubina, 2016; Park, Alber-Morgan, & Fleming, 2011). When parents are involved in identifying what skills their children need to learn (and, just as important, what they do not need to learn), the hard work teachers expend is more likely to produce outcomes with real significance in the lives of children and their families. Ultimately, families must live with the outcomes of decisions made by individualized education program (IEP) teams (Giangreco et al., 2011). Over the course of a child's years in school, a great many educators and other professionals will come and go, but family is a constant in the child's life.

Understanding Families of Children with Disabilities

Learning Outcome 3.2 Describe challenges, characteristics, and roles of families of children with disabilities.

Teachers and families working together for the benefit of a child with disabilities make a powerful team. To work together, they must communicate with one another and respect each other's responsibilities and challenges. Families are dynamic, multigenerational systems of interrelated, interdependent elements (Sun, 2016). Each element affects the child, and the child affects each element. Thus, understanding how a child's disability influences

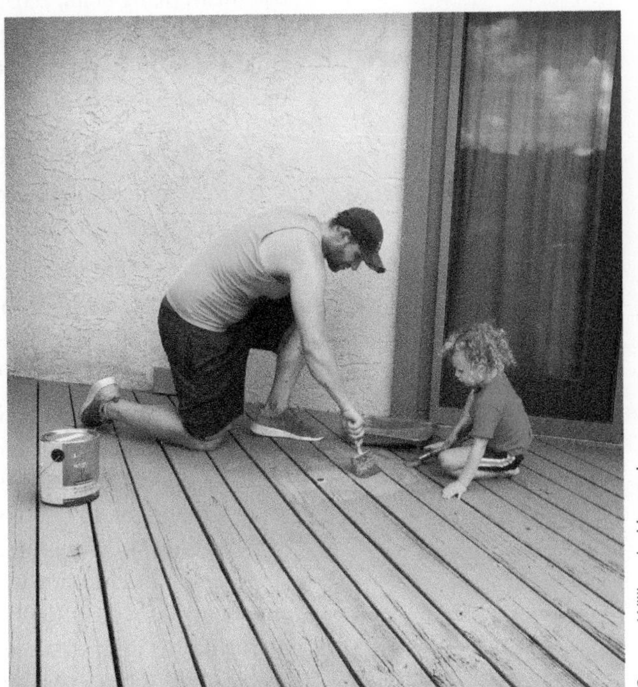

A parent is a child's first teacher.

Source: William L. Heward

the family system and the many interrelated roles of parenthood is an important initial step for effective partnerships with families.

Pearson eText
Video Example 3.1
A disability diagnosis evokes a wide range of emotions in parents.

Family Responses to Disability

The birth of a baby is an emotionally powerful, joyous event that simultaneously brings new challenges and responsibilities. The birth of a child with disabilities, or the onset or diagnosis of a disability, is a traumatic "change in plans" that brings additional challenges and stresses (Van Riper, 2007). Early research on parents' responses to having children with disabilities identified mostly negative outcomes as parents went through three stages of adjustment some call a grief cycle: confronting, adjusting, and accepting or adapting (e.g., Anderegg et al., 1992; Blacher, 1984; Ferguson, 2003). First, parents experience a period of emotional crisis characterized by shock, denial, and disbelief. This initial reaction is followed by a period of alternating feelings of anger, guilt, depression, shame, lowered self-esteem, rejection of the child, and overprotectiveness. Eventually, parents reach a third stage in which they accept and adapt to their child's disability. Firsthand reports by parents describe a similar sequence of experiences (e.g., Boushey, 2001; Holland, 2006).

Poyadue (1993) suggested a stage beyond acceptance that involves appreciation of the positive aspects of family life with a child who has a disability. Many parents report not only coping successfully with the challenges posed by having a child with a disability but also experiencing benefits to the family (Beighton & Wills, 2017; Kayfitz et al., 2010; Lalvani, 2008). For example, Patterson and Leonard (1994) interviewed couples whose children required intensive home care routines because of chronic and complex health care needs and found roughly equal numbers of positive and negative responses. Positive responses included increased closeness among couples and stronger family bonds. In another study, the majority of 1262 parents of children with disabilities agreed with the following statements: "The presence of my child is very uplifting. Because of my child, I have many unexpected pleasures. My child is the reason I am a more responsible person" (Behr et al., 1992, p. 26). As the mother of a child with Down syndrome in another study noted: "[People] think you're overwhelmed.... They think if you're a family with a disabled kid that you, your family, doesn't have fun ... I disagree totally. We have a lot of fun" (Lalvani, 2008, p. 441).

Pearson eText
Video Example 3.2
A special education teacher helped Tyler's father develop a hopeful outlook for his son.

After a period of uncertainty, most families of children with disabilities reestablish healthy family functioning. With strength and resilience, parents determine to do whatever they can to meet their children's needs and to move forward with an enlightened sense of optimism (King et al., 2009; Zechella & Raval, 2018). Figure 3.1 shows a five-stage "resilience model" that identifies experiences and tasks for parents as they move from learning of their child's disability through acceptance and appreciation. Kochhar-Bryant (2008) developed this model based on the following:

- Parents and family members are the best sources of knowledge about their child.
- Parents' resilience may not be immediately appreciable but should be identified and supported.
- Parents are engaged in a continuous adjustment process that can be facilitated by sensitive, caring professionals.

The Many Roles of the Exceptional Parent

Parenting any child demands tremendous physical and emotional energy. Hart and Risley (1995), who conducted a longitudinal study of 42 families with young children, noted, "All the babies had to be fed, changed, and amused. As we went from one home to another we saw the same activities and lives centered on caregiving... . Most impressive of all that the parents had in common was the continual and incredible challenge a growing child presents" (pp. 53, 55).

Parents of children with disabilities, however, experience added physical, emotional, and financial stress (Reilly et al., 2012). Although educators who are not parents of children with disabilities cannot possibly know the 24-hour, 7-day reality of being the parent of such a child (Hutton & Caron, 2005), they should strive to understand as much as possible how a child with special needs affects (and is affected by) the family system. In addition to

FIGURE 3.1 A Resilience Model Toward Family Strength

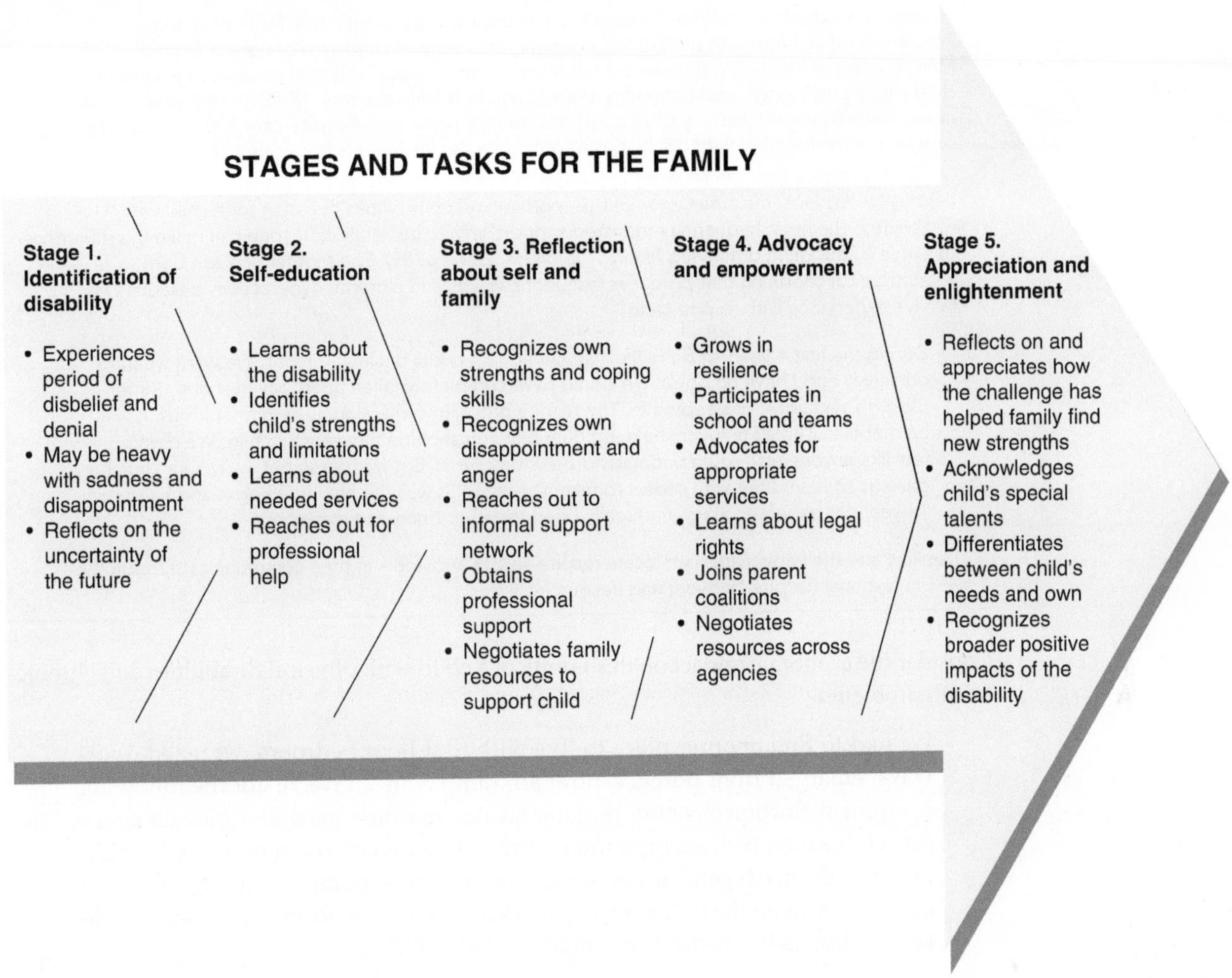

STAGES AND TASKS FOR THE FAMILY

Stage 1. Identification of disability	Stage 2. Self-education	Stage 3. Reflection about self and family	Stage 4. Advocacy and empowerment	Stage 5. Appreciation and enlightenment
• Experiences period of disbelief and denial • May be heavy with sadness and disappointment • Reflects on the uncertainty of the future	• Learns about the disability • Identifies child's strengths and limitations • Learns about needed services • Reaches out for professional help	• Recognizes own strengths and coping skills • Recognizes own disappointment and anger • Reaches out to informal support network • Obtains professional support • Negotiates family resources to support child	• Grows in resilience • Participates in school and teams • Advocates for appropriate services • Learns about legal rights • Joins parent coalitions • Negotiates resources across agencies	• Reflects on and appreciates how the challenge has helped family find new strengths • Acknowledges child's special talents • Differentiates between child's needs and own • Recognizes broader positive impacts of the disability

Source: From Kochhar-Bryant, C. A. (2008). *Collaboration and system coordination for students with special needs: From early childhood to the postsecondary years* (p. 213). Upper Saddle River, NJ: Merrill/Prentice Hall. Used by permission of Pearson Education, Inc.

providing love and affection, parents of children with disabilities fulfill at least nine other varied and demanding roles.

CAREGIVER Caring for any child is a demanding task, but the additional caregiving requirements of children with disabilities can cause added stress (Phillips, Conners, et al., 2017; Quintero & McIntyre, 2010). And the level of care needed by some children with severe disabilities or chronic health conditions can be nonstop:

> Mike sleeps when he wants to, mostly during the day. He sleeps with a heart monitor on which alarms several times per night, because he stops breathing frequently. Usually I'm up by 8:00 and often cannot go to bed until 12:00 or 1:00 because of Mike's feedings, medication. It's hard to fit all of this into a day and still have time for sleep (Bradley et al., 1992).

Although many parents receive help from extended family members and friends in caring for a child with disabilities, the amount and level of help are often insufficient. **Respite care** can reduce the mental and physical stress on parents and families created by the day-to-day responsibilities of caring for a child with disabilities (Strunk, 2010) (Figure 3.2).

PROVIDER Food, clothing, housing, transportation, health care, child care, not to mention music lessons, sports, and hobbies: It takes a lot of money to raise a child. The U.S. Department of Agriculture estimates the cost to raise a child from birth through age 17 is $233,610 (Lino et al., 2017). Providing for a child with disabilities means additional expenses.

FIGURE 3.2 Respite: Support for Families.

Parents of nondisabled children frequently hire others to care temporarily for their children. For parents of children with disabilities, however, the range of child care options is limited. Many parents of children with severe disabilities identify the availability of reliable, high-quality child care as their single most pressing need (Warfield & Hauser-Cram, 1996). In response to this need, many communities have developed respite care programs. **Respite care** is the short-term care of a family member with disabilities to provide relief for parents from caretaking duties.

Quality respite care can reduce the mental and physical stress on parents and families created by the day-to-day (in some cases, moment-to-moment) responsibilities of caring for a child with disabilities. The most frequently requested support service by families,"respite can make the difference between a struggling or thriving family" (Solomon, 2007, p. 39). The mother of a son born with a neurological condition that produces frequent seizures and extreme hyperactivity describes her family's experience with respite care:

> During the first 4 years of Ben's life, we averaged 4 hours of sleep a night. We were wearing ourselves out; I have no doubt we would have completely fallen apart. My husband, Roger, used his vacations for sleeping in. The respite program came along just in time for us. It was hard at first. There's an overwhelming guilt that you shouldn't leave your child. We didn't feel like anyone else could understand Ben's problems. But we had to get away. Our church gave us some money, with orders to take a vacation. It was the first time Roger and I and our 12-year-old daughter, Stacy, had really been together since Ben was born.

Families and their advocates can locate respite service providers in their communities through the ARCH National Respite Network and Resource Center.

Consider the economic impact on this family of a child with physical disabilities and chronic health problems:

> We had to find another place to live with first floor bedroom, widened doorways, enlarged front porch, central air, ramp, van.... We've got the following equipment: Suction machine, portable suction machine, generator for emergency power, hospital bed, air pressure mattress, wheelchair, room monitor, humidifier, bath chair, oxygen, air cleaner, gastronomy tube pump, breathing treatment machine. And all the following expenses have gone up: formula, diapers, appliances, utility bills, medications (Bradley et al., 1992).

It is not just families of children with physical disabilities or health conditions who face financial burdens. Many parents of children with learning and behavior problems pay thousands of dollars each year for specific treatments, behavior intervention programs, and therapy. Although some families receive financial assistance from federal, state, or local agencies, these sources seldom cover the costs (National Conference of State Legislatures, 2018; Worcester et al., 2008). On top of the additional expenses, families of children with disabilities often have reduced income because one parent works part time instead of full time or must withdraw from the workforce altogether to care for the child (Davenport & Eidelman, 2008; Solomon, 2007).

TEACHER Most children learn many skills without anyone teaching them. Children with disabilities, however, often do not acquire new skills naturally or independently. In addition to learning systematic teaching techniques (McConnell & Kubina, 2016; Ozcan & Cavkaytar, 2009), some parents must learn to use and/or teach their children to use special equipment and assistive devices such as hearing aids, braces, wheelchairs, and adapted eating utensils (Parette et al., 2010).

COUNSELOR All parents are counselors in the sense that they contend with their children's changing emotions and attitudes. But parents of a child with disabilities must also deal with their child's feelings that result from his or her particular disability: "Will I still be deaf when I grow up?" "I'm not playing outside anymore; they always tease me." "Why can't I go swimming like the other kids?" Parents play a critical role in how a child with disabilities views himself. Their interactions can help develop an active, engaged child who confidently tries new experiences or a withdrawn child with negative attitudes toward himself and others.

BEHAVIOR SUPPORT SPECIALIST All parents are challenged and frustrated from time to time by their children's noncompliance and misbehavior. But the frequency and severity of challenging behaviors exhibited by some children with disabilities can make it nearly impossible for their families to experience and enjoy normal routines of daily life (Fox et al., 2002). Turnbull and Ruef (1996) interviewed 14 families with children with intellectual disabilities who frequently exhibited problem behavior. The children's problem behavior fell into one of two domains, according to the behavior's impact on the child and the family: dangerous behavior (e.g., "He punches his face a lot on the jaw line—his cheek bone, his mouth, occasionally his forehead.... He will eventually bleed from his mouth.") and difficult behavior (e.g., "When I am around him it is constant noise. He talks or squawks. By afternoon I am frazzled.") (p. 283). Such behavior demands specialized and consistent treatment, and some parents must become skilled in behavior-support techniques to achieve a semblance of normal family life (e.g., Park, Alber-Morgan, & Cannella-Malone, 2011).

Source: Robin Nelson/PhotoEdit

Brothers and sisters without disabilities often have special needs and concerns related to their sibling's disability.

PARENT OF SIBLINGS WITHOUT DISABILITIES Children are deeply influenced by having a brother or a sister with special needs; the nature of that influence, however, is varied. Some studies have found negative effects, such as a higher incidence of emotional or behavioral problems (Vanegas & Abdelrahim, 2016) or resentment or jealousy (Hutton & Caron, 2005), in siblings of children with disabilities. But researchers have also reported many instances of siblings displaying nurturing and affection toward siblings with disabilities (Hannah & Midlarsky, 2005; Moyson & Roeyers, 2011). Research on peer-mediated interventions shows that a brother or sister can help a sibling with disabilities learn new social skills in the home (Kryzak & Jones, 2017; Zhang & Wheeler, 2011). The positive relationship between a sibling and a brother or sister with disabilities often lasts well into adulthood (Orsmond & Seltzer, 2000).

Brothers and sisters of a child with disabilities often have concerns about their sibling's disability, including uncertainty regarding the cause of the disability and its effect on them, uneasiness about the reactions of friends, and a feeling of being left out or being required to do too much for the child with disabilities (Moyson & Roeyers, 2011). Parents play key roles in determining the nature of the relationship between their children and the extent to which their children without disabilities are happy and well adjusted (Quintero & McIntyre, 2010).

PARTNER AND/OR CO-PARENT Having a child with disabilities can put stress on a marriage or other co-parenting relationship. Specific stressors can be as diverse as arguing over who is to blame for the child's disability; disagreeing about expectations for the child's behavior; and spending so much time, money, and energy on the child with disabilities that little is left for each other (Brobst et al., 2009; Meadan et al., 2010; Vanegas & Abdelrahim, 2016). It is a mistake, however, to assume that a child with disabilities has a negative effect on marital relationships. Many families of children with disabilities experience average to above-average levels of marriage adjustment (e.g., Wieland & Baker, 2010), and studies have found that a child with disabilities can strengthen a marriage in part because of a couple's shared commitment to the child (Bauer, 2008; Scorgie & Sobsey, 2000).

INFORMATION SPECIALIST Grandparents, aunts and uncles, neighbors, the school bus driver: All of these people can be important influences on a child's development. Although most parents can reasonably expect their children to receive certain kinds of treatment from significant others, many parents of children with disabilities know they cannot depend on appropriate actions and reactions from others. These parents must try to ensure that other people interact with their child in ways that support their child's dignity, acceptance, opportunities for learning, and maintenance of adaptive behaviors. One mother of a child with Down syndrome describes her response to anyone who stares at her son: She looks the person squarely in the eye and says, "You seem interested in my son. Would you like to meet him?" (Schulz, 1985, p. 6). This usually ends the staring and often creates an opportunity to provide information or begin a friendship.

ADVOCATE Although involvement in their child's education is desirable for all parents, it is a must for parents of children with disabilities. They must acquire special knowledge (e.g., about different kinds of related services) and learn special skills (e.g., how to participate effectively in IEP meetings). They must consistently and firmly present their concerns and wishes regarding learning goals, placement options, and career development opportunities for their children (Lindstrom et al., 2007; Wright & Wright, 2006). They must often advocate for effective educational services and opportunities for their children in a society that devalues people with disabilities (Vanegas & Abdelrahim, 2016). As one mother put it: "If I don't do it, he's going to get lost out there. And so I've got to button up my boot straps and make sure that I know everything that I need to know about this, and take the bull by the horns" (King et al., 2009, p. 58).

Understanding and Respecting Cultural Differences

Learning Outcome 3.3 Examine cultural backgrounds, beliefs, and linguistic practices that can impede parent involvement and identify ways school personnel can help families feel welcome and appreciated.

Cultural and linguistic differences between professionals and families can serve as barriers to family involvement. Teachers who fail to recognize and respect differences between their own cultural perspectives and the values and beliefs of families are prone to biased and faulty judgments about parents that weaken the parent–teacher partnership.

The demands and challenges faced by families who have less formal education, live in poverty, or are isolated from the dominant American culture may prevent them from becoming actively involved in school partnerships. The literature on culturally diverse families supports the following notions (Araujo, 2009; Banks & Banks, 2016; Brandon & Brown, 2009; Cartledge et al., 2000; Correa et al., 2011; Gollnick & Chinn, 2013; Olivos, 2009).

Pearson eText
Video Example 3.3
Families living in poverty may need various supports to maximize their children's potential. https://www.youtube.com/watch?v=sel65jIFRZw&index=5&list

MANY FAMILIES LIVE IN POVERTY In 2016, 19% of all children in the United States were living in poverty, and 41% of children were considered "low income" (Koball & Jiang, 2018). The situation is worse for children with disabilities; children who are Black, Hispanic, or American Indian; and children whose parents are immigrants (Koball & Jiang, 2018). In 2000, Fujiura and Yamaki reported that 28% of children with disabilities lived below the federal poverty line, and material hardships for families raising children with disabilities have worsened since then (Parish et al., 2008).

MANY FAMILIES ARE ENGLISH-LANGUAGE LEARNERS (ELLS) In fall 2017, 5 million ELLs (10.1% of the school population) were enrolled in U.S. schools (U.S. Department of Education, 2020b). For many parents of these children, interactions with the schools are difficult at best or practically nonexistent. Schools should provide materials both in the native language and in English and preferably communicate with the family directly through home visits or by telephone.

IF FAMILIES ARE UNDOCUMENTED IMMIGRANTS, THEY MAY FEAR INTERACTING WITH AUTHORITIES Building families' trust and cooperation, even if they are undocumented immigrants, is important. The special educator's role is not to engage in the activities of the Office of Immigration and Naturalization Services. The school's focus must be educating children.

FAMILIES FROM MANY CULTURAL BACKGROUNDS TEND TO BE FAMILY ORIENTED Extended family members—*compadres* or *padrinos* (godparents) in Hispanic cultures, for instance—may play important roles in child rearing and family decisions. A child's disability or even a mild language problem may be an extremely personal subject for discussion with outsiders, and families may seek solutions for problems within the family structure. Educators should respect this informal kinship system of support and understand that schooling may represent a much more formal and impersonal support service for some families. The close, insular aspect of a family is a strength that helps the family function and cope with the stresses sometimes associated with raising a child with a disability (Bailey et al., 1999a; Rueda et al., 2005).

FAMILIES MAY HAVE DIFFERENT EXPERIENCES WITH AND VIEWS ABOUT DISABILITY In some Hispanic cultures, for example, parents may believe that God sent the child with disabilities to them as a gift or blessing; others may believe the child was sent as a test or a punishment for previous sins. In studies on Latino families, parents acknowledged transforming their lives since the birth of their child by becoming better parents (Bailey et al., 1999a, 1999b). Many Native American cultural/tribal groups do not consider the birth of a child with a disability to be a negative or tragic event. Health and physical characteristics that might be defined as disabilities in mainstream culture may be framed as special strengths rather than deficiencies. "Native American societies have an uncanny gift for tolerance" (Boyd-Ball, 2007, n.p.).

Although previous studies have reported the existence of folk beliefs and alternative treatments for disabilities in some cultural groups, others have found that in Puerto Rican and Mexican families such beliefs are not prevalent (Bailey et al., 1999a, 1999b). Families reported knowing about religious or superstitious explanations for disabilities but did not believe them to be true of their own children. They reported that some family members (usually the elders) might believe that to cure the child, the family must seek traditional or religious healing methods (Bailey et al., 1999a, 1999b; Zechella & Raval, 2018). However, most families interviewed used Western medicine to treat their children with disabilities (Bailey et al., 1999a, 1999b); in fact, some moved to the United States to access services and treatment for their children (Zechella & Raval, 2018).

MANY PARENTS HAVE HAD NEGATIVE EDUCATION EXPERIENCES OF THEIR OWN In some cases, these parents have fallen victim to racial and linguistic discrimination by the schools. Negative feelings toward home–school interaction are often strengthened when schools communicate with parents only to share bad news about their children.

THE EDUCATIONAL SYSTEM—THE SPECIAL EDUCATION SYSTEM, IN PARTICULAR—MAY BE INTIMIDATING TO THE FAMILY Although this may be true for any family, regardless of cultural or linguistic background, for a non–English-speaking family or one that has less formal schooling, a professional's use of educational jargon may be especially intimidating. Some families may even put the professional on a pedestal and, believing the professional is the expert, not question or comment on their own wishes for their child's education.

Pearson eText
Video Example 3.4
Culture affects students' and families' perspectives about school.

Although it is important that professionals understand the cultural and linguistic practices of the community and families they serve, an important caveat must be stated: Just as professionals should refrain from making assumptions about how the parents of a child with a disability feel based on some model or theory of adjustment, educators must also avoid the error of assuming that all members of a cultural or ethnic group share the same experiences, values, or beliefs.

Practitioners should assume that all parents are "life educated" and bring "funds of knowledge" to the parent–professional partnership. **Funds of knowledge** refers to families' strengths, resources, and insights. All families have "historically accumulated and culturally developed bodies of knowledge and skills essential for household or individual functioning and well-being" (Moll et al., 1992, p. 133). To learn about and capitalize on families' funds of knowledge, Johnson (2004) suggests that teachers

- Invite students' families and other community members into the classroom.
- Visit families' homes.
- Spend time in the communities where their students live.
- Develop lessons around students' funds of knowledge.
- Plan class projects that explore families' cultural practices.

Changing Needs as Children Grow

Another way to increase our understanding of how a child with disabilities might affect his or her family and vice versa is to examine the likely impact of the child's and family's changing needs at various ages (Turnbull et al., 2015). Table 3.1 identifies some of the major issues and concerns that parents and siblings face during four life-cycle stages and suggests strategies for supporting families at each stage. And the demands of parenting a child with disabilities often do not end when the child reaches adulthood. Many parents in their 70s and 80s continue to care for their adult children with disabilities (Pryce et al., 2017).

Developing and Maintaining Family–Professional Partnerships

Turnbull and colleagues (2015) define a family–professional *partnership* as

> A relationship in which families (not just parents) and professionals agree to build on each other's expertise and resources, as appropriate, for the purpose of making and implementing decisions that will directly benefit students and indirectly benefit other family members and professionals (p. 161).

To better understand the characteristics of effective family–professional partnerships, Blue-Banning et al. (2004) conducted in-depth focus groups and interviews with 137 adult family members of children with and without disabilities and 53 professionals. The participants represented a wide range of ethnic groups and socioeconomic levels and resided in Kansas, North Carolina, and Louisiana. Results suggested partnerships are facilitated by professional behaviors clustered around six dimensions: communication, commitment, equality, skills, trust, and respect.

The study by Blue-Banning and colleagues (2004) gives empirical support to something that educators have long known but too seldom practice: Effective home–school partnerships are characterized by family members and professionals jointly pursuing shared goals in a climate of mutual respect and trust. Indeed, "interpersonal factors—such as equitable involvement in decision-making, a problem-solving-oriented meeting style, a transparent

TABLE 3.1 Issues faced by family members during four life-cycle stages of a person with disabilities and ways that professionals can help

	LIFE-CYCLE STAGES	
	BIRTH AND EARLY CHILDHOOD	**CHILDHOOD**
Issues for parents	• Discovering and coming to terms with exceptionality • Obtaining an accurate diagnosis • Informing siblings and relatives • Locating early intervention services • Participating in IFSP meetings • Seeking to find meaning in the exceptionality • Clarifying a personal ideology to guide decisions • Addressing issues of stigma • Identifying positive contributions of exceptionality • Setting great expectations	• Establishing routines to carry out family functions • Adjusting emotionally to educational implications • Clarifying issues of inclusion vs. special class placement • Advocating for inclusive experiences • Participating in IEP conferences • Locating community resources • Arranging for extracurricular activities • Developing a vision for the future
Issues for siblings	• Less parental time and energy for sibling needs • Feelings of jealousy because of less attention • Fears associated with misunderstandings about exceptionality	• Division of responsibility for any physical care needs • Limited family resources for recreation and leisure • Informing friends and teachers • Possible concern about younger sibling surpassing older • Issues of attending the same school • Need for basic information on exceptionality
Enhancing successful transitions	• Advise parents to prepare for the separation of the preschool child by periodically leaving the child with others. • Facilitate gathering of information about and visiting of preschools in the community. • Encourage participation in parent-to-parent programs. (Veteran parents are matched in one-to-one relationships with parents who are just beginning the transition process.) • Familiarize parents with possible school (elementary and secondary) programs, career options, or adult programs so they have an idea of future opportunities.	• Provide parents with an overview of curricular options. • Ensure that IEP meetings provide an empowering context for family collaboration. • Encourage participation in parent-to-parent matches, workshops, or family support groups to discuss transitions with others.

(Continued)

TABLE 3.1 (Continued)

	LIFE-CYCLE STAGES	
	ADOLESCENCE	**ADULTHOOD**
Issues for parents	• Adjusting emotionally to possible chronicity of exceptionality • Identifying issues of emerging sexuality • Dealing with physical and emotional changes of puberty • Addressing possible peer isolation and rejection • Planning for career/vocational development • Arranging for leisure and recreation activities • Expanding child's self-determination skills • Planning for postsecondary education	• Addressing supported employment and living options • Adjusting emotionally to any adult implications of dependency • Addressing the need for socialization opportunities outside the family • Initiating career choice or vocational program • Planning for possible need for guardianship
Issues for siblings	• Overidentification with sibling • Greater understanding of differences in people • Influence of exceptionality on career choice • Dealing with possible stigma and embarrassment • Participation in sibling training programs • Opportunity for sibling support groups	• Possible issues of responsibility for financial support • Addressing concerns regarding genetic implications • Introducing new in-laws to exceptionality • Need for information on career and living options • Clarify role of sibling advocacy • Possible issues of guardianship
Enhancing successful transitions	• Assist families and adolescents to identify community leisure activities. • Incorporate into the IEP skills that will be needed in future career and vocational programs. • Visit or become familiar with a variety of career and living options. • Develop a mentor relationship with an adult with a similar exceptionality and an individual who has a career that matches the student's strengths and preferences.	• Provide preferred information to families about guardianship, estate planning, wills, and trusts. • Assist family members in transferring responsibilities to the individual with an exceptionality, other family members, or service providers as appropriate. • Assist the young adult or family members with career or vocational choices. • Address the issues and responsibilities of marriage and family for the young adult.

IEP (individualized education program), IFSP (individualized family service program).

Sources: Adapted from Turnbull, A., & Turnbull, H., Erwin, E. J., Soodak, L. C., & Shogren, K. A. (2015). *Families, professionals, and exceptionality: Positive outcomes through partnership and trust* (7th ed., p. 108); and Turnbull, A. P., & Turnbull, H. R. (1990, 1997, 2001). *Families, professionals, and exceptionality: Collaborating for empowerment* (2nd ed., pp. 134–135; 3rd ed., p. 149; 4th ed., p. 173). Upper Saddle River, NJ: Pearson. Used by permission.

process, and feeling respected...may be important determinants of parents' satisfaction with meetings and subsequent services" (Slade et al., 2018, p. 254). Families receive supports in the form of knowledge and resources that empower them to participate as full partners, and professionals receive input from families that helps them be more effective teachers.

HLP3 Collaborate with families to support student learning and secure needed services.

Culturally Responsive Services for Families

Educators can increase the involvement by families from culturally and linguistically diverse backgrounds with strategies such as the following (Araujo, 2009; Brandon & Brown, 2009; Francis et al., 2017; Harry, 2008; Rodriguez et al., 2014):

- Have native-speaking staff members make initial contacts.
- Provide trained, culturally sensitive interpreters during parent–teacher conferences and IEP and IFSP meetings.
- Conduct meetings in family-friendly settings.
- Identify and defer to key decision makers in the family.
- Recognize that families from some cultures may view time differently from the way school personnel do and schedule meetings accordingly.
- Provide transportation and child care to make it easier for families to attend school-based activities.
- Ask questions to learn more about the culture and experiences of families.

HLP2 Organize and facilitate effective meetings with professionals and families.

CULTURAL RECIPROCITY Educators should also work toward **cultural reciprocity**, understanding how differing values and belief systems may influence families' perspectives, wishes, and decisions. For example, a special educator who views disability as a physical phenomenon that can be assessed and treated objectively may have difficulty developing an effective partnership with parents who view disability as a blessing or a punishment that is to be treated from a spiritual perspective (Bailey et al., 1999a; Harry et al., 1999).

FIGURE 3.3 Building Cultural Reciprocity

Professionals who seek to make a difference for children must be willing to take the initiative in building a bridge between the cultures of diverse families and the culture of schools. To build this bridge, Beth Harry recommends that professionals initiate a two-way process of information sharing and understanding called *cultural reciprocity*. The process is recursive, meaning that each step informs the others.

- **Step 1.** Identify the cultural values embedded in your interpretation of a student's difficulties or in a recommendation for service. Ask yourself which values underlie your recommendation. Next, analyze experiences that have contributed to your holding of these values. Consider the roles of nationality, culture, socioeconomic status, and professional education in shaping your values.
- **Step 2.** Find out whether the family being served recognizes and values your assumptions and, if not, how family members' views differ from yours.
- **Step 3.** Acknowledge and give explicit respect to any cultural differences identified and fully explain the cultural basis of your assumptions.
- **Step 4.** Through discussion and collaboration, determine the most effective way of adapting your professional interpretations or recommendations to the value system of this family.

Harry points out that "by developing your own cultural self-awareness, you are able to recognize the cultural underpinnings of your professional practice. This, in turn, enables you to facilitate conversations with the families." Through the process, families also acquire knowledge about the special education system, which supports them in making informed decisions about services. "With cultural reciprocity, we find not only better relationships, but more reasonable goals that are implemented."

Source: Adapted from ERIC/OSEP Special Project. (2001). *Family involvement in special education* (Research Connections in Special Education, no. 9, pp. 4–5). Arlington, VA: ERIC Clearinghouse on Disabilities and Gifted Education.

Recognizing differences between our own perspectives and those of people from other cultures and ethnic groups requires careful examination of our own cultural background and belief system. "Understanding that our own beliefs and practices are but one cultural variation should make it easier to respect, and therefore to serve, the wide diversity of families whose children are served by special education programs" (Harry, 2003, p. 138). See Figure 3.3, "Building Cultural Reciprocity."

Principles of Effective Communication

Ongoing two-way communication is the key operational element of the family–professional partnership. The family members in the study by Blue-Banning and colleagues (2004) said they needed frequent communication, but they also highlighted the importance of the quality of communication. "Family members stressed that communication should be honest and open, with no hidden information and no 'candy-coating' of bad news" (p. 173). Family members and professionals emphasized the need for two-way communication, stating that both professionals and parents should listen carefully and nonjudgmentally to what each has to say. One father stated it like this: "The first thing is to listen to us . . . because we know our kids better than anybody. . . . I think some of these people have preconceived notions about everything. . . . So if I tried to say to them [professionals] something, it'd be LISTEN TO ME" (p. 175).

When asked to voice their perceptions of and preferences for interactions with education professionals, a group of parents of children with autism said they wanted frequent, honest, and open communication between home and school (Stoner et al., 2005). "Parents wanted to be informed of achievements, but they also wanted to know of any problems that the teachers had encountered" (p. 46). Wilson (1995) recommends five principles for effective communication between educators and parents.

ACCEPT PARENTS' STATEMENTS Conveying verbal and nonverbal acceptance of parents' statements tells parents their input is valued. Parents are more likely to speak freely and openly when they believe that what they say is respected. Acceptance means conveying "I

Transition: Next Year Is Now

Culturally Responsive Transition Planning

The convergence of three factors obliges special educators to employ culturally responsive transition planning strategies.

Poor postschool outcomes for marginalized groups. Students of color, English-language learners, and students from low socioeconomic status (SES) backgrounds are less likely to experience success (e.g., enroll in postsecondary education, find meaningful paid employment) when they leave high school than are White, native-English-speaking, high-SES students (Musu-Gillette et al., 2016; Newman et al., 2011). These postschool outcome gaps are even more pronounced for students with disabilities (Newman et al., 2011).

Decreased parent involvement as students get older. As students progress through school, parent involvement typically declines (Child Trends, 2013). Given that parent involvement is a strong predictor of positive postschool outcomes for youth with disabilities (Test et al., 2009), all educators, even those working with secondary-age students, should strive to engage families.

Cultural mismatch between families/students and school personnel. As the student population in U.S. schools becomes more culturally, linguistically, and economically diverse, school personnel remain a homogenous group—predominantly White and female (National Center for Education Statistics, 2019b).

What Is Culturally Responsive Transition Planning?

Culturally responsive transition planning requires teachers to understand their biases, to listen to and collaborate closely with families, to facilitate student engagement in their own planning, and to support the dreams and hopes of students and their families—even when they differ from those of the teacher (Greene, 2014). Teachers who practice culturally responsive transition planning should consider the communication and collaboration suggestions made throughout this chapter and seek answers to these questions:

- How can I help families transmit their language, values, and cultural practices to their child, while helping the student prepare for success in the wider community?
- How can I promote student independence and self-determination when those goals clash with the family's values? Autonomy (e.g., independent living) may not be a high-priority goal in some family-oriented cultures.
- How will I prepare youth to interact with authorities (e.g., immigration agents, police officers) in ways that balance self-advocacy and personal safety?
- What community supports are available to my students' families? Are those supports accessible? Do they provide culturally responsive services?
- What should I teach my students about eye contact, expectations and rules about social distancing, concepts of time, and work ethic when I prepare students for job interviews and other "real world" interactions with adults? Are my expectations congruent with my students' cultural values?

Additional considerations for culturally responsive transition planning can be found in Povenmire-Kirk et al. (2015) and Suk et al. (2020).

understand and appreciate your point of view." It does not mean the teacher must agree with everything a parent says.

LISTEN ACTIVELY A good listener pays attention to content, noting who said it and how, and responds in a genuine manner. For example, in an IEP conference attended by extended family members, an educator should notice if a grandparent seems to be speaking for the child's parents or if the mother and father express different opinions about an issue through tones of voice or body language. An active listener not only comprehends, interprets, sorts, and analyzes what the speaker says but also responds to the speaker's message with animation

FIGURE 3.4 Example of Communication Problems Between an Active and a Passive Listener.

ACTIVELY LISTENING PARENT	PASSIVELY LISTENING PRESCHOOL TEACHER
"I would very much like to have my child use his communication board on a more regular basis. Currently, he becomes very frustrated because he can't tell us what he needs." The parent frowns and looks sad.	"All the students in my class are able to speak. We will have the speech/language pathologist work with Andy so that he can speak as well." The teacher is fiddling with papers she needs for her next parent conference.
"Perhaps you didn't read Andy's file carefully. His cerebral palsy is so involved that he is not able to make any understandable speech sounds. We have already had him evaluated by a speech therapist at St. Luke's, and they created the communication board for him so he could develop his language skills." The parent shakes her head and pushes a catalogue of language devices toward the childcare provider.	(Still looking at her other papers.) "We have an excellent speech/language pathologist. She will have Andy talking in no time. Andy can work with her during circle time since that is oral and Andy wouldn't be able to participate."
"We don't want Andy to miss out on circle time. He loves to be a part of the group. We can choose appropriate pictures to put on his communication board so he can respond with the rest of the children. He gets very frustrated when he is not allowed to be with the rest of the students." The parent's shoulders tighten, and she leans forward, thumping the catalogue of language devices to emphasize the use of the communication board.	"Oh, we don't let the children bring toys to the circle. He has to be able to speak up like everyone else. Also, I've been meaning to talk to you about his behavior. He has been refusing to cooperate with our group activities. I'd like to send him to time out when this happens."
(She gives a big sigh.) "As I said, he gets very frustrated when he isn't able to communicate and when he isn't a part of the group. I don't think time out would be the right answer for this problem."	"Well, if you don't allow us to control his behavior, I don't know how Andy is ever going to be able to be a part of our class." She looks at her watch, ready to end the meeting.
"We seem to have a different understanding of Andy's problems. Perhaps we need to meet as a team again, so the speech-language pathologist can also be involved. I'm concerned that you are not addressing Andy's communication needs." The parent's face is red, and her hands are shaking as she pulls the catalogue back into her bag. The parent takes a deep breath, pulls her bag over her shoulder, and leaves, shaking her head as she goes.	"That would be fine, because I have another parent coming now and can't talk any longer. It has been a pleasure meeting with you today." The childcare provider smiles and shakes the parent's hand as she shuffles her papers together and heads toward the door to greet the next parent.

Source: Adapted from Howard, V. F., Williams, B. F., & Lepper, C. (2010). *Very young children with special needs: A foundation for educators, families, and service providers* (4th ed., p. 71). Upper Saddle River, NJ: Pearson. Used by permission.

and interest (Howard et al., 2014; Thistle et al., 2015). Figure 3.4 illustrates the kind of communication problems that occur when only one party is actively listening.

QUESTION EFFECTIVELY Teachers should ask mostly open-ended questions when communicating with parents. An open-ended question such as "What did Shareena do with her homework project last week?" is more likely to evoke an informative reply from parents than is the closed-ended question "Is Shareena having trouble with her homework?" which might result in a "yes" or "no" response. Questions to parents should not focus solely on problems or deficits, and teachers must respect families' desire to keep some things private and "in the family" (Turnbull et al., 2015).

ENCOURAGE It is important for parents to hear good news about their son or daughter. Describing or showing parents specific instances of their child's good behavior or improved performance encourages parental involvement.

STAY FOCUSED Although greetings and some small talk are desirable before getting down to business, conversations between parents and teachers should focus on the child's educational program and progress. Educators must be sensitive to cultural differences and conversational styles of individual families (Gonzalez-Mena, 2017; Lynch & Hanson, 2011), but they must also notice when small talk is drifting from the purpose at hand so they can refocus the conversation.

Identifying and Breaking Down Barriers to Parent–Teacher Partnerships

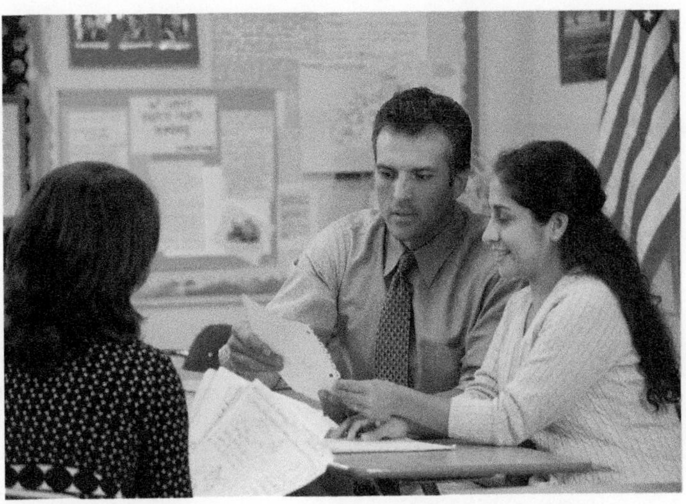

Source: Areil Skelley/Getty Images

Parent-teacher communication is enhanced when teachers identify and breakdown barriers.

Let's face it: Parents and teachers do not always communicate effectively and cooperate with one another. Sometimes they seem to be on opposite sides, battling over what each thinks is best for the child. The child, unfortunately, never wins that battle. She needs to have the people responsible for the two places where she spends most of her life—home and school—work together to make those environments consistent with and supportive of her job of learning.

PROFESSIONAL ROADBLOCKS TO COMMUNICATION Parents' and teachers' assumptions about and attitudes toward one another are sometimes counterproductive. Teachers sometimes complain that parents are uninterested, uncooperative, or hostile. Parents may complain that educators are negative, unavailable, or patronizing. We should examine factors that cause friction between parents and teachers, not to assign fault but to identify what we can change and improve. Professionals who recognize that some of their own behaviors may diminish the potential for productive partnerships with parents are in a better position to change their actions and obtain the benefits that such relationships can provide (Hanhan, 2008; Matuszny et al., 2007).

Although educators cannot directly change the attitudes of parents, they can—and, as professionals, must—identify and eliminate personal behaviors that may serve as barriers to communication with families. Some professionals hold stereotypes and false assumptions about what parents of children with disabilities must be feeling and what they must need (Dyson, 1996; Voltz, 1994). Such attitudes often lead to poor relationships between families and professionals. We should not be surprised if parents feel intimidated, confused, hostile—or terminate their involvement altogether—when professionals interact with them in any of the following ways:

- *Treating parents as vulnerable clients instead of equal partners.* Professionals who see parents only as people who need their help make a grave mistake. This dynamic is particularly troubling when a White teacher approaches families of color as needing to be "saved." Teachers must recognize all families as valuable contributors and act accordingly.
- *Keeping professional distance.* Most professionals in human services develop some degree of distance to avoid getting too involved with a client—supposedly to maintain objectivity and credibility. But aloofness or coldness in the name of professionalism has hindered or terminated many parent–teacher relationships. Parents must believe that the educators working with their children really care about them (Nelson et al., 2004).
- *Treating parents as if they need counseling.* Some professionals make the faulty assumption that having a child with disabilities causes a parent to need therapy or parent education. A mother of a child who attended a preschool for students with developmental delays described her frustration: "Everybody who came here was aimed at me. Everybody is telling me 'You need parent counseling.' I mean, I have lived for 30 years. I never needed help and all of a sudden I need help on how to do this and help on how to do that. I feel like they are saying John is not the problem, I am the problem" (Rao, 2000, p. 481).
- *Blaming parents for their child's disability.* Some parents do feel responsible for their child's disability and, with a little encouragement from a professional, can be made to feel completely guilty (Broomhead, 2013). Productive parent–professional relationships focus on collaborative problem solving, not blame.
- *Disrespecting parents as less intelligent.* Teachers sometimes give too little recognition to parents' information and suggestions. They consider parents too biased, too involved, or too

unskilled to make useful observations (Lake & Billingsley, 2000). "They treat me like I'm uneducated. They break down things into real small pieces and then ask me to repeat things. I have gone to nursing school. I can read. Maybe they met other people who cannot read but they can ask me 'Rose, can you read?' They treat you like you are a child" (Rao, 2000, p. 481).

- *Treating parents as adversaries.* Some teachers expect the worst whenever they interact with parents. Even when that attitude can be partially explained by previous unpleasant encounters with unreasonable parents, it usually becomes a self-fulfilling prophecy and is at best a negative influence on new relationships.
- *Labeling parents.* Some educators are eager to label parents. If parents disagree with a diagnosis, they are in denial; if parents refuse a suggested treatment, they are resistant; and if parents insist that something is wrong with their child despite test evidence to the contrary, they are anxious (Sonnenschein, 1981).

CONFLICT RESOLUTION Not all ineffective parent–teacher relationships are caused by professional mishandling. Some parents are genuinely difficult to work with or unreasonable. Parents sometimes fight long and hard for services for their child. But after securing services, the parents continue their intense advocacy, and even minor issues become major confrontations. One mother stated, "For years I have scrapped and fought for services. Now I come on like gangbusters over issues that are really not that important. I don't like what has happened to me. I've ended up to be an aggressive, angry person" (Bronicki & Turnbull, 1987, p. 10).

Although some teachers voice concern that parents of children with disabilities are unrealistic and make too many demands of schools (e.g., Chesley & Calaluce, 1997), most recognize these parents, similar to all parents, are simply advocating for the best possible educational services and outcomes for their children. When someone sees things differently from us and we both have vested interests in the outcome, we often attempt to resolve our differences through argument. Although a teacher may "win" an argument with parents—if one defines winning as forcing parents to agree verbally or simply give up their perspective—arguing is rarely a useful tool in a partnership.

Dialoguing. Dialoguing is an approach to conflict resolution in which both parties try to see each other's point of view. Gonzalez-Mena (2017) points out differences between a dialogue and an argument:

- The object of an argument is to win; the object of a dialogue is to gather information.
- The arguer tells; the dialoguer asks.
- The arguer tries to persuade; the dialoguer seeks to learn.
- The arguer tries to convince; the dialoguer wants to discover.
- The arguer sees two opposing views and considers hers the valid or best one; the dialoguer is willing to understand multiple viewpoints (p. 160).

Most of us are better arguers than dialoguers—probably because we have had much more practice with the former. We tend to argue first and think rationally later. But later might be too late if in "winning" the argument, we have damaged the relationship. Gonzalez-Mena (2017) recommends the RERUN approach—reflect, explain, reason, understand, and negotiate:

- **Reflect.** Acknowledge what you perceive the other person is thinking or feeling. If you understand what the person is feeling, you might say, "I think you're looking at it this way." If you perceive that the other person is very emotional, acknowledge your perception: "You sound really upset." These two openers are invitations to talk more. People who know their feelings and thoughts are received and accepted are more likely to be open to listening—if not right away, eventually.
- **Explain.** Explain your perspective concisely. But do not lecture. We have two ears and one mouth—a reminder that we should listen twice as much as we talk.
- **Reason.** The explanation of your perspective should include the reason you believe or feel the way you do.

- **Understand.** Next comes the hardest part. Tune in to both your own and the parent's thoughts and feelings and try to understand the situation from both points of view. You do not have to say anything out loud at this point; just be sure you have clarity. You may have to talk inwardly to yourself to get it. Self-reflection is an important part of the process. When you think you understand, you're ready for the next step.
- **Negotiate.** Try brainstorming together until you can find a mutually satisfying solution. Don't give up. Refuse to take an either–or attitude. If you don't get stuck in a dualistic frame of mind, you can probably find a third or fourth solution that differs from or combines both of your stances on the matter. (Adapted from Gonzalez-Mena, 2017, p. 162.)

Additional suggestions for effective communication and conflict resolution with parents can be found in Dyches et al. (2012); McLamed and Reiman (2017); and Mueller and Vick (2018).

Home–School Communication Methods

Learning Outcome 3.4 Describe principles of effective communication between educators and families, and contrast several common modes of home–school communication.

No single method of communication will be effective or even appropriate with every parent and family. By making a variety of communication avenues available to families, teachers can increase the number of families they reach and the frequency and quality of communications. Some families prefer face-to-face interactions; others appreciate receiving written messages or phone calls; still others feel more comfortable communicating with teachers through email messages (Stuart, Flis, & Rinaldi, 2006). Teachers should have a variety of both one-way and two-way communication strategies in their toolkits and should ask parents which methods of communication they prefer. Featured Teacher Joshua Hoppe agrees: "Embracing parents' preferred means of communication is crucial. I have some parents who respond only to face-to-face contact, others who prefer exchanging written notes, some who prefer phone conversations, and some who prefer exchanging emails and text messages." Table 3.2 summarizes some effective forms of home–school communication.

Face-to-Face Communication

PARENT–TEACHER CONFERENCES Although open houses and informal chats during pick-up and drop-off are examples of face-to-face interactions teachers may have with families, parent–teacher conferences provide for more extensive, in-depth communication. In a face-to-face meeting, teachers and parents can exchange information and coordinate their efforts to assist the child with disabilities in school and at home. Unfortunately, parent–teacher conferences

TABLE 3.2 Methods of home–school communication

MODE	ONE-WAY METHODS	TWO-WAY METHODS
Face to face	• Video messages • Video posts	• Informal, spontaneous meetings • Parent–teacher conferences (including video conferences and home visits) • IEP and IFSP meetings
Text	• Happy grams • Letters • Newsletters • Websites • Bulletin boards • App-delivered messages	• Home–school reporting forms or assignment planners • Dialogue notebooks • Home–school contracts • Emails • Text messages (via phone or classroom communication app)
Voice	• Voicemails • Hotlines	• Phone calls

IEP, individualized education program; IFSP, individualized family service plan.

FIGURE 3.5 Outline for a Parent–Teacher Conference

Conference Outline

Date Oct. 12, 2021 Time 4:30 - 5:30

Student's Name Jeremy Wright
Parents' Name(s) Barbara and Tom Wright
Teacher's Name Tim G.
Other Staff Present None
Objectives for Conference: (1) Show graph of J's reading progress, (2) find out about spelling program, (3) get parents' ideas: intervention for difficulties on playground/in gym, (4) share list of books for leisure reading

Student's Strengths
- good worker academically, wants to learn
- excited about progress in reading fluency

Area(s) Where Improvement Is Needed:
- continue w/spelling @ home
- arguments & fighting w/other kids

Questions to Ask Parents:
- Interactions w/friends while playing in neighborhood?
- How would they feel about f'dback from classmate re: playground/gym behavior?
- Consequences?

Parents' Responses/Comments:
- very pleased w/reading - want to build on it.
- wondering how long w/in-home spelling?
- willing to give rewards @ home: playground/gym

Examples of Student's Work/Interactions:
- graph of corrects/errors per min.: reading
- weekly pre- & post-test scores: spelling.

Current Programs and Strategies Used by Teacher:
- reading: silent read, two 1-min. time trials, self-charting comprehension practice
- spelling: practice w/tape recorder, self-checking

Suggestions for Parents:
- continue spelling games (invite friends)
- Show interest in/play fantasy games (Dung. & Dragons) w/J

Suggestions from Parents:
- Try using some high-interest spelling words (e.g., joust, castle)
- Matt & Amin could help with playground/gym program

Follow-up Activities: (Agreed to in conf)

Parents:
- Continue to play spelling game 2 nights per week
- Take J to library for adventure books

Teacher:
- Ask J for high-interest words & use 3-4 in his weekly list.
- Develop peer intervention strategy w/Matt, Amin & J (group contingency?)

Date to Call for Follow-up: Oct. 26 (Tuesday) ______ (check when called)

are often stiff, formal affairs with anxious teachers and worried parents wondering what bad news they will hear this time. With some thoughtful planning and a systematic approach, however, teachers can improve productivity and comfort for all participants.

HLP2 Organize and facilitate effective meetings with professionals and families.

Preparing for the Conference. Preparation is the key to an effective parent–teacher conference. It entails establishing specific objectives for the conference, reviewing a record of the student's recent assessments or grades, selecting examples of the student's work, creating a graph or chart showing progress, and preparing an agenda for the meeting (Dardig, 2008; Washburn & Billingsley, 2019).

Figure 3.5 shows an outline that teachers can use to prepare an agenda for and record notes on a parent–teacher conference.

Conducting the Conference. The child's classroom is an appropriate setting for most parent–teacher conferences because it provides ready access to student records and curriculum materials and reminds the teacher and parents that the purpose of the conference is to work together to improve the child's education. In some cases, it may be appropriate to hold the conference in the family's home, a community setting (e.g., public library), or via videoconferencing (e.g., Zoom, Skype, FaceTime). Wherever parent conferences are held, the area should be conducive to partnership interactions. Teachers should not sit behind their desks, creating a barrier between themselves and the parents, or have parents sit in undersized children's chairs.

A four-step sequence for conducting parent–teacher conferences recommended by Stephens and Wolf (1989) more than 30 years ago remains sound advice today:

1. *Build rapport*. Establishing mutual trust and the belief that the teacher really cares about the student is important to a good parent–teacher conference. A minute or two devoted to relevant small talk helps build rapport. Instead of beginning with a superficial statement about the weather or traffic, the teacher might comment on some recent news or community event that is likely to be of interest to the family or their child.
2. *Obtain information*. As suggested earlier, teachers should use open-ended questions that cannot be answered with a simple yes or no. For example, "Which school activities has Felix mentioned lately?" is better than "Has Felix told you what we've been doing in school?" The first question encourages parents to provide more information; the teacher is trying to build a conversation, not preside over a question-and-answer session. Throughout the conference, the teacher should show genuine interest in listening to parents' concerns, avoid dominating the conversation, and stay focused on the purpose of the meeting. Teachers should refrain from making gestures, facial expressions, and other forms of "body language" that suggest frustration, suspicion, confrontation, or defensiveness. Above all, professionals should not make comments that lecture ("Do you realize . . ."), criticize or judge ("That was a mistake . . ."), or threaten ("Unless you take my advice . . .") (Fiedler et al., 2007; Hanhan, 2008).
3. *Provide information*. The teacher should give parents concrete information about their child in jargon-free language. The teacher should share examples of schoolwork and data on student performance—what the student has already learned and what he needs to learn next. If the student has made insufficient progress, the teacher and parents should discuss ways to improve.
4. *Summarize and follow up*. The conference should end with a concise summary of the discussion and any decisions that were made. The teacher should review strategies agreed on during the conference and indicate which party will carry out each strategy. Some teachers record notes on a laptop computer during the conference and at the conclusion of the meeting print a copy so that parents will also have a record of what was said or agreed to.

HLP5 Interpret and communicate assessment information with stakeholders to collaboratively design and implement educational programs.

Detailed suggestions for planning and conducting parent–teacher conferences can be found in Dardig (2008), Hanhan (2008), Kroth and Edge (2007), and Washburn and Billingsley (2019). These strategies are relevant for all types of parent–teacher meetings. However, IEP, IFSP, and transition planning meetings, which are discussed in Chapters 2, 14, and 15, respectively, entail additional procedural requirements.

Pearson eText
Video Example 3.5
Teachers should know what they say and do during parent-teacher conferences leaves a lasting impression on parents.

VIDEO SHARING Not surprisingly, face time with families will almost always be a form of two-way communication. However, there may be times when a teacher wants to share information via video. For instance, a teacher may post on YouTube or on her class website a video explanation of how to complete an upcoming homework assignment. Or if a student is absent, a teacher may video record a lesson and send it directly to the student.

Written Communication

Face-to-face meetings should not be the sole means of home–school communication. Written messages, especially when part of a systematic program of ongoing information exchange, can be an effective way to maintain home–school communication. Teachers should never rely on written messages, regardless of their form, as the sole method of communicating with parents. Educators must also be sensitive to the cultural and linguistic backgrounds and educational levels of parents (Al-Hassan & Gardner, 2002). A study of parents' rights documents published by state departments of education found that only 4% to 8% of the materials were written at the recommended reading level for parents (Fitzgerald & Watkins, 2006). Up to 50% of the documents were written at the college reading level or higher, and "nearly all lacked additional organizational and textual features that would make them more readable" (p. 507). Similarly, Lo (2014) found most IEPs were written at high school or college reading levels. If parents must spend a great deal of time trying to understand the

FIGURE 3.6 Daily Behavior Report Card

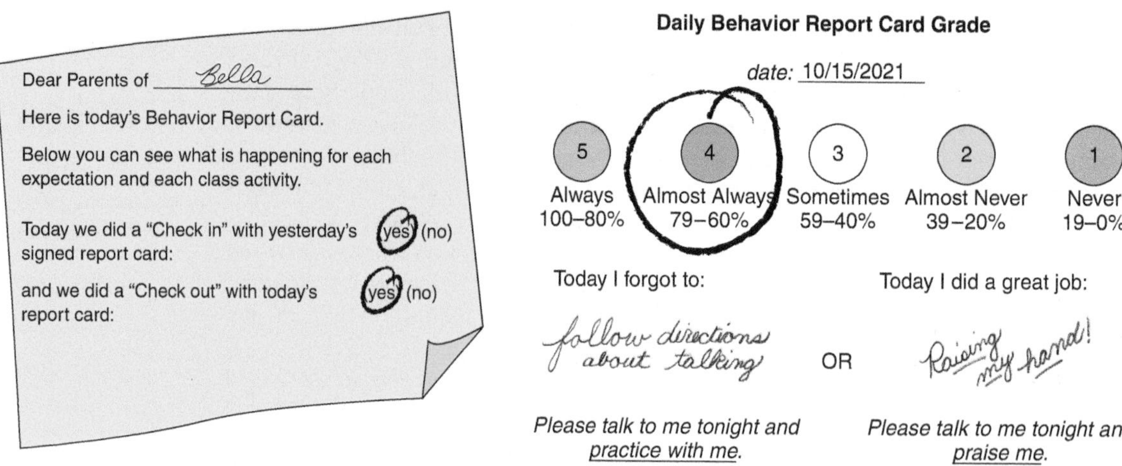

Dear Parents of *Bella*

Here is today's Behavior Report Card.

Below you can see what is happening for each expectation and each class activity.

Today we did a "Check in" with yesterday's signed report card: (yes) (no)

and we did a "Check out" with today's report card: (yes) (no)

Daily Behavior Report Card Grade

date: 10/15/2021

5	4	3	2	1
Always 100–80%	Almost Always 79–60%	Sometimes 59–40%	Almost Never 39–20%	Never 19–0%

Today I forgot to: *follow directions about talking*

OR

Today I did a great job: *Raising my hand!*

Please talk to me tonight and practice with me.

Please talk to me tonight and praise me.

Time Period / Expectation	Math	Science	Social Studies	Language Arts
Be prepared	5 4 3 2 1	5 4 3 2 1	5 4 3 2 1	5 4 3 2 1
Be respectful	5 4 3 2 1	5 4 3 2 1	5 4 3 2 1	5 4 3 2 1
Raise hands when you need help	5 4 3 2 1	5 4 3 2 1	5 4 3 2 1	5 4 3 2 1
Eyes on teacher	5 4 3 2 1	5 4 3 2 1	5 4 3 2 1	5 4 3 2 1
Follow directions	5 4 3 2 1	5 4 3 2 1	5 4 3 2 1	5 4 3 2 1

Teacher's Initials: *KV* Student's Initials: *B* Parent's Initials: *DS*

Source: From Electronic Daily Behavior Report Card (E Dbrc): A Web Based System for Progress Monitoring by Tufan Adiguzel, Denise Soares, and Kimberly Vannest.

written messages from their child's school, they may view those messages as a nuisance and be discouraged from active involvement in their child's education.

Pearson eText

Video Example 3.6

Positive home–school communication contributes to the rewards of being a special educator.

TWO-WAY HOME–SCHOOL REPORTING FORMS Teachers can build a two-way, parent–teacher communication system around a reporting form or a notebook that the child carries between home and school. A standard form or checklist such as the one shown in Figure 3.6 can inform parents about their child's homework assignments, behavior in the classroom, and progress on IEP goals (Mires & Lee, 2017; Vannest et al., 2010; Vannest et al., 2011). Parents sign the form to indicate they have received it and can use the form to provide information or request assistance from the teacher(s). To be most effective, home–school communication forms should be simple to use, with spaces for teachers and parents to circle or check responses and to write short notes to one another.

DIALOGUE NOTEBOOKS Home–school dialogue notebooks offer another form of written communication between parents and teachers (Davern, 2004; Hagiwara & Shogren, 2019). Teachers and parents write observations about the child's behavior or progress each day and write comments or questions to each other. Dialogue notebooks are time consuming but are very effective with some families. In describing a notebook system a teacher used to communicate regularly with the parents of children with emotional and behavioral disorders, Williams and Cartledge (1997) emphasize the importance of being organized, persistent, and flexible in expectations for parent participation.

HOME–SCHOOL CONTRACTS A home–school contract specifies parent-delivered rewards for the child contingent on the child's behavior or academic performance in the classroom. For example, Kerr and Nelson (2010) describe a home–school contract developed by the teacher and parents of a child who disrupted a daily academic "warm-up" activity with singing and other attention-getting behavior. The parents agreed to help their son with textbook reading each night so he was prepared for the warm-up activity and to buy him a ticket for the high school football game each week he completed all of the warm-ups correctly. Home–school contracts use parent-delivered rewards, build in parent recognition and praise of the child's accomplishments, and involve the teacher and parents together in a positive program to support the child's learning.

ELECTRONIC MESSAGING Educators and families are increasingly communicating with one another via email, text messaging, and "Internet-based" options (Blau & Hameiri, 2017; Bouffard, 2008). Classroom communication apps, such as BuzzMob, ClassDojo, HomeworkNOW, and Remind, offer another avenue for increasing and improving teacher–parent communication. This type of communication may be most efficient because it allows for such quick responding, which is particularly important for time-sensitive matters. As Featured Teacher Joshua Hoppe notes, written exchanges can also serve as important documentation: "The parents of one of my students were having problems with him at home. They sent detailed emails about what was happening that I reviewed and responded to on a Saturday morning. These emails provided a record of what we tried and what the results were. We reviewed this information at team meetings and used it as a basis for further collaboration."

HAPPY GRAMS AND SPECIAL ACCOMPLISHMENT LETTERS The simplest type of home–school written message is a brief note informing parents of a positive accomplishment by their child. Many teachers regularly send students home with such "happy grams," giving parents an opportunity to praise the child at home and stay abreast of activities at school. A letter to parents detailing the accomplishment of an important milestone or special achievement by their child is an excellent way to build a partnership. For an example of such a letter and suggestions for developing a system for writing them, see *Teaching & Learning*, "Parent Appreciation Letters."

CLASS NEWSLETTERS AND WEBSITES Class newsletters and websites are additional methods of fostering home–school communication. Although producing a newsletter or designing a website requires a lot of work, it can be worth the effort. A one- or two-page monthly newsletter can provide parents information that is too long or detailed to give over the telephone. A newsletter is also an excellent way to recognize parents who participate in various activities. Featuring student-produced stories, photos, and news items in a class newsletter or website transforms a teacher task into an enjoyable and meaningful learning activity for the entire class. Englund (2009) details procedures for designing a website where parents can access an e-portfolio of their child's progress.

Telephone Communication

PHONE CALLS Regular telephone calls can be an effective and efficient way to maintain home–school communication and parent involvement. A brief conversation that focuses on a child's positive accomplishments lets parents and teachers share the child's success and recognize each other's contributions. Short, positive calls from the teacher also reduce parents' fear that calls from school always indicate a problem. Teachers should call each child's parents at least once every 2 or 3 weeks and should ask parents what times they prefer to receive calls. Keeping a log helps to maintain the schedule and reminds teachers of any necessary follow-up.

VOICEMAIL AND HOTLINES Voicemails and hotlines are a convenient, low-cost technology for home–school communication. By recording daily messages on a hotline, teachers can give parents a great deal of information for relatively little cost. Parents can call and listen at their convenience, literally 24 hours a day. Recorded telephone messages can provide schoolwide and classroom-by-classroom information, share good news (e.g., citizen of the month), serve as a homework hotline (Dardig, 2008), and provide parents with suggestions for working with their children at home (Heward et al., 1991). Parent callers can also leave messages to pose questions, offer suggestions for the teacher, and so on.

TEACHING & LEARNING

Parent Appreciation Letters

By Jill C. Dardig

What Is a Parent Appreciation Letter? Once in a while, I receive a thank-you note from a student. Sometimes these notes are handwritten; nowadays most are emailed. No matter what the mode of transmission, getting one of these letters really makes my day—a little positive recognition goes a long way!

Like teaching, parenting can be a challenging and exhausting enterprise, especially when parenting a child whose special needs require extended energy and intensive support. In addition, many parents of children with disabilities have a history of receiving negative or problem-oriented letters and phone calls from school concerning their child. And when they do, these parents may feel that their children's difficulties reflect poorly on them, making their jobs as parents even more stressful.

What can a teacher do to recognize and show appreciation for the efforts, endurance, and successes of parents of children with special needs? A parent appreciation letter, which celebrates their child's achievement, whether big or small, is a wonderful way to tell parents that you share in their joy when their child takes a step forward and to congratulate them on their contribution to this happy event (Figure 3.7).

How Do You Write Appreciation Letters? Set up a "Special Accomplishments Chart" to record special achievements of all the students in your class on an ongoing basis. (See Figure 3.8 for an example.) Keep the chart on a clipboard or in a notebook in a handy place in your classroom.

FIGURE 3.7 Parent Appreciation Letter

Wingate Middle School
123 Lone Pine Road
Anytown, OH
512-555-1908

Dear Mr. and Mrs. Diaz,

I've been so proud of Lee these past few weeks! He has made consistent progress in managing his frustration and choosing appropriate ways to solve problems.

On several occasions Lee ran into some challenging workbook assignments and calmly moved on to the next sections that he could complete more easily. Then he went back to the skipped sections and was able to work out the solutions by himself.

On other occasions Lee politely asked me for assistance, which I gladly gave him.

Perhaps the best moment was when Lee encouraged a classmate to stay calm and cool in a difficult social situation.

Thank you both for your support in helping Lee make good behavioral choices both in school and at home. His progress will certainly help him adapt well to the high school setting next year.

Sincerely,

Yoko McCoy

Yoko McCoy
Special Education Teacher
ymccoy@wingate.K12.org

Source: Reprinted by permission from Jill C. Dardig.

FIGURE 3.8 Special Accomplishments Chart

STUDENT	ACCOMPLISHMENT AND SIGNIFICANCE	DATE	LETTER SENT TO PARENTS?
Laura-preschool	Put her coat on without help and quickly while in her wheelchair before recess; this may seem like a small thing, but it's a big step towards her achieving independence and fitting in with her peers.	10/6	Yes, 10/6
Martha—2nd grade	Inserted and kept her hearing aid in and turned on to proper volume every day without reminders; this enables her to comprehend instructions and lesson content; she's on top of everything this week!	10/6	Yes, 10/6
Akeelah—4th grade	Spelling test improvement—earned 100% on advanced grade-level tests 3 weeks in a row in a subject she had been struggling with; she showed motivation and commitment to study every day at school and at home—her regular class teacher noted this progress.	10/6	Not yet
Carlo—7th grade	Orientation & mobility—using his cane, Carlo successfully traveled from resource room to inclusion class on a different floor of the school building by himself; I know he's working on independent travel at home and out in the community; he expressed pride in his accomplishment and has mentioned that he may not need a buddy to accompany him to the restroom and lunchroom anymore!	10/9	Not yet
Lee—8th grade	Social behavior—on several occasions, chose appropriate option (calmly moved on to the next section, came back later to work on difficult problem) when frustrated with written work, then tried again and was successful; politely asked teacher for help on another occasion; also helped a classmate make an appropriate choice; these behaviors will serve him well next year in high school.	10/15	Yes, 10/15
Branden—sophomore in high school	Vocational—at nursing home work-study placement, increased speed and accuracy of serving lunches to residents; served entire floor in a half hour and still had time for some very nice conversations with the residents (they love and appreciate Branden and his nice sense of humor); got a rave review from his supervisor, possible future career?	10/16	Yes, 10/19
Jordan—senior in high school	Excelled in our math unit on handling checking and savings accounts; these skills will be so useful for her in the near future; she expressed an interest in having an actual bank account and learning more about budgeting.	10/16	Not yet

Source: Reprinted by permission from Jill C. Dardig.

Each week or two, use the chart to help you select one or more students whose parents will receive a parent appreciation letter. Each letter should state its purpose, identify and provide some interesting detail about the student's achievement, explain the importance of the achievement, thank the parents for helping their child succeed in school, and provide a link between the current accomplishment and future successes. If you send a parent appreciation letter by surface mail or with the student (rather than by email), don't be surprised if your student tells you that the letter is on the refrigerator door at home for the entire family to enjoy.

Regardless of the mode of parent–teacher communication or differences in cultural experiences and language backgrounds of the participants, educators should follow the suggestions shown in Figure 3.9 in their interactions with parents and families. Contrast these 10 guidelines with the professional roadblocks to communication described earlier.

FIGURE 3.9 Ten Guidelines for Communicating with Parents and Families

1. ***Don't assume that you know more about the child, his needs, and how those needs should be met than his parents do.*** If you make this assumption, you will usually be wrong and, worse, miss opportunities to obtain and provide meaningful information.
2. ***Junk the jargon.*** Educators whose speech is laced with technical terminology will have difficulty communicating effectively with parents (or with anyone else, for that matter). Speak in clear, everyday language and avoid the "alphabet soup" of special education (e.g., FAPE, IFSP, MFE).
3. ***Don't let assumptions and generalizations about parents and families guide your efforts.*** Do not assume a parent is in the *x*, *y*, or *z* stage of adjustment and therefore needs *a*, *b*, or *c* type of support or program. If you are genuinely interested in what a father or mother feels and wants, and you should be, ask.
4. ***Be sensitive and responsive to the cultural and linguistic backgrounds of parents and families.*** The information and support services desired by families from diverse cultural and ethnic groups vary, and majority educators must work to be sensitive to those differences.
5. ***Don't be defensive or intimidated.*** Unless you are the parent of a child with disabilities, you cannot ever really know what parenting a child with disabilities is like. But as a trained teacher, you do know something about helping children with disabilities learn. That's your job; it's what you do every day. Offer families the knowledge and skills you have without apology and welcome their input.
6. ***Refer families to other professionals when needed.*** As a teacher, you interact with parents and families in an effort to improve the child's educational progress. You are not a marriage counselor, therapist, or financial advisor. If a parent or a family member indicates the need for non–special education services, offer to refer him or her to professionals and agencies qualified to provide them.
7. ***Help parents strive for a realistic optimism.*** Children with disabilities and their families benefit little from professionals who are doom-and-gloom types or who minimize the significance of a disability. Help parents analyze, plan, and prepare for their child's future.
8. ***Start with something parents can be successful with.*** When parents show an interest in helping their child at home, don't set them up to fail by giving them complicated materials, complex instructions, and a heavy schedule of nightly tutoring. Begin with something simple that is likely to be rewarding to the parent and the child.
9. ***Respect a parent's right to say no.*** Most educators are eager to share what they know and to help families plan and carry out shared teaching goals. But professionals sometimes "fail to recognize the more basic needs of families, one of which is to not need a professional support person! . . . there comes a time when parents and other members of the family wish to be left alone" (J. S. Howard et al., 2005, p. 124).
10. ***Don't be afraid to say, "I don't know."*** Sometimes parents will ask questions that you cannot answer or request services you cannot provide. A mark of a true professional is knowing the limits of your expertise and when you need help. It is okay to say, "I don't know." Parents will think more highly of you.

Other Forms of Parent Involvement

Learning Outcome 3.5 Discuss a variety of strategies for engaging parents of children with disabilities.

Lim's (2008) definition of parent involvement as "any activities that are provided and encouraged by the school and that encourage parents in working on behalf of their children's learning and development" (p. 128) is a good one because it recognizes the wide variety of forms and levels at which parent involvement can occur and focuses on benefits for the child. Parents as tutors, parent education and training programs, and support groups represent three different types of parent involvement with a common purpose of educational benefits for children.

Parents as Tutors

HLP16 Use explicit instruction.

For children with disabilities, the casual routines of everyday life at home and in the community may not provide enough practice and feedback to teach them important skills. Many parents of exceptional children have responded to this challenge by systematically teaching their children at home. And, particularly in the midst of a global pandemic, parents are increasingly taking an active role in teaching their children, whether or not they have disabilities. See *Teaching & Learning*, "Parents as Tutors."

The majority of parents who participate in systematic home tutoring programs describe the experience as positive for them and their children. A mother and father wrote: "We really enjoyed teaching M. to tell time, and he enjoyed working with us. He learned so quickly and we were so happy and proud to see the progress he was making. We have two other children. Doing this program allowed us to spend time alone with M" (Donley & Williams, 1997, p. 50).

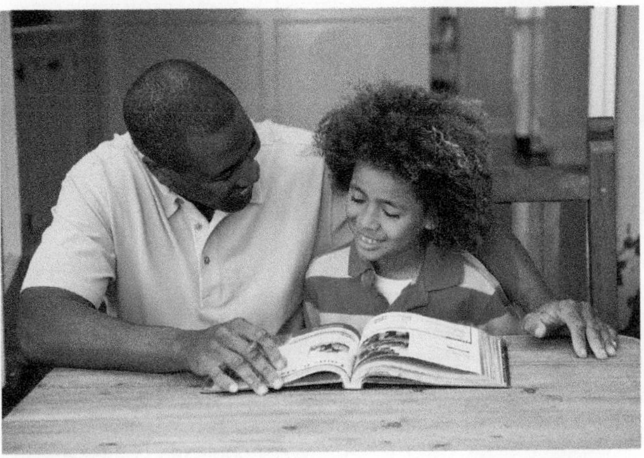
Source: Ronnie Kaufman/Larry Hishowitz/ Blend Images/Alamy

Teachers can provide families with resources and support that enhance student learning.

Parents who wish to tutor their children at home should be helped to do so. Teachers should recognize, however, that not all parents want to teach their children at home. Some parents may think that home tutoring will compete with other activities in the home and negatively affect their family's overall quality of life (Parette & Petch-Hogan, 2000). Others may not have the time to learn and use the necessary teaching skills. Professionals must not interpret such situations as indications that parents do not care enough about their children.

Parent Education and Training Programs

Education for parenting is not new; such programs date back to the early 1800s. Parent education can serve a variety of purposes and occur in different formats: from one-time-only events that inform parents of a new school policy, to make-it-and-take-it workshops in which parents make instructional materials to use at home (e.g., a math facts practice game), to multiple-session programs on IEP or IFSP planning or behavior support strategies. Research shows benefits of systematic parent education and training, particularly in programs that teach parents ways to interact with their children (Bearss et al., 2015; Schultz et al., 2011). Teachers are well positioned to point parents in the right direction when families are struggling with challenging behavior at home. Examples of high-quality parent training programs include The Kazdin Method (Kazdin, 2009), Incredible Years (http://www.incredibleyears.com), and RAPID Skills Training (Simmons, 2019). Parent training programs are often led by teachers or other professionals (e.g., community social workers), but they can also be self-directed (e.g., parents can enroll in a free on-line course or can purchase a manual to guide them through the parenting techniques).

Parent Support Groups

Many parents just want opportunities to connect with one another—to support each other in their journeys of parenting children with disabilities (Hsiao, 2018). Educators can work with parents to form such groups informally or help parents connect to established programs, such as Parent to Parent (P2P USA, 2018). Parent to Parent helps parents of children with disabilities become reliable allies for one another by providing them opportunities to receive support from a parent who has experienced similar circumstances and challenges. Experienced trained "support parents" are carefully matched in a one-to-one relationship with parents who have been newly referred to the program.

Educators who want to form parent support groups should involve parents in planning and conducting the groups as much as possible (Kroth & Edge, 2007; Turnbull et al., 2015). Educators can use both open and closed needs assessment procedures to determine what parents want from a parent group. An *open needs assessment* consists of questions such as these:

The best family time for my child is when we _____.
I will never forget the time that my child and I _____.
When I take my child to the store, I am concerned that she will _____.
The hardest thing about having a special child is _____.
I wish I knew more about _____.

A *closed needs assessment* asks parents to select from a list of topics they would like to learn more about. For example, educators can give parents a list of topics (e.g., bedtime behavior, interactions with siblings, homework, making friends, planning for the future) and ask them to select any topic that is a concern or interest. Parents' and families' needs and preferences can also be assessed with an instrument that combines open and closed format items (Matuszny et al., 2007).

TEACHING & LEARNING

Parents as Tutors

Well-conducted home-based parent tutoring can enhance a child's educational progress and give enjoyment to both child and parent.

What Is a Parents-as-Tutors Program? Parents become their children's tutors when they systematically teach self-help and daily living skills (e.g., Cavkaytar & Pollard, 2009), assist their children with homework (Patton et al., 2001), provide home-based academic instruction to supplement classroom instruction (McConnell & Kubina, 2016; Resetar et al., 2006), or teach language and communication skills (Cooke et al., 2009; Park, Alber-Morgan, & Canella-Malone, 2011). Teachers can build a parents-as-tutors program by training parents in tutoring skills, providing instructional materials that can be used at home, and supporting parents as they try tutoring at home. For some families, providing instructional materials requires advocacy on their behalf, particularly for online instruction. Without devices and reliable Internet access, families are at a significant disadvantage when educating their children at home, thereby widening socioeconomic-based achievement gaps.

How Do You Plan for a Parents-as-Tutors Program? Teachers who wish to help parents tutor their children at home should provide parents with the following guidelines:

Pearson eText
Video Example 3.7
Effective parent tutors set a positive tone, arrange frequent response opportunities, and provide feedback and encouragement.

- *Keep sessions short.* Aim for 10- to 20-minute sessions, 3 or 4 days per week.
- *Make the experience positive.* Parents should praise their child's attempts.
- *Provide frequent opportunities for the child to respond.* Tutoring materials and activities should evoke numerous responses from the child rather than require the child to attend passively to a great deal of explanation and demonstration by the parent.
- *Keep responses to the child consistent.* By praising the child's correct responses (materials and activities at the child's appropriate instructional level are a must) and providing a consistent, unemotional response to errors (e.g., "Let's read that word again, together"), parents can prevent the frustration and negative results that can occur when home tutoring is mishandled.
- *Use tutoring to practice and extend skills already learned in school.* For example, parents can use spelling or vocabulary words from school as the questions or items for adapted board games (Wesson et al., 1988), or parents can practice math facts with flashcards.
- *Keep a record.* Similar to classroom teachers, parents can never know the exact effects of their tutoring without data. A daily record enables both parents and child to see gradual progress that might be overlooked if subjective opinion is the only basis for evaluation. Most children do make progress under guided instruction, and a record documents that progress, perhaps providing the parent with an opportunity to see the child in a new and positive light.

Parent Tutoring Record

Date October 15, 2021 Subject/Activity Math/Addition Flashcards

What we're aiming for 30 corrects in 1 minute

Highest 1-minute check out so far 17 corrects in 1 minute

Last session's check out 15 corrects in 1 minute

Today's goals and results

- Practice goal 10 min on-task practice Met?  Yes No
- Check out 20 corrects Result 21 (Yay!!) Charted? Yes No

Carmen's rewards

- Practice 5 bonus tokens
- Check out 5 bonus tokens
- Both goals met 10 bonus tokens + 15 minutes of screen time

How Much Family Involvement?

It is easy to get carried away with a good concept, especially one such as parent and family involvement, which has so much promise for positive outcomes. But teachers and other professionals who provide special education services must not take a one-sided, unidirectional view of parent involvement. Sometimes the time and energy required for parents to participate in home-based tutoring programs or parent education groups cause stress among family members or guilt if the parents cannot fulfill teachers' expectations (Callahan et al., 1998; Turnbull et al., 2015).

Kroth and Edge (2007) describe the "mirror model" for parent involvement (see Figure 3.10), which recognizes that parents have a great deal to offer as well as a need to receive services from special educators. The model gives parents an equal part in deciding what services they need and what assistance they might provide to professionals or other parents. The top half of the model assumes that professionals have certain information, knowledge, and skills that they should share with parents to help them with their children. The bottom half of the model assumes that parents have information, knowledge, and skills that can help professionals be more effective in educating their children. The model assumes that not all parents need everything professionals have to offer and that no parent should be expected to provide everything. All parents should be expected to provide and obtain information, most will be active participants in IEP planning, and fewer will participate in or contribute to workshops and extended parent education groups.

Parents and family are the most important people in a child's life. Skilled and caring teachers should be next in importance. Working together, teachers, parents, and families can and do make a difference in the lives of exceptional children.

FIGURE 3.10 Mirror Model for Parent Involvement

Professional services for parents		
	Few	In-depth workshops and/or therapy groups
	Some	Parent education workshops
	Most	Placement committee meetings, Individualized Education Program (IEP) conferences, parent meetings on how to participate, class handouts, phone calls, home visits, report in conferences, information on workshops available
	All	Information on consent to test and place; information on criteria to place; due process procedures; information on tests and other school records pertaining to child; information on how to participate on placement committees and IEP conferences; information on services available
Parental services for professionals and parents		
	All	Information on child and family that pertains to educational programming; information on needed services
	Most	Input into placement decisions and IEP decisions; assist on field trips; support on agreed-upon programs; feedback to professionals
	Some	Parent advocates for other parents; parent advisory groups; task force members on curriculum; volunteer help in classrooms
	Few	Parent-to-parent programs; workshop leaders

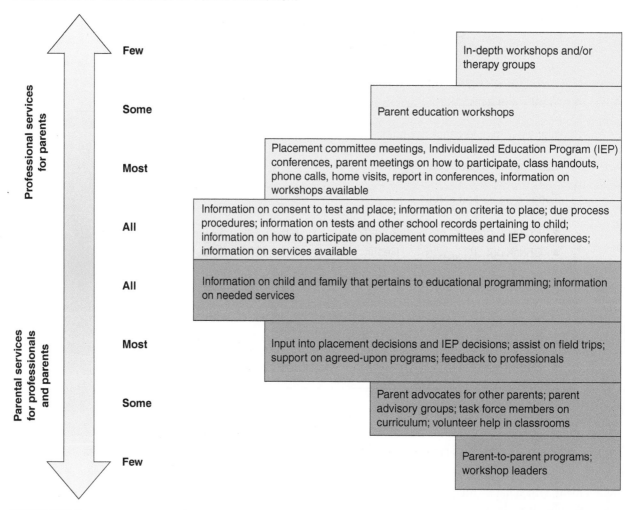

Source: Adapted from "The Mirror Model of Parental Involvement" by R. L. Kroth (1980) *Pointer, 25*(1), 18-22) and *Communicating with parents and families*, 4th Edition, by R. L. Kroth and D. Edge. Copyright © 2007 by Kroth and Edge.

ADVICE FROM THE FEATURED TEACHER by Joshua Hoppe

Collaborating with Parents and Families

Source: Joshua Hoppe

The most effective special educators create and nourish strong and comfortable partnerships with the families of their students. They do so by building rapport, communicating and listening effectively, and respecting where families are coming from in their wishes for their children.

Facilitate Meaningful Communication

- ***Take initiative.*** Consider it your job to keep lines of communication open. Call just to update parents on what is happening in school and see how everything is going at home. If parents feel you care about them and their child, you are well on your way to nourishing a partnership.
- ***Use everyday, straightforward language.*** When I first started teaching, I was nervous about my role. Wanting to sound knowledgeable and authoritative, I used far too much jargon when speaking with parents. This created a communication barrier. Take the core concepts and frameworks you have learned in school to inform what you are saying, but say them as you would in a real world conversation.

- ***Listen fully to what parents are saying.*** Parents know their children better than anyone. By listening to them, you will gain a wealth of information. When parents feel you really listen to them, they feel comfortable telling you their dreams and concerns for their child's future.
- ***Get an interpreter when needed.*** If you cannot communicate with a parent in his or her native language, find someone who can. I was lucky enough to have a colleague from the Philippines who helped me communicate with a parent from the Philippines. If you are not so fortunate to have a resource this easily accessible, you will have to branch out. Investigate district resources and find an interpreter.

Respect Families' Cultural Beliefs and Practices

- ***Learn how cultural differences affect families' participation in school activities and make adaptations.*** The religious beliefs of one of my students did not include celebrating birthdays or holidays. Rather than eliminate holiday-themed activities altogether or exclude the child while the rest of my students enjoyed them, I spoke with the child's mother and found her reasonable and easy to work with. We decided that whenever a planned activity compromised the family's religious beliefs, we would come up with an adaptation to remove any connections the family objected to. For example, if the other kids were making an Easter basket, she would make a spring basket.
- ***Understand how cultural differences may influence parents' perceptions.*** I had a student whose impulsivity and inattention to task severely hampered learning. Doctors recommended medication, but his mother refused because her cultural belief was that taking medication might cause her son to become possessed by demons. Although I did not agree with her belief, I respected it, and we worked on other means of providing environmental support and shaping appropriate behavior. It is now a few years later, and her son has made tremendous progress without medication.
- ***Draw the line with respect to cultural practices and seek compromise.*** One student's family had a cultural belief about discipline that involved spanking the child with objects. This boy's extremely challenging behaviors frustrated and caused great stress for the family, and they employed this method to control his behavior at home. When the student came to school with bruises, I had to intercede. I initiated a call to Child Protective Services, and the school intervened. We were able to express that her cultural view of discipline was her right but that a student showing up to school with bruises crossed a line. I worked with the family to develop a solution. We created a self-monitoring sheet for the student to rate himself on following behavioral expectations. I taught him how to use the sheet at school, and he took it home each day for his mother to sign. If he did well for the entire day, he received a reward at home. If he exhibited certain challenging behaviors, he was unable to engage in a preferred activity at home that evening. By adding these interventions to her parenting style, this mother was able to rely more on positive reinforcement to achieve desirable changes in behavior.

Key Terms and Concepts

cultural reciprocity

funds of knowledge

respite care

Summary

Support for Family Involvement

- Three factors are responsible for the increased emphasis on parent and family involvement in special education: parent advocacy, legislative mandates, and educators' desire to increase their effectiveness.
- A successful parent–teacher partnership benefits the professional; the parents; and, most important, the child.

Understanding Families of Children with Disabilities

- Families are dynamic, multigenerational systems wherein the child has an effect on all others in the system, and all other members of the family have an effect on the child. Educators must strive to understand how a child's disability might influence the family system and the many interrelated roles of parenthood.

- Many parents experience similar emotions and challenges as they react and adjust to the birth or diagnosis of a child with a disability (e.g., shock, denial, grief, reflection, advocacy, appreciation).
- After a period of uncertainty, most families of children with disabilities exhibit strength and resilience, reestablish healthy family functioning, and become determined to do whatever they can to meet their children's needs.
- Parents of children with disabilities fulfill at least nine roles and responsibilities: caregiver, provider, teacher, counselor, behavior support specialist, parent of siblings without disabilities, partner/co-parent, information specialist and trainer for significant others, and advocate for school and community services.
- Differences in the cultural beliefs and linguistic practices of professionals and families often serve as barriers to parent involvement.
- A child's disability affects parents and siblings in different ways during the different life-cycle stages of the family.
- Respite care—the temporary care of an individual with disabilities by nonfamily members—is a critical support for many families of children with severe disabilities.

Developing and Maintaining Family–Professional Partnerships

- Understanding differences between our own perspectives and those of people from other cultures and ethnic groups requires careful examination of our own cultural background and belief system.
- Five principles of effective communication between educators and parents are accepting what is being said, active listening, questioning appropriately, encouraging, and staying focused.
- Attitudes of and behaviors by professionals that serve as barriers to communication with parents and families include making assumptions about the services and information that parents need, treating parents as clients or adversaries instead of partners, keeping professional distance, acting as if parents need counseling, blaming parents for their child's disability or performance, disrespecting parents' suggestions, and labeling parents who don't act as professionals believe they should.
- Dialoguing is an approach to conflict resolution in which both parties try to see each other's point of view.
- The most common modes of home–school communication are parent–teacher conferences, written messages, telephone calls, voicemail, and hotlines. Teachers are using class newsletters, websites, email, and apps to communicate with families with increasing frequency and effectiveness.
- Ten guidelines for communicating with parents of children with disabilities are:
  - Don't assume you know more about a child than the parents do.
  - Junk the jargon and speak in plain, everyday language.
  - Don't let assumptions or generalizations guide your efforts.
  - Be sensitive and responsive to cultural and linguistic differences.
  - Don't be defensive toward or intimidated by parents.
  - Refer families to other professionals when needed.
  - Help parents strive for a realistic optimism.
  - Start with something that parents can be successful with.
  - Allow and respect parents' right to say "no."
  - Don't be afraid to say, "I don't know."
- Many parents can help teach their child with disabilities.
- Parents and professionals should work together in planning and conducting parent support and education groups.
- Parent-to-parent groups provide new parents of children with disabilities support from parents who have experienced similar circumstances and challenges.
- The mirror model of parent involvement assumes that not all parents need everything professionals have to offer and that no parent should be expected to participate in every form of school involvement.

Chapter 4

Intellectual Disabilities

Source: SolStock/E+/Getty Images

Learning Outcomes

After reading this chapter and completing the embedded activities, you should be able to

4.1 List three diagnostic criteria to qualify for special education services under the Individuals with Disabilities Education Act category of intellectual disabilities and name widely used instruments for assessing intellectual functioning and adaptive behavior.

4.2 Describe common characteristics of students with intellectual disabilities and explain how these characteristics are relevant to planning and delivering instruction.

4.3 Identify factors that might account for the wide differences in the prevalence of intellectual disabilities within the school-age population across states and school districts, and list some of the causes of intellectual disabilities.

4.4 Describe key elements of instruction for teaching academic, functional, and self-determination skills to students with intellectual disabilities.

4.5 Identify factors that should guide planning and placement decisions for individuals with intellectual disabilities.

Education, Teaching Credentials, and Experience

- *B.A., criminal justice, Medaille College, 2000*
- *M.Ed., special education, D'Youville College, 2010*
- *Certifications: New York, special education, 7–12; social studies, 7–12*
- *12 years of teaching experience*

To learn more about the cooperative learning structures Madonna uses, such as Kagan's Quiz-Quiz-Trade, Stand Up-Hand Up-Pair Up, and Fan-N-Pick (Kagan & Kagan, 2009), see *Teaching & Learning,* "Cooperative Learning," later in this chapter.

Featured Teacher

Madonna Wilburn

Riverside Institute of Technology, Buffalo Public Schools, Buffalo, NY

Source: Keyonna D. Wilson

Being a special education teacher is the most rewarding job! I love seeing students graduate and move on to the next stage of their lives. Some of my most special moments are watching my students graduate, especially those who had low expectations of themselves and for whom others held low expectations. I feel proud of the accomplishments my students make along the way—writing an essay, reading a paragraph, interacting appropriately with other students, complimenting others, self-advocating, and obtaining employment. I celebrate all of these accomplishments with my students. It is an honor to be a part of helping students reach their big goals.

Teaching special education is also a very challenging job. You wear many hats. In addition to a teacher, I sometimes feel like I am mother, sister, aunt, drill sergeant, counselor, psychologist, clergy, a shoulder to cry on, dress code enforcer, nutrition provider, comedian, and the list could go on. When a student needs something to make it through the day, week, or year, you address it as best you can.

Last year, I taught about 70 students throughout the school day in a combination of separate classes and inclusive co-teaching settings. This year I teach 20 students with intellectual disabilities, learning disabilities, and ADHD in a separate classroom. My students range in age from 14 to 21 years and are in 9th and 12th grade. But regardless of their age, grade, or disability, I have found the most effective instructional strategies are those that require active student participation. Student engagement is the key to success for all my students. One of my favorite ways to facilitate this engagement is with the Kagan cooperative learning structures. When my students are engaged, they not only learn the content but also connect with each other and have fun; this motivates them to learn even more.

THE HISTORY OF SPECIAL EDUCATION IS DEEPLY ROOTED in the education and treatment of people with intellectual disabilities. In the United States, the first public school special education classes were for children with intellectual disabilities. The first federal legislation on special education provided funds for training professionals to prepare teachers for children with intellectual disabilities. This chapter presents the complex concept of intellectual disability and introduces instructional practices that have greatly improved educational outcomes for students with intellectual disabilities.

Definitions

Learning Outcome 4.1 List three diagnostic criteria to qualify for special education services under the Individuals with Disabilities Education Act category of intellectual disabilities and name widely used instruments for assessing intellectual functioning and adaptive behavior.

Various terms for and definitions of intellectual disability have been proposed, adopted, and debated over the years. In early times, people with severe cognitive deficits were labeled *idiots* (derived from a Greek word meaning "people who did not hold public office"). In the 19th century, the label *imbecile* (derived from the Latin word for "weak and feeble") indicated a less severe degree of intellectual disability. The terms *feebleminded* and *simpleton* were eventually added to refer to people with mild intellectual disability (Clausen, 1967). Although grossly inappropriate and stigmatizing today, each of those terms was used by professionals in medicine, psychology, and education to refer to people with intellectual disabilities. Over the years, *mental deficiency* (Doll, 1941) and, later, *mental retardation* (Heber, 1961) were introduced and considered appropriate terminology. In 2007, the American Association on Mental Retardation changed its name to the American Association on Intellectual and Developmental Disabilities (AAIDD). Consistent with the practice of most special educators today, this text uses the term *intellectual disabilities*, except for instances when the terminology itself is being discussed.

First, we will look at the traditional and still most commonly used approach to defining and classifying intellectual disability as an inherent trait within the individual. Then we will examine the most recent conception of intellectual disability as a state of functioning reflecting the fit between a person's capabilities and environment.

IDEA Definition

The Individuals with Disabilities Education Act (IDEA) defines **intellectual disability** as "significantly subaverage general intellectual functioning, existing concurrently with deficits in adaptive behavior and manifested during the developmental period, that adversely affects a child's educational performance" (34 CFR, §300.8[c][6]).

The definition specifies three criteria for a diagnosis of intellectual disability. First, "significantly subaverage intellectual functioning" must be demonstrated. The word *significant* refers to a score of 2 or more standard deviations below the mean on a standardized intelligence test (an IQ [intelligence quotient] score of approximately 70 or less; intelligence testing is discussed later in the chapter). Second, an individual must also have significant difficulty with tasks of everyday living (adaptive behavior). Third, the deficits in intellectual functioning and adaptive behavior must occur during the developmental period to help distinguish intellectual disability from other disabilities (e.g., impaired intellectual performance caused by traumatic brain injury). A child who exhibits substantial limitations in intellectual functioning and adaptive behavior will automatically meet the IDEA requirement that the disability "adversely affects a child's educational performance."

AAIDD Definition

The AAIDD (2019) definition of intellectual disability specifies significant limitations in both intellectual functioning and adaptive functioning and stipulates that the disability originates before the age of 18 years. Drawing a distinct difference from the traditional view of intellectual disability as an inherent trait or permanent condition, the AAIDD considers an individual's functioning in the context of the individual's present environment and the supports needed to improve it. Five assumptions are essential to understanding and applying the definition for diagnosis and classification:

1. Limitations in present functioning must be considered within the context of community environments typical of the individual's age, peers, and culture.
2. Valid assessment considers cultural and linguistic diversity as well as differences in communication, sensory, motor, and behavioral factors.

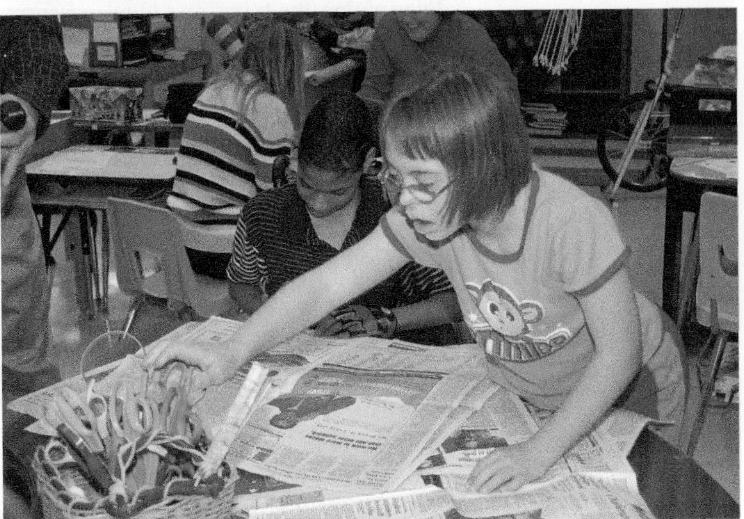

Although Kaitlyn needs extensive supports in some areas of life functioning, she needs only limited supports in other areas.

Source: Laura Bolesta/Blendon/Pearson Allyn and Bacon/Merrill Education

Pearson eText
Video Example 4.1
"Don't limit me!"https://www.youtube.com/watch?v=YOwDfnoek6E#t=26

3. Within the individual, limitations often coexist with strengths.
4. The purpose of describing limitations is to develop a profile of needed supports.
5. With appropriate personalized supports over a sustained period, the life functioning of the person with intellectual disability generally will improve. (AAIDD Ad Hoc Committee on Terminology and Classification, 2010, p. 1)

Supports are defined as "resources and strategies that aim to promote the development, education, interests, and personal well-being of a person and that enhance individual functioning" (AAIDD Ad Hoc Committee, 2010, p. 18). Supports needed by a student with intellectual disability are identified during the individualized education program (IEP) process. For adults, an interdisciplinary team can use the AAIDD's Supports Intensity Scale to develop a profile of the types and intensity of needed supports (Thompson et al., 2017).

Classification of Intellectual Disabilities

Through the last half of the 20th century, intellectual disabilities were classified by their degree of intellectual impairment—mild, moderate, severe, and profound—each level encompassing a range of IQ scores (see Table 4.1).

TABLE 4.1 Traditional classification of intellectual disabilities by IQ score

LEVEL	IQ SCORE
Mild	50–55 to ~70
Moderate	35–40 to 50–55
Severe	20–25 to 35–40
Profound	Below 20–25

For many years, students with intellectual disabilities were classified as *educable mentally retarded (EMR)* or *trainable mentally retarded (TMR)*, the terms referring to mild and moderate levels of intellectual disability, respectively. This two-level classification system did not include children with severe and profound intellectual disabilities because they were often denied a public education and were likely to reside in state-operated institutions. *EMR* and *TMR* are archaic and inappropriate terms today: offensive, stigmatizing, and suggesting predetermined achievement limits.

Today clinicians and researchers apply descriptors (mild, moderate, severe, profound) to designate levels of intellectual disability but base their classification on a person's adaptive behavior rather than IQ score. The shift recognizes the central role of adaptive behavior in determining the types and levels of supports a person needs, the inexactness of intelligence testing, and the importance of clinical judgment in diagnosis and classification (American Psychiatric Association, 2013; Luckasson & Schalock, 2015).

Identification and Assessment

Assessing Intellectual Functioning

Intellectual functioning is assessed by an IQ test administered by a school psychologist or other trained professional. IQ tests consist of a series of questions (e.g., vocabulary, similarities), problem-solving tasks (e.g., mazes, block designs), memory, and other items assumed to require certain degrees of intelligence to answer or solve correctly. The child's performance on each set of test items is entered into a formula that yields a score representing the child's overall IQ.

IQ tests are *standardized tests*; that is, the same questions and tasks are always presented in a prescribed way, and the same scoring procedures are used each time the test is administered. IQ tests are also norm-referenced. During its development, a **norm-referenced test** is administered to a large sample of people selected at random from the population for whom

FIGURE 4.1 Theoretical Distribution of IQ Scores on the Normal Curve

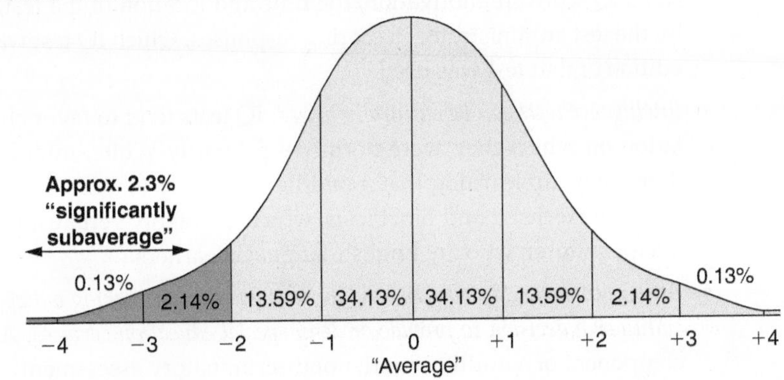

the test is intended. Developers use the scores of people in the norming sample to represent the general distribution of scores throughout that population.

IQ scores seem to be distributed throughout the population according to a phenomenon called the *bell-shaped curve*, or **normal curve**, shown in Figure 4.1. A mathematical concept called **standard deviation** describes how a particular score varies from the mean, or average, of all the scores in the norming sample. Test developers apply an algebraic formula to the scores achieved by the norming sample to determine what value equals 1 standard deviation for that test. A child's IQ test score can then be described in terms of how many standard deviations above or below the mean it is. Theoretically, an equal number of people score above and below the mean, and about 2.3% of the population falls 2 or more standard deviations below the mean.

The AAIDD's criterion for "significant limitations of intellectual functioning" is an IQ score approximately 2 standard deviations below the mean, which is a score of 70 or below on two widely used intelligence tests, the Wechsler Intelligence Scale for Children (WISC-V) (Wechsler, 2014) and the Stanford-Binet Intelligence Scales (Roid, 2003). The IQ cutoff score of 70 is intended as a guideline and should not be interpreted as a hard-and-fast requirement. A higher IQ score of 75 or more may also be associated with intellectual disabilities if, according to a clinician's judgment, the child exhibits deficits in adaptive behavior thought to be caused by impaired intellectual functioning.

Although IQ tests have been widely criticized, when administered and interpreted properly, they provide useful information. IQ tests can identify an overall deficit in cognitive functioning, and IQ score is a strong predictor of school achievement. Because IQ tests are composed largely of verbal and academic tasks—the same things a child must master to succeed in school—they correlate highly with school achievement.

Although the major intelligence tests are among the most carefully constructed and researched psychological assessment instruments available, they are far from perfect. Educators should be aware of the following considerations (Kritikos et al., 2018; Overton, 2016; Salvia et al., 2017):

- *Intelligence is a hypothetical construct.* No one has ever seen a thing called *intelligence;* we infer it from observed performance. We assume it takes more intelligence to perform some tasks at a given age than it does to perform others.
- *An IQ test measures only how a child performs at one point in time on the items included on the test.* An IQ test samples a small portion of an individual's skills and abilities; we infer from that performance how a child might perform on other tasks and in other situations.
- *IQ scores can change significantly.* IQ scores often increase over time, particularly in the 70 to 80 range, where diagnostic decisions are not so clear cut (Whitaker, 2008; Whitaker & Gordon, 2012). Examiners are hesitant to diagnose intellectual disability on the basis of an IQ score that might increase after a period of intensive, systematic intervention.

- *Intelligence testing is not an exact science.* Among the many variables that affect a person's IQ score are motivation, the time and location of the test, inconsistency or bias by the test administrator in scoring responses, which IQ test was selected, and which edition of that test was used.
- *Intelligence tests can be culturally biased.* IQ tests tend to favor children from the population on which they were normed—primarily White, middle-class children. Some items may tap learning that a middle-class child is more likely to have experienced. Both the Wechsler and Binet tests, which are highly verbal, are especially inappropriate for children who are English-language learners.
- *An IQ score should never be used as the sole basis for making a diagnosis of intellectual disability or a decision to provide or deny special education services.* An IQ score is just one component of a multifactored, nondiscriminatory assessment.
- *An IQ score should not be used to determine IEP objectives.* A student's performance on criterion-referenced tests of curriculum-based knowledge and skills is a more appropriate and useful source of information for IEP objectives.

Assessing Adaptive Behavior

Pearson eText
Video Example 4.2
An auction is a fun way to practice and learn adaptive behavior.

Adaptive behavior is "the collection of conceptual, social, and practical skills that have been learned and performed by people in order to function in their everyday lives" (AAIDD, 2020). Examples include the following:

- *Conceptual skills*—using language for speaking, reading, writing; using number concepts such as those involved in counting and telling time
- *Social skills*—getting along with others, being a responsible group member, solving social problems, following rules and obeying laws, avoiding being victimized
- *Practical skills*—activities of daily living, such as dressing, toileting, and food preparation; job skills; health care; traveling in the community; following schedules; maintaining one's health and safety; making purchases; and using the phone (adapted from AAIDD, 2020)

Systematic assessment of adaptive behavior is important for reasons beyond the diagnosis of intellectual disabilities. The adaptive skills exhibited by a person with intellectual disabilities are critical factors in determining the supports required for success in school, work, community, and home environments (Tassé et al., 2012). Numerous assessments for adaptive behavior have been developed. Most consist of a series of questions that a teacher, parent, or caregiver answers. Three frequently used instruments for assessing adaptive behavior by school-age children are described next.

VINELAND ADAPTIVE BEHAVIOR SCALES A frequently used instrument for assessing adaptive behavior by school-age children is the Vineland Adaptive Behavior Scales (Sparrow et al., 2016). This assessment can be used with individuals from birth through adulthood and consists of questionnaires typically completed by a teacher and parent or other caregiver.

ADAPTIVE BEHAVIOR DIAGNOSTIC SCALE The Adaptive Behavior Diagnostic Scale (ABDS) assesses three domains—conceptual, social, practical—and may be used with children age 2 through 21 years (Pearson et al., 2016).

AAIDD DIAGNOSTIC ADAPTIVE BEHAVIOR SCALE The Diagnostic Adaptive Behavior Scale (DABS), designed for use with individuals from 4 to 21 years old, includes a cutoff point at which an individual is considered to have significant limitations in adaptive behavior (Tassé et al., 2017). Thus, the DABS provides critical information on determining a diagnosis of intellectual disability.

The relative nature of social adjustment and competence makes measurement of adaptive behavior difficult. Actions considered appropriate in one situation or by one group may not be in another situation or by another group. No universal agreement exists concerning the adaptive behaviors everyone should exhibit. As with IQ tests, cultural bias can be a problem in adaptive behavior scales; for instance, an item on some scales requires a child to tie a laced shoe, but some children have never had shoes with laces.

Characteristics

Learning Outcome 4.2 Describe common characteristics of students with intellectual disabilities and explain how these characteristics are relevant to planning and delivering instruction.

Intellectual disability is seldom a time-limited condition. Although some children with intellectual disabilities make tremendous advancements in adaptive skills—some to the point of functioning independently and no longer being served under any disability category—most are affected throughout their life span.

Many children with mild intellectual disabilities are not identified until they enter school; some, not until the second or third grade, when more difficult academic work is required. Most students with mild intellectual disabilities learn basic academic skills and vocational and daily living skills well enough to support themselves independently or semi-independently in the community.

Children with moderate intellectual disabilities show significant delays in development during their preschool years. As they grow older, discrepancies in overall intellectual development and adaptive functioning generally grow wider between these children and their age-matched peers without disabilities. People with moderate intellectual disabilities are more likely to have health and behavior problems than are individuals with mild intellectual disabilities.

Children with severe or profound intellectual disabilities are almost always identified at birth or shortly afterward. Most of these infants have significant central nervous system damage, and many have additional disabilities or health conditions (Heikua et al., 2005). Chapter 12 describes the characteristics and education of students with multiple disabilities.

Positive Attributes

Descriptions of the learning characteristics and adaptive behavior of individuals with intellectual disabilities focus on limitations and deficits and paint a picture of a homogeneous group of people whose most important characteristics revolve around the absence of desirable traits. But individuals with intellectual disabilities are a huge and diverse group composed of people with highly individual personalities (Haywood, 2006; J. D. Smith & Mitchell, 2001a, 2001b). All children and adults with intellectual disabilities display positive characteristics; many show tenacity and curiosity in learning, get along well with others, and are positive influences on those around them (Bauer, 2008; Niemiec et al., 2017; Reiss & Reiss, 2004).

Cognitive Functioning and Learning

Cognitive functioning and learning characteristics of individuals with intellectual disabilities include slow learning rates, poor memory, attention problems, difficulty maintaining and generalizing what they have learned, and poor motivation.

LEARNING RATE Children with intellectual disabilities acquire new knowledge and skills at rates well below those of children without disabilities. A frequently used measure of learning rate is *trials to criterion*—the number of practice or instructional trials needed before a student can respond correctly without prompts or assistance at some specified criterion. For example, although a child without disabilities may require just two or three trials to discriminate between two geometric forms, a child with intellectual disabilities may need 20 to 30 or more trials to learn the same discrimination.

Because students with intellectual disabilities learn more slowly than their peers, some educators have assumed that instruction should be slowed down to match the lower rate of learning. Research has shown, however, that students with intellectual disabilities, similar to all learners, benefit from participating in lively paced instruction with frequent response opportunities (e.g., Browder et al., 2018).

Source: Katelyn Metzger/Merrill Education

Like all children, those with intellectual disabilities have challenges and positive attributes.

MEMORY Students with intellectual disabilities have difficulty remembering information. As would be expected, the more severe the cognitive impairment, the greater the memory problems. Students with intellectual disabilities have difficulty with *working memory*, the ability to remember one thing while performing another task (Lanfranchi et al., 2012), as well as short-term memory, the ability to recall and use information that was encountered just a few seconds to a couple of hours earlier (Henry, 2008). For example, they may have difficulty remembering a specific sequence of job tasks an employer stated a few minutes before.

Children with intellectual disabilities take longer than do their age-matched peers without disabilities to recall information and have more difficulty managing larger amounts of cognitive information at one time (Bergeron & Floyd, 2006). Early researchers suggested that after people with intellectual disabilities learned a specific item of information sufficiently to commit it to *long-term memory*—information recalled after a period of days or weeks—they retained that information about as well as people without cognitive disabilities (Belmont, 1966; Ellis, 1963).

Some promising research has focused on teaching children with intellectual disabilities metacognitive or executive control strategies, such as rehearsing and organizing information into related sets, which many children without disabilities learn to do naturally (Carlin et al., 2005). Students with intellectual disabilities do not tend to use such strategies spontaneously but can be taught to do so, with improved performance on memory-related and problem-solving tasks as an outcome (Merrill, 2005).

ATTENTION Efficient learners attend to critical features of a task (e.g., to the outline of geometric shapes instead of dimensions such as their color or position on the page). Students with intellectual disabilities are typically slower to attend to relevant features of a learning task than are students without disabilities (Merrill, 2005) and instead may focus on distracting irrelevant stimuli (Carlin et al., 2007; Dickson et al., 2006). In addition, individuals with intellectual disabilities often have difficulty sustaining attention to learning tasks (Sun et al., 2019). These attention problems compound and contribute to a student's difficulties in acquiring, remembering, and generalizing new knowledge and skills.

Effective instructional design for students with intellectual disabilities must systematically control for the presence and saliency of critical stimuli as well as the presence and effects of distracting stimuli. After initially directing a student's attention to the most relevant feature of a simplified task and reinforcing correct responses, the teacher can gradually increase the task's complexity and difficulty. A student's attention to relevant stimuli will improve as she succeeds (Huguenin, 2000).

GENERALIZATION AND MAINTENANCE Children without disabilities often apply what they have learned in the classroom in other settings and continue to do so over time, even without explicit instruction. In contrast, many students with disabilities, particularly those with intellectual disabilities, do not transfer, or generalize, newly learned knowledge and skills to settings or situations that differ from the conditions where they learned those skills. Discovering and refining strategies and tactics that promote the generalization and maintenance of learning by individuals with intellectual disabilities is one of the most important and challenging areas of contemporary research in special education.

MOTIVATION Some students with intellectual disabilities exhibit an apparent lack of interest in learning or in problem-solving tasks (Glidden & Switzky, 2006). Some individuals with intellectual disabilities develop *learned helplessness*, which describes an individual's expectation of failure, regardless of his efforts, based on experiences of repeated failure. In an attempt to minimize or offset failure, the person may set extremely low expectations for himself and not appear to try very hard. Faced with a difficult task or problem, some individuals with intellectual disabilities quickly give up and turn to or wait for others to help them (Fidler, Hepburn, et al., 2005). Some acquire a problem-solving approach called *outer-directedness*, which describes an individual's distrust of her own responses to situations and reliance on others for assistance and solutions (Fidler, Philofsky, et al., 2005).

Rather than an inherent characteristic of intellectual disabilities, the apparent lack of motivation may be the product of frequent failure and prompt dependency acquired as the result of others' caretaking. After experiencing success, individuals with intellectual disabilities do not differ from people without intellectual disabilities on measures of outer-directedness (Bybee & Zigler, 1998). Teaching self-determination skills to students with intellectual disabilities can help them become motivated, self-reliant problem solvers who act on their world rather than wait to be acted on (Fowler et al., 2007; Shogren, Toste, et al., 2017; Wehmeyer et al., 2012). See Figure 4.2.

Teaching students to take responsibility for their learning is an important component of self-determination. Teaching students with disabilities to recruit assistance from teachers is one strategy for helping them succeed in regular classrooms and take an active role in their education. Craft et al. (1998) taught four fourth graders with intellectual disabilities to recruit their teacher's attention while they worked on spelling assignments in a regular classroom. The students learned to show their work to the teacher two to three times per session and say things such as, "How am I doing?" or "Look, I'm all finished!" Recruitment training, which was conducted in the resource room, increased the frequency of each student's recruiting, the frequency of teacher praise, the percentage of worksheet items completed, and the accuracy of the students' work. After the study, the general education teacher remarked, "They fit in better, they were more a part of the group, and they weren't being disruptive because they were working" (p. 408). To learn more about this strategy for teaching students to take an active role in their learning, see *Teaching & Learning*, "'Look, I'm All Finished!' Recruiting Teacher Attention" in Chapter 6.

FIGURE 4.2 What Is Self-Determination?

If you listed what you think students with intellectual disabilities need most to transition successfully from high school to their adult life, what would be on that list? It would, most likely, look something like this:

- Job skills and workplace supports
- Independent living and community inclusion skills
- Postsecondary education and training
- Transportation
- Health care
- Friends, family, and supports

Those (and other items) are all, obviously, important to enable students with intellectual disabilities to become independent, self-sufficient young adults. Another item that should be on the list may not be as obvious. Research has shown that students with disabilities, including students with intellectual disabilities, who are more self-determined when they leave high school, achieve more positive employment, independent living, and quality-of life outcomes than do their peers with disabilities who are less self-determined.

What does "being self-determined" mean? Self-determined people *act* in ways that enable them to set and attain goals, make decisions, solve problems, advocate on their own behalf, and generally improve the quality of their lives. Self-determined people act on their preferences and interests and not on coercion or someone else's preferences and interests. There's more to being self-determined, though, than simply doing what you want rather than what someone else wants. Self-determined behavior is not just acting to gratify instant needs or acting recklessly for short-term pleasure; it is acting consciously and with intention based on one's preferences and interests to choose; make decisions; advocate; and, generally, self-govern and self-regulate one's behavior in pursuit of one's goals.

Source: Paula Solloway/Alamy stock Photo

Self-determination may be the most important factor in ensuring a good quality of life for students with intellectual disabilities as they transition to adulthood.

Self-determination is too often equated with acting without help to "control" one's own life. People with intellectual disabilities have limitations in their capacity to "control" their lives by making complex decisions or solving difficult problems. The important point to understand is that being self-determined does *not* require doing things independently; rather, it is about making things happen in one's life by acting volitionally and being a causal agent. Even if a student cannot independently make a decision, for example, she can be actively supported to engage in the decision-making process, and if the student needs others' support to make that decision, she can still be "self-determined" as long as the ultimate decision takes into account, to the maximum degree practicable, the student's preferences, interests, beliefs, values, skills, abilities, and long-term goals.

Source: Adapted from M. L. Wehmeyer (2013), Self-determination: The most natural support. In W. L. Heward, *Exceptional Children: An Introduction to Special Education* (10th ed., pp. 132–133). Pearson Education, Upper Saddle River, NJ.

Adaptive Behavior

By definition, children with intellectual disabilities have substantial deficits in adaptive behavior. These limitations can take many forms and tend to occur across domains of functioning. Limitations in self-care and daily living skills and social relationships are common characteristics of individuals with intellectual disabilities.

SELF-CARE AND DAILY LIVING SKILLS Most individuals with intellectual disabilities who require extensive supports must learn basic self-care skills such as dressing, eating, and hygiene. The coronavirus pandemic has made handwashing and mask wearing critically important daily living skills. Direct instruction and environmental supports such as added prompts and simplified routines are necessary to ensure that deficits in these adaptive areas do not seriously limit quality of life.

Most people with mild intellectual disabilities learn to take care of their basic needs, but they often benefit from training in self-management skills to achieve the levels of performance necessary for independent living and successful employment (e.g., Grossi & Heward, 1998).

HLP9 Teach social behaviors.

SOCIAL RELATIONSHIPS Making and sustaining friendships and personal relationships presents significant challenges for many children with intellectual disabilities. Poor communication skills, inability to recognize the emotional state of others, unusual behaviors, and lack of access to social situations can lead to social isolation (Callus, 2017; Matheson et al., 2007). It is difficult at best for someone who is not a professional educator or paid caretaker to want to spend the time necessary to get to know a person who interrupts frequently, does not maintain eye contact, strays from the conversational topic, and stands too close. Standing too close may have made conversational partners feel uncomfortable in the past, but in the time of COVID-19 social distancing is a life-saving skill. Teaching social and interpersonal skills to students with intellectual disabilities is one of the most important functions of special education (Agran et al., 2016; Hart et al., 2014). See *Transition: Next Year Is Now*, "Teaching Soft Skills to Prepare Students for the Future."

Behavioral Excesses and Challenging Behavior

Students with intellectual disabilities are more likely to exhibit behavior problems than are children without disabilities. Although youth with mild or borderline intellectual disabilities exhibit more antisocial behavior than do adolescents without disabilities (Douma et al., 2007; Schuiringa et al., 2017), in general, the more severe the intellectual impairment, the higher the incidence and severity of problem behavior. Difficulty accepting criticism, limited self-control, and unusual and inappropriate behaviors such as aggression or self-injury are observed more often in children with intellectual disabilities than in children without disabilities. Some genetic syndromes associated with intellectual disabilities tend to include atypical and maladaptive behavior. For example, some children with Prader-Willi syndrome (described in Table 4.2) engage in self-injurious, obsessive-compulsive behavior, and **pica** (eating nonnutritive substances such as string, hair, or dirt) (Ali, 2001; O'Brien, 2019).

The incidence of mental illness and behavior disorders in children and adolescents with intellectual disabilities is three to four times higher than that of the general population (Munir, 2016). One third of individuals with intellectual disabilities served by state developmental disability agencies in the United States have mental illnesses, and 39% needed support to manage self-injurious, disruptive, and/or destructive behavior (National Association of State Directors of Developmental Disabilities Services, 2019). Although comprehensive guidelines are available for treating psychiatric and behavioral challenges of people with intellectual disabilities (Rush & Francis, 2000), much more research is needed on how best to support this population (Koslowski et al., 2016; Tasse et al., 2019).

Transition: Next Year Is Now

Teaching Soft Skills to Prepare Students for the Future

What Are Soft Skills and Why Are They Important?

In contrast to the technical skills (i.e., "hard skills") needed to perform a job task, "soft skills" are those that allow people to get along with co-workers and complete projects. Individuals with soft skills may be described as reliable, friendly, responsible, hard-working, and flexible, so it is not surprising that soft skills are valued by employers (Robles, 2012). In fact, these skills have been identified as more important than technical skills or academic skills for finding and keeping a job (Casner-Lotto & Barrington, 2006; Cunningham & Villaseñor, 2014). For individuals with disabilities, limited soft skills have been identified as a key barrier to employment (Riesen et al., 2014).

Teaching Students to UPGRADE Their Performance

Clark et al. (2020) developed a systematic approach for teaching employment-related soft skills to youth with a range of disabilities, including intellectual disability, autism, and other developmental disabilities. Students improved their soft skills in areas targeted for intervention (e.g., attitude and cooperation) and generalized those skills to new, untaught areas (e.g., teamwork) (Clark et al., 2018; Clark & Test, 2020; Clark et al., 2019). Students also improved their ability to self-evaluate their performance, and their newly acquired soft skills improved their overall job performance.

How Do I Teach UPGRADE?

Teachers can implement the following seven steps to teach a student to self-monitor and improve soft skills:

1. Evaluate the student's performance across several soft skill areas and share those evaluations with the student. The UPGRADE program includes scoring guides or rubrics for communication skills, reliability, attitude and cooperation, teamwork, productivity, and quality of work.
2. Help the student identify an area to target and set a goal in that area (using the evaluations completed in Step 1).
3. Introduce the UPGRADE mnemonic and procedures to the student (see Step 4).
4. Have the student complete a task (academic, social, daily living, or vocational) in the school or a community setting.
5. Guide the student through the UPGRADE steps:
   - U = You (student) grade your own performance with the rubric used in Step 1
   - P = Professional (teacher, employer) evaluates performance (again with the same rubric) and shares evaluation with the student
   - G = Graph both scores and compare them, noting any discrepancies
   - R = Restate the goal and determine whether or not it was met
   - A = Acknowledge what you did well
   - D = Decide what you can do better next time to meet the goal
   - E = Execute improvements next time to meet the goal
6. Monitor your student's performance across all soft skill areas and move on to a new one when the student is ready.
7. Provide opportunities for the student to practice these new skills in different settings, with different people, and under a range of different circumstances. In other words, promote generalization!

HLP21 Teach students to maintain and generalize new learning across time and settings.

TABLE 4.2 Some prenatal conditions associated with intellectual disabilities

SYNDROME	DEFINITION AND CAUSE	REMARKS AND CHARACTERISTICS
Down syndrome	Caused by chromosomal abnormality; most common of three major types is trisomy 21, in which the 21st set of chromosomes is a triplet rather than a pair. Most often results in moderate level of intellectual disability, although some individuals function in mild or severe range. Affects about 1 in 691 live births; incidence of Down syndrome increases with age of mother to approximately 1 in 30 for women at age 45 years.	Best-known and well-researched biological condition associated with intellectual disability; estimated to account for 5%–6% of all cases. Characteristic physical features: short stature; flat, broad face with small ears and nose; upward-slanting eyes; small mouth with short roof, protruding tongue may cause articulation problems; hypotonia (floppy muscles); heart defects common; susceptibility to ear and respiratory infections.
Fetal alcohol spectrum disorders (FASDs)	FASDs include fetal alcohol syndrome (FAS), alcohol-related neurodevelopmental disorder (ARND), and alcohol-related birth defects. The mother's excessive alcohol use during pregnancy has toxic effects on the fetus, including physical defects and developmental delays. Children with FAS may have abnormal facial features, growth problems, and difficulty with learning and attention. Children with ARND may have intellectual disabilities.	A leading cause of intellectual disability, FASDs have an incidence higher than that of Down syndrome and cerebral palsy. In addition to cognitive impairments, some children experience sleep disturbances, motor dysfunctions, hyperirritability, aggression, and conduct problems. Although risk of FASDs is highest during the first trimester of pregnancy, pregnant women should avoid drinking alcohol at any time.
Fragile X syndrome	A triplet, repeat mutation on the X chromosome interferes with production of the FMR-1 protein, which is essential for normal brain functioning; majority of males experience mild to moderate intellectual disability in childhood and moderate to severe deficits in adulthood; females may carry and transmit the mutation to their children but tend to have fewer disabilities than affected males.	Affects approximately 1 in 4000 males; the most common inherited cause of intellectual disability and the most common clinical type of intellectual disability after Down syndrome. Characterized by social anxiety and avoidance (avoiding eye contact; tactile defensiveness; turning the body away during face-to-face interactions; and stylized, ritualistic forms of greeting); preservative speech often includes repetition of words and phrases.
Phenylketonuria (PKU)	Genetically inherited condition in which a child is born without an important enzyme needed to break down an amino acid, phenylalanine, found in many common foods; failure to break down this amino acid causes brain damage that often results in aggressiveness, hyperactivity, and severe intellectual disability.	Widespread screening has virtually eliminated intellectual disability resulting from PKU in the United States. By analyzing the concentration of phenylalanine in a newborn's blood plasma, doctors can diagnose PKU and treat it with a special diet. Most children with PKU who receive a phenylalanine-restricted diet have normal intellectual development.
Prader-Willi syndrome	Caused by deletion of a portion of chromosome 15. Infants have hypotonia (floppy muscles) and may have to be tube fed. The initial phase is followed by development of insatiable appetite; constant preoccupation with food can lead to life-threatening obesity if food seeking is not controlled. Affects 1 in 10,000 to 25,000 live births.	Associated with intellectual and learning disabilities; behavior problems common: impulsivity, aggressiveness, temper tantrums, obsessive-compulsive behavior; some forms of self-injurious behavior, such as skin picking; delayed motor skills, short stature, small hands and feet, underdeveloped genitalia.
Williams syndrome	Caused by deletion of material on the seventh chromosome; cognitive functioning ranges from normal to moderate levels of intellectual disability.	Distinctive facial features including a broad forehead, a short nose, full cheeks, and a wide mouth; outgoing and social; lack of reserve toward strangers; often also have attention-deficit/hyperactivity disorder (ADHD) and/or anxiety.

Sources: AAIDD Ad Hoc Committee on Terminology and Classification (2010); Beirne-Smith et al. (2015); Centers for Disease Control and Prevention (2019a, 2019b); Dimitropoulos et al. (2001); Fidler et al. (2007); National Down Syndrome Society (2020); National Institutes of Health (2020).

Prevalence

Learning Outcome 4.3 Identify factors that might account for the wide differences in the prevalence of intellectual disabilities within the school-age population across states and school districts, and list some of the causes of intellectual disabilities.

Many factors contribute to the difficulty of estimating the number of people with intellectual disabilities. Some of these factors include changing definitions of intellectual disabilities, the schools' reluctance to label children with mild intellectual impairment, and the changing status of children with mild intellectual disabilities (some are declassified during their school careers; others are no longer identified after leaving school). Historically, the federal government estimated the prevalence at 3% of the general population, although recent analyses find little objective support for this figure. If prevalence figures were based solely on IQ scores, 2.3% of the population theoretically would have intellectual disabilities (see Figure 4.1).

Basing prevalence estimates on IQ scores only, however, ignores the other necessary criteria for intellectual disabilities—deficits in adaptive functioning and the need for supports. Some professionals believe that if adaptive behavior is included with intellectual ability when estimating prevalence, the figure drops to about 1% (Cervantes et al., 2019). In fact, two national studies estimated the prevalence of intellectual disabilities at 0.78% (Larson et al., 2001) and 1.27% of the U.S. population (Fujiura, 2003).

In the 2018–2019 school year, approximately 423,215 students age 6 to 21 years received special education under the disability category of intellectual disabilities (U.S. Department of Education, 2020a). These students represented about 6.7% of all children in special education. Intellectual disability is the fifth-largest disability category after learning disabilities, speech or language impairments, other health impairments, and autism.

Prevalence rates vary greatly from state to state. For example, the prevalence of intellectual disabilities as a percentage of the school-age population in 2018–2019 ranged from a low of 0.22% (Colorado) to a high of 1.95% (West Virginia) (U.S. Department of Education, 2020a). Such differences in prevalence stem in large part from the widely differing criteria for identifying students with intellectual disabilities (McNicholas, 2018; Scullin, 2006). Prevalence figures also vary considerably among districts within a given state (Hetzner, 2007).

Causes

More than 350 risk factors associated with intellectual disabilities have been identified (Dykens et al., 2000). Approximately 35% of cases have a genetic cause, another third involve external trauma or toxins, and etiology remains unknown for another third of cases (Heikua et al., 2005; Szymanski & King, 1999). Nevertheless, knowledge of etiology is critical to efforts designed to lower the incidence of intellectual disabilities and may have implications for some educational interventions (Hodapp & Dykens, 2007; Vissers et al., 2016).

Figure 4.3 lists etiologic factors associated with intellectual disabilities that the AAIDD categorizes as **prenatal** (occurring before birth), **perinatal** (occurring during or shortly after birth), or **postnatal** (occurring after birth). Each of these etiologic factors can be classified further as biomedical or environmental (social, behavioral, educational). However, a combination of biological and environmental factors is often involved in individual cases of intellectual disabilities, making specific determination of etiology extremely difficult (Heikua et al., 2005; van Karnebeek et al., 2005).

BIOMEDICAL CAUSES Researchers have identified specific biomedical causes for about two thirds of individuals with severe levels of intellectual disabilities (Batshaw et al., 2019). Table 4.2 describes the most common prenatal conditions that often result in

FIGURE 4.3 Etiologic Risk Factors for Intellectual Disabilities

Timing	Biomedical	Social	Behavioral	Educational
Prenatal	1. Chromosomal disorders 2. Single-gene disorders 3. Syndromes 4. Metabolic disorders 5. Cerebral dysgenesis 6. Maternal illnesses 7. Parental age	1. Poverty 2. Maternal malnutrition 3. Domestic violence 4. Lack of access to prenatal care	1. Parental drug use 2. Parental alcohol use 3. Parental smoking 4. Parental immaturity	1. Parental cognitive disability without supports 2. Lack of preparation for parenthood
Perinatal	1. Prematurity 2. Birth injury 3. Neonatal disorders	1. Lack of access to birth care	1. Parental rejection of caretaking 2. Parental abandonment of child	1. Lack of medical referral for intervention services at discharge
Postnatal	1. Traumatic brain injury 2. Malnutrition 3. Meningoencephalitis 4. Seizure disorders 5. Degenerative disorders	1. Impaired child caregiver 2. Lack of adequate stimulation 3. Family poverty 4. Chronic illness in the family 5. Institutionalization	1. Child abuse and neglect 2. Domestic violence 3. Inadequate safety measures 4. Social deprivation 5. Difficult child behaviors	1. Impaired parenting 2. Delayed diagnosis 3. Inadequate early intervention services 4. Inadequate special educational services 5. Inadequate family support

Source: *Intellectual Disability: Definition, Classification, and Systems of Supports* (11th ed.) by AAIDD Ad Hoc Committee on Terminology and Classification (p. 60). Copyright 2010 by American Association on Intellectual and Developmental Disabilities. Reproduced with permission of AAIDD.

intellectual disabilities. The term *syndrome* refers to a number of symptoms or characteristics that occur together and provide the defining features of a given condition. **Down syndrome** and **fragile X syndrome** are the two most common genetic causes of intellectual disabilities (Cregenzán-Royo et al., 2018; Roberts et al., 2005). As a result of the Human Genome Project and other advances in the field of genetics, it has been estimated that intellectual disabilities are caused by more 750 different genetic disorders (Hodapp & DesJardin, 2002).

It is important to understand that none of the risk factors shown in Figure 4.3 or Table 4.2 *is* intellectual disability. These conditions, diseases, and syndromes are commonly associated with intellectual disabilities, but they may or may not result in significant limitations in both intellectual and adaptive functioning that define intellectual disabilities. "Because intellectual disability is characterized by impaired functioning, its etiology is whatever causes this impairment in functioning" (AAIDD Ad Hoc Committee, 2010, p. 61). Any risk factor, whether it is low birth weight or Down syndrome, causes intellectual disability only when it results in impaired functioning sufficient to meet the criteria for diagnosis.

Some of the health conditions and disorders shown in Table 4.2 require special education and related services as disabilities in their own right or are causes of other disabilities whether or not intellectual disability is also involved. A number of these conditions are discussed in Chapter 9 (cytomegalovirus, meningitis, rubella) and Chapter 11 (diabetes, epilepsy, head injuries, hydrocephalus, muscular dystrophy, spina bifida).

ENVIRONMENTAL CAUSES Individuals with mild intellectual disabilities, those who require less intensive supports, make up 85% to 90% of all people with intellectual disabilities. The vast majority show no evidence of organic pathology—no brain damage or other biological problem. When no biological risk factor is evident, the cause is presumed to be *psychosocial disadvantage*, environmental influences such as poverty, minimal opportunities to develop early language, child abuse and neglect, or chronic social or sensory deprivation. Professionals sometimes use the term *intellectual disability of cultural-familial origin* when referring to the result of a poor social environment early in the child's life (AAIDD Ad Hoc Committee, 2010).

Although no direct evidence proves that social and environmental deprivation causes intellectual disability, researchers generally believe that these influences cause many cases of mild intellectual disabilities. Empirical support for the influence of poverty is found in research showing that children who live in poverty have a higher than normal chance of being diagnosed with intellectual disabilities (Le Menestrel, Duncan, & National Academies of Sciences, Engineering, and Medicine, 2019).

Prevention

Medical advances have reduced the incidence of intellectual disabilities caused by some of the known biological factors. Probably the biggest single preventive strike against intellectual disabilities (and many other disabling conditions, including blindness and deafness) was the development of an effective rubella vaccine in 1962. When **rubella** (German measles) is contracted by mothers during the first 3 months of pregnancy, it causes severe damage in 10% to 40% of unborn children. Fortunately, this cause of intellectual disabilities can be eliminated if women are vaccinated for rubella before becoming pregnant.

Advances in medical science have enabled doctors to identify certain genetic influences associated with intellectual disabilities. Screening procedures and diagnostic tests can detect genetic disorders during pregnancy. Noninvasive screening procedures, such as ultrasonography and serum screening, are routinely provided to women whose pregnancies are considered at risk for a congenital disability. Maternal serum screening measures the amount of alpha-fetoprotein and other biochemical markers in the mother's bloodstream for disabilities such as Down syndrome and spina bifida.

Diagnostic tests, such as amniocentesis and chorionic villi sampling, can confirm the presence of various disorders associated with intellectual disabilities. **Amniocentesis** requires withdrawing a sample of fluid from the amniotic sac surrounding the fetus during the second trimester of pregnancy (usually the 15th to 20th week). Fetal cells are removed from the amniotic fluid and grown in a cell culture for about 2 weeks. A chromosome and enzyme analysis is then performed to identify the presence of about 80 specific genetic disorders before birth. Many of these disorders, such as Down syndrome, are associated with intellectual disabilities.

In **chorionic villi sampling (CVS)**, a small amount of chorionic tissue (a fetal component of the developing placenta) is removed and tested. CVS can be performed earlier than amniocentesis (during the 8th to 10th week of pregnancy). Because fetal cells exist in relatively large numbers in the chorion, they can be analyzed immediately without waiting 2 to 3 weeks for them to grow.

Amniocentesis and CVS are invasive procedures that carry risk of miscarriage ranging from about 5 to 10 per 1000 procedures (Mujezinovic & Alfirevic, 2007). A recently developed simple blood test that detects fetal DNA and RNA in the mother's bloodstream in the first trimester (Papageorgiou et al., 2011; Wright & Burton, 2009) can determine a baby's sex and the presence of numerous genetic and chromosomal abnormalities. The test can be done as early as 5 weeks into the pregnancy and is reported to be 100% accurate.

Women who are at risk for giving birth to a baby with a disability on the basis of the parents' genetic backgrounds are commonly referred for **genetic counseling** (Blesson & Cohen, 2019; Roberts et al., 2002). Genetic counseling is a discussion between a specially trained medical counselor and the prospective parents about the possibility that they may give birth to a child with disabilities. To read discussions of ethical considerations of genetic testing for disabilities, see Bauer (2008), Beirne-Smith and colleagues (2015), Jamal et al., (2019), and Kuna (2001).

Newborn screening tests for inherited conditions and biomedical risk factors are mandatory in every state. The Secretary of the Department of Health and Human Services recommends states screen for 35 core and 26 secondary disorders (U.S. Department of Health and Human Services, 2020). A simple blood test administered to virtually every baby born in the United States has drastically reduced the incidence of intellectual disabilities caused by **phenylketonuria (PKU)**. By analyzing the concentration of phenylalanine in a newborn's blood plasma, doctors can diagnose PKU and treat it with a phenylalanine-restricted diet. Most children with PKU who receive treatment have normal intellectual development.

Toxic exposure through maternal substance abuse such as alcohol and environmental pollutants (e.g., lead poisoning) are two major causes of intellectual disabilities that can be prevented with education and training.

Educational Approaches

Learning Outcome 4.4 Describe key elements of instruction for teaching academic, functional, and self-determination skills to students with intellectual disabilities.

The search for effective methods for educating students with intellectual disabilities began in France more than 200 years ago, when Jean Marc Gaspard Itard kept a detailed diary of his efforts to teach a young boy who was found in the woods and thought to be a feral child. Itard showed that systematic intervention could produce significant gains with a child thought to be incapable of learning (Itard, 1806/1962).

Since Itard's time, researchers and practitioners working with students with intellectual disabilities have developed numerous methods of specialized instruction, some of which have contributed to improved practice in all other areas of education. Similarly, efforts by early advocates on behalf of children and adults with intellectual disabilities blazed trails for advocacy groups representing individuals with other disabilities. Some key historical events and their implications for the education and treatment of children and adults with intellectual disabilities are highlighted in Figure 4.4.

Curriculum Goals

What do students with intellectual disabilities need to learn? Too often in the past, children with mild intellectual disabilities were presented with a slowed or watered-down version of the general education curriculum that focused largely on traditional academic subjects. For

FIGURE 4.4 Key Historical Events in the Education of Children with Intellectual Disabilities

Date	Historical Event	Educational Implication
1806	Jean Marc Gaspard Itard published an account of his work with Victor, the Wild Boy of Aveyron.	Itard showed that intensive treatment could produce significant learning. Many consider Itard the father of special education.
1848	Edouard Seguin, who had studied and worked under Itard, helped establish the Pennsylvania Training School.	This was the first educational facility for people with intellectual disabilities in the United States.
1850	Samuel Gridley Howe began the School for Idiotic and Feeble Minded Youth.	This was the first publicly funded residential school in the United States.
1896	The first public school class for children with intellectual disabilities began in Providence, RI.	This began the special class movement, which grew to 1.3 million children in 1974, the year before IDEA.
1905	Alfred Binet and Theodore Simon developed a test in France to screen students not benefiting from general education classrooms.	The test enabled empirical identification of students with intellectual disabilities and contributed to the growth of the special class movement.
1916	Lewis Terman, of Stanford University, published the Stanford-Binet Intelligence Scale in the United States.	Most schools adopted IQ testing as a means of identifying children with below-average general intelligence.
1935	Edgar Doll published the Vineland Social Maturity Scale.	The scale provided a standardized method for assessing a person's adaptive behavior, which later became part of the definition of intellectual disabilities.
1950	Parents formed the National Association for Retarded Children (known today as The Arc).	The Arc remains a powerful and important advocacy organization for people of all ages with intellectual disabilities.
1958	National Defense Education Act (PL 85–926) enacted.	Provided funds for training professionals to train teachers of children with intellectual disabilities.
1959	AAMR published its first manual on the definition and classification of mental retardation, with diagnosis based on an IQ score of 1 standard deviation below the mean (approximately 85).	Many students were identified in the borderline category of mental retardation and served in special classes for "slow learners" or EMR students.
1961	John F. Kennedy established the first President's Panel on Mental Retardation. (Today, the President's Committee for People with Intellectual Disabilities.)	The panel's first report (Mayo, 1962) made recommendations that helped guide national policy with respect to intellectual disabilities (e.g., citizenship, education, prevention).
1969	Bengt Nirje published a key paper defining normalization. Wolf Wolfensberger championed normalization in the United States.	Normalization became a leading philosophy guiding the development and delivery of educational, community, vocational, and residential services for people with intellectual disabilities.
1973	American Association on Mental Retardation (AAMR) published a revised definition that required a score on IQ tests of 2 standard deviations below the mean (≈70 or less) and concurrent deficits in adaptive behavior.	This eliminated the category of borderline intellectual disabilities.
1992	AAMR published "System '92," a radically different definition of mental retardation with a classification system based on intensities of supports.	New definition and classification system generated cautious support by some and concern by others.
2007	AAMR changed its name to the American Association on Intellectual and Developmental Disabilities (AAIDD) and replaced the term *mental retardation* with *intellectual disability*.	According to the AAIDD, the term *intellectual disability* (a) reflects current practices that focus on functional behaviors and contextual factors; (b) provides a logical basis for providing individualized supports due to its social-ecological framework; (c) is less offensive to people with disabilities; and (d) is more consistent with international terminology.
2010	"Rosa's Law" (PL 111-256) signed by President Barack Obama in October 2010.	Amends language in federal statutes by replacing all references to "mental retardation" and "mentally retarded individual" to " intellectual disability" and "individual with an intellectualdisability. "Law named after 9-year-old girl with Down syndrome, who fought with her parents to have a similar law passed in home state of Maryland.

example, a group of children with mild intellectual disabilities might spend several weeks learning the 50 states and their capitals. Students with more severe intellectual impairments often spent hours putting pegs into pegboards and sorting plastic sticks by color because educators believed these isolated skills were developmental prerequisites for more meaningful activities. Unfortunately, knowing that Boise is the capital of Idaho or being able to sort by color did not help these students function more capably.

Wiser curricular decisions combined with increasingly effective instructional techniques and supports are enabling many students with intellectual disabilities to participate meaningfully in the general education curriculum (Soukup et al., 2007; Wehmeyer, 2006).

ACADEMIC CURRICULUM All students with intellectual disabilities should receive instruction in reading, writing, and math (e.g., Cannella-Malone et al., 2015; Copeland & McDonnell, 2020; Everhart et al., 2011; Rivera & Baker, 2013). Functional academics are "the most useful parts" of reading, writing, arithmetic, and science for the student (Browder & Spooner, 2006). Choosing functional academic targets is not as simple as it might seem. The most useful part of writing for one student (e.g., making a grocery list) may not be functional for another student (e.g., writing the number of items packaged on the job). Careful observation of a student's current routines will reveal the skills he requires or could use often. Teachers should also consider the skills future environments are likely to require.

Teachers must guard against the faulty assumption that a traditional academic skill cannot be functional because it is not a typical activity or learning outcome for students with intellectual disabilities. For example, although *crystal* and *limestone* would not appear on any lists of functional sight words, a student with a rock collection might find the words extremely functional (Browder, 2000).

Source: Paula Solloway/Alamy stock Photo

Students with intellectual disabilities benefit from instruction in functional academics.

Complete immersion in the academic curriculum, however, can be a restrictive and ineffective education for a student with intellectual disabilities. Care must be taken that a student's involvement in the academic portions of the general education curriculum does not limit opportunities to learn the skills needed to function independently and successfully in current and future environments.

FUNCTIONAL CURRICULUM Learning functional curriculum content increases a student's independence, self-direction, health and fitness, and enjoyment in everyday school, home, community, and work environments. Special educators have taught students with intellectual disabilities a wide range of practical skills, such as using public transportation (Price et al., 2018), shopping (Bouck et al., 2017), ATM use (Barczak, 2019), ordering in a restaurant (Mechling et al., 2005), cooking and food safety (Kellems et al., 2016; Madaus et al., 2010), and leisure and sports skills (Cannella-Malone et al., 2016; Lo, Burk, & Anderson, 2014). Bouck (2011) provides content analysis of 10 commercially available functional curriculum models for secondary students with mild to moderate intellectual disabilities.

Teachers determine whether a particular knowledge or skill is functional by answering questions such as:

- Will learning this knowledge or skill help the student be more independent and successful in his home, school, or community?
- Will failure to learn this knowledge or skill have negative consequences for the student?

The ultimate approach to determining if a given skill qualifies as functional curriculum is to contemplate this question from the student's perspective: "Will I need it when I'm 21?" (Beck et al., 1994). The answer to this question is critical because when educators fail to relate curriculum for a student with intellectual disabilities to outcomes with direct relevance to

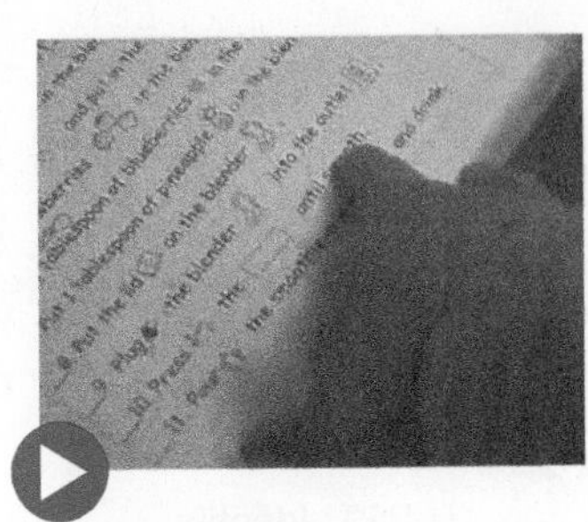

Pearson eText
Video Example 4.3
Students with intellectual disabilities need instruction in functional academics and daily living skills.

that student's eventual independence and quality of life, "years of valuable opportunities for meaningful learning can be wasted" (Knowlton, 1998, p. 96).

Neither teachers nor students should view decisions about what to teach as either academic or functional. General and special educators who teach students with intellectual disabilities should seek to align the academic and functional curricula in ways that allow each student to benefit as much as possible from access to the general education curriculum while learning from a personalized curriculum of functional skills across life domains (Browder et al., 2006). Examples of lessons blending effective instruction of both functional skills and academic goals can be found in Collins et al. (2010). See also the *Teaching & Learning* feature in Chapter 12, "Embedding Academic Content into Functional Skill Instruction."

As students with intellectual disabilities reach middle and high school, learning functional skills that will help them transition to adult life in the community becomes especially critical. Several models and taxonomies of adult functioning provide frameworks from which to build functional curriculum activities (Bambara et al., 2020). For example, Life Skills Instruction includes 147 major life demands that are associated with a variety of specific life skills and organized around six domains of adult functioning (Cronin et al., 2007).

SELF-DETERMINATION Self-determined learners set personal goals, plan steps for achieving those goals, choose and implement a course of action, evaluate their performance, and make adjustments in what they are doing to reach their goals. Learning self-determination skills can serve as a curriculum goal in its own right as well as a means to help students achieve other learning outcomes (see Figure 4.2).

Self-determination entails a complex set of skills and is a lofty goal for any student. However, students with intellectual and other disabilities can learn to be more self-determined, and those who do are more likely to achieve IEP goals and transition successfully from school to adult life (Shogren, Garnier Villarreal, et al., 2017; Shogren et al., 2015). Numerous research-based practices can enhance the knowledge and skills that enable students to be more self-determined (Cobb et al., 2009). For example, the Self-Determined Learning Model of Instruction (Wehmeyer et al., 2012) teaches students to engage in a self-regulated problem-solving process that includes setting goals, creating plans to address those goals, and self-assessing their progress toward those goals.

Relatedly, a substantial literature base shows that students with intellectual disability can learn to self-regulate behavior or self-direct learning when taught skills such as self-instruction, self-monitoring, self-prompting, and self-evaluation (e.g., Clark et al., 2019; Cullen & Alber-Morgan, 2015; Miller & Taber-Doughty, 2014; Rouse et al., 2014). For example, Agran et al. (2002) taught four middle school students with intellectual disabilities a four-step problem-solving sequence to achieve self-set goals related to their participation and success in the general education classroom. The students were taught to (a) verbalize, "What is the problem?" and to say out loud what it was (e.g., "I need to say at least one sentence during class."); (b) ask, "What can I do about it?" and verbalize the proposed solution; (c) implement the proposed solution; and (d) ask, "Did that fix the problem?"

Instructional Methods

Students with intellectual disabilities learn best when their teachers use instructional methods derived from empirical research, such as the following practices:

HLP11 Identify and prioritize long- and short-term learning goals.

- Assess each student's present levels of performance to identify and prioritize the most important instructional targets.
- Define and task-analyze the new knowledge or skills to be learned.
- Design instructional materials and activities that provide frequent opportunities to respond during guided and independent practice.

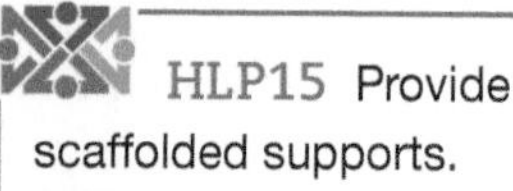

HLP15 Provide scaffolded supports.

- Provide and then fade prompts and cues until the student responds independently to naturally occurring stimuli.
- Provide systematic consequences for student performance in the form of contingent reinforcement, instructional feedback, and error correction.

- Incorporate fluency-building activities into lessons.
- Use strategies to promote the generalization and maintenance of newly learned skills.
- Conduct direct and frequent measurements of student performance and use those data to inform instructional decisions.

Some of these components of effective instruction are described here; others are discussed in subsequent chapters.

TASK ANALYSIS **Task analysis** means breaking down complex or multistep skills into smaller, easier-to-learn subtasks. The subskills or subtasks are then sequenced, either in the natural order in which they are typically performed or from easiest to most difficult. Assessing a student's performance on a sequence of task-analyzed subskills helps pinpoint where instruction should begin. Figure 4.5 shows the task analysis and data collection form a teacher developed for her student, Cara, to use her school locker. See *Teaching & Learning*, "Task Analysis."

ACTIVE STUDENT RESPONSE Decades of research in general and special education have revealed and underscored the positive relationship between students' active engagement with academic tasks and their achievement (see reviews by Hattie, 2012; States et al., 2019). High rates of active participation are important for all learners but particularly important for students with disabilities: "The pedagogical clock continues to tick mercilessly, and the opportunities for these students to advance or catch up diminish over time" (Kame'enui, 1993, p. 379).

HLP18 Use strategies to promote active student engagement.

Researchers have used terms such as *academic learning time* (Fisher et al., 1980), *opportunities to respond* (Greenwood et al., 1984), and *active student responding* (Heward, 1994) to refer

FIGURE 4.5 Task analysis and data collection form for a student using her school locker

Student: Cara **Task:** Using hallway key locker **Teacher:** Sandie Trask-Tyler
Goal: Cara will independently put/secure her book bag, jacket, and personal belongings in her hallway locker when arriving at school with 100% accuracy, 4/5 consecutive sessions

Date →	9/8	9/10	9/11	9/12	9/13	9/16						
1. Carry belongings to locker key hook board	–	–	V	✓	✓	✓						
2. Lift key off hook	–	–	G	✓	✓	✓						
3. Take key and belongings out classroom door and turn left in the hallway	✓	✓	✓	✓	✓	✓						
4. Walk to the front of her locker	✓	✓	✓	✓	✓	✓						
5. Insert key into the lock on her locker	–	–	P	✓	✓	✓						
6. Turn key 90° to the right	–	–	P	G	✓	✓						
7. Lift black locker handle	–	–	P	P	V	✓						
8. Open locker door	✓	✓	✓	✓	✓	✓						
9. Put book bag in locker	✓	✓	✓	✓	✓	✓						
10. Put jacket in locker	–	–	V	✓	✓	✓						
11. Put other personal items in locker	–	–	NA	V	✓	✓						
12. Make sure items are fully inside locker	–	–	P	V	✓	✓						
13. Close locker door	✓	✓	✓	✓	✓	✓						
14. Turn key upright, 90° to the left	–	–	P	G	V	✓						
15. Pull key from lock	–	–	P	G	✓	✓						
16. Take key back to the classroom	–	✓	✓	✓	✓	✓						
17. Place the key back on the hook	–	–	V	✓	✓	✓						
Total Independent Steps	5	6	6	11	15	17						
Baseline/Teach	B	B	T	T	T	T						

Baseline/Probe Sessions: ✓ correct, – incorrect
Teaching Sessions: ✓ independent correct, **B** = baseline, **G** = gestural/visual prompt correct, **P** = physical guidance prompt correct, **T** = teach, **V** = verbal prompt correct

Source: Reprinted by permission from Sandie Trask-Tyler.

Pearson eText
Video Example 4.4
Cara performs each step of the task analysis shown in Figure 4.5.

TEACHING & LEARNING

Task Analysis

What Are the Component Steps of a Task Analysis? When developing a task analysis, teachers can use one or more of the methods described here to identify the component steps or subskills.

Observe competent performers. Watch someone doing the skill correctly and write down what the person does. The task analysis shown in Figure 4.5 was developed by watching what two independent students did when using their hallway lockers. If the skill or activity is an extended, complex task, a video record of someone executing it could help with identifying the steps.

Perform the task yourself. If the task to be analyzed is fairly straightforward and one you do often, do it yourself and write down or voice each step into a recorder as you perform it. This is how Cara's teacher created the task analysis for making microwave popcorn shown in Figure 4.6. Although simple on the surface, this technique may be more difficult than it seems, especially for everyday tasks. Be careful—it's easy to omit steps.

Ask an expert. When the task analysis will guide instruction for skills or activities students will need to perform in a competitive environment (e.g., a job), seek input from experts. There are many ways to change bed linens or clear dishes from the table after eating; some are more efficient and appropriate in certain environments. If teaching young adults to strip and make

Pearson eText
Video Example 4.5
Cara's teacher created a task analysis to guide her instruction for making popcorn.

Figure 4.6 Task Analysis and Data Collection Form for Making Microwave Popcorn

Student: Cara **Task:** Make Microwave Popcorn **Teacher:** Sandie Trask-Tyler

Goal: Cara will independently and safely make microwave popcorn 3 consecutive sessions.

Date →								
1. Open the cabinet door								
2. Locate the microwave popcorn box								
3. Pick up the box and put it on the counter								
4. Open the box and take out 1 package								
5. Put the popcorn box back in the cabinet								
6. Close the cabinet door								
7. Tear/pull open the plastic wrapping								
8. Take popcorn out of the plastic wrapping								
9. Locate trash can								
10. Throw away wrapper								
11. Walk to microwave								
12. Open microwave door								
13. Put popcorn in microwave correct side up								
14. Close microwave oven door								
15. Press popcorn button								
16. Wait until the microwave shuts off								
17. Open the microwave door								
18. Put on oven mitts								
19. Remove popcorn from microwave using mitts								
20. Put popcorn on counter								
21. Take off oven mitts (put on microwave)								
22. Close microwave door								
Total Independent Steps								
Baseline/Teach/Probe								

Baseline/Probe Sessions: ✓ correct, – incorrect
Teaching Sessions: ✓ independent correct, **V** = verbal prompt correct, **G** = gestural/visual prompt correct, **P** = physical guidance prompt correct

beds or bus tables as job training for a hotel or restaurant job, observe and interview professional room attendants and table bussers.

How Do You Validate the Task Analysis? Ask a colleague to perform each step of your task analysis exactly as written and provide no additional instructions or prompts. As you watch your colleague, it will be immediately evident if any steps are missing or not logically sequenced. This exercise will inform revisions of the task analysis so that it is accurate.

Why Do You Individualize the Task Analysis? Task analyses must be individualized, according to the age, cognitive skills, and motor abilities of the student. The detail and sometimes sequence of steps most effective for one student may differ from what another student needs to achieve the same outcome. Some students may need a task to be broken down into smaller steps, or they may need additional prompts using assistive devices in the environment to complete the task.

to this important variable. **Active student response (ASR)** occurs when a student makes a detectable, lesson-specific response. Given a lesson's purpose, words read, sentences written, algebra problems answered, lengths and weights measured, musical notes played, historical figures named, or chemical compounds analyzed may count as ASR. *Count* is key because the basic measure of ASR is the number of responses by a student during an observed period of instruction.

When other key variables are held constant (e.g., quality of curriculum materials, prerequisite skills, motivation), an ASR-rich lesson will result in more learning than will a lesson in which students make few or no responses. Research-based methods for increasing ASR for all students, including those with intellectual and other disabilities, include choral responding (Menzies et al., 2017), response cards (Schnorr et al., 2016), and classwide peer tutoring (Maheady et al., 2006). Learn more about choral responding, response cards, and classwide peer tutoring in the *Teaching & Learning* features in Chapters 2 and 6.

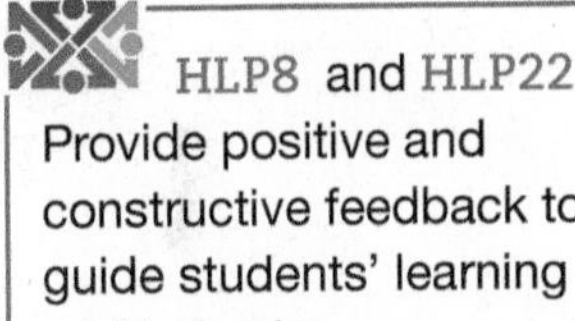
HLP8 and HLP22 Provide positive and constructive feedback to guide students' learning and behavior.

SYSTEMATIC FEEDBACK Instructional feedback—information provided to students about their performance—falls into two broad categories: (a) praise and other forms of confirmation or **positive reinforcement** for correct responses and (b) error correction for incorrect responses. Feedback is most effective when it is specific, immediate, positive, frequent, and differential (comparing the student's present performance with past performance, e.g., "You read 110 words today, Jermon. That's five more than yesterday.").

A special type of feedback called *instructive feedback* can increase the efficiency of instruction for students with intellectual and other disabilities (Werts et al., 1996). When giving feedback on students' responses to targeted items, the teacher intentionally provides "extra information." For example, after a student correctly reads the word *corn,* the teacher might say, "Right, this word is *corn*; corn is a vegetable." The instructive feedback is the statement "corn is a vegetable." Several studies have found that instructive feedback does not impede students' acquisition of the target information and that students learn much of the additional information (e.g., Carroll & Kodak, 2015; Loughery et al., 2014; Werts et al., 2011).

Using feedback effectively is one of the most important skills for teachers. Effective teachers change both the focus and the timing of their feedback as students progress from initial attempts at learning a new skill through practicing a newly acquired skill. When a student is first learning a new skill or content knowledge, feedback should follow each response (see Figure 4.7). Feedback during this **acquisition stage of learning** should focus on the accuracy and form of the student's response (e.g., "Very good, Kathy. Two quarters equal 50 cents."). Providing feedback after each response in the acquisition stage reduces the likelihood that students will practice errors by responding in the absence of feedback.

When a student begins to perform a new skill with some consistent accuracy (at minimum, correct responses outnumber errors), she should begin making a series of responses before the teacher provides feedback. During this **practice stage of learning**, feedback

FIGURE 4.7 Feedback Within a Series of Instructional Trials During the Acquisition and Practice Stages of Learning

Acquisition Stage of Learning

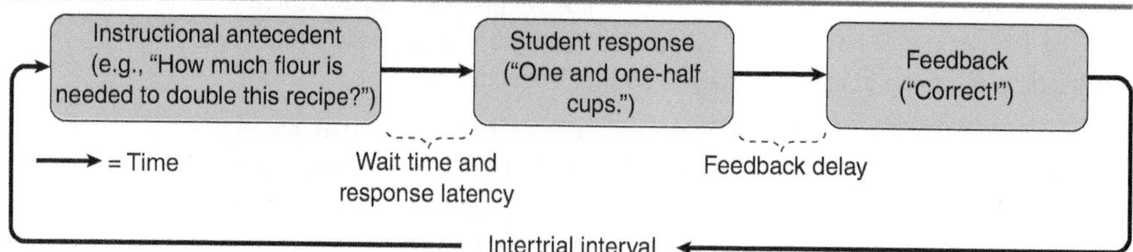

Practice Stage of Learning

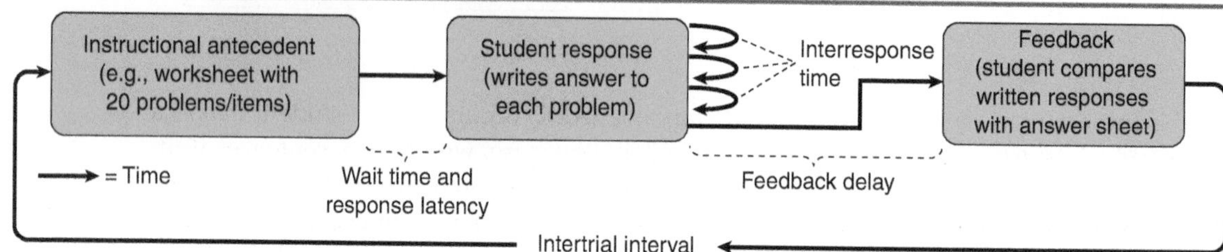

Notes: *Wait time* is the time between the teacher's presentation of a question or problem and a signal that the student may respond; *latency* is the elapsed time between a signal to respond and the student's initiation of the response; *interresponse time* is the time between two consecutive responses.

should emphasize the correct rate at which the student performed the target skill (e.g., "Way to go, Dominique! You correctly answered 28 problems in 1 minute."). Feedback after each response during the practice stage may impede the student's opportunity to develop fluency.

TRANSFER OF STIMULUS CONTROL Trial-and-error learning is inefficient and can be frustrating for any student; for students with intellectual disabilities, it is likely to be a complete waste of time. Instead of waiting to see whether the student will make a correct response, the effective teacher provides a prompt (e.g., physical guidance, verbal directions, pictures, prerecorded auditory prompts) that makes a correct response very probable (Dogoe & Banda, 2009). The teacher reinforces the correct response, repeats the prompt, and reinforces another correct response. The teacher then gradually and systematically withdraws response prompts so that the student's responding comes under the stimulus control of natural cues that occur in the learner's everyday environment.

HLP21 Teach students to maintain and generalize new learning across time and settings.

GENERALIZATION AND MAINTENANCE Instruction is of little value if students do not use what they have learned for successful functioning in school, home, community, and workplace settings. **Generalization** and **maintenance** refer to the extent to which students use prior learned knowledge and skills in relevant settings over time. Researchers have identified and continue to develop strategies and tactics for promoting generalization and maintenance (Cooper et al., 2020). Three of these strategies are described briefly here:

Teach the full range of stimulus conditions and response requirements. When introducing a new skill, it is not possible to teach every variation of how the student should perform the skill in all settings and situations. Differences in environmental stimuli across settings and situations may require the skill to be performed in different ways. For this reason, teachers must thoughtfully select examples and non-examples that represent a range of possible situations the student is likely to encounter inside and outside the classroom. For example, when learning to bus tables in a school cafeteria for possible work in a restaurant, students should learn to discriminate which tables to clear from a variety of situations: empty tables, people still eating, empty table but food on plate, personal belongings left behind, and so on (Horner et al., 1986).

Make the instructional setting similar to the generalization setting. If the generalization setting differs greatly from the setting where teaching takes place, the student may not perform the new behavior. One tactic for combating this problem entails incorporating as many features typical of the generalization setting as possible into the teaching situation. For example, making part of the classroom resemble a store to help students practice making purchases is one way to program common stimuli across instructional and generalization settings.

Another tactic is to teach students to use a contrived common stimulus in the instructional setting, which they can then transport to the generalization setting where it prompts or assists performance of the target skill. For example, students can practice ordering meals at a mock-up fast food counter in their classroom by pointing to icons of food items on a small card; they can use that card to order independently at community restaurants (van den Pol et al., 1981). Rowe and Test (2013) taught students to make purchases with debit cards in a classroom setting with a simulated debit card machine and picture prompt cards. Although the students in this study were able to generalize to the community setting without a contrived common stimulus, students who struggle with generalization could learn to use picture prompt cards to assist with their debit card purchases in the community.

Community-based instruction—teaching in the actual setting where students will ultimately use their new skills—increases the probability of generalization and maintenance. A review of 23 research studies, however, showed that simply conducting instruction in the community is no guarantee of generalization and maintenance (Walker et al., 2010). Poorly designed instruction will be ineffective regardless of where it is conducted. And community-based instruction can be expensive and typically is not available on a daily basis. Morse and Schuster (2000) found that 2 days per week of community-based instruction supplemented by simulation training in the classroom were effective for teaching students with intellectual disabilities to shop for groceries. Similarly, Cihak et al. (2004) compared effectiveness and efficiency of simulated and community-based instruction. They found that combining simulated instruction with community-based instruction was more efficient than either approach by itself.

Maximize contact with naturally occurring contingencies reinforcement. The most basic strategy for promoting generalization and maintenance is to increase the probability that a student's performance of a newly learned skill will be reinforced in the natural environment (e.g., the regular classroom, the playground, the community, recreational and work settings) (Baer, 1999). Teachers can accomplish this by (a) teaching functional skills that students need and that the people in the natural environment are likely to value and (b) teaching students to perform new skills with sufficient accuracy and fluency to produce reinforcement in the natural environment.

DIRECT AND FREQUENT MEASUREMENT Teachers should verify the effects of their instruction by measuring student performance directly and frequently. Measurement is *direct* when it objectively records the learner's performance of the behavior of interest in the natural environment for that skill. Measurement is *frequent* when it occurs on a regular basis; ideally, measurement should take place as often as instruction occurs.

> HLP6 Use student assessment data, analyze instructional practices, and make necessary adjustments that improve student outcomes.

When teachers fail to collect direct and frequent measures of their students' performance, they are prone to two mistakes: (a) continuing ineffective instruction even though no real learning has occurred and (b) discontinuing or changing an effective program of instruction because subjective judgment detects no improvement (Heward, 2005). Without counting, would you know if a student's reading has improved from 70 words read correctly per minute to 80 words per minute?

Placement Options

Learning Outcome 4.5 Identify factors that should guide planning and placement decisions for individuals with intellectual disabilities.

Children with mild intellectual disabilities were traditionally educated in self-contained classrooms in the public schools, and students with moderate and severe intellectual disabilities were routinely placed in special schools. Today many children with intellectual disabilities are educated in regular classrooms. However, although there has been progress toward educating students with intellectual disabilities in less restrictive environments, Brock (2018) found no evidence of a continued trend toward inclusion in recent years. Indeed, during the 2018–2019 school year, the percentages of students with intellectual disabilities educated in various settings were identical to the percentages reported for the 2012–2013 school year. Specifically, in both of these school years, 17% of students with intellectual disabilities were educated in general education classrooms, with 27% being served in resource room programs and 49% in separate classes (U.S. Department of Education, 2014, 2020a). About 7% of students with intellectual disabilities are educated in separate schools, residential facilities, or home or hospital environments.

Sometimes a number of small neighboring school districts pool their resources to offer a special school program for students with moderate, severe, and profound intellectual disabilities. However, some special educators believe that separate schools prohibit students from obtaining an education in the least restrictive environment and that all children should attend their local neighborhood schools regardless of the type or severity of their disability (e.g., Stainback & Stainback, 1996; Taylor, 2005).

As you learned in Chapter 2, simply placing a child with disabilities in a regular classroom does not mean that the child will be receive an appropriate and effective instruction or be accepted socially. However, special and general educators working together have developed programs and methods for teaching students with intellectual disabilities alongside their classmates without disabilities. Systematically planning for the student's inclusion in the classroom through team games and collaborative learning and group investigation projects and directly training all students in specific skills for interacting with one another are just some of the methods for increasing the chances of a successful general education class placement (Doyle & Giangreco, 2013; King-Sears et al., 2015; Salend, 2016).

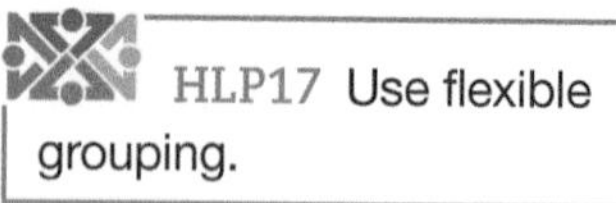
HLP17 Use flexible grouping.

Peer tutoring, cooperative learning (see *Teaching & Learning,* "Cooperative Learning"), friendship training, and peer buddy programs can also promote the instructional and social inclusion of students with intellectual disabilities (Brock et al., 2020; Carter et al., 2016; Gillies, 2016; Miller, Cooke, et al., 2003; Hart Barnett & Whalon, 2014). See *Teaching & Learning,* "Peer Helpers: Including Students with Severe Disabilities," in Chapter 12.

TEACHING & LEARNING

Cooperative Learning

Why Should Teachers Use Cooperative Learning Strategies? Cooperative learning is an approach to teaching that involves students working together to achieve a goal or accomplish a task. When cooperative learning activities are well designed and implemented, students have opportunities to engage with content, receive feedback on their learning, and practice their social skills. Cooperative learning activities are adaptable to a range of content, settings, and age groups, making them a viable instructional option for any teacher. However, teachers must be wary: Simply having students "work together" does not ensure they will learn the content or gain the social benefits of working alongside their peers.

How Do I Use Cooperative Learning in the Classroom? Many approaches to cooperative learning have been documented as effective, including peer tutoring, reciprocal teaching, and Kagan structures (Hattie, 2012; Kagan & Kagan, 2009). A number of common characteristics define these effective practices:

- *Individual accountability*—Each member of the group is held responsible for learning. Students with intellectual disabilities who receive a modified curriculum may be learning different, or adapted, content, but the activity must be designed to allow them to show their learning.

- *Group accountability*—Although each student is responsible for learning, the group is also responsible for helping others in the group learn. This positive interdependence requires students to work together to achieve the goal (Gillies, 2016).
- *Clear structure and directions*—An effective cooperative learning activity will include structured procedures, clear directions (both verbal and in writing; Kagan & Kagan, 2009), and explicit instruction in *how* to follow the procedures. This includes modeling, practice, and feedback!
- *Teacher monitoring*—While the students are working together, the teacher must actively monitor to (a) ensure all students are engaged and learning, (b) provide praise to reinforce students' following directions and learning new skills, and (c) prompt students to celebrate each other's successes.

Kagan and Kagan (2009) have developed and tested numerous structures for implementing cooperative learning. For instance, in Numbered Heads Together, students work together to arrive at a consensus answer to a question or problem. Although all students work together to solve the problem, only one student per group (the one whose number is called) is responsible for standing up and reporting the answer to the class. Because the students don't know which number will be called, they all have to be ready to report. Several studies have documented that Numbered Heads Together is effective across a range of settings and student populations (Hunter et al., 2015).

In Find the Fiction, students write three statements related to the subject they are studying, read those statements to their teammates, and then have teammates guess which statement is not true ("fiction"). In Quiz-Quiz-Trade, students use flashcards to quiz a partner and give feedback; they trade roles (other partner quizzes with his or her set of cards), and then they trade cards and move to a new partner. This allows them to be in both the student role and teacher role for several sets of flashcards. Featured Teacher Madonna Wilburn uses Quiz-Quiz-Trade to review vocabulary words and concepts in her social studies class. She loves Kagan structures because "students get up out of their seats and interact with ALL students in the classroom" and they provide "a way for students to think about a topic and share their knowledge with each other."

Pearson eText
Video Example 4.6
Numbered Heads Together is a cooperative learning activity that combines peer support and individual accountability.

Students with intellectual disabilities often benefit from similar programs for students who are not disabled. During the early elementary grades, students with intellectual disabilities as well as their chronological-age peers need instruction in basic academic skills. During this period, most students with intellectual disabilities benefit from full or partial inclusion in general education classroom settings.

The relative appropriateness of spending the entire school day in a regular classroom changes for some students as they move from the elementary grades to high school, when opportunities for community-based instruction in vocational and life skills are critical (Bouck, 2011; Hartman, 2009). As it is for any student with disabilities, the extent to which the regular classroom is the most appropriate placement for a student with intellectual disabilities can only be determined by considering the student's individual needs. "School inclusion can then be seen as a means (as opposed to just a goal unto itself) toward the ultimate objective of community inclusion and empowerment" (Polloway et al., 1996, p. 11).

Source: David Mager/Pearson Education

Most students with intellectual disabilities benefit from evidence-based instruction in inclusive classrooms.

Acceptance and Membership

Since the early 1970s, the principle of **normalization** has provided a conceptual foundation and touchstone for improving the life experiences of people with intellectual disabilities. The concept originated in Scandinavia but was first described in an American publication by Nirje (1969) in a book published by the President's Committee on Mental Retardation. Nirje's idea of normalization contained "eight planks": a normal rhythm of the day; a normal routine of life (e.g., living in one place and working in another); a normal rhythm of the year (e.g., observing holidays, personal religious days, and relaxation days); a normal developmental experience of the life cycle (e.g., experiencing the settings and atmospheres enjoyed by typical peers); valuing individual choices (e.g., allowing the dignity and freedom to fail); living in a sexual world; normal economic standards; and living, learning, and recreating in the same community facilities others enjoy (Perske, 2004).

Wolfensberger (1972), one of the first and best known champions of normalization in the United States, wrote that the principle refers to the use of progressively more normal settings and procedures "to establish and/or maintain personal behaviors which are as culturally normal as possible" (p. 28). Normalization is not a technique or a set of procedures but an overriding philosophy. It says that people with intellectual disabilities should, to the greatest extent possible, be both physically and socially integrated into everyday society regardless of their degree or type of disability.

Although the principle of normalization has helped individuals with intellectual disabilities who are physically present in many school, community, and work settings today, it has not gained them acceptance and true membership (Lemay, 2006). Wolfensberger (1983) proposed the concept of social role valorization (SRV) as a necessary and natural extension of the normalization principle.

> The key premise of SRV is that people's welfare depends extensively on the social roles they occupy: People who fill roles that are positively valued by others will generally be afforded by the latter the good things of life, but people who fill roles that are devalued by others will typically be badly treated by them. This implies that in the case of people whose life situations are very bad, and whose bad situations are bound up with occupancy of devalued roles, then if the social roles they are seen as occupying can somehow be upgraded in the eyes of perceivers, their life conditions will usually improve, and often dramatically so (Wolfensberger, 2000, p. 105).

Perhaps the greatest current expression and extension of the normalization and SRV concept in special education can be found in the growing movement toward teaching self-determination skills to individuals with intellectual disabilities.

One of the most important things that special educators can do is to help students with intellectual disabilities identify their goals and provide the instruction and supports that will enable them to pursue those goals. As support for self-determination and social role valorization grows among both educators and the public, the time draws nearer when all people with intellectual disabilities will experience the benefits of valued membership in integrated school, community, and employment settings.

ADVICE FROM THE FEATURED TEACHER by Madonna Wilburn

- Seek out a really good mentor in special education. Develop a friendship with them, see what resources they are using, and even shadow them throughout the day. Many administrators will help facilitate this relationship if you just ask.
- Never be afraid to ask questions. For example, when collaborating with co-teachers, ask what specific parts you will take in planning, delivering lessons, grading, providing accommodations.
- Read as much as you can and keep yourself up to date on the latest, most effective pedagogy in education, especially special education.

Source: Keyonna D. Wilson

- Get organized. It will make your life easier. Keep color-coded binders to keep track of meetings, students' class schedules, IEPs, BIPs, and progress reports.
- Create systems to help you collaborate with other teachers. Keep extra blank progress reports sheets so they are ready to send to teachers. Create easy-to-read sheets for classroom teachers that outline each student's IEP so teachers have easy access and can easily understand what the IEP requires. Make sure teachers know their students' goals and prompt them to give you evidence as to whether or not students are meeting their goals.
- Data collection and analysis have become a big part of the education world, so plan on collecting data and keeping good records of goals, progress, attendance, parent communication, and communication between you and teachers. Collect evidence of student work and keep it as a record of student progress.
- Develop a set of rules, expectations, and procedures for everything you do and want the students to do in your classroom.
- Create a positive behavior system in your classroom. In my class students can earn tickets for attendance, being polite, participating, completing homework, and doing well on tests. I try to "catch" them doing good; even in the halls, students know that if other teachers compliment them, they will earn a ticket.
- Be creative and resourceful. I am always on the lookout for materials I can use in my classroom, at teacher stores, dollar stores, garage sales. These items can be yarn, baskets, hangers, paints, scrapbooking paper, glue, poster, buttons. If it is cheap enough, I buy it, and I eventually find a creative way to use it.
- Keep in mind that every parent wants their child to succeed. Communication can be difficult, especially if parents' cultural expectations are different from those of the teachers, but try not to let that get in the way of collaborating with families. Special education language in itself can be very confusing. Find out what languages the parents speak and make sure information is communicated to them in that language. Also find out about the cultural backgrounds of each of your students; this will help with relationship building.
- Find out and use what communication modes your families prefer. This could be phone calls, email, text messages, the student's notebook, or a take-home folder. It is also helpful to find out the best time of the day and day of the week to communicate with families.
- Don't get overwhelmed by the big goal; instead celebrate the small daily and weekly achievements and trust they will add up to the big goal. Most learning and behavior improvement comes from consistently implementing solid instruction and reinforcement, day in, day out. What happens on one day is likely to have little impact, so if you or your students have a bad day, don't be discouraged. Remember it is what you do every day—not one day—that matters most. Keep moving forward.

Key Terms and Concepts

acquisition stage of learning
active student response (ASR)
adaptive behavior
amniocentesis
chorionic villi sampling
Down syndrome
fragile X syndrome
generalization
genetic counseling
intellectual disability
maintenance
normal curve
normalization
norm-referenced test
perinatal
phenylketonuria (PKU)
pica
positive reinforcement
postnatal
practice stage of learning
prenatal
rubella
standard deviation
task analysis

Summary

Definitions

- The Individuals with Disabilities Education Act (IDEA) defines *intellectual disability* as significantly subaverage general intellectual functioning existing concurrently with deficits in adaptive behavior and manifested during the developmental period that adversely affects a child's educational performance.
- The American Association on Intellectual and Developmental Disabilities (AAIDD) defines intellectual disability as significant limitations in both intellectual functioning and adaptive behavior as expressed in conceptual, social, and practical adaptive skills. This disability originates before age 18 years.
- The traditional and still sometimes used method of classifying intellectual disabilities consists of four degrees or levels of intellectual impairment determined by IQ score: mild, moderate, severe, and profound.
- Today, most clinicians and researchers apply the same four descriptors to designate levels of intellectual disability but base their classification on a person's adaptive behavior rather than IQ score.

Identification and Assessment

- An IQ test consists of a series of questions (e.g., vocabulary, similarities), problem solving (e.g., mazes, block designs), memory, and other tasks assumed to require certain amounts of intelligence to answer or solve correctly.
- IQ scores seem to be distributed throughout the population according to a phenomenon called the *normal curve*. Theoretically, about 2.3% of the population falls 2 or more standard deviations below the mean, which the AAIDD calls "significantly subaverage."
- The IQ cutoff score of 70 is only a guideline and should not be interpreted as a hard-and-fast requirement. An IQ score of 75 or higher may be associated with intellectual disability if, according to a clinician's judgment, the child exhibits deficits in adaptive behavior thought to be caused by impaired intellectual functioning.
- Because IQ tests include many verbal and academic tasks—the same things a child must master to succeed in school—they correlate highly with school achievement.
- Adaptive behavior consists of the conceptual, social, and practical skills that people need to function in their everyday lives.
- Systematic assessment of adaptive behavior is important because the exhibited adaptive skills—as well as the nature and severity of maladaptive behaviors—of a person with intellectual disabilities are critical factors in determining the nature and degree of supports required for success in school, work, community, and home environments.
- Most instruments for assessing adaptive behavior consist of a series of questions answered by someone familiar with the individual.
- Measuring adaptive behavior has proven difficult, in large part because of the relative nature of social adjustment and competence: Behavior considered appropriate in one situation or by one group may not be appropriate in or by another.

Characteristics

- All children and adults with intellectual disabilities display positive attributes, such as tenacity and curiosity in learning, getting along well with others, and being a positive influence on those around them.
- Children with mild intellectual disabilities may experience substantial performance deficits only in school. Their social and communication skills may be normal or nearly so. They are likely to become independent or semi-independent adults.
- Most children with moderate intellectual disabilities show significant developmental delays during their preschool years.
- Most children with severe and profound intellectual disabilities are identified at birth or shortly thereafter and may have additional disabilities or health conditions.
- The cognitive functioning of students with intellectual disabilities is characterized by
  - memory deficits, especially working memory and short-term memory;
  - limited use of metacognitive or executive control strategies such as rehearsing and organizing information;
  - slower learning rate compared to that in typically developing age-mates;
  - trouble attending to relevant features of a learning task, perhaps focusing instead on distracting irrelevant stimuli, and often difficulty sustaining attention;
  - difficulty generalizing and maintaining newly learned knowledge and skills;
  - expecting failure regardless of their efforts (learned helplessness); and
  - distrusting their own responses to situations and relying on others for assistance and solutions (outer-directedness).
- Children with intellectual disabilities have substantial deficits in adaptive behavior across domains of functioning. Limitations in self-care skills and social relationships as well as behavioral excesses are common.

Prevalence

- Theoretically, 2.3% of the population would score 2 standard deviations or more below the norm on IQ tests, but this does not account for adaptive behavior, the other criterion for diagnosis of intellectual disability. Many experts cite an incidence figure of approximately 1% of the total population.

- During the 2018–2019 school year, approximately 6.7% of all students receiving special education did so under the category of intellectual disabilities.

Causes and Prevention

- Hundreds of causes and risk factors associated with intellectual disabilities have been identified.
- Risk factors for intellectual disabilities are classified by when they occur (i.e., prenatal, perinatal, or postnatal) and whether they are biomedical or environmental (social, behavioral, educational).
- Biomedical causes are identified for about two thirds of individuals with severe and profound levels of intellectual disabilities.
- Although etiology is unknown for most individuals with mild intellectual disabilities, psychosocial disadvantage in early childhood is suspected in many cases.
- Vaccines, amniocentesis, chorionic villi sampling, genetic counseling, and early screening tests have reduced the incidence of intellectual disabilities caused by some genetic disorders.

Educational Approaches

- Students with intellectual disabilities need instruction in basic academic skills that are required or could be used often in their current and future environments.
- Curriculum should focus on functional skills that will help students succeed in self-care, vocational, domestic, community, and leisure domains.
- Major components of explicit systematic instruction are task analysis, active student response, systematic feedback, transfer of stimulus control from teacher-provided cues and prompts to natural stimuli, programming for generalization and maintenance, and direct and frequent measurement of student performance.

Placement Options

- During the 2018–2019 school year, approximately 17% of students with intellectual disabilities were educated in regular classrooms; 27% in resource rooms; 49% in separate classrooms; and about 7% in separate schools, residential facilities, or home or hospital environments.
- During the early elementary grades, many students with intellectual disabilities benefit from full or partial inclusion in regular classroom settings.
- Strategies for facilitating successful placement in a general education class include planning for the student's inclusion through team games, collaborative learning, and group investigation projects and by directly training all students in specific skills for interacting with one another.
- The relative appropriateness of inclusion in the regular classroom changes for some students with intellectual disabilities as they move from the elementary grades to the secondary level, when opportunities for community-based instruction in vocational and life skills are critical.
- How much time a student with intellectual disabilities spends in a regular classroom should be determined by that student's individual needs.
- The principles of normalization, social role valorization, and self-determination are important in helping people with intellectual disabilities achieve acceptance and membership in society.

Chapter 5
Learning Disabilities

Source: Anthony Magnacca/Merrill Education

Learning Outcomes

After reading this chapter and completing the embedded activities, you should be able to

5.1 Define learning disabilities and list three criteria most states use to identify students with learning disabilities.

5.2 List characteristics and causes of learning disabilities.

5.3 Identify the prevalence of learning disabilities and describe assessments used to identify students with learning disabilities and monitor their progress.

5.4 Describe evidence-based strategies for teaching reading, writing, math, and content knowledge to students with learning disabilities.

5.5 Compare and contrast typical placements and supports for students with learning disabilities.

Featured Teacher

Amaris Johnson

The Jackie Robinson School, New York City District 29, St. Albans, New York

Source: Amaris Johnson

I teach 24 fifth graders in a full-time inclusion classroom where I co-teach with a general education teacher. My co-teacher and I share the common goal of providing the best instruction to our students; we are a cohesive unit. Being a special educator in an integrated co-teaching classroom does not mean you are restricted to only working with the students who have IEPs in your classroom. This allows me to not only support students on my caseload but also identify and support other students who need intervention. I also collaborate with the school counselor, physical therapist, occupational therapist, speech therapist, school psychologist, and school social worker.

Successful co-teaching requires a commitment to well-established routines for communication, collaboration, and documenting student progress. For instance, I use a "performance binder" for each student, which allows me to track their goals on a weekly basis and communicate progress to other professionals and parents. I also involve my students in monitoring their own progress. When I return assignments, students have 5 minutes to track their progress on their graphs and set a goal for next time. Next, students have 5 minutes to share with each other their successes and goals. Table monitors then gather binders, and the classroom president leads a conversation about each group's progress toward their goals.

Having students complete exit tickets is another way I monitor their progress. At the end of a lesson, students write answers to a few questions about what they have learned. This routine helps my students stay focused on the learning objectives and gives me the data I need to plan future instruction.

I help my students reach their goals by teaching them learning strategies. For instance, in math, I use schema-based instruction during parallel teaching. This approach teaches students to use the following strategy steps: Identify problem type (change problem/compare problem), demonstrate how to organize information using a diagram, translate information in the diagram into a number sentence, plan to solve the problem, and then solve the problem. Exit tickets at the end of these lessons enable students to showcase their understanding of the problem using a schematic drawing, a number sentence, and a written explanation.

What I enjoy most about being a special educator is developing close-knit relationships with my students and their parents. An important part of my job is being an advocate for families in my community, informing them of the services and resources they and their children are eligible for, and ensuring their voices are heard and valued.

One of my most meaningful contributions as a special educator was helping establish positive behavior interventions and supports (PBIS) at my school. As a credentialed special education teacher and Board Certified Behavior Analyst (BCBA), I helped lead the PBIS initiative that teaches prosocial behavior to all students. My BCBA training enabled me to help the PBIS team develop clear definitions of schoolwide behavior expectations and to convince them of how critical positive reinforcement is for helping students meet those expectations.

Being a special educator is no easy feat, and on some days, the low points overshadow the good, but once the smoke clears, you can see that your efforts have made a difference. Being a special educator is an incredibly rewarding job.

Education, Teaching Credentials, and Experience

- *A.A. and Liberal Arts, Nassau Community College, 2008*
- *B.A in Psychology, Queens College, 2012*
- *M.A. in Teaching, Queens College CUNY, 2017*
- *Certifications/credentials: New York, Childhood Education, 1–6; New York, Students with Disabilities, 1–6; Board Certified Behavior Analyst*
- *2 years of teaching experience*

By THE LATE 1950s MOST PUBLIC SCHOOLS HAD ESTABLISHED special education programs (or at least offered some type of special service) for children with intellectual disabilities, physical disabilities, sensory impairments, and emotional or behavioral disorders. But there remained a group of children with serious learning challenges who did not fit the existing categories of exceptionality. Although these students appeared capable, they had serious difficulties learning basic academic skills and subjects. Because the schools at that time had no programs for these children, parents seeking help for their children turned to physicians and psychologists. By the 1960s, professionals in the medical field concluded the children's learning problems were caused by neurological abnormalities they termed *brain damage, minimal brain dysfunction, neurological impairment, perceptual handicap, dyslexia,* and *aphasia.*

Samuel Kirk coined the term *learning disabilities* in a 1963 address to an audience of parents whose children were experiencing serious difficulties learning to read, write, spell, or solve math problems. The parents liked the term and that very evening voted to form the Association for Children with Learning Disabilities. Today, the organization's name is Learning Disabilities Association of America (LDA), and it is a powerful advocacy group for people with learning disabilities. In 1968, the Council for Exceptional Children (CEC) established the Division for Learning Disabilities. Some key historical events and their implications for the education of children with learning disabilities are highlighted in Figure 5.1.

FIGURE 5.1 Historical Events in the Field of Learning Disabilities

DATE	HISTORICAL EVENT	EDUCATIONAL IMPLICATIONS
1920s–1940s	Research by Alfred Strauss and others (Cruickshank, Doll, Kephart, Kirk, Lehtinen, Werner) with children with intellectual disabilities and brain injury at the Wayne County Training School in Michigan found relationships between brain injury and disorders that interfered with learning: perceptual disorders, perseveration, disorders of conceptual thinking, and behavioral problems such as hyperactivity and impulsivity.	In the book *Psychopathology and Education of the Brain-Injured Child,* Strauss and Lara Lehtinen (1947) recommended strategies for relieving perceptual and conceptual disturbances of children with brain injury and thus reducing their symptomatic learning problems.
1950s–1960s	By the early 1950s, most public schools had established special education programs for children with intellectual disabilities, sensory impairments, physical disabilities, and behavioral disorders. But there remained a group of children who were having serious learning problems at school, yet did not fit into any of the existing categories of exceptionality. They did not "look" disabled; the children seemed physically intact, yet they were unable to learn certain basic skills and subjects at school.	In searching for help with their children's problems, parents turned to other professionals—notably doctors, psychologists, and speech and language specialists. Understandably, these professionals viewed the children from the perspectives of their respective disciplines. As a result, terms such as *brain damage, minimal brain dysfunction, neurological impairment, perceptual handicap, dyslexia,* and *aphasia* were often used to describe and to account for the children's learning and behavior problems.
1963	The term *learning disabilities* was coined by Samuel Kirk in an address to a group of parents whose children were experiencing serious difficulties in learning to read, were hyperactive, or could not solve math problems.	The parents liked the term and, that very evening, voted to form the Association for Children with Learning Disabilities (ACLD).
1966	A national task force identified 99 different characteristics of children with *minimal brain dysfunction* (the term used at the time) reported in the literature (Clements, 1966).	The inherent danger in such lists is a tendency to assume that each of those characteristics is exhibited by *all* of the children considered to be in the category. This danger is especially troublesome with learning disabilities, because the children who make up the category are an extremely heterogeneous group.
Mid-1960s–1970s	The concept of process, or ability, testing grew out of the belief that learning disabilities are caused by a basic underlying difficulty of the child to process, or use, environmental stimuli in the same way that children without disabilities do. Two of the most widely used process tests used for diagnosing and assessing learning disabilities were developed during this time: the Illinois Test of Psycholinguistic Abilities (ITPA) (Kirk, McCarthy, & Kirk, 1968) and the Marianne Frostig Developmental Test of Visual Perception (Frostig, Lefever, & Whittlesey, 1964).	The ability training approach dominated special education for children with learning disabilities, from the field's inception through the 1970s. The three most widely known ability training approaches were psycholinguistic training, based on the ITPA; the visual-perceptual approach (Frostig & Horne, 1973); and the perceptual-motor approach (Kephart, 1971).

(Continued)

FIGURE 5.1 (Continued)

DATE	HISTORICAL EVENT	EDUCATIONAL IMPLICATIONS
1968	The National Advisory Committee on Handicapped Children drafted and presented to Congress a definition of learning disabilities.	This definition was later incorporated into IDEA and used to govern the dispersal of federal funds for support of services to children with learning disabilities.
1968	The Division for Children with Learning Disabilities (DCLD) was established within the Council for Exceptional Children (CEC).	DCLD has become the largest division of CEC.
1969	The Children with Learning Disabilities Act (part of PL 91–230) was passed by Congress.	This legislation authorized a 5-year program of federal funds for teacher training and the establishment of model demonstration programs for students with learning disabilities.
Late 1970s–early 1980s	Reviews of research showing the ineffectiveness of psycholinguistic training (Hammill & Larsen, 1978), the visual-perceptual approach (Myers & Hammill, 1976), and perceptual-motor approaches (Kavale & Mattison, 1983) are published.	Process testing and ability training gradually gave way to increased use of a skill training approach. If a student has not learned a complex skill and has had sufficient opportunity and wants to succeed, a skill trainer would conclude that the student has not learned the necessary prerequisite skills and provides direct instruction and practice on those prerequisite skills.
1975	Congress passed the Individuals with Disabilities Education Act (PL 94-142)	Learning disabilities were included as one of the disability categories in IDEA.
1980s and 1990s	Research on instructional design, content enhancements, and learning strategies provides additional knowledge on effective teaching methods for students with learning disabilities.	Skill training approach supplemented with increased emphasis on helping students with learning disabilities have meaningful contact with the general curriculum.
2001	In response to concerns about the large number of children identified as learning disabled, the U.S. Office of Special Education sponsored a Learning Disabilities Summit in Washington, DC.	Nine white papers were developed on topics such as diagnostic decision making, classification models, early identification, and the nature and legitimacy of learning disabilities as a disability. Recommendations included in these papers play an influential role in how learning disabilities are treated in the reauthorization of IDEA in 2004.
2004	IDEA Improvement Act of 2004 changes the rules for determining whether a child has a specific learning disability. Schools are no longer required to document a severe discrepancy between achievement and intellectual ability and may instead use an identification process based on a child's responsiveness to research-based intervention.	Schools using a responsiveness to intervention (RTI) model provide systematic help for all students struggling with basic skills (usually reading) in the early grades. Referral for special education evaluation and possible diagnosis of a learning disability is reserved for students who fail to make satisfactory progress after one or two 10- to 12-week trials of intensive small-group intervention using research-based instructional programs.

In some ways, the area of learning disabilities has brought out both the worst and the best that special education has to offer. It has served as a breeding ground for fads and miracle treatments ("New Diet Regimen Cures Learning Disabilities!"). At the same time, some of special education's most innovative and productive researchers have devoted their careers to the study and treatment of learning disabilities, and many instructional strategies first developed for students with learning disabilities have influenced and benefited the entire field of education.

Definitions

Learning Outcome 5.1 Define learning disabilities and list three criteria most states use to identify students with learning disabilities.

Many definitions of learning disabilities have been proposed and debated over the years. The federal definition in the Individuals with Disabilities Education Act (IDEA) and a definition proposed by the National Joint Committee on Learning Disabilities (NJCLD) have had the most influence on educational practice. Additionally, the term *specific learning disorder* defined by the American Psychiatric Association is used by physicians in clinical practice.

Federal Definition

IDEA regulations define **specific learning disability** as follows:

(i) General. Specific learning disability means a disorder in one or more of the basic psychological processes involved in understanding or in using language, spoken or written, that may manifest itself in the imperfect ability to listen, think, speak, read, write, spell, or to do mathematical calculations, including conditions such as perceptual disabilities, brain injury, minimal brain dysfunction, dyslexia, and developmental aphasia.

(ii) Disorders not included. Specific learning disability does not include learning problems that are primarily the result of visual, hearing, or motor disabilities, of intellectual disability, of emotional disturbance, or of environmental, cultural, or economic disadvantage. (34 *CFR* 300.8(c)(10))

OPERATIONALIZING THE FEDERAL DEFINITION When using the federal definition to identify students with learning disabilities, most states require three criteria:

1. A severe discrepancy between the student's intellectual ability and academic achievement
2. An exclusion criterion—the student's difficulties are not the result of another known condition that can cause learning problems
3. A need for special education services

Ability–Achievement Discrepancy. Children with learning disabilities exhibit an unexpected difference between their general ability and achievement. According to federal guidelines that accompanied the original IDEA, only children with a "severe discrepancy between achievement and intellectual ability" were to be identified with learning disabilities (U.S. Office of Education, 1977). Children experiencing minor or temporary academic difficulties should not be identified with learning disabilities.

Before IDEA 2004, the most common practice for identifying children with learning disabilities was to determine if a severe discrepancy existed between their expected and actual achievement. This involved comparing a student's score on an IQ test with his or her score on a standardized achievement test. If the student scored in the average range or above on the IQ test and substantially below average on the achievement test, he or she was determined eligible for special education services under the learning disabilities category. Although such a comparison seems simple on the surface, in practice, it is fraught with problems (Alphonso & Flanagan, 2018).

First of all, the discrepancy criterion may preclude early identification because children in the early grades may not yet have a large enough IQ–achievement discrepancy to qualify for special education services. To fulfill the discrepancy criterion, schools must wait for students to fail before providing services.

Another problem is lack of empirical evidence that measuring the discrepancy between IQ and achievement test scores accurately and consistently identifies students with learning disabilities (Fletcher et al., 2019). Considering the limitations of IQ testing (see Chapter 4) and the wide variety of achievement tests available, the lack of consistency in applying the discrepancy criterion is not surprising. The federal government proposed several mathematical formulas for determining a severe discrepancy. All of the proposed formulas were eventually rejected, and the final rules and regulations for IDEA did not contain a specific definition of nor formula for determining a severe discrepancy. This confusion and disagreement about exactly how a severe discrepancy should be determined led to states and school districts using widely differing procedures to identify students with learning disabilities (Alphonso & Flanagan, 2018). Recognizing the problems inherent in the discrepancy approach, Congress significantly changed the way that states could determine a child's eligibility for special education under the specific learning disabilities category when it reauthorized IDEA in 2004:

> When determining whether a child has a specific learning disability . . . a local educational agency shall not be required to take into consideration whether a child has a severe discrepancy between achievement and intellectual ability. . . . [And] a local educational agency may use a process that determines if the child responds to scientific, research-based intervention as a part of the evaluation procedures (PL 108-466, Sec. 614[b][6][A–B]).

This approach to identifying students with learning disabilities, called **response to intervention (RTI)**, shifts identification from a "wait-to-fail" model to one of early identification and prevention (Young & Johnson, 2019). RTI uses a multi-tiered system of support (MTSS) to identify students with learning disabilities. MTSS consists of multiple tiers of increasing intensity, "the more intense the students' needs, the more intense the instruction and time for instruction and intervention" (Blackburn & Witzel, 2018, p. 4). This system identifies students with learning disabilities by examining how well they respond to increasingly more intensive evidence-based academic interventions.

Exclusion. The IDEA definition of learning disabilities includes significant learning problems that are not "primarily the result" of other conditions that can impede learning, such as another recognized disability or lack of opportunity to learn because of cultural factors, environmental or economic disadvantage, or limited English proficiency. The word *primarily* in the definition recognizes that a learning disability can coexist with other disabilities; in that case, however, the student typically receives services under the other disability category.

Need for Special Education. Students with learning disabilities show specific and severe learning problems despite standard educational efforts and therefore need specially designed instruction to meet their unique needs. This criterion is meant to avoid the overidentification of children who have not had the opportunity to learn. Such children should progress satisfactorily as soon as they receive effective instruction at a curricular level appropriate to their current skills.

For more comprehensive information on IDEA 2004 regulations for the identification of specific learning disabilities, see Office of Special Education and Rehabilitation Services (2006).

NJCLD Definition

The NJCLD is composed of representatives from 11 organizations committed to the education and welfare of individuals with learning disabilities. The NJCLD (1991) believes that the federal definition of learning disabilities contains several inherent weaknesses:

- *Exclusion of adults.* The federal definition refers only to *"children."* Learning disabilities occur across the developmental life span.
- *Reference to "basic psychological processes."* This phrase invites debate on how to teach students with learning disabilities, a curricular issue, not a definitional one.
- *Inclusion of spelling as a learning disability.* Spelling can be subsumed under "written expression."
- *Inclusion of obsolete terms.* Terms such as *minimal brain dysfunction, perceptual impairments,* and *developmental aphasia* have proven difficult to define and only add confusion to the definition.
- *Wording of the exclusion clause.* The IDEA definition suggests that learning disabilities cannot occur along with other disabilities. However, a person may have a learning disability along with another disability but not *because of* another disability.

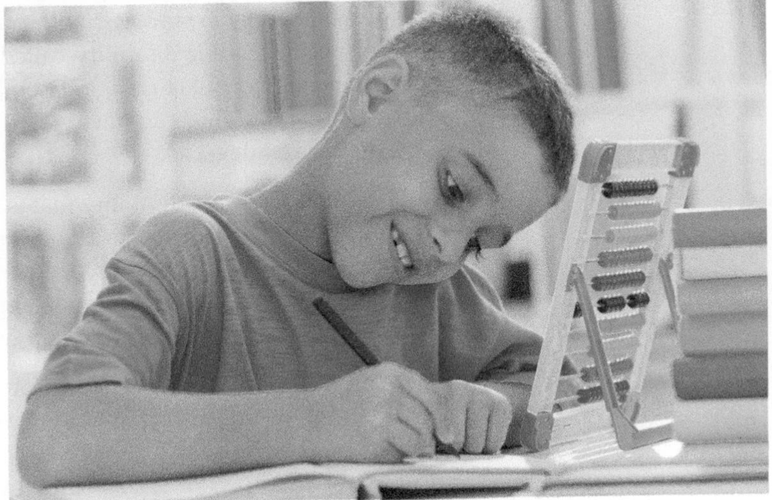

Source: VP Photo Studio/Shutterstock

Students with learning disabilities have significant learning problems that are not the result of another disability or lack of opportunity to learn.

In response to the problems it saw with the federal definition, the NJCLD (1991) developed its own definition, which was updated in 2016:

> *Learning disabilities* is a general term that refers to a heterogeneous group of disorders manifested by significant difficulties in the acquisition and use of listening,

speaking, reading, writing, reasoning, or mathematical abilities. These disorders are intrinsic to the individual, presumed to be due to central nervous system dysfunction, and may occur across the life span. Problems in self-regulatory behaviors, social perception, and social interaction may exist with learning disabilities but do not by themselves constitute a learning disability. Although learning disabilities may occur concomitantly with other disabilities (for example, sensory impairment, intellectual disabilities, emotional disturbance), or with extrinsic influences (such as cultural or linguistic differences, insufficient or inappropriate instruction), they are not the result of those conditions or influences. (p. 1).

American Psychiatric Association Definition

The American Psychiatric Association (APA) uses the term *specific learning disorders* instead of *learning disabilities*. In 2013, the APA revised its definition of learning disorders in the fifth edition of the *Diagnostic and Statistical Manual of Mental Disorders* (DSM-5). The DSM-5 defines *specific learning disorder* as a neurodevelopmental disorder that impedes learning of academic skills. Students who are diagnosed with a specific learning disorder perform well below average in reading, writing, or mathematics. In contrast to previous APA definitions, the DSM-5 definition no longer uses the discrepancy criterion for diagnosis.

Characteristics

Learning Outcome 5.2 List characteristics and causes of learning disabilities.

Learning disabilities are associated with problems in listening, reasoning, memory, attention, selecting and focusing on relevant stimuli, and the perception and processing of visual or auditory information. These perceptual and cognitive processing difficulties are assumed to be the underlying causes of the following characteristics students with learning disabilities experience, either individually or in combination: reading problems, written language deficits, math underachievement, poor social skills, attention deficits and hyperactivity, behavior problems, and low self-esteem or self-efficacy.

Reading Problems

Difficulty reading is by far the most common characteristic of students with learning disabilities—80% to 90% of all children identified with learning disabilities are referred for special education because of reading problems (Fletcher et al., 2019). Children who have not acquired basic reading skills in the early grades tend to fall further and further behind their peers, not only in reading but in general academic achievement as well (Young et al., 2018). A specific reading disability, called *dyslexia*, is a persistent deficit that is a "neurobiological, developmental, language-based learning disability that affects individuals' ability to learn to read" (Roitch & Watson, 2019, p. 81). The International Dyslexia Association (2002) defines **dyslexia** as

> a specific learning disability that is neurobiological in origin. It is characterized by difficulties with accurate and/or fluent word recognition and by poor spelling and decoding abilities. These difficulties typically result from a deficit in the phonological component of language that is often unexpected in relation to other cognitive abilities and the provision of effective classroom instruction.

Many children with learning disabilities experience severe difficulties with phonological and phonemic awareness. **Phonological awareness** "refers to an awareness of the sound structure (syllables, phonemes) of spoken language" (Kilpatrick, 2015, p. 4). The most important aspect of phonological awareness for learning to read is **phonemic awareness**, the knowledge that words consist of separate sounds, or phonemes, and the ability to manipulate these individual sound units. In their literature review, Lam and McMaster (2014) identified phonemic awareness, word identification skills, and fluency as consistent predictors of responsiveness to early reading intervention. A child with phonemic awareness can manipulate sounds in the following ways.

- *Orally blend sounds to make words* (e.g., "What word do you have if you put these sounds together: /c/, /aaaa/, /t/?"—*cat*).
- *Isolate sounds at the beginning, middle, and ending of words* (e.g., "What is the first sound in *rose*?"—/rrrrr/).
- *Segment a word into sounds* (e.g., "Say the sounds in the word *sat*"—/ssss/—/aaaa/—/t/).
- *Manipulate sounds within a word* (e.g., "What word do you have if you change the/ssss/in *sat* to/mmmm/?"—*mat*) (adapted from Simmons et al., 2011, p. 54).

Pearson eText
Video Example 5.1
Phoneme segmentation fluency is a strong predictor of reading proficiency.

In addition to being able to hear and manipulate sounds, skilled readers quickly recognize individual words. The ability to rapidly read individual words advances comprehension in at least two ways. First, faster readers encounter more words and idea units and thereby have the opportunity to comprehend more. Second, when students are not struggling to decode words, they "are able to devote greater cognitive resources to higher-level cognitive processes" (Spencer & Wagner, 2018, p. 3).

Source: Laura Bolesta/Millennium/Pearson Allyn and Bacon/Merrill Education

Children who receive explicit instruction in letter-phoneme relationships and blending are more likely to become good readers than children who are encouraged to memorize words or makes guesses based on context and pictures.

In a study with more than 425,000 participants, Spencer et al. (2014) found first through third graders with deficiencies in reading comprehension also had poor decoding skills and limited vocabulary. The researchers concluded that reading comprehension problems are the result of deficits in word recognition. Additionally, Spencer and Wagner (2018) found oral language skills are a better predictor of reading comprehension than word reading skills. Either way, most students with learning disabilities experience reading comprehension problems (Berkeley & Larson, 2018; Fletcher et al., 2019).

Comprehension deficits become more problematic when students are expected to independently read increasingly advanced material in middle and high school (Vaughn et al. 2011). See Chapter 15, *Teaching & Learning*, "When Secondary Students Can't Read."

Written Language Deficits

The National Center for Educational Statistics (2012) reported that only 27% of the nation's 8th and 12th graders scored at or above proficient in writing. Considering the large percentage of all students who struggle with writing, it is not surprising that most students with learning disabilities are also poor writers. Students with learning disabilities perform significantly lower than their age-matched peers without disabilities on all written expression tasks, including handwriting, spelling, punctuation, vocabulary, grammar, and expository writing (Fletcher et al., 2019; Graham et al., 2017). Some students with learning disabilities are competent readers but extremely poor writers.

Students with learning disabilities seldom use self-regulation strategies such as setting goals or organizing ideas. As a result, they tend to produce poorly organized compositions containing a few underdeveloped ideas. Figure 5.2 shows a story written by Sean, a 10-year-old student, when shown an illustration of prehistoric cavemen. Sean's oral reading of his story reveals a huge disparity between his written and oral language abilities. Fortunately, most students with learning disabilities improve their writing when provided with explicit instruction on specific writing skills and strategies, frequent opportunities to practice, and systematic feedback (e.g., Alber-Morgan et al., 2007; Harris et al., 2016).

FIGURE 5.2 Written Language Sample from a 10-Year-Old Student with Learning Disabilities

Sean's Written Story	Sean's Oral Reading of His Story
A loge tine ago they atene a cosnen they head to geatthere on fesee o One day tere were sane evesedbeats all gaseraned tesene in cladesn they hard a fest for 2 meanes.	A long time ago there were ancient cave men. They had to get their own food. One day there were some wildebeests. They all gathered them and killed them. They had a feast for two months.

Source: Courtesy of Timothy E. Heron, The Ohio State University.

Math Underachievement

Children with learning disabilities progress with math skills "about 1 year for every 2 years in school but plateau by age 10 or 12" (Jitendra et al., 2018, p. 189). Numerical reasoning and calculation pose major problems for many students with learning disabilities; they perform lower than typically achieving students on every type of math problem at every grade level and have particular difficulty retrieving number facts and solving story problems (Fletcher et al., 2019).

These deficits may be related to working memory, "how we temporarily manipulate and store information during thinking and reasoning tasks" (Baddeley, 2000, p. 1). Researchers have identified working memory problems as a strong predictor of mathematics deficiencies (e.g., Fanari et al., 2019). As with reading and writing, research shows that explicit instruction that incorporates guided practice, fluency training, and feedback can improve the math performance of students with learning disabilities (e.g., Fletcher et al., 2019).

Pearson eText Video Example 5.2
Students with learning disabilities have varied experiences with making friends. http://www.youtube.com/watch?v=P0nX2q2Q_Fg

Poor Social Skills

Students with learning disabilities are prone to interpersonal problems. Poor social skills often lead to rejection, low social status, unpleasant interactions with teachers, difficulty making friends, and loneliness—all of which are experienced by many students with learning disabilities regardless of classroom placement (Pullen et al., 2017).

Poor social skills of some students with learning disabilities may be the result of how they interpret social situations relative to their own experiences and their inability to perceive the nonverbal affective expressions of others (Meadan & Halle, 2004). Researchers who studied messages by children on a website for people with learning disabilities found "rare instances" when children described positive social relationships (e.g., "I have lots of friends"), but the children overwhelmingly expressed social difficulties (Raskind et al., 2006). Additionally, one study found that although most students with learning disabilities are part of social groups in school, their social status was consistently lower than that of their typically developing peers (Estell et al., 2008). To address the social skills deficits of many students with learning disabilities, researchers have developed social skills training curricula that teach self-awareness and friendship-making skills such as reading and using appropriate body language, listening and conversation skills, dealing with teasing, and managing anger (e.g., Guiler, 2011; Halloran, 2019).

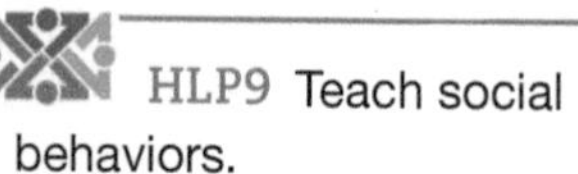
HLP9 Teach social behaviors.

Attention Deficits and Hyperactivity

Some students with learning disabilities have difficulty attending to a task or display high rates of hyperactivity. Children who persistently exhibit these problems may be diagnosed with attention-deficit/hyperactivity disorder (ADHD). Researchers report a 45.1% degree of **comorbidity** (two conditions occurring in the same individual) between learning disabilities and ADHD (DuPaul et al., 2013). Compared to students with learning disabilities alone, students with comorbid learning disabilities and ADHD score lower on letter and word identification tasks, teachers' ratings of reading levels, and parents' reports of social skills (Wei et al., 2014). ADHD is described in detail in Chapter 11.

Challenging Behavior

Researchers have consistently found a higher-than-usual incidence of challenging behavior among students with learning disabilities (Grigorenko et al., 2019; Mather et al., 2015). A comparative study of more than 600 adolescents with and without learning disabilities found a higher frequency of risk-taking behaviors such as smoking, marijuana use, delinquency, acts of aggression, and gambling among youth with learning disabilities (McNamara & Willoughby, 2010). Although research clearly shows increased behavior challenges among children with learning disabilities, it is not known whether the academic deficits or the behavior challenges cause the other difficulty or whether both are products of other causal factors. It is important to note that many children with learning disabilities exhibit no challenging behavior.

Regardless of the interrelationships of these characteristics, teachers and other caregivers responsible for planning educational programs for students with learning disabilities need skills for addressing social and behavioral difficulties as well as academic deficits. These important teaching skills are described in Chapter 6.

Low Self-Esteem or Self-Efficacy

Students with learning disabilities are more likely to report lower levels of self-efficacy, mood, effort, and hope than are their peers without learning disabilities (Cavioni et al., 2017; Musetti et al., 2019). Whether this tendency for negative self-perception is an inherent characteristic of learning disabilities or the result of a painful history of frustration and disappointment with academic and social situations is not known.

The Signature Characteristic

Although students with learning disabilities are an extremely heterogeneous group, it is important to remember "the signature characteristic of students with learning disabilities is severe low achievement despite generally effective instruction and intelligence in the normal range" (L.S. Fuchs et al., 2015, p. 135). The difference between what students with learning disabilities "are expected to do and what they can do… grows larger and larger" over time (Deshler et al., 2001, p. 97). The performance gap becomes especially noticeable and disabling in the middle and secondary grades, when the academic growth of many students with disabilities plateaus.

Although an objective awareness of the learning and behavior problems faced by children with learning disabilities is necessary for effective intervention, teachers should not focus solely on students' deficits. It is equally—or perhaps even more—important to

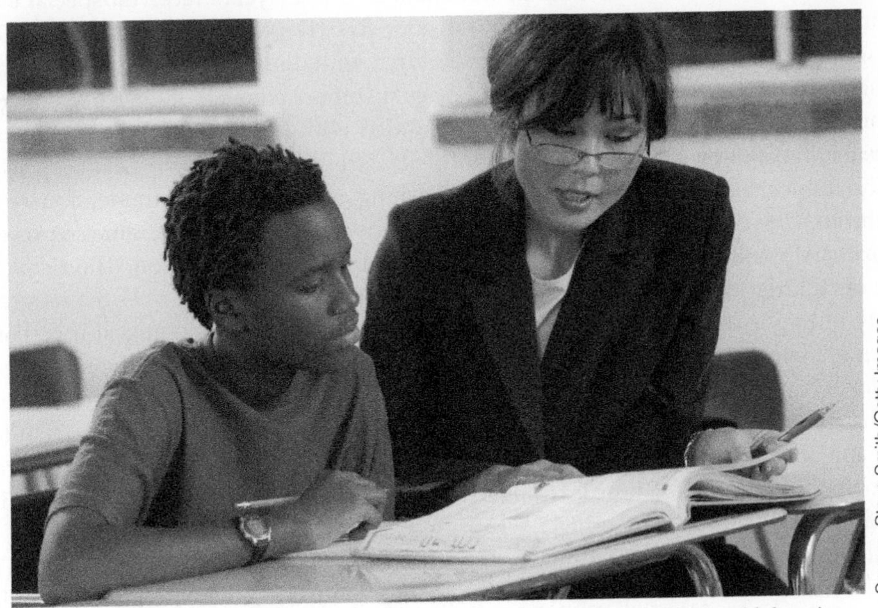

Source: Steve Smith/Getty Images

Teachers should recognize and nurture the positive qualities of their students with learning disabilities.

FIGURE 5.3 The Importance of Maintaining a Positive Focus

Tom Lovitt was a pioneer in the education of children's learning disabilities and one of the field's more productive teachers and scholars. His carefully conducted research and thoughtful writing have spanned five decades and dealt with virtually every aspect of special education. In one of his classic books on teaching children with learning problems, *In Spite of My Resistance . . . I've Learned from Children,* Lovitt (1977) wrote that, all things being equal, a teacher who imparts many skills to many children is good, and one who does not is not. After all, teaching is helping children learn new things.

Although Lovitt consistently declared that the development of children's academic and social skills is the primary purpose for teachers and students to come together, he also warned us not to become so concerned with fixing everything we believe is wrong with the student that we forget about recognizing and building upon all that is positive.

> We teachers, in all good faith, set out to remediate as many of the "shortfalls" as possible so that youth with learning disabilities will be as normal and wonderful as we are. We should reconsider this total remedial approach to learning disabilities. One reason for considering an alternative should be obvious if we thought of a day in the life of a student with learning disabilities. First, the teacher sets out to remediate his reading, then his math, and then his language, social skills, and soccer playing. Toward the end of the day, she attempts to remediate his metacognitive deficits. That lad is in a remediation mode throughout the day. Is it any wonder that some of these youngsters have self-concepts, self-images, self-esteems, and attributions that are out of whack?
>
> We should spend some time concentrating on these youngsters' positive qualities. If a girl is inclined toward mechanics, or a boy to being a chef, we should nurture those skills. And if a child doesn't have a negotiable behavior, we should locate one and promote it. I can't help but think that if every youngster, LD or otherwise, had at least one trade, skill, or technique at which he or she was fairly competent, that would do more for that youngster's adjustment than would the many hours of remediation to which the child is subjected. Perhaps that accent on the positive would go a long way toward actually helping the remediation process. If children knew they could excel in something, that might help them become competent in other areas as well.

(T. C. Lovitt, August 7, 2011, personal communication). Reprinted by permission from Thomas C. Lovitt.

recognize and value the strengths (e.g., useful skills, positive personality traits) and interests of each child and help that child maintain a positive outlook (see Figure 5.3).

Prevalence

Learning Outcome 5.3 Identify the prevalence of learning disabilities and describe assessments used to identify students with learning disabilities and monitor their progress.

Learning disabilities make up by far the largest of all special education categories. During the 2018–2019 school year, 2.38 million students age 6 to 21 years received special education under the specific learning disability category (U.S. Department of Education, 2020a). This figure represents 38% of all school-age children with disabilities and about 3.6% of the total school-age population. Across grade levels, disproportionately higher percentages of African American and Latino students are identified with learning disabilities, and males outnumber females by 3 to 1 (Cortiella & Horowitz, 2014).

The number of students identified with learning disabilities grew tremendously from 1976 through the 2002–2003 school year, until students with learning disabilities represented approximately half of all school-age children receiving special education. The rising incidence of children with learning disabilities fueled the ongoing debate over the nature and validity of the learning disability category and led some scholars to suggest it be considered an epidemic (Swanson, 2000). Recent years have seen a decrease in the identification rates for learning disabilities. From 2002 to 2011, the number of students served under the learning disability category decreased by 18%. Possible reasons for this decline include the expansion of early intervention, improvements in reading instruction in general education classrooms, and the shift in how learning disabilities are identified (e.g., RTI) since the reauthorization of IDEA in 2004 (Cortiella & Horowitz, 2014).

Although some believe the number of children identified with learning disabilities indicates the true extent of the disability, others contend that too many low achievers—children without a disability who are doing poorly in school because they have not received effective instruction—have been improperly diagnosed, placing a severe strain on the limited resources available to serve those students challenged by a true disability.

Causes

In most cases, the cause (etiology) of a child's learning disability is unknown. Many causes have been proposed, reflecting the diverse characteristics of students with learning disabilities. Just as there are different types of learning disabilities (e.g., language, math, reading), there are likely to be different causes. Three classes of suspected causes include brain damage or dysfunction, heredity, and environmental factors.

Brain Damage or Dysfunction

Some professionals believe all children with learning disabilities have some type of neurological injury or dysfunction. This belief is inherent in the NJCLD's position that learning disabilities are "presumed to be due to central nervous system dysfunction" (p. 19). Neuroimaging technologies such as magnetic resonance imaging (MRI) and functional magnetic resonance imaging (fMRI) have enabled researchers to identify differences of activation patterns (i.e., function) on specific brain regions between individuals with and without reading and language disabilities performing phonological processing tasks (e.g., Miller, Sanchez, & Hynd, 2003; Richards, 2001). Other studies have found the brain structure of some children with reading disabilities differs slightly from that of children without disabilities (Langer et al., 2019). Collectively, neuroimaging research has been reasonably consistent in revealing functional or structural differences (or both) of individuals with dyslexia (e.g., Peters et al., 2018). When compared with typical readers, students with dyslexia show an overactivated anterior system and two underactivated posterior systems, an activation pattern researchers call the *neural signature* of dyslexia (Shaywitz, 2003).

This research holds promise for understanding the neurobiological bases of dyslexia and other specific learning disabilities. However, we do not yet know how and to what extent the brain's neural networks are affected by the child's experiences (i.e., learning) and vice versa (McGowan et al., 2019). Thus, we do not know whether neurobiological factors associated with learning disabilities are contributors to the learning problems of children, the product of an unstimulating environment, or a combination of the two. However, growing evidence suggests that intensive remedial reading instruction can reduce differences in the ways the brains of children with reading disabilities and those of children without reading problems are activated (Berringer, 2019). For example, Shaywitz and colleagues (2004) reported that an average of 105 hours of individual tutoring that focused on the **alphabetic principle** (how letters and combinations of letters represent the small segments of speech called *phonemes*) and oral reading fluency practice not only improved children's reading fluency but also "facilitated the development of the neural systems that underlie skilled reading" (p. 933).

Special educators should refrain from placing too much emphasis on theories linking learning disabilities to brain damage or brain dysfunction. There are three major reasons for such caution. First, not all children with learning disabilities display clinical (medical) evidence of brain damage, and not all children with brain damage have learning disabilities. Second, assuming a child's learning problems are caused by brain dysfunction may serve as a built-in excuse for continuing to provide ineffective instruction. When a student with suspected brain damage fails to learn, his teachers may be quick to presume the brain dysfunction prevents him from learning and slow to analyze and change instructional variables. Third, whether a child's learning disability results from brain injury or other central nervous system dysfunction will not, given our present state of knowledge, alter the form or intensity of instructional interventions.

Heredity

Siblings and children of people with reading disabilities have a slightly greater-than-normal likelihood of having reading problems. Growing evidence indicates that genetics may account for some family links with reading disabilities (Landi & Purdue, 2019; Olson et al., 2019). Research has located possible chromosomal loci for the genetic transmission of phonological deficits that may predispose a child to reading problems later (Landi & Purdue, 2019).

Experiential Factors

Although virtually impossible to document as a primary cause of learning disabilities, environmental factors—particularly impoverished living conditions early in children's lives and limited exposure to effective instruction in school—undoubtedly contribute to the learning problems experienced by many children. The tendency for learning disabilities to run in families also suggests a correlation between environmental influences on children's early development and subsequent achievement in school. Evidence for this relationship can be found in longitudinal research such as that conducted by Hart and Risley (1995), who found that infants and toddlers who received infrequent communication exchanges with their parents were more likely to show deficits in vocabulary, language use, and intellectual development before entering school.

Another experiential factor that is likely to contribute to children's learning problems is the quality of instruction they receive. Even though many schools are adopting RTI models of instruction, students may not be receiving effective Tier 1 instruction. Many special educators today believe Siegfried Engelmann (1977) was correct when he asserted that the vast majority of "children who are labeled 'learning disabled' exhibit a disability not because of anything wrong with their perception, synapses, or memory, but because they have been seriously mistaught" (pp. 46–47).

Although the relationship between the absence of effective instruction and learning disabilities is not clear, a great deal of evidence shows that most students' learning problems can be remediated by intensive doses of explicit instruction. It would be naive, however, to think that the achievement problems of all children with learning disabilities are caused entirely by inadequate instruction. Nevertheless, from an educational perspective, intensive, systematic instruction should be the intervention of first choice for all students with learning disabilities.

> HLP4 Use multiple sources of information to develop a comprehensive understanding of a student's strengths and needs.

Identification and Assessment

Assessments commonly used to identify students with learning disabilities include a combination of standardized intelligence and achievement tests, criterion-referenced tests, curriculum-based measurement (CBM), and direct and daily measurement.

Intelligence and Achievement Tests

Standardized IQ tests and individual achievement tests are typically administered during the referral process to determine eligibility for special education services under the learning disabilities category. These tests are widely used as diagnostic tools with children with learning disabilities because a discrepancy between general intellectual ability and achievement remains a primary factor in determining eligibility for special education services (Alphonso & Flanagan, 2018). These norm-referenced tests are constructed so that one student's score can be compared with the scores of other students of the same age who have taken the test. (See Chapter 4 for a discussion of intelligence tests.) Widely used standardized tests for assessing overall academic achievement include the Iowa Tests of Basic Skills (Hoover et al., 2007), the Woodcock-Johnson IV Tests of Achievement (Schrank et al., 2014), and the Wechsler Individual Achievement Test III (Wechsler, 2009). Scores on these and similar tests are commonly reported as grade-level equivalents; a score of 3.5, for example, means that the student's score equals the average score of the students in the norm group who were halfway through the third grade.

Some norm-referenced tests measure achievement in specific academic areas. Frequently administered reading achievement tests include the Test of Reading Comprehension, Fourth Edition (Brown et al., 2008) and Woodcock Reading Mastery Tests Third Edition (Woodcock, 2011). Norm-referenced tests that assess mathematics achievement include KeyMath-3 (Connolly, 2007) and the Test of Mathematical Abilities, Third Edition (Brown et al., 2012).

Criterion-Referenced Tests

Criterion-referenced tests differ from norm-referenced tests in that a child's score on a criterion-referenced test is compared with a predetermined criterion, or mastery level, rather than with normed scores of other students. The value of criterion-referenced tests is they identify specific skills the child has already learned and skills that require instruction. A criterion-referenced test widely used by special educators is the Brigance Comprehensive Inventory of Basic Skills (Brigance, 2010), which includes nearly 400 criterion-referenced assessments in reading, language arts, and math. Some commercially distributed curricula now include criterion-referenced test items for use as both a pretest and a posttest. The pretest assesses the student's entry level to determine which aspects of the program she is ready to learn; the posttest evaluates the effectiveness of the program. Criterion-referenced tests can be, and often are, informally developed by classroom teachers.

Curriculum-Based Measurement

Any measurement system must be valid and reliable. Repeatedly putting a ruler in a pot of water might yield a reliable measure of 3 inches, but it would not produce a valid measure of the water's temperature. As silly as this example might seem, measures used in education too often assess something other than the skills students need to progress in the curriculum. **Curriculum-based measurement (CBM)** (also called *progress monitoring*) entails measuring the growth of students' proficiency in the core skills that contribute to success in school (Hosp et al., 2016). CBM is a **formative assessment** method in that it provides information on student learning as instruction takes place over time. By contrast, results of a **summative assessment** generally do not inform instruction because it is conducted after instruction has been completed (e.g., at the end of a grading period or school year). CBM probes are brief, reliable assessments that indicate proficiency of basic skills such as reading, spelling, or math. For example, a CBM probe for oral reading fluency requires counting the number of words a student reads correctly in a 1-minute timing. Because oral reading fluency is a valid predictor of general reading skills, a student meeting grade level expectations for reading rate is likely to be a proficient reader.

> **HLP6** Use student assessment data, analyze instructional practices, and make necessary adjustments that improve student outcomes.

CBM entails multiple, ongoing, fluency-based measures of student performance over time and visual inspection of graphed student data as the basis for instructional decision making (Figure 5.4). To make instructional decisions, the teacher creates a graph and draws an aim line from the student's baseline performance (e.g., 20 wpm) to the student's end-of-the-term goal (e.g., 100 wpm). If the student is making timely progress toward his goal, his weekly probe scores will be at or above the aim line. If the student is progressing too slowly to meet the goal, a change of instruction is indicated.

FIGURE 5.4 Example of a CBM Graph

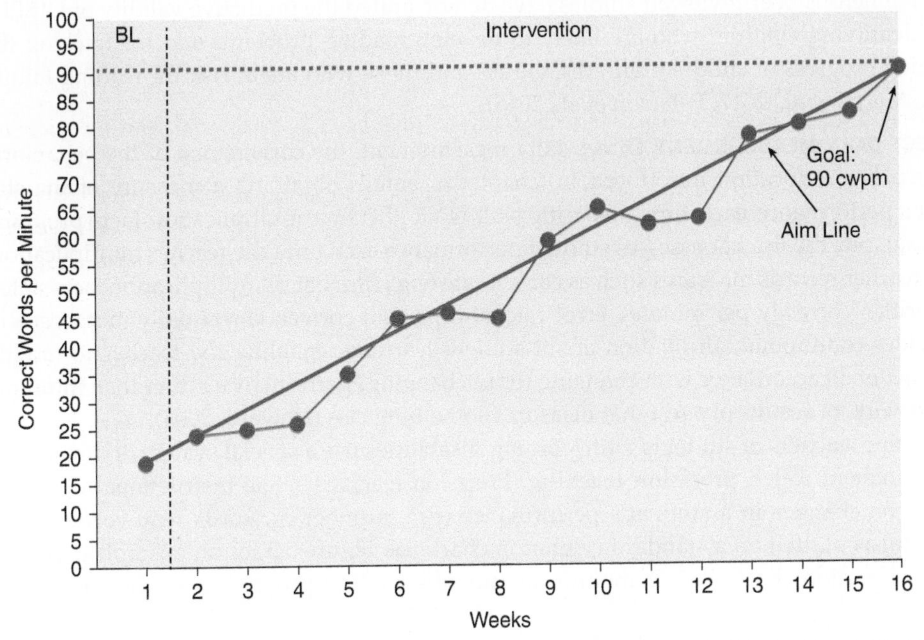

CBM measures are easy to administer and score; cost and time efficient; and, perhaps most important, sensitive to small, incremental changes in student performance over time (Hessler & Konrad, 2008). The Dynamic Indicators of Basic Early Literacy Skills (DIBELS) is a set of valid and reliable curriculum-based measures with these attributes (University of Oregon, 2018–2019). DIBELS was developed to be an efficient indicator of key reading skills to enable the early identification of children at risk for reading difficulties and to assess the effects of interventions designed to prevent such failure. DIBELS consists of a set of 1-minute fluency measures used to regularly monitor the development of prereading and early reading skills. Research has demonstrated that children who meet or exceed the benchmark goal for each measure are likely (odds greater than 80%–90%) to become proficient readers (Good et al., 2011).

Detailed guidelines and tools for conducting CBM are available at the websites of the Center on Multi-Tiered System of Supports and the Research Institute on Progress Monitoring. The most recent version, DIBELS Next, consists of several individual measures and a composite score as follows (University of Oregon, 2018–2019):

Pearson eText
Video Example 5.3
Oral reading fluency assessments are important for identification and progress monitoring.

- *First Sound Fluency.* The assessor says a series of words, and the student pronounces the first sound for each word.
- *Letter Naming Fluency.* The assessor shows the student a sheet of letters and prompts the student to name them.
- *Phoneme Segmentation Fluency.* The assessor says whole words, and the student says the individual sounds in each word.
- *Nonsense Word Fluency.* The assessor presents the student with a list of VC and CVC nonsense words (e.g., *ov, sig, rav*) to pronounce.
- *DIBELS Oral Reading Fluency.* The student reads a grade level passage aloud for 1 minute and the assessor records the number of correct and incorrect words read per minute.
- *Daze (DIBELS Maze).* The assessor provides a reading passage in which some words are replaced by a multiple-choice box that includes the original word and two distractors. While reading the passage silently, the student selects the word in each box that best fits the meaning of the sentence.
- *Composite Score.* A combination of multiple DIBELS scores, the composite score provides the best overall estimate of a student's reading proficiency. The scores used to calculate the composite vary by grade and time of year.

Numerous peer-reviewed studies have demonstrated the predictive validity of DIBELS for identifying children who are likely to develop reading problems and for tracking the reading progress of children with disabilities and those who are at risk for reading failure (e.g., Morris et al., 2017; Peterson et al., 2018).

DIRECT DAILY MEASUREMENT Direct daily measurement, the cornerstone of the behavioral approach to education introduced in Chapter 4, entails obtaining a measure of the student's performance each time a specific skill is taught. In a multiplication facts program, for example, the teacher assesses student performance each time she teaches multiplication. The teacher records measures such as correct rate (e.g., number of multiplication facts stated or written correctly per minute), error rate, and percent correct. Direct daily measurement provides continuous information about student learning, enabling the teacher to modify instruction in accordance with changing (or unchanging) performance rather than intuition, guesswork, or results of a test that measures something else (Heward, 2003).

Some teachers of students with learning disabilities use a special system of direct daily measurement called **precision teaching**. Precision teachers make instructional decisions based on changes in a student's performance (e.g., number of words read correctly per minute) as plotted on a standard celeration chart. See Figure 5.5 for an example of a standard celeration chart used to monitor a student's reading progress over the course of 8 weeks.

In Figure 5.5, the student's data show upward trends of correct response rates and downward trends of incorrect response rates. In addition to showing how much a student is learning, the slope of the trend lines show how fast a student is learning. Detailed information about and resources for precision teaching are described by Kubina and Yurich (2012).

Identifying Learning Disabilities with Response to Intervention

The basic premise of RTI is that a low-achieving student's response to increasingly intensive, scientifically validated instruction can reveal whether the student's learning difficulties are the result of insufficient instruction or of a disability for which special education is needed. RTI has two functions: identification and prevention. A child's failure to progress in response to scientifically validated instruction eliminates instructional quality as a viable explanation for poor academic growth and suggests evidence of a disability (Fuchs et al., 2012). Children who respond favorably to RTI's increasingly intensive instruction benefit from the preventive aspect of the approach.

O'Connor and colleagues (2013) found that one third of students with learning disabilities were not identified until they reached fourth grade. RTI can help schools identify students with learning disabilities earlier and reduce the number of children incorrectly

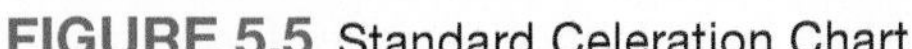

FIGURE 5.5 Standard Celeration Chart

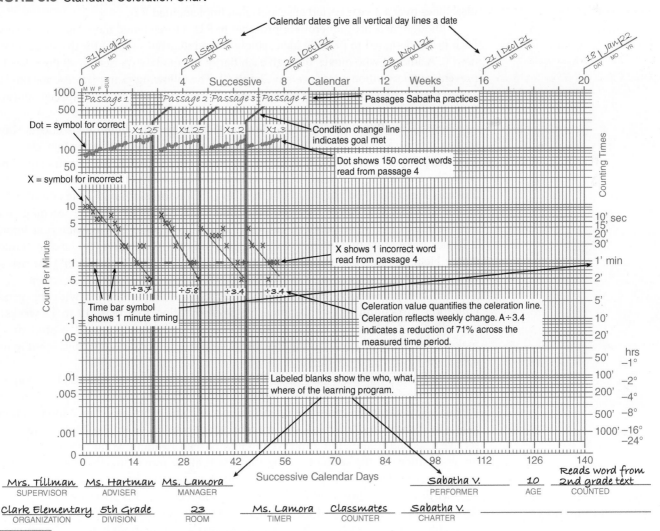

Source: Courtesy of Rick Kubina, Penn State University.

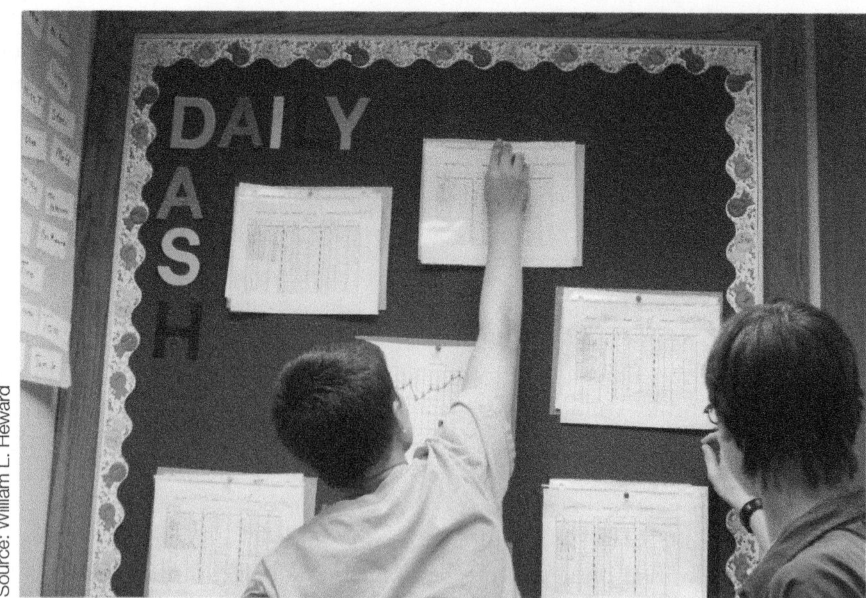

Source: William L. Heward

Self-recording direct and daily measures of their academic performance increases students' involvement and responsibility in their own learning.

identified. Torgesen (2009) reported a substantial drop in identification rates for learning disabilities over a 3-year period at schools that implemented RTI.

Although there are numerous approaches to RTI, a three-tiered model is most common. Each tier is designed to provide increasingly more intensive support for the students who need it. A student who moves through each tier of the model experiences all three levels of preventive intervention introduced in Chapter 1. The following examples describe how RTI can be used to prevent reading problems and identify children who need special education for reading disabilities.

Tier 1: Core Programming in the General Education Classroom. All students should receive evidence-based curriculum and instruction in the general education classroom. Frequent progress monitoring in the form of CBM tracks the performance of students whose scores on a screening test (e.g., DIBELS) fall below benchmarks for critical reading skills. Students are considered at risk if both their level of performance and their rate of growth on the CBM are well below those of their classmates. Examples of Tier 1 teaching strategies include explicit instruction, choral responding (see Chapter 2), classwide peer tutoring (Chapter 2), response cards (Chapter 6), and guided notes (see *Teaching & Learning*, "Guided Notes: Helping All Students Succeed in the General Education Curriculum"). At-risk students who struggle during Tier 1 instruction receive supplemental Tier 2 instruction.

Tier 2: Supplemental Interventions. Students who are struggling with the general education curriculum receive an intensive fixed-duration trial (e.g., 10 to 12 weeks) of small-group supplemental tutoring using a research-validated program. A student who makes satisfactory progress during this intensive prevention trial is not considered to have a disability.

L. S. Fuchs and Fuchs (2007a, 2007b) have recommended using a **dual discrepancy criterion** that designates a student as nonresponsive only when the student (a) fails to make adequate growth in the presence of instruction and (b) completes Tier 2 intervention(s) below the benchmark criteria. A student who is not responsive to Tier 2 intervention may receive a second trial of Tier 2 intervention (with modifications to the intervention based on observations of the student during the first trial) or move directly to a multifactored evaluation to determine the presence of disability and special education eligibility.

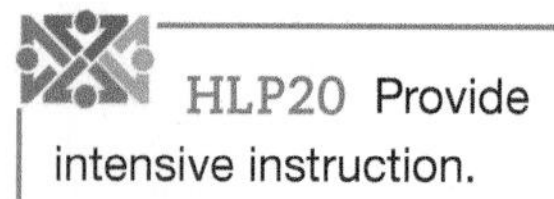
HLP20 Provide intensive instruction.

Tier 3: Intensive Intervention. In most RTI models, Tier 3 is special education. Some special educators recommend that students who do not make progress with small-group intervention in Tier 2 receive intensive individualized interventions before a determination of special education eligibility (e.g., Reschly, 2005).

TEACHING & LEARNING

Guided Notes: Helping All Students Succeed in the General Education Curriculum

What Are Guided Notes? Guided notes are teacher-prepared handouts that "guide" a student through a lecture with standard cues and specific spaces in which to write key facts, concepts, or relationships. To complete their guided notes, students must respond throughout the lecture by listening, looking, thinking, and writing about the lesson's content. In addition to requiring students to actively respond to curriculum and improving retention of course content, guided notes can help students easily identify important information and produce an accurate set of notes to study. When teachers use guided notes, they must prepare the lesson or lecture carefully, and they are more likely to stay on task with the lecture's content and sequence. Teachers can use guided notes for teaching a wide range of skills and content across the curriculum.

Guided Notes for a Lesson on Clouds Completed by an Elementary Student with Learning Disabilities

Clouds

Directions: Follow along with your teacher and fill in your guided notes.

What Are Clouds?

★ Clouds are tiny drops of condensing water vapor or ice crystals that settle on particles of dust in the atmosphere.

What Are the Different Kinds of Clouds?

★ Although there are many different types of clouds, there are three main types:

Types of Clouds
Cirrus
Cumulus
Stratus

How Do I Know What Type of Clouds Are in the Sky?

- Cirrus clouds
  - Most common
  - Usually made of ice crystals
  - Look like feathers
  - Thin and wispy

Draw a picture of a cirrus cloud.

- Cumulus clouds
  - White and puffy
  - Look like cotton balls
  - Usually predict fair weather but can develop into cumulonimbus clouds which may produce rain, lightning, strong winds, and hail

Draw a picture of a cumulus cloud.

How Do You Make Guided Notes? Guided notes can support the presentation of virtually any academic content or skill area. The following are general guidelines for creating guided notes.

- Examine existing lecture outlines to identify the most important course content that students must learn. Include all facts, concepts, and relationships students are expected to learn on GNs.
- Provide background information on the GNs so that students' note taking focuses on the important facts, concepts, and relationships they need to learn. Don't require students to write too much.
- Delete the key facts, concepts, and relationships from the lecture outline, leaving the remaining information to provide structure for students' note taking. Insert cues such as asterisks, bullets, and blank lines to show students where, when, and how many facts or concepts to write.
- Intersperse questions into the GNs and opportunities for other forms of active student responding during the lesson. Stop lecturing from time to time and ask a series of questions, to which the students answer chorally or with response cards (see Chapters 2 and 6), referring to their GNs for answers as needed.
- Provide students who need additional accommodations modified versions of GNs. For example, teachers can provide students with GNs that require less writing to help students keep up with fast-moving lessons.

Figure 5.6 illustrates how teachers may use progress monitoring data in a three-tier RTI model. The figure shows three students from the same second grade classroom have different instructional needs. When monitoring progress using CBM, decision rules specify that a change of instruction is indicated if three consecutive data points fall below the aim line. Dontai's baseline (i.e., before instruction) oral reading fluency (ORF) is 62 correct words per minute (CWPM) (see Panel A). His teacher creates an aim line that shows the overall rate of progress needed to reach an ambitious goal of 94 CWPM in 16 weeks. Because Dontai's ORF is in the average to above-average range, his teacher administers CBM probes every other week. These CBM data points cluster along Dontai's aim line, demonstrating that Tier 1 instruction is effective and no change of instruction is needed.

Based on Theo's below-average baseline ORF of 35 (see Panel B), his teacher decides to conduct weekly CBM probes and sets a 16-week ORF goal of 50 CWPM. Measures of Theo's performance during Tier 1 instruction yield three consecutive data points below his aim line, triggering a decision rule to change instruction. So, in addition to Tier 1 instruction, Theo's teacher implements supplemental Tier 2 instruction in a small group arrangement three to four times per week. Progress monitoring indicates that Tier 2 instruction is effective because Theo is now on track to achieve his goal.

Because Shelly's baseline ORF of 17 CWPM is well below average (Panel C), her teacher set a 16-week goal of 28 CWPM and monitors her progress more closely with twice-weekly CBM probes. During Tier 1 instruction, Shelly had three consecutive data points below her aim line, so she received supplemental Tier 2 intervention. Shelly started to improve with Tier 2 instruction and then performed below her aim line on three consecutive biweekly probes. Shelly's Tier 3 intervention included daily individual tutoring that put her back on track.

Potential benefits and goals of RTI include the following (Alber-Morgan, 2010; Blackburn & Witzel, 2018):

- Early intervention for struggling learners
- Reduction in the number of students referred for special education, especially culturally diverse learners

FIGURE 5.6 Monitoring Progress Using RTI

Panel A: Dontai responds well to Tier 1 instruction.

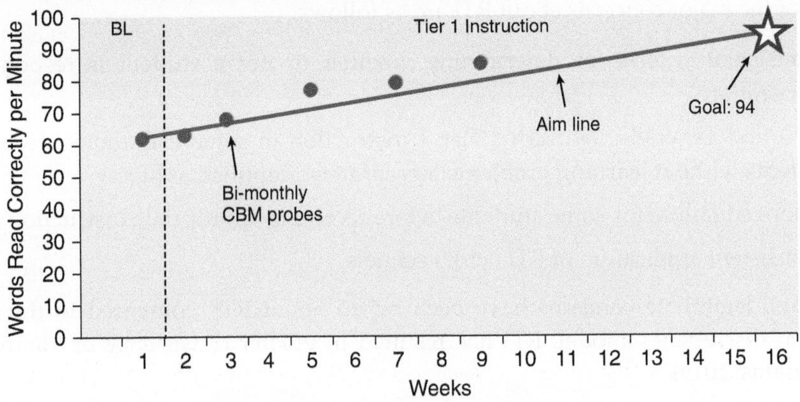

Panel B: Theo needs Tier 2 instruction and responds well to it.

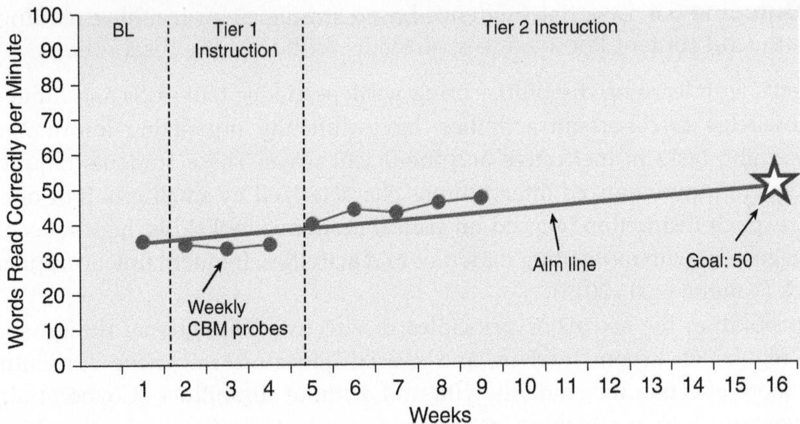

Panel C: Shelly needs Tier 3 instruction and responds well to it.

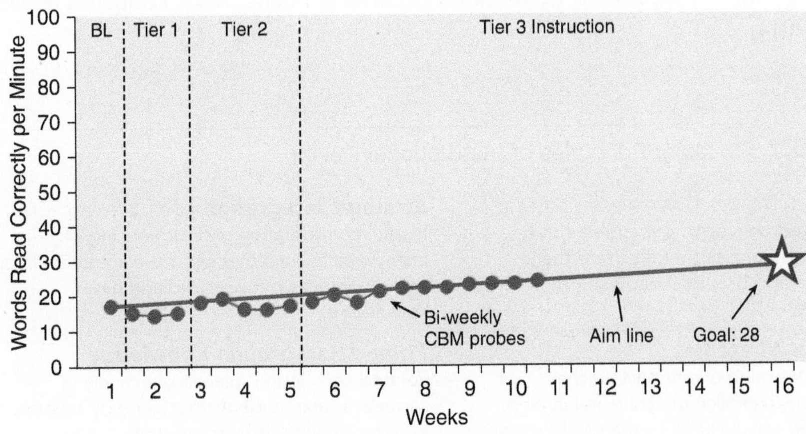

- Provision of more instructionally useful data than those provided by traditional methods of assessment and identification
- Increased likelihood that students can access differentiated instruction and high-quality instruction in the general education classroom by stipulating the use of evidence-based instructional practices
- Service to all students with achievement problems so that only those students who fail to respond to multiple levels of intervention receive a learning disability diagnosis

RTI guidelines and resources are available at the following websites: National Center on Response to Intervention, the National Research Center on Learning Disabilities, and the RTI Action Network.

Some of the major concerns about RTI are as follows:

- Inconsistent criteria for determining whether or not a student is responding to intervention
- Weak and generally ineffective Tier 1 instruction in some classrooms, resulting in students without learning problems inaccurately identified as at risk
- Prolonged failure for some students before receiving appropriate instruction
- Inconsistent application of RTI across schools

Although legitimate concerns have been raised about RTI, compared to the ability–achievement discrepancy model, RTI has resulted in greater consistency of identification (Maki & Adams, 2019).

Educational Approaches

Learning Outcome 5.4 Describe evidence-based strategies for teaching reading, writing, math, and content knowledge to students with learning disabilities.

Many students with learning disabilities bring weak academic tool skills and limited background knowledge to classroom activities, have difficulty organizing information, and approach learning tasks in ineffective and inefficient ways. These students require intensive and frequent individualized interventions characterized by small group or one-to-one instruction, explicit instruction focused on critical academic tool skills, high rates of active student engagement with motivating materials and activities, frequent practice, and systematic feedback (Vaughn et al., 2014).

By incorporating the six major principles of effective instructional design shown in Figure 5.7, regular classroom teachers and special educators can make curriculum and instruction more effective for students with and without disabilities (Coyne et al., 2011). Other interventions such as matching instruction to students' auditory, visual, or kinesthetic learning styles and using cognitively focused instruction (e.g., "brain gym" exercises, attention training) are not supported by research (Kearns & Fuchs, 2013; Landrum & McDuffy-Landrum, 2014).

FIGURE 5.7 Six Major Principles of Instructional Design

Big Ideas
Highly selected concepts, principles, rules, strategies, or heuristics that facilitate the most efficient and broadest acquisition of knowledge.

Conspicuous Strategies
Sequence of teaching events and teacher actions that make explicit the steps in learning. They are made conspicuous by the use of visual maps or models, verbal directions, full and clear explanations, and so forth.

Mediated Scaffolding
Temporary support for students to learn new material. Scaffolding has faded over time.

Strategic Integration
Planful consideration and sequencing of instruction in ways that show the commonalities and differences between old and new knowledge.

Primed Background Knowledge
Related knowledge, placed effectively in sequence, that students must already possess in order to learn new knowledge.

Judicious Review
Sequence and schedule of opportunities learners have to apply and develop facility with new knowledge. The review must be adequate, distributed, cumulative, and varied.

Source: From Kame'enui, E. J., Carnine, D. W., & Dixon, R. C. (2011). Introduction. In M. D. Coyne, E. J. Kame'enui, & D. W. Carnine (Eds.), *Effective teaching strategies that accommodate diverse learners* (4th ed., p. 13). © 2011. Reproduced by permission of Pearson Education, Inc., Upper Saddle River, NJ.

Explicit instruction and learning strategy instruction are two highly effective and empirically validated approaches to designing and delivering instruction for students with learning disabilities (e.g., Gajria & Jitendra, 2016; Hughes et al., 2017; Swanson & Hoskyn, 1998). Explicit instruction is a systematic approach for guiding "through the learning process with clear statements about the purpose and rationale for learning the new skill, clear explanations and demonstrations of the instructional target, and supported practice with feedback until independent mastery has been achieved" (Archer & Hughes, 2011, p. 1). Explicit instruction includes directions, modeling, guided practice, active student responding with frequent feedback, and independent practice. Decades of empirical research have documented the effectiveness of explicit instruction for teaching students with learning disabilities (e.g., Hughes et al., 2017).

HLP16 Use explicit instruction.

Teaching learning strategies also produces successful outcomes for students with learning disabilities. A learning strategy is defined as "an individual's approach to a learning task. A strategy includes how a person thinks and acts when planning, executing, and evaluating performance on a task and its outcomes" (Deshler & Lenz, 1989, p. 205). Learning strategies instruction has produced successful outcomes for elementary and high school students' reading comprehension, written expression, mathematics, study skills, note-taking skills, and listening skills (e.g., Ennis & Losinski, 2019; Jozwik et al., 2019; Nordness et al., 2019; Ray et al., 2018). Teaching a learning strategy consists of having students memorize a series of steps (usually in the form of a mnemonic) for accomplishing a task (e.g., writing a paragraph), and providing guided practice until the student can apply the strategy independently.

HLP14 Teach cognitive and metacognitive strategies to support learning and independence.

For examples of mnemonic learning strategies and how to teach them, see *Transition: Next Year Is Now*, "Learning Strategies for Transitioning to College."

Transition: Next Year Is Now

Learning Strategies for Transitioning to College

Among the 200,000 students with learning disabilities who begin college each year, only about 34% graduate from a 4-year degree program within 8 years of their high school graduation (NCES, 2019). To increase the likelihood of success in college, transition planning must include teaching skills that enable students to learn and study independently. Successful college students take accurate notes, comprehend what they read, demonstrate their learning through written expression, study effectively, and answer questions correctly on tests.

In addition to being effective for elementary and high school students, learning strategies instruction is effective for college students with disabilities (e.g., MacArthur et al., 2015; Song & Ferretti, 2013; Torres & Black, 2018). Teaching students with learning disabilities to use learning strategies while they are still in high school can provide them with critical preparation for college. The following examples of learning strategies would be beneficial for college-bound students.

SKILL AREA	LEARNING STRATEGY	STEPS
Reading Comprehension	TRAP (Hagaman & Casey, 2017).	***Think*** before you read ***Read*** a paragraph ***Ask*** yourself the main idea and details ***Put*** the main idea in your own words
Note Taking	CUES (Boyle, 2013)	***Cluster*** information ***Use*** cues from instructor ***Enter*** vocabulary words into notes ***Summarize*** main ideas
Paragraph Writing	NOW! (Konrad, 2017)	***Name*** your topic ***Organize*** your details ***Wrap*** it up and restate the topic

(Continued)

SKILL AREA	LEARNING STRATEGY	STEPS
Studying	FLASH (Konrad & Alber-Morgan, 2020)	***Find*** your materials (figure out what's going to be on the test) ***Look*** for important words, phrases, ideas in your notes and books ***Add*** a question or important vocabulary term to one side of each card and add corresponding answers to the other side ***Study*** the flashcards ***Have*** someone quiz you
Taking Tests	SPLASH (Reid et al., 2013)	***Skim*** the test ***Plan*** your strategy ***Leave*** out tough questions ***Attack*** questions you know ***Systematically*** guess ***Housecleaning*** (check that all the questions are answered)

Self-regulated strategy development is a systematic method for teaching learning strategies. The stages are as follows: Develop background knowledge needed to accomplish the strategy, discuss the strategy, model the strategy, memorize the strategy, support the strategy, and establish independent practice (Harris & Graham, 2018). For example, the TRAP strategy is a mnemonic for the following steps: (1) Think before you read, (2) Read a paragraph, (3) Ask yourself the main idea and two details, and (4) Put the main idea and details in your own words. When using self-regulated strategy development for TRAP, the teacher assesses and teaches background knowledge for accomplishing the reading comprehension strategy, discusses the strategy with the student (what it is, how it will benefit the student), and then models the strategy. The student then memorizes the mnemonic steps and practices the strategy using less challenging reading passages before moving on to more challenging passages. After the teacher provides guided practice with frequent feedback, the student engages in independent practice of the strategy. Finally, the teacher encourages generalization by discussing with students the variety of situations in which they should use the strategy and then directing students to use the strategy outside the classroom. More information about self-regulated strategy development can be found at the IRIS Center website: http://iris.peabody.vanderbilt.edu/module/srs/.

Explicit instruction and learning strategies are effective in isolation, but teachers who combine these approaches will likely have the best student outcomes. Additionally, both approaches are characterized by the six major principles of effective instruction (see Figure 5.7) and can be applied across all academic skills and content. The following sections describe specific explicit instruction and learning strategy interventions for teaching reading, writing, mathematics, and content area knowledge to students with learning disabilities.

Reading

Extensive research over the past several decades has produced more than 2000 peer-reviewed scientific articles about early reading acquisition and reading difficulties (e.g., Bursuck & Damer, 2015; King-Sears & Bowman-Kruhm, 2010; Vaughn & Wanzek, 2014). This research reveals a great deal about the nature of children's reading disabilities and the kind of interventions most effective in preventing and remediating reading problems—interventions such as explicit instruction of phonemic awareness, letter–phoneme relationships, and sounding out words.

Pearson eText
Video Example 5.4
"This word rhymes with *mop*. Sound it out."

Figure 5.8 shows key principles of effective beginning reading instruction. Direct Instruction reading programs, such as SRA/McGraw-Hill's Reading Mastery (Engelmann & Bruner, 2008) and Corrective Reading (Engelmann et al., 2008), typically use explicit instruction and incorporate the key principles in Figure 5.7. DI programs teach complex reading skills in small steps that progressively build on previous learning. Instructional design and delivery are consistent with the tenets of explicit instruction, including frequent active student responding and feedback. (see *Teaching & Learning*, "Direct Instruction for Reading").

When students can decode words, teachers can focus more on reading fluency by having students read passages repeatedly during brief timings (see Chapter 1, *Teaching & Learning*, "It's Good To Go Fast!"). Repeated reading interventions have been demonstrated to be effective for students with learning disabilities (Stevens et al., 2017).

FIGURE 5.8 Research-Based Principles of Early Reading Instruction

1. **Begin teaching phonemic awareness directly in kindergarten.** Many children and adults who cannot read are not aware of phonemes. If phonemic awareness does not develop by age 5 or 6, it is unlikely to develop later without instruction. Activities such as the following help develop children's phonemic awareness:
   - *Phoneme deletion.* What word would be left if the /k/ sound were taken away from *cat*?
   - *Word-to-word matching.* Do *pen* and *pipe* begin with the same sound?
   - *Phoneme counting.* How many sounds do you hear in the word *cake*?
   - *Odd word out.* What word starts with a different sound: *bag, nine, beach, bike*?

   Teachers should start teaching phonemic awareness before beginning instruction in letter–phoneme relationships and continue phonemic awareness activities while teaching the letter–phoneme relationships.

2. **Teach each letter–phoneme relationship explicitly.** Only about 40 to 50 letter–sound relationships are necessary to read. Telling children explicitly what single sound a given letter or letter combination makes will prevent reading problems better than encouraging children to figure out the sounds for the letters by giving clues. Many children have difficulty figuring out the individual letter–phoneme correspondences if they hear them only in the context of words and word parts. Therefore, teachers should separate phonemes from words for instruction. For example, the teacher shows the children the letter *m* and says, "This letter says /mmm/."

   A new phoneme and other phonemes the children have learned should be practiced for about 5 minutes each day in isolation. The rest of the lesson should use these phonemes in words and stories composed of only the letter–phoneme relationships the children have learned in isolation up to that point.

3. **Teach frequent, highly regular letter–sound relationships systematically.** To teach systematically means coordinating the introduction of the letter–phoneme relationships with the material the children are asked to read. The words and stories should be composed of only the letter–phoneme relationships the children have learned. The order of the introduction of letter–phoneme relationships should be planned to allow reading material composed of meaningful words and stories as soon as possible. For example, if the first three letter–phoneme relationships the children learn are /a/, /b/, /c/, the only real word the children can read is *cab*. But if the first three letter–phoneme relationships are /m/, /a/, /s/, the children can read *am, Sam, mass, ma'am*.

4. **Show children exactly how to sound out words.** After children have learned two or three letter–phoneme relationships, teach them how to blend the sounds into words. Show them how to move sequentially from left to right through spellings as they sound out each word. Every day practice blending words composed of only the letter–phoneme relationships the children have learned.

5. **Give children connected, decodable text to practice the letter–phoneme relationships.** Children need extensive practice in applying their knowledge of letter–sound relationships to reading. The most effective integration of phonics and reading occurs with *decodable text*—text composed of words that use the letter–phoneme relationships the children have learned to that point and a limited number of sight words that have been systematically taught. As the children learn more letter–phoneme relationships, the texts become more sophisticated.

   Texts that are less decodable do not integrate phonological knowledge with actual reading. For example, "*The dog is up*" is the first sentence children read in one meaning-based program with an unintegrated phonics component. The sound–letter relationships the children had learned up to this point were /d/, /m/, /s/, /r/, /t/. By applying their phonics knowledge, the children could read only "_________ d_________ _________ _________." But if children have learned /a/, /s/, /m/, /b/, /t/, /h/, /f/, /g/, /i/, they can read "*Sam has a big fist.*" The sentence is 100% decodable because the phonics component has been integrated properly into the child's real reading.

   Text that is less decodable requires children to use prediction or context to figure out words. Although prediction is valuable in comprehension for predicting the next event or predicting an outcome, it is not useful in word recognition. The use of predictable text rather than decodable text might allow children to use prediction to figure out a passage. However, the strategy does not transfer to real reading. Predictable text gives children false success. While such success may motivate many children, ultimately they will not be successful readers if they rely on text predictability to read.

6. **Use interesting stories to develop language comprehension.** Research does not rule out the use of interesting, authentic stories to develop language comprehension. But it does recommend not using these stories as reading material for nonreaders. Teacher-read stories play an important role in building children's oral language comprehension, which ultimately affects their reading comprehension. Story-based activities should be structured to build comprehension skills, not decoding skills.

   During the early stages of reading acquisition, children's oral language comprehension level is much higher than their reading comprehension level. The stories teachers read to children to build their comprehension should be geared to their oral language comprehension level. The material used to build children's decoding should be geared to their decoding skills, with attention to meaning. Teachers should teach comprehension strategies and new vocabulary using orally presented stories and texts that are more sophisticated than the early decodable text the children read. The teacher should read these stories to the children and discuss the meaning with them. After the children become fluent decoders, they can apply these comprehension strategies to their own reading.

Source: Adapted from Grossen, B. (2006). Six principles for early reading instruction. In W. L. Heward, *Exceptional children: An introduction to special education* (8th ed., pp. 186–188). Upper Saddle River, NJ: Pearson.

TEACHING & LEARNING

Direct Instruction for Reading

What Is Direct Instruction? An Internet search of *direct instruction* yields hundreds of definitions. Most of them read like this: a teacher-directed teaching method in which the teacher stands in front of a classroom and uses lectures or demonstrations to present academic content to students. In stark contrast is Direct Instruction, with a capitalized D and I. Direct Instruction (DI) was created by Siegfried Engelmann and Wesley Becker at the University of Illinois in the 1960s and further developed by Engelmann, Doug Carnine, Ed Kame'enui, Jerry Silbert, and others at the University of Oregon.

Steadfast belief in the motto "If the student hasn't learned, the teacher hasn't taught" motivated Engelmann and colleagues to craft rigorously designed and field-tested programs for teaching reading, math, writing, spelling, and thinking skills to children. A DI program is not published until the lowest performing students master at least 90% of the skills taught in the program.

Pearson eText
Video Example 5.5
"What word refers to a large field in Africa?"

A first-time observer of a well-taught DI lesson is immediately struck by the high energy level: The rapid pacing, the teacher's verbal and visual signals, and the students responding in unison stand out readily from typical teaching methods. The casual observer, however, is seldom aware of the sophisticated instructional design that is the heart of DI.

What Are the Components of DI? Two major rules underlie DI: "Teach more in less time" and "Control the details of the curriculum." The goal is to include all necessary and sufficient components for the lesson's success, and nothing extraneous. A brief introduction to some of those components follows (Barbash, 2012; Carnine et al.; Engelmann & Carnine, 1982; Watkins & Slocum, 2003).

Logical Content Analysis DI programs are designed based on the finding that if children could respond perfectly to a small set of carefully engineered tasks, they would generalize their learning to new untaught examples and situations. For example, children who learn to spell 600 word parts called *morphographs* and 3 rules for connecting them can spell 12,000 words. Children who rehearse the 600 word parts and 3 rules to a level of automaticity can spell any of the 12,000 words with ease.

Clear Communication. To prevent students from learning misrules because of the way concepts are introduced (e.g., triangles are blue, the numerator is always greater than the denominator), instructional examples are selected and sequenced to avoid ambiguity and yield maximum generalization to untaught examples. To learn the limits or boundaries of a concept, students respond to examples and nonexamples that are *similar to one another except for the critical feature* that makes them different. To learn the range of a concept, students identify examples that *differ from one another as much as possible* yet still illustrate the concept.

Scripted Lessons. Scripts enable teachers to deliver the lesson as designed and devote full attention to their students' performance. Just 'reading the script' will not teach students anything. Even though DI programs are carefully tested and scripted, there is nothing simple about using them successfully. Good DI teachers must learn special presentation techniques and make many 'on-the-fly' decisions in response to the children's performance.

Student Engagement. Good DI teachers generate high rates of active student response by having students respond in unison to a rapidly paced series of teacher-presented items (See Chapter 2 *Teaching & Learning,* "Choral Responding: Good Noise in the Classroom") and interspersing individual turns within group responses.

Immediate Feedback. Effective DI teachers praise correct responses, and DI lessons are designed so that 70% of students' first-time responses are correct. They also correct errors immediately via a *model-lead-test* procedure that enables the student(s) who erred to respond correctly and independently. "The major difference between the average Reading Mastery I teacher, who teaches *most* of the children, and the outstanding teacher, who teaches *all* of the children, is the ability to correct" (Engelmann & Bruner, 1995, p. 11). A good DI teacher does not move to the next task in a lesson (or from one lesson to the next) until all students have demonstrated their mastery of the current task (or lesson).

What Is the Evidence for DI? When asked, "How do you know it's working?" kindergarten teacher Kim Calloway's compelling reply, "They're reading. Every year they're reading," is powerful, first-hand testament to DI's effectiveness. There is also more scientific research demonstrating DI's effectiveness than is found for any other model of instruction.

From 1967 to 1977, the federal government sponsored Project Follow Through, which compared 22 different models of instruction in the largest education experiment ever conducted—more than 200,000 children in 178 high-poverty communities participated (Watkins, 1997). DI was the clear winner across the board. Not only did children in the DI classrooms make the greatest gains in academic achievement, catching up to or even surpassing national norms on several arithmetic, reading, and language skills, but also children in DI programs had the highest scores on measures of self-concept, higher even than the programs designed to enhance self-concept.

In the half-century since Project Follow Through, hundreds of studies have found DI produces consistently strong effects with students. Hattie's (2009) synthesis of the results of 304 Direct Instruction (DI) studies including more than 42,000 children obtained an effect size of 0.82, larger than any other curriculum or instructional program studied. Stockard and colleagues' 2018 meta-analysis of 328 studies (Stockard et al., 2018) found consistent, statistically significant positive academic achievement outcomes that were greater when students had more exposure to the method, and that showed little decline over time.

To learn more about DI and how to improve the effectiveness of any lesson by incorporating DI principles of instructional design and delivery, see also Heward and Twyman (2021) and the National Institute for Direct Instruction (2017).

Pearson eText
Video Example 5.6
"They're reading."

In addition to basic decoding and fluency skills, children with learning disabilities also need reading comprehension instruction. Evidence-based practices for teaching reading comprehension include answering questions, using self-questioning to monitor comprehension, completing graphic organizers, examining text structure, and summarizing (e.g., Alber-Morgan & Joseph, 2013; Gajria & Jitendra, 2016; Rouse-Billman & Alber-Morgan, 2019). Examples of mnemonic learning strategies that utilize several of these practices include TWA (Think before reading, Think while reading, and Think after reading; Johnson et al., 2011); ART (Ask, Read with alertness, Tell; McCallum et al., 2011); and KWL (What I know, What I want to know, What I learned; Cantrell et al., 2000). Self-questioning is another effective strategy in which students monitor their reading comprehension by stopping at the end of each paragraph to ask and answer a question about the content (e.g., Rouse et al., 2014; Rouse-Billman & Alber-Morgan, 2019).

Writing

Writing is a complex skill that requires a synthesis of handwriting (or keyboarding), basic mechanics (i.e., spelling, grammar, punctuation), and clear expression or communication of ideas. As students advance through school, they are increasingly required to produce more writing to demonstrate their learning. Explicit instruction that includes specific directions, modeling, guided practice, and independent practice is effective for teaching writing to students with learning disabilities (e.g., Datchuk, 2017; Walker et al., 2005). An important component for the success of explicit instruction is frequent and specific feedback.

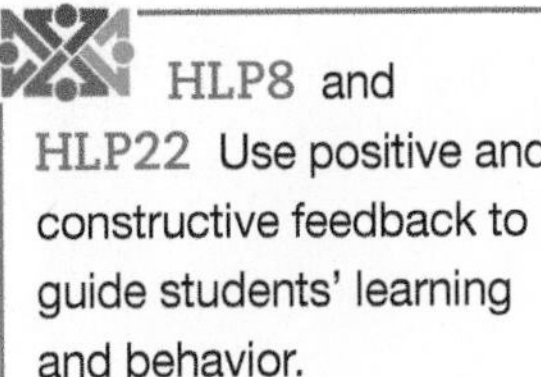

HLP8 and HLP22 Use positive and constructive feedback to guide students' learning and behavior.

Direct instruction writing programs, such as *Expressive Writing* (Engelmann, 2004), *Reasoning and Writing* (Engelmann & Silbert, 2001), and *REWARDS Writing* (Archer et al., 2008), provide explicit instruction on the component skills of writing and the synthesis of those component skills. For example, in *Expressive Writing 1*, students begin forming simple sentences by looking at a picture and writing what the picture shows. After advancing through all of the lessons, students are able to write paragraphs, punctuate sentences correctly, and stay on topic. *Expressive Writing 2* is designed for students who can write a paragraph but struggle with clarity, variation of sentence types, and correct punctuation.

In addition to explicit instruction, learning strategies have also produced successful outcomes for students' written expression. In their meta-analysis of writing interventions for students with learning disabilities, Gillespie and Graham (2014) found strategy instruction to be the most effective for teaching complex writing skills such as planning, organizing, and drafting. Teachers can use self-regulated strategy development to teach mnemonic writing strategies to students with learning disabilities (see *Transition: Next Year Is Now,* "Learning Strategies for Transitioning to College"). Mnemonic learning strategies have been developed and researched for a variety of composition types. For example, POW-TREE is a strategy for persuasive writing and stands for Pick my idea, Organize my thoughts/notes, Write and say more–Topic sentence (tell what you believe), Reasons (3 or more), Ending (wrap it up), Examine (have I included all the parts?) (Sandmel et al., 2009). C-SPACE is a strategy for narrative writing and stands for Character, Setting, Problem, Action, Conclusion, and Emotion (Graham & Harris, 1992).

Math

Based on decades of research, Jayanthi et al. (2008) made the following recommendations for teaching mathematics to students with learning disabilities: Use explicit instruction, teach learning strategies for problem solving, provide many teaching examples, have students verbally state the steps as they solve problems and make visual representations (i.e., draw pictures), provide continuous assessment to inform instructional decisions, and use peer-mediated instruction (e.g., classwide peer tutoring, cooperative learning groups).

Explicit instruction of math concepts includes clear modeling of problem solving using thinking aloud to explain each step, providing multiple examples, and providing immediate feedback (Jayanthi et al., 2008). Examples of commercial DI math programs using explicit instruction include Direct Instruction Mathematics (Stein et al., 2018), Corrective Mathematics (McGraw-Hill, 2004), and Connecting Math Concepts (McGraw-Hill, 2013).

Many studies have also shown the benefit of using a **concrete-representational-abstract sequence** when introducing new concepts. When using explicit instruction, math lessons that progress in a concrete-representational-abstract sequence are beneficial for elementary and secondary students with learning disabilities (Bouck et al., 2018; Milton et al., 2019). At the concrete stage, students use manipulatives such as place value blocks, Unifix cubes®, and counters. For example, manipulating place value blocks helps students understand what happens when solving problems requiring regrouping. Once students demonstrate competence at the concrete stage, they move to the representational stage when they examine or draw pictures of objects representing the math problems. In the abstract stage, the students use only numbers to solve problems.

As with reading and writing, learning strategies are also effective for improving math performance of students with learning disabilities. Mnemonic learning strategies have been developed for a range of different computation and application skills (Boon et al., 2019). For example, a strategy for solving addition problems with regrouping is RENAME (Miller & Kaffar, 2011), which stands for Read the problem, Examine the ones column (10 or more, go next door), Note ones in the ones column, Address the tens column (10 or more, go next door), Mark tens in the tens column, and Examine and note hundreds; exit with a quick check. A strategy for solving story problems is RIDE (Mercer et al., 2011), which stands for Read the problem correctly, Identify the relevant information, Determine the operation and unit for expressing the answer, and Enter the correct numbers. Featured Teacher Amaris Johnson uses schema-based instruction (Cook et al., 2019) to teach her students a learning strategy for solving word problems. "This method is especially effective because it allows my students to verbalize their thinking so I can determine if they truly understand the number story."

Content Areas

When lectures and assigned readings become the primary means for accessing academic content in middle and high school, the classroom becomes an especially frustrating and difficult place for students with learning disabilities. The teacher talks and assigns a portion of a high-vocabulary, content-dense textbook, and students are responsible for obtaining, remembering, and using the information later (usually on a quiz or exam). A combination of poor reading, listening, note-taking, and study skills, compounded by a limited store of background knowledge, makes obtaining needed information from reading, lectures, and homework assignments a daunting task for students with learning disabilities.

Teachers can use content enhancements to assist students with these challenges and increase success in content areas such as science and social studies. ***Content enhancement*** is a general term for a wide range of techniques teachers use to enhance the organization and delivery of curriculum content so that students can better access, interact with, comprehend, and retain that information (Bulgren et al., 2007). Content enhancements explicitly show how content area concepts and ideas are related. Providing advance organizers, visual displays, and reading materials with key concepts highlighted are simple ways of enhancing content.

HLP13 Adapt curriculum tasks and materials for specific learning goals.

Teaching students to use mnemonic devices, such as HOMES (Huron, Ontario, Michigan, Erie, Superior), to remember academic content is an effective content enhancement (Lubin & Polloway, 2016). Content enhancements often helpful to students with learning disabilities include graphic organizers, guided notes, and note-taking strategies.

Graphic Organizers. *Graphic organizers* are visual-spatial arrangements of information containing words or concepts connected graphically that help students see meaningful hierarchical, comparative, and sequential relationships (Ciullo et al., 2015; Ellis & Howard, 2007; Ives, 2007). Graphic organizers can be used for vocabulary instruction, content area concepts, and reading comprehension. For example, story maps (i.e., visual representations of the elements of a narrative story) can help students with learning disabilities improve their comprehension (Alves et al., 2015; Boon et al., 2015).

Computer-based graphic organizers are another good option for students with learning disabilities. Ciullo and Reutebuch (2013) found computer-based graphic organizers to be effective for students with learning disabilities on their social studies and written expression outcomes but found that graphic organizers would likely not be as effective in the absence of explicit instruction and guided practice. Good examples of graphic organizers can be found online. Teacher Vision, Learning Point Associates, the North Central Regional Education Laboratory (NCREL), Education Oasis, and Enchanted Learning all have grade-level and discipline-specific graphic organizers for classroom use. Visual displays can be effective for teaching abstract concepts to students with disabilities. For example, the visual maps in Figure 5.9 help students see how the "big idea" of convection operates in similar fashion across a number of applications.

Guided Notes. **Guided notes** are teacher-prepared handouts that provide an outline of the lecture content, which students complete during class by writing in key facts, concepts, or relationships (Konrad et al., 2011). A variation of guided lecture notes, *structured reading worksheets*, are teacher-prepared supplements that help students study and comprehend assigned reading from content-rich textbooks by prompting them to find and write key points (Alber et al., 2002). Numerous studies have found that students at all achievement levels in elementary through postsecondary classrooms perform better on tests of content retention when they used guided notes (e.g., Jimenez et al., 2014; Konrad et al., 2009; Kourea et al., 2019). See *Teaching & Learning*, "Guided Notes: Helping All Students Succeed in the General Education Curriculum."

Note-Taking Strategies. Many secondary teachers consider the ability to take good notes a key skill for success in high school and beyond. Because content classes at the middle and secondary levels tend to be delivered in traditional lecture format, an emphasis on note taking qualifies as a "signature practice" for engaging and supporting all students in challenging content learning (Morocco et al., 2006). Good note takers focus on important content, organize the information, and create a written product from which to study for tests.

The listening; language; working memory; and, in some cases, motor skill deficits of many students with learning disabilities make it difficult for them to identify what is important during a lecture and write it down correctly and quickly enough to keep up. While trying to choose and write one point in a notebook, the student with learning disabilities

FIGURE 5.9 Simple Visual Maps Showing How the "Big Idea" of Convection Applies Across Applications

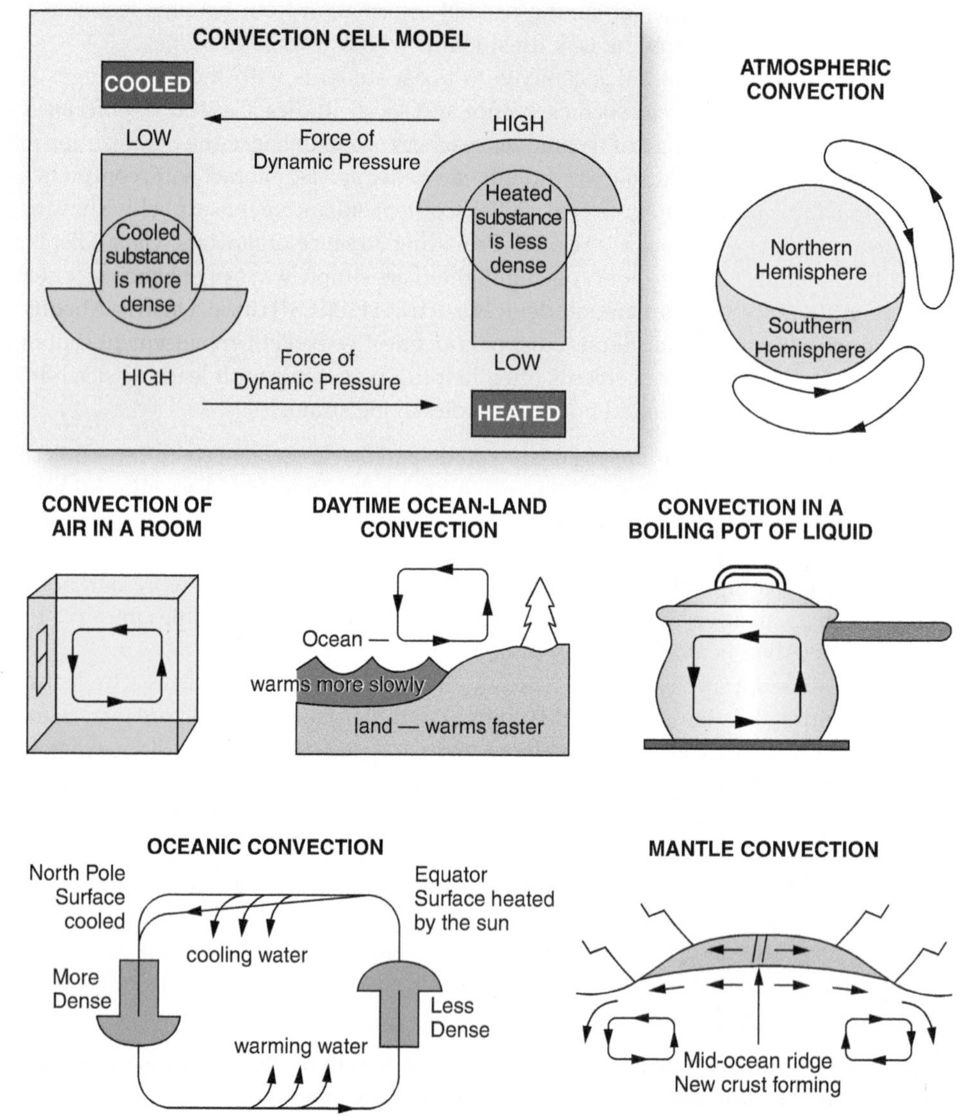

Source: From Grossen, B., Carnine, D. W., Romance, N. R., & Vitale, M. R. (2011). Effective strategies for teaching science. In M. D. Coyne, E. J. Kame'enui, & D. W. Carnine (Eds.), *Effective teaching strategies that accommodate diverse learners* (4th ed., p. 189). © 2011. Reproduced by permission of Pearson Education, Inc., Upper Saddle River, NJ.

might miss the next two points. One study found that middle school students with learning disabilities accurately recorded only 13% of science lecture content (Boyle, 2010).

Strategic note taking involves specially designed note paper containing cues such as: "What do you already know about this topic?" or "List new vocabulary and terms" that help students organize information and combine new knowledge with prior knowledge. In one study, middle school students who were trained to use strategic note taking performed better than students who used conventional note taking on measures of note-taking completeness and accuracy, immediate recall, and comprehension of the lecture content (Boyle, 2013).

Nonacademic Needs

The defining characteristic of students with learning disabilities is low academic achievement despite average or above-average intelligence, and the educational approaches in this chapter focus on teaching academic skills. However, many students with learning disabilities also have social skills deficits, behavior problems, and attention difficulties. When developing

IEPs, teams must also address these nonacademic needs. See Chapter 6 for educational approaches for teaching social skills and addressing challenging behavior, and see Chapter 11 for educational approaches related to difficulties with attention and hyperactivity.

Placement Options

Learning Outcome 5.5 Compare and contrast typical placements and supports for students with learning disabilities.

Regular Classroom

IDEA requires that students with disabilities be educated with students without disabilities, have access to the core curriculum to the maximum extent possible, and be removed from the general education classroom only to the extent their disability necessitates. During the 2018–2019 school year, 72% of students with learning disabilities were educated in regular classrooms for at least 80% of the school day (U.S. Department of Education, 2020a).

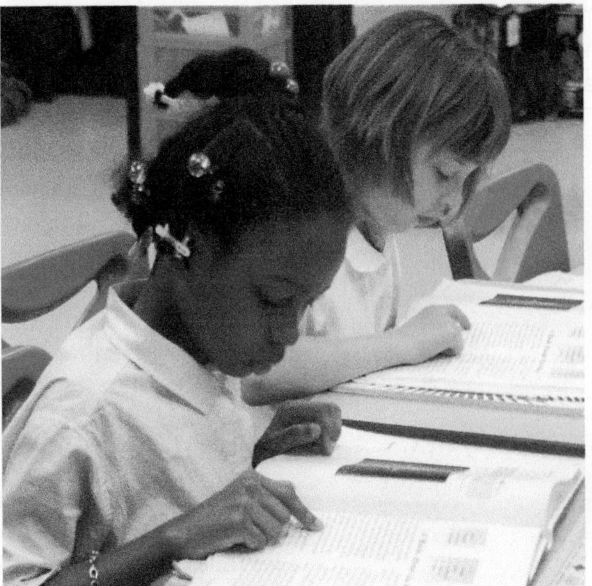
Source: Katelyn Metzger/Great Western Academy/Pearson Allyn and Bacon/Merrill Education

The success of students with learning disabilities in the regular classroom requires evidence-based curriculum and instruction.

Research on the academic achievement of students with learning disabilities in inclusive classrooms is mixed. Some studies have reported better learning outcomes for students with learning disabilities in regular classrooms than in pull-out programs (e.g., Rea et al., 2002; Rojewski et al., 2015; Tremblay, 2013). For example, Tremblay (2013) compared outcomes of 158 students with learning disabilities attending either an inclusion with co-teaching classroom or a solo teacher special education classroom. The students in the inclusive classrooms outperformed the students in the special education classrooms in reading, writing, and attendance. In another study, Rojewski et al. (2015) found that students with LD who spent more than 80% of the school day in an inclusive general education classroom were twice as likely to enroll in postsecondary education compared to students who spent less time in inclusive classrooms.

Other studies have reported disappointing achievement results for students with learning disabilities in the general education classroom (e.g., Schumm et al., 2000); concerns about inadequate instruction (e.g., Chard & Kame'enui, 2000); teachers' limited understanding of the learning needs of students with LD (DeSimone & Parmar, 2006); and poor acceptance by teachers, peers, or both (e.g., Cook, 2001). Advocates of full inclusion for students with learning disabilities contend that pull-out services such as resource rooms and special class placement stigmatize students, damage their self-concept, and limit opportunities to develop relationships with typical peers (e.g., Hornby, 2015).

HLP13 Adapt curriculum tasks and materials for specific learning goals.

Teachers can help students with learning disabilities succeed in inclusive classrooms by using whole-class evidence-based practices that increase opportunities for active student responding accompanied by frequent and specific feedback (e.g., response cards, choral responding, cooperative learning groups). Teachers can supplement whole-class activities by adapting the instructional materials and curriculum based on individual learning needs. Material and task adaptations may include the following: simplifying task directions, altering the amount of material assigned, altering the difficulty level of the material, and highlighting relevant information (Alber-Morgan et al., 2019).

In some school districts, a consultant teacher may provide support to general education classroom teachers and other staff members who work directly with students with learning disabilities. The consultant teacher helps the general education teacher select assessment devices, curriculum materials, and instructional activities. The consultant may even demonstrate teaching methods or behavior management strategies. An advantage of this model is that the consultant teacher works with several teachers and thus indirectly serves many children. A drawback is that most consultant teachers have little direct contact with students.

Resource Room

A resource room is a specially staffed and equipped classroom where students with learning disabilities come for one or several periods during the school day to receive individualized instruction. A resource room teacher serves an average of 20 students with disabilities, although the number of students served at one time is generally fewer than 10 or 12. During the 2018–2019 school year, 21% of students with learning disabilities attended a resource room 20% to 60% of the school day (U.S. Department of Education, 2020a). Resource room teachers are certified special educators whose primary role is providing intensive, individualized instruction on academic skills, social skills, and learning strategies.

HLP1 Collaborate with professionals to increase student success.

Students typically attend regular classrooms for most of the school day and come to the resource room for one or more periods of specialized instruction in skill areas in which they need the most support. In addition to teaching students with learning disabilities, the resource teacher also works closely with each student's general education teacher(s) to suggest and help plan each student's program in the general education classroom.

Some advantages of the resource room model are (a) students do not lose their identity with their general education class peer group; (b) students can receive the intensive, individualized instruction they need every day; and (c) flexible scheduling allows the resource room to serve a fairly large number of students. Some disadvantages of resource rooms are they (a) require students to spend time traveling between classrooms, (b) may result in inconsistent instructional approaches between settings, and (c) can make it difficult to determine whether and how students should be held accountable for what they missed while out of the general education classroom.

Separate Classroom

During the 2018–2019 school year, 4.7% of students with learning disabilities attended a separate classroom more than 60% of the school day (U.S. Department of Education, 2020a). In a separate classroom, a special education teacher is responsible for all educational programming for 8 to 12 students with learning disabilities. The academic achievement deficiencies of some children with learning disabilities are so severe that they need full-time placement in a setting with a specially trained teacher. In addition, poor work habits and inappropriate social behaviors make some students with learning disabilities candidates for the separate classroom, where distractions can be minimized and individual attention emphasized. As noted in Chapter 2, IEP teams are not to view a student's placement in a separate classroom (or any other educational setting) as permanent. A student should be placed in a separate classroom only after legitimate and supported attempts to serve her effectively in less restrictive environments have proven unsuccessful.

ADVICE FROM THE FEATURED TEACHER by Amaris Johnson

Prioritize Student Success

Source: Amaris Johnson

- ***Keep students priority number one.*** Teaching is much more than just delivering math, reading, and science lessons. You must also be a counselor, mentor, and advocate. Even when overwhelmed by deadlines and expectations, keep your students' success at the forefront of everything you do.
- ***Establish clear routines.*** Students need teachers who are consistent with structure, routines, and consequences. What are the first things the students will see, hear, and do when they enter your classroom? How will they hang their backpacks, where will they place the papers, how

should they get your attention? Clear routines allow students the security of knowing what to expect and allow you to accomplish other tasks as your students gain independence.

- ***Help students take ownership of their goals.*** Although student progress is the teacher's responsibility, you will achieve success more efficiently by putting the student in the driver's seat. Share progress monitoring data with students to help them develop self-awareness of their strengths and needs, set ambitious goals, and self-monitor their progress toward reaching those goals. I find that when students take ownership of their learning, they accomplish their goals and develop a sense of pride.

Communicate Effectively with Families

- ***Listen to families.*** When working with families from culturally and linguistically diverse backgrounds, it is especially important to listen to their concerns. At times I believe I know what is best for the child. However, after learning about a family's experiences and values, I can merge my professional expertise with the family's perspectives, all for the benefit of the child.
- ***Ask open-ended questions.*** Parents need to know you are working with their child's best interest at heart and the only way to truly do that is gather information about their concerns. Ask open-ended questions and offer advice only when you fully understand the problem.
- ***Illustrate learning goals with real-world examples.*** When discussing students' goals, use real-world scenarios. For example, when explaining why learning place value is important, I relate it to using money when shopping. Reminding parents how the decimal separates dollars (ones, tens, hundreds) from cents (hundredths) helps them understand how socially relevant a place value goal can be for their child.
- ***Use a variety of formats to communicate with parents.*** When communicating with parents, I make phone calls, use FaceTime, send text messages and emails, and make home visits. I also use ClassDojo (www.classdojo.com) to keep parents informed of their child's behavior and performance as well as share photos and videos of classroom activities.

Be a Team Player

- ***Discuss preferences and non-negotiables.*** Before the school year starts, meet with your co-teacher to get on the same page. Be frank about your personal preferences and non-negotiables in the classroom. Consider ways to combine your ideas in a mutually beneficial way that will ultimately provide the most benefit to your students.
- ***Listen to each other.*** Both co-teachers should feel as if they have an equal voice in classroom decisions, so it is imperative to actively listen to each other and express yourselves in a respectful manner. Effectively communicating both preferences and concerns with your co-teacher can result in the epitome of teamwork.
- ***Observe successful team teachers.*** An activity that can generate productive discussion with your co-teacher is observing successful co-teachers in action, either in person or by using online resources. This will provide you and your teaching partner with opportunities to see aspects of co-teaching that you may not have considered and to discuss their potential relevance to and/or feasibility in your own classroom.

Key Terms and Concepts

alphabetic principle
comorbidity
concrete-representational-abstract sequence
criterion-referenced tests
curriculum-based measurement (CBM)
dual discrepancy criterion
dyslexia
formative assessment
guided notes
phonemic awareness
phonological awareness
precision teaching
response to intervention (RTI)
specific learning disability
summative assessment

Summary

Definitions

- *Specific learning disability* is defined in IDEA as a disorder in one or more of the basic psychological processes involved in understanding or in using language, spoken or written, which may manifest in an imperfect ability to listen, think, speak, read, write, spell, or perform mathematical calculations and is not caused by a sensory, motor, or intellectual disability; an emotional disturbance; or environmental or economic disadvantage.
- In operationalizing this definition, most states require three criteria: (a) a severe discrepancy exists between the student's intellectual ability and academic achievement, (b) the student's difficulties are not the result of another known condition that can cause learning problems, and (c) the student needs special education services to succeed in school.

Characteristics

- Difficulty reading is the most common characteristic of students with learning disabilities. It is estimated that 90% of all children identified with learning disabilities are referred for special education services because of reading problems.
- Many students with learning disabilities show one or more of the following characteristics: written language deficits, math underachievement, poor social skills, attention deficits and hyperactivity, challenging behavior, and low self-esteem or self-efficacy.
- The fundamental, defining characteristic of students with learning disabilities is specific and significant achievement deficits in the presence of adequate overall intelligence.
- In addition to their academic and social skills deficits, students with learning disabilities possess positive attributes and interests that teachers should identify and try to strengthen.

Prevalence

- Learning disabilities make up the largest disability category in special education. Students with learning disabilities represent 34% of all school-age students receiving special education.
- About three times as many boys as girls are identified as having learning disabilities.
- Some educators believe the high prevalence of learning disabilities results from the overidentification and misdiagnosis of low-achieving students.

Causes

- Although the actual cause of a specific learning disability is seldom known, suspected causes include brain damage, heredity, and environmental factors.
- Specific regions of the brains of some individuals with reading and language disabilities show abnormal activation patterns during phonological processing tasks.
- Genetics may account for some family links with dyslexia. Research has located possible chromosomal loci for the genetic transmission of phonological deficits that may predispose a child to reading problems later.
- Environmental factors—particularly impoverished living conditions early in a child's life and poor instruction—are likely contributors to the achievement deficits of many children with learning disabilities.

Identification and Assessment

- Four forms of assessment are frequently used with students with learning disabilities:
  - Norm-referenced tests compare a child's score with the scores of age mates who have taken the same test.
  - Criterion-referenced tests, which compare a child's score with a predetermined mastery level, are useful in identifying specific skills the child has learned as well as skills that require instruction.
  - Curriculum-based measurement (CBM) is a formative assessment method that measures a student's progress in the actual curriculum in which she is participating.
  - Direct and daily measurement involves assessing a student's performance on a specific skill each time it is taught.
- Response to intervention (RTI) assesses a low-achieving student's response to increasingly intensive, scientifically validated instruction to determine whether the student's learning difficulties are the result of poor or insufficient instruction or of a disability for which special education is needed. A child's failure to progress in response to scientifically validated instruction eliminates instructional quality as a viable explanation for poor academic growth and suggests evidence of a disability. Children who respond favorably to RTI's increasingly intensive instruction benefit from the preventive aspect of the approach.

Educational Approaches

- Students with learning disabilities require intensive and frequent individualized interventions characterized by small group or one-to-one instruction, explicit instruction focused on critical academic tool skills, high rates of active student engagement with motivating materials and activities, frequent practice, and systematic feedback.
- Research does not support matching instruction to students' learning styles and using cognitively focused instruction (e.g., "brain gym" exercises, attention training).

- Strategy instruction teaches students learning strategies so they can guide themselves successfully through specific tasks or general problems.
- Evidence-based practices for teaching reading comprehension include answering questions, using self-questioning to monitor comprehension, completing graphic organizers, examining text structure, and summarizing.
- Self-regulated strategy development is an effective intervention for teaching writing skills such as planning, organizing, and drafting to students with learning disabilities.
- Elementary and secondary students with learning disabilities benefit from math instruction that progresses in a concrete-representational-abstract sequence.
- Content enhancements, such as graphic organizers and visual displays, guided notes, and note-taking strategies, modify the organization and delivery of curriculum content so that students can better access, interact with, comprehend, and retain the information.

Placement Options

- About two thirds of students with learning disabilities are educated in regular classrooms.
- In some schools, a consultant teacher helps regular classroom teachers work with children with learning disabilities.
- In the resource room, a special educator provides intensive, individualized instruction to students for one or more periods in the academic or social skill areas in which they need the most help.
- Many researchers and advocates for students with learning disabilities do not support full inclusion because it would eliminate the continuum of service delivery options.
- Where a student is taught is not as important as the quality of instruction that the student receives.

Chapter 6

Emotional or Behavioral Disorders

Source: ChameleonsEye/Shutterstock

Learning Outcomes

After reading this chapter and completing the embedded activities, you should be able to

6.1 Compare and contrast definitions of emotional disturbance.

6.2 Describe characteristics and causes of emotional or behavioral disorders.

6.3 Identify the prevalence of emotional disturbance and describe assessments used to identify students with emotional or behavioral disorders.

6.4 Name and give examples of scientifically supported strategies for educating students with emotional or behavioral disorders.

6.5 Compare and contrast typical placements and supports for students with emotional or behavioral disorders.

Featured Teacher

Michelle Nielson-Pugmire

Vae View Elementary, Davis County School District, Farmington, UT

Source: Eastman Adams Photography

I am lucky enough to wake up every day and do what I love. I teach in one of two self-contained special education classrooms located in a Title 1 elementary school. I teach all academic core standards as well as bridge academic and social skills gaps. All my students receive services for one or more of the following exceptional needs: emotional or behavioral disorders, learning disabilities, autism, and other health impairments. We address a variety of challenging behaviors in my class: oppositional defiance, anger issues, and attention-seeking or avoidance behaviors. My students' academic skill levels range from kindergarten to seventh grade. Some students remain in my class throughout the day; others spend part of each school day in regular classrooms with same-age peers. My overriding goal is for all my students to achieve success in regular education settings.

Our class motto is: "I am free to make choices, but I am not free from the consequences of the choices I make." Both positive and negative behaviors are recorded throughout the day, and students can earn or lose privileges based on their behavior. I have high behavior and academic expectations for my students.

My classroom uses a token economy in which students earn class money for appropriate behavior, for generalizing previously taught skills, and for meeting personal goals (behavioral and academic). Students use their class money to purchase rewards from our class store such as skip homework passes, skip assignment passes, sitting in the teacher's chair, iPad time, teaching the class for 10 minutes, pulling a prank (teacher approved), treasure chest (one edible and one non-edible), and extra recess. I change the rewards frequently based on students' interests. Sometimes we hold a surprise auction, spin for a mystery motivator, or hold a dice roll.

To help with classroom management and parent communication, I use a daily planner. At the end of each day, students record in their daily planners what academic subjects they worked on, assigned homework, and an overall rating of their daily behavior. After each student discusses his or her self-behavior ratings with me, we agree on accuracy, and I add any notes for parents and initial the planner. Students take their planners home, obtain a parent's signature, and return them the next day. Parents can write questions, concerns, and suggestions for me.

I love how out of the box my students are, and I embrace the daily challenge of figuring out how they think. My class is extremely diverse, and we accept one another for our differences. My students know and understand they are in my class for a reason, and we all have different strengths and weaknesses. It is a safe place where failures are accepted (as we learn from our failures), it is OK to be ourselves, make mistakes, use our strengths to help others, and work on our weaknesses. I have high expectations which the students in my class meet and often exceed. My students are amazing and I learn as much from them as they do me.

Education, Teaching Credentials, and Experience

- *B.S., elementary and special education, Weber State University, 2009*
- *Utah Level 2 Professional Educator License in elementary grades 1–8 and in special education mild/moderate disabilities K–12*
- *9 years of teaching exceptional needs students with a focus on students with emotional and behavioral disorders*
- *5 years as a professional learning community coach for 3rd–6th SPED learning centers*
- *Schoolwide Social Skills Instructor*
- *DSD Teacher Mentor Leader for new SPED Teachers*

Content Extension 6.1

A daily planner completed by Michelle's students.

CHILDHOOD SHOULD BE A HAPPY TIME: a time to play, make friends, and learn—and for most children, it is. But some children's lives are in constant turmoil. Some children strike out at those around them, sometimes with disastrous consequences. Others are so withdrawn they seem to be in their own worlds. In either case, playing with others, making friends, and learning all the things a child must learn are extremely difficult for these children. These are children with emotional or behavioral disorders (EBD).

Many children with emotional or behavioral disorders are disliked by their classmates and teachers; even their siblings and parents may reject them. A child with behavioral disorders may be difficult to be around, and attempts to befriend him (most are boys) often lead to rejection, verbal abuse, or even physical attack. Although most children with emotional or behavioral disorders are of sound mind and body, their noxious or withdrawn behavior is as serious an impediment to their learning as are the intellectual, sensory, and physical disabilities that challenge other children.

Definitions

Learning Outcome 6.1 Compare and contrast definitions of emotional disturbance.

A widely accepted definition of emotional or behavioral disorders is lacking for numerous reasons. First, disordered behavior is a social construct; no clear agreement exists about what constitutes good mental health. All children behave inappropriately at times. How often, with how much intensity, and for how long must students exhibit challenging behavior before they are considered to have a behavior disability? Second, different theories of emotional disturbance use concepts and terminology that do little to promote consistency across definitions. Third, behavioral expectations and norms vary considerably across ethnic and cultural groups. Finally, emotional or behavioral disorders sometimes occur in conjunction with other disabilities, making it difficult to determine whether one condition is an outcome or the cause of the other.

Of the many proposed definitions of emotional or behavioral disorders, the definition in the Individuals with Disabilities Education Act (IDEA) and one proposed by a coalition of professional associations concerned with children with challenging behavior have had the most influence in special education.

Federal Definition

Emotional disturbance is one of the IDEA disability categories under which a child is eligible to receive special education services. IDEA defines **emotional disturbance** as

i. [a] condition exhibiting one or more of the following characteristics over a long period of time and to a marked degree that adversely affects educational performance:

   A. An inability to learn that cannot be explained by intellectual, sensory, and health factors;
   B. An inability to build or maintain satisfactory interpersonal relationships with peers and teachers;
   C. Inappropriate types of behavior or feelings under normal circumstances;
   D. A general pervasive mood of unhappiness or depression; or
   E. A tendency to develop physical symptoms or fears associated with personal or school problems.

ii. Emotional disturbance includes schizophrenia. The term does not apply to children who are socially maladjusted, unless it is determined that they have an emotional disturbance under paragraph (i) of this section. (PL 108-446, 20 *CFR* §300.8[c][4])

At first glance, this definition may seem straightforward enough. It identifies three conditions that must be met: *chronicity* ("over a long period of time"), *severity* ("to a marked degree"), and *difficulty in school* ("adversely affects educational performance"); and it lists five types of problems that qualify. But in fact, the federal definition is extremely vague. What do terms such as *satisfactory* and *inappropriate* really mean? Differing degrees of teacher tolerance for student behavior (An et al., 2019; Maag, 2016), differences between teachers' and parents' expectations for student behavior (Olson et al., 2018), and the fact that expectations for behavior vary across cultures (Walker & Gresham, 2014) make the referral and identification of students with emotional or behavioral disorders a highly subjective process.

How does one determine which challenging behaviors indicate "social maladjustment," and which indicate true "emotional disturbance"? Many children experiencing significant difficulties in school because of their behavior are ineligible for special education under IDEA because their problems are considered to be "merely" conduct disorders or discipline problems (Sadeh & Sullivan, 2017). The federal definition was derived from a single study conducted by Eli Bower (1960) in the Los Angeles County schools more than 60 years ago. Bower never intended to make a distinction between emotional disturbance and social maladjustment. Indeed, he stated that the five components of the definition (see "A–E" above) were, in fact, meant to be indicators of social maladjustment (Bower, 1982).

It is difficult to imagine a child who is sufficiently socially maladjusted to have received that label but who does not display one or more of the five characteristics included in the federal definition. The IDEA definition seemingly excludes children on the very basis for which they are included. The definition's illogical criterion for ineligibility, the dated and arbitrary list of the five characteristics, and the subjective wording that enables school districts not to serve many children with behavior challenges have produced strongly voiced criticism (Forness & Kavale, 2000; O'Neill, 2006).

CCBD Definition

In response to the problems with the federal definition, the Council for Children with Behavioral Disorders (CCBD, 2000) drafted a new definition using the term *emotional or behavioral disorder*. The CCBD definition was later adopted by the National Mental Health and Special Education Coalition (a group of 30 education, mental health, and child advocacy organizations) and subsequently submitted to the U.S. Congress as a proposed replacement for the IDEA definition. The CCBD definition of **emotional or behavioral disorder** reads as follows:

> 1. The term "emotional or behavioral disorder" means a disability that is characterized by emotional or behavioral responses in school programs so different from appropriate age, cultural, or ethnic norms that the responses adversely affect educational performance, including academic, social, vocational, or personal skills; more than a temporary, expected response to stressful events in the environment; consistently exhibited in two different settings, at least one of which is school-related; and unresponsive to direct intervention in general education, or the condition of the child is such that general education interventions would be insufficient.
> 2. The term includes such a disability that coexists with other disabilities.
> 3. The term includes a schizophrenic disorder, affective disorder, anxiety disorder, or other sustained disorder of conduct or adjustment, affecting a child if the disorder affects educational performance as described in paragraph (1). (p. 6)

> Advantages of this definition, according to the CCBD (2000), are that it clarifies the educational dimensions of the disability; focuses on the child's behavior in school settings; places behavior in the context of appropriate age, ethnic, and cultural norms; and increases the possibility of early identification and intervention. Perhaps most important, the revised terminology and definition do not require "meaningless distinctions between social and emotional maladjustment, distinctions that often waste diagnostic resources when it is already clear that serious problems exist" (p. 7).

Characteristics

Learning Outcome 6.2 Describe characteristics and causes of emotional or behavioral disorders.

Children with emotional or behavioral disorders are characterized primarily by behavior that falls significantly beyond cultural and age group norms on either of two dimensions: externalizing and internalizing. Either pattern of abnormal behavior adversely affects academic achievement and social relationships.

Externalizing Behaviors

The most common behavior pattern of children with emotional or behavioral disorders consists of externalizing behaviors. In the classroom, children with **externalizing behaviors** frequently get out of their seats; yell, talk out, and curse; disturb peers; hit or fight; ignore

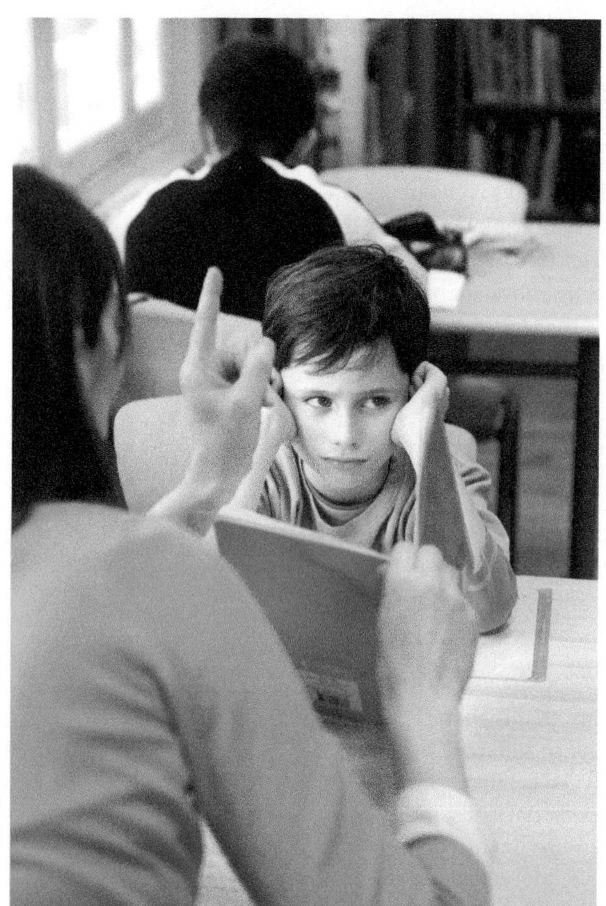
Source: Burger/Phanie/Alamy Stock Photo

Noncompliance is a common externalizing behavior.

the teacher; complain and argue excessively; steal; lie; destroy property; have temper tantrums, and are noncompliant (Walker, 1997; Walker & Gresham, 2014).

Rhode et al. (2020) describe noncompliance as the "kingpin" behavior around which other behavioral excesses revolve, defined as "not following a direction within a reasonable amount of time. Most of a Tough Kid's arguing, tantrums, fighting, or rule breaking is secondary to avoiding requests or required tasks" (p. 10). Antisocial, noncompliant children "can make our teaching lives miserable and single-handedly disrupt a classroom" (Rhode et al., 2020, p. 9).

All children sometimes cry, disrupt others, and refuse to comply with requests of parents and teachers. Children with emotional or behavioral disorders do so with disturbing frequency, and their antisocial behavior often occurs with little or no apparent provocation. Aggression takes many forms—verbal abuse toward adults and other children, destructiveness and vandalism, and physical attacks on others. These children seem to be in continuous conflict with those around them. It is no wonder that children with emotional or behavioral disorders find it difficult to establish and maintain friendships.

Many believe that most children who exhibit deviant behavioral patterns will grow out of them with time and become normally functioning adults. Although this optimistic outcome may hold true for some children who exhibit problems such as withdrawal, fears, and speech impairments (Rutter, 1976), research indicates that it is not so for children who display consistent patterns of aggressive, coercive, antisocial, or delinquent behavior (e.g., Espelage et al., 2018; McCoy et al., 2018). The best single predictor of delinquency in adolescence is a pattern of antisocial behavior at a young age. Children who enter adolescence with a history of aggressive behavior stand a very good chance of dropping out of school, being arrested, abusing drugs and alcohol, and having marginalized adult lives (Mitchell et al., 2019).

Internalizing Behaviors

Some children with emotional or behavioral disorders are anything but aggressive. Their challenge is not engaging in enough social interaction. They are said to exhibit **internalizing behaviors**. Although children who consistently act immature and withdrawn do not present the threat to others that antisocial children do, their behavior is a serious impediment to their development. These children seldom play with others their own age. They lack the social skills needed to make friends and have fun, and they often retreat into daydreams and fantasies. Some are extremely fearful of certain things without reason (i.e., phobia), frequently complain of being sick or hurt, and go into deep bouts of depression (Dart et al., 2019). Obviously, such behavior limits a child's chances to take part in, learn from, and enjoy typical school and leisure activities. Table 6.1 describes the most common types of anxiety disorders and mood disorders seen in school-age children.

Because children who exhibit the internalizing behaviors may be less disturbing to classroom teachers than those who exhibit externalizing behaviors, they are in danger of not being identified (Splett et al., 2019). Happily, the outlook is fairly good for children with mild or moderate degrees of withdrawn and immature behavior who are fortunate enough to have competent teachers and other school professionals responsible for their development. Carefully targeting social and self-determination skills and systematically arranging opportunities for and reinforcing those behaviors often prove successful (e.g., Zirkus & Morgan, 2020).

It is a grave mistake, however, to believe that children with emotional disorders characterized by internalizing behaviors have only mild and temporary problems. The severe anxiety and mood disorders some children experience cause pervasive impairments to their

TABLE 6.1 Types of anxiety, mood, and other emotional disorders in children

CONDITION	CHARACTERISTICS AND SYMPTOMS	REMARKS
Anxiety Disorders	Maladaptive emotional state or behaviors caused by excessive and often irrational fears and worries.	
Generalized anxiety disorder	Excessive, unrealistic worries, fears, and tension that lasts 6 months or more; in addition to chronic anxiety, symptoms include restlessness, fatigue, difficulty concentrating, muscular aches, insomnia, nausea, excessive heart rate, dizziness, and irritability.	Excessive worrying interferes with normal activities. Children tend to be very hard on themselves, striving for perfection, sometimes redoing tasks repeatedly; they may also seek constant approval or reassurance from others. Usually affects children between the ages of 6 and 11 years.
Phobias	Intense fear of a specific object or situation (e.g., snakes, dogs, or heights); level of fear is inappropriate to the situation and is recognized by the person as being irrational; can lead to the avoidance of common, everyday situations.	Most phobias can be treated successfully with behavior therapy techniques such as systematic desensitization (gradual and repeated exposure to feared object or situation while relaxing) and self-monitoring.
Obsessive/ compulsive disorder (OCD)	Persistent, recurring thoughts (obsessions) that reflect exaggerated anxiety or fears; typical obsessions include worry about being contaminated, behaving improperly, or acting violently. The obsessions may lead an individual to perform a ritual or routine (compulsions)—such as washing hands, repeating phrases, or hoarding—to relieve the anxiety caused by the obsession.	OCD most often begins in adolescence or early adulthood. Most individuals recognize their obsessions are irrational and that the compulsions are excessive or unreasonable. Behavioral therapy is effective in treating most cases of OCD; medications are often effective.
Anorexia nervosa	Refusal to maintain body weight at or above a minimally normal weight for age and height. Obsessive concern with body weight or shape. Intense anxiety about gaining weight or becoming fat, even though severely underweight. Two subtypes: restricting food intake by starving oneself down to an abnormal weight and binge eating or purging.	Anorexia and bulimia (see below) are primarily disorders of females, particularly adolescent girls. Early in the course of anorexia, the person often denies the disorder. Depression, anxiety, compulsive exercise, social withdrawal, obsessive/compulsive symptoms, and substance abuse are often associated with eating disorders.
Bulimia nervosa	Recurrent episodes of (a) binge eating (eating in a discrete period of time an amount of food much larger than most people would eat under similar circumstances while feeling that one cannot stop eating) and (b) inappropriate compensatory behavior to prevent weight gain (e.g., self-induced vomiting, misuse of laxatives or other medications, fasting, excessive exercise).	Preoccupation with weight and shape and excessive self-evaluation are primary symptoms of both anorexia and bulimia. Many patients demonstrate a mixture of both anorexic and bulimic behaviors.
Posttraumatic stress disorder (PTSD)	Prolonged and recurrent emotional reactions after exposure to a traumatic event (e.g., sexual or physical assault, unexpected death of a loved one, natural disaster, witnessing or being a victim of acts of war or terrorism). Symptoms: flashbacks and nightmares of the traumatic event; avoiding places or things related to the trauma; emotional detachment from others; and difficulty sleeping, irritability, or poor concentration.	Individual and group counseling and support activities can be helpful. Teachers can help by providing an environment in which the child with PTSD feels safe, and positive social attention for the child's involvement with normal activities.
Selective mutism	Consistent failure to speak in specific social situations, despite speaking normally in other situations. Not due to lack of knowledge or skill with language or better explained by a communication disorder (e.g., stuttering).	Treatment uses positive approach: reinforcement for approximations of speaking (e.g., nonspeech vocalizations, participation in class activities) and no attention or punishment for not speaking.
Mood Disorders	Impaired functioning caused by episodes of abnormally depressed or elevated emotional state.	
Depression	Pervasive sad mood and sense of hopelessness. Symptoms include social withdrawal; irritability; feelings of guilt or worthlessness; inability to concentrate; loss of interest in normal activities; drastic change in weight, appetite, or sleeping pattern; prolonged crying bouts; recurring thoughts of suicide. Several symptoms must occur over a period of time and not be temporary, reasonable responses to life circumstances (e.g., grief over death of a family member).	Researchers estimate that 15% to 20% of adolescents experience depression at one time or another; girls are twice as likely as boys to be depressed. Depression is often overlooked in children, especially when externalizing behavioral disorders overshadow symptoms. Teachers should be attentive for signs of possible depression and refer students for evaluation.
Bipolar disorder (formerly called *manic-depressive disorder*)	Alternating episodes of depressive and manic states. During manic episodes, person is in an elevated mood of euphoria—a feeling of extraordinary elation, excitement—and exhibits three or more of the following symptoms: excessive egotism; very little sleep needed; incessant talkativeness; rapidly changing thoughts and ideas in uncontrolled order; easily distracted; agitated, "driven" activities; and participation in personally risky activities. The peak age at onset of first symptoms falls between the ages of 15 and 19 years. Five years or more may elapse between the first and second episodes, but time periods between subsequent episodes usually narrow.	Some patients are reluctant to participate in treatment because they find the experience of mania very enjoyable. Patients often recall this experience and minimize or deny entirely the devastating features of full-blown mania or the demoralization of a depressive episode. Regular patterns of daily activities, including sleeping, eating, physical activity, and social or emotional stimulation, may help. Medications are often effective in treating acute episodes, preventing future episodes, and providing stabilizing moods between episodes.

(Continued)

TABLE 6.1 (Continued)

CONDITION	CHARACTERISTICS AND SYMPTOMS	REMARKS
Other Disorders		
Schizophrenia	A severe psychotic disorder characterized by delusions, hallucinations (hearing voices), unfounded fears of persecution, disorganized speech, catatonic behavior (stupor and muscular rigidity), restricted range and intensity of emotional expression (affective flattening), reduced thought and speech productivity, and decreased initiation of goal-directed behavior. Onset typically occurs during adolescence or early adulthood. Most people with schizophrenia alternate between acute psychotic episodes and stable phases with few or no symptoms.	Although no cure exists, most children with schizophrenia benefit from a variety of treatments, including antipsychotic medication, behavioral therapy, and educational interventions such as social skills training. The general goals of treatment are to decrease the frequency, severity, and psychosocial consequences of psychotic episodes and to maximize functioning between episodes.
Tourette syndrome	An inherited neurological disorder characterized by motor and vocal tics (repeated and involuntary movements) such as eye blinking, facial grimacing, throat clearing or sniffing, arm thrusting, kicking, or jumping. About 15% of cases include coprolalia (repeated cursing, obscene language, and ethnic slurs). Symptoms typically appear before age 18 years; males affected three to four times more often than females. Many students also have attention problems, impulsiveness, compulsions, ritualistic behaviors, and learning disabilities.	Tics are experienced as irresistible; the student may seek a secluded spot to release symptoms after delaying them. Tics are more likely during periods of stress and decrease with relaxation or when focusing on an absorbing task. Tolerance and understanding of symptoms are of paramount importance to students; untimed exams (in a private room if vocal tics are a problem) and permission to leave the classroom when tics become overwhelming are often helpful.

Sources: American Psychiatric Association (2013); American Speech-Language-Hearing Association (2020a); Anxiety Disorders Association of America (2020); Kauffman and Landrum (2018); Morris and March (2004); Rutherford, Quinn, and Sathur (2007); Tourette Syndrome Association (2020).

educational performance and can threaten their very existence. Indeed, without identification and effective treatment, the extreme emotional disorders of some children can lead to self-inflicted injury or even death from substance abuse, starvation, or suicidal behavior (Adrian et al., 2019; Spirito & Overholser, 2003).

Academic Achievement

Most students with emotional or behavioral disorders perform 1 or more years below grade level academically. Studies of the academic achievement of students with emotional or behavioral disorders have reported dismal outcomes such as the following (Mitchell et al., 2019; Popham et al., 2019; Siperstein et al., 2011):

- Two thirds do not pass grade-level competency exams.
- They are more likely to receive grades of D and F than are students with other disabilities.
- Achievement deficits tend to worsen as students grow older.
- They have the highest absenteeism rate of any group of students.
- Only one in three leaves high school with a diploma or certificate of completion compared with 50% of all students with disabilities and 76% of all youth in the general population.

The strong relationship between challenging behavior and low academic achievement is reciprocal (Kremer et al., 2016; Savage et al., 2017). Disruptive and defiant behavior interrupts instruction and limits participation in classroom activities and assignment completion. This lack of engagement with the curriculum may result in failure to learn. The problem is further exacerbated by ineffective instruction from teachers who are unaware of or unable to address the student's academic skills deficits. The student becomes frustrated, which leads to misbehavior in the form of avoidance and escape that in turn causes the student to fall yet further behind academically (Feldman et al., 2017; Payne et al., 2007). See *Transition: Next Year Is Now,* "It's Cool to Stay in School," for recommendations about how to help students who are at risk for dropping out of school.

In addition to the challenges to learning caused by their behavioral excesses and deficits, many students with emotional or behavioral disorders have learning disabilities or language delays (or both), which compound their difficulties in mastering academic skills and content (Bichay-Awadalla et al., 2019; Chow & Wehby, 2018). Providing frequent opportunities for active responding can improve the academic achievement of students with emotional or behavioral disorders while decreasing their disruptive behaviors.

Choral responding is one effective and low-cost way to increase student engagement in academic instruction; see *Teaching & Learning,* "Choral Responding: Good Noise in the Classroom" (Chapter 2).

Transition: Next Year Is Now

It's Cool to Stay in School

Of all students receiving special education services, students with EBD are at the highest risk for dropping out of school. In fact, 35% dropped out during the 2016–2017 school year (U.S. Department of Education, 2020c). By examining the predictors of success for students with EBD, teachers can identify and implement effective interventions that will help these students become successful and motivated to stay in school.

Davis and Cumming (2019b) identified four categories of predictors, including individual skill-related predictors (e.g., self-determination, self-advocacy, independent living skills), family-related predictors (e.g., parent involvement and expectations), school-based predictors (e.g., inclusion in regular classrooms), and community-based predictors (e.g., interagency collaboration, work experiences). Teachers and school staff can intervene on each of these predictors to increase the likelihood of positive outcomes and graduation for students with emotional or behavioral disorders.

Individual

Teachers can provide direct instruction on self-determination and self-advocacy (see Chapters 4 and 15), embed self-determination objectives in lessons in the general education curriculum, teach students to self-monitor their performance (see Chapter 11), and focus on social skills specifically related to the student's interactions in a variety of classroom and vocational settings.

Family-Related

Teachers and school staff can help families set personal, professional, and community goals for the student and help parents understand the importance of high expectations. Teachers can also identify and encourage families to take advantage of available resources that will help them help support their child's success. Chapter 3 provides suggestions for collaborating with families.

School-Based

Teachers should communicate high expectations to their students and provide instruction in "soft skills" required by employers, such as being a team player, displaying leadership skills, showing flexibility, communicating effectively, listening actively, and being a good problem-solver. (See *Transition: Next Year Is Now*: "Teaching Soft Skills to Prepare Students for the Future" in Chapter 4.) Additionally, students at risk for dropping out of school should be provided with vocational opportunities such as job shadowing, internships, and mentoring (e.g., Check & Connect: http://checkandconnect.umn.edu/). Most important, teachers and support staff must help students feel connected to the school community and work to establish caring relationships with students.

Community-Based

Teachers should connect their students with opportunities for paid employment and community activities such as sports or social clubs.

Students who stay in school and graduate have a much better chance of finding post-school success. Teachers must work tirelessly to identify and build upon the individual, family-based, school-based, and community-based assets each student brings to school.

Pearson eText
Video Example 6.1
With support from caring teachers and transition planning, students with emotional or behavioral disorders are more likely to stay in school.

Intelligence

Many more children with emotional or behavioral disorders score below the mean on IQ tests than do children without disabilities. Whether a greater percentage of children with emotional or behavioral disorders are less intelligent than children without disabilities is difficult to say. An IQ test measures how well a child performs certain tasks at the time and place the test is administered. It is almost certain the disruptive behavior a child with emotional or behavioral disorders exhibits has interfered with past opportunities to learn many of the tasks included on the test. Rhode and colleagues (2020) estimate students actively attend to the teacher and to assigned work approximately 85% of the time but students with behavioral disorders are on task only about 60% or less of the time. This difference in on-task behavior can have a dramatic impact on learning. Off-task and disruptive behavior frequently produce teacher attention, which can have the unintended effect of reinforcing the undesired behavior. One research-based strategy for breaking this pattern is teaching students to obtain attention for appropriate behavior. See *Teaching & Learning*, "'Look, I'm All Finished!' Recruiting Teacher Attention."

TEACHING & LEARNING

"Look, I'm All Finished!" Recruiting Teacher Attention

Why Should Students Learn to Recruit Teacher Attention? Preparing a student with disabilities for inclusion in a regular classroom should include explicit instruction in classroom survival skills such as staying on task during a lesson, following teachers' directions, and completing assigned seatwork.

These skills are likely to enhance any student's acceptance and success in the classroom. Because teachers value such "good student" behaviors, students are also likely to receive teacher praise and attention for exhibiting them (Lane et al., 2019; Lane et al., 2006).

Many students with disabilities are experts at getting teacher attention. Unfortunately, that attention is often for the wrong behavior. Disruptive behavior combined with academic skill deficits makes many students with disabilities prone to negative interactions with teachers in general education classrooms. Teaching students to politely recruit positive teacher attention for academic efforts can reverse this pattern of negativity.

Classrooms are busy places, and teachers can easily overlook students who need attention and support, especially low-achieving students who are still, quiet, and docile. A disruptive student is more likely to get teacher attention than is the student who is working quietly and productively. By politely recruiting their teachers' attention and assistance, students with disabilities can function more independently and actively influence the quality of instruction they receive.

Students with intellectual disabilities (Craft et al., 1998; Rouse et al., 2014), learning disabilities (Wolford et al., 2001), and emotional or behavioral disorders (Lo & Cartledge, 2006) have learned to recruit teacher and peer attention for academic and vocational skills.

Who Should Be Taught to Recruit? Politely obtaining teacher assistance is a valuable skill for any student, but it is particularly important for these children:

Withdrawn Willamena seldom asks a teacher anything. She's so quiet and well behaved that her teachers sometimes forget she's in the room. Withdrawn Willamena is a prime candidate for recruitment training.

In-a-Hurry Harry is half-done with a task before his teacher finishes explaining it. Racing through his work makes him the first to turn it in. But his work is error filled and often incomplete, so Harry doesn't hear much praise from his teacher. Harry would benefit from recruitment training that includes self-assessment and self-correction.

Shouting Shelly has just finished her work, and she wants her teacher to look at it—right now! Shelly doesn't raise her hand; she gets her teacher's attention—and disrupts most of her classmates—by shouting across the room. Shelly should be taught appropriate ways to gain teacher attention.

Pestering Pete raises his hand, waits quietly for his teacher to come to his desk, and politely asks, "Have I done this right?" But he repeats this routine so often that his teachers grow weary of it, and positive teacher attention often turns into reprimands. Recruitment training for Pete should teach him to limit the number of times he cues his teachers for attention.

Teaching Students to Recruit Reinforcement The following steps are recommended for teaching students to recruit reinforcement, positive teacher attention, and feedback.

1. **Select Target Behaviors.** Identify target behaviors that are likely to be reinforced by the teacher, such as coming to class on time, turning in homework, speaking politely, completing class work, paying attention during instruction, or helping a peer.
2. **Teach Self-Assessment.** Teach students to evaluate their work before they recruit the teacher's attention. Students will be more likely to receive positive teacher attention if their efforts are complete and accurate.
3. **Teach Appropriate Recruiting.** Teach students to recruit attention by using a hand raise and waiting quietly (or the typical procedure in your specific setting). Teach students to recruit when the teacher is available, ask for feedback in a polite manner, and thank the teacher for the feedback. Finally, teach students to limit the number of times they recruit the teacher's attention (e.g., 2 to 3 times in a 20-minute independent work period).
4. **Model and Role-Play.** Practice the recruiting sequence by providing directions, modeling, role playing, and feedback.
5. **Promote Generalization and Maintenance.** Strategies for promoting generalized outcomes include using unpredictable and delayed reinforcement, reminding students to recruit, asking other teachers to reinforce your students' recruiting efforts, and teaching students to self-record their recruiting responses. (For more information on teaching students to recruit teacher attention, see Alber and Heward [2000]).

Social Skills and Interpersonal Relationships

Developing and maintaining interpersonal relationships during childhood and adolescence is an important predictor of future adjustment. As might be expected, students with emotional or behavioral disorders are often rejected by peers and experience great difficulty in making and keeping friends (McDonald & Gibson, 2018; Pereira & Lavoie, 2018). The findings of a study (Schonert-Reichl, 1993) comparing the social relationships of secondary students with behavioral disorders with those of same-age peers without disabilities are typical of much of the published literature on social skills of students with emotional or behavioral disorders: Students with behavioral disorders reported lower levels of empathy toward others, participation in fewer curricular activities, less frequent contacts with friends, and lower quality relationships than were reported by their peers without disabilities (Crum et al., 2016; Martin-Key et al., 2017).

Involvement with Juvenile Justice System

Students with emotional or behavioral disorders are about three times more likely to be arrested than students with other disabilities (Lipscomb et al., 2017). More than one third of students with emotional or behavioral disorders are arrested during their school years (Wagner & Newman, 2012). In 2018, U.S. law enforcement agencies arrested 728,280 persons under age 18; females committed 30% of all offenses. (Office of Juvenile Justice and Delinquency Prevention [OJJDP], 2020.)

Arrest rates for juveniles increase sharply during the middle school years. This pattern probably reflects both the greater harm adolescents can cause to society by their inappropriate behavior and the fact that younger children are often not arrested (and therefore do not show up on the records) for committing the same acts that lead to the arrest of an older child. Younger children, however, are being arrested, and they are committing serious crimes. Youth younger than 15 years of age, for example, accounted for 29% of all violent crime arrests in 2018 (OJJDP, 2020).

Most juvenile offenders are *recidivists* (repeat offenders). A report of chronic offenders in Lane County, Oregon, found that 15% of juvenile offenders committed 64% of all new crimes by juveniles (Wagner, 2009). A study of serious adolescent offenders making the transition to young adulthood estimated recidivism rates of 75% to 80% (Brame et al., 2018). An encouraging finding from a longitudinal study of 1354 serious adolescent offenders found that most youth who commit felonies greatly reduce their rate of offending over time (Mulvey, 2011). This study also found that longer stays in juvenile detention facilities do not reduce recidivism and community-based supervision after release from detention is effective in reducing repeat offenses.

Prevalence

Learning Outcome 6.3 Identify the prevalence of emotional disturbance and describe assessments used to identify students with emotional or behavioral disorders.

Prevalence estimates for emotional or behavioral disorders in children have varied tremendously. A widely cited review of epidemiological studies conducted over a span of nearly 40 years and ending in the mid 1990s (Roberts et al., 1998) found a prevalence rate of 22% for mental health problems in children from preschool through secondary school. Using criteria that included a mental health diagnosis and significant impairment in one or more life domains, Costello et al. (2006) found a prevalence rate of approximately 12%. Forness and colleagues (2012) analyzed nine prevalence studies conducted from 1995 to 2010 and found a mean prevalence rate of 12% for moderate to severe emotional or behavioral disorders. The Centers for Disease Control and Prevention (2013) reports that 13% to 20% of children in the United States experience a mental disorder in a given year.

Most prevalence studies count the number of individuals who meet diagnostic criteria at the time of the study. Such *point prevalence* studies ask teachers to identify students in their classes who display challenging behavior at that point in time. Many children exhibit inappropriate behavior for short periods, and such one-shot surveys or screenings will identify them. Research indicates that at least 3% to 6% of school-age children have emotional or behavioral problems that are sufficiently serious and persistent to warrant intervention (Kauffman & Landrum, 2018). Annual reports from the federal government, however, show that far fewer children are being served than the most conservative prevalence estimates. The number of children age 6 to 21 years who received special education under the IDEA category of emotional disturbance during the 2018–2019 school year represented about 0.5% of the school-age population (U.S. Department of Education, 2020a).

Gender

More than three fourths of children identified for special education because of emotional or behavioral disorders are boys (Wagner, Kutash, et al., 2005). Boys identified with emotional or behavioral disorders are likely to have externalizing disorders in the form of antisocial, aggressive behaviors (Furlong et al., 2004). Although girls with emotional or behavioral disorders are more likely to show internalizing disorders such as anxiety and social withdrawal, research shows that girls may have problems with aggression and antisocial behavior as well (Talbott & Thiede, 1999).

Causes

The behavior of some children with emotional or behavioral disorders is so self-destructive and apparently illogical that it is difficult to imagine how they got that way. We shake our heads in bewilderment and ask, "Where did that behavior come from?" Numerous theories and conceptual models have been proposed to explain abnormal behavior (Kauffman & Landrum, 2018; Webber & Plotts, 2008). Regardless of the model used to view emotional or behavioral disorders, suspected causes can be grouped into two major categories: biological and environmental.

Biological Factors

BRAIN DISORDERS Many individuals who have brain disorders experience problems with behavior. Brain disorders are the result of either *brain dysgenesis* (abnormal brain development) or *brain injury* (caused by influences such as disease or trauma that alter the structure or function of a brain that had been developing normally up to that point). (Traumatic brain injury is discussed in Chapter 12.) The vast majority of children with emotional or behavioral disorders, however, show no evidence of brain disorder or injury.

GENETICS Evidence indicates genetic links to some forms of emotional or behavioral disorders (Holz et al., 2018). The disorder with the strongest research support for a genetic link is schizophrenia, a severe and debilitating form of mental illness characterized by auditory hallucinations (hearing voices), delusions, unfounded fears of persecution, and disordered speech. A massive collaborative study of mental illness involving more than 300 scientists from 35 countries compared the genetic makeup of 37,000 people with schizophrenia with 113,000 individuals without the condition and found 108 distinct locations in the human genome associated with schizophrenia (O'Donovan et al., 2014). Estimates of the prevalence of schizophrenia and related psychotic disorders in the United States is 0.25% to 0.64% (National Institute of Mental Health, 2020). A family history of schizophrenia is associated with a higher risk of developing schizophrenia, mood disorders, and delusional disorders (Chou et al., 2017).

TEMPERAMENT Temperament refers to a person's behavioral style or typical way of responding to situations. Because physiological differences or markers are associated with differences in infants' temperament, it is considered an inborn biological influence (Kagan, 2018). An infant who seldom cries but smiles and coos when passed from one person to another is said to have an easygoing temperament. In contrast, an infant who is distractible, frequently fusses, and withdraws from new situations might be said to show signs of a difficult temperament.

Some research shows an easy or positive temperament is correlated with resilience to stress (Smith & Prior, 1995) and a difficult temperament at an early age increases the likelihood of behavior challenges in adolescence (Maltby et al., 2019). In one study, children with an inhibited temperament style characterized by withdrawing from novel situations, playing alone, and spending time on the periphery of social action in the second year of life were more likely to develop social phobias and symptoms of anxiety by age 13 (Schwartz et al., 1999).

Although a child's temperament is unlikely in itself to cause emotional or behavioral disorders, it may predispose the child to problems by interacting with environmental factors, such as making parenting interactions more difficult (Nelson et al., 2007; Sirois et al., 2019). Thus, certain events that might not produce challenging behavior in a child with an easygoing temperament might result in disordered behavior by the child with a difficult temperament (Holden, 2019; Sanson et al., 2018).

Environmental Factors

Three primary environmental factors contribute to the development of conduct disorder and antisocial behavior: (a) an adverse early rearing environment, (b) an aggressive pattern of behavior displayed when entering school, and (c) social rejection by peers. Considerable evidence shows these causal factors occur in sequence (Thornton & Frick, 2018). The settings in which these events occur are home, school, and the community.

HOME The relationship children have with their parents, particularly during the early years, is critical to the way they learn to behave. Parents who treat their children with love, are sensitive to their children's needs, and provide praise and attention for desired behaviors tend to have children with positive behavioral characteristics (e.g., Reuben et al., 2016). Children with emotional or behavior challenges are more likely to come from homes in which parents are inconsistent disciplinarians, use harsh and excessive punishment, spend little time engaged in prosocial activities with their children, do not monitor the whereabouts and activities of their children, and show little love and affection for good behavior (Fairchild et al., 2019; Fishbein et al., 2019).

Because of the correlation between parental child-rearing practices and challenging behavior, some mental health professionals have been quick to pin the blame for children's behavior challenges on parents. But the parent–child relationship is dynamic and reciprocal; the behavior of the child affects the behavior of the parent just as much as the parent's actions affect the child's actions. Therefore, blaming parents for their child's emotional or behavior challenges is neither practical nor proper. Instead, professionals must work with parents to help them systematically change certain aspects of the parent–child relationship in an effort to prevent and modify those problems (Helton & Alber-Morgan, 2018; Park, Alber-Morgan, & Fleming, 2011).

SCHOOL School is where children spend the largest portion of their time outside the home. Therefore, it makes sense to observe carefully what occurs in schools in an effort to identify factors that may contribute to challenging behavior. Also, because most children with emotional or behavioral disorders are not identified until they are in school, it seems reasonable to question whether school contributes to the development of behavioral disorders. Educational practices that contribute to the development of emotional or behavioral challenges include ineffective instruction that results in academic failure, unclear rules and expectations for appropriate behavior, inconsistent and punitive discipline practices, infrequent teacher praise and approval for academic and social behavior, and failure to individualize instruction to accommodate diverse learners or to implement culturally responsive practices (Crocket et al., 2018; Gage, Scott, et al., 2018; Mitchell et al., 2019).

Source: Radius Images/Design Pics/Alamy Stock Photo

Well-intentioned but ill-timed teacher attention can reinforce challenging behavior.

A teacher's actions can unintentionally maintain and actually strengthen deviant behavioral patterns. Consider the all-too-common interaction between teacher and student illustrated in Figure 6.1. It begins with a teacher's request that the student ignores and follows a predictable and escalating sequence of teacher pleas and threats that the student counters with excuses, arguments, and eventually a full-blown tantrum. The escalating aggression and tantrumming become so aversive to the teacher that she withdraws the task demand (thereby reinforcing and strengthening the student's disruptive behavior) so the student will stop tantrumming (thereby reinforcing

FIGURE 6.1 Coercive Pain Control

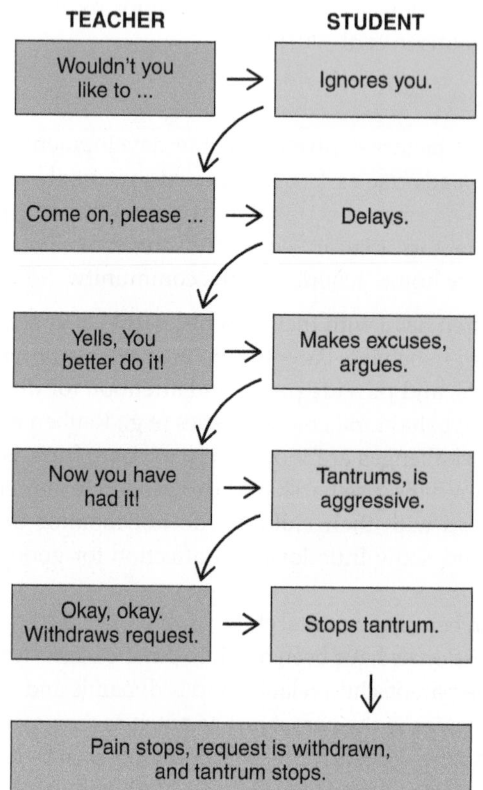

Source: Reprinted from Rhode, G., Jensen, W. R., & Williams, H. K. (2020) *The tough kid book: Practical classroom management strategies* (3rd ed., p. 11). Eugene, OR: Ancora Publishing. Used with permission.

the teacher's withdrawing the request). This process teaches the child to argue, make excuses, tantrum, destroy property, and even use physical aggression to get what he wants.

COMMUNITY Students associating with peers who exhibit antisocial behavior are likely to experience trouble in the community and at school. Gang membership, drug and alcohol abuse, and deviant sexual behavior are community factors that contribute to the development and maintenance of an antisocial lifestyle (Connolly & Jackson, 2019; Walker & Gresham, 2014).

A Complex Pathway of Risks

It is impossible to identify a single factor or isolated event as the cause of a child's emotional or behavioral disorder. Most chronic behavior challenges are the accumulated effect of exposure to a variety of family, neighborhood, school, and societal risk factors. The greater the number of risk factors and the longer a child's exposure to them, the greater the probability the child will experience negative outcomes (Merrick et al., 2017). Figure 6.2 illustrates this pattern of antisocial behavior development as originally conceived by Gerald Patterson and his colleagues (Patterson, 1982; Patterson et al., 1992). Although the interplay of these risk

FIGURE 6.2 The Path to Long-Term Negative Outcomes for Children and Youth Who are at Risk for School Failure, Delinquency, and Violence

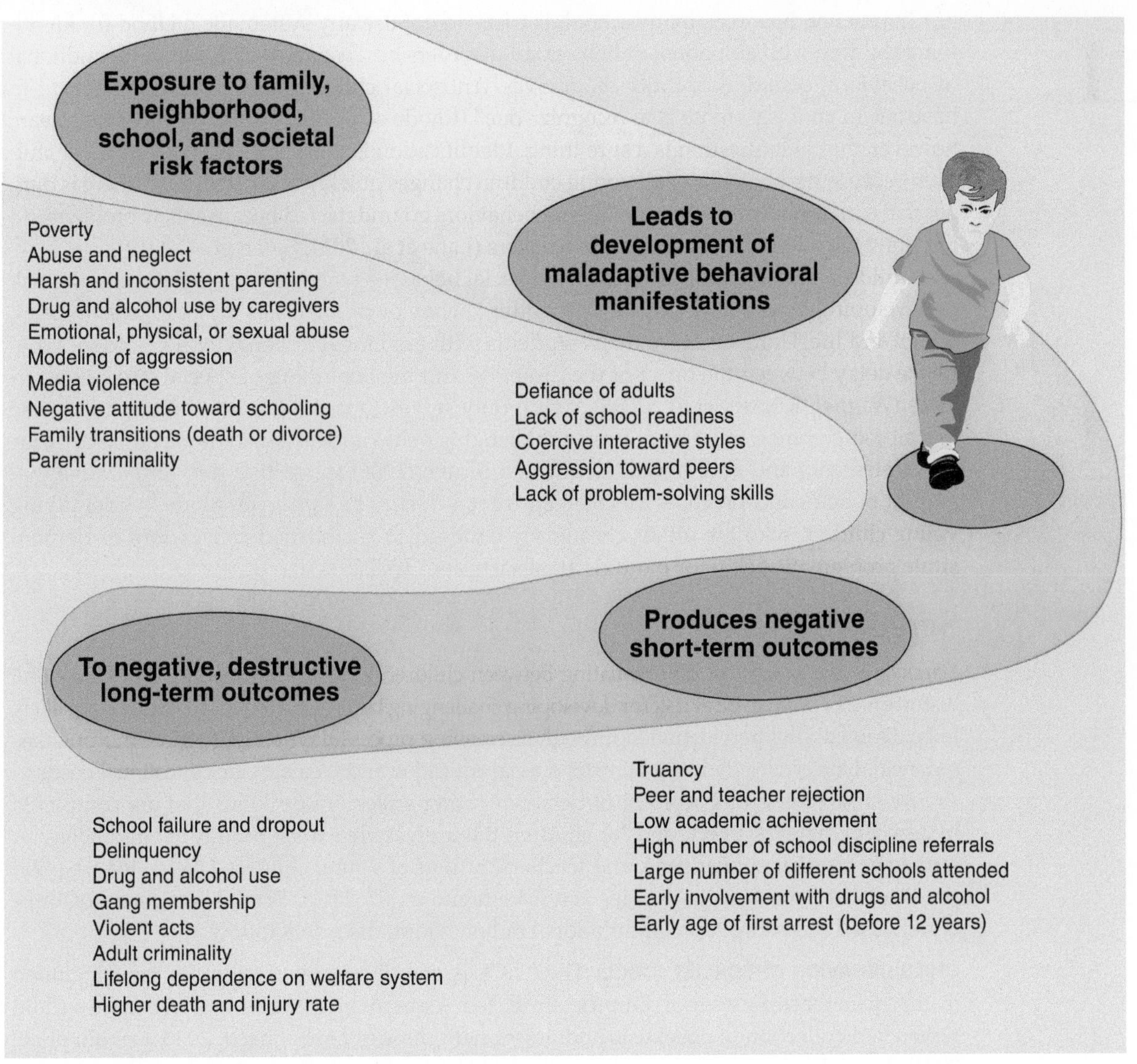

Source: Walker, H. M., Sprague, J. R. (1999). The Path to School Failure, Delinquency, and Violence: Causal Factors and Some Potential Solutions. Intervention in School and Clinic Vol. 35(2), pp. 67–73. Copyright © 1999 by Hammill Institute on Disabilities. Reprinted by permission of SAGE Publications, Inc.

factors is complex and the specific contribution of any given risk factor cannot be determined, the outcome is, sadly, highly predictable.

Although knowledge of these risk factors provides information necessary for planning and implementing prevention programs (Conroy, 2016; Fagan et al., 2020), precise knowledge of etiology is not required to effectively treat children's existing behavior challenges. Attempting to determine the extent to which various factors in a child's past are responsible for current challenging behaviors is "an impossible and quite unnecessary task. Disruptive child behavior can be changed very effectively without knowing the specific, original causes for its acquisition and development" (Walker, 1997, p. 20).

Identification and Assessment

HLP4 Use multiple sources of information to develop a comprehensive understanding of student's strengths and needs.

Assessment of emotional or behavioral disorders, as with all disabilities, should answer four basic questions concerning special education services:

1. Who might need help?
2. Who really does need help (who is eligible)?
3. What kind of help is needed?
4. Is the help benefiting the student?

In practice, however, many school districts do not use any systematic method for identifying children with emotional or behavioral disorders because most children with emotional or behavioral disorders identify themselves. Antisocial children seldom go unnoticed: "To have one in your classroom is to recognize one" (Rhode et al., 2020, p. 9). This does not mean, however, that identification is a sure thing. Identification is more difficult with younger children because the behavior of all young children changes quickly and often. Also, there is danger that some children with internalizing behaviors go undetected because their problems do not draw the attention of parents and teachers (Lane et al., 2014; Splett et al., 2019).

Children who display patterns of antisocial behavior when entering school run the risk of developing more serious and long-standing behavior problems as they progress through school and life. Unfortunately, many students with emotional or behavioral disorders experience delay between the onset of the disability and the beginning of special education services (Wagner, Kutash, et al., 2005), which only serves to make it more difficult to reverse this all-too-common trajectory of early challenging behavior leading to tragic outcomes during adolescence and adulthood. Conroy and Brown (2006) stated that it is "imperative that current policies and practices be changed from a *reactive* to a *proactive* mode by identifying young children who are either chronically exposed to established risk factors or demonstrate problematic behavior patterns at an early age" (p. 225).

Screening Tests

Screening is the process of differentiating between children who either show signs of behavioral disturbance or seem to be at risk for developing challenging behavior from those who are not likely to be disabled. Children identified through a screening process then undergo more thorough assessment to determine their eligibility for special education and their specific educational needs.

Most screening tools consist of behavior rating scales or checklists that are completed by teachers, parents, peers, and/or children themselves. Teachers' ratings of child behavior tend to be consistent over time, and teachers' ratings of young children's behavior are good predictors of behavior at an older age (Montague et al., 2011). Brief descriptions of three widely used screening tests for emotional or behavioral disorders follow.

CHILD BEHAVIOR CHECKLIST (CBCL) The CBCL is one of several assessment tools included in the Achenbach System of Empirically Based Assessment (ASEBA), a widely used and researched collection of checklists and assessment devices (Achenbach, 2020; Konold et al., 2004). This school-age version comes with teacher report, parent report, and self-report forms and can be used with children age 6 through 18 years. The teacher's report form includes 112 items (e.g., "sudden changes in mood or feelings," "not liked by other pupils") that are rated on a 3-point scale: "not true," "somewhat or sometimes true," or "very true or often true." The CBCL also includes items representing social competencies and adaptive functioning such as getting along with others and acting happy.

BEHAVIORAL AND EMOTIONAL RATING SCALE (BERS) The BERS assesses a student's strengths in 52 items across five areas of functioning: interpersonal strengths (e.g., reacts to disappointment in a calm manner), family involvement (e.g., participates in family activities), intrapersonal strengths (e.g., demonstrates a sense of humor), school functioning (e.g., pays attention in class), and affective strengths (e.g., acknowledges painful feelings of others) (Epstein, 2004). Data from a strength-based assessment such as the BERS may be used to present positive attributes of students in individualized education program (IEP) meetings, as an aid in writing IEP goals and objectives, and as an outcome measure to document a student's progress on strength-related IEP goals and objectives (Epstein et al., 2001).

SYSTEMATIC SCREENING FOR BEHAVIORAL DISORDERS (SSBD) The SSBD employs a three-step multiple gating screening process for progressively narrowing down the number of children suspected of having serious behavior challenges (Walker et al., 2014). In Gate I, classroom teachers rank order every student in their classrooms according to behavioral profiles on two dimensions: externalizing problems and internalizing problems. The top three students on each teacher's list progress to Gate II, the Critical Events Index.

Critical events are behaviors of high salience and concern even if their frequency is low. Any occurrence of these target behaviors is an indicator of major disruption of social-behavioral adjustment processes in school. The 33 items that make up the Critical Events Index include externalizing behaviors such as "is physically aggressive with other students" and "makes lewd or obscene gestures" and internalizing behaviors such as "vomits after eating" and "has auditory or visual hallucinations." Students who exceed normative criteria on the Critical Events Index advance to Gate III of the SSBD, which consists of direct and repeated observations during independent seatwork periods in the classroom and on the playground during recess. Children who meet or exceed cutoff criteria for either or both observational measures are referred to child study teams for further evaluation to determine their eligibility for special education.

Direct Observation and Measurement of Behavior

In assessment by direct observation and measurement, the actual behaviors causing concern about a child are clearly specified and observed in the settings where they normally occur (e.g., in the classroom, on the playground) (Lewis et al., 2014). The measurable dimensions of behavior include frequency, duration, latency, topography, and magnitude (Figure 6.3).

FIGURE 6.3 Five Measurable Dimensions of Behavior

FREQUENCY OR RATE: how often a particular behavior occurs, usually expressed as a count per standard unit of time (e.g., 6 talkouts per minute). All children cry, get into fights with other children, or sulk from time to time; yet we are not apt to think of them as emotionally disturbed. A primary difference between children with behavioral disorders and other children is the frequency with which these behaviors occur.

DURATION: how long a child engages in a given activity (e.g., worked on math problems for 12 minutes). The amount of time children with behavioral disorders engage in certain activities is often markedly different—longer or shorter—from that of other children. For example, most young children have temper tantrums, but the tantrums generally last no more than a few minutes. A child with emotional or behavioral disorders may tantrum for more than an hour at a time. The problem may also be one of too short a duration—for example, a child who does not stick to an academic task for more than a few seconds at a time.

LATENCY: the time that elapses between the opportunity to respond and the onset of the behavior. The latency of a child's behavior may be too long (e.g., several minutes elapse before he begins to comply with a teacher's request) or too short (e.g., the child immediately begins screaming and tantrumming at the slightest provocation or frustration, thus having no time to consider more appropriate alternative behaviors).

TOPOGRAPHY: the physical shape or form of behavior. Some children with emotional or behavioral disorders emit behaviors that are seldom, if ever, seen in typical children (e.g., setting fires, hurting animals). These behaviors may be maladaptive, bizarre, or dangerous to the child or others.

MAGNITUDE: the force or intensity with which behavior is emitted. The magnitude of a child's responses may be too little (e.g., talking in a volume so low that she cannot be heard) or too much (e.g., slamming the door).

The advantage of assessing and describing emotional or behavioral disorders in terms of these dimensions is that identification, design of intervention strategies, and evaluation of treatment effects can all revolve around direct and objective measurement.

This approach leads to a direct focus on the child's problem—the behavior that is adversely affecting the child's life—and ways of dealing with it, such as strengthening a desired alternative behavior as opposed to concentrating on some presumed (and unreachable) problem within the child. Detailed procedures for observing and measuring behavior can be found in Cooper et al. (2020).

Functional Behavior Assessment

HLP10 Conduct functional behavioral assessments to develop individual student behavior support plans.

Functional behavior assessment (FBA) is a systematic process for gathering information to understand why a student may be engaging in challenging behavior. FBA results are used to generate hypotheses about what the behavior's function, or purpose, is for the student. Two common functions of problem behavior are (a) to get something the student wants (positive reinforcement) (e.g., hitting other students produces attention from the teacher) and (b) to avoid or escape something the student doesn't want (negative reinforcement) (e.g., disruptive behavior when the teacher presents academic tasks results in task removal).

Knowledge of a behavior's function can point to the design of an appropriate and effective **behavior intervention plan (BIP)**, a required IEP component for all students with disabilities whose school performance is adversely affected by behavioral issues. For example, knowing that a student's tantrums are maintained by teacher attention suggests a different intervention than one indicated for challenging behavior maintained by escape from academic tasks. The research literature contains numerous examples of using FBA to guide the successful intervention for extremely challenging and disruptive behavior (e.g., Gage et al., 2012; Miltenberger et al., 2019; Ruiz & Kubina, 2017). FBA entails one or more of three assessment methods: indirect assessment, direct assessment, and functional analysis (Peterson & Neef, 2020).

INDIRECT FUNCTIONAL BEHAVIOR ASSESSMENT The easiest and quickest form of FBA involves asking teachers, parents, and others who know the child well about the circumstances that typically surround the occurrence and nonoccurrence of the problem behavior and the reactions the behavior usually evokes from others. A number of instruments for conducting indirect FBA via structured interview, questionnaire, or checklist have been published (e.g., the Motivation Assessment Scale [Durand & Crimmins, 1992]; Questions About Behavioral Function [Paclawsky et al., 2000]). One widely used empirically validated tool for indirect FBA, the Functional Assessment Interview, includes a student-assisted form so students can serve as their own informants (O'Neill et al., 2015). The interview questions the informant to identify behavior(s) that cause trouble for the student at school, describe the student's class schedule and its relation to challenging behavior, rate the intensity of behaviors across class periods and times of day, describe the situation in which the challenging behavior typically occurs (e.g., difficult, boring, or unclear material; peer teasing; teacher reprimands), and describe the events that often follow the behavior and may function to maintain it.

HLP5 Interpret and communicate assessment information with stakeholders to collaboratively design and implement educational programs.

DESCRIPTIVE FUNCTIONAL BEHAVIOR ASSESSMENT Descriptive FBA entails direct observation of the challenging behavior under naturally occurring conditions. Using a technique called **ABC recording**, an observer records a temporally sequenced account of each occurrence of the challenging behavior(s) in the context of the antecedent conditions and events and consequences for those behaviors as those events unfold in the student's natural environment. This assessment technique is so named because it obtains information on (a) the antecedent events that occasion or trigger challenging behavior (e.g., transitions from one classroom or activity to another, task difficulty), (b) the nature of the behavior itself (e.g., frequency, duration, topography), and (c) the consequences that may function to maintain the behavior (e.g., teacher attention, withdrawal of task demands).

The results of indirect and direct FBAs are often combined to obtain a picture of function. Figure 6.4 shows the hypothesized functions of aggression, property destruction, and tantrums by Brian, a 13-year-old student diagnosed with oppositional defiant disorder and attention-deficit/hyperactivity disorder as determined by the results of a Functional Assessment Interview and ABC recording. In some cases, the results of an indirect and/or

FIGURE 6.4 Hypothesized Functions of Aggression, Property Destruction, and Tantrums by a 13-Year-Old Student Diagnosed with Oppositional Defiant Disorder and Attention-Deficit/Hyperactivity Disorder

Antecedent	Behavior	Consequence	Function
When adult or peer attention is diverted from Brian . . .	he engages in a variety of problem behaviors, which result in . . .	attention from adults and peers.	Gain attention from adults and peers
When Brian's access to preferred toys and activities is restricted . . .	he engages in a variety of problem behaviors, which result in . . .	gaining access to preferred toys and activities.	Gain access to preferred toys and activities
When Brian is required to perform difficult or undesirable tasks . . .	he engages in a variety of problem behaviors, which result in . . .	the tasks being removed.	Escape from difficult and/or nonpreferred tasks

Source: From Neef, N. A., & Peterson, S. M. (2007). Functional behavior assessment. In J. O. Cooper, T. E. Heron, & W. L. Heward, *Applied behavior analysis* (2nd ed., p. 515). Upper Saddle River, NJ: Pearson Education, Inc. Used by permission.

descriptive FBA lead to an effective treatment plan. Revealing the controlling variables for many chronic challenging behaviors, however, requires a functional analysis.

FUNCTIONAL ANALYSIS Functional behavior assessment might also include a **functional analysis**, the experimental manipulation of several antecedent or consequent events surrounding the target behavior in an attempt to verify the hypothesized functions of the behavior (Bell & Fahme, 2018; Slayton & Hanley, 2018). The same or similar antecedent conditions and consequences identified through indirect and descriptive FBA are used in a functional analysis, but the variables are manipulated in a controlled setting rather than the natural environment. This allows better control of the variables, and the safety of the child and others can be ensured. Only highly trained personnel such as Board Certified Behavior Analysts (BCBAs) who have attained appropriate consents from parents or guardians and have ensured that adequate safeguards are in place to protect the student and others from any harm should conduct functional analyses (Hanley, 2012; Steege et al., 2019).

A functional analysis confirmed and clarified the hypothesized functions of the student's challenging behaviors and led to the design of a successful multicomponent intervention shown in Figure 6.5.

Educational Approaches

Learning Outcome 6.4 Name and give examples of scientifically supported strategies for educating students with emotional or behavioral disorders.

Curriculum Goals

What should students with emotional or behavioral disorders be taught? An obvious but only partially correct answer is that students with externalizing behaviors should learn to control their aggression and that those with internalizing behaviors should learn to have fun and make friends. However, if programs serving children with emotional or behavioral disorders treat maladaptive behavior at the expense of academic instruction, students who already possess deficient academic skills will fall even further behind their peers. Special education for students with emotional or behavioral disorders must include effective instruction on the academic and social skills required for success in school, community, and vocational settings.

ACADEMIC SKILLS Systematic instruction in reading, writing, and math is as important to students with emotional or behavioral disorders as it is to any student who hopes to function successfully in school and society. The academic course schedules of nearly all secondary students with emotional or behavioral disorders closely resemble those of students in the general population. Nearly all secondary school youth with emotional or behavioral disorders take English, math, social studies, and science classes.

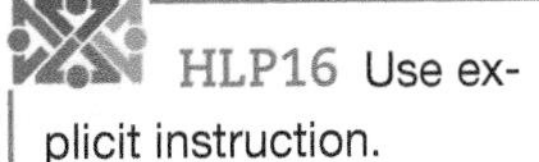
HLP16 Use explicit instruction.

FIGURE 6.5 Interventions for Attention and Escape Functions of Aggression, Property Destruction, and Tantrums by a 13-Year-Old Student Diagnosed with Oppositional Defiant Disorder and Attention-Deficit/Hyperactivity Disorder

ATTENTION FUNCTION			
Intervention	**Antecedent**	**Behavior**	**Consequence**
Teach a new behavior	When adult or peer attention is diverted from Brian . . .	he will raise his hand and say, "Excuse me . . ."	and adults and peers will provide attention to Brian.
Teach a new behavior	When adult or peer attention is diverted from Brian . . .	he will self-monitor his appropriate independent work and match teacher recordings . . .	and the teachers will provide him with one-on-one time if he meets a specific criterion.
Change the antecedent	During independent work times, adults will provide attention to Brian every 5 minutes . . .	to increase the probability that Brian will appropriately work independently . . .	which will increase adult opportunities to praise and attend to appropriate behavior.
Change the antecedent	Allow Brian to play with peers during leisure times . . .	to increase the probability that Brian will play appropriately . . .	which will increase adult opportunities to praise appropriate behavior and for peers to respond positively.

ESCAPE FUNCTION			
Intervention	**Antecedent**	**Behavior**	**Consequence**
Teach a new behavior	When Brian is required to perform a difficult or undesirable task . . .	he will ask, "May I take a break now?" . . .	and the teacher will allow Brian to take a break from the task.
Change the reinforcement contingency	When Brian is required to perform difficult or undesirable tasks . . .	and he engages in a variety of problem behaviors . . .	he will be required to continue working on the task and the time out intervention will be discontinued.

Source: From Neef, N. A., & Peterson, S. M. (2007). Functional behavior assessment. In J. O. Cooper, T. E. Heron, & W. L. Heward, *Applied behavior analysis* (2nd ed., p. 517). Upper Saddle River, NJ: Pearson Education, Inc. Used by permission.

Until recently, relatively few studies on academic interventions with students with emotional or behavioral disorders appeared in the peer-reviewed research literature (Maggin, Wehby, & Gilmour, 2016; McKenna, Shin, et al., 2019). However, increasing awareness of the crucial role effective instruction plays in the treatment of children with emotional or behavioral disorders is leading to more research on curriculum and instruction (Campbell et al., 2018). Fortunately, this research shows that students with emotional or behavioral disorders make excellent progress when provided with explicit, systematic instruction (e.g., Garwood et al., 2020; Wehby & Lane, 2019).

Good instruction is the foundation for effective behavior management in the classroom. Teachers must communicate high expectations to students with emotional or behavioral disorders, provide appropriately challenging tasks and frequent opportunities to respond, and resist the temptation of assigning easier tasks to avoid outbursts.

HLP9 Teach social behaviors.

SOCIAL SKILLS Many students with emotional or behavioral disorders have difficulty maintaining a conversation, expressing their feelings, participating in group activities, and responding to failure or criticism in positive and constructive ways. They often get into fights and altercations because they lack the social skills needed to handle or defuse provocations. The slightest snub, bump, or misunderstood request—which would be laughed off or ignored by most children—can precipitate an aggressive attack by some students.

Learning the social and nonacademic skills teachers expect is especially important for children with emotional or behavioral disorders. A survey of 717 teachers across grade levels identified the following five skills as critical to success in regular classrooms (Lane et al., 2006):

- Controls temper in conflict situations with peers
- Controls temper in conflict situations with adults
- Follows or complies with directions
- Attends to teacher's instructions
- Easily transitions from one classroom activity to another

Many studies on teaching social skills to students with emotional or behavioral disorders have been published. A review by Hutchins et al. (2019) concluded that social skills training is generally effective and is an essential component of a comprehensive program for students with emotional or behavioral disorders. Featured Teacher Michelle Nielson-Pugmire agrees: "Basic social skills such as waiting to take one's turn or politely asking for help aren't just important for school; they're imperative for success in life. I use explicit instruction and role-play every day to teach social skills."

Numerous social skills curricula and training programs have been published, such as the following:

- *Taking Part: Introducing Social Skills to Children* (Cartledge & Kleefeld, 2009) helps students in preschool through third grade learn social skills in six units: making conversation, communicating feelings, expressing oneself, cooperating with peers, playing with peers, and responding to aggression and conflict.
- *The Prepare Curriculum: Teaching Prosocial Competencies* (Goldstein, 2000) is designed for students who are aggressive, withdrawn, or otherwise deficient in social competencies. Activities and materials for middle and high school students are provided in 10 areas, such as problem solving, anger control, stress management, and cooperation.
- *The Walker Social Skills Curriculum* includes ACCEPTS: A Curriculum for Children's Effective Peer and Teacher Skills (Walker, McConnell, et al., 1988) for children in grades K to 6 and ACCESS: Adolescent Curriculum for Communication and Effective Social Skills (Walker, Todis, et al., 1988) for students at the middle and high school levels.
- *The Tough Kid Social Skills Book* includes tools and strategies to help teachers, school psychologists, counselors, and behavior analysts teach skills such as recognizing and expressing feelings, joining in, solving arguments, dealing with teasing, and accepting "No" (Sheridan, 2010).

Regardless of the social skills targeted, instruction should include modeling of examples and nonexamples, opportunities for role playing, guided practice with feedback, and strategies to promote generalization to the natural environment (D. H. Anderson et al., 2018; Gresham & Elliot, 2014; Hutchins et al., 2019).

HLP21 Teach students to maintain and generalize new learning across time and settings.

Research-Based Teaching Practices

A four-phase review process to identify scientifically supported teaching methods for students with emotional or behavioral disorders revealed these strategies (Lewis et al., 2004):

- Teacher praise (reinforcement)
- High rates of active student response (ASR)
- Explicit instructional practices, including direct instruction
- Schoolwide positive behavior support, functional assessment-based individual plans, and self-management

Pearson eText
Video Example 6.2
"Thank you for working quietly."

Explicit instruction was introduced and described in Chapters 2 and 5. Functional behavior assessment was explained earlier in this chapter. Teacher praise, schoolwide positive behavioral support, and self-management are described in the remainder of this section. Proactive, positive classroom management and the use of peer mediation and support are also described.

TEACHER PRAISE Social approval, often conveyed through verbal praise, is a powerful reinforcer for most people. The original experimental demonstrations of the power of adults' social attention as reinforcement for children's behavior took place in a series of studies designed by Montrose Wolf and carried out by the preschool teachers at the University of Washington's Institute of Child Development in the early 1960s (e.g., Allen et al., 1964; Johnston et al., 1966). Describing those early studies, Risley (2005) wrote:

> We had never seen such power! The speed and magnitude of the effects on children's behavior in the real world of simple adjustments of something so ubiquitous as adult attention was astounding. Forty years later, social reinforcement (positive attention, praise, "catching them being good") has become the core of most American advice and training for parents and teachers—making this arguably the most influential discovery of modern psychology (p. 280).

Numerous studies since have demonstrated the positive effects of contingent praise on the behavior of preschoolers (e.g., Hester et al., 2009) and school-age students with and without disabilities (e.g., Downs et al., 2019; Kranak et al., 2017; Markelz & Taylor, 2016; O'Handley et al., 2020). Yet many educators do not realize that the systematic use of contingent praise and attention may be the most powerful motivational and classroom management tool they have (Flora, 2004). Teacher praise and attention are especially important for students with learning and behavior challenges.

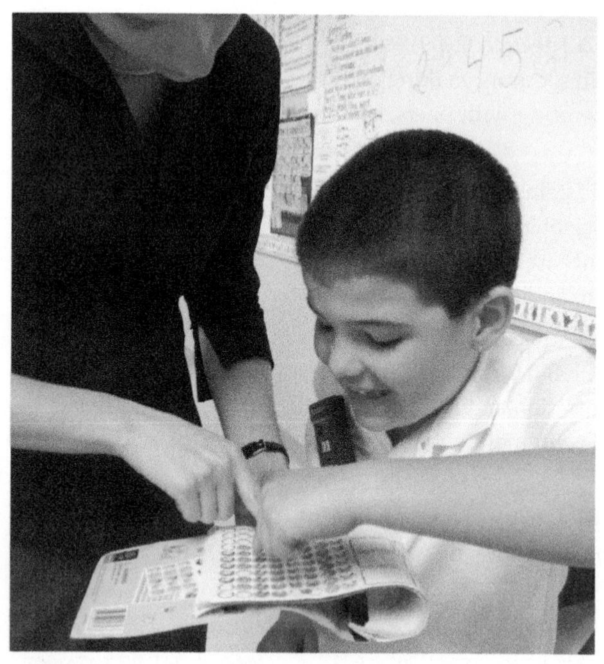

Source: Katelyn Metzger/Great Western Academy/Pearson Allyn and Bacon/Merrill Education

Systematic teacher praise and attention for desired behavior is a powerful classroom management and instructional tool.

Despite its documented effectiveness in increasing academic performance and desired student behaviors, studies in general and special education classrooms over the past three decades have consistently found very low rates of teacher praise (e.g., Flores et al., 2018; Jenkins et al., 2015). Especially discouraging are studies reporting that teachers reprimand students with emotional or behavioral disorders much more frequently than they praise them (Caldarella et al., 2020a; Royer et al., 2019). Scott et al. (2011) found that teachers directed reprimands or negative feedback to students with challenging behaviors at a rate of 6 per hour while praising those same students 1.2 times per hour. Although reprimands may temporarily suppress disruptive behavior (Alber & Heward, 2000), a longitudinal study of 149 teachers and 311 students considered at risk for emotional or behavioral disorders found reprimands ineffective in decreasing misbehavior over time or increasing academic engagement (Caldarella et al., 2020b). Figure 6.6 provides some tips for increasing teacher praise.

FIGURE 6.6 Tips for Increasing Teacher Praise

Stay on the lookout for behavior worthy of praise. Even the most unskilled and unruly student is correct or obedient sometimes. Don't miss these critical teaching moments.

Contrive opportunities for students to do something well just so you can give approval. For example, an easy way to provide a low-achieving student with an opportunity to succeed in front of classmates is to ask a question for which you are certain the student knows the answer and then call on the student.

Don't worry about sounding wooden and unnatural at first. Teachers are often concerned their students will think they are not being genuine. Practice four or five varied praise statements. Providing specific praise and approval is similar to any other skill: You'll get better with practice.

Prompt yourself to praise. Mark reminders in your lesson plan or play an audio recording of randomly spaced beeps. Each time you see or hear a prompt, look for a student or group behaving well and praise that behavior. Apps such as R+Remind and iPraiseU can also prompt praising.

Self-monitor your praising. Set a goal to give a certain number of praise statements during a class period and count them by marking tallies or moving pennies from one pocket to another. Start small and gradually increase your daily goal as your praising skills improve.

Don't worry about overpraising. Of all the mistakes a teacher can make, frequently praising students' good academic and social behaviors is unlikely to be one of them.

Note: Additional ideas for increasing the frequency and effectiveness of teacher praise can be found in Allday et al. (2012); Fullerton et al. (2009); Keller and Duffy (2005); Musti-Rao and Haydon (2011); and Stormount and Reinke (2009).

> HLP18 Use strategies to promote active student engagement.

ACTIVE STUDENT RESPONDING Lessons in which students actively participate produce more learning and less misbehavior than do lessons in which students respond occasionally or passively attend. Scott et al. (2011) conducted more than 1200 observations of students with and without behavior challenges in elementary and secondary classrooms and found teachers used group instruction formats 63% of the time and students were not actively engaged 61% of their time in class. And group instruction is the common instruction format in the regular classroom regardless of grade level (Hollo & Hirn, 2015).

Group instruction, whether with an entire class or small groups, presents teachers with five major tasks: maintaining students' attention, giving each student sufficient opportunities to respond, providing feedback for students' responses, monitoring students' learning, and preventing and addressing disruptive behavior. Teaching practices that enable all students in the class or group to respond simultaneously offer one solution to all of these problems. Research and teachers' experience support the effectiveness and practicality of several such techniques, chief among them classwide peer tutoring (see Chapter 2), guided notes (see Chapter 5), choral responding (see Chapter 2), and response cards (Owiny et al., 2018). See *Teaching & Learning* "Response Cards: Everyone Participates."

SCHOOLWIDE POSITIVE BEHAVIORAL INTERVENTIONS AND SUPPORTS (SWPBIS) Traditionally, discipline in the schools has emphasized the use of punishment in an effort to control the misbehavior of specific students. Not only are such strategies generally ineffective for decreasing behavior problems and increasing school safety (Curwin et al., 2018), they also do not teach students desired, prosocial behaviors. The development of SWPBIS represents a tremendous advance in achieving student discipline and establishing positive school climate. SWPBIS uses a multi-tiered system of supports (MTSS) framework of organizational systems and research-based, scientifically validated interventions for establishing a positive school culture and teaching and supporting appropriate behaviors that enable the academic and social behavior success of all students (Chitiyo & May, 2018; Gage, Whitford, & Katsiyannis, 2018; Horner & Sugai, 2015). More than 7000 schools in the United States are currently implementing SWPBIS. A wide range of resources and training materials to help schools implement SWPBIS are available at the Center on Positive Behavioral Interventions & Supports website.

TEACHING & LEARNING

Response Cards: Everyone Participates

What Are Response Cards? Similar to choral responding described earlier, **response cards (RCs)** are a research-based alternative to one-student-at-a-time participation. RCs are cards, signs, or items that students hold up to display their answers to teacher-posed questions or problems. Numerous studies evaluating the effects of RCs with general and special education students at the elementary, middle, and secondary levels have produced a similar pattern of findings. In addition to increased participation and learning outcomes (Cakiroglu, 2014; Didion et al., 2020; Duchaine et al., 2018; Hott & Brigham, 2020), studies have found improved on-task behavior and decreases in the frequency of disruptions and inappropriate behavior when students used RCs (e.g., Goodnight, Whitley, & Brophy-Dick, 2019; Horn, 2010; Lambert et al., 2006; Schnoor, Freeman-Green & Test, 2016).

With *preprinted RCs*, students select the card with the answer of their choice. Examples include yes/true and no/false cards, colors, traffic signs, molecular structures, and parts of speech. Students can also use a single RC with multiple answers printed on clearly marked sections (e.g., protein, fat, carbohydrate, vitamin, and mineral in a lesson on healthful eating habits). Students hold up their cards with closed fingers or a clothespin indicating their answers.

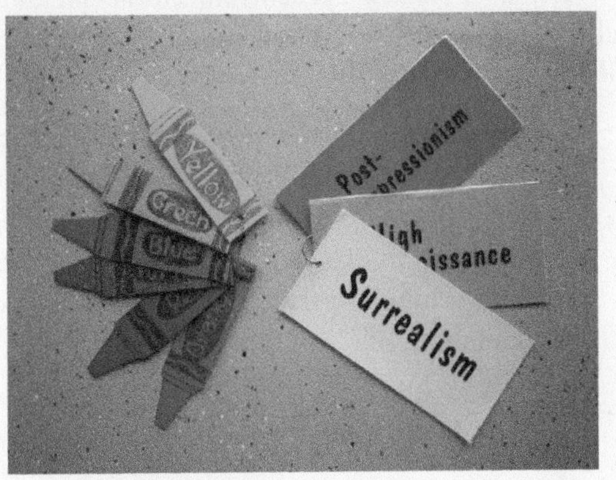

Source: William L. Heward

Preprinted response cards.

Pearson eText
Video Example 6.3
Response cards increase student engagement, decrease disruptions, and improve learning.

With *write-on RCs*, students mark their answers on blank cards that they erase between learning trials. Write-on RCs can be custom made for specific subject matter. For example, music students might mark notes on an RC that has permanent treble and bass clef scales; students in a driver's education class could draw where their car should go on RCs with permanent streets and intersections.

Teachers can make a set of 40 durable write-on RCs from a sheet of white laminated bathroom board (available from builders' supply stores). Dry-erase markers are available at most office supply stores, and paper towels or tissues will easily wipe the RCs clean.

How Do You Use Response Cards?

Suggestions for All Types of Response Cards

- Model several trials and have students practice using their RCs.
- Give clear cues when students are to hold up and put down their cards.
- Maintain a lively pace throughout the lesson; keep intervals between trials short.
- Tell students to look at their classmates' RCs if they need a hint; it's not cheating.

Suggestions for Using Preprinted Response Cards

- Design the cards to be easy to see (e.g., consider size, print type, colors).
- Make the cards easy for students to manipulate and display (e.g., put answers on both sides of the cards; attach a group of related cards to a ring).
- Begin instruction on new content with a small set of cards (perhaps only two), gradually adding cards as students' skills improve.

Suggestions for Using Write-On Response Cards

- Limit language-based responses to one to three words.
- Keep a few extra markers on hand.
- Be sure students do not hesitate to respond because they are concerned about making spelling mistakes: (a) provide several practice trials with new terms before the lesson begins; (b) write new terms on the board and tell students to refer to them during the lesson; or (c) use the "don't worry" technique: tell students to try their best, and misspellings will not count against them.
- Let students draw on their RCs for a few minutes after the lesson as a reward for good behavior and participation.

Additional tips for using response cards, including digital tools and apps similar to response cards, can be found in Twyman and Heward (2018).

SWPBIS is conceptualized and implemented from a prevention perspective, with a continuum of instructional interventions and behavioral supports that become more targeted and intensive as indicated by students' needs (Sugai & Horner, 2020). Most implementations entail three tiers of supports (see Figure 6.7.)

Tier 1—Primary Prevention: Universal Supports for All Students. All teachers and school staff participate in a team effort to teach appropriate behavior to all students across all school settings within the school.

- *State and define behavioral expectations.* School personnel identify a small number of positively framed rules such as Be respectful, Be responsible, and Be safe, and develop specific examples of behavioral expectations for each rule (e.g., being respectful in class means raising your hand when you want to speak or get help. During lunch or in the hall, being respectful means using a person's name when you talk to him or her.).
- *Teach behavioral expectations.* School personnel teach behavioral expectations to all students in the building using an explicit, systematic format: Present the rule; discuss

FIGURE 6.7 Continuum of Schoolwide Positive Behavioral Support

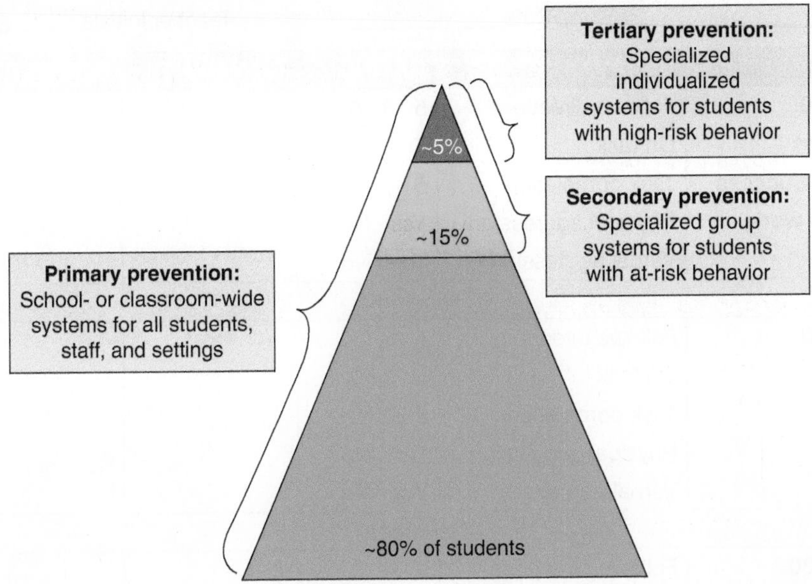

Source: Figure adapted from SCHOOL WIDE POSITIVE BEHAVIOR SUPPORT: IMPLEMENTERS' BLUEPRINT AND SELF ASSESSMENT, 2010, by Rob Horner and George Sugai for the OSEP Center on Positive Behavioral Interventions and Support, www.pbis.org. Copyright © 2010 by Horner and Sugai. Reprinted with permission.

the rationale for the rule; and describe, model, and rehearse examples until students demonstrate fluent performance.

- *Acknowledge and reward appropriate behaviors.* School personnel acknowledge and reward appropriate behaviors on a regular basis. Some schools do this through formal systems (tickets, rewards); others do it through social events. Schools strive to establish a ratio of four positive adult interactions with students for every one that is negative.
- *Correct behavioral errors.* When students violate behavioral expectations, personnel provide clear procedures for showing them their behavior was unacceptable and preventing their unacceptable behavior from contacting inadvertent rewards.

Pearson eText
Video Example 6.4
There are many fun and creative ways to acknowledge and reward appropriate behaviors.

All teachers and school staff teach and reward desired student behavior, apply clearly defined consequences for rule violations, and participate in ongoing data analysis to improve the system. Well-implemented universal supports are usually effective for about 80% to 85% of students.

Tier 2—Secondary Prevention: Targeted Interventions for Students with At-Risk Behavior. In a typical school, about 15% to 20% of students will require more focused behavioral support because of chronic misbehavior and minor rule violations. Tier 2 supports are often delivered in a small-group format. Check in/check out (CICO) is an example of a research-based tier 2 intervention. The basic components of CICO are (a) a brief meeting at the beginning of the day to set behavioral goals, (b) a point card on which teachers record points based on the student's meeting defined criteria and give the student feedback at different times during the day (see Figure 6.8), (c) a brief meeting at the end of the day to review how the day went, and (d) rewards for earning a predetermined number of points (Crone et al., 2020). Positive effects on students' social behavior and academic performance have been reported (Toms et al., 2018).

HLP6 Use student assessment data, analyze instructional practices, and make necessary adjustments that improve student outcomes.

Tier 3—Tertiary Prevention: Intensive, Individualized Interventions for Students with High-Risk Behavior. Students who exhibit serious challenging behaviors such as major rule violations that put the student or others in danger, or who are unresponsive to secondary-level interventions—or about 5% of students in most schools—require intensive, individualized interventions and ongoing behavioral supports.

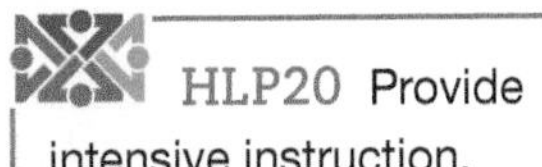
HLP20 Provide intensive instruction.

FIGURE 6.8 Example of Check-In/Check-Out Recording Form

Student ____________ Date ____________ Teacher Initials ____________

TIME	BEHAVIORS	RATING*	COMMENTS	BONUS PTS**
8:45–9:00	Follows directions	5 3 0		
Breakfast	On task	5 3 0		
Road to Success	Task completion	5 3 0		
Morning work	Physical aggression	Yes No		
	Verbal aggression	Yes No		
		Transition		
9:15–9:30	Follows directions	5 3 0		
DIBELS	On task	5 3 0		
LA/Math	Task completion	5 3 0		
	Physical aggression	Yes No		
	Verbal aggression	Yes No		
		Transition		
9:30–10:30	Follows directions	5 3 0		
LA/Math	On task	5 3 0		
Assessments	Task completion	5 3 0		
	Physical aggression	Yes No		
	Verbal aggression	Yes No		
		Transition		
10:30–11:00	Follows directions	5 3 0		
PE	On task	5 3 0		
	Task completion	5 3 0		
	Physical aggression	Yes No		
	Verbal aggression	Yes No		
11:20–12:05	Follows directions	5 3 0		
Lunch	Physical aggression	Yes No		
	Verbal aggression	Yes No		
		Transition		
1:00–1:20	Follows directions	5 3 0		
Clean up	On task	5 3 0		
Read aloud	Task completion	5 3 0		
Bus	Physical aggression	Yes No		
	Verbal aggression	Yes No		

*__Rating:__ 5 = 1 or no warning, 3 = 2 warnings, 0 = 3 or more warnings.
Physical aggression: no instances of hitting, punching, throwing objects, inappropriate gestures, and so on.
Verbal aggression: no instances of yelling, swearing, whining, arguing loudly, crying, name calling, and so on.
Leaving class: Did he leave class without permission?
** **Bonus points for participation and on task behavior!**

Source: Courtesy of Michelle Nielson-Pugmire.

These supports may also include wraparound services outside school to address quality-of-life issues. A team conducts a functional behavior assessment (described earlier) and creates an individualized behavioral intervention plan (BIP). Dunlap and colleagues (2010) provide numerous tips and research-based strategies for creating and implementing BIPs within a SWPBIS system.

SELF-MANAGEMENT Many children with emotional or behavioral disorders believe they have little control over their lives. Things just seem to happen to them, and being disruptive is their means of reacting to an inconsistent and frustrating world. These students can learn responsibility and achieve self-determination through **self-management**—making responses to increase or decrease future frequency of a target behavior one wishes to change. Self-management is also an important tool for promoting generalization and maintenance of outcomes.

Of the many forms of self-management, self-monitoring and self-evaluation are the most widely used and most researched. **Self-monitoring** is a relatively simple procedure in which individuals observe their own behavior and record the occurrence or nonoccurrence of a specific target behavior. Individuals using **self-evaluation** compare their performance against a predetermined standard or goal. With both strategies, a self- or teacher-delivered reward may be contingent upon meeting performance criteria.

More than 40 peer-reviewed studies have demonstrated that students with challenging behavior can use self-monitoring and self-evaluation to regulate social and academic behavior (see Bruhn et al., 2015). Detailed procedures and materials for teaching self-monitoring and other self-management skills to students can be found in Bruhn et al. (2015); Clark et al. (2019); and Joseph and Konrad (2009). KidTools and KidSkills, free software programs that teach children to create and use self-management tools, can be downloaded at the KidTools website (http://kidtools.cepel.org). Also see *Teaching & Learning*, "Self-Monitoring Helps Students Do More Than Just Be On-Task" in Chapter 11.

PROACTIVE, POSITIVE CLASSROOM MANAGEMENT Teachers of students with emotional or behavioral disorders must design and manage classroom environments that decrease antisocial behavior and increase the frequency of positive teacher–student interactions as a basis for building positive behavior and academic success.

Pearson eText
Video Example 6.5
Students of all ages and skill levels benefit from clear expectations and consistent daily routines.

This is a very tall order. Fortunately, teachers can turn to a strong base of clearly defined, evidence-based practices for guidance on effective classroom management (e.g., Kerr & Nelson, 2010; Rhode et al., 2020; Scarlett, 2015; Sprick, 2009).

Proactive strategies are interventions that anticipate and prevent problems before they occur. "It is much more difficult to remediate the problems caused by a Tough Kid than to prevent them. Once a teacher has lost the management tempo in a classroom and things are out of control, it is difficult to regain control" (Rhode et al., 2020, p. 41).

Proactive strategies include the following: structuring the physical environment of the classroom (e.g., have the students with the most challenging behaviors sit nearest the teacher [Bicard, Ervin, Bicard, & Baylot-Casey, 2012]), establishing clear rules and expectations for appropriate behavior (Nagro et al., 2019), planning lessons and managing transitions to minimize downtime, providing students with opportunities to make choices (Green et al., 2011; Wehby & Lane, 2019), presenting instruction to students in ways that increase the probability of compliance (Lee et al., 2008), keeping students actively engaged during instruction (Heward, 2019), praising and positively reinforcing desired behavior (Marchant & Anderson, 2012), and anticipating and addressing challenging behaviors before they occur (Ennis et al., 2013).

Teachers of students with emotional or behavioral disorders must be skilled in using behavior change strategies such as *shaping, contingency contracting, extinction* (ignoring disruptive behavior), *differential reinforcement of alternative or incompatible behavior, response cost* (a loss of reinforcers as a consequence for misbehavior, like a fine), *time-out* (restricting a student's access to reinforcement for a brief time following an inappropriate behavior), and *overcorrection* (requiring restitution beyond the damaging effects of the antisocial behavior, such as cleaning all of the desks as a consequence for a child writing on his own desk) (Cooper et al., 2020). These techniques should not be implemented as isolated interventions but incorporated into an overall instructional and classroom management plan that includes the previously mentioned proactive strategies and perhaps a **token economy** or **level system** in which students access greater independence and more privileges as they demonstrate increased behavioral control (Ivy et al., 2017; Pritchard et al., 2018).

Featured Teacher Michelle Nielson-Pugmire's students self-record positive and negative behaviors on individual daily level sheets. Some students begin each day at the entry level and earn privileges; others are on a color-keyed level system where they gain or lose privileges based on their behavior.

Content Extension 6.2

The Levels System

The lev[illegible] is a colored coded system and is based around privileges earned and lost, blue [illegible] with the most privileges and white being without privileges.

Blu[illegible]

- -A[illegible]ular and special education classes
- -Attends all recesses
- -Can fulfill class jobs
- -Can choose daily work during daily work time
- -Can attend Friday's class store, movie, and or activity
- -Can receive free time on computers/iPad
- -Receives class money for being on blue at the end of the day
- -Level blue for 3 days in a row receives a free mystery motivator spin.

Yellow Level Privileges

- Attends all regular and special education classes
- Can fulfill class jobs
- Free time at desk only (no computer/iPad)
- Can choose daily work during daily work time
- Can attend Friday's class store, movie, and or activity
- 5 minutes of recess (5 minutes of each recess on a spot)
- Students can earn class tokens/money during this time for observing and following class rules and expectations

Red Level Privileges

- Receives all instruction in the learning center setting
- No Recess privileges (Run laps, Exercise)
- Teacher chooses daily work
- Eat Lunch in seat away
- No class store, movie, or activity privileges
- *No other privileges* (field trips, extra regular education activities, assemblies, etc.)
- Students can earn class tokens/money for observing and following class rules and expectations

Featured Teacher Michelle Nielson-Pugmire's level systems.

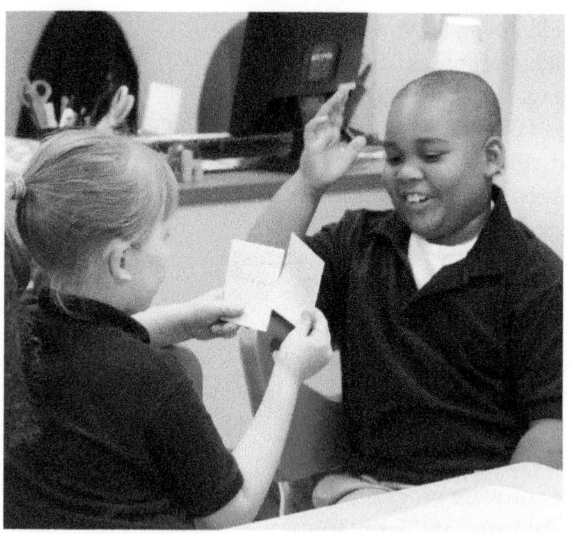
Source: Katelyn Metzger/Great Western Academy/Pearson Allyn and Bacon/Merrill Education

Peer tutoring provides structured opportunities to practice social skills while working on academic goals.

PEER MEDIATION AND SUPPORT The power of the peer group can be an effective means of producing positive changes in students with emotional or behavioral disorders. Strategies for teaching peers to help one another replace inappropriate behaviors with positive alternative behaviors include the following:

- *Peer monitoring.* Teach peers to observe a peer's behavior and provide the peer with feedback (Hatzenbuhler et al., 2019).
- *Positive peer reporting.* Teach, encourage, and reinforce students for reporting each other's positive behaviors (Dillon et al., 2019; Murphy & Zlomke, 2014).
- *Peer tutoring.* Allow students with emotional or behavioral disorders and their peers to serve as tutors for one another; this provides all students opportunities to practice social skills (Wang et al., 2013).
- *Peer support and confrontation.* Train peers to acknowledge one another's positive behaviors and suggest or model appropriate alternative responses when inappropriate behavior occurs (Braun & Bierman, 2020).

Implementing a peer support, or group process, model is much more complicated than bringing together a group of children and hoping they will benefit from positive peer influence. Most children with serious emotional or behavioral disorders have not been members of successfully functioning peer groups in which appropriate behavior is modeled and valued, nor have many such children learned to accept responsibility for their actions. The teacher's first and most formidable challenge is promoting group cohesiveness. Although group process treatment programs take many forms, most incorporate group meetings and group-oriented contingencies.

Group meetings can take place throughout the day. During a planning meeting each morning the group reviews the day's schedule, each member states a behavioral goal for the day, peers provide support and suggestions to one another for reaching their goals, and the group agrees on a collective goal for the day. At the end of each day group members discuss how well they met their individual and group goals, and each member gives and receives positive peer comments. Problem-solving meetings take place whenever any group member, including the teacher, wants to discuss a problem.

Group contingencies specify rewards and privileges that will be enjoyed by the group if the behavior of group members meets certain criteria (Helton & Alber-Morgan, 2020; McKenna & Flower, 2014). Popkin and Skinner (2003) conducted an interesting application of a group contingency with students with emotional or behavioral disorders. The researchers wrote *spelling* and a performance criterion on each of a set of 30 index cards (e.g., 5 cards with 75%, 8 cards with 80%, and 5 cards with 95%). At the end of the school day, the teacher randomly selected one of the cards. If the students' average performance as a class exceeded the criterion shown on the card, the entire group received a reward. The students who had been doing well in spelling improved (e.g., B students became A students), and the students who had done poorly showed large increases in their performance (e.g., failing students earned As and Bs). After several weeks, the researchers added similar sets of cards to the deck for *mathematics* and *grammar*. Students contributed ideas for the rewards and helped determine the criteria for earning them.

HLP7 Provide a consistent, organized, and respectful learning environment.

Fostering Strong Teacher–Student Relationships

In addition to academic and behavior management skills, the teacher of children with emotional or behavioral disorders must establish healthy and positive child–teacher relationships. William Morse (1985), one of the pioneers in the education of children with emotional or behavioral disorders, identified two important affective characteristics necessary for teachers to relate effectively and positively to students with behavior challenges: differential acceptance and empathetic relationship.

Differential acceptance means the teacher can receive and witness frequent and often extreme acts of anger, hate, and aggression from children without responding similarly. This is much easier said than done. But the teacher of students with emotional or behavioral disorders must view disruptive behavior for what it is—behavior that reflects the student's past frustrations and conflicts with himself and those around him—and try to help the child learn better ways of behaving. Acceptance should not be confused with approving or condoning antisocial behavior; the child must learn that he is responding inappropriately. Instead, this concept calls for understanding without condemning.

Having an *empathetic relationship* with a child refers to a teacher's ability to recognize and understand the many nonverbal cues that often are the keys to understanding the individual needs of children with emotional or behavioral disorders. Teachers should communicate directly and honestly with their students. Many of these children have already had experiences with supposedly helpful adults who have not been honest with them. Children with emotional or behavioral disorders can quickly detect someone who is not genuinely interested in their welfare.

Teachers of children with emotional or behavioral disorders must also realize that their actions serve as a powerful model. Therefore, it is critical that teachers' actions and attitudes be mature and demonstrate self-control. At the same time, teachers who take themselves too seriously risk overreacting to emotionally charged situations with students and risk burnout (Abrams, 2005). Teachers should use an appropriate sense of humor to build relationships with students, defuse conflict, engage learners, and help manage their own stress levels (Gilliam, 2019). Kennedy and Haydon (2020) describe a variety of strategies for developing high-quality student-teacher relationships.

Content Extension 6.3

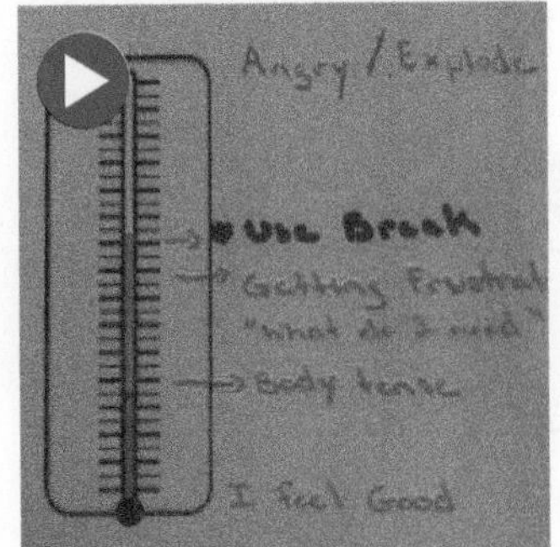

Featured Teacher Michelle Nielson-Pugmire's students learn to gauge their frustration level and decide when they need to take a break.

Focus on Alterable Variables

The twofold task of the teacher of children with emotional or behavioral disorders is helping students (a) replace antisocial and maladaptive behaviors with more socially appropriate behaviors and (b) acquire academic knowledge and skills. The frequent displays of antisocial behavior, the absence of appropriate social skills, and the academic deficits many students with emotional or behavioral disorders exhibit make this a staggering challenge. The challenge is all the more difficult because the teacher can never control (or even know) all the factors affecting a student's behavior. Typically, a host of contributing factors exists over which the teacher can exert little or no influence (e.g., delinquent friends with whom the student associates before and after school). But it does little good to bemoan the student's past (which no one can alter) or to use all of the negative factors in the student's current life that cannot be changed as an excuse for failing to help the student in the classroom.

Special educators should focus their attention and efforts on the aspects of a student's life that they can effectively control. Bloom (1980) used the term *alterable variables* to refer to things that both make a difference in student learning and can be affected by teaching practices. Alterable variables include key dimensions of curriculum and instruction, such as the amount of time allocated for instruction, the sequence of activities within the overall lesson, the pacing of instruction, the frequency with which students actively respond during instruction, how and when students receive praise or other forms of reinforcement for their efforts, and the manner in which errors are corrected. The teachers who focus on the identification and systematic management of alterable variables are those most likely to make a difference in the lives of children with emotional or behavioral disorders.

Placement Options

Learning Outcome 6.5 Compare and contrast typical placements and supports for students with emotional or behavioral disorders.

Students with emotional or behavioral disorders are served across the continuum of educational placements. During the 2018–2019 school year, approximately 49% of school-age children with emotional or behavioral disorders were educated in regular classrooms, 17%

in resource rooms, 17% in separate classrooms, 12% in special schools, 1% in correctional facilities, 1% in residential schools, and 1% in home or hospital placements (U.S. Department of Education, 2020a). Although the trend in recent years has been for increased placement of students with emotional or behavioral disorders in regular classrooms, about 40% of all students in this disability category are educated in separate classrooms, special schools, and residential facilities.

The relatively high proportion of students with emotional or behavioral disorders who are served in more restrictive settings compared with students in most other disability categories probably reflects the fact that only students with the most severe behavior challenges are identified and served. As a result, most students receiving special education because of emotional or behavioral disorders have serious, long-standing challenges that require intensive interventions in highly structured environments (Maggin et al., 2016). Consistent implementation of the specialized supports and programming needed by these students can be very difficult in regular classrooms (McKenna, Solis, et al., 2019).

HLP13 Adapt curriculum tasks and materials for specific learning goals.

A major challenge of educating students with emotional or behavioral disorders is arranging an environment that supports learning academic and social skills at acceptable rates and protects the safety of all students. Supporters of full inclusion believe the regular classroom can be made into such an environment for all students with disabilities. Some positive outcomes have been reported for students with emotional or behavioral disorders in regular classrooms. For example, a study comparing middle school students who spent the entire school day in separate classrooms with students who participated in various classes in regular classrooms for at least 1 hour per day found that the students who spent part of the day in regular classrooms had better academic records and better work habits than did the students who spent the entire day in special classes (Meadows et al., 1994). Although these results seem to support the contention that students with emotional or behavioral disorders should be educated in regular classrooms, the authors point out that the students included in regular classrooms did not exhibit the extreme aggression, lack of self-control, or degree of withdrawal that the students who stayed in the separate classrooms did. They also noted that placement in regular classrooms typically represents "a major reduction, ... if not a complete cessation, of differential programming" (p. 178). That is, the general education teachers did not make instructional or management accommodations to meet the needs of the students with behavior challenges. Without specialized instruction or accommodations, it is hard to imagine how students with severe emotional or behavioral disorders would receive an appropriate education in the regular classroom.

Although it supports educating students with emotional or behavioral disorders in the general education classroom when their individual needs can be met, the CCBD does not believe the general education classroom is the most appropriate placement for all students with emotional or behavioral disorders.

> CCBD supports a full continuum of mental health and special education services for children and youth with emotional or behavioral disorders. We believe that educational decisions depend on individual student needs. Consequently, ... CCBD does not support the notion that all, . . . students with emotional or behavioral disorders are always best served in general education classrooms (CCBD, 1993, p. 1).

Meticulous planning, coordination, and needed support are often unavailable to make inclusion effective. When an IEP team makes the decision to place a student with emotional or behavioral disorders in a regular classroom or to transition a student from a more restrictive setting to the regular classroom, it is imperative that the student and the general education teacher be prepared before and supported after the placement. Preparation includes identifying the social and academic expectations in the general education classroom, assessing the student's current social and academic skills against those expectations, teaching the student additional skills needed to meet those expectations, and in-service training for the teacher on special techniques of behavior management (State et al., 2019). Support after the general class placement should include a crisis intervention support plan and ongoing consultation and in-class modeling and intervention by a special educator trained to work with students with behavioral disorders (Simpson, 2004a).

Challenges, Achievements, and Advocacy

Special education for students with emotional or behavioral disorders faces a number of critical and ongoing issues. A continuing concern of many advocates for children with emotional or behavioral disorders is revising the federal definition of this disability so that all children with emotional and behavioral challenges that adversely affect their educational performance are eligible to receive the special education and related services they need. Although IDEA mandates that all children with disabilities receive an individualized program of special education and related services, in practice, determination of whether a child is disabled under the category of emotional disturbance is often more a function of a school district's available resources to provide needed services than a function of the child's actual needs for such services.

Despite public concern over school safety and youth violence and widespread recognition that antisocial behavior is a chronic disabling condition that exacts tremendous social and financial costs for society, we do little to prevent it. Instead of intervening early when problems are small and more likely to respond to intervention, we wait until children are older and their antisocial behavior is well established and much more difficult to change (Bierman et al., 2020). The knowledge and tools for early detection and prevention are available (e.g., Hartman et al., 2017; Walker et al., 2009). What is needed is the national resolve and commitment of resources sufficient for a large-scale program of early detection and prevention.

These issues, as well as many others, have been recognized, discussed, and debated for decades. And all will likely remain problems well into the future. Although the challenges faced by those who work with and advocate for students with emotional or behavioral disorders appear daunting and unrelenting, the field has experienced significant advances and successes to help guide the future.

The field has identified specific program components and instructional practices that, when used in combination, are likely to result in successful outcomes for students with emotional or behavioral disorders (Farmer et al., 2020; Maggin et al., 2016). Some of those achievements and best practices have been described in this chapter. We must now work diligently to close the gap between what is known about effective special education for students with emotional or behavioral disorders and what those students experience each day in the classroom.

ADVICE FROM THE FEATURED TEACHER

by Michelle Nielson-Pugmire and Kimberly Rich

Working with Students with Emotional or Behavioral Disorders

Source: Eastman Adams Photography

Kimberly Rich was my mentor when I first started teaching, and years later, we still collaborate.

Build a Rapport Classwide and Individually

- ***Be Sincere and Honest.*** Ask yourself, "Would you, could you work for or learn from someone who was insincere or untrustworthy?" The first step in building rapport is trust. We as teachers must be straightforward, sincere, and trustworthy.

- ***Get to know your students individually.*** I hold morning meetings where each student and teacher receives a minute to share anything they want. When their minute ends, each student lets me know on a scale of 1 to 10 how they are feeling that morning (1 being rough and 10 being fantastic). I use the information gleaned during these meetings to understand which students may need a little extra that day, what issues need to be dealt with, who may need to be pulled out of their shell and to spark up one-on-one conversations when time permits or is made.
- ***Play.*** It is important to set time aside to play games that your students choose. Sometimes when I see my students playing line tag or foursquare, just hanging out, or playing an imaginary game they have creatively conjured up, I will ask if I can join in. Other times we will create and play a game together.

Be Consistent

- ***Teach classroom procedures.*** Determine and teach classroom procedures and expectations clearly right from the beginning. Have students repeat these at the beginning of each day, reminding them what you expect from them. Praise students regularly for following classroom procedures, routines, and rules.
- ***Follow through on contingent delivery of consequences.*** Students learn to trust you if you are consistent with them. If students earn a privilege, make sure they get it; if they lose a privilege, make sure they lose it. This will increase the effectiveness of your behavior management.

Stay in Control

- ***Don't take it personally.*** Children with emotional or behavioral disorders will lash out at you just because you're there. It's best to respond in a neutral manner to prevent an escalation of challenging behavior. Never take personally anything students say or do.
- ***Let students see how you react to failure and frustration.*** The classroom can be stressful at times. When you stay in control during stressful situations, you provide a positive role model for your students. Also, model for your students that it's OK to be wrong. Deliberately make a mistake; your students will notice and when they do, show them how to handle making a mistake appropriately.
- ***When you make a mistake with a student—and you will—apologize.*** Be sincere and honest about whatever the mistake is and apologize. I teach my kiddos if they make a mistake to own it and learn from it. I can expect no less from myself.

Keep and Use Your Sense of Humor

- ***Laugh at yourself now and then.*** It is very difficult to work with students who have many academic and behavior needs. Your students need to see you enjoying yourself.
- ***Create a sunshine folder.*** Collect and/or write down funny things kids have said or done, great thoughts, or things students have given to you that put a smile on your face. When you've had a rough day, pull the folder out.

Key Terms and Concepts

ABC recording
behavior intervention plan (BIP)
emotional disturbance
emotional or behavioral disorder
externalizing behaviors
functional analysis
functional behavior assessment (FBA)
group contingencies
internalizing behaviors
level system
response cards
self-evaluation
self-management
self-monitoring
token economy

Summary

Definitions

- No single, widely used definition of emotional or behavioral disorders exists. Most definitions require a child's behavior to differ markedly (extremely) and chronically (over time) from current social or cultural norms.
- Many leaders in the field do not like the definition of "emotional disturbance" in IDEA because students who are "socially maladjusted" are not eligible for special education services.
- The CCBD proposed a definition of emotional or behavioral disorders as a disability characterized by "behavioral or emotional responses in school programs so different from appropriate age, cultural, or ethnic norms that they adversely affect educational performance."

Characteristics

- Children with externalizing behaviors exhibit antisocial and aggressive behavior.
- Children with internalizing behaviors are withdrawn and lack social skills needed to interact effectively with others.
- As a group, students with emotional or behavioral disorders perform academically 1 or more years below grade level.
- A large number of students with emotional or behavioral disorders also have learning disabilities or language delays.
- Students with emotional or behavioral disorders generally score slightly below average on IQ tests.
- Many students with emotional or behavioral disorders have difficulty developing and maintaining interpersonal relationships.
- About one third of students with emotional or behavioral disorders are arrested during their school years.

Prevalence

- Estimates of the prevalence of behavioral disorders vary tremendously. Credible studies indicate that 3% to 6% of students have emotional and behavior challenges that warrant special education.
- Far fewer children with emotional or behavioral disorders are receiving special education than the most conservative prevalence estimates.

Causes

- Biological factors related to development of behavioral disorders include brain disorders, genetics, and temperament.
- Environmental etiologic factors occur in the home, school, and community.
- Although knowledge of causes is necessary for planning and implementing prevention programs, effective intervention and treatment of children's existing behavior challenges do not require precise knowledge of etiology.

Identification and Assessment

- Systematic screening should be conducted as early as possible to identify children who are at risk for developing serious patterns of antisocial behavior.
- Most screening instruments consist of behavior rating scales or checklists completed by teachers, parents, peers, or children themselves.
- Direct observation and measurement of specific challenging behaviors within the classroom can indicate whether and for which behaviors intervention is needed. Five measurable dimensions of behavior are rate, duration, latency, topography, and magnitude.
- Functional behavior assessment (FBA) is a systematic process for gathering information to discover a behavior's function, or purpose, for the student. Two major functions of challenging behaviors are (a) to get something the student wants (positive reinforcement) and (b) to avoid or escape something the student doesn't want (negative reinforcement).
- Results of FBA can point to the design of an appropriate and effective behavior intervention plan (BIP).

Educational Approaches

- Students with emotional or behavioral disorders require systematic instruction in social skills and academics.
- Schoolwide positive behavioral interventions and supports (SWPBIS) uses a multi-tiered system of supports (MTSS) framework to establish a positive school culture and promote the academic and social success of all students. SWPBIS entails universal supports for all students; targeted interventions for students with at-risk behavior; and intensive, individualized interventions for students with high-risk behavior.
- A good classroom management system uses proactive strategies to create a positive, supportive, and noncoercive environment that promotes prosocial behavior and academic achievement.
- Self-management skills can help students develop control over their environment, responsibility for their actions, and self-direction.
- Group process approaches use the influence of the peer group to help students with emotional or behavioral disorders learn to behave appropriately.
- Two important affective traits for teachers of students with emotional or behavioral disorders are differential acceptance and empathetic relationship.
- Teachers should concentrate their resources and energies on alterable variables—those things in a student's environment

that the teacher can influence that make a difference in student learning and behavior.

Placement Options

- Although the trend in recent years has been for increased placement of students with emotional or behavioral disorders in regular classrooms, 40% of all students in this disability category receive their education in separate classrooms, special schools, and residential facilities.
- Comparing the behavioral and academic progress of students with emotional or behavioral disorders in different educational placements is difficult because students with milder disabilities are included first and more often, whereas students who exhibit more severe behavioral disturbances tend to remain in more restrictive placements.
- When a student with emotional or behavioral disorders is placed in a regular classroom, it is imperative that the student and the general education teacher be prepared before and supported after the placement.

Challenges, Achievements, and Advocacy

- Two of the most pressing challenges for the field of emotional or behavioral disorders are (a) ensuring that all students with emotional or behavior challenges that adversely affect their educational performance receive special education services, and (b) developing large-scale programs of early detection and prevention.

Chapter 7
Autism Spectrum Disorder

Source: Pearson/Alberto Viglietta

Learning Outcomes

After reading this chapter and completing the embedded activities, you should be able to

7.1 Describe the defining features of autism spectrum disorder (ASD).

7.2 List factors that might account for the increase in the prevalence of ASD in recent years and how the search for causes of autism has changed from the first reports of the disability to today.

7.3 Explain why valid and reliable tools for early screening and diagnosis of ASD are so critical.

7.4 Describe several evidence-based strategies for teaching students with ASD and specify what distinguishes them from unproven, faddish approaches.

7.5 List advantages and disadvantages of providing educational services for children with ASD in regular classrooms.

Education, Teaching Credentials, and Experience

- *B.S. in Human Development and Family Studies, University of Utah, 2014*
- *M.Ed. in Early Childhood Special Education, University of Utah, 2017*
- *Certifications/credentials: Special Education, birth to age 5, Utah Department of Education*
- *3 years as a paraprofessional in a classroom for preschoolers with ASD*
- *6 years as lead teacher in a classroom for preschoolers with ASD*

Content Extension 7.1

Independent task materials used by Katelyn's students.

Featured Teacher

Katelyn Johnson

Woodrow Wilson Elementary School, Granite School District, Salt Lake City, Utah

Source: Kurns Photography

When my younger brother was diagnosed with autism at age 3, I automatically assumed the dual roles of protector and teacher. I remember bragging about my "artistic" brother. I had no idea what autism was, but I was right about having a special brother! Some things might be different and more difficult for him, but with high expectations and good instruction he showed us he was capable of reaching ambitious goals.

My formal experience as a special educator began as a paraprofessional in a preschool classroom for children with autism. I was awed by the classroom teacher's skills and the environment she managed—she remains a trusted mentor today. When that teacher moved to another building, I was hired for her position. My classroom is an implementation site for the Autism Support Services: Education, Research, and Training (ASSERT) program developed by Dr. Thomas Higbee at Utah State University. Using strategies and tactics from applied behavior analysis (ABA), ASSERT builds each student's skills in structured one-to-one instruction and promotes generalization of those skills to group activities in naturalistic settings.

Independence is required for success. Everything we do is geared toward helping our preschoolers become more independent. Some of the daily activities I use to promote independence are work bins, task bags, and activity schedules. We always teach students how to complete an activity before having them do it independently, and we provide a motivating reinforcer when they are finished. I use errorless learning to teach students how to follow a schedule and to complete an activity. Once a student shows they are capable of following a schedule and completing a task, I gradually remove my support, so the student has the opportunity to be completely independent. I have a couple designated areas in my classroom where students know they are required to complete the tasks 100% independently. Being self-sufficient not only helps them at school but at home as well.

Successful transition to a regular classroom is the ultimate goal for my students. To help reach that goal, my paraprofessionals and I relentlessly focus on teaching social skills needed to interact appropriately with typically developing peers. A student with autism who lacks those skills is unlikely to experience success in an inclusive classroom. For example, all students should have the expectation of turn-taking when playing with their peers. To teach this, we task analyze turn-taking into multiple smaller skills, such as demonstrating appropriate eye contact, using words to describe a step (e.g., "your turn"), asking for a turn, keeping hands still during a peer's turn, and waiting patiently. When learning how to play a game, sequentially chaining all the steps together is a great example of how to start small, then build to the full skill set. To promote generalization, I make sure students practice these skills in small groups with a range of peers. Each year I do social skills groups with my students. These are great opportunities for practice! Although I individualize them to meet students' specific needs, I hope to turn it into a program the whole preschool department can use to reach all students.

One reason I love this profession so much is the tremendous variety of students I get to work with. Each child represents a new and exciting challenge.

NOT SO LONG AGO, THE PROGNOSIS FOR CHILDREN WITH AUTISM was extremely poor, with problems of daily living persisting into adulthood and requiring intensive supervision and supports for more than 90% of individuals (Bristol et al., 1996). The good news is that research has improved our understanding of autism, and effective education and treatment are producing a much better quality of life for children and adults with autism.

In the span of a couple decades, autism moved from being a relatively unrecognized disability, even within the field of special education, to one of widespread interest in education and society in general. Still, much remains unknown about the disability. Richard Simpson (2004b), who, like most people, was "both fascinated and spellbound" (p. 137) by children with autism when he first began working with them, has written:

> In spite of the extraordinary recent media coverage and other attention that autism has received, it continues to have the same mystique that it had when I first entered the field. That is, in spite of significant advancements in treating and understanding individuals with autism spectrum disorders, the disability remains a mystery. Even when viewed through a disability lens, individuals with ASD are a particularly challenging and enigmatic group. (p. 138)

Although people with autism have no doubt always been part of the human community, the condition was not described or named until 1943, when Leo Kanner, a psychiatrist at Johns Hopkins Hospital in Baltimore, published case reports on a group of 11 children. He wrote that the children displayed behaviors that differed "so markedly and uniquely from anything reported so far, that each case merits ... a detailed consideration of its fascinating peculiarities" (Kanner, 1943, p. 217). The children Kanner described, eight boys and three girls, shared the following characteristics:

- Difficulty relating to others in a typical manner
- Extreme aloneness that seemed to isolate the child from the outside world
- Resistance to being picked up or held by parents
- Significant speech deficits, including mutism and echolalia
- In some cases, exceptional memorization skills
- Early specific food preferences
- Monotonous, obsessive desire for repetition and sameness
- Bizarre, repetitive behavior such as rocking back and forth and spinning objects
- Explosive temper tantrums
- Lack of imagination and few spontaneous behaviors such as typical play
- Normal physical appearance

Kanner (1943) concluded that this group of characteristics, especially the "inability to relate themselves in the ordinary way to people and situations" (p. 242), constituted a pathogenic syndrome. He called this condition *early infantile autism*.

Unaware of Kanner's work, Hans Asperger, a pediatrician in Vienna, used the term *autistic psychopathology* in 1944 to describe a behavioral syndrome he found among a group of older children and adolescents (Wing, 1998). Asperger's "little professors" (as he called them) had good language skills and often above-average to superior intelligence, but they were socially naive and inappropriate and used odd intonation and body language while giving monologues about specialized interests.

Definitions

Learning Outcome 7.1 Describe the defining features of autism spectrum disorder (ASD).

Many of the behavioral deficits and excesses first reported by Kanner and Asperger are key diagnostic criteria in contemporary definitions of **autism spectrum disorder**, a neurodevelopmental disorder marked by persistent deficits in social communication and interaction and restricted, repetitive patterns of behavior and interests.

IDEA Definition of Autism

When Congress reauthorized the Individuals with Disabilities Education Act (IDEA) in 1990 (PL 101-476), autism was added as a disability category under which children were entitled to special education. IDEA defines the disability as follows:

i. *Autism* means a developmental disability affecting verbal and nonverbal communication and social interaction, generally evident before age three, that adversely affects a child's educational performance. Other characteristics often associated with autism are engagement in repetitive activities and stereotyped movements, resistance to environmental change or change in daily routines, and unusual responses to sensory experiences.
ii. Autism does not apply if a child's educational performance is adversely affected primarily because the child has a serious emotional disturbance as defined in paragraph (c) (4) of this section.
iii. A child who manifests the characteristics of autism after age three could be identified as having autism if the criteria in paragraph (c) (1) (i) of this section are satisfied. (34 *CFR*, Part 300 §300.8[c][1][i–iii] [August 14, 2006])

The DSM Definition of Autism Spectrum Disorder

The American Psychiatric Association's *Diagnostic and Statistical Manual of Mental Disorders* (DSM) is a handbook used by physicians, psychologists, and licensed therapists in the United States to diagnose mental, behavioral, and developmental disorders. Many secondary school students receiving special education today under the IDEA disability category of autism were diagnosed with one of four pervasive developmental disorders—autistic disorder, Asperger's disorder, childhood disintegrative disorder, or pervasive developmental disorder not otherwise specified (PDD-NOS)—per the DSM-IV (American Psychiatric Association, 2000). The disorders were differentiated from one another primarily by the age of onset and the severity of various symptoms, with autistic disorder the most severe form and Asperger syndrome the mildest form.

The DSM-5 (American Psychiatric Association, 2013) subsumes all four disorders under ***autism spectrum disorder***, with the following diagnostic criteria.

- *Persistent deficits in social communication and social interaction* across contexts, as manifested by the following:
  - Problems with social-emotional reciprocity, sharing interests, initiating or reacting normally to social interactions
  - Deficits in using and understanding nonverbal communicative behaviors (e.g., body language, eye contact, gestures, facial expression)
  - Difficulties developing and maintaining relation-ships, adapting behavior to changing social contexts, making friends; lack of interest in peers
- *Restricted, repetitive patterns of behavior, interests, or activities*, demonstrated by at least two of the following:
  - Stereotyped or repetitive motor movements, object use, or speech
  - Insistence on sameness, inflexibility with regard to routines, or ritualized patterns of behavior
  - Highly restricted, fixated interests that are abnormal in intensity or focus
  - Hyper- or hypo-reactivity to sensory input or unusual interest in sensory aspects of the environment

Source: Pavel L/Shutterstock

A child with autism might focus his attention on one object or activity for hours.

Symptoms must be present in early childhood, cause significant impairment in social, occupational, or other important areas of current functioning, and are not explained by intellectual disability or developmental delay (adapted from American Psychiatric Association, 2013, pp. 50–51).

The DSM-5 assigns one of three levels of severity for ASD based on the amount of support required to counteract the limitations and impairments to everyday functioning as a result of the disorder.

Characteristics

As you read the characteristics of children with ASD, remember these important points: Some children on the spectrum are very severely affected in most or all domains of everyday functioning, but others are only mildly affected. Although many children with ASD behave in similar ways, any two children on the spectrum may be more distinguished by their differences than by their similarities. "There is no single behavior that is always typical of autism and no behavior that would automatically exclude an individual child from a diagnosis of autism" (National Research Council, 2001, p. 11). Autism advocate Stephen Shore said it best: "If you've met one individual with autism, you've met one individual with autism" (Magro, 2020).

Impaired Social Interactions

Many children with autism exhibit extreme aloofness. Parents often report their attempts to cuddle and show affection to the child are met with a profound lack of interest by the child. The child seems not to know or care whether he is alone or in the company of others. The child seldom uses social gestures such as showing and pointing things out to others or waving and nodding her head at others.

Children with ASD often have difficulty perceiving the emotional state of others, expressing emotions, and forming attachments and relationships. Some theorists and researchers attribute the problems exhibited by children with autism in social situations to deficits in **theory of mind**, the intuitive ability to distinguish and interpret one's own and other people's thoughts, motives, and beliefs (Happé, 2003; Korkmaz, 2011). "In brief, having a theory of mind is to be able to reflect on the contents of one's own and other's minds" (Baron-Cohen, 2001, p. 3).

Effectively taking the perspective of others includes the abilities to distinguish differences between appearance and reality and to understand that others may hold "false beliefs" based on their experiences and social context. The Sallie-Anne task is a classic false-belief test (Baron-Cohen et al., 1985) wherein students watch as two characters, Sallie and Anne, observe a doll being placed in a box. Sallie then leaves the room, and Anne moves the doll to a cabinet. Sallie then returns to room, and the students are asked where Sallie will look for the doll. At about age 4 years, typically developing children will realize Sallie thinks the doll is still in the box. Many children with autism will say Sallie will look for the doll in the cabinet.

The inability to infer another person's thoughts and feelings may be one reason some children with autism talk incessantly about obscure topics in which others have no interest (Southall & Campbell, 2015). Researchers are developing a variety of interventions for teaching perspective taking and other theory of mind skills to children with autism (e.g., Lovett & Rehfeldt, 2014; Peterson & Thompson, 2018).

Young children with ASD often show deficits in **joint attention**, a social communication skill children typically begin to display in infancy. Joint attention is evident when two people use gestures and gaze to share, follow, or direct each other's attention to interesting objects or events. A typically developing child looks where someone else is looking, as when a child notices his mother has turned her head to look at something and does the same, or when a child turns his head or eyes in the direction someone is pointing. Joint attention allows the young child and another person to interact with their shared environment in the same frame of reference, an important factor in the development of language and social skills.

Deficits in joint attention help explain why children with autism have difficulty learning by observing others. To learn how to help students with autism develop joint attention and learn by observation, see DeQuinzio et al. (2018); Kourassanis-Velasquez & Jones (2019); Meindl & Cannella-Malone (2011); and Tekin-Iftar & Birkan, 2010).

Source: Laura Bolesta/Merrill Education

Mustafa's teacher uses a token board to remind him to use his speech and social skills to ask for help.

Communication and Language Deficits

Some children with autism do not speak, although they may hum or occasionally utter simple sounds. The speech of many who do talk consists largely of **echolalia**—verbatim repetitions of what people around them have said—and noncontextual, stereotyped utterances without any apparent communicative purpose. Echolalia may be immediate or delayed. For example, a 7-year-old boy with autism repeated throughout the day phrases he had heard from movies, cartoons, television shows, announcers of sporting events, and teachers during math instruction:

> "Hermione, we need to go find Harry!"
> "Hi, Squidward!"
> "Angelica, help me!"
> "Today's Noggin show was brought to you by your good friends at McDonald's."
> "Jeff Gordon rounds the far outside turn!"
> "Add five; carry the one." (Murphy, 2003, p. 22)

Some children with ASD have an impressive vocabulary but do not use it in appropriate or useful ways. A common characteristic of children with autism is the concrete or literal processing of verbal information. They understand straightforward cause-and-effect relationships and questions that have a definite answer more easily than they do abstract concepts, idioms, metaphors, sarcasm, or humor.

Repetitive, Ritualistic, and Unusual Behavior Patterns

Some children with autism engage in repetitive behaviors and ritualistic routines that are strikingly conspicuous. They may exhibit **stereotypy**, which is persistent and repetitive motor or vocal behaviors that do not serve any apparent function such as rocking their bodies when in a sitting position, twirling around, flapping their hands, flicking their fingers, sniffing at the air, or humming a set of three or four notes over and over again. For some individuals, the repetitive movement produces self-stimulation (e.g., sounds, sights, vestibular, and other sensations) that functions as automatic reinforcement to maintain the behavior (Lanovaz et al., 2011).

Many people without disabilities also engage in stereotypies, but they do so in privacy and at a far lower frequency than that of individuals with autism. A child with autism may spend hours at a time gazing at her cupped hands, staring at lights, spinning objects, clicking a ballpoint pen, and so on. These behaviors not only dominate much of the child's time, making it difficult at best to participate in and learn from lessons, but they are social stigma that inhibit others from interacting with the child in a normal way.

Insistence on Sameness

Many children with autism are inflexible with routines. They may insist on having all their books and pencils arranged in exactly the same way and get very upset if anything is moved. They may rigidly follow seemingly nonfunctional routines or habits, such as using a certain route to walk to and from their desk and other classroom locations, drinking only from a particular cup, or unwrapping a candy bar in a tedious and idiosyncratic manner. Even slight changes in their routines at home or in the classroom can trigger explosive "meltdowns" in some children.

Verbal children with autism may show this desire for sameness in a preoccupation with a certain subject or area of interest to the exclusion of all others. These children may talk incessantly about one topic, regardless of how bored their listeners are with it, and show no interest in anything else. They may ask the same question over and over, regardless of the reply.

Some educators view the intense preoccupation by students with ASD with their favorite obsessions as an eccentric foible at best and as an impediment to developing social relationships and engaging with the academic curriculum at worst. However, encouraging students' involvement with their special interest areas, be it tarantulas or thermometers, can lead to positive outcomes and strengths in other areas of functioning (Winter-Messiers et al., 2007). See *Teaching & Learning*, "Behavior Traps: Turning Obsessions to Motivational Gold."

Unusual Responsiveness to Sensory Stimuli

About 70% to 80% of individuals with autism react atypically to sensory stimulation (Simpson et al., 2019). This takes the form of over- and underresponsiveness to sensory stimulation. An *overresponsive* (hypersensitive) individual may not be able to tolerate certain sounds, being touched or the feel of certain textures, or foods with certain smells or tastes.

An *underresponsive* (hyposensitive) child appears oblivious to sensory stimulation to which most people react. Some children with autism do not seem to feel pain in a normal way. Some underresponsive children will spin around and around, rock back and forth, or rub and push things hard into their skin, perhaps to create additional forms or higher intensities of stimulation (Gabriels et al., 2008).

It is not uncommon for an individual with autism to display a combination of both over- and underresponsiveness—for example, being hypersensitive to tactile stimulation but unresponsive to many sounds. The child's responses (or lack thereof) to sensory stimulation may be highly variable across settings or situations and from day to day or even moment to moment. Fortunately, some fairly simple interventions (e.g., gradually increasing the intensity of stimulation until the person can habituate or get used to the sensation [Koegel et al., 2004)]) have been shown to help reduce fearful and avoidance responses to sensory stimulation by individuals with autism (Stiegler & Davis, 2010).

Cognitive Functioning

Autism spectrum disorder occurs across the full range of intellectual abilities. A national survey of 8-year-old children with ASD found that 42% had average or above-average IQ scores and 33% of children with ASD also meet the diagnostic criteria for intellectual disability (Centers for Disease Control and Prevention, 2020a). Some professionals use the terms *low-functioning autism* and *high-functioning autism* to differentiate individuals with and without intellectual disabilities.

Many children with autism have deficits in cognitive tasks and skills collectively called **executive functioning**, the ability to regulate one's own behavior, such as planning and goal setting, cognitive and behavioral flexibility, inhibition, working memory, and selective attention (Montgomery et al., 2012).

Uneven skill development is a common characteristic of ASD. About 10% of children exhibit "splinter skills," areas of relatively superior performance that are unexpected compared to other domains of functioning (Heaton et al., 2008). For example, a child may draw very well or remember things that were said a week before but have no functional language and refrain from eye contact.

Some individuals with autism exhibit **savant syndrome**, possessing remarkable talent in a particular area such as memorization, mathematical calculations, music, or drawing while functioning at the intellectually disabled level in most or all other areas. Although the term *autistic savant* is often used to refer to this phenomenon, only about half of people with savant syndrome have autism, and half have other forms of intellectual or developmental disabilities, central nervous system injury, or disease (Treffert, 2014). The amazing betting calculations performed by Raymond in the movie *Rain Man* are illustrative of savant syndrome (although Kim Peek, the man on whom the movie character was based, did not have autism; Brogaard, 2012).

Pearson eText
Video Example 7.1
Individuals with savant syndrome have remarkable abilities, such as phenomenal visual memory and attention to detail. https://www.youtube.com/watch?v=bsJbApZ5GF0

Extraordinary cases of *prodigious* savant syndrome occur when the skill exhibited by an individual with autism surpasses that even seen in the general population (Hughes et al., 2018). A well-known example is the artist Stephen Wiltshire, who draws hyper-detailed cityscapes from memory.

HLP21 Teach students to maintain and generalize new learning across time and settings.

TEACHING & LEARNING

Behavior Traps: Turning Obsessions to Motivational Gold

What Are Behavior Traps? Do you have an activity, hobby, or interest that you find so fascinating and fun you could spend hours on it without getting bored or tired of it? Are you so obsessed with this interest that you keep going back to it every chance you get? If so, you may have been ensnared by a **behavior trap**. Baited with virtually irresistible reinforcers, behavior traps can produce substantial, long-lasting behavior changes. For example, if you love to dance, you might dance every day to different music at different times of the day in different places with different people. All of this practice leads to learning new dances and ever-more sophisticated dance moves. The more adept you become, the more you enjoy dancing, which makes you dance even more.

Many students with autism have special areas of interest (SIAs) that can be used as motivation for teaching a wide range of academic, social, and functional skills. For example, if a student hates reading but loves Captain America, his teacher can use Captain America comic books as a tool for reading instruction. Here's how a teacher created a behavior trap that capitalized on a fifth grader's obsession with baseball cards:

> Carlos experiences school as tedious and unrewarding. But he does find solace in his baseball cards, often studying, sorting, and playing with them in class. His teacher, Ms. Greene, long ago lost count of the number of times she had to stop an instructional activity to separate Carlos and his beloved baseball cards. Then one day, when she approached Carlos' desk to confiscate his cards in the middle of a lesson on alphabetization, Ms. Greene discovered Carlos had already alphabetized all the left-handed pitchers in the National League! Ms. Greene realized she'd found the secret to sparking Carlos' academic development.
>
> Carlos was both astonished and thrilled to learn Ms. Greene not only let him keep his baseball cards at his desk, but also encouraged him to "play with them" during class. Before long, Ms. Greene had incorporated baseball cards into learning activities across the curriculum. In math, Carlos calculated batting averages; in geography, he located the hometown of every major leaguer born in his state; and in language arts, he wrote letters to his favorite players requesting an autographed photo. Carlos began to make significant gains academically, and an improvement in his attitude about school was also apparent (Alber, S. R., Heward, W. L. (1996). "GOTCHA!" Twenty-Five Behavior Traps Guaranteed to Extend Your Students' Academic and Social Skills. Intervention in School and Clinic Vol. 31(5), pp. 285-289. Copyright © 1996 by Hammill Institute on Disabilities. Reprinted by permission of SAGE Publications, Inc.).

How Can I Use Behavior Traps?

1. **Identify the SIA.** This is the easiest assessment a teacher will ever conduct. The objects, events, people, or activities that qualify as SIAs are known to anyone who has spent any time with the child. Tyler Lewis, the young man with autism you met in Chapter 1, loved maps when he was a boy; he endlessly talked about, looked at, and drew maps.
2. **Incorporate the SIA across the curriculum.** Tyler's fascination with maps could be integrated easily into math, reading, writing, science, and social studies lessons.
3. **Make "getting caught" easy.** The student doesn't have to earn his way into a behavior trap. Free access to the SIA will lure the student into the trap. Provide materials needed to engage in the SIA and prompt the student to use them in ways that incorporate the targeted skills (e.g., "That's an interesting map, Tyler. Would you show me how many different types of structures are identified on it?").
4. **Start small and use the trap judiciously.** Use the SIA to help the student improve skills with which he has experienced some success and then gradually add new skills. Even though Tyler is crazy about maps, requiring him to write a 10-page research report on the topic (especially if his writing skills are poor) could destroy the effectiveness of maps as behavior trap bait. Better to begin by asking Tyler to label and classify his favorite map components, then write brief descriptions about them, then compare and contrast the functions of the components,

and so on. In time, Tyler may write reports with all the detail of an experienced cartographer. Figure 7.1 shows examples of behavior trap activities across curriculum areas for a student whose SIA is horses.

5. **Don't be in a hurry to eliminate the SIA.** Remember you're not trying to eliminate the student's interest but rather use it to motivate the student to learn new skills, which may eventually lead to other interests.
6. **Involve the target student's peers.** Encourage peers to participate in SIA-related curriculum activities. Peer involvement gives the target student opportunities to practice social and language skills. A bonus may be that peers acquire interest in and useful knowledge about their classmate's SIA.
7. **Periodically change the curriculum areas and activities associated with the SIA.** Although a student may not tire of his SIA outside the trap, an SIA may lose its effectiveness as bait if a trap focuses solely on a single curriculum area or activity.
8. **Evaluate.** Look for improvements in the skills and knowledge the behavior trap was designed to "catch." Collect data on the amount of time the student actively engages with the SIA-related curriculum, the completion and accuracy of academic products, and the student's comments. The student's behavior will suggest ways that an ineffective trap can be revised. Over time, the student's interest in the curriculum area(s) baited with the SIA may grow to the point where the trap is no longer necessary. To learn more about behavior traps, see Alber and Heward (1996).

FIGURE 7.1 Behavior Trap Planning Sheet

Student *Monique* Special Interest Area(s)—The Bait *Horses*

CURRICULUM AREA	SETTING THE TRAP	ONCE INSIDE THE TRAP
Reading: comprehension	*Place colorful books about horses on the bookshelf.*	*Monique will select a book about horses, read it, and retell her three favorite parts.*
Math: applying formulas	*Show video of horse races.*	*Monique will apply Distance = Rate x Time to calculate distance, rate, and time given two of the three variables for a horse race.*
Science: classification	*Display photos and/or models of different breeds and types of horses and close relatives (ponies, mules).*	*Monique will create a biological classification chart showing the kingdom, phylum, class, order, family, genus, and species for horses.*
Social Studies: historical timelines	*Show video of last three Triple Crown winners.*	*Using the Internet, Monique will research and draw a timeline (1900 to 1948) illustrating important events related to equestrian competition.*
Social interaction & communication skills: asking questions	*Take a field trip to a stable or farm.*	*Prepare questions to ask professional who professionals who work with horses.*

Many children with ASD exhibit *overselectivity*, the tendency to focus on a minute feature of an object or a person rather than the whole. For example, if shown a guitar for the first time, a child might focus on the sound hole and not consider anything else about the instrument, such as its size, shape, other parts, or even the sound it makes. This overselectivity interferes with the child's understanding of what a guitar is—the totality of its parts and function. The tendency to overselect hinders learning new concepts and interferes with the child's ability to interpret relevant meaning from the environment. The tendency to attend to individual details rather than integrate them into a gestalt or "big picture" is a key element of a neuropsychological theory in autism called *weak central coherence* (Noens & van Berckelaer-Onnes, 2005).

Obsessive attention on a specific object or activity is another characteristic often seen in individuals with ASD. This focused attention may last for a long time and can be very difficult to break. For instance, if a child with autism has focused her attention on trains, she may continually choose to play with trains and resist playing with other toys. Focused attention may impede the child's ability to shift attention to other people or activities, such as a parent who is entering the room or another child who is attempting to join her play.

Some children with autism possess a strong aptitude for rote memory for certain things. For example, a child with autism may be able to name all of baseball's Cy Young Award winners since 1956 and repeat the script of an entire movie verbatim. Yet the same child may not recall what he did during recess or remember the sound the letter *k* makes.

Challenging Behavior

Some children with autism exhibit challenging behavior in the form of property destruction, aggression toward others, and even self-injury. Parents often describe their children's aggression as "constant" or "never ending" and that the "cumulative fatigue was almost unbearable" (Hodgetts et al., 2013, p. 169).

Many individuals with autism experience sleep problems, such as delayed onset of sleep, brief sleep duration, and night walking. Said one parent: "We never slept. You're always listening for him. He was a wanderer and would get into trouble and light fires and leave and unlock the house" (Hodgetts et al., 2013, p. 169). Food and eating problems are also common in children with ASD. Some children have extremely narrow food preferences, often sensory based (e.g., refusing foods of certain textures); some refuse to eat altogether; and some choke, gag, and spit out food (Bandini et al., 2017). Some children with autism engage in **pica**, the compulsive, recurrent consumption of nonfood items (e.g., paper, dirt, pebbles, hair). Stiegler (2005) cited the following account of one parent's experience with his child's pica:

> Over the last couple years we have pulled out of [our son's] throat: a set of keys, large bulldog clips, sticks, rocks, wads of paper, opened safety pins, wire (from the screen). Plus add the stuff that he gets down before we can get it out: magnets from the fridge, Barbie parts, paper, money, paper clips, etc. (Menard, 1999, n.p.).

The high-intensity and sometimes dangerous behaviors of some children with autism create tremendous stress on parents and can lead to family dysfunction if not brought under control (Osborne & Reed, 2009). Thompson (2009) details practical, research-based interventions to prevent severe emotional outbursts and other behavior problems by children with autism in home, school, and community settings.

Asperger Syndrome

At the mild end of the autism spectrum is **Asperger syndrome**. Although Asperger syndrome is no longer recognized as a separate diagnostic category in the DSM, many students receiving special education still carry the diagnosis, and numerous organizations and researchers focus their efforts on individuals with Asperger syndrome. The most distinctive feature of Asperger syndrome is impairment in social areas, particularly an inability to understand how to interact with others. Deficits in the use of nonverbal behaviors related to social interaction such as eye gaze, facial expression, gestures, body posture, and personal space are common. Children with Asperger syndrome do not have general language delay, and most have average or above-average intelligence.

Some professionals use the term "high-functioning autism" to describe these individuals (Ozonoff et al., 2015). Following are other characteristics many individuals with Asperger syndrome exhibit (Attwood, 2008; Autism Society, 2019; Smith Myles et al., 2014):

- Intense interest in a particular subject, often atypical things or parts of things (e.g., deep-fat fryers, ZIP codes, washing-machine motors), to the exclusion of everything else
- Clumsiness, difficulty with fine- and/or gross-motor activities
- Inflexible adherence to routines

- Fascination with maps, globes, and routes
- Superior rote memory; tendency to amass many related facts
- Speech and language impairments in the areas of semantics, pragmatics, and prosody (volume, intonation, inflection, and rhythm); pedantic, odd speech patterns; formal style of speaking
- Difficulty understanding others' feelings
- Extensive vocabulary, reading commences at an early age
- Perfectionist; frustrated when asked to submit work they believe is below standard

Difficulty reading other people's feelings makes developing romantic relationships especially hard for teens and young adults with Asperger syndrome. Their peculiarities and social skills deficits make it difficult for children with Asperger syndrome to develop and maintain friendships. Because they are highly verbal and often have superior intelligence, students with Asperger syndrome are often misdiagnosed as having obsessive-compulsive disorder or attention-deficit/hyperactivity disorder (ADHD).

Positive Attributes and Strengths of Students with Autism Spectrum Disorder

Pearson eText Video Example 7.2
Many individuals with autism are affectionate and caring.

After reading descriptions of the social and communication impairments, skill deficits, and behavioral excesses exhibited by individuals with ASD, it is easy to overlook their strengths and positive attributes. Not all individuals with ASD are unattached to those around them or consistently behave in a stilted or inappropriate manner. Many children with autism are loving and caring, thoughtful and creative. Recall Tyler Lewis, the young man with autism you met in Chapter 1? Tyler has many positive qualities and enthusiastically talks about his interests and accomplishments. Tyler's family has three dogs, and a dog with a disability has become Tyler's favorite.

As we might expect, a noticeable difference exists between descriptions of autism by people with and without the condition (Grandin, 1995; Kluth, 2004; Willey, 2003). Although people without disabilities tend to focus on the social, communication, and cognitive differences compared with typical functioning, many people with autism and Asperger syndrome have described positive features associated with their disability.

Temple Grandin (2006) describes some of the positive aspects of the way she experiences autism, as follows:

> I think in pictures and sounds. I don't have the ability to process abstract thought the way that you do. Here's how my brain works: It's like the search engine Google for images. If you say the word "love" to me, I'll surf the Internet inside my brain. Then, a series of images pops into my head. What I'll see, for example, is a picture of a mother horse with a foal, or I think of "Herbie the Lovebug," scenes from the movie *Love Story* or the Beatles song, "Love, love, all you need is love . . . ."
>
> [O]ne of the features of being autistic is that I'm good at synthesizing lots of information and creating systems out of it.
>
> Some people might think if I could snap my fingers I'd choose to be "normal." But I wouldn't want to give up my ability to see in beautiful, precise pictures. I believe in them. (n.p.)

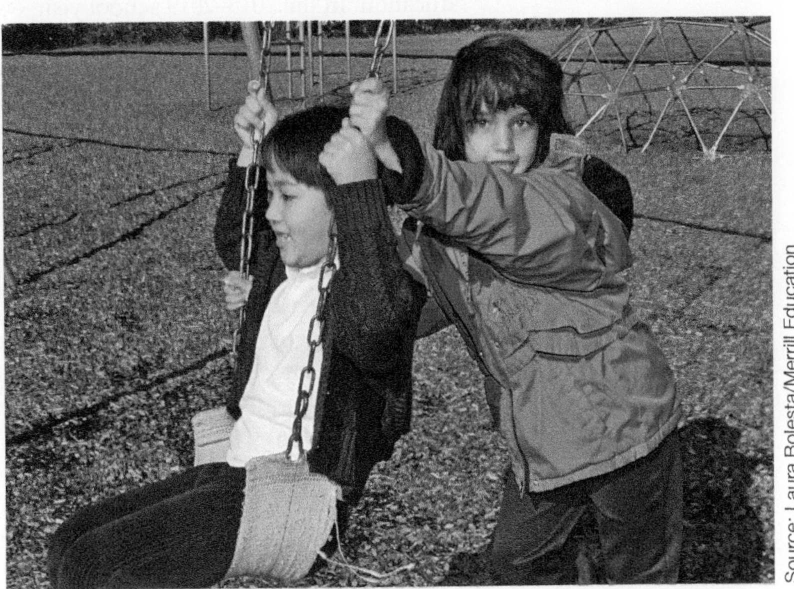

Source: Laura Bolesta/Merrill Education

Teachers should recognize and build on the positive attributes and strengths of children with autism spectrum disorders.

Greta Thunberg, the Swedish teenager whose school strike for climate sparked a worldwide movement to decrease carbon emissions, discovered her special interest in climate change when she was just 9 years old and could not understand why everyone wasn't similarly obsessed with preventing it (Silberman, 2019). Thunberg, a 2020 Nobel Peace Prize nominee, calls Asperger syndrome her "superpower" and says it has helped her in life:

> It makes me different, and being different is a gift, I would say. It also makes me see things from outside the box. I don't easily fall for lies, I can see through things. If I would've been like everyone else, I wouldn't have started this school strike, for instance. (BBC News, 2019)

Prevalence

Learning Outcome 7.2 List factors that might account for the enormous increase in the prevalence of ASD in recent years and how the search for causes of autism has changed from the first reports of the disability to today.

Once considered a rare disorder, autism today is far more common than childhood cancer, Down syndrome, or diabetes. The reported incidence of autism has increased dramatically in recent years. Since the Centers for Disease Control and Prevention (CDC) reported in 2000 that about 1 in 150 children in the United States had been identified with ASD, the incidence rate has since been revised upward seven times to 1 in 54 children in 2020 (CDC, 2020a).

The CDC's latest estimate is based on data from 2016 on both 8-year-old and 4-year-old children that show more children are being evaluated and identified with autism at younger ages. "Some of the increase in autism prevalence might be due to the way children are identified, diagnosed, and receiving services in their communities. The increase may also reflect reductions in racial differences in identification of autism, as this is the first ADDM Network report to identify black 8-year-olds with autism as having the same rates as white children" (CDC, 2020b).

The rise in autism prevalence is an international phenomenon, with studies from Asia, Europe, and North America reporting approximate prevalence rates of between 1% and 2%, including a recent study in South Korea showing 2.6% (Chiarotti & Venerosi, 2020). ASD is more than four times as common in boys and occurs in all racial, ethnic, and socioeconomic groups.

Autism is now the fourth-largest and the fastest growing disability category in special education. In the 2018–2019 school year, 663,844 students age 6 to 21 and 92,990 preschoolers received special education services under the IDEA category of autism (U.S. Department of Education, 2020a). This number of school-age children is 8.4 times the number of school-age students with autism served during 2000–2001. As was the case with the increase in the number of children diagnosed with learning disabilities from the early 1980s through the turn of the century, the factors responsible for the dramatic increase in the number of children receiving special education under the autism category are unclear. The increase is likely attributable to a confluence of factors, including greater awareness of ASD, changes in federal and state policy and law favoring better identification and reporting of autism, improved screening and assessment procedures, greater availability of services for the diagnostic category, greater acceptance of the label by parents and educators, and changes in the diagnostic criteria to a spectrum of related disorders that includes children with milder forms of autism who would not have been identified previously (Mazumdar et al., 2013; Taylor, 2006). Another contributing factor may be diagnosis shift; as the number of students with autism has increased, the numbers in the disability categories of learning disabilities, emotional or behavioral disorders, and intellectual disabilities have all decreased in recent years.

Some experts believe, however, all of these factors together do not account for the total increase in the prevalence of autism and an increase in the true incidence of ASD has occurred (Blaxhill, 2004; Hertz-Picciotto & Delwiche, 2009). Regardless of causes, the increased number of children being identified with ASD presents a public health and educational challenge for society and schools that must develop the infrastructure and expertise to serve them. It also heightens the need for research into causes of autism and for development of ever more effective treatments.

Causes

Autism is a neurodevelopmental disorder with no medical or physiological markers. About 85% of cases are *idiopathic*, meaning the cause is unknown (National Human Genome Research Institute, 2019). As Schreibman (2005) noted, "When a definite etiology for a disorder is unknown, theories of etiology proliferate. Nowhere is that more apparent than in the field of autism" (p. 75). So many causes of autism have been proposed over the years that "it's a dull month without a new cause for autism" (Rutter, 2002).

From the 1950s to the mid-1970s, many professionals believed that parental indifference to the emotional needs of their children caused autism. This notion may have had its beginnings in Kanner's (1943) observations that many of the parents of his original "autistic" group were preoccupied and that "there were very few really warmhearted fathers and mothers" (p. 50).

During the 1950s and 1960s, Bruno Bettelheim perpetuated the notion that autism could be attributed to inadequate parenting. Bettelheim's (1967) theory of *psychogenesis* claimed that autism was an outcome of uninterested, cold parents who were unable to develop an emotional bond with their children. Mothers of children with autism were called "refrigerator mothers" and led to believe they had caused their children's disability. Such blame creates a great deal of guilt on top of the grief already experienced when parents find their toddler exhibiting the disturbing behavioral markers of autism. Although a causal link between parenting style and autism has never been discovered, the misconception still receives media attention from time to time, and many parents must battle the unnecessary guilt associated with that initial blame (Association for Science in Autism Treatment, 2020).

So, if parental practices are not a factor, what then does cause autism? Scientists are not sure, but current research focuses on three sources: neuropathology, genetic inheritance, and environmental toxins.

Neuropathology

Recent research shows a clear biological origin for autism in the form of abnormal prenatal and postnatal brain development, structure, or neurochemistry (DiCicco-Bloom et al., 2006; Potvin & Ratto, 2019; Schultz et al., 2006). Although the precise neurobiological mechanisms associated with autism have not been discovered, "it is clear that autism reflects the operation of factors in the developing brain" (National Research Council, 2001, p. 11). Studies of brain function point out differences in processing in different regions of the brain but also possible differences in connectivity.

Genetic Factors

Autism clearly has a genetic component: Having one child with autism greatly increases the chances of having another child with autism. A study of 1.5 million families in the United States with 2 children, the eldest diagnosed with ASD, found rates of reoccurrence of ASD in younger male children of 12.9% if the older sibling with ASD was male and 16.7% if the older sibling was female (Palmer et al., 2017). The rates of recurrence of ASD among female children were 7.6% if the affected sibling was female and 4.2% if male. The authors concluded, "An older female sibling with ASD is associated with greater risk of recurrence in the younger sibling compared with an older diagnosed male sibling, and male siblings are more likely to experience recurrence than female siblings regardless of the sex of the diagnosed sibling" (p. 1107).

A study of Swedish children born from 1982 to 2007 found siblings of a child with ASD have 10-fold the normal risk of also developing the disorder, cousins twice as likely (Sandin et al., 2014). Studies of identical twins have reported that if one child has ASD, then the other will be affected about 36% to 95% of the time (National Institute of Neurological Disorders and Stroke [NINDS], 2020). Autism risk also increases in children born to older parents.

Numerous genetic links with autism have been identified, but scientists still do not completely understand their causal relationships. The largest genetic sequencing study reported to date found 102 genes linked to risk for autism. ASD genes alter early development broadly; others appear more specific to ASD (Satterstrom et al., 2020).

About 10% of children with autism have a genetic and chromosomal disorder such as Down syndrome, fragile X syndrome, or tuberous sclerosis (DiGuiseppi et al., 2010; Zafeiriou et al., 2013). Research of families in which only one child has ASD helps identify whether genetic changes are being passed from parents to child or whether genetic changes exist in the child alone. Gene mutations found only in children with ASD and not in their parents or siblings, called a *de novo mutation*, may be linked to ASD (Anderson, 2014).

Most individuals with ASD have no genetic history of autism, suggesting that random, rare, and possibly multiple gene mutations are likely to affect a person's risks. However, a genetic factor is not the singular cause because if one identical twin has autism, the other twin may not. Because identical twins share the same genes, some other factor or combination of factors must be at work. The current theory among autism genetics researchers supports the idea of complex inheritance. This means multiple genetic factors are likely involved, which in combination may predispose an individual to developing autism. There is still much research to be done to determine the potential role of environmental factors on spontaneous mutations and how that influences ASD risk (NINDS, 2020).

Environmental Factors

In addition to the presence of a necessary, but currently still unknown, combination of autism-related genes, exposure to certain environmental factors may lead to the development of autism in some children (Modabbernia et al., 2017). Raz and colleagues (2015) found that expectant mothers exposed to high levels of air pollution in the form of particulate matter from vehicles, power plants, and fires, particularly in the third trimester, were more likely to have a child with autism than expectant mothers living in cleaner areas. Exposure to air pollution during developmental years may also play a role. A study of 279 children with autism and 245 typically developing children in California found that children with autism were three times more likely to have been exposed to higher levels of regional air pollution and to diesel exhaust particles from living near freeways in their first year of life than the typical children (Volk et al., 2013).

Toxic chemicals can harm the developing human brain. A review of the literature by Grandjean and Landrigan (2014) identified 11 industrial chemicals (e.g., lead, methylmercury, polychlorinated biphenyls, arsenic, toluene, manganese) as developmental neurotoxicants with potential links to autism and other neurodevelopmental disabilities. The authors postulated that "even more neurotoxicants remain undiscovered" and that "chemicals in existing use and all new chemicals must therefore be tested for developmental neurotoxicity" (p. 330).

Most people who have been exposed to environmental risk factors do not develop ASD. As with genes, it is likely that a combination of environmental factors is involved in increasing risk for ASD. Genes and environmental factors may be interrelated by a process called *epigenetics*, whereby an environmental factor changes the normal activity of certain genes (Lyall et al., 2017; NINDS, 2020).

Research continues to bring us closer to revealing causes of autism, which in turn may lead to prevention and more effective treatments. Research has also eliminated several suspected causes of autism, such as parenting practices and vaccinations (see Figure 7.2).

In 1998, an English physician, Andrew Wakefield, suggested the measles, mumps, and rubella (MMR) vaccine damaged children's gastrointestinal system, which led to regressed development and autism. Wakefield's hypothesis received tremendous media coverage worldwide. Worried parents elected not to have their children vaccinated, which in turn caused a spike in MMR diseases in children, including several deaths.

No research has found a connection between the mumps-measles-rubella (MMR) vaccine (or vaccines containing thimerosal, a mercury-based preservative that prevents bacterial

FIGURE 7.2 Vaccines Do Not Cause Autism

In 1998, an English physician, Andrew Wakefield, suggested the measles, mumps, and rubella (MMR) vaccine insulted children's gastrointestinal system, which led to regressed development and autism. Wakefield's hypothesis received tremendous media coverage worldwide. Worried parents elected not to have their children vaccinated, which in turn caused a spike in MMR diseases in children, including several deaths.

No research has found a connection between the MMR vaccine (or vaccines containing thimerosal used for protection against diphtheria, tetanus, pertussis, and hepatitis B) and autism (American Academy of Pediatrics, 2013). A study of more than 95,000 children who have older siblings with and without autism spectrum disorder (ASD) found "no harmful association between MMR vaccine receipt and ASD even among children already at higher risk for ASD" (Jain et al., 2015, p. 1534)

Numerous questions about the legitimacy of the study on which Wakefield derived his "gut theory" of autism (Wakefield et al., 2008) led to an investigation by Britain's General Medical Council, which discovered that Wakefield had a financial conflict of interest with a lawyer planning to bring suit against vaccine manufacturers for causing autism (Deer, 2010). *The Lancet*, the British medical journal that had published the article, retracted the paper (Editors of *The Lancet*, 2010). Accounts of the Wakefield MMR vaccine scare by Ahearn (2010) and Deer (2010) provide vivid examples of why public policy and personal decisions regarding health and education should be informed by reliable science.

growth) and autism (American Academy of Pediatrics, 2018). A meta-analysis of five cohort studies involving 1,256,407 children and five case-control studies involving 9920 children were included in this analysis, which revealed no relationship between vaccination and autism (Taylor et al., 2014). A study of more than 95,000 children who have older siblings with and without autism spectrum disorder (ASD) found "no harmful association between MMR vaccine receipt and ASD even among children already at higher risk for ASD" (Jain et al., 2015, p. 1534). Research has also found no evidence for a connection between increased risk for ASD and the Tdap vaccination given to pregnant women whose infants are at highest risk of death after pertussis infection (Becerra-Culqui et al., 2018).

Numerous questions about the legitimacy of the study on which Wakefield derived his "gut theory" of autism (Wakefield et al., 2008) led to an investigation by Britain's General Medical Council, which discovered that Wakefield had a financial conflict of interest with a lawyer planning to bring suit against vaccine manufacturers for causing autism (Deer, 2010). *The Lancet*, the British medical journal that had published the article, retracted the paper (Editors of *The Lancet*, 2010). Accounts of the Wakefield MMR vaccine scare by Ahearn (2010) and Deer (2010) provide vivid examples of why public policy and personal decisions regarding health and education should be informed by reliable science.

Identification and Assessment

Learning Outcome 7.3 Explain why valid and reliable tools for early screening and diagnosis of ASD are so critical.

Because the specific neurobiological causes of autism are not known, no medical test for ASD is available. Determining whether a child has an ASD is based on professional assessment of behavioral characteristics per the DSM.

The parents of 21 children diagnosed with autism reported that the average age of their child when they first recognized something was wrong was 15 months (Hutton & Caron, 2005). The changes in behavior associated with autism may be gradual or quite sudden, as shown in the following parent's account reported by Fleischmann (2004):

> It wasn't a gradual change that happened. It was an Invasion of the Body Snatchers experience. One day he looked the same and that's the only way I recognized him. He no longer made eye contact, spoke, sang, interacted .... He screamed and cried and stayed awake and stomped and hid under mattresses and pillows and ate dirt (p. 39).

Autism can be reliably diagnosed at 18 months, and researchers are pursuing reliable methods for detecting warning signs in children as young as 6 months (Jones & Klin, 2013; Landa et al., 2007). One study reported that functional neuroimaging of a high-risk 6-month-old predicted a diagnosis of autism at 24 months of age with 96% accuracy (Emerson et al., 2017). Early diagnosis enables early intervention, which correlates with dramatically better outcomes than are typically obtained when intervention begins later in the child's life.

Unfortunately, an analysis of two U.S. surveys found that one third to one half of children with autism are formally diagnosed after age 6 years (Sheldrick et al., 2017). Parents who described their children's ASD as severe reported age-at-identification means of 3.7 and 4.5 years; children of parents who described their children's ASD as mild were identified at average ages 5.6 and 8.6 years. A study of 1420 families of children with ASD indicated an average wait time of 3 years between parents' first concerns and receiving a diagnosis of ASD (Oswald et al., 2017).

Screening

Many parents of children with autism report their baby developed in typical fashion for the first year or more, acquiring some meaningful communication skills and enjoying cuddling and hugging. But then between 12 and 15 months of age, the child began showing oversensitivity to certain sounds or touch; no longer seemed to understand even simple words or gestures; and became increasingly withdrawn, aimless, and perseverative (Wetherby et al., 2004). Sometimes the early warning signs appear well before the baby's first birthday. When they do appear during the first year of life, they usually are not in the form of delays in major motor milestones (Landa et al., 2007). Many babies who are later diagnosed with autism often sit, crawl, and start to walk on time but show delayed or unusual development in social and communication domains.

Signs that warrant concern during the first year and a half of life include lack of pointing or gestures, infrequent or poor-quality imitation of the caregiver's facial expressions, no single words by 16 months, lack of smiling, not responding to their name when called, lack of joint attention (e.g., not looking at what parent looks at or points to), and loss of previously acquired language or social skills at any age (Hyman et al., 2020; Kalb et al., 2010). In addition to these early markers, very young children with ASD may engage in repetitive and stereotyped patterns of specific behaviors by, for example, repeating certain behaviors over and over; saying scripted verses from familiar videos or TV shows again and again; or showing obsessive interest in certain objects, activities, or parts of objects.

The American Academy of Pediatrics recommends all children be screened with a standardized autism-specific screening tool at 18 and again at 24 months of age to identify children whose development may have regressed (Hyman et al., 2020). Brief descriptions of three widely used ASD screening instruments follow. More information about the early warning signs of autism and other developmental disorders can be found at the CDC "Learn the Signs. Act Early" website and at Autism Navigator (2020), which include a video glossary of early symptoms in toddlers.

Source: AISPIX/Shutterstock

Autism-specific screening tools detect early warning signs of autism, such as lack of joint attention, the failure to look at what a parent looks or points at.

MODIFIED CHECKLIST FOR AUTISM IN TODDLERS (M-CHAT-R/F) The M-CHAT-R/F (Robins et al., 2009) is an expanded American version of the original CHAT, which was developed in the United Kingdom (Baron-Cohen et al., 1992). A free online screening tool, the M-CHAT-R/F consists of 20 yes-or-no questions parents or guardians answer, such as the following:

- If you point at something across the room, does your child look at it? (For example, if you point at a toy or an animal, does your child look at the toy or animal?)

- Does your child play pretend or make-believe? (For example, pretend to drink from an empty cup, pretend to talk on a phone, or pretend to feed a doll or stuffed animal?)
- Does your child make unusual finger movements near his or her eyes? (For example, does your child wiggle his or her fingers close to his or her eyes?)
- When you smile at your child, does he or she smile back at you?
- Does your child try to copy what you do? (For example, wave bye-bye, clap, or make a funny noise when you do?)

When the M-CHAT results indicate the child may not be developing like other children of the same age, parents are encouraged to review the findings with their pediatrician or have a developmental evaluation with a specialist (or both). About half of children classified as at-risk by the M-CHAT-R/F are subsequently diagnosed with ASD (Robins et al., 2015).

SOCIAL COMMUNICATION QUESTIONNAIRE (SCQ) The SCQ is a 40-item screening tool a parent or other primary caregiver completes in less than 10 minutes (Rutter et al., 2003). The SCQ was developed for screening children age 4 years and older, and research shows decreased accuracy with younger children (Chestnut et al., 2017). Barnard-Brak et al. (2016) suggested that the SCQ may be more appropriate for screening children in the later years of primary school and a screening instrument such as the M-CHAT be used for toddlers.

AUTISM SPECTRUM SCREENING QUESTIONNAIRE (ASSQ) The ASSQ is a 27-item checklist parents and teachers complete when screening for Asperger syndrome and other high-functioning ASDs in children (Ehlers et al., 1999).

Diagnosis

Children who fail screening tests or whose parents or caregivers have reason for concern undergo a complete diagnostic evaluation. A professional with expertise in autism, typically a developmental pediatrician, psychologist, psychiatrist, or neurologist, should give an autism diagnosis. Following are brief descriptions of several rating scales, observation checklists, and diagnostic interviews that have been developed to aid the examiner's evaluation of a child suspected of having ASD. Professionals and parents should remember, however, that no single test or assessment device is fail proof, especially when diagnosing a disability with such a wide range of expression.

CHILDHOOD AUTISM RATING SCALE (CARS-2) The CARS is one of the most widely used instruments for diagnosing autism in children age 2 years and older. It consists of a 15-item rating scale completed by the clinician based on information from a parent report, records, and direct observation of the child (Schopler et al., 2010).

AUTISM DIAGNOSTIC INTERVIEW—REVISED (ADI-R) AND AUTISM DIAGNOSTIC OBSERVATION SCHEDULE (ADOS-2) The ADI-R is a semi-structured interview of the primary caregivers of a child or adult suspected of having autism (Rutter et al., 2003). A trained examiner conducts a detailed interview with the child's primary caregiver, typically requiring at least 2 hours to complete. Questions cover communication, social development, and play; repetitive and restrictive behaviors; behavior problems; and family characteristics. Results from the ADI-R ideally are supplemented by the ADOS-2, which entails a trained examiner working with the child in a prescribed set of interactions designed to evoke behaviors characteristic of autism (Lord et al., 2000). Many researchers consider the ADOS-2 to be the "gold standard" for diagnostic instrument for autism (Camodeca et al., 2020).

ASPERGER SYNDROME DIAGNOSTIC SCALE (ASDS) The ASDS is designed to identify Asperger syndrome in children age 5 through 18 years (Smith Myles et al., 2000). It consists of 50 yes-or-no items that can be answered by parents, family members, teachers, speech-language pathologists, psychologists, and other professionals familiar with the child. The ASDS yields a quotient that predicts the likelihood the individual has Asperger syndrome. Camodeca et al. (2020) tested the utility of the ASDA for identifying autism spectrum disorder per DSM-5 diagnostic criteria and found inconsistent results. These researchers concluded that ASDS might best be used as a screener to prioritize cases for ASD assessment.

Educational Approaches

Learning Outcome 7.4 Describe several evidence-based strategies for teaching students with ASD and specify what distinguishes them from unproven, faddish approaches.

Children with autism are among the most challenging students to teach. They may focus on irrelevant stimuli while seeming oblivious to instructional stimuli; show little or no apparent interest in their teachers and peers; and with little or no warning have a "meltdown" that includes aggression, property destruction, self-injury, or all three. Seldom does a child with autism progress without an education that is truly special. Such children require instruction that is meticulously planned, skillfully delivered, and continually evaluated and analyzed for its effectiveness. Here is the good news: Working together, researchers and practitioners have discovered practices that significantly improve educational outcomes for children with autism.

In this section we examine the importance of early intervention, introduce applied behavior analysis as a fundamental source of science-based teaching practices, and describe several instructional strategies for teaching children with autism. Figure 7.3 identifies some key events in the history of understanding and educating children with ASD.

FIGURE 7.3 Key Historical Events in the Education of Children with Autism Spectrum Disorder

DATE	HISTORICAL EVENT	EDUCATIONAL IMPLICATIONS
1911	Eugen Bluer, a Swiss psychiatrist, coins the term *autism*—from the Greek word, *autos* (self)—to describe patients with schizophrenia who actively withdrew from social contact.	When used later to name a condition in children who displayed behaviors similar to Bluer's patients, the term *autism* implied that children purposely withdrew from those around them.
1943	Leo Kanner, a child psychiatrist at Johns Hopkins University, describes the characteristics of a childhood disorder he calls *early infantile autism*.	Kanner's observation that "there were very few really warmhearted fathers and mothers" may have caused some to speculate that indifferent, nonresponsive parents were -responsible for the disorder.
1944	Hans Asperger, an Austrian pediatrician with a special interest in "psychically abnormal" children, publishes a paper describing a pattern of behavior based on his work with more than 400 children with "autistic psychopathy."	The combination of behaviors and abilities he described later came to be known as Asperger syndrome.
1965	The Autism Society is founded (originally National Society for Autistic Children).	The Autism Society promotes services and information that maximize quality of life and dignity for individuals and families living with autism.
1967	Bruno Bettelheim's book, *An Empty Fortress*, advances the notion that children with autism purposively withdrew into their own worlds because of cold and uncaring parents.	Bettelheim's theory that "refrigerator mothers" caused autism led to professional blaming of parents and devastating guilt.
1981	Lorna Wing publishes an article in Great Britain in which the term *Asperger syndrome* is used for the first time.	Wing's seminal paper generated renewed interest in Asperger syndrome, especially in Europe.
1987	Ivar Lovaas publishes results of the Young Autism Project, in which children with autism participated in an intensive early intervention program of one-to-one behavioral treatment for an average of 40 hours per week for 2 years or more before age 4 years.	This was the first study to show that early, intensive, behavioral intervention could enable some children with autism to achieve normal functioning. It gave hope to parents and provided researchers and practitioners with principles on which to build.
1990	Individuals with Disabilities Education Act (IDEA) Amendments of 1990 (PL 101-476)	Autism added as a disability category under which children are entitled to special education.
1993	Catherine Maurice's *Let Me Hear Your Voice: A Family's Triumph Over Autism* is published.	This powerful account of a mother's efforts to find help for her two children raised worldwide attention to the importance of science-based autism treatments.
1994	Asperger syndrome is officially recognized in the *Diagnostic and Statistical Manual of Mental Disorders* (DSM-IV) as a pervasive developmental disability within the autism spectrum.	This created increased awareness of Asperger syndrome among clinicians, researchers, and educators.
1994	The National Alliance for Autism Research (NAAR) is founded, the first organization in the United States dedicated to promoting research seeking to identify causes and potential biomedical cures for autism.	NAAR-funded research has been leveraged into more than $48 million in autism research awards by the National Institutes of Health and other funding sources and has led to advances in the neurosciences and other scientific fields.
1998	The Association for Science in Autism Treatment (ASAT) is founded.	The ASAT's mission is to educate parents, professionals, and policymakers by disseminating accurate, scientifically sound information about autism and its treatment and by combating inaccurate or unsubstantiated information.

(Continued)

FIGURE 7.3 (Continued)

DATE	HISTORICAL EVENT	EDUCATIONAL IMPLICATIONS
2000	The Behavior Analyst Certification Board begins credentialing Board Certified Behavior Analysts (BCBA).	The BACB gives parents, schools, and agencies assurance that a BCBA has achieved a certain level of knowledge/skills regarding effective and ethical practice of applied behavior analysis (ABA).
2002	Council for Exceptional Children's (CEC) Division on Developmental Disabilities (DDD) renamed Division on Autism and Developmental Disabilities (DADD).	Special educators with interests in ASD have a centralized source of information and a voice within CEC.
2005	Autism Speaks founded with $25 million by grandparents of a child with autism.	Autism Speaks is the nation's largest autism science and advocacy organization, dedicated to funding research into the causes, prevention, treatments and a cure for autism; increasing awareness of ASD; and advocating for the needs of individuals with ASD and their families.
2006	The Interactive Autism Network (IAN) is established at the Kennedy Krieger Institute.	IAN Community is an online library and meeting place where everyone concerned with autism spectrum disorders (ASDs) can learn more about autism research. IAN Research matches willing individuals with ASDs and their families with appropriate local and national research projects.
2006	Combating Autism Act of 2006 (PL 109-416)	Authorized nearly $1 billion over more than 5 years to combat autism through research, screening, early detection, and early intervention, increasing federal spending on autism by at least 50%. It includes provisions relating to the diagnosis and treatment of persons with ASD and expands biomedical research on autism, including a focus on possible environmental causes.
2009	National Autism Center publishes results of its National Standards Project, a review of existing research literature by expert panel to identify evidence-based treatment approaches for autism.	The NAC also published a handbook for educators and parents outlining specific evidence-based program components, procedures, and implementation strategies.
2013	The American Psychiatric Association published revised definition of ASD in the DSM-5.	Autistic disorder and Asperger disorder are subsumed within ASD; three levels of severity are added, depending on the extent of supports needed for everyday functioning.
2017	*Endrew F. v. Douglas Country School District*	In a case brought by the parents of a boy with autism, the Supreme Court ruled unanimously that IEPs must be reasonably calculated to enable children to make progress relative to their unique circumstances (Yell & Bateman, 2017).
2019	Autism CARES Act of 2019 (PL 116-60)	Reauthorization of Combating Autism Act increases annual funding to more than $369 million through 2024 by 2019.

Critical Importance of Early Intensive Behavioral Intervention

Ivar Lovaas and his colleagues at the University of California, Los Angeles, provided the first evidence for the potential of systematic early intervention to improve the lives of children with autism (Lovaas, 1987; Smith et al., 1997; Smith & Lovaas, 1998). In 1987, Lovaas reported the results of a study in which 19 children with autism received an early intensive behavioral intervention (EIBI) program of one-to-one treatment averaging 40 hours per week for 2 years or more before age 4 years. Intervention also included parent training and inclusion in a preschool setting with typically developing children. Compared with a group of 19 similar children at age 7 years, the children in the EIBI group had gained an average of 20 IQ points and made major advances in educational achievement. Nine of the children had moved from first to second grade in regular classrooms and were considered well adjusted by their teachers.

Follow-up evaluations of the same group of 19 children several years later, at the average age of 11.5 years, showed the children had maintained their gains (McEachin et al., 1993). In particular, 8 of the 9 "best-outcome" children were considered "indistinguishable from average children on tests of intelligence and adaptive behavior" (p. 359). Although some have raised important questions about the validity and generality of this research (e.g., Gresham & MacMillan, 1997a, 1997b), replications of the "UCLA model," including a study in which children were randomly assigned to EIBI or an alternate intervention, have produced similar results (Cohen et al., 2006; Smith et al., 2000).

The work of Lovaas and colleagues was a landmark accomplishment in the education of children with autism (Baer, 2005). First, they discovered and validated at least some of the factors that can be controlled to help children with autism achieve normal functioning in regular classrooms. Second, the dramatic improvements in the children's social, communication, and cognitive functioning helped spur wide-ranging interest and research funding for a disorder for which custodial care was thought to be the only option. Third, the successful outcomes provided a legitimate basis for hope and encouragement for parents and teachers desperate to learn how to help children with autism.

Applied Behavior Analysis

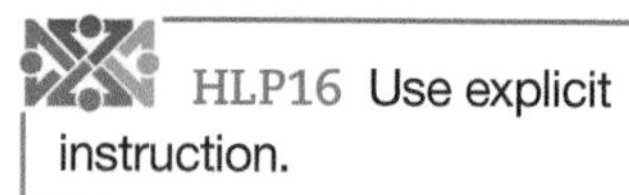
HLP16 Use explicit instruction.

The teaching methods used in the Lovaas early intervention project were derived from **applied behavior analysis (ABA)**. ABA provides a scientific approach to designing, conducting, and evaluating instruction based on empirically verified principles describing functional relationships between events in the environment and behavior change (i.e., learning) (Cooper et al., 2020). Behavioral principles and tactics such as positive reinforcement, shaping, and chaining are used to teach children to acquire skills in a planned, systematic manner. Children receive repeated opportunities to practice and use their new skills across the day, with different settings, people, and situations.

Treatments based on other models can yield beneficial outcomes for children with autism. For example, an intervention derived from developmental psychology and designed to improve joint attention and symbolic play enhanced mother–child interactions and raised children's scores on standardized tests of IQ and language (Kasari et al., 2006). However, no other treatment approach for children with autism has the amount or quality of scientific evidence documenting its effectiveness than does treatment informed by ABA (Eldevik et al., 2010; Larsson, 2013). Research also shows that eclectic intervention programs consisting of a mix of components from different treatment models are not as effective as programs based on ABA (e.g., Eikeseth et al., 2002; J. S. Howard et al., 2014; McMahon & Cullinan, 2016).

The National Professional Development Center on Autism Spectrum Disorders conducted the most extensive review of the autism education and treatment literature to date. More than 150 expert reviewers examined 1090 articles published in peer-reviewed journals from 1990 to 2011 (Wong et al., 2014; Wong et al., 2015). The results indicated that 27 intervention practices were determined to have sufficient scientific support to be considered evidence based. The evidence-based practices consist of interventions that are fundamental ABA techniques (e.g., reinforcement, extinction, prompting), assessment and analytic techniques that are the basis for intervention (e.g., functional behavior assessment, task analysis), and combinations of primarily behavioral practices used in a routine and systematic way that fit together as a replicable procedure (e.g., functional communication training, pivotal response training) (Wong et al., 2014, p. 19).

Teaching parents of children with autism behavioral strategies such as use of visual schedules, positive reinforcement, planned ignoring, and techniques to promote compliance and daily living skills can relieve parental stress (Bearss et al., 2015; Iadarola et al., 2018). Helton and Alber-Morgan (2018) offer advice for helping parents understand ABA.

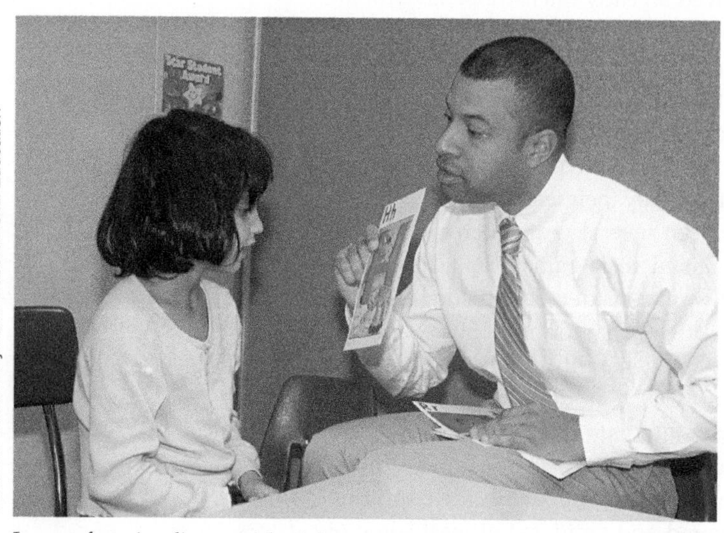
Source: Pearson Allyn and Bacon/Merrill Education

Lessons featuring discrete trial training are an important part of Ayah's school day.

Although many parents and practitioners have advocated for ABA programs and services for children with autism, misunderstandings about what ABA is and is not are widespread (Boutot & Hume, 2012; Heward, 2005; Keenan & Dillenberger, 2020). One of the most common misconceptions is that ABA consists only of **discrete trial training (DTT)**, one-on-one sessions during which a teacher presents a routinized sequence of contrived learning trials to a child. For example, the teacher presents instruction (e.g., "Touch the spoon"), the child responds, and receives reinforcement for a correct response. Each sequence of antecedent stimulus, child response, and consequence (or feedback) is a learning trial, as illustrated in the top half of Figure 4.7.

As Donald Baer (2005), one of the founders of ABA, pointed out,

> The discrete trial method of teaching, or DTT, is as old as teaching and much older than education. It can be described as follows:
>
> 1. The teacher prepares a set of problems to present to a student one at a time.
> 2. This sequence is usually in an optimum order for teaching and learning, to the best of the teacher's ability.
> 3. The student responds or fails to respond to each problem.
> 4. The teacher responds to each of the student's responses or nonresponses, rewarding or acknowledging correct responses; ignoring, correcting, or reproving incorrect responses; and either ignoring or prompting responses after nonresponses.
> 5. The cumulative effect of this teaching is to impart a new set of integrated facts, a concept, or a skill.
>
> It is commonly used in school classrooms for teaching any subject matter. DTT is the method of Socratic dialogue, it is often how law students are taught their most useful skills, and it is often how medical interns are taught clinical and diagnostic skills (p. 10).
>
> [DTT] is used in countless variations. Whether DTT is drudgery or sublimely informative depends not on its format, but on how skillfully the teacher has prepared what the student will encounter and how skillfully the teacher can answer whatever response to the encounters the student may make (p. 24).

DTT is not ABA, and ABA can be done without DTT. However, DTT plays an important role in ABA-based programming for children with autism, and it is a method all teachers should know how to use with a high degree of skill. It is also important to know that DTT is just one type of teaching arrangement. ABA-based programming uses a variety of procedures to help individuals with autism acquire and generalize new skills. The following is a partial list of practices derived from ABA for teaching students with autism:

- Reinforcement strategies to shape new behavior (Fonger & Malott, 2019), promote and maintain adaptive responses (Brosh et al., 2018; Kranak et al., 2017), and increase variability in children's behavior (Silbaugh & Facomata, 2019).
- Strategies for shifting control over a student's responses from contrived stimuli used during instruction to naturally occurring stimuli in the student's environment (Garcia-Albea et al., 2014).
- Alternative forms of communication such as the Picture Exchange Communication System (PECS) (Doherty et al., 2018; see Chapter 8).
- Teaching practices for spoken and written language based on a functional analysis of verbal behavior (Sundberg, 2020).
- Generative instruction such as matrix training (Axe & Sainato, 2010) and equivalence-based instruction (Miguel & Kobari-Wright, 2013).
- Peer-mediated interventions for building academic and social skills (Sperry et al., 2010; Watkins et al., 2015).
- Strategies to increase active student responding during group instruction (Bondy & Tincani, 2018).
- Behavioral skills training for a wide range of social, personal, and employment related skills (see *Transition: Next Year Is Now,* "Behavioral Skills Training for Job/Employment Skills").
- Self-management tactics (Beaver et al., 2017; Rosenbloom et al., 2019).
- Methods of errorless discrimination learning (Jerome et al., 2007).
- Functional analysis of challenging behavior (Hanley et al., 2014).
- Functional communication training (Tiger et al., 2008).

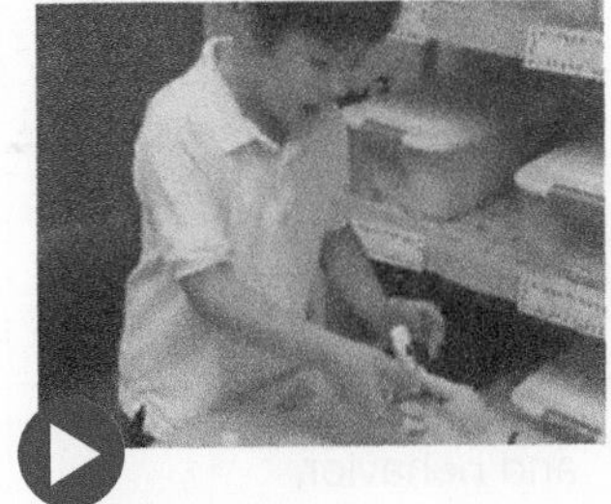

Pearson eText
Video Example 7.3
Skillful teachers embed motivating opportunities for students to use their emerging language skills.

HLP10 Conduct functional behavioral assessments to develop individual student behavior support plans.

Transition: Next Year Is Now

Behavioral Skills Training for Job/Employment Skills

"What do you want to be when you grow up?" Getting and keeping a job is a nearly universal goal instilled in most of us from very early in life. Over time, we learn to understand the importance of paid employment for independence, personal fulfillment, and quality of life. These benefits of having a job are the same for individuals with and without disabilities.

Obtaining and maintaining employment is a complex process requiring a synthesis of many important skills. Before the job even starts, individuals need to find a job that fits their interests and skill set, learn to fill out a job application, and acquire interviewing skills. Once hired, in addition to the skills required for the job itself, successfully employed people need social skills (e.g., interacting politely with co-workers), self-advocacy skills (e.g., asking for help from a supervisor), and self-management skills (e.g., getting to work on time). *Next Year Is Now* boxes throughout this text describe strategies for teaching these employment skills and others to students with disabilities.

Pearson eText
Video Example 7.4
In addition to doing their job well, successful and happy employees interact positively with supervisors and co-workers and ask for help when they need it.

Behavior Skills Training

Behavior skills training (BST) is an evidence-based practice that entails instruction, modeling, role playing, rehearsal, and feedback. BST has been used to teach a wide range of social and vocational skills to learners with and without disabilities (e.g., Morgan & Wine, 2018; Ryan et al., 2019; Stocco et al., 2017). And Parsons et al. (2013) used BST to teach human service staff how to use BST!

The following illustrates how Roberts et al. (2020) used BST to teach job interview skills (i.e., answering interview questions, asking questions at an interview, and demonstrating appropriate body language) to young adults with autism.

1. *Describe the skill and rationale for learning it.* "Today we are going to learn how to...[name the skill]. It is important to learn this skill because... [provide rationale]. Remember to... [clearly and succinctly describe the rule or strategy you are teaching]."
2. *Model the skill.* "Watch me as I show you how to [name the skill]." Perform the skill or the first step for more complex skills. For social skills, make sure the modeling includes both roles.
3. *Role-play the skill with the student.* "Let's practice this skill together." Assign the student the "role" and set the scene for the role-play (e.g., "You are being interviewed by the manager at the grocery store. I'll be the manager."). Then provide the stimuli (e.g., interview questions) to which the student must respond.
4. *Provide feedback.* During role-play, provide real-time feedback. Make sure feedback is precise. Look for opportunities to provide ample praise in addition to error correction.

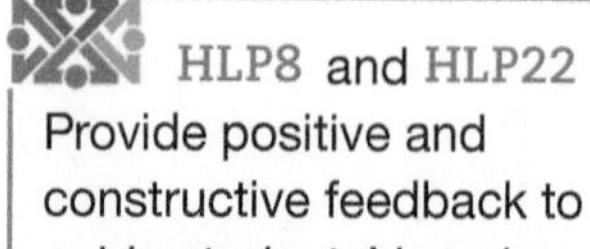

HLP8 and HLP22 Provide positive and constructive feedback to guide students' learning and behavior.

Building on Skills

Gradually fade your support during role playing to move the student toward independent mastery of the skills. Continue to provide opportunities for practice and continue delivering supportive and corrective feedback. Program for generalization and maintenance by using the following strategies.

- Teach multiple examples (e.g., ask the same interview question in varied ways).
- Teach students how to respond to negative feedback or comments from an interviewer (e.g., "That was a poor answer. You don't seem very interested in this job.").
- Provide practice in authentic settings (e.g., community-based instruction; see Chapters 12 and 15).
- Give students a self-monitoring tool to help them track their performance in a range of settings (see *Teaching & Learning,* "Self-Monitoring Helps Students Do More Than Just Stay on Task" in Chapter 11).

HLP21 Teach students to generalize new learning across time and settings.

Visual Supports: Helping Students with Autism Cope with Social Situations and Increase Their Independence in the Classroom

Visual supports encompass a wide variety of interventions that involve visual cues and prompts that help students perform skills with greater independence and accuracy (Cohen & Gerhardt, 2015). Visual activity schedules and social stories are two strategies for students with ASD that entail visual supports.

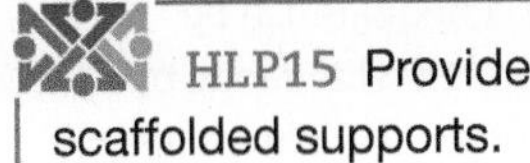

HLP15 Provide scaffolded supports.

HLP13 Adapt curriculum tasks and materials for specific learning goals.

VISUAL ACTIVITY SCHEDULES A visual activity schedule is a visual prompt showing a sequence of activities within a daily routine (e.g., math, learning centers, reading, snack) or a series of steps for completing one task (e.g., get ready for lunch: Clean up toys, wash hands, sit at the table, eat your lunch). Numerous studies have shown that students with autism can be taught to use picture activity schedules to select and carry out a sequence of activities in the classroom (e.g., Gauvreau & Schwartz, 2013; Pierce et al., 2013). Activity schedules have also helped adolescents learn social and transition-related skills (Banda & Grimmett, 2008). Schedules can be linked to include peers without disabilities in group activities and games (Broadhead et al., 2014). See *Teaching & Learning,* "Visual Activity Schedules: Promoting Independence for Students with Autism."

TEACHING & LEARNING

Visual Activity Schedules: Promoting Independence for Students with Autism

Why Are Visual Activity Schedules Important for Students with Autism? Visual activity schedules help students to stay on task and achieve greater independence with functional and academic skills. Visual schedules are important for children with autism because they provide structure and routine, promote self-sufficiency, facilitate smooth transitions from one activity to the next, provide structure for down time, help students understand what activities are associated with different physical spaces, and promote social interactions and communication skills. Children who learn to use visual activity schedules no longer require a teacher or a parent to tell them when to initiate one activity and when to move on to the next. Beyond a simple prompting tool, a visual schedule can be a significant means of building independence and self-determination. Visual activity schedules may be used with students of all ages.

How Do I Implement Visual Activity Schedules?

1. **Select Activities to Include**
   - For a schedule showing steps for completing one task, create a task analysis for the student to follow. For example, when teaching students to request teacher feedback after completing prevocational tasks (e.g., mail sorting), the steps on their picture schedule may include the following: "Do your work, look at picture, check your work and fix, raise hand, and quietly wait for the teacher" (Rouse et al., 2014, p. 316).
   - For schedules showing daily routines, identify the important tasks and the sequence. For example, the schedule shown here the following behaviors in sequential order: Find your circle, Sit on floor, Quiet hands, Eyes on teacher, and Ready to listen.
   - When preparing the activity schedule of a daily routine, intersperse high-effort activities with fun activities. Seeing a fun activity coming up next may be motivating and help the student stay on task.
   - Build choice making into the child's activity schedule. Students can help decide which activities to include in the schedule, when they would like to do them, and what rewards they would like to earn for completing tasks.

Pearson eText
Video Example 7.5
Visual schedules can be designed in wide range of formats to meet students' individual needs. https://www.youtube.com/watch?v=YNfnuuATlkA

2. Determine Schedule Format and Medium

- Depict activities with photos, icons, objects, words, or combination. The schedule should suit the child's needs. For example, what format is the child likely to understand most clearly when upset?
- Video clips of the student or a peer performing each step or activity may be helpful.
- Horizontal, vertical, flip chart, on ring, or combination. Will the schedule be located in a stationary position or be portable? On a mobile device?

3. Construct the Schedule

- Make a card that illustrates each step of the task or each sequential activity in a daily routine. Represent each task or step with words (i.e., the name of the step) and a picture (e.g., photograph, clip art, icons, or drawings).
- Place Velcro on the back of each card and attach a Velcro strip to a clipboard, binder, or laminated card on the student's desk. This allows the student to remove the task card each time the task is completed.
- Consider adding additional strips of Velcro to the schedule for tokens and a visual reminder of the reward a student is working for. (See Vincent's picture activity schedule from Chapter 12 for an example.)
- Digital activity schedules make use of video clips and presentation software (e.g., Reinert et al., 2020; Stromer et al., 2006), which students can access from a computer, mobile device, or specialized assistive technology devices.

4. Teach the Student How to Use the Schedule

- Model for the student (a) checking the schedule, (b) completing the next activity or step task shown by the schedule, (c) recording that the activity or step task has been completed, and (d) doing the next activity or step on the schedule.
- Prompt the student through each step, providing praise and corrective feedback.
- Gradually fade your prompts and feedback to promote the student's independent use of the schedule.
- Assess the student's performance with the schedule to determine if any adjustments need to be made.
- Detailed information on making activity schedules and teaching students to use them can be found in Cohen and Gerhardt (2015) and McClannahan and Krantz (2010).

Source: Courtesy of Ananda Aspen and Liza Stack, California Autism Professional Training and Information Network.

This check-off schedule helps Joey get ready for circle time

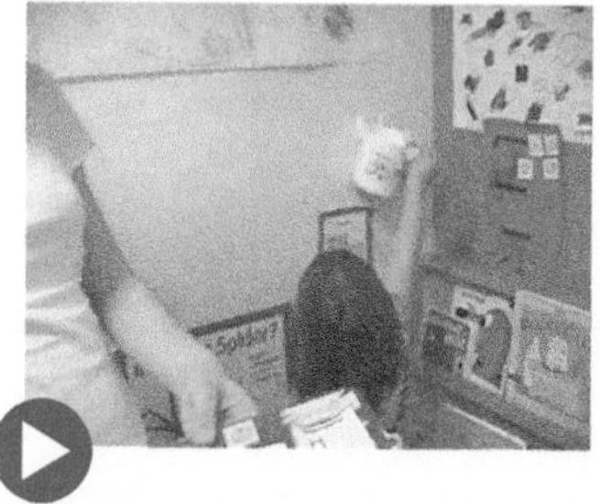

Pearson eText
Video Example 7.6
Visual schedules help preschoolers with and without disabilities develop independence.

SOCIAL STORIES Learning to tolerate change and how and when to use communication and social interaction skills within the typical rules that govern social situations is a major challenge for many students with autism. **Social stories** explain social situations and concepts and the expected behaviors of the people involved in a format understandable to an individual with ASD. Teachers and parents can use social stories to describe a situation and expected behaviors, explain simple steps for achieving certain goals or outcomes, and teach new routines and anticipated actions (Gray & Attwood, 2010). Engaging children in social stories before an event or activity can decrease their anxiety, improve their behavior, and help them understand the event from others' perspectives.

HLP9 Teach social behaviors.

Social stories are written at the student's level of comprehension and usually contain four basic types of sentences written from the perspective of the student:

- Descriptive sentences identify the contextual variables of the target situation. Example: I can't interrupt when others are having a conversation or are busy with something.
- Perspective sentences describe the reactions and feelings of others about the situation. Example: Interrupting makes people angry because you stop them from talking, and they might forget what they were talking about.
- Directive sentences describe the desired behavior with respect to a specific social cue or situation. Example: If it's extremely important, I can tap the person on the shoulder and say, "Excuse me." Otherwise, I must be patient and wait until they're finished.
- Affirmative sentences express shared beliefs or reference a rule or law about the situation to reassure the individual. Example: Everyone deserves to talk without being interrupted. (Examples adapted from Morris, 2020.)

Social stories are usually constructed with one sentence per page. Photographs or line drawings depicting key information and important aspects of the events are sometimes added to illustrate the sentence on each page (Figure 7.4). Comic book conversation is a modification of a social story that uses pictures, simple figures, and comic strip components such as speech bubbles instead of text (Glaeser et al., 2003). Social stories containing self and peer video models can be presented via computers and smartboards (Sansosti & Powell-Smith, 2008; Xin & Sutman, 2011).

Several studies have reported improvements in children's behavior after systematic exposure to social stories. For example, Ivey et al. (2004) found that three 5- to 7-year-old boys with autism increased their independent and appropriate participation in novel activities when parents read social stories to the children once a day for 5 days before the events. However, the research base for social stories is limited, and the mechanisms for how social stories affect behavior are not fully understood. Based on their review of 28 published studies on social stories, Test et al. (2011) concluded that social stories could not be considered an evidence-based practice. Leaf and colleagues (2015) examined 41 studies on the effects of social stories on individuals with autism and found that the majority of studies provided only partial demonstration or no demonstration that the social story procedure was responsible for behavior change. And Kassardjian et al. (2014) reported that "doing nothing" was as effective in teaching targeted social skills to a group of three children with autism as was reinforcing, attending to, and answering comprehension questions about social stories.

Nevertheless, sufficient positive results for social story interventions have been reported in the peer-reviewed literature that the method may be considered a promising practice (Kokina & Kern, 2010). Social stories are most effective when part of a multicomponent intervention that includes elements such as video modeling, response prompts, script fading, feedback, reinforcement, and self-recording of desired behaviors (Gül, 2016; Halle et al., 2016; Kurt & Kutlu, 2019; Sansosti & Powell-Smith, 2008). For example, Crozier and Tincani (2005) found that a social story supplemented by occasional verbal prompts (e.g., "Remember to raise your hand when you want to talk to a teacher," p. 153) was more effective than the social story alone. Special education teachers should use formative data collection to determine whether the practice is effective for individual students.

FIGURE 7.4 Social Story About Waiting in the Lunch Line at the School Cafeteria with Pictures Illustrating the Text

At my school, students eat lunch in the cafeteria.
p. 1
The cafeteria can be very crowded at lunch.
p. 2
When I go to the cafeteria, I get my tray and stand at the end of the line. I stay in line and wait with everyone else to get my lunch.
p. 3
When I have to wait I can think of other things. I can think of a song or my favorite book.
p. 4
Soon it will be my turn and I can choose my lunch.
p. 5
Waiting in line is hard but I try my best to wait calmly. Everyone feels good when people wait their turn.
p. 6

Source: From Crozier, S., & Sileo, N. M. (2005). Encouraging positive behavior with social stories: An intervention for children with autism spectrum disorders. *Teaching Exceptional Children, 37*(6), p. 30. Used by permission.

HLP19 Use assistive and instructional technologies.

TECHNOLOGY Smartboards, computers, and tablets with high-speed Internet access, three-dimensional printers, and a wide variety of peripheral devices are increasingly common sights in classrooms. Today's students, including many with autism, are expert users of mobile devices in their personal lives and want to be connected at school as well (Twyman, 2014). Each of these "hard" technologies can accelerate and enhance learning for all students but only when used wisely to deliver well-designed *instructional technology* (i.e., the program, the software) (Layng & Twyman, 2014).

When selecting educational apps for a smartphone or tablet, teachers should look for the following.

- *Clearly specified learning outcomes:* The app directly matches or supports the child's IEP goals or progress in the general curriculum. Content is king, no matter how sleek, slick, and fun an app or software program is.
- *High rates of active student responding:* The app provides plenty of opportunities for the learner to practice the skills related to the learning objective.
- *Differential feedback:* The app provides immediate feedback after both correct and incorrect answers; the feedback is noticeably different for correct versus incorrect answers.
- *Adaptive difficulty:* The difficulty of the material increases and decreases automatically, depending on the learner's performance.
- *Mastery based:* The learner is required to achieve mastery of the current skill set before being allowed to progress to the next level.
- *Performance reports:* Learner performance data are reported with enough detail for a teacher or parent to target problem areas.
- *Usability:* The app should be easy to use, with simple instructions (either textual or graphic) of how to interact with the interface. Images and sounds should be relevant to the learning activity, not distracting for the learner. The app's reading level should be appropriate for the lowest age of learner identified. (Criteria for apps adapted from Mahon [2014] and Twyman [2014].)

How not to select apps for classroom or home learning: Price, developer's description, user reviews, or popularity. For example, Balefire Labs purchased the top 10 paid apps in the Education category on iTunes and reviewed them.

> Here's what we learned: Anyone who is basing their purchasing of apps on popularity rankings, expecting them to be high quality educationally, is in trouble. As we have said before, if you are just looking for apps that are fun or to keep your kids occupied when you are at a restaurant or in the car, many of these apps are probably fine. But just be aware that that's what most of these apps are ... entertainment. And bear this in mind if you're using those Top Charts to choose educational apps for your kids! (Balefire Labs, 2013, n.p.)

Distinguishing Unproven Treatments from Evidence-Based Practices

Although the popularity of unproven interventions has always been a problem in special education, the tremendous range of behavioral deficits, excesses, and peculiarities children with ASD manifest has made the field especially fertile ground for the proliferation of treatments promising remediation or cure. The Interactive Autism Network (2011) reported that families were using 381 different autism treatments and that children were receiving an average of 5 treatments simultaneously (One child received 56 concurrent treatments!). In another study, parents reported that their children with autism were receiving 7 simultaneous treatments (Green et al., 2006).

Many treatments claiming to help children with autism are backed by little or no scientific evidence. Taking megadoses of vitamins and diet supplements; wearing weighted vests; having one's skin brushed; using a platform swing; spending time in a room with colorful, flashing lights and soothing sounds; and intravenous infusions of purified porcine secretin are just some of the widely used autism treatments for which little or no credible research exists (Metz et al., 2015; Murdock et al., 2014; Sniezyk & Zane, 2015; Williams et al., 2009, Zimmerman et al., 2019). Facilitated communication provides an especially troubling example of the extent to which an unproven treatment can become common practice.

FACILITATED COMMUNICATION **Facilitated communication (FC)** is a process by which a communication partner, called a facilitator (most often a teacher or therapist; sometimes a friend or parent), provides physical support to assist an individual who cannot speak or whose speech is limited to typing on a keyboard or pointing at pictures, words, or other symbols on a communication board. Facilitated communication was developed in Australia for use with people with cerebral palsy (Crossley, 1988). It was brought to the United States by Douglas Biklen (1990), who claimed that FC produced sophisticated language in people with intellectual disabilities and autism, suggesting an "undisclosed literacy" consistent with "normal intellectual functioning."

Despite the absence of any rigorous, scientific evidence to support those claims, FC was soon being widely implemented in special education and adult programs serving individuals with disabilities. During the 1990s, many state education and developmental disability agencies and school districts hired FC experts and sent their teachers to be trained in the new technique. Many children and adults with disabilities were "facilitated" on a daily basis.

Although some educators and many parents raised questions from the beginning about the efficacy and appropriateness of FC and asked for data supporting its use, many more were too excited about the promises of this new wonder therapy to ask many questions. But as the uniformly negative results of carefully controlled empirical studies on FC accumulated (e.g., Oswald, 1994; Simpson & Myles, 1995; Wheeler et al., 1993), more began to question its use. Research designed to validate FC repeatedly demonstrated either facilitator influence (correct or meaningful language is produced only when the facilitator "knows" what should be communicated) or no unexpected language competence compared with the participants' measured IQ or a standard language assessment (for a review, see Jacobson et al., 2016).

In light of the overwhelming scientific evidence showing the communication attributed to individuals with severe disabilities during FC was influenced by the facilitator, several prominent professional organizations passed resolutions or position statements cautioning that FC is unproven and that no important decisions should be made regarding a student's or client's life that are based on the process unless authorship can be confirmed (e.g., American Association on Mental Retardation, 1994; American Psychological Association, 1994). Numerous studies since then have failed to produce any credible scientific support for FC and have produced a great deal of evidence against it (see Holehan & Zane, 2020; Mostert, 2010; Schlosser et al., 2019).

Why tell the story of a technique clearly discredited by peer-reviewed research decades ago? Now reemerged under new names (e.g., supported typing, saved by typing, rapid prompting method) by its advocates, FC continues to be used in various schools and programs serving children with autism and other developmental disabilities (Institute on Communication and Inclusion at Syracuse University, 2020).

WHY ARE UNPROVEN AUTISM TREATMENTS SO POPULAR? Parents and teachers of children with autism are easy targets for interventions that promise cures. As many authors and families have noted, who among us, parent or teacher, wouldn't look for anything that might help (Maurice & Taylor, 2005; Zane, 2011)? To read one parent's perspectives on the anguish of trying to separate unsubstantiated claims from scientifically validated treatments for her two children, read Content Extension 7.2 "The Autism Wars."

Content Extension 7.2

The Autism Wars by Catherine Maurice.

Educators are equally susceptible, often gullibly so, to testimonials, advertised promises, and pseudoscientific "evidence" (Kauffman, 2011; Stephenson & Carter, 2011). And instead of using legitimate measures of learning to evaluate a curriculum or instructional method, some programs consider staff and students' reports of "having fun" a measure of success (Downs & Downs, 2010). Schools and programs that adopt unproven autism treatments not only risk wasting financial resources and encouraging parents to cling to unrealistic expectations based on claims made for those treatments; they also risk slowing, or even harming, students' progress (Zane et al., 2008).

How can professionals discriminate innovative interventions for autism that hold promise for effectiveness from those based on exaggerated claims, fads, ideology, and pseudoscience? They should stay abreast of developments in autism treatment research from credible sources that base their conclusions and recommendations on peer-reviewed science and that have no ideological bent or financial interest favoring a particular treatment or approach.

The knowledgeable selection of an evidence-based treatment from those that are fashionable and false is a necessary but insufficient step in providing the most effective education for children with autism. A poorly implemented treatment, no matter how much research supports it, is unlikely be very effective. Teachers should learn as much as they can about a new instructional practice and then implement it with as much professional care and fidelity as possible. Finally, and perhaps most important, regardless of the source and amount of research supporting a particular practice, teachers should collect direct and frequent measures of student learning to evaluate its effects on their students.

Placement Options

Learning Outcome 7.5 List advantages and disadvantages of providing educational services for children with ASD in regular classrooms.

During the 2018–2019 school year, approximately 40% of students with autism were educated in regular classrooms, 18% were served in resource room programs, and 33% were in separate classes (U.S. Department of Education, 2020a). About 9% of students with autism attended special schools or residential facilities.

Regular Classroom

Students with autism are increasingly placed in regular classrooms for the purpose of improved social integration. Under the right conditions, students with autism become "accepted, visible members" of peer groups (Boutot & Bryant, 2005). A strong argument for educating children with autism in inclusive settings is that socially competent children are an essential ingredient for peer-mediated interventions, an evidence-based practice for children with autism (Wong et al., 2015).

Although some children who have received EIBI make a smooth transition to public school classrooms, many others struggle mightily with the demands of a new and highly complex environment. Perhaps the biggest shock for a child with autism who has transitioned from an EIBI program to a public school classroom is going from being the star of the show with multiple adults focusing on meeting his individual needs from moment to moment to being part of a group of 20 or more students. As children move from kindergarten into the primary grades, meaningful progress in academics is added to social interaction.

Forty-one autism experts—educators, clinicians, and researchers who together had more than 500 years of experience teaching children with ASD—were asked to name the three or four most important skills needed by a student with ASD for success in the regular classroom (Heward, 2011). Their answers to this informal survey encompassed a wide range of challenges and issues and included skills such as transitioning from one activity to another without fuss, being able to retain large amounts of auditory information, dealing with thin schedules of adult attention and reinforcement, and managing self-care skills such as toileting and eating. The collective wisdom of these experts, determined by tallying how many of them mentioned a given skill, is that success in the regular classroom for a student with ASD depends on the child's ability to reliably do the following:

- Display near-zero levels of challenging behavior.
- Participate and learn in group lessons.
- Complete assigned tasks independently (or with minimal teacher assistance).
- Interact with peers appropriately.
- Comply with classroom rules and follow the teacher's directions.
- Get the teacher's attention and assistance appropriately.

Source: Lori Whitley/Winterset Elementary/Pearson Allyn and Bacon/Merrill Education

Javan's active participation in group lessons helps him benefit from instruction in the regular classroom.

The classroom skills a student with ASD needs are not fundamentally different from those expected of any student. Doing all of the above is a tall order for any child with autism but an especially difficult challenge for children on the severe end of the autism spectrum. There are, however, good reasons for optimism. Teachers' implementation of evidence-based practices for preventing challenging behavior and replacing it with adaptive responses (e.g., C. M. Anderson et al., 2018; Dunlap et al., 2019) are enabling many children with autism to spend increasing portions of the school day in inclusive classrooms. And early intervention programs are increasingly aware of teaching children how to participate effectively in group lessons before they transition to classrooms (e.g., Charania et al., 2010).

Pearson eText
Video Example 7.7
Successful inclusion requires collaborative planning and execution.

Researchers have developed and continue to refine evidence-based practices that special and general education teachers can use to help children with ASD learn each of these skill areas (Wong et al., 2015). An advantage of many of these practices is that they can be applied with all students in the class, not just those with ASD. It is easier for a teacher to implement the same technique with the entire class than it is do something "special" for a student with disabilities while doing something different with the rest of the class. Improved student behavior and academic performance, especially if the teacher sees all or most students in the classroom benefiting, increases the likelihood of the teacher continuing to use the intervention.

Techniques teachers can implement with the entire class and that have been shown to help students with ASD learn the skills they need to be successful in regular classrooms include choral responding and response cards for participating in group instruction (Heward, 2019), self-management (Southall & Gast, 2011) for completing assigned tasks and following rules and directions, collaborative learning activities such as classwide peer tutoring (Kamps et al., 1994) for interacting appropriately with classmates, and teaching children how to recruit teacher attention or assistance (see Alber & Heward, 2000).

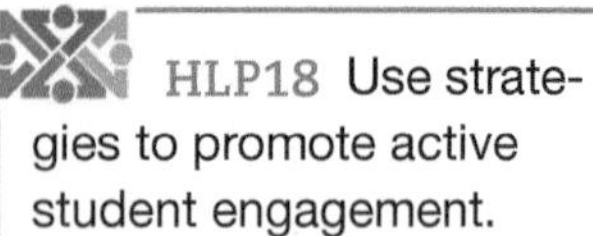

HLP18 Use strategies to promote active student engagement.

Teaching & Learning features elsewhere in this text explain how to start using choral responding, response cards, and classwide peer tutoring and how to teach children to self-monitor and recruit teacher attention. Although more research is needed to refine and improve the effectiveness of all of these strategies, teachers can use these tools to help students with ASD.

Resource and Special Classrooms

The regular classroom is not the least restrictive environment for all students with ASD. Many children at the severe end of the autism spectrum are best served in a setting where they can receive a highly individualized program of intensive, specialized instruction focused on the social/communication, self-control, and independence skills necessary for maximal benefit from placement in a regular classroom. "To assign children with autism who do not possess those skills to the usual public school classroom is to assign them to regression" (Baer, 2005, p. 9).

Pearson eText
Video Example 7.8
Practice with typically developing peers in the resource room makes generalization to the regular classroom more likely.

Because instructional time is such a precious commodity for students with disabilities, it must be used wisely. Because the potential is high for significant improvements in functioning by children with autism who receive early intensive behaviorally based education and treatment, the phrase "make every minute count" is more than just a slogan. In addition to using words such as *intensive, specialized,* and *focused,* invoking the word *urgent* is not an exaggeration when describing the special education needed by children with autism. Many students with autism spend a portion of each school day in the regular classroom with same-age peers and part of the day in a resource room where they receive intensive, specialized instruction focused on their IEP goals and objectives.

Instruction in a resource room or special class typically features a high frequency of instructional trials per minute; careful specification of and planning for transferring the control of students' responses from teacher-contrived antecedent and consequent stimuli to naturally occurring events; specific strategies for promoting the generalization of newly learned skills to the regular classroom, the community, and the home; continuous recording of data on each child's performance of targeted skills; and daily review of those data as the basis for making curricular and instructional decisions.

Providing supplemental or booster lessons in the resource room using the same curriculum materials the students encounter in the regular classroom can enhance students' success with those materials in the regular classroom. A resource room can provide an effective setting in which to conduct small-group learning activities with peers from the regular classroom. Bringing general classroom peers into the resource room to practice new skills can make generalization to the regular classroom more natural and likely.

As it should be for any child with disabilities, the question of *where* a child with autism receives special education should be determined only after identifying *what* evidence-based practices and related services are necessary to meet the student's individual needs. As one parent of a child with autism noted, "My goal for my son is not necessarily education in the least restrictive environment but *life* in the least restrictive environment" (Letso, 2013, p. 4).

ADVICE FROM THE FEATURED TEACHER by Katelyn Johnson

Keep the "Special" in Special Education

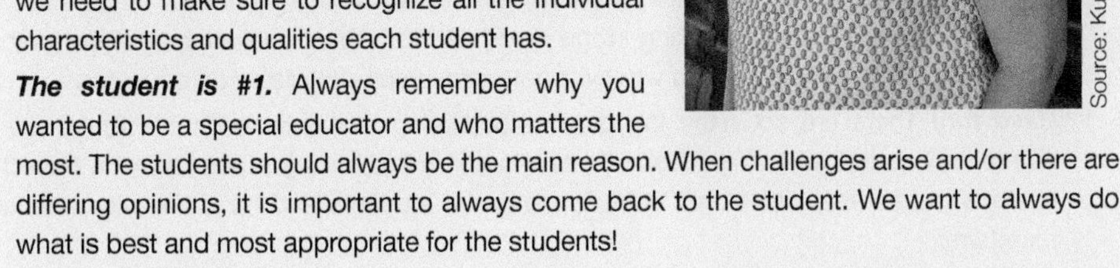

Source: Kurns Photography

- ***Individualize.*** Remember that even though the students in your class might have the same diagnosis or classification this does not mean they are the same. Every student is different, and it is important to treat them differently. Just because one intervention worked for one student does not mean the same intervention will work for a different student. Students might have very similar characteristics, but as educators we need to make sure to recognize all the individual characteristics and qualities each student has.
- ***The student is #1.*** Always remember why you wanted to be a special educator and who matters the most. The students should always be the main reason. When challenges arise and/or there are differing opinions, it is important to always come back to the student. We want to always do what is best and most appropriate for the students!
- ***Evidence-based practices.*** Others might have different ideas that you would have never thought of but would work great in your class or for a specific student. Trainings seem boring and waste of time (and yes, some might be), but if you go in with the right attitude, you might learn new things that you can implement in your class. As educators we have several types of resources provided to us. Keep learning, go to trainings, learn new strategies, seek out support, and get different ideas. We aren't supposed to know everything; we need to reach out to others.
- ***Practice-based evidence.*** Collect your own evidence. Even with evidence-based practices, not all students will respond positively. The only way you'll really know if something is working is if you gather your own "practice-based evidence" with each student.

Play as a Team

- ***Parents.*** Parents face challenges that we as teachers don't fully understand. We send the kids home at the end of the day, but parents are ALWAYS dealing with challenges that come with having a child with a disability. Be nice to parents. Respect parents. Try to put yourself in their shoes and realize they might be doing the best they can. I always try to start with an open mind and fresh start with each and every parent I work with, even if I have heard those really bad stories from previous teachers. I think if you can build a good relationship with the parents it is a positive environment for the student and yourself!
- ***Paraprofessionals.*** I will say this until I am blue in the face, but teamwork is so important. I COULD NOT do this job without the help and support of the paraprofessionals on my team. They are key players in making sure things run smoothly and correctly. I have learned that if I

put the time and energy into training them and providing them with the resources to help them succeed, then I have some of the strongest members on my team. I have also learned that they respect the job, the students, and me more if they are treated with the respect they deserve!

Stay Positive

- ***Believe in yourself.*** There will be hard times, but you can't give up. You will run into different challenges, and at that time it seems overwhelming, like you want to give up. But you have to remember that you went into this career for a reason. Dig deep and remind yourself of that reason. Once you are handling the challenging situations and move forward, you will look back and realize how strong you are! Sometimes the best form of medicine for me is to just cry out all the frustration and show up the next day ready to try again.
- ***Learn from your mistakes.*** Every year presents its own challenges and the first year might seem really hard, but that does not mean every year will be that hard. Each year you will grow and learn from your successes, mistakes, and other people. Everyone is going to make mistakes, and that's okay as long as you move forward and learn from them. What isn't okay is dwelling on your mistakes and letting them define you. Don't let the first few years of teaching define who you are as a teacher and DON'T GIVE UP! I promise each year will become easier and easier because you will face the challenges with a confidence you didn't have the prior years.
- ***Create a healthy support system.*** It's easy to get stuck on the negative and challenges that come with it. There is the stereotypical "faculty room talk" that focuses on all the negative and bad in this field. DON'T GET STUCK IN THAT CYCLE! Find a healthy support system that focuses on the positives. Recognize the challenges but use your support system as a way to move through the challenges and find solutions. As my nana used to always tell me, "If all you look for is negative then all you will find is the negative. Look for the positive and you will find the positive." Working in this field has PLENTY of challenges but the way you look at them and handle them is what will determine your attitude as an educator.
- ***Have fun!*** There are so many fun parts about being a special educator. Enjoy the fun moments, be silly, and laugh. Sometimes when you are having a bad day, the best thing to do is to remember to laugh! Have fun with the students and have fun with your team members.

Key Terms and Concepts

applied behavior analysis (ABA)
Asperger syndrome
autism spectrum disorder
behavior trap
discrete trial training
echolalia
executive functioning
facilitated communication
joint attention
pica
savant syndrome
social stories
stereotypy
theory of mind

Summary

Definitions

- Autism spectrum disorder (ASD) is a neurodevelopmental disorder of childhood marked by persistent deficits in social communication and interaction and by restricted, repetitive patterns of behavior and interests.
- Asperger syndrome is marked by impairments in all social areas, particularly an inability to understand how to interact socially. Children with Asperger syndrome do not have general language delay, and most have average or above-average intelligence.

Characteristics

- Some children with ASD are severely affected in most or all domains of functioning, but others are only mildly affected.
- Impaired social interactions include difficulty in perceiving the emotional state of others, expressing emotions, and forming attachments and relationships, as well as deficits in joint attention (e.g., not looking at what a parent looks at).
- Some children with ASD do not speak. Echolalia is common among those who do talk.
- Children with ASD tend to exhibit concrete or literal processing of verbal information and have difficulty understanding the social meanings of language.
- A diagnosis of ASD can be made for a child with severe or profound intellectual disabilities as well as for one who is intellectually gifted.
- Many children with ASD exhibit the following cognitive and learning characteristics:
  - Overselectivity—the tendency to focus on a minute feature of an object or a person rather than the whole.
  - Obsessive attention on a specific object or activity for long periods of time.
  - Strong aptitude for rote memory for certain things but difficulty recalling recent events.
  - Uneven skill development—areas of relatively superior performance that are unexpected compared to other domains of functioning.
  - Unusual responsiveness to sensory stimuli: overresponsiveness (hypersensitivity)—for example, intense dislike of certain sounds, being touched, or the feel of certain textures—and/or underresponsiveness (hyposensitivity)—for example, no reaction to stimuli that are painful to most people.
  - Obsessiveness about having everything in their environment stay the same and becoming very upset when items are moved or when routines change.
  - Stereotypic and self-stimulatory behaviors, such as rocking their bodies when in a sitting position, twirling around, flapping hands, flicking fingers, or spinning things.
  - Aggressive and self-injurious behavior.
- Very rarely, autism savant syndrome—an extraordinary ability in a specific area or skill while functioning at the intellectual disabilities level in all other areas.
- Some people with ASDs have described positive aspects of their disability, such as sensitivity to detail and intense interest in topics, which can improve functioning in some environments.

Prevalence

- Although once considered a rare disorder, recent studies show autism occurs in about 1% of all children.
- Boys are affected about four to five times more often than are girls.
- Reasons for the dramatic increase in the incidence of ASD are not clear but may include greater awareness of the disability, more widespread screening and better assessment procedures, increased availability of services via the disability category, great acceptance of label by parents, diagnostic shift, and an actual increase in the true incidence of the disability.

Causes

- For many years, it was widely thought that parents who were indifferent to the emotional needs of their children caused autism. However, no causal link between parental personality and autism has been ever discovered.
- Recent research shows a clear biological origin for autism in the form of abnormal brain development, structure, or neurochemistry.
- Some experts believe certain genes may make a child more susceptible to autism but that exposure to certain environmental factors may lead to the development of the disorder in some individuals.

Identification and Assessment

- No medical test for ASD is available; a diagnosis is most often made according to criteria in the DSM.
- Autism can be reliably diagnosed at 18 months of age, with research currently developing methods for detecting warning signs in children at 6 months of age.
- Screening babies for early warning signs of autism is critical because early diagnosis is correlated with dramatically better outcomes.
- Signs that warrant concern during the first 18 months of life include lack of pointing or gestures, infrequent or poor imitation, no single words by 16 months, lack of smiling, not responding to name, lack of joint attention, and loss of previously acquired language or social skills.

Educational Approaches

- Children with autism are among the most difficult to teach of all students; they require instruction that is carefully planned, meticulously delivered, and continually evaluated and analyzed.
- Although the prognosis for children with autism was traditionally extremely poor, early intensive behaviorally based education and treatment have helped many children achieve communication, language, and social skills so they can succeed in regular classrooms.
- Among the many treatments and therapies available for helping children with autism, interventions based on applied behavior analysis (ABA) have the most consistent research evidence supporting their effectiveness.
- Discrete trial training (DTT) is an important part of ABA-based programming for children with autism. However, DTT

alone does not constitute ABA, and ABA can be done without DTT.

- ABA programming uses a variety of procedures to help individuals with autism acquire and generalize new skills, such as strategies for shifting stimulus control, the Picture Exchange Communication System (PECS), peer-mediated interventions, functional assessment, and naturalistic teaching strategies, to name a few.
- Visual activity schedules—a series of images, photos, icons, or video clips depicting activities a child can perform, presented in sequence—can help children with autism independently select and carry out a sequence of activities in the classroom, home, or community.
- Social stories, when combined with other effective interventions, such as modeling, response prompts, and feedback, can decrease a child's anxiety about an event, improve behavior, and help the child understand events from the perspective of others.
- Most treatments promising to cure or relieve the symptoms of autism are based on little or no scientific evidence.
- Autism treatments should be chosen based on a review of the scientific evidence for their effectiveness, implemented with fidelity, and evaluated by direct and frequent measures of student learning.

Placement Options

- Approximately 40% of students with ASD are educated in regular classrooms, 18% in resource rooms, 33% in separate classrooms, and 9% in special schools or residential facilities.
- According to one group of autism experts, success in the regular classroom for a student with ASD depends on the child's ability to
  - Display near-zero levels of challenging behavior.
  - Participate and learn in group lessons.
  - Complete assigned tasks independently (or with minimal teacher assistance).
  - Interact with peers appropriately.
  - Comply with classroom rules and follow the teacher's directions.
  - Get the teacher's attention or assistance appropriately.
  - Instruction in a resource room or other specialized setting should feature a high frequency of instructional trials, procedures for transferring control to naturally occurring stimuli, strategies for promoting the generalization and maintenance of newly learned skills, and daily review of data on each child's performance for making curricular and instructional decisions.
- Regardless of the setting, the presence of socially competent children is helpful because peer-mediated interventions are among the most effective types of interventions for teaching communication and social skills to children with ASD.
- Whatever the child's educational placement, parent involvement and consistency between home and school are critical components for optimal learning.

Chapter 8

Communication Disorders

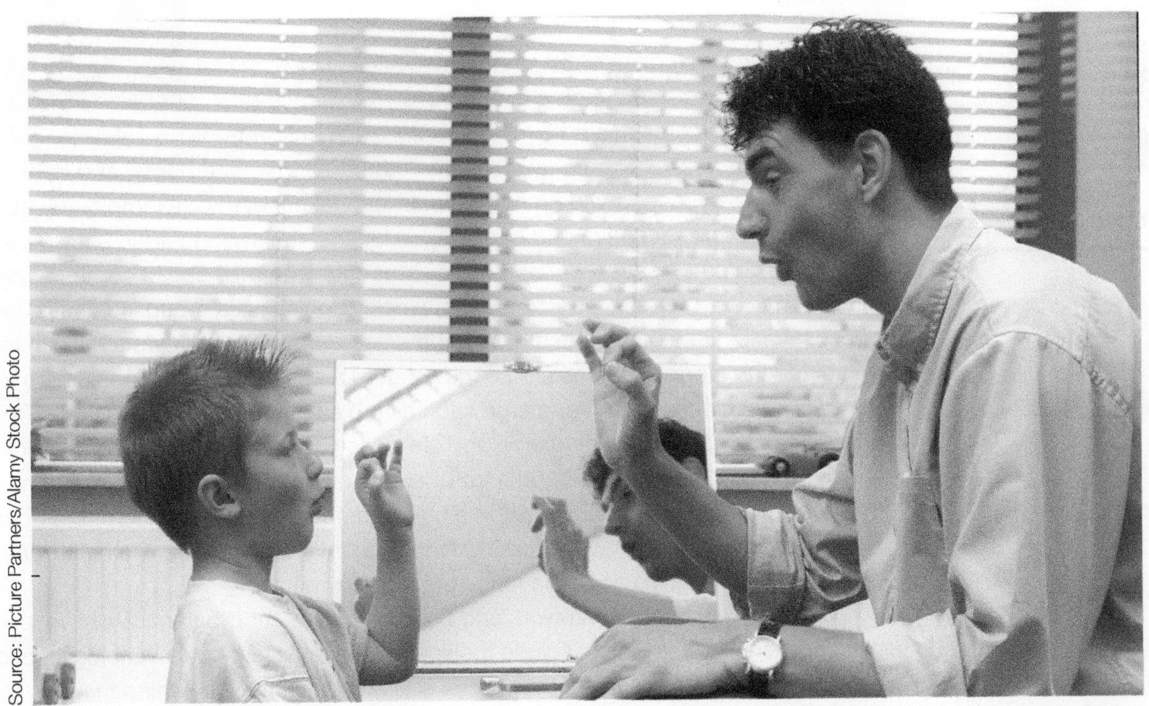

Source: Picture Partners/Alamy Stock Photo

Learning Outcomes

After reading this chapter and completing the embedded activities, you should be able to

8.1 Define communication, language, and speech, and describe typical and atypical speech and language development.

8.2 Describe characteristics of various receptive and expressive communication disorders and identify the prevalence of children who receive services under the speech or language impairment category.

8.3 Describe and identify causes of speech and language impairments and list the major components of a comprehensive evaluation used to detect the presence and extent of a communication disorder.

8.4 Identify the basic goals and common elements of effective interventions for speech-sound errors and language disorders.

8.5 Explain how the speech-language pathologist's role changes as a function of the setting where a child with communication disorders is served.

Education, Teaching Credentials, and Experience

- *B.A. in English, Hofstra University in May 2007*
- *M.A. in Speech-Language Pathology, Hofstra University in August 2012*
- *Certifications: State of Delaware, Speech Language Pathologist; ASHA, Certificate of Clinical Competence in Speech-Language Pathology*
- *7 years of teaching experience*

Featured Teacher

Emily Pickard

Sussex Consortium, Cape Henlopen School District, Lewes, Delaware

Source: Coleen Brittingham

I currently provide speech and language services to 25 ninth to twelfth graders ranging in age from 14 to 21 years. Most of my students have autism, but I also teach students with classifications of emotional disability, other health impairments, and deaf/blind. My students represent a wide range of instructional needs. For example, my students with severe receptive and expressive deficits may require augmentative and alternative communication (AAC), and my students with mild social communication deficits may only need to participate in a weekly social skills group. Typically, my direct services take place in a small-group classroom setting. However, since incidental teaching opportunities are so important, I also work on communication with my students in natural environments such as job sites and field trips. Most of my students participate in a vocational and life skills program. Our vocational program is wonderful. Our students spend a lot of time working at their job sites, and many businesses in our community welcome our students to work with them. In addition to assisting our students with working independently on job sites, we help transition them to adult agencies and gain long-term employment.

We have very strong teamwork and collaboration in our program. We have team meetings every week, which include the speech therapist, school psychologist, occupational therapist and, of course, the special education teacher. One thing that has helped our school tremendously with writing IEPs is a half-day planning meeting in which the whole team works together on the IEP document. We also send the document home a few days in advance so parents are able to review it before coming into the meeting. As a parent myself, I can only imagine how overwhelming it would be to walk into a room of sometimes 10 to 15 people to discuss my child. I think it's really important not only to take time going over the student's strengths in depth but also to comment on some personal things about the child as well, such as "I love having John in my class," "John makes us laugh every day," or "He has such a great personality." These types of comments go a long way toward building rapport with parents and getting their buy-in. I am also a believer in skipping the jargon when talking with parents. If you just speak directly, kindly, and in layman's terms, most parents will respond very well to you.

I use a variety of teaching methods in my lessons and a lot of visual supports. Some of my students use the picture exchange communication system (PECS) as their main form of expressive communication. Others require visual schedules to assist with independent transitions to the next activity. We often use visual task analyses for activities such as completing a job task or following a recipe.

Some students use scripts to assist them with what to say in challenging situations. For example, one of our students was having difficulty communicating with his job coach so we created some basic scripts for his vocational binder, including phrases such as, "I'm finished." "Can you check my work?" "What can I do next?" I also use role playing and video modeling to teach social skills. Recently I was doing a social skills lesson about understanding our strengths and flaws. I wanted the students to realize that it is okay to not be good at everything, and to be proud of what they *are* good at. One student raised her hand and said, "Miss Emily, should we add a 'not yet' column? For example, I'm working really hard on math, and not giving up, but I'm

Content Extension 8.1

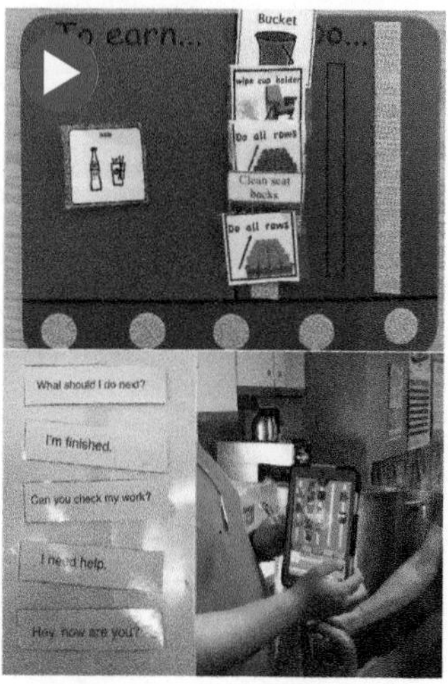

Visual supports used by Emily's students.

not good at it yet." This was such a proud moment for me because the student was thinking deeply about what I was trying to teach, and also demonstrating the ability to identify something that she isn't good at—at least not yet.

I can honestly say my job is never boring. There is always a moment of "I've never heard/seen that before!" We have the opportunity to be such a vital, important part of not only a child's life, but a whole family's life. I love interacting with people, and I not only get to interact with many children, but also other professionals and families on a daily basis.

COMMUNICATION IS SO FUNDAMENTAL TO THE HUMAN EXPERIENCE that we cannot stop communicating even when we want to. You may decide to say nothing, but sometimes saying nothing communicates a great deal. Still, imagine trying to go through an entire day without speaking. How would you make contact with other people? You would be frustrated when others did not understand your needs and feelings. By the end of the day, besides feeling exhausted from trying to make yourself understood, you might even start to question your ability to function adequately in the world.

Although relatively few people with communication disorders are completely unable to express themselves, an exercise such as the one just described would increase your awareness of some of the problems and frustrations children and adults with communication disorders face every day. Children who cannot express their desires, thoughts, and feelings are certain to encounter difficulties in their schools and communities. When communication disorders persist, it may be hard for children to learn and develop and to form satisfying relationships with other people.

Definitions

Learning Outcome 8.1 Define communication, language, and speech, and describe typical and atypical speech and language development.

Before we define communication disorders, a discussion of some basic terms is necessary.

Communication

Communication is the interactive exchange of information, ideas, feelings, needs, and desires. Each communication interaction includes three elements: (a) a message, (b) a sender who expresses the message, and (c) a receiver who responds to the message. Although communication most often involves at least two participants, each playing the dual roles of speaker and listener, intraindividual communication occurs when the same person is both sender and receiver of the same message (e.g., when we talk to ourselves or write a note to remind ourselves to do something later). In addition to enabling some degree of control in a social environment, communication serves several important functions, particularly between teachers and children.

NARRATING Children need to be able to tell (and follow the telling of) a story—a sequence of related events connected in an orderly, clear, and interesting manner. Five-year-old Cindy tells her teacher, "I had a birthday party. I wore a funny hat. Daddy made a cake, and Mommy took pictures." Fourteen-year-old Ian tells the class about the events leading up to the Selma-to-Montgomery marches.

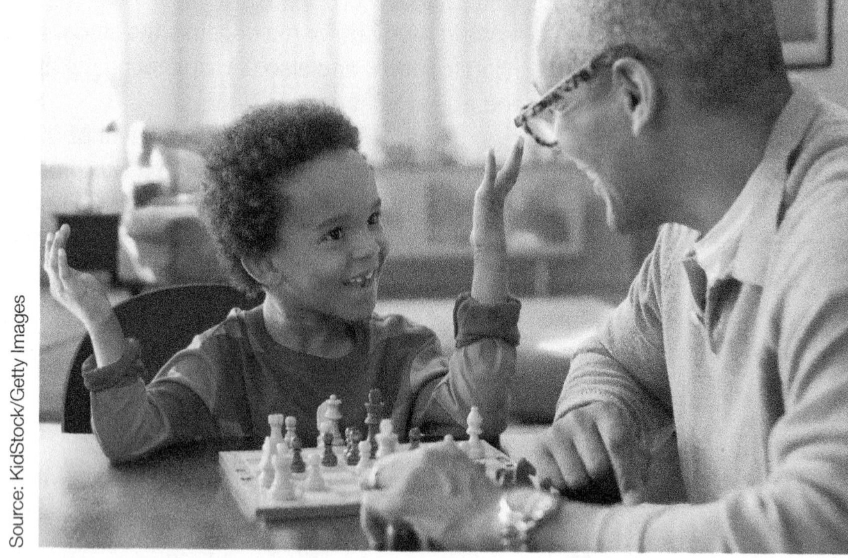
Source: KidStock/Getty Images

Good communicators use nonlinguistic cues such as body posture and gestures and pragmatic conversational skills such as turn taking.

EXPLAINING AND INFORMING Teachers expect children to interpret the explanations of others in speech and writing and to put what they understand into words so their listeners or readers will be able to understand it. In a typical classroom, children must frequently respond to teachers' questions: "Which number is larger?" "How do you suppose the story will end?" "Why do you think Barack Obama was a great president?"

REQUESTING Children are expected to communicate their wishes and desires to others in socially appropriate ways. A child who has learned to state requests clearly and politely is more likely to get what she wants and less likely to engage in inappropriate behavior to communicate her needs.

EXPRESSING It is important for children to express their personal feelings and opinions and to respond to the feelings of others. Speech and language can convey joy, fear, frustration, humor, sympathy, and anger. A child writes, "I have just moved. And it is hard to find a friend because I am shy." Another tells her classmates, "Guess what? I have a new baby brother!" Through such communicative interactions, children gradually develop a sense of self and an awareness of other people.

Although speech and language form the message system most often used in human communication, spoken or written words are not necessary for communication to occur. Both paralinguistic behaviors and nonlinguistic cues play major roles in human communication. *Paralinguistic behaviors* include speech modifications (e.g., variations in stress, pitch, intonation, rate of delivery, pauses) and nonlanguage sounds (e.g., "oohh," laughter) that change the form and meaning of the message. *Nonlinguistic cues* include body posture, facial expressions, gestures, eye contact, head and body movement, and physical proximity. Some researchers estimate that two thirds or more of the information in some face-to-face interactions may be communicated by nonspeech means (Burgoon et al., 2010).

Language

A **language** is a formalized code used by a group of people to communicate with one another. All languages consist of a set of abstract symbols—sounds, letters, numbers, elements of sign language—and a system of rules for combining those symbols into larger units. Languages are dynamic; they grow and develop as tools for communication as the cultures and communities of which they are part change. More than 7000 living languages are spoken in the world (Lewis, 2015).

No matter what language is spoken, the symbols and rules governing language are essentially arbitrary. There is no logical, natural, or required relationship between a set of sounds and the object, concept, or action it represents. The word *whale*, for example, brings to mind a large mammal that lives in the sea; but the sound of the word has no apparent connection with the creature. *Whale* is merely a symbol we use for this particular animal. A small number of *onomatopoeic words*—such as *pop, buzz*, and *hiss*—sound like what they represent, but most words have no such relationship. Likewise, a few hand positions or movements in American Sign Language are *iconic*: They look like the object or event they represent (e.g., tipping an imaginary cup to one's lips is the sign for *drink*).

FIVE DIMENSIONS OF LANGUAGE There are five dimensions of language that define its *form* (phonology, morphology, syntax), *content* (semantics), and *use* (pragmatics). **Phonology** refers to the linguistic rules governing a language's sound system. Phonological rules apply to the sequence and combination of sounds of a given language. A **phoneme** is a speech sound that differentiates word meanings. For example, only the initial phoneme prevents the words *pear* and *bear* from being identical, yet in one case, we think of a fruit and in the other a large animal. The English language uses 42 to 46 phonemes (Small, 2016).

Morphology refers to a language's basic units of meaning and how those units are combined into words. **Morphemes**, the smallest elements of language that carry meaning, can be sounds, syllables, or whole words. *Free morphemes* can stand alone (e.g., *fit, slow*). *Bound morphemes* do not carry meaning by themselves; they are grammatical markers that change the meaning of words when attached to free morphemes (e.g., *un*fit, slow*ly*). The word *baseballs* consists of two free morphemes (*base* and *ball*) and one bound morpheme (*s*).

Syntax is the system of rules governing the meaningful arrangement of words. If morphemes could be strung together in any order, language would be an unintelligible tangle of words. Syntactical rules are language specific (e.g., Japanese and English have different rules), and they specify acceptable (i.e., grammatical) relationships among subject, verb, object, and other sentence elements. The meaning of a sentence cannot be derived from the congregate meanings of the individual words; it is found in the interactive meanings of those words based on their grammatical and sequential relationships with one another. For example, "Help my chicken eat" conveys a meaning very different from "Help eat my chicken."

Semantics concerns the meaning of words and combinations of words. The semantic knowledge of competent language users includes vocabulary and concept development, connotative meanings by context (*hot* refers to temperature when discussing the weather but something else when talking about an athlete's recent performance), categories (*collies* and *beagles* are *dogs*), and relationships among words (such as antonyms and synonyms).

Pragmatics governs the social use of language. There are three kinds of pragmatic skills: (a) *using language* for different purposes (e.g., greeting, informing, demanding, promising, requesting), (b) *changing language* according to the needs of a listener or situation (e.g., talking differently to a baby than to an adult, giving background information to an unfamiliar listener, speaking differently in a classroom than on a playground), and (c) *following rules* for conversations and storytelling (e.g., taking turns, staying on topic, rephrasing when misunderstood, standing at an appropriate distance during conversations, using facial expressions and eye contact) (American Speech-Language-Hearing Association, 1993/2020). Pragmatics vary across and within cultures, and good communicators understand and respect the rules of their communication partners.

DIALECTS Before entering school, most children have learned patterns of speech and language appropriate to their families and communities. The way each of us speaks is the result of a complex mix of influences, including race and ethnicity, socioeconomic status, education, occupation, geographical region, and peer group identification. Every language contains a variety of forms, called **dialects**, that result from historical, linguistic, geographic, and sociocultural factors. Each dialect shares a common set of rules with the standard language. Standard American English (as used by most teachers, in textbooks, and on newscasts) is an idealized form seldom used in everyday conversation. As it is spoken in North America, English includes at least 10 regional dialects (e.g., Appalachian English, Southern English, New York dialect, Central Midland) and several sociocultural dialects (e.g., Black English, Latino English) (Wolfram & Schilling, 2015).

> The dialect spoken by any given group of people is neither superior nor inferior to the dialect spoken by any other group of people... There are dialects of English spoken by many people and dialects spoken by fewer people, but number of speakers does not indicate superiority or correctness. Every dialect of English is linguistically correct within the rules that govern it, and every dialect of English is as valid as any other. (Fahey et al., 2019, p. 344).

Speech

Speech is the oral production of language. Although speech is not the only vehicle for expressing language (gestures, manual signing, pictures, and written symbols are also used), it is the fastest, most efficient method of communication by language. Speech sounds are the product of four separate but related processes (Fahey et al., 2019): *respiration* (breathing provides the power supply for speech), *phonation* (the production of sound when the vocal folds of the larynx are drawn together by the contraction of specific muscles, causing the air to vibrate), *resonation* (the sound quality of the vibrating air, shaped as it passes through the throat, mouth, and sometimes nasal cavities), and *articulation* (the formation of specific, recognizable speech sounds by the tongue, lips, teeth, and mouth). Figure 8.1 shows the organs used to produce speech sounds.

Speech is one of the most complex human behaviors. Fahey et al. (2019) describe just some of what happens in speaking a single word, *statistics*.

> The tip of the tongue is lifted from a resting position to an area on the roof of the mouth just behind the upper teeth called the alveolar ridge to produce the *s* sound. The tongue is pressed against the alveolar ridge hard enough to produce constriction but not so hard as to stop the airflow altogether. As the speaker slowly contracts the muscles of exhalation under precise control, air is forced between the tip of the tongue and the alveolar ridge. Leaving the tongue in the same area, the speaker now presses a little harder to stop the airflow and then quickly releases the contact for the production of the *t* sound. The tongue drops to a neutral position and the vocal folds in the larynx vibrate to produce the vowel *a*. The speaker turns off the voice and lifts the tongue to the alveolar ridge for the next *t*, then vibrates the vocal folds for the vowel *i* while the tongue stays in a forward but slightly lowered position. The speaker turns voicing off again

FIGURE 8.1 Speech Organs

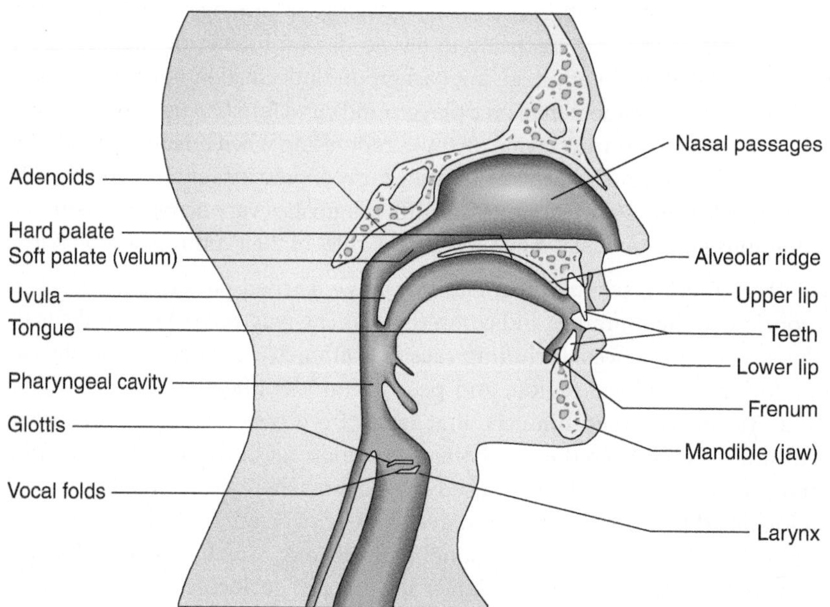

> and moves the tongue to the alveolar ridge yet again to produce the controlled constriction for the next *s*, followed by increased pressure to stop the airflow and release it for the *t*. The voice is turned on one more time and the tongue lowered to a neutral position for the *i*, and then turned off as the tongue arches to the back of the mouth where it contacts the velum, or fleshy part of the roof of the mouth, for the *k*. Finally, the tongue tip darts to the alveolar ridge for the production of the final *s* sound.
>
> All of this occurs in the production of *one* word! (p. 7)

Most languages begin in spoken form, the product of people talking with each other. Writing is a secondary language form that uses graphic symbols to represent the spoken form. There is no one-to-one correspondence, however, between **graphemes** (print symbols or letters) and phonemes. For example, in English the grapheme "e" represents two different phonemes in words like "pet" and "peat" and is unspoken but alters the sound of another grapheme in words like "pike."

Typical Speech and Language Development

Language learning is a remarkable process and one not fully understood. Despite the enormous complexity of speech and language, most children, without any formal instruction, learn to talk during the first few years of life, and most follow a predictable sequence in the acquisition of speech and language skills.

Knowledge of the speech and language milestones helps professionals determine whether a particular child is simply developing language at a slower than usual rate or whether the child shows an atypical pattern of language development. Figure 8.2 identifies some key indicators of typical speech and language development. The ages at which children acquire certain speech and language skills are not rigid and inflexible. Children's early environments and opportunities vary widely, and all of these factors exert tremendous influence on language development.

As the descriptions in Figure 8.2 indicate, words and sentences spoken by children differ from adult forms. Children who use structures such as "All gone sticky" and "Where he is going?"; pronunciations such as "cwackers" and "twuck"; or word forms such as "comed," "goed," or "sheeps" gradually learn to replace them with acceptable forms. These early developmental forms drop out as the child matures, usually without intervention or instruction (Fahey et al., 2019; Owens & Farinella, 2019). Children often produce speech sounds inconsistently. The clarity of a sound may vary according to factors such as where the sound occurs in a word and how familiar the word is to the child.

A major longitudinal study has provided a great deal of information about the social and linguistic environment in which typical children learn to talk. Hart and Risley (1995, 1999) conducted monthly hour-long observations of children from 42 diverse families over a period of 2½ years. The researchers recorded everything said by, to, and around each of the children during unstructured activities in their daily lives at home. Of the many interesting results of this landmark study, two findings are especially notable. First, children between the ages of 11 and 36 months are exposed to a tremendous amount of spoken language. "Perhaps most striking of all our findings… was the sheer amount of children's exposure to talk and interaction among the people around them. Over the years of observation, we regularly recorded an average of 700–800 utterances per hour within the children's hearing" (Hart & Risley, 1999, p. 34).

Second, children who are learning to talk practice their new skill relentlessly, actively participating in thousands of learning trials every day. They say words again and again, they repeat what they hear, they describe things, they talk to themselves while playing, they say what they want, they ask questions, and they respond to questions. After the children in the Hart and Risley study said their first word at an average age of 11 months, their number of

FIGURE 8.2 Overview of Typical Language Development

Birth to 6 months

- Infant first communicates by crying, which produces a reliable consequence in the form of parental attention.
- Different types of crying develop—a parent can often tell from the baby's cry whether she is wet, tired, or hungry.
- Comfort sounds—coos, gurgles, and sighs—contain some vowels and consonants.
- Comfort sounds develop into babbling, sounds that in the beginning are apparently made for the enjoyment of feeling and hearing them.
- Vowel sounds, such as /i/ (pronounced "ee") and /e/ (pronounced "uh"), are produced earlier than consonants, such as /m/, /b/, and /p/.
- Infant does not attach meaning to words she hears from others but may react differently to loud and soft voices.
- Infant turns eyes and head in the direction of a sound.

7 to 12 months

- Babbling becomes differentiated before the end of the first year and contains some of the same phonetic elements as the meaningful speech of 2-year-old infants.
- Baby develops inflection—her voice rises and falls.
- She may respond appropriately to "no," "bye-bye," or her own name and may perform an action, such as clapping her hands, when told to.
- She will repeat simple sounds and words, such as "mama."

12 to 18 months

- By 18 months, most children have learned to say several words with appropriate meaning.
- Pronunciation is far from perfect; baby may say "tup" when you point to a cup or "goggie" when she sees a dog.
- She communicates by pointing and perhaps saying a word or two.
- She responds to simple commands such as "Give me the cup" and "Open your mouth."

18 to 24 months

- Most children go through a stage of echolalia, in which they repeat, or echo, the speech they hear. Echolalia is a normal phase of language development, and most children outgrow it by about the age of 2½ years.
- There is a great spurt in acquisition and use of speech; baby begins to combine words into short sentences, such as "Daddy bye-bye" and "Want cookie."
- Receptive vocabulary grows even more rapidly; at 2 years of age, she may understand more than 1,000 words.
- Understands such concepts as "soon" and "later" and makes more subtle distinctions between objects such as cats and dogs and knives, forks, and spoons.

2 to 3 years

- The 2-year-old child talks, saying sentences such as "I won't tell you" and asking questions such as "Where my daddy go?"
- She participates in conversations.
- She identifies colors, uses plurals, and tells simple stories about her experiences.
- She can follow compound commands such as "Pick up the doll and bring it to me."
- She uses most vowel sounds and some consonant sounds correctly.

3 to 4 years

- The normal 3-year-old child has lots to say, speaks rapidly, and asks many questions.
- She may have an expressive vocabulary of 900–1,000 different words, using sentences of three to four words.

(Continued)

FIGURE 8.2 (Continued)

- Sentences are longer and more varied: "Cindy's playing in water"; "Mommy went to work"; "The cat is hungry."
- She uses speech to request, protest, agree, and make jokes.
- She understands children's stories; grasps such concepts as funny, bigger, and secret; and can complete simple analogies such as "In the daytime it is light; at night it is . . . "
- She substitutes certain sounds, perhaps saying "baf" for "bath" or "yike" for "like."
- Many 3-year-olds repeat sounds or words ("b-b-ball," "l-l-little"). These repetitions and hesitations are normal and do not indicate that the child will develop a habit of stuttering.

4 to 5 years

- The child has a vocabulary of more than 1,500–2,000 words and uses sentences averaging five words in length.
- She begins to modify her speech for the listener; for example, she uses longer and more complex sentences when talking to her mother than when addressing a baby or a doll.
- She can define words such as "hat," "stove," and "policeman" and can ask questions such as "How did you do that?" or "Who made this?"
- She uses conjunctions such as "if," "when," and "because."
- She recites poems and sings songs from memory.
- She may still have difficulty with consonant sounds such as /r/, /s/, /z/, and /j/ and with blends such as "tr," "gl," "sk," and "str."

After 5 years

- Language continues to develop steadily, although less dramatically, after age 5.
- A typical 6-year-old uses most of the complex forms of adult English and has an expressive vocabulary of 2,600 words and a receptive understanding of more than 20,000 words.
- Most children achieve adult speech sound production by age 7.
- Grammar and speech patterns of a child in first grade usually match those of her family, neighborhood, and region.

Sources: Adapted from ASHA (2015b); Hart and Risley (1999); Hulit et al. (2015); Owens (2016); Reed (2012).

utterances per hour increased steadily. On average, at 19 months of age, the children became talkers: Their frequency of utterances containing recognizable words had grown to exceed the frequency of nonword utterances. At 28 months, the children became speakers: Their frequency of talking matched their parents'. At age 3 years, the children said an average of 1400 words per hour using an average of 232 different words per hour and almost 20,000 total words in a 14-hour waking day.

Pearson eText
Video Example 8.1
"Let us talk!" https://www.youtube.com/watch?v=F9HWlIQ1nZE

The Bridging the Word Gap National Research Network is a consortium of more than 100 researchers, practitioners, and policymakers with a shared mission of bridging the "30 million word gap," referring to the vast difference in the number of words that some children from poverty backgrounds hear by age 4 years compared with the experiences of more affluent children.

Communication Disorders Defined

ASHA defines a **communication disorder** as "an impairment in the ability to receive, send, process, and comprehend concepts or verbal, nonverbal and graphic symbol systems. A communication disorder may be evident in the processes of hearing, language, and/or speech" (1993/2020).

To be eligible for special education services, a child's communication disorder must have an adverse effect on learning. The Individuals with Disabilities Education Act (IDEA) defines *speech or language impairment* as "a communication disorder, such as stuttering, impaired articulation, a language impairment, or a voice impairment that adversely affects a child's educational performance" (34 *CFR*, Part 300 §300.8[c][11]).

Similar to all disabilities, communication disorders vary widely by degree of severity. Some children's speech and language deviate from those of most children to such an extent that they have serious difficulties with learning and interpersonal relationships. Children who cannot make themselves understood or who cannot comprehend ideas spoken to them by others experience a significant disadvantage in virtually all aspects of education and personal adjustment. A severe communication disorder may lead others—teachers, classmates, people in the community—to erroneously believe the child does not care about the world around him or simply has nothing to say (Downing et al., 2015).

Specialists in the field of communication disorders make a distinction between speech impairments and language impairments. A child may have a speech impairment, a language impairment, or both.

SPEECH IMPAIRMENTS A widely used definition considers speech to be impaired "when it deviates so far from the speech of other people that it (a) calls attention to itself, (b) interferes with communication, or (c) provokes distress in the speaker or the listener" (Van Riper & Erickson, 1996, p. 110). Three basic types of **speech impairments** are articulation disorders (errors in the production of speech sounds), fluency disorders (difficulties with the flow or rhythm of speech), and voice disorders (problems with the quality or use of one's voice). Each is discussed later in the chapter.

It is important to keep the speaker's age, education, and cultural background in mind when determining whether speech is impaired. A 4-year-old girl who says, "Pwease weave the woom" would not be considered to have a speech impairment, but a 40-year-old woman would surely draw attention to herself with that pronunciation because it differs markedly from the speech of most adults. A traveler unable to articulate the /l/ sound would not be clearly understood when he tries to buy a bus ticket to Lake Charles, Louisiana. A male high school student with an extremely high-pitched voice might be reluctant to speak in class for fear of being mimicked and ridiculed by his classmates.

Many children have mild to moderate speech impairments. Their speech can usually be understood, but they may mispronounce certain sounds or use immature speech, similar to that of younger children. These problems often disappear as a child matures. If a mild or moderate articulation problem does not improve over an extended period or if it has an adverse effect on the child's interaction with others, referral to a speech-language pathologist (SLP) is indicated (Owens, 2016).

LANGUAGE DISORDERS A **language disorder** is "impaired comprehension and/or use of spoken, written, and/or other symbol systems. The disorder may involve (1) the form of language (phonology, morphology, and syntax), (2) the content of language (semantics), and/or (3) the function of language in communication (pragmatics) in any combination" (ASHA, 1993/2020).

Some children have serious difficulties in understanding language or expressing themselves through language. A child with a **receptive language disorder** may struggle learning the days of the week in proper order or following a sequence of commands such as "Pick up the paint brushes, wash them in the sink, and then put them on a paper towel to dry." A child with an **expressive language disorder** may have a limited vocabulary for her age, say sounds or words in the wrong order (e.g., "hostipal," "aminal," "wipe shield winders"), and use tenses and plurals incorrectly (e.g., "Them throwed a balls"). Children with an expressive language disorder may or may not also have difficulty with receptive language. For instance, a child may be able to count out six pennies when asked and shown the symbol 6, but she may not be able to say "six" when shown the symbol. In that case, the child's difficulty is expressive rather than receptive.

Characteristics

Learning Outcome 8.2 Describe characteristics of various receptive and expressive communication disorders and identify the prevalence of children who receive services under the speech or language impairment category.

Speech-Sound Errors

Four basic kinds of speech-sound errors occur:

- *Distortions.* A speech sound is distorted when it sounds more like the intended phoneme than another speech sound but is conspicuously wrong. The /s/ sound, for example, is relatively difficult to produce; children may produce the word "sleep" as "schleep," "zleep," or "thleep." Some speakers have a lisp; others a whistling /s/. Distortions can cause misunderstanding, although parents and teachers often become accustomed to them.
- *Substitutions.* Children sometimes substitute one sound for another, as in saying "train" for "crane" or "doze" for "those." Children who substitute sounds are often certain they have said the correct word and may resist correction. Sound substitutions can cause considerable confusion for the listener.
- *Omissions.* Children may omit certain sounds, as in saying "cool" for "school." They may drop consonants from the ends of words, as in "pos" for "post." Most of us leave out sounds at times, but an extensive omission problem can make speech unintelligible.
- *Additions.* The addition of extra sounds makes comprehension difficult. For example, a child might say "buhrown" for "brown" or "hamber" for "hammer."

Traditionally, all speech-sound errors by children were identified as articulation problems and thought to be relatively simple to treat. *Articulation* refers to the movement of muscles and speech organs necessary to produce various speech sounds. Research during the past two decades, however, has revealed that many speech-sound errors are not simply a function of faulty mechanical operation of the speech apparatus but are directly related to problems in recognizing or processing the sound components of language (phonology) (Schwartz & Marton, 2011).

ARTICULATION DISORDERS A child with an **articulation disorder** is not able to produce a given sound because that sound is not in his repertoire. A severe articulation disorder is present when a child pronounces so many sounds poorly that his speech is unintelligible most of the time; even the child's parents, teachers, and peers cannot easily understand him. The child with a severe articulation disorder may say, "Yeh me yuh a da wido," instead of "Let me look out the window," or perhaps "Do foop is dood" for "That soup is good." The fact that articulation disorders are prevalent does not mean that teachers, parents, and specialists should regard them as simple or unimportant. On the contrary, an articulation disorder severe enough to interfere significantly with intelligibility is a debilitating communication problem, and articulation disorders are not necessarily easy to diagnose and treat effectively (e.g., Bauman-Waengler, 2020; Pindzola et al., 2016).

PHONOLOGICAL DISORDERS A child with a **phonological disorder** has the ability to produce a given sound but does so inconsistently; she produces the same sound correctly in some instances and incorrectly in others. Children with phonological disorders are apt to experience problems in academic areas, and they are especially at risk for difficulties in reading (Hayiou-Thomas et al., 2017) and writing (Puranik & Lonagan, 2017).

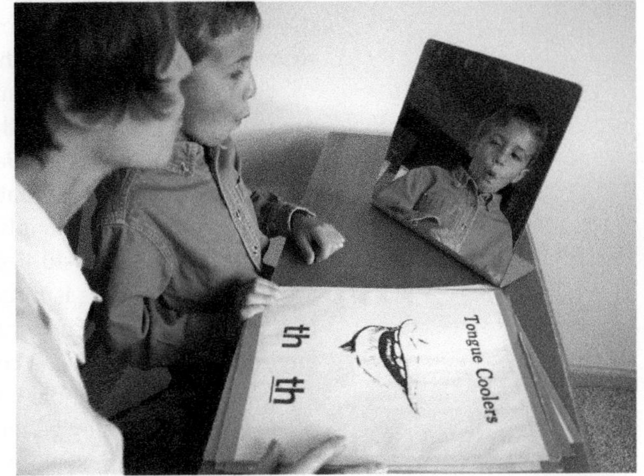

Source: Christina Kennedy/PhotoEdit

Special education for this student with a speech disorder includes intensive intervention sessions with a speech-language pathologist.

FIGURE 8.3 Distinguishing Articulation and Phonological Disorders

Articulation Disorder

- Difficulty with only a few sounds, with limited effect on intelligibility
- Consistent misarticulation of specific sounds
- Sound errors are motoric
- Co-existing communication disorders possible but not as likely as with phonological disorders

Phonological Disorder

- Multiple sound errors with obvious impairment of intelligibility
- Inconsistent misarticulation of sounds
- Can motorically produce sound but not in appropriate places
- Errors consistent with a phonological process (e.g., final consonant deletion, making an error on a sound in one position but producing that sound correctly in another position, as in omitting "t" in "post" but producing "t" in "time")
- Other language delays likely

Sources: Adapted from Haynes and Pindzola (2012); Sunderland (2004); Schwartz and Marton (2011).

Determining whether a speech-sound error is primarily an articulation or a phonological disorder is important because the treatment goals and procedures differ. Clinicians use the general indicators for differentiating between articulation disorders and phonological disorders shown in Figure 8.3.

Fluency Disorders

Typical speech makes use of rhythm and timing. Words and phrases flow easily, with certain variations in speed, stress, and pauses. The speech of children with **fluency disorders** is characterized by atypical continuity, smoothness, rate, and effort. "These disfluencies may be accompanied by physical tension, negative reactions, secondary behaviors, and avoidance of sounds, words, or speaking situations." (ASHA, 2020b).

STUTTERING The best known (and in some ways least understood) fluency disorder is **stuttering**, a condition marked by rapid-fire repetitions of consonant or vowel sounds, especially at the beginnings of words, prolongations, hesitations, interjections, and complete verbal blocks (Owens & Farinella, 2019). Developmental stuttering is considered a disorder of childhood in contrast to neurogenic stuttering, which occurs after childhood and is typically caused by neurological disease or trauma (Owens & Farinella, 2019). The onset of developmental stuttering is usually between the ages of 2 and 5 years, with 75% occurring before age 3.5 years (Owens & Farinella, 2019). Longitudinal research studies support a high likelihood of natural recovery from stuttering by the time children are 8 years of age (Yairi & Ambrose, 2013).

Stuttering is far more common among males than females, and it occurs more frequently among twins. It is believed that approximately 3 million people in the United States stutter (Stuttering Foundation, 2019a). The incidence of stuttering is about the same in all Western countries: Regardless of what language is spoken, about 1% of the general population has a stuttering problem at any given time. The causes of stuttering remain unknown, although the condition has been studied extensively with some interesting results. A family member of a person who stutters is three to four times more likely to stutter than the family member of a person who does not stutter. It is not known whether stuttering results from genetics, environmental factors, or a combination of both (Yairi & Seery, 2014).

Stuttering is situational; that is, it appears to be related to the setting or circumstances of speech. A child may be more likely to stutter when talking with people whose opinions matter most to him, such as parents and teachers, and in situations such as being called on to speak in front of the class. Most people who stutter are fluent about 90% of the time

TEACHING & LEARNING

Helping Students Who Stutter

Almost all children who stutter show significant improvements in fluency during intensive therapy sessions supervised by SLPs. In the absence of supportive classroom and home environments, these improvements are of limited value. Many teachers are unsure of how to act with students who stutter. Here are a few general guidelines.

Create a Good Speech Environment

- *Speak in a calm, unhurried style.* Calm, steady speech will have a more positive effect on the student than telling her to "slow down" or "relax."
- *Create silences in your interactions.* Pause at appropriate places in conversation to help create a relaxed communication environment, a slower rate of speech, and a more natural speech cadence.
- *Model typical nonfluencies.* Use typical interjections ("um" or "ah"), occasional whole-word or phrase repetitions, and pauses. Knowing that fluent speakers also exhibit nonfluencies can help reduce the student's fear of speaking.
- *Establish conversational rules.* Interruptions may distract the student and increase nonfluencies. Teach all class members to take turns talking and to be good listeners.

Value What the Student Says

- *Listen actively.* Active listening, which includes restating what the student has said, tells the student his message is important. Replace absentminded "uh-huhs" and generic statements (e.g., "Good talking!") with content-specific comments (e.g., "Yes, Johnny, that is a large blue truck.").
- *Show acceptance of what the child expresses rather than how it is said.* Ask the student to repeat only the parts of the utterance you did not understand rather than those that were nonfluent. This request shows you are listening to the student and his message is important.
- *Follow the student's conversational lead.* Speech will more likely be fluent if the student can talk about areas of interest.

Don't Rush the Student

- *Don't anticipate what the student wants to say.* Let the student work through stuttering moments on her own; don't finish the utterance for her.
- *Don't say "slow down," "relax," or "take a breath."* Although well-intentioned, such comments may make it even more difficult for a student to speak fluently.
- *Maintain eye contact.* You may not intend to communicate that you are rushing the student, but your body language and gestures (e.g., looking away, nodding quickly, hand motions) may indicate you are in a hurry.

Provide Positive Support and Feedback

- *Ask the student what strategies she uses to speak more fluently and how you can help.* It is okay to speak openly and individually with the student about her stuttering. You might help the student create a self-reflection and advice sheet like the one shown in Figure 8.4.
- *Provide specific and encouraging feedback.* Praise fluency frequently (e.g., "That flowed well!") and intersperse corrective feedback in one-on-one interactions after you have a good rapport with the student (e.g., "That was a little choppy. Do you want to try again?").

Guidelines adapted from: American Speech-Language-Hearing Association (2019b); Everling (2013); and The Stuttering Foundation (2019a).

HLP8 and HLP22
Provide positive and constructive feedback to guide students' learning and behavior.

Pearson eText
Video Example 8.2
Students who stutter need supportive teachers and peers.
https://www.youtube.com/watch?v=KKG2UM_5F_Y

FIGURE 8.4 Personal Reflection and Advice Sheet

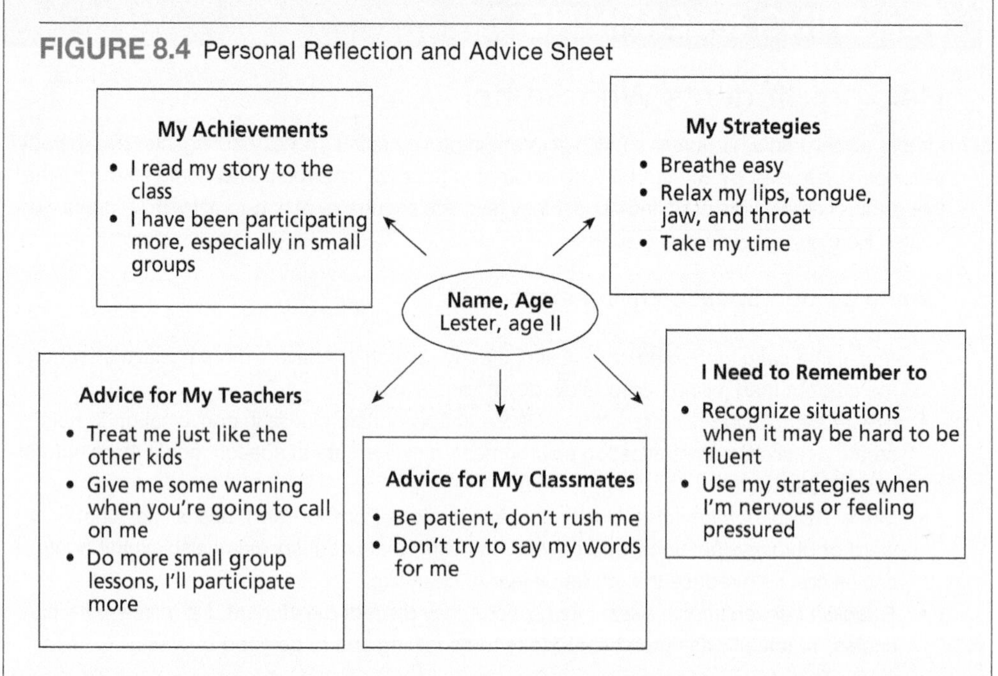

(Stuttering Foundation, 2019a); a child with a fluency disorder may not stutter at all when singing, talking to a pet, or reciting a poem in unison with others. Reactions and expectations of parents, teachers, and peers clearly have an important effect on any child's personal and communicative development.

CLUTTERING A type of fluency disorder known as **cluttering** is characterized by excessive speech rate, repetitions, extra sounds, mispronounced sounds, and poor or absent use of pauses. The clutterer's speech is garbled to the point of unintelligibility. "Let's go!" may be uttered as "Sko!" and "Did you eat?" collapsed to "Jeet?" (Yairi & Seery, 2014). Whereas the stutterer is usually acutely aware of his fluency problems, a clutterer may be oblivious to his disorder.

Voice Disorders

Voice is the sound produced by the larynx. A voice is considered normal when its pitch, loudness, and quality are adequate for communication and it suits a particular person. A **voice disorder** is characterized by "the abnormal production and/or absences of vocal quality, pitch, loudness, resonance, and/or duration, which is inappropriate for an individual's age and/or sex" (ASHA, 1993/2020).

Voice disorders are more common in adults than in children. Considering how often some children shout and yell without any apparent harm to their voices, it is evident the vocal cords can withstand heavy use. In some cases, however, a child's voice may be difficult to understand or may be considered unpleasant (Sapienza et al., 2011). *Dysphonia* describes any condition of poor or unpleasant voice quality.

The two basic types of voice disorders involve phonation and resonance. A *phonation disorder* causes the voice to sound breathy, hoarse, husky, or strained most of the time. In severe cases, there is no voice at all. Phonation disorders can have organic causes, such as growths or irritations on the vocal cords, but hoarseness most frequently comes from chronic vocal abuse, such as yelling, imitating noises, or habitually talking while anxious or tense. Misuse of the voice causes swelling of the vocal folds, which in turn can lead to growths known as *vocal nodules, nodes,* or *polyps.* A breathy voice is unpleasant because it is low in volume and fails to make adequate use of the vocal cords.

A voice with a *resonance disorder* is characterized by either too many sounds coming out through the air passages of the nose (*hypernasality*) or, conversely, not enough resonance of the nasal passages (*hyponasality*). A hypernasal speaker may be perceived as talking through her nose or having an unpleasant twang. A child with hyponasality (sometimes called *denasality*) may sound like he has a chronic cold or a stuffed nose even when he does not.

Language Disorders

Language disorders involve problems in one or more of the five dimensions of language: phonology, morphology, syntax, semantics, or pragmatics. Language disorders are usually classified as either receptive or expressive. As described previously, a *receptive* language disorder interferes with the understanding of language. A child may, for example, be unable to comprehend spoken sentences or follow a sequence of directions. An *expressive* language disorder interferes with the production of language. The child may have a very limited vocabulary; may use incorrect words and phrases; or may not speak at all, communicating only through gestures. A child may have good receptive language when an expressive disorder is present or may have both expressive and receptive disorders in combination. Educators sometimes use the term *language learning disability (LLD)* to refer to children with significant receptive or expressive language disorders.

To say that a child has a language delay does not necessarily mean that the child has a language disorder. As Reed (2017) explains, a *language delay* implies that a child is slow to develop linguistic skills but acquires them in the same sequence as typically developing children do. Generally, all language features are delayed at about the same rate. A *language disorder*, however, suggests a disruption in the usual rate or sequence in which specific language skills emerge. For example, a child who consistently has difficulty responding to who, what, and where questions but who otherwise displays language skills appropriate for her age would likely be considered to have a language disorder.

Children with serious language disorders are almost certain to have problems in school and with social development. They frequently play a passive role in communication. Children with impaired language are less likely to initiate conversations than are their peers. When asked questions, their replies rarely provide new information related to the topic. It is often difficult to detect children with language disorders; their performance may lead people to mistakenly classify them with disability labels such as intellectual disabilities, hearing impairment, or emotional disturbance, when in fact these descriptions are neither accurate nor appropriate.

Children with oral language problems are also likely to have reading and writing disabilities (DeThorne et al., 2010; Fahey et al., 2019; Kim et al., 2015; Owens & Farinella, 2019). The problem is compounded because many children with speech-language delays are "treatment resistors" to generally effective early literacy interventions (Al Otaiba, 2001).

Prevalence

Estimates of the prevalence of communication disorders in children vary widely. Reliable figures are hard to come by because investigators often use different definitions of speech and language disorders and sample different populations. In the 2018–2019 school year, about 1,036,790 children age 6 to 21 years received special education and related services under the IDEA's disability category "speech or language impairment" (U.S. Department of Education, 2020a). This number represented 16.4% of all students with disabilities who received special education services and 1.6% of the school-age population. Speech or language impairment is the second-largest disability category after learning disabilities.

The number of children with speech and language impairments is much higher than the number of children who receive services under the speech or language impairment category. Approximately 50% of children who receive special education services because of another primary disability (e.g., intellectual disabilities, learning disabilities, hearing impairments) also have communication disorders (Hall et al., 2001).

Speech and language impairments are more prevalent among males than females and are about the same in each of the major geographical regions of the United States.

Approximately two thirds of school-age children served by SLPs are boys (Hall et al., 2001). The percentage of children with speech and language disorders decreases significantly from the earlier to the later school grades.

Causes

Learning Outcome 8.3 Describe and identify causes of speech and language impairments and list the major components of a comprehensive evaluation used to detect the presence and extent of a communication disorder.

There are many types of communication disorders with numerous possible causes. A speech or language impairment may be *organic*—that is, attributable to damage, dysfunction, or malformation of a specific organ or part of the body. Most communication disorders, however, are not considered organic but are classified as functional. A *functional communication disorder* cannot be attributed to a specific physical condition, and its origin is not clearly known.

Causes of Speech Impairments

Examples of physical factors that frequently result in speech impairments are **cleft palate**, paralysis of the speech muscles, absence of teeth, craniofacial abnormalities, enlarged adenoids, and traumatic brain injury. **Dysarthria** is the collective name for a group of speech disorders caused by neuromuscular impairments that affect the movements necessary for proper respiration, phonation, resonation, articulation, or prosodic aspects of speech (Duffy, 2013). Lack of precise motor control needed to produce and sequence sounds causes distorted and repeated sounds. An organic speech impairment may be a child's primary disability, or it may be secondary to other disabilities, such as cerebral palsy or intellectual disabilities.

Causes of Language Disorders

Factors that can contribute to language disorders in children include developmental and intellectual disabilities, autism, traumatic brain injury, child abuse and neglect, hearing loss, and structural abnormalities of the speech mechanism (Rosenbaum & Simon, 2015).

Some severe disorders in expressive and receptive language result from injury to the brain. **Aphasia** describes a loss of the ability to process and use language. Aphasia is one of the most prevalent causes of language disorders in adults, most often occurring suddenly after a cardiovascular event (e.g., stroke). Head injury is a significant cause of aphasia in children. Aphasia may be either expressive or, less commonly, receptive. Children with mild aphasia have language patterns very similar to those of typically developing children but may have difficulty retrieving certain words and tend to need more time than usual to communicate. Children with severe aphasia, however, are likely to have a markedly reduced storehouse of words and language forms.

Research indicates that genetics may contribute to communication disorders (Tomblin, 2017). Scientists in Britain have discovered a gene area that affects speech (Porterfield, 1998), and other researchers have reported genetic links to phonological disorders (Uffen, 1997) and stuttering (Yairi, 1998).

Environmental influences also play an important part in delayed, disordered, or absent language. The communication efforts of some children are reinforced; other children, unfortunately, are punished for talking, gesturing, or otherwise attempting to communicate. A child who has little stimulation at home and few chances to speak, listen, explore, and interact with others will probably have little motivation for communicating and may well experience delays in language development.

Identification and Assessment

"Don't worry; she'll grow out of it."
"Speech therapists can't help a child who doesn't talk."
"He'll be all right once he starts school."

These are common examples of misguided and inaccurate yet widely held attitudes toward communication disorders. Although some children who experience mild speech impairments or language delays do get better without intervention, many do not. To avoid the consequences of unrecognized or untreated speech and language impairments, it is especially important for children to receive professional assessment and evaluation services.

Screening and Teacher Observation

In some school districts, SLPs screen the spoken language abilities of all kindergarten children. These screenings might involve norm-referenced tests, informal assessments the SLP develops, and questionnaires or checklists for parents and teachers (Justice & Redle, 2014; Owens & Farinella, 2019). Classroom teachers also play an important role in identifying children who may have speech and language impairments. Teachers can use a checklist such as the one in Figure 8.5 to identify children with whom the SLP can conduct individualized screening for possible communication disorders. Children who fail a speech and language screening test are candidates for a systematic, in-depth evaluation.

FIGURE 8.5 A Checklist for Identifying Possible Language Impairment in the Classroom

Directions: The following behaviors may indicate that a child in your classroom has a language impairment that is in need of language intervention. Please check the appropriate items.

_____ Child mispronounces sounds and words.

_____ Child omits word endings, such as plural *-s* and past tense *-ed*.

_____ Child omits small, unemphasized words, such as auxiliary verbs or prepositions.

_____ Child uses an immature vocabulary; overuses empty words, such as "one" and "thing"; or seems to have difficulty recalling or finding the right word.

_____ Child has difficulty comprehending new words and concepts.

_____ Child's sentence structure seems immature or overreliant on forms, such as subject–verb–object. It's unoriginal, dull.

_____ Child has difficulty with one of the following:

_____ Verb tensing	_____ Articles	_____ Auxiliary verbs
_____ Pronouns	_____ Irreg. verbs	_____ Prepositions
_____ Word order	_____ Irreg. plurals	_____ Conjunctions

_____ Child has difficulty relating sequential events.

_____ Child has difficulty following directions.

_____ Child's questions are often poorly formed.

_____ Child has difficulty answering questions.

_____ Child's comments are often off topic or inappropriate for the conversation.

_____ There are long pauses between a remark and the child's reply or between successive remarks by the child. It's as if the child is searching for a response or is confused.

_____ Child appears to be attending to communication but remembers little of what is said.

Source: Robert E. Owens, Jr. *Language Disorders: A Functional Approach to Assessment and Intervention*, 6e. Published by Pearson.

Evaluation Components

HLP4 Use multiple sources of information to develop a comprehensive understanding of a student's strengths and needs.

Testing procedures vary according to the suspected type of disorder. Often the specialist conducts broad screenings to detect areas of concern and then moves to more detailed evaluation in those areas. Most examiners use a variety of assessment devices and approaches to obtain as much relevant information as possible to inform diagnostic decisions and treatment plans. A comprehensive evaluation to detect the presence and extent of a communication disorder would likely include the following components:

- *Case history and physical examination.* Most professional speech and language assessments begin by documenting the child's case history. This typically involves completing a biographical form that includes information such as the child's birth and developmental history, health record, scores on achievement and intelligence tests, and adjustment to school. Parents may be asked when the child first crawled, walked, uttered words, and began playing with other children. The specialist carefully examines the child's mouth, noting any irregularities in the tongue, lips, teeth, palate, or other structures that may affect speech production. If the child has an organic speech problem, the child is referred for possible medical intervention.
- *Articulation.* The specialist assesses speech errors and records sounds pronounced incorrectly, types of mispronunciations, and number of errors. Examples of articulation tests include the Photo Articulation Test (Lippke et al., 1997) and the Goldman-Fristoe Test of Articulation—2 (Goldman & Fristoe, 2000).
- *Hearing.* The child's hearing is assessed to determine whether a hearing problem is causing the suspected communication disorder. Audiometry, a formal procedure for testing hearing, is discussed in Chapter 9.
- *Phonological awareness and processing.* Competent speakers and users of language can distinguish the presence and absence of speech sounds, differences between and among sounds, and when individual sounds begin and end. They can remember language sounds and reproduce them at a later time. Children without such phonological awareness and processing skills not only have problems with receptive and expressive spoken language but also have great difficulties in learning to read. Phonological processing measures include the Test of Phonological Awareness (Torgeson & Bryant, 2004) and the Comprehensive Test of Phonological Processing (Wagner et al., 1999).
- *Overall language development and vocabulary.* The amount of vocabulary a child has acquired is generally a good indicator of language competence. Frequently used tests of vocabulary include the Peabody Picture Vocabulary Test—4 (Dunn & Dunn, 2006) and the Comprehensive Receptive and Expressive Vocabulary Test (Wallace & Hammill, 2002). An overall language test, such as the Test of Language Development (Hammill & Newcomer, 2008) or the Clinical Evaluation of Language Fundamentals (Semel et al., 2003), assesses the child's understanding and production of language structures (e.g., important syntactical elements such as the concept that conjunctions show relations between the sentence elements they connect).
- *Assessment of language function.* In his account of language and communication, B. F. Skinner (1957; Sundberg, 2020) emphasized the circumstances surrounding the various functions of communication (e.g., requesting, naming) rather than the structure and form of language (e.g., words and sentences). Skinner's analysis of verbal behavior has led to advances in the assessment and treatment of language

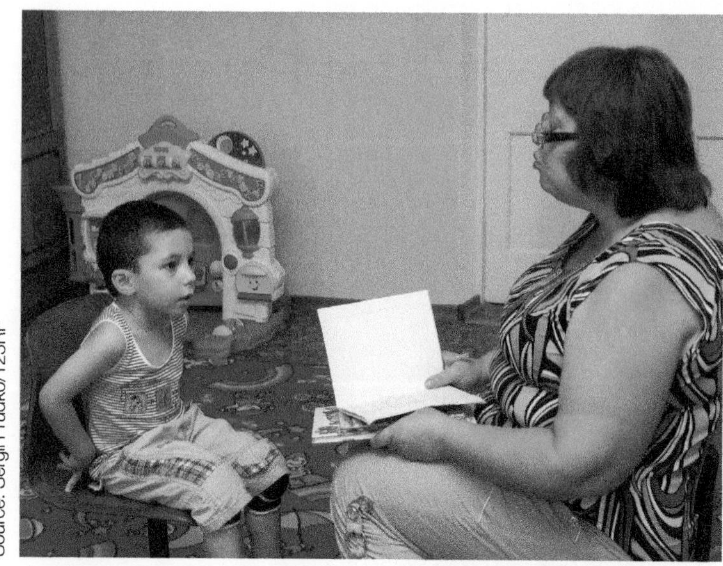

Source: Sergii Prudko/123RF

A comprehensive evaluation of communication disorders includes assessment of expressive and receptive speech and language skills.

and communication disorders. The *Verbal Behavior Milestones Assessment and Placement Program* (VB-MAPP) is an assessment tool based on Skinner's analysis (Sundberg, 2008). This test identifies a student's strengths and weaknesses across the different language functions and compares them with the language and communication skills of typically developing children. The VB-MAPP also includes a Barriers Assessment that identifies 24 possible barriers that might be preventing a child from making progress (e.g., prompt dependency, weak motivation) and a Transition Assessment that can help to identify a child's overall educational needs.

- *Language samples.* An important part of any evaluation for communication disorders is obtaining accurate samples of the child's expressive speech and language. The examiner considers factors such as intelligibility and fluency of speech, voice quality, and use of vocabulary and grammar. Some SLPs use structured tasks to evoke language samples, such as asking a child to describe a picture, tell a story, or answer a list of questions. Most specialists, however, use informal conversation to obtain language samples, believing that the child's language sample will be more representative if the examiner uses natural conversation rather than highly structured tasks (Hadley, 1998). Open-ended questions such as "Tell me about your family" are suggested rather than yes–no questions or questions that can be answered with one word, such as "What color is your car?" To ensure a complete and accurate record of the talk and to reduce distractions for the child caused by note taking, examiners usually make an audio recording of the child's talking.
- *Observation in natural settings.* Observation and measurement of children's language use in social contexts and everyday activities are important elements of assessment for communication disorders. It is imperative that the observer sample the child's communication behavior across various settings rather than limit it to a clinic or an examining room. A parent–child observation is frequently arranged for young children. The specialist provides appropriate toys and activities and requests the parent to interact with the child in typical fashion.

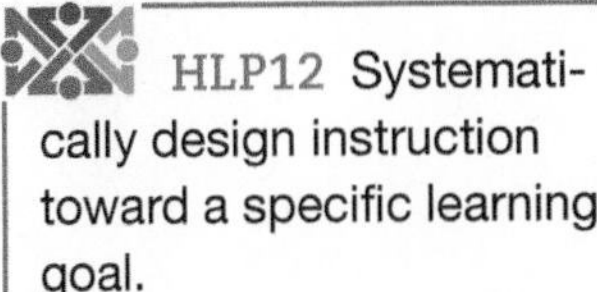
HLP12 Systematically design instruction toward a specific learning goal.

Because of the large volume of assessment information obtained, some SLPs use computer programs to organize and analyze the data. The SLP then develops a treatment plan in cooperation with the child's parents and teachers to set up realistic communication objectives and determine the methods that will be used.

Assessment of Communication Disorders in Children Whose First Language Is Not English or Who Use Nonstandard English

It is often difficult to distinguish between a student whose learning and communication problems result from a disability and a student whose primary need is systematic, culturally responsive instruction. Proper assessment of the speech-language skills of children from diverse cultural, linguistic, and socioeconomic backgrounds poses a difficult challenge for language-majority educators (Hoff, 2013). See *Teaching & Learning,* "When Is a Difference a Disability?"

For children who are learning English, determining their communicative competence requires careful assessment of the child's language proficiency in both the first and second languages (L1 and L2) combined with an analysis of authentic conversational behavior (Cheng, 2012). Culturally and linguistically diverse students and those who speak a nonstandard dialect should not be diagnosed with a speech-language disorder if "problems" are observed only in English and not in their first language (or dialect). A student with a genuine language impairment will experience difficulties in both L1 and standard English (Roseberry-McKibbin, 2007).

Best practices in assessing speech and language competence of children who do not speak standard English as their first language include assessments of basic interpersonal communication skills (BICS) and cognitive academic language proficiency (CALP) (Roseberry-McKibbin, 2018). BICS is a set of language skills required in everyday face-to-face communication situations (e.g., conversing about the weather); CALP refers to proficient use of language specific to academic learning situations (e.g., "Compare formal and functional properties of sand and granite"). A typical English-language learner (ELL) needs about 2 years under ideal conditions to develop BICS to a level similar to that of native speakers, and achieving a similar level of performance with CALP may require 5 to 7 years (Cummins, 2002).

IDEA requires that assessment for the purpose of identifying children with disabilities be conducted in the child's native language. Although a few standardized language proficiency tests are available in languages other than English (McLaughlin & Lewis, 2008), translation or adaptation of tests into other languages poses certain problems (e.g., Rhodes et al., 2005). For instance, depending on the family's country of origin, a Spanish-speaking child may use any one of five distinct words to describe a kite: *cometa, huila, volantin, papalote,*

TEACHING & LEARNING

When Is a Difference a Disability?

Educators must be careful not to confuse communication differences with delayed or disordered speech and language. It should not be surprising that students who are English-language learners and students whose first language is English but who speak a nonstandard dialect often perform poorly on formal tests of English speech and language. The results of formal language tests should never be the sole basis for diagnosing a speech or language impairment.

A child who uses a dialect different from the dominant culture of the school should not be treated as having a communication disorder. If the teacher does not accept natural communication differences among children and mistakenly assumes that a speech or language impairment is present, problems may arise in the classroom and during parent–teacher communication (Reed, 2017). However, some children with communication differences have communication disorders within their dialects, and such impairments must not be overlooked (Cheng, 2012; Payne, 2011). Figure 8.6 provides a list of questions for teachers to ask to distinguish difference from disability.

FIGURE 8.6 Questions to Help Teachers Distinguish Communication Difference from Disability

STUDENT CHARACTERISTIC	TEACHERS SHOULD ASK	IF THE ANSWER IS NO, THEN...
Alejandro does not follow directions.	Does he follow directions in his first language?	Alejandro may have attention, memory, and/or behavior challenges associated with a disability.
Madoka mispronounces the /th/ sound.	Is /th/ a standard sound in her first language?	Madoka probably does not have a speech disorder; she may need instruction and practice in producing unfamiliar sounds. If her language uses a different alphabet, she will need extra support connecting English graphemes and phonemes.
Ephraim has difficulty reading sight words.	Does he know the meanings of the words when they are spoken?	Ephraim may have more difficulty reading words that are not in his spoken vocabulary. If he continues to struggle learning the meanings of words, he may have attention and/or memory challenges associated with a disability.
Lefki's handwriting is illegible.	Is she able to produce legible writing in her first language?	Lefki may have fine motor and/or attention deficits associated with a disability.
Ashkii does not make eye contact with teachers or participate in class discussions.	Are eye contact and child-adult conversations culturally appropriate in the child's home culture?	Given that Ashkii's behaviors are consistent with his community's norms, his behavior should not automatically be interpreted as disrespectful, inappropriate, or related to a disability.
Julieta frequently disrupts lessons.	Is she disruptive when receiving instruction in her first language?	Julieta's disruptions may be motivated by escape from fatigue and/or frustration with attempts to communicate in a second language.

A student with a genuine language impairment will exhibit difficulties in both his first language (L1) and Standard American English. Teachers can assist SLPs in language assessments in the following ways:

- Supplement standardized assessments with direct observations of a student's communicative behaviors in natural settings where he can use the language of his choice.
- Seek input from a teacher of ELL students if there is not one already on the multidisciplinary team.
- Pay close attention to the family's use of language; this may provide clues for determining if a language difference is actually a disorder.
- Learn which speech sounds may be difficult for students because they are not used in their first language (e.g., /j/ in Spanish, /b/ in Chinese; Klingner & Eppolito, 2014).

HLP1 Collaborate with professionals to increase student success.

and *chiringa* (DeAvila, 1976). Thus, although translation of tests and other materials into a child's native language may be helpful in many instances, educators must take care to avoid inaccurate translations.

Educational Approaches

Learning Outcome 8.4 Identify the basic goals and common elements of effective interventions for speech-sound errors and language disorders.

Speech-language pathologist is the preferred term for a school-based professional with primary responsibility for identifying, evaluating, and providing therapeutic services to children with communication disorders. As a key member of a child's IEP team, the SLP's goal is to correct the child's speech and language problems or to help the child achieve the maximum communicative potential, which may involve compensatory techniques and augmentative and alternative means of communication. Speech-language pathology addresses both organic and functional causes and encompasses practitioners with numerous points of view who use a wide range of intervention techniques.

YouTube

Pearson eText
Video Example 8.3
Assessing students' ability to repeat nonsense syllables can help SLPs differentiate language differences from language disorders. https://www.youtube.com/watch?v=Czbg78bFwYM

Some SLPs use structured exercises and drills to correct speech sounds; others emphasize speech production in natural language contexts. Some prefer to work with children in individual therapy sessions; others believe group sessions are advantageous for language modeling and peer support. Some SLPs encourage children to imitate the therapist's speech; others have the child listen to recordings of his own speech. Some specialists follow a structured, teacher-directed approach in which they precisely prompt, reinforce, and record targeted speech and language behaviors; others use less structured methods. Some SLPs focus on a child's expressive and receptive communication; others devote attention to other aspects of the child's behavior and environment, such as developing self-confidence and improving interactions with parents and classmates.

Treating Speech-Sound Errors

A general goal of specialists in communication disorders is to help the child speak as clearly and pleasantly as possible so that listeners will focus on the child's message rather than how he says it.

ARTICULATION ERRORS The goals of therapy for articulation problems are acquisition of correct speech sound(s), generalization of the correct sound(s) to all settings and contexts (especially the classroom), and maintenance of the correct sound(s) after therapy has ended.

Articulation therapy involves discrimination and production activities. *Discrimination activities* teach the child to detect differences between similar sounds (e.g., the /t/in *tape*, the /k/in *cape*) and to differentiate between correct and distorted

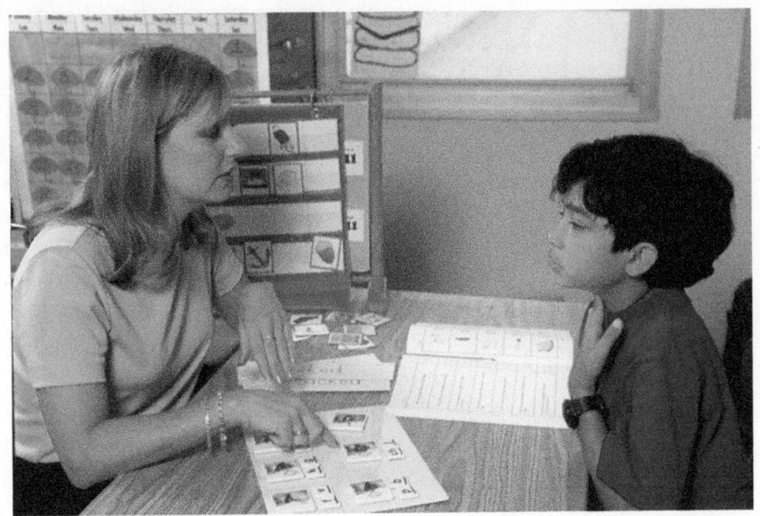

Source: Mary Kate Denny/PhotoEdit

SLPs use auditory, visual, and tactile feedback to help children improve their speech.

speech sounds. The SLP provides auditory, visual, and tactile feedback to help the child learn to match his speech to that of a standard model. A generally consistent relationship exists between children's ability to recognize sounds and their ability to articulate them correctly.

Production is the ability to produce a given speech sound alone and in various contexts. Therapy emphasizes the repetitive production of sounds in various contexts, with special attention to the motor skills needed for articulation. The SLP may have the child carefully watch how to produce sounds and then use a mirror to monitor his own speech production. Children are expected to accurately produce problematic sounds in syllables, words, sentences, and stories. They may record their own speech and listen carefully for errors. Therapy progresses from the child producing simple sounds in isolation; then in syllables, words, phrases, sentences, and structured conversation; and finally in unstructured conversation. Teachers and parents can assist by providing good speech models, reinforcing improved performance, and encouraging the child to talk.

Pearson eText
Video Example 8.4
Hand signals and visual prompts can help students correctly articulate speech sounds.

PHONOLOGICAL ERRORS When a child's spoken language includes phonological errors, therapy helps the child identify the error pattern(s) and produce more linguistically appropriate sound patterns (Barlow, 2001). For example, a child who frequently omits final consonants might learn to recognize the difference between minimally contrastive words—perhaps using a set of cards with the words *sea, seed, seal, seam,* and *seat*. Activities are constructed to reward the child for following directions (e.g., "Pick up the *seal* card") and speaking clearly enough for the therapist to follow his directions (e.g., the child directs the SLP to give him the *seat* card). To respond correctly, the child must attend to and use the information in the final consonant sound.

Children who struggle with phonological awareness can often articulate specific sounds but may not use those sounds in proper linguistic context. Although the distinction between articulation errors and phonological errors is important, many children with communication disorders have problems with both. The therapeutic approaches for articulation and phonological disorders are not incompatible and can be used together for some children.

Treating Fluency Disorders

People who stutter have been subjected to countless treatments—some of them unusual, to say the least. Past treatments included holding pebbles in the mouth, talking out of one side of the mouth, eating raw oysters, speaking with the teeth clenched, taking alternating hot and cold baths, and speaking on inhaled rather than exhaled air (Ham, 1986). For many years, it was widely thought that stuttering was caused by a tongue that was unable to function properly. As a result, early physicians often prescribed ointments to blister or numb the tongue or even suggested the removal of portions of the tongue through surgery!

The application of behavioral principles has strongly influenced contemporary practice in the treatment of fluency disorders. Therapists using this methodology regard stuttering as learned behavior and seek to replace it by establishing and encouraging fluent speech. One example of a behaviorally based stuttering treatment approach is the Lidcombe Program, which trains parents to ignore their child's stuttering initially and reinforce fluent utterances with frequent praise (e.g., "That was smooth talking!") (Packman et al., 2014). Onslow et al. (2003) found that studies evaluating the effectiveness of the Lidcombe Program with more than 750 children worldwide have reported a 95% success rate.

Children may learn to manage their stuttering by deliberately prolonging certain sounds or by speaking slowly to get through a "block." They may increase their confidence and fluency by speaking in groups, where pressure is minimized and successful speech is positively reinforced. They may learn to monitor their own speech and to reward themselves for periods of fluency (Manning & Dilollo, 2018). They may learn to speak to a rhythmic beat or with the aid of devices that mask or delay their ability to hear their own speech. Audio recorders are often used for drills, simulating conversations, and documenting progress.

Children often learn to control their stuttering and produce increasingly fluent speech as they mature (Ramig & Pollard, 2011). No single method of treatment has been recognized as most effective. Stuttering frequently decreases when children enter adolescence, regardless of which treatment method was used. Often, the problem disappears with no treatment at all. Results from studies of the phenomenon of spontaneous recovery from stuttering have reported that 65% to 80% of children diagnosed as stutterers apparently outgrow or get over their dysfluencies without formal intervention (Yairi & Ambrose, 2013). Nevertheless, an SLP should be contacted when a child exhibits signs of stuttering or when the parents are concerned about speech fluency. Although some children who stutter improve without help, many do not. Early intervention may prevent the child from developing a severe stutter. In its initial stages, stuttering can almost always be treated successfully by teachers, parents, and an SLP working together. See *Teaching & Learning,* "Helping Students Who Stutter."

Treating Voice Disorders

A thorough medical examination should always be sought for a child with a voice disorder. Surgery or other medical interventions can often treat organic causes. In addition, SLPs often recommend environmental modifications; a person who is consistently required to speak in a noisy setting, for example, may use a small microphone to reduce vocal straining and shouting. Most interventions for voice disorders, however, entail direct vocal rehabilitation to help the child produce more acceptable and efficient speech. Voice therapy often begins with teaching the child to listen to his own voice and identify the aspects that need to be changed. Depending on the type of voice disorder, vocal rehabilitation may include activities such as exercises to increase breathing capacity, relaxation techniques to reduce tension, vocal hygiene (e.g., drink fluids, avoid excessive throat clearing, vocal rest), and procedures to increase or decrease the loudness of speech (Sapienza et al., 2011).

Because many voice problems are attributable to vocal abuse, interventions derived from applied behavior analysis can be used to help children and adults break habitual patterns of vocal misuse. For example, a child might self-monitor the number of vocal abuses he commits in the classroom or at home, receiving rewards for gradually lowering the number of vocal abuses over time.

Treating Language Disorders

Treatments for language disorders are also extremely varied. Recognizing children must have something they *want* to communicate, some therapists focus on precommunication activities that encourage the child to explore and that make the environment conducive to the development of receptive and expressive language. And because children learn through imitation, it is important for the teacher or specialist to speak clearly, use correct inflections, and provide a rich variety of words and sentences.

Children with very limited spoken language might be taught how to orally "read" pictures as a language enhancement activity (Alberto & Fredrick, 2000). Teachers can use storyboards and song boards with pictures illustrating language: The teacher places and removes pictures from the board as she tells the story or points to the appropriate picture while singing a line (Skau & Cascella, 2006). Children with language impairments might develop written language skills by exchanging email letters with pen pals (Harmston et al., 2001).

VOCABULARY BUILDING Vocabulary has been called the building block of language (Dockrell & Messer, 2004). Children with language disorders have a limited store of words to call upon. SLPs and classroom teachers use a wide variety of techniques to build students' vocabulary, including graphic organizers, mnemonics, and learning strategies described in Chapter 5. Foil and Alber (2003) recommend that teachers use the following sequence to help students learn new vocabulary:

1. Display each new word, pronounce it, say the meaning of the word, and have students repeat it.
2. Provide and have students repeat multiple examples of the word used in context.
3. Connect the word and its meaning to students' current knowledge and prompt students to describe their experiences related to the word.
4. Provide multiple opportunities for students to use the word in context during guided practice and provide feedback on their responses. [Insert margin note:]
5. Help students discriminate between words with similar meanings but subtle differences (e.g., *separate* and *segregate*).
6. Assign independent practice activities; challenge students to select new vocabulary words to learn independently.

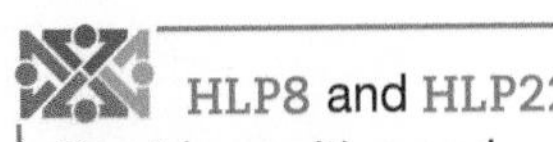
HLP8 and HLP22
Provide positive and constructive feedback to guide students' learning and behavior.

7. Prompt students to use their new vocabulary in varied settings and situations, provide praise and other forms of reinforcement when students' speech and writing contain new vocabulary, and have students self-record how often they use new vocabulary.

HLP21 Teach students to maintain and generalize new learning across time and settings.

NATURALISTIC STRATEGIES Speech-language pathologists are increasingly using naturalistic interventions to help children develop and use communication skills. Naturalistic approaches were developed as an alternative to didactic language interventions because children often experienced difficulties in generalizing new skills from structured teaching settings to everyday contexts. In contrast to didactic teaching approaches, which use contrived materials and activities (e.g., pictures, puppets) and massed trials to teach specific skills, naturalistic interventions, often called *milieu* or *incidental teaching,* take advantage of

FIGURE 8.7 Six Strategies for Increasing Naturalistic Opportunities for Language Teaching

1. **Interesting materials.** Students are likely to communicate when things or activities in the environment interest them. *Example:* James laid quietly on the rug, with his head resting on his arms. Ms. Davis sat at one end of the rug and rolled a big yellow ball right past James. James lifted his head and looked around for the ball.
2. **Out-of-reach materials.** Students are likely to communicate when they want something that they cannot reach. *Example:* Mr. Norris lifted a drum off the shelf and placed it on the floor between Judy and Annette, who were both in wheelchairs. Mr. Norris hit the drum three times and then waited, looking at his two students. Judy watched and clapped her hands together. Then, she reached for the drum with both arms outstretched.
3. **Inadequate portions.** Students are likely to communicate when they do not have the necessary materials to carry out an instruction. *Example:* Mr. Robinson gave every student except Mary a ticket to get into the auditorium for the high school play. He told his students to give their tickets to the attendant. Mr. Robinson walked beside Mary toward the entrance. When Mary reached the attendant, Mr. Robinson paused and looked at Mary. She pointed to the tickets in his hand and signed "give me." Mr. Robinson gave her a ticket and she handed it to the attendant, who said, "Thank you. Enjoy the play."
4. **Choice making.** Students are likely to communicate when they are given a choice. *Example:* Peggy's favorite pastime is listening to tapes on her tape recorder. On Saturday morning, Peggy's father said to her, "We could listen to your tapes" (pointing to the picture of the tape recorder on Peggy's communication board) "or we could go for a ride in the car" (pointing to the picture of the car). "What would you like to do?" Peggy pointed to the picture of the tape recorder. "OK, let's listen to this new tape you like," her father said as he put the tape in and turned on the machine.
5. **Assistance.** Students are likely to communicate when they need assistance in operating or manipulating materials. *Example:* Tammy's mother always places three clear plastic containers with snacks (cookies, crackers, popcorn) on the kitchen table before Tammy returns from school. When Tammy arrives home and is ready for a snack, she goes to the table and chooses what she wants. The containers are hard to open, so Tammy usually brings the container with her chosen snack to her mother. Her mother responds to this nonverbal request by modeling a request form that specifies Tammy's choice (e.g., "Open popcorn.").
6. **Unexpected situations.** Students are likely to communicate when something happens that they do not expect. *Example:* Ms. Esser was helping Kathy put on her socks and shoes after rest time. After assisting with the socks, Ms. Esser put one of the shoes on her own foot. Kathy stared at the shoe for a moment and then looked up at her teacher, who was smiling. "No," laughed Kathy, "my shoe."

Source: From Kaiser, A. P., & Grim, J. C. (2006). Teaching functional communication skills. In M. E. Snell & F. Brown (Eds.), *Instruction of students with severe disabilities* (6th ed., p. 464). Upper Saddle River, NJ: Pearson Education, Inc. Reprinted by permission.

naturally occurring activities throughout the day to provide motivation and opportunities for a child to use language skills. Naturalistic approaches occur in the context of typical conversational interchanges that follow the child's interests and attention.

However, good naturalistic teaching does not require the teacher to wait patiently to see whether and when opportunities for meaningful and interesting language use by children occur (Christensen-Sandfort & Whinnery, 2013). Naturalistic interventions involve structuring the environment to create numerous opportunities for desired child responses (e.g., holding up a toy and asking, "What do you want?") and structuring adult responses to a child's communication (e.g., the child points outside and says, "Go wifth me" and the teacher says, "Okay, I'll go with you"). Effective milieu teaching more closely resembles a conversation than a structured instructional episode (Kaiser & Grim, 2006). Environments where language teaching takes place should be designed to catch students' interest and increase the likelihood of communicative interactions that can be used for teaching purposes. Figure 8.7 shows six strategies for arranging environments to create naturally occurring language teaching opportunities.

No matter what the approach to treatment, children with language disorders need to be around children and adults with something interesting to talk about. Educators assumed for many years that a one-to-one setting was the most effective format for language intervention. Emphasis was on eliminating distracting stimuli and focusing a child's attention on the desired communication task. Today, it is generally recognized that language is an interactive, interpersonal process and that educators should use naturally occurring intervention formats to expose children with language disorders to a wide range of experiences, contexts, and people that cannot be replicated in one-to-one therapy.

Augmentative and Alternative Communication

HLP19 Use assistive and instructional technologies.

Augmentative and alternative communication (AAC) refers to a diverse set of strategies and methods to assist individuals who cannot meet their communication needs through speech or writing. AAC entails three components (ASHA, 2019b):

- A representational symbol set or vocabulary
- A means for selecting the symbols
- A means for transmitting the symbols

Each of the three components of AAC may be unaided or aided. *Unaided AAC techniques* do not require a physical aid or device. They include oral speech, gestures, facial expressions, general body posture, and manual signs. Of course, individuals without disabilities use a wide range of unaided augmentative communication techniques. *Aided AAC techniques* of communication involve an external device or piece of equipment. AAC devices range from no-tech (e.g., paper and pencil) to low-tech (e.g., the child pushes a switch to transmit a single word or phrase) to high-tech electronic equipment (e.g., computerized voice-output device).

Pearson eText Video Example 8.5
AAC includes speech-output devices like Katrina's.

Individuals who do not speak so that others can understand must have access to vocabulary that matches as nearly as possible the language they would use in various situations if they could speak. Da Fonte and Boesche (2019) suggest that decisions about what to include in a student's augmentative vocabulary should take into account the following:

- Vocabulary that peers in similar situations and settings use
- What communication partners (e.g., teachers, parents) think will be needed
- Vocabulary the student is already using in all modalities
- Contextual demands of specific situations

SYMBOL SETS AND SYMBOL SYSTEMS After selecting the vocabulary for an AAC system, the educator must choose or develop a collection of symbols to represent the vocabulary. Symbol sets are graphic, which means that the symbols look like the object or concept they represent as much as possible. Numerous *symbol sets* are available both commercially and free. These sets are a collection of pictures or drawings in which each symbol has one or more specified meanings, from which a person's AAC vocabulary might be constructed.

Using software programs such as Mayer-Johnson's Boardmaker, teachers can create individualized sets of communication symbols. Symbol sets may also be homemade, consisting of photos, pictures, and perhaps words and the alphabet.

Content Extension 8.2

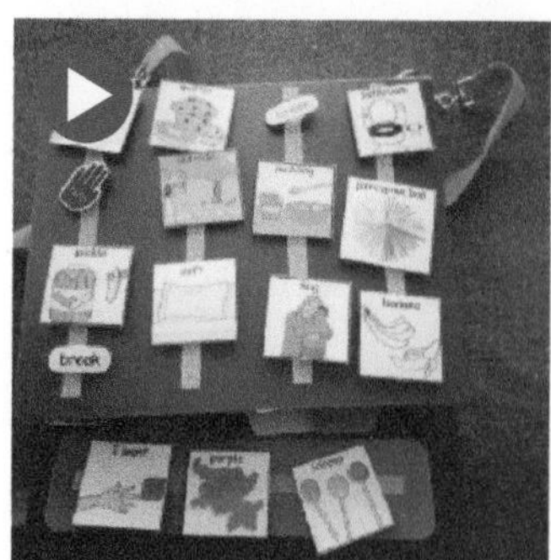

Read about using PECS to teach functional communication skills.

The Picture Exchange Communication System (PECS) is an AAC strategy that teaches nonverbal users to request highly motivating items and activities by giving a picture of the item or activity to a communicative partner. Users advance to a PECS communication book containing picture vocabulary and a sentence strip for constructing more complex language (e.g., "I see a car."). When the PECS training structure is implemented with fidelity, most children quickly acquire functional communication and some begin to initiate spoken words (e.g., Cagliani et al., 2017; Chua & Poon, 2018; Gilroy et al., 2018; Lamb et al., 2018; Park, Alber-Morgan, & Cannella-Malone, 2011).

In contrast to symbol sets, *symbol systems* are structured around an internal set of rules that govern how new symbols are added to the system. One of the best-known symbol systems is Blissymbolics, an international graphical language of more than 4000 symbols, first developed for use by people with physical disabilities (Blissymbolics Communication International, 2019). Bliss characters combine multiple symbols to create new meanings (e.g., "school" is communicated by selecting the symbols "house-gives-knowledge"). Simple shapes are used to keep the symbols easy and fast to draw. Because many Blissymbolics are abstract, however, and do not look like the concept they represent, some individuals have difficulty learning the system.

SELECTING THE SYMBOLS Students select symbols in augmentative communication by direct selection, scanning, or encoding responses (Da Fonte & Boesche, 2019). *Direct selection* involves pointing to the symbol one wishes to express with a finger or fist or sometimes with a wand attached to the head or chin. With a limited number of selections widely spaced from one another, the user can select symbols by "eye pointing." *Scanning* techniques present choices to the user one at a time, and the user makes a response at the proper time to indicate which item or group of selections she wants to communicate. Scanning can be machine or listener assisted (e.g., the listener may point to symbols one at a time while watching for the user's eye blink, which signals selection). *Encoding* involves giving multiple signals to indicate the location of the symbol or the item to be selected. Usually, the user makes a pair of responses that directs the listener to a specific printed message on a reference list. In a display in which symbols are organized by color and number, for example, a student can first touch one card (to select the red group of messages) and then make a second pointing response to indicate which number message in the red group is intended.

TRANSMITTING THE SYMBOLS After determining a meaningful vocabulary and an appropriate symbol set, consider which method of transmitting the symbols is best for the student. An ever-more sophisticated variety of AAC devices offer a wide range of alternatives for transmitting communication symbols. Software developers have created numerous AAC apps for smartphones, such as the iPhone and Android, and for portable tablets, such as the iPad. Dedicated communication aids—such as the Dynavok Maestro and Prentke Romich Intro Talker—offer computerized speech selection and transmission and a large vocabulary that can be individualized for the user.

Despite the high-tech "arms race" among developers and providers of computer-based AAC systems, one of the most common and effective AAC tools is the *communication board*, a flat area (often a tray or a table attached to a wheelchair) on which the symbols are arranged for the user to select. A student may have a basic communication board of common words, phrases, numbers, and so forth, for use across many situations. A student may also have various situational boards, or miniboards, with specific vocabulary for certain situations (e.g., at a restaurant, in science class). Students can also transport and display symbols in a wallet or a photo album. Although the student's use of AAC technology—whether it is scanning a sophisticated digital array or handing a picture card to a peer—often appears to take center stage, "When the focus is on successful communication, the form is reduced to its proper place of being a means toward an end, rather than the end itself" (DeThorne et al., 2014, p. 45).

Pearson eText
Video Example 8.6
Selecting the right AAC device requires teamwork, systematic evaluation, and ongoing monitoring.

Placement Options

Learning Outcome 8.5 Explain how the speech-language pathologist's role changes as a function of the setting where a child with communication disorders is served.

During the 2018–2019 school year, approximately 88% of children with speech or language impairments were served in the regular classroom for at least 80% of the school day (U.S. Department of Education, 2020a). A wide variety of service delivery models for students with communication disorders are used within and across educational placement options. Variations of all these models exist, and many schools and SLPs serve children using combinations of two or more of the following models.

Monitoring

The SLP monitors or checks on the student's speech and language performance in the regular classroom. This option is often used just before a student is dismissed from therapy.

Pull-Out

The traditional and still most prevalent model of service delivery is the pull-out approach, sometimes called *intermittent direct service.* SLPs spend two thirds of their time working with a child individually or with small groups of up to three children (ASHA, 2014). Depending on the needs of the individual child, pull-out may involve sessions of up to 1 hour 5 days per week. School-based SLPs work with a median caseload of 48 students each month. Most students receiving services from school-based SLPs meet with the SLP at least two times a week, most often for 21- to 30-minute sessions. The classroom teacher and SLP collaboratively determine activities and materials for each child's speech and language therapy sessions.

Many SLPs believe it is impossible to adequately serve a child with speech or language impairments with an isolated, pull-out approach (two or three 30-minute sessions each week with a specialist) (Harn et al., 1999). Because communication is seen as occurring most meaningfully in the natural environment, remedial procedures are increasingly carried out in the regular classroom during ongoing routines rather than in a special speech room. See *Transition: Next Year Is Now,* "Teaching Self-Advocacy to Students with Communication Challenges" on p. 254.

Collaborative Consultation

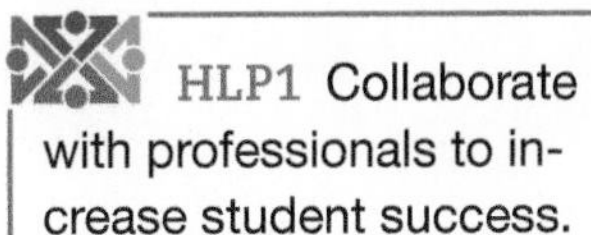
HLP1 Collaborate with professionals to increase student success.

Increasingly, communication disorders specialists serve as consultants for regular and special education teachers (and parents) rather than spending most of their time providing direct services to individual children. SLPs who work in school settings more often function as team members concerned with children's overall education and development.

The SLP often provides training and consultation for the general education classroom teacher, who may do much of the direct work with a child with communication disorders. The specialist concentrates on assessing communication disorders, evaluating progress, and providing materials and techniques; and encouraging teachers and parents to follow the guidelines.

Classroom or Curriculum Based

Increasingly, SLPs are working as educational partners in the classroom, mediating between students' communication needs and the communication demands of the academic curriculum. SLPs report devoting about one fourth of their time to helping teachers integrate language and speech goals into daily curriculum activities. The advantage is that services are brought to the child and the teacher, and communication connections with the curriculum are made more directly. See *Transition: Next Year Is Now,* "Teaching Self-Advocacy to Students with Communication Challenges?"

Transition: Next Year Is Now

Teaching Self-Advocacy to Students with Communication Challenges

Self-advocacy skills enable students with disabilities to request support in a variety of situations in school and other environments throughout adulthood (Test et al., 2005). However, self-advocacy may be especially challenging for individuals with disabilities transitioning from previous school experiences that reinforced their passivity and dependence (Roberts et al., 2016). Because self-advocacy predicts improved school retention and successful outcomes in adulthood (Roberts et al., 2016), it is essential for students with disabilities to learn self-advocacy skills and engage in many practice opportunities (Paradiz et al., 2018).

Featured Teacher Emily Pickard, agrees, "Self-advocacy is such a key area and so critical for our students to learn! Often, self-advocacy skills can prevent conflicts and challenging behaviors when the student is able to self-advocate appropriately." Emily designs self-advocacy instruction to address specific needs based on real situations her students encounter. For example, during a social skills lesson, a student reported that he did not understand the ratings he received from his job coach and was upset about his evaluation. He said the job coach was sometimes too critical of him and stayed too close to him at his job sites. Emily suggested that he bring up his concerns to his job coach in a non-confrontational manner. Then she scheduled a meeting with the job coach and the student to discuss and resolve this concern. Prior to the meeting, Emily implemented a lesson to prepare this student to self-advocate with his job coach.

Featured Teacher Emily Pickard's Self-Advocacy Role-Playing Lesson

Objective. The student will role play "I feel..." statements to communicate concerns.

With this group of students and their skill level, many of my lessons are conversational in nature. I use a white board to write notes based on what students are telling me. I also use direct questions about the problem, possible solutions, and ways to communicate their concerns.

Opening the lesson/Rationale. Open the lesson by getting students' responses to the following questions: What is the problem? Can you give me a specific example of a time when you felt this way? How do you think the job coach will feel when you approach her? What will happen after you talk to her?

Modeling. Sometimes I use other staff members to model the behavior. I would say something like, "Mrs. Ramirez and I have been having difficulty working together because sometimes I think she can be bossy. We are going to have a conversation about it and communicate our feelings." Mrs. Ramirez and I would then model appropriate use of "I feel" statements.

Role playing. The following is an example of a role playing script.

Student: Job coach, I feel uncomfortable when you talk to me harshly (State the problem with an "I feel" statement).

Staff: I didn't know you felt that way. What can I do differently? (Ask for specifics of what the student would like to see happen.)

Student: I would like it if you talked to me positively.

Feedback. I like to keep these lessons light and conversational. For example, when the student began saying, "Job coach, this just isn't working out," I stopped him and laughed and told him that it sounded like he was breaking up with her. He laughed too and tried again. If a student is really struggling with what to say, I would use a visual prompt on the board of a script with blanks. "I feel _____ when you _____."

Assessment. Observation during role play and during interaction with the job coach.

Other examples of self-advocacy skills that Emily teaches her transitioning students include:

- Using appropriate solutions when challenging situations at school or work arise (i.e., confide in and request assistance from a trusted adult, use a coping strategy to calm down, use self-advocacy to express feelings)

- Increasing involvement in their own IEP planning
- Meeting with the transition specialist to discuss continued education opportunities that will be available after leaving school
- Inquiring with current job sites to ask about the potential of maintaining employment upon exiting school

As self-advocacy skills are needed throughout life, it is important to plan for generalization so students are prepared for a wide variety of situations over time. Emily provides the following suggestions for programming for generalization of self-advocacy skills.

- Take advantage of incidental teaching opportunities. Look for other naturally occurring situations throughout the student's typical day in which self-advocacy skills are needed (e.g., getting incorrect change at lunch).
- Present students with challenging situations with both familiar and unfamiliar staff. For example, challenge a student who seldom says no by having a staff member he trusts ask him to break the rules. "Hey John, the boys' bathroom is full, why don't you use the girls'?" We also have had unfamiliar staff approach students in community and ask the student to come with them somewhere.
- Assign students to tasks that are nonpreferred at job sites, or do not even assign them a task. This challenges the students to express their opinion in an appropriate manner. We teach students compliance really well—sometimes too well. Students will have to learn as adults to speak up when they are not satisfied and communicate what they would prefer instead.
- Use writing activities or goals to address self-advocacy skills. Have students meet with the vocational coordinator to talk about future job options, learn how to call to set up transportation and travel independently to and from work, and attend their IEP meeting to discuss what they would like to work on.

After directly teaching students many examples of how to self-advocate across situations they will typically encounter throughout their day, assess their generalization by providing them with novel situations in which to perform self-advocacy skills.

HLP21 Teach students to maintain and generalize new learning across time and settings.

Training classroom teachers and parents to promote children's speech and language development has become an increasingly important aspect of SLPs' responsibilities. A growing controversy among some members of the SLP profession is the extent to which services for students with speech and language impairments provided in general education classrooms should take "a therapeutic focus" versus an "educational focus" (Prelock, 2000a, 2000b). Although providing services in inclusive models is encouraged, some SLPs express concern that this arrangement waters down speech and language therapy. Ehren (2000) discusses these concerns and suggests that SLPs can preserve their role identity and the integrity of services provided by maintaining a therapeutic focus and sharing the responsibility for student success with classroom teachers. Featured Teacher Emily Pickard agrees: "My job is to work on communication with my students, and support my teacher and team in any way I can related to communication."

Separate Classroom

Students with the most severe communication disorders are served in special classrooms for children with speech or language impairments. During the 2018–2019 school year, approximately 4% of children with speech or language impairments were served in separate classrooms (U.S. Department of Education, 2020a).

Community Based

In community-based models, speech and language therapy is provided outside the school, usually in the home. This model is most often used with preschoolers and sometimes for students with severe disabilities, with an emphasis on teaching functional communication skills in the community. Featured Teacher Emily Pickard's students spend time learning important skills in community settings. "Our Vocational program is AMAZING. Our students are out on job sites constantly, and our community is wonderful about helping us find places that fit their needs."

ADVICE FROM THE FEATURED TEACHER by Emily Pickard

Source: Coleen Brittingham

- ***No reinforcer, no lesson.*** Everybody is reinforced by something different. If you don't know what reinforces a student, keep trying until you figure it out. Take the time to build trust by being the Grandma for a few days when a student is just getting to know you—noncontingent reinforcement, lots of love, no demands. If a student goes through even just a few days of this type of reinforcement from you they will be happy to do the task you want them to complete; they know you hold the goodies!
- ***Fake it till you make it.*** Do you have a meeting with a parent who intimidates you? Is your supervisor coming to observe you? Just trying to make it through the day? Put on your confident face. Fake it till you make it means just that. You have been well educated to do your job and you can do it, quite well.
- ***Tomorrow is a new day.*** You have everything planned for a perfect lesson. You know what you are going to teach, have your visuals ready and prepared, and know how to differentiate for each student. However, something goes wrong. The lesson goes downhill and you're not sure why. That's OK. You can go home, and think it over and try again tomorrow. You will do better, and so will your students. Not every lesson is going to be a home run.
- ***Add the "boop boop."*** My first supervisor had this fun little trick she used with every child she saw. She made sure she had a clear beginning, middle, and end of each lesson and that the kids knew what those were. When a child would come to her room, she would sing a hello greeting song and at the end add in a "boop boop!" with a knock on the table. Every kid laughed, every time. This sets up lessons for success because of the structure, but it also made the children happy to be there and let them know it would be fun. Win-win!
- ***Have fun with your students.*** The same supervisor who taught me about the "boop boop" also taught me that kids are just funny. People are funny. Don't be afraid to have fun with your students. For children who struggle to understand amusing social interactions, identify it for them. You laugh, they laugh, and you let them know, "That's funny!"
- ***Gain trust from your team.*** My job is to work on communication with my students and support my teachers and team in any way I can. There are teachers I have worked with over several years who trust me, rely on me, and tell me what they are really thinking. This year, I began working with a teacher who didn't let me know when he needed help. As a team, we made an effort to joke with him and build a relationship with him. He slowly began opening up more and more, and recently he has been asking for help and using us as resources. We had to gain his trust and build rapport with him—just like we do with our students.
- ***Be mindful of all children's backgrounds.*** When you are meeting with a family that requires an interpreter, make sure you have one present. When using a home–school communication book, make sure the parents receive and understand the written messages you're sending them. Recently, I had a long-term substitute teacher join the team. She realized that one Spanish-speaking parent was not able to understand the messages in the home–school communication book. This bothered her, and she said to the team, "I just want her to know what a delight her daughter is to have in this class." She began using Google Translate so the student's mother could gain more information shared about her child's day. I am sure this meant a lot to the family.

- ***Be honest. Be kind. Be gentle.*** I try to always think about how I would feel if I was the parent on the other side of the table. Our team had an IEP meeting for a ninth grader with autism who had been receiving services since kindergarten. Since it was his eligibility year, he received new assessments. His results indicated low expressive and receptive language and social communication deficits. As I was presenting this report, I looked over at his mother and saw that she was tearful. I stopped and profusely apologized. I had not realized that, even after all these years, it was still difficult for her. Since then, I have really worked on my approach to families. I try to make sure that I am gentle when delivering difficult information. I don't think we should ever sugar-coat a child's challenges, but we must be kind and gentle when communicating about them to families.

Key Terms and Concepts

aphasia
articulation disorder
augmentative and alternative communication (AAC)
cleft palate
cluttering
communication
communication disorder
dialects
dysarthria
expressive language disorder
fluency disorder
graphemes
language
language disorder
morphemes
morphology
phoneme
phonological disorder
phonology
pragmatics
receptive language disorder
semantics
speech
speech impairments
stuttering
syntax
voice disorder

Summary

Definitions

- *Communication* is any interaction that transmits information. Narrating, explaining, informing, requesting, and expressing are major communicative functions.
- A *language* is an arbitrary symbol system that enables a group of people to communicate. Each language has rules of phonology, morphology, syntax, semantics, and pragmatics that describe how users put sounds and ideas together to convey meaning.
- *Speech* is the oral production of language; it is the fastest and most efficient method of communication by language.
- Typical language development follows a relatively predictable sequence. Most children learn to talk and use language without any formal instruction; by the time they enter first grade, their grammar and speech patterns match those of the adults around them.
- A *communication disorder* is "an impairment in the ability to receive, send, process, and comprehend concepts or verbal, nonverbal and graphic symbol systems" (ASHA, 1993/2020).
- A child has a speech impairment if the child's speech draws unfavorable attention to itself, interferes with the ability to communicate, or causes social or interpersonal problems.
- The three basic types of speech impairments are articulation disorders (errors in the production of speech sounds), fluency disorders (difficulties with the flow or rhythm of speech), and voice disorders (problems with the quality or use of one's voice).
- Some children have trouble understanding language (receptive language disorders), others have trouble using language to communicate (expressive language disorders), and still others have language delays.
- Speech or language differences based on cultural or regional dialects are not communication disorders. However, children who use a different dialect may also have speech or language disorders.

Characteristics

- Four basic kinds of speech-sound errors exist: distortions, substitutions, omissions, and additions.
- A child with an articulation disorder cannot produce a given sound physically.
- A child with a phonological disorder can produce a given sound and does so correctly in some instances but not at other times.
- Stuttering, the most common fluency disorder, is marked by rapid-fire repetitions of consonant or vowel sounds,

especially at the beginnings of words, prolongations, hesitations, interjections, and complete verbal blocks.

- A voice disorder is characterized by abnormal vocal quality, pitch, loudness, resonance, or duration for the speaker's age and sex.
- Language impairments involve problems in phonology, morphology, syntax, semantics, or pragmatics; they are usually classified as either receptive or expressive.

Prevalence

- About 1.6% of school-age children receive special education for speech and language impairments, the second-largest disability category under IDEA.
- Nearly twice as many boys as girls have speech impairments.
- Children with articulation and spoken language problems represent the largest category of speech-language impairments.

Causes

- Although some speech and language impairments have physical (organic) causes, most are functional disorders that cannot be directly attributed to physical conditions.

Identification and Assessment

- Assessment of a suspected communication disorder may include some or all of the following components: (a) case history and physical examination, (b) articulation test, (c) hearing test, (d) auditory discrimination test, (e) phonological awareness and processing, (f) vocabulary and overall language development test, (g) assessment of language function, (h) language samples, and (i) observation in natural settings.

Educational Approaches

- Speech-language pathologists (SLPs) use a wide range of techniques for identifying, evaluating, and providing therapeutic services to children. These include structured exercises and drills as well as individual and group therapy sessions.
- A general goal of treating speech-sound errors is to help the child speak as clearly as possible. Addressing articulation and phonological errors involves discrimination and production activities. Fluency disorders can be treated with the application of behavioral principles and self-monitoring, although many children recover spontaneously.
- Voice disorders can be treated surgically or medically if the cause is organic. Most remedial techniques offer direct vocal rehabilitation. Behavioral principles help break habitual patterns of misuse.
- Language disorder treatments vary widely. Precommunication activities encourage exploration of expressive language. SLPs connect oral language to literacy components of the curriculum. Naturalistic interventions disperse learning trials throughout the natural environment and normal conversation.
- Augmentative and alternative communication may be aided or unaided and consists of three components: a representational symbol set or vocabulary, a means for selecting the symbols, and a means for transmitting the symbols.

Placement Options

- The vast majority of children with speech and language problems (88%) attend regular classes for most of the day.
- ASHA recognizes seven service delivery models: monitoring, pull-out, collaborative consultation, classroom or curriculum based, separate classroom, community based, and combination.

Chapter 9

Deafness and Hearing Loss

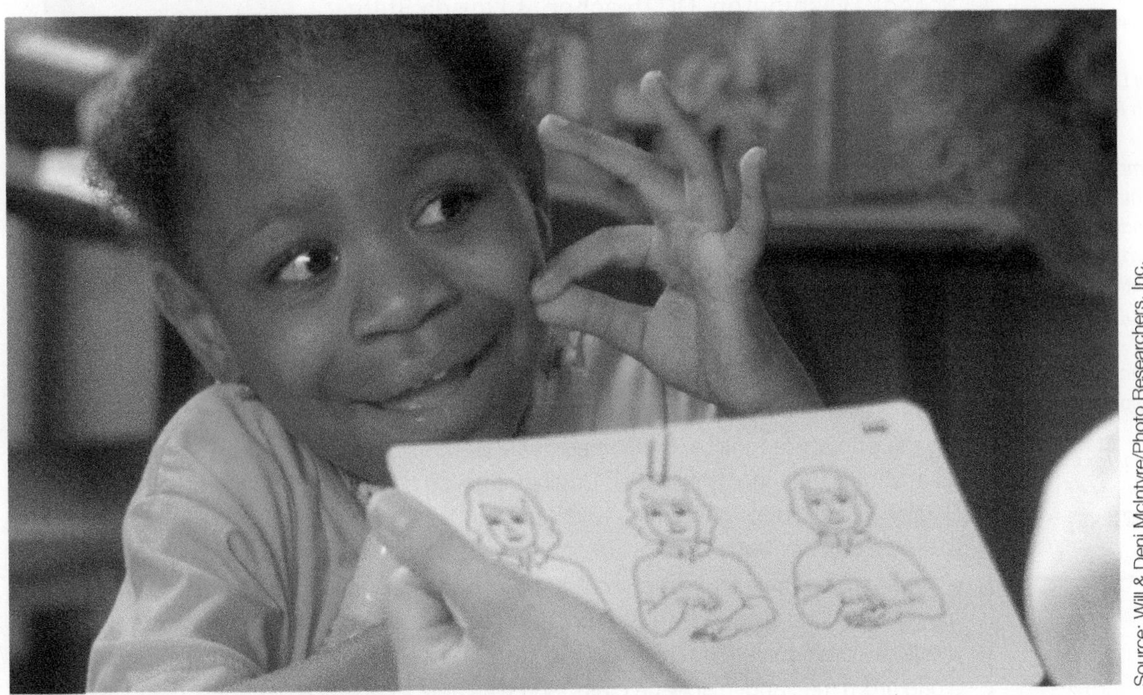

Source: Will & Deni McIntyre/Photo Researchers, Inc.

Learning Outcomes

After reading this chapter and completing the embedded activities, you should be able to

9.1 Define and distinguish between deafness and hard of hearing.

9.2 Identify the estimated prevalence of children who are deaf or hard of hearing and describe types and causes of hearing loss.

9.3 Describe assessments for identification of deafness and hearing loss.

9.4 Identify technologies and supports used by students who are deaf and hard of hearing to amplify, supplement, or replace sound.

9.5 Compare and contrast approaches to educating children who are deaf and hard of hearing and describe how placement options can influence their opportunities.

Education, Teaching Credentials, and Experience

- *B.S., elementary education, Gallaudet University, 1993*
- *M.Ed, Deaf Education/Deaf Studies, Lamar University, 2017*
- *M.Ed. Educational Leadership, University of North Florida, 2019*
- *Florida, Hearing-impaired Education, Elementary Education K–6; ESOL Endorsement*
- *National Board Certification, special education: deaf and hard of hearing, 2005 to present*
- *25 years of experience teaching students with special needs*
- *Florida State School for the Deaf and Blind Teacher of the Year 2002–2003 and 2018–2019*

Featured Teacher

Jessica Stultz

Principal of Kendall Demonstration Elementary School, Washington, DC (teacher at Florida State School for the Deaf and Blind during production of this edition)

Source: Jessica Stultz

I teach reading, spelling, language arts, science, social studies, and mathematics to fifth graders with severe to profound hearing loss. Most of my students were born into Deaf families in which both parents are Deaf and American Sign Language (ASL) is the primary language of the household. My goals are to give students the academic and social skills needed to progress to middle school and beyond, provide a supportive and fun classroom environment, and help students make new friends and discover new interests. In our classroom, we embrace responsibility, cooperation, and respect.

Research shows that when using English and ASL simultaneously, one language takes precedence over the other. Oftentimes, ASL is weakened with English becoming the primary language. It is imperative that deaf children receive ASL in its entirety, as a whole language, not broken English. English should be respected as well; I teach English visually through reading and writing.

As a teacher who is deaf, I am often my students' role model. A parent told me that she was thrilled her child developed into a strong deaf individual after one year in my classroom. I had "warned" this parent that I do not use SimCom and I use ASL as my mode of communication. This child received full access to her education through ASL alone (from me), and in speech class, she was able to practice her speech and listening skills with spoken English. As a result, the parent informed me that she believed her child became a "whole" person, and was able to better interact with her deaf peers. I received a similar response from another parent who told me her son discovered ASL as a true language and became comfortable with his deaf identity. He continued to use his speech but would not use spoken English and ASL at the same time, thus avoiding compromising either language. Parents who understand this concept are priceless.

As a teacher who is fond of storytelling, I am a strong believer in the power of using ASL to tell a good story. It is extremely important for the teacher of the deaf to be a skilled orator, storyteller, and ASL user. This is a powerful strategy in gaining student interest in reading and all other subjects (such as in social studies when teaching a history tidbit or in math to describe a story problem). I remember fondly, high school students coming to me years later (I had taught them in elementary school) about the Magic Tree House series. Several students were still very excited about it, letting me know they could read this series on their own (third-grade level books) because they could visualize the stories while reading in English. One student told me, "I love Magic Tree House because with you them, it was like watching a movie." These students were reading below grade level, but with ASL storytelling, the students could really enjoy the books. The impact of these reading experiences followed students throughout their school years.

I founded a performing arts troupe for elementary students in the fall of 2010. As an after-school program, *Eyes Alive!* introduces students to theatrical arts opportunities and ties in ASL storytelling and Deaf culture with skits and short plays. About 30 deaf and hard of hearing students from first through fifth grade produce ASL skits, ASL poetry, and mimes. In 2012, *Eyes Alive!* released our first feature film, "The Wizard of Oz," which has nearly a million views on YouTube. A few years ago, we produced "Snow White and the Seven Dwarves" and three of Aesop's fables. Recently we released "Nursery Rhymes in ASL." I am very proud of this program, of what it gives to the students and to the sign language community.

Pearson eText
Video Example 9.1
Jessica's students enjoyed the opportunity to produce and act in "Snow White."
https://www.youtube.com/watch?v=0rnSLwG7zvc

A SIGHTED PERSON CAN SIMULATE BLINDNESS by closing her eyes or donning a blindfold, but it is virtually impossible for a hearing person to turn off her ears. Throughout life, all hearing animals obtain information about their world, from all directions, 24 hours a day. When a twig snaps behind us, we don't have to turn and look to know that we are not alone.

In addition to its tremendous survival advantage, hearing plays the lead role in the natural, seemingly effortless manner by which most children acquire speech and language. Hearing infants as young as 1 month of age can discriminate speech sounds (Hulit et al., 2015). By the time they are 1 year old, hearing children produce many of the sounds of their language and speak their first words. In contrast, for children who cannot hear speech sounds, learning a spoken language is anything but natural or effortless.

Definitions

Learning Outcome 9.1 Define and distinguish between deafness and hard of hearing.

Children who are deaf and hard of hearing receive special education and related services under the federal disability category of hearing impairments. The Individuals with Disabilities Education Act (IDEA) defines **deafness** and **hearing loss** as follows:

> Deafness means a hearing loss that is so severe that the child is impaired in processing linguistic information through hearing, with or without amplification, [and] that adversely affects a child's educational performance (PL 108-446, 20 U.S.C. §1401 [2004], 20 *CFR* §300.8[c][3]).
>
> Hearing loss means a loss in hearing, whether permanent or fluctuating, that adversely affects a child's education performance but that is not included under the definition of deafness in this section (PL 108-446, 20 U.S.C. §1401 [2004], 20 *CFR* §300.8[c][5]).

Most special educators distinguish between children who are deaf and those who are hard of hearing. A child who is deaf cannot use hearing to understand speech. Even with a hearing aid, the hearing loss is too great to allow a deaf child to understand speech through the ears alone. Although most deaf people perceive some sounds through **residual hearing**, they use vision as the primary sensory mode for learning and communication.

Children who are **hard of hearing** can use their hearing to understand speech, generally with the help of a hearing aid. The speech and language skills of a child who is hard of hearing, although they may be delayed or deficient, are developed mainly through the auditory channel.

Many deaf people do not view themselves as disabled and consider *hearing loss* an inappropriate and demeaning term because it suggests a deficiency or pathology. Similar to other cultural groups, members of the Deaf community share a common language and social practices (Goldblatt & Most, 2018; Kemmery & Compton, 2014). When the cultural definition of hearing loss is used, *Deaf* is spelled with a capital *D*, just as an uppercase letter is used to refer to a French, Japanese, or Jewish person. Although person-first language is the appropriate way to refer to individuals with disabilities, people who identify with the **Deaf culture** generally prefer terms such as *teacher of the Deaf*, *school for the Deaf*, and *Deaf person*.

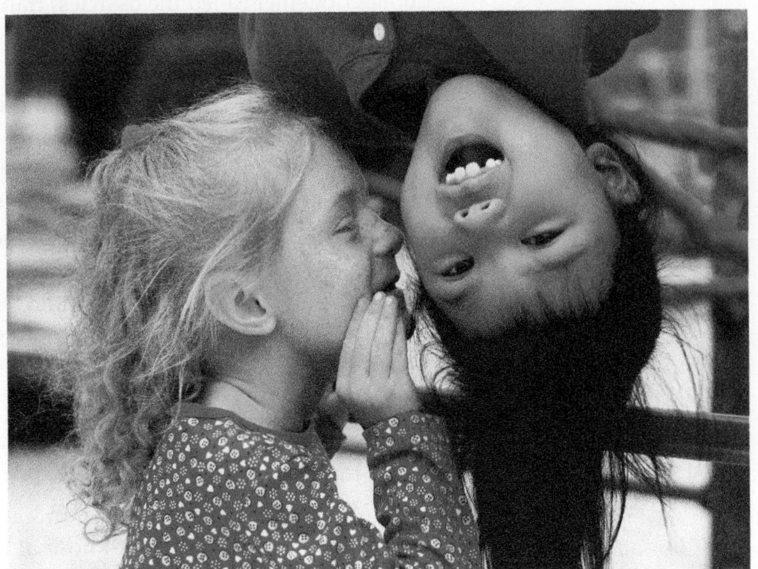

Source: Silver Burdett Ginn

Hearing plays the lead role in the natural, almost effortless manner by which most children acquire speech and language.

FIGURE 9.1 Basic Anatomy of the Human Ear

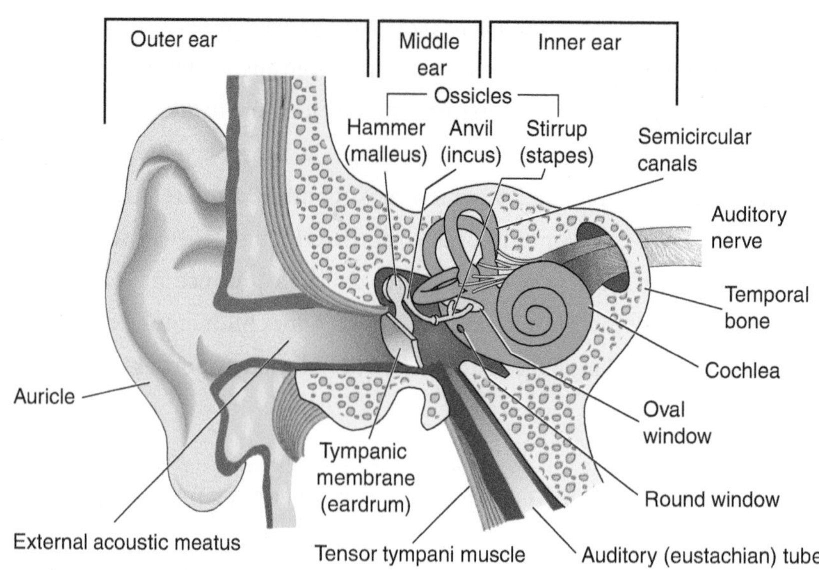

How We Hear

Audition, the sense of hearing, is a complex and not completely understood process. The ear gathers sounds (*acoustical energy*) from the environment and transforms that energy into a form (*neural energy*) the brain can interpret. Figure 9.1 shows the major parts of the human ear. The *outer ear* consists of the external ear and the auditory canal. The part of the ear we see, the **auricle** (or *pinna*), funnels sound waves into the **auditory canal (external acoustic meatus)** and helps distinguish the direction of sound.

When sound waves enter the external ear, they are slightly amplified as they move toward the **tympanic membrane** (eardrum). Pressure variations in sound waves move the eardrum in and out. These movements of the eardrum change the acoustical energy into mechanical energy, which is transferred to the three tiny bones of the *middle ear* (*hammer, anvil*, and *stirrup*). The base (*footplate*) of the third bone in the sequence, the stirrup, rests in an opening called the *oval window*, the place where sound energy enters the inner ear. The vibrations of the three bones (together called the **ossicles**) transmit energy from the middle ear to the inner ear.

The *inner ear*, the most critical and complex part of the entire hearing apparatus, is covered by the *temporal bone*, the hardest bone in the entire body. The inner ear contains the **cochlea**, the main receptor organ for hearing, and the *semicircular canals*, which control the sense of balance. The cochlea, named for its resemblance to a coiled snail shell, consists of two fluid-filled cavities that contain 30,000 tiny hair cells arranged in four rows. Energy transmitted by the ossicles moves the fluid in the cochlea, which in turn stimulates the hair cells. Each hair cell has approximately 100 tiny spines, called *cilia*, at the top. When the hair cells are stimulated, they displace the fluid around them, which produces minute electrochemical signals that are transmitted along the auditory nerve to the brain. High tones are picked up by the hair cells at the basal, or lowest turn of the cochlea; low tones stimulate hair cells at the apex, or top, of the cochlea.

The Nature of Sound

Sound is measured in units that describe its intensity and frequency. Both dimensions of sound are important in considering the needs of a child who is deaf or hard of hearing. The intensity or loudness of sound is measured in **decibels (dB)**. Zero dB represents the smallest sound a person with normal hearing can perceive, which is called the *zero hearing-threshold level (HTL)*, or **audiometric zero**. Larger decibel numbers represent increasingly louder sounds on a ratio scale in which each increment of 10 dB is a 10-fold increase in intensity. A low whisper 5 feet away registers about 10 dB; conversational speech 10 to

20 feet away ranges from 20 to 50 dB. Traffic on a city street produces sound at about 70 dB. Sounds of 125 dB or louder cause pain to most people.

The frequency, or pitch, of sound is measured in cycles per second, or **hertz (Hz)**; 1 Hz equals 1 cycle per second. Pure tones consist of one frequency only. Speech and most environmental sounds are complex tones containing different frequencies. The lowest note on a piano has a frequency of about 30 Hz, middle C about 250 Hz, and the highest note about 4000 Hz. The human ear can detect sounds ranging from approximately 20 to 20,000 Hz. Although a person who cannot hear very low sounds (e.g., a foghorn) or very high sounds (e.g., a piccolo) may experience some inconvenience, the person will encounter no significant problems in the classroom or everyday life. An individual with a severe hearing loss in the speech range, however, is at a great disadvantage in acquiring and using a spoken language.

The frequency range most important for hearing spoken language is 500 to 2000 Hz, but some speech sounds have frequencies below or above that range. For example, the /s/ phoneme (as in the word *sat*) is a high-frequency sound, typically occurring between 4000 and 8000 Hz (Northern & Downs, 2014). A student whose hearing loss is more severe at the higher frequencies will thus have particular difficulty in discriminating the /s/ sound. Conversely, phonemes such as /dj/ (the sound of the *j* in *jump*) and /m/ occur at low frequencies and are more problematic for a student with a low-frequency hearing loss. As you might expect, a student with a high-frequency hearing loss tends to hear men's voices more easily than women's voices.

Characteristics

Any discussion of characteristics of students who are deaf or hard of hearing should include three qualifications. First, students who receive special education because of hearing loss constitute an extremely heterogeneous group (Karchmer & Mitchell, 2011). It is a mistake to assume that a commonly observed behavioral characteristic or average level of academic achievement is representative of all children with hearing loss.

Second, many factors influence the effects of hearing loss on a child's communication and language skills, academic achievement, and social and emotional functioning, including the type and degree of hearing loss, the age at onset, the attitudes of the child's family, opportunities to acquire a first language (whether through speech or sign), and the presence or absence of other disabilities.

Third, generalizations about how deaf people are supposed to act and feel must be viewed with extreme caution. If professionals do not have an understanding of intercultural interactions between Deaf and hearing people, they are "quite likely to try to fit Deaf people into standard frames, categories, and assumptions about persons with a handicap or affliction, rather than view the Deaf person as one who speaks a different language and belongs to a different culture" (Singleton & Tittle, 2000, p. 221). Featured Teacher Jessica Stultz asserts, "Audism is an attitude of superiority based on the ability to hear or behave in the manner of one who hears. It promotes the belief that life without hearing is futile and miserable and results in negative stigma toward anyone who does not hear. If I could change one thing about special education, I would eradicate audism."

English Literacy

A child with a hearing loss—especially a prelingual loss of 90 dB or greater—is at a significant disadvantage for acquiring English language skills. From early infancy, hearing children typically acquire a large vocabulary and knowledge of grammar, word order, idiomatic expressions, subtle shades of meaning, and many other aspects of verbal expression by listening to others and to themselves. A child who, from birth or soon after, cannot hear the speech of other people will not learn speech and language spontaneously, as do children with normal hearing. Because reading and writing involve graphic representations of a phonologically based language, a deaf child who has not benefited from exposure to a rich grammatical model of spoken English must strive to decode, comprehend, and produce text based on a language for which she may have little or no understanding. How does one teach letter–sound correspondence, a critical component of reading, to children who cannot hear? *Visual phonics*, a multisensory system of hand cues and

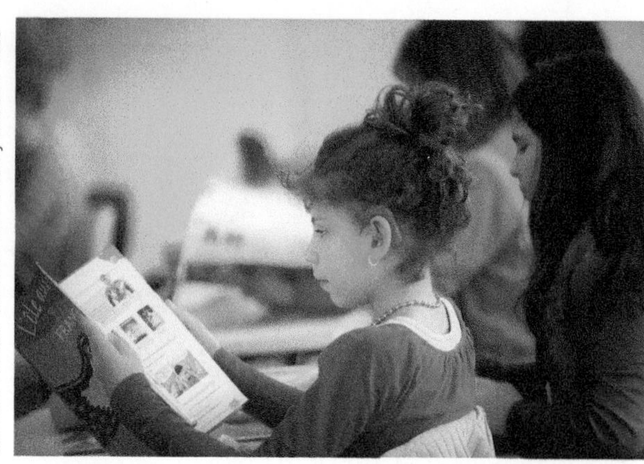
Source: Amelie-Benoist/BSIP/Alamy Stock Photo

Because hearing loss imposes challenges to acquiring literacy, explicit, systematic, and intensive reading instruction is especially important.

written symbols that represent sounds, is a promising approach. Using visual phonics, young children were able to learn initial sounds, syllable segmentation, and letter–sound correspondence (Tucci & Easterbrooks, 2015).

Students with hearing loss have smaller vocabularies compared to peers with normal hearing (Haliday et al., 2017), and the gap widens with age (American Speech-Language-Hearing Association [ASHA], 2018). Children with hearing loss, more so than other children, learn concrete words such as *tree, run,* and *book* more easily than abstract words such as *honesty, later,* and *compressed.* They also have difficulty with function words such as *the, an, are,* and *a.*

They may omit word endings, such as *-s, -ed,* or *-ing.* Because the grammar and structure of English often do not follow logical rules, a person with prelingual hearing loss must exert a great deal of effort to read and write with acceptable form and meaning. For example, if the past tense of *talk* is *talked,* then why doesn't *go* become *goed*? If the plural of *man* is *men,* then shouldn't the plural of *pan* be *pen*? Learning words with multiple meanings is difficult. It is not easy to explain the difference between the expressions "He's beat" (tired) and "He was beaten" to a person who has never had normal hearing.

Many deaf students have difficulty differentiating questions from statements and understanding and writing sentences with passive voice ("The assignment was given yesterday") and relative clauses ("The gloves I left at home are made of leather"). They typically compose sentences that are short, incomplete, or improperly arranged. The following sentences written by elementary deaf students illustrate some of the writing problems attributable to not hearing the spoken language:

Bobby is walked.
The boy sees a brown football on the hold hand.
The trees is falling a leaves.
The happy children is friending.

Speaking

Atypical speech is common in many children who are deaf or hard of hearing. On top of all of the challenges hearing loss poses to learning the vocabulary, grammar, and syntax of English, not being able to hear one's own speech makes it difficult to assess and monitor it. The speech of some children who are deaf and hard of hearing is difficult to understand because they omit quiet speech sounds they cannot hear, such as /s/, /sh/, /f/, /t/, and /k/. Some speak too loudly or not loudly enough. Their speech may be abnormally high pitched or sound mumbled because of improper stress or inflection.

Academic Achievement

Students who are deaf and hard of hearing continue to lag behind their general education peers in academic achievement (Hrastinski & Wilbur, 2016; Qi & Mitchell, 2012; Shaver et al., 2011). Most children with hearing loss have difficulty with all areas of academic achievement, especially reading and math (Bull et al., 2018; Werfel, 2017). Studies of the academic achievement of students with hearing loss have routinely found them to lag far behind their hearing peers, and the gap in achievement between children with normal hearing and those with hearing loss usually widens as they get older (ASHA, 2018).

Academic performance must not be equated with intelligence. Deafness imposes no limitations on the cognitive capabilities of individuals, and some deaf students read very well and excel academically (Karchmer & Mitchell, 2011; Williams & Finnegan, 2003). The problems that deaf students often experience in education and adjustment are largely attributable to inadequate development of a first language as well as a mismatch between the demands of spoken and written English and the students' ability to understand and communicate in English.

Social Functioning

Children with severe to profound hearing loss often report feeling isolated, without friends, and unhappy in school, particularly when their socialization with other children with hearing loss is limited. These social problems appear to be more frequent in children with mild or moderate hearing loss than in those with severe to profound losses (ASHA, 2018). Weiner et al. (2013) reported that deaf students are bullied at a significantly higher rate than hearing students.

Children with hearing loss are more likely to have behavioral difficulties in school and social situations than are children with normal hearing. In their meta-analysis, Stevenson et al. (2015) found that students with hearing impairments scored consistently higher on emotional and behavioral difficulties than hearing children, especially in the area of peer relationships.

Children and adults who are deaf frequently express feelings of depression, withdrawal, and isolation (Batten et al., 2014; Wolters et al., 2014), particularly those with acquired hearing loss (Connolly et al., 2006). Research has not provided clear insights into the effects of hearing loss on behavior; however, it appears that the extent to which a child with hearing loss successfully interacts with family members, friends, and people in the community depends largely on others' attitudes and the child's ability to communicate in some mutually acceptable way (Ita & Friedman, 1999).

Prevalence

Learning Outcome 9.2 Identify the estimated prevalence of children who are deaf or hard of hearing and describe types and causes of hearing loss.

Approximately 15% of American adults (37.5 million people) report some trouble hearing (National Institute on Deafness and Other Communication Disorders [NIDCD], 2016). Males are more likely than females to experience hearing loss. The majority of all people with hearing loss are 65 years of age or older. About 2 to 3 of every 1000 children are born deaf or hard of hearing (NIDCD, 2016).

During the 2018–2019 school year, 64,359 students age 6 to 21 years received special education services under the disability category of hearing impairment (U.S. Department of Education, 2020a). This represents 1% of all school-age students who received special education services and about 0.1% of the student population. The actual number of school-age children with hearing loss in special education programs is somewhat higher because some children with hearing loss are counted under another primary disability category (e.g., intellectual disabilities, multiple disabilities, deaf-blind). It is not known precisely the percentage of these students who are deaf or hard of hearing. A national survey of deaf or hard-of-hearing students found that 39% had severe or profound hearing loss and that 40% had another disabling condition (Gallaudet Research Institute, 2013).

Types and Causes of Hearing Loss

Types and Age of Onset

Hearing loss is classified by the affected region of the auditory system. A **conductive hearing impairment**, as its name implies, involves a problem with the conduction, or transmission, of sound vibrations to the inner ear. A conductive hearing loss results from abnormalities or complications of the outer or middle ear. A buildup of excessive wax in the auditory canal can cause a conductive hearing loss, as can a disease that leaves fluid or debris. Some children are born with incomplete or malformed auditory canals. Conductive hearing loss can occur if the eardrum or ossicles do not move properly. Surgery or other medical treatment can often correct a conductive hearing loss, and hearing aids are usually beneficial.

Whereas **sensory hearing impairment** indicates damage to the cochlea, **neural hearing impairment** is attributed to abnormality of the auditory nerve pathway. Both types are often subsumed by the term *sensorineural hearing impairment*. Hearing aids may not help people with sensorineural hearing impairments because the electromechanical energy corresponding to sound is delivered to the brain in distorted fashion or not delivered at all. Surgery or medication cannot correct most sensorineural hearing loss. Any combination of conductive, sensory, and neural hearing loss is called a *mixed hearing impairment*.

Hearing loss is also either *unilateral* (present in one ear only) or *bilateral* (present in both ears). Most deaf and hard-of-hearing students have bilateral losses, although the degree of loss may not be the same in both ears. Children with unilateral hearing loss generally learn speech and language without major difficulties, although they tend to have problems localizing sounds and listening in noisy or distracting settings.

It is important to consider the age of onset—whether a hearing loss is **congenital** (present at birth) or **acquired** (appears after birth). The terms **prelingual hearing loss** and **postlingual hearing loss** identify whether a hearing loss occurred before or after the development of spoken language. A child who cannot hear the speech of other people from birth or soon after will not learn speech and language spontaneously. To approximate the experience of a child who is deaf from birth, watch a television program in a language you do not speak with the sound turned off. You would face the double problem of being unable to read lips and understand an unfamiliar language. Prelingual deafness imposes tremendous challenges to comprehending and producing spoken language.

A child who acquires a hearing loss after speech and language are well established, usually after age 2 years, has educational needs very different from those of a child who is prelingually deaf. Whereas the educational program for a child who is prelingually deaf usually focuses on acquisition of language and communication, the program for a child who is postlingually deaf usually emphasizes the maintenance of intelligible speech and appropriate language patterns.

Causes of Congenital Hearing Loss

Although more than 400 causes of hearing loss have been identified, a national survey of more than 23,000 deaf and hard-of-hearing students found that the cause was undetermined in 57% of cases (Gallaudet Research Institute, 2013).

GENETIC FACTORS About half of all congenital deafness is attributed to genetic abnormalities (Debonis & Donohue, 2008). More than 200 types of genetically caused deafness have been identified. Genetic hearing loss may be autosomal dominant, autosomal recessive, or X-linked (related to the sex chromosome). *Autosomal dominant hearing loss* exists when one parent, who carries the dominant gene for hearing loss and typically has a hearing loss, passes the gene on to the child. In this case, each offspring has a 50% probability of receiving the gene and having a hearing loss. The probability is higher if both parents have the dominant gene or if both grandparents on one side of the family have hearing loss due to genetic causes. About 20% of inherited deafness is the result of dominant inheritance.

Approximately 80% of inherited hearing loss is caused by *autosomal recessive hearing loss*, in which both parents typically have normal hearing and carry a recessive gene. In this case, there is a 25% probability that each child will have a hearing loss. Because both parents usually have normal hearing and no other family members have hearing loss, there is no prior expectation that the child may have a hearing loss. Because most hereditary deafness is the result of recessive genetic traits, a child of two deaf people has only a slightly increased risk of deafness because it is unlikely the same genetic syndrome affected both parents (Northern & Downs, 2014).

In *X-linked hearing loss*, the mother carries the recessive trait for hearing loss on the sex chromosome and passes it on to male offspring but not to females. X-linked transmission accounts for about 2% to 3% of hereditary hearing loss. Hearing loss is a characteristic of more than 400 genetic syndromes, such as Down syndrome, Usher syndrome, Treacher Collins syndrome, and Waardenburg syndrome (Todd, 2015).

MATERNAL RUBELLA Although rubella (also known as German measles) has relatively mild symptoms, it can cause deafness, vision loss, heart disorders, and a variety of other serious disabilities in a developing child when contracted by a pregnant woman, particularly during the first trimester. A major rubella epidemic in the United States and Canada in 1963 to 1965 accounted for more than 50% of the students with hearing loss in special education programs in the 1970s and 1980s. Since an effective vaccine was introduced in 1969, the incidence of hearing loss caused by rubella has decreased significantly.

CONGENITAL CYTOMEGALOVIRUS Congenital cytomegalovirus (CMV) is a common viral infection, and most people infected with it experience minor symptoms such as respiratory infections that soon disappear. Approximately 1 in 150 children are born with congenital CMV, and 10% to 20% of those may later develop conditions such as developmental disabilities, visual impairment, and, most often, hearing loss (Korver et al., 2017). At present, no prevention or treatment for CMV exists. However, a blood test can determine if a woman of childbearing age is at risk for developing an initial CMV infection during pregnancy.

PREMATURITY It is difficult to precisely evaluate the effects of prematurity on hearing loss, but early delivery and low birth weight are more common among children who are deaf than among the general population.

Causes of Acquired Hearing Loss

OTITIS MEDIA A temporary, recurrent infection of the middle ear, **otitis media** is the most common medical diagnosis for children. Nearly 90% of all children will experience otitis media at least once, and about one third of children younger than age 5 years have recurrent episodes (Bluestone & Klein, 2007). Left untreated, otitis media can result in a buildup of fluid and a ruptured eardrum, which causes permanent conductive hearing loss.

MENINGITIS The leading cause of postlingual hearing loss is meningitis, a bacterial or viral infection of the central nervous system that can, among its other effects, destroy the sensitive acoustic apparatus of the inner ear. Children whose deafness is caused by meningitis generally have profound hearing loss. Difficulties in balance and other disabilities may also be present.

MÉNIÈRE'S DISEASE A disorder of the inner ear, Ménière's disease is characterized by sudden and unpredictable attacks of vertigo (dizziness), fluctuations in hearing, and *tinnitus* (the perception of sound when no outside sound is present). In its severest form, Ménière's disease can be incapacitating. Little is understood about the mechanisms underlying the condition, and at present, no reliable treatment or cure exists. Ménière's disease most often occurs between the ages of 40 and 60 years (Minor et al., 2004).

NOISE EXPOSURE Repeated exposure to loud sounds is a common cause of hearing loss. It is estimated that 15% of Americans age 20 to 69 have noise-related permanent hearing loss. Noise-induced hearing loss (NIHL) caused by chronic exposure to recreational and occupational noise often occurs gradually, and the person may not realize his hearing is being damaged until it is too late. Sources of noise that can cause NIHL include motorcycles, jet aircraft, target shooting, leaf blowers, and amplified music, all emitting sounds from 120 dB to 150 dB. Prolonged or repeated exposure to noise above 85 dB can cause hearing loss. The louder the sound, the shorter the time needed for NIHL to occur (NIDCD, 2017a).

Identification and Assessment

Learning Outcome 9.3 Describe assessments for identification of deafness and hearing loss.

Assessment of Infants

Newborns respond to sounds by startling or blinking. At a few weeks of age, infants with normal hearing can listen to quiet sounds, recognize their parents' voices, and pay attention to their own gurgling and cooing sounds. All infants, hearing and deaf alike, babble. In children with normal hearing, vocalizations containing a minimum of one consonant and one vowel sound, called *canonical babbling*, emerge between 7 and 12 months of age (Bass-Ringdahl, 2010). Children who are deaf tend to stop babbling and vocalizing because they cannot hear themselves or their parents, but the baby's increasing silence may go unnoticed for a while and then be mistakenly attributed to other causes.

The Joint Committee on Infant Hearing (2013) recommends that all infants be screened by 1 month of age. Today a "1-3-6" model of Early Hearing Detection and Intervention

FIGURE 9.2 Some Expected Auditory Behaviors During Baby's First Year

Birth to 3 Months

- Startles to loud noises
- Coos and makes pleasurable gurgling sounds
- Turns toward voices
- Quiets down or smiles when spoken to
- Stirs or awakens from sleep to a relatively close loud sound

4 to 6 Months

- Engages in vocal play when alone; gurgles
- Babbles with speechlike sounds
- Turns eyes toward direction of sounds
- Notices toys that make sounds
- Laughs and chuckles

7 Months to 1 Year

- Responds differently to a cheerful voice versus an angry voice
- Responds to music or singing
- Vocalizes emotions
- Babbling acquires inflection and contains short and long groups of speech sounds ("tata, upup, bibibi")
- Tries to imitate the speech sounds of others
- Turns head in the direction of the source of a sound
- Ceases activity when parent's voice is heard
- Responds to own name and requests such as "Want more?" or "Come here."
- Uses a few words (e.g., *mama* or *dada, doggie*) by first birthday

programs in most states is working toward the goal of having all babies screened by 1 month, diagnosed by 3 months, and enrolled in early intervention programs no later than 6 months of age. The two most widely used methods of screening for hearing loss in infants measure physiological reactions to sound. With *auditory brain stem response*, sensors placed on the scalp measure electrical activity as the infant responds to auditory stimuli. In *otoacoustic emission* screening, a tiny microphone placed in the baby's ear detects the "echoes" of hair cells in the cochlea as they vibrate to sound (Ross & Levitt, 2000).

Even when an infant passes screening in the hospital, hearing loss can develop later. Figure 9.2 lists some common auditory behaviors of infants with normal hearing. An infant who fails to demonstrate these responses may have a hearing loss, and an audiological exam is recommended.

Pure-Tone Audiometry

Source: Marmaduke St. John/Alamy Stock Photo

An audiometer generates tones of precise intensity and frequency.

A procedure called *pure-tone audiometry* is used to assess the hearing of older children and adults. The test determines how loud sounds at various frequencies must be for the child to hear them. The examiner uses an **audiometer**, an electronic device that generates pure tones at different levels of intensity and frequency. Most audiometers deliver tones in 5-dB increments from 0 to 120 dB, with each decibel level presented in various frequencies, usually starting at 125 Hz and increasing in octave intervals (doubling in frequency) to 8000 Hz. The child, who receives the sound either through earphones (air conduction) or through a bone vibrator (bone conduction), is instructed to press a button when he hears a sound and to release it when he hears no sound. To obtain a hearing level on an

FIGURE 9.3 Audiogram for a Student with a Severe Hearing Loss

Severe Loss (71 to 90 dB)

Brante:

- Can hear voices only if they are very loud and 1 foot or less from her ear
- Wears a hearing aid, but it is unclear how much she gains from it
- Can distinguish most vowel sounds but hears only a few consonants
- Can hear a door slamming, a vacuum cleaner, and an airplane flying overhead
- Communicates by speech and signs
- Must always pay close visual attention to a person speaking with her
- Splits her school day between a special class and a regular classroom with an educational interpreter

Audiogram for Brante, who has a severe hearing loss

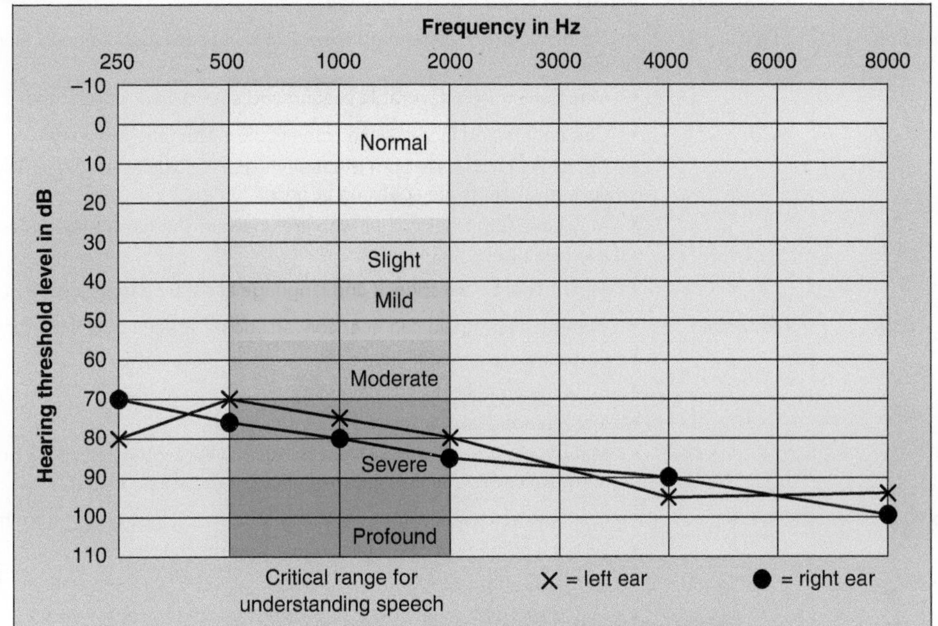

audiogram, the child must detect a sound at that level at least 50% of the time. For example, a child who has a 60-dB hearing loss cannot detect a sound until it is at least 60 dB loud. The examiner plots the results of the test on a chart called an **audiogram** (Figure 9.3).

Speech Reception Test

A complete hearing exam includes testing a person's detection and understanding of speech sounds. A list of phonetically balanced one- and two-syllable words is presented at different decibel levels. The **speech reception threshold (SRT)**, the lowest decibel level at which the individual can repeat half of the words, is measured and recorded for each ear.

Alternative Audiometric Techniques

Several alternative techniques have been developed for testing the hearing of very young children and individuals with severe disabilities who may not understand and follow conventional audiometry procedures. In **play audiometry**, the examiner directs the child to perform simple but distinct activities, such as picking up a toy or putting a ball into a cup whenever she hears the signal, either pure tones or speech. A similar procedure is **operant conditioning audiometry** in which the child receives a token or candy when she pushes a button in the presence of a light paired with a sound. Sometimes the sound is presented without the light. If the child pushes the button in response to the sound alone, the examiner knows the child can hear that sound. **Behavior observation audiometry** is a passive assessment procedure in which the examiner observes the child's reactions to sounds. A sound is presented at an increasing level of intensity until a response, such as head turning, eye blinking, or cessation of play, is reliably observed.

Classification of Hearing Loss

Hearing loss is usually described by the terms *slight*, *mild*, *moderate*, *severe*, and *profound*, depending on the average hearing level, in decibels, across the frequencies most important for understanding speech (500 to 2000 HZ). Figure 9.4 lists some of the impacts of levels of hearing loss on speech and language and classroom supports that may be needed. It is important to recognize, however, that no two children have exactly the same pattern of hearing, even if their responses

Content Extension 9.1

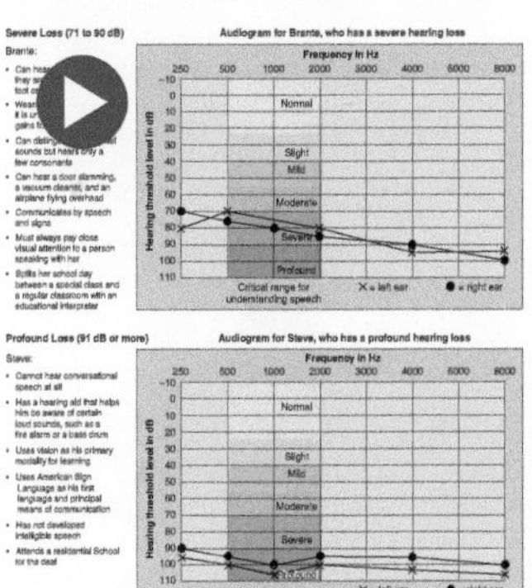

Audiograms for students with mild to profound hearing loss.

FIGURE 9.4 Classification of Hearing Loss, Effects on Speech and Language, and Probable Educational Needs

Degree of Hearing Loss	Classification	Impact on Speech and Language
27 to 40 dB	Slight	• No difficulty understanding speech in quiet settings, but noisy environments pose problems to learning • May benefit from favorable seating and sound field amplification
41 to 55 dB	Mild	• Can understand face-to-face conversation with little difficulty • Misses much of classroom discussion—particularly when the speaker cannot be seen clearly or several students are speaking at once • May have some classmates who are unaware she has a hearing loss • Benefits from a hearing aid • Most benefit from speech and language assistance from a speech-language pathologist
56 to 70 dB	Moderate	• Without hearing aid can hear conversational speech only if it is near, loud, and clear • Finds it extremely difficult to follow group discussions • Full-time amplification is necessary • Speech noticeably impaired but intelligible • Many benefit from time in a special class where intensive instruction in language and communication can be provided
71 to 90 dB	Severe	• Can hear voices only if they are very loud and 1 foot or less from her ear • Wears a hearing aid, but it is unclear how much it helps • Can hear loud sounds such as a slamming door, vacuum cleaner, and airplane flying overhead • May distinguish most vowel sounds but few if any consonants • Communicates by speech and sign • May split school day between a special class and a regular classroom with an educational interpreter
91 dB or more	Profound	• Cannot hear conversational speech • Hearing aid enables awareness of certain very loud sounds, such as a fire alarm or a bass drum • Vision is primary modality for learning • American Sign Language likely to be first language and principal means of communication • Has not developed intelligible speech • Most require full-time program special education program for students who are deaf

on a hearing test are similar. Just as an intelligence test cannot provide sufficient information to plan a child's educational program, the special education needs of a child who is deaf or hard of hearing cannot be determined from an audiometric test alone. Children hear sounds with differing degrees of clarity, and the same child's hearing ability may vary from day to day. Some children with very low levels of measurable hearing can benefit from hearing aids and can learn to speak. In contrast, some children with less measurable hearing loss do not function well through the auditory channel and rely on vision as their primary means of communication.

Technologies and Supports

Learning Outcome 9.4 Identify technologies and supports used by students who are deaf and hard of hearing to amplify, supplement, or replace sound.

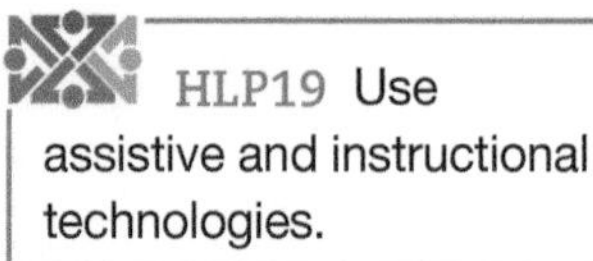
HLP19 Use assistive and instructional technologies.

Technologies That Amplify or Provide Sound

It was once assumed that people who were deaf simply did not hear at all, but nearly all deaf children have some degree of residual hearing. Modern technology for amplifying and clarifying sound enable many children with severe and profound hearing loss to use their residual hearing productively.

HEARING AIDS A hearing aid is similar to a miniature public address system, with a microphone, an amplifier, a receiver, and controls to adjust volume and tone. Hearing aids come in a variety of designs and can be worn behind the ear, in the ear, completely in the ear canal, on the body, or incorporated into eyeglass frames. Children can wear hearing aids in one or both ears (monaural or binaural aids). Whatever its shape, power, or size, a hearing aid picks up sound, magnifies its energy, and delivers this louder sound to the user's middle ear.

Early versions indiscriminately amplified all sounds and were ineffective for most children with sensorineural hearing loss. Today's digital programmable hearing aids employ computer microchips that distinguish and separate speech sounds from background noise and deliver a clear, distortion-free signal that differentially amplifies selected frequencies tailored to the user's individual pattern of hearing loss. The user can select preprogrammed settings for optimal listening in different environments, such as a classroom or outdoors.

The earlier in life a child is fitted with an appropriate hearing aid, the more likely she will learn to use hearing for communication and awareness (Tomblin et al., 2015). Today, it is not unusual to see infants and preschoolers wearing hearing aids; the improved listening conditions become an important part of the young child's speech and language development. To derive maximum benefit from a hearing aid, a child should wear it throughout the day.

GROUP ASSISTIVE LISTENING DEVICES Group assistive listening devices can solve the problems caused by distance, noise, and reverberation in the classroom. In most systems, a radio link is established between the teacher and the children with hearing loss, with the teacher wearing a small microphone transmitter (often on the lapel, near the lips) and each child wearing a receiver that doubles as a personal hearing aid. An FM radio frequency is usually employed, and wires are not required, so the teacher and students can move freely around the classroom.

Pearson eText Video Example 9.2
FM systems enable students with hearing loss to distinguish their teacher's voice from distracting sounds. https://www.youtube.com/watch?v=ln8NHzVfJkQ

COCHLEAR IMPLANTS Unlike hearing aids, which deliver amplified sound to the ear, a **cochlear implant** bypasses damaged hair cells and stimulates the auditory nerve directly. The implant is surgically placed under the skin behind the ear. An implant has four basic parts: an external *microphone*, which picks up sound from the environment; an external *speech processor*, which selects and arranges sounds picked up by the microphone; a *transmitter*; and a *receiver/stimulator*, which receives signals from the speech processor and converts them into electric impulses. *Electrodes* collect the impulses from the stimulator and send them directly to the brain via the auditory nerve (Figure 9.5).

FIGURE 9.5 Internal and External Components of a Cochlear Implant

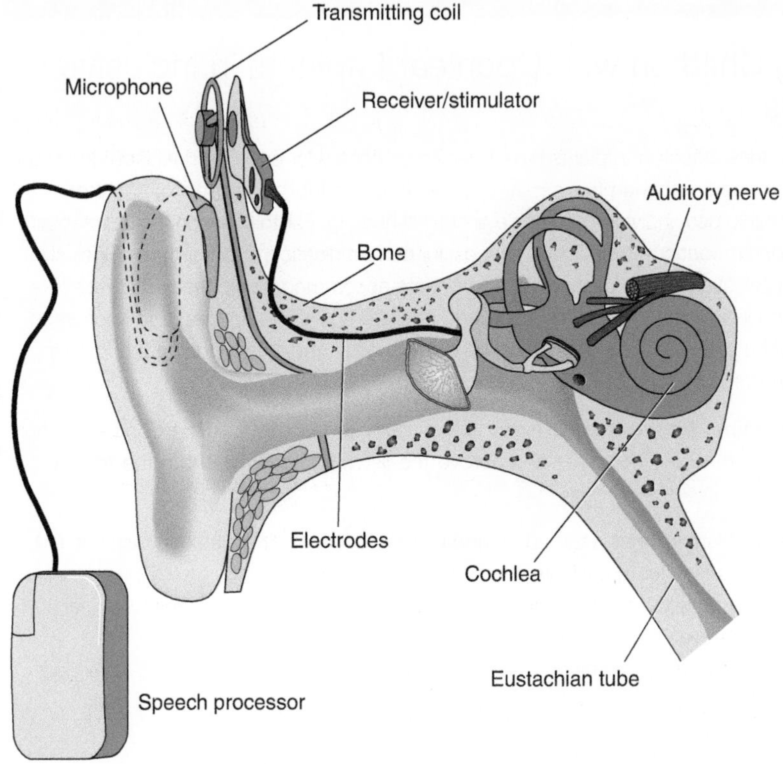

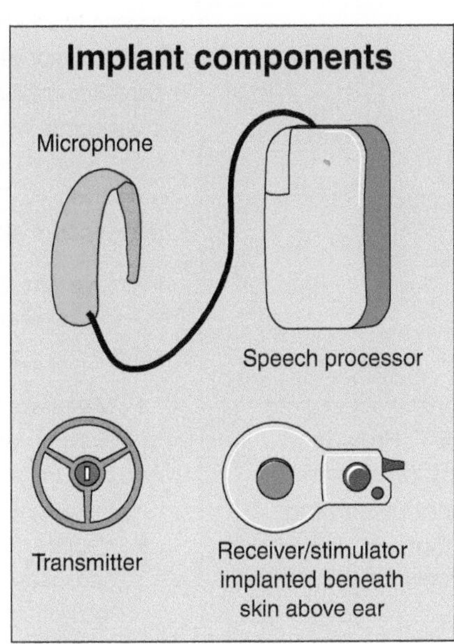

The FDA approved cochlear implants in 1990 for children age 2 to 17, and for children as young as 12 months in 2000 (NIDCD, 2017b). Cochlear implant surgery usually takes 2 to 3 hours, and the child stays overnight in the hospital. About 4 weeks later, the child returns to the implant center for initial activation of the device and tune-up sessions over 2 to 3 days. As of the end of 2012, approximately 324,200 people worldwide had received cochlear implants, including 38,000 children and 58,000 adults in the United States (NIDCD, 2017b). A national survey found that 15% of deaf and hard-of-hearing students had cochlear implants (Gallaudet Research Institute, 2013). Additionally, about 40% of children who are born profoundly deaf receive cochlear implants (NIDCD, 2017b).

A cochlear implant does not restore or create normal hearing. It can, however, give deaf individuals a useful auditory understanding of the environment and help them understand speech. When coupled with intensive postimplantation therapy, cochlear implants can help young children acquire speech, language, cognitive, and social skills. Although many questions about cochlear implants remain to be answered, initial research reports have described significant improvements in receptive and expressive speech and language skills in children with cochlear implants compared to peers without cochlear implants (e.g., Marschark et al., 2018; Schorr et al., 2008, 2009). Additionally, optimal speech perception, language acquisition, and speech production were evident for children receiving cochlear implants prior to 12 months of age (Deltman et al., 2016). Academic outcomes for students with cochlear implants vary widely, and a recent study of word and world knowledge by deaf college students with and without cochlear implants found virtually no difference between the groups, with hearing students still outperforming both groups (Convertino et al., 2014). See *Teaching & Learning*, "Supporting Children with Cochlear Implants in Inclusive Classrooms."

Tremendous controversy surrounds cochlear implants (National Association of the Deaf, 2000). Some members of the Deaf community vehemently oppose cochlear implants and consider the procedure to be a form of genocide of the Deaf culture (e.g., Hyde & Power, 2006; Komesaroff, 2007). Featured Teacher Jessica Stultz contends: "For the most part, the Deaf community has grown to accept cochlear implants. However, members of the Deaf community oppose medical doctors advising parents against ASL for their Deaf child with a cochlear implant."

HLP7 Provide a consistent, organized, and respectful learning environment.

TEACHING & LEARNING

Supporting Children with Cochlear Implants in Inclusive Classrooms

In the past few decades, cochlear implants have been revolutionary for enabling deaf individuals to access the auditory world. Although this assistive technology continues to advance, cochlear implants do not yet enable deaf individuals to achieve normal hearing. For this reason, teachers must provide further accommodations to facilitate successful communication and learning in inclusive classrooms. When selecting and implementing appropriate accommodations, teachers must take steps to improve the listening and visual environment, facilitate social interactions, and encourage self-advocacy. Teachers can support their students with cochlear implants by doing the following (Davenport & Alber-Morgan, 2016; Stith & Drasgow, 2005).

Improve the Listening Environment. Noisy classrooms are challenging environments for hearing important information. Teachers can improve the listening environment in the following ways:

- Make sure the cochlear implant is turned on and working correctly. If the student uses an FM system, wear the transmitter that allows direct access to your voice.
- Seat the student to achieve optimal auditory access to the instructional activities (i.e., near the teacher or whomever is speaking).
- Reduce distracting noises by keeping the classroom door closed; using rugs, wall coverings, and curtains to reduce reverberation; and attaching felt padding or cut open tennis balls to the bottoms of chair legs.

Improve the Visual Environment. Deaf children with cochlear implants rely on the visual environment for a great deal of information.

- Make sure the lighting in the classroom is good quality so students can easily see instructional materials without fatigue.
- Get the student's attention before speaking. Make sure the student is looking at you when you are giving instructions. Additionally, provide directions before passing out materials for activities so the student is not attempting to attend to both the materials and the teacher simultaneously.
- Be sure to face the student when speaking and keep your hands or any other objects from covering your face.

Facilitate Peer Interactions. Communication challenges can certainly affect the quality of interactions with peers in inclusive classrooms. Teachers can improve peer interactions in the following ways.

- Teach the student to recognize when communication breakdowns occur and to ask for clarification when talking to a peer (e.g., "I didn't understand that; would you please repeat it?").
- Create frequent opportunities for peer interactions in a variety of classroom arrangements and activities throughout the day (e.g., center time, paired instructional activities). A peer buddy arrangement can be a fun way to encourage positive peer interactions.
- Use modeling and role playing to directly teach social interaction skills with peers, such as conversational turn-taking, asking for and offering help, or inviting a peer to play a game.

Encourage Self-Advocacy. Teach children with cochlear implants to self-advocate, for example, by asking a speaker to repeat a message they did not hear, reporting when their equipment is not working, and moving during instruction so they can better see and hear who is speaking. See Chapter 8, *Transition: Next Year Is Now*, "Teaching Self-Advocacy to Students with Communication Challenges."

Pearson eText
Video Example 9.3
Like all students, those with cochlear implants benefit from active engagement, frequent and immediate feedback, and teacher enthusiasm.

Supports and Technologies That Supplement or Replace Sound

SIGN LANGUAGE INTERPRETERS *Interpreting*—signing the speech of a teacher or other speaker for a person who is deaf—began as a profession in 1964 with the establishment of the Registry of Interpreters for the Deaf (RID). The organization was initially composed mostly of freelance interpreters, who interpret primarily for deaf adults in situations such as legal or medical interactions.

Sign language interpretation (sometimes called *transliteration*) has enabled many deaf and hard-of-hearing students to successfully complete college and other postsecondary education programs. The use of educational interpreters for deaf and hard-of-hearing students in elementary and secondary classrooms has increased (Monikowski & Winston, 2011). An interpreter must provide the deaf or hard-of-hearing student with all speech and other auditory information in the classroom, a formidable task for even the most highly skilled interpreter.

A skilled interpreter in the classroom is no guarantee that students with hearing loss will receive and participate in accurate communication. Garay (2003) recommends teaching deaf students how to use interpreters effectively—for example, how to let interpreters know when they do not understand something and how to appropriately and effectively indicate when they have something to ask the teacher or contribute to the class discussion.

SPEECH-TO-TEXT TRANSLATION Computer-aided speech-to-text translation increases access to live presentations, such as public or classroom lectures.

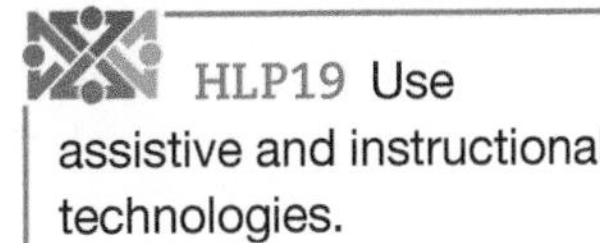

HLP19 Use assistive and instructional technologies.

An example of this technology is the C-Print speech-to-text service developed at the National Technical Institute for the Deaf (NTID) at the University of Rochester (Stinson et al., 2014). Using a shorthand code, a trained captionist types the teacher's lecture and students'

Source: Can Do Canines

Hearing dogs alert deaf people to important sounds such as alarms.

comments into a laptop computer. Special software translates the code (e.g., typing "kfe" produces "coffee"), and the text appears on a screen or a student's personal laptop computer monitor about 3 seconds after the words are spoken. The text display remains on the screen for approximately 1 minute, which provides students with much more time to consider the words than using an interpreter or speechreading would. The system provides a meaning-for-meaning (not verbatim) translation of the lecture, which would be impossible at speech rates of 150 words per minute. Captionists eliminate redundancies, identify key points, and condense information on the fly, keeping as close as possible to the original. Text files can be saved, edited, and printed after class.

Technically, sign language *interpretation* means translating spoken English into American Sign Language (ASL), which has its own vocabulary and syntax. *Transliteration* is the use of sign in the same word order as spoken English.

TELEVISION, VIDEO, AND MOVIE CAPTIONING Most programming today on commercial and public network television is captioned (printed text appears at the bottom of the screen, similar to watching a film with subtitles). Since 1993, a federal law has required that all new televisions sold in the United States be equipped with an internal device that allows the user to position captions anywhere on the screen. Many videos and movies are captioned, and an ever-increasing number of movie theaters are offering a captioning system called Rear Window. Captions from an LED panel at the back of the theater are projected on an adjustable, clear Lucite panel attached to the viewer's seat.

TEXT TELEPHONES The telephone presented a major barrier to people with hearing impairments in employment and social interaction until acoustic couplers made it possible to send immediate messages over conventional telephone lines in typed or digital form. Text telephones (TTs)—also called TTYs (teletypes) or TDDs (telecommunication devices for the deaf)—enable the user to send a typed message over telephone lines to anyone else who has a TT. As a result of the Americans with Disabilities Act, TTs are now available in most public places such as airports and libraries. Every state has a relay service that enables TT users to communicate with a person on a conventional telephone via a sign language interpreter who relays the messages. Relay numbers are published in every phone directory.

Pearson eText
Video Example 9.4
Klara's hearing dog improves quality of life for the whole family. https://www.youtube.com/watch?v=SpvexELg750

COMPUTER TECHNOLOGY Ever-improving personal computer and mobile digital technologies have opened and expanded avenues of communication and connectivity for people with hearing impairments. Smartphones and other mobile devices enable people who are deaf to text message, email, surf the Web, and participate in social media.

ALERTING DEVICES Some individuals who are deaf or hard of hearing use special devices to alert them to certain sounds or events. For example, to signal the doorbell, a fire alarm, or an alarm clock, a sound- or vibration-sensitive switch can be connected to a flashing light or to a vibrating device. Hearing dogs are trained to alert a deaf person to important sounds in the environment (Guest et al., 2006).

Educational Approaches

Learning Outcome 9.5 Compare and contrast approaches to educating children who are deaf and hard of hearing and describe how placement options can influence their opportunities.

Over the years, many philosophies, theories, and specialized methods and materials have been developed for teaching children who are deaf. Most of these approaches have been enthusiastically promoted by their advocates and critically denounced by others. Indeed, for more than

FIGURE 9.6 Key Historical Events in the Education of Students Who Are Deaf or Hard of Hearing

DATE	HISTORICAL EVENT
Late 16th century	Pedro Ponce de Leon (1520–1584), an Augustinian monk and scholar, established a school for the deaf children of noble families in Spain.
18th century	Schools for children who were deaf were established in England, France, Germany, Holland, and Scotland. Both oral and manual methods of instruction were used.
Early 19th century	The prevailing philosophy that people who were deaf could not benefit from oral instruction led to segregation in asylums or special sanctuaries.
1817	Thomas Gallaudet and Laurent Clerc opened the American Asylum for the Education of the Deaf and Dumb (renamed the American School for the Deaf) in Hartford, CT. Some consider Clerc the father of deaf education in the United States.
1864	Gallaudet University (then called the National College for the Deaf and Dumb) was founded.
Mid- to late 19th century	Oral approaches dominated to such a great degree that the use of sign language in schools was officially prohibited at an international conference in 1880. This era marked the beginning of what some have called "the Hundred Years' War" over what methods of communication are best for deaf children.
Mid- to late 20th century	Enrollments in residential schools for children with hearing loss declined sharply because most students whose deafness was caused by the rubella epidemics of the 1960s left high school, and public school programs became more widely available.
1960s	Research by linguist William Stokoe at Gallaudet showed that sign language used by the deaf community was a legitimate language in its own right. What had been called "the Sign Language" was given a new name, American Sign Language (ASL).
1968	Congress funded the National Technical Institute for the Deaf (NTID) at the Rochester Institute of Technology.
1970s	The majority of deaf education programs adopted total communication (TC) as the method of communication and instruction. Although TC is still used frequently today, it has not raised the academic achievement of deaf students.
1986	Concerned over academic and employment outcomes of deaf students, Congress established the Commission on Education of the Deaf (CED) with the Education of the Deaf Act of 1986.
1988	Students at Gallaudet University protested the hiring of a hearing president at their college. The Deaf President Now movement galvanized the Deaf community; increased awareness in hearing society of concerns and issues facing the Deaf culture; and led to the hiring of Gallaudet's first deaf president, I. King Jordan.
1989	The U.S. Food and Drug Administration approved cochlear implant surgery as a means of bypassing the inner ear and providing a sense of sound directly through the auditory nerve for those with sensorineural hearing loss. Many in the Deaf community view cochlear implants as a threat to the existence of their language and culture.
1990s	The Deaf community increased its activism and self-advocacy, especially with regard to ASL as a Deaf child's first language.
2010	Attendees at the International Congress on Education of the Deaf (ICED) unanimously passed a statement formally rejecting the 1880 edict that had banned sign language in school programs for the deaf.

100 years, people have waged an impassioned debate over how best to teach children who do not hear. Figure 9.6 highlights some key historical events in deaf education. For interesting historical accounts of deaf education, see Scheetz (2012), Van Cleve (2007), and Winzer (2009). Most programs for students who are deaf and hard of hearing emphasize one of three approaches: the oral/aural approach, total communication, or the bilingual-bicultural approach (Estabrooks et al., 2016).

Oral/Aural Approaches

Educational programs with an oral/aural emphasis view speech as essential if students who are deaf are to function in the hearing world. Training in producing and understanding speech and language is incorporated into virtually all aspects of the child's education. A purely oral approach without any manual communication was used widely in the United States before the 1970s. Today, about one fourth of special schools and educational programs for students who are deaf or hard of hearing identify themselves as solely oral/aural programs. However, with rising numbers of deaf and hard-of-hearing children educated in regular classrooms, the actual proportion educated orally is increasing. Speech is the primary communication mode in classrooms attended by 52% of deaf and hard-of-hearing students (Gallaudet Research Institute, 2013).

A child who attends a program with an oral emphasis typically uses several means to develop residual hearing and the ability to speak as intelligibly as possible. Auditory, visual, and tactile methods of input are frequently used. Much attention is given to amplification,

Source: BL/BSIP SA/Alamy Stock Photo

A combination of amplification and auditory training can help a child make the most of his residual hearing.

auditory training, speechreading, the use of technological aids, and, above all, talking. A few schools maintain a purely oral environment and may even prohibit children from pointing, using gestures, or spelling out words to communicate. Children in these programs are required to express themselves and learn to understand others through speech alone. Other programs emphasize speech and listening skills but also use and encourage a variety of approaches to help students produce and understand spoken language.

Educators who use an oral approach acknowledge that teaching speech to deaf children is difficult, demanding, and time consuming for the teachers, the parents, and—most of all—the students. The rewards of successful oral communication, however, are worth the effort. And indeed, most students with hearing loss can learn speech well enough to communicate effectively with hearing people. The best results are attained by students enrolled in comprehensive oral programs or integrated most of the school day into general education programs (Paul & Whitlow, 2011).

AUDITORY LEARNING Listening makes up 45% of daily communication for adults, and children spend up to 60% of the school day in situations when they are expected to be listening effectively (Crandell & Smaldino, 2001). Many children with hearing loss have much more auditory potential than they use, and their residual hearing can be improved in the context of actual communication and daily experiences. All children with hearing loss, regardless of whether their preferred method of communication is oral (speech) or manual (signs), should receive training and practice with improving their listening skills.

Auditory training for the young child with hearing loss begins by teaching awareness of sound. Parents might direct their child's attention to sounds such as a doorbell ringing or water running. They might then focus on localization of sound—for example, by hiding a radio somewhere in the room and encouraging the child to look for it. Discrimination of sounds is another important part of auditory training; a child might learn to notice the differences between a man's voice and a woman's voice, between a fast song and a slow song, or between the words *rack* and *rug*. Identification of sounds comes when a child can recognize a sound, word, or sentence through listening.

Auditory training should focus on teaching the child to learn to listen and to learn by listening instead of simply learning to hear (Erber, 2011; Ling, 2002). Advocates of auditory learning contend that the first three levels of auditory training—detecting, discriminating, and identifying sounds—are important but insufficient for developing the student's residual hearing. Auditory learning emphasizes a fourth and highest level of listening skills: the comprehension of meaningful sounds.

> HLP3 Collaborate with families to support student learning and secure needed services.

Practitioners of an approach called *auditory-verbal therapy* conduct some sessions in which a child is required to use only hearing to recognize sounds and words without looking at the speaker's lips (Estabrooks et al., 2016). Parental involvement is critical to success as auditory training opportunities are integrated into family and social activities as well as in school (Dornan et al., 2010). In actual practice, however, the child gains useful information from vision and the other senses to supplement the information received from hearing. Consequently, all senses should be developed.

Speechreading is the process of understanding a spoken message by observing the speaker's lip movements, facial expressions, eye movements, and body gestures. Some sounds are readily distinguished by watching the speaker's lips. For example, whereas the word *pail* begins with the lips in a shut position, the lips are somewhat drawn together and puckered at the corners for the word *rail*. Paying careful attention to a speaker's lips may help an individual with hearing loss derive important clues—particularly if the individual also can gain additional information through residual hearing, signs or gestures, facial expressions, and the situation.

Speechreading, however, is extremely difficult and has many limitations. About half of all English words have some other words that appear the same in pronunciation; that is, although they sound quite different, they look alike on the lips. Words such as *bat*, *mat*, and *pat*, for example, look exactly alike and simply cannot be discriminated by watching the speaker's lips. To complicate matters, visual clues may be blocked by a hand, a pencil, a mustache, or a face mask. Many speakers are virtually unintelligible through speechreading; they may seem not to move their lips at all. In addition, it is extremely tiring to watch lips for a long time, and it may be impossible to do so at a distance, such as during a lecture. Walker (1986) estimates that even the best speechreaders detect only about 25% of what is said through visual clues alone; "the rest is contextual piecing together of ideas and expected constructions" (p. 19).

Despite the problems inherent in speechreading, it can be a valuable tool in a deaf or hard-of-hearing person's communication repertoire (Paul & Whitlow, 2011). When deaf people practice speechreading via computer-assisted video instruction, their speechreading skills can improve (Sims & Gottermeier, 1995).

CUED SPEECH **Cued speech** supplements oral communication with a visual system of hand signals that represent 40 phonemes of spoken English. The hand signals must be used in conjunction with speech; they are neither signs nor manual alphabet letters and cannot be read alone. Eight hand shapes identify consonant sounds, and four locations around the chin identify vowel sounds. A hand shape coupled with a location gives a visual indication of a syllable. Cued speech helps students identify syllabic and phonetic features of speech that cannot be distinguished through speechreading. According to Orin Cornett, who developed the system in 1964, cued speech does not disrupt the natural rhythm of speech (Cornett & Daisey, 2001). Some research shows that students taught with cued speech develop reading and spelling at levels comparable to those of hearing children (Hage & Leybaert, 2006).

TOTAL COMMUNICATION As Scheetz (2012) points out, **total communication** refers to an educational philosophy as well as to a mode of communication. Advocates use a variety of forms of communication to teach English to students with hearing loss. Practitioners of total communication (also called "SimCom") maintain that the simultaneous presentation of English language by speech and manual communication (signing and fingerspelling) makes it possible for children to use either one or both types of communication (Hawkins & Brawner, 1997). Following its introduction as a teaching philosophy in the 1960s, total communication became the most widely used method of instruction in schools for the deaf. Today, about 29% of students who are deaf and hard of hearing attend classrooms where speech and manual sign are the primary language and mode of communication (Gallaudet Research Institute, 2013).

MANUALLY CODED ENGLISH Teachers who practice total communication speak as they sign and make a special effort to follow the form and structure of spoken English as closely as possible. Several English-based sign systems have been designed for educational purposes, with the intention of facilitating the development of reading, writing, and other language skills in students with hearing loss. *Manually coded English* refers to several educationally oriented sign systems, such as Signing Essential English (commonly known as SEE I) (Anthony, 1971), Signing Exact English (SEE II) (Gustafson et al., 1980), and Signed English (Bornstein, 1974). Although manually coded English borrows many signs and incorporates some of the features of ASL, it follows Standard English usage and word order. Unfortunately, deaf students must often learn to use two or more sign language systems, depending on the person with whom they are communicating.

FINGERSPELLING **Fingerspelling** is used to spell out proper names for which no signs exist and to clarify meanings. Fingerspelling is an integral part of ASL and an important aspect of becoming bilingual in English and ASL (Sehyr et al., 2017). It consists of 26 distinct hand positions, one for each English letter. A one-hand manual alphabet is used in the United States and Canada (Figure 9.7). Some manual letters—such as *C*, *L*, and *W*—resemble the shape of printed English letters, whereas others—such as *B*, *F*, and *S*—have no obvious similarity. As in typewriting, each word is spelled out letter by letter.

Deaf babies' first attempts at fingerspelling emerge shortly after their first birthday, and their first fingerspelled word occurs at 2 years of age (Erting et al., 2000). Fingerspelling can help deaf and hard-of-hearing students with reading by providing a link to spoken and written English (Alawad & Musyoka, 2018).

FIGURE 9.7 The Manual Alphabet Used to Fingerspell English in United States and Canada

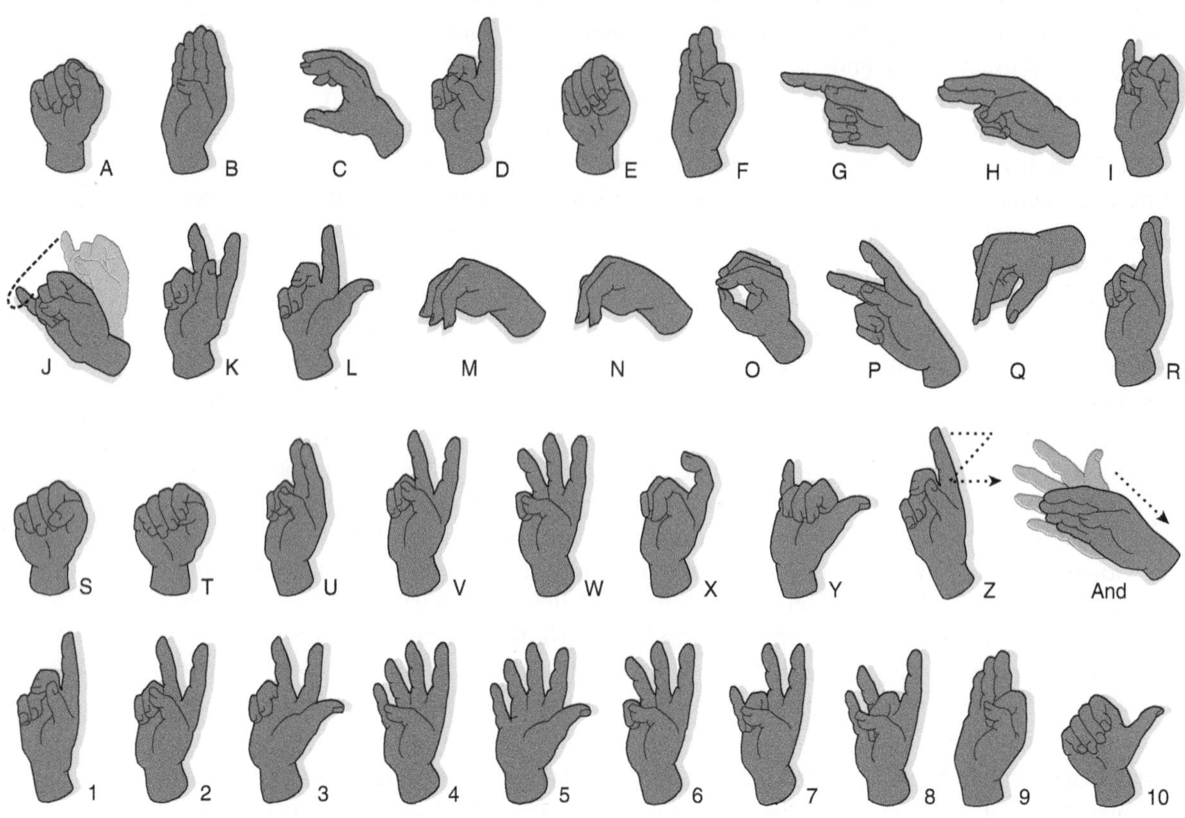

American Sign Language and the Bilingual-Bicultural Approach

American Sign Language (ASL) is the language of the Deaf culture in the United States and Canada. Although the sign languages used by deaf speakers were once thought to be non-languages (alinguistic), work by the linguist William Stokoe (Stokoe, 1960; Stokoe et al., 1995) showed that ASL is a distinct language in its own right rather than a variation of spoken English. ASL is a visual-spatial language in which the shape, location, and movement pattern of the hands; the intensity of motions; and the signer's facial expressions all communicate meaning and content. Because ASL has its own rules of phonology, morphology, syntax, semantics, and pragmatics, it does not correspond to spoken or written English (Valli et al., 2011). Articles, prepositions, tenses, plurals, and word order are expressed differently from English. It is as difficult to make precise word-for-word translations between ASL and English as it is to translate many world languages into English word for word.

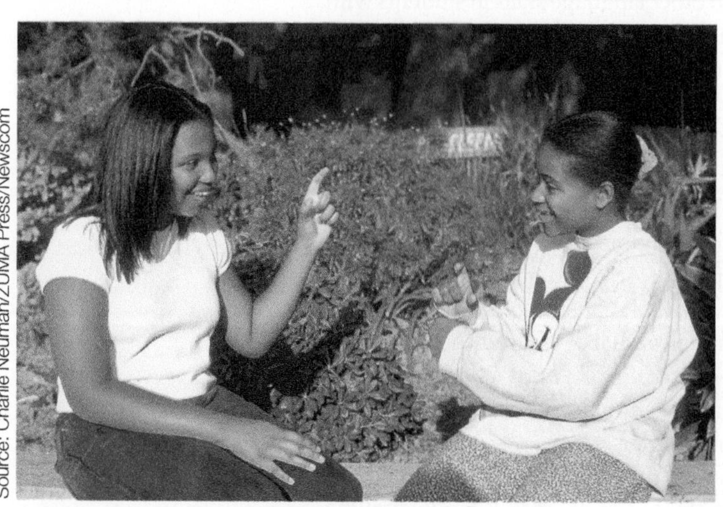
Source: Charlie Neuman/ZUMA Press/Newscom

American Sign Language (ASL) is a complete language with its own vocabulary, syntax, and grammatical rules.

Some ASL signs are *iconic;* that is, they convey meaning through hand shapes or motions that look like or appear to imitate or act out their message. In making the sign for "cat," for example, the signer seems to be stroking feline whiskers on her face; in the sign for "eat," the hand moves back and forth toward and away from the mouth. Most signs, however, do not resemble the objects or actions they represent. If ASL were simply a form of pantomime, then most nonsigners would be able to understand it with relative ease. But the vast majority of signs cannot be guessed by people who are unfamiliar with sign language.

Featured Teacher Jessica Stultz explains: "ASL is completely separate and distinct from English. While every language has ways of signaling different functions, such as asking a question rather than making a statement, languages differ in how this is done. For example, English speakers ask a question by raising the pitch of their voice; ASL users ask a question by raising their eyebrows, widening their eyes, and tilting their bodies forward."

During the 1990s, the Deaf community and a sizeable number of both hearing and deaf special educators began calling for ASL to be the language of instruction (Baker & Baker, 1997; Drasgow, 1998). They believe that ASL provides a natural pathway to linguistic competence and that English is better learned in the context of a **bilingual-bicultural (bi-bi) approach** after the child has mastered his native or first language (ASL) (Baker, 2011). Proponents of this model view deafness as a cultural and linguistic difference, not a disability, and recognize ASL as the deaf child's first language. The National Association of the Deaf (2018) believes that "deaf and hard of hearing infants should be given the opportunity to acquire ASL as early as possible, in addition to the opportunity to access and acquire the spoken language(s) used by their families through the use of assistive technologies and other strategies" (n.p.).

Pearson eText
Video Example 9.5
The bilingual-bicultural approach helps deaf students learn their first language, ASL, and their second language, English. https://www.youtube.com/watch?v=RHoIRuo0ng4

The goal of the bilingual-bicultural education approach is to help deaf students become bilingual adults who are competent in their first language, ASL, and who can read and write with competence in their second language, English. About 15% of deaf and hard-of-hearing students attend classrooms where ASL is the primary language and mode of communication (Gallaudet Research Institute, 2013).

The theoretical argument for bilingual education is that students who have a solid foundation in their first language (L1) will be able to use their literacy-related L1 skills as a springboard for learning the second language (L2) (Marschark et al., 2014). Deaf infants and toddlers from families where ASL is the primary language achieve language development milestones at about the same rate as hearing children do with spoken language (Emmorey, 2002; Goldin-Meadow, 2003). Children from deaf families enter school ready to learn because as infants and toddlers, they learn their first language through communicating with family members (Marschark et al., 2006). Research showing a correlation between early exposure to ASL and improved English literacy (Yoshinaga-Itano, 2006) provides empirical support for the bilingual-bicultural approach.

Mayer and Akamatsu (1999), however, question the extent of L1–L2 interdependence when the two languages under consideration are a native sign language and the written form of an oral language. They also point out the logical inconsistency and danger of not providing deaf students with direct instruction and practice in bottom-up literacy skills such as phonics. Although there is solid philosophical and theoretical reasoning for a bilingual-bicultural approach and many programs have been implemented—Scheetz (2012) reports that 19 state schools for the deaf identify their programs as bilingual—research on effectiveness and long-term program outcomes is needed (DeLana et al., 2007). In one study of more than 150 deaf students enrolled for at least 4 years in a bilingual program, the students achieved academic growth measures in reading and math that outperformed a nationally normed group of grade-level peers consisting mostly of hearing students (Lange et al., 2013).

Which Approach for Whom?

Educators, scientists, philosophers, and parents—both hearing and deaf—have for many years debated the most appropriate instructional methods for children who are deaf. The controversy continues today. In the past, however, fundamental disagreement focused on the extent to which deaf children should express language through speech and perceive the communication of others through speechreading and residual hearing. Today, the debate has switched to which language—English or ASL—should be a deaf child's first language.

Different children communicate in different ways. Some deaf children, unfortunately, have experienced deep frustration and failure because of rigid adherence to an oral-only program. They have left oral programs without having developed a usable avenue of communication. Equally unfortunate is the fact that other children have not been given an adequate opportunity to develop their auditory and oral skills because they were placed in educational programs that did not provide good oral instruction. In both cases, children have been unfairly penalized. Every child who is deaf should have access to an educational program that uses a communication method best suited to that child's unique abilities and needs (Marschark, 2007). Mahshie (1995) recommends letting the child choose the first language:

> In environments where the Deaf child encounters both spoken and signed language separately—as whole languages—during the course of natural interactions, it has become apparent to both parents and professionals that the child will be the guide regarding his or her predisposition toward a more oral or more visual language. In this win-win situation, the choice of a first language is clearly the child's (p. 73).

Early and continued access to language and the communication modality best suited to individual needs and preferences, effective instruction with meaningful curriculum, and self-determination are the keys to increasing the number of deaf or hard-of-hearing people

Transition: Next Year Is Now

Making Friends in Middle School

Going to middle school from elementary school is a transition for everyone. Thoughtful preparation for this big step can lay the groundwork for successful transitions into and throughout adulthood. When Featured Teacher Jessica Stultz prepares her fifth graders for middle school, she stresses the importance of building positive social relationships. Her advice is relevant to all elementary students transitioning to middle school.

- **Act friendly.** Middle school is a great opportunity to make new friends. Smile a lot; be kind and courteous to others. Compliment people without being annoying or fake. Always keep your head held high, and never cross your arms over your chest or scowl because that makes you seem mean and unfriendly.
- **Join a club or activity.** Joining an activity group or club can really increase your friendship circle. And who knows, you might have a talent for something you aren't even aware of, and you may develop a new skill.
- **Just say hi!** Go up to someone you would like to get to know and say "Hi" and offer a compliment or ask him a few questions. Be sure to smile, but don't feel the need to be over-the-top friendly or happy.
- **Take care of yourself.** Eat healthy, take regular showers/baths, and wash your face. A little hygiene can make all the difference.
- **No drama.** Drama is around every corner in middle school. One little something said on IM, text message, or Facebook can ruin your reputation and destroy friendships. Be neutral if two groups of people who are your friends start fighting. Stay away from people who start drama. Also, don't gossip. Don't spread gossip. Don't listen to gossip.
- **Avoid negative peer pressure.** Peers can have a great deal of influence over choices students make in middle school, and social pressure from peers is difficult to resist. To avoid giving into peer pressure, find friends with similar interests and be assertive (e.g., tell friends what you like and what you don't like). Don't use alcohol or other drugs. Avoid situations that can get you in trouble (e.g., skipping school). Talk with trusted adults about situations you do not understand or that make you feel uncomfortable, such as bullying.

HLP1 Collaborate with professionals to increase student success.

Visiting the middle school can help elementary students feel less anxious about the transition. Students can benefit a great deal from the collaboration between elementary and middle school teachers. Together teachers can plan a field trip and provide opportunities for students to learn about and feel comfortable with going to middle school.

Prior to the visit, pair elementary students with middle school students to be pen pals. Students can introduce themselves in their letters; ask questions; and write about their interests, concerns, and experiences. Students who have met as pen pals will likely be very excited to meet each other in person on the day of the visit. Middle school students might also send a welcome and advice letter to the elementary students.

During the visit, middle school students meet, greet, and show their pen pals around the school. They can explain school routines; introduce their new friends to teachers, school staff, and other students; and answer questions about life as a middle schooler. Another way to welcome transitioning elementary students is having the middle school students prepare a presentation about middle school academics, school clubs, activities, and special events. Activities like this have the potential to alleviate any worries students have and inspire them to look forward to going to middle school.

who can access and enjoy the full spectrum of educational, social, vocational, and recreational opportunities society has to offer.

Placement Options

In most areas of the United States today, parents of deaf and hard-of-hearing students can choose between local public school programs and residential schools. The majority of students who are deaf or hard of hearing are educated in local public schools: 63% in regular classrooms, 15% in resource rooms, and 11% in separate classrooms. About 8% of deaf and hard-of-hearing students are educated in special schools, 2% in separate residential schools for the deaf, and 1.5% in private schools (U.S. Department of Education, 2020). Compared with deaf and hard-of-hearing students in regular public school classrooms, deaf and hard-of-hearing students who attend special schools are more likely to have greater levels of hearing loss and to use ASL (Shaver et al., 2014).

The question of where students who are deaf should be educated has produced some research evidence—and much strong opinion—in support of both inclusive and separate settings (Cerney, 2007; Schick et al., 2014). As Bat-Chava (2000) notes, where a child who is deaf is educated also influences the child's cultural identity. In schools where oral English is the language of instruction, supplemented by fingerspelling and English-based sign systems, students are more likely to view hearing loss as a disability. Schools where ASL is the language of instruction foster the perspective of Deaf culture.

Instruction and support services typically provided to deaf and hard-of-hearing students in regular classrooms leave much to be desired. Cawthon (2001) found that elementary teachers in inclusive classrooms directed about half as many utterances to deaf students as they did to hearing students and that educational interpreters were critical factors in how well the deaf students understood and participated in classroom discourse and learning activities. Recent national surveys found that only about 14% of all school-age deaf and hard-of-hearing students reported receiving interpreting service as an instructional support (Gallaudet Research Institute, 2013), and just 45% of secondary students with severe or profound hearing loss who were included in regular classrooms were provided interpreting services (Shaver et al., 2011).

The skill level of an educational interpreter plays a critical role in the success and appropriateness of a regular classroom placement for students who are deaf. After finding that about 60% of 2100 educational interpreters across the United States had inadequate skills, researchers concluded that "many deaf and hard-of-hearing students receive interpreting services that will seriously hinder reasonable access to the classroom curriculum and social interaction" (Schick et al., 2006, p. 3).

While acknowledging many deaf students benefit from regular classroom placements, all of the professional and parent organizations involved with educating students who are deaf have issued position statements strongly in favor of maintaining a continuum of placement options (e.g., Commission on Education of the Deaf, 1988; National Association of the Deaf, 2002). As one respected leader in the field of deaf education noted, including a deaf child in a classroom with hearing children may actually have an exclusionary effect that isolates the child academically and socially because of unequal access to the curriculum (Moores, 1993).

As with all learners, we should never overlook the most fundamental factor in determining how successful a student will be in a regular classroom (or any other placement): quality of instruction. After studying the math achievement of 215 secondary students with hearing loss who were either in self-contained classrooms or included in regular classrooms with or without an interpreter, Kluwin and Moores (1989) concluded, "Quality of instruction is the prime determinant of achievement, regardless of placement" (p. 327). See *Teaching & Learning,* "Help Me Succeed in Your Classroom: Tips from Deaf Students."

TEACHING & LEARNING

Help Me Succeed in Your Classroom: Tips from Deaf Students

Why Is It Important to Listen to Deaf Students Talk about Their School Experiences Most deaf students are educated by hearing teachers in classrooms of predominantly hearing peers. Although these teachers and peers are well intentioned, some may lack empathy because they experience the world from a hearing person's perspective. Featured Teacher Jessica Stultz asked a group of deaf students at her school to describe their experiences in regular classrooms and how teachers can help them. Fifth grader Paisley noted, "I felt lonely and left out because whenever I tried to communicate, they [peers] would respond in a way that I didn't understand." Seventh grader Victoria said, "It can be overwhelming for me, and I do not always understand what is being taught." Taking the time and effort to listen to the voices of deaf children will make you a better teacher. Seventh grader Ty affirmed, "My favorite teacher always teaches with a smile. She is very passionate about what she teaches us and makes sure we understand what is being taught."

Pearson eText
Video Example 9.6
"My favorite teacher always teaches with a smile."

What Can I Learn by Listening to Deaf Students? Jessica's students make the following recommendations.

- Learn which mode of communication the student prefers and use that mode consistently.
- Be positive, friendly, patient, and encouraging.
- Provide individual attention.
- Make sure your students understand what you are teaching and provide them with positive and corrective feedback.
- When deaf students have difficulties with peers, intervene and help them problem solve.

The following are additional tips from older students (DeafTEC, n.d.):

- Supplement your lectures with a lot of visuals (e.g., PowerPoint slides).
- Provide instructional materials in advance so students have time to review and build background knowledge prior to the lesson.
- Make sure you are facing the students when you talk to them.
- Be available to provide extra review and clarification of the material after class. Make sure students know you are open to providing them extra time and assistance.
- Get to know your students; listen to them and they will tell you what they need.

Postsecondary Education

The percentage of students with hearing loss who attend postsecondary educational programs has risen dramatically since the 1980s. About half of all deaf or hard of hearing people complete at least some college (Garberoglio et al., 2019). The oldest and best known is Gallaudet University in Washington, DC, which offers a wide range of undergraduate and graduate programs in the liberal arts, sciences, education, business, and other fields. The NTID, located at the Rochester Institute of Technology, provides wide-ranging programs in technical, vocational, and business-related fields such as computer science, hotel management, photography, and medical technology. Both Gallaudet and NTID are supported by the federal government, and each enrolls approximately 1500 students who are deaf or hard of hearing.

ADVICE FROM THE FEATURED TEACHER by Jessica Stultz

Don't Try to Save the World: Teach

Source: Jessica Stultz

- ***Don't try to "save the world" or be a child's savior.*** Children do not need your sympathy or heroism; they need and deserve your expertise, compassion, and commitment to their success.
- ***Start off the year strong.*** On the first day of school, you will be setting the tone for the rest of the school year. Be clear about rules and expectations from the start. Do not confuse the student with frequent changes in behavior strategies. Be consistent and the rest of the year will breeze by.
- ***Stay composed in stressful situations.*** Avoid becoming frustrated, but if you do, don't let your students see it. Students remember years later a teacher who was grumpy or often foul tempered.
- ***Do the unexpected.*** Don't get stuck in a rut. Surprise your students with a variety of stimulating lessons, projects, and hands-on activities without compromising classroom management and evidence-based instructional approaches. Give your students something positive to talk about at home.

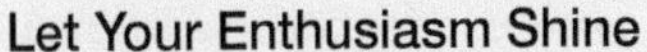

Let Your Enthusiasm Shine

- ***Be an actor.*** Love of the subject you're teaching is so important for inspiring enthusiasm in your students. If long division bores you, don't let your students know that! Be an actor!
- ***Encourage laughter.*** An excellent teacher keeps her students' attention without using fear. Encourage a lot of laughter in your classroom.
- ***Be compassionate.*** Develop strong rapport with students through understanding and sensitivity. Show them that you genuinely care.
- ***Stay alert.*** Anticipate students' difficulties in understanding content or anticipate their feelings of anxiety to prevent meltdowns or crises. Stay one step ahead.

Keep Asking, Keep Learning

- ***Use your mentor.*** Your mentor can be a valuable resource who will reduce the stress of being a new teacher. You can ask your mentor to provide you with feedback, ideas, reminders, and samples of lesson plans.
- ***Be a forever student.*** Accept constructive feedback, and always seek ways to improve. Professional training is ongoing. Keep up-to-date with issues, subjects, materials, and technology.

Key Terms and Concepts

acquired
American Sign Language (ASL)
audiogram
audiometer
audiometric zero
audition
auditory canal (external acoustic meatus)
auditory training
auricle
behavior observation audiometry
bilingual-bicultural (bi-bi) approach
cochlea
cochlear implant
conductive hearing impairment
congenital
congenital cytomegalovirus
cued speech
Deaf culture
deafness
decibels (dB)
fingerspelling
hard of hearing
hearing loss
hertz (Hz)

neural hearing impairment
operant conditioning audiometry
ossicles
otitis media
play audiometry
postlingual hearing loss
prelingual hearing loss
residual hearing
sensory hearing impairment
speech reception threshold
speechreading
total communication
tympanic membrane

Summary

Definitions

- Hearing loss exists on a continuum from mild to profound, and most special educators distinguish between children who are deaf and those who are hard of hearing. A deaf child cannot understand speech through the ears alone. A hard-of-hearing child can use hearing to understand speech, generally with the help of a hearing aid.
- Many Deaf people do not view hearing loss as a disability. Similar to other cultural groups, members of the Deaf community share a common language (ASL) and social practices.
- Sound is measured by its intensity (decibels [dB]) and frequency (Hertz [Hz]); both dimensions are important in considering the special education needs of a child with a hearing loss. The frequencies most important for understanding speech are 500 to 2000 Hz.

Characteristics

- Deaf children—especially those with a prelingual hearing loss of 90 dB or greater—are at a great disadvantage for acquiring English literacy skills.
- The speech of many children with hearing loss may be difficult to understand because they omit speech sounds, speak too loudly or softly, speak in a high pitch, speak with limited inflection, or speak too quickly or too slowly.
- As a group, students who are deaf and hard of hearing lag far behind their hearing peers in academic achievement, and the achievement gap usually widens as they get older.
- Children with severe to profound hearing loss often report feeling isolated and unhappy in school, particularly when their socialization with other children with hearing loss is limited.
- Many individuals who are deaf choose membership in the Deaf community and culture.

Prevalence

- Students with hearing loss represent 1% of all school-age students receiving special education.

Types and Causes of Hearing Loss

- Hearing loss is described as conductive (outer or middle ear) or sensorineural (inner ear) and unilateral (in one ear) or bilateral (in both ears).
- A prelingual hearing loss occurs before the child has developed speech and language; a postlingual hearing loss occurs after that time.
- Causes of congenital hearing loss include, but are not limited to, genetic factors, maternal rubella, congenital cytomegalovirus (CMV), and prematurity.
- Causes of acquired hearing loss include otitis media, meningitis, Ménière's disease, and noise exposure.

Identification and Assessment

- Auditory brain stem response and otoacoustic emission are two methods of screening for hearing loss in infants.
- A formal hearing test generates an audiogram, which graphically shows the intensity of the faintest sound an individual can hear 50% of the time at various frequencies.
- Hearing loss is classified as slight, mild, moderate, severe, or profound, depending on the degree of hearing loss.

Technologies and Supports

- Technologies that amplify or provide sound include hearing aids, assistive listening devices, and cochlear implants.
- Technologies and supports that supplement or replace sound include educational interpreters, speech-to-text translation, television captioning, text telephones, and alerting devices.

Educational Approaches

- The oral/aural approach views speech as essential if students are to function in the hearing world; much emphasis is given to amplification; auditory training; speechreading; the use of technological aids; and, above all, talking.

- Total communication uses speech and simultaneous manual communication via signs and fingerspelling in English word order.
- In the bilingual-bicultural approach, deafness is viewed as a cultural and linguistic difference, not a disability, and American Sign Language (ASL) is used as the language of instruction.

Placement Options

- About 63% students who are deaf or hard of hearing are educated in regular classrooms; of the others, approximately 15% attend resource rooms, 11% are served in separate classrooms, 8% go to special schools, and 2% attend residential programs.
- All of the major professional and parent organizations involved in deaf education have issued position statements strongly in favor of maintaining a continuum of placement options.
- Access to the language and communication modality best suited to individual needs and preferences, effective instruction with meaningful curriculum, and self-advocacy are the keys to improving the future for people who are deaf or hard of hearing.

Chapter 10

Blindness and Low Vision

Source: Katelyn Metzger/Merrill Education

Learning Outcomes

After reading this chapter and completing the embedded activities, you should be able to

10.1 Describe how blindness and low vision affect learning, motor development, and social interaction.

10.2 Identify types and causes of visual impairments and explain why it is important for teachers to know about the types of visual impairments affecting children in their classrooms.

10.3 Compare educational goals and instructional methods for children with low vision and children who are blind.

10.4 Define expanded core curriculum and explain its importance for children with visual impairments.

10.5 Explain how the educational placement of students with visual impairments can affect their opportunities to learn the expanded core curriculum of nonacademic skills necessary for overall success in life.

Featured Teacher

Cecelia Peirano

Ohio State School for the Blind, Columbus, OH

Source: Cecelia Peirano

I teach eight fifth and sixth graders with visual impairments, age 10 to 13 years. My students' academic abilities vary greatly; two of my students are deaf-blind, one is an English-language learner, and one has been identified as gifted. Two of my students attend their public school for half of each school day and come to me for the other half of the day.

The success of students with visual impairments requires an incredible amount of time and energy. In addition to tackling the general academic curriculum and attending physical education, music, and art classes, they receive specialized instruction in the expanded core curriculum unique to students with visual impairments: braille, listening skills, orientation and mobility, social skills, visual efficiency, and technology.

Today's technology is wonderful for students with visual impairments and their teachers. It gives students many opportunities to be included in regular activities with their sighted peers and the skills they will need to join the job market as teenagers or adults. Accessing print material has always been difficult for students with visual impairments, but technology has definitely leveled the playing field.

Students with low vision can learn to use closed-circuit televisions, ZoomText, pocket viewers, iPads, and many additional pieces of equipment to read, enlarge, store, and manipulate print, access computers, or have material read to them. Students who use braille can access and respond to instructional material with notetakers, JAWS or other screen readers, refreshable braille displays, and special keyboards for smartphones or tablets, and the list goes on! Students just soak up all the information available through new technology, and our students with visual impairments need to be a part of it!

Teachers can also make curriculum more accessible with programs that translate print to braille, such as Duxbury, or by transmitting whiteboard material directly to students' computers, notetakers, and iPads, where they can read, enlarge, or listen to what the teacher is writing on the board. Teachers and students can also download books or presentations to these devices as well.

Some of the most effective adaptations to curriculum and instruction are low tech. In math, for example, students need more manipulatives and hands-on time to explore concepts. The materials need to be enlarged or made tactually accessible. In addition to Nemeth, the braille code for math, modifications for math instruction include three-dimensional objects, tactile graphics, talking calculators, computers with assistive software, and extended time.

There is a great joy in teaching a child how to explore a tactile map and having him realize he has traveled from Ohio to Florida, and adapting a science lesson that leads to a student's smile when she finally understands how gas molecules expand when heated. I had one student, Casey, who always turned his head toward me, grinned, and said, "Oh, now I get it!" That says it all!

Education, Teaching Credentials, and Experience

- *B.A., elementary education, The Ohio State University, 1977*
- *M.A., visual impairment, K–12, The Ohio State University, 1978*
- *Ohio Professional Elementary, 1–8; Professional Special Education, Visually Impaired, K–12; National Board Certification, Exceptional Needs Specialist, Vision, 2004, 2014*
- *41 years of experience teaching students with visual impairments*
- *Ohio District 6 Teacher of the Year, 2020*

Content Extension 10.1

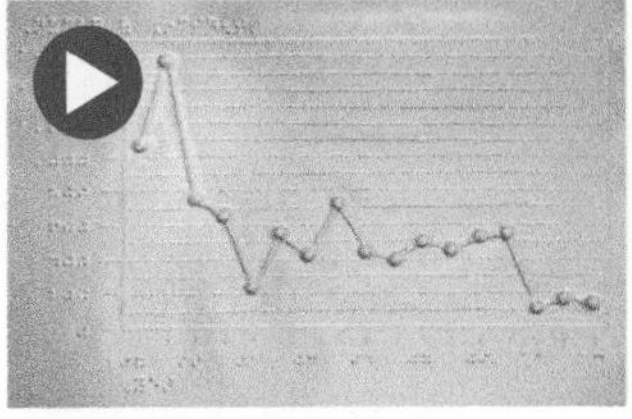

A tactile graph used by Featured Teacher Cecilia's students.

SIXTEEN-YEAR-OLD MARIA IS A BRIGHT COLLEGE-BOUND STUDENT who has been totally blind since birth. She took a series of intellectual and psychological tests and performed well, scoring at about her expected age and grade level. Something unusual happened, however, on one of the test items. The examiner handed Maria an unpeeled banana and asked, "What is this?" Maria took several guesses but could not answer correctly. The examiner was astonished, as were Maria's teachers and parents. After all, this section of the test was intended for young children. Even though Maria had eaten bananas many times, she had missed out on an important aspect of the banana experience: She had never held and peeled a banana by herself.

This true story illustrates the tremendous importance of vision in providing information about our world. Although students with visual impairments may learn to make good use of their other senses as channels for contacting the environment, they do not totally compensate for absence of vision. Touch and taste cannot tell a child about things that are far away or even just beyond her arms' reach. And although hearing provides considerable information about the near and distant environment, it seldom provides information that is as complete, continuous, or exact as the information people obtain from seeing their surroundings.

Vision plays a critical role in the classroom. Sighted students routinely use several important visual skills. They focus on different objects and shift their vision from near to far as needed. They exercise good hand-to-eye coordination, maintain visual concentration, discriminate among colors and letters, see and interpret many things simultaneously, and remember what they have seen. Children with visual impairments have deficits in one or more of these abilities. As a result, they need special equipment, adaptations, or both.

Definitions

Unlike other disabilities covered by the Individuals with Disabilities Education Act (IDEA), visual impairment has both legal and educational definitions.

Legal Definitions of Blindness

The statutory definition of blindness is based on visual acuity and field of vision. **Visual acuity**—the ability to clearly distinguish forms or discriminate among details—is most often measured by reading letters, numbers, or other symbols from the Snellen eye chart. The familiar phrase "20/20 vision" does not, as some people think, indicate perfect vision; it simply means at a distance of 20 feet, the eye can see what a normally seeing eye sees at that distance. As the bottom number increases, visual acuity decreases.

Legal blindness is defined as visual acuity of 20/200 or less in the better eye with the use of a corrective lens (Social Security Administration, 2019). If Jane has 20/200 vision, she needs to stand at a distance of 20 feet to see while wearing her glasses what a normally sighted person can see from 200 feet. In other words, Jane must get much closer to see things clearly, making it difficult to use her vision in many everyday situations. But many children with visual acuity of 20/200 or even 20/400 succeed in the classroom with special help. Some students' visual acuity is so poor they cannot perceive fine details at any distance, even while wearing glasses or contact lenses. An individual whose visual acuity in the better eye after correction falls between 20/70 and 20/200 is considered **partially sighted** for legal and governmental purposes.

When gazing straight ahead, a normal eye can see objects within a range of approximately 160 to 170 degrees. A person whose **field of vision** is restricted to an area no greater than 20 degrees is considered legally blind. Some people with **tunnel vision** describe their perception as viewing the world through a narrow tube; they may have good central vision but poor peripheral vision at the outer ranges of the visual field. Conversely, some eye conditions make it impossible for people to see things clearly in the center of the visual field but allow relatively good peripheral vision. Because a person's visual field often deteriorates gradually over a period of years, a thorough visual examination should always include measurement of the visual field as well as visual acuity. Figure 10.1 shows what a person might see with normal or poor visual acuity or a limited field of vision.

Children who are legally blind are eligible to receive a wide variety of educational services, materials, and benefits from governmental agencies. They may, for example, obtain Talking Books and playback devices from the Library of Congress. Their schools may be able to obtain books and educational materials from the American Printing House for the Blind because the federal government allots states and local school districts a certain financial allowance for each student who is legally blind. A person who is legally blind is also entitled to vocational training, free U.S. mail service, and an income tax exemption. To learn more about services available to people with visual impairments, visit the websites of the American Printing House for the Blind and the American Foundation for the Blind.

The legal definition of blindness is not especially useful for teachers. Some children who do not meet the criteria for legal blindness have visual impairments that require special education. Other students who are legally blind have little or no need for special education services.

FIGURE 10.1 A Street Scene as It Might Be Viewed by People with 20/20 Vision (a), 20/200 Visual Acuity (b), and Restricted Fields of Vision (c and d)

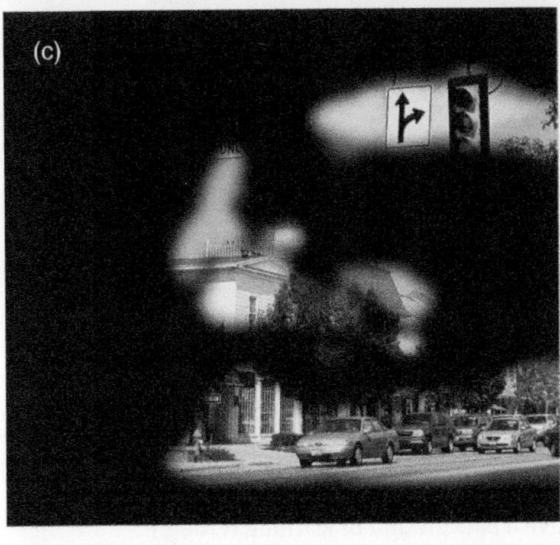

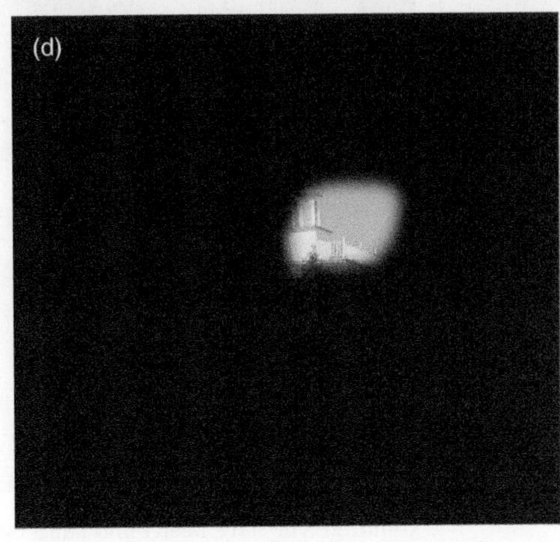

Educational Definitions of Visual Impairment

The definition of **visual impairment** in IDEA emphasizes the relationship between vision and learning:

> Visual impairment including blindness means an impairment in vision that, even with correction, adversely affects a child's educational performance. The term includes both partial sight and blindness. (20 USC §1401 [2004], 20 *CFR* §300.8[c][13])

Students with visual impairments display a wide range of visual abilities—from total blindness to relatively good vision. The precise measurements of visual acuity and visual field used to determine legal blindness have limited relevance for educators. Instead, educators classify students with visual impairments based on the extent to which they use vision and tactile and auditory senses for learning.

Pearson eText
Video Example 10.1
Students who are blind use their sense of touch to learn about the world. https://www.youtube.com/watch?v=yBhqIWxrRYc

- A student who is *totally blind* receives no useful information through the sense of vision and uses tactile and auditory senses for all learning.
- A child who is *functionally blind* has so little vision that she learns primarily through the tactile and auditory senses; however, she may be able to use her limited vision to supplement the information her other senses perceive and to assist with certain tasks (e.g., moving through the classroom).
- A child with **low vision** uses vision as a primary means of learning but supplements visual information with tactile and auditory input.

Age at Onset

Similar to other disabilities, visual impairment can be congenital (present at birth) or adventitious (acquired). Most visual impairments of school-age children are congenital. A child who has been blind since birth has a different perception of the world than does a child who lost his vision at age 12 years. Whereas the first child has a background of learning through hearing, touch, and the other nonvisual senses, the second child also has a large background of visual experiences on which to draw. Most people who are adventitiously blind retain a visual memory of things they saw. This memory can be helpful in a child's education; an adventitiously blind child may, for instance, remember the appearance of colors, maps, and printed letters. At the same time, however, a child who is adventitiously blind may have greater need for emotional support and acceptance than a child who does not have to adjust to the loss of vision (Wahl et al., 2006).

Source: Scott Cunningham

Children who have been blind since birth have a background of learning through hearing, touch, and other nonvisual senses.

Characteristics

Learning Outcome 10.1 Describe how blindness and low vision affect learning, motor development, and social interaction.

Cognition and Language

This chapter began with a story about a bright teenager without sight who could not identify the object she was holding as a banana. Maria had eaten bananas many times, she could spell and read the word *banana*, and she could explain the best climate for growing bananas. But because she'd never held and unpeeled a banana, Maria could not identify it.

Vision enables children to organize and connect different experiences, connections that help make the most of those experiences. Children who are blind perform more poorly than sighted children do on cognitive tasks requiring comprehension or relating different items of information. Impaired or absent vision makes it difficult for children to understand the connections between experiences. "It is as though all the educational experiences of the blind child are kept in separate compartments" (Kingsley, 1997, p. 27).

Sighted children without other disabilities are constantly learning from their experiences and interactions with their environment. As they move about, sight provides a steady stream of detailed information about their environment and about relationships among things in that environment. Without any effort on their part or on the part of others, children with normal sight acquire great stores of useful knowledge from everyday experiences. Visual impairments, however, preclude most such incidental learning.

Ferrell (2006) described what two children, one with normal vision and one with limited vision, might learn from their everyday experiences with a family pet. When a child with normal vision hears a cat meow and sees its mouth open, he relates the sound to the cat. When he pets the cat, he feels soft fur and sees the cat's entire body simultaneously. A child with visual impairments hears the meow but cannot see what is producing it; he can feel its soft fur but can feel only part of the cat at a time. If he gets scratched, the paw comes out of and returns to nowhere. This makes learning even simple concepts such as "cats have tails" and "bananas are smooth" difficult.

Abstract concepts, analogies, and idiomatic expressions can be particularly difficult for children who cannot see. Jeanna Mora Dowse (2009), a teacher of students with visual impairments, described how an occupational therapist (OT) told a preschool child who was blind and taking his time walking to a therapy session to "Shake a leg!" The child stopped walking, shook his right leg, and continued walking as slowly as before. The OT then explained "shake a leg" means "move faster." There is no evidence these learning challenges restrict the potential of children with visual impairments. They do, however, magnify the importance of repeated, direct contact with concepts through nonvisual senses (Ferrell & Spungin, 2011).

Motor Development and Mobility

Blindness or severe visual impairment often leads to deficits in motor development and increased risk of falls (Sadowska et al., 2017). Vision plays four important functions in the acquisition of motor skills: (a) motivation, (b) spatial awareness, (c) protection, and (d) feedback (Houwen et al., 2009). A significant portion of the purposeful movements of fully sighted babies involves reaching for things they see. The child's efforts to grasp objects strengthen muscles and improve coordination, which in turn enables more effective movement. The absence of clear vision, however, reduces the baby's motivation to move. For a child who is blind, the world is no more interesting when sitting up and turning her head from side to side than it is when she is lying on the floor.

Vision provides critical information on the distance of objects and direction of movement. A child without clear vision may move less often because movements in the past have resulted in painful contact with the environment. The continuous feedback vision provides enables the child to correct errors and improve precision of movement. Together, the spatial

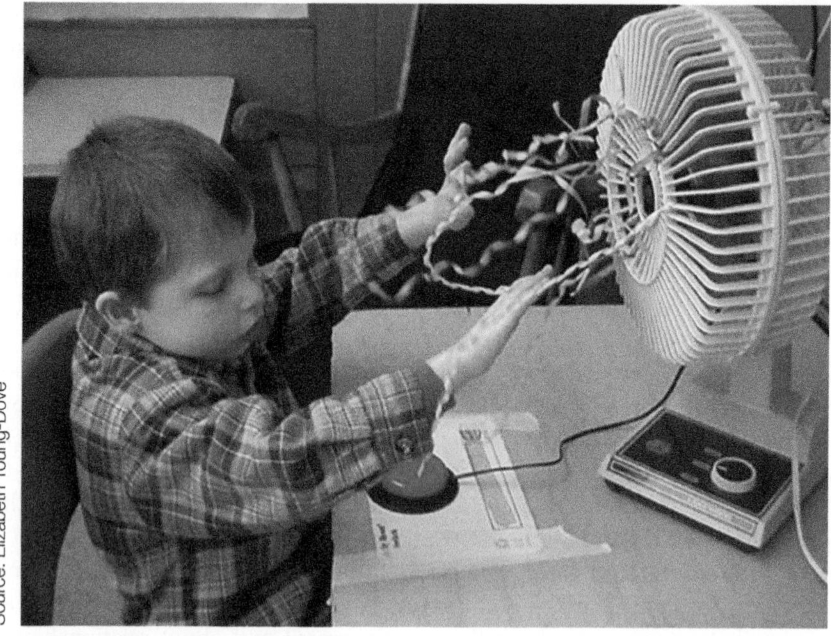

Source: Elizabeth Young-Dove

By pushing the button that turns the fan on and off, Morgan uses his sense of touch to learn the concept of cause and effect. Children with visual impairments rely on their nonvisual senses to learn.

awareness and feedback functions of vision enable a sighted child to observe and imitate the movements of others (Brambring, 2007; Haibach et al., 2014). Even children with low vision can have poorer motor skills than do children who are sighted (Haegele et al., 2015). Their gross motor skills, especially balance, are weak. They frequently cannot imitate motor activities and may be less likely to take risks moving through space (Bouchard & Tétreault, 2000). Parents' concern for their children's safety may also contribute to reduced opportunities for physical exploration and activity (M. E. Stuart et al., 2006).

Social Adjustment and Interaction

Compared with typically sighted children, children with visual impairments play and interact less during free time and are often delayed in the development of social skills (Celeste, 2006; Zebehazy & Smith, 2011). Although many adolescents with visual impairments have best friends, many also struggle with social isolation, must work harder than their sighted peers to make and maintain friendships, and are at higher risk for mental health challenges as adults (Augestad, 2017; Jessup et al., 2018; Lifshitz et al., 2007). Students with visual impairments may not be invited to participate in group activities such as going to a ball game or a movie because sighted peers assume they are not interested. Over time students with visual impairments and their sighted age mates have fewer and fewer shared experiences and common interests as bases for conversation, social interactions, and friendships.

Rosenblum (2000) identifies several issues influencing the limited social involvement of many adolescents with visual impairments. Because of the low incidence of the disability, many children with visual impairments cannot benefit from peers or adult role models who are experiencing the same challenges. Social isolation becomes particularly pronounced for many teenagers with visual impairments when sighted peers obtain drivers' licenses.

Another factor contributing to social difficulties is the inability to see and respond to the social signals of others, which reduces opportunities for reciprocal interactions (Campbell, 2007). During a conversation, for example, a student who is blind cannot see her conversation partner's gestures, facial expressions, and body language. This hampers the blind student's understanding of the conversation partner's message. Her failure to respond with socially appropriate eye contact, facial expressions, and gestures suggests lack of interest in her partner's communicative efforts and makes it less likely the individual will seek out her company in the future.

Some individuals with visual impairments engage in repetitive body movements or other behaviors such as body rocking, eye pressing and poking, hand flapping, and head weaving. These behaviors were traditionally referred to in the visual impairment literature as "blindisms" or "blind mannerisms" (Kingsley, 1997). *Stereotypic behavior* (stereotypy) is a more clearly defined term that is also more appropriate: Some sighted children exhibit such behaviors, and they do not occur among all children who are blind (Gense & Gense, 1994).

Although not usually harmful, stereotypic behavior can place a person with visual impairments at a great social disadvantage because these actions may call negative attention to the person. It is not known why many children with visual impairments engage in stereotypic behaviors, though the vestibular stimulation produced by the behaviors is a suspected source of reinforcement (Bak, 1999). Behavioral interventions such as self-monitoring and differential reinforcement of incompatible behaviors have helped individuals with visual impairments reduce stereotypic behaviors such as repetitive body rocking or head drooping during conversation (McAdam et al., 1993).

Many people who have lost their sight report the biggest difficulty socially is contending with attitudes and behavior of sighted people. Many people hold myths, misconceptions, and overgeneralizations about people who are blind (Garber & Huebner, 2017). These beliefs inhibit our ability to recognize those with visual impairments as individuals, each of whom has unique strengths, needs, dreams, and challenges.

Prevalence

Although the National Center for Health Statistics (2017) reported nearly 27 million Americans age 18 and older have trouble seeing, visual impairment requiring special education is a low-incidence disability. Children with visual impairments constitute a very small percentage of the school-age population—fewer than 2 children in 1000. Even when viewed as a percentage of the population of students who receive special education services, the prevalence of visual impairments is very small: Only about 1 in 250 school-age children with individualized education programs (IEPs) are served under the disability category of visual impairment. During the 2018–2019 school year, approximately 24,169 children age 6 to 21 years received special education services under the IDEA category visual impairments (U.S. Department of Education, 2020a).

Many students with visual impairments have one or more additional disabilities and are served and counted under other disability categories, such as deaf-blindness and multiple disabilities. Thus, the number of students with visual impairments is much larger than the data reported for IDEA. The American Printing House for the Blind (2018) reported that 64,634 children from birth through grade 12 were eligible for services for visual impairment in fiscal year 2019.

Types and Causes of Visual Impairments

Learning Outcome 10.2 Identify types and causes of visual impairments and explain why it is important for teachers to know about the types of visual impairments affecting children in their classrooms.

How We See

Effective vision requires proper functioning of three anatomical systems of the eye: the optical system, the muscular system, and the nervous system. Figure 10.2 shows a simplified diagram of the eye. The eye's optical system collects and focuses light energy reflected from objects in the visual field. As light passes through the eye, several structures bend, or refract, the light to produce a clear image. The light first hits the *cornea*, the curved transparent membrane that protects the eye (much as an outer crystal protects a watch face). It then passes through the *aqueous humor*, a watery liquid that fills the front chamber of the eye. Next the light passes through the *pupil*, a circular hole in the center of the colored *iris*; the pupil

FIGURE 10.2 Basic Anatomy of the Human Eye

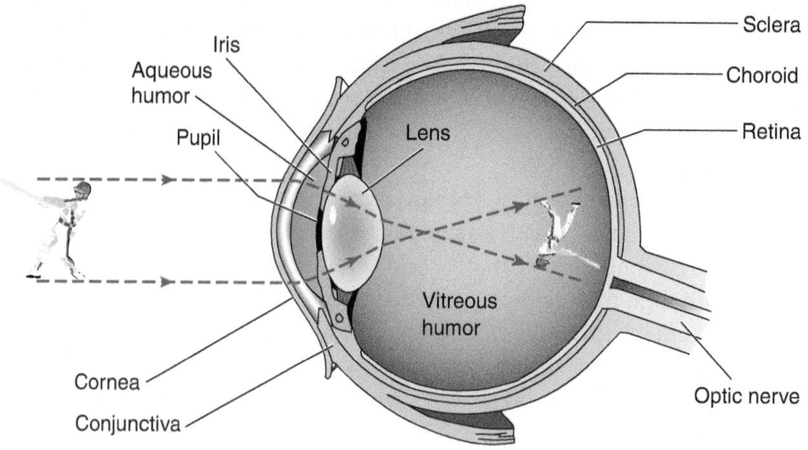

contracts or expands to regulate the amount of light entering the eye. The light then passes through the *lens*, a transparent, elastic structure. After light passes through the *vitreous humor*, a jellylike substance that fills most of the eye's interior, it reaches the innermost layer of the eye, the *retina*. This multilayered sheet of nerve tissue at the back of the eye is similar to the film in a camera: To see a clear image, the light rays must come to a precise focus on the retina.

The eye's muscular system enables **ocular motility**, the eye's ability to move. Six muscles attached to the outside of each eye enable it to search, track, converge, and fixate on images. These muscles also play a significant part in depth perception (**binocular vision**), the ability to fuse the separate images from each eye into a single, three-dimensional image. Inside the eye, tiny muscles adjust the shape of the lens, making it thicker or thinner, so the eye can bring objects at different distances into sharp focus.

The eye's nervous system converts light energy into electrical impulses and transmits that information to the brain, where it is processed into visual images. The retina consists of millions of light receptors called *cones* and *rods*. The cones enable detection of color and detail necessary for tasks such as reading and are located in the center of the retina and function best in good light. The rods, which are responsible for peripheral vision, detection of movement, and vision in dim light, are distributed around the periphery of the retina. The optic nerve carries the electrical messages from the cones and rods directly to the visual cortex at the base of the brain.

Causes of Visual Impairments

Damage or disturbances to any part of the eye's optical, muscular, or nervous systems can result in impaired vision. Causes of visual impairments are grouped into three broad categories: refractive errors, structural impairments, and cortical visual impairments.

REFRACTIVE ERRORS **Refraction** is the process of bending light rays when they pass from one transparent structure into another. As just described, the normal eye refracts, or bends, light rays so that a clear image falls directly on the retina. However, for many people—perhaps half the general population—the size and shape of the eye prevent the light rays from focusing clearly on the retina. In **myopia**, or nearsightedness, the eye is longer than normal from front to back, causing the image to fall in front of the retina instead of exactly on it. A child with myopia can see near objects clearly; but more distant objects, such as a chalkboard or a movie screen, are blurred or not seen at all (see Figure 10.1). The opposite of myopia is **hyperopia**, commonly called farsightedness. A *hyperopic eye* is shorter than normal, preventing the light rays from converging on the retina. A child with hyperopia has difficulty seeing near objects clearly but can focus well on more distant objects. Glasses or contact lenses can compensate for many refractive errors by changing the course of light rays to produce as clear a focus as possible.

STRUCTURAL IMPAIRMENTS Visual impairments can be caused by poor development of, damage to, or malfunction of one or more parts of the eye's optical or muscular systems. Cataracts and glaucoma are two of the numerous causes of visual impairment resulting from damage or disintegration of the eye itself. A **cataract** is cloudiness in the lens that blocks the light necessary for seeing clearly. **Glaucoma** is abnormally high pressure within the eye caused by disturbances or blockages of the fluids that normally circulate within the eye. Central vision and peripheral vision are impaired or lost entirely when the increased pressure damages the optic nerve (see Figure 10.1).

Dysfunction of the muscles that control and move the eyes can make it difficult or impossible for a child to see effectively. **Nystagmus**, a rapid, involuntary, back-and-forth movement of the eyes in a lateral, vertical, or rotary direction, can cause problems in focusing and reading. **Strabismus** is an inability to focus on the same object with both eyes because imbalance of the eye muscles creates an inward or outward deviation of one or both eyes. If left untreated, strabismus and other disorders of ocular motility can lead to permanent loss of vision.

CORTICAL VISUAL IMPAIRMENTS Some children with visual impairments have nothing wrong with their eyes. The term **cortical visual impairment (CVI)** refers to reduced visual functioning due to known or suspected damage to or malfunction of the parts of the brain that interpret visual information. Causes of CVI include insufficient oxygen at birth (anoxia), head injury, brain maldevelopment such as hydrocephalus, and infections of the central nervous system. Visual functioning may fluctuate depending on environment, lighting conditions, and activities. Some children with CVI use their peripheral vision, some are photophobic, some are attracted to bright light, and some gaze at lights or the sun.

Pearson eText
Video Example 10.2
Students with cortical visual impairment like Katrina benefit from a variety of high- and low-tech assistive devices.

Table 10.1 summarizes some of the most common types and causes of visual impairments. Although a teacher seldom needs detailed knowledge concerning the etiology of a student's visual impairment, understanding how the visual impairment affects the student's classroom performance is important. It is useful to know, for example, Traci's cataracts make it difficult for her to read under strong lights, Derek has only a small amount of central vision in his right eye, or Naoko will need to administer eye drops to relieve the pressure caused by her glaucoma before leaving on a class field trip.

Educational Approaches

Learning Outcome 10.3 Compare educational goals and instructional methods for children with low vision and children who are blind.

Educators have developed numerous specialized teaching methods and curriculum materials to overcome the obstacles to learning presented by blindness and low vision. Recent advances in technology have greatly increased access to the general education curriculum and academic success for students with visual impairments. As one high school student who is blind remarked, "By taking advantage of technology around me, I am able to have an education equal to my sighted peers" (Leigh & Barclay, 2000, p. 129). However, the education of students with visual impairments is a field with a rich history of more than 150 years, and today's developments were made possible by the contributions of many teachers and researchers (Geruschat & Corn, 2006; Moore, 2006). Figure 10.3 highlights key historical events and their implications for the education of students with visual impairments.

Specialized Instruction for Students Who Are Blind

Because they must frequently teach skills and concepts that sighted children acquire through vision, teachers of students who are blind must help their students gain as much information as possible through the nonvisual senses (Chen & Downing, 2006a, 2006b; Salisbury, 2008). For example, a child who is blind may hear a bird singing but gets no concrete idea of the bird itself from the sound alone. A teacher interested in teaching such a student about birds might plan a series of

TABLE 10.1 Types and causes of visual impairments

CONDITION	DEFINITION AND CAUSE	REMARKS AND IMPLICATIONS
Albinism	Lack of pigmentation in eyes, skin, and hair; results in moderate to severe visual impairment by reducing visual acuity and causing nystagmus; heredity	Children with albinism almost always have photophobia, making the eyes extremely sensitive to light; eye fatigue may occur during close work.
Amblyopia	Reduction in or loss of vision in the weaker eye from lack of use; caused by strabismus, unequal refractive errors, or opacity of the lens or cornea	Close work may result in eye fatigue, loss of place, or poor concentration; seating should favor the functional eye.
Astigmatism	Distorted or blurred vision caused by irregularities in the cornea or other surfaces of the eye that produce images on the retina not in equal focus (refractive error)	Loss of accommodation when objects are brought close to the face; avoid long periods of reading or close tasks that cause discomfort; child may have headaches and fluctuating vision.
Cataract	Blurred, distorted, or incomplete vision caused by cloudiness in the lens; most often the result of aging but also caused by injury, malnutrition, or rubella during pregnancy, glaucoma, retinitis pigmentosa, or heredity	Avoid glare of any kind; light source behind child; good contrast between print and paper; variation in near and distant tasks can prevent tiring.
Color deficiency or color blindness	Difficulty distinguishing certain colors; red–green confusion is most common; caused by absent or malformed cones, macular deficiency, or heredity	Usually not educationally significant; teach alternative ways to discriminate objects usually identified by color (e.g., tags for clothing colors, position of red and green on traffic lights).
Cortical visual impairment (CVI)	Impaired vision caused by damage to or malfunction of the visual cortex or optic nerve (or both); causes include anoxia, head injury, and infections of the central nervous system; many children with CVI have additional disabilities, such as cerebral palsy, seizure disorders, or intellectual disabilities	Visual functioning may fluctuate depending on lighting conditions and attention; vision usually does not deteriorate; improvement sometimes occurs over a period of time; some children with CVI use their peripheral vision; some are photophobic; some are attracted to bright light; may fail to blink at threatening motions; visual images should be simple and presented singly.
Diabetic retinopathy	Impaired vision as a result of hemorrhages and growth of new blood vessels in the area of the retina due to diabetes; a leading cause of blindness in adults	Provide good lighting and contrast; magnification; pressure to perform can affect blood glucose.
Glaucoma	Abnormally high pressure within the eye caused by disturbances or blockages of fluids that normally circulate within the eye; vision is impaired or lost entirely when increased pressure damages the retina and optic nerve	Fluctuations in visual performance may frustrate child; be alert to symptoms of pain; administer eye drops on schedule; child may be subjected to teasing because of bulging eyes.
Hyperopia (farsightedness)	Difficulty seeing near objects clearly but able to focus on distant objects; caused by a shorter than normal eye that prevents light rays from converging on the retina (refractive error)	Loss of accommodation when objects are brought close to the face; avoid long periods of reading or close tasks that cause discomfort.
Macular degeneration	Central area of the retina gradually deteriorates, causing loss of clear vision in the center of the visual field; common in older adults but fairly rare in children	Tasks such as reading and writing are difficult; prescribed low-vision aid or closed-circuit TV; provide good illumination; avoid glare.
Myopia (nearsightedness)	Distant objects are blurred or not seen at all but near objects are seen clearly; caused by an elongated eye that focuses images in front of the retina (refractive error)	Encourage child to wear prescribed glasses or contact lenses; for near tasks, child may be more comfortable working without glasses and bringing work close to face.
Nystagmus	Rapid, involuntary, back-and-forth movement of the eyes, which makes it difficult to focus on objects; when the two eyes cannot focus simultaneously, the brain avoids a double image by suppressing the visual input from one eye; the weaker eye (usually the one that turns inward or outward) can actually lose its ability to see; can occur on its own but is usually associated with other visual impairments	Close tasks for extended period can lead to fatigue; some children turn or tilt head to obtain the best focus; do not criticize this.
Retinitis pigmentosa (RP)	The most common genetic disease of the eye; causes gradual degeneration of the retina; first symptom is usually difficulty seeing at night followed by loss of peripheral vision; heredity	High illumination with no glare; contrasting visual field causes difficulties scanning and tracking, skills necessary for tasks such as reading; teach student to locate visual objects with systematic search grid; because RP is progressive, curriculum should include mobility training, especially at night, and braille training if the prognosis is loss of sight.
Retinopathy of prematurity (ROP)	Caused by administering high levels of oxygen to at-risk infants; when the infants are later removed from the oxygen-rich incubators, the change in oxygen levels can produce an abnormally dense growth of blood vessels and scar tissue in the eyes, leading to visual impairment and often total blindness	High illumination, magnifiers for close work; telescopes for distance viewing; child may have brain damage resulting in intellectual disability or autism spectrum disorder that require additional services.
Strabismus	Inability to focus on the same object with both eyes because of an inward or outward deviation of one or both eyes; caused by muscle imbalance; secondary to other visual impairments	Classroom seating should favor the stronger eye; some students may use one eye for distance tasks and the other for near tasks; frequent rest periods may be needed during close work; may need more time to adjust to unfamiliar visual tasks.

Sources: Adapted from American Foundation for the Blind (2020a, b); American Optometric Association (2020); Lighthouse International (2020); and Miller and Menacker (2013).

FIGURE 10.3 Key Historical Events in the Education and Treatment of People with Visual Impairments

DATE	EVENT/IMPLICATIONS
1784	Shocked at seeing people who were blind performing as jesters or begging on the streets of Paris, Victor Hauy resolved to teach them more dignified ways of earning a living. He started the first school for children who were blind. The success of Hauy's students influenced the establishment of other residential schools in Europe in the early 19th century .
1821	Samuel Gridley Howe founded the Perkins School for the Blind, the oldest and best-known residential school for students who are blind. Many methods and materials for teaching students with visual impairments were developed at Perkins. Anne Sullivan and her famous pupil, Helen Keller, spent several years at Perkins.
1829	Louis Braille, a student at a Paris school for children who were blind, published the first draft of a tactile method of reading. Braille's system of embossed six-dot cells proved the most efficient method of reading by touch and remains the primary means of literacy for the blind today.
1862	The Snellen chart was developed by a Dutch ophthalmologist. The chart provides a fast, standardized test of visual acuity and is still used today as a visual screening tool .
1900	The first public school class for children who were blind opened in Chicago.
1909/1913	The first classes for children with low vision began in Cleveland and Boston. Children with low vision were educated in special "sight-saving classes" in which all instruction was conducted orally.
1932	The Library of Congress made Talking Books available to any person who is legally blind.
1938	The first itinerant teaching program for children with visual impairments attending regular classrooms began in Oakland, California. This marked the beginning of the long and relatively successful history of including children with visual impairments in regular classrooms.
1940s–1950s	Thousands of children became blind or severely visually impaired by retinopathy of prematurity. Because residential schools could not accommodate the influx of visually impaired children, public school programs for students with visual impairments became more widely available in the 1950s and 1960s.
1944	Richard Hoover developed a system for teaching orientation and mobility (O&M) skills that featured a long white cane. This system and the "Hoover cane" became standard parts of the curriculum for students with visual impairments.
1951	The Perkins brailler was invented.
Mid-1960s	Natalie Barraga published research showing that children with low vision do not lose their remaining sight by using it and that visual functioning can be improved by use. Barraga's (1964, 1970) work was instrumental in ending the sight-saving classes attended by children with low vision for more than 50 years.
1970s	Development of the Kurzweil Reading Machine, the world's first text-to-speech optical scanning machine, provided access to print materials not available in braille, large-print, or recorded formats. The Kurzweil set the stage for a continuing explosion of technological advancements that have benefited the lives of many people with visual impairments.
1997	The Individuals with Disabilities Education Act mandated that O&M services be provided to any student with a disability who needs them.
1996/2004	The American Foundation for the Blind published/revised the "expanded core curriculum" of nonacademic skills needed by blind and visually impaired students for overall success in life (Hatlen, 2011).

activities that have the student touching birds of various species and manipulating related objects such as eggs, nests, and feathers. The student might assume responsibility for feeding a pet bird at home or in the classroom. Through such experiences, the child with visual impairments can gradually obtain a more thorough and accurate knowledge of birds than she could if her education were limited to reading books about birds, memorizing vocabulary, or feeling plastic models.

BRAILLE Braille is the primary means of literacy for people who are blind. **Braille** is a tactile system of reading and writing in which letters, words, numbers, and other systems are made from arrangements of raised dots (Figure 10.4). The Nemeth code consists of braille symbols for mathematical and scientific notation.

In some ways, braille is similar to the shorthand or stenography court reporters use. A set of 189 abbreviations, called *contractions,* saves space and permits faster reading and writing. For example, when the letter *r* stands by itself, it means *rather*. The word *myself* in braille is written *myf*. Frequently used words, such as *the, and, with,* and *for*, have their own special contractions. For example, the *and* symbol appears four times in the following sentence:

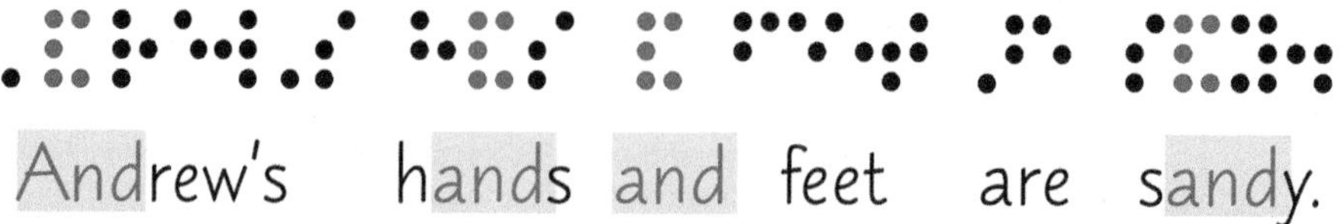

Students who are blind can read braille much more rapidly than they can read the raised letters of the standard alphabet. The speed of braille reading varies a great deal from student to student; however, it is usually much slower (about 100 words per minute for good braille readers) than reading print (Stanfa & Johnson, 2015). Most children who are blind are introduced to braille as preschoolers. Rather than have the child learn to write out every word, letter by letter, and later unlearn this approach, teachers introduce contractions early in the program (Wormsley, 2004). Of course, it is important for the child to eventually learn the correct spelling of words, even if not every letter appears in braille.

Children generally learn to write braille by using a **brailler**, a six-keyed mechanical device that somewhat resembles a typewriter. Although it usually takes several years for children to become thoroughly familiar with braille, it is no more difficult than learning to read print for sighted children. Koenig (2006) suggests that a child who says braille is difficult to read has probably heard an adult say so.

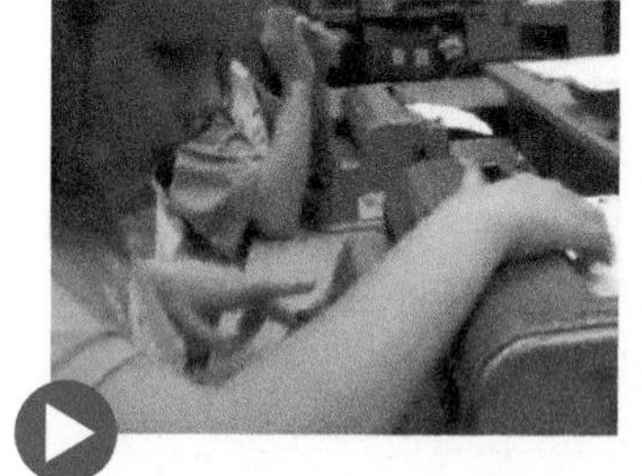

Pearson eText
Video Example 10.3
The brailler is a six-keyed device that punches raised braille dots on special paper.

Braille Technological Aids. Most braille books are large, expensive, and cumbersome. It can be difficult for students to retrieve information quickly when they must tactilely review many pages of braille books or notes. Technological developments have made braille more efficient, thus enabling students who are blind to function more independently in regular classrooms, universities, and employment settings.

BrailleNote, a portable device with a standard Perkins-style keyboard, can translate braille into synthesized speech or print, display downloaded books or text files in braille, and access Web pages, and it has calculator and calendar features. The Mountbatten Pro Brailler is an electronic brailler that is easier to use than the manual, mechanical brailler

FIGURE 10.4 The Braille System for Representing Numbers and Letters

The six dots of the braille cell are arranged and numbered thus: 1 4 / 2 5 / 3 6

The capital sign, dot 6, placed before a letter makes it a capital. The number sign, dots 3, 4, 5, 6, placed before a character makes it a figure and not a letter.

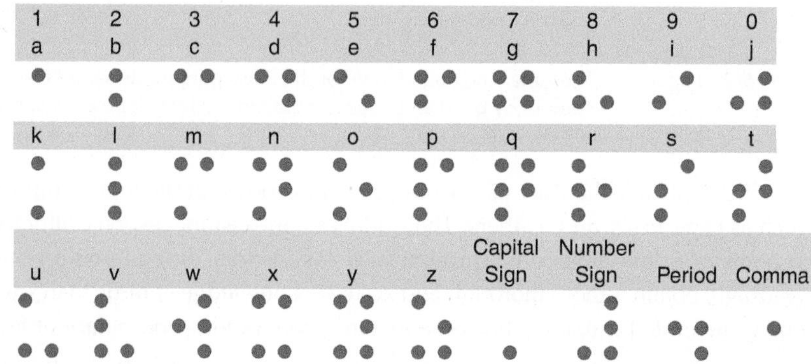

Source: National Library Service for the Blind and Physically Handicapped, Library of Congress, Washington, DC.

(Cooper & Nichols, 2007). Braille embossers print braille from digital text; some printers produce pages with both braille and print formats, enabling readers who are blind or sighted to use the same copy.

TACTILE AIDS AND MANIPULATIVES Manipulatives have long been recognized as effective tools for teaching beginning mathematics skills to elementary students. When using manipulatives such as Cuisenaire rods, sighted students use length and color to distinguish the various numerical values of the rods. Belcastro (1993) developed a set of rods that enables students who are blind to quickly identify different values by feeling the lengths and tactile markings associated with each. Other math manipulatives commonly used include braille math blocks, Digi-Blocks, and APH tools to enhance number system concepts, as well as Tack-Tiles® Braille Systems.

HLP13 Adapt curriculum tasks and materials for specific learning goals.

One mathematical aid for students who are blind is the Cranmer abacus. Long used in Japan, the abacus has been adapted to assist students who are blind in learning number concepts and making calculations. Manipulation of the abacus beads is particularly useful in counting, adding, and subtracting. Osterhaus (2011) provides detailed descriptions of materials and practical strategies for teaching math to students who are blind and visually impaired.

For more advanced mathematical functions, the student is likely to use the Speech-Plus talking calculator, a small electronic instrument that performs most of the operations of any standard calculator. It "talks" by voicing entries and results aloud and also presents them visually in digital form. This is only one of many instances in which the development of synthetic speech technology has helped people who are blind. Talking clocks and spelling aids are also available. Osterhaus (2011) provides detailed descriptions of materials and practical strategies for teaching math to students who are blind and visually impaired.

In science and social studies, several adaptations encourage students who are blind to use their tactile and auditory senses for firsthand manipulation and discovery (Chen & Downing, 2006a; Ross & Johnson, 2017; Wild & Koehler, 2017). Examples are embossed relief maps and diagrams, three-dimensional (3D) models, and electronic probes that give an audible signal in response to light. The SAVI/SELPH (Science Activities for the Visually Impaired/Science Enrichment for Learners with Physical Handicaps) projects at the University of California, Berkeley, have developed curricula with manipulative materials that enable students with visual impairments to participate in learning activities along with normally sighted students.

Content Extension 10.2

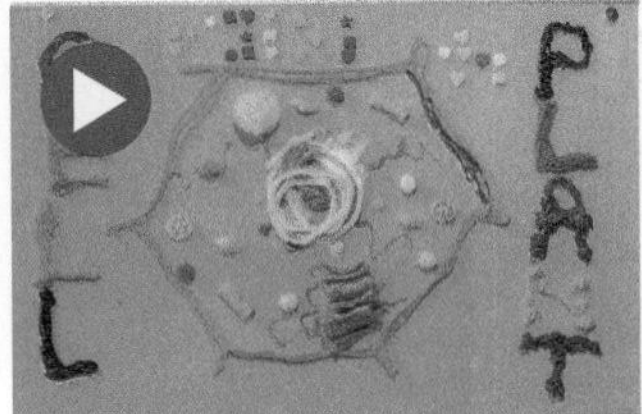

Tactile models of plant and animal cells made by Featured Teacher Cecelia Peirano's students.

Tactile books created by attaching objects to the pages of a simple and sturdy book can help young children who are blind or have severe visual impairments acquire book concepts and early literacy skills (Holbrook et al., 2017). Each page of a tactile book includes braille or print related to the artifacts on the page.

The ever-increasing sophistication and decreasing cost of 3D printers have ushered in an exciting way for teachers to obtain tactile books and models (Jo et al., 2016). The Tactile Picture Books Project at the University of Colorado is creating a library of tactile books that anyone with access to a 3D printer will be able to reproduce (Kim et al., 2014).

HLP19 Use assistive and instructional technologies.

TECHNOLOGICAL AIDS FOR READING PRINT Many students with visual impairments are auditory readers. Character recognition software converts printed or electronic text into spoken words. For example, the Kurzweil 1000 is a sophisticated computer-based reading system that uses an optical-character recognition system to scan and read text with synthetic speech. The user can regulate the speed, have the machine spell out words letter by letter if desired, and even choose from a variety of natural-sounding voices that can be modified to suit individual preferences.

Pearson eText
Video Example 10.4
Assistive technology enables children with visual impairments to enjoy a wide range of activities. https://www.youtube.com/watch?v=IcUNnnwFm4g

ACCESS TO COMPUTERS AND MOBILE DEVICES Assistive technology that provides access to personal computers and mobile devices has opened tremendous opportunities for education, employment, communication, and leisure enjoyment by individuals with visual impairments. These technologies include hardware and software that magnify screen images and speech-recognition software that enables the user to tell the computer what to do and software that converts text files to synthesized speech.

Pearson eText
Video Example 10.5
3D models help children with visual impairments understand science concepts.
https://www.youtube.com/watch?v=NpSQG6d2DsI

Keyboarding is an important means of communication among children who are blind and their sighted classmates and teachers and is also a useful skill for further education and employment. Instruction in keyboarding should begin as early as feasible in the child's school program. Handwriting is seldom taught to students who are totally blind, with the noteworthy exception of learning to sign one's name for tasks such as maintaining a bank account, registering to vote, and applying for a job.

Featured Teacher Cecelia Peirano underscores the importance of learning keyboarding: "Keyboarding is necessary for students to access technology; we start teaching keyboarding in first grade. Our students use the Talking Typer program available from the American Printing House for the Blind. It uses the touch typing method with both auditory and large-print capabilities. Don't use large-print, braille or adaptive keyboards unless the student has a physical disability. Students just need to feel the raised marks on the *f* and *j* keys on all standard keyboards. Because they don't try to look at the keyboard, my totally blind students are almost always my best typists."

Specialized Instruction for Students with Low Vision

What does a child with low vision actually see? It is difficult for us to know. Even when two children share the same cause of visual impairment, it is unlikely that they see things in exactly the same way. And each child may see things differently at different times (Guerette et al., 2011). Between 75% and 80% of school-age children enrolled in educational programs for students with visual impairments have some potentially useful vision. Learning by students with low vision need not be restricted to the nonvisual senses, and they generally learn to read print.

Curriculum development and instructional planning for children with low vision should be guided by the following basic premises about low vision and its effects on a person (Corn & Erin, 2010; Corn et al., 2004):

- *Children with congenital low vision view their visual experiences as whole.* Although it may be proper to speak of residual vision in reference to those who experience adventitious low vision, those with congenital low vision do not have a normal vision reference. They view the world with all of the vision they have ever had.
- *Children with low vision generally view the environment as stationary and clear.* Although there are exceptions, the belief that people with low vision live in an impressionistic world in which they are continuously wanting to clear the image is a misconception.
- *Low vision offers a different aesthetic experience.* Low vision may alter an aesthetic experience, but it does not necessarily produce a lesser one.
- *Vision is not always the most efficient or preferred method of functioning.* For some tasks, the use of vision alone or in combination with other senses may reduce one's ability to perform. For example, using vision may not be the most efficient method for determining how much salt has been poured on one's food.
- *Those who have low vision may develop a sense of visual beauty, enjoy their visual abilities, and use vision to learn.*

VISUAL EFFICIENCY *Functional vision* and **visual efficiency** are related terms denoting how well a person uses whatever vision he has (Corn & Lusk, 2010). Visual efficiency cannot be determined or predicted by clinical measures of visual acuity or visual field. Some children with severe visual impairments use the limited vision they have very capably. Other children with relatively minor visual impairments function poorly as visual learners; they may even behave as though they were blind.

Visual skills include awareness (visually sensing the presence of objects or movement), fixating or locating (aligning one or both eyes on a stationary object), scanning (searching for an object or person among multiple visual stimuli), tracking (visually following a moving object), gaze shifting (shifting fixation from one object to another), discriminating (visually determining differences between and among stimuli), visual sequencing (detecting the sequence in which objects appear, leave, or move in the visual field), and eye–hand coordination (Erin & Topor, 2010; Shaw & Trief, 2009). Students with visual impairments who have acquired these skills enjoy enhanced autonomy and choice in the range of activities they can perform independently in home, school, vocational, and community environments. The fundamental premises underlying the development of visual efficiency is that functional vision is learned behavior (and therefore teachable) and that children must be actively involved in using their own vision (Corn & Erin, 2010).

> HLP12 Systematically design instruction toward a specific learning goal.

Merely furnishing a classroom with attractive things for children to see is not sufficient. Without training, children with low vision may be unable to derive much meaningful information through vision. Forms may be perceived as vague masses and shapeless, indistinct blobs. Children with low vision need systematic training in visual recognition and discrimination to learn to use their visual impressions intelligently and effectively, to make sense out of what they see (Li, 2004; Lueck, 2004).

> HLP21 Teach students to maintain and generalize new learning across time and settings.

Functional vision instruction should occur within the context of meaningful activities throughout the student's daily schedule and not be isolated to "visual stimulation sessions" (Ferrell & Spungin, 2011) (see Figure 10.5).

OPTICAL DEVICES Many ophthalmologists and optometrists specialize in the assessment and treatment of low vision. A professional examination can help determine which types of optical aids, if any, can benefit a particular child with low vision. These special devices might include glasses and contact lenses, small handheld telescopes, and magnifiers placed on top of printed pages. Such aids cannot give normal vision to children with visual impairments but may help them perform better at certain tasks, such as reading small print or seeing distant objects.

Optical aids are usually specialized rather than all-purpose, and children whose vision is extremely limited are more likely to use monocular (one-eye) than binocular (two-eye) aids, especially for seeing things at a distance. Juanita might, for example, use her glasses for reading large print, a magnifier stand for reading smaller print, and a monocular telescope for viewing the chalkboard. A usual disadvantage of corrective lenses and magnifiers is the more powerful they are, the more they tend to distort or restrict the peripheral field of vision. Some field-widening lenses and devices are now available for students with limited visual fields. These include prisms and fish-eye lenses designed to make objects appear smaller so a greater area can be perceived on the unimpaired portions of a student's visual field.

Source: Katelyn Metzger/Pearson Allyn and Bacon/Merrill Education

Most optical aids are designed for special purposes. Brennan uses his monocular telescope to focus on distance targets for independent travel.

Closed-circuit television systems are used in some classrooms to enable students with low vision to read regular-sized printed materials. These systems usually include a sliding table on which a book is placed, a television camera with a zoom lens mounted above the book, and a television monitor nearby. The student can adjust the size, brightness, and contrast of the material and can select either an ordinary black-on-white image or a negative white-on-black image, which many students prefer. The teacher may also have a television monitor that lets him see the student's work without making repeated trips to the student's desk. A disadvantage of closed-circuit television systems is they are usually not portable, so a student who uses television as a primary reading medium is largely restricted to a specially equipped classroom or library. Many students with low vision use ZoomText, a computer program that enlarges and enhances images and text on their computer screens.

FIGURE 10.5 Embedding Opportunities to Use Functional Visual Skills Throughout the Day

The following are examples of embedding opportunities to use and develop functional visual skills throughout the daily schedule for Kevin, an 8-year-old boy with cortical visual impairment caused by a car accident when he was 3 years old. Immediately after the accident, he bumped into almost everything as if he were totally blind. Kevin now attends to and fixates on objects when asked and walks around obstacles most of the time but has difficulty locating items he needs or asked of him. Kevin likes to smile, especially at familiar faces, but tends to close his eyes when things do not seem to interest him.

PLACE AND TIME	ACTIVITY AND VISUAL SKILLS NEEDED
At home: breakfast	Kevin is asked to find a glass of orange juice. The juice is placed at the 10 o'clock position. After he masters this skill, the glass will be placed at a different location such as at the 2 o'clock position. Changing the position of the glass requires Kevin to "scan" for it rather than getting it from a fixed location. *Visual skills involved*: localization, visual attending, scanning, and eye–hand coordination
At school: second period math class	Kevin is working on counting tangible objects, such as coins, to 10 and one-to-one correspondence. When he counts coins accurately, he is rewarded with another coin. Increasing the contrast of the objects will make it easier for Kevin to find them. Quarters will be placed on a dark piece of construction paper and the pennies on the light-colored desktop. *Visual skills involved*: localization, visual attending, shift attention, scanning, and eye–hand coordination (while he pushes each coin to the side as he counts)
Community: grocery store	While grocery shopping, Kevin is brought to the cereal aisle and asked to find his favorites. *Visual skills involved*: localization, visual attending, and scanning
Community: orientation and mobility lesson in residential area	While riding in the car, the instructor encourages Kevin to describe what he observes (e.g., other passing vehicles, pedestrians). When traveling on the sidewalk, the instructor asks him to talk about what he sees (e.g., a stop sign, a fence, a flower bed). *Visual skills involved*: localization, visual attending, scanning, and tracking

Source: Courtesy of Alicia Li, Department of Special Education, Eastern Michigan University.

Recent advances in computer and optical technologies have led to the development of augmented reality or virtual reality devices (Lahav et al., 2015). These lightweight, head-mounted devices track the position of the user's head and project the desired images onto beam-splitting optics that allow the user to see an overlay or superimposed image on the environment (Feiner, 2002). One augmented reality system for people with low vision, called Nomad, uses a high-resolution laser to project an image directly onto the user's retina. Studies have shown that Nomad can function as a substitute computer monitor (Kleweno et al., 2001) and users can read print with the device (Goodrich et al., 2004). More recently, electronic smart glasses (e.g., eSight) have begun making their way to the marketplace.

READING PRINT Students with low vision use three basic approaches for reading print: (a) approach magnification (reducing the distance between the eye and the page of print from 40 cm to 5 cm results in 8× magnification), (b) lenses (optical devices), and (c) large print. Many books and other materials are available in large print for children with low vision. The American Printing House for the Blind produces books in 18-point type. Some states and other organizations produce large-type materials; but the size and style of the print fonts, spacing, paper, and quality of production vary widely. The sentence you are reading now is set in 10-point type. Here are four commonly used large-print sizes:

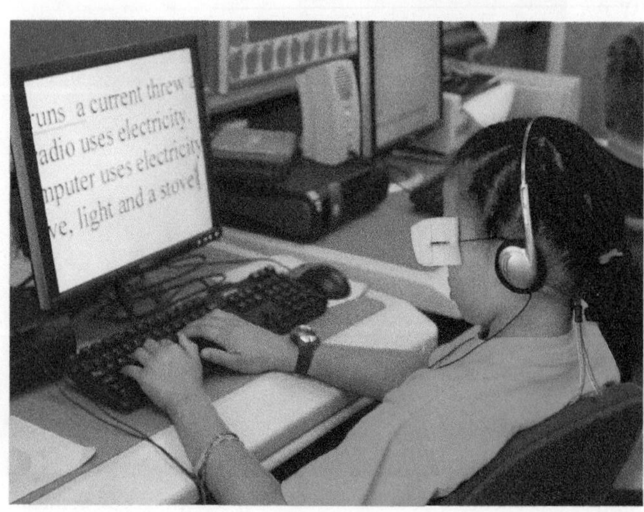

Source: Katelyn Metzger/Pearson Allyn and Bacon/Merrill Education

Many students with visual impairments benefit from software that enlarges print and images.

This is 14-point type.

This is 18-point type.

This is 20-point type.

This is 24-point type.

Although print size is an important variable, other equally important factors to consider are the print quality of the material, the font or typeface, the contrast between print and page, the spacing between lines, and the illumination of the setting in which the child reads (Griffin et al., 2002; Russell-Minda et al., 2007). Educators generally agree that a child with visual impairments should use the smallest print size that she can read comfortably. A child may be able to transfer from large print to smaller print as reading efficiency increases, just as most normally sighted children do. Figure 10.6 compares advantages and disadvantages of large-print materials and optical devices.

Pearson eText
Video Example 10.6
Featured Teacher Cecelia Peirano's students use various strategies and tools to access text during reading instruction.

Most children with low vision learn to read regular-sized print with or without the use of optical aids. This makes a much wider variety of materials available and eliminates the added cost of obtaining large-print books or enlarging texts with special duplicating machines. Additionally, regular-sized print books are easier to store and carry around than are large-print books. Some children with visual impairments are dual-media learners, who learn to use both print and braille simultaneously (Lusk & Corn, 2006a, 2006b).

Teachers can accommodate the slower reading rates of most children with low vision by (a) providing 1½ to 2 times as much time as sighted children need for reading, (b) ensuring sufficient time to study and using auditory reading aids such as Talking Books or text-to-speech computer software if time is not available, and (c) allowing extra time on tests (Gompel et al., 2004).

CLASSROOM ADAPTATIONS Minor classroom adaptations, such as proper lighting, can be very important for students with low vision. Although most classrooms have adequate lighting, adjustable lamps and dimmer switches are helpful for some children. Willings (2020) details lighting arrangements helpful to students with low vision. Many students benefit from desks with adjustable or tilting tops so they can read and write at close range without leaning over and casting a shadow. Encouraging children to experiment with lighting will help them find arrangements that work best for them

FIGURE 10.6 Advantages and Disadvantages of Large-Print Materials and Optical Devices for Readers with Low Vision

LARGE-PRINT MATERIALS	OPTICAL DEVICES
Advantages	**Advantages**
• Little or no instruction is needed to use a large-print book or other materials • A low vision clinical evaluation is not needed • Students carry large-print books like other students carry books in their classes • Digital text can be enlarged to optimal font size for individual readers • Funds for large-print books come from school districts that may require parental or other funding for optical devices	• Access to regular print materials in and outside the classroom (e.g., magazines, menus, labels, price tags) • Lower cost per student than large-print materials • Lighter and more portable than large-print books • Always at hand; no ordering or waiting for production or availability • Users have access to distant print and objects, such as chalkboards, signs, and people • Support transition to adult life when most reading material is available in regular size print
Disadvantages	**Disadvantages**
• Because fewer words can be seen at once, more difficult to read with a smooth sweep of eye movements • Imperfect print enlarged by photocopy often fuzzy • Many large-print books only produced in black and white • Fractions, captions, diagrams, maps, and other graphics may be hard to read when smaller than 18-point type • Size and weight make can make large-print books difficult to handle, fit in desks or lockers, and carry about • Not as readily available after the school years • Dependence on large print may reduce student's ability to use regular print independently	• Prescription of an optical device requires clinical evaluation • Funding for clinical evaluation and optical device must be obtained • Instruction in proper use of the optical devices is needed • The cosmetics of optical devices may cause self-consciousness • User must tolerate any optical problems associated with the optics of devices (e.g., limited field, loss of contrast)

Source: Adapted from Corn and Ryser (1989); Swenson (2013); and Willings (2015).

(Sticken & Kapperman, 2010). Writing paper should have a dull finish to reduce glare; an off-white color such as buff or ivory is generally better than white. Worksheets photocopied on colored paper can be difficult for students with low vision to use; if needed, an instructional assistant or a classmate can first go over the worksheet with a dark pen or marker. Some teachers have found it helpful to give chairs with wheels to students with low vision so they can easily move around the chalkboard area or other places in the classroom where instruction is taking place without constantly getting up and down. Teachers can make many other modifications using common sense and considering the needs of individual students. See *Teaching & Learning,* "Setting Up a Classroom for Students with Visual Impairments."

HLP13 Adapt curriculum tasks and materials for specific learning goals.

Expanded Core Curriculum

Learning Outcome 10.4 Define *expanded core curriculum* and explain its importance for children with visual impairments.

In addition to communication and sensory skills such as reading and writing braille, functional vision skills, and assistive technology, the *expanded core curriculum* for students with visual impairments includes orientation and mobility, listening skills, social interaction skills, independent living skills, recreation and leisure skills, and career education (Allman et al., 2014).

ORIENTATION AND MOBILITY *Orientation* is knowing where you are, where you are going, and how to get there by interpreting information from the environment. *Mobility* is moving safely and efficiently from one point to another. Although the two sets of skills are complementary, orientation and mobility are not the same. A person can know where he is but not be able to move safely in that environment, and a person may be mobile but become disoriented or lost.

Orientation and mobility (O&M) instruction is considered a related service by IDEA and is included in the IEPs of virtually all children with significant visual impairments. O&M specialists have developed many specific techniques (e.g., trailing, squaring off, using arms as bumpers) and mobility devices (e.g., a shopping cart, a suitcase on wheels) to teach students with visual impairments to understand their environment and maneuver through it safely and effectively (Griffin-Shirley & Trusty, 2017; Jacobson, 2013).

HLP7 Establish a consistent, organized, and respectful learning environment.

TEACHING & LEARNING

Setting Up a Classroom for Students with Visual Impairments

Ms. Milton has just found out that two students with visual disabilities will be joining her class. Evan is blind, and Emily has low vision. Their IEPs say they should be seated in the front of the room. Emily needs a larger desk for equipment and access to an electrical outlet. Ms. Milton had already put all of the students' desks in groups because she wants her students to do a lot of group work this year.

Earlier this morning, a deliveryman arrived with boxes of equipment from the special education department. Looking at this stack of strange devices, Ms. Milton realizes she doesn't even know the names of most of this equipment, let alone how to use it. Ms. Milton wonders what resources she can consult to learn about this equipment and how to set up her classroom to safely and effectively meet Evan and Emily's needs. To find out what Ms. Milton learned, click on the link and complete the tutorial.

http://iris.peabody.vanderbilt.edu/module/v01-clearview/#content

Source: The IRIS Center, Peabody College at Vanderbilt University and Claremont Graduate University.

For most students, more time and effort are spent on orientation training than on learning specific mobility techniques. It is extremely important that from an early age, children with visual impairments learn basic concepts that will familiarize them with their own bodies and their surroundings. For example, they must learn that the place where the leg bends is called a "knee" and that rooms have walls, doors, windows, corners, and ceilings. Perla and O'Donnell (2004) stress the importance of systematically teaching students to respond to orientation and mobility obstacles and puzzles as problem-solving opportunities so they will not have to depend on others every time they find themselves in a novel environment.

Cane Skills. The long cane is the most widely used device by adults with severe visual impairments who travel independently. The traveler does not tap the cane but sweeps it lightly in an arc while walking to gain information about the path ahead (Kim & Emerson, 2014). Properly used, the cane serves as both a bumper and a probe. It acts as a bumper by protecting the body from obstacles such as parking meters and doors; it is also a probe to detect in advance things such as drop-offs or changes in travel surface (e.g., from grass to concrete or from a rug to a wooden floor).

Pearson eText
Video Example 10.7
Orientation and mobility instructors help children learn how to use a long cane to navigate their environment.

Even though mastery of cane skills can do much to increase a person's independence and self-esteem, cane use requires physical effort and poses certain disadvantages (Gitlin et al., 1997). Canes cannot detect overhanging obstacles such as tree branches and provide only fragmentary information about the environment, particularly if the person who is blind is in new or unfamiliar surroundings.

Preschool children benefit from the services of an O&M specialist, but there is disagreement over which, if any, mobility device is most suitable for initial use by very young children. Professionals recognize the long cane's benefits of increased protection and confidence while traveling but question whether preschoolers can handle the motor and conceptual demands of long cane use. These concerns have led to the development of a variety of alternative mobility devices, including modified and smaller canes such as the Connecticut precane, kiddie canes, and canes with T-bar handles (American Printing House for the Blind, 2020).

Guide Dogs. About 2% of people with visual impairments travel with the aid of guide dogs (Guiding Eyes for the Blind, 2019). Similar to a cane traveler, a guide dog user must have good O&M skills to select a route and be aware of the environment. The dog wears a special harness and has been trained to follow several verbal commands, provide protection from obstacles, and ensure the traveler's safety. Guide dogs are especially helpful when a person must travel complicated or unpredictable routes, as in large cities. Several weeks of intensive training at special guide dog agencies are required before the person and the dog can work together effectively (Guerette & Zabihaylo, 2010). Guide dogs are not usually available to children younger than 16 years of age or to people with multiple disabilities. Young children, however, should have exposure to and positive experiences with dogs so they are comfortable with them and can make informed choices later about the possibilities of working with a guide dog.

Although owning a guide dog is a major responsibility and sometimes inconvenient, many owners report increased confidence and independence in traveling and say their dogs often serve as icebreakers for interactions with sighted people (Lane et al., 2016). However, guide dogs are not pets but working companions for their owners, and sighted people should not pet a guide dog without first obtaining the owner's permission or take hold of the dog's harness because this might confuse the dog and the owner.

Sighted Guides. Most people who are blind find it necessary to rely occasionally on the assistance of others. The **sighted guide technique** is a simple method of helping a person with visual impairments to travel:

- When offering assistance to a person who is blind, speak in a normal tone of voice and ask, "May I help you?" This helps the person locate you.
- Do not grab the person's arm or body. Permit him to take your arm.

- The person with visual impairment should lightly grasp the sighted person's arm just above the elbow and walk half a step behind in a natural manner. Young children might hold on to the index finger or pinky of an adult sighted guide.
- The sighted person should walk at a normal pace, describing curbs or other obstacles and hesitating slightly before going up or down. Never pull or push a person who is blind.
- Do not try to push a person who is blind into a chair. Simply place his hand on the back of the chair, and the person will seat himself.

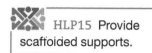

HLP15 Provide scaffolded supports.

When students with visual impairments are in regular classrooms, it may be a good idea for one of the students and the O&M specialist to demonstrate the sighted guide technique to classmates. To promote independent travel, however, overreliance on the sighted guide technique should be discouraged after the student has learned to get around the classroom and the school.

Electronic Travel Aids. A variety of electronic travel aids facilitate the orientation and mobility of individuals with visual impairments. The laser beam cane converts infrared light into sound as the light beam strikes objects in the traveler's path. Different levels of vibration in the cane signal relative proximity to an obstacle. Other electronic travel aids are designed for use in conjunction with a standard cane or guide dog. The Mowat Sensor is a flashlight-sized device that bounces ultrasound off objects and gives the traveler information about the distance and location of obstacles through changes in vibration. The SonicGuide, which is worn on the head, converts reflections of ultrasound into sounds of varied pitch, amplitude, and tone that enable the traveler to determine distance, direction, and characteristics of objects in the environment.

Recent research has developed accessible and affordable global positioning system (GPS) technologies and other way-finding products for people with visual impairments that can announce present location, interpret traffic signals, read street signs, give distance and direction information, and more (Marston et al., 2007; Ponchillia et al., 2007).

Whatever the preferred method of travel, most students with visual impairments learn to negotiate familiar places, such as school and home, on their own. Many students with visual impairments can benefit from learning to use a systematic method for obtaining travel information and assistance with street crossing. Good orientation and mobility skills have many positive effects. A child with visual impairments who can travel independently is likely to develop more physical and social skills and more self-confidence than will a child who must continually depend on other people to get around. Good travel skills also expand a student's opportunities for employment and independent living (Cmar et al., 2018; Wolffe & Kelly, 2011). See *Transition: Next Year Is Now,* "High-Tech Tools for Independence."

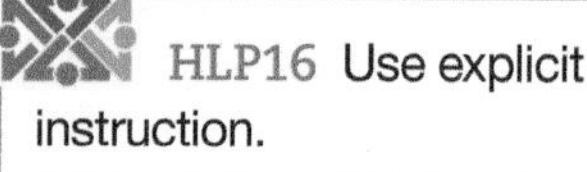
HLP16 Use explicit instruction.

LISTENING SKILLS Children with visual impairments, especially those who are blind, must obtain an enormous amount of information by listening. Vision is thought to be the coordinating sense, and it has been estimated that 80% of information received by a normally sighted person comes through the visual channel (Arter, 1997). Children who are blind must use other senses, predominately touch and hearing, to contact and comprehend their environment. A widely held misconception is that people who are blind automatically develop a better sense of hearing to compensate for their loss of sight. Children with visual impairments do not have a super sense of hearing, nor do they necessarily listen better than their normally sighted peers do. It is more accurate to say that, through proper instruction and experiences, children with visual impairments learn to use their hearing more efficiently (Koenig, 2006).

The systematic development of listening skills is a crucial component of the educational program of every child with visual impairments. Listening is not the same thing as hearing; it is possible to hear a sound without understanding it. Listening involves being aware of sounds, discriminating differences in sounds, identifying the source of sounds, and attaching meaning to sounds (Ferrell & Spungin, 2011).

Transition: Next Year Is Now

High-Tech Tools for Independence

Fortunately, we live in an age in which technology advances are making it feasible for people with visual impairments to live more independently than ever. Teachers of students with visual impairments should start introducing children to these tools early and explicitly teach students how to use them as they start moving toward transition to adult roles.

Tools for Getting Around Town

Individuals with visual impairments who have effective tools for helping them get out of their houses and into the community will have more opportunities for work and community engagement. Indeed, those with high levels of self-efficacy related to transportation are more likely to be employed (Cmar et al., 2018). Soundscape, BlindSquare, and Ariadne are examples of GPS-enabled apps available to help people with visual impairments navigate from location to location. Some of these apps give turn-by-turn directions, descriptions of landmarks and street names, and other auditory cues to help users know where they are and where they are headed. Individuals with visual impairments may also find public transportation apps helpful as well as apps that allow them to access on-demand transportation networks, such as Lyft or Uber. Navigating in unfamiliar indoor environments can be challenging as well. Clew (http://www.clewapp.org/) is an app that allows users to retrace their paths to help them return to starting locations with voice directions and haptic feedback.

Tools for Daily Living

Ordinary daily living skills, such as shopping, cooking, and self-care, can be challenging for individuals with visual impairments. Smartphone apps, such as Be My Eyes (Kristensen & Wilberg, 2015) and BeSpecular (BeSpecular, 2016), enable blind people to request assistance with daily living tasks from a network of volunteers who have downloaded the app. A person uses video or photos to show volunteers what they need help with. For instance, a person may enter a request for help identifying the expiration date on a carton of milk or color coordination on an outfit. The app confirms if a volunteer is available and creates a connection between the two. The sighted helper describes what the blind person is filming, and they solve the problem by working together (e.g., "Now I see the carton. It says sell by June 14."). Seeing AI is an "intelligent camera app" (https://www.microsoft.com/en-us/seeing-ai/) that can read text (including handwriting), describe colors, recognize people, read bar codes, and identify currency. Other types of apps that can help individuals with visual impairments with their daily living tasks include grocery store apps, mobile banking apps, digital assistants (e.g., "Alexa"), on-demand food delivery apps (e.g., DoorDash), and apps to help locate items (e.g., TrackR, Tile).

Featured Teacher Cecelia Peirano recommends the following steps when introducing a new high-tech tool to students with visual impairments:

1. Engage your student with a problem or challenge. (How can you travel to the store independently? What if you were being dropped off at the front of a building and needed to find your way to a specific room and back?)
2. Discuss the specific need or purpose and introduce the app that will fill that need.
3. Have the students explore the app by running their fingers over it and checking it out independently.
4. Take the students step by step through the app.
5. Give students specific tasks to practice using the app.
6. Have students practice using the app in smaller to larger environments (class, school, neighborhood, community, downtown).
7. Compare and contrast it to other apps and their capabilities.
8. Give scenarios for the students to select the best app.
9. Cecelia's colleague, Dan Kelley, adds that it is important to teach students to be careful with information shared via apps. For example, if you want to use Be My Eyes for help with reading mail, you need to be sure you're not inadvertently sharing credit card numbers!

HLP19 Use assistive and instructional technologies.

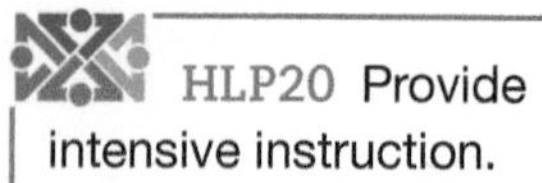 HLP20 Provide intensive instruction.

Learning-to-listen activities can take an almost unlimited variety of forms. Young children, for example, might learn to discriminate between sounds that are near and far, loud and soft, high pitched and low pitched. A teacher might introduce a new word into a sentence and ask the child to identify it or ask children to clap each time a key word is repeated. In the "shopping game," a child begins by saying, "I went to the store and I bought ______." Each player repeats the whole list of items purchased by previous students and then adds his or her own item to the list (Arter, 1997). It is important to arrange the rules of such games so that children who fail to remember the list are not eliminated, which would result in fewer opportunities to practice for the children with the weakest listening and auditory memory skills. Older students might practice higher order listening skills such as identifying important details in the presence of distracting background noises, differentiating between fact and opinion, or responding to verbal analogies (Barclay, 2012).

Students with visual impairments, particularly in high school, make frequent use of recorded materials. In addition to using recordings of texts, lectures, and class discussions, students with visual impairments and their teachers can obtain on a free-loan basis thousands of recorded books and magazines and playback equipment through the Library of Congress, the American Printing House for the Blind, the Canadian National Institute for the Blind, Recordings for the Blind, and various other organizations. A listener can process auditory information at more than twice the speed of the average oral reading rate of about 120 words per minute (Aldrich & Parkin, 1989). With practice, students can listen to accelerated and compressed speech at speeds of up to 275 words per minute without affecting comprehension (Arter, 1997). The Book Port Plus, a portable player/recorder available from the American Printing House for the Blind (2016), lets the user adjust the playback rate and sound quality of recorded text and includes a speech-compression feature that electronically shortens the length of selected words.

FUNCTIONAL LIFE SKILLS A higher percentage of students with *visual impairments* graduate from high school than students served under any other disability category (U.S. Department of Education, 2020c). But some special educators have expressed concern that efforts to help students with visual impairments match the academic achievement of their sighted age mates too often comes at the expense of sufficient opportunities to learn daily living and career skills (Lohmeier, 2005; Sacks et al., 1998). Specific instruction and ongoing supports should be provided to ensure that students with visual impairments learn skills such as cooking, personal hygiene and grooming, shopping, financial management, transportation, and recreational activities that are requisites for an independent and enjoyable adulthood (Corn & Erin, 2000; Kaufman, 2000; Rosenblum, 2000). Teaching certain life skills is especially important in the time of COVID. People with visual impairments are at increased risk because they have to touch more surfaces to learn and navigate, depend on others making social distancing difficult, rely on public transportation, and may have comorbid health impairments that increase the probability of developing symptoms (United States Association of Blind Athletes, 2020).

HLP19 Use assistive and instructional technologies.

Individuals with disabilities are increasingly using assistive technology to maximize their independence and quality of life. A variety of self-operated prompting technologies can help them enjoy independence in domestic, community, and employment settings (Cullen & Alber-Morgan, 2015). To find out how three secondary students challenged by blindness and intellectual disabilities used a self-operated auditory prompting system to prepare some of their favorite snack foods, see *Teaching & Learning*, "I Made It Myself, and It's Good!" But keep in mind, technology only works when it is being used, as Featured Teacher Cecelia Peirano advises: "Teachers need to stay current on what devices would benefit each student, get training to use it, and then teach them to use it. I can't tell you how many students have transferred into our school with equipment they've had for years that has been stored in a closet."

TEACHING & LEARNING

"I Made It Myself, and It's Good!": Increasing Independence with Self-Operated Auditory Prompts

Why Use Self-Operated Auditory Prompts? Steve, Lisa, and Carl wanted to cook, but intellectual disabilities made remembering complicated tasks, such as recipes, extremely difficult. Picture cookbooks or color-coded recipes, used successfully with learners with intellectual disabilities (e.g., Book et al., 1990), were not an option. Steve, Lisa, and Carl also had no functional vision or braille skills. Because their teacher wanted them to function as independently as possible as adults, her challenge was finding a method that would work not only on directly trained recipes but for new recipes they might encounter as adults in the future. Based on previous research, she decided to create and evaluate the effectiveness of a portable auditory prompting device.

How Can Teachers Use Self-Operated Auditory Prompts (SOAPS)? To determine how to set up SOAPS, begin by task analyzing the recipes, starting with some of the students' favorite snack foods. Next, use a phone or tablet to audio record each step (e.g., "Open the bag of cake mix by tearing it at the tab") and record a "beep" at the end of each direction.

Next, teach all students how to operate the device and have them practice starting and stopping it each time they hear a beep. (For tips on how to teach students with visual impairments to use new technology, see Featured Teacher Cecelia Peirano's suggestions in *Transition: Next Year Is Now,* "High-Tech Tools for Independence.") Instruction for each recipe step should include verbal praise for correct responses and least-to-most prompting (e.g., verbal, physical, and hand-over-hand guidance) following errors.

Provide several practice trials each school day until the student can independently perform all steps. Depending on the difficulty of the task and the individual student, the number of trials needed to master a recipe might range from 10 to 40. If students are making the same types of errors repeatedly (e.g., spilling liquids), be sure to provide supplemental instruction (e.g., teaching them to use fingers to feel how much liquid they are pouring).

The ultimate evaluation of any cook is in the food he makes. Does it taste good? An error on any one of several crucial steps in the 27-step task analysis for making microwave cake (e.g., not stirring the egg into the batter) would be a cake no one would want to eat. Before training, none of Steve's attempts with the recipes could be eaten, but all of his posttraining attempts were edible. After learning three trained recipes, Steve used SOAPS to successfully prepare five untrained recipes on 12 of 14 tries. Lisa and Carl enjoyed similar results. The self-operated feature of the system puts the students in control, thereby increasing the probability of independent functioning and level of self-determination. As Carl remarked when giving a piece of microwave cake he had just made to his girlfriend, "I made it myself, and it's good!"

Additional suggestions for creating SOAPS can be found in Savage (2014).

Source: Lisa, Carl, and Steve's story based on "Teaching young adults with developmental disabilities and visual impairments to use tape-recorded recipes: Acquisition, generalization, and maintenance of cooking skills" by S. A. Trask-Tyler, T. A., Grossi, & W. L. Heward. *Journal of Behavioral Education,* 1994, Vol. 4, pp. 283–311.

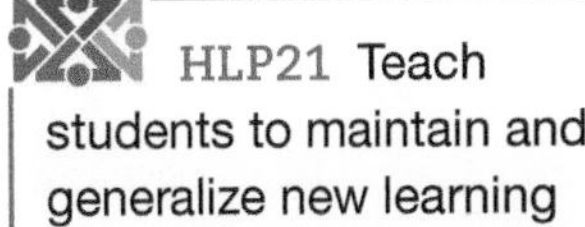
HLP21 Teach students to maintain and generalize new learning across time and settings.

Pearson eText Video Example 10.8
Accommodations such as a "beep ball" enable individuals who are blind to enjoy a range of recreation and leisure activities. https://www.youtube.com/watch?v=yJjxI04NVI4&list=PLONBNiNoSE7D29EWEZniS7R_fUnKb2fra&index=1

Placement Options

Learning Outcome 10.5 Explain how the educational placement of students with visual impairments can affect their opportunities to learn the expanded core curriculum of nonacademic skills necessary for overall success in life.

In the past, most children with severe visual impairments were educated in residential schools. Today, however, the vast majority of students with visual impairments are educated in public schools: 68% of all school-age students with visual impairments receive their education in regular classrooms, 12% attend resource rooms for part of each day, and 9% are served in separate classrooms (U.S. Department of Education, 2020a). The remaining 11% receive their education in other placements, including residential schools.

Inclusive Classroom and Itinerant Teacher Model

Students with visual impairments were among the first students with disabilities to be included in regular classrooms. Although Cruickshank (1986) suggested that "the blind child is perhaps the easiest exceptional child to integrate into a regular grade in the public schools" (p. 104), successful inclusion requires a full program of individualized special education and related services.

Most students with visual impairments in regular classrooms receive support from itinerant teacher-consultants, sometimes called *vision specialists*. These specially trained teachers may be employed by the school district; a nearby residential school; or a regional, state, or provincial education agency. Although their roles and caseloads vary widely, most itinerant teacher-consultants have some or all of the following responsibilities (Olmstead, 2005):

- Help identify the child's current level of performance, learning goals and objectives, and need for related services as a member of the IEP team.
- Collaborate with the general education teacher on curricular, instructional, and environmental modifications according to the child's individual needs.
  See *Teaching & Learning*, "Setting Up a Classroom for Students with Visual Impairments."
- Provide direct instruction on compensatory skills (e.g., braille, listening, keyboarding).
- Obtain or prepare specialized learning materials (e.g., math manipulatives).
- Adapt reading assignments and text-based curriculum material into braille, large-print, or audio-recorded form.
- Initiate and maintain contact with various agencies that provide services for children with visual impairments.
- Make referrals for low-vision aids and services, and train students in the use and care of low-vision aids.
- Provide information to and consult with parents and other school personnel.

> HLP13 Adapt curriculum tasks and materials for specific learning goals.

> HLP1 Collaborate with professionals to increase student success.

The itinerant teacher-consultant may or may not provide instruction in O&M. Some schools, particularly in rural areas, employ dually certified teachers who are also O&M specialists. Other schools employ one teacher for educational support and another for O&M training. Students on an itinerant teacher's caseload may range from infants to young adults and may include children who are blind, those with low vision, and those with multiple disabilities.

The amount of time the itinerant teacher-consultant or resource room teacher spends with a student who attends classes in the regular classroom varies considerably. Some students may be seen every day because they require a great deal of specialized assistance. Others may be seen weekly, monthly, or even less frequently because they can function well in the regular classroom with less support.

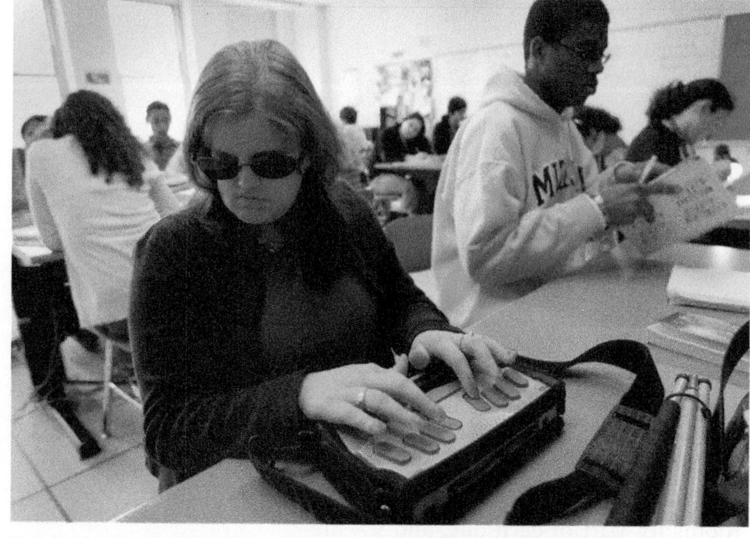

Source: Kuni Takahashi/MCT/Newscom

Success in the regular classroom for students with visual impairments depends on collaboration between the vision specialist and classroom teacher.

For inclusion to succeed, a child with visual impairments needs a skilled and supportive general education teacher. This was underscored by a study that asked adolescents to assess the impact of visual impairments on their lives (Rosenblum, 2000). All 10 students in the study attended public school regular classrooms for at least 50% of the school day. Several students reported that a general education teacher made it difficult for them to use disability-specific skills such as braille or computerized speech output in the classroom. ("It took him about a quarter to get the stuff [tests and worksheets] to the braillist in the first place" [p. 439].) Other participants reported that insensitive teachers caused them to feel humiliation and frustration about having a visual impairment. ("The science teacher wanted me to identify rocks by a visual method, and I told her I can't. She goes, 'Well, you're going to have to if you

FIGURE 10.7 Supporting Students with Visual Impairments in the Regular Classroom

Although each student with a visual impairment is unique and requires a specially designed set of accommodations and modifications to meet her own academic and social goals, teachers should follow some fundamental guidelines when working with any student who relies on nonvisual senses for communication and learning. Using the following tips and techniques will increase the effectiveness of your communication with students who have visual impairments and encourage and promote their confidence and independence.

Communicate with Clarity and Respect

- Always state the name of the student you are speaking to in the classroom. The student with a visual impairment will not notice eye contact.
- Indefinite pronouns such as *this*, *that* and *there* can be confusing to students with visual impairments. It is better to name specific items, events, or people.
- Individuals with visual impairments frequently make idiomatic references to sight, and it is okay for their teachers and peers to do so also: e.g., "Do you see what I mean?" or "Let's take a look at this next sentence."
- Always give a verbal warning when you are about to hand something to a student with visual impairments. This avoids unnecessary surprises and helps the student respond efficiently.
- Include specific spatial references when giving your student directions. For example, telling the student, "The book is on your left," or "The desk is 10 feet in front of you," is better than saying, "It's over there," or "It's near the table."
- When writing or drawing on the board, describe your actions verbally in a manner useful for all students in the class. Be sure not to talk down to the student with a visual impairment.
- Introduce yourself by name when meeting your student outside the classroom. Do not assume that he will recognize your voice, and do not ask, "Guess who this is?"
- When you are about to leave the student's vicinity, tell him that you are going.
- When you need to physically show your student how to do something, use the hand-under-hand technique. Have the student place her hands on top of yours so she can feel the movement of your hands. This is usually more effective than placing your hands over the student's hands.

Expect and Enable Independence

- If students are expected to perform jobs or responsibilities in your classroom, be sure also to assign a meaningful job to your students with visual impairments.
- Allow students with visual impairments time to obtain and put away materials. If a student had to use glue and scissors for an activity, make sure she returns those items to their proper places. Although it is often much easier to get and put away materials for students with visual impairments, it is critical that they learn to become self-sufficient and pick up after themselves.
- Peers are often the most effective and efficient teachers of social skills. Cooperative groups are a great way for students with visual impairments to learn important social skills.
- Always make safety a priority, but do not overprotect students with visual impairments. Hands-on experiences are the best way for a student to learn new concepts.
- Provide real-life experiences whenever possible. When on a school field trip, give the student with a visual impairment sufficient time to explore her environment.

Source: Adapted from Jeanna Mora Dowse (2009), who worked for many years as an itinerant teacher of students with visual impairments in two school districts in Apache County, Arizona.

want to get a good grade'" [p. 439].) Several other participants reported that general education teachers treated them like younger children. ("The teachers talk to me differently like I'm more of a 6 year old rather than a 13 year old" [p. 43].) Figure 10.7 provides tips for supporting a student with visual impairments in the regular classroom.

Some vision professionals resist noncategorical special education programs for students with visual impairments. They argue it is unrealistic to expect general education teachers or teachers trained in other areas of special education to be competent in specialized techniques such as braille, O&M, and visual efficiency (American Foundation for the Blind, 2004). The Council for Exceptional Children's Division of Visual Impairments recognizes a student's need for instruction in the expanded core curriculum may require different educational placements at various times during the student's school years (Huebner et al., 2006).

The following suggestions for teachers of students with low vision are from The Vision Team, a group of specialists in visual impairment who work with general education teachers in 13 school districts in Hennepin County, Minnesota.

- Using the eyes does not harm them. The more children use their eyes, the greater their efficiency will be.
- Holding printed material close to the eyes may be the best way for the child with low vision to see. It will not harm the eyes.
- Although eyes cannot be strained from use, the eyes of a child with low vision may tire more quickly. A change of focus or activity helps.

- Copying is often a problem for the child with low vision. The child may need a shortened assignment or more time to do classwork.
- It is helpful if the teacher verbalizes as much as possible while writing on the chalkboard or using the overhead projector.
- One of the most important things a child with low vision learns in school is to accept the responsibility of seeking help when necessary rather than waiting for someone to offer help.
- In evaluating quality of work and applying discipline, the teacher best helps the child with low vision by using the same standards that he uses with other children.

Residential Schools

About 3% of school-age children with visual impairments attend residential schools (U.S. Department of Education, 2020a). The current population of residential schools consists largely of children with visual impairments with additional disabilities, such as intellectual disabilities, hearing impairment, behavioral disorders, and cerebral palsy. (See Chapter 12 for information on children with multiple disabilities, including those who are deaf-blind.) Some parents cannot care for their children adequately at home; others prefer the greater concentration of specialized personnel, facilities, and services that a residential school usually offers.

Parents and educators who support residential schools for children with visual impairments frequently point to the leadership such schools have provided over a long period and their range of services. These supporters argue that a residential school can be the least restrictive environment for some students with visual impairments and multiple disabilities. Among the advantages cited are specialized curriculum and equipment, participation in extracurricular activities, individualized instruction, small classes, and improved self-esteem.

As with any other point in the continuum of educational settings, placement in a residential school should not be regarded as permanent. Many children with visual impairments move from residential schools into public schools (or vice versa) as their needs change. Some students in residential schools attend nearby public schools for part of the school day. Most residential schools encourage parent involvement and have recreational programs that bring students with visual impairments into contact with sighted peers. Independent living skills and vocational training are important parts of the program at virtually all residential schools.

Residential schools also play an important role in outreach, including training teachers of children with visual impairments (McMahon, 2014) and serving as resource centers for instructional materials. Some residential schools offer short-term training to students with visual impairments who attend regular public schools. One example is a summer workshop emphasizing braille, mobility, and vocational training.

Featured Teacher Cecelia Peirano teaches at a residential school and explains, "My students are both day students from the surrounding area and residential students from across the state. They participate in rigorous academics and state tests as well as special programs and technology specifically for students with visual impairments. When making placement decisions, parents and school districts must consider where each student's individual needs can best be met."

Pearson eText
Video Example 10.9
To foster independence, teachers of students with visual impairments should encourage self-awareness and promote self-advocacy.
https://www.youtube.com/watch?v=oWUo9AMaS2A

Equal Opportunity and the Right to Be Different

Similar to other groups of individuals with disabilities, people with visual impairments have become increasingly aware of their rights as citizens and consumers. They are fighting discrimination based on their disabilities and experiencing the benefits of self-determination (Agran et al., 2007; Koestler, 2004). Many people—even some special educators who work with students with visual impairments—underestimate their students' capacities and deny them a full range of occupational and personal choices. The future should bring a shift away from some of the vocations and settings in which people with visual impairments have traditionally worked (e.g., piano tuning, rehabilitation counseling) in favor of a more varied range of employment opportunities.

In describing the importance of the expanded core curriculum, Hatlen (2000) tells of a prominent blind woman who, when asked, "What is it that blind people want from society?" replied, "The opportunity to be equal and the right to be different."

What did this woman mean by two remarks that seem diametrically opposite? Perhaps she meant that print and braille are equal, but very different; that the need for independent travel is similar for sighted and blind persons, but the skills are learned very differently by blind people; and that concepts and learning that occur for sighted people in a natural, spontaneous manner require different learning experiences for blind persons. Perhaps she was emphasizing that blind persons should have the opportunity to learn the same knowledge and skills as sighted people, but that their manner of learning will be different (p. 779).

ADVICE FROM THE FEATURED TEACHER by Cecelia Peirano

Supporting Your Students with Visual Impairments

Communicate

Source: Cecelia Peirano

- Be specific when communicating with your students, their parents, and professionals.
- Use the student's name when you are speaking only to him or her, directional words to give specific locations, and descriptive language to avoid confusion. For example, "Seth, please place your science assignment in the basket to the left of the pencil sharpener" will give you better results than "Put your paper over there."
- When meeting with aides, teachers, or other professionals, give specific instructions—written, if possible—about what your student needs. That way if the meeting is interrupted or cut short, you will have left clear directions for what your student needs in your absence.

Prepare Well Ahead of Time

- Be prepared with materials ahead of time so your students spend class time as active participants.
- Encourage other staff to get all materials to you ahead of time so they can be put into the appropriate format, such as braille, large print, or an auditory file. You will also have to gather any manipulatives, make tactile graphics, and review any material that will need additional explanation. This might be the case if students are being introduced to Southeast Asia or the periodic table.
- Schedule meeting times that work for the staff involved. They will be more likely to have a quick conference to pass on lesson plans or information that helps in preparing material for your student if they know exactly when you're coming.
- Try to agree on specific schedules and responsibilities while collaborating with the entire staff involved with your student. This will avoid confusion if the student will be missing class for O&M or other special services and has assignments to make up. A good resource is *Classroom Collaboration* (Hudson, 1997), which is written specifically for working with students with visual impairments.

Let Students Struggle a Bit

- Provide your students with the skills and confidence to be independent.
- Expect your students to have the same responsibilities as other students and provide them with the tools to do so successfully. For example, if they need to take the lunch count, help them set up a notetaker file to prepare the information needed.
- Students learn new skills by trying difficult tasks. Sit on your hands if you need to; don't reach in and do it for them. As they discover new methods, provide just enough help that they can then continue on in the process.
- Find ways to increase social interactions with peers. Peer interaction and group projects can be great for all types of social skills and confidence building because sometimes you need to hear it from a good friend!

Key Terms and Concepts

binocular vision
braille
brailler
cataract
cortical visual impairment
field of vision
glaucoma
hyperopia
legal blindness
low vision
myopia
nystagmus
ocular motility
orientation and mobility (O&M)
partially sighted
refraction
sighted guide technique
strabismus
tunnel vision
visual acuity
visual efficiency
visual impairment

Summary

Definitions

- Legal blindness is defined as visual acuity of 20/200 or less in the better eye after correction with glasses or contact lenses or a restricted field of vision of 20 degrees or less.
- An educational definition classifies students with visual impairments based on the extent to which they use vision and auditory or tactile means for learning.
- A student who is totally blind receives no useful information through the sense of vision and must use tactile, auditory, and other nonvisual senses for all learning.
- A child who is functionally blind has so little vision that she learns primarily through the auditory and tactile senses; however, she may be able to use her limited vision to supplement the information her other senses perceive.
- A child with low vision uses vision as a primary means of learning.
- The age at onset of a visual impairment affects a child's educational and emotional needs.

Characteristics

- Children with severe visual impairments do not benefit from incidental learning that normally sighted children acquire in everyday experiences and interactions with the environment.
- Visual impairment often leads to delays or deficits in motor development.
- Some students with visual impairments experience social isolation and difficulties in social interactions because of limited common experiences with sighted peers; inability to see and use eye contact, facial expressions, and gestures during conversations; or stereotypic behaviors.
- The behavior and attitudes of sighted people can be unnecessary barriers to the social participation of individuals with visual impairments.

Prevalence

- Visual impairment is a low-incidence disability affecting fewer than 2 of every 1000 children in the school-age population. About half of all students with visual impairments have additional disabilities.

Types and Causes of Visual Impairment

- The eye collects light reflected from objects and focuses the objects' image on the retina. The optic nerve transmits the image to the visual cortex of the brain. Difficulty with any part of this process can cause vision problems.
- Refractive errors mean the size and shape of the eye prevent the light rays from focusing clearly on the retina.
- Structural impairments are visual impairments caused by poor development of, damage to, or malfunction of one or more parts of the eye's optical or muscular systems.
- Cortical visual impairment (CVI) refers to decreased vision or blindness caused by damage to or malfunction of the parts of the brain that interpret visual information.

Educational Approaches

- Braille—a tactile system of reading and writing in which letters, words, numbers, and other systems are made from arrangements of embossed six-dot cells—is the primary means of literacy for students who are blind.
- Students who are blind may also use special equipment to access standard print through touch, reading machines, and prerecorded materials.
- Children with low vision should be taught to use their vision as much and as efficiently as possible.
- Students with low vision use three basic methods for reading print: magnification, optical devices, and large print.

- Students who are blind or have severe visual impairments need instruction in orientation (knowing where they are, where they are going, and how to get there) and mobility (moving safely and efficiently from one point to another).
- Systematic development of listening skills is an important component of the educational program of every child with visual impairments.
- The curriculum for students with visual impairments should also include systematic instruction in functional living skills such as cooking, personal hygiene and grooming, shopping, financial management, transportation, and recreational activities.

Placement Options

- Three of four children with visual impairments spend at least part of each school day in regular classrooms with sighted peers.
- In many districts, a specially trained itinerant vision specialist provides support for students with visual impairments and their general education teachers.
- Some large school districts have resource room programs for students with visual impairments.
- About 3% of children with visual impairments, especially those with other disabilities, attend residential schools.

Chapter 11

Attention-Deficit/Hyperactivity Disorder, Health Impairments, and Physical Disabilities

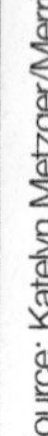
Source: Katelyn Metzger/Merrill Education

Learning Outcomes

After reading this chapter and completing the embedded activities, you should be able to

11.1 Define attention-deficit/hyperactivity disorder (ADHD) and describe the most common treatment options for ADHD.

11.2 Define other health impairments and orthopedic impairments, and explain why the number of children served under these categories of the Individuals with Disabilities Education Act is smaller than the actual number of children who have health impairments or physical disabilities.

11.3 List and describe the types and causes of health conditions and physical impairments seen most frequently in school-age children.

11.4 Discuss the importance of a "parallel curriculum" for students with health impairments or physical disabilities.

11.5 Explain why the continuum of educational services and placement options is especially critical for students with health impairments or physical disabilities.

Featured Teacher

Dave Martinez

Cherokee County School District, Canton, GA

Source: Amy Aenchbacher

I teach physical education to students with disabilities from elementary through high school. I also help general physical educators include students with disabilities in their classes. As an adapted physical educator, I am responsible for designing individualized physical education programs that align with state and national standards. I strive to create programs that promote involvement in community recreation and leisure activities and lead students to active and healthy lifestyles as adults. An inclusive afterschool program for students with orthopedic impairments created with a colleague is one example.

Isaiah, a former student of mine, received special education services in a self-contained class. He enjoyed being physically active and participated in my inclusive physical education class and the Special Olympics program I coordinated. Isaiah committed to the 8 weeks of training required of all Special Olympians. His favorite sports were bowling, swimming, and basketball. I remember how proud Isaiah's parents were when he won a bronze medal for swimming. One day his mother told me Isaiah wanted a letter jacket just like the high school football players. This inspired me to convince our school district's athletic department to give Special Olympians the opportunity to earn a varsity letter from their respective high schools.

I've worked with students with a range of significant disabilities and challenges. In every case, I'm reminded of an important lesson learned in my training program: My students can do anything; they may just need to do it differently. I am constantly amazed at what my students are able to do when the multidisciplinary team comes together and the environment is arranged for success.

Education, Teaching Credentials, and Experience

- *B.S. and M. A., physical education/adapted physical activity, University of South Florida, 1994 and 1998; Ed.S., coaching pedagogy/physical education, Valdosta State University, 2019*
- *Certifications: Georgia health and physical education (PK–12); adapted physical education specialist (National Consortium for Physical Education for Individuals with Disabilities); adaptive recreation and sports specialist (Blaze Sports); certified inclusion fitness trainer (American College of Sports Medicine & National Center on Health, Physical Activity, and Disability)*
- *26 years of teaching experience*

Content Extension 11.1

Cherokee County Special Olympics

Varsity Letter Requirements

Cherokee County Special Olympics is committed to the highest ideals of sport and expects all athletes to honor sports and Special Olympics. To be eligible to receive a varsity letter, Special Olympics athletes must participate in a Special Olympics sport for a minimum of two seasons while in high school and exhibit the following:

Sportsmanship

- Practice positive sports behaviors
- Respect other athletes, coaches, and officials
- Refrain from using bad language
- Refrain from insulting other persons
- Refrain from fighting with other athletes, coaches, volunteers or staff

Training and Competition

- Attend practices and competitions
- Learn and follow the rules of the sport
- Obey and respect coaches and game officials
- Participate to best ability while training, divisioning, and competing

Personal Responsibilities

- Refrain from making inappropriate or unwanted physical, verbal or sexual advances on others
- Refrain from using alcohol, smoking or taking illegal drugs while representing Cherokee County Special Olympics at training sessions, competition or during Games
- Refrain from taking drugs for the purpose of improving performance
- Obey all laws and Cherokee County Special Olympics rules

Varsity letters are presented to eligible athletes during the Special Olympics sports banquet.

Featured Teacher Dave's flyer about earning a varsity letter through Special Olympics.

CHILDREN WITH ATTENTION-DEFICIT/HYPERACTIVITY DISORDER, health impairments, and physical disabilities are an extremely varied population. Their disabilities may be mild, moderate, or severe. Some have highly visible health conditions or impairments; others appear no different from the typical child. Some children with special health care needs are extremely restricted in their activities and intellectual functioning; others have no major limitations on what they can do and learn. Children may have a single impairment or a combination of disabilities. They may have lived with a disability since birth or have acquired it recently. Some disabilities are always present; others occur only from time to time. Over an extended period, the degree of disability may increase, decrease, or remain about the same.

Natalie has undergone long periods of hospitalization and finds it difficult to keep up with her academic work. Gary takes medication that controls his seizures most of the time, but it also tends to make him drowsy in class. Janella tires easily and attends school only 3 hours per day. Ken does his schoolwork in a specially designed chair that helps him sit more comfortably in the classroom.

As you can see, the students whose special education needs we consider in this chapter have a great many individual differences. Although general statements about some physical disabilities and health conditions are appropriate, a host of variables determines the effects on the child and his educational needs. These variables include the degree and severity of the impairment, age of onset, and environmental context. Thus, general information and suggested guidelines form the basic content of this chapter.

Attention-Deficit/Hyperactivity Disorder

Learning Outcome 11.1 Define attention-deficit/hyperactivity disorder (ADHD) and describe the most common treatment options for ADHD.

Although everyone has difficulty attending at times (attention deficit), and we all sometimes engage in high rates of purposeless or inappropriate movement (hyperactivity), a child who consistently exhibits these behavioral traits may be diagnosed with **attention-deficit/hyperactivity disorder (ADHD)**. For children with ADHD, their inability to stay on task, impulsive behavior, and fidgeting impairs their learning and increases unsatisfactory interactions with others.

Although the last decade of the 20th century witnessed an explosion of interest in ADHD, historical references to the symptoms that are diagnosed as ADHD today suggest that such children have been with us for centuries (Barkley, 2015; Conners, 2000). The first published account of the disorder in the medical or scientific literature appeared in 1902, when British physician George Still described Still's disease. Still believed children who were restless and exhibited problems maintaining attention had a "defect of moral control" that he presumed to be the result of brain injury or dysfunction. Over the years, researchers have used a variety of terms to refer to this combination of behavioral symptoms: *postencephalitic disorder* in the 1920s, *brain damage syndrome* in the 1940s, *minimal brain dysfunction* in the 1960s, and *hyperkinetic impulse disorder of children* in the 1970s (Mather & Goldstein, 2001). Because medical science has found no clear-cut evidence of brain damage, emphasis in defining and diagnosing the condition has focused and relied on the description and identification of a combination of behavioral symptoms.

Definition and Diagnosis

"The essential feature of attention-deficit/hyperactivity disorder (ADHD) is a persistent pattern of inattention and/or hyperactivity-impulsivity that interferes with functioning or development" (American Psychiatric Association, 2013, p. 61). Symptoms include the following:

- *Inattention*—not attending to details, difficulty sustaining attention to tasks or activities, does not seem to listen, not following through on instructions (e.g., starts a task but soon gets sidetracked), difficulty organizing tasks and activities (e.g., work is messy and disorganized), dislikes tasks that require sustained mental effort, frequently loses things, easily distracted, often forgetful
- *Hyperactivity and impulsivity*—fidgeting, restlessness, runs about or climbs on furniture, often excessively loud or noisy, often "on the go" as if "driven by a motor," talks excessively, blurts out answers, difficulty waiting to take his or her turn, interrupts others, acts without thinking (e.g., starts a task without reading or listening to instructions), impatient, rushes through tasks, has difficulty resisting temptations. (Adapted from American Psychiatric Association, 2013.)

To be diagnosed with ADHD, a child must have exhibited six or more of these symptoms for at least 6 months in two or more environments, with the onset of several symptoms by age 12 years. These symptoms must interfere with the child's functioning in social, academic, or occupational tasks and not be the result of another mental disorder (e.g., mood disorder, anxiety disorder).

Depending on the constellation of symptoms, one of three ADHD subtypes is assigned: combined presentation (inattention and hyperactivity/impulsivity), predominantly inattentive presentation, or predominantly hyperactivity-impulsive presentation. Approximately 55% of children with ADHD have been diagnosed with the combined type, 27% with the predominantly inattentive subtype, and 18% with the hyperactive-impulsive subtype (Wilens et al., 2002).

Deficits in executive function have been hypothesized as a primary characteristic of children with ADHD (Barkley, 2015; Brocki et al., 2010). Executive function consists of "those self-directed actions needed to choose goals and to create, enact, and sustain actions toward those goals, or more simply as self-regulation to achieve goals" (Barkley, 2012, p. 60). Major components of executive function are working memory (i.e., ability to hold and use information while engaging in an activity), mental flexibility (i.e., ability to adapt to changing circumstances), and self-control (i.e., ability to resist impulses) (Center on the Developing Child, 2020).

The diagnostic criteria for ADHD are highly subjective. For example, what is the basis for deciding whether a child is "often 'on the go'"? And how does one determine whether a child who avoids or dislikes schoolwork or homework does so because of an attention deficit as opposed to one of many other possible reasons? A child regarded by one physician as not having ADHD may very well be diagnosed by another as having it. Because no valid, independent test for ADHD exists, diagnosis rests on information obtained from parents and teachers.

A checklist parents and teachers may use as a starting point for determining whether or not a child has ADHD [https://www.cdc.gov/ncbddd/adhd/documents/adhdfactsheetenglish.pdf].

Eligibility for Special Education

Students with ADHD can be served under the other health impairment category if the outcome of the disorder is a "heightened alertness to environmental stimuli that results in limited alertness with respect to the educational environment that adversely affects academic performance" (20 USC §1401 [2004], 20 *CFR* §300.8[c][9]). However, many children with ADHD are served under other disability categories. Researchers estimate 16% to 31% of children identified with learning disabilities and 25% to 56% of those identified with emotional disturbance also have ADHD (Xin et al., 2014).

Many children with ADHD who are not served under the Individuals with Disabilities Education Act (IDEA) receive services under Section 504 of the Rehabilitation Act. As discussed in Chapter 1, Section 504 is a civil rights law that provides certain protections for people with disabilities. Under Section 504, schools may be required to develop and implement accommodation plans to help students with ADHD succeed in the regular classroom. Accommodation plans ("504 Plans") often include such adaptations as extended time on tests, preferential seating, additional teacher monitoring, shortened assignments, tasks broken into smaller chunks, and monitoring effects of medication on the child's behavior in school.

HLP13 Adapt curriculum tasks and materials for specific learning goals.

Prevalence

Although the American Psychiatric Association (2013) estimates the prevalence of ADHD at 5% of school-age children, the Centers for Disease Control and Prevention (CDC, 2020c) reports that 9.4% of children have been diagnosed with ADHD, and some researchers have found that up to 15% of the school population meets criteria for ADHD (Rowland et al., 2015). Boys are diagnosed with ADHD at a rate more than two times than that of girls (CDC, 2020a). A typical classroom has one or two children either diagnosed with ADHD or presenting the problems typically associated with ADHD.

An analysis of how diagnostic criteria, prevalence, and treatment of ADHD have changed over time [http://www.cdc.gov/ncbddd/adhd/documents/timeline.pdf].

A series of rulings by the U.S. Department of Education in the 1990s made students with ADHD eligible for special education under IDEA's other health impairments (OHI) category. As a result, child count data reported by the states for the OHI category increased greatly. A large proportion of the children who receive special education services under the OHI category are diagnosed with ADHD.

Academic Achievement and Comorbidity with Other Disabilities

Most children with ADHD struggle in the classroom. Compared with their peers, children with ADHD score lower on achievement tests in reading, mathematics, spelling, and writing; earn lower grades in school; and have more difficulty with skills that support academic achievement, such as organization and planning (DuPaul & Langberg, 2015). Many children with ADHD also have other disabilities. For instance, about 6 in 10 children with ADHD have at least one other mental, emotional, or behavioral disorder (CDC, 2020a). Many children with learning disabilities, intellectual disabilities, autism spectrum disorders, tic disorders, and obsessive-compulsive disorder are identified as having ADHD (American Psychiatric Association, 2013; Rowland et al., 2015; Schnoes et al., 2006).

Causes

The causes of ADHD are not well understood. Similar patterns of behavior leading to the diagnoses of ADHD in two different children will likely be caused by completely different factors (Gresham, 2002; Maag & Reid, 1994). Although many consider ADHD a neurological disorder, no clear and consistent evidence links brain damage or dysfunction to the behavioral symptoms of ADHD. Research using neuroimaging technologies has shown some individuals with ADHD have structural or biochemical differences in their brains (e.g., Cherkasova & Hechtman, 2009; Sowell et al., 2003). However, not all individuals diagnosed with ADHD have brains that appear different from those of individuals without ADHD. And some people without ADHD have brain structures similar to those with ADHD.

Genetic factors may place individuals at a greater than normal risk for ADHD (Willcutt et al., 2000); ADHD tends to run in families (Barkley, 2017), and it is associated with a wide range of genetic disorders and diseases (Levy et al., 2006). For example, individuals with fragile X syndrome, Turner syndrome, and Williams syndrome (see Chapter 4) frequently have attention and impulsivity problems. Symptoms of ADHD are also associated with conditions such as fetal alcohol syndrome, prenatal exposure to cocaine, and lead poisoning.

Treatment

The two most widely used treatment approaches for children with ADHD are behaviorally based interventions and medication.

HLP7 Provide a consistent, organized, and respectful learning environment.

BEHAVIORALLY BASED INTERVENTIONS Interventions derived from applied behavior analysis provide teachers and parents with practical strategies for teaching and living with children with ADHD (DuPaul et al., 2016). These methods include positive reinforcement for on-task behavior, modifying assignments and instructional activities to promote success, and systematically teaching self-control. Teacher-administered interventions for children with ADHD include restructuring the environment (e.g., seating the child close to the teacher and breaking assignments into small, manageable chunks), providing frequent opportunities to actively respond within ongoing instruction, and providing differential consequences for behavior (e.g., positive reinforcement such as praise and tokens for appropriate behavior, ignoring inappropriate behavior, and time-out or response cost for inappropriate behavior) (CDC, 2020d; Harlacher et al., 2006; Nolan & Filter, 2012). Interventions based on functional assessment of off-task, disruptive, and distracting behavior by students with ADHD (e.g., Whitford et al., 2013) and parent training programs (CDC, 2020d; Daley et al., 2018) have also proven effective.

HLP10 Conduct functional behavior assessments to develop individual student behavior support plans.

Given that impulsivity adversely affects learning for many students with ADHD, an important line of research is exploring how to teach self-regulation skills. Research has demonstrated children with ADHD can learn to self-regulate their behavior and reduce impulsiveness (Alsalamah, 2017; Reid et al., 2005). Neef et al. (2001) demonstrated children with

ADHD can learn self-control when treatment regimens are directly tied to assessment. Correspondence training, another effective practice, teaches students using "do–say" verbal statements about what they have done previously and "say–do" statements describing what they plan to do (e.g., Shapiro et al., 1998). For instance, the teacher may ask the child to verbalize what he plans to do next and then provide a reward if the student then engages in the behavior he verbalized.

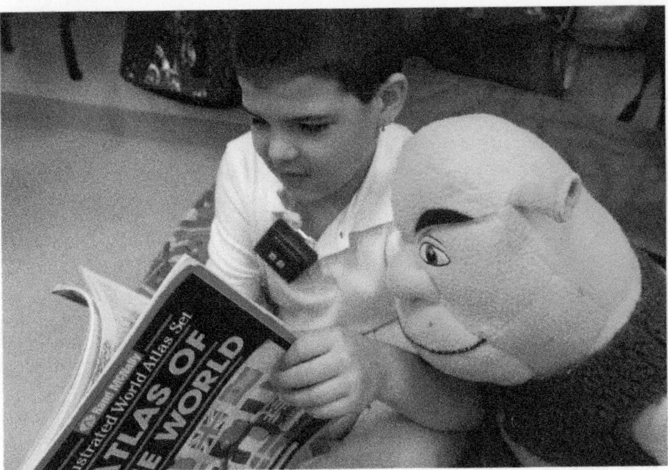

Source: Katelyn Metzger/Pearson Allyn and Bacon/Merrill Education

Since learning to self-monitor his behavior, Brandon is more on-task and productive.

Teaching students to self-monitor their behavior is another way to promote self-regulation. Self-monitoring is a relatively simple procedure in which individuals observe their behavior systematically and record the occurrence or nonoccurrence of a specific behavior. Self-monitoring has helped students with and without disabilities stay on task (Alsalamah, 2017; Wills & Mason, 2014), decrease disruptions (Bruhn & Watt, 2012), improve their performance in a variety of academic subject areas (Alsalamah, 2017; Wolfe et al., 2000), and complete homework assignments (Falkenberg & Barbetta, 2013). In addition to improving the target behavior, self-monitoring enables students to achieve a form of self-determination by taking responsibility for their learning.

Asking a child with ADHD to self-monitor whether he is on task and productive may seem a bit like asking the fox to guard the hen house. How can a student with ADHD pay attention to his own paying attention? Isn't he likely to forget? And if he does remember, what will keep him from recording that he was on task even if he wasn't? Although these are understandable concerns, research has shown self-monitoring to be an effective intervention for students diagnosed with ADHD (e.g., Alsalamah, 2017; Lo & Cartledge, 2006; Wills & Mason, 2014). See *Teaching & Learning,* "Self-Monitoring Helps Students Do More Than Just Stay on Task."

MEDICATION Prescription stimulant medication is the most common intervention for children with ADHD. Methylphenidate, sold under the trade name Ritalin, is the most frequently prescribed medication for ADHD. Other stimulants such as dextroamphetamine (Dexedrine), dextroamphetamine sulfate (Adderall), methamphetamine hydrochloride (Desoxyn), and pemoline (Cylert) are also widely prescribed.

The number of children prescribed medication for ADHD has increased tremendously since the late 1980s, when it was estimated 700,000 children received medication for ADHD.

TEACHING & LEARNING

Self-Monitoring Helps Students Do More Than Just Stay on Task

Why Teach Self-Monitoring Skills? Teaching students to self-monitor is a powerful way to improve not only their attention to task but also the productivity and quality of their work. Following are suggestions based on more than 30 years of research on self-monitoring. For a review of principles and strategies for self-monitoring, see Cooper et al. (2020). Detailed procedures and materials for teaching students self-monitoring and other self-management skills are described in Joseph and Konrad (2009) and Rafferty (2010).

How to Get Started

1. **Specify the target behavior and performance goals.** In general, students should self-monitor specific academic or social tasks (e.g., having materials ready for class, participating in class discussions, answering math problems) instead of an on-task behavior such as "paying attention." On-task behavior does not necessarily result in a collateral increase in productivity. By contrast,

when productivity increases, improvements in on-task behavior almost always occur. However, a student whose persistent off-task and disruptive behaviors create problems for him or others in the classroom may benefit more from self-monitoring on-task behavior, at least initially. Collaborate with students to select target behaviors and set performance goals.

Pearson eText
Video Example 11.1
Self-monitoring tools help Brandon stay on task.

2. **Select or create materials that make self-monitoring easy.** Simple paper-and-pencil recording forms, wrist counters, hand-tally counters, and countdown timers can make self-monitoring easy and efficient. Self-recording forms consisting of nothing more than a series of boxes or squares are often effective. At various intervals, the student might write a + or −, circle *yes* or *no*, mark an × through a smiling face or sad face, or record tally marks for the number of target responses made during a just-completed interval. "High-tech" self-monitoring options are also available (e.g., "SCORE IT"; Vogelgesang et al., 2016).
3. **Provide supplementary cues.** Although the self-monitoring device or form itself provides a visual reminder to self-monitor, additional prompts or cues are often helpful. Prompts should be frequent at the beginning of a self-monitoring intervention and gradually reduced in number as the student becomes accustomed to self-monitoring. Auditory prompts in the form of prerecorded beeps or tones can cue self-monitoring. For example, Todd et al. (1999) had a student place a check mark next to *yes* or *no* under the heading "Was I paying attention?" each time the student heard a prerecorded tone that sounded at random intervals.

   Tactile prompts can also signal self-recording moments. The MotivAider is a small, battery-operated device the user can program to vibrate at fixed or variable time intervals. Flaute et al. (2005) describe 20 ways for using a MotivAider to improve behavior and productivity in the classroom.
4. **Provide explicit instruction.** Self-monitoring is easy, but simply telling students how to do it won't work. Model examples and nonexamples of the target behavior and how and when to record it, provide repeated opportunities to practice, and give praise and corrective feedback.
5. **Reinforce accurate self-monitoring.** Although self-monitoring often positively affects behavior even when inaccurate, accurate self-monitoring is desirable, especially when self-recorded data will be used for self-evaluation or self-administered rewards. One effective method for increasing the accuracy of self-monitoring is rewarding students when their self-recorded data match the teacher's data. Check students' data frequently at the beginning of a

Source: Courtesy of Ya-yu Lo, University of North Carolina Charlotte.

self-monitoring program and then gradually reduce the number of checks to a random check every now and then.

6. **Reward improvements in the target behavior.** Self-monitoring is often part of an intervention package that includes reinforcement for meeting self- or teacher-selected performance goals.
7. **Encourage self-evaluation.** Self-evaluation entails comparing one's performance with a predetermined goal or standard. Show the student how to self-evaluate and make self-evaluative statements (e.g., "That was my best score ever. Excellent!" "I missed my goal by two problems. I'll work harder tomorrow.").
8. **Evaluate the program.** Take data on the student's behavior for several days before the student begins self-monitoring. Use these data as a baseline against which to compare the data you obtain during the first several sessions of self-monitoring.

By 1995, the number had more than doubled to 1.6 million children (Safer et al., 1996). The CDC (2014) estimated the percentage of *all* children age 4 to 17 years receiving medication for ADHD had increased from 4.8% in 2007 to 6.1% in 2011. Piper et al. (2018) reported children in the United States are significantly more likely to take medication for ADHD than are children in other countries.

When prescribed and monitored by a competent physician, Ritalin has proven to be a safe and often effective intervention (Multimodal Treatment Study Group, 1999). Reviews of controlled studies show 65% to 75% of school-age children diagnosed with ADHD respond positively to stimulants, at least in the short term; 25% to 30% show either no response or a negative response (Connor, 2015). A positive response typically includes a reduction in hyperactivity, increased attention and time on task, increased academic productivity, and improvements in general conduct. Although teachers and parents generally report favorable outcomes for children who are taking stimulant medication, common side effects include insomnia, decreased appetite, headaches, weight loss, decrease of positive affect, and irritability. These side effects usually subside and can often be controlled with a reduction in dosage (Goldstein & Goldstein, 1998).

Mather and Goldstein (2001) believe "the immediate short-term benefits of stimulant medications far outweigh the liabilities and thus appear to justify the continued use of these medications in the treatment of ADHD" (p. 63). Based on their assessment of two meta-analyses of medication studies, Forness et al. (2000) suggest it is unwise and could be considered malpractice not to include drug therapy as part of a comprehensive treatment program for children with ADHD.

No clear evidence indicates stimulant medications lead to improved academic achievement (e.g., better grades and scores on achievement tests) (Flora, 2007; Rajeh et al., 2017). A longitudinal study that followed children with ADHD who had taken Ritalin for 4 years found the children did not make gains in either specific or general areas of academic achievement from the first through the fifth grade (Frankenberger & Cannon, 1999). Some professionals have voiced concerns that educators and parents rely too much on medical interventions (Flora, 2007; Northup et al., 2001). They view drug treatment as an inappropriate, easy way out that might produce short-term improvements in behavior but long-term harm. The Clinical Practice Guidelines of the American Academy of Pediatrics (2011) state that behavioral interventions should be considered first for preschool children; for older children, particularly adolescents, medication should be prescribed in conjunction with behavioral interventions.

Because the diagnosis of ADHD often leads to the prescription of stimulant medication, it is important that teachers have valid knowledge of the condition and its treatment. Unfortunately, educators hold many misconceptions about ADHD and its treatment by stimulant medication. Snider et al. (2003) asked 145 teachers to rate how much they agreed or disagreed with 13 statements about ADHD and its treatment by stimulant medication. All of the questions were either true or false on the basis of scientific research, and more than half of the teachers answered only 5 of the 13 questions correctly (see Figure 11.1). Sources of information for educators and parents on safe and effective use of stimulant medication in treating children are DuPaul and Stoner (2014) and the *ADHD Parents Medication Guide* (2013).

FIGURE 11.1 Percentage of Classroom Teachers Who Correctly Rated Statements About Attention-Deficit/Hyperactivity Disorder and Its Treatment by Stimulant Medication

ITEM	PERCENTAGE CORRECT
ADHD is the most commonly diagnosed psychiatric disorder of childhood. (*True*)	58
There are data to indicate that ADHD is caused by a brain malfunction. (*False*)	10
ADHD symptoms (e.g., fidgets, does not follow through on instruction, easily distracted) may be caused by academic deficits. (*True*)	63
Stress and conflict in the student's home life can cause ADHD symptoms. (*True*)	71
Diagnosis of ADHD can be confirmed if stimulant medication improves the child's attention. (*False*)	33
Stimulant medication use may decrease the physical growth rate (i.e., height) of students. (*True*)	38
Stimulant medication use may produce tics in students. (*True*)	45
Adderall, Ritalin, and Dexedrine have abuse potential similar to Demerol, cocaine, and morphine. (*True*)	46
The long-term side effects of stimulant medications are well understood. (*False*)	67
Over time, stimulant medication loses its effectiveness. (*True*)	46
While on stimulant medication, students exhibit similar amounts of problem behaviors as their normally developing peers. (*False*)	27
Short-term studies show that stimulant medication improves the behaviors associated with ADHD. (*True*)	86
Studies show that stimulant medication has a positive effect on academic achievement in the long run. (*False*)	6

Note: Statements were rated using a 5-point Likert-type scale (1 = *strongly disagree* to 5 = *strongly agree*). Percentage correct indicates percentage of respondents who answered 4 or 5 to an item that was true and 1 or 2 to an item that was false.

Source: Figure from "Teacher Knowledge of Stimulant Medication and ADHD" by Linda Arrowood, Tracey Busch and Vickie E. Snider, from REMEDIAL AND SPECIAL EDUCATION, January 2003, Volume 24(1). Copyright © 2003 by Arrowood et al. Reprinted with permission by SAGE publications.

Definitions of Health Impairments and Physical Disabilities

Learning Outcome 11.2 Define other health impairments and orthopedic impairments, and explain why the number of children served under these categories of the Individuals with Disabilities Education Act is smaller than the actual number of children who have health impairments or physical disabilities.

Children with health conditions and physical disabilities who require special education are served under two IDEA categories: other health impairments (OHI) and orthopedic impairments.

> **Other health impairment** means having limited strength, vitality, or alertness, including a heightened alertness to environmental stimuli, that results in limited alertness with respect to the educational environment, that—
>
> i. Is due to chronic or acute health problems such as asthma, attention deficit disorder or attention deficit hyperactivity disorder, diabetes, epilepsy, a heart condition, hemophilia, lead poisoning, leukemia, nephritis, rheumatic fever, sickle cell anemia, or Tourette syndrome; and
> ii. Adversely affects academic performance. (20 USC §1401 [2004], 20 *CFR* §300.8[c][9])
>
> A severe **orthopedic impairment** adversely affects a child's educational performance. The term includes impairments caused by a congenital anomaly (e.g., clubfoot, absence of some member, etc.), impairments caused by disease (e.g., poliomyelitis, bone tuberculosis), and impairments from other causes (e.g., cerebral palsy, amputations, and fractures or burns that cause contractures). (20 USC §1401 [2004], 20 *CFR* §300.8[c][8])

Although IDEA uses the term *orthopedic impairment,* children with physical disabilities may have orthopedic impairments or neuromotor impairments. An orthopedic impairment involves the skeletal system—bones, joints, limbs, and associated muscles. A **neuromotor**

impairment involves the central nervous system, affecting the ability to move, use, feel, or control certain parts of the body. Although orthopedic and neuromotor impairments are two distinct and separate types of disabilities, they may cause similar limitations in movement. Many of the same educational, therapeutic, and recreational activities are appropriate for students with orthopedic and neuromotor impairments (Best et al., 2010). And a close relationship exists between the two types. For example, a child who cannot move her legs because of damage to the central nervous system (neuromotor impairment) may develop disorders in the bones and muscles of the legs (orthopedic impairment), especially if she does not receive proper therapy and equipment.

Note in each IDEA disability definition the common clause: *that adversely affects a child's educational performance.* A child is entitled to special education services if her educational performance is adversely affected by a health-related condition or a physical disability. Most health impairments and physical disabilities that require special education are **chronic conditions**—that is, they are long lasting and most often permanent (e.g., cerebral palsy is a permanent disability that will affect a child throughout her life). By contrast, an **acute condition**, although it may produce severe and debilitating symptoms, is of limited duration (e.g., a child with pneumonia will experience symptoms, but the disease itself is not permanent). Some children with chronic health conditions or physical disabilities experience flare-ups or episodes of acute symptoms (e.g., a child with cystic fibrosis may experience periods of acute respiratory difficulties).

Prevalence

Studies of the number of children with health impairments and physical disabilities have produced hugely diverse findings. A national survey found about 13% of the U.S. population experience limitations in daily activities due to chronic health conditions (Lucas & Benson, 2019; van der Lee et al., 2007). Sexson and Dingle (2001) estimate that chronic medical conditions affect up to 20% of school-age children in the United States. Whatever the actual number, researchers widely accept that the incidence of chronic health conditions has increased considerably in recent decades. In 1960, data showed that just 1.8% of American children and adolescents had a chronic health condition that limited their activities compared with 7% in 2004 (Perrin et al., 2007).

Clearly, health impairments and physical disabilities affect many children's lives. During the 2018–2019 school year, however, only around 33,516 children between the ages of 6 and 21 years received special education services under the orthopedic impairments disability category compared with approximately 1,025,953 children served under OHI (U.S. Department of Education, 2020a). These two disability categories represent approximately 0.5% and 16.2% of all children receiving special education services, respectively.

Two factors make the actual number of children with health conditions and physical disabilities much higher than the number of children receiving special education services under these two IDEA categories. First, numerous children have chronic health conditions or physical impairments that do not adversely affect their educational performance enough to warrant special education. Second, because physical and health impairments often occur with other disabilities, children may be counted under other categories, such as multiple disabilities, speech impairment, or intellectual disabilities. For example, for the purpose of special education eligibility, a diagnosis of intellectual disabilities may take precedence over a diagnosis of physical impairment.

Types and Causes

Learning Outcome 11.3 List and describe the types and causes of health conditions and physical impairments seen most frequently in school-age children.

Literally hundreds of health conditions and physical impairments can adversely affect educational performance. Here we address those encountered most frequently in school-age children. Extensive discussions of the many health conditions and physical impairments that may result in the need for special education can be found in Batshaw et al. (2019) and Best et al. (2010).

Epilepsy

Whether we are awake or asleep, our brains are continually astir with electrical activity. When abnormal electrical discharges in the brain cause a disturbance of movement, sensation, behavior, or consciousness, a *seizure* has occurred. Some have compared the event to "an engine misfiring or to a power surge in a computer" (Hill, 1999, p. 231). Anyone can have a seizure. It is common for a seizure to occur when someone has a high fever, drinks excessive alcohol, or experiences a blow to the head.

When seizures occur chronically and repeatedly, the condition is known as a *seizure disorder* or, more commonly, **epilepsy**. Epilepsy is not a disease, and it constitutes a disorder only while a seizure is actually in progress. It is estimated that 1.2% of the U.S. population has epilepsy (CDC, 2020e).

The cause of approximately 30% of epilepsy cases is identified from among at least 50 different conditions known to result in seizure activity, such as cerebral palsy; infections of the brain or central nervous system; metabolic disorders such as hypoglycemia, genetics, and alcohol or lead poisoning; an underlying lesion caused by scar tissue from a head injury; high fever; an interruption in blood supply to the brain; and rough handling of a baby (shaken-baby syndrome) (Lowenthal, 2001; Zelleke et al., 2019). Epilepsy can occur at any stage of life but usually begins in childhood. A wide variety of psychological, physical, and sensory factors can trigger seizures in susceptible people—for example, fatigue; excitement; anger; surprise; hyperventilation; hormonal changes (as in menstruation or pregnancy); withdrawal from drugs or alcohol; and exposure to certain patterns of light, sound, or touch.

Many misconceptions about epilepsy circulated in the past, and some remain prevalent even today (e.g., it is contagious; it is a form of mental illness; while having a seizure, a person may swallow his tongue) (Epilepsy Foundation of America, 2020a; Kanner & Schafer, 2006). Negative public attitudes, in fact, may be as harmful to people with epilepsy as the condition itself. During a seizure, a dysfunction in the brain's electrochemical activity causes temporary loss of muscle control. Between seizures, most of the time, the brain functions normally. There are several types of seizures.

The **generalized tonic-clonic seizure** (formerly called *grand mal*) is the most conspicuous and serious type of seizure. The affected child usually has little or no warning a seizure is about to occur; the muscles become stiff, and the child loses consciousness and falls to the floor. Then the entire body shakes violently as the muscles alternately contract and relax. Saliva may exude from the mouth, the legs and arms may jerk, and the bladder and bowels may empty. In most cases, contractions diminish in 2 to 3 minutes, and the child either goes to sleep or regains consciousness in a confused or drowsy state. Generalized tonic-clonic seizures may occur as often as several times a day or as seldom as once a year. They are more likely to occur during the day than at night. A tonic-clonic seizure, although very frightening to someone who has never witnessed one, is not a medical emergency unless it lasts a very long time or if one seizure occurs right after another without a return to consciousness between seizures.

Pearson eText
Video Example 11.2
Learn what to do when a child has a seizure. https://www.youtube.com/watch?v=hLeSlQS9g2c

An **absence seizure** (previously called *petit mal*) is far less severe than the generalized tonic-clonic type but may occur much more frequently—as often as 100 times per day in some children. Usually a brief loss of consciousness occurs, lasting from a few seconds to half a minute or so. The child may stare blankly, flutter or blink her eyes, grow pale, and drop whatever she is holding. She may be mistakenly viewed as daydreaming or not listening. The child may or may not be aware she has had a seizure, and no special first aid is necessary.

A **complex partial seizure** (also called *psychomotor*) may appear as a brief period of inappropriate or purposeless activity. The child may smack her lips, walk about aimlessly, or shout. Although she may appear to be conscious and even respond to spoken directions, the child is unaware of her unusual behavior. A complex partial seizure usually lasts 2 to 5 minutes, after which the child has amnesia about the entire episode.

A **simple partial seizure** is characterized by sudden jerking motions with no loss of consciousness. Partial seizures may occur weekly, monthly, or just once or twice a year. During seizures, the teacher should keep dangerous objects out of the child's way and, except in emergencies, should not try to physically restrain him.

Many children experience a warning sensation, called an *aura*, a short time before a seizure. The aura takes various forms: distinctive feelings, sights, sounds, tastes, and even smells. The aura can be a useful safety valve enabling children to leave the class or group before the seizure occurs. Some children report that the warning the aura provides helps them feel more secure and comfortable.

In some children, absence and partial seizures may go undetected for long periods. An observant teacher can be instrumental in identifying the presence of a seizure disorder and referring the child for appropriate medical help. The teacher can also assist parents and physicians by noting both the effectiveness and the side effects of any medication. With proper medical treatment and support of parents, teachers, and peers, most students with seizure disorders lead full and normal lives. Antiepileptic drugs control seizures in 70% of individuals with epilepsy (Epilepsy Foundation of America, 2020b). Some children require such heavy doses of medication, however, their learning and behavior are adversely affected, and some medications have undesirable side effects, such as fatigue, nausea, slurred speech, lack of appetite, and thickening of the gums. All children with seizure disorders benefit from a realistic understanding of their condition and accepting attitudes by teachers and classmates (Schafer & DiLorio, 2006). Although a student with a seizure disorder may be uncomfortable about letting friends know about the condition, classmates should be aware, so they will know how to—and how *not* to—respond in the event of a seizure (Mittan, 2009).

HLP3 Collaborate with families to support student learning and secure needed services.

Diabetes

Diabetes is a chronic disorder of metabolism that affects an estimated 34.2 million people of all ages in the United States, or 10.5% of the population (CDC, 2020f). Without proper medical management, a child with diabetes cannot obtain and retain adequate energy from food. Not only does the child lack energy, but untreated diabetes affects many important body parts (particularly the eyes and the kidneys). Early symptoms include thirst, headaches, weight loss (despite a good appetite), frequent urination, and cuts that are slow to heal.

Children with **type 1 diabetes** (formerly called *juvenile diabetes* or *early-onset diabetes*) have insufficient insulin, a hormone the pancreas produces that is necessary for the metabolism of glucose, a form of sugar produced when food is digested. Children with diabetes must follow a specific, physician-prescribed diet and receive daily injections of insulin under the skin. Most children with diabetes learn to inject their own insulin—in some cases as frequently as four times per day.

The most common form of diabetes, **type 2 diabetes**, results from insulin resistance (the body failing to properly use insulin), combined with relative insulin deficiency. Type 2 diabetes occurs most often in adults, but there have been recent significant increases in the incidence of type 2 diabetes in children (Mayer-Davis et al., 2017).

Teachers who have a student with diabetes in their classrooms should learn to recognize symptoms of both too little and too much sugar in the child's bloodstream and ensure the child receives the appropriate treatment for each condition (Getch et al., 2007). *Hypoglycemia* (low blood sugar), also called *insulin reaction* or *diabetic shock*, can result from taking too much insulin, unusually strenuous exercise, or a missed or delayed meal (insulin and exercise lower blood sugar and food raises it). Symptoms of hypoglycemia include faintness, dizziness, blurred vision, drowsiness, and nausea. The child may appear irritable or have a marked personality change. In most cases, giving the child some form of concentrated sugar (e.g., sugar cube, fruit juice, candy bar) ends the insulin reaction within a few minutes. The child's doctor or parents should inform the teacher and school health personnel of the appropriate foods to give in case of insulin reaction.

Hyperglycemia (high blood sugar) is more serious; it indicates too little insulin is present and the diabetes is not under control. Its onset is gradual rather than sudden. Symptoms of hyperglycemia, sometimes called *diabetic coma*, include fatigue; thirst; dry, hot skin; deep, labored breathing; excessive urination; and fruity-smelling breath. A doctor or nurse should be contacted immediately if a child displays such symptoms.

Asthma

Asthma is a chronic lung disease characterized by episodic bouts of wheezing, coughing, and difficulty breathing. An asthmatic attack is usually triggered by allergens (e.g., pollen, certain foods, pets), irritants (e.g., cigarette smoke, smog), exercise, or emotional stress. The result is a narrowing of the airways in the lungs, which increases resistance to the airflow in and out of the lungs and makes it harder for the individual to breathe. The severity of asthma varies greatly, from mild coughing to extreme difficulty breathing that requires emergency treatment. Many children with asthma experience normal lung functioning between episodes. Asthma is the most common lung disease of children, affecting approximately 8% of all children (Asthma and Allergy Foundation of America, 2020). The causes of asthma are not completely known, but most consider it the result of an interaction of heredity and environment.

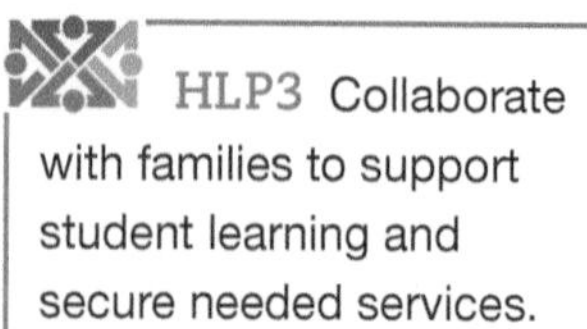
HLP3 Collaborate with families to support student learning and secure needed services.

Primary treatment for asthma begins with a systematic effort to identify stimuli and environmental situations that trigger attacks. Asthma can be controlled effectively in most children with a combination of medications and limiting exposure to known triggers. Most children whose breathing attacks are induced by physical exercise can still enjoy physical exercise and sports through careful selection of activities (e.g., swimming generally provokes less exercise-induced asthma than running) and/or taking certain medications before rigorous exercise. Although asthma is biochemical in origin, emotional stress can also be a factor. Periods of psychological stress or intense emotional responses increase the likelihood of asthmatic attacks, and asthmatic episodes produce more stress. Treatment often involves an asthma teaching program in which children and their families learn ways to reduce and cope with emotional stress.

Pearson eText
Video Example 11.3
All teachers should maintain "asthma-friendly" classrooms.
https://www.youtube.com/watch?v=trr7a1JlAzQ

Asthma accounts for more hospitalizations than any other childhood disease and is the leading cause of school absenteeism. Chronic absenteeism makes it difficult for a child with asthma to maintain performance at grade level, and homebound instructional services may be necessary. The majority of children with asthma who receive medical and psychological support, however, successfully complete school and lead normal lives. The classroom teacher can play an important role in reducing the impact of asthma by working cooperatively with parents and medical personnel to minimize contact with provoking factors and constructing a plan to assist the child during attacks.

Autosomal Recessive Disorders

Children inherit autosomal recessive disorders when two copies of an abnormal gene are present, one from each parent (U.S. National Library of Medicine, 2020a). Such disorders are rare, but three of the most common are cystic fibrosis, sickle cell disease, and Tay-Sachs disease.

CYSTIC FIBROSIS **Cystic fibrosis** is a disease in which the body's exocrine glands excrete thick mucus that blocks the lungs and parts of the digestive system. Cystic fibrosis occurs predominantly in White people, but it can affect all races. Children with cystic fibrosis often have difficulty breathing and are susceptible to pulmonary disease (lung infections). Malnutrition and poor growth are common characteristics of children with cystic fibrosis because of pancreatic insufficiency that causes inadequate digestion and malabsorption of nutrients, especially fats. Affected children often have large and frequent bowel movements because food is only partially digested. Getting children with cystic fibrosis to consume enough calories is critical to their health and development.

Medications prescribed for cystic fibrosis include enzymes to facilitate digestion and solutions to thin and loosen the mucus in the lungs. Children with cystic fibrosis undergo daily physiotherapy in which the chest is vigorously thumped and vibrated to dislodge mucus followed by positioning the body to drain loosened secretions. During vigorous physical exercises, some children may need help from teachers, aides, or classmates to clear their lungs and air passages.

Although the life expectancy of people with cystic fibrosis used to be very short—in the 1950s, few children with cystic fibrosis lived to attend elementary school—the prognosis for affected children continues to improve. More than half of the cystic fibrosis population today is age 18 years and older, and the median predicted age of survival is in the mid-40s (Cystic Fibrosis Foundation, 2020).

SICKLE CELL DISEASE **Sickle cell disease** affects the ability of red blood cells to carry oxygen; the sickle-shaped cells do not easily move through the blood, causing blockages that lead to several complications. Sickle cell disease is most common in people of African descent but may affect people of all racial and ethnic backgrounds. Children with sickle cell disease are at risk for episodes of severe pain, serious infections, organ damage, acute chest syndrome (a condition similar to pneumonia), and stroke.

Treatments for children with sickle cell disease vary according to their symptoms (CDC, 2020g). Common treatments include blood transfusions, medication, and increasing fluid intake. For children with sickle cell disease, physicians emphasize the prevention of various symptoms. For instance, pain crises may be prevented or lessened by avoiding high altitudes or extreme (too hot or too cold) temperatures. Preventive measures for helping children avoid infection are particularly important, including following food safety guidelines, practicing thorough hand washing, and vaccinating on schedule.

TAY-SACHS DISEASE **Tay-Sachs disease** progressively destroys nerve cells in the brain and spinal cord (U.S National Library of Medicine, 2020b). Tay-Sachs disease is more common in people of Ashkenazi Jewish descent but may affect children of any ethnicity. Symptoms generally begin to appear in infancy and include loss of motor skills, seizures, loss of vision and hearing, and intellectual disability. This disease is considered fatal; most children do not live beyond 5 years of age.

HIV and AIDS

Human immunodeficiency virus (HIV) can lead to **acquired immune deficiency syndrome (AIDS)**. A person with AIDS cannot resist and fight off infections because of a breakdown in the immune system. Opportunistic infections such as tuberculosis, pneumonia, and cancerous skin lesions attack the person's body, grow in severity, and ultimately result in death. Although no vaccine or cure exists for AIDS, advances in antiretroviral drug treatment have dramatically reduced mortality rates.

HIV, which is found in an infected person's bodily fluids (blood, semen, vaginal secretions, and breast milk), is transmitted from one person to another through sexual contact and blood-to-blood contact (e.g., intravenous drug use with shared needles, transfusions of unscreened contaminated blood). Women can transmit HIV to their children during pregnancy, birth, or breastfeeding (CDC, 2020h).

Because of fear generated by misconceptions about the spread of the disease, some school districts have barred children with HIV/AIDS from attending school in defiance of the IDEA principle of zero reject. However, saliva, nasal secretions, sweat, tears, urine, and vomit do not transmit HIV unless those fluids contain blood (CDC, 2020h). A child with HIV/AIDS in the classroom presents no undue health risks to other children. Children with HIV/AIDS cannot legally be excluded from attending school unless they are deemed a direct health risk to other children (e.g., exhibit biting behavior, have open lesions).

Parents are not required to inform the school their child has HIV (or any other medical or health condition). All teachers and school personnel should be trained in **universal precautions**, a set of standard safety techniques that interrupt the chain of infection spread by potential biohazards such as blood and bodily fluids. Universal precautions include safe administration of first aid for a cut, nosebleed, or vomiting.

For recommendations on developing and implementing an HIV/AIDS prevention and education curriculum for students with disabilities, see Sileo (2005). For an excellent overview of the importance of universal precautions, including step-by-step guidelines for proper methods of putting on and removing protective gloves, cleaning up potentially contaminated areas in the classroom, and proper handwashing, see Edens et al. (2003).

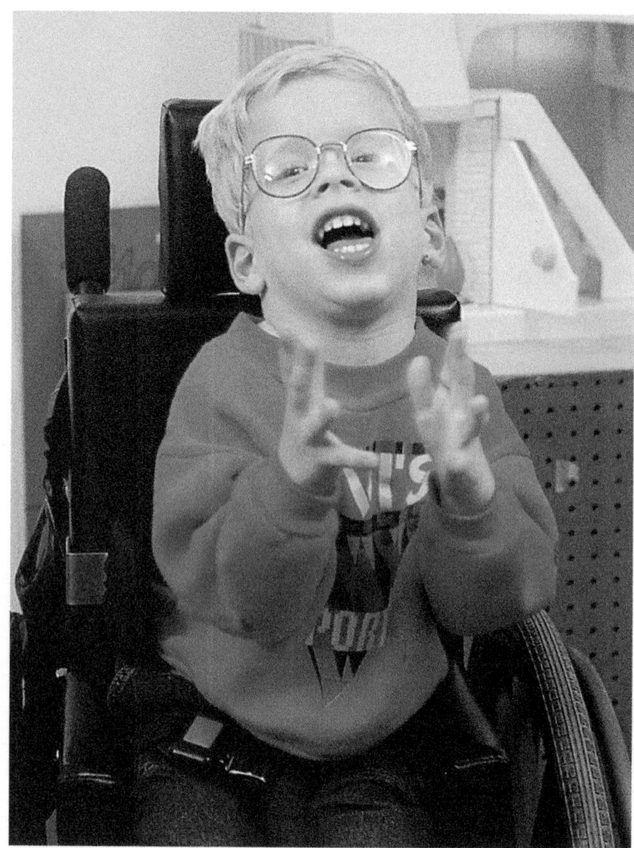
Source: Scott Cunningham/Pearson Allyn and Bacon/Merrill Education

Although cerebral palsy affects Joey's control over his movements, it has not dampened his enthusiasm and determination for learning.

Cerebral Palsy

Cerebral palsy—a disorder of movement and posture—is the most prevalent physical disability in school-age children, affecting roughly 3 in 1000 children (CDC, 2020i). Cerebral palsy is a permanent condition resulting from a lesion to the brain or an abnormality of brain growth. Many diseases can affect the developing brain and lead to cerebral palsy. Children with cerebral palsy experience disturbances of voluntary motor functions that may include paralysis, extreme weakness, lack of coordination, involuntary convulsions, and other motor disorders. They may have little or no control over their arms, legs, or speech, depending on the type and degree of impairment. More severe forms of cerebral palsy are often diagnosed in the first few months of life. In many cases, however, cerebral palsy is not detected until the child is 2 to 3 years old, when parents notice their child is having difficulty balancing or standing. The motor dysfunction usually does not get progressively worse as a child ages. Cerebral palsy can be treated but not cured. It is not a disease; not fatal; not contagious; and in the great majority of cases, not inherited.

Between 23% and 44% of children with cerebral palsy have cognitive impairments, ranging from mild to severe (Odding et al., 2006). Sensory impairments are also common in children with cerebral palsy; 5% to 15% have hearing loss (Nehring, 2010), and 60% to 70% have impaired vision, particularly strabismus (Odding et al., 2006). No clear relationship exists between the degree of motor impairment and the degree of intellectual impairment (if any) in children with cerebral palsy (or other physical disabilities). Whereas a student with mild motor impairment may experience severe developmental delays, a student with severe motor impairments may be intellectually gifted (Willard-Holt, 1998).

The causes of cerebral palsy are varied and not clearly known. It has most often been attributed to the occurrence of injuries, accidents, or illnesses that are *prenatal* (before birth), *perinatal* (at or near the time of birth), or *postnatal* (soon after birth) and that result in decreased oxygen to low-birth-weight newborns. Factors most often associated with cerebral palsy are intellectual disabilities of the mother, premature birth (gestational age of 32 weeks or less), low birth weight, and a delay of 5 minutes or more before the newborn's first cry.

Because the location and extent of brain damage are so variable in individuals with cerebral palsy, a diagnosis of the condition is not descriptive of its effects. Cerebral palsy is classified in terms of the affected parts of the body and by the nature of its effects on muscle tone and movement (Best & Bigge, 2010). The term *plegia* (from the Greek "to strike") is used in combination with a prefix indicating the location of limb involvement:

- *Monoplegia*—only one limb (upper or lower) is affected.
- *Hemiplegia*—two limbs on same side of the body are involved.
- *Triplegia*—three limbs are affected.
- *Quadriplegia*—all four limbs (both arms and legs) are involved; movement of the trunk and face may also be impaired.
- *Paraplegia*—only legs are impaired.

- *Diplegia*—impairment primarily involves the legs, with less severe involvement of the arms.
- *Double hemiplegia*—impairment primarily involves the arms, with less severe involvement of the legs.

Cerebral palsy is also classified by its effects on muscle tone (hypertonia or hypotonia) and quality of movement (athetosis or ataxia) (Johnson et al., 2019). Approximately 50% to 60% of all individuals with cerebral palsy have *spastic cerebral palsy,* which is characterized by tense, contracted muscles (**hypertonia**). Their movements may be jerky, exaggerated, and poorly coordinated. They may be unable to grasp objects with their fingers. When they try to control their movements, they may become even jerkier. If they can walk, they may use a scissor gait, standing on the toes with knees bent and pointed inward. Deformities of the spine; hip dislocations; and contractures of the hand, elbow, foot, and knee are common.

Athetosis occurs in about 20% of all individuals with cerebral palsy. Children with *athetoid cerebral palsy* make large, irregular, twisting movements they cannot control. When they are at rest or asleep, little or no abnormal motion occurs. An effort to pick up a pencil, however, may result in wildly waving arms, facial grimaces, and extension of the tongue. These children may not be able to control the muscles of their lips, tongue, and throat and may drool. They may also seem to stumble and lurch awkwardly as they walk. At times their muscles may be tense and rigid; at other times, they may be loose and flaccid. Extreme difficulty in expressive oral language, mobility, and activities of daily living often accompanies this form of cerebral palsy.

Ataxia is the primary type of involvement in 1% to 10% of cases of cerebral palsy. Children with *ataxic cerebral palsy* have a poor sense of balance and hand use. They may appear to be dizzy while walking and may fall if not supported. Their movements tend to be jumpy and unsteady, with exaggerated motion patterns that often overshoot the intended objects. They seem to be constantly attempting to overcome the effect of gravity to stabilize their bodies.

Rigidity and *tremor* are additional but much less common types of cerebral palsy. Children with the rare rigidity type of cerebral palsy display extreme stiffness in the affected limbs; they may be fixed and immobile for long periods. Rhythmic, uncontrollable movements mark tremor cerebral palsy; the tremors may actually increase when the children attempt to control their actions. Because most children with cerebral palsy have diffuse brain damage, pure types of cerebral palsy are rare. Children may be described as having *mixed cerebral palsy,* consisting of more than one of these types, particularly if their impairments are severe.

Most infants born with cerebral palsy have **hypotonia**, or weak, floppy muscles, particularly in the neck and trunk. When hypotonia persists throughout the first year without being replaced with spasticity or athetoid involvement, the condition is called *generalized hypotonia.* Children with hypotonia typically have low levels of motor activity, are slow to make balancing responses, and may not walk until 30 months of age. Children with severe hypotonia must use external support to achieve and maintain an upright position.

Cerebral palsy is a complex condition most effectively managed through the cooperative involvement of physicians, teachers, physical therapists (PTs), occupational therapists (OTs), communication specialists, counselors, and others who work directly with children and families. Regular exercise and careful positioning in school settings help children with cerebral palsy move as fully and comfortably as possible and prevent or minimize progressive damage to muscles and limbs. Most children with cerebral palsy can learn to walk, although many need to use wheelchairs, braces, and other assistive devices, particularly for moving around outside the home. Orthopedic surgery may increase range of motion or obviate complications such as hip dislocations and permanent muscle contractions.

Spina Bifida

Congenital malformations of the brain, spinal cord, or vertebrae are known as *neural tube defects.* The most common neural tube defect (approximately 3 in 10,000 live births in the United States per year) (CDC, 2020j) is **spina bifida**, a condition in which the vertebrae do not enclose the spinal cord. As a result, a portion of the spinal cord and the nerves that control muscles and feeling in the lower part of the body fails to develop normally. Of the three types of spina bifida, the mildest form is **spina bifida occulta**, in which only a few vertebrae are malformed, usually in the lower spine. The defect is usually not visible externally. Approximately 15% of people in the United States have spina bifida occulta, but because they experience few or no symptoms, very few ever know they have it (Spina Bifida Association, 2020a). If the flexible casing (meninges) that surrounds the spinal cord bulges through an opening in the infant's back at birth, the condition is called **meningocele**. These two forms do not usually cause any loss of function for the child.

In **myelomeningocele**—the most common and most serious form of spina bifida—the spinal lining, spinal cord, and nerve roots all protrude. The protruding spinal cord and nerves are usually tucked back into the spinal column shortly after birth. This condition carries a high risk of paralysis and infection. In general, the higher the location of the lesion on the spine, the greater the effect on the body and its functioning.

About 70% to 90% children born with myelomeningocele develop **hydrocephalus**, the accumulation of cerebrospinal fluid in tissues surrounding the brain. Left untreated, this condition can lead to head enlargement and severe brain damage. Hydrocephalus is treated by the surgical insertion of a **shunt**, a one-way valve that diverts the cerebrospinal fluid away from the brain and into the bloodstream. Replacements of the shunt are usually necessary as a child grows older. Teachers who work with children who have shunts should be aware that blockage, disconnection, or infection of the shunt may result in increased intracranial pressure. They should heed warning signs such as drowsiness, vomiting, headache, irritability, seizures, and change in personality because a shunt malfunction, blockage, or infection can be life threatening (Paff et al., 2018; Spina Bifida Association, 2020b). Shunts can be removed from many school-age children when the production and absorption of cerebrospinal fluid are brought into balance.

Spina bifida usually results in some degree of paralysis of the lower limbs. Most children with spina bifida have good use of their arms and upper body (although some children experience fine-motor problems). They usually walk with braces, crutches, or walkers; they may use wheelchairs for longer distances. Some children need help dressing and toileting; others manage these tasks on their own.

Because the spinal defect usually occurs above where the nerves that control the bladder emerge from the spinal cord, most children with spina bifida have urinary incontinence and need to use a *catheter* (tube) or bag to collect their urine. Medical personnel teach **clean intermittent catheterization (CIC)** to children with urinary complications so they can empty their bladders at convenient times (Lehr & Harayama, 2016; Singh et al., 2018). Effective with both boys and girls, CIC works best if used every 2 to 4 hours and does not require an absolutely sterile environment (McLone & Ito, 1998).

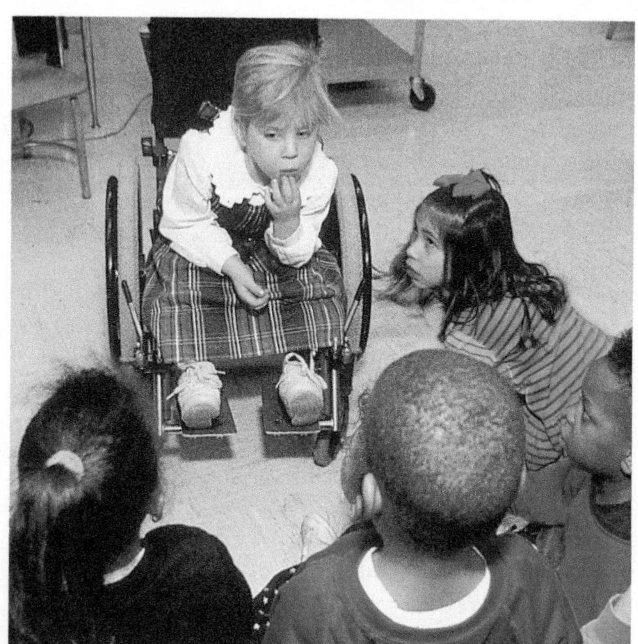
Source: Scott Cunningham/Pearson Allyn and Bacon/Merrill Education

Self-catherization enables Kristine's independence.

Muscular Dystrophy

Muscular dystrophy refers to a group of about 40 inherited diseases marked by progressive *atrophy* (wasting away) of the body's muscles. **Duchenne muscular dystrophy (DMD)** is the most common and most severe type. DMD affects only boys (1 in 3500 male births), but about one third of cases are the result of genetic mutation in families with no history of the disease (Best, 2010a). Muscle weakness is usually evident between the ages of 2 and 6 years, when the child begins to experience difficulty in running or climbing stairs. The child may walk with an unusual gait, showing a protruding stomach and hollow back. The calf muscles of a child with muscular dystrophy may appear unusually large because the degenerated muscle has been replaced by fatty tissue.

Children with muscular dystrophy often have difficulty getting to their feet after lying down or playing on the floor. They may fall easily. By age 10 to 14 years, the child loses the ability to walk; the small muscles of the hands and fingers are usually the last to be affected. Treatment focuses on maintaining function of unaffected muscles for as long as possible, facilitating ambulation, helping the child and the family cope with limitations imposed by the disease, and providing emotional support and counseling to the child and the family (Hill, 1999). Regular physical therapy, exercise, and use of appropriate aids and appliances can help children maintain a good deal of independence. The child should be encouraged to be as active as possible. However, a teacher should be careful not to lift a child with muscular dystrophy by the arms: Even a gentle pull may dislocate the child's limbs.

At this time, no known treatment exists to stop or reverse any form of muscular dystrophy. Although some cases may be mild and progress very slowly, enabling the person to live into adulthood with only moderate disability, muscular dystrophy is often fatal in adolescence or young adulthood (Muscular Dystrophy Coordinating Committee, 2020). Death often results from heart failure or respiratory failure caused by atrophied chest muscles. For discussions of how classroom teachers can help themselves, classmates, and parents cope with the death of a student, see Munson and Hunt (2005) and Lehr and Harayama (2016). Additional tips and resources, including videos and modules, are available from The Coalition to Help Grieving Students (https://grievingstudents.org/).

Spinal Cord Injuries

Spinal cord injuries are usually the result of a lesion to the spinal cord caused by a penetrating injury (e.g., a gunshot wound), stretching of the vertebral column (e.g., whiplash during an auto accident), fracture of the vertebrae, or compression of the spinal cord (e.g., a diving accident). Motor vehicle accidents (39%), falls (32%), acts of violence (14%), and sports (8%) are the most common causes of spinal cord injuries (National Spinal Cord Injury Statistical Center, 2020). Injury to the spinal column is generally described by letters and numbers indicating the site of the damage; for example, a C5 to C6 injury means the damage has occurred at the level of the fifth and sixth cervical vertebrae, a flexible area of the neck susceptible to injury from whiplash and diving or trampoline accidents. A T12 injury refers to the 12th thoracic (chest) vertebra and an L3 to the 3rd lumbar (lower back) area. In general, paralysis and loss of sensation occur below the level of the injury. The higher the injury on the spine and the more the injury (lesion) cuts through the entire spinal cord, the greater the paralysis.

Students who have sustained spinal cord injuries usually use wheelchairs for mobility. Motorized wheelchairs, although expensive, are recommended for those with **quadriplegia** (also called *tetraplegia*), but children with **paraplegia** can use self-propelled wheelchairs. Children with quadriplegia may have severe breathing problems because chest muscles, which normally govern respiration, are affected. Most children with spinal cord injuries lack bladder and bowel control and need to follow a careful management program to maintain personal hygiene and avoid infection and skin irritation.

Rehabilitation programs for children and adolescents who have sustained spinal cord injuries usually involve physical therapy, the use of adaptive devices for mobility and independent living, and psychological support to help them adjust to a sudden disability. Personal care attendants (PCAs) assist many individuals who have spinal cord injury with activities of daily living. Adolescents and adults are often particularly concerned about sexual function. Even though most spinal cord injuries do affect sexuality, with understanding partners and positive attitudes toward themselves, many people with spinal cord injuries enjoy satisfying sexual relationships (Byzek, 2001).

Characteristics of Children with Health Impairments and Physical Disabilities

The characteristics of children with health impairments and physical disabilities are so varied that attempting to describe them is nearly impossible. Some children with health conditions have chronic but relatively mild health conditions; others have extremely limited endurance and vitality, requiring sophisticated medical technology and around-the-clock support to maintain their very existence. One student with cerebral palsy may need few special modifications in curriculum, instruction, or environment, but the severe limitations in movement and intellectual functioning another student with cerebral palsy experiences may require a wide array of curricular and instructional modifications, adaptive equipment, and related services. And a given health or physical condition may take markedly different trajectories. For example, treatment of cancer may prolong and enhance the life of a child, lead to complete remission of the disease, or have few or no positive effects on a child's life.

These variables render lists of learning and behavioral characteristics of children with health impairments or physical disabilities highly suspect at best. Nevertheless, two cautiously qualified statements can be made concerning the academic and socioemotional characteristics of children with physical disabilities and health impairments. First, although many students with health impairments or physical disabilities achieve well above grade level, as a group, these students function below grade level academically. In addition to the neuromotor and orthopedic impairments that may hamper their academic performance, the daily health care routines and medications some children must endure have negative side effects on academic achievement. For example, Kiriakopoulos (2018) described how the mother of a 15-year-old teenager with epilepsy helps teachers understand the effects of seizures and medication on a student's school performance.

> I tell them, "Imagine you have the flu. Plus, you've taken a nighttime cold medicine. You head off to school and must perform on par all day, feeling awful, and do all of your work. In addition to that, the teacher pats you on the back and speaks to you the whole time to encourage you along. Now, write the alphabet backwards with your non-dominant hand, while swinging your opposite foot backwards in a circle." Kids with epilepsy take medication every day that makes them feel that way.

The educational progress of some children is also hampered by frequent and sometimes prolonged absences from school for medical treatment when flare-ups or relapses require hospitalization.

Second, as a group, students with health impairments or physical disabilities perform below average on measures of social-behavioral skills. Coster and Haltiwanger (2004) reported classroom teachers and other school professionals, such as PTs and OTs, rated more than 40% of the 62 elementary students with physical disabilities below mean on six of seven social-behavioral tasks considered necessary for optimal functioning and learning in school (e.g., following social conventions, compliance with adult directives, positive interaction with peers and adults, constructive responses to feedback, and personal care awareness).

Coping emotionally with a chronic health impairment or physical disability presents a major problem for some children (Antle, 2004; Kanner & Schafer, 2006). Maintaining peer relationships and a sense of belonging to the group can be difficult for a child who must frequently leave the instructional activity or the classroom to participate in therapeutic or health care routines. Prolonged absences my create anxiety about fitting in at school (Olsen & Sutton, 1998). Students with health impairments and physical disabilities frequently identify concerns about physical appearance as reasons for emotional difficulties and feelings of depression (Sexson & Dingle, 2001).

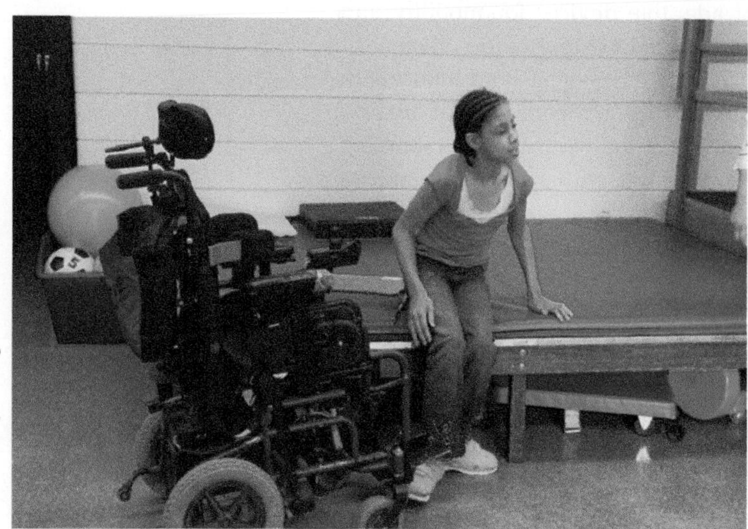

Source: Katelyn Metzger/Merrill Education

The severity, age of onset, and visibility of health impairments and physical disabilities affect development and behavior.

Variables Affecting the Impact of Health Impairments and Physical Disabilities on Educational Performance

Many factors must be considered in assessing the effects of a physical disability or health impairment on a child's development and behavior. A physical impairment or medical condition can limit a child's ability to engage in age-appropriate activities, mobility, cognitive functioning, social and emotional development, sensory functioning, and communication across a continuum ranging from normal functioning (no impact) to extremely impaired. A minor or transient health or physical impairment is not likely to have lasting effects, but a severe, chronic impairment can greatly limit a child's range of experiences. In addition to the severity with which the condition affects different areas of functioning, two particularly important factors are age of onset and visibility.

AGE OF ONSET Some conditions are congenital (present at birth); other conditions are acquired during the child's development as a result of illness, accident, or unknown cause. As with all disabilities, it is important for the teacher to be aware of the child's age at the time he acquired the health or physical impairment. A child who has not had the use of his legs since birth may have missed out on some important developmental experiences, particularly if he did not receive early intervention services. In contrast, a teenager who suddenly loses the use of her legs has likely had a normal range of experiences throughout childhood but may need considerable support from her parents, teachers, specialists, and peers in adapting to life with this newly acquired impairment.

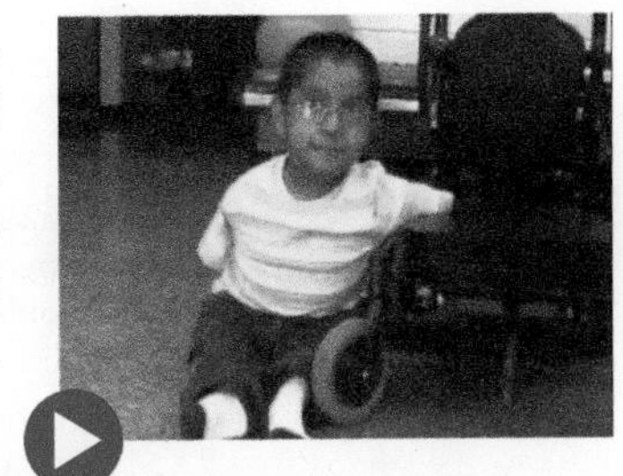

Pearson eText
Video Example 11.4
Jose's parallel curriculum includes learning how to use his special wheelchair.

VISIBILITY Physical impairments and health conditions range from highly conspicuous to invisible. How children think about themselves and the degree to which others accept them often are affected by the visibility of a condition. Some children use a variety of special orthopedic appliances, such as wheelchairs, braces, crutches, and adaptive tables. They may ride to school on a specially equipped bus or van. In school, they may need assistance using the toilet or may wear helmets. Although such special devices and adaptations help children meet important needs, they make the physical impairment more visible, which makes the child look even more different from her classmates without disabilities.

FIGURE 11.2 Key Historical Events in the Education of Children with Physical Disabilities and Health Impairments

DATE	HISTORICAL EVENT	EDUCATIONAL IMPLICATIONS
1893	Industrial School for Crippled and Deformed Children is established in Boston.	This was the first special institution for children with physical disabilities in the United States (Eberle, 1922).
Circa 1900	The first special classes for children with physical impairments begin in Chicago.	This was the first time children with physical disabilities were educated in public schools (La Vor, 1976).
Early 1900s	Serious outbreaks of tuberculosis and polio occur in the United States.	This led to increasing numbers of children with physical impairments being educated by local schools in special classes for the "crippled" or "delicate" (Walker & Jacobs, 1985).
Early 20th century	Winthrop Phelps demonstrates that children can be helped through physical therapy and the effective use of braces. Earl Carlson (who himself had cerebral palsy) was a strong advocate of developing the intellectual potential of children with physical disabilities through appropriate education.	The efforts of these two American physicians contributed to increased understanding and acceptance of children with physical disabilities, and to recognition that physical impairment did not preclude potential for educational achievement and self-sufficiency.
Early 20th century to 1970s	Decisions to "ignore, isolate, and institutionalize these children are often based on mental incompetence presumed because of physical disabilities, especially those involving communication and use of upper extremities" (Conner, Scandary, & Tullock, 1988, p. 6).	Increasing numbers of children with mild physical disabilities and health conditions were educated in public schools. Most children with severe physical disabilities were educated in special schools or community agencies (e.g., the United Cerebral Palsy Association).
1975	PL 94-142 mandates a free appropriate public education for all children with disabilities and requires schools to provide related services (e.g., transportation services, physical therapy, school health services) necessary for students to be educated in the least restrictive environment.	No longer could a child be denied the right to attend the local public school because there was a flight of stairs at the entrance, bathrooms were not accessible, or school buses were not equipped to transport wheelchairs. The related services provision of IDEA transformed schools from "solely scholastic institutions into therapeutic agencies" (Palfrey, 1995, p. 265).

(Continued)

FIGURE 11.2 (Continued)

DATE	HISTORICAL EVENT	EDUCATIONAL IMPLICATIONS
1984	The Supreme Court rules in *Independent School District v. Tatro* that schools must provide intermittent catheterization as a supportive or related service if necessary to enable a student with disabilities to receive a public education.	The *Tatro* ruling expanded the range of related services that schools are required to provide and clarified the differences between school health services, which can be performed by a nonphysician, and medical services, which are provided by physicians for diagnostic or eligibility purposes.
1984	The World Institute on Disability is cofounded by Ed Roberts, an inspirational leader for self-advocacy by people with disabilities.	This was a major milestone in the civil rights and self-advocacy movement by people with disabilities.
1990	Americans with Disabilities Act (ADA; PL 101-336) is passed.	The ADA provides civil rights protections to all people with disabilities in private sector employment and mandates access to all public services, accommodations, transportation, and telecommunications.
1999	The U.S. Supreme Court rules in *Cedar Rapids v. Garret F.* that a local school district must pay for the one-on-one nursing care for a medically fragile student who required continuous monitoring of his ventilator and other health-maintenance routines.	The decision reaffirmed and extended the Court's ruling in the 1984 *Tatro* case that schools must provide any and all health services needed for students with disabilities to attend school, as long as performance of those services does not require a licensed physician.
2004	The Improving Access to Assistive Technology Act of 2004 (PL 108-364) is signed into law. Third time Congress amends and extends provisions of the Technology-Related Assistance for Individuals with Disabilities Act of 1988.	Congress funds an Assistive Technology Act Project (ATAP) in each state to assist people with disabilities in obtaining AT services throughout their entire life spans. ATAP activities include product demonstrations; AT device loan programs; financing assistance; and public awareness regarding the availability, benefits, and costs of AT. For more info, go to www.resna.org/taproject.

The visibility of some physical disabilities may cause other children and adults to underestimate the child's abilities and limit opportunities for participation. By contrast, many health conditions such as asthma or epilepsy are not visible so others may not realize that the child needs accommodations. The fact that the child functions normally most of the time supports this misperception (Best, 2010b).

Educational Approaches

Learning Outcome 11.4 Discuss the importance of a "parallel curriculum" for students with health impairments or physical disabilities.

Special education of children with health impairments and physical disabilities in the United States has a history of more than 100 years (Figure 11.2). Although some students can fully access and benefit from education with minimal accommodations, the intensive health and learning needs of other students require a complex and coordinated array of specialized instruction, therapy, and related services. In addition to progressing in the general education curriculum to the maximum extent possible, many students with health impairments or physical disabilities also need intensive instruction in a "parallel curriculum" on "coping with their disabilities" (Bowe, 2000, p. 75). Similar in function to the "expanded core curriculum" for students with visual impairments, the parallel curriculum for students with health impairments and physical disabilities includes increasing independence by self-administering special health care routines; using adaptive methods and assistive technologies for mobility, communication, and daily-living tasks; and learning self-determination and self-advocacy skills. See *Transition: Next Year Is Now,* "Self-Management Tools for Adult Success."

Transition: Next Year Is Now

Self-Management Tools for Adult Success

Children with health impairments and physical disabilities grow up to be adults with many of the same challenges they faced in school. For instance, adults who were diagnosed with ADHD as children continue to struggle with executive function deficits and may have difficulty continuing on to college or finding and keeping a job (Uchida et al., 2018). And after high school, in many cases, young adults are out on their own, learning to manage their schedules, appointments, medications, and treatments independently. Fortunately, high-tech self-management tools are helping adults with health and physical disabilities live more independently than ever.

Instruction in middle and high school should give students access to such tools and opportunities to practice using them for time management and productivity, keeping up with treatments and medications, and managing health and wellness.

HLP19 Use assistive and instructional technologies.

Time Management and Productivity

With so many time management and productivity apps on the market, there is likely one that will help students who struggle with executive function skills. For instance, "Todoist" and "Wunderlist" allow users to create and organize to-do lists, prioritize tasks, monitor progress to completion, and set reminders to get things done. Timer apps, such as "Timeglass" or simply the timer and stopwatch on students' smartphones, come in handy when teaching students how to monitor how they spend their time or to encourage them to get a task (or step within a task) done quickly.

Keeping up with Appointments, Treatments, and Medications

Keeping up with just one medication can be a challenge, but many individuals with physical disabilities or health impairments are managing multiple medications and treatments. For instance, an individual with cerebral palsy may have physical therapy, occupational therapy, and speech appointments to manage as well as medications to take and therapies to implement at home. Good medication management apps, such as "Medisafe" and "MyTherapy: Medication Reminder," not only remind users to take their medication but can also assist with automatic prescription refills and sharing information with others (e.g., medical providers, family members) (Salgado et al., 2018). Apps can also make self-monitoring symptoms, treatments, and triggers for many health conditions easier (e.g., "Seizure Tracker," "DiabetesConnect," "Asthma Buddy").

Self-managing Health and Wellness

Healthy eating, exercise, and other good health habits are important for everyone, but they can be critical for individuals with physical and health impairments. Mobile technology can play a role in helping individuals manage these habits. Some health conditions require special diets. For example, individuals with epilepsy may be on a ketogenic diet and can use a food or macronutrient counter app such as "My Fitness Pal" or "Carb Manager" to help them self-monitor their food intake. Individuals with spinal cord injuries, other physical disabilities, and even ADHD may benefit from physical activity, so they may find apps such as "Fitbit" or "JEFIT" helpful for self-monitoring their exercise. Students can learn to self-manage a range of other good health habits, including hygiene, sleep, screen time, and hydration. For instance, people with sickle cell disease need to drink ample water to prevent and manage symptoms, so apps like "Daily Water" or "Aqualert" can prompt and reinforce water drinking.

When deciding which apps to share with students, keep in mind components of effective instruction. For instance, Tomaseone et al. (2018) reviewed behavior change techniques designed to improve physical activity for adults with spinal cord injuries. Common components of effective behavior change self-management interventions included explicit instruction on how to perform the behavior, goal setting, problem solving, action planning, and social support. Select apps that incorporate some or all of these elements. It is also important to recognize that preference for self-management tools is highly individualized. Encourage students to practice using a variety of tools to find one that works for them (Tomaseone et al., 2018).

YouTube

Pearson eText
Video Example 11.5
For students with health impairments, successful transition to adulthood includes learning to manage treatments and medications.
https://www.youtube.com/watch?time_continue=2&v=RDGyHzUXlSo

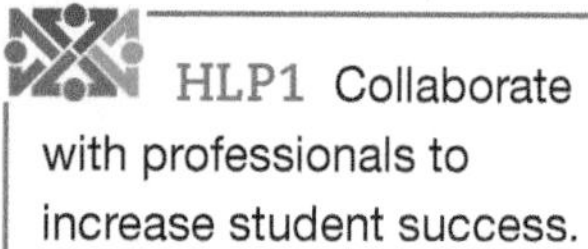
HLP1 Collaborate with professionals to increase student success.

Teaming and Related Services

The transdisciplinary team approach has special relevance for students with health impairments and physical disabilities. No other group of exceptional children comes into contact, both in and out of school, with as many different teachers, physicians, therapists, and other specialists. Because the medical, educational, therapeutic, vocational, and social needs of these students are often complex, educational and health care personnel must openly communicate and cooperate with one another. Two particularly important members of the team for many children are the PT and the OT. Each is a licensed health professional who has completed a specialized training program.

Pearson eText
Video Example 11.6
Kavana works with her physical therapist to build strength and improve her posture.

PHYSICAL THERAPISTS **Physical therapists (PTs)** focus on the development and maintenance of motor skills, movement, and posture. They may prescribe specific exercises to help a child increase control of muscles and use specialized equipment, such as braces, effectively. Massage and prescriptive exercises are perhaps the most frequently applied procedures, but physical therapy can also include swimming, heat treatment, special positioning for feeding and toileting, and other techniques. PTs encourage children to be as motorically independent as possible; help develop muscular function; and reduce pain, discomfort, and long-term physical damage. They may also suggest sitting positions and activities in the classroom and devise exercise or play programs that children with and without disabilities can enjoy together.

OCCUPATIONAL THERAPISTS **Occupational therapists (OTs)** focus on children's participation in activities, especially those related to self-help, employment, recreation, communication, and aspects of daily living (e.g., dressing, eating, personal hygiene). An OT may help a child learn (or relearn) motor behaviors such as drinking from a modified cup, buttoning clothes, tying shoes, pouring liquids, cooking, and typing on a computer keyboard. These activities can enhance a child's physical development, independence, vocational potential, and self-concept. OTs conduct specialized assessments and make recommendations to parents and teachers regarding the use of appliances, materials, and activities at home and school. Many OTs also work with vocational rehabilitation specialists to help students find secure work and independent living options for students after they complete educational programs. To find out how a PT and an OT worked with a third-grade student with spastic cerebral palsy and other members of the student's IEP team to support five learning outcomes, see Szabo (2000).

OTHER SPECIALISTS Other specialists who frequently provide instruction and related services to children with physical disabilities and health impairments include the following:

- *Speech-language pathologists (SLPs)* provide speech therapy, language interventions, oral motor coordination (e.g., chewing and swallowing), and augmentative and alternative communication (AAC) services.
- *Adapted physical educators* provide physical education activities designed to meet the individual needs of students with disabilities.
- *Recreation therapists* provide instruction in leisure activities and therapeutic recreation.
- *School nurses* provide specific health care services to students, monitor students' health, and inform individualized education program (IEP) teams about the effects of medical conditions on students' educational programs.
- *Prosthetists* make and fit artificial limbs.
- *Orthotists* design and fit braces and other assistive devices.
- *Orientation and mobility specialists* teach students to navigate their environment as effectively and independently as possible.
- *Biomedical engineers* develop or adapt technology to meet a student's specialized needs.
- *Health aides* carry out medical procedures and health care services in the classroom.
- *Counselors and medical social workers* help students and families adjust to disabilities.

Environmental Modifications

Environmental modifications are frequently necessary to enable a student with health or physical impairments to participate more fully and independently in school.

HLP7 Provide a consistent, organized, and respectful learning environment.

Environmental modifications include adaptations to provide increased access to a task or an activity, changing the way instruction is delivered, and changing how a task is done (Best et al., 2010; Heller et al., 1995). Although barrier-free architecture is the most publicly visible type of environmental modification for making community buildings and services more accessible, some of the most functional adaptations require little or no cost:

- Install paper-cup dispensers near water fountains so students in wheelchairs can use them.
- Move a class or an activity to an accessible part of a school building so a student with a physical impairment can participate.
- Provide soft-tip pens that require less pressure for writing.
- Provide a head-mounted pointer stick and keyboard guard that enable a student with limited fine-motor control to strike one computer key at a time.
- Change desks and tabletops to appropriate heights for students who are very short or who use wheelchairs.

TEACHING & LEARNING

P.E. Is for Everyone!

Why Should P.E. Be a Part of Every Child's Experience? All children benefit from the physical activity, social experiences, and fun P.E. has to offer; however, some students with gross motor or developmental disabilities require accommodations or modifications to the general physical education curriculum. Adapted physical education (APE) is physical education modified for students with disabilities.

How Is P.E. Adapted for Students with Disabilities? Appropriate and effective APE has much in common with other special education services discussed throughout this book:

- ***Instructional decisions are individualized.*** Goals, objectives, teaching methods, accommodations, and modifications are selected to meet each student's individual needs. Some students, for instance, need adapted equipment. Juan, one of Featured Teacher Dave Martinez's students, has an IEP objective that focuses on learning to bowl using a ramp and a modified ball. Juan wants to participate in Dave's Special Olympics program and is nearing the age of eligibility to do so. Learning to use this equipment not only helps Juan participate in PE at school but will also help prepare him for a community-based recreation activity.
- ***Services are delivered in a continuum of placements.*** APE may take place in a regular physical education class or in a separate setting, depending on the needs of the student. Juan uses modified bowling equipment in the school's gymnasium alongside peers without disabilities who are also learning to bowl.
- ***Services are delivered collaboratively.*** APE teachers are members of the multidisciplinary team. Children who receive APE often need related services, such as physical therapy, occupational therapy, or speech/language therapy, so APE teachers often collaborate, consult, and co-teach with PTs, OTs, and SLPs. Dave and the regular PE teacher sometimes co-teach lessons during Juan's PE class, and sometimes his PT contributes to lessons as well.
- ***Data are continuously collected and carefully analyzed to drive instruction.*** APE teachers task analyze the skills they're teaching and engage in frequent data collection to monitor students' progress toward objectives. Featured Teacher Dave Martinez uses various mobile applications to help him collect data. For instance, a high-speed camera app allows him to capture action, such as Juan's bowling, and analyze student performance frame by frame. He is then able to share these picture data with Juan's parents at IEP meetings to show the progress he is making.

HLP11 Identify and prioritize long- and short-term learning goals.

HLP1 Collaborate with professionals to increase student success.

- Provide a wooden pointer to enable a student to reach the upper buttons on an elevator control panel.
- Modify response requirements by allowing written responses instead of spoken ones or vice versa.

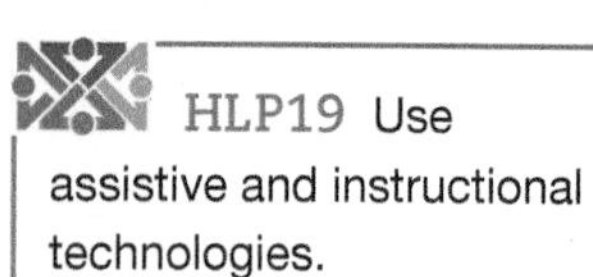
HLP19 Use assistive and instructional technologies.

Assistive Technology

Although the term *technology* often conjures up images of sophisticated computers and other hardware, technology includes any systematic method based on scientific principles for accomplishing a practical task or purpose. IDEA defines **assistive technology** as both assistive technology devices and the services needed to help a child obtain and effectively use the devices.

> *Assistive technology device* means any item, piece of equipment, or product system, whether acquired commercially off the shelf, modified, or customized, that is used to increase, maintain, or improve the functional capabilities of a child with a disability. The term does not include a medical device that is surgically implanted or the replacement of such device (20 USC §1401 [2004], 20 *CFR* §300.5).

> *Assistive technology service* means any service that directly assists a child with a disability in the selection, acquisition, or use of an assistive technology device (20 USC §1401 [2004], 20 *CFR* §300.6).

Individuals with physical disabilities use both low-tech assistive devices (e.g., adapted eating utensils, a "grabber" or "reacher" that enables a person in a wheelchair to reach items on a shelf) and high-tech assistive devices (e.g., computerized synthetic speech devices, electronic switches activated by eye movements) for a wide variety of purposes, including mobility, performance of daily living skills, improved environmental manipulation and control, better communication, access to computers, recreation and leisure, and enhanced learning (Best et al., 2010; Dell et al., 2016). IEP team members should not view a student's acquisition and use of assistive technology as an educational outcome in itself but as a means of increasing the student's independence and access to various activities and opportunities.

Some students cannot move freely from place to place without the assistance of a mobility device. Many children as young as 3 to 5 years old can learn to explore their environment with freedom and independence in "energy efficient, creative, wheeled scooter boards and wheeled go-carts that provide mobility without restricting upper or lower extremity functions" (Evans & Smith, 1993, p. 1418). Adapted bicycles enable children with disabilities to enjoy the thrill of bicycle riding and reap the health benefits (Klein et al., 2005).

Advances in wheelchair design have made manual chairs lighter and stronger, powered chairs have been adapted for use in rural areas, and new environmental controls have put wheelchair users into contact with both immediate and distant parts of their world. A student should not be described as being "confined to a wheelchair." This expression suggests the person is restrained or even imprisoned. Most students who use wheelchairs leave them from time to time to exercise, travel in an automobile, or lie down. The preferred language is "has a wheelchair" or "uses a wheelchair to get around."

New technological aids for communication are used increasingly by children whose physical impairments prevent them from speaking clearly. For students who can speak but have limited motor function, voice input/output products enable them to access computers. Such developments allow students with physical impairments to communicate expressively and receptively with others and take part in a wide range of instructional programs. Many individuals with physical disabilities use telecommunications technologies to expand their world, gain access to information and services, and meet new people. Many children and adults with disabilities use email, Facebook, and other social media to communicate with others, make new friends, and build and maintain relationships.

Technology can seldom be pulled off the shelf and serve a student with disabilities with maximum effectiveness. Before purchasing and training a child to use any assistive technology device, the IEP team should carefully consider certain characteristics of the child and the potential technologies that might be selected as well as the impact of using those technologies on the child's family (Alper & Raharinirina, 2006; Parette & Brotherson, 1996). An assessment of the child's academic skills, social skills, and physical capabilities should help identify the goals and objectives for the technology and narrow down the kinds of devices that may be effective.

The team should also determine the child's preferences for certain types of technology. The IEP team should then consider the characteristics of potentially appropriate technologies, including availability, simplicity of operation, initial and ongoing cost, adaptability to meet the child's changing needs, and the device's reliability and repair record. A good example of an IEP team individualizing assistive technology for a student with cerebral palsy is shown in Video Example 8.6. Bausch and Ault (2008) detail how IEP teams can design an assistive technology implementation plan to ensure devices are used and have their intended outcomes.

HLP6 Use student assessment data, analyze instructional practices, and make necessary adjustments that improve student outcomes.

Animal Assistance

Animals can help children and adults with physical disabilities in many ways. Nearly everyone is familiar with guide dogs, which can help people who are blind travel independently. Another recent and promising approach to the use of animals by people with disabilities is the helper or service dog. Depending on a person's needs, dogs can be trained to carry books and other objects (in saddlebags), pick up telephone receivers, turn light switches on or off, and open doors. Dogs can also assist with balance and support—for example, to help a person propel a wheelchair up a steep ramp or stand up from a seated position. Additionally, dogs can be trained to contact family members or neighbors in an emergency. Monkeys also have been trained to serve as personal care attendants for people with disabilities.

In addition to providing practical assistance and enhancing the independence of people with disabilities, animals also have social value as companions. People frequently report their helper animals serve as icebreakers in opening up conversations and contacts with people without disabilities in the school and community.

YouTube

Pearson eText
Video Example 11.7
Helping Hands trains monkeys to assist people with spinal cord injuries.
https://www.youtube.com/watch?v=vRzp9O9Qc1o

Special Health Care Routines

Many students with health or physical impairments require specialized procedures such as taking prescribed medication or self-administering insulin shots, CIC (described earlier in this chapter), tracheotomy care, ventilator or respirator care, and managing special nutrition and dietary needs. These special health-related needs are prescribed in an **individualized health care plan (IHCP)**, which is included as part of the student's IEP. In addition to general information describing the history, diagnosis, and assessment data relevant to the condition, the IHCP "includes precise information about how to handle routine healthcare procedures, physical management techniques, and medical emergencies that may arise while the child is at school" (Getch et al., 2007, p. 48). Teachers and school personnel must be trained to safely administer the health care procedures they are expected to perform (Heller et al., 2000). In-depth information on health care procedures, including sample IHCP objectives, task analysis, and teaching techniques, can be found in Heller et al. (2008).

Often, well-meaning teachers, classmates, and parents tend to do too much for a child with a health or physical impairment. It may be difficult or time consuming for the child to learn to care for his own needs, but the confidence and skills gained from independent functioning are well worth the effort in the long run (Lehr & Harayama, 2016). Students who learn to perform all or part of their daily health care needs increase their ability to function independently in nonschool environments and lessen their dependence on caregivers (Betz & Nehring, 2007; Collins, 2007).

Service dogs assist with daily living tasks and provide companionship.

IMPORTANCE OF POSITIONING, SEATING, AND MOVEMENT Proper positioning, seating, and regular movement are critical for children with physical disabilities. Proper positioning and movement promote muscle and bone development and help maintain healthy skin. In addition to these health benefits, positioning can influence how children with physical disabilities are perceived and accepted by others. Simple adjustments can contribute to improved appearance and greater comfort and increased health for children with physical disabilities (Best et al., 2010; Cantu, 2004):

- Good positioning results in alignment and proximal support of the body.
- Stability positively affects use of the upper body.
- Stability promotes feelings of physical security and safety.
- Good positioning distributes pressure evenly and provides comfort for seating tolerance and long-term use.
- Good positioning can reduce deformity.
- Positions must be changed frequently.

Proper seating helps combat poor circulation, muscle tightness, and pressure sores and contributes to proper digestion, respiration, and physical development. Be attentive to the following (Heller et al., 2008):

- The face should be forward, in midline position.
- The shoulders should be in a midline position, not hunched over.
- The trunk should be in a midline position; maintain normal curvature of the spine.
- A seatbelt, pommel or leg separator, or shoulder and chest straps may be necessary for shoulder or upper trunk support and upright positions.
- Pelvic position: Hips as far back in the chair as possible and weight distributed evenly on both sides of the buttocks.
- Foot support: Both feet level and supported on the floor or wheelchair pedals.

Skin care is a major concern for many children with physical disabilities. Caregivers should check the skin underneath braces or splints daily to identify persistent red spots that indicate an improper fit. Someone should perform skin checks at least twice daily. Students who can conduct self-checks of their skin should be taught to do so. Use of a long-handled mirror can reduce the student's dependence on others for this self-care task (Ricci-Balich & Behm, 1996). A health care professional should be contacted if any spot does not fade within 20 minutes after the pressure is relieved (Rapport et al., 2016). Students who can use their arms should be taught to perform "chair pushups" in which they lift their buttocks off the seat for 5 to 10 seconds. Doing chair pushups every 30 to 60 minutes may prevent pressure sores. Children who cannot perform pushups can shift their weight by bending forward and sideways.

LIFTING AND TRANSFERRING STUDENTS To prevent the development of pressure sores and help students maintain proper seating and positioning, teachers must know how to move and transfer students with physical disabilities. Teachers should follow routines for lifting and transferring a child with disabilities that entail standard procedures for each child for (a) making contact with the child, (b) communicating what is going to happen in a manner the child can understand, (c) preparing the child physically for the transfer, and (d) requiring the child to participate in the routine as much as possible (Stremel et al., 1990). Figure 11.3 shows an example of an individualized routine for lifting and carrying a preschool child with cerebral palsy and spastic quadriplegia. Posting charts and photos of recommended positions for individual students can remind teachers and other staff to use proper transferring and positioning techniques.

Independence and Self-Esteem

All children, whether or not they face the challenges presented by a chronic health condition or physical disability, need to develop respect for themselves and feel they have a valued place in their families, schools, and communities. Effective teachers encourage children to

FIGURE 11.3 Example of a Routine for Lifting and Carrying a Child with Physical Disabilities

Name: Susan **Date:** 5/12/2010

Lifting and Carrying Routine

Follow these steps each time you pick Susan up from the floor or move her from one piece of equipment to another or move her in the classroom from one location to another.

Step	Activity	Desired Response
Contacting	Touch Susan on her arm or shoulder and tell her you are going to move her from _________ to _________.	Wait for Susan to relax.
Communicating	Tell Susan where you are going and show her a picture or object that represents where she is going. For example, show her her coat and say, "We are going outside now to play."	Wait for Susan to respond with facial expressions and vocalizations. (Try not to get her so hyped that she becomes more spastic.)
Preparing	Make sure Susan's muscle tone is not stiff before you move her. Use deep pressure touch with a flat hand on her chest area to help relax her.	Wait to make sure that Susan's body is relaxed and in alignment (as much as possible).
Lifting	Place Susan in a sitting position and lift her from sitting unless she is in the stander, where she will need to be lifted from standing. Tell her that you are going to lift her. Put your arms around Susan's back and under her knees and bend her knees to her chest so that you maintain her in a flexed position.	Wait for Susan to reach her arms forward toward you and facilitate at her shoulders if she does not initiate reach within 10 seconds.
Carrying	Turn Susan away from you so that she is facing away and can see where you are moving. Lean her back against your body to provide support and hold her with one arm under her hips with her legs in front. If her legs become stiff, use your other arm to hold her legs apart by coming under one leg and between the two legs to hold them gently apart.	Susan will be able to see where she is going and can use her arms to indicate location (grossly).
Repositioning	Put Susan in the next position she is to use for the activity. Tell her what is happening; "Music is next, and you are going to sit on the floor so you can play the instruments with Jilly and Tommy."	Susan is ready to participate in the next activity.

Source: From Campbell, P. H. (2010). Addressing motor disabilities. In M. E. Snell & F. Brown (Eds.), *Instruction of students with severe disabilities* (7th ed., p. 362).

develop a positive, realistic view of themselves and their physical conditions. They enable the children to experience success; accomplishment; and, at times, failure. They expect the children to meet reasonable standards of performance and behavior. They help children cope with disabilities wherever possible and realize that, beyond their impairments, these children have many qualities that make them unique individuals.

Students with physical limitations should be encouraged to develop as much independence as possible (Angell et al., 2010; Enright, 2000). Nevertheless, most people with physical disabilities find it necessary to rely on others for assistance at certain times and in certain situations. Effective teachers can help students cope with their disabilities, set realistic expectations, and accept help gracefully when it is needed.

Many people with disabilities report their hardware (e.g., wheelchairs, prosthetic limbs, communication devices) creates a great deal of curiosity and leads to frequent, repetitive questions from strangers. Learning how to explain their disabilities and respond to questions can be an appropriate component of educational programs for some children. They may also benefit from discussing concerns such as when to ask for help from others and when to decline offers of assistance.

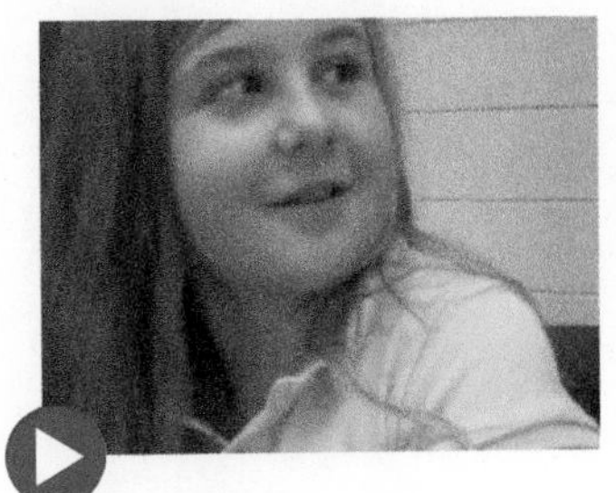

Pearson eText
Video Example 11.8
Charlotte is learning to walk with her new prosthesis.

Many self-help groups are available for people with disabilities. These groups help provide information and support to children affected by similar disabilities. It is usually encouraging for a child and parent to meet and observe capable, independent adults who have disabilities, and worthwhile helping relationships can be established. Teachers can promote self-knowledge and self-confidence in their students with physical disabilities by introducing them to such adults and groups. Some self-advocacy groups operate centers for independent living, which emphasize adaptive devices, financial benefits, access to jobs, and provision of personal care attendants.

Placement Options

Learning Outcome 11.5 Explain why the continuum of educational services and placement options is especially critical for students with health impairments or physical disabilities.

For no group of exceptional children is the continuum of educational services and placement options more relevant than for students with special health needs and physical impairments. Most children with health or physical impairments spend at least part of the school day in regular classrooms. During the 2018–2019 school year, about 67% of students with OHIs and about 54% of those who received special education services under the category of orthopedic impairment were educated in regular classrooms (U.S. Department of Education, 2020a). The percentage of students in each disability category served in resource rooms was 20% and 16%, respectively.

Many children with health impairments and physical disabilities are also served in special classes. In 2016, about 8% of all students with OHI and 22% of those who received special education services under the category of orthopedic impairments were educated in separate classrooms (U.S. Department of Education, 2020a). Special classes usually provide smaller class sizes; more adapted equipment; and easier access to the services of professionals such as physicians, PTs and OTs, adapted physical educators, and specialists in communication disorders and therapeutic recreation. Some districts build or adapt school buildings especially for students with physical disabilities.

Some children with the most severe impairments are served in homebound or hospital education programs. If a child's medical condition necessitates hospitalization or treatment at home for a lengthy period (generally 30 days or more), the local school district is obligated to develop an IEP and provide appropriate educational services to the child through a qualified teacher. Some children need home- or hospital-based instruction because their life support equipment cannot be made portable.

A **technology-dependent student** is "one who needs both a medical device to compensate for the loss of a vital body function and substantial and ongoing nursing care to avoid death or further disability" (Office of Technology Assessment, 1987, p. 3). Educators also use the term *medically fragile* to refer to students "who are in constant need of medical supervision to prevent life-threatening situations" (Katsiyannis & Yell, 2000, p. 317). As Lehr and McDaid (1993) pointed out, however, many of these children are "survivors of many adverse conditions, who in fact are not fragile at all, but remarkably strong to be able to rebound from periods of acute illness" (p. 7).

Home and hospital settings are usually regarded as the most restrictive placements because little or no interaction with students without disabilities is likely. Most large hospitals and medical centers employ educational specialists who cooperate with the hospitalized student's home school district in planning and delivering instruction. Itinerant teachers or tutors hired by the school district visit homebound children regularly. Some school programs use closed-circuit TV to enable children to see, hear, and participate in class discussions and demonstrations from their beds.

One should not assume that a technology-dependent child cannot be educated in the public schools. After examining the experiences of 77 families of children who are ventilator assisted, the authors of a study on the educational placements of such children concluded "barriers to the integration of these children into school-based programs are attitudinal more than technological" (Jones et al., 1996, p. 47).

Related Services in the Classroom

We will likely see a continuation of the trend to serve children with health and physical impairments in regular classrooms as much as possible. Therapists and other related service and support personnel will come into classrooms to assist teachers, children, and classmates.

Including students with physical impairments and special health care needs in regular classrooms, however, has raised several controversial issues. Many questions center on the extent to which teachers and schools should be responsible for a child's physical health care needs. Some educators and school administrators believe services such as catheterization, tracheotomy care, and tube feeding are more medical than educational and should not be the school's responsibility. The expense of such services, the training and supervision of personnel, and the availability of insurance pose potential problems for school districts. Similar questions have been raised with regard to the assistive devices and special therapeutic services children may need to access and benefit from a public education. For example, who should bear the cost of an expensive computerized communication system for a child with cerebral palsy—the parents, the school, both, or some other agency?

Two landmark U.S. Supreme Court cases have made clear the government's position. In *Irving Independent School District v. Tatro* (1984), the Court decided a school district was obligated to provide CIC to a young child with spina bifida. The Court considered catheterization to be a related service, necessary for the child to remain in the least restrictive educational setting and able to be performed by a trained layperson.

Cedar Rapids Community School District v. Garret F. (1999) involved nursing care for a middle school student who was paralyzed in a motorcycle accident at the age of 4 years and could breathe only with an electric ventilator or by someone pumping an air bag attached to his tracheotomy tube. In addition to having someone monitor and check the settings on his ventilator, Garret required continuous assistance with his tracheotomy, positioning in his wheelchair, catheterization, assessments of his blood pressure, and assistance with food and drink. Garret's mother had used money from insurance and a settlement with the motorcycle company to hire a nurse to care for his medical needs. When Garret reached middle school, his mother asked the school district to assume the cost of his physical care during the school day. The school district refused, believing it was not responsible under IDEA for providing continuous nursing care. The Supreme Court agreed with lower courts that the nursing services were related services because Garret could not attend school without them and ruled the school district had to pay for continuous one-on-one nursing care. These two rulings used what is known as a "bright-line test" for making decisions about related services (Katsiyannis & Yell, 2000). A bright-line test is clearly stated and easy to follow. The bright-line test established in the *Tatro* case and upheld by the *Garret* case is if a licensed physician is required to perform a service, the school district is not responsible for paying for it. If a nurse or a health aide can perform the service, even if it is medical in nature, it is considered a related service the school district must provide under IDEA to give the child access to a free appropriate public education. You can find reviews and discussions of special education law and legal precedents concerning the schools' responsibility for providing assistive technology and special health care services in Wright and Wright (2006) and Yell (2019a).

Inclusive Attitudes

Acceptance is a basic need of all children. How parents, teachers, classmates, and others react to children with health impairments or physical disabilities is at least as important as the disability itself. Turner-Henson et al. (1994) conducted interviews with parents of children with chronic illnesses and reported one third (34.5%) of the parents had experienced specific incidences of discrimination concerning their children. Although the study did not focus on schools, more than half (55%) of the problems parents cited occurred at school (e.g., child excluded from parties because of food limitations; teacher thinks child is faking low blood sugar). Peers were the second-most common source of discrimination (36%). Indeed, children with disabilities are at higher risk of bully victimization, and one study found that children with ADHD are at greatest risk compared to other disability groups (Blake et al., 2016). Many children with health impairments or physical disabilities experience excessive pity and overprotection; others are bullied, stared at, teased, and excluded (Pinquart, 2017; Pivik et al., 2002). Featured Teacher Dave Martinez works to encourage peer acceptance by using peer facilitators in his APE classes. He explains, "This allows for more individualized instruction for students with disabilities while promoting acceptance of differences among students without disabilities."

The classroom can be a useful place to discuss disabilities and encourage understanding and acceptance of a child with a health impairment or physical disability. Some teachers find simulation or role-playing activities helpful. Classmates might, for example, have the opportunity to use wheelchairs, braces, or crutches to expand their awareness of some barriers a classmate with physical disabilities faces. Factual information can also help build a general understanding. Classmates should learn to use accurate terminology and offer the correct kind of assistance when needed.

ADVICE FROM THE FEATURED TEACHER by Dave Martinez

Source: Amy Aenchbacher

Promoting the Success of Students with Special Health Care Needs and Physical Disabilities

Collaborate with Multidisciplinary Team Members

- ***Keep lines of communication open and positive.*** I schedule frequent (weekly, biweekly, or monthly) meetings with everyone on the team to keep the communication process flowing.
- ***Welcome others into your teaching space.*** I invite professionals from other disciplines (e.g., OTs and PTs) to join my physical education class and provide their services during my lesson. This transdisciplinary approach allows us to observe and learn from each other and to work together to better support our students' individual needs.
- ***Attend school- and district-wide meetings.*** Go beyond attending required faculty meetings, and participate in building and district-wide events. This is a great way to stay connected with colleagues and contribute to the school community.

Individualize

- ***Look beyond labels.*** Students with health impairments and physical disabilities are a very diverse group. Standardized approaches just won't work with everyone. It is easy to focus on a student's disability label, but the label doesn't tell the whole story. Learn what each child needs to be successful.
- ***Identify and build on each student's strengths.*** It's easy to focus on a child's skill deficits or visible disabilities, but every child has strengths and interests. Focus on your students' strengths and unique capabilities; doing so will facilitate a learning environment that is accepting of all students.
- ***Get to know your students and their families.*** Communicate with your students, parents, and other family members to identify what recreational and leisure time activities are valuable and relevant in the home and community. You can then create a program focused on the specific skills necessary to recreate in the home with family members and in the community with peers.

Go Beyond the School Walls and the School Day

- ***Be an advocate for your students.*** My school district does an excellent job inviting me to IEP and multidisciplinary team meetings. However, in many school districts, this is not always the case. Therefore, physical education (which includes adapted physical education) may not be documented in the IEP. APE teachers are responsible for advocating for quality physical education programming; therefore, it may be necessary to schedule a meeting with an administrator or special education facilitator. During the meeting, the APE specialist can highlight the requirements of IDEA as related to physical education. It may also be helpful for the APE specialist to bring documentation to support his or her advocacy efforts.
- ***Get involved in extracurricular activities and make community connections.*** I coordinate the Special Olympics program in my community, and I encourage the students enrolled in my

adapted physical education classes to participate. Doing so enables them to further develop their sport skills and personal fitness levels. Furthermore, I initiated a program in my school district that enables Special Olympics athletes the ability to earn varsity letters and attend school sports banquets at the end of each season. I am currently in the process of creating a wheelchair track and field team for high school students with physical disabilities. These nonacademic programs encourage positive equal-status relationships while promoting social acceptance for students with disabilities.

- ***Get active in state and national professional associations.*** I currently serve as the Georgia State Coordinator of the Adapted Physical Education National Standards Committee, and I serve as an expert for the Voices for Healthy Kids School Health Policy Consortium. This type of involvement helps me stay connected with others in the field and stay up-to-date on the latest research, which ultimately benefits my students.

Key Terms and Concepts

absence seizure
acquired immune deficiency syndrome (AIDS)
acute condition
assistive technology
asthma
ataxia
athetosis
attention-deficit/hyperactivity disorder (ADHD)
cerebral palsy
chronic conditions
clean intermittent catheterization
complex partial seizure
cystic fibrosis
diabetes
Duchenne muscular dystrophy
epilepsy
generalized tonic-clonic seizure
human immunodeficiency virus (HIV)
hydrocephalus
hypertonia
hypotonia
individualized health care plan
meningocele
muscular dystrophy
myelomeningocele
neuromotor impairment
occupational therapist (OT)
orthopedic impairment
other health impairment
paraplegia
physical therapist (PT)
quadriplegia
shunt
sickle cell disease
simple partial seizure
spina bifida
spina bifida occulta
Tay-Sachs disease
technology-dependent student
type 1 diabetes
type 2 diabetes
universal precautions

Summary

Attention-Deficit/Hyperactivity Disorder

- To be diagnosed with attention-deficit/hyperactivity disorder (ADHD), a child must consistently display six or more symptoms of inattention or hyperactivity-impulsivity for a period of at least 6 months.
- Students with ADHD are eligible for special education under the other health impairment (OHI) category if their symptoms adversely affect their academic performance. Many children with ADHD who meet eligibility requirements for special education are served under other disability categories, most often emotional disturbance or learning disabilities. Some children with ADHD are eligible for services under Section 504 of the Rehabilitation Act.
- The prevalence of ADHD is estimated to be 5% to 15% of all school-age children.
- Boys are much more likely to be diagnosed with ADHD than are girls.
- Genetic factors may contribute to a greater than normal risk of an ADHD diagnosis. ADHD is associated with a wide range of genetic disorders.
- Some individuals with ADHD have structural or biochemical differences in their brains that may play a causal role in their behavioral deficits and excesses.
- Behavioral interventions for students with ADHD include reinforcing on-task behavior, modifying assignments and instructional activities to promote success, and teaching self-control strategies.

- Stimulants are the most frequently prescribed medication for children with ADHD. About 65% to 75% of children with ADHD respond positively to stimulants, at least in the short term. Common but usually manageable side effects of stimulant medications include insomnia, decreased appetite, headaches, weight loss, and irritability.
- The use of stimulant medications with children is controversial. Some professionals believe the benefits outweigh the liabilities and drug therapy should be part of a comprehensive treatment program for children with ADHD. Other professionals are concerned stimulant medications have few long-term benefits and educators and parents rely too heavily on medical interventions.

Definitions of Health Impairments and Physical Disabilities

- Children with health impairments and physical disabilities are eligible for special education under two disability categories of IDEA: other health impairments and orthopedic impairments.
- Orthopedic impairments involve the skeletal system; neuromotor impairments involve the nervous system. Both are frequently described in terms of the affected parts of the body.
- Physical disabilities and health impairments may be congenital or acquired, chronic or acute.

Prevalence

- In 2018–2019, about 17% of all children who received special education services were served under the disability categories of other health impairments and orthopedic impairments. This figure does not include children with physical or health impairments who are served under other disability categories or who do not require special education services.

Types and Causes

- Epilepsy produces disturbances of movement, sensation, behavior, or consciousness.
- Diabetes is a disorder of metabolism that can often be controlled with insulin.
- Children with cystic fibrosis, sickle cell disease, asthma, HIV/AIDS, and other chronic health conditions may require special education and other related services, such as health care services and counseling.
- Cerebral palsy is a permanent condition arising from impairment to the brain and causing disturbances in voluntary motor functions.
- Spina bifida is a congenital condition that may cause loss of sensation and severe muscle weakness in the lower part of the body. Children with spina bifida can usually participate in most classroom activities but need assistance in toileting.
- Muscular dystrophy is an often fatal disease marked by progressive *atrophy* (wasting away) of the body's muscles.
- Spinal cord injuries are caused by a penetrating injury, stretching of the vertebral column, fracture of the vertebrae, or compression of the spinal cord and usually result in some form of paralysis below the site of the injury.

Characteristics

- Age of onset and visibility of the impairment are two important factors to consider when assessing the effects of a health condition or physical impairment on a child's development and behavior.

Educational Approaches

- Most children with health impairments and physical disabilities require services from an interdisciplinary team of professionals.
- Physical therapists (PTs) use specialized knowledge to plan and oversee a child's program for making correct and useful movements. Occupational therapists (OTs) focus on a child's participation in activities that will be useful in self-help, employment, recreation, communication, and other aspects of daily living.
- Modifications to the physical environment and classroom activities can enable students with health and physical impairments to participate more fully in the school program.
- An assistive technology device is any piece of equipment a child with disabilities uses to increase, maintain, or improve functional capabilities.
- Animals, particularly dogs and monkeys, can assist people with physical disabilities in various ways.
- Students should be taught to manage their personal health care routines, such as clean intermittent catheterization and self-administration of medication.
- Proper positioning and seating are important for children with physical disabilities. All teachers and other school staff should follow a standard routine for lifting and moving children with physical disabilities.
- How parents, teachers, classmates, and others react to a child with physical disabilities is as important as the disability itself.
- Students with physical limitations should be encouraged to develop as much independence as possible. Effective teachers

help students cope with their disabilities, set realistic expectations, and accept help gracefully when needed.

- Children with health impairments and physical disabilities can gain self-knowledge and self-confidence by meeting capable adults with disabilities and joining self-advocacy groups.

Placement Options

- Well over 50% of students with physical impairments and chronic health conditions are served in regular classrooms.
- Special classes usually provide smaller class size, more adapted equipment, and easier access to the services of professionals such as physicians, PTs and OTs, and specialists in communication disorders and therapeutic recreation.
- Some technology-dependent children require home- or hospital-based instruction because their life support equipment cannot be made portable.
- The education of students with health and physical impairments in regular classrooms has raised several controversial issues, particularly regarding the provision of medically related procedures in the classroom.
- Successful reentry of children who have missed extended periods of school because of illness or disease requires preparation of the child, parents, classmates, and school personnel.

Chapter 12

Low-Incidence Disabilities: Multiple Disabilities, Deaf-Blindness, and Traumatic Brain Injury

Source: Many Hats Media

Learning Outcomes

After reading this chapter and completing the embedded activities, you should be able to

12.1 Define multiple disabilities, deaf-blindness, and traumatic brain injury, and describe characteristics of individuals with these diabilities.

12.2 State why it is difficult to identify the exact number of students with severe disabilities, and list some of the biological causes of severe disabilities.

12.3 Explain why a curriculum based on typical developmental stages and milestones is inappropriate for students with severe and multiple disabilities and suggest an appropriate alternative perspective.

12.4 Describe effective teaching strategies for educating students with severe and multiple disabilities.

12.5 List advantages and disadvantages of regular classroom placement for students with severe and multiple disabilities.

Featured Teacher

Carey Creech-Galloway

Conkwright Elementary School, Clark County Public Schools, Winchester, Kentucky

Source: Belle Galloway

I enjoy the student-centered approach and individual programming that occur in special education. I must continually try to achieve the most beneficial balance of functional skills and academic curriculum. That and the incredibly varied student ability levels keep me on my toes. To be an effective teacher of students with severe disabilities requires organization, flexibility, and knowledge of systematic instructional strategies.

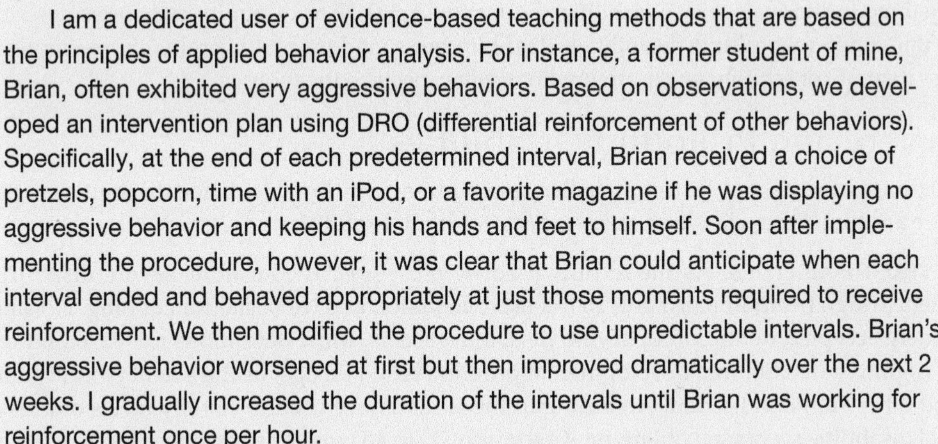

I am a dedicated user of evidence-based teaching methods that are based on the principles of applied behavior analysis. For instance, a former student of mine, Brian, often exhibited very aggressive behaviors. Based on observations, we developed an intervention plan using DRO (differential reinforcement of other behaviors). Specifically, at the end of each predetermined interval, Brian received a choice of pretzels, popcorn, time with an iPod, or a favorite magazine if he was displaying no aggressive behavior and keeping his hands and feet to himself. Soon after implementing the procedure, however, it was clear that Brian could anticipate when each interval ended and behaved appropriately at just those moments required to receive reinforcement. We then modified the procedure to use unpredictable intervals. Brian's aggressive behavior worsened at first but then improved dramatically over the next 2 weeks. I gradually increased the duration of the intervals until Brian was working for reinforcement once per hour.

An important part of being an evidence-based educator is collecting and graphing data. Each of my students receives intensive instruction on a minimum of six to eight instructional objectives each school day, so I may be collecting data on up to 50 individualized education program (IEP) objectives. Monitoring progress is very challenging even with computer-based software. Whenever possible, I group students with similar objectives in small groups, which helps with data collection. Over time I have fine-tuned my data collection methods to include not only paper and pencil data forms but also Google Forms that capture data in real time. These forms have made it easy to view data quickly in a spreadsheet and create a graph in minutes.

I cannot stress enough how important direct and frequent measurement is when teaching students with severe disabilities. It gives information about each student's level of independence and allows the teacher to make data-based decisions. For example, I may have a student learning to use a communication board to request items. At the beginning of the school year, that student may require physical or model prompts, but by school year's end, only verbal prompts are required. This is a huge amount of progress that may not be evident without data collection.

In addition to behavior intervention plans and data collection, there are so many considerations for students with significant disabilities: lesson plans, IEP goals and objectives, related services schedules, training classroom support personnel, family communication, alternate assessments, and medical emergency plans. A colleague and I developed a Multiple and Severe Disabilities Classroom Checklist to help teachers keep track of all of the moving parts that make up a classroom program for students with multiple and severe disabilities.

Education, Teaching Credentials, and Experience

- *B.S. and M.Ed., Special Education: Moderate and Severe Disabilities, University of Kentucky, 2004 and 2011*
- *Kentucky, teaching exceptional children, moderate and severe disabilities, K–12*
- *Kentucky, teacher consultant in program for exceptional children, K–12*
- *16 years as a special education teacher*

Pearson eText
Video Example 12.1
Featured Teacher Carey relies on evidence-based teaching techniques.

Content Extension 12.1

CLASSROOM CHECKLIST*

...urce Classrooms for Students with Multiple/Severe Disabilities

...ON PLANS COMPLETED (for whole week)

- ... student's goals and objectives and daily "I Can" statements.
- ...e standard(s) for that week (from alternative or extended standards).
- ...te how instruction is tied to core content and/or how it will increase students' independence.
- Include behavioral objectivesand reinforcement schedule.
- List instructional procedures and data collection methods.
- Make lesson plans available in a binder, on a clipboard, or in a folder.

CLASSROOM ENVIRONMENT TO SUPPORT INSTRUCTION

- Be positive and treat all learners with dignity and respect.
- Arrange classroom toallow monitoring of students from all areas of theroom.
- Arrange classroom to support multiple instructional formats (areas for 1:1, small-group, and large-group instruction; areas for quiet or leisure time).
- Arrange classroom topromotegeneralization and independance.
  - Students'personal spaces are labeled appropriately.
  - Materials and work areas are clearly defined andaccessibleto all students.
- Make sure dassroom is clean, materials are stored neatly,and materials and work areas are easily accessible. Provide designated places for data binders, work systems, completed work to be turned in, make up work, recreation activities, etc. Labelthem and arrange for easy access.
- Aim for a high ratio of praise to reprimands/corrections (5:1 or higher).
- Provide visual supports (e.g., timers, visual schedules, class wide reinforcement systems).

SCHEDULES POSTED IN CLASSROOM

- Make sure posted schedules are visible to students and staff.
- Post the following:
  - Schedule for each student to follow throughout the school day (in their mode of communication)
    - Provide picture schedule, object schedule, work schedule broken down for each task... whatever works best for the student
    - Teach the student to check and follow the schedule throughout the day
    - Reference the schedule frequently

Multiple/Severe Disabilities Classroom Checklist developed by Featured Teacher Carey Creech-Galloway and Lorraine Thomas.

FIRST GRADER EMILY IS LEARNING TO FEED HERSELF with a spoon. A teacher shows 13-year-old Terrence that when first meeting someone, a handshake is more appropriate than a hug. Having recently returned to school after hospitalization from a head injury he sustained in a swimming pool accident, 11th grader Anthony uses a hallway map to navigate between classes. Manuela, who is 20 years old, is learning to ride a city bus to her afternoon job bussing tables at a diner. Emily, Terrence, Anthony, and Manuela need special education to learn everyday activities that most of us take for granted.

Definitions

Learning Outcome 12.1 Define multiple disabilities, deaf-blindness, and traumatic brain injury, and describe characteristics of individuals with these disabilities.

The term *low-incidence disabilities* refers to disabilities that do not occur very often. Combined, the three Individuals with Disabilities Education Act (IDEA) disability categories described in this chapter—multiple disabilities, deaf-blindness, and traumatic brain injury—represent less than 3% of school-age children who receive special education.

Severe and Profound Disabilities

The impairments and learning challenges children with low-incidence disabilities experience are sometimes classified as severe or profound disabilities.

SEVERE DISABILITIES. As the term is used by most special educators, **severe disabilities** refers to significant impairments in intellectual, motor, and/or social functioning. No single widely accepted definition of severe disabilities exists. Most definitions are based on tests of cognitive functioning, developmental progress based on age, or the extent of educational and other supports needed. According to the system once used to classify levels of intellectual disabilities, a person obtaining IQ scores of 35 to 40 would be considered to have severe intellectual disabilities. In practice, however, many individuals who score in the moderate range (IQ scores of 40 to 55) are considered to have severe disabilities.

A developmental approach to defining severe disabilities was once common. For example, Justen (1976) defined students with severe disabilities as individuals "age 21 and younger who are functioning at a general developmental level of half or less than the level which would be expected on the basis of chronological age" (p. 5). Today special educators realize that developmental levels have little relevance to this population and instead emphasize that a student with severe disabilities, regardless of age, is one who needs instruction in basic skills that most children without disabilities acquire in the first 5 years of life.

The organization TASH (formerly The Association for Persons with Severe Handicaps) describes the people for whom it advocates as

> people with significant disabilities and support needs who are most at risk for being excluded from society; perceived by traditional service systems as most challenging; most likely to have their rights abridged; most likely to be at risk for living, working, playing and learning in segregated environments; least likely to have the tools and opportunities necessary to advocate on their behalf; and are most likely to need ongoing, individualized supports to participate in inclusive communities and enjoy a quality of life similar to that available to all people. (TASH, 2020)

Source: Many Hats Media

Students with severe disabilities need intensive, systematic instruction to learn basic skills.

PROFOUND DISABILITIES. Students with **profound disabilities** have "serious and dramatic impairments that may include significant or complete sensory impairment, severe cognitive impairments, severe physical disabilities, chronic health conditions, and sometimes terminal illness" (Ferguson et al., 1996, p. 100). Although IQ scores of 20 to 25 and below typically result in a classification of profound intellectual disabilities, traditional intelligence tests are virtually useless with children who have profound disabilities. Imagine the difficulty, as well as the inappropriateness, of giving an IQ test to a student who cannot hold up his head or point, let alone talk. If tested, such students tend to be assigned IQ scores at the extreme lower end of the continuum. Knowing that a student has an IQ of 25, however, is of no value in designing an appropriate educational program.

Special educators who serve children with the most significant disabilities have generated very little debate over definitional issues compared with their colleagues in intellectual disabilities, learning disabilities, and emotional and behavioral disorders. This is a reflection of two inherent features of severe or profound disabilities. First, a definition that delineates precisely who is and is not to be identified by the terms is unnecessary because the characteristics of students with the most significant disabilities are less ambiguous than for other disability categories. Second, the tremendous diversity of learning and physical challenges students with severe or profound disabilities experience renders any single set of descriptors inadequate.

Multiple Disabilities

IDEA defines **multiple disabilities** as

> concomitant impairments (such as intellectual disability–blindness, intellectual disability–orthopedic impairment), the combination of which causes such severe educational needs that they cannot be accommodated in special education programs solely for one of the impairments. Multiple disabilities does not include deaf-blindness (20 §1401 [2004], 20 *CFR* §300.8[c][7]).

Deaf-Blindness

IDEA defines **deaf-blindness** as

> concomitant hearing and visual impairments, the combination of which causes such severe communication and other developmental and educational needs that they cannot be accommodated in special education programs solely for children with deafness or children with blindness (20 U.S.C. §1401 [2004], 20 *CFR* §300.8[c][2]).

Although the term *deaf-blind* implies the absence of hearing and vision, the vast majority of children with deaf-blindness have some functional hearing, vision, or both. The combined effects of the dual impairments severely impede learning, communication, motor and mobility skills, and social behavior.

Traumatic Brain Injury

When it was originally passed, IDEA did not mention the needs of children who have experienced head trauma or coma. However, when Congress amended the law in 1990 (PL 101-476), it added traumatic brain injury (TBI) to the disability categories under which children could be eligible for special education services. IDEA defines **traumatic brain injury** as

> an acquired injury to the brain caused by an external physical force, resulting in total or partial functional disability or psychosocial impairment, or both, that adversely affects a child's educational performance. Traumatic brain injury applies to open or closed head injuries resulting in impairments in one or more areas, such as cognition; language; memory; attention; reasoning; abstract thinking; judgment; problem-solving; sensory, perceptual, and motor abilities; psychosocial behavior; physical functions; information processing; and speech. Traumatic brain injury does not apply to brain injuries that are congenital or degenerative, or to brain injuries induced by birth trauma (20 §1401 [2004], 20 *CFR* §300.8[c][12]).

Head injuries are classified by the type of injury (open or closed), by the kind of damage sustained by the brain, and by the location of the injury. An **open head injury** is the result of penetration of the skull, such as that caused by a bullet or a forceful blow to the head with a

FIGURE 12.1 Parts of the Brain and Some of their Functions

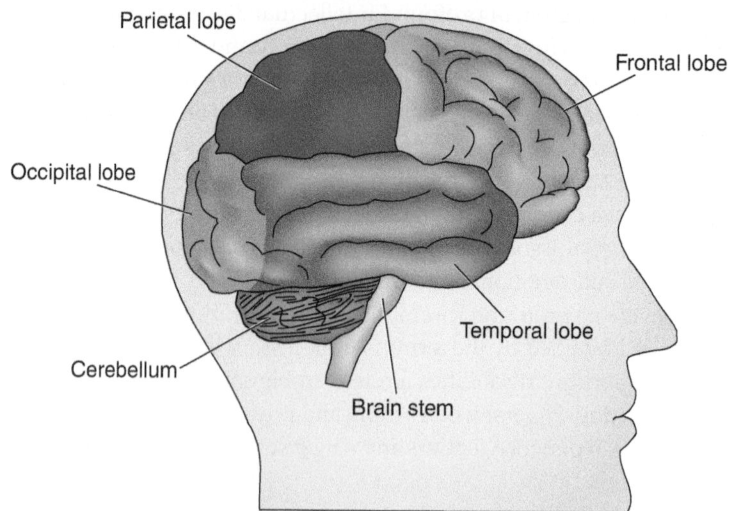

Frontal lobe

- Emotions
- Expressive language
- Word associations
- Memory for habits and motor activities
- Problem solving
- Reasoning

Parietal lobe

- Integration of different senses
- Location for visual attention
- Location for touch perception
- Manipulation of objects

Occipital lobe

- Vision

Cerebellum

- Balance and equilibrium
- Some memory for reflex motor acts

Brain stem

- Regulates body functions (e.g., breathing, heart rate, swallowing)
- Reflexes to seeing and hearing (e.g., startle response)
- Controls autonomic nervous system (e.g., sweating, blood pressure, digestion, internal temperature)
- Affects level of alertness

Temporal lobe

- Hearing
- Speech
- Memory acquisition
- Categorization of objects

hard or sharp object. Open head injuries that are not fatal often result in the loss of behavioral or sensory functions controlled by the part of the brain where the injury occurred (Figure 12.1).

The most common type of head injury does not involve penetration of the skull. A **closed head injury** occurs when the head hits or is hit by an object with such force that the brain slams against the inside of the cranium. The rapid movement and impact tears nerve fibers, or axons, breaking connections between different parts of the brain.

The effects of TBI on learning and behavior are determined by the severity of the injury and the part of the brain that sustained damage. A mild brain injury results in a *concussion*, a brief loss of consciousness (from a few seconds to several minutes) without any subsequent complications or damage. Even a mild concussion, however, is often followed by postconcussion syndrome, which can include temporary headaches, dizziness, and fatigue. Repeated mild TBIs over a period of months or years can result in cumulative neurological and cognitive deficits. Repeated mild TBIs occurring within a short period of time (i.e., hours, days, or weeks) can be catastrophic or fatal (Centers for Disease Control and Prevention, 2020k).

Contusions (bruising, swelling, bleeding) usually accompany a moderate brain injury. Blood vessels in the brain may also rupture, causing a *hematoma* (blood clot) that may grow, putting pressure on vital brain structures. A moderate brain injury usually results in loss of consciousness lasting 30 minutes to 24 hours followed by several days or weeks of confusion. Individuals who sustain a moderate brain injury experience significant cognitive and behavioral impairments for many months. Most, however, make a complete or nearly complete recovery (Vu et al., 2011).

Severe head trauma almost always results in a *coma*, a state of prolonged unconsciousness lasting days, weeks, or even longer. A person in a coma cannot be awakened and makes no meaningful response to external stimulation. In addition to brain contusions, hematomas, or damage to nerve fibers, a person with severe brain injury may have experienced **anoxia** (loss of oxygen to the brain). Although many people with severe brain injuries make significant improvements during the 2 years postinjury and continue to improve at a gradual pace for many years, most will have permanent physical, behavioral, and/or cognitive impairments (Vu et al., 2011).

Characteristics of Students with Low-Incidence Disabilities

Multiple and Severe Disabilities

Definitions and lists of characteristics used to describe the children within a disability category have limited meaning at the level of the individual student. And, of course, it is at the individual level where relevant instructional decisions are made. As you read about the various physical, behavioral, and learning characteristics of students with multiple and severe disabilities, keep in mind that this is the most heterogeneous group of all exceptional children. As Westling et al. (2021) point out, the differences among students with severe disabilities are greater than their similarities.

Most students with severe disabilities exhibit significant deficits in intellectual functioning. The majority have more than one disability. Many need special services and supports because of any combination of motor impediments; communication, visual, and auditory impairments; or seizure disorders.

Although some people with profound disabilities are able to achieve semi-independent functioning with some tasks of daily living, most are nonambulatory, and some are unresponsive to sensory stimuli. Round-the-clock support and care are required. Students with profound disabilities are sometimes described in terms of their "behavior states" or alertness levels: sleep states (asleep-inactive, asleep-active), indeterminate states (drowsy, daze), and awake states (inactive-alert, awake, active-alert, awake-active or stereotypy, crying or agitated) (Arthur, 2004).

Even with the best available methods of diagnosis and assessment, it is often difficult to identify the nature and intensity of a child's disabilities. Some children, for example, do not respond in any apparent way to visual stimuli, such as bright lights or moving objects. Is this because the child is blind as a result of eye damage, or is the child's unresponsiveness a feature of profound intellectual disability caused by brain damage? Such questions arise frequently in planning educational programs for students with the most significant disabilities.

Although each student presents a unique combination of physical, intellectual, and social characteristics, the following are frequently observed:

- *Slow acquisition of new skills.* Compared with other students with disabilities, those with severe disabilities learn at a slower rate, learn fewer skills, and have extreme difficulty learning abstract concepts.
- *Poor generalization and maintenance of new skills. Generalization* refers to the performance of a skill in settings or under conditions different from those in which the skill was learned initially. *Maintenance* refers to the continued use of a skill after instruction has been terminated. Without instruction that has been meticulously planned and implemented to facilitate generalization and maintenance, students with severe disabilities seldom show such outcomes.
- *Limited communication skills.* Almost all students with severe disabilities have difficulty expressing themselves and understanding others. Some cannot talk or gesture meaningfully and might not respond when communication is attempted.
- *Impaired motor development.* Many children with severe disabilities have limited physical mobility. Many cannot walk; some cannot stand or sit up without support. They are slow to perform such basic tasks as rolling over, grasping objects, and holding up

their heads. Physical impairments and health conditions are common (van Timmeren et al., 2017). Treatment of medical conditions and health problems results in frequent and often extended absences from school (Zijlstra & Vlaskamp, 2005).

- *Deficits in self-help skills.* Some children with severe disabilities cannot independently care for their most basic needs, such as dressing, eating, toileting, and maintaining personal hygiene. They often require special training involving prosthetic devices or adapted skill sequences to learn these basic skills.
- *Infrequent social interactions and constructive behavior.* Children without disabilities and those whose disabilities are less severe typically play with other children, interact with adults, and seek out information about their surroundings. Because of their physical, cognitive, and communicative limitations, some children with the most significant disabilities seldom engage in typical behaviors that would initiate interactions from others, such as waving, smiling, and pointing (Nijs & Maes, 2014). They may appear to be unaware of their surroundings and may not show normal emotions. It may be difficult to capture the attention of or evoke any observable response from a child with profound disabilities.
- *Stereotypic behavior.* Some children with severe disabilities engage in behaviors that are ritualistic (e.g., rocking, waving fingers in front of face, putting fingers in mouth), self-stimulatory (e.g., grinding teeth), or vocally stereotypic (e.g., humming, repeating nonsense sounds words). Some children with severe disabilities also display dystonic postures (e.g., head tilting, spastic stretching of arms or legs).
- *Challenging behavior.* Some children with severe disabilities engage in self-injurious behavior or aggressive outbursts (e.g., throwing and destroying materials, hitting or biting others). In addition to safety issues, the high frequency with which some children emit these challenging behaviors interferes with instruction aimed at teaching more adaptive behaviors and with acceptance and functioning in integrated settings (Poppes et al., 2010).

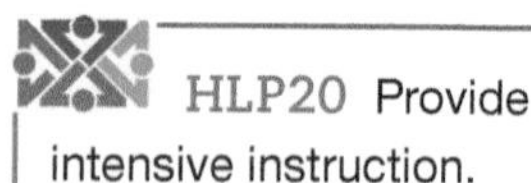
HLP20 Provide intensive instruction.

The one defining characteristic of students with the most significant disabilities is that they exhibit significant and obvious deficits in multiple life-skill or developmental areas. These students require "extensive repeated individualized instruction and support that is not of a temporary or transient nature" and use "substantially adapted materials and individualized methods of accessing information in alternative ways to acquire, maintain, generalize, demonstrate and transfer skills across multiple settings" (Kansas Department of Education, 2018, p. 1).

IDEA mandates that all children are entitled to a free appropriate public education in the least restrictive environment no matter how complicated or challenging their learning, behavioral, or medical needs may be. However, some individuals have questioned whether children with profound disabilities can benefit from education. To read one viewpoint, see Figure 12.2.

Source: AMELIE-BENOIST/BSIP/Alamy Stock Photo

Despite intense challenges, students with severe disabilities can be persistent, cheerful, and interested in the world around them.

Despite the intense challenges their disabilities impose, many students with severe disabilities exhibit warmth, persistence, determination, cheerfulness, a sense of humor, sociability, and various other desirable traits. Like Featured Teacher Carey Creech-Galloway, many special educators derive great satisfaction teaching students with severe disabilities and observing their progress in school, home, and community settings.

Deaf-Blindness

Many students who are deaf and blind exhibit some of the same characteristics as those with multiple and severe disabilities described earlier. The cognitive ability of individuals who are deaf-blind range from giftedness (e.g., Helen Keller) to profound intellectual impairment. More than 90% of children who are deaf-blind have one or

FIGURE 12.2 Are All Children Educable?

Some people question the wisdom of spending large amounts of money, time, and human resources attempting to educate children who have such profound disabilities that they may never be able to function independently. Some would prefer to see resources spent on children with higher apparent potential—especially when economic conditions limit the quality of educational services for all children in the public schools. "Why bother with children who fail to make meaningful progress?" they ask.

Our knowledge of the learning and developmental processes of individuals with severe and profound disabilities is still primitive and incomplete. We do know, however, that children with severe disabilities can benefit from intense and "customized" special education (Smith et al., 2001). Even when a student shows little or no progress, it would be wrong to conclude that the student is incapable of learning. Instead, our teaching methods may be imperfect, and the future may bring improved methods and materials to enable that student to learn useful skills. No matter how severe their disabilities, all children have the right to the best possible public education society can offer them.

No one knows for certain the true learning potential of children whose disabilities are complex and pervasive. We do know that students with the most severe disabilities will go no farther than we let them; it is up to us to open doors and to raise our sights, not to create additional barriers.

The late Don Baer, a pioneer in the development of effective teaching methods for people with disabilities, offered this perspective on the debate over who may or may not be educable:

> Some of us have ignored both the thesis that all persons are educable and the thesis that some persons are uneducable, and instead have experimented with ways to teach some previously unteachable people. Over a few centuries, those experiments have steadily reduced the size of the apparently ineducable group relative to the obviously educable group. Clearly, we have not finished that adventure. Why predict its outcome, when we could simply pursue it, and just as well without a prediction? Why not pursue it to see if there comes a day when there is such a small class of apparently ineducable persons left that it consists of one elderly person who is put forward as ineducable. If that day comes, it will be a very nice day. And the next day will be even better.

(D. M. Baer, February 15, 2002, Personal communication to W. L. Heward)

more additional disabilities: 64% have cognitive impairments, 58% also have physical disabilities, and 51% have complex health care needs (National Center on Deaf-Blindness, 2020).

Although a few students with deaf-blindness excel academically and are remarkably independent (Phillips et al., 2013; Watt, 2020), the overall situation is sobering. Results of a national study of youth with disabilities showed that on standardized achievement measures of reading and math, students who are deaf-blind outperformed only students with multiple disabilities and intellectual disabilities (Wagner et al., 2006). The same study found that 95% of students who are deaf-blind have "very low" functional skills (e.g., activities of daily living, motor skills, social interaction and communication, community living) and that most age-appropriate functional skills were "extremely difficult or impossible to perform" for 69% of deaf-blind students (p. 39).

Pearson eText
Video Example 12.2
Children who are deaf-blind, like all children, need to experience new adventures. https://www.youtube.com/watch?v=7d2d5nB3QOs

Many children who are deaf-blind engage in various forms of self-stimulatory behavior (e.g., body rocking, hand flapping). These behaviors may result from sensory deprivation or boredom, provide useful proprioceptive input about spatial location of a child's body, and self-regulate arousal levels (Belote & Maier, 2014).

Because students with dual sensory impairments may not initiate interactions or respond to the efforts of others to gain their attention, they appear passive or even noncompliant. The unresponsiveness of a child with deaf-blindness can lead parents and caregivers to do things for the child that inadvertently contribute to his passivity and communication difficulties. With increasingly fewer opportunities and no requirements to exert control over his environment, "learned helplessness" may develop, and the child becomes a passive recipient of care (Pease, 2000).

Traumatic Brain Injury

Although not always visible and sometimes seemingly minor or inconsequential, TBI is complex. The symptoms vary widely depending on the severity of the injury, its extent and site, the age of the child at the time of the injury, and time passed since the injury.

Pearson eText
Video Example 12.3
Effects of traumatic brain injury vary widely. https://www.youtube.com/watch?v=lBOo2a2BWMI

Brain injuries cause impairments that fall into three main categories: (a) physical and sensory changes (e.g., lack of coordination, spasticity of muscles); (b) cognitive impairments

FIGURE 12.3 Possible Signs and Effects of Traumatic Brain Injury

Physical and sensory changes

- Chronic headaches, dizziness, light headedness, nausea
- Vision impairments (e.g., double vision, visual field defects, blurring, sensitivity to light)
- Hearing impairment (e.g., increased sensitivity to sound)
- Alterations in sense of taste, touch, and smell
- Sleep problems (e.g., insomnia, day/night confusion)
- Stress-related disorders (e.g., depression)
- Poor body temperature regulation
- Recurrent seizure activity
- Poor coordination and balance
- Reduced speed of motor performance and precision of movement

Cognitive changes and academic problems

- Difficulty keeping up with discussions, instructional presentations, note taking
- Difficulty concentrating or attending to task at hand (e.g., distractible, confused)
- Difficulty making transitions (e.g., home to school, class to class, switching from fractions to decimal problems on same math worksheet)
- Inability to organize work and environment (e.g., difficulty keeping track of books, assignments, lunch box)
- Problems in planning, organizing, pacing tasks and activities
- Extremely sensitive to distraction (e.g., unable to take a test in a room with other students)
- Tendency to perseverate; inflexibility in thinking
- Impairments in receptive oral language (e.g., difficulty following directions; misunderstanding what is said by others)
- Inability to perceive voice inflections or nonverbal cues
- Impairments in reading comprehension
- Impairments in expressive oral or written language (e.g., aphasia, difficulty retrieving words, poor articulation, slow speech, difficulty in spelling or punctuation)

Social, emotional, and behavioral problems

- Chronic agitation, irritability, restlessness, or anxiety
- Increased aggressiveness
- Impaired ability to self-manage; lowered impulse control; poor anger control
- Difficulty dealing with change (i.e., rigid); poor coping strategies
- May overestimate own ability (often evidenced as "bragging")
- Decreased insight into self and others; reduced judgment
- Decreased frustration tolerance; frequent temper outbursts and overreactions to events
- May talk compulsively and excessively
- Inability to take cues from the environment (often leading to socially inappropriate behavior)

Source: Adapted from Hill, J. L. (1999). *Meeting the needs of children with special physical and health care needs* (pp. 259–260). Upper Saddle River, NJ: Merrill/Prentice Hall. © 1999 by Merrill/Prentice Hall. Used by permission.

(e.g., short- and long-term memory deficits, difficulty maintaining attention, language problems); and (c) social, behavioral, and emotional problems (e.g., mood swings, self-centeredness, lack of motivation) (Figure 12.3). TBI can cause epilepsy (see Chapter 11) and increase the risk of brain disorders that become more prevalent with age, such as Alzheimer's and Parkinson's diseases.

Prevalence of Low-Incidence Disabilities

Learning Outcome 12.2 State why it is difficult to identify the exact number of students with severe disabilities, and list some of the biological causes of severe disabilities.

Multiple Disabilities

Because no definition of severe disabilities is universally accepted, no accurate and uniform figures on prevalence exist. Estimates of the prevalence of severe disabilities range from 0.1% to 1% of the school-age population (Kleinert et al., 2015).

Because "severe disabilities" is not an IDEA disability category, the number of students with severe disabilities cannot be determined from the data supplied by the U.S. Department of Education. Students who have severe disabilities are served and reported under several disability categories, including intellectual disability, multiple disabilities, other health impairments, autism, deaf-blindness, and TBI. In the 2018–2019 school year, approximately 126,697 school-age children received special education under the IDEA disability category of multiple disabilities (U.S. Department of Education, 2020a).

Deaf-Blindness

Deaf-blindness is a very low-incidence disability. Before the passage of IDEA in 1975, fewer than 100 children with dual-sensory impairments were receiving specialized education services, virtually all of which were located at residential schools for children who are blind. Although only 1,425 school-age children were served under the deaf-blindness disability category in the 2018–2019 school year (U.S. Department of Education, 2020a), a national census counted 10,638 children with deaf-blindness from birth through age 18 years (National Center on Deaf-Blindness, 2019). The discrepancy exists because many students who are deaf-blind receive services under other disability categories, most commonly multiple disabilities, hearing impairment, or visual impairment.

Traumatic Brain Injury

Nearly 3 million people sustain a TBI each year in the United States (Centers for Disease Control and Prevention, 2020k). Of those, about 288,000 will be hospitalized, and 56,800 will die. TBI is the leading cause of death in children and the most common acquired disability in childhood. It is estimated that 5.3 million Americans have a long-term need for help in performing activities of daily living as a result of TBI (Brain Injury Association of America, 2020).

Despite the sobering statistics on head injuries, the number of children receiving special education under the category of TBI is quite small. In 1991–1992, the first school year after TBI was added to IDEA as a separate disability category, only 330 school-age children were served nationally. By the 2018–2019 school year, the number had increased to 25,344 (U.S. Department of Education, 2020a).

What accounts for the huge difference between the incidence of TBI and the number of children served? First, the vast majority of children's head injuries are mild and do not adversely affect educational performance to warrant special education. Second, the human brain has a remarkable capacity to naturally compensate for and recover from injury (Vu et al., 2011). Third, many students with mild brain injuries are identified and served under another disability category, most likely learning disabilities or emotional disturbance. Nevertheless, special educators and neurologists are concerned that schools fail to identify many children with mild TBI who would benefit from special education and related services (Deidrick & Farmer, 2005).

Causes of Low-Incidence Disabilities

Multiple and Severe Disabilities

Severe intellectual disabilities can be caused by a wide variety of conditions, largely biological, that may occur before (prenatal), during (perinatal), or after (postnatal) birth. In almost every case, a brain disorder is involved. Brain disorders are the result of either *brain dysgenesis* (abnormal brain development) or *brain damage* (caused by influences that alter the structure or function of a brain that had been developing normally up to that point).

A significant percentage of children with severe disabilities are born with chromosomal abnormalities, such as Down syndrome, or with genetic or metabolic disorders that can cause serious problems in physical or intellectual development. Complications of pregnancy—including prematurity, Rh incompatibility, and infectious diseases the mother contracts—can cause severe disabilities. A pregnant woman who uses drugs, drinks alcohol excessively, or is poorly nourished has a greater risk of giving birth to a child with severe disabilities. Down syndrome, fragile X syndrome, and fetal alcohol syndrome can be identified as the cause of about one third of all cases of moderate, severe, and profound intellectual disability (see Chapter 4) (Shapiro & Batshaw, 2019).

Severe disabilities also may develop later in life from brain injury caused by automobile and bicycle accidents, falls, assaults, or abuse. Malnutrition, neglect, ingestion of poisonous substances, and certain diseases that affect the brain (e.g., meningitis, encephalitis) also can cause severe disabilities. Although hundreds of medically related causes of severe disabilities have been identified, in many cases, the cause cannot be clearly determined.

Traumatic Brain Injury

Common causes of closed head injuries are car and bicycle accidents, falls, and sports accidents. Acts of violence such as gunshot wounds, domestic violence, and child abuse cause about 20% of brain injuries. *Shaken-baby syndrome* is a form of TBI caused by violent shaking of an infant. Explosive blasts from combat or terrorist attacks cause TBI in military personnel and civilian victims.

Deaf-Blindness

Causes of deaf-blindness that are present or occur around the time a child is born include prematurity, infections during pregnancy such as cytomegalovirus and toxoplasmosis, complications during childbirth, and numerous congenital syndromes. Deaf-blindness may also be acquired in childhood or during adulthood due to causes such as meningitis or brain injury.

CHARGE syndrome, a genetic pattern of birth defects with an incidence of about 1 in every 8000 to 10,000 births worldwide, is an extremely complex condition that involves hearing loss, vision loss, and balance problems for most affected children (CHARGE Syndrome Foundation, 2020). CHARGE syndrome is the most commonly identified genetic cause of deaf-blindness (National Center on Deaf-Blindness, 2020).

Usher syndrome—a group of genetic conditions that involves both hearing loss and retinitis pigmentosa, a progressive, degenerative eye disease (see Chapter 10)—is another common cause of deaf-blindness. The most common type is Type I, which consists of profound congenital deafness with retinitis pigmentosa and severe balance problems. Type II consists of moderate to severe hearing loss, retinitis pigmentosa, and no balance problems. Children born with Type III Usher syndrome have normal hearing at birth, progressive hearing loss in childhood or the early teens, and night vision problems often developing in the teen years (National Center on Deaf-Blindness, 2020).

Educational Approaches

How does one go about teaching students with the most significant disabilities? To answer this question requires consideration of two fundamental and interrelated questions: What skills should be taught? What instructional methods should be used?

Although answers to these questions must be determined for all students with special educational needs, they have enormous importance for students whose ability to learn in the absence of skillfully designed and delivered instruction is extremely limited.

Curriculum: What Should Be Taught?

Learning Outcome 12.3 Explain why a curriculum based on typical developmental stages and milestones is inappropriate for students with severe and multiple disabilities and suggest an appropriate alternative perspective.

Because students with the most significant disabilities learn more slowly and acquire a much smaller set of skills than any group of students, deciding what to teach them is of paramount importance. For many years, a student's "mental age," as determined by norm-referenced tests, was the primary factor in the selection of curriculum content and teaching activities. This practice led to an emphasis on activities thought to be essential prerequisites for higher level skills because children of a given age typically demonstrated these skills. As a result, students with severe disabilities spent years sorting blocks by color, touching body parts on cue, and placing wooden pegs in pegboards. These contrived activities contributed little, if any, value to the student's daily functioning (Figure 12.4).

If developmental age is a poor basis for determining curriculum content for students with severe disabilities, what factors should drive those decisions? Of the many factors to consider, functionality and age-appropriateness should be at the top of the list.

FIGURE 12.4 My Brother Darryl: A Case for Teaching Functional Skills

Eighteen years old, Darryl has been in school for 12 years. He has had a number of years of "individualized instruction." Darryl can now do lots of things he couldn't do before:

- He can put 100 pegs in a board in less than 10 minutes with 95% accuracy, but he can't put quarters into a vending machine.
- Upon command, he can touch his nose, shoulder, leg, hair, ear. He is still working on wrist, ankle, and hips, but he can't blow his nose when needed.
- He can do a 12-piece Big Bird puzzle with 100% accuracy and color an Easter bunny and stay in the lines. He prefers music but has never been taught to use a radio or record player.
- He can now fold primary paper in half and even quarters, but he can't sort clothes, white from colors, for washing.
- He can roll Play-Doh and make wonderful clay snakes, but he can't roll bread dough and cut out biscuits.
- He can string beads in alternating colors and match them to a pattern on a Dynamic Learning Map card, but he can't lace his shoes.
- He can sing his ABCs and tell me the names of all the letters in the alphabet with 80% accuracy when they are presented on a card in upper case, but he can't tell "Men's" room from "Ladies'" when we go to McDonald's.
- He can be told it's cloudy or rainy and take a black felt cloud and put it on the day of the week on an enlarged calendar (with assistance), but he still goes out in the rain without a raincoat or hat.
- He can identify with 100% accuracy 100 different Peabody Picture Cards by pointing, but he can't order a hamburger by pointing to a picture or gesturing.
- He can walk on a balance beam forward, sideways, and backward, but he can't walk up the steps of the bleachers unassisted in the gym or go to basketball games.
- He can count to 100 by rote memory, but he doesn't know how many dollars to pay the waitress for a $2.59 McDonald coupon special.
- He can put a cube in the box, under the box, beside the box, and behind the box, but he can't find the trash bin in McDonald's and empty his trash into it.
- He can sit in a circle with appropriate behavior and sing songs and play "Duck Duck Goose," but nobody else in his neighborhood his age seems to want to do that.

I guess he's just not ready yet.

Written by Preston Lewis, a curriculum specialist in the Kentucky Department of Education.

FUNCTIONALITY Functional skills are immediately useful to a student. They are required in the student's daily activities and valued by people in the settings where these activities occur. Dressing oneself, preparing a snack, riding a bus, purchasing items from vending machines, and responding appropriately to common sight words in community settings are functional skills for many students with severe disabilities. Functional skills mean less dependence on others and enable more meaningful participation in current and future educational, domestic, work, and community environments. Brown and colleagues (1982) suggested the following tests for determining the functionality of a particular skill: If the student could not perform the task, (a) would someone else have to do it for the student, and (b) could the student function as an adult without the skill?

AGE-APPROPRIATENESS Students with severe disabilities should participate in activities that are appropriate for their same-age peers without disabilities. Age-appropriate behaviors are expected in most settings, and they are modeled and valued by peers without disabilities. As a result, age-appropriate skills are more likely to be practiced and reinforced, and thus maintained in the student's repertoire, than are behaviors typical of a much younger child. Having teenagers sit on the floor and play clap-your-hands games is stigmatizing and discourages integration. Such activities also contribute to the perception by some that students with severe disabilities are eternal children. Teaching secondary students with severe disabilities how to play video games and operate an iPad would give them more age-appropriate recreation and leisure skills.

CURRICULUM AREAS IEP teams for students with severe disabilities should consider the following curriculum areas: self-care, communication, literacy, recreation and leisure, choice making, and the general education academic curriculum.

Self-care Students with severe disabilities often struggle with even the most basic self-care skills. Learning to care for oneself promotes independence and should be of utmost importance to those involved in educating a student with severe disabilities. IEP goals may target skills related to personal hygiene, home safety, food preparation, and safety in the community (Bambara et al., 2020). It is important to embed self-care skills throughout each school day and to collaborate with parents and caregivers in home and community settings to promote maintenance and generalization (Burns & Thompson, 2014).

HLP3 Collaborate with families to support student learning and secure needed services.

Communication Communication is an essential quality of human life. As you learned in Chapter 8, communication enables us to express our needs and desires; obtain and provide information; and, most important, form and maintain relationships with others. Communication does not develop naturally or easily for children with severe and multiple disabilities. Communicative efforts by an infant with severe and multiple disabilities may be subtle or unusual and thus difficult for parents and caregivers to identify and interpret (Chen, 2014). At the same time, the infant may not even perceive that his parents and caregivers are gesturing, talking, or signing to him.

Early research and training in communication for people with severe disabilities focused on remediation of specific forms of communication, such as the production of speech sounds, words, and descriptive phrases. However, methods used to teach communication skills to these students have changed significantly in recent years. Three perspectives regarding the nature of communication have helped shape contemporary research and instructional practices (Downing, 2011; Johnston & Blue, 2020; Stremel, 2008); these changes encompass shared meanings, modes of communication, and function:

1. **Communication occurs when communication partners establish shared meanings.** The responsibility for successful communication rests with both partners. However, shared meaning is more likely when the partner who is relatively more skilled uses the principles of responsive interaction, such as following the lead of the less skilled communicator, balancing turns between conversation partners, and responding with interest and affect.
2. **Communication is independent of the specific form or mode that is used.** Speech is usually a desirable goal, and many students with severe disabilities learn to understand and produce spoken language. But the sensory, motor, and cognitive limitations of some students with severe disabilities keep them from learning to speak intelligibly even after intensive and extensive instruction. Many students who do not acquire speech are successful users of augmentative and alternative communication (AAC), including gestures, various sign language systems, communication boards, Picture Exchange Communication Systems (PECS), and electronic communication aids. (See Chapter 8 for a detailed description of AAC.)
3. **Communication must "work" for the child by influencing the behavior of others.** Communication is functional when it enables a child to do things such as tell people what to do, get help, convey social pleasantries ("Hi," "Bye"), show interest in an activity, protest, express an emotional or physical state, make a choice, and request or report information (Cascella & McNamara, 2005).

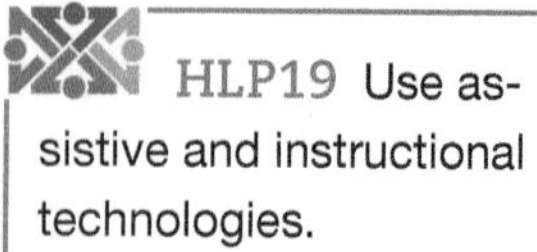
HLP19 Use assistive and instructional technologies.

Literacy Because it provides increased access to information and further learning, literacy is important for all students. For many years, educators, including many *special* educators, assumed students with severe disabilities would not benefit from instruction in reading and math. Recent research, however, has shown that even children who communicate on a presymbolic level can benefit from instruction in early literacy skills (e.g., Browder et al., 2012; Browder et al., 2011).

Pearson eText
Video Example 12.4
Simple supplemental pictures can help students with significant disabilities develop literacy skills.

Diane Browder (2013), a pioneer in development of early literacy instruction for children with significant disabilities, described a visit to a classroom where an elementary-aged child was learning the book version of the movie *Toy Story*. At one point, the teacher, Bree Jimenez, asked her visitor to hold up a board of pictures for the child to see, then asked, "When did Buzz Lightyear first come into the story?" The girl leaned over to a picture of a cake symbolizing a birthday party and blew on it indicating Buzz Lightyear first came into the story during a birthday party. "That girl reads now," said Browder.

Browder (2013) writes, "Whether teaching students academic content in general or special education, creating accessible versions of the text that other students will read is a good place to begin. For example, the chapter of a novel may be summarized in a simple paragraph. Pictures may be used to help students track the text as a teacher or peer reads the passage aloud" (p. 432). Featured Teacher Carey Creech-Galloway uses pictures to help her students develop literacy skills: "Students with severe disabilities acquire and generalize language quicker when words are paired with pictures.

Pairing pictures with print is especially important when teaching young students, but secondary students also benefit from this strategy—just make sure the pictures are age-appropriate." Carey coauthored a study that found that eText embedded instructional supports such as pictorial examples and nonexamples and animated coaches who provided response prompts helped high school students with multiple disabilities learn science content (Knight et al., 2018).

Recreation and Leisure Most children develop the ability to play and later to occupy themselves constructively during their free time. But children with severe disabilities may not learn to enjoy recreation and leisure skills without explicit instruction and supports. Teaching appropriate recreational and leisure skills helps students with severe disabilities interact socially, maintain their physical health and motor skills, and become more involved in community activities. Many people with severe disabilities do not use their unstructured time appropriately; rather than participate in enjoyable pursuits, they may spend excessive time sitting, wandering, or looking at television. Recreation and leisure are now acknowledged as an extremely important part of the curriculum for students with severe disabilities, and a variety of instructional programs and adapted equipment have been developed.

In one study, middle school students with intellectual disabilities learned to play a card game with instruction that included peer tutoring and simultaneous prompting (Fetko et al., 2013). Students in this study not only learned to play the card game but also had opportunities to socialize with peers and learn science facts. Changing the way team games are played can enable an individual with severe disabilities to participate in team sports. Figure 12.5 shows how equipment and rule modifications enabled a 10th-grade student with cerebral palsy and severe intellectual disabilities to play basketball in a way that maintained the integrity of the game for players without disabilities. For information and guidelines for selecting and teaching recreation, leisure, and sport activities, see Bambara et al. (2020), Block (2016), and Chapter 11.

Making Choices Imagine going through an entire day without being able to make a choice, any choice at all. Someone else—a teacher, a staff person, a parent—will decide what you will wear, what you will do next, what you will eat for lunch, whom you will sit next to, and so on throughout the day, every day. In the past, students with severe disabilities had few opportunities to express preferences and make choices; they were simply cared for and taught to be compliant. It was easier and faster to complete a task for a person with severe disabilities than it was to teach her the task. Such treatment deprives the individual of potentially valuable learning experiences and fosters learned helplessness.

Today special educators recognize opportunities to choose and the ability to make choices as quality of life issues for their students. These teachers can use their students' preferences to design and deliver more effective instruction. Educators are increasing efforts to help students with severe disabilities express their preferences and make decisions about

FIGURE 12.5 Example of Equipment and Rule Modifications Enabling a Student with Severe and Multiple Disabilities to Participate Meaningfully in a Team Sport

David and Basketball

David is a tenth-grade student with cerebral palsy and severe mental retardation. He moves around in his wheelchair with full support from others. One of David's Individualized Education Program objectives addresses participation in recreational activities that include a movement of picking up and throwing a ball.

In basketball games, two types of baskets are placed side by side: one has a higher rim, and the other has a lower rim. To ensure David's essential involvement in the game, which basket his team can use depends totally on the degree of effort David makes. During a basketball game, David engages in picking up and throwing a basketball to make an adapted shot outside of the basketball court. Each time he successfully makes an adapted shot, his team is allowed to use the lower basket.

Thus, David's efforts to throw a ball are converted momentarily and proportionally into the height of a basket. In this way, he can assist team players without disabilities who are not good at shooting in making more successful shots. Therefore, David is considered an active participant in an essential part of the basketball game.

Source: Ohtake, Y. (2004). Meaningful inclusion of all students in team sports. *Teaching Exceptional Children, 37*(2), 25. Reprinted with permission.

matters that will affect them (Tullis et al., 2011). For example, a child might be presented with pictures of two activities and asked to point to the one she would rather do. Another might be asked, "Whom would you like for your partner?" Or the teacher might say, "Should we do this again?" Of course, in presenting such choices, the teacher must be prepared to accept whichever alternative the student selects and to follow through accordingly.

Researchers have discovered ways to help people with severe disabilities indicate whether they want to participate in daily routines and activities (Lancioni et al., 2006); express preferences for what foods they will purchase and eat (Cooper & Browder, 1998); and make choices regarding leisure activities (Kreiner & Flexer, 2009), where they would like to live (Faw et al., 1996), and the kinds of jobs they would like (Agran & Krupp, 2011).

General Education Curriculum IDEA requires that all students with disabilities have access to the general curriculum taught to students without disabilities. State standards specify expected learning outcomes by grade level for each content area. For example, according to Common Core State Standards for Mathematics, a first grader is expected "to represent and solve problems involving addition and subtraction," and a fifth grader should be able to "perform operations with multi-digit whole numbers and with decimals to hundredths." IDEA and No Child Left Behind require students with disabilities to participate in statewide assessments of student learning. Most students with severe disabilities participate in alternate assessments as measures of their progress on state standards (see Chapter 2).

Featured Teacher Carey Creech-Galloway is an active contributor to the emerging research literature exploring ways that teachers can design lessons that blend effective instruction of both functional skills and academic goals (Collins, Evans, et al., 2010; Collins, Karl, et al., 2010). For example, Carey taught four adolescents with moderate and severe disabilities to apply the Pythagorean theorem to solve real-life scenarios (e.g., sewing, using a ladder) and to additional novel problems on the state alternative assessment test (Creech-Galloway et al., 2013).

Two basic strategies for combining functional and academic content are (a) embedding core academic content into functional activities (Karl et al., 2013) and (b) adding functional applications to instructional objectives based on core content standards (Collins et al., 2011). See *Teaching & Learning*, "Embedding Core Academic Content into Functional Skill Instruction."

SELECTING AND PRIORITIZING INSTRUCTIONAL TARGETS Students with severe disabilities present numerous skill deficits, which are often compounded by challenging behavior. Each of these skill deficits and behavioral challenges could (but not necessarily should) be targeted as an IEP goal. It is nearly impossible, however, to design and implement a teaching program to address simultaneously all of the learning needs of a student with severe disabilities. Selecting and prioritizing instructional objectives is one of the greatest responsibilities a special educator undertakes as an IEP team member.

Accurate predictions of how much any particular skill—functional or academic—ultimately will contribute to a student's overall quality of life are difficult to make. In many cases, we simply do not know how useful a new skill or bit of knowledge will prove to be. But when deciding which academic standards to incorporate into a student's program, common sense and, most of all, the student's best interests must rule the day. "Some skills are more fundamental than those required by the general education curriculum" (Kaufman et al., 2020, p. 29), and as Ayers and colleagues (2011) note, "there is no reasonable way to integrate Chaucer and volcanoes into a community-based lesson related to paying for a meal in a restaurant" (p. 15).

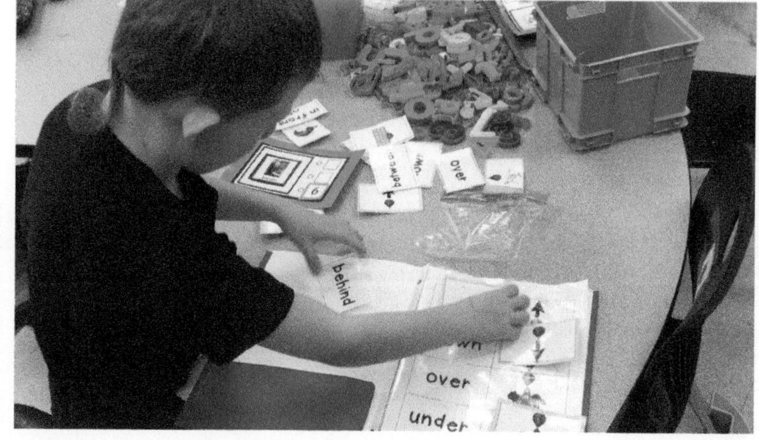

Source: William L. Heward

Each day Brandon chooses from among several activities to practice functional skills.

A functional approach must remain a priority when developing curriculum for students with severe disabilities. Whichever skills are targeted for instruction, they ultimately need to be

TEACHING & LEARNING

Embedding Core Academic Content into Functional Skill Instruction

Why Should Educators Embed Core Content into Functional Skill Instruction? There is no question that emphasis on functional skills is important for students with severe and multiple disabilities. However, since the 1997 reauthorization of IDEA, greater emphasis has been placed on access to the general curriculum for all students. It is becoming increasingly clear that students, even those with severe disabilities, can learn academic skills. Featured Teacher Carey Creech-Galloway agrees, "We know the importance of teaching our students skills in their natural environment. We also know that systematic instruction enables our students to acquire academic skills such as identifying story elements, using a set of data to answer questions, measuring, and making comparisons between concepts. Embedding academic core content into functional skills increases the likelihood students will acquire and maintain those skills."

How Do I Embed Core Content into Functional Skills Lessons? Before embedding academic instruction into functional skills, teachers must first determine the functional skill they will be teaching (e.g., food preparation, doing laundry), which should be selected based on students' IEP goals. Next, Carey recommends the following steps suggested by Collins, Karl, et al. (2010).

HLP12 Systematically design instruction toward a specific learning goal.

1. *Determine core content and instructional objectives*. After you have identified the functional skill you're targeting, identify academic content areas and standards to embed into instruction. Write an observable, measurable instructional objective for each core content area you will be embedding. See Figure 12.6.
2. *Plan with instructional context in mind*. Consider where instruction will take place and who will be providing it (e.g., general education teacher, special education teacher, paraeducator, peers). Carefully schedule instructional opportunities across materials, adults, peers, and settings. Plan to teach multiple exemplars and carefully choose instructional materials that are real world, in the student's mode of communication, and with adaptations that facilitate independence. See the third column of the planning sheet for examples.
3. *Select evidence-based teaching methods*. Determine which evidenced-based practices you will use to teach the skill. For example, time delay prompting is an evidenced-based practice for teaching both functional and core content skills to students with moderate and severe disabilities. Select procedures that are precise, are easy to implement within daily instruction, and provide good data for making instructional decisions. See the third column of the planning sheet for examples.
4. *Strategically embed opportunities for nontargeted skill acquisition*. Find opportunities to incorporate nontargeted information during instruction. For example, you may be teaching the student first to identify a solid, liquid, or gas in a picture. While you are teaching that information, you can add that we can melt solids to turn them into a liquid, or we can bring water to a high temperature to create a gas. You can use pre- and post-tests to determine whether your student has acquired essential nontargeted information throughout instruction.
5. *Collect and graph data daily*. This will help you make timely instructional decisions such as whether to add or remove prompts, provide more teaching trials, or use more descriptive praise. Create detailed data collection forms so you can reflect students' skill mastery (or lack thereof).
6. *Assess generalization and maintenance*. After the student acquires a skill, conduct brief assessment probes for generalization and maintenance. Assess the student's performance of that skill in different settings, using different materials, and in the presence of different people. This will allow you to pinpoint academic areas that need additional instruction or strategies that enable the student to maintain the skill and generalize across settings.

HLP6 Use student assessment data, analyze instructional practices, and make necessary adjustments that improve student outcomes.

FIGURE 12.6 Planning Sheet for Embedding Core Content Objectives into Functional Skills Instruction

Student Mae H. **Grade:** 7th

Functional Domain Using public transportation

Functional Skill Taking the city bus

IEP Goal When given a destination, bus schedule, and $5.00, Mae will take the bus to that destination, completing 100% of task analysis steps with no prompting.

Core Content Standard	Instructional Objectives	Lesson Plan Ideas (Context & Evidence-Based Methods)
Math: Solve real-world and mathematical problems involving the four operations with rational numbers.	When given the cost of bus fare for one ride and the cost of a 5-ride pass, Mae will determine which option is more cost efficient with 100% accuracy across three sessions.	• Classroom simulations with real money and real bus passes; use and systematically fade response prompts • Choice-making activity—allow students to choose which option they prefer, and then take community trips to exercise choice (let the consequences do the teaching)
English/ Language Arts: Demonstrate command of standard English grammar when writing and speaking.	When presented with a social situation related to riding the bus (e.g., greeting the driver, asking for help with fare or directions), Mae will speak clearly and demonstrate standard English conventions on 4 out of 5 trials.	• Classroom simulations to role-play verbal interactions with bus driver and others on the bus • Community trips; gradually fade prompts • Teach Mae to use a picture activity schedule for bus riding
Science: Demonstrate knowledge of the hydrologic cycle.	When presented with a diagram of the hydrologic cycle and terms such as "condensation" and "evaporation," Mae will point to the corresponding portion of the cycle on 4 out of 5 trials.	• Check the weather before taking community trips; discuss the hydrologic cycle in the context of the day's weather • Choice-making activity—allow Mae to choose what to wear and pack after checking the weather
Social Studies: Demonstrate map-reading skills.	When presented with a bus map of the city, Mae will identify where she wants to go, trace the bus route to that location, and name the cardinal direction from her starting point to that location with 100% accuracy across 2 trials.	• Practice tracing bus routes to various locations (starting with simple routes and gradually moving to more complex ones) • Create a compass rose; have students place their home in the center and then identify landmarks around the city for each of the cardinal directions • Use time delay procedures to teach parts of map and compass rose

meaningful for the learner and her family. A variety of person-centered planning methods are available to help IEP teams work with the individual and family members to identify and prioritize the relative significance of skills or learning activities (e.g., Giangreco et al., 2011; Shogren, Wehmeyer, et al., 2017).

Figure 12.7 shows a form on which an IEP team summarized the outcomes of various assessments and IEP goal recommendations for a student with severe disabilities in an inclusive classroom setting.

Instructional Methods: How Should Students with Severe and Multiple Disabilities Be Taught?

Learning Outcome 12.4 Describe effective teaching strategies for educating students with severe and multiple disabilities.

Concern for the well-being of students with severe disabilities and ensuring their access to meaningful curricular content and extracurricular activities are important. By themselves, however, concern and access are not enough. To learn effectively, students with severe disabilities

FIGURE 12.7 Summary of Assessment, Personalized Curriculum Needs, and IEP Recommendations for a Student with Severe Disabilities

Summary of Ecological Assessment for an Individualized Education Program (IEP)

Student's Name: Roddie Sprankle Date: May 26, 2021

Planning Team: Roddie, Ms. Sprankle (Roddie's mother), Ms. Durham (current special education teacher), Mr. Lindquist (current physical therapist), Mr. Adzima (special education teacher at Colby), Ms. Gomez (principal of Colby), Ms. Townsend (third-grade teacher at Colby), Ms. Karpowicz (math and computer teacher at Colby), Mr. Preston (language arts teacher at Colby)

1. **Background on Student**
   Roddie Sprankle is an 8-year-old boy who has traumatic brain injury as the result of an accident at age 5 years. Roddie made a remarkable recovery from the accident and has continued to show important progress over the past 3 years. He can now walk with a walker and speak in short phrases. Last year Roddie mastered writing a cursive signature and putting on his jacket. He made good progress on learning sight words and some math facts, which he often practiced using computer software. Roddie did not learn to initiate conversation. Although he talks more this year, his comments are often difficult to comprehend as he searches for the words he wants to use. He also made little progress on reading phrases. A prior evaluation by a neurologist, Dr. Hauster, notes that Roddie needs continued training in memory strategies and cognitive stimulation.
2. **Person-Centered Planning with Student and Family**
   Roddie's mother's priorities are that he (1) be treated well by other students (social inclusion); (2) continue to learn life skills, given his excellent progress this year in learning to put on his jacket; and (3) be taught reading. Roddie has expressed an interest in trying out the cafeteria. Currently, he eats in his special education classroom with only five other students present.
3. **Encouraging Student Self-Determination**
   Roddie has been learning goal setting and decision making this year. He has presented the planning team with a photo album of his preferences, which he placed in rank order. His top five include food (tacos, hamburgers, French fries), working on the computer, playing computer games, swimming at the YMCA, and music. He has also presented the team with his goals, which include being able to walk without his walker and getting his own computer.
4. **Development of Personalized Curriculum**
   Because Roddie has emerging functional academic skills, these can be used to create curricular parallels in general education. Expanding his sight word vocabulary, teaching him to read and write short phrases, and helping him build on his knowledge of math facts by learning to add are important priorities. These skills should be embedded in as many academic subjects as possible (e.g., learning sight word vocabulary in math). Roddie also has priority needs related to communication, self-direction, social interaction skills, and motor development that can be taught within the typical classroom.
5. **Recommendations for the IEP**
   The team has determined that the priorities for Roddie's IEP include (1) functional academics (Roddie wants this work to be computer assisted), (2) continued improvement of his balance and fine-motor skills (Roddie's priority is to walk without his walker), (3) initiation of conversations, (4) self-direction (goal setting, self-managed seatwork), and (5) mastery of personal care skills. Roddie will spend most of his day in Ms. Townsend's third grade classroom and will receive specially designed instruction from Mr. Adzima and a teaching assistant. He will also receive individual assistance for toileting and individual physical therapy sessions based on his preference for privacy in these activities.

Source: Courtesy Diane M. Browder, University of North Carolina Charlotte. Used by permission.

need more than love, care, and a supportive school environment. They seldom acquire complex skills through imitation and observation alone; they are not likely to blossom on their own.

Because their skill deficits and learning problems are so significant, students with severe disabilities need instruction that is intensive, carefully planned, systematically executed, and continuously monitored for effectiveness.

Collectively, the authors of leading texts on teaching students with severe disabilities recommend that teachers attend to the following components of an instructional program (e.g., Browder et al., 2020; Brown et al., 2020; Collins, 2012; Westling et al., 2021):

> HLP4 Use multiple sources of information to develop a comprehensive understanding of a student's strengths and needs.

- *Assess current level of performance.* Precise assessment of current performance is necessary to determine which skills to teach and at what level instruction should begin. Unlike traditional assessments, which rely heavily on standardized scores and developmental levels, assessment of students with severe disabilities emphasizes each learner's ability to perform specific, observable behaviors under specific conditions. Can Keeshia hold her

Source: William L. Heward

Response prompts and physical guidance help students learn new skills.

head up without support? For how many seconds? Under what conditions? In response to what verbal or physical signals? Assessment should not be a one-shot procedure but take place at different times, in different settings, and with different people. The fact that a student with severe disabilities does not demonstrate a skill at a particular time or place does not mean she is incapable of demonstrating that skill.

- *Clearly define the skill to be taught.* "Carlos will feed himself" is too broad a goal for many students with severe disabilities. A more appropriate statement might be "When applesauce is placed on Carlos's spoon, he will put the spoon in his mouth within 5 seconds." A clear statement like this enables the teacher and other observers to determine whether Carlos attains this objective. If, after repeated trials, he has not, a different method of instruction should be tried.
- *Break down the skill into component steps.* Effective teachers of students with severe disabilities use **task analysis** (see Chapter 4) to break down a skill into a series of specific, observable steps. Assessment of student performance on each step of the task analysis helps the teacher determine where to begin instruction. She can systematically teach each required step until the student can accomplish the entire task independently. Without this sort of structure and precision in teaching, a great deal of valuable time is likely to be wasted.

Pearson eText
Video Example 12.5
Featured Teacher Carey Creech-Galloway's lessons demonstrate the essence of special education: individually planned, specialized, intensive, goal-directed instruction.

- *Determine how the learner will actively participate in the lesson.* Active engagement and repeated practice, important elements of effective instruction for all students, are crucial for learners with severe disabilities. Some students with severe disabilities can participate in the same way that typical students might, such as using response cards in a lesson on number identification (Skibo et al., 2011). Active participation by some students, however, requires alternative response modes or topographies—for example, an adapted mouse for selecting choices of vocabulary words on a computer screen or eye gaze to indicate yes/no picture symbols in a shared reading lesson (Fenlon et al., 2010). For students with profound disabilities, even a single response (e.g., small movement of the hand or head, eye gaze) requires extensive effort and, in some cases, adaptive equipment. Therefore, the multidisciplinary team must work together to prepare students for meaningful engagement in instruction (Smith et al., 2001).
- *Provide response prompts.* It is important for the child to know what action or response is expected. A prompt can be verbal; the teacher might say, "Bev, say, 'apple,'" to indicate what Bev must do before she will receive an apple. A prompt can be physical; the teacher might point to a light switch to indicate that Bev should turn on the light. The teacher also may need to demonstrate an activity many times and to guide the child physically through some or all of the tasks required in the activity.

HLP 8 and HLP22 Provide positive and constructive feedback to guide students' learning and behavior.

- *Provide immediate feedback.* Students with severe disabilities must receive immediate and clear information about their performance, including reinforcement for correct responses (e.g., praise statement and giving child access to preferred toy for 5 seconds) and corrective feedback for errors and nonresponses (e.g., "No, that's not it" in a calm voice and repeating the response prompt) (e.g., Leaf et al., 2011). It is critical to identify effective reinforcers for students with severe disabilities. Unfortunately, it is not always easy to determine what items or events motivate a noncommunicative child. Many teachers devote extensive efforts attempting to find out which items and activities will function as reinforcers for a particular child, and they keep careful records of what is and is not effective. For descriptions of methods for assessing stimuli that may serve as reinforcers for students with severe and profound disabilities, see Cannella-Malone, Sabielney, et al. (2013).

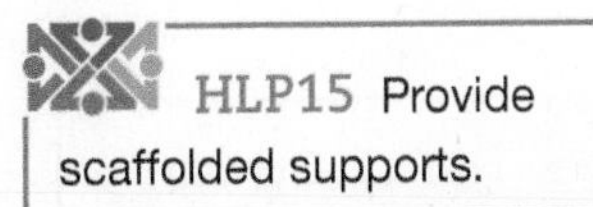

HLP15 Provide scaffolded supports.

- *Gradually withdraw response prompts.* Contrived prompts must be withdrawn so that a student's correct responses come under control of naturally occurring stimuli. **Time delay** is an evidence-based teaching tactic for transferring control from instructional prompts to natural stimuli (Browder et al., 2009). For detailed information on time delay and other methods for delivering and fading instructional prompts to students with severe disabilities, see Collins (2012) and Brown et al. (2020).
- *Promote generalization and maintenance.* Effective teachers ensure that their students can perform targeted skills in different settings and with different instructors, cues, and materials before concluding with confidence that the student has acquired and generalized a skill. Several strategies for facilitating generalization are discussed in Chapter 4. Authentic materials help promote generalization to real-life situations and should be used whenever possible. For example, students learning to make purchases should practice with real money instead of simulated bills and coins. Using naturalistic teaching strategies and conducting instruction in community-based instruction is one of the best ways to facilitate a student's generalization and maintenance of important skills (Steere & DiPipi-Hoy, 2012). See *Transition: Next Year Is Now,* "It's Not Just a Field Trip: Community-Based Instruction."

  Descriptions of strategies and tactics for helping students generalize and maintain what they have learned can be found in Cooper et al. (2020) and Westling et al. (2015).

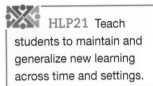

HLP21 Teach students to maintain and generalize new learning across time and settings.

- *Directly and frequently assess student learning.* Learning by students with severe disabilities most often occurs in very small steps, progress that may be missed without objective measurement. Learning is shown most clearly when some measure of student performance is collected each time the skill is taught. Recording a student's performance of each step of a task-analyzed skill or routine is needed (e.g., see Collins, Karl, et al., 2010, and Figure 4.5 in Chapter 4).

HLP6 Use student assessment data, analyze instructional practices, and make necessary adjustments that improve student outcomes.

Transition: Next Year Is Now

It's Not Just a Field Trip: Community-Based Instruction

What Is Community-Based Instruction and Why Should I Do It?

As suggested by its name, community-based instruction (CBI) is teaching and learning that occurs in community settings. Depending on the skills being targeted, CBI can take place just about anywhere—a grocery store, a restaurant, or even a trampoline park. However, as fun as these instructional outings may be, as Featured Teacher Carey Creech-Galloway notes, CBI is not merely a field trip.

Teaching with CBI has many advantages, the most important of which is it allows students to practice skills in real-life settings—the settings where they will be expected to use those skills. This improves students' chances of generalizing skills beyond the classroom, allows teachers to assess what specific challenges may arise in novel settings, and gives students chances to develop social connections in the community (Barczak, 2019).

Pearson eText
Video Example 12.6
Practicing in real-life settings helps students generalize skills beyond the classroom.

How Do I Implement CBI?

Always begin with students' goals. Featured Teacher Carey looks at the skills her students are working on, the core content standards for alternate assessment, and overall unit instruction that is occurring within her classroom while planning her community-based instruction. She notes, "I try to create each CBI experience to correspond with work we are doing in the classroom... CBI can address skills in all areas: communication, OT/PT objectives, training in the community environment for students with VI or HI, academic, social, behavior, functional... CBI, like all good instruction, is focused, intentional, and targets specific goals and objectives."

HLP12 Systematically design instruction toward a specific learning goal.

Consider what types of community settings would give students opportunities to practice some of these skills. Try to maximize efficiency by asking yourself if there is a way to address several students' IEP goals and/or goals across a range of domains. Featured Teacher Carey has taken her elementary students to the ballet, a local gymnastics and tumbling gym, a state park for a Halloween celebration, and the local grocery store. "We worked on skills in all of these settings: locating survival signs and environmental signs in the community; crossing the street; making a purchase; following a picture schedule/routine for a task; using AAC devices to express wants and needs; PT and OT goals such as stamina, flexibility, range of motion, and fine-motor skills; counting money; telling time; following two-step directions; and many behavioral and social goals weaved in between."

Make logistical arrangements. This includes working with businesses to determine the best days and times for your visits, getting administrative and parental permissions, arranging transportation, and making sure all the adult helpers (e.g., related service providers, paraprofessionals, parent chaperones) understand their roles.

HLP20 Provide intensive instruction.

Prepare at school. In the weeks leading up to community-based instructional outings, after you have identified target skills, prepare students by providing intensive instruction on those target skills with intentional planning for generalization. Use varied photos and videos to show students a range of examples of the target skill being performed in a variety of settings. Provide students practice and role-play opportunities with a range of people within the classroom and around the school building. When possible, provide simulated instruction by arranging the classroom setting and materials to reflect the natural setting as much as possible (Barczak, 2019). See Chapter 4 for more on simulated instruction for CBI.

HLP21 Teach students to maintain and generalize new learning across time and settings.

Don't forget your data sheets! Community settings are perfect locations to collect generalization data. Bring any data sheets you use in your classroom that align with skills you are targeting in the community. For each generalization probe, note whether the student was able to perform the skill independently or with prompting. If the student needs a lot of prompting in the community, that will help you recognize the need for more generalization training in your classroom—as well as more community-based instruction.

Ways to Make CBI Even More Effective

Enlist support from related service providers. You'll want to bring along other adults to assist you on your outings; why not be strategic about it and co-plan with your related service providers? Carey addresses speech, language, fine-motor, and gross-motor skills in many of her CBI outings. She carefully plans with the speech-language pathologist, the occupational therapist, and the physical therapist so they can provide instruction and collect data across a range of skills.

Carey recommends using what you learn from your CBI outings to improve your classroom instruction and assessment. For instance, while out in the community, it is a great time to "troubleshoot that task analysis you thought was perfect in the classroom but then when you see the student perform a skill in the community you see gaps." Identifying these gaps will help you provide accommodations in the moment (in the community) but will also help you as you prepare upcoming lessons in your classroom.

Carey understands that for her students next year really is now. Don't wait until high school to begin instruction in the community!

PARTIAL PARTICIPATION The principle of **partial participation**, first described by Baumgart and colleagues (1982), acknowledges that even though some individuals with severe disabilities cannot independently perform all steps of a given task or activity, they often can learn to perform selected components or an adapted version of the task. Partial participation helps learners be more active in a task, make more choices in how the task will be carried out, provide more control over the activity, and fulfill valuable roles in the classroom or community (Giangreco et al., 2020; Udvari-Solner et al., 2004). Ongoing evaluation determines when various components of assistance can be faded or eliminated (McDonnell et al., 2020).

Similar to any instructional strategy or technique, partial participation can be misused. Ferguson and Baumgart (1991) describe four types of misapplications of partial participation: (a) *passive participation*—the learner is present but not actively participating; (b) *myopic participation*—the student's participation is limited to only some parts of the activity, which are chosen for the convenience of others; (c) *piecemeal participation*—partial participation and the accompanying concepts of functional, activity-based, age-appropriate curriculum activities are used only part of the time; and (d) *missed participation*—in trying to help students become independent, the point of partial participation is missed altogether.

POSITIVE BEHAVIORAL SUPPORT In the not-too-distant past, a student who engaged in hand mouthing and stereotypic head weaving may have had his arms put in splints while a teacher manipulated his head up and down for several minutes. A student who tantrummed or screamed may have been "treated" by being sprayed with water mist or given an extended seclusion time-out from instruction. A student who repeatedly struck out at others was restrained and held motionless on the floor for several minutes. Little evidence exists for the therapeutic value of these "treatments," especially the use of restraint and seclusion. The Council for Exceptional Children's official policy is that "Physical restraint or seclusion procedures should be used in school settings only when the physical safety of the child or youth or others is in immediate danger" (Council for Exceptional Children, 2009, p. 2).

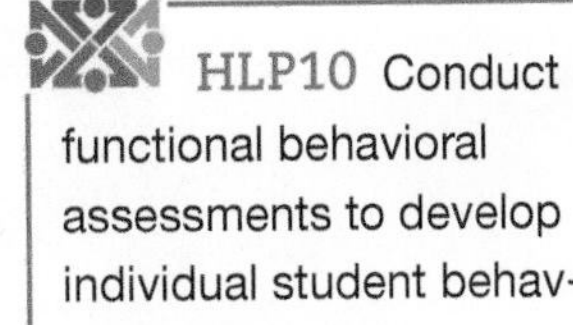
HLP10 Conduct functional behavioral assessments to develop individual student behavior support plans.

Positive behavioral support begins with a functional assessment of the problem behavior (see Chapter 6). Results of functional assessments guide the development of positive behavior support plans. For example, functional assessments conducted by Roscoe et al. (2010) revealed that aggressive outbursts during instructional activities by a 13-year-old student with multiple disabilities were maintained by teacher attention in the form of preferred conversational topics (e.g., zoo, dogs). This information led to the design of a function-based intervention that decreased the child's aggression by teaching her a socially accepted alternative behavior (pointing to an "I want to talk" card) to access highly preferred conversation topics.

Compared with interventions that do not consider the function of problem behavior, treatments informed by functional assessment are more likely to produce durable improvements in behavior, less restrictive in nature, and more likely to be accepted by practitioners and parents (Hanley, 2012; Slaton et al., 2017). School districts' teaching and support staffs increasingly include Board Certified Behavior Analysts (BCBAs). Training and supervised experience in applied behavior analysis enables BCBAs to safely and expertly conduct functional assessments, interpret the results, and design and evaluate research-based interventions (Behavior Analyst Certification Board, 2020).

Challenging behaviors such as noncompliance, aggression, acting out, and self-injury can sometimes be reduced in frequency or prevented altogether through relatively simple environmental modifications of curriculum or the way in which learning activities are conducted. For example:

- Provide students with a choice of tasks or a task sequence (Zelinsky & Shadish, 2018).
- Intersperse easy or high-probability tasks or requests with more difficult items or low-probability requests (Common et al., 2019; Wood et al., 2018).
- Teach children to respond to a call of their names and group calls (e.g., "everyone") (Beaulieu et al., 2012).
- Maintain a rapid pace of instruction (Tincani & De Mers, 2016).
- Use a response-prompting procedure that results in few errors (O'Neill et al., 2018).
- Provide reinforcement on a fixed or variable schedule independent of behavior (C. L. Phillips et al., 2017).
- Provide access to leisure items, activities, and attention (Cannella-Malone et al., 2008; Wood et al., 2018).

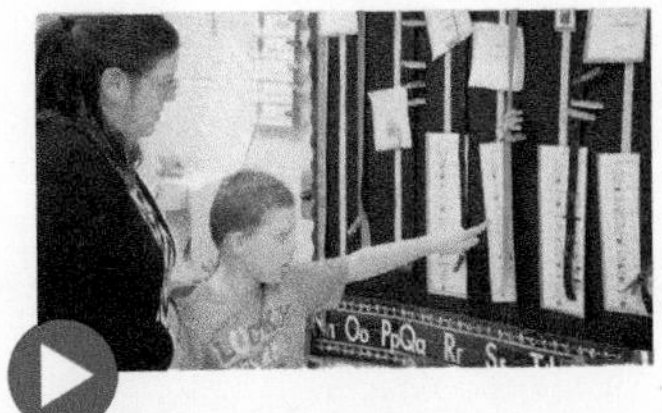
Pearson eText
Video Example 12.7
Effective classroom management systems depend on positive reinforcement, student ownership, and consistency.

SMALL-GROUP INSTRUCTION For many years, it was thought that one-to-one instruction was the only effective teaching arrangement for students with severe disabilities. The rationale was that one-to-one teaching minimized distractions and increased the likelihood the student would respond only to the teacher. Although such teaching formats enable the intensive, systematic instruction that is effective for students with severe disabilities, well-designed and executed small-group instruction can also be effective and has many advantages (Brown et al., 2020; Hunt et al., 2020):

- Skills learned in small-group instruction may be more likely to generalize to group situations and settings.
- Small-group instruction provides opportunities for social interaction and reinforcement from peers that are missed when a student is taught alone and isolated from other students.
- Small-group instruction provides opportunities for incidental or observational learning from other students.
- In some instances, small-group instruction may be a more cost-effective use of the teacher's time.

Pearson eText
Video Example 12.8
Well-designed and skillfully executed small-group instruction is effective and efficient.

Teachers can enhance the effectiveness of small-group instruction for all students by

- Ensuring that students possess basic prerequisite skills such as (a) sitting quietly for a period of time, (b) maintaining eye contact, and (c) following simple instructions or imitating simple responses.
- Encouraging students to listen and watch other group members and then praise them for doing so.
- Making instruction interesting by keeping individual turns short, giving all members turns, and using demonstrations and a variety of materials.
- Using methods that produce high rates of active student response, such as choral responding and response cards (see Chapter 6), which enable every student in the group to respond to each instructional trial.
- Teaching at a lively pace (i.e., keeping time between learning trials very brief).
- Involving all members by using multilevel instruction individualized to each student's targeted skills and mode of response.
- Using partial participation and material adaptation to enable all students to respond.
- Eliminating unnecessary teacher talk and limiting the amount or length of student response in a single turn.

Special Considerations for Students with Deaf-Blindness

An educational program for children who are deaf is often inappropriate for a child who also has limited vision because many methods of instruction and communication rely heavily on the use of sight. In contrast, programs for students with visual impairments usually require good hearing because much instruction is auditory. Although most students with dual sensory impairments can make use of information presented in visual and auditory modalities, when used in instruction, these stimuli must be enhanced and the students' attention directed toward them.

Tactile teaching techniques involving the sense of touch are used to supplement the information obtained through visual and auditory modes (Chen, 2014). Students who are deaf-blind use a variety of hand-to-hand communication methods (Bruce et al., 2016; Hersh, 2013)

- *Tactile sign language*: The deaf-blind person holds the other person's hands or wrists and feels the movements as he or she signs.
- *Manual alphabets*: The speaker signs each letter on the listener's flat palm.
- *Block alphabet (Spartan)*: The speaker draws block capital letters onto the listener's palm.
- *Finger braille*: The speaker types braille code onto the fingers of the listener.

Communication is achieved only with great difficulty by people who are deaf-blind and requires effort on the part of communication partners. Teachers can help students who depend on hand-to-hand methods to receive information and express their knowledge, desires, opinions, and emotions by making their hands accessible, using hand-under-hand touch to respond to child's explorations and expressions of feeling, imitating the child's hand actions by moving hands under or alongside the child's, and playing interactive hand games (Miles, 2003).

According to Lane (2003), the challenge for teachers of students who are deaf-blind is finding ways to alter daily interactions that are attuned to vision and hearing to be attuned to touch. "Braille did just that when he invented his code of the alphabet; the deafblind community did just that when it adapted communication in ASL [American Sign Language] to the tactual modality. However, nothing less than all types of human interactions must be rethought in this way" (p. 12).

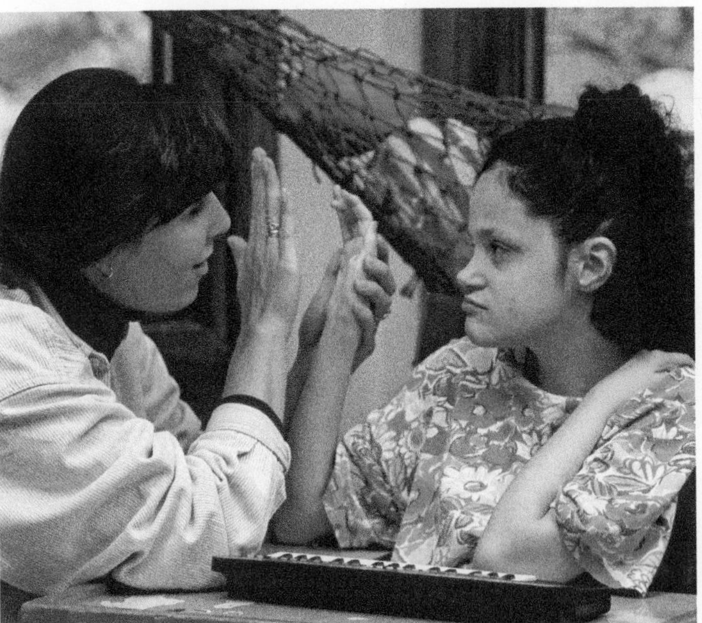

Source: Scott Cunningham/Pearson Allyn and Bacon/Merrill Education

Tactile stimuli play a critical role in instruction for students with deaf-blindness.

Special Educational Considerations for Students with Traumatic Brain Injuries

Many of the curricular and instructional approaches for students with severe or multiple disabilities also apply to students with brain injuries; however, teachers and IEP teams have several additional considerations. Recovery from a brain injury is a long and unpredictable process. A student might make excellent progress, then regress to an earlier stage, and then make a rapid series of gains. Individuals with brain injuries sometimes reach plateaus in their recovery during which no improvements occur for some time. A plateau does not signal the end to functional improvement. Ylvisaker (2005) recommends that the child return to school when she is physically capable, can respond to instructions, and can sustain attention for 10 to 15 minutes.

Students who have been hospitalized with head injuries reenter school with deficits from their injuries compounded by their extended absence from school. Students with head injuries are likely to require comprehensive programs of academic, psychological, and family support. IEP goals and services may need to be reviewed and modified as often as every 30 days because of the dramatic changes in behavior and performance by some children during the early stages of recovery. Educators can assist students with TBI by doing the following (Babikian & Asarnow, 2009; Deidrick & Farmer, 2005; Schilling & Getch, 2012; Vu et al., 2011):

- Decrease course load or number of assignments to be completed at the same time.
- Break assignments into smaller chunks.
- Schedule academic instruction during peak performance periods; provide frequent breaks and adequate rest. Chronic fatigue may necessitate a reduced class load and shortened school day.
- Rehearse social situations in advance and provide explicit instructions and prompts about social interactions such as maintaining socially accepted body space and tone of voice.
- Provide clear, uncomplicated instructions; break multistep instructions into simplified steps.
- Pair auditory instructions with visual cues.
- Have a teacher, counselor, or aide meet with the student at the beginning and end of each school day to review the day's schedule, keep track of assignments, and monitor progress.
- Have a peer to help the student move efficiently from class to class, and permit early dismissal from class to allow time to get to the next room.

HLP9 Teach social behaviors.

- Include adapted physical education for students who have difficulties with mobility, balance, or coordination.
- Provide behavior management or counseling interventions to help with poor judgment, impulsiveness, overactivity, aggression, destructiveness, and socially uninhibited behavior students with head injury often experience.
- Record lectures, assign a note taker, and allow extra time to take tests.

Placement Options

Learning Outcome 12.5 List advantages and disadvantages of regular classroom placement for students with severe and multiple disabilities.

What is the most appropriate educational setting for a student with severe disabilities? This important question continues to be the subject of much debate and discussion (Giangreco, 2020; Giangreco et al., 2020; Kauffman et al., 2020; Kleinert et al., 2015).

Where Are Students with Low-Incidence Disabilities Being Educated?

A national survey of nearly 40,000 students across 15 states found that fewer than 3% of students with the most significant disabilities had regular classroom as their primary placement, and just 4.3% were served in resource rooms (Kleinert et al., 2015). Approximately 14% of students with multiple disabilities receive instruction in the regular classroom, 18% receive instruction in a resource room, 45% receive instruction in a separate class, and 23% receive instruction in special schools or other settings (U.S. Department of Education, 2020a).

For deaf-blind students, approximately 26% receive instruction in regular classrooms, 13% in resource rooms, 36% in separate classes, and 25% in special schools and other settings (U.S. Department of Education, 2020a).

For students with TBI, approximately 51% receive instruction in regular classrooms, 21% in resource rooms, 20% in separate classes, and 8% in special schools and other settings (U.S. Department of Education, 2020a).

Benefits of Neighborhood Schools

Lou Brown (who has long championed the inclusion of people with severe disabilities in integrated school, vocational, and community settings) and his colleagues at the University of Wisconsin made a strong case for why students with severe disabilities should attend the same school they would attend if they did not have disabilities:

> The environments in which students with severe intellectual disabilities receive instructional services have critical effects on where and how they spend their postschool lives. Segregation begets segregation. We believe that when children with intellectual disabilities attend separate schools, they are denied opportunities to demonstrate to the rest of the community that they can function in integrated environments and activities; their peers without disabilities do not know or understand them and too often think negatively of them; their parents become afraid to risk allowing them opportunities to learn to function in integrated environments later in life; and taxpayers assume they need to be sequestered in segregated group homes, enclaves, work crews, activity centers, sheltered workshops, institutions, and nursing homes (Brown et al., 1989a, p. 1).

Brown and his colleagues offered four reasons why students with severe disabilities should be educated in neighborhood schools. First, when students without disabilities go to an integrated school with peers who have disabilities, they are more likely to develop a greater acceptance of diversity and are likely to function responsibly as adults in a pluralistic society (Downing et al., 2004). Second, integrated schools are more meaningful instructional environments (Fisher & Meyer, 2002). Third, parents and families have greater access to school activities when children are attending their home schools. Fourth, attending one's home school provides greater opportunities to develop a wide range of social relationships (Zambo, 2010). Although each rationale has received various types and levels of research support in the literature (Ryndak & Fisher, 2007), the benefits of inclusion on social skills and relationships have the most extensive empirical support.

SOCIAL RELATIONSHIPS Establishing and maintaining a network of social relationships is one of the most important goals of inclusive educational practices for students with severe disabilities. Table 12.1 presents examples of 11 kinds of social relationships that might develop between students with severe disabilities and their peers without disabilities when they attend the same school.

Pearson eText
Video Example 12.9
Inclusion provides students with multiple and severe disabilities access to the general curriculum and opportunities for positive social interaction.

Including students with multiple and severe disabilities in regular classrooms provides opportunities for positive social interactions and the development of friendships, as this elementary teacher described:

> I think him just being here is a great opportunity for communication because he's getting to interact. The other kids want to hold his hand, they want to speak to him, they want to sit beside him. His being in the mainstream setting just provides him with other students that want to talk to him and that want to be his friend (De Bortoli et al., 2012, p. 242).

Simply placing students in neighborhood schools and regular classrooms does not necessarily result in support from peers:

> There's not a lot of interaction between the mainstream students and him. None of the other students seem to want to even attempt the "high fives," a big communication tool. So, there's that divide in that respect (De Bortoli et al., 2012, p. 242).

Educators have developed a wide variety of strategies for promoting social interactions and friendship. One strategy is teaching the student with disabilities a specific skill for initiating and maintaining interaction. For example, Hughes and colleagues (2011) taught five high school students with significant disabilities to use communication books to initiate conversations with

HLP9 Teach social behaviors.

TABLE 12.1 Social relationships that can develop between students with severe disabilities and their peers without disabilities when they attend the same school

SOCIAL RELATIONSHIP	EXAMPLE
Peer tutor	Leigh role-plays social introductions with Margo, providing feedback and praise for Margo's performance.
Eating companion	Jennifer and Lucas eat lunch with Linda in the cafeteria and talk about their favorite music groups.
Art, home economics, industrial arts, music, physical education companion	In art class, after students are instructed to paint a sunset, Tom sits next to Dan and offers suggestions and guidance about the best colors to use and how to complete the task.
Regular class companion	A fifth-grade class is doing a "Know Your Town" lesson in social studies. Ben helps Karen plan a trip through their neighborhood.
During-school companion	Students "hang out" and interact on a social level: After lunch and before the bell for class rang, Molly and Aliyah go to the student lounge for a soda.
Friend	David, a member of the varsity basketball team, invites Alejandro, a student with severe disabilities, to his house to watch a game on TV.
Extracurricular companion	Sarah and Winona prepare their articles for the school newspaper together and then work on the layout in the journalism lab.
After-school-project companion	The sophomore class has decided to build a float for the homecoming parade, so Jordan and Maria work on it together after school and on weekends.
After-school companion	On Saturday afternoon, Mike and Bill go to the shopping mall.
Travel companion	David walks with Alejandro when he wheels from last-period class to the gym, where Alejandro helps the basketball team as a student manager.
Neighbor	Parents of students without disabilities in the neighborhood regularly exchange greetings with Audrey when they are at school, around the neighborhood, at local stores, at the mall, or at the grocery.

Source: Table adapted from "The Home School: Why Students with Severe Disabilities Must Attend the Schools of Their Brothers, Sisters, Friends, and Neighbors" by L. Brown, from JOURNAL FOR THE ASSOCIATION FOR PERSONS WITH SEVERE HANDICAPS, 1987, Volume 14.

Source: Bill Aron/PhotoEdit

Friendships between students with and without disabilities are more likely to develop when they share classroom experiences.

general education students who had expressed interest in interacting with students with disabilities. Each page of a student's communication book contained a Picture Communication Symbol (Mayer-Johnson, 2008) and printed text to depict an age-appropriate question or statement related to school events, sports, and recreational interests (e.g., "What kind of music do you like?").

Still other approaches involve changes in the roles and responsibilities of instructional faculty, such as collaborative teaching teams (Dettmer et al., 2012; Ryndak et al., 2020).

Many strategies for facilitating the inclusion of students with severe disabilities are compatible with one another, and programs typically incorporate multiple, concurrent methods for identifying and providing supports for students, their peers, and their teachers.

Other strategies focus on teaching classmates without disabilities to initiate social contacts during free time, cooperative learning, or peer tutoring and peer buddy activities (Brock et al., 2020; Copeland et al., 2004; Sartini et al., 2013). See *Teaching & Learning,* "Peer Helpers: Including Students with Severe Disabilities."

How Much Time in the Regular Classroom?

Although research has clearly shown the social benefits of inclusion for students with disabilities, as well as for their peers without disabilities, the effects of full inclusion on the attainment of IEP goals are not yet known. Although the functional IEP goals and objectives for students with severe disabilities can be embedded within the academic instruction in the regular classroom, doing so meaningfully is often very difficult, especially at the secondary level. Making the most effective use of available instructional time is critical to students who by definition require direct, intensive, and "customized" instruction to acquire basic skills that students without disabilities learn without instruction.

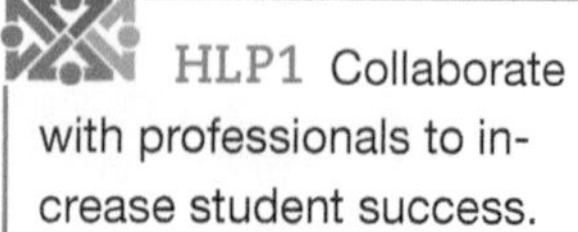
HLP1 Collaborate with professionals to increase student success.

A major challenge for both special and general educators is to develop models and strategies for including students with severe disabilities in regular classroom activities without sacrificing their opportunities to acquire, practice, and generalize the functional skills they need most.

The question of how much time students with severe disabilities should spend in the regular classroom is an important one. Although a few full-inclusion advocates might argue that every student with disabilities should have a full-time placement in a regular classroom regardless of the nature of her educational needs, most special educators probably would agree with Brown and colleagues (1991), whose position is that students with severe disabilities should be based in the same schools and classrooms they would attend if they did not have disabilities.

Pearson eText
Video Example 12.10
Peer helper programs benefit students with and without disabilities.

TEACHING & LEARNING

Peer Helpers: Including Students with Severe Disabilities

What Are Peer Helpers, and Why Are They Important? Peer helpers (or peer buddies) are students without disabilities who interact with students with disabilities to increase their social engagement and quality of life. Students with severe disabilities are often isolated from their peers without disabilities. With a peer helper program, students with disabilities can feel more included, have access to models of appropriate social skills, and form friendships (Hughes & Carter, 2006). Additionally, participating in a peer helper program benefits students without disabilities who develop empathy, responsibility, and appreciation of diversity (Brock et al., 2020).

Setting Up A Peer Helper Program Featured Teacher Carey Creech-Galloway suggests the following steps for getting a peer helper program started at the elementary level:

1. **Collaborate with general education teachers to select peer helpers.** Peer helpers are same-grade peers without disabilities who demonstrate good citizenship, a willingness to help, and a desire to form authentic relationships with students with disabilities.
2. **Determine what types of supports the peer will provide.** For example, will the peer helper walk with the student to and from different classrooms, assist the student with academic or nonacademic work while in class, or sit with and help the student in the cafeteria?
3. **Train the peer helpers.** Specifically, Carey focuses on teaching the helpers to prompt and provide help only after the student with disabilities has tried the task independently. Be sure the peer helper knows when and how to ask an adult to intervene.
4. **Monitor students and peer helpers.** Monitor (via observation and feedback from other teachers) students as they engage in activities together. Check in with the peer helpers to provide feedback and to make sure they are feeling comfortable and confident. Make adjustments to schedules and pairings as needed.

At the high school level, developing a peer helper program might be a bit more formal. Hughes et al. (2013) recommend the following steps for starting a high school peer buddy program.

1. **Develop a peer buddy course.** This gives students time and space to interact and develop peer buddy relationships.
2. **Publicize your peer buddy program.** Share information about your course at staff meetings, during morning announcements, and in newsletters. Actively seek out nominations for peer buddies by talking to school counselors and teachers.
3. **Select and match peer buddies.** Invite students to visit special education classrooms, interview them, and have them complete an application to find out about their interests and experiences. Use this information to create peer buddy matches.
4. **Train peer buddies.** Begin with an orientation to teach awareness, sensitivity, and communication techniques. Then teach peer buddies to model, prompt, and reinforce specific skills. Prepare peer buddies for the range of challenging behaviors they may observe, and provide tips for addressing them.
5. **Provide feedback.** Gather information via observations, peer buddy reflective journals, and regular meetings with peer buddies. Provide positive feedback on what is going well and make suggestions for improvement.
6. **Find creative ways to build and sustain your program.** Plan a variety of activities to build on the relationships that have developed in the course. For instance, peer buddy programs can be expanded to include clubs, athletic events, and community-based instruction.

> There are substantial differences between being based in and confined to regular education classrooms. "Based in" refers to being a member of a real class, where and with whom you start the school day, you may not spend all your time with your class, but it is still your group and everyone knows it.... It is our position that it is unacceptable for students with severe disabilities to spend either 0% or 100% of their time in regular education classrooms.... How much time should be spent in regular classes? Enough to ensure that the student is a member, not a visitor. A lot, if the student is engaged in meaningful activities. Quite a bit if she is young, but less as she approaches 21. There is still a lot we do not know (pp. 40, 46).

The Challenge and Rewards of Teaching Students with Severe and Multiple Disabilities

Teachers—special as well as general educators—who are providing instruction to students with severe and multiple disabilities can rightfully be called pioneers on an exciting new frontier of education. In 1984, Orelove stated that professionals who were involved in educating students with severe disabilities could "look back with pride, and even awe, at the advances they have made. In a relatively brief period, educators, psychologists, and other professionals have advocated vigorously for additional legislation and funds, extended the service delivery model into the public schools and community, and developed a training technology" (p. 271).

Although significant progress has been made in the several decades since Orelove's positive assessment, a great deal more can and must be accomplished. Future research must increase our understanding of how students with severe disabilities acquire, maintain, and generalize functional skills. As we develop more effective techniques for changing behavior, they must be balanced with concern for the personal rights and dignity of individuals with severe disabilities. Current and future teachers of students with severe disabilities have the opportunity to be at the forefront of those developments.

Teaching students with severe disabilities is difficult and demanding. The teacher must be well organized, firm, and consistent. She must be able to manage a complex educational operation, which usually involves supervising paraprofessional aides, student teachers, peer tutors, and volunteers. The teacher must be knowledgeable about one-to-one and small-group instruction formats and be able to work cooperatively with general education teachers and related-services professionals. She must maintain accurate records and constant planning for the future needs of her students. Effective communication with parents and families, school administrators, vocational rehabilitation personnel, and community agencies is also vital.

Students with the most severe disabilities sometimes give little or no apparent response, so their teachers must be very sensitive to small changes in behavior. The effective teacher is consistent and persistent in designing and implementing strategies to improve learning and behavior. The effective teacher should not be too quick to remove difficult tasks or requests that result in noncompliance or misbehavior. It is better to teach students to request assistance and to intersperse tasks that are easy for the student to perform.

There is a difference between either expecting miracles or being passively patient and simply working each day at the job of designing, implementing, and evaluating systematic instruction and supports. It can be a mistake to expect a miracle:

> In the beginning, we were expecting a sudden step forward, that we might somehow turn a cognitive, emotional, or social key inside the child's mind that would produce a giant leap ahead.... Such a leap would have been so gratifying, and it would have made our work so much easier. But it never happened. Instead, progress followed a slow, step-by-step progression, with only a few and minor spurts ahead from time to time. We learned to settle in for hard work (Lovaas, 1994, n.p.).

Some might consider it undesirable to work with students with severe and multiple disabilities because of the extent of their behavioral challenges and learning problems. Yet teaching students who require instruction at its very best can offer many highly rewarding teaching experiences. Much satisfaction can be felt in teaching a child to feed and dress herself independently; helping a student make friends with peers without disabilities; and supporting a young adult's efforts to live, travel, and work as independently as possible in the community. Both the challenge and the potential rewards of teaching students with severe disabilities are great.

ADVICE FROM THE FEATURED TEACHER

by Carey Creech-Galloway

Develop a Schedule and Stick to It

- Begin developing a schedule by using the school's master schedule to fill in the lunch times, grade level content times, recess, specials or electives, and any times in the day that cannot be changed that the student will participate in the general education setting. This

Source: Belle Galloway

will help you see what time is available to pull students for specially designed instruction or (if you are lucky enough to have the staff support and time) when you may push into the general education setting.

- List all of the students' IEP objectives and related services first and other activities that have set times during the school day. Schedule the students, instructional assistants, and the teacher all on the same schedule so that they all know their responsibilities for that block of time.
- List the student(s) and instructor and the goal or activity for that time period. You may even want to list the materials needed until your paraprofessionals become familiar with your expectations. Don't forget to have several generalization activities on hand so that students have an opportunity to apply the concepts taught during direct instruction.

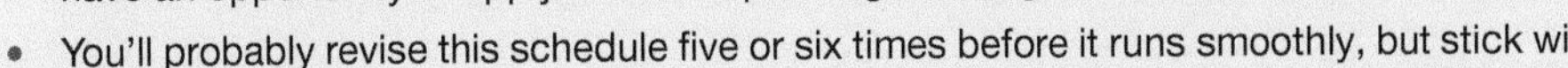

- You'll probably revise this schedule five or six times before it runs smoothly, but stick with it!

Get Organized with Your Instructional Data

- Develop a system for keeping each student's instructional data organized. You could begin with a binder with each IEP objective on a tab with the data sheet and graph behind the tab. You can organize this per student or per IEP objective if that applies (e.g., all students working on brushing teeth in one binder).
- Secondary teachers may find it more beneficial to break into instructional groups per the IEP goals first and then set up group instruction binders that contain the probe data collection, data collection sheets for the skills being taught, graphs for each student's performance, and a list of instructional materials required.
- Take some data each time you provide instruction on an IEP objective because you need the data to make decisions on instruction. As one of my University of Kentucky professors told me, "If you aren't taking data on the skill, why teach it?"

Embed Functional Skills Instruction Throughout the School Day

- To maintain functional skills or independent living skills, the student needs opportunities during the day to practice these skills when they may occur naturally.
- With an increasing emphasis on core content instruction, it is important for teachers of students with moderate and severe disabilities to keep in mind long-term and transition goals for their students so they can increase their independence.
- Start with a list of daily living skills and which students need to work on these skills. List any vocational skills, cooking skills, community living skills, or recreation and leisure skills that your students may need in the future. Target two or three skills for each student and schedule time during the day for those skills to be taught. For example, you could embed some of those skills in the following routines and activities: brushing teeth after lunch, wiping tables at the end of the day, preparing breakfast for another student, and sorting items in the school bank.

Collaborate with General Education Teachers

- Meet with the teachers individually, if possible, and determine how you will communicate—whether through a paraprofessional, a peer tutor, email, or weekly meetings.
- Set clear goals for your students in the general education setting. Talk with the general education teachers about what opportunities there are in their classroom for your student to participate and discuss how work will be modified.
- Have a plan for times when the general education classroom is not appropriate for your students—for example, the entire class is taking a standardized test or the schedule is changed for some reason.

- Look at each student's IEP goals and determine when these goals could be worked on in the general education setting.
- Be flexible. Plan lessons that are focused on measurable, observable outcomes and look at how to teach core content skills in a functional way. Remember you can—and should—use systematic instructional strategies to teach core content objectives as well as functional skills.

Key Terms and Concepts

anoxia
closed head injury
deaf-blindness
multiple disabilities
open head injury
partial participation
profound disabilities
severe disabilities
task analysis
time delay
traumatic brain injury

Summary

Definitions

- Students with multiple disabilities have concomitant impairments that cannot be accommodated in special education programs solely for one of the impairments. The impairments and learning challenges children with multiple disabilities experience are sometimes classified as severe or profound disabilities.
- Students with severe disabilities need instruction in basic skills that most children without disabilities acquire without instruction in the first 5 years of life.
- TASH defines people with severe disabilities as individuals "who require ongoing support in more than one major life activity in order to participate in an integrated community and enjoy a quality of life similar to that available to all citizens."
- Students with profound disabilities have pervasive delays in all domains of functioning at a developmental level no higher than 2 years.
- Students with deaf-blindness cannot be accommodated in special education programs designed solely for students with hearing or visual impairments. Although the vast majority of children who are deaf-blind have some functional hearing, vision, or both, the dual impairments severely impede learning.
- The Individuals with Disabilities Education Act (IDEA) defines traumatic brain injury (TBI) as an acquired injury to the brain caused by an external physical force, resulting in total or partial functional disability, psychosocial impairments, or both, that adversely affects a child's educational performance.

Characteristics

- Students with multiple and severe disabilities need instruction in many basic skills that most children without disabilities learn without help. These children may show some or all of the following behaviors or skill deficits: slow acquisition rates for learning new skills, difficulty generalizing and maintaining newly learned skills, severe deficits in communication skills, impaired physical and motor development, deficits in self-help skills, infrequent constructive behavior and interaction, and frequent inappropriate behavior.
- Despite their intense challenges, students with severe disabilities often exhibit many positive characteristics, such as warmth, humor, sociability, and persistence.
- Despite their limitations, children with the most significant disabilities can and do learn.
- More than 90% of children who are deaf-blind have one or more additional disabilities: 64% have cognitive impairments, 58% also have physical disabilities, and 51% have complex health care needs. Cognitive ability of students with deaf-blindness can range from profound intellectual disability to giftedness.
- Brain injuries cause impairments that fall into three main categories: (a) physical and sensory changes (e.g., lack of coordination, spasticity of muscles); (b) cognitive impairments (e.g., short- and long-term memory deficits, difficulty maintaining attention, language problems); and (c) social, behavioral, and emotional problems (e.g., mood swings, self-centeredness, lack of motivation).

Prevalence

- Estimates of the prevalence of severe disabilities range from 0.1% to 1% of the population.
- Together, children served under the IDEA disability categories of multiple disabilities, TBI, and deaf-blindness represent fewer than 3% of all children who receive special education.

Causes

- Brain disorders, which are involved in most cases of severe intellectual disabilities, are the result of either brain dysgenesis (abnormal brain development) or brain damage (caused by influences that alter the structure or function of a brain that had been developing normally up to that point).
- Severe and profound disabilities most often have biological causes, including chromosomal abnormalities, genetic and metabolic disorders, complications of pregnancy and prenatal care, birth trauma, and later brain damage.
- In about one sixth of all cases of severe disabilities, the cause cannot be clearly determined.
- Causes of deaf-blindness include prematurity, infections during pregnancy, complications during childbirth, and numerous congenital syndromes (e.g., Usher syndrome). Deaf-blindness may also be acquired in childhood or during adulthood due to causes such as meningitis or brain injury.
- TBI in children is usually the result of car and bicycle accidents, falls, accidents during contact sports, or shaken-baby syndrome.

Educational Approaches

- A curriculum based on typical developmental milestones is inappropriate for most students with severe disabilities.
- Students with severe disabilities must be taught skills that are functional, age-appropriate, and directed toward current and future environments.
- Students with severe disabilities should be taught choice-making skills.
- The emphasis of research and training in communication for people with severe disabilities has shifted from instruction of specific forms of communication to a focus on functional communication in any mode that enables communication partners to establish shared meanings.
- Some students with severe disabilities use augmentative and alternative systems of communication (AAC), such as gestures, various sign language systems, pictorial communication boards, Picture Exchange Communication Systems (PECS), and electronic communication aids.
- Students with severe disabilities should be taught age-appropriate recreation and leisure skills.
- Because each student with severe disabilities has many learning needs, teachers must carefully prioritize and choose IEP objectives and learning activities that will be of most benefit to the student and his family.
- Effective instruction of students with the most significant disabilities is characterized by:
  - Precise assessment of the student's current level of performance
  - Clearly defined target behaviors
  - Ordering of skills in a logical sequence
  - Clear prompts or cues for student response
  - Immediate feedback and reinforcement
  - Strategies that promote generalization and maintenance
  - Direct and frequent measurement of the student's progress
- Partial participation is both a philosophy for selecting activities and a method for adapting activities and supports to enable students with severe disabilities to actively participate in meaningful tasks they cannot perform independently.
- Teachers of students with severe disabilities must be skilled in positive, instructionally relevant strategies for assessing and dealing with challenging and problem behaviors.

Placement Options

- Research has shown that integrated small-group instructional arrangements with students with severe disabilities can be effective.
- Students with severe disabilities are more likely to develop social relationships with students without disabilities if they attend their home school and are included in the regular classroom.

Challenge and Rewards

- Although the initial reactions of many general education teachers who have a student with severe disabilities placed in their classrooms are negative, these apprehensions and concerns often transform into positive experiences as the student becomes a regular member of their classroom.
- Teachers must be sensitive to small changes in behavior. Effective teachers are consistent and persistent in evaluating and changing instruction to improve learning and behavior.
- Working with students who require instruction at its very best can be highly rewarding to teachers.

Chapter 13
Gifted and Talented

Source: Laurence Gough/Shutterstock

Learning Outcomes

After reading this chapter and completing the embedded activities, you should be able to

13.1 Describe various definitions of giftedness.

13.2 Identify characteristics of gifted and talented students.

13.3 Describe guidelines for identifying gifted students.

13.4 Explain how teachers provide appropriate instruction for gifted and talented students.

13.5 Identify and describe placement options for gifted and talented students.

Featured Teacher

Jennifer Sheffield

Franklin-Simpson Edge Academy, Franklin, Kentucky

Source: Allison Grace Thompson

I teach at Franklin-Simpson Edge Academy, an enrichment program for gifted students. Edge Academy directly serves 50 gifted fourth- and fifth-grade students. My school district serves a total population of around 3000 students and is located in a small town in a rural county in south central Kentucky. Our student population is approximately 78% White, 12% African American, 5% Hispanic, 5% two or more races, and 1% Asian; and 66% of our students qualify for free or reduced lunch.

Students at Edge Academy alternate among full class instruction, independent work, and flexible groupings based upon their abilities and interests. I try to provide my students with opportunities to use similar processes and methodologies used by professionals in various STEM fields (science, technology, engineering, mathematics). In science lab, students ask research questions, design and conduct experiments, collect and analyze data, and report results. They learn how challenging it can be to isolate and manipulate just one variable while holding constant all other variables, how bias can come into play when interpreting results, and the importance of replication for believability.

I try to create open-ended learning opportunities that do not limit student achievement to a teacher-created ceiling. Although I plan lessons with specific learning objectives in mind, I always leave room for students to go beyond them. Oftentimes I do NOT post or share explicitly stated learning goals or objectives that tell my students what they're "supposed" to be getting out of a lesson. Instead, I let actual learning experience guide their discovery. When students have time to think, talk, and work without me trying to control every step of the process, they often come up with deeper connections than I'd anticipated when I initially designed the lesson.

For example, I presented the classic math challenge, Sessa's chessboard, to my students. The challenge is to figure out how many grains of rice Sessa would have on the 64th square of a chessboard, if he was given 1 grain for the first square of the chessboard, doubled to 2 for the second, doubled to 4 for the third, and so on. The students worked with calculators alone or in groups and were free to share ideas with each other. Their calculators eventually displayed scientific notation (which none of the students knew how to interpret at the time), adding another layer of discovery. My actual learning goal wasn't for the students to find the exact numerical answer, but to introduce a discussion of scientific notation and how and why we use it—but in a fun way!

I am passionate about gifted education. My goal is to make school into the experience many GT kids hunger for: a place to enjoy learning, a place where it's cool to be enthusiastic about insects, astronomy, dinosaurs, computer coding, poetry, solving crazy tough math problems... whatever! I love seeing my students come bounding off the school bus in the morning, full of energy with smiles on their faces, excited and ready to share ideas and get to work. I am grateful to teach in a school district that values gifted education and encourages differentiated curriculum and personalized learning experiences for all students.

Education, Teaching Credentials, and Experience

- *B.A. in art, University of Louisville, 1993*
- *M.A.T. in elementary education, Bellarmine University, 2003*
- *Ed.S. in Gifted Education and Talent Development, Western Kentucky University, 2018*
- *Certifications: Kentucky, elementary education (K–5), Gifted Endorsement, Gifted Education Coordinator*
- *12 years of teaching experience*

Content Extension 13.1

Featured Teacher Jennifer's students complete the Sessa's chessboard math challenge.

THE STUDY OF EXCEPTIONAL CHILDREN largely focuses on students with disabilities—children who require individualized programs of specially designed instruction and related services to benefit from education. Gifted and talented (GT) students also need special education. Traditional curriculum and methods of instruction do not provide the advanced and unique challenges gifted students require to obtain maximum benefit from education. Developing the abilities and talents of these exceptional children is the mission of special educators who work with GT students. Featured Teacher Jennifer Sheffield suggests that teaching GT students might be a good fit if you

- have a curious mind and love to learn—you will always be learning something new to stay abreast of things in a GT classroom.
- don't mind completely rearranging lesson plans on the fly when students' questions and discussion take things on a new and interesting turn.
- don't mind that a 9-year-old child not only knows more about a subject than you do but also likes to challenge and fact check you all day, every day.
- enjoy watching kids jump up and down waving their calculators in the air when they solve another insanely complicated math problem.
- haul a dead horseshoe crab's exoskeleton home from your beach vacation and your car smells like a dead fish stuffed into a teenager's tennis shoe for the entire 12-hour drive home. You don't mind because "all my kids are going to totally freak out when they see this thing!"
- understand that a child with an extremely high IQ is just as likely to forget her lunch box as any other student.
- don't mind sitting next to a student at lunch who recites the entire plot of the sci-fi book he just read, verbatim, for 20 minutes straight.
- you have a good sense of humor, coupled with a generous and tolerant appreciation for the humor of others, including puns, sarcasm, bad vocal impressions, and the occasional slapstick performance.

If GT is your calling, you won't want to teach anything else!

Definitions

Learning Outcome 13.1 Describe various definitions of giftedness.

Intelligence, creativity, and talent have been central to definitions of giftedness proposed over the past century. Lewis Terman (1925) defined gifted individuals as those who score in the top 2% on standardized tests of intelligence. Guilford (1967) called for the identification of people with creative potential. Witty (1951) described GT children as those "whose performance is consistently remarkable in any potentially valuable area" (p. 62). The current and still-evolving definitions of GT children continue to reflect these three elements—intelligence, creativity, and special talents.

Federal Definitions

The first federal definition of GT students appeared in a 1972 report to Congress titled *Education of the Gifted,* by then U.S. commissioner of education Sydney Marland:

> [T]he term "gifted and talented children" means children, and whenever applicable, youth, who are identified at the preschool, elementary, or secondary level as possessing demonstrated or potential high performance capabilities in areas such as intellectual, creative, specific academic, or leadership ability or in the

> performing and visual arts and who by reason thereof require services or activities not ordinarily provided by the school.... [G]ifted and talented will encompass a minimum of 3 to 5 percent of the school population (p. 5).

The Marland definition encompassed multiple forms of giftedness in addition to superior intellectual ability and had significant influence on states' definitions.

The current federal definition, first promulgated in the Jacob K. Javits Gifted and Talented Students Education Act of 1988 (PL 100-297) as part of the Elementary and Secondary Education Act and the No Child Left Behind Act of 2001, reads as follows:

> Students, children, or youth who give evidence of high achievement capability in areas such as intellectual, creative, artistic, or leadership capacity, or in specific academic fields, and who need services and activities not ordinarily provided by the school in order to fully develop those capabilities (P.L. 107-110 (Title IX, Part A, Definition 22) (2002); 20 USC 7801(22) (2004)).

The most recent version of the Elementary and Secondary Education Act (i.e., Every Student Succeeds Act of 2015) added new provisions in which states must specify their plan to improve the ability for school personnel to identify and provide instruction to gifted and talented students based on their needs.

National Association for Gifted Children

The National Association for Gifted Children (NAGC, 2010) defines gifted individuals as

> those who demonstrate outstanding levels of aptitude (defined as an exceptional ability to reason and learn) or competence (documented performance or achievement in top 10% or rarer) in one or more domains. Domains include any structured area of activity with its own symbol system (e.g., mathematics, music, language) and/or set of sensorimotor skills (e.g., painting, dance, sports) (p. 1).

Gifted students display an exceptionally rapid rate of learning compared with other students of the same age, experience, and environment. As children reach adolescence, the primary characteristics of their giftedness are achievement and high motivation in a specific domain. Additionally, "Giftedness exists in every demographic group and personality type. It is important that adults look hard to discover potential and support gifted children as they reach for their personal best" (NAGC, 2020a, n. p.).

Other Contemporary Definitions

Contemporary conceptions of giftedness balance theoretical with practical elements emphasizing problem solving; talents that are culture, context, and domain related; and the influence of sustained, deliberate practice on the realization of exceptional talent. These views are evident in the definitions of GT students by Joseph Renzulli, Jane Piirto, and June Maker.

RENZULLI'S THREE-TRAIT DEFINITION Renzulli (1978) defines giftedness as the product of an interaction among three clusters of human traits: (a) above-average general intellectual abilities, (b) high level of task commitment, and (c) creativity. Figure 13.1 illustrates how ability (demonstrated or potential), task commitment, and creative expression are jointly applied to general and specific performance areas. Similar to the most recent federal definition, Renzulli's definition casts a wide net; it provides a great deal of freedom in determining who is capable of high potential for GT performance.

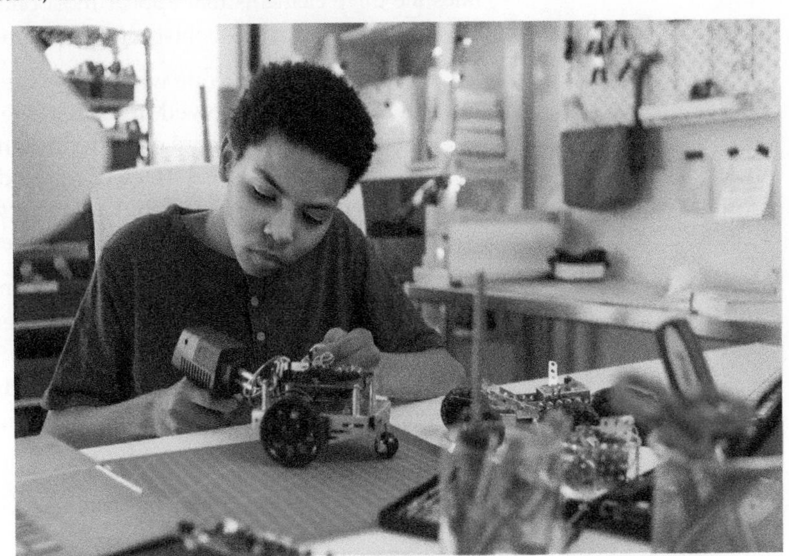

Source: SDI Productions/E+/Getty Images

Many gifted students display superior memory, observational skills, curiosity, creativity, and the ability to learn academic content with minimal repetition.

FIGURE 13.1 Renzulli's Three-Trait Definition

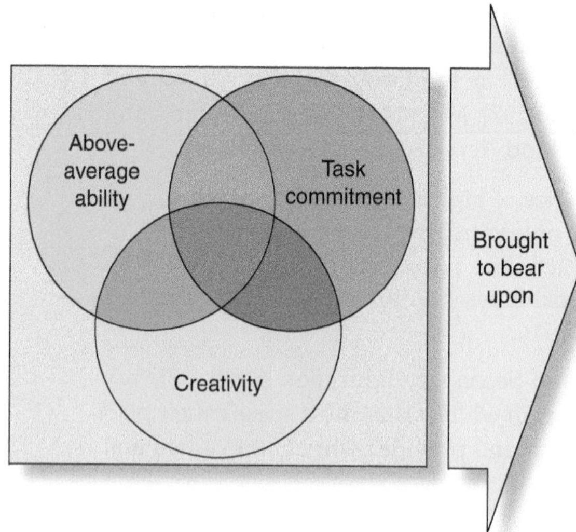

General Performance Areas

Mathematics • Visual Arts • Physical Sciences • Philosophy • Social Sciences • Law • Religion • Language Arts • Music • Life Sciences • Movement Arts

Specific Performance Areas

Cartooning • Astronomy • Public Opinion Polling • Jewelry Design • Map Making • Choreography • Biography • Filmmaking • Statistics • Local History • Electronics • Musical Composition • Landscape Architecture • Chemistry • Demography • Microphotography • City Planning • Pollution Control • Poetry • Fashion Design • Weaving • Play Writing • Advertising • Costume Design • Meteorology • Puppetry • Marketing • Game Design • Journalism • Electronic Music • Child Care • Consumer Protection • Cooking • Ornithology • Furniture Design • Navigation • Genealogy • Sculpture • Wildlife Management • Set Design • Agricultural Research • Animal Learning • Film Criticism • and so on

Source: Figure adapted from "What Makes Giftedness? Reexamining a Definition" by Joseph S. Renzulli, from PHI DELTA KAPPAN, 1978, Volume 60.

PIIRTO'S TALENT DEVELOPMENT CONCEPT Piirto (2007) defines gifted individuals as

> individuals who, by way of having certain learning characteristics such as superior memory, observational powers, curiosity, creativity, and the ability to learn school-related subject matters rapidly and accurately with a minimum of drill and repetition, have a right to an education that is differentiated according to those characteristics (p. 37).

Piirto believes giftedness in children becomes apparent early and those children should be served from preschool through college. Although gifted students may or may not become producers of knowledge or creators of innovation, their education should give them the background to become adults who do produce knowledge or make new artistic and social contributions.

MAKER'S PROBLEM-SOLVING PERSPECTIVE Maker's perspective of giftedness and talent incorporates the three elements that appear most often in contemporary definitions: high intelligence, advanced creativity, and sophisticated problem-solving skills. She characterizes a gifted person as

> a problem solver—one who enjoys the challenge of complexity and persists until the problem is solved in a satisfying way. Such an individual is capable of: a) creating a new or more clear definition of an existing problem, b) devising new and more efficient or effective methods, and c) reaching solutions that may be different from the usual, but are recognized as being effective, perhaps more effective, than previous solutions (Maker, 1993, p. 71; also see Maker, 2005).

By recognizing special talents and emphasizing an understanding of the role of opportunity as well as environmental and personality factors, these and other contemporary conceptions of giftedness and talent—such as Sternberg's (2007) triarchic theory of intelligence, Gagné's (2003) differentiated model of giftedness and talent, and Gardner's (2006) theory of multiple intelligences—are radical departures from earlier definitions that focused primarily on high IQ.

State-by-State Definitions

Many states have incorporated aspects of the 2001 federal definition into their definitions of giftedness and talent. Although the general intelligence element prevails across states' definitions of giftedness and talent (46 states consider superior ability or potential as giftedness), different states feature other aspects of special abilities and performance: specific academic ability (32 states), creativity (27 states), visual and performing arts talent (23 states), advanced leadership capacity (22 states), and motivation (4 states) (NAGC, 2020b). Four states currently have no official definition of GT students.

Characteristics

Learning Outcome 13.2 Identify characteristics of gifted and talented students.

Pearson eText
Video Example 13.1
Featured Teacher Jennifer Sheffield's students explain what it is like to be gifted and offer advice for teachers.

Giftedness encompasses a wide range of abilities, skills, and traits. Some students have special talents but rarely do they match widely held stereotypes and myths about giftedness. These students may not be outstanding in academics, but they may have exceptional abilities in areas such as music, dance, art, or leadership. Gifted and highly talented individuals are found across gender, cultural, economic, linguistic, and disability groups (NAGC, 2020a). Learning and intellectual characteristics of many GT children include superior ability to (Bildiren, 2018; Clark, 2013; Rimm et al., 2018):

- Rapidly acquire, retain, and use large amounts of information
- Relate one idea to another
- Make sound judgments
- Appreciate multiple and opposing points of view
- Perceive the operation of large systems of knowledge
- Acquire and manipulate abstract symbol systems
- Create novel solutions to problems by reframing the question

Highly gifted students show advanced neuromotor and neurosensory development at an early age. Additionally, highly gifted students "show unusually fast processing speed in problem-solving tasks, an exceptional ability to transfer problem-solving skills to new situations, and strong metacognitive abilities" (Jung & Gross, 2014, p. 307). Many highly gifted children—those with IQ scores 3 standard deviations or greater above the mean (IQ >145)—exhibit the following characteristics (Clark, 2009; Silverman, 1995):

- Intense intellectual curiosity
- Perfectionism and need for precision
- Learning with great intuitive leaps
- Intense need for mental stimulation and challenge
- Rapid and thorough comprehension of concepts, essential elements, and underlying structures
- Superior ability to convey broad ideas and synthesize commonalities
- Appreciation of complexity
- Early moral and existential concerns
- Tendency toward introversion, independence, and isolation

Many gifted children have a highly developed sense of moral judgment, fair play, compassion, and empathy for others for their age (Roeper & Silverman, 2009). As a result, teachers and parents may find themselves in heated discussions with gifted children over issues such as why adults litter or why politicians want to cut aid programs for older and poor individuals (Rimm et al., 2018).

Some discussions and lists of the characteristics of gifted children portray only strengths and virtues. The very attributes by which we identify gifted children, however, can cause or contribute to a multitude of challenges (Missett, 2014; Mofield & Parker Peters, 2015). For example, strong verbal ability may be evident in gifted students who talk themselves out of troublesome situations or who dominate class discussions, and high curiosity may appear aggressive or snoopy to others. Educators need substantive preparation in gifted education to avoid unrealistic stereotypes or letting students' shortcomings be used to deny gifted education assessment and services (e.g., Anderson & Martin, 2018).

Source: Newscom

The unique abstract style of Alexandra Nechita, shown here at age 16 years, was evident when she was 4 years old.

Creativity

Some scholars consider creative ability central to the definition of giftedness (e.g., Luria et al., 2016; Silvia, 2015). In general, creativity refers to producing original ideas that change the way others think or behave (Cross & Coleman, 2014). Based on their review of 90 creativity studies, Plucker et al. (2004) defined creativity as "the interaction among aptitude, process, and environment by which an individual or group produces a perceptible product that is both novel and useful as defined within a social content" (p. 90). One of the earliest models of creativity was developed by J. P. Guilford (1967, 1987), who conceptualized creativity as divergent thinking consisting of the following dimensions, which can be assessed using The Torrence® Tests of Creative Thinking (Torrence, 2018).

- *Fluency:* produces many ideas
- *Flexibility:* offers a wide variety of ideas, unusual ideas, and alternative solutions
- *Novelty or originality:* uses words in unique ways, uses low-probability words and responses, and has innovative ideas
- *Elaboration:* provides details
- *Synthesizing ability:* links together unlikely ideas
- *Analyzing ability:* organizes ideas into larger, inclusive patterns
- *Ability to reorganize or redefine existing ideas:* transforms an existing object into one of different design, function, or use
- *Complexity:* manipulates many interrelated ideas

Creativity is quite subjective and heavily dependent on context and culture (Luria et al., 2016). Many creative individuals may come from economically disadvantaged backgrounds; they tend to be resourceful students who find a way to use their imagination and lack of resources to think outside the box (see Grantham et al., 2011).

Clark (2013) suggests that the purpose of creativity is "to recognize and bring forth that which is new, diverse, advanced, complex, and/or previously unknown so that humankind can experience life as fuller, richer, and/or more meaningful" (p. 124). Although many GT individuals become scientists, inventors, writers, and great artists and performers, they have no obligation to do so—this may not be their interest, passion, or goal.

After studying highly creative individuals in various fields, Piirto (2011) concluded that (a) specific behaviors in childhood are predictive of creativity in each field, (b) the emergence of talent in various domains occurs in a developmental sequence, and (c) the importance of IQ scores should be minimized and subsumed into a more contextual view of children performing tasks in specific domains. The relationship between intelligence (IQ) and creativity is debatable, and testing for creative potential is often invalid and unreliable (Lemons, 2011).

Precociousness

Pearson eText
Video Example 13.2
Alexandra Nechita is a creatively gifted artist who was a precocious child.
https://www.youtube.com/watch?v=6P7ulm0p_ug

Gifted and talented children often display precociousness—creativity, talents, or intellectual abilities that are highly advanced for their age (Lubinski, 2016). For example, 6-year-old Janie has just completed her report on the solar system for class tomorrow. She looks out her bedroom window and wonders what might be happening on the countless planets that orbit all of those stars. She thinks about the circumstances that made life possible on planet Earth. Although most students write school reports and wonder about extraterrestrial life, Janie is functioning years ahead of her peers. She writes in complete sentences, expresses herself exceptionally well, and has a powerful urge to know the answers to many and varied questions.

FIGURE 13.2 Profiles of Two Gifted and Talented Students, Both Age 10 Years and in Fifth Grade

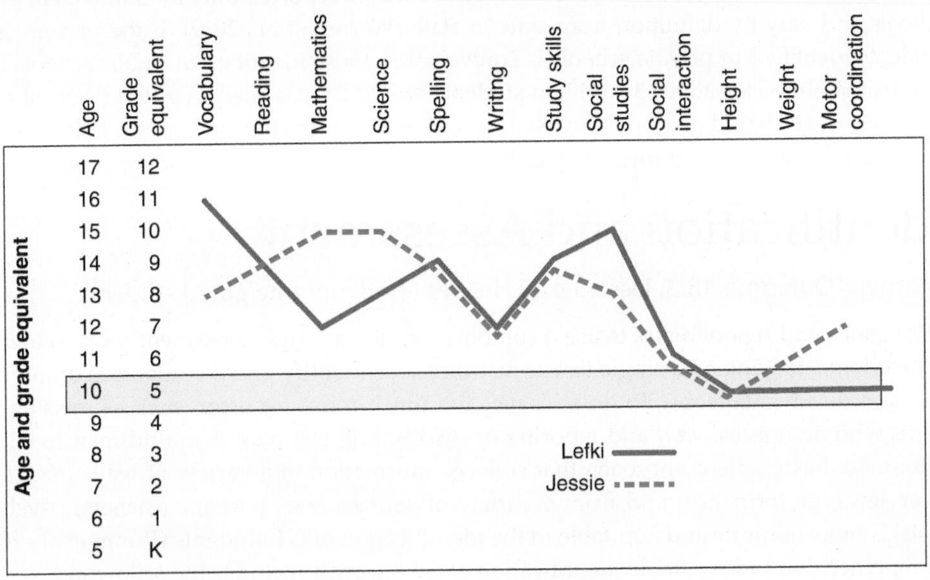

Individual Differences Among Gifted and Talented Students

Awareness of individual differences is essential to understanding gifted students. Similar to all children, gifted children show both inter- and intraindividual differences. An *interindividual* difference exists when two students earn different scores on the same test. A student who obtains a high score on a reading achievement test and a much lower score on a math achievement test shows an *intraindividual* difference between the two areas of performance. Intraindividual differences are also evident when a child with high intelligence or achievement is less mature emotionally or socially. A graph or profile of any student's abilities would reveal some high points and some lower points; scores would not be the same across all dimensions. **Asynchrony** is a term used to describe disparate rates of intellectual, emotional, social, and physical growth or development some gifted children display.

A gifted student's overall pattern of performance, however, is often well above average for the student's grade, age, or experience. As shown in Figure 13.2, Lefki performs higher in vocabulary and social studies than Jessie; however, Jessie shows higher performance in science and mathematics than Lefki. Each student also has intraindividual differences in scores. For example, Lefki has the vocabulary of an 11th grader but scores at a 7th-grade equivalent in mathematics; Jessie scored grade equivalents of 10th grade in science and mathematics and 7th grade in writing. All students, including those who are gifted, have relative strengths and weaknesses.

Prevalence

If giftedness were defined solely on the basis of superior cognitive ability as evidenced by IQ scores, then, theoretically, 2.3% of the general population would be gifted by virtue of an IQ score 2 standard deviations or more above the mean (roughly 130). The same theoretical approach predicts that about 1 in 1000 people would be highly gifted by attaining an IQ score of 145 (3 standard deviations above the mean), and roughly 1 in 10,000 would be considered exceptionally or profoundly gifted (an IQ score of 160, at 4 standard deviations above the mean).

Not only is intelligence testing a theoretically thorny, inexact, and biased process (particularly when applied to children from cultural and linguistic backgrounds different from those with whom the tests were normed), but the concept of giftedness also encompasses special talents and the potential for intellectual, creative, and superior performance. Some prevalence estimates of giftedness range as high as 10% to 15% of the school-age population (Belanger & Gagné, 2006).

There are about 3.2 million school-age gifted students in the United States (U.S. Department of Education, Office for Civil Rights, 2013). Data on the number of gifted and talented students identified in K–12 schools are imprecise because data are reported only for students in public schools and vary by definition from state to state (Worrell et al., 2019). If the percentage of students identified in private schools is equivalent to those identified in public schools (e.g., approximately 6.5%), about 3.7 million students would be classified as gifted (Worrell et al., 2019). However, based on population statistics, White and Asian American students are overrepresented in gifted programs, whereas Black and Latino students are underrepresented.

Identification and Assessment

Learning Outcome 13.3 Describe guidelines for identifying gifted students.

Most states and school districts use a combination of tests and assessment tools to identify GT students. Relying on a single test or instrument to identify gifted students is uninformative and disadvantageous. To do so leaves too much room for error, such as missing students who do not test well and ignoring or discounting test bias. A multidimensional and multimodal assessment approach that collects information in a variety of ways (e.g., tests, interviews, performance) and from a variety of sources (e.g., parents, teachers, psychologists) is more accurate and equitable in the identification of GT students (Rimm et al., 2018). Comprehensive and equitable identification of GT students includes the following:

HLP4 Use multiple sources of information to develop a comprehensive understanding of a student's strengths and needs.

- Group and individual intelligence tests
- Achievement tests
- Proficiency or state tests
- Portfolios of student work
- Student performances or products
- Teacher nomination
- Parent, family, or caregiver nomination
- Self-nomination
- Peer nomination
- Extracurricular or leisure activities

Equity-minded professionals in gifted education recommend a comprehensive and proactive approach for identifying gifted students who require specialized services (e.g., Peters & Engerrand, 2016). Clark (2013) describes such an approach based on a model first developed by the California Association for Gifted Children. The "progressive filtering" approach refines a large pool of potentially gifted students down to a smaller, formally identified group. The time-consuming and thorough process entails developing a large pool of potentially gifted students (screening); testing, consulting, and analyzing data (development of profile and case study); making identification and placement decisions (committee meeting for consideration; placement in gifted program); and developing an appropriate educational program.

As part of a multidimensional assessment for creatively gifted students, Sternberg (2018) recommends educators include a way to measure student attitudes and how willing they are to defend their ideas in the face of criticism and keep their composure during these kinds of challenges. Sternberg (2017) also recommends using the ACCEL (Active Concerned Citizenship and Ethical Leadership) model to identify gifted students based on how they respond to questions about problems such as climate change, autocratic governments, and global pandemics.

Multidimensional screening involves collecting and examining teacher reports, student inventories, and work samples and perhaps the administration of group achievement or group or individual intelligence tests. Figure 13.3 shows questions a teacher might ask about a child's classroom behavior as part of the screening process. In many states, the coordinator of gifted services at the district or regional level determines whether the screening results indicate a potential for giftedness and justify further assessment. If so, the coordinator asks parents

FIGURE 13.3 Questions That Can Help Teachers Identify Students Who May Be Gifted and Talented

Does the child

- Ask a lot of questions?
- Show a lot of interest in progress?
- Have in-depth information on many things?
- Often want to know why, why not, or how something is so?
- Become unusually upset at injustices?
- Seem interested in and concerned about social or political problems?
- Often have a better reason for not doing what you want done than you have for asking her or him to do it?
- Refuse to drill on spelling, mathematics, facts, flash cards, or handwriting?
- Criticize others for dumb ideas?
- Become impatient if work is not "perfect"?
- Seem to be a loner?
- Seem bored and often have nothing to do?
- Complete only part of an assignment or project and then take off in a new direction?
- Stick to a subject long after the class has gone on to other things?
- Seem restless and leave his or her seat often?
- Daydream?
- Seem to understand easily?
- Like solving puzzles and problems?
- Have his or her own idea about how something should be done? And stay with it?
- Talk a lot?
- Love metaphors and abstract ideas?
- Love debating issues?

This child may be showing giftedness through cognitive ability.

Does the child

- Show unusual ability in some area—maybe reading or mathematics?
- Show fascination with one field of interest? And manage to include this interest in all discussion topics?
- Enjoy meeting or talking with experts in this field?
- Get answers correct but find it difficult to tell you how?
- Enjoy graphing everything? Seem obsessed with probabilities?
- Invent new obscure systems and codes?

This child may be showing giftedness through academic ability.

Does the child

- Try to do things in different, unusual, imaginative ways?
- Have a really zany or odd sense of humor?
- Enjoy new routines or spontaneous activities?
- Love variety and novelty?
- Create problems with no apparent solutions? And enjoy asking you to solve them?
- Love controversial and unusual questions?
- Have a vivid imagination?
- Seem never to proceed sequentially?

This child may be showing giftedness through creative ability.

Does the child

- Organize and lead group activities? Sometimes take over?
- Enjoy taking risks?
- Seem cocky, self-assured?
- Enjoy decision making? Stay with that decision?
- Synthesize ideas and information from a lot of different sources?

This child may be showing giftedness through leadership ability.

Does the child

- Seem to pick up skills in the arts—music, dance, drama, or painting, for example—without instruction?
- Invent new techniques? Experiment?
- See minute detail in products or performances?
- Have high sensory sensitivity?

This child may be showing giftedness through visual or performing arts ability.

Source: From Barbara Clark, *Growing Up Gifted*, 8th ed. (p. 185), © 2013. Reproduced by permission of Pearson Education, Inc., Upper Saddle River, NJ.

if they would like to refer their child for more extensive testing. The next step is developing an assessment portfolio that includes parent or caregiver interviews, an individual intelligence test, achievement tests in specific content areas, and creativity tests. The coordinator compiles, organizes, and presents these data to a placement committee for consideration. The committee determines if the student qualifies for or would benefit from gifted education services and what type of program would best suit the student's particular pattern of giftedness. The parents or caregivers are an integral part of this meeting and have to agree with the results and placement decisions the committee develops. If the student qualifies for placement in a gifted program, the gifted education teacher or person in charge of the program initiates the appropriate services.

Multicultural Assessment and Identification

The underrepresentation of African American, Hispanic/Latino, and Native American students in gifted education programs is a persistent and pervasive problem (Ford et al., 2016; Peters & Engerrand, 2016). For decades, reports and census studies have shown these three groups are consistently underrepresented in gifted education (e.g., Worrell et al., 2019). Low rates of referrals because of educators' low expectations and the use of culturally biased tests and instruments are primarily to blame (Castellano & Frazier, 2011; Rimm et al., 2018; Worrell et al., 2019).

Many youth from traditionally marginalized cultural and linguistic groups have not had the extensive opportunities to develop a broad pattern of gifts and talents, but they have often developed special abilities within a particular domain. Current best practices for identifying GT students from diverse racial and cultural groups involve a multifactored, or multidimensional and multimodal, assessment process that meets the following criteria (Castellano & Frazier, 2011; Clark, 2013; Ford et al., 2016):

- Identifies students with a goal of inclusion rather than exclusion
- Gathers data from multiple sources providing both objective and subjective information (e.g., parent interviews, individual intelligence testing, performance on group problem-solving tasks, motivational and behavioral factors, and individual conferences with candidates)
- Uses a combination of formal and informal testing techniques, including teacher input, family input, and the results of intelligence tests and achievement tests
- Begins identification procedures as early as possible
- Uses unconventional or nontraditional measures involving arts and aesthetic expression, such as dance, music, and creative writing, as well as nonverbal measures
- Uses information gathered during the screening and identification process to help determine the curriculum, programs, and services

Maker (1996, 2005) developed an assessment procedure to identify gifted children from different racial and cultural groups, called DISCOVER (Discovering Strengths and Capabilities while Observing Varied Ethnic Responses). DISCOVER presents a series of five progressively more complex problems that provide children various ways to demonstrate their problem-solving competence by interacting with the content and with one another. Maker (2005) states that assessment emphasizing problem solving instead of formal tests of acquired knowledge can "level the playing field" by enabling students who solve problems on a daily basis to demonstrate their abilities.

> "Little Claudia," a 5-year-old Mexican American girl, who was responsible for dressing her 2-year-old brother and making sure he was taken to daycare before she went to kindergarten class, had extensive practice in problem solving. However, she was not exposed to advanced knowledge through visits to museums or a home environment with many sources of information, nor was she given opportunities to produce sophisticated products through special courses, lessons, or other opportunities afforded to children from middle and upper socioeconomic status (SES) families. Many children from diverse economic, geographic, and cultural groups face challenges similar to Little Claudia's (p. 12).

Maker (2001, 2005) reports positive results from using the DISCOVER model to assess the problem-solving abilities of African American, Navajo, Tohono O'odham, and Mexican American students. The process (a) identifies children who closely represent the cultural characteristics of their communities; (b) identifies similar percentages of children from various ethnic, cultural, linguistic, and economic groups; (c) is equally effective for identifying boys and girls; and (d) enables identified students placed in enrichment programs to make gains equal to or greater than those of students identified by traditional standardized tests.

Some schools identify gifted learners with assessments that do not require the use of verbal symbol systems, such as The Raven's Standard Progressive Matrices Test (Raven et al., 1983) and the Naglieri Nonverbal Ability Test–2nd Edition (Naglieri, 2007). Naglieri and Ford (2005) assert that traditional intelligence and achievement tests penalize students from low-socioeconomic backgrounds and traditionally marginalized cultural groups who have not had the opportunity to learn the vocabulary required for success on such tests.

Identifying underrepresented GT children is just the beginning. In the absence of high-quality, culturally responsive instruction, culturally and racially diverse GT students may "distance" themselves from the gifted label and be hesitant to enter and unwilling to stay in a gifted education program (Ford, 2010; Henfield et al., 2008). To address this problem, educators need formal training in both gifted education and multicultural education.

Gifted and Talented Girls

Impediments to the identification and advancement of GT girls and women come in many forms, including cultural barriers; testing bias; gender-role stereotyping; and conflicts among career, marriage, friends, and family (Reis, 2013). Historically, gifted girls have been underrepresented in gifted programs and discouraged from pursuing interests and careers in science and math. Although equity for women continues to improve, progress has been slow due to pervasive and consistent bias in our culture. For example, "When raters evaluate college essays, job applications, grant applications, portfolios, or tenure reviews, identical materials receive higher ratings when a male name rather than a female name is attached to the materials" (Rimm et al., 2018, p. 292). Teachers in gifted education also demonstrate this bias. When presented with identical vignettes, teachers consistently rated those labeled as "male" higher than those labeled as "female" (Bianco et al., 2011). Additionally, teachers recommended 77% of the "male" vignettes to the gifted program compared to 54% of the "female" vignettes (Bianco et al., 2011). Even when gifted girls are identified and excel in school, their achievements often do not transfer to their careers in adulthood (Kerr et al., 2012). Conflicts about role definitions, self-concept, academic choices, and a lack of family and general community support for female achievements continue to be key concerns for GT girls (Clark, 2013; Reis, 2013).

Gifted and Talented Boys

Even though White boys have historically outscored girls on most achievement tests (Boothe, 2004), GT boys also experience many challenges in school. For example, nonathletic or sensitive boys may be teased or alienated by other children (Rimm et al., 2018). To fit in socially, GT boys may intentionally underachieve or behave in inappropriate ways to gain peer acceptance and avoid being ostracized or bullied (Kerr et al., 2012). Disapproval and negative stereotyping may discourage creatively talented boys from pursuing careers in the arts. To gain social approval, they may feign interest in traditionally masculine activities, such as sports, letting their artistic talents and desires go unfulfilled.

Gifted and Talented Students with Disabilities

It surprises many people to learn that students with disabilities can also be GT. Some disabilities, such as learning disabilities, may mask giftedness on test scores and in classroom academic performance; giftedness may also mask a disability (Baldwin et al., 2015). The combination of giftedness and disability presents a complicated set of behaviors and attitudes that confuse and challenge educators and parents (Reis et al., 2014). Students with dual exceptionalities whose giftedness goes unidentified are especially likely to underachieve or even drop out of school (Mayes & Moore, 2016).

Pearson eText
Video Example 13.3
Twice-exceptional students need special education for their disabilities and giftedness.

The number of students with disabilities who are also gifted is difficult to determine, but it is estimated that about 360,000 students in U.S. schools are twice exceptional (National Education Association, 2006). Factors impeding the identification of gifted students who have disabilities may include low self-esteem, lack of motivation, poor organization skills, disruptive behavior, and poor concentration skills (Kalbfleisch, 2013). Baldwin et al. (2015) recommend building on students' interests, implementing adaptations and accommodations that address the strengths and learning needs, and supporting students socially and emotionally.

King (2005) recommended that teachers support the social and emotional needs of twice-exceptional students by doing the following:

- Promote students' self-understanding and self-acceptance with objective information about their disabilities and their strengths.
- Encourage students to succeed and enlist support of parents and other teachers in this endeavor.
- Teach strategies for coping with frustration.
- Monitor the emotions that accompany students' frustrations and perceived failures and provide counseling if needed.
- Help students establish and maintain friendships.

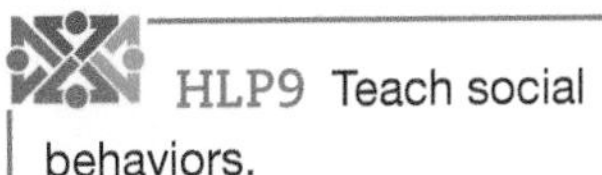

HLP9 Teach social behaviors.

Source: Scott Cunningham/Pearson Allyn and Bacon/Merrill Education

Gifted children with disabilities should have daily opportunities to develop their talents and enjoy the feelings of success.

- Help parents understand their child's giftedness and disability, emphasizing the child's potential.
- Make students aware of their potential and encourage them not to sell themselves short when setting future goals and career planning.
- Provide adult mentors who are also twice exceptional.

An appropriate education for gifted students with disabilities requires what Neu (2003) terms a *dually differentiated* curriculum that recognizes and "meets the needs of students who exhibit two contradictory sets of learning characteristics by creating a balance between nurturing the students' strengths and compensating for their learning deficits" (p. 158). The special education and related services implemented to meet the student's needs that result from the disability do not exceed the student's need to be challenged in the domain(s) of giftedness and talent.

Educational Approaches

Learning Outcome 13.4 Explain how teachers provide appropriate instruction for gifted and talented students.

The overall goal of educational programs for GT students should be the fullest possible development of each child's demonstrated and potential abilities. In addition to maximum academic achievement, exemplary programs help students develop feelings of self-worth, self-sufficiency, and pride in one's identity; civic responsibility; and vocational and avocational competence. In the broadest sense, then, the educational goals for gifted students do not differ from those for any child. Some additional specific educational outcomes, however, are especially important for GT students.

Gifted students need both content knowledge and the opportunity to develop and apply that knowledge effectively. They need curriculum content with relevance and depth and instruction at a pace sensitive to their background knowledge and how quickly they learn.

Experts agree all programs for gifted students should have the following characteristics (Piirto, 2007; Rimm et al., 2018; Tomlinson et al., 2009; Van Tassel-Baska, 2013):

- *Academically rigorous.* Gifted students need a relevant and academically rigorous curriculum, especially within the regular classroom, where most are educated.
- *Thematic and interdisciplinary.* GT students should be exposed to the structure, terminology, and methods of various disciplines. Gifted students thrive on big ideas and enjoy learning the connections among interdisciplinary concepts. Connecting the lesson or content, when applicable, to sociology, anthropology, medicine, science, language arts, history, the arts, music, and so on, helps gifted students to make connections in various subject areas and to appreciate the complexity of the topic they are studying.
- *Responsive to and respectful of gifted students' learning characteristics.* GT students are characterized by "their ability to learn at a faster rate; their ability to think abstractly about content that is challenging; their ability to think productively, critically, creatively, and analytically; and their ability to constantly and rapidly increase their store of knowledge, both knowledge of facts and knowledge of processes and procedures" (Piirto, 2007, p. 429).

When developing appropriate curriculum, the most important concern is to match students' specific abilities, potentials, and interests with a qualitatively different curriculum.

Curriculum Differentiation

Differentiation is a broad term referring to customizing teaching environments, curricula, and instructional practices to create appropriately different learning experiences for students with different needs, interests, readiness, and learning profiles (Kaplan, 2019). The reality that gifted learners differ in meaningful ways is the guiding premise of differentiation. The main objective is to engage learners in lessons appealing to differing interests, using varied rates of instruction, and providing varied degrees of complexity within and across a challenging and conceptually rich curriculum. Research shows that well-planned differentiated instruction produces higher achievement for all students (Tomlinson, 2017). Meaningful curriculum differentiation for GT students requires that educators recognize the individual strengths of these learners and acknowledge the inadequacy of the regular curriculum to meet those needs (Kaplan, 2019).

Acceleration and Enrichment

Effective teachers differentiate by adjusting the pace, breadth, and depth of curriculum in ways that respect and capitalize on gifted students' individual learning differences. **Acceleration** is the general term for a variety of methods for increasing the speed with which a student progresses through school. A form of acceleration called **curriculum compacting** involves compressing instructional content that students have already mastered so they have more time for enrichment. **Enrichment** enables students to probe or study specific subject matter, a topic of interest, or a discipline in greater detail and depth than would occur in the standard curriculum.

ACCELERATION Early admission (to kindergarten, middle school, high school, or college), grade skipping, self-paced instruction, curriculum compacting, telescoping curriculum (i.e., completing a course within a short time period, resulting in grade advancement), concurrent or dual enrollment in high school and college, advanced placement (AP), and credit by examination are some of the most commonly used *grade acceleration* practices (Rimm et al., 2018). A fourth grader taking a ninth-grade math class would be an example of *subject acceleration*. A variety of acceleration options should be available at each stage of a student's development, from early entrance to kindergarten through early college enrollment (Lupkowski-Shoplik et al., 2018).

One common concern is that early admission and grade skipping will lead to social or emotional problems because the child will be in a classroom with older students who are more advanced physically and emotionally. Some educators and parents are also concerned that GT students will suffer from the pressure to achieve at higher levels and will burn out or lose their excitement for learning. Although these concerns are understandable, when acceleration is done properly, few, if any, socioemotional or achievement problems result (Assouline et al., 2014; Rimm et al., 2018). In 2004, the Templeton Foundation published a major report on acceleration with the somewhat hyperbolic title *A Nation Deceived* (Colangelo et al., 2004). It detailed cases in which acceleration solved the curriculum problems of bright children, showing that many educators' concerns about acceleration may be unfounded. As a result of this report, which was featured on the front page of many newspapers across the country, many states and school districts have formulated acceleration policies that allow students to receive an education at their intellectual and academic levels rather than age level.

CURRICULUM COMPACTING Many GT students have already mastered much of the content of the general education curriculum when the school year begins. Compacting instructional content and materials gives academically able students more time to work on appropriately challenging tasks. Curriculum compacting includes assessing students' knowledge and skills to determine which content is removed from their curriculum and replaced with more advanced or in-depth content (Reis et al., 2016). When pretesting academically talented students, teachers should present the most difficult problems or content first. Students who can solve the most difficult problems do not need to waste their time solving the easier ones.

For curriculum compacting to be effective, teachers must have an extensive understanding of the curricular content and not only condense the material but also modify its presentation, create more meaningful instruction, and evaluate that instruction for individual students. For example, Juan's teacher, Mr. Dominguez, suspects that Juan has already mastered most of the fourth-grade mathematics curriculum, and some fifth- and sixth-grade level math concepts as well. To discover if Juan is a good candidate for curriculum compacting, Mr. Dominguez first determines the scope and sequence of the mathematics problems that Juan should be able to do in the fifth and sixth grades. Then he constructs an evaluation process that will accurately determine at what level Juan can perform the mathematics problems. If Juan has mastered the content and strategies of the higher-level math, then Mr. Dominguez must design and provide replacement activities that are a more challenging and productive use of Juan's time. Featured Teacher Jennifer Sheffield underscores this important point: "Gifted students repeatedly doing work they already know how to do is NOT practice makes perfect; it's running in place academically."

ENRICHMENT Students engage in enrichment when they probe or study specific subject matter, a topic of interest, or a discipline in greater detail and depth than would occur in the standard curriculum. Independent study, mentorships, and shadowing are widely used methods for enrichment. Enrichment may be the most commonly applied strategy general education teachers use to differentiate curriculum for GT students.

The most successful enrichment activities accomplish both process- and content-related goals (Rimm et al., 2018). *Process goals* entail the development of skills such as creative thinking and problem solving; *content goals* entail the additional enhanced and nuanced knowledge about the topic of interest.

Teachers can present topics of investigation from the ongoing classroom activities or from beyond the limits of the day-to-day instructional offerings. Allowing GT students to help define the area of interest and independently access a variety of information and materials facilitates the development of competencies and skills. Enrichment is not "do your own thing" without structure or guidance; students should not be turned loose on a random, haphazard project. Rather, projects should have a basic framework that defines the purpose, direction, and outcomes. Teachers must provide guidance when necessary to keep students working efficiently.

The Schoolwide Enrichment Model (SEM) attempts to meet the needs of GT students in general education classrooms (Renzulli & Reis, 2013). The first step of SEM is identifying a talent pool of high-ability students (usually 10% to 15% of the school's enrollment) by using a multifactored assessment approach that includes achievement tests, teacher and peer nominations, and creativity assessments. After they are identified, students can take part in specialized services, many of which are also available and appropriate for other learners in the same classroom. Renzulli and Reis (2013) described some of the relevant features of SEM:

- Teachers assess talent pool students to identify individual interests and to encourage further development and exploration of their interests in various ways.
- Teachers offer curriculum compacting to all eligible students. Redundant or repetitious information and materials are eliminated from the general education curriculum.
- Teachers offer three types of enrichment activities to students: Type I, general exploratory experiences; Type II, purposefully designed instructional methods and materials; and Type III, advanced-level studies with greater depth and complexity.

All children in the talent pool participate in Type I and Type II enrichment activities. Only students who show serious interest in a specific topic advance into Type III investigators. Students are never compelled to begin Type III projects; the level remains an open option for them. SEM also includes a Total Talent Portfolio, a collection of student work focusing on strengths, used to make instructional decisions (Renzulli & Reis, 2013).

ACCELERATE OR ENRICH? Whether acceleration or enrichment is the most appropriate strategy for differentiation depends on the subject matter and the student. Some curriculum material, such as reading or social studies, readily lends itself to enrichment. By the time a GT student is in the fourth grade, she probably will have mastered the skills of reading; enrichment with more complex reading material is a way to differentiate. In contrast, subjects such as mathematics and world languages are ideally suited to acceleration because of their sequential nature. In mathematics, the subject matter proceeds from arithmetic to algebra to calculus and so on. A child must learn to add before subtracting and must learn to multiply before dividing. A first grader who is fluent with the basic arithmetic operations will benefit little from several more years of adding, subtracting, multiplying, and dividing.

Although acceleration and enrichment are often viewed as separate options for talented students, the two strategies are intertwined. Enrichment broadens the curriculum and includes material that is not in the general education course of study. However, acceleration often involves advanced material also not contained in the general education course of study. Any curriculum differentiation technique that involves advanced placement or potential course credit (e.g., in an AP course) is acceleration; any strategy that supplements or goes beyond the standard grade-level curriculum that does not entail advanced placement or potential credit is enrichment.

Differentiating Instruction in the Classroom

Reis and Renzulli (2015) suggest five dimensions of differentiation teachers should consider when individualizing instruction for GT students: content, instructional strategies, the classroom, products, and the teacher.

HLP13 Adapt curriculum tasks and materials for specific learning goals.

- *Content.* Provide students with appropriately challenging content that is aligned with their specific interests.
- *Instructional Strategies.* Identify student preferences for instructional delivery such as working in groups, working alone, learning through discussion, or learning through different types of projects.
- *Classroom.* Create and manage a learning environment that appeals to GT students such as introducing guest speakers, using various types of technology, arranging field trips, and implementing variations of flexible grouping.
- *Products.* Allow students to create products that demonstrate their learning in their preferred style of expression such as through writing, demonstrations, and group or individual presentations.
- *Teacher.* Decide how to differentiate by considering interests, abilities, and preferred modes of expression, and "accept the freedom, flexibility, and creativity to implement this process in the classroom" (Reis & Renzulli, 2015, p. 3).

Methods for differentiation within the regular classroom can include using Bloom's taxonomy and tiered lessons as frameworks for modifying questions and creating instructional activities. Inquiry-based learning, problem-based learning, project-based learning, and leadership training are additional ways to differentiate instruction.

USING BLOOM'S TAXONOMY FOR QUESTIONS AND ASSIGNMENTS Bloom and his colleagues (Bloom et al., 1956; Krathwohl, 2002) formulated a taxonomy of educational objectives that has been very useful for differentiating curriculum. The original **Bloom's taxonomy** contains six levels or types of cognitive understanding: knowledge, comprehension, application, analysis, synthesis, and evaluation. In a revised version of the taxonomy, active verbs replaced nouns. Specifically, knowledge is now *remember,* comprehension is *understand,* application is *apply,* analysis is *analyze,* synthesis is *create,* and evaluation is *evaluate* (Anderson et al., 2001).

Teachers most often ask knowledge (remember, recall) and comprehension (understand) questions. Figure 13.4 illustrates how Bloom's taxonomy could guide the types of questions asked and possible student products in a unit based on the Cinderella story. Although both average and high-ability students should have learning opportunities at all levels of Bloom's taxonomy, opportunities and expectations to work at the advanced levels of the taxonomy are especially important for academically gifted students. It is a mistake, however, to think that GT learners do not need instructional activities at the lower levels of the taxonomy (Clark, 2013; Ford, 2011). To analyze, evaluate, and create meaningful concepts and relationships, students must first remember and understand basic information about the topic.

TIERED LESSONS A **tiered lesson** provides different extensions of the same basic lesson for groups of students of differing abilities. For example, after the teacher presents a basic

FIGURE 13.4 Using Bloom's Taxonomy as a Guide for Differentiating Instruction Based on the Cinderella Story

Level	Common Verbs to Use to Phrase Questions	Example from the Cinderella Story	Possible Student Products
Remember	know, collect, cite, repeat, recall, define, enumerate, list, name, label, tell, recount, relate, specify, memorize, identify	1. How many stepsisters did Cinderella have? 2. Do you recall what the slipper was made of?	Test, list, definition, fact, reproduction
Understand	restate, recognize, locate, summarize, explain, report, convert, discuss, express, retell, describe, identify, translate, estimate	1. Discuss the events on the night of the ball 2. Describe what happened to the pumpkin	Same as for knowing level
Apply	exhibit, apply, dramatize, solve, employ, practice, compute	1. Make an exhibit of the ball gowns Cinderella's two sisters and stepmother wore 2. Dramatize what happened when the Prince came to Cinderella's house with the glass slipper	Illustration, diagram, map, diary, model, collection, diorama, puzzle
Analyze	interpret, categorize, dissect, analyze, classify, diagram, outline, compare, group, arrange, contrast, examine, inventory, subdivide	1. Compare and contrast Cinderella's treatment by her stepmother and by the Prince 2. Examine why the stepmother was so cruel to Cinderella	Questionnaire, survey, report, graph, chart, outline
Evaluate	judge, criticize, prove, decide, assess, revise, appraise, estimate, rate, evaluate, determine, conclude	1. Prove that Cinderella deserves to go to the ball 2. Determine what would have happened if Cinderella had run away but had not lost her slipper	Panel discussion, evaluation scale, report, survey, editorial, verdict, recommendation
Create	compose, propose, produce, invent, imagine, formulate, create, design, predict, construct, improve, develop, rearrange	1. Compose a song that Cinderella would sing while she did her work in the cinders 2. Design Cinderella's ball gown; chariot; slippers	Formula, invention, film, new game, story, poem, art product, machine, advertisement

Source: Jane Piirto, © 2007. Used with permission.

lesson to the whole class, three groups of students might work on follow-up activities or assignments at basic, middle, and high difficulty levels. Figure 13.5 shows an example of a tiered lesson using riddles to promote thinking and problem-solving skills.

Content Extension 13.2

"A Sticky Situation"

Mr. Ba[illegible] Mrs. Sheffield are trying to decide which type of glue to purchase for GEMS Academy. One commercial claims that Gooey Glue is the strongest, but another insists that Sticky Goo is the best. Gooey Glue is a liquid glue and Sticky Goo is a gel. Your task is to design an experiment to test both glues and decide which one really is the strongest.

So far you have been given the following materials:

Bottle of Gooey Glue
Bottle of Sticky Goo
Popsicle sticks
Toothpicks
Gram Weights

You *do not* have to use all materials listed. Also, think carefully about what *other* tools or materials you may need to effectively conduct your experiment.

Create an experimental design plan to test both glues.

Inquiry-based learning lab sheets created by Featured Teacher Jennifer Sheffield.

INQUIRY-BASED LEARNING **Inquiry-based learning** is an evidence-based practice for teaching science that engages students in asking research questions, planning investigations, collecting and analyzing data, deriving explanations, and communicating their findings (Adams & Pierce, 2014; Furtak et al., 2012). Herron (1971) developed a model of inquiry that requires students to work more independently at each of four progressive levels.

At Level 1, Confirmation/Verification, the teacher provides the research question, the procedure, and the solution. Featured Teacher Jennifer Sheffield refers to Level 1 as "Science Recipes" because "if you follow the directions for the experiment, you should get the predicted result. You can learn new things doing this, but it isn't really an experiment—you're just following a science recipe to get the desired, pre-determined outcome." At Level 2, Structured Inquiry, the teacher provides the research question and the procedure, and students generate the results. During Guided Inquiry (Level 3), the students generate the procedures and solution. The most independent level is Open Inquiry (Level 4), during which students generate the question, the procedure, and the results. Jennifer Sheffield's students

FIGURE 13.5 A Tiered Lesson Using Riddles

Author: Ms. Erin Morris Miller (National Research Center/Gifted and Talented)	**Author's e-mail:** HOTLINX@virginia.edu
Curriculum area(s): math, science, social studies	Grade Level: 3
Time required: 30 minutes	Instructional gr ouping: heterogeneous

Overview
This is a thinking skills lesson to help students practice thinking openly and flexibly. Use this lesson as a mental warm-up session before beginning a challenging lesson that requires the students to think flexibly or counterintuitively. Use this lesson to prepare the students for times when making assumptions would be bad. Examples: solving word problems in math, finding patterns in math, drawing conclusions from reading selections, and making decisions during a unit on economy. (Idea inspired by a high school advanced placement calculus teacher, Fred Pence, who began class with a puzzle to get students in the mood to problem solve. The concept was adapted for younger students.) In this lesson, students first solve a riddle as a whole class and then divide into small groups to solve additional riddles. Groups are formed according to the students' readiness to read and understand difficult vocabulary. Each group works independently as the teacher moves from group to group, facilitating discussions.

Standards
This lesson helps students develop the skills necessary to achieve any standard that involves problem solving. Examples include math and science problems as well as dilemmas in social studies and analysis of literature.

Materials
There are three levels of riddles. Level 1 consists of three simple riddles, level 2 consists of one medium-hard riddle, and level 3 consists of one difficult riddle.

As a result of this lesson, students should
know . . .
Riddles are written puzzles.
understand . . .
Riddles require people to think creatively.
Riddles require people to not make assumptions.
be able to do . . .
Solve riddles.

Preassessment
One main difference between the riddles is the difference in the vocabulary involved. Groups should be formed based on the students' verbal proficiency.

Basic riddles
What can go up a chimney down but can't go down a chimney up? (an umbrella)

If a rooster laid a brown egg and a white egg, what kind of chicks would hatch? (None. Roosters don't lay eggs!)

What needs an answer but doesn't ask a question? (the phone)

Medium-hard riddle
I can sizzle like bacon,
I am made with an egg,
I have plenty of backbone but lack a good leg,
I peel layers like onions but still remain whole,
I can be long like a flagpole yet fit in a hole.
What am I?
(a snake)

Challenging riddle
This thing devours all,
Birds, beasts, trees, flowers,
Gnaws iron, bites steel,
Grinds hard stones to meal,
Slays kings, ruins towns,
And beats high mountains down.
(time) (by J. R. R. Tolkien)

start at the Structured Inquiry level and then quickly transition to the Guided and Open Inquiry levels as they design and carry out their own experiments.

PROBLEM-BASED LEARNING In **problem-based learning** students work together in small groups to seek solutions to real world problems. The problems engage students' curiosity and initiate learning of subject matter. The Integrated Curriculum Model developed at The Center for Gifted Education at William & Mary features problem-based lessons in language arts, mathematics, science, and social studies.

Source: Jennifer Sheffield

Letting students choose the problems they wish to study and how they will go about their investigations is one method for differentiating curriculum for students with outstanding academic abilities.

A real world problem serves as the basis for each of the science units, and understanding and applying the concept of systems compose the overarching theme. These units give students experience in collecting, organizing, analyzing, and evaluating data and communicating their findings and ideas to others. The problem-based language arts units feature change as the overarching theme; the social studies units focus on the concept of interdependence. Problem-based units are used by teachers in almost 20 countries and have been adopted by the American Embassy Schools and the Department of Defense Schools. Although the problem-based units were developed for GT students, they can be used with students at all ability levels by modifying the activities to match students' skills and interests.

Letting students choose the problems they wish to study and how they will go about their investigations constitute one method for differentiating curriculum for students with outstanding academic abilities.

PROJECT-BASED LEARNING In **project-based learning**, students work together for an extended period of time to investigate an authentic question and produce a product or presentation designed to answer that question (Buck Institute, 2020). Project-based learning is a recursive process that provides students valuable opportunities to think critically, create, and communicate as they explore open-ended questions like the following: "How can we solve the problem of homelessness?" "How can communities restructure policing to ensure social justice and safety for all?" "How can we motivate people to follow public health guidelines such as mask wearing and social distancing?" Small groups of students collaboratively plan and create a project while the teacher facilitates engagement, monitors progress, and provides ongoing feedback. After students present their projects, they receive teacher and peer feedback and engage in self-evaluation. Researchers report positive effects on comprehension, retention of content, problem-solving skills, and critical thinking skills for students who engage in project-based learning (Finkelstein et al., 2010; Holm, 2011). See *Teaching & Learning,* "The Two PBLs: Problem-Based Learning and Project-Based Learning."

TEACHING LEADERSHIP SKILLS Many definitions of giftedness include the ability to lead effectively. Leadership skills include inspiring others, directing activities, proposing agreeable compromises, and keeping a group organized (Bean, 2010). Bisland (2004) recommends teaching younger children leadership skills by reading and discussing biographies of inspiring leaders, examining traits of leaders in children's literature, and creating individual reference books of leaders. Rimm et al. (2018) recommend teaching students about the traits of effective leaders, providing opportunities for students to engage in leadership roles, and teaching component leadership skills. Gifted students can benefit from leadership activities such as coordinating schoolwide and community projects, organizing extracurricular activities, and mentoring peers in their schools. Cross-age mentoring opportunities can help gifted students develop lasting leadership skills and the disposition to guide, support, and inspire others (Besnoy & McDaniel, 2016).

Differentiation Outside the Classroom

For some students with outstanding talent, activities outside the classroom are the most significant and rewarding components of their education.

INTERNSHIP AND MENTOR PROGRAMS The role of mentorship in developing talent and creativity has been recognized since the Middle Ages. The importance of mentors cannot be overestimated in certain artistic and scientific fields, where the development of both conceptual and performance skills is critical to success. Mentors are also critically important for low-income and culturally different students (Olszewski-Kubilius & Clarenbach, 2014). Internship and mentor programs expose gifted students to a powerful combination of proven educational strategies—modeling, guided practice, feedback, and reinforcement of important behaviors—in real world settings (Callahan & Dickson, 2014). See *Transition: Next Year Is Now,* "Mentors for Gifted Students," for suggestions about how to establish mentoring relationships.

SPECIALIZED COURSES Specialized courses and workshops are offered in many communities through arts and cultural venues, museums, and recreation centers. These courses, which may or may not award high school or college education credits, provide a rich variety of opportunities for students to encounter mentors, make new friends, and explore concepts that may not be available in the confines of the school curriculum.

JUNIOR GREAT BOOKS This is a highly structured educational program in which students read selections from several areas, including classics, philosophy, fiction, and poetry, and then discuss their meaning with teachers. Teachers must undergo special training and use specific questioning techniques designed to evoke high-quality responses from the students.

TEACHING & LEARNING

The Two PBLs: Problem-Based Learning and Project-Based Learning

Featured Teacher Jennifer Sheffield uses both *problem-based* and *project-based learning*. Each approach focuses on real problems and authentic goals, with problem-based learning emphasizing the problem-solving process and project-based learning emphasizing the product.

How Do You Teach Problem-Based Learning? Jennifer presents "an ill-defined and compelling problem to which there is no simple solution (e.g., How can we sustainably feed 9 billion humans? Should we give up electricity to save our planet?). Students then explore multiple sources of information supporting the different viewpoints of various stakeholders as they try to determine the best course of action. Students explore controversial issues for which there are no easy or right answers, which often leads to fantastic class discussions and deep insights."

How Do You Teach Project-Based Learning? "When planning project-based learning activities, I ask myself: What content do I want the students to learn? Do I have the same content goals for all students? What products will the students be able to create? What processes will students use? Will students work individually, with partners, or in small groups? How much flexibility is allowed?

"Project-based learning is used for many of our special interest labs (SILS). Students complete a survey to indicate which lab they would like to join. For example, the Machine Dissection lab requires student partners to dissect a piece of technology, such as a laptop computer or printer. Partners document their process, identify the machine's key parts and their functions, research the history and development of the machine, and explain its significance to society. The partners then create a presentation to share what they have discovered."

The following are examples of SILS that require students to create a product.

- Roller Coaster Physics groups build scale models of functional roller coasters and compete in a contest measuring speed and "thrill factor."
- Three-dimensional (3D) printing or computer-aided design groups create computer models to scale and print plastic 3D models.
- iMovie groups script, direct, and produce movies.

Feedback and Revision. "After receiving peer feedback on the content and aesthetics of their presentations, students have the option of refining and resubmitting their products. Critically reviewing their classmates' presentations often gives students ideas for improving their own work."

Self-Reflection. "Following the presentations, I encourage my students to reflect on what they learned, what they would seek to improve next time, what lingering questions they have, and what they learned about themselves."

Content Extension 13.3

Featured Teacher Jennifer Sheffield's PBL activity on sustainable food production.

Transition: Next Year Is Now

Mentors for Gifted Students

Why Do Gifted Students Need Mentors?

Many gifted students show wide-ranging talents, interests, and ambitions in several different academic and creative domains. Having wide-ranging interests, although generally beneficial, can present challenges when preparing gifted students for transition beyond high school. Mentors can help gifted students make informed career decisions by providing them with authentic in-depth opportunities to learn about a profession. In fact, students who reported having high-quality mentoring experiences were more like to report career certainty (Lunsford, 2011).

What Makes a Mentoring Program Effective?

Effective mentoring programs match students and mentors based on mutual interests. Together the mentor and student may establish goals for a project, identify specific experiences to pursue, set a timeline for a project, engage in regular meetings over a period of months, and evaluate progress. Upon completion of a mentor-guided project, the gifted student can present (or co-present) the findings to peers in school or even at professional conferences. For example, if a gifted student is matched with a university professor, the student could attend the professor's research team or lab meetings with college students, develop research projects under the direction of the professor, and disseminate the findings in the form of conference presentations or publications.

Matching Students to Mentors

Setting up a mentoring relationship involves identifying student interests, preparing students to be mentored, locating a good match, and evaluating the mentorship.

Identify Student Interests

Teachers can identify student interests by having the student complete an interest questionnaire and/or interviewing the student. Questions may include some of the following:

- What topic is especially interesting to you?
- Why are you interested in this topic?
- What experiences have you had related to your topic of interest?
- What are your goals for a mentoring experience?
- How might a mentor help you reach your goals?

Prepare Students for Mentoring

Social skills go a long way to making the mentoring relationship successful. Teachers can model appropriate interactions and role-play discussions in which the gifted student proposes ideas and practices being receptive to feedback. Additionally, teachers can prepare students by helping them begin to identify possible projects (e.g., research or community action projects), and then project goals, objectives, and timelines.

Locate Mentors

Some schools may already have mentoring networks in place. In this case, use the school district's procedures for assigning mentors. For schools that do not have a mentoring network in place, teachers can start a mentoring program, which requires administrative support, community outreach, and mentor training. See Ball (2018) for recommendations for developing a mentoring program within a school district.

If a mentoring network is not available through the school district, teachers can also provide parents with information that will help them identify appropriate mentors. Options may include contacting faculty at a local university, contacting professionals at local industries, or contacting a mentoring organization for gifted students. Online mentoring is a viable option for students in rural areas or locations where human resources related to their interests may not be readily available. Technology options for distance mentoring, such as video conferencing, emailing, file-sharing arrangements (e.g., Google docs), and instant messaging, can provide a bridge of communication for mentors and mentees who live in different geographical locations. The following websites match gifted students with mentors.

National Mentoring Partnership	http://www.mentoring.org/
iMentor	https://imentor.org/
UConn Mentor Connection	https://mentor.education.uconn.edu/
National Mentoring Resource Center	https://nationalmentoringresourcecenter.org/
U.S. Department of Education Mentoring Resource Center	https://www.edmentoring.org/index.html
Mentored Pathways	https://www.mentoredpathways.org/
Institute for Educational Advancement	https://educationaladvancement.org/programs/iea-explore/explore-mentors/
Million Women Mentors	https://www.millionwomenmentors.com/about

Students from underrepresented groups might benefit from being matched with mentors who are from the same cultural or socioeconomic background or the same gender. For example, female students might benefit from the guidance of female mentors who can help them understand and deal with the challenges presented as a minority in a particular career field.

Have Students Evaluate Mentors

Throughout the mentoring process, students should keep a journal of their experiences and reflect on what they are learning. At the end of the mentoring experience, students can also evaluate the projects (e.g., Did I meet my objectives? To what extent is this project a contribution? What would I change if I did this project again? Is this the right career direction for me?). In addition, students can participate in exit interviews and opinion surveys to provide the mentors with feedback for improving future mentoring relationships.

SUMMER PROGRAMS Summer programs offer short-term, intensive learning experiences in specific intellectual or artistic domains such as environmental studies, space and aeronautical studies, and music. Many colleges and universities offer summer programs aimed at GT students from underrepresented groups.

INTERNATIONAL EXPERIENCES New Zealanders have a cultural rite of passage wherein they pack a bag and travel in modest fashion to the far reaches of the planet. The "trek" gives people from a remote Pacific island nation an exceptional opportunity to see and touch the world in intimate fashion. An international curricular experience can merge the excitement of exploration with the demands of a structured learning experience. Programs such as the International Baccalaureate Program offer academic credit for studies at participating educational agencies around the world.

Placement Options

Learning Outcome 13.5 Identify and describe placement options for gifted and talented students.

Educators have grouped students based on their abilities since the earliest days of schooling. These groups were often informal, consisting of two or more students who could keep pace with each other during subject matter instruction.

Ability grouping, teaching GT students in homogeneous groups with their intellectual and academic peers or in heterogeneous groups of students encompassing a wide range of abilities, has generated considerable debate and strong opinions over the years. Social injustices and upheavals have resulted in increased calls for equity—and hence, heterogeneous grouping—in many of society's institutions. But virtually all leaders in the field of gifted education believe that *flexible* grouping that does not result in tracking helps students reach their full potential.

The NAGC (2009) states that "[g]rouping gifted children is one of the foundations of exemplary gifted education practice" (p. 1) and contends that the many myths surrounding ability grouping for gifted students—that it damages the self-esteem of struggling students, creates an elitist group who think too highly of themselves, and is undemocratic and even racist at times—have no research support. The NAGC believes grouping is usually necessary to achieve the "least restrictive

Source: Jennifer Sheffield

In cluster ability grouping, students within a heterogeneous class are grouped for instruction in each subject area according to their achievement.

environment" for gifted students to learn, and it affords schools the most effective and efficient means to provide the differentiated curriculum and instruction the students need. Gifted programs use a variety of grouping practices for both full- and part-time gifted education programming.

Full-Time Grouping Options

SPECIAL SCHOOLS Special high schools for gifted students began in the early 20th century with the establishment of Stuyvesant High School in New York City. The establishment of the Hunter College High School for Gifted Girls came even earlier. The Hunter College Elementary School for gifted students opened in 1941. Children are selected for admission to these schools on the basis of competitive examinations and scores on individual IQ tests. Special schools—public, private, and charter—for students identified as gifted continue to exist in communities across the United States.

Many large urban school systems operate magnet schools with curricula emphasizing various themes. For example, many districts have language immersion schools, schools that focus on visual and performing arts, and special schools for mathematics and science. Although not all these schools are designed specifically for students identified as gifted, students who have a special talent or interest may find these options appealing.

SPECIAL CLASSROOMS The primary advantage of the self-contained classroom is that all curriculum and instruction can be focused on the needs of GT students. Other advantages of self-contained classrooms are that students are more likely to work at a pace commensurate with their abilities, and membership in a class of intellectual equals may challenge some gifted students to excel even further. The self-contained classroom model may also be more efficient because gifted education teachers do not have to move from classroom to classroom or school to school to serve students.

In addition to sharing many of the disadvantages of self-contained classrooms for students with disabilities (e.g., limited opportunity to interact with peers in general education), self-contained classroom programs for GT students must often deal with the stigma of being viewed as elitist. Some districts may be too small to support the self-contained classroom option, even multi-age or across-grade-level classes.

HLP17 Use flexible grouping.

CLUSTER ABILITY GROUPING In **cluster ability grouping**, the five to eight highest performing students at a given grade level learn together as a group in a regular classroom of mixed-ability students. A teacher with training in gifted education provides specialized instruction to that cluster group. Cluster grouping enables gifted students to receive intensive differentiated curriculum within an inclusive environment.

Research shows that gifted students educated with full-time ability grouping options gain from 1.3 to 2 years' academic growth per year and show small but positive gains in social maturity, self-efficiency, self-esteem, and motivation (Rogers, 2006). Gifted elementary students who participate in cluster grouping achieve better in reading and math than non–cluster-grouped gifted students (Gentry, 2014). Additionally, cluster grouping has resulted in teachers identifying more high-achieving students from culturally diverse backgrounds (Brulles et al., 2012).

Part-Time Grouping Options

RESOURCE ROOM OR PULL-OUT PROGRAM Some educators believe that the resource room, or pull-out model, is the best option for serving GT students. Pull-out programs offer many of the advantages of self-contained classrooms but also pose several challenges. Administrators and teachers in schools with resource room or pull-out services for GT students should recognize that these children do not stop being gifted when they leave the resource room. Although the learning opportunities provided in the resource room may be of the highest quality, the need to differentiate curriculum for gifted students in the regular classroom during the rest of the school day remains.

TEACHING & LEARNING

High-Ability Cooperative Learning Groups

Many gifted students enjoy working in cooperative learning groups where they can challenge each other intellectually and develop social interaction and leadership skills (Diezman & Watters, 2001; Huss, 2006).

What Are Cooperative Learning Groups? Cooperative learning groups are small teams of students collaboratively completing academic tasks, solving problems, and achieving common goals. Well-designed cooperative learning groups promote development of academic and social skills.

How Do You Teach Cooperative Learning Group Lessons? Jennifer Sheffield recommends the following guidelines.

Step 1. Present a hook. Begin with a hook to get students excited about what they're going to do: a brainstorming activity, an analysis of an image, a riddle, a goofy skit, a video short—anything fun and intriguing! To introduce a flight and rocketry lesson, I use a ping pong ball "launcher" made from a bendy straw and a funnel. I ask a couple of students to blow into the straw to see how far they can launch the ping pong ball. The ball doesn't budge because of Bernoulli's principle, but the kids don't know that. Then everyone makes a launcher and we start exploring the science behind it.

Source: Jennifer Sheffield

Step 2. Give directions. Provide directions for the assignment and answer students' questions. Teach students to acknowledge and encourage participation and input from each member of the group. Welcome suggestions from groups for process or products that may vary from the original assignment. Letting groups pursue their own twist if it's reasonable is a good way to promote student ownership of their learning.

Step 3. Have students self-select their groups. Give students 2 or 3 minutes to decide with whom they want to work. Each group should contain members with complementary skills: creative students with organized students, analytical students with intuitive students, good writers with good talkers, and so on. When the groups are set, don't assign individual roles (e.g., leader, spokesperson, recorder); let the students make those decisions.

Step 4. Provide time limits. Provide a time frame for the activity but be flexible. I tell my students it's OK if they don't always finish on time; they can share their ideas with the class and explain that they are still working on another facet of their presentation. Early finishers can observe other groups and return to their projects if they get some new ideas. When projects require multiple class sessions, students can request conferences with me to ask questions and get feedback.

Step 5. Monitor progress. Circulate about the room and listen to groups' discussions, encourage students to elaborate on their ideas, answer questions, and provide feedback as needed. When a group struggles with leadership or organization, I'll ask questions like, "What do you think might help your group get finished?" or "Do you have ideas for integrating all of your group members' contributions?" If necessary,

Pearson eText
Video Example 13.4
Featured Teacher Jennifer Sheffield uses cooperative learning groups to teach students about environmental sustainability.

I'll mention strategies other groups have used, such as everyone working independently for 10 minutes and then bringing their ideas back for a group discussion.

Step 6. Provide sharing time. Sharing allows students to learn from each other and take pride in their contributions. My students use Google Docs, Edmodo, Spiderscribe, Prezi, Glogster, iMovie, and podcasts to present what they learned, created, and discovered. During sharing time, students give each other constructive feedback on their presentations and revise their work if necessary.

Step 7. Encourage reflection. After sharing their work with the class, I ask students to discuss the experience with each other (in pairs or small groups) and characterize their contributions as positive, negative, or neutral and explain their reasoning. Students should discuss their reflections with each other with minimal direction from me.

CLUSTER PERFORMANCE GROUPING In *cluster performance grouping*, the teacher groups students within the same heterogeneous class for instruction in each subject area according to their achievement. The most common form of within-class grouping is regrouping by subject; students are generally grouped into three or more levels, with increasingly advanced study material provided at each level.

LIKE-ABILITY COOPERATIVE LEARNING GROUPS When the teacher uses cooperative learning activities, the three to four highest ability students are grouped together and assigned a differentiated learning task with differentiated expected outcomes and assessment criteria. See *Teaching & Learning*, "High-Ability Cooperative Learning Groups."

Research shows small, positive gains in academic, social, and self-esteem measures for gifted students in part-time ability grouping options. Students can achieve more than a year's academic growth when the learning activities in these options focus on extensions of the general curriculum or on critical thinking or creative production (Rogers, 2006).

Although ability grouping options can facilitate the provision of differentiated curriculum and instruction for GT learners, educators must realize that just putting students into like-ability or performance groups is insufficient. What matters most is what happens in the groups rather than grouping itself. Challenging curriculum, well-designed lessons, effective instructional practices, and a respectful learning environment are needed to get the most out of any grouping arrangement.

Consulting Teacher Model

HLP1 Collaborate with professionals to increase student success.

Most GT students are served in regular classrooms. If the school district has a program for GT students, a teacher with special training in gifted education provides direct and indirect support for the general education teacher. Working in consultation with the general education teacher, this special educator—sometimes called a *facilitator*, a *consulting teacher*, or an *intervention specialist for the gifted*—might provide specialized instruction in science, math, the humanities, or other subjects to flexibly grouped students. This educator may work with a high-ability reading or math group while the rest of the class works in these domains. The educator may mentor independent projects, design special learning centers, plan special field trips, and help students prepare for academic competitions.

An advantage of the consultant teacher model is that the gifted education teacher is no longer isolated and alone, working in the resource room or pull-out classroom without knowledge of what the students are doing in their home classrooms. Instead, the consultant teacher is in partnership with general education teachers, collaborating on curriculum planning teams as they plan multilevel lessons.

Another important advantage of this model is that students of all ability levels in the regular classroom can benefit from smaller student–teacher ratios; multitiered lessons; and learning activities on creativity, critical thinking, or study strategies that the gifted specialist teaches to the whole class.

Many schools, however, do not have a gifted education specialist, and general education teachers are responsible for differentiating curriculum for students with advanced educational needs. We cannot stress this enough: To most effectively understand, teach, and challenge GT students, teachers, counselors, and other educators must be formally trained. Unfortunately, most colleges and universities do not offer course work or degrees in gifted education.

Gifted and talented students from all walks of life need an appropriate education; they need differentiated curriculum, instructional strategies, materials, and experiences that will enable them to realize their potential. There are new approaches and perspectives concerning the manner in which these students are identified and how services are delivered that reflect insights into the way humans develop, learn, and create. These innovations promise a brighter future for students with gifts and talents—a future that will benefit the world in which they live.

ADVICE FROM THE FEATURED TEACHER by Jennifer Sheffield

Be Flexible

Source: Allison Grace Thompson

To be an excellent GT educator, you need to be flexible, open minded, nonjudgmental, creative, and willing to try things that will stretch your comfort level.

- ***Give lots of choices.*** Differentiate content, process, and product. This doesn't have to be complicated. For example, a student doing a compare and contrast activity could complete a Venn diagram comparing/contrasting three subjects instead of just two, to add complexity. Give students choices for ways to demonstrate what they know—videos, podcasts, presentations, models, skits, diagrams and charts, poems, etc.
- ***Be open to suggestions.*** Whatever's in your lesson plan, GT students will think of about 15 ideas of how to do it another way. Don't be married to your written plans; if a better suggestion comes along, don't be afraid to try it! Empower students to create their own optimum learning experiences.
- ***Avoid arbitrary time constraints.*** Let the students' engagement in the lesson guide your flow, especially if it's a lesson you've never taught before—how could you know how long a good discussion on the topic might take? GT kids *hate* having to quit working on an engaging task or end a discussion right in the thick of things. Trust your ability as a facilitator to gauge when it's time to move on the next stage of your lesson. If high-quality learning is going on, let it happen.

Create a Safe Environment for Risk Taking

Encourage students to take academic risks. Share stories of great scientific discoveries that have resulted from accidents, mistakes, and misconceptions. Help students understand that every failure is an opportunity to learn and try again. If you never fail, you're not taking any risks; and if you're not taking risks, you're just coasting along and not pushing yourself enough to make any real growth.

- ***Model and foster a growth mindset.*** It's OK for kids to get frustrated while working on a difficult task. Communicate that challenging projects can be frustrating because they take a great deal of time, energy, and focus. Let kids know that conquering a tough task will make them feel awesome and provide a sense of true achievement; self-confidence is built from accomplishing things that take effort versus things that are easy.

- ***Celebrate spectacular failures.*** A student's model rocket catches fire, a small group's lab experiment goes wrong, the lesson you spent so much time preparing implodes—everyone should be able to laugh at and learn from their mistakes. Smile and comment about what a great bad idea that was! It's good for students to see their teacher recover from failures with good humor and reflect upon what to try next time.
- ***Provide clear rules for discussions.*** GT kids are often very passionate about their ideas and can be emotionally sensitive. Make your classroom a safe place to have deep and meaningful discussions without angry accusations, hurt feelings, and tears. Communicate clear rules for what is acceptable (and what isn't) for class discussions, including nonverbal behaviors like eye rolling.

Be Supportive

Being a GT student can be an isolating experience. GT students can benefit a great deal from showing them that you care and are advocating for them.

- ***Show students you care.*** Attend your students' extracurricular events whenever you can. I have 160 students, and there is no way I could make every soccer game, swim meet, play performance, etc. However, I do make a special effort to show up at an extracurricular activity of any student with whom I've had difficulty building a positive relationship. It sends the message to the student and parents that you care about the child as a person, not just his or her performance in the classroom as a student.
- ***Advocate for gifted and talented students.*** Be an active voice for GT students in your school. Make sure your students' accomplishments are highlighted on district or school websites and make contacts within your local media outlets (newspaper, television stations, etc.) and invite them to your classroom whenever you're doing something especially interesting. Create good PR—you never know where your strongest supporters in the community may come from.

Explore Online Resources

There is a wealth of high-quality, no-cost educational resources available online related to the social, emotional, and academic needs of gifted students. Take advantage of these resources!

- ***Stay current.*** Follow gifted education organizations, researchers, and educators you respect on Twitter as a quick way to stay current on curriculum ideas, online resources and apps, educational research, and other available resources related to supporting and educating gifted students.
- ***Take advantage of available listservs in your state for gifted educators.*** These are often hosted by state universities. It's a great way to make sure you don't miss out on local and regional opportunities for professional development and competitions or events for students that may be of interest. You will also build a readily accessible network of teachers and GT Coordinators with whom to ask questions and share resources.

Key Terms and Concepts

ability grouping
acceleration
asynchrony
Bloom's taxonomy
cluster ability grouping
curriculum compacting
differentiation
enrichment
inquiry-learning
problem-based learning
project-based learning
tiered lesson

Summary

Definitions

- The federal government defines gifted and talented (GT) children as those who demonstrate evidence of high-achievement capability in areas such as intellectual, creative, artistic, or leadership capacity or in specific academic fields and who need services and activities not ordinarily provided by the school to fully develop these capabilities.
- The National Association for Gifted Children (NAGC) defines gifted individuals as those who demonstrate outstanding levels of aptitude (exceptional ability to reason and learn) or competence (documented performance or achievement in the top 10% or rarer) in one or more domains.
- Renzulli's definition of giftedness is based on the traits of above-average general abilities, high-level task commitment, and creativity.
- Piirto defines gifted individuals as having superior memory, observational powers, curiosity, creativity, and ability to learn.
- Maker defines the GT student as a problem solver who can create a new or clearer definition of an existing problem, devise new and more efficient or effective methods, and reach solutions that may differ from the usual.

Characteristics

- Learning and intellectual characteristics of GT students include the ability to
  - Rapidly acquire, retain, and use large amounts of information.
  - Relate one idea to another.
  - Make sound judgments.
  - Appreciate multiple and opposing points of view.
  - Perceive the operation of large systems of knowledge.
  - Acquire and manipulate abstract symbol systems.
  - Solve problems by reframing the question and creating novel solutions.
- Characteristics of highly gifted students with IQs of 145 and above include
  - Intense intellectual curiosity
  - Fascination with basic words and simple ideas
  - Perfectionism and need for precision
  - Learning with great intuitive leaps
  - Intense need for mental stimulation and challenge
  - Difficulty conforming to the thinking of others
  - Early moral and existential concerns
  - Tendency toward introversion
- Many gifted children are highly creative. Although there is no standard definition of creativity, most researchers and educators agree that fluency, flexibility, originality, and elaboration are important dimensions.
- Gifted students display both inter- and intraindividual differences. *Asynchrony* is a term used to describe disparate rates of intellectual, emotional, social, and physical growth or development displayed by some gifted children.

Prevalence

- There are about 3.2 million school-age gifted students in the United States.
- Some prevalence estimates of giftedness range as high as 10% to 15% of the school-age population.

Identification and Assessment

- Comprehensive and equitable identification of GT students includes a combination of intelligence tests; achievement measures; checklists; teacher, parent, community, and peer nominations; self-nomination; and leisure interests.
- Some states or school districts use a progressive filtering process to identify students for gifted education services that refines a large pool of potentially gifted students down to a smaller, formally identified group.
- African American, Hispanic American, and Native American students are underrepresented in gifted education programs and advanced placement classes.
- Identification instruments, policies, and procedures must not be discriminatory or biased; they must be valid and reliable for all groups and take into account cultural, linguistic, and economic differences.
- Maker's DISCOVER procedure can be used to equitably identify GT students from different cultural groups and low-socioeconomic-status backgrounds.
- It is estimated there are 360,000 "twice exceptional" (i.e., gifted with a disability) students in U.S. schools.
- Teachers of gifted students with disabilities must strive for a balance between nurturing the students' strengths and teaching and providing accommodations and supports to meet the needs resulting from their disabilities.

Educational Approaches

- Curricula for GT students should be academically rigorous, thematic and interdisciplinary, and responsive to the learning characteristics of gifted students.
- *Differentiation* refers to a variety of strategies for providing curricula and instructional practices appropriate to the different needs, interests, readiness, and learning profiles of students.
- *Acceleration* is the general term for a variety of methods for increasing the speed with which a student progresses through the curriculum or school.

- *Curriculum compacting* involves compressing instructional content so students have time to work on more challenging materials.
- *Enrichment* means probing or studying a subject in greater depth than would occur in the general education curriculum.
- The Schoolwide Enrichment Model is a plan for whole-school improvement that not only attempts to meet the needs of GT students within the regular classroom but also is meant to be used with other students in the class.
- Bloom's taxonomy of educational objectives provides a framework for differentiating curriculum by asking questions and assigning activities that require students to demonstrate different types of knowledge.
- Tiered lessons provide extensions of the same basic lesson for groups of students of differing abilities.
- Inquiry-based learning is an evidence-based practice for teaching science that engages students in asking research questions, planning investigations, collecting and analyzing data, deriving explanations, and communicating their findings.
- Problem-based learning is a collaborative problem-solving activity that challenges students to seek solutions to real world problems.
- Project-based learning is an instructional activity in which students work together for an extended period of time to investigate an authentic question and produce a project (e.g., a product or presentation) that answers the question.
- Gifted educators recommend a wide range of leadership activities that include learning about leadership in the classroom, interacting with leaders, and engaging in opportunities to be a leader.
- Options for learning outside school include internships and mentorships, special courses and workshops in the community, Junior Great Books, summer programs, competitions and fairs, and international experiences.

Educational Placement Alternatives and Ability Grouping

- Grouping gifted students is usually the "least restrictive environment" for their learning and affords schools an effective and efficient means to provide differentiated curriculum and instruction.
- Full-time options for ability grouping—teaching GT students in homogeneous groups composed of their intellectual and academic peers—include special schools, special classrooms, and cluster ability groups within regular classrooms.
- Part-time options for ability grouping include resource rooms or pull-out programs, cluster performance grouping, and like-ability cooperative learning groups.
- Most GT students are served in regular classrooms. A consultant teacher trained in gifted education often helps the general education classroom teacher plan and deliver specialized instruction.

Chapter 14

Early Childhood Special Education

Source: Susan Chiang/Getty Images

Learning Outcomes

After reading this chapter and completing the embedded activities, you should be able to

14.1 Explain why early intervention is critical for young children with disabilities.

14.2 Identify the key elements of individualized family service plans (IFSPs) and explain how they differ from individualized education programs (IEPs).

14.3 List and describe the purposes and types of assessment used in early childhood special education.

14.4 Describe how a play activity or an everyday routine can become a specially designed learning opportunity for a preschooler with disabilities.

14.5 List and briefly describe service delivery options for young children and identify advantages and disadvantages of each type.

Education, Teaching Credentials, and Experience

- *B.S., physical education, MidAmerica Nazarene University, 1999*
- *M.Ed., early childhood special education, University of Kansas, 2003*
- *Idaho State, professional teaching certificate, special education, pre K–3*
- *16 years as an early childhood special education teacher and 2 years of paraprofessional work in a self-contained special education preschool classroom*

Featured Teacher

Mark Fraley

Source: Breanne Fraley

Skyway Elementary School

Vallivue School District • Caldwell, ID

I teach 22 preschoolers who have been found eligible to receive special education services following a process that involves a child find screening, a consent to assess, an evaluation report, and eligibility determination. Each of my students falls into one of the disability categories, most often developmental delay or language impairment. I do have students who are on the autism spectrum and several who have multiple disabilities. I work alongside a terrific team composed of two educational assistants, a speech-language therapist, a school psychologist, an occupational therapist, a physical therapist, and supportive administrators. The way we work together as a team helps us keep student needs always at the forefront.

On a typical school day, we start off with reviewing our daily routine so students are aware of the activities and how the day will proceed. Having a structured routine is very beneficial for young children; predictability limits anxiety and brings a level of reassurance that helps them thrive in the classroom. For students who are on the autism spectrum, we provide a visual schedule that enables them to make successful transitions. In planning the day, I consider striking a balance between teacher-led and child-led activities, high energy versus quiet listening, and highly motivating work versus a less preferred type of work. I look for my students to participate fully and implement accommodations as needed.

Collaborating with families is critical for student success. I make my classroom a welcoming place from day one by inviting the families to participate in volunteer opportunities and visits. Upon arrival at school, we talk with families and see how their children's day has started. Did they sleep well? Did they eat a good breakfast? Are they in a good mood? Significant communication delays prevent many of my students from providing a satisfactory answer when their parents ask, "What did you do in school today?" To help with that, I create take-home sheets by importing the day's photos from my digital camera to my classroom computer, pasting a few of the most telling shots on a PowerPoint, and making copies on a printer in the school work office.

I take countless pictures during the school year. These photos are a powerful, effective form of communication that lets parents and families see what their children do in school. I get so excited when seeing families celebrate their children's progress, when they begin seeing new possibilities that were originally crushed with a diagnosis or a traumatic event.

Content Extension 14.1

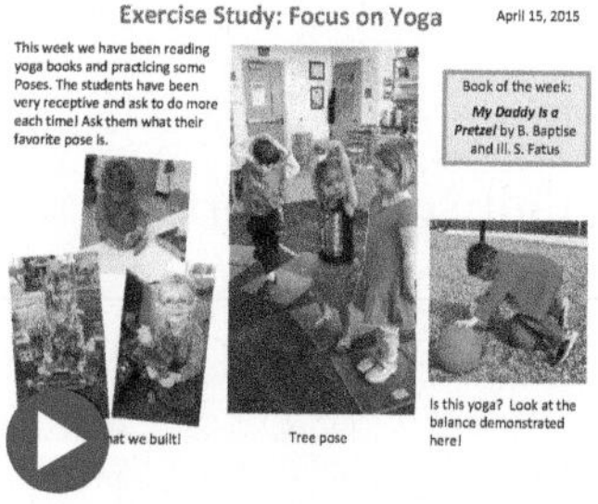
Exercise Study: Focus on Yoga April 15, 2015

This week we have been reading yoga books and practicing some Poses. The students have been very receptive and ask to do more each time! Ask them what their favorite pose is.

Book of the week: *My Daddy Is a Pretzel* by B. Baptise and ill. S. Fatus

Tree pose

Is this yoga? Look at the balance demonstrated here!

Example of Featured Teacher Mark's take-home sheets.

FROM THE MOMENT THEY ARE BORN TO THE DAY THEY ENTER SCHOOL, children learn a phenomenal amount. Most children grow and develop in relatively predictable ways, learning to move about their world, communicate, and play. Typical rates and patterns of child development, however, contrast sharply with the progress of many young children with disabilities. For young children with disabilities to master many skills that most children acquire naturally, they need carefully planned and implemented early childhood special education services.

The Importance of Early Intervention

Learning Outcome 14.1 Explain why early intervention is critical for young children with disabilities.

The earlier intervention begins, the better. The human brain develops most rapidly and dynamically during the first few years of life (Hodal, 2018). In fact, 80% of brain development occurs by age 2, after which the brain continues to reorganize, fine-tune, and remodel the major circuits and networks already in place (Gilmore et al., 2018). The growing body of neuroimaging research demonstrates how pivotal early learning environments are for long-lasting cognitive and social development (Follari, 2019; Levitt & Eagleson, 2018). Early positive experiences build the foundation for a lifetime of learning, whereas early negative experiences have the opposite effect (Bredecamp, 2020; Follari, 2019). The first years of life are even more critical for children with disabilities, who, with each passing month, risk falling even further behind their typically developing age mates. Early and intensive intervention can greatly ameliorate the many challenges of disabilities.

What Is Early Intervention?

In the early childhood and special education literature, the term *early intervention* often refers only to services provided to infants and toddlers from birth through age 2 years. *Early childhood special education* refers to special education and related services provided to preschoolers age 3 to 5 years. Early intervention consists of a comprehensive system of therapies, educational, nutritional, child care, and family supports, all designed to reduce the effects of disabilities or prevent the occurrence of learning and developmental problems later in life for children presumed to be at risk for such problems.

Does Early Intervention Work?

Hundreds of studies have been conducted to determine how well early intervention works. We'll look at a few of those studies here. First, we'll consider two of the earliest examples of what Guralnick (1997) calls first-generation research—studies that sought to answer the question: "Does early intervention make a difference for children and their families?" Then we'll look at two examples of second-generation research studies designed to discover what factors make early intervention more or less effective for particular groups of children.

SKEELS AND DYE The earliest and one of the most dramatic demonstrations of the potential impact of early intervention was conducted by Skeels and Dye (1939). They found that one-to-one attention and intensive stimulation with 1- to 2-year-old children with intellectual disabilities resulted in IQ gains and eventual independence and success as adults compared to similar children who received adequate medical and health services but no individual attention. Although the Skeels and Dye study can be justly criticized for its lack of tight experimental methodology, it challenged the widespread belief at the time that intelligence was fixed and that little could be expected from intervention efforts. This study served as the catalyst for many subsequent investigations into the effects of early intervention.

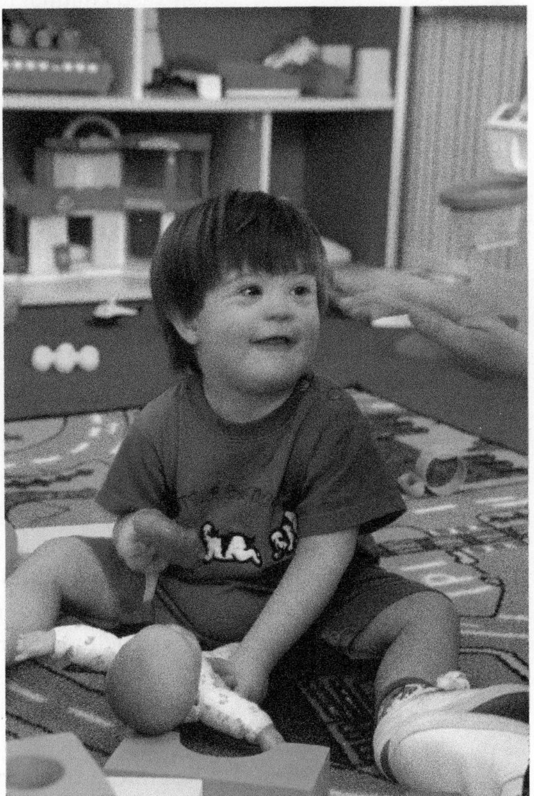

Source: Bill Aron/PhotoEdit

The first years of life are critical for all children and especially so for children with disabilities.

THE MILWAUKEE PROJECT The goal of the Milwaukee Project was to reduce the incidence of intellectual disabilities through a program of parent education and infant stimulation for children considered at risk for developmental delay because of their mothers' levels of intelligence (IQs below 70) and conditions of poverty (Garber & Heber, 1973). The mothers received child care training and learned how to interact with and stimulate their children through play. Beginning before the age of 6 months, the children also participated in an infant stimulation program conducted by trained teachers. By the age of 3½ years, the experimental children tested an average of 33 IQ points higher than did a control group of children who did not participate in the program.

Although the Milwaukee Project was criticized for its research methods (e.g., Page, 1972), it did offer some evidence that a program of maternal education and early infant stimulation can reduce the incidence of intellectual disabilities caused by psychosocial disadvantage. Psychosocial disadvantage, a combination of social and environmental deprivation early in a child's life, is believed to be a major cause of mild intellectual disabilities (see Chapter 4).

Pearson eText
Video Example 14.1
The Abecedarian study showed the powerful and lasting effects of early education.
http://www.youtube.com/watch?v=8YyZ8FkFsK4

THE ABECEDARIAN PROJECT The Abecedarian Project is one of the longest running and most carefully controlled and respected studies on early intervention ever conducted in the United States. It was an experiment to test whether intellectual disabilities caused by psychosocial disadvantage could be prevented by intensive, early education preschool programs (in conjunction with medical and nutritional supports) beginning shortly after birth and continuing until children enter kindergarten (Campbell & Ramey, 1994). The 57 children randomly assigned to the experimental group received intensive and prolonged early intervention: 5 days per week of full-day preschool for 50 weeks per year. The 54 children in the control group received supplemental medical, nutritional, and social services, and some attended a child care center, but they received no daily early educational intervention. Outcome measures were assessed for both groups at multiple points in time. By age 3 years, children in the early intervention group scored higher on IQ tests than did the children in the control group; at age 12 years, in addition to higher IQ scores, the early intervention participants had achieved better reading and mathematics scores and were 50% less likely to have failed a grade. They also had better outcomes as adults in cognitive functioning, academic skills, educational attainment, employment, parenthood, and social adjustment. In a recent review of results from three randomized control trials based on the Abecedarian Approach, Ramey (2018) affirmed that cognitive disabilities can be prevented with high-quality early intervention. Additionally, the most disadvantaged children received the greatest benefits from early intervention (Ramey, 2018).

THE INFANT HEALTH AND DEVELOPMENT PROGRAM The Infant and Health Development Program (IHDP) provided early intervention services to infants who were born prematurely and at low birth weight (less than 2500 g, or about 5½ lb), two conditions that place children at risk for developmental delays (Ramey et al., 1992). This large-scale study involved nearly 1000 children and their families in eight locations throughout the United States. Early intervention specialists conducted home visits for newborns through age 3 years. Because of health problems associated with prematurity and low birth weight, the children did not begin attending the center-based early education program until 12 months of age and continued until age 3 years. Improvements in intellectual functioning were noted, with babies of comparatively higher birth weight showing increases similar in magnitude to those found in the Abecedarian Project.

The IHDP study found a positive correlation between how much children and their families participated in early intervention and the intellectual development of the children. At age 3 years, the percentages of children with IQ scores in the intellectual disabilities range were 17% for the control group, 13% for those with low participation, 4% for medium participation, and less than 2% for high participation. Children in the high participation group had an almost ninefold reduction in the incidence of intellectual disabilities compared with control group children and a sixfold reduction compared with children in the low-participation group.

Studies such as the Abecedarian Project and IHDP provide strong evidence that children at risk for developmental delays and poor school outcomes respond favorably to systematic early intervention. Factors highly related to outcome effectiveness of these programs include intensity of the intervention and level of participation by the children and their families. Not surprisingly, young children with developmental disabilities receiving higher dosages of early intervention services showed more growth in communication, socialization, and daily living skills than peers receiving less intensive intervention (Woodman et al., 2018).

SUMMARIZING THE RESEARCH BASE Decades of empirical research have established early intervention systems that substantially benefit children and families (Guralnick, 2019). Numerous methodological problems make it difficult to conduct early intervention research in a scientifically sound manner. Among the problems are the wide disparities among children in the developmental effects of their disabilities; the tremendous variation across early intervention programs in curriculum focus, teaching strategies, duration, and intensity of services; and the ethical concerns of withholding intervention from some children to obtain a control group for comparison purposes (Fargus-Malet et al., 2010; Guralnick, 2005).

Despite these problems, most educators agree with Guralnick's (2005) conclusion that on balance, the research evidence shows comprehensive, experientially based early intervention enhances the development of young children who already exhibit delays and helps children who are at risk for developmental delays by preventing these delays entirely or by minimizing their magnitude.

Our national policymakers also believe that early intervention produces positive results for young children with disabilities, those who are at risk for developmental delays, and their families. Citing research and testimony from families, Congress identified the following outcomes for early intervention in the Individuals with Disabilities Education Improvement Act of 2004:

Pearson eText
Video Example 14.2
Changing the first 5 years of a child's life changes everything.
https://www.youtube.com/watch?v=GbSp88PBe9E

1. to enhance the development of infants and toddlers with disabilities, to minimize their potential for developmental delay, and to recognize the significant brain development that occurs during a child's first 3 years of life;
2. to reduce the educational costs to our society, including our Nation's schools, by minimizing the need for special education and related services after infants and toddlers with disabilities reach school age;
3. to maximize the potential for individuals with disabilities to live independently in society;
4. to enhance the capacity of families to meet the special needs of their infants and toddlers with disabilities; and
5. to enhance the capacity of State and local agencies and service providers to identify, evaluate, and meet the needs of all children, particularly minority, low-income, inner city, and rural children, and infants and toddlers in foster care (PL 108-446, USC 1431, Sec. 631[a]).

The Individuals with Disabilities Education Act, Early Intervention, and Early Childhood Special Education

Learning Outcome 14.2 Identify the key elements of individualized family service plans (IFSPs) and explain how they differ from individualized education programs (IEPs).

Since 1975, Congress has enacted five bills reauthorizing and amending the original Individuals with Disabilities Education Act (IDEA). The second of those bills, PL 99-457, has been called the most important legislation ever enacted for young children with developmental delays (Shonkoff & Meisels, 2000). Before passage of this law, Congress estimated that states served at most about 70% of preschool children with disabilities, and systematic early intervention services for infants and toddlers with disabilities from birth through age 2 years were scarce or nonexistent in many states. PL 99-457 mandated preschool services for children with disabilities age 3 to 5 years and included a voluntary incentive grant program for early intervention services to infants and toddlers and their families.

Early Intervention for Infants and Toddlers

If a state chooses to provide comprehensive early intervention services to infants and toddlers and their families—all 50 states do—it can receive federal funds under IDEA's early intervention provisions. Each state receives federal funds under this program based on the number of children from birth through age 2 years in the state's general population. In 2017, approximately 3.1% of the population of infants and toddlers, about 388,694, were served nationally (U.S. Department of Education, 2018). IDEA mandates early intervention services for any child younger than 3 years of age who

- **i.** needs early intervention services because of developmental delays, as measured by appropriate diagnostic instruments or procedures, in 1 or more of the areas of cognitive development, physical development, communication development, social or emotional development, or adaptive development; or
- **ii.** has a diagnosed physical or medical condition that has a high probability of resulting in developmental delay (PL 108-446, 20 USC 1432, Sec. 632[5]).

Thus, states receiving IDEA funds for early intervention services must serve all infants and toddlers with developmental delays or established risk conditions. Each state may also, at its discretion, serve at-risk infants and toddlers "who would be at risk of experiencing a substantial developmental delay if early intervention services were not provided" (PL 108-446, 20 USC 1432, Sec. 632[1]). Although not required to do so, states may also use IDEA funds to provide early intervention services to infants and toddlers who fall under two types of *documented risk*, biological and environmental. States may provide early intervention services for young children experiencing any of the following:

- *Developmental delays* are significant delays or atypical patterns of development. Each state's definition of developmental delay must be broad enough to include all disability categories covered by IDEA, but children do not need to be classified or labeled according to those categories to receive early intervention services.
- *Established risk conditions* include diagnosed physical or medical conditions that almost always result in developmental delay or disability. Examples are Down syndrome, fragile X syndrome, fetal alcohol spectrum disorder, brain or spinal cord damage, sensory impairments, and maternally transmitted acquired immune deficiency syndrome (AIDS).
- *Biological risk conditions* include pediatric histories or current biological conditions (e.g., significantly premature birth, low birth weight) that result in a greater than usual probability of developmental delay or disability.
- *Environmental risk conditions* include factors such as extreme poverty, parental substance abuse, homelessness, abuse or neglect, and parental intellectual impairment, which are associated with a higher than normal probability of developmental delay.

> HLP3 Collaborate with families to support student learning and secure needed services.

INDIVIDUALIZED FAMILY SERVICE PLAN IDEA requires that early intervention service for infants and toddlers be delivered according to an **individualized family service plan (IFSP)** developed by a multidisciplinary team that includes the child's family. An IFSP must include the following eight elements:

1. a statement of the infant's or toddler's present levels of physical development, cognitive development, communication development, social or emotional development, and adaptive development, based on objective criteria;
2. a statement of the family's resources, priorities, and concerns relating to enhancing the development of the family's infant or toddler with a disability;
3. a statement of the measurable results or outcomes expected to be achieved for the infant or toddler and the family, including preliteracy and language skills, as developmentally appropriate for the child, and the criteria, procedures, and timelines used to determine the degree to which progress toward achieving the results or outcomes is being made and whether modifications or revisions of the outcomes or services are necessary;

4. a statement of the specific early intervention services based on peer-reviewed research, to the extent practicable, necessary to meet the unique needs of the infant or toddler and the family, including the frequency, intensity, and method of delivering services;
5. a statement of the natural environments in which early intervention services will appropriately be provided, including a justification of the extent, if any, to which the services will not be provided in a natural environment;
6. the projected dates for initiation of services and the anticipated length, duration, and frequency of services;
7. the identification of the service coordinator from the profession most immediately relevant to the infant's or toddler's or family's needs (or who is otherwise qualified to carry out all applicable responsibilities under this part) who will be responsible for the implementation of the plan and coordination with other agencies and persons, including services; and
8. the steps to be taken to support the transition of the toddler with a disability to preschool or other appropriate services (PL 108-446, 20 USC 1436, Sec. 636[d]).

Because IFSPs are developed to support infants and toddlers, they differ from IEPs in several important ways:

- Center on the family as the constant and most important factor in the child's life.
- Define the family as the recipient of early intervention services rather than the child alone.
- Focus on the natural environments where the child and family live, extending services beyond formal settings such as preschools to everyday routines in the home and community.
- Include interventions and services provided by a variety of health and human service agencies in addition to education.

The IFSP must be evaluated once a year and reviewed with the family at 6-month intervals, or sooner if requested by the family. Recognizing the critical importance of time for infants with disabilities, IDEA allows early intervention services to begin before the IFSP is completed if the parents give their consent. Figure 14.1 shows portions of an IFSP developed with and for the family of a 26-month-old child with disabilities.

Special Education for Preschoolers

IDEA requires states to provide special education services to all children with disabilities age 3 to 5 years. The regulations governing these programs are similar to those for school-age children, with the following exceptions:

- Preschoolers do not have to be diagnosed with a disability (e.g., intellectual disability orthopedic impairment) to receive services. They may instead receive services under the eligibility category developmental delay.
- IEPs for preschoolers must include a section with suggestions and information for parents.
- Local education agencies may elect to use a variety of service delivery options (home-based, center-based, or combination programs), and the length of the school day and year may vary.
- The state education agency must administer preschool special education programs, but it may contract services from other agencies to meet the requirement of a full range of services. For example, many preschoolers with disabilities are served in community-based Head Start programs.

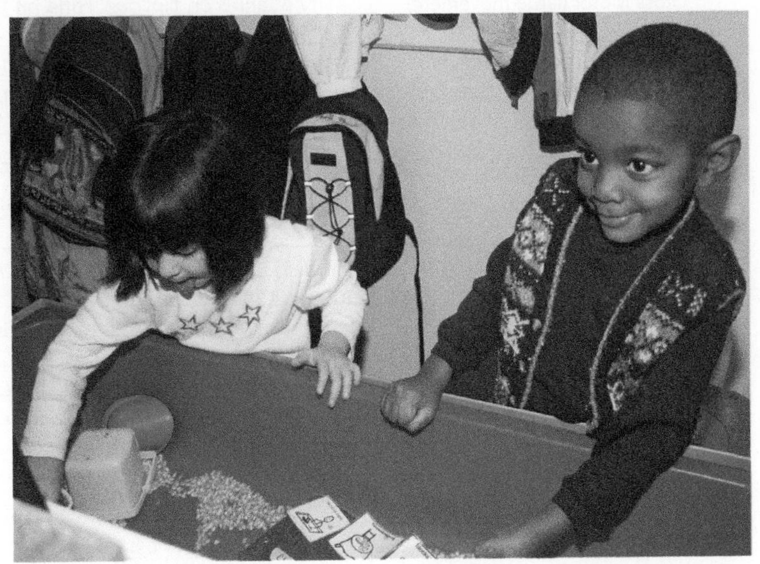

Source: Laura Bolesta/Merrill Education

IDEA requires states to provide special education to all children with disabilities ages 3 to 5 years.

FIGURE 14.1 Portion of an Individualized Family Service Plan Written with the Family of a 26-Month-Old Child with Disabilities

INDIVIDUALIZED FAMILY SERVICE PLAN (IFSP) for Children Birth to Three Years SANTA CLARA COUNTY

Child's name: Cathy Rae Wright Birth Date: 11-15-09 Age: 26 months Sex: F

Parent(s)/Guardian(s): Martha and Gary Wright Address: 1414 Coolidge Drive Cupertino Zip: 95014

Home phone: 398-2461 **Work phone:** 554-2490 **Primary language of the home:** English **Other languages** ______

Date of this IFSP 1/15/12 **Projected periodic review** 7/15/12 (at 6 months or before) **Projected annual review** 1/15/13 **Tentative IFSP exit** 11/15/12

Service Coordinator Name	Agency	Phone	Date Appointed	Date Ended
Sandy Drohman	Regional Center	408-461-2192	12/10/08	/ /

Family's strengths and preferred resources (With the family, identify the family strengths and the resources they might find helpful in addressing family concerns and priorities.) Mr. and Mrs. Wright are well-educated and constantly seek additional information about Cathy's condition. They are anxious to help Cathy in any way possible. Mrs. Wright's family is very supportive. They provide child care for Cathy's older brother.

Because of Cathy's tendency to be medically fragile, Mr. and Mrs. Wright prefer a home-based early intervention program. They appreciate receiving written materials to help them understand how to work with Cathy. Mrs. Wright wants to be home when the home visitor comes so she can learn from her.

Family's concerns and priorities (With the family, identify major areas of concerns for the child with special needs and the family as a whole.) Mr. and Mrs. Wright are very concerned about Cathy's delays in walking, using her fingers to pick up things, and in talking with other children. They also worry about her small size. Cathy is their second child and was born at 24 weeks gestation. Mr. and Mrs. Wright would like to have more information on the issues of prematurity and they would like to find an appropriate support group for themselves.

CHILD'S STRENGTHS AND PRESENT LEVELS OF DEVELOPMENT

With the family, identify what the child can do and what the child is learning to do. Include family and professional observations in each of the following areas:

PHYSICAL *Based on parent report and HELP Strands

Health Cathy is said by her parents to be healthy but is very petite. Her parents are working with a nutritionist to help Cathy gain weight.

Vision Cathy has had corrective surgery for strabismus.

Hearing She has had numerous ear infections and currently has tubes in her ears.

Gross Motor (large movement) Cathy stands on tiptoes, runs on toes, makes sharp turns around corners when running, walks upstairs with one hand held.

Fine Motor (small movement) Cathy grasps crayon adaptively and points with index finger; imitates horizontal strokes, builds 6 block tower, turns pages one at a time; has trouble picking up small objects.

COGNITIVE (responsiveness to environments, problem-solving) Cathy finds hidden object; attempts and succeeds in activating mechanical toy; demonstrates use of objects appropriate for age.

COMMUNICATION (language and speech)

RECEPTIVE (understanding) Cathy points to body parts when asked; obeys two-part commands.

EXPRESSIVE (making sounds, talking) Cathy names 8 pictures, interacts with peers using only gestures; attempts to sing songs with words.

SOCIAL/EMOTIONAL (how relates to others) Cathy expresses affection, is beginning to obey and respect simple rules, tends to be physically aggressive.

ADAPTIVE/SELF-HELP (sleeping, eating, dressing, toileting, etc.) Cathy can put on socks and shoes, verbalizes need to use the toilet, but is not potty trained, feeds self.

DIAGNOSIS (if known) ______

(Continued)

FIGURE 14.1 (Continued)

INDIVIDUALIZED FAMILY SERVICE PLAN (IFSP) for Children Birth to Three Years SANTA CLARA COUNTY

Child's name: Cathy Rae Wright

IFSP OUTCOMES

With the family, identify the goals they would like to work on in the next six months. These should be directly related to the family's priorities and concerns as stated on page one.

OUTCOME: Cathy will increase her attempts to vocally communicate in order to make her needs known and to positively interact with others.

	Service Type (Individual = I Group = G) Location	Frequency of sessions Length of each session	Start Date	End Date (anticipated)	Responsible Agency/ Group Including payment arrangements (if any)
Strategy or activity to achieve the outcome (Who will do what and when will they do it?) AIM Infant Educator will model for Mr. and Mrs. Wright techniques to solicit Cathy's vocalization efforts. ***Criteria*** (How will we know if we are making progress?) Increased vocalization will be observed by parents and infant educator.	I — Home-based infant program	1 hour each week	1-23-12	11-10-12	AIM (funded by SARC) Family
Strategy or activity to achieve the outcome (Who will do what and when will they do it?) Mrs. Wright will take Cathy to play with neighborhood children and will invite children to her home. She will encourage play and vocalization. ***Criteria*** (How will we know if we are making progress?) Mrs. Wright will observe and note extent of interaction.	G — Home and in the neighborhood	once each week for at least 30 minutes	2-1-12	ongoing	Mrs. Wright
Strategy or activity to achieve the outcome (Who will do what and when will they do it?) Cathy will be assessed by a speech pathologist by 2-15-12 and followed on an as needed basis. ***Criteria*** (How will we know if we are making progress?) A follow-up report will be submitted.	I — Regional Center Speech and Language Clinic	1 hour play-based assessment	2-15-12	as needed	Sandy Drohman will make arrangements (funded by SARC)

OUTCOME: Mr. and Mrs. Wright will join Parents Helping Parents in order to receive peer parent support and learn more about Cathy's condition.

	Service Type	Frequency / Length	Start Date	End Date	Responsible Agency/Group
Strategy or activity to achieve the outcome (Who will do what and when will they do it?) Sandy Drohman will provide all referral information to Mr. and Mrs. Wright and will accompany them to their first meeting if they desire. ***Criteria*** (How will we know if we are making progress?) Mr. and Mrs. Wright will find satisfaction in increased support and knowledge.	G — Parents Helping Parents	(up to parents' discretion)			Sandy Drohman Mr. and Mrs. Wright Parents Helping Parents
Strategy or activity to achieve the outcome (Who will do what and when will they do it?) AIM Infant Educator will assist Mr. and Mrs. Wright in obtaining additional information about Cathy's condition. ***Criteria*** (How will we know if we are making progress?) Mr. and Mrs. Wright will express satisfaction over the assistance received in becoming more informed.	I — Home	ongoing	2-1-12	11-10-12	AIM Infant Educator

Source: Adapted from Adapting Early Childhood Curricula for Children With Special Needs by Ruth E. Cook, Diane M. Klein, and Deborah Chen, 9th ed. (pp. 73–77).

Screening, Identification, and Assessment

HLP4 Use multiple sources of information to develop a comprehensive understanding of a student's strengths and needs.

Learning Outcome 14.3 List and describe the purposes and types of assessment used in early childhood special education.

Determining eligibility for special education services and planning an appropriate individualized program requires a comprehensive assessment in which data are gathered from multiple sources assessing all domains of the child's development (McAfee et al., 2016). Assessment and evaluation in early childhood special education are conducted for the following purposes (Division for Early Childhood, 2014; Wortham & Hardin, 2020).

- *Screening:* Quick, easy-to-administer tests to identify children who may have a disability and who should receive further testing
- *Determining eligibility for services:* In-depth, comprehensive assessment from multiple sources to assess all major areas of development
- *Individualized planning:* Curriculum-based, criterion-referenced assessments to determine a child's current skill level, identify IFSP or IEP objectives, and plan intervention activities
- *Monitoring progress:* Curriculum-based, criterion-referenced measures to monitor progress on IFSP or IEP objectives
- *Measuring child outcomes:* Curriculum-based, criterion-referenced, and comprehensive developmental assessments to evaluate child growth and program effectiveness

Screening

Before young children and their families can be served, the children must be identified. Some children's disabilities are so significant that no test is needed. Generally, the more severe a disability, the earlier it is detected. In the delivery room, medical staff can identify certain physical disabilities and health impairments, such as microcephaly and cleft palate, as well as most instances of Down syndrome. Within the first few weeks, other physical conditions such as paralysis, seizures, or rapidly increasing head size can signal possible disabilities. But most children who experience developmental delays are not identifiable by obvious physical characteristics or behavioral patterns, especially at very young ages. This is where screening comes into play.

THE APGAR SCALE The Apgar scale, which measures the degree of *asphyxia* (oxygen deprivation) an infant experiences during birth, is administered to virtually all babies born in U.S. hospitals. The test administrator—nurse, nurse anesthetist, or pediatrician—evaluates the newborn twice on five physiological measures: heart rate, respiratory effort, response to stimulation, muscle tone, and skin color. The child is given a score of 0, 1, or 2 on each measure according to the criteria described on the scoring form (see Figure 14.2).

The first administration of the test, conducted 60 seconds after birth, measures how the baby fared during the birth process. If the newborn receives a low score, the delivery room staff takes immediate resuscitation action. The test is given again 5 minutes after birth. At that point, a total score of 0 to 3 (out of a possible 10) indicates severe asphyxia, 4 to 6 moderate asphyxia, and 7 to 10 mild asphyxia. Some stress is assumed on all births, and the 5-minute score measures the success of any resuscitation efforts. A 5-minute score of 6 or less indicates follow-up assessment to determine what is causing the problem and what interventions may be needed. The Apgar scale has been shown to identify high-risk infants—those with a greater than normal chance of developing later problems.

NEWBORN BLOOD TEST SCREENING Some form of newborn screening is mandated in all states, but the components of the newborn screen vary from state to state. Phenylketonuria (PKU) is screened in all states. It causes severe intellectual disabilities, which can be easily prevented if the condition is detected before symptoms develop and the child is treated with a special diet. Testing is also done for *hypothyroidism*, which can likewise lead to intellectual disabilities if not detected early. Affected individuals are treated with supplemental thyroid hormone.

FIGURE 14.2 The Apgar Evaluation Scale

			60 sec.	5 min.
Heart rate	Absent Less than 100 100 to 140	(0) (1) (2)	1	2
Respiratory effort	Apneic Shallow, irregular Lusty cry and breathing	(0) (1) (2)	1	1
Response to catheter stimulation	No response Grimace Cough or sneeze	(0) (1) (2)	1	2
Muscle tone	Flaccid Some flexion of extremities Flexion resisting extension	(0) (1) (2)	1	2
Color	Pale, blue Body pink, extremities blue Pink all over	(0) (1) (2)	0	1
	Total		4	8

The American College of Medical Genetics (2004) submitted a report to the Federal Health Resources and Services Administration identifying national standards for state newborn screening programs. The report identified a core of 29 conditions and 25 secondary conditions for which test results should be reported. Currently, there are 35 core conditions and 26 secondary conditions targeted for screening (U.S. Department of Health and Human Services, 2018). States may also screen for conditions beyond the 61 listed. All states and the District of Columbia have newborn screening programs, but the conditions screened for vary across states.

Screening tests require a few small drops of blood collected from each newborn, usually taken in the hospital 24 to 48 hours after birth. This is done by a heel stick and spotting a few small drops of blood on a paper card, which is then sent for laboratory analysis that tests for as many as 30 congenital conditions or diseases that can lead to physical and health problems, sensory impairments, or developmental delays. Other common testing includes (but is not limited to) biotinidase deficiency, congenital adrenal hyperplasia, congenital hypothyroidism, cystic fibrosis, sickle cell disease, maple syrup urine disease, and galactosemia and hemoglobinopathy (diseases of the red blood cells).

DEVELOPMENTAL SCREENING TESTS The Denver II (Frankenburg & Dodds, 1990) is a widely used screening test for developmental delays. Designed for children from 2 weeks to 6 years of age, the test uses direct observation of the child and parent reports. The Denver II assesses 125 skills arranged in four developmental areas: gross motor, fine motor–adaptive, language, and personal-social. Each test item is represented on the scoring form by a bar showing at what ages 25%, 50%, 75%, and 90% of typically developing children can perform that skill. The child is allowed up to three trials per item. A child's performance on each item is scored as "pass" or "fail" and then interpreted as representing "advanced," "OK," "caution," or "delayed" performance by comparing the child's performance with those of the same age in the standardized population. The Denver II was designed to fit the schedule of well-baby visits recommended by the American Academy of Pediatrics. The Brigance Early Childhood Screens (2013) is another widely used screening tool designed to identify delays in language, motor, self-help, social-emotional, and cognitive skills.

Pearson eText
Video Example 14.3
Knowledge of developmental milestones helps families and professionals identify and address delays. https://www.youtube.com/watch?v=KrUNBfyjlBk

No one observes a child more often and with more interest than the child's parents. Recognizing this fact, early childhood specialists have developed numerous screening tools for parent use. One such tool is the Ages and Stages Questionnaires (ASQ-3) (Squires & Bricker, 2009). The ASQ-3 includes 11 questionnaires that the parents complete when the child is 4, 6, 8, 12, 16, 18, 20, 24, 30, 36, and 48 months old. Each questionnaire consists of 30 items covering

5 areas of development: gross motor, fine motor, communication, personal-social, and adaptive. Many of the items include illustrations to help the parents evaluate their child's behavior.

Determining Eligibility for Services

When the results of a screening test raise suspicion of disability or developmental delay, the child may be referred for comprehensive assessment to determine eligibility for services. Comprehensive assessment includes observation, interviews, and diagnostic tests in each of the following developmental domains (McAfee et al., 2016; Wortham & Hardin, 2020).

- *Motor development.* The ability to move one's body and manipulate objects within the environment provides a critical foundation for all types of learning. Motor development involves improvements in strength, flexibility, endurance, and eye-hand coordination and includes gross-motor movement and mobility (e.g., walking, running, throwing) and fine-motor control (e.g., cutting with scissors, tying a shoe).
- *Cognitive development.* Children use cognitive skills when they sort or count objects, remember things they have done in the past, plan and make decisions about what they will do in the future, integrate newly learned information with previously learned knowledge and skills, solve problems, and generate novel ideas.
- *Communication and language development.* Children use communication and language skills when they receive information from others, share information with others, and use language to effectively control the environment. This domain encompasses all forms of communicative development, including the ability to respond nonverbally with gestures, smiles, or actions and the acquisition of spoken language—sounds, words, phrases, sentences, and so on.
- *Social and emotional development.* Children who have developed competence in social skills share toys and take turns, cooperate with others, and resolve conflicts. Children should feel good about themselves and know how to express their emotions and feelings.
- *Adaptive development.* Self-care and adaptive skills, such as dressing and undressing, eating, toileting, tooth brushing, and hand washing, enable young children to function independently across multiple environments, which provides and enhances opportunities for additional kinds of learning.

Pearson eText
Video Example 14.4
Parents play an important role in developmental assessment. https://www.youtube.com/watch?v=EHNnfjoDVME

Generally, these five developmental domains are broken down into specific, observable tasks and sequenced in the order in which most children learn them. Some tasks correspond with specific ages at which the majority of children can perform them. This arrangement allows the examiner to note significant delays or gaps as well as other unusual patterns in a child's development. The developmental domains are not mutually exclusive; there is considerable overlap across domains and across skills within a specific domain. Most activities in everyday settings involve using skills from multiple domains. For example, playing marbles with someone requires skills from the motor, cognitive, communication, and social domains.

Two widely used tests for diagnosing developmental delays are the Battelle Developmental Inventory (BDI-2) (Newborg, 2005) and the Bayley Scales of Infant and Toddler Development–III (Bayley, 2005). The Battelle can be administered to children with and without disabilities, from birth through age 7 years, 11 months, and it has adapted testing procedures for use with children with different disabilities. The Bayley III evaluates development in cognition, language, social-emotional motor, and adaptive behavior in infants and toddlers from 1 to 42 months.

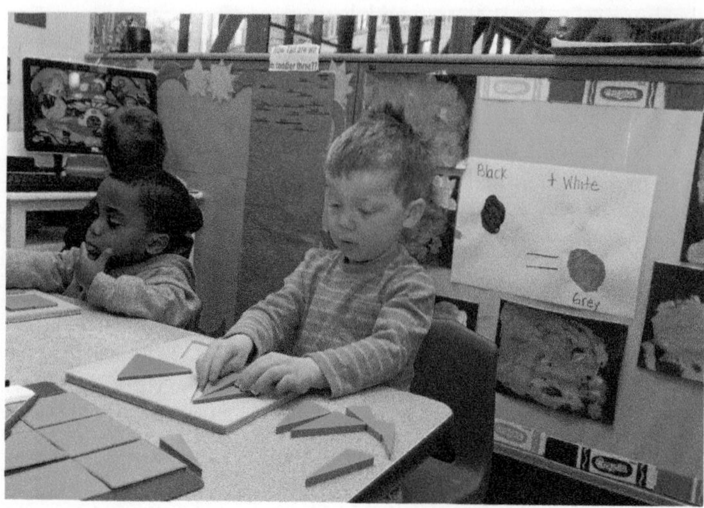

Source: Annie Fuller/Transportation Daycare Center/Pearson Allyn and Bacon/Merrill Education

Early childhood special education assessment and intervention must address all developmental domains.

Program Planning and Monitoring Progress

Effective individual program planning must be guided by accurate and sensitive progress monitoring measures. Results of brief and frequent assessments should drive decisions about selection of objectives, mastery criteria, and intervention strategies. The process of assessment and intervention is ongoing and recursive. For example, if data show the student is not progressing as expected, the teacher can immediately modify the intervention procedures. Ongoing assessment helps teachers make timely decisions about the effectiveness of their teaching, resulting in better student outcomes. Featured Teacher Mark Fraley agrees: "The data I gather in my classroom shed light onto what skills are beginning to emerge and how I can help support these developing skills through thoughtfully planned activities and lessons."

HLP6 Use student assessment data, analyze instructional practices, and make necessary adjustments that improve student outcomes.

Individual Growth and Development Indicators

Wolery and Ledford (2014) recommend using **Individual Growth and Development Indicators (IGDIs)** and direct systematic observation to monitor student progress. IGDIs are sensitive indicators of progress administered repeatedly to determine growth over time and to show a child's responsiveness to intervention. Examples of IGDIs include The Early Communication Indicator (Walker & Carta, 2010); The Early Social Indicator (Carta & Greenwood, 2010); and Picture Naming, Rhyming, Alliteration, and Segment Blending (Missall & McConnell, 2010).

Direct Systematic Observation

Direct systematic observation consists of watching a child for specific behaviors or skills and recording the child's performance. Direct observation is useful for understanding behavior, evaluating development, monitoring progress, and guiding instructional practices (Wortham & Hardin, 2020). Direct observation requires the teacher to clearly identify and define the behavior, the context for collecting data (e.g., during free play, during circle time), and the dimension of behavior to record (e.g., accuracy, frequency, duration). For example, a teacher may record the frequency of social initiations toward another peer during free play or the duration of on-task behaviors during center time. For multiple-step skills such as washing hands or brushing teeth, the teacher can create a task analysis of the steps and record the number of steps completed correctly (see Chapter 4).

Curriculum and Instruction in Early Childhood Special Education

Learning Outcome 14.4 Describe how a play activity or an everyday routine can become a specially designed learning opportunity for a preschooler with disabilities.

Curriculum and Program Goals

Programs in early childhood special education should be designed and evaluated with respect to the following outcomes or goals.

- *Support families in achieving their own goals.* Although the child with special needs is the focal point, a major function of early intervention is helping families achieve the goals most important to them. Families function as a system, and separating the child from the system results in limited and fragmented outcomes (Baily et al., 2012).
- *Promote maximum child independence and mastery.* Early childhood special education seeks to minimize the extent to which children depend on others and differ from their age mates. To achieve this goal, intervention strategies should promote active engagement; initiative and autonomy (choice making, self-directed behavior); and self-sufficiency with age-appropriate tasks in many typical routines and situations.

In situations when independence is not safe, possible, or practical, support and assistance should be provided to enable the child to participate as much as she can.

- *Promote development in all important domains.* Successful early intervention programs help children make progress in each of the developmental areas previously described. Because young children with disabilities are already behind their peers, early childhood special educators should use instructional strategies that lead to rapid learning. Efficient instruction enables the child to perform closer to typical developmental levels and allows time to address additional goals and objectives. See *Transition: Next Year Is Now,* "It's Never Too Early to Have a Job: Classroom Jobs for Preschoolers."

HLP9 Teach social behaviors.

- *Build and support social competence.* Social skills, such as learning to get along with others and making friends, are among the most important skills anyone can learn. Most children learn such skills naturally, but many children with disabilities do not learn to interact effectively and properly just by playing with others.

HLP21 Teach students to maintain and generalize new learning across time and settings.

- *Facilitate generalization of learned skills.* Typically, children use what they have learned in one situation at other places and times. But many children with disabilities have extreme difficulty remembering and using previously learned skills in other situations.
- *Prepare and assist children for typical life experiences with their families, in school, and in their communities.* Early intervention should be characterized by the principle of normalization; that is, services should be provided in settings that are as similar to the typical settings where young children without disabilities play and learn as is possible. A large and growing body of published research demonstrates the benefits of inclusive practices for children with disabilities and their families and suggests strategies for effective inclusion programs (e.g., Kemp et al., 2013; Odom et al., 2011; Stanton-Chapman & Brown, 2015).
- *Help children and their families make smooth transitions.* A transition occurs when a child and his family move from one early intervention program or service delivery mode to another. For example, program transitions typically occur at age 3 years when a child with disabilities moves from a home-based program to an early childhood special education classroom and again at age 5 years when the child moves from a preschool classroom to a regular kindergarten classroom. Preparing and assisting children and their families for smooth transitions ensures continuity of services, minimizes disruptions to the family system, and is another important way for promoting the success of young children with disabilities as they move into more normalized environments (Rous & Hallum, 2012).
- *Prevent or minimize the development of future problems or disabilities.* Early intervention programs that serve at-risk infants and toddlers are designed with prevention as their primary goal.

A joint position statement by the Council for Exceptional Children's Division for Early Childhood and the National Association for the Education of Young Children on the value of inclusion and how it can be used to improve early childhood services can be found at the Frank Porter Graham Child Development Institute website.

Developmentally Appropriate Practice

Virtually all early childhood educators—whether their students have disabilities or not—believe that learning environments, teaching practices, and other components of programs serving young children should be based on what is typically expected of and experienced by children of different ages and developmental stages (e.g., Gestwicki, 2016; Kostelnik et al., 2019; Morrison, 2018). **Developmentally appropriate practice (DAP)** is a philosophy and set of practice guidelines based on that belief. According to the National Association for the Education of Young Children (NAEYC, 2009), DAP is a framework of principles and guidelines that outline practice "that promotes young children's *optimal* learning and

Transition: Next Year Is Now

It's Never Too Early to Have a Job: Classroom Jobs for Preschoolers

The calendar helper stepped up, grabbed the star wand, and pointed to each number as she counted up to today's date, "9, 10, 11, 12." I replied, "Great job, calendar helper! You are using big numbers now! I remember when you could count only to 3!" After returning to her seat at circle, her smile beamed with a sense of accomplishment.

Why Give Preschoolers Classroom Jobs?

Classroom jobs play an important role in student learning. In addition to providing opportunities to practice a wide variety of skills across developmental areas, classroom jobs can also shape positive social interactions and give added incentives to participate in daily routines. Classroom jobs give children opportunities to contribute to the classroom community, learn the value of work, and develop responsibility and a sense of purpose that set the stage for future employment pursuits.

What Types of Classroom Jobs Should Preschoolers Do?

The following are examples of classroom jobs that Featured Teacher Mark Fraley uses with his preschool students.

- *Calendar helper.* The calendar helper identifies the month, day of the week, and date, and leads the class in reading numbers patterns and guessing which one is next.
- *Line leader.* The line leader is called to line up first. The student stands on a letter X that is taped to the floor near the door and is expected to follow hallway rules.
- *Weather helper.* The weather helper looks out the window to see what the weather is and then relays this information to the class.
- *Snack helper.* The snack helper hands out placemats and napkins and gets snack items ready for the classroom.
- *Music helper.* The music helper selects a song during the circle time from a list of teacher-selected songs.

What Are Ways to Manage Classroom Jobs in Your Classroom?

Mark Fraley makes the following suggestions for managing classroom jobs:

- Create a job board that includes a picture and word description of the job along with a place to assign a name or student photo.
- As an alternative to assigning everyone a different job, consider using a "Star Student" method. In this approach, one student—the Star Student—is selected to perform several jobs. The day's Star Student benefits from focused attention and opportunities to help throughout various daily routines. This gives an element of predictability that young children thrive on.
- Classroom jobs can also be used when collaborating with related-service providers. For example, one of Mark's students was working on clothing vocabulary. Mark and the speech and language therapist decided to create a classroom job that was heavily influenced by this need—a fashion helper job, which simply asks one student to describe his clothing choice (or a friend's clothing choice) for that day. This job became really popular in Mark's classroom and remains an important part of each day.
- One aspect of classroom jobs that is important to think about involves how young children learn about the world around them from enacting familiar roles. Classroom jobs provide a playful platform through which they can be similar to the grown-ups in their lives. I often find students who want to imitate teachers and therefore want to use the same wording, actions, and materials.

Mark Fraley offers the following suggestions for making classroom jobs a positive experience:

- Be consistent in how the job is performed and what is expected.
- Use visuals! Providing pictures with instructions gives the support many children need.
- Don't just reward the performing part of the job; praise children who are actively listening and remaining engaged while their peer is on the job.
- Use real-life examples or demonstrations when possible. For example, show a video clip of a meteorologist from a local news channel as a model.
- Share with the family how their child took responsibility for the classroom job and encourage the family to find jobs the child can do at home. This makes families happy!

development" (p. 1). Developmentally appropriate practice rests on core principles that early childhood educators should consider in their decision making (NAEYC, 2009):

- *Knowledge must inform decision making.* Practitioners must know about (a) child development and learning, (b) each child as an individual, and (c) the social and cultural contexts each child lives in.
- *Goals must be challenging and achievable.* Learning and development are most likely to occur when new experiences build on what a child already knows and is able to do and when those experiences also entail the child stretching a reasonable amount in acquiring new skills, abilities, or knowledge.
- *Teaching must be intentional to be effective.* Good teachers are intentional in everything they do—setting up the classroom, planning curriculum, making use of various teaching strategies, assessing children, interacting with them, and working with their families.

Although most early childhood special educators view the NAEYC's DAP guidelines as the foundation on which to provide early intervention, they also recognize that young children with disabilities need specially designed, individualized instruction (i.e., special education) (Cook et al., 2020; Division for Early Childhood, 2014). Researchers and practitioners in early childhood special education have developed effective methods for incorporating instruction aimed at children's IFSP and IEP goals into the context of the typical play and preschool activities of young children. For example, sociodramatic play with dolls, stuffed animals, and puppets is a developmentally appropriate practice that provides opportunities for children to learn language and literacy skills (Morrison, 2018). To learn how puppets can help preschoolers with disabilities learn language skills, see *Teaching & Learning,* "Using Puppets in the Early Childhood Classroom."

TEACHING & LEARNING

Using Puppets in the Early Childhood Classroom

by Mary D. Salmon, Stacie McConnell, Diane M. Sainato, and Rebecca Morrison

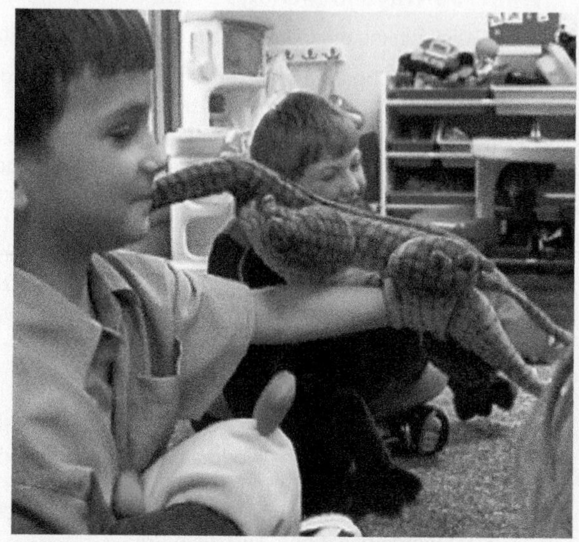

Why Use Puppets? Most young children are delighted by puppets. Their vivid colors, interesting textures, and larger-than-life expressions encourage curiosity and heighten attention among all children, including those with a range of developmental disabilities. Puppets' physical characteristics, overstated smiles or frowns, and motivational appeal make them valuable tools in early childhood classrooms.

When and How Should You Use Puppets? Teachers can use puppets during circle time, transitions, and sociodramatic play. Teachers can also use puppets to help children address emotions.

Circle Time

- The teacher or a child can be the puppeteer, leading the class during calendar time.
- Dress a large, full-bodied puppet in child-sized clothing for a lesson on weather concepts. Spice up his wardrobe with a variety of hats, sunglasses, and mittens as well as attire appropriate for all types of weather.

- Teaching classroom rules is an important and ongoing process. To increase impact, designate a puppet to teach these common procedures: "Rule Bunny says, 'Play nicely with your friends,' or 'Put materials away neatly.'"
- Puppets can read stories, sing songs, lead "Simon Says," and model a variety of motor skills.

Transitions

- A puppet can shake a bell or ring a chime to indicate when it is time to clean up or move to the next activity.
- Having a puppet lead the way to the next activity can capture the attention of a busy (and noisy) group of youngsters.
- Children can take turns using a puppet to ready the class for special activities. Line leaders can guide the class to the library, gym, or music or art class, using a puppet to improve group attention.
- Puppets can model appropriate clean-up behaviors, such as placing blocks in a bin or putting away art materials.

Sociodramatic Play and Social Skills

- Simple hand puppets along with a few accessories (e.g., hats, badges) can assume different roles, such as salesclerk, police officer, or firefighter.
- Many characters from favorite books are available as puppets. Children can act out their favorite story and become any character they wish.
- Combine favorite stories with representative puppets to teach appropriate social behaviors. For example, use *The Rainbow Fish* by Marcus Pfister to teach sharing.

Dealing with Emotions

- Puppets can make emotions "larger than life." Use them to demonstrate appropriate emotional responses while watching or acting out short skits.
- A child may be more inclined to express her feelings through a puppet. Teachers can role-play with a puppet to demonstrate appropriate classroom expectations and behavior.

Pearson eText Video Example 14.5
Puppets can help children develop play and social skills.

Selecting IFSP and IEP Goals and Objectives

HLP11 Identify and prioritize long- and short-term learning goals.

The breadth of activities that young children typically engage in provides an almost unlimited number of possibilities for instructional goals and objectives. Early childhood special educators can judge the value of potential IFSP or IEP goals and objectives according to the following quality indicators (e.g., Boavida et al., 2014; Ridgley et al., 2011):

1. *Functionality.* A functional skill (a) increases the child's ability to interact with people and objects in her daily environment and (b) may have to be performed by someone else if the child cannot do it.
2. *Generality.* In this context, a skill has generality if it (a) represents a general concept as opposed to a particular task; (b) can be adapted and modified to meet the child's disability; and (c) can be used across different settings, with various materials, and with different people.
3. *Instructional context.* The skill should be easily integrated into the child's daily routines and taught in a meaningful way that represents naturalistic use of the skill.
4. *Measurability.* A skill is measurable if its performance or a product produced by its performance can be seen, felt, or heard. Measurable skills can be counted or timed and enable objective determination of learning progress.

Content Extension 14.2

Featured Teacher Mark Fraley's gingerbread man scavenger hunt.

Teachers can address individual IEP objectives in the context of engaging whole-class activities that address each of the above quality indicators. Featured Teacher Mark Fraley created an activity in which his students followed clues around the building to find the gingerbread men they baked earlier that day. "R will make eye contact with adults as he communicates each time (prompts or cue cards may be needed)" and "G will walk down the hall while holding the class line-up rope with minimal support" are examples of individual objectives.

HLP13 Adapt curriculum tasks and materials for specific learning goals.

Instructional Adaptations and Modifications

Similar to their colleagues who teach school-age students with disabilities, early childhood special education teachers must be competent with a wide range of evidence-based instructional strategies and tactics. Modifications and adaptations of the physical environment, materials, and activities are often sufficient to support successful participation and learning. Such modifications range from subtle, virtually invisible supports (e.g., changing the duration or sequence of activities, using a child's preferences as a conversation topic while playing) to more obvious interventions and support (e.g., providing the child with an adaptive device, teaching peers to prompt and reward participation) (Cook et al., 2020; Deris & DiCarlo, 2013).

Teachers should identify adaptations and modifications within the context of specific activities throughout the day. For example, Barton et al. (2011) recommend the following adaptations for circle time.

- Progressively increase the amount of time the child must participate in circle time.
- Use picture schedules and timers so the child knows the sequence of activities and when circle time is over.
- Embed preferred activities and choices.
- Teach a peer buddy to help the child participate.
- Provide explicit instruction of imitation.
- Have an adult provide hand-over-hand assistance initially and then fade prompts when the child becomes more independent.

YouTube

Pearson eText
Video Example 14.6
Featured Teacher Mark Fraley's trapeze activity targets skills in several developmental domains.
https://www.youtube.com/watch?v=AJVaW_ICx58

TEACHING PLAY Play provides natural contexts through which young children with disabilities can learn and practice social and communication skills, language skills, problem-solving skills, and cognitive skills (Bredecamp, 2019; Cook et al., 2020; Dennis & Stockall, 2015). Although playing is critical for learning, many young children with disabilities do not engage in play and may need systematic interventions, such as play expansions, visually structured tasks, and least-to-most prompting, to develop play behaviors.

Play expansions increase the variety and complexity of play behaviors and spoken language by young children with disabilities (Barton et al., 2019; Barton et al., 2018; Frey & Kaiser, 2011). When using play expansions, the teacher first imitates the child's play and then models additional or more advanced actions. For example, if the child puts one block on top of another, the teacher does the same and then stacks two more blocks close to the first stack and tops both stacks with a long block. As the child imitates and expands his play actions, the teacher provides descriptive language of the child's actions and reinforcement (e.g., "You're making two stacks of blocks. And a roof, too!").

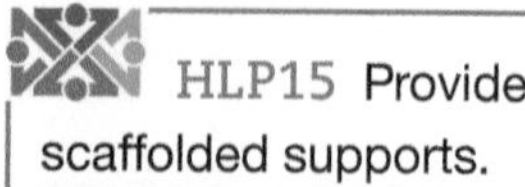
HLP15 Provide scaffolded supports.

Designing visually structured tasks that prompt students through a play sequence is another way to teach and support play skills (Hampshire & Hourcade, 2014). The teacher can provide a mini picture schedule that shows the steps of a play task or arrange the play materials in sequential order from left to right. For example, the mini schedule could show the sequence for building a block structure or placing toy farm animals into different areas of the farm.

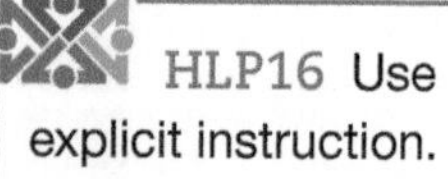
HLP16 Use explicit instruction.

Another way to directly teach play skills is using a sequence of least-to-most prompts (e.g., Barton & Pavilanis, 2012; Davis-Temple et al., 2014). With least-to-most prompts, the teacher systematically increases support until the child can perform the behavior. For example, to teach a child to pretend to feed a baby doll with a bottle, the first prompt might be showing the child a picture of a doll drinking from a bottle, followed by physically modeling bottle feeding the doll; then using a verbal prompt ("your turn to feed the baby"); and finally, physically guiding the child's hands. The teacher withdraws the prompts as the child becomes more independent. When children engage in free play independently, teachers can embed frequent opportunities for social interaction and collaborative problem solving (Martin et al., 2015; Ramani & Brownell, 2014). Direct instruction of play skills should culminate with frequent interactive play experiences with peers.

PEER-MEDIATED INTERVENTIONS Peer-mediated interventions enlist the support of peers without disabilities to engage and support children with disabilities. Preschool peers can model positive behaviors or specific skills, prompt interactive language and play skills, and reinforce target skills. Directly teaching peers to interact with children with disabilities during play or other activities results in increased quantity and quality of social interactions and language production for children with disabilities (Katz & Girolametto, 2013; Stanton-Chapman & Brown, 2015; Watkins et al., 2015). Peers without disabilities can be taught to play with a child with disabilities, share toys, and initiate conversations.

Teachers can combine social narratives with peer-mediated instruction to increase prosocial behaviors of preschoolers with disabilities (Harjusola-Webb et al., 2012). Social narratives are brief stories told for the purpose of teaching a specific prosocial behavior. For example, the teacher tells a story about children taking turns while playing a game and checks their understanding before the students play a game in which they must take turns. To learn how Featured Teacher Mark Fraley encourages interactions between preschoolers with and without disabilities, see *Teaching & Learning*, "Peer-Mediated Instruction in Inclusive Preschool Classrooms."

TEACHING & LEARNING

Peer-Mediated Instruction in Inclusive Preschool Classrooms

What Is Peer-Mediated Instruction? When teachers provide opportunities for children to teach one another, they are using peer-mediated instruction. Mark Fraley uses peer-mediated instruction throughout the school day to help his students develop their social, language, academic, and motor skills and to help them achieve their IEP goals.

How Do You Use Peer-Mediated Instruction? Mark provides the following suggestions for facilitating successful peer-mediated learning opportunities.

- *Target easily attainable skills.* Select skills students are likely to succeed with in the first few attempts. For example, in the block area, I model how to build a simple structure (e.g., arch, road, bridge). Then I give some of the materials to one student and some to the other student and tell them to build the structure together.
- *Create motivating activities.* For a student who has difficultly interacting with peers, have him distribute letters to classmates with simply a sticker sealed inside. Being a deliverer of good news can produce positive interactions with peers. Consider individual preferences when selecting activities. One of my students loves to launch things with a plastic spoon taped to the edge of table and watch them fly. I gave a set of plastic bugs to another

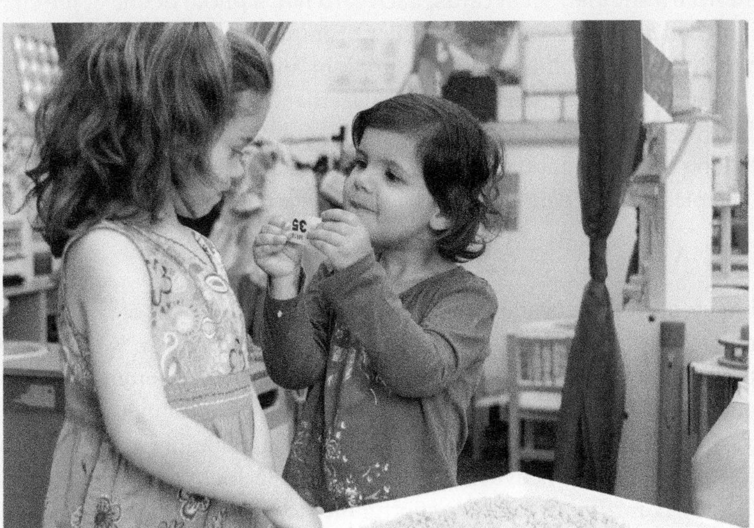
Source: Mark Fraley

Pearson eText
Video Example 14.7
Featured Teacher Mark Fraley prompts and encourages peer-mediated instruction.
https://www.youtube.com/watch?v=S6_Woum_jGo

student and asked him to give them to "John" one at a time. The idea is that "John" could associate the fun of watching these bugs fly with a peer interacting with him.

- *Embed opportunities for social interaction.* Create jobs that require cooperation and embed them within daily routines. For example, assign two snack helpers; one is in charge of placemats, and the other is responsible for napkins. What happens when napkins are put down first? This takes a little communication and cooperation.
- *Select appropriate peer models.* Identify good peer models by observing children during free play time. Children who gravitate toward others naturally and have a knack for listening tend to make good peer models and persevere through tough challenges.
- *Guide peer models.* Teach the peer models to use language consistent with what you are using. For example, if you are working on having a student learn to sign the request "more," you want the peer model to know the sign, model the sign, and understand that when the target student signs "more," you should make a very big deal about it. For more information on peer-mediated instruction, see Chapter 12, *Teaching & Learning*, "Peer Helpers: Including Students with Severe Disabilities."

Pearson eText
Video Example 14.8
Effective early childhood special educators embed learning opportunities in classroom routines and activities throughout the day.

EMBEDDED LEARNING OPPORTUNITIES One effective method for incorporating intentional instruction into typical preschool activities is called **embedded learning opportunities**. The concept is based on the premise that although quality early childhood programs offer opportunities for learning throughout the day, many children with disabilities need additional guidance and support to benefit from these opportunities (Davenport & Johnston, 2015; Ledford et al., 2017). Therefore, teachers should look and plan for and plan ways to embed brief, systematic instructional interactions that focus on children's IEP objectives in the context of naturally occurring classroom activities. Figure 14.3 shows a teacher's plan for embedding learning opportunities in daily routines such as arrival to school, free play, and snack time.

Featured Teacher Mark Fraley says, "Snack time is a wonderful activity for embedding learning opportunities in multiple domains: social-communicative skills such as requesting, asking and responding to questions, and appropriately getting someone's attention; fine-motor skills such as eating with a spoon and drinking from a cup; and adaptive skills such as cleaning up and washing hands." A creative and effective example of embedding language learning opportunities into mealtimes was reported by Robinson et al. (1999). Each child was seated at the table in front of a placemat showing a picture of a food item, a cartoon character, an animal, and something silly (e.g., a cat wearing glasses and reading a book) (Figure 14.4). Twelve different placemats were used in the study, and each child sat before a different one each day. At first, the teacher played "The Talking Game" with the children while they ate breakfast in the school lunchroom. The children took turns picking an index card from a shuffled set of cards. Each card had a photo of one of the children in the group. After a child selected a card, the teacher prompted him to say something to the child pictured on the card. If the child could not think of anything to say, the teacher prompted him to talk about one of the pictures on his placemat. After several weeks, the teacher no longer used the index cards and stopped prompting the children's interactions. The children continued talking with one another during mealtimes at rates higher than they had before, often using the pictures on their placemats as conversation starters.

Preschool Activity Schedules

Early childhood special education teachers face the challenge of organizing the day into a schedule that meets each child's individual learning needs and provides children with many opportunities to explore the environment and communicate with others. The schedule should include a balance of child-initiated and planned activities, large- and small-group activities, active and quiet times, and indoor and outdoor activities; it should allow easy transition from activity to activity (Cook et al., 2020). In short, the schedule should provide a framework for maximizing children's opportunities to develop new skills and practice what they have learned while remaining manageable and flexible (Johnson et al., 2015).

FIGURE 14.3 Plan for Embedding Opportunities in Daily Routines

Embedded Learning Opportunities Objective-by-Activity Planning Matrix

Child's Name LISA (L) **Date:** ________

Objective / **Activities**	Social Increase tolerance for proximity to peers. Acknowledge peers using social communications.	Language Increase functional communication (requests).Increase use of spoken vocabulary.	Motor Develop motor planning and accuracy to increase efficiency and independence in play and daily routines.	Preacademic Enjoy looking at books. Develop alphabetic principle; understand relationship of print to language.	Self-Help/ Independence Move through daily routine without prompts. Use utensils and cup for self-feeding without assistance.
Arrival Transition Cue: Natural cue to play area	Teacher (T) greets L and provides imitative prompt for L to say "Good morning" to peer.	T uses pause-and-wait strategy to encourage L to request help taking off her backpack.	T uses physical scaffolding to help L hang jacket and backpack on hook.	T says, "Find your cubby," directing L's attention to name/picture card on the cubby.	T uses backward-chaining procedure to help L motor plan her sequence of entering room, placing items in her cubby, and walking to play area.
Free Play Transition Cue: Lights on/off for cleanup	T helps L tolerate proximity of peers by inviting peer to sit on mat at a comfortable distance from L, commenting to L, "It's great to have a friend to play with, isn't it!"	T uses violation-of-routines strategy by placing L's favorite musical toy out of sight. When L approaches teacher and vocalizes. her distress, T immediately says, "Oh my—let's find your music box!"	If L has difficulty activating a toy she has selected, T provides (then fades) physical prompts.	T directs L's attention to labels on lego bins and plastic dinosaur bins, encouraging choice.	T waits for L to select toy.
Circle Transition Cue: "Let's line up for recess" (T points to door)	T allows L to remain outside the circle until all children are settled, then moves her closer to the group, prompting her to "show me where you'd like to sit."	T uses verbal imitative prompt for L to request her favorite song, "Little Red Caboose, "by saying, "Train song" (L already uses the word *train* when playing with the train in the block area).	For songs with motions, T provides physical prompts as needed. During an active dancing activity, L is allowed to move away from the circle if she prefers.	T makes sure L's favorite storybook is one of the story choices during circle time. T does not ask L to come to the front of the circle but places three name cards directly in front of her, asking her to "find your name; LI-SA," exaggerating the /li/ sound at the beginning of the word, saying, "Lisa begins with L."	T prompts L to move toward the circle area only if necessary. T waits until all other children are seated. If L still does not move toward the circle area, T directs L's attention to table closest to circle, if neccessary taking her to that spot. (see "Social" goals)

Source: Adapted from ADAPTING EARLY CHILDHOOD CURRICULA FOR CHILDREN WITH SPECIAL NEEDS by Ruth E. Cook, Diane M. Klein, and Deborah Chen, 9th ed (p. 342). Copyright © 2016. Reprinted by permission of Pearson Education, Inc., Upper Saddle River, NJ.

A Supportive Physical Environment

The physical arrangement of the classroom must support the planned activities. Designing an effective preschool classroom requires thoughtful planning to ensure that play areas and needed materials are accessible to and safe for all students, boundaries between areas minimize distractions, and, most important, the environment makes children want to explore and play. Suggestions for setting up a preschool classroom include the following (Cook et al., 2020; Morrison, 2018):

- Organize the classroom into several different well-defined areas to accommodate different kinds of activities (e.g., quiet play, messy play, dramatic play, constructive play, active play).
- Arrange quiet activities together, away from avenues of traffic, and loud activities together.
- Equip each area with abundant, appropriate materials that are desirable to children.

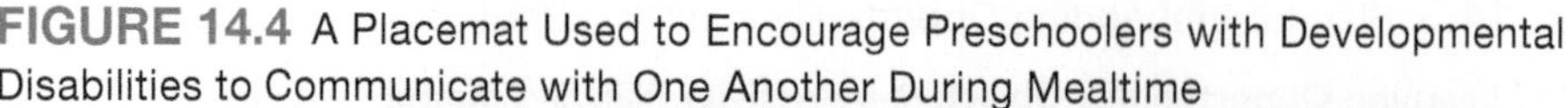

FIGURE 14.4 A Placemat Used to Encourage Preschoolers with Developmental Disabilities to Communicate with One Another During Mealtime

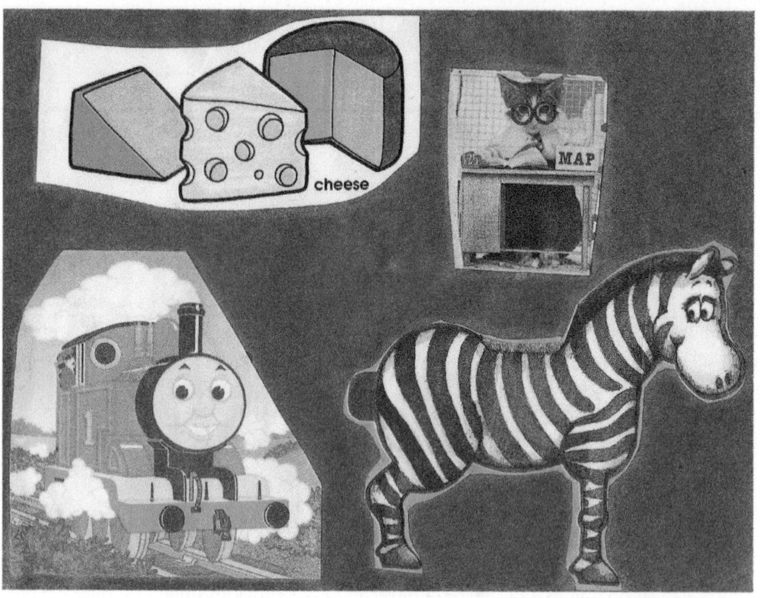

Source: Courtesy of Diane M. Sainato, The Ohio State University.

- Place materials where children can access them easily and independently.
- Have an open area, perhaps a large rug, to conduct large-group activities such as circle time and story reading.
- Label or color code all storage areas so assistants and volunteers can easily find needed materials.
- Arrange equipment and group areas so that students can move easily from one activity to another. Clearly identify work areas with pictures or color codes.
- Provide lockers or cubbies for students' belongings, Add picture cues to help students find their lockers.

Service Delivery Options for Early Intervention

Learning Outcome 14.5 List and briefly describe service delivery options for young children and identify advantages and disadvantages of each type.

Early intervention services are delivered in a variety of settings, depending on the age of the child and the type and intensity of supports she and her family need. Hospitals are frequently the setting for early intervention services for infants and newborns with significant disabilities. Most early childhood special education services, however, are provided in the child's home, in a center- or school-based facility, or in a combination of both settings. Young children with mild developmental delays are often served by itinerant special education teachers in general education preschool settings.

Hospital-Based Programs

Low-birth-weight and other high-risk newborns who require specialized health care are placed in neonatal intensive care units (NICUs). NICUs include a variety of professionals, such as neonatologists who provide medical care for infants with special needs, nurses who provide ongoing medical assistance, psychologists and social workers who help parents and families with emotional and financial concerns, and infant education specialists who promote interactions between parents and infants.

Home-Based Programs

Home-based programs are built around family involvement and support. The parents typically assume primary responsibility as caregivers and teachers for their child with disabilities. They are usually supported by an early intervention specialist who visits the home regularly. Home visitors (or home teachers or home advisors, as they are called in some programs) are specially trained paraprofessionals. They may visit as frequently as several times a week but probably no less than a few times a month. They sometimes carry the results of their in-home evaluations back to supervisors, who may recommend changes in the program.

Home-based early intervention programs have several advantages:

- The home is the child's natural environment, and parents can often give more time and attention to the child than even the most adequately staffed center or school.
- Other family members, such as siblings and grandparents, have more opportunity to interact with the child during instruction and socially. These significant others can play important roles in the child's growth and development.
- Home learning activities and materials are more likely to be natural and appropriate.
- Parents who are actively involved in helping their children learn and develop have an advantage over parents who feel guilt, frustration, or defeat at their seeming inability to help their children.
- Home-based programs can be less costly to operate.

Home-based programs, however, can have disadvantages:

- Because home-based programs place so much responsibility on parents, they are not effective with all families. Not all parents are able or willing to spend the time required to teach their children, and some who try are not effective teachers.
- A large and growing number of young children do not reside in the traditional two-parent family—especially children with teenage mothers who are single and poor. It is unlikely that a young mother struggling with the realities of day-to-day survival will be able to meet the added demands of involvement in a home-based early intervention program (Turnbull et al., 2015).
- Children in home-based programs may not receive as wide a range of services as they would in a center-based program, where they can be seen by a variety of professionals. (Note, however, that the services of professionals such as physical therapists, occupational therapists, and speech-language therapists are sometimes provided in the home.)
- The child may not receive sufficient opportunities for social interaction with peers.

Center-Based Programs

Center-based programs provide early intervention services in a special educational setting outside the home. The setting may be in a school, a special day care center, or part of a hospital complex. Some centers provide a wide range of services for children with varying types and degrees of disabilities, combining services of professionals from several different fields.

Center-based programs encourage social interaction among children, and many integrate children with and without disabilities into child care or preschool classes. Some children attend a center each weekday for all or most of the day; others may come less frequently, although most centers expect to see each child at least once a week. Most centers offer parent education programs. (Some programs require parents to attend training sessions.) Virtually all effective programs for young children with disabilities recognize the critical need to involve families and welcome them in every aspect of the program.

Center-based programs generally offer four advantages that are difficult to build into home-based efforts:

- A team of specialists from different fields has an increased opportunity to directly observe each child and collaborate in planning, implementing, and evaluating the effectiveness of interventions.

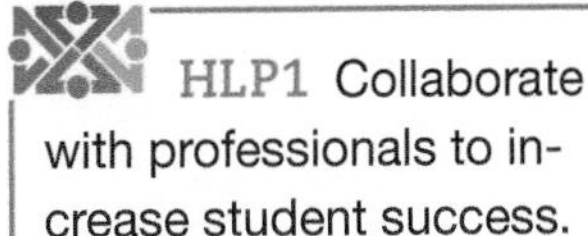
HLP1 Collaborate with professionals to increase student success.

- The intensive instruction and related services that can be provided in a center-based program are especially important for children with severe disabilities.
- The opportunity for interaction with typically developing peers makes center programs especially effective for some children.
- Most parents involved in center programs feel some relief at the support they get from the professionals who work with their child and from other parents with children at the same center.

Disadvantages of center-based programs include the expense of transportation, the cost and maintenance of the center itself, and the possibility of less direct parent involvement than in home-based programs.

Combined Home-Center Programs

Many early intervention programs combine center-based activities and home visitation. Few center programs take children for more than a few hours a day or more than 5 days per week. But because young children with disabilities require more intervention than a few hours a day, many programs combine the intensive help of a variety of professionals in a center with the continuous attention and care of parents at home. Coordinated intervention carried out in both home and center environments offers many of the advantages of the two types of programs and negates some of their disadvantages.

Families: Most Important of All

HLP3 Collaborate with families to support student learning and secure needed services.

The success of efforts to prevent disabilities in children and to identify, assess, and intervene with children who have special needs as early as possible requires the training, experience, and cooperation of a wide range of professionals. Current best practice guidelines for early childhood services call for a transdisciplinary approach to the delivery of related services in which parents and professionals work together to assess needs, develop the IFSP or IEP, provide services, and evaluate outcomes (Division for Early Childhood, 2014).

Of all the people needed to make early intervention work, parents and families are the most important. Given enough information and support, parents can help prevent many risks and causes of disabilities—before pregnancy, before birth, and certainly before a child has gone months or years without help. Given the chance and support, parents can take an active role in determining their children's educational needs and goals. And given some guidance, training, and support, many parents can teach their children at home and even at school.

Successful programs for young children with disabilities take great care to involve parents. Parents are the most frequent and constant observers of their children's behavior. They usually know better than anyone else what their children need, and they can help educators set realistic goals. They can report on events in the home that outsiders might never see—for instance, how a child responds to other family members. They can monitor and report on their children's progress at home, beyond the more controlled environment of the early intervention center or preschool. In short, parents can contribute to their children's programs at every stage—assessment, planning, classroom activities, and evaluation. Many parents even work in preschool classrooms as teacher aides, volunteers, or other staff members.

But in our efforts to involve parents, we must recognize that although professionals come and go, parents and families are in it for the long haul. In their focus to help young children attain important developmental milestones, it is easy for early childhood professionals to overlook that parents are just beginning a lifetime of commitment and responsibility.

As Hutinger et al. (1983) aptly reminded us nearly 40 years ago, we must not forget that early childhood is supposed to be a fun, happy time for children and for the adults who are fortunate enough to work with them.

> Part of our mission as professionals in the field of early childhood special education is to possess an art of enjoyment ourselves and to help instill it in the young children and families with whom we work.
>
> Early childhood comes but once in a lifetime.... Let's make it count!

ADVICE FROM THE FEATURED TEACHER by Mark Fraley

Use Child-Centered Teaching Tactics

Source: Breanne Fraley

Children learn by playing. If a child is on the floor playing with building blocks, I sit on the floor and simply join her. This shows I value her as a person and respect what she has to say or contribute. When I am at the student's level, I follow her lead. By allowing students to self-direct their learning to a certain degree, it is easy to find what they are interested in and plan activities that incorporate these things. The following tips can help increase student learning and enjoyment during child-centered activities.

- ***Give students choices.*** I use a choice board that contains photos of each learning center and Velcro-backed pictures of the students. Each child sticks his picture next to the center of his choice.
- ***Don't ask too many questions during play.*** Asking questions is not only intrusive to play but also changes my role from play partner to test giver. How much fun is it to play with a test giver? Not much! Instead, I'll make comments like a sports broadcaster: "I see you are building a green tower with long rectangle blocks. It is very tall!"
- ***Let students make and learn from their mistakes.*** I used to get upset when my students responded incorrectly or took too long to complete a task. I have to remember that young children, especially those with developmental disabilities, need many, many opportunities to master a skill. Allowing room for mistakes gives them a chance to try another strategy or method. It is fun as a teacher to make a mistake in front of students, such as trying to put the wrong lid on a bin during clean-up. Your students will see this and step in to help or guide you as you have taught them through problem solving. Making mistakes can also encourage more communication opportunities as they will need to request items or identify the problem.

Create an Organized and Predictable Environment

Preschool classrooms are busy places with many activities occurring simultaneously throughout the day. Posting your plans and intentions reduces the chance of conflicts with staff or parents over misunderstandings of who was supposed to be doing what, with whom, and when. When a conflict occurs or if there is breakdown in the way services are delivered, posted schedules can be a reference tool to review and troubleshoot.

- ***Create a master activity schedule.*** The master schedule shows what activities everyone in your classroom, professionals and children, should be doing during each time period of the day. One matrix hanging on my classroom wall indicates the roles that all members of the teaching team—my instructional assistants, the speech-language pathologist, physical therapists, and occupational therapists—are to assume throughout the day (e.g., lead teacher, collector of child performance data). Another matrix makes it easy for parents and classroom volunteers to quickly see what's going on and how they might help.
- ***Display visual schedules for your students.*** Make a poster of your daily routine with pictures, icons, and words your students can understand. Transitions can be challenging times for young children, and a visual reference of what is going to happen next can guide them to more independent functioning. Some students benefit from an individualized visual schedule they can carry with them.

Collect Data from Multiple Sources

All teachers should collect data to assess student learning and evaluate their teaching. For special education teachers, direct and frequent measurement of student progress on IEP goals and objectives is not just good practice; it is required by law. Over the years, I have learned the value of obtaining data from a wide variety of sources and how to do so efficiently. Here are a few of those approaches:

- ***Find easy ways to monitor progress.*** I keep counts of important student behaviors, such as social initiations or academic responses, with tally marks on a piece of masking tape placed on my leg or shirt. I also list activities on specifically designed data sheets kept on a clipboard next to each classroom center or activity area so I can mark the number, type, and prompt level of responses by students.

- ***Write anecdotal observations.*** Anecdotal observations can provide important information about the context of the student's learning and behavior. I write anecdotal observations of student accomplishments on note cards kept in a folder beside my desk.
- ***Use technology to record permanent products.*** I take digital photos throughout the day of where students spend their time and how they are interacting with peers. Additionally, I video record my circle time and other instructional activities group times to review my teaching and student performance.

Working with Other Professionals

The early childhood classroom can be a very busy one when you look at the number of professionals who can be involved at one time. Collaboration is a must in order to keep a focus on student needs and to get the most out of the time students are receiving interventions. How does one collaborate effectively with other IEP team members? Here are a few tips:

- ***Respect everyone's schedule and keep an organized calendar.*** Due to time constraints, with many scheduled meetings and trainings, it is important to be sensitive to your team members' commitments.
- ***Utilize your team members' strengths.*** By getting to know what they excel at and enjoy investing their time in, you will find that projects get completed and work gets done in a positive and productive way.
- ***Keep a relaxed approach when not dealing with critical elements.*** The nature of working with intense, repetitive, and sometimes harmful behaviors that students display can lead to a tense and stressful classroom environment. The demands of the job are high. When possible, find ways to be playful, use humor, and breathe when the classroom is not on high alert.
- ***Celebrate the little victories.*** Remember that adults also benefit from verbal and specific praise as it relates to their contribution to the classroom.

Key Terms and Concepts

developmentally appropriate practice
embedded learning opportunities
Individual Growth and Development Indicators
individualized family service plan (IFSP)
play expansions

Summary

The Importance of Early Intervention

- Early intervention consists of educational, nutritional, child care, and family supports designed to reduce the effects of disabilities or prevent the occurrence of developmental problems later in life for children at risk for such problems.
- Research has documented that early intervention can provide both intermediate and long-term benefits for young children with disabilities and those at risk for developmental delay. Benefits include the following:
  - Gains in physical development, cognitive development, language and speech development, social competence, and self-help skills
  - Prevention of secondary disabilities
  - Reduction of family stress
  - Reduced need for special education services or placement during the school year
  - Saving society the costs of additional educational and social services that would be needed later without early intervention
  - Reduced likelihood of social dependence in adulthood
  - Increased effectiveness of early intervention when it begins as early in life as possible and is intensive and long lasting

The Individuals with Disabilities Education Act, Early Intervention, and Early Childhood Special Education

- States that receive IDEA funds for early intervention services must serve all infants and toddlers from birth through age 2 years with developmental delays or established risk conditions. At their discretion, states may serve infants and toddlers who are at risk for acquiring disabilities because of certain biological or environmental risk conditions.
- Early intervention services for infants and toddlers are family centered, transdisciplinary, and described by individualized family service plans (IFSPs).
- The Individuals with Disabilities Education Act (IDEA) requires states to provide special education services (via individualized education programs [IEPs]) to all preschool children with disabilities, age 3 through 5 years.
- Preschool children do not have to be identified and reported under disability categories to receive services.

Screening, Identification, and Assessment

- Screening involves quick, easy-to-administer tests to identify children who may have a disability and who should receive further testing.
- Diagnosis requires in-depth, comprehensive assessment of all major areas of development to determine a child's eligibility for early intervention or special education services.
- Program planning uses curriculum-based, criterion-referenced assessments to determine a child's current skill level, identify IFSP or IEP objectives, and plan intervention activities.
- Evaluation uses curriculum-based, criterion-referenced measures to determine progress on IFSP or IEP objectives and evaluate a program's effects.
- Many early intervention programs are moving away from assessments based entirely on developmental milestones and are incorporating curriculum-based assessment in which each item relates directly to a skill included in the program's curriculum. This provides a direct link among testing, teaching, and program evaluation.

Curriculum and Instruction in Early Childhood Special Education

- Early intervention and education programs for children with special needs should be designed and evaluated according to these outcomes or goals:
  - Support families in achieving their own goals.
  - Promote child engagement, independence, and mastery.
  - Promote development in all important domains.
  - Build and support social competence.
  - Facilitate the generalized use of skills.
  - Prepare for and assist children with normalized life experiences in their families, schools, and communities.
  - Help children and their families make smooth transitions.
  - Prevent or minimize the development of future problems or disabilities.
- Developmentally appropriate practices provide a foundation or context from which to build individualized programs of support and instruction for children with special needs.
- IEP and IFSP objectives for infants and young children should be evaluated according to their functionality, generality, instructional context, measurability, and relation between short- and long-range goals.
- Embedded learning opportunities are brief, systematic instructional interactions that focus on a child's IEP objectives in the context of naturally occurring classroom activities. They are an effective method for incorporating specialized instruction into typical preschool activities.
- Teaching play and using peer-mediated instruction can help children build skills across all development domains.
- A preschool activity schedule should maximize children's opportunities to develop new skills and practice what they have learned previously while remaining manageable and flexible.
- How activities are scheduled and organized affects the interaction between children with and without disabilities.
- Suggestions for setting up a preschool classroom include the following:
  - Organize the classroom into different, well-defined areas to accommodate different kinds of activities.
  - Locate quiet activities together, away from avenues of traffic, and locate loud activities together.
  - Equip each area with appropriate and desirable materials.
  - Locate materials where children can retrieve them without help from adults.
  - Have an open area for large-group activities.
  - Label or color code all storage areas.
  - Arrange equipment and group areas so that students can move easily from one activity to another.
  - Provide lockers or cubbies for students.

Service Delivery Options for Early Intervention

- In hospital-based programs, early intervention services are provided to low-birth-weight and other high-risk newborns in neonatal intensive care units (NICUs).
- In home-based programs, a child's parents act as the primary teachers, with regular training and guidance from a teacher or specially trained paraprofessional who visits the home.
- In center-based programs, a child goes to the center for instruction, although the parents are usually involved. Center programs allow a team of specialists to work with the child and enable the child to meet and interact with other children.
- Many programs offer the advantages of both models by combining home visits with center-based programming.
- Parents and families are the most important people in an early intervention program. They can act as advocates, participate in educational planning, observe their children's behavior, help set realistic goals, work in the classroom, and teach their children at home.

Chapter 15

Transition to Adulthood

Source: SolStock/E+/Getty Images

Learning Outcomes

After reading this chapter and completing the embedded activities, you should be able to

15.1 Compare postschool outcomes for young adults with disabilities with those of their peers without disabilities.

15.2 Define transition services as outlined in the Individuals with Disabilities Education Act, and describe components of a transition IEP.

15.3 Provide examples of evidence-based predictors and practices for improving postschool outcomes in postsecondary education.

15.4 Provide examples of evidence-based predictors and practices for improving postschool outcomes in employment.

15.5 Provide examples of evidence-based predictors and practices for improving postschool outcomes in independent living.

Featured Teacher

Michael Craig

Charles Drew Transition Center, Detroit Public Schools, Detroit, MI

Source: Andrew Craig

I have spent the majority of my career teaching students in Detroit Public Schools, and these past few years have been the most exciting. At Charles Drew Transition Center, I teach in the horticulture program, a unique vocational center for students, age 18 to 26, with moderate to severe cognitive impairments, visual impairments, hearing impairments, physical disabilities, autism, and multiple disabilities. Our goal is to teach work skills that lead to the possibility of employment, independence, and full inclusion into community life.

But our program is so much more than a work skills program! I started and now run the country's largest school market garden program, The Gardens at Drew, which serves the dual purpose of providing hands-on vocational horticulture training for students with disabilities and filling a huge void in our area of the city by providing access to fresh, locally grown produce for our school families. We provide produce for students through the school lunch program, for parents at our in-school farm stand, and for the community at large through donations to food pantries and through sales at Detroit's Food Hub, Eastern Market, and fine restaurants.

Instruction takes place in a variety of settings—in a classroom, in one of our many hoophouses, on our 3-acre farm, and throughout the rest of our campus, where we provide landscaping opportunities for learning. Students learn the entire process of hydroponic growing, from seeding plugs and inserting them into grow light units to germinate; to taking the plugs and inserting them into the hydroponic units; to harvesting, sorting, and bagging produce for delivery.

Family involvement and community engagement are keys to our success. One of our parents is a gardener and provided us with cuttings from her own fig trees. We have taken those cuttings and currently have them growing under lights in our classroom. We've created multiple lessons around these plants and purchased a food dehydrator to make healthy snacks from the resulting produce. Another parent recently toured our program and inquired about support for her church's garden. This parent happened to work at a landscape irrigation company and was able to arrange a donation of irrigation supplies and installation support for the irrigation of all our outside growing beds. This has resulted in water savings, instructional time saving, and greater productivity. Through my involvement in our Grandparents Association, there is now a large growing area for our grandparents to grow produce and have the ability to work side by side with their student family members.

I am so proud of the work we do, but I don't do it alone. It is the collaborative effort of students, families, community partners, social workers, behavior specialists, and other support staff that makes the Drew Horticulture Program the largest school market garden in the country, and, more importantly, a program in which all students, regardless of their disabilities, are able to participate and achieve.

Education, Teaching Credentials, and Experience

- *B.S., elementary education, 1993, Eastern Michigan University*
- *M.Ed., educational leadership, 2005, Wayne State University*
- *Certifications: elementary education, language arts, social science, special education (cognitive impairments), school administration, advanced master gardener*
- *27 years of teaching experience: 13 years as an elementary teacher and 14 as a special education teacher*
- *Michigan Educator of the Year, 2015*

HELPING YOUTH WITH DISABILITIES ACHIEVE the quality of life they desire as adults is the ultimate goal of special education. But transitioning from high school to the privileges and responsibilities of adulthood, a challenge for most young people, is especially difficult for youth with disabilities. Skill deficits, limited opportunities created by low expectations or discrimination, and the absence of needed supports are just some of the obstacles to successful transition to adulthood many youth with disabilities face.

What Happens When Students with Disabilities Leave High School?

Learning Outcome 15.1 Compare postschool outcomes for young adults with disabilities with those of their peers without disabilities.

Do they find work? Where do they live? Are they happy? How do their experiences compare with those of people without disabilities?

Numerous studies of graduates and leavers of secondary special education programs provide enlightening information on their experiences as young adults. The largest, most comprehensive studies of adult adjustment by youth with disabilities after they leave secondary special education programs are the two National Longitudinal Transition Studies (NLTS1 and NLTS2) funded by the U.S. Office of Special Education Programs. NLTS1 assessed and monitored changes in the lives of 8000 youths with disabilities who left U.S. secondary special education programs from 1985 through 1987. NLTS2 was a 10-year study of the experiences of a nationally representative sample of more than 11,000 youth with disabilities who were in at least seventh grade and receiving special education services in the 2000–2001 school year as they moved from secondary school into adult roles.

High School Completion

Students who do not complete high school are likely to face more difficulties in adult adjustment than those who do. Students with disabilities who do not complete high school face lower levels of employment, reduced access to postsecondary education and training opportunities, higher rates of problems involving the criminal justice system, and lower levels of community participation (Sanford et al., 2011). The graduation rate for students with disabilities is approximately 60%, significantly lower than the 80% graduation rate for the general population (Stetser & Stillwell, 2014), although dropout rates vary significantly by state and by disability category (U.S. Department of Education, 2020c). Efforts to improve school completion by students with disabilities should focus on alterable variables that correlate with lower dropout rates, such as effective academic instruction, interventions that target school engagement, helping build positive student–teacher relationships, and social skills instruction (Doren et al., 2014). See Chapter 6, *Transition: Next Year Is Now,* "It's Cool to Stay in School."

Postsecondary Education

Attending college improves the likelihood of employment, raises earning potential, and increases job satisfaction, even for those who do not earn a degree (Kang et al., 2018; Pew Research Center, 2014). Going to college is no longer a fantasy for individuals with disabilities; it is a reality occurring with greater frequency. In the 2015–2016 academic year, 19.4% of students enrolled in postsecondary education were identified with disabilities (U.S. Department of Education, 2019). Data from NLTS2 showed that enrollment in postsecondary education programs by former high school special education students more than doubled from 19% in 1990 to 46% in 2005 (Newman et al., 2010). Although increasing numbers of students with disabilities are attending college, they continue to be less likely than their peers without disabilities to enroll. Enrollment in postsecondary programs by NLTS2 participants varied widely by disability category, ranging from 29% of students with intellectual disabilities to 75% of students with hearing impairment (Newman et al., 2011).

Postsecondary education may be even more important for people with disabilities than it is for individuals without them because it significantly improves their chances of meaningful employment. Among adults with disabilities, only 10% of those who leave high school without a diploma participate in the labor force; participation increases to 17.2% for those who have completed high school and to 26.2% for those with some postsecondary education (Bureau of Labor Statistics, 2020). For individuals with disabilities who obtain a 4-year degree, participation in the labor force rises to 30.5%.

Individuals with disabilities who complete a postsecondary education—whether it is a certificate from a technical training program, a 2-year associate's degree from a community college, or a 4-year bachelor's degree—enjoy increased vocational options and greater lifetime earnings. Overall, college graduates can expect to enjoy better health, greater self-confidence, increased career options, higher level problem-solving skills, improved interpersonal relationships, and more community involvement (Madaus, 2006; Mayhew et al., 2016; Pew Research Center, 2014). They will also be less dependent on parents and governmental benefits than will individuals who do not pursue postsecondary education (Pew Research Center, 2014; Turnbull et al., 2003).

Postsecondary education options are increasing for students with significant disabilities such as intellectual disabilities, autism, and multiple disabilities. Some school districts allow dual enrollment wherein students who require special education services after 18 years of age receive the remainder of their high school education at community colleges, universities, or vocational-technical schools (Institute for Community Inclusion, 2019). These programs enable youth with moderate and severe disabilities to continue their education in a more age-appropriate learning environment and to participate in some aspects of traditional college life, including class attendance, recreation and social activities, and paid employment opportunities (Grigal et al., 2013). Most programs offer a combination of college classes, basic or functional skills classes, and job experiences. "Think College" is an organization that is working to increase and improve postsecondary education options for individuals with intellectual disabilities. Their website offers many resources, including articles, tip sheets, and a database of hundreds of postsecondary programs across the United States (https://thinkcollege.net/).

Pearson eText
Video Example 15.1
More than ever, young people with disabilities are achieving the dream of going to college. https://www.youtube.com/watch?v=n_VK7RLK9J0

Although the range and availability of services offered by colleges and universities for students with disabilities have increased greatly in recent years, graduation rates for students with disabilities remain well below those of students without disabilities (Wagner, Newman, et al., 2005).

Employment

The NLTS2 found that 57% of youth with disabilities were working for pay outside the home during the first 4 years after leaving high school compared with a 66% employment rate among same-age youth in the general population (Newman et al., 2009). Employment outside the home by students with disabilities who had completed high school (received a diploma or certification of completion) was 61% versus 41% for noncompleters. The three most common jobs held by youth with disabilities were food service worker (17%), skilled laborer (11%), and cashier (10%).

Slightly more than half (58%) of young adults with disabilities who are employed have full-time jobs. Youth with disabilities out of high school for 1 to 4 years earn an average hourly wage of $8.20 compared with $9.20 per hour earned by youth in the general population. Only 44% of working youth with disabilities receive any employment benefits such as health insurance, sick leave, or paid vacation.

Individuals with disabilities are significantly less likely to be employed, especially as they get older, compared with those without disabilities. Kang et al. (2018) reported 33% of individuals with disabilities age 16 to 64 were employed versus 77% of individuals without disabilities. Adults with intellectual, developmental, or multiple disabilities are even less likely to be employed. Exceedingly high unemployment rates for individuals with disabilities are a major factor for the persistently high poverty rates for adults with disabilities (Houtenville, 2013).

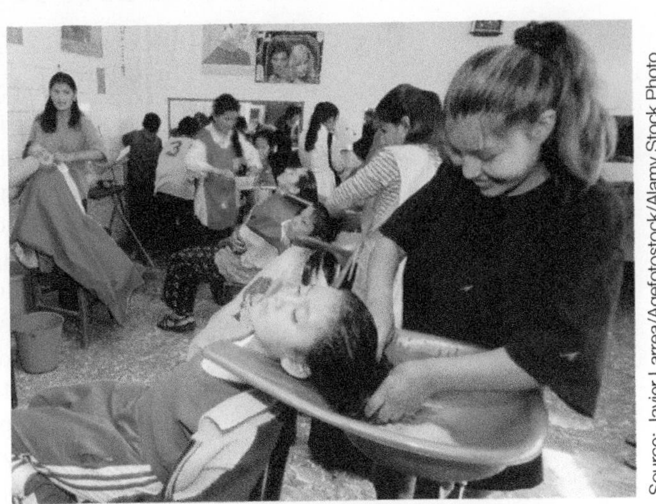
Source: Javier Larrea/Agefotostock/Alamy Stock Photo

Elena's after-school job gives her a sense of autonomy and connectedness with the community.

Community Involvement

Successful adulthood involves much more than holding a job; it also includes being an active, independent member of society. Independence for an adult includes the ability to participate in society, work, have a home, raise a family, and share the joys and responsibilities of community life (Ferguson & Ferguson, 2016). Adults with disabilities face numerous obstacles in day-to-day living that affect where and how they live, their use of community resources, and opportunities for social interaction.

Just about half (49%) of young adults in NLTS2 had participated in an organized social activity outside work or school in the preceding year, from lessons or classes outside school (22%) and a volunteer community service activity (25%), to a community group of some kind (31%). As with other postschool outcome measures, community participation varied greatly by disability, ranging from 82% of youth with visual impairments having taken part in at least one social activity to 28% of youth with intellectual disabilities.

Young adults with disabilities encounter the criminal justice system at a higher rate than same-age peers without disabilities. Overall, 28% of out-of-high-school youth in NLTS2 had been arrested, a rate more than double that of youth in the general population (12%). The percentage of out-of-high-school youth by disability category ranged from a high of 62% of those with emotional or behavioral disorders to 3% of those with orthopedic impairments.

The postschool outcomes summarized here represent improvements over findings of earlier studies (e.g., NLTS1). That's the good news. Unfortunately, far too many youth with disabilities leave high school to discover, to their dismay and discouragement, that "the fiscal and logistical demands of daily life [are] far more complex than what they learned in functional math, home-economics, or life skills classes... [and that the] protective nature of their experiences in special education had left them ill-prepared for the real world" (Knoll & Wheeler, 2005, pp. 502–503). And it is not just students with major cognitive limitations or severe physical, sensory, or behavioral disabilities who find adjusting to life after high school difficult. Youth with high-incidence disabilities face significant challenges in many aspects of adult life (Newman et al., 2011; Rojewski et al., 2014).

It is clear that many secondary students and recent school leavers with disabilities do not view themselves as ready for adulthood. Only about 60% of NLTS2 youth age 15 to 19 years reported they thought of themselves as being able to handle challenges or feeling "useful and important" (Wagner et al., 2007). Well-planned transition services can make a difference for these youth (Newman et al., 2016).

The Individuals with Disabilities Education Act and Transition Services

Learning Outcome 15.2 Define *transition services* as outlined in the Individuals with Disabilities Education Act, and describe components of a transition IEP.

Congress first included funding for transition services for youth with disabilities when it amended the Individuals with Disabilities Education Act (IDEA) in 1983 (PL 98–199). In 1984, Madeleine Will, director of the U.S. Office of Special Education and Rehabilitation Services, proposed a transition services model that encompassed three levels of service—generic, time-limited, and ongoing support—each conceptualized as a bridge from secondary special education to adult employment (Will, 1986).

Although Will's "bridges model" of school-to-work transition showed the federal government recognized the need to improve employment outcomes for individuals with disabilities, many special educators thought it was too limited. Halpern (1985) wrote that it is a mistake to focus on adult employment as the sole purpose of transition services: "Living successfully in one's community should be the primary target of transitional services" (p. 480). Halpern proposed a transition model that directed Will's generic, time-limited, and ongoing support services toward helping youth with disabilities adjust to adult life in the community in three domains: (a) quality of residential environment, (b) adequacy of social and interpersonal network, and (c) meaningful employment. Halpern's view that secondary education for students with disabilities must focus on all domains of adult functioning greatly influenced subsequent amendments to IDEA. These amendments have made transition services a central component of special education designed to achieve the national goal of "equality of opportunity, full participation, independent living, and economic self-sufficiency for individuals with disabilities" (IDEA 2004, Sec. 614[d][2][D][5]).

Transition Services

IDEA defines **transition services** as

> A coordinated set of activities for a child with a disability that is designed to be within a results-oriented process, that is focused on improving the academic and functional achievement of the child with a disability to facilitate the child's movement from school to post-school activities, including postsecondary education, vocational education, integrated employment (including supported employment), continuing and adult education, adult services, independent living, or community participation (20 USC § 1401 [602][34]).

Transition Planning

Beginning no later than the first individualized education program (IEP) to be in effect when the child is 16 years old (or 14 years old in some states) and updated annually thereafter, each child's IEP must contain the following:

1. appropriate measurable postsecondary goals based upon age-appropriate transition assessments related to training, education, employment, and, where appropriate, independent living skills;
2. transition services (including courses of study) needed to assist the child in reaching those goals (20 USC § 1401 (614) [d][1][A][8]).

This transition-focused IEP, or simply **transition IEP**, details the curricular programming and other supports to help the student transition successfully to adult life (Mazzotti et al., 2009; Szidon et al., 2015). The purpose of the transition IEP is "to ensure that all of our students step into the adult life they desire. This doesn't mean locking a student into a life plan. It means that each student will leave high school recognizing her personal strengths, knowing where to turn for support, and looking toward adult life with confidence" (Horvath, 2006, p. 603).

Developing the Transition IEP

IDEA 2004 and the regulations governing its implementation require IEP teams to follow a specific transition planning process (Figure 15.1).

AGE-APPROPRIATE TRANSITION ASSESSMENT Age-appropriate transition assessment is the all-important initial and ongoing component of transition planning. The purpose is to help the student answer the following questions (NSTTAC, 2013):

HLP4 Use multiple sources of information to develop a comprehensive understanding of a student's strengths and needs.

- What are my talents and interests?
- What do I want in life, now and in the future?
- What are some of life's demands that I can meet now?
- What are the main barriers to getting what I want from school and my community?
- What are my options in the school and community for preparing me for what I want to do, now and in the future?

The transition IEP team should use a combination of formal and informal assessment methods to determine the student's strengths, needs, preferences, and interests in current and future work, education, domestic, and social environments.

Informal assessments include interviews, direct observations, anecdotal records, curriculum-based assessments, interest inventories, preference assessments, and job-site evaluations. Formal measures include standardized assessments of adaptive behavior, independent living, academic skills, interests, preferences, career development, and self-determination.

FIGURE 15.1 Steps in the Transition-Planning Process

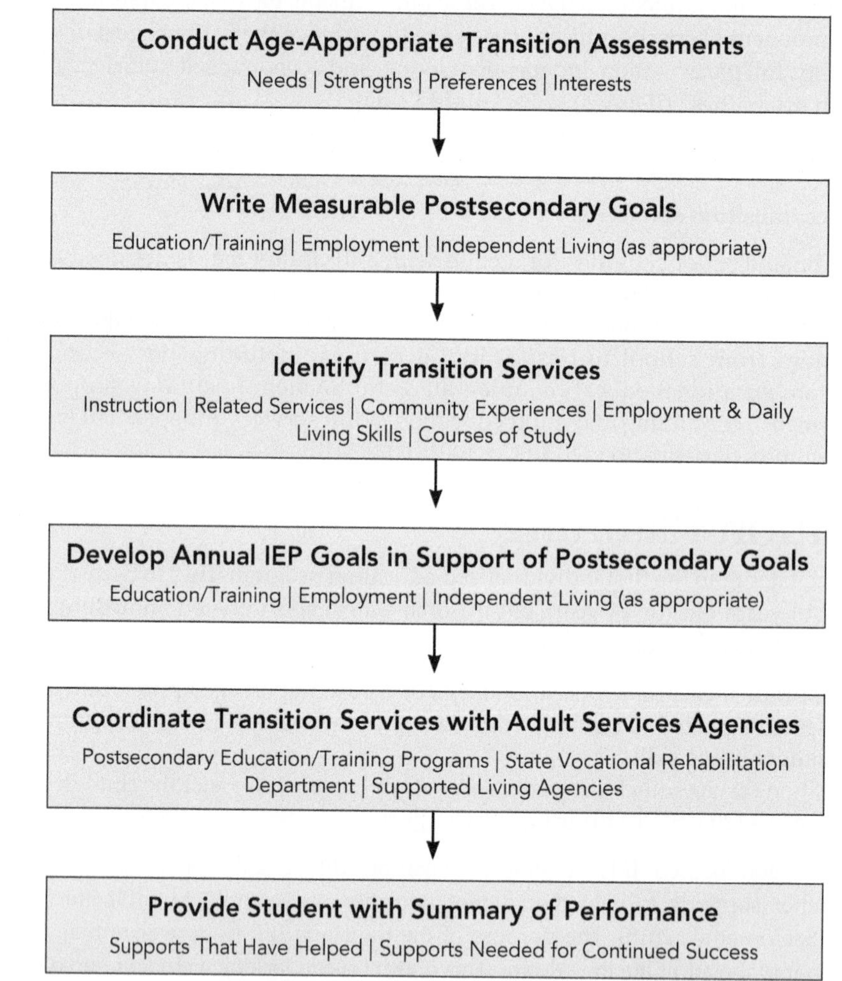

Conduct Age-Appropriate Transition Assessments
Needs | Strengths | Preferences | Interests
Write Measurable Postsecondary Goals
Education/Training | Employment | Independent Living (as appropriate)
Identify Transition Services
Instruction | Related Services | Community Experiences | Employment & Daily Living Skills | Courses of Study
Develop Annual IEP Goals in Support of Postsecondary Goals
Education/Training | Employment | Independent Living (as appropriate)
Coordinate Transition Services with Adult Services Agencies
Postsecondary Education/Training Programs | State Vocational Rehabilitation Department | Supported Living Agencies
Provide Student with Summary of Performance
Supports That Have Helped | Supports Needed for Continued Success

Source: Adapted from the Center for Change in Transition Services, Seattle University, and Mazzotti et al. (2009).

The Transition Assessment and Goal Generator (TAGG; Martin et al., 2015) is a norm-referenced online assessment tool for secondary students with mild to moderate disabilities who have postsecondary education or employment goals (or both). There are three versions of TAGG, to be completed by the student (grade 4.8 reading level), family members (reading level 5.7), and professionals (reading level 10.4), respectively. Items derive from research-identified indicators of postsecondary education and employment in eight constructs: strengths and limits, disability awareness, persistence, interacting with others, goal setting and attainment, employment, student involvement in IEP, and support community. Users may read, listen to audio recordings, or watch American Sign Language videos of the TAGG instructions and items. The TAGG automatically builds a graphic profile of results across constructs by users, a summary statement, lists of strengths and needs, and suggested IEP annual transition goals matched to Common Core State Standards. Greene (2018) provides a list of several age-appropriate transition assessments (with URLs to access related resources) across several domains (e.g., academic, self-determination, health care).

HLP11 Identify and prioritize long- and short-term learning goals.

MEASURABLE POSTSECONDARY GOALS Postsecondary goals are "generally understood to refer to those goals that a child hopes to achieve after leaving secondary school (i.e., high school)" (IDEA 2004 Part B Regulations, §300.320[b]).

IDEA requires that each student's IEP contain at least one postsecondary goal in education or training; one in employment; and, when appropriate for the student, one in independent living (i.e., life skills in the following domains: leisure/recreation, home and personal care, and community participation).

FIGURE 15.2 Postsecondary Goals for Three High School Students

Student	Education/Training	Employment	Independent Living
Allison—18-year-old student with learning disabilities	Allison will obtain a 4-year degree from a liberal arts college with a major in child development.	After college, Allison will be employed in the field of early childhood education.	N/A
Jodi—17-year-old student with mild intellectual disabilities	The fall after high school, Jodi will attend the Customer Service Representative course offered through the Pathways to Employment program at Central Piedmont Community College.	Within 3 months after graduation, Jodi will be competitively employed, working 20 or more hours, in the retail industry with time-limited supports of a job coach.	After high school, Jodi will assume responsibility for a share of living expenses by saving money earned at work and following a budget set by Jodi and her parents.
Kevin—18-year old student with significant intellectual disabilities; plans to stay in school until age 21 years to obtain 3 more years of services	Immediately after graduation, Kevin will participate in habilitative and functional skill training through CAP services and will attend courses designed to provide specialized academic, functional, and occupational preparation for individuals with disabilities (two times per week) at the community college.	Within 3 months of graduation, Kevin will obtain a supported employment position that allows him to work to his maximum stamina and incorporates the use of assistive technology.	Immediately following graduation, Kevin will participate in one to two age-appropriate community and individual community-based activities per week related to horticulture, socialization with young adults, animals, and music.

Source: Adapted from *National Technical Assistance Center on Transition (NTACT): Student Case Study Examples & Non-Examples*. Charlotte: University of North Carolina, National Technical Assistance Center on Transition. Available at https://transitionta.org/transitionplanning

A measurable postsecondary goal must contain a time frame, a clear behavior, and a situation. For example, "The summer after leaving high school, Lynn will obtain a part-time position working in a pet store." Figure 15.2 shows examples of postsecondary goals for three students: Allison, Jodi, and Kevin.

Parent and family involvement, important throughout a student's transition from school to adult life, is particularly helpful during assessment and determining of postsecondary goals (Ankeny et al., 2009; Cavendish et al., 2017).

Person-centered planning, which entails a variety of strategies and activities for determining the desires, concerns, hopes, and dreams of individuals with disabilities and their families, can be an excellent way to engage students and families in the transition process (e.g., Mazzotti et al., 2015; Michaels & Ferrara, 2005).

COURSES OF STUDY An important part of transition planning is identifying the type of course work students will need in high school to help them best prepare for their postsecondary goals. A student whose postsecondary education goal is to major in biology at a 4-year university is likely going to need different coursework in high school than a student who is planning to obtain an associate's degree in welding. In some states, different types of course work will lead to different types of exit documents (e.g., certificates, diplomas), so IEP teams should incorporate graduation goals into their planning as well.

Pearson eText
Video Example 15.2
Students who lead their own IEP meetings learn to be self-advocates.

TRANSITION SERVICES AND ACTIVITIES The services section of the transition IEP describes a coordinated set of transition-related strategies and activities in the areas of instruction, employment, community experiences, independent living, related services, and, if necessary, daily living and functional vocational assessment. For each postsecondary goal, the IEP team identifies at least one instructional strategy, experience, or activity to assist the student in reaching it. For instance, Mazzotti and colleagues (2009) described the following transition services to support a student's postsecondary goals of completing a welding course and gaining a job as an entry-level welder: job safety instruction, community-based experiences related to automotive construction, and work experience with a local welder. The IEP team must also identify the person or agency responsible for implementing each service and the timeline for these responsibilities.

Pearson eText
Video Example 15.3
Important transition activities are as varied as students' goals—from job shadowing to grocery shopping to trying on a sweatshirt while visiting a community college.

Answers to questions such as the following should guide decisions about transition services and activities (Cavendish et al., 2017; Flexer et al., 2013; Grossi, 2013; Sitlington et al., 2010; Test, 2012; Wehman & Kregel, 2020):

- What are the student's strengths? How can the student build on those strengths to facilitate a successful transition?
- What skills does the student need to develop or improve to make progress toward postsecondary goals?
- Will the student seek a regular high school diploma? If so, what course of study and proficiency tests are required?
- Is the student likely to remain in high school through the maximum age of eligibility for special education services? If so, what curriculum and experiences will be needed after age 18?
- In what school and community activities will the student participate?
- Has the student expressed interest in a particular kind of work or career? If not, what can the team do to help her explore career possibilities and discover her aptitudes and preferences?
- What supports in the student's current and future environments are necessary for the desired postschool outcomes to become reality?
- What evidence exists for the services and interventions we are recommending?

ANNUAL IEP GOALS For each postsecondary goal, there must be at least one supporting annual IEP goal. Figure 15.3 shows IEP goals supporting the postsecondary goals for Allison, Jodi, and Kevin. IEP goals can be linked to more than one postsecondary goal. For example, Allison's IEP goal to improve her algebra skills supports her postsecondary goals of attending college and obtaining a job in early childhood education.

HLP1 Collaborate with professionals to increase student success.

COLLABORATION AND COORDINATION Interdisciplinary teaming and interagency collaboration are vital to planning and delivering effective transition services for secondary students (Povenmire-Kirk et al., 2018).

Successful, seamless transition requires the coordination, delivery, and transfer of services from the secondary school program to receiving agencies (e.g., employers, postsecondary education programs, residential service providers). Although work-study and vocational training programs for students with disabilities and vocational rehabilitation services for adults with disabilities have long existed in every state, systematic communication and coordination of services among schools and community-based adult service agencies are relatively new phenomena with varying degrees of success from state to state and community to community.

Although interagency cooperation is critical to successful transition, IDEA gives special education the ultimate responsibility for implementing transition goals and activities. Secondary special educators play key roles in the lives of transition-age students with disabilities. Teachers such as Michael Craig (this chapter's Featured Teacher) serve as role models and mentors, help youth with disabilities successfully complete high school, connect them to the world of work, and encourage self-directed decision making (Lindstrom et al., 2011).

SUMMARY OF PERFORMANCE IDEA requires that a summary of performance (SOP) be provided to each student who exits special education services by graduation or by exceeding the age of eligibility. The SOP describes the student's academic achievement and functional

FIGURE 15.3 Annual IEP Goals Aligned with Postsecondary Goals Shown in Figure 15.2

Student	Annual IEP Goal
Allison—18-year-old student with learning disabilities	Allison will develop algebra skills, as measured by her homework completion and quiz scores, by using a planner to record assignments, prepare questions for class, and record formulas for study in the Algebra II course during her senior year. This is an appropriate transition-related IEP goal because • developing algebra skills in her Algebra II course is consistent with Allison's post-secondary goal of attending a four-year liberal arts university; and • Allison's employment goal is contingent upon her completion of college; therefore, annual goals that support her college completion also support her employment goal.
Jodi—17-year-old student with mild intellectual disabilities	Given explicit instruction on balancing a checkbook, Jodi will demonstrate how to write a check, make checking account deposits and withdrawals, and balance a checkbook, four out of six opportunities during the duration of her IEP. This is an appropriate transition-related IEP goal because • it focuses directly on Jodi's postsecondary goal of sharing living expenses and following a budget.
Kevin—18-year-old student with significant intellectual disabilities	Given the GoTalk20+ augmentative communication device and weekly community practice, Kevin will independently use the device to communicate a desire for an item in community settings, including restaurants and ticket counters, using single words with 80% accuracy. This is an appropriate transition-related IEP goal because • Kevin is not able to use a GoTalk20+ effectively, and learning to do so will prepare him to participate in a habilitative and vocational training program, recreational opportunities, and educational opportunities after high school; • learning to use a GoTalk20+ effectively will prepare Kevin to incorporate assistive technology use in future employment; and • communicating choices will prepare Kevin for the goal of participating in leisure activities that interest him.

Source: Adapted from *National Technical Assistance Center on Transition (NTACT): Student Case Study Examples & Non-Examples*. Charlotte: University of North Carolina, National Technical Assistance Center on Transition. Available at https://transitionta.org/transitionplanning.

performance; makes specific recommendations of what the student should do to continue progressing toward his or her goals; and identifies the kinds of community-based education or training, vocational, and independent living agencies and services that may have a role in helping the student achieve those goals.

As with every step of transition planning, students should take an active role in developing their SOPs (Morgan et al., 2017). Students who work with their IEP teams to identify which supports and services have been most helpful and which ones will most likely be needed from adult agencies after they leave school may be more able to self-advocate for services.

Evidence-Based Predictors and Practices

Learning Outcome 15.3 Provide examples of evidence-based predictors and practices for improving postschool outcomes in postsecondary education.

Evidence-based practices in secondary transition fall into two broad categories: (a) predictors—features of schools and programs that predict improved postschool outcomes, and (b) practices—classroom-level interventions determined to be effective for secondary youth with disabilities (Haber et al., 2016; Mazzotti et al., 2016; Test et al., 2015). Effective

TABLE 15.1 Predictors for successful transition

PREDICTOR	POSTSECONDARY EDUCATION	EMPLOYMENT	INDEPENDENT LIVING
Career Awareness	✓	✓	
Community Experiences		✓	
Decision Making	✓	✓	
Goal Setting	✓	✓	
High School Diploma		✓	
Inclusion in General Education	✓	✓	✓
Interagency Collaboration	✓	✓	
Occupational Courses	✓	✓	
Parent Expectations	✓	✓	✓
Parental Involvement		✓	
Program of Study		✓	
Self-Determination	✓	✓	
Self-Care	✓	✓	✓
Social Skills	✓	✓	
Student Support	✓	✓	✓
Transition Program	✓	✓	
Travel Skills		✓	
Vocational Education	✓	✓	
Work Experience	✓	✓	✓
Work Study		✓	

Source: Adapted from *National Technical Assistance Center on Transition (NTACT): Post-school Success*. Charlotte: University of North Carolina, National Technical Assistance Center on Transition. Available at https://www.transitionta.org/postschool.

transition planning relies on both! Fortunately, as illustrated in Tables 15.1 and 15.2, these predictors and practices often positively affect more than one skill or postschool outcome area, so they are a good investment. Table 15.1 summarizes the predictors and the postschool outcome areas for which they predict improvement. Table 15.2 shows the practices and skills they target, some of which have been addressed in earlier chapters, as they reflect principles of effective instruction and high-leverage practices across skills, settings, and ages. As such, a practice not identified as "evidence-based" for a given outcome area or target skill may still be quite effective. Teachers should use professional wisdom and student data to determine whether or not to adopt and then continue using a practice.

Postsecondary Education

PREDICTORS Students with disabilities are more likely to enroll in postsecondary education if they have had inclusive experiences (i.e., general education curriculum in regular classrooms), work experience, and other career-related experiences. Instruction in high school should focus on self-determination skills (including self-advocacy, goal setting, and decision making), academic skills, independent living skills, and social skills (Rowe et al., 2015).

Finally, transition to postsecondary education is more probable when students have support—a "network of people (e.g., family, friends, educators, and adult service providers) who provide services and resources in multiple environments to prepare students to obtain their annual transition and postsecondary goals aligned with their preferences, interests, and needs" (Rowe et al., 2015, p. 123).

PRACTICES Given the importance of strong academic skills for transition to postsecondary education, secondary teachers should prioritize instruction in these skills for students planning to go on to college. This includes providing them with an increasingly rigorous curriculum as they progress through school and employing effective teaching practices described throughout this book—especially explicit instruction and strategy instruction.

TABLE 15.2 Evidence-based practices for secondary students

PRACTICE	MATH	READING	SCIENCE	SOCIAL STUDIES	FUNCTIONAL/ DAILY LIVING SKILLS	JOB SKILLS	STUDENT INVOLVEMENT IN THE IEP	GENERAL GOAL ATTAINMENT	DROPOUT PREVENTION
Anchored Instruction	✓								
Chaining					✓				
Check and Connect							✓		✓
Community-based Instruction					✓				
Computer-assisted Instruction						✓			
Direct Instruction		✓							
Graduated Sequence of Instruction	✓								
Graphic Organizers and Concept Mapping		✓	✓	✓					
Mnemonics and Strategy Instruction	✓	✓	✓						
One-more-than Strategy					✓				
Peer-assisted Instruction	✓	✓	✓	✓					
Prompting Techniques					✓	✓			
Published Curricula (e.g., Self-Directed IEP)							✓		
Repeated Reading		✓							
Schema-based Instruction	✓								
Self-Determined Model of Instruction								✓	
Self-management Instruction	✓	✓			✓				
Simulations					✓				
Structured Inquiry			✓						
Time Delay Procedures			✓		✓	✓			
Touch Math	✓								
Video Modeling					✓				

Source: Adapted from *National Technical Assistance Center on Transition (NTACT): Effective Practices and Predictors*. Charlotte: University of North Carolina, National Technical Assistance Center on Transition. Available at https://www.transitionta.org/effectivepractices.

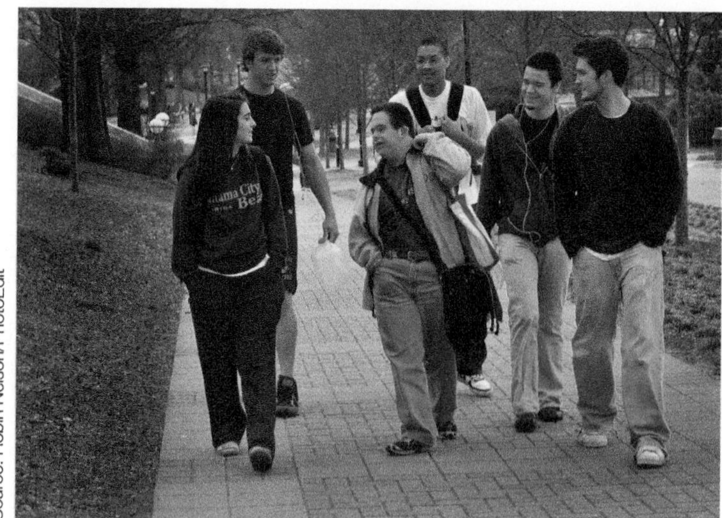
Source: Robin Nelson/PhotoEdit

Attending college is an attainable post-secondary goal for many students with disabilities.

Indeed, all of the practices listed in Table 15.2 can be enhanced when the teacher provides explicit instruction, arranges multiple opportunities for students to practice with immediate feedback, and equips students with learning strategies to move them toward independence.

In addition, students transitioning to postsecondary education need a range of other skills. For instance, good social skills are critical for success, not only in college but at work and in every area of adult life as well (Clark et al., 2018; Clark et al., 2019; Gear et al., 2011; Jantz, 2011). Wenzel and Rowley (2010) describe a semester-long course that helps college students with Asperger syndrome learn critical social skills for survival and success on campus.

HLP9 Teach social behaviors.

Students should receive instruction in and opportunities to practice self-determination skills, such as goal setting, planning, self-management, and self-advocacy as well. This includes practice in identifying themselves as a student with a disability, learning about which accommodations and supports they need for academic success in high school, and practice requesting these supports at the postsecondary level.

TEACHING & LEARNING

When Secondary Students Can't Read

Preparing students for postsecondary education—and life in general—includes ensuring they become readers. Students who are not proficient readers are more likely to drop out of high school (Carlson, 2013), interact with the juvenile justice system (Pyle et al., 2016), and have challenges in all areas of life (e.g., health, employment; DeWalt et al., 2004). Once students begin to struggle with reading, over time, their reading skills may weaken even further because they avoid reading. Certainly, early intervention is critical for reading, but we should not give up on older students who did not acquire fundamental reading skills in the early years. Evidence suggests with appropriate intervention, older students can improve their reading skills (Solis et al., 2014).

HLP14 Teach cognitive and metacognitive strategies to support learning and independence.

Components of Effective Reading Instruction for Secondary Students Research on teaching older students who struggle with reading indicates teachers should do the following (Hougen, 2014; Kim et al., 2017; Solis et al., 2014):

- Teach both decoding and comprehension strategies. For decoding, instruction should focus on strategies for attacking multi-syllabic words. Comprehension strategies include summarizing, paraphrasing, self-questioning, and self-monitoring.
- Use explicit instruction, including modeling, frequent practice, and feedback.
- Provide frequent opportunities to read and use reading material that builds background knowledge and supports vocabulary and content learning (e.g., science, social studies).
- Make deliberate efforts to engage and motivate students. This includes finding reading material that is personally relevant to the students.
- Do not give up! Instruction must be intensive and persistent. It may take several years for an older student to catch up.

What About Students with Significant Disabilities? All students should receive access to reading instruction and literacy opportunities. There is a growing body of evidence that students with intellectual disabilities can learn a range of literacy skills and access the general education curriculum when given explicit instruction, adapted texts, assistive technology, and other supports (Knight et al., 2018; Spooner & Browder, 2015).

Certainly, reading skills that help students with intellectual disabilities access the general curriculum are important; however, such instruction should not take place at the expense of functional skills. For example, youth with disabilities should learn functional reading skills, such as how to evaluate the credibility of information presented on a Web page when they are navigating the Internet (Delgado et al., 2019), how to read words (and their meanings) associated with their job or place of employment (Storey & Miner, 2017), and how to apply the range of literacy skills needed to grocery shop (Douglas et al., 2018).

Beyond academic and functional skills, older students should also be given opportunities to learn that reading is a leisure skill and can be a vehicle for social engagement. The Next Chapter Book Club (Next Chapter Book Club, 2019) is an example of a structured activity that promotes literacy, community inclusion, and social connectedness for individuals with intellectual disabilities. A small group of individuals with intellectual disabilities and two volunteer facilitators gather in a local bookstore or café to read and discuss a book. Members take turns reading aloud, while the others follow along. NCBC members choose the book they want to read and decide how they want to run their club, which also gives members opportunities to practice self-determination and self-advocacy.

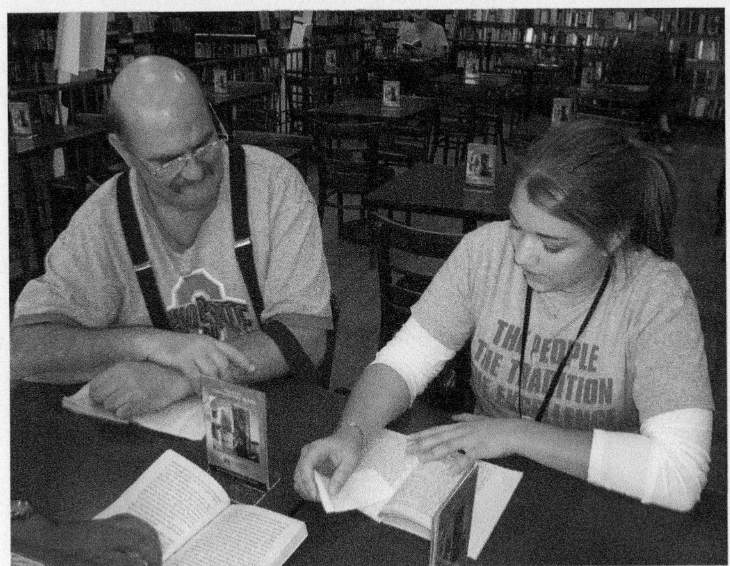

Source: Tom Fish

Volunteer facilitators use a variety of strategies to help Next Chapter Book Club members enjoy reading.

Many college students, with and without disabilities, use high-tech tools to help them find success. High school teachers should prepare students for transition by using evidence-based practices, such as explicit instruction, to teach students to use such tools. Francis et al. (2018) describe 10 apps high school teachers can use to support transition to college. These apps cover five important domains—academic, social, independent living, executive function, and mental health—all of which are essential for postsecondary education. See Chapter 11, *Transition: Next Year Is Now,* "Self-Management Tools for Adult Success."

Employment

Learning Outcome 15.4 Provide examples of evidence-based predictors and practices for improving postschool outcomes in employment.

Individuals with disabilities who have jobs report a higher quality of life than their unemployed counterparts (Lindsay et al., 2018). Besides economic benefits, work offers opportunities for social interaction and skill enhancement, and builds a sense of pride and self-satisfaction.

All young adults face important questions about what to do with their lives—attend college or technical school, work as a bricklayer or an accountant—but for people without disabilities, answering those questions involves choosing from a number of options. By contrast, young adults with disabilities typically have fewer options. Occupational choices decrease when the person with disabilities has limited skills; they decrease even more

Source: William L. Heward

Comprehensive transition services and activities helped Tyler Lewis obtain and keep a job he loves.

because of the nature of the disability and diminish still further because of employers' prejudices and misconceptions about people with disabilities. For most adults with disabilities, obtaining and holding a job are major life challenges and goals.

PREDICTORS Most importantly, experiences in high school must include opportunities to engage in work-related activities (Storey, 2019). This includes developing students' career awareness, providing access to occupational courses, and giving students real work experiences (e.g., internships, job shadowing). Other predictors include community experiences, access to general education curriculum and regular classrooms, parent involvement, interagency collaboration, and student support networks. To improve employment outcomes, instruction should focus on academic skills, self-determination, independent living skills, and social skills (Rowe et al., 2015). Additionally, the curriculum must stress functional skills; that is, students must learn skills actually needed by employers (Swedeen et al., 2010). Many employers who hire young adults with disabilities view instruction of academic skills as "minimally important" (Moon et al., 2011). Students with disabilities must also receive ample opportunities to learn the social and interpersonal skills expected of employees in integrated work sites (Gear et al., 2011; Hughes et al., 2008). Finally, community-based work experience and job skills instruction should begin as early as age 10 years for students with severe disabilities and occur for progressively extended periods as students near graduation. Research shows a positive correlation between paid work experiences during the last 2 years of high school and postschool employment and total earnings (e.g., Carter et al., 2011; Mazzotti et al., 2013).

Pearson eText
Video Example 15.4
Students benefit from both paid and unpaid work experiences.

PRACTICES Designing work-based experiences is critical for setting the stage for successful transition to employment, but what happens in these experiences—and the role of the teacher or transition specialist—is just as important. While on community work sites, students should receive explicit instruction on specific job skills, ways to increase production rates, and transportation to and from employment sites.

Students should experience community jobs that match their vocational interests. Martin et al. (2008) describe how a 17-year-old student with moderate intellectual disabilities used vocational assessment software to select an entry-level job he would like to observe or try. The process includes choice making, planning, trying out a job, and evaluating the experience.

Although students should train and work in the community whenever possible so they learn "the communication, behavior, dress and other codes critical for success in integrated environments ... [and] to get to and from important places on time or to produce consistently" (Brown et al., 1999, p. 6), classroom-based simulation training can be an effective supplement (Lattimore et al., 2006). For example, a student who has a job folding towels at a local gym would likely benefit not only from on-the-job training and support but also from classroom practice folding towels and other skills needed for success on the job.

Developing and operating a school-based business enterprise can help high school students learn functional academic, work, problem-solving, and social skills. Lindstrom et al. (1997) describe four school-based businesses that students with disabilities in several high schools in Oregon helped develop and operate: an espresso and baked-goods bar, a take-out meals operation, a mail-order seed business, and a winter produce garden. Students in Featured Teacher Michael Craig's horticulture program help run a market garden, which allows them to practice a range of skills needed for postsecondary success. See *Transition: Next Year Is Now,* "Sowing Seeds for Successful Transition: The Gardens at Drew."

Pearson eText
Video Example 15.5
"It's all about learning on the job." https://www.youtube.com/watch?v=7kn6MT-hf_w

Secondary students with moderate and severe disabilities should also spend an increasing amount of time experiencing and receiving instruction at actual community job sites. Regardless of setting, instruction in employment skills should be explicit and should include prompting procedures, such as least-to-most prompting (e.g., Riesen & Jameson, 2018) and systematic time-delay methods (e.g., Horn et al., 2019). Prompts should be gradually faded as students acquire more proficiency with the targeted skills.

CAREER EDUCATION: A K–12 JOURNEY Researchers have developed numerous models for employment-related transition services (e.g., Kochhar-Bryant & Greene, 2009; Martin et al., 2008; Sitlington et al., 2010; Wehman & Kregel, 2020). Each of these models stresses the importance of career education at an early age, students choosing goals, a functional secondary school curriculum that includes real work experiences in integrated job sites, systematic coordination between schools and adult service providers, and parental involvement and support. As you have seen throughout this book in the *Transition: Next Year Is Now* feature, transition-focused planning is relevant for all children with exceptionalities and their families and should begin early.

The Council for Exceptional Children's Division on Career Development and Transition recommends beginning career development and transition services for children with disabilities in the elementary grades (Blalock et al., 2003). Developing career awareness and vocational skills early does not mean placing 8-year-old children on job sites for training. Appropriate work-related curriculum and instructional objectives should be selected at each age level (Cease-Cook et al., 2015; Wandry et al., 2013; Wehman, 2011). For example, elementary school students might sample different types of jobs through classroom responsibilities such as watering plants, cleaning chalkboards, or taking messages to the office. Middle school students should begin to spend time at actual community job sites, with an increasing amount of in-school instruction devoted to the development of associated work skills, such as following a schedule, staying on task, and adjusting to changes in plans (Wehman & Kregel, 2020). Figure 15.4 shows examples of transition-related curriculum activities in the domestic, community, leisure, and vocational domains that might be incorporated into a student's IEP across the span from elementary school through high school.

COMPETITIVE EMPLOYMENT Virtually all special educators who have studied the transition of secondary special education students to adult life believe that improving competitive employment outcomes will require significant curriculum revisions and improved coordination of school and adult vocational habilitation services (e.g., Flexer et al., 2013; Sitlington et al., 2010; Wehman, 2011a). Federal law defines **competitive employment** as

FIGURE 15.4 Examples of Transition-Related Curriculum Activities Across Grade Levels

	DOMESTIC	COMMUNITY	LEISURE	VOCATIONAL
Elementary	• Grooming • Put away clean clothes • Keep room uncluttered • Feed pet • Clear table • Dust • Vacuum • Answer telephone • Make bed • Make sandwich	• Buy nutritious snack • Use proper table etiquette • Learn to make emergency calls • Open bank account	• Play video games • Take turns • Practice conversational skills (i.e., listening, subject matter etc.) • Share • Make friends • Ride bike • Play little league sport	• Make choices • Tell time • Complete assignment on time • Wait calmly • Show concern for others • Introduce self to others • Answer telephone • Ask for permission to leave table
Middle school	• Take care of personal clothes • Straighten bathroom after use • Use microwave oven to prepare simple meal • Wash and clean inside of car • Sweep floors • Water plants • Take phone messages • Learn emergency and first aid procedures	• Make small personal purchases • Deposit money in bank account • Cross street with stop light	• Attend dance class • Take swimming lessons • Join club • Search the internet • Attend event out with a friend	• Set a schedule • Follow a schedule • Set alarm clock • Introduce others • Remain calm if plans are altered • Keep a to do list • Organize paperwork • Stay focused on tasks
High school	• Handle family laundry • Prepare more complicated meals • Initiate and do things that have to be done • Fix and maintain things (e.g., replace lightbulbs, clean coffeemaker) • Auto care (e.g., gas, oil) • Lawn maintenance	• Shop for week's groceries • Learn how to solve problems (e.g., lodge complaints) • Comparison shop • Balance bank statement • Control impulse buying	• Volunteer • Go to school sports events • Shop with friends • Go out to eat with friends • Hang out at friend's house • Go on a date • Make new friends	• Perform patient transport duties at hospital • Perform stocking at large retailer • Perform food preparation at hotel restaurant

Source: Table courtesy of Paul Wehman (2011a).

work in a competitive labor market on a full- or part-time basis in an integrated setting that earns at or above the federal minimum wage, but not less than the customary wage and level of benefits paid by the employer for the same or similar work performed by individuals who are not disabled (Workforce Innovation and Opportunity Act, 2014).

Supported Employment. Supported employment helps adults with severe disabilities, who have historically been unemployed or restricted to sheltered settings, earn real wages for real work. Supported employment means

> (i) Competitive employment in an integrated setting with ongoing support services for individuals with the most severe disabilities—(A) For whom competitive employment has not traditionally occurred or for whom competitive employment has been interrupted or intermittent as a result of a severe disability; and (B) Who, because of the nature and severity of their disability, need intensive supported employment services from the designated State unit and extended services after transition in order to perform this work; or (ii) Transitional employment for individuals with the most severe disabilities due to mental illness. (34 *CFR* 363.6 [c][2][iv])

Supported employment has grown rapidly since its inception. In 1986, fewer than 10,000 individuals were working in federally assisted supported employment demonstration projects in 20 states. Just 2 years later, the supported employment movement had grown to a total of 32,342 participants nationally; the cumulative wages these workers earned grew from $1.4 million to $12.4 million in the 15 states that reported earnings data (Wehman et al., 1989). In 2009, 117,638 people with disabilities were working through supported employment (Braddock et al., 2011). Supported employees earned more than $750 million in annual wages in 1995, many becoming taxpayers for the first time in their lives. Vermont's supported employees earned an average hourly wage of $8.59 in 2009 (Braddock et al., 2011). A statewide study in Maryland found that average weekly earnings of individuals placed in supported employment was 3.5 times greater than the earnings of individuals in sheltered work environments ($134.33 compared with weekly wages of $40.69) (Conley, 2003; see also the Association for Persons in Supported Employment's website).

The success of supported employment depends in large part on job development—the identification and creation of community-based employment opportunities for individuals with disabilities (Griffin et al., 2007)—and adoption of a "place then train" rather than a "train then place" model (Wehman et al., 2018, p. 133). Given that individuals with disabilities are more likely to struggle with generalization of skills to new contexts, allowing individuals to learn on the job improves their chances of success.

Effective supported employment also relies on an **employment specialist**. The employment specialist is key to making a supported work program effective. Sometimes called a *job coach* or *employment consultant*, the employment specialist is a community-based professional who works in a nonprofit job placement program, a public vocational or adult services program, or a secondary special education program.

In a typical supported employment program, the employment specialist serves as the primary source of support for the employee with disabilities. Although the job coach gradually reduces the level of direct, onsite training and support, this model of outside assistance has several inherent drawbacks (Mank et al., 1998; Simmons & Flexer, 2013; Trach, 2008):

- The arrival and presence of the job coach can disrupt the natural work setting.
- The supported employee may perform differently in the presence of the job coach.
- The job coach's presence can limit interactions between the supported employee and co-workers without disabilities.
- It is difficult for an employment specialist to be sensitive to the changing demands of a job over time.

Source: Amelie-Benoist/BSIP/AGE Fotostock

Employment specialists provide supports that enable people with significant disabilities to do real work for real pay.

- The cost for an employment specialist who must travel to the job site is higher and the efficiency of the approach is lower than one that takes advantage of the natural interactions of co-workers.
- Given an always-on-call job coach, employers and co-workers may be less inclined to figure out and implement natural solutions to problems.
- Problem solving by the job coach may work against the supported employee's learning to solve problems and assume responsibility for her performance.

Natural Supports. The role of the employment specialist has evolved from one of primary supporter for the employee with disabilities to one of working with the employer and co-workers to help identify, develop, and facilitate typical or indigenous supports of the workplace. Rogan et al. (1993) define natural supports as "any assistance, relationships or interactions that allow a person to secure or maintain a community job ... in a way that corresponds to the typical work routines and social interactions of other employees" (p. 275). Figure 15.5 provides descriptions of seven categories of natural supports identified by Rogan (1996).

FIGURE 15.5 Seven Types of Natural Supports for Assisting a Person with Disabilities to Obtain and Maintain a Job

Organizational supports involve the preparation and organization of activities in the job setting, including, but not limited to, scheduling, order of tasks, and locations of materials. Supported employment professionals may be uneasy requesting such supports from employers, but the reality is that employers provide similar accommodations regularly to employees without disabilities. Examples include:

- All necessary supplies are moved to a storage area accessible to the supported employee.
- The supervisor adjusts the supported employee's schedule to accommodate the public bus schedule. For example, Brad needs wheelchair-accessible transportation to get to and from work. The paratransit system is unreliable on the weekends, so his supervisor excuses him from weekend shifts.
- The supervisor works with the employment consultant to carve out job responsibilities that will be most appropriate for the supported employee.

Physical supports involve the design and function of physical objects and equipment in a job setting, whether technical or nontechnical. These supports can range from the simplest jig to specialized computer equipment. Examples include:

- Greg's boss purchases mail pouches, which he attaches to Greg's wheelchair every morning. Greg collects recyclables in the pouches.
- The supported employee purchases an augmentative communication device through vocational rehabilitation.

Social supports involve interactions with other individuals. Although social supports often include individuals in the work environment, they can involve individuals from any environment that affects the supported employee's outcomes at work. Examples include:

- With help from the supervisor, John's employment consultant identifies a coworker who has similar interests with John and requests that the coworker take breaks with John occasionally.
- A neighbor gives the supported employee a ride to and from work.

Training supports involve the extension of personal competence and skill through direct training and instruction. The most common training support used in supported employment is direct training by a job coach. Examples of other training supports include:

- A coworker receives consultation from an employment specialist on suggested training activities and then provides training to the supported employee.
- A supported employee shadows a coworker performing the job that she is to perform.

Social service supports involve accessing professional and nonprofessional disability-related services. Examples include:

- The supported employee uses Social Security Plan for Achieving Self-Support (PASS) to pay for transportation to and from work.
- A residential service provider assists the supported employee in finding an apartment near a bus line.

Community supports involve accessing community agencies and services that are available to all individuals. Examples include:

- The supported employee uses public transportation to get to and from work.
- The supported employee takes adult education courses to upgrade his skills.

Personal and family supports involve accessing family and personal resources. These supports often fall into another category, but the category itself is important as a reminder that a supported employee and his or her family or personal network often hold the answers to addressing many of the support needs that are identified. Examples include:

- The supported employee joins a self-advocacy group to learn to better advocate for herself at work.
- Family members provide employment referrals to the job seeker and the job developer.

Source: Adapted from Trach, J. S. (2008). Natural supports in the workplace and beyond. In F. R. Rusch (Ed.), *Beyond high school: Preparing adolescents for tomorrow's challenges* (2nd ed., pp. 259–261). Reproduced by permission of Pearson Education, Inc., Upper Saddle River, NJ.

Natural Cues and Self-Management. The belief that employees with disabilities should be taught independence in the workplace has gained widespread acceptance among supported employment professionals and spawned exciting and promising research in the use of natural cues and self-management. A natural cue is an existing feature of the work environment the employee can see, hear, touch, or smell and use as a signal for what to do next (Inge & Moon, 2006). For example, clocks or whistles may signal it is time to go to a job station, co-workers' stopping work and leaving the job station might be the prompt for break time, and a growing pile of dirty dishes should cue an increased rate of dishwashing. The employment specialist's role shifts from training the employee to perform job-related vocational and social skills to teaching him how to detect and respond independently to the naturally occurring cues in the workplace. When those cues do not prompt the desired behavior, the supported employee can be taught to respond to contrived cues, such as picture prompts depicting individual steps in a multistep task (Cihak et al., 2008) or prerecorded verbal prompts interspersed within favorite music the employee might listen to on a personal audio player (Grossi, 1998; Mechling, 2007).

Self-monitoring can also be effectively used in employment training. Research has shown that teaching employees with disabilities to self-monitor (observe and record one's performance) and self-evaluate (compare self-monitored performance with a goal or production criterion) increases their job productivity and independence (Clark et al., 2018; Clark et al., 2019; Gilson et al., 2017; Storey, 2007). Clark et al. (2019) taught students to evaluate their performance with UPGRADE, a package that includes explicit instruction in self-evaluation and goal setting. Students showed improvements on a range of target skills, including work quality, productivity, and teamwork. To learn more about UPGRADE, see Chapter 4, *Transition: Next Year Is Now,* "Teaching Soft Skills to Prepare Students for the Future." Mobile devices, such as phones and tablets, are making it even easier for individuals with disabilities to learn a range of skills, including employment skills; self-monitor their performance; and generalize skills to new environments and tasks (Cannella-Malone, Brooks, et al., 2013; Cullen et al., 2017).

HLP21 Teach students to maintain and generalize new learning across time and settings.

SHELTERED EMPLOYMENT **Sheltered employment** refers to work by people with disabilities at an accredited occupationally oriented facility, a **work center** (formerly called "sheltered workshop"), operated by a private nonprofit agency. Work centers employ people with disabilities certified under special provisions of federal minimum wage laws by the Wage and Hour Division, U.S. Department of Labor, which allows work centers to pay hourly wages based on the employee's productivity. Work centers determine prevailing wage rates for similar work done by experienced workers in the surrounding community. For example, an employee producing 50 units per hour, compared with a competitive hourly standard of 100 units, would be paid 50% of the prevailing wage rate for that job. There are over 300,000 individuals with disabilities working for sub-minimum-wage pay at such centers in the United States (National Council on Disability [NCD], 2018d).

Most special educators and related employment services professionals no longer consider sheltered employment an appropriate transition outcome for young adults with disabilities (NCD, 2018d; Targett & Wehman, 2011). The theoretical purpose of work centers is to train individuals in skills that will enable them to obtain competitive employment; however, few work center employees are ever placed in jobs in the community, and many who are placed do not keep their jobs for long (Rogan et al., 2002) and earn less money than similarly matched individuals who do not work in these centers first (Cimera et al., 2012).

Many professionals believe the poor competitive employment record of work centers reflects the inherent limitations of these sites rather than the employment potential of people with disabilities (Migliore et al., 2008). Sheltered employment has been called a dead-end street for individuals with intellectual disabilities (Frank & Sitlington, 1993).

Recent initiatives give reason for optimism, as they have underscored the limitations of sheltered employment and include provisions for moving toward competitive employment. For instance, the Workforce Innovation and Opportunity Act (WIOA, 2014) was passed to increase competitive integrated employment options and eliminate use of sub-minimum wages. WIOA also requires that a portion of vocational rehabilitation funds be used to support students with disabilities in transitioning from high school to postsecondary education or employment. In addition, several states have adopted "Employment First" policies that recognize integrated competitive employment as the preferred option over sheltered employment (APSE, 2020).

Transition: Next Year Is Now

Sowing Seeds for Successful Transition: The Gardens at Drew

Featured Teacher Michael Craig is literally sowing seeds to help his students transition successfully to postsecondary roles. His school-based enterprise, The Drew Horticulture Program and The Gardens at Drew, serves the dual purpose of providing hands-on vocational horticulture training for students with disabilities while filling a void in the surrounding community by providing access to fresh, locally grown produce.

Setting up a school-based enterprise can be challenging, but with some time, careful planning, and teamwork, students and the community can reap the benefits. Follow these steps to set up your own school-based enterprise (Lindstrom et al., 1997; Public Schools of North Carolina, 2019):

1. **Form a team of professionals and students who are invested in building a business.** This includes making sure you have administrative support.
2. **Assess the needs of the community (school community or surrounding local community).** What products or services do people want or need? Fresh vegetables, coffee, car detailing, school supplies? Surveys and interviews are good ways to gather such information.
3. **Select a product or service to sell.** Use the assessment data you have gathered to choose a product consumers will want!
4. **Develop a business plan that includes a budget, advertising strategies, and a staffing plan.** Featured Teacher Michael also cautions, "Plan for the sustainability of your program. With funding dwindling or non-existent, teachers need to be relentless in efforts to maintain and grow their programs. Writing grants, soliciting corporate support, and accepting donations from local business leaders are some ways to enable programs to continue to operate for years to come."
5. **Purchase supplies and equipment needed to run the business.** Seek out donations if possible.
6. **Start running the business.** Keep in mind Featured Teacher Michael advice: "Not everything goes exactly as planned, and students make mistakes. Know this will happen, plan for it, and teach so students learn from it. Learn to laugh!"
7. **Keep in mind the primary purpose of the business is to teach students skills.** Use students' IEPs and grade-level standards to determine which academic, social, communication, and vocational skills you will target while running the enterprise. Plan instruction accordingly.
8. **Engage in ongoing evaluation.** Are students meeting their goals? Is the business bringing in enough money to pay for itself? Are customers satisfied? Make changes as needed. Featured Teacher Michael has found program evaluation helpful, noting, "Two years ago, I noticed a distinct drop in student motivation during the winter months when weather dictated learning inside in the classroom. The following year, we added indoor hydroponics to give students opportunities to continue engaging in meaningful work, even during the winter."

Independent Living and Community Participation

Learning Outcome 15.5 Provide examples of evidence-based predictors and practices for improving postschool outcomes in independent living.

Where one lives determines a great deal about how one lives. It influences where a person can work; what community services and resources will be available; who her friends will be; what opportunities for recreation and leisure exist; and, to a great extent, what feelings of self and place in the community will develop.

At one time, the only place someone with severe disabilities could live, if she did not live with family, was a large, state-operated institution. Most of these institutions in the United States were founded in the 19th or early 20th century, when it was generally believed people with intellectual disabilities could not be educated. Large custodial institutions (some housed 1000 or more people with intellectual and other disabilities) kept people with disabilities segregated from the rest of society; they were never designed to help people learn to live in the community. In the 1960s and 1970s, these institutions underwent intense criticism for their inability to provide individualized residential services in a comfortable, humane, and normalized environment (Blatt, 1976; Kugel & Wolfensberger, 1969). The complaints were not leveled against the concept of residential programs; there will probably always be people whose disabilities are so severe that they require the kind of 24-hour support a residential facility can offer. The problem lies with the inherent inability of institutional environments to allow people to experience a normal lifestyle. For a glimpse into the inhumane conditions at one institution, revisit the Pennhurst video from Chapter 1.

Deinstitutionalization—the movement of people with disabilities out of large institutions and into smaller, community-based living environments such as group homes or apartments—has been an active reality over the past four decades. The number of people with intellectual and developmental disabilities living in large state institutions has decreased steadily from a high of 194,650 in 1967 to 32,909 people in 2009 (Lakin et al., 2011). As of January 2010, more than half of 354 state institutions and residential units for people with intellectual and developmental disabilities that have been operating within the previous 50 years had been closed, and as of 2015, 13 states had closed all of their institutions (Lulinski et al., 2018).

Lakin and colleagues (2011) reviewed 36 studies of the outcomes of deinstitutionalization for nearly 5000 people with intellectual disabilities. They found 31 of the studies indicated generally positive outcomes for residents, and studies that specifically assessed changes in social skills, language and communication skills, self-care and domestic skills, and community-living skills after leaving large institutions to live in the community "overwhelmingly showed positive outcomes." They concluded that "to overlook such substantial and consistent findings cannot be easily justified in either public policy or treatment practices" (p. 4). The organization TASH (2000) has a resolution on deinstitutionalization calling for the termination of residential facilities.

SUPPORTED LIVING Despite improvements, barriers to independent living persist. Personal safety, household skills, and medication assistance are the most common barriers cited by caregivers (Reed et al., 2014). But with the right supports, attitudes, and instruction, these barriers can be overcome. Based on the belief that residential placements must be adapted to the needs of the person with disabilities, not vice versa, **supported living** helps people with disabilities live in the community as independently and normally as possible. Similar to the way supported employment provides ongoing, individualized supports to help a person with disabilities perform meaningful work in a community-based job setting, supported living entails a personalized network of various types and levels of natural supports.

Klein (1994) explains what supported living is by describing what it is not. There are no criteria for participation (e.g., people in this program must be able to cook for themselves, have a physical disability, need more or less than 3 hours per day of attendant care, have visual impairments). Supported living is not based on readiness and movement through a continuum. Participation in traditional residential services is based on a professional's assessment of the person's readiness or ability to live in a particular program, and a person must perform well (learn new skills on her individual habilitation plan) in order to move to the next, less restrictive rung on the continuum. A 2009 survey of state departments of developmental disabilities found that 246,822 people with intellectual and developmental disabilities were participating in supported living in the United States (Braddock et al., 2011).

PREDICTORS Research has not identified as many predictors of independent living as it has for postsecondary education or employment; fortunately, those that have been identified overlap with the other postschool outcome areas, so focusing on the following predictors does not have to be a burdensome addition. Students have higher rates of independent living if they have had inclusive experiences in school, real work experience, instruction in independent living skills, and student support (Mazzotti et al., 2016). For instance, programs should be structured to

TEACHING & LEARNING

Self-Directed Video Prompting for Transition

by Eliseo Jimenez and Helen I. Cannella-Malone

Since Desmond was a young child, his IEP team has focused on teaching him daily living skills. Now that he is of transition age, Desmond is learning to use a research-based strategy, self-directed video prompting, to learn a range of independent living skills (Cullen & Alber-Morgan, 2015).

What Is Self-Directed Video Prompting? Using video prompting, students operate a mobile device to watch a brief video clip of someone doing the next step of a task they want to complete. They do that step and then watch the next video prompt.

How Do You Plan for Self-Directed Video Prompting? Teachers who want to use self-directed video prompting should follow these steps:

1. *Select a high-interest, functional task.* Microwave popcorn is one of Desmond's favorite snacks, and he wanted to learn to make it. His mom made it for him after school almost every day, so she was very interested in targeting this skill.
2. *Task analyze the skill.* Review Figure 15.6, a task analysis for making microwave popcorn.

FIGURE 15.6 Task Analysis for Making Microwave Popcorn

1
Take Plastic Off And Throw Away
2
Put Popcorn In Microwave
3
Close Microwave
4
Start Microwave
5
Take Popcorn Out Of Microwave
6
Open Bag
7
Pour Popcorn Into Bowl
8
Throw Away Bag

Source: Helen I. Cannella-Malone, The Ohio State University.

Pearson eText
Video Example 15.6
Self-directed video prompting helps students develop independent living skills.

Pearson eText
Video Example 15.7
Each video clip shows a step in the task analysis for making popcorn shown in Figure 15.6. https://www.youtube.com/playlist?list=PLz26Mu5AGsKsDW6bE2PN-IfDfnZvDSJUz

3. *Create a series of brief videos of someone performing each step of the task analysis.*
4. *Upload (or create) the videos on a mobile device.* Teachers can use mobile apps, such as inPromptu, Go Talk Now, iPrompts, and My Pictures Talk, to create video prompts.
5. *Have the student watch the video of the first step of the task and then perform it.* Repeat this process for each step. The teacher may operate the mobile device during this phase.
6. *Explicitly teach the student to provide his own video prompts with the mobile device.* Use less intrusive prompting (e.g., modeling, verbal prompts) for students who are already familiar with mobile devices and more intrusive prompting (e.g., physical prompts) for students who are not familiar with mobile devices. Promote independence by fading prompts as quickly as possible, using student data as your guide.
7. *Promote generalization.* When the student can use video prompts to complete the task independently, extend video prompting across settings and tasks. For instance, after Desmond learned to make popcorn in the classroom, he used self-directed video prompting to make his favorite snack in the staff lounge at his community job site. His teacher then taught him to use self-directed video prompting for doing his laundry and riding the city bus to work.

About the Authors Eliseo Jimenez is a faculty member in intellectual disabilities at Georgia State University, and Helen Cannella-Malone is a faculty member in the special education and applied behavior analysis program at The Ohio State University.

provide students opportunities to practice financial planning, self-help, cooking, home maintenance, accessing community resources (including transportation), and self-determination.

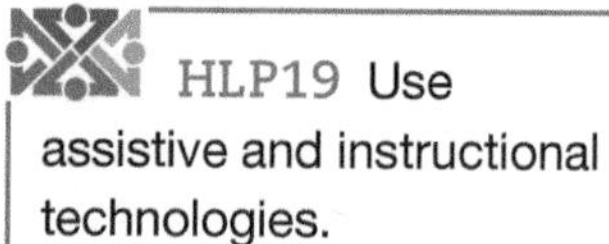

HLP19 Use assistive and instructional technologies.

PRACTICES Preparing students to live independently includes teaching them a range of functional skills, encompassing, but not limited to, financial literacy, banking, shopping, cooking, home maintenance, communication, social skills, self-care, and recreation and leisure skills. Fortunately, an extensive body of research has shown that students, even those with significant disabilities, can learn these types of daily living skills. In both community-based and simulated settings, teachers can use time-delay procedures (see Chapter 4); prompting techniques (including video prompting; see *Teaching & Learning*, "Self-Directed Video Prompting for Transition"); and video modeling (Test et al., 2015). For example, Kellems et al. (2018) compared prompting with static pictures to video prompting and found both were effective for teaching a variety of life skills to students with autism spectrum disorders.

Recreation, Leisure, and Social Engagement

Recreation, enjoyable use of leisure time, and social engagement are important components of a self-satisfying adult life. Most of us take our ability to pursue such outcomes for granted. We benefit from a lifetime of learning how to play, how to enjoy personal hobbies or crafts, and how to form friendships and romantic relationships.

Pearson eText
Video Example 15.8
Transition plans should include recreation and leisure activities that promote social engagement, friendship and fun.

RECREATION AND LEISURE Recreation and leisure activities do not come easily for many adults with disabilities, however. Using community recreational resources requires transportation; the physical ability and skills to play the game; accessible places and equipment; and, usually, other willing and able friends with whom to play. Alone or in combination, these factors severely limit the recreation and leisure activities available to many adults with disabilities (Ginis et al., 2016; Matheson et al., 2007; Merrells et al., 2018). Because of these problems, the majority of community-based recreation and leisure experiences for many adults with disabilities are segregated outings. Too often, the so-called leisure activities for adults with disabilities consist of watching television, listening to music in the solitude of their rooms, and spending discretionary time socially isolated (Strand & Kreiner, 2005).

Recreation and leisure skills instruction is a critical curriculum component for school-age children with disabilities. Juarez et al. (2010) describe how numerous games, hobbies, crafts, and projects can be adapted to become enjoyable, worthwhile leisure-time pursuits for people with disabilities. Areas they suggest include music appreciation and study, photography, card games, collecting, and nature study. Suggestions are also available for adapting leisure activities for young adults who are deaf-blind, such as using permanent tactile prompts (e.g., attaching fabric to the flipper buttons of a pinball machine), adequately stabilizing materials, enhancing the visual or auditory input provided by the materials (e.g., using large-print, low-vision playing cards), and simplifying the requirements of the task (e.g., raising the front legs on a pinball machine to reduce the speed with which the ball approaches the flippers).

Active recreation that includes physical exercise not only can increase life satisfaction for an adult with disabilities but also can help the person maintain a job by improving overall vitality and health condition (Ispen, 2006). Learning appropriate recreation and leisure skills is particularly important for adults with severe disabilities (Bambara et al., 2020). Most people with severe disabilities have ample free time, but many do not use it constructively and may instead engage in inappropriate behaviors such as body rocking, hand flapping, or bizarre vocalizations. A number of studies have demonstrated how to teach recreation and leisure skills to individuals with moderate and severe intellectual disabilities (e.g., Seward et al., 2014; Spriggs et al., 2017; Walker et al., 2010). In one interesting demonstration of age-appropriate instruction, four adults with moderate intellectual disabilities learned to order drinks in an Irish pub (O'Reilly et al., 2000).

Recreation and leisure activities involving secondary students with disabilities and their classmates without disabilities are especially valuable for all parties involved (Hughes et al., 2002). Participating in community recreation and leisure activities with an adult with disabilities is an excellent way for prospective teachers to appreciate the value of a functional curriculum for school-age students and in the process perhaps make a good friend (Dardig, 2006). To learn about one such program, read about the Next Chapter Book Club within *Teaching & Learning,* "What About Secondary Students Who Can't Read?"

SOCIAL ENGAGEMENT Everyone should have opportunities for social activities and access to friends and companionship. Because social relationships do not form easily for many youth with disabilities, transition teachers should be deliberate about teaching social skills (see Chapter 6) and planning opportunities for social engagement. Best Buddies is a nonprofit organization dedicated to helping school-age students, college students, and adults with intellectual and developmental disabilities establish one-to-one friendships with same-age peers without disabilities. (To learn more, visit the Best Buddies website: https://www.bestbuddies.org/.)

In addition to social skills instruction, youth with disabilities may need help navigating the more complex relationships, including romantic relationships, that begin forming in young adulthood. Youth with disabilities should not be excluded from opportunities to learn about sexuality and enjoy intimate relationships. However, dating and romantic involvement can be particularly challenging for youth with disabilities. Secondary transition planning teams should take into consideration students' needs in regard to intimate relationships. Baer and Daviso (2013) suggest several skills related to maintaining such relationships, such as showing affection appropriately, asking someone for a date, and avoiding unwanted pregnancy and sexually transmitted diseases. They caution, however, that teaching such skills must be done with care and consideration to respect families' values and to address students' specific needs. Travers, Tincani, et al. (2014) reviewed the literature on sexuality education for youth with intellectual disabilities and found that despite a clear need for such education, there is unfortunately very little research in this area. They found only one study focused on youth younger than the age of 18 years, which likely indicates that youth with intellectual disabilities are entering adulthood unprepared to make informed decisions about intimate relationships and sexual health.

The Ultimate Transition Goal: A Better Quality of Life

Significant strides have been made in the lives of many adults with disabilities. Tens of thousands of people who previously were relegated to institutions and other segregated settings now live in real homes in regular neighborhoods. Many who never had an opportunity to learn meaningful job skills go to work each day and bring home a paycheck. But living in a community-based residence and having a job in an integrated setting do not translate automatically into a better life. People with disabilities consistently report a lower quality of life in comparison to those without disabilities (Kessler Foundation/National Organization on Disability, 2010; van Heijst & Geurts, 2015).

Most advocates and professionals now realize what people with disabilities have long understood: Inclusion in typical employment, housing, and recreation settings is a necessary first step, but the only truly meaningful outcome of human service programs is an improved quality of life. How would you judge the quality of life for a woman who always sits alone during lunch and breaks at work because she has not developed a social relationship with any of her co-workers?

And what about the quality of life for a young man who lives in a group home in a residential neighborhood but whose only "friends" are the paid staff responsible for supervising him on his weekly trip to the shopping mall and who seldom gets to choose what he will eat for dinner or when he will go to bed? One measure of the quality of a person's life is the extent to which he can make choices. The choices we make play a significant role in defining our individual identities—from everyday matters, such as what to eat or wear, to the choices we make on larger matters, such as where to live or what kind of work to do (Ferguson & Ferguson, 2016).

Misguided and Limiting Presumptions

A continuing problem for many adults with disabilities is lack of acceptance as full members of our society, with all the rights, privileges, and services granted to any citizen. We have made progress (witness the litigation and legislation on behalf of people with disabilities discussed throughout this book), but we still have a long way to go. Courts can decree and laws can require, but neither can alter the way in which individuals treat people with disabilities.

Most adults with disabilities believe the biggest barriers to full integration into society are not inaccessible buildings or the actual restrictions imposed by their disabilities but the differential treatment of them by people without disabilities. Just as the terms *racism* and *sexism* indicate prejudiced, discriminatory treatment based on race and gender, **ableism** describes biased reactions toward people with disabilities. Those reactions are not based on an individual's qualities or performance but on a presumption of what a person with a disability must feel or be like because of the disability (Bogdan & Biklen, 1977). When asked how people generally react toward them, 28% of adults with disabilities in a national survey reported that people act as if they are sorry for them, 27% said they are treated differently, and 14% said people tend to avoid further contact with them (Kessler Foundation/National Organization on Disability, 2010). People with severe disabilities in this study were much more likely to describe negative experiences than were those with mild or moderate disabilities.

Only when a man or a woman with a disability is allowed to be simply an ordinary person—given the opportunity to strive and perhaps succeed but also allowed the freedom and dignity to strive and sometimes fail—can full membership and participation in society become a reality. Only then can people with disabilities enjoy a quality of life that citizens without disabilities take for granted.

Self-Advocacy and Self-Determination

Advocacy on behalf of children and adults with disabilities has had a tremendous impact, especially during the past 30 years. Indeed, most of the pervasive changes in education, employment opportunities, and residential services have occurred because of the efforts of advocates. Family members, friends, professionals, and attorneys have traditionally undertaken advocacy for people with disabilities.

Increasingly, people with disabilities are asserting their legal and human rights, challenging the view that they are incapable of speaking for themselves. An interesting finding from NLTS2 was that 67% of age-eligible young adults with disabilities had registered to vote compared with only 58% of 18- to 24-year old young adults in the general population. Perhaps most conspicuous has been the self-advocacy of individuals with physical disabilities, who have been highly effective in their lobbying as part of the independent living movement. Individuals with sensory impairments have also engaged in successful self-advocacy. A striking example was Gallaudet University students' refusal in 1988 to accept the appointment of a hearing president who did not know American Sign Language. People with intellectual disabilities have engaged in little self-advocacy, perhaps because many have not learned to recognize when their rights are being violated and because they lack the verbal skills to advocate on their own behalf. Evidence indicates, however, that people with intellectual and developmental disabilities are beginning to use Internet resources and tools to further their civil rights (Zubal-Ruggieri, 2007).

Still a Long Way to Go

In general, the quality of life for most adults with disabilities is better today than it has ever been. Not only do more adults with disabilities live, work, and recreate in community-based, integrated environments, but more adults with disabilities have also acquired or are acquiring the personal, social, vocational, and leisure skills that enable them to enjoy the benefits of those settings. But *more* people with disabilities is not the same as *all* people with disabilities. And individuals don't live life "in general"; they experience specific instances of joy and sadness, success and failure. There is still a long way to go.

Pearson eText
Video Example 15.9
The ultimate measure of special education's success is quality of life.

The quality of life for someone who now has his own bedroom in a group home and works for wages in a sheltered work center is appreciably better than it was before he left the institution, where he ate and slept communally and his "work" consisted of an endless series of arts-and-crafts projects. But do the unacceptable standards of the past mean that a relatively better quality of life today is therefore good? Would it be good enough for you?

ADVICE FROM THE FEATURED TEACHER by Michael Craig

Source: Andrew Craig

- Don't be afraid to seek out collaborations with and advice from local, state, and national experts.
- Remember that teaching includes wearing many hats. In my work, I'm not only a teacher but a farmer, businessman, grant writer, and marketer.
- Develop solid relationships with parents and students, so everyone can talk honestly about the student's future upon exit from high school. Be transparent and clear about what's working and what isn't.
- Implement backward planning with the IEP, working from a student's exit from school to postsecondary goals to the present time, with stated goals and objectives that will chart a path to success.
- Don't reinvent the wheel. If an effective curriculum already exists, see if you can purchase it and adapt it for your students as needed. For instance, I combine the Life Centered Career Education curriculum (LCCE) with the Chicago Botanic Garden's *Gardening as a Social Enterprise: Including People with Disabilities* approach. Although I still have to adapt lessons to meet my students' needs, I have a great starting point with these two curricula.
- Embed learning opportunities in a variety of settings and teach more than one skill at a time. Ask yourself, "What other skills can my students be working on right now?" There are always ways to combine communication skills, social skills, vocational skills, and academic skills. Be strategic!
- Make sure to check in regularly with other professionals providing services to your students. This serves two purposes: (1) gathering of important information to help guide your instruction, and (2) sending the message that you are an involved teacher, which may increase others' sense of accountability for serving your students.
- Give students meaningful experiences in authentic environments. My students know the tomatoes they're growing today will end up in salads and sauces all around our city tomorrow. This helps motivate them and prepares them to generalize skills beyond our school setting.

Key Terms and Concepts

ableism
competitive employment
deinstitutionalization
employment specialist
sheltered employment
supported living
transition IEP
transition services
work center

Summary

What Happens When Students with Disabilities Leave High School?

- The high school graduation rate for students with disabilities is significantly lower than the graduation rate for the general population (60% vs. 80%).
- The National Longitudinal Transition Study-2 (NLTS2) found that youth with disabilities enroll in postsecondary education at a much lower rate than their peers without disabilities, and enrollment rates vary widely by disability category.
- Data from the NLTS2 indicate that of youth with disabilities working for pay outside the home during the first 4 years after leaving high school, 58% were employed full time, and 44% received benefits.
- Adults with disabilities are significantly more likely to live in poverty than those without disabilities.
- About half (49%) of young adults in NLTS2 had participated in some type of community social activities outside work or school in the preceding year.
- More than twice as many out-of-high-school youth with disabilities in NLTS2 had been arrested (28%) than had youth in the general population (12%).

The Individuals with Disabilities Education Act and Transition Services

- Will's "bridges model" for transition from high school to adult employment encompasses three levels of support—generic, time-limited, and ongoing—depending on the student's needs.
- Halpern's view that secondary special education must help students with disabilities achieve maximum success in all domains of adult functioning greatly influenced amendments to the Individuals with Disabilities Education Act (IDEA).
- Transition services are a coordinated set of activities designed to assist a child with disabilities to achieve postsecondary goals in education or training; employment; and, when appropriate, independent living.

Transition Planning

- Beginning no later than age 16 years, each child's IEP must contain measurable postsecondary goals based on age-appropriate transition assessments and a description of the transition services needed to assist the child in reaching those goals.
- IDEA regulations stipulate the following transition-planning process:
  - Conduct an age-appropriate transition assessment.
  - Write measurable postsecondary goals.
  - Identify an appropriate course of study for the student.
  - Identify transition services.
  - Develop annual individualized education program (IEP) goals that align with postsecondary goals.
  - Coordinate transition services with adult services agencies.
  - Provide the student with a summary of performance.

Evidence-Based Predictors and Practices

- Participation in postsecondary education significantly improves chances of meaningful employment for people with disabilities.
- Predictors of participation in postsecondary education include inclusive experiences; work experience and other career-related experiences; instruction in self-determination, academic, independent living, and social skills; and a student support network.
- Evidence-based practices to support transition to postsecondary education include explicit instruction and strategy instruction that focus on academics, self-determination, and social skills.
- Predictors of successful transition to work include developing students' career awareness, providing access to occupational courses, and giving students real work experiences (e.g., internships, job shadowing). Other predictors include inclusive experiences in school and the community; parent involvement; interagency collaboration; student support networks; and instruction in academic, self-determination, independent living, and social skills.
- Evidence-based practices to support transition to employment include explicit instruction on specific job skills, ways to increase production rates, transportation to and from employment sites, and social skills. Techniques such as prompting, systematic time delay, and computer-assisted (e.g., phone apps) instruction have proven effective in teaching a range of skills needed for success on the job.
- Supported employment recognizes that many adults with severe disabilities require ongoing support to obtain and hold a job. Supported employment is characterized by performance of real, paid work in regular, integrated work sites; it requires ongoing support from a supported work specialist.

- The role of the employment specialist has evolved from one of primary supporter for the employee with disabilities to one who works with the employer and co-workers to create innovative and natural support networks.
- Self-monitoring, self-evaluation, self-instruction, and learning how to respond to natural cues are four ways that employees with disabilities can increase their independence and productivity in the workplace.
- Although many adults with severe disabilities work in sheltered work centers, this is no longer considered an appropriate employment option.
- Supported living is an approach toward helping people with disabilities live in the community as independently and normally as they can by providing a network of various kinds and levels of natural supports.
- Learning to participate in age-appropriate recreation, leisure activities, and adult relationships is necessary for a satisfying lifestyle.
- Individuals with disabilities should not be excluded from opportunities to learn about sexuality and to explore intimate relationships.

The Ultimate Transition Goal: A Better Quality of Life

- Many adults with disabilities continue to face lack of acceptance as full members of society.
- Ableism—discriminatory treatment and biased reactions toward someone with a disability—occurs on personal, professional, and societal levels. It must be eliminated before normalization can become a reality for every man and woman with a disability.
- People with disabilities have begun to assert their legal rights, challenging the view that they are incapable of speaking for themselves.

Postscript

Developing Your Own View of Special Education

ALL INTRODUCTORY TEXTBOOKS contain a great deal of information, and in that respect, this book is no different from any other. We hope, however, you have gained more than a collection of basic facts and information about special education and learners with exceptionalities. We hope you have examined your own attitudes toward and relationships with children and adults with disabilities. We began this book by sharing 10 beliefs that underlie our personal, but by no means unique, view of special education. We restate those beliefs here:

- People with disabilities have a fundamental right to live and participate in the same settings and programs—in school, at home, in the workplace, and in the community—as do people without disabilities.
- People with disabilities have the right to self-determination.
- Special education must expand the effectiveness of its early identification and prevention efforts.
- Special education must do a better job of helping students with disabilities transition from school to adult life.
- Special education must continue to improve its cultural competence and promote social justice.
- School and family partnerships enhance the meaningfulness and the effectiveness of special education.
- The work of special educators is most effective when supplemented by the knowledge and services of all the helping professions.
- All students have the right to an effective education.
- Teachers must demand effectiveness from the curriculum materials and instructional tools they use.
- The future for people with disabilities holds great promise.

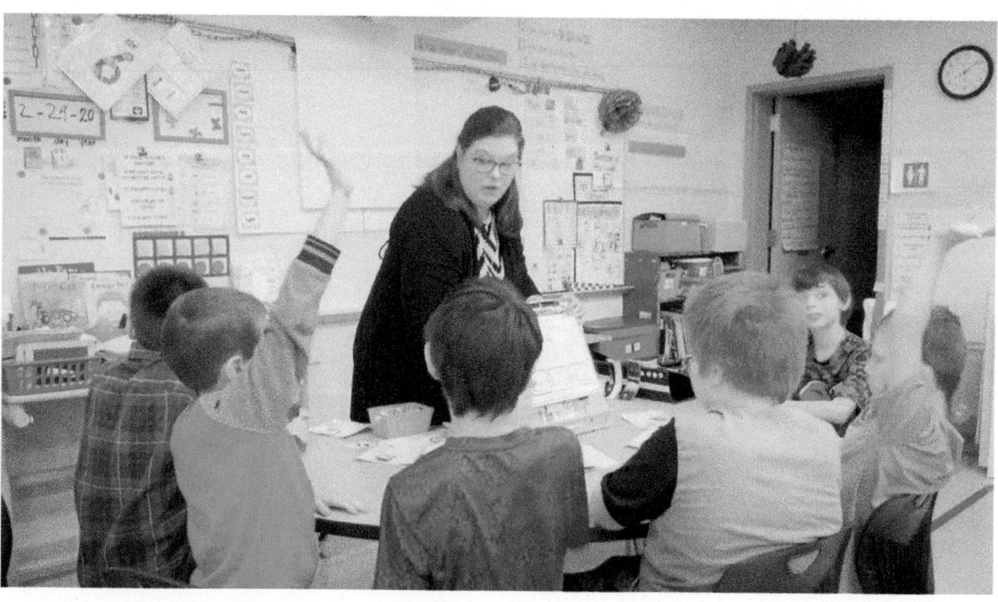

As a Special Educator

If you are a prospective special educator, view special education as a profession and yourself as a professional in the making. A professional commands knowledge and specific skill sets such as those exemplified by the extraordinary teachers featured in this text. Becoming a special educator will make you different from people without your professional training. This has nothing to do with arrogance and everything to do with recognizing that students with disabilities depend on their teachers' developing and responsibly using as much professional competence as they can muster.

Obtaining an objective understanding of the nature and scope of a special educator's responsibilities is the first step toward professional competence. Special education is serious business. The learning problems faced by students with disabilities are real, and they require intensive and systematic instruction. Be wary of the notion that disability is merely a socially constructed phenomenon, that all children with disabilities would be successful and happy learners if others simply viewed them more positively. This romantic ideology is seldom promoted by people with disabilities or by their parents and families. Children with disabilities have skill deficits and difficulties in acquiring and generalizing new knowledge and skills—real learning challenges that cannot be deconstructed away. They need and deserve effective special education.

When others learn of your desire and commitment to teach children with exceptional educational needs, they might remark how "wonderful" or "patient" you must be. Good intentions are fine, but desire and commitment are only first steps. What learners with disabilities need most are teachers who are in some ways impatient—impatient with curriculum, instructional methods, and policies that do not help their students learn. So, here is our recommendation to you as a future teacher: Don't be patient; be effective.

You will increase your effectiveness by using only curriculum and instructional methods backed by sound, peer-reviewed research evidence. Special education research has produced a significant and reliable knowledge base of effective teaching practices. Although this research has not discovered everything we need to know about teaching exceptional students—many important questions remain unanswered—today's special educators are supported by a research base that includes instructional strategies and tactics that did not exist when the Education of All Handicapped Children Act was signed into law in 1975.

When considering a new curriculum, program, or instructional method, ask these questions:

- Has this program been tested in the classroom? What measures of student performance were used to evaluate this program?
- What evidence shows that this program works? Does the program efficiently produce measurably superior student outcomes?
- Is the program culturally responsive?
- Has any research on this program been published in peer-reviewed journals?
- Does any evidence suggest the program will succeed if modified to meet the skill levels and ages of my students?

Educating students with disabilities has always presented teachers with complex and difficult challenges. And today's special education teachers are expected to do more than ever before. For example, special educators must help ensure students' access to the general education curriculum while teaching them the functional skills needed for daily living and successful transition from school to adult life in the community and workplace.

Prepare yourself for meeting these challenges as best you can. Demand relevant, up-to-date information and hands-on practical experiences from your teacher education program. Continue your education and professional development throughout your career. Stay abreast of advances in special education. Read professional journals, actively participate in in-service training opportunities, and attend professional conferences. Even better, conduct research on instructional methods, systematically collect data on the student outcomes, and share the results of your research with colleagues through presentations and publications.

Special education is not a grim, thankless business. Quite the opposite! As you learned from featured teachers Danielle, Keisha, Joshua, Madonna, Amaris, Michelle, Katelyn, Emily, Jessica, Cecelia, Dave, Carey, Jennifer, Mark, and Michael, special education is an exciting, dynamic field that offers personal satisfaction and feelings of accomplishment unequaled in many professions. Welcome aboard!

As a Community Member

If being a special education teacher is not in your plans, use what you have learned from this text as a member of an inclusive community. The degree of success and happiness a person with disabilities enjoys in the normal routines of everyday life is not determined solely by their skills and abilities. In large measure, the integration of people with disabilities into contemporary society depends on the attitudes and actions of citizens with little knowledge of or experience with exceptional learners. How can people come to accept and support a group they do not know?

Society controls who enters and who is kept out, much as a gatekeeper lets some visitors pass but refuses others. For a particular individual, society's gatekeeper may have been a physician who urged parents to institutionalize their child or a teacher who resisted having difficult-to-teach students in her classroom. It may have been an employer who refused to hire workers with disabilities. It may have been a social worker, a school board member, a voter.

How society views people with disabilities influences how individual members of the community respond. For several decades, society's views have changed gradually for the better—changed by people who believe exclusion and denial of opportunities are primitive, unfair, and ultimately detrimental to everyone. But to have maximum impact, the movement toward integration and opportunities described in this book must ultimately translate into personal terms for those who do not choose careers in special education. People with disabilities and people without disabilities experience certain aspects of life differently, but we are more like one another than we are different. And the conclusion we hope you have reached is this: Every child and adult with disabilities must be treated as an individual, not as a member of a category or a labeled group.

In Sum

Viewing every individual with disabilities as a person first may be the most important step in building more inclusive schools and communities. And although changing our attitudes does not diminish disabilities, it will give us a new outlook—a more objective and positive one. This view allows us to see exceptional people as people who have both strengths to be celebrated and built upon and needs to be addressed—and how we respond to students' strengths and needs is the essence of special education.

Glossary

ABC recording A form of direct observation often used as a part of functional behavior assessment. The observer records a descriptive, temporally sequenced account of all behaviors of interest and the antecedent conditions and consequences for those behaviors as those events occur in the student's natural environment.

ability grouping Placing students with similar levels of achievement and skill into the same classes or instructional groups.

ableism Differential treatment of people with disabilities based on presumptions of what a person with a disability must feel or be like because of the disability.

absence seizure A type of epileptic seizure in which the individual loses consciousness, usually for less than half a minute; can occur very frequently in some children.

acceleration An educational approach that provides a child with learning experiences usually given to older children; most often used with gifted and talented children.

acquired immune deficiency syndrome (AIDS) A fatal illness in which the body's immune system breaks down. At present, there is no known cure for AIDS or a vaccine for the virus that causes it. See *human immunodeficiency virus*.

acquisition stage of learning The initial phase of learning when the student is learning how to perform a new skill or use new knowledge; feedback should focus on the accuracy and topography of the student's response. Compare with *practice stage of learning*.

active student response (ASR) A student's active participation during instruction; measured by counting the number of observable responses made to an ongoing lesson or to curriculum materials.

acute condition A serious, but not permanent, state of illness or injury; contrast with *chronic*.

adaptive behavior Conceptual, social, and practical skills that people have learned in order to function in their everyday lives; refers to typical performance of people without disabilities in meeting the expectations of everyday environments.

adaptive device Any piece of equipment designed to improve the function of a body part. Examples include standing tables and special spoons for use by people with weak hands or poor muscle control.

alphabetic principle The understanding that words are composed of letters that represent sounds and the ability to pronounce and blend the sounds of letters into words (decoding) and to recode sounds into letters (spelling).

American Sign Language (ASL) A visual-gestural language with its own rules of syntax, semantics, and pragmatics; does not correspond to written or spoken English. ASL is the language of the Deaf culture in the United States and Canada.

amniocentesis The insertion of a hollow needle through the abdomen into the uterus of a pregnant woman. Used to obtain amniotic fluid to determine the presence of genetic and chromosomal abnormalities. It also confirms the gender of the fetus.

anoxia A lack of oxygen severe enough to cause tissue damage; can cause permanent brain damage and intellectual disability.

aphasia The loss of speech functions; often, but not always, refers to inability to speak because of brain lesions.

applied behavior analysis (ABA) "The science in which tactics derived from the principles of behavior are applied systematically to improve socially significant behavior and experimentation is used to identify the variables responsible for behavior change" (Cooper et al., 2020, p. 19).

articulation disorder Abnormal production of speech sounds.

Asperger syndrome A developmental disorder characterized by normal cognitive and language development with impairments in all social areas, repetitive and stereotypic behaviors, preoccupation with atypical activities or items, pedantic speech patterns, and motor clumsiness; included in autism spectrum disorders.

assistive technology "Any item, piece of equipment, or product system, whether acquired commercially off the shelf, modified, or customized, that is used to increase, maintain, or improve the functional capabilities of children with disabilities" (the Individuals with Disabilities Education Act regulations, 34 CFR § 300.5).

asthma A respiratory condition characterized by recurrent episodes of wheezing, coughing, and difficulty breathing.

asynchrony A term used to describe the disparate rates of intellectual, emotional, and physical growth or development characteristic of many gifted and talented children.

at risk A term used to refer to a child who is not currently identified with a disability but is considered to have a greater than usual chance of developing a disability.

ataxia A poor sense of balance and body position and lack of coordination of the voluntary muscles; characteristic of one type of cerebral palsy.

athetosis A type of cerebral palsy characterized by large, irregular, uncontrollable twisting motions. The muscles may be tense and rigid or loose and flaccid. Often accompanied by difficulty with oral language.

attention-deficit/hyperactivity disorder (ADHD) A diagnostic category of the American Psychiatric Association for a condition in which an individual exhibits excessive inattention, impulsivity, and/or hyperactivity.

audiogram A graph of the faintest level of sound a person can hear in each ear at least 50% of the time at each of several frequencies, including the entire frequency range of normal speech.

audiologist A professional who specializes in the evaluation of hearing ability and the treatment of impaired hearing.

audiology The science of hearing.

audiometer A device that generates sounds at specific frequencies and intensities; used to examine hearing.

audiometric zero The smallest sound a person with normal hearing can perceive; also called the *zero hearing-threshold level (HTL)*.

audition The act or sense of hearing.

auditory canal (external acoustic meatus) The part of the ear that slightly amplifies and transports sound waves from the external ear to the middle ear.

auditory training A program that works on listening skills by teaching individuals with hearing impairments to make as much use as possible of their residual hearing.

augmentative and alternative communication (AAC) A diverse set of nonspeech communication strategies and methods to assist individuals who cannot meet their communication needs through speech; includes sign language, symbol systems, communication boards, and synthetic speech devices.

auricle The external part of the ear; collects sound waves into the auditory canal.

autism See *autism spectrum disorder*.

autism spectrum disorder A developmental disability characterized by persistent deficits in social communication and social interaction and by restricted, repetitive, and stereotypic patterns of behavior, interests, and activities. Symptoms are present in early childhood.

behavior observation audiometry A method of hearing assessment in which an infant's reactions to sounds are observed; a sound is presented at an increasing level of intensity until a response, such as head turning, eye blinking, or cessation of play, is reliably observed.

behavior trap Effective behavior traps include four essential features: (a) They are "baited" with virtually irresistible reinforcers that "lure" the student to the trap; (b) only a low-effort response already in the student's repertoire is necessary to enter the trap; (c) once inside the trap, the student is motivated by interrelated contingencies of reinforcement to acquire, extend, and maintain targeted academic and/or social skills; and (d) they can remain effective for a long time because students show few, if any, satiation effects (see Cooper et al., 2020, p. 740).

behavioral intervention plan (BIP) A statement of specific strategies and procedures to prevent the occurrence of a child's challenging behavior and intervene when necessary; based on results of a functional behavior assessment. Required in the individualized education program for all students with disabilities whose school performance is adversely affected by challenging behavior.

bilingual-bicultural (bi-bi) approach An approach to teaching students who are deaf in which American Sign Language (ASL) is used as the child's native language and English is taught as a second language; also stresses teaching of Deaf culture.

binocular vision Vision using both eyes working together to perceive a single image.

blind Having either no vision or only light perception; learning occurs through other senses.

blindness, legal See *legal blindness*.

Bloom's taxonomy A hierarchy of educational objectives consisting of six types of cognitive understanding: (a) remember, (b) understand, (c) apply, (d) analyze, (e) create, and (f) evaluate. Can be used as a framework for differentiating curriculum by asking questions and assigning activities that require students to demonstrate different types of learning.

braille A system of writing letters, numbers, and other language symbols with a combination of six raised dots. A person who is blind reads the dots with his fingertips.

brailler A six-keyed device for writing braille.

cataract Clouding of the crystalline lens of the eye that results in a reduction or loss of vision.

cerebral palsy Motor impairment caused by brain damage, which is usually acquired during the prenatal period or during birth. Can involve a wide variety of symptoms (rigidity, spasticity, and tremor; see also *ataxia, athetosis*) and range from mild to severe. Neither curable nor progressive.

choral responding (CR) Students responding orally in unison to a series of questions or problems presented by the teacher. An evidence-based tactic for increasing student engagement and learning during group instruction.

chorionic villi sampling (CVS) A procedure for prenatal diagnosis of chromosomal abnormalities that can be conducted during the first 8 to 10 weeks of pregnancy; fetal cells are removed from the chorionic tissue, which surrounds the fetus, and directly analyzed.

chronic condition A long-lasting, often permanent condition; contrast with *acute*.

clean intermittent catheterization A clean (not sterile) catheter (tube) is inserted into the urethra and advanced into the bladder; the catheter remains in place until urine is released into a bag.

cleft palate A congenital split in the palate that results in an excessive nasal quality of the voice. Can often be repaired by surgery or a dental appliance.

closed head injury Caused by the head hitting a stationary object with such force that the brain slams against the inside of the cranium; stress of this rapid movement and impact pulls apart and tears nerve fibers, or axons, of the brain.

cluster ability grouping An instructional arrangement in which a small group of the highest performing students at a given grade level learn together as a group in a regular classroom of mixed-ability students.

cluttering A type of fluency disorder in which speech is very rapid, with extra sounds or mispronounced sounds; speech may be garbled to the point of unintelligibility; compare with *stuttering*.

cochlea Main receptor organ for hearing located in the inner ear; tiny hairs within the cochlea transform mechanical energy into neural impulses that then travel through the auditory nerve to the brain.

cochlear implant A surgically implanted device that converts sound from the environment into electric impulses that are sent directly to the brain via the auditory nerve. Enables some people who are deaf to achieve a useful auditory understanding of the environment and to understand speech.

communication An interactive process requiring at least two parties in which messages are encoded, transmitted, and decoded by any means, including sounds, symbols, and gestures.

communication disorder "An impairment in the ability to receive, send, process, and comprehend concepts or verbal, nonverbal, and graphic symbols systems. A communication disorder may be evident in the processes of hearing, language, and/or speech" (American Speech-Language-Hearing Association, 1993).

comorbidity Two or more conditions occurring in the same person (e.g., learning disabilities and attention-deficit/hyperactivity disorder).

competitive employment Full- or part-time work in a competitive labor market in an integrated setting, at or above the federal minimum wage, but not less than the customary wage and level of benefits paid by the employer for the same or similar work performed by individuals who are not disabled.

complex partial seizure A type of seizure in which an individual experiences a brief period of inappropriate or purposeless activity (also called *psychomotor seizure*). Usually lasts from 2 to 5 minutes, after which the person has amnesia about the entire episode.

concrete-representational-abstract sequence The logical sequence for teaching math using first objects (concrete), then pictures (representational), then numbers (abstract).

conductive hearing impairment Hearing loss caused by obstructions in the outer or middle ear or malformations that interfere with the conduction of sound waves to the inner ear. Can often be corrected surgically or medically.

congenital Any condition that is present at birth.

congenital cytomegalovirus (CMV) A common virus that infects most people worldwide; can remain alive but dormant in the body for life; usually harmless, but in a very small percentage of children infected at birth, CMV may later develop and lead to various conditions, including intellectual disability; visual impairment; and, most often, hearing impairment.

content enhancement A general term for a wide range of techniques teachers use to enhance the organization and delivery of curriculum content so that students can better access, interact with, comprehend, and retain that information. Examples include advance organizers, visual displays, graphic organizers, and guided notes.

continuum of alternative placements A range of placement and instructional options for children with disabilities. Often depicted as a pyramid, with placements ranging from the regular classroom at the bottom to special schools, residential facilities, and homebound or hospital placements at the top. The Individuals with Disabilities Education Act requires school districts (local education agencies) to provide a continuum of alternative placements to meet the individual needs of students with disabilities.

cortical visual impairments (CVI) Decreased vision or blindness caused by known or suspected damage or malfunction of the parts of the brain that interpret visual information.

criterion-referenced test A test constructed so that a child's score can be compared with a predetermined criterion, or mastery level; contrast with *norm-referenced test*.

cued speech A method of supplementing oral communication by adding cues in the form of eight different hand signals in four different locations near the chin.

cultural reciprocity A two-way process between professionals and families of information sharing, understanding, and respecting how their differing values and belief systems may influence perspectives, wishes, and decisions. Requires careful examination of each party's own cultural background and belief system.

curriculum compacting Compressing instructional content that students have already mastered so they have more time for enrichment.

curriculum-based measurement (CBM) A type of formative evaluation consisting of frequent measures of a student's progress in learning the objectives that comprise the curriculum in which the student is participating.

cystic fibrosis An inherited disorder that causes a dysfunction of the pancreas and mucus, salivary, and sweat glands. Cystic fibrosis causes severe, long-term respiratory difficulties. No cure is currently available.

deaf Having a hearing loss severe enough so that speech cannot be understood through the ears alone, even with a hearing aid; some sounds may still be perceived.

Deaf culture Shared language (in the United States, American Sign Language [ASL]), social practices, literature, and beliefs of the Deaf community; members do not view deafness as a disability.

deaf-blindness Any combination of hearing and visual impairments that causes such severe communication, developmental, and educational needs that the individual cannot be accommodated in a special education program designed solely for children with hearing impairments or visual impairments.

deafness See *deaf*.

decibel (dB) The unit of measure for the relative intensity of sound on a logarithmic scale beginning at zero. Zero decibels refers to the faintest sound a person with normal hearing can detect.

deinstitutionalization The movement of individuals with disabilities, especially people with intellectual disabilities, from large institutions to smaller, community-based residences and work settings.

developmentally appropriate practice A philosophy and guidelines for practice based on the belief that the learning environments, teaching practices, and other components of programs that serve young children should be based on typical expectations and experiences for children of different ages and developmental stages.

diabetes A chronic disease in which the body does not produce or properly use insulin, a hormone needed to convert sugar, starches, and other food into energy (see *type 1 diabetes, type 2 diabetes*).

dialects A variety within a specific language; can involve variation in pronunciation, word choice, word order, and inflected forms.

differentiation Customizing environments, curricula, and instructional practices to create appropriately different learning experiences for students with different needs, interests, readiness, and learning profiles.

disability A condition characterized by functional limitations that impede typical development as the result of a physical or sensory impairment or difficulty in learning or social adjustment.

disproportionate representation When a particular group receives special education at a rate significantly higher or lower than would be expected based on the proportion of the general student population that group represents.

Down syndrome A chromosomal anomaly that often causes moderate to severe intellectual disability, along with certain physical characteristics such as a large tongue; heart problems; poor muscle tone; and a broad, flat bridge of the nose.

dual discrepancy criterion A criterion for identifying a student as unresponsive in a response to intervention (RTI) approach when the student (a) fails to make adequate growth in the presence of instruction and (b) completes Tier 2 intervention(s) below the benchmark criteria (Fuchs & Fuchs, 2007a).

Duchenne muscular dystrophy The most common form of muscular dystrophy, a group of long-term diseases that progressively weaken and waste away the body's muscles.

due process A set of legal steps and proceedings carried out according to established rules and principles; designed to protect an individual's constitutional and legal rights.

duration (of behavior) The measure of how long a person engages in a given activity.

dysarthria A group of speech disorders caused by neuromuscular impairments in respiration, phonation, resonation, and articulation.

dyslexia A specific language-based disorder of constitutional origin characterized by difficulties in single-word decoding, usually reflecting insufficient phonological processing. These difficulties, which are not the result of generalized developmental disability or sensory impairment, are often unexpected in relation to age and other cognitive and academic abilities and severely impair the individual's ability to read (Orton Dyslexia Society Research Committee, 1994).

echolalia The repetition of what other people have said as if echoing them; characteristic of some children with delayed development, autism, and communication disorders.

embedded learning opportunities Incorporating intentional and systematic instruction into naturally occurring classroom routines (e.g., snack time, clean up).

emotional disturbance A disability defined in the Individuals with Disabilities Education Act as a condition exhibiting one or more of the following characteristics over a long period of time and to a marked degree that adversely affects educational performance: inability to build or maintain satisfactory interpersonal relationships, inappropriate types of behavior or feelings under normal circumstances, a general pervasive mood of unhappiness or depression, or a tendency to develop physical symptoms or fears associated with personal or school problems. Many professionals prefer the term *emotional or behavioral disorders*.

emotional or behavioral disorder A disability characterized by emotional or behavioral responses in school programs so different from appropriate age, cultural, or ethnic norms that the responses adversely affect educational performance. Contrast with *emotional disturbance*.

employment specialist A community-based professional who works in a nonprofit job placement program, a public vocational or adult services program, or a secondary special education program to support employees with disabilities. Sometimes called a *job coach* or *employment consultant*.

enrichment An educational approach that provides a child with extra learning experiences that the standard curriculum would not normally include. Most often used with gifted and talented children.

epilepsy A condition marked by chronic and repeated seizures, disturbances of movement, sensation, behavior, or consciousness caused by abnormal electrical activity in the brain (see *generalized tonic-clonic seizure, complex partial seizure, simple partial seizure,* and *absence seizure*). Can usually be controlled with medication, although the drugs may have undesirable side effects. May be temporary or lifelong.

exceptional children Children whose performance deviates from the norm, either below or above, to the extent that special education is needed.

executive functioning Regulating one's own behavior, such as planning and goal setting, cognitive and behavioral flexibility, inhibition, working memory, and selective attention.

expressive language disorder A language impairment that interferes with the production of language; contrast with *receptive disorder.*

externalizing behaviors Antisocial, disruptive behaviors (e.g., aggression, noncompliance, property destruction) characteristic of many children with emotional or behavioral disorders.

facilitated communication (FC) A type of augmentative communication in which a "facilitator" provides assistance to someone in typing or pointing to vocabulary symbols; typically involves an alphanumeric keyboard on which the user types out a message one letter at a time. Also called *supported typing.* No credible research supports FC as a viable intervention.

field of vision The expanse of space visible with both eyes looking straight ahead, measured in degrees; 160 to 170 degrees is considered normal.

fingerspelling The manual alphabet used to spell out proper names for which no signs exist and to clarify meanings; an integral part of American Sign Language (ASL).

fluency The combination of accuracy and speed that characterizes highly skilled performance; often measured by the number of responses per minute.

fluency disorder A speech disorder characterized by atypical rate, rhythm, and repetitions in sounds, syllables, words, and phrases; see *stuttering, cluttering.*

formative assessment Any type of ongoing evaluation of student performance or learning that occurs as instruction takes place over time; results can be used to modify instruction to make it more effective.

fragile X syndrome A chromosomal abnormality associated with mild to severe intellectual disability. Thought to be the most common known cause of inherited intellectual disabilities.

free appropriate public education (FAPE) As guaranteed by the Individuals with Disabilities Education Act, schools must provide each qualifying child with disabilities a program of education and related services individually designed to meet that child's unique needs and from which the child receives educational benefit, including being prepared for further education, employment, and independent living.

functional analysis Experimental manipulation of antecedent or consequent events representing those observed in the child's natural environment to verify their function in either triggering or maintaining challenging behavior.

functional behavior assessment (FBA) A systematic process of gathering information about the purposes (functions) a problem behavior serves for an individual; that information then guides the design of interventions. FBA entails one or more of three assessment methods: indirect assessment (structured interviews with significant others), direct assessment (systematic observations), and functional analysis (see *functional analysis*).

functional curriculum Knowledge and skills that some students with disabilities must learn to achieve as much success and independence as they can in school, home, community, and employment settings. Examples include dressing, toileting, making a purchase, and preparing a snack.

funds of knowledge Families' strengths, resources, and insights on which teachers should capitalize in order to be most effective.

generalization The extent to which previously learned knowledge or skill either occurs under conditions different from those under which it was originally learned or is performed in a different but functionally equivalent manner. Situation or setting generalization occurs when a student performs a behavior in the presence of stimuli other than those that were present originally. Response generalization occurs when a person performs behaviors that were never directly trained but have the same effect on the environment as the original trained behavior.

generalized tonic-clonic seizure The most severe type of seizure, in which the individual has violent convulsions, loses consciousness, and becomes rigid. Formerly called *grand mal seizure.*

genetic counseling A discussion between a specially trained medical counselor and people who are considering having a baby about the chances of having a baby with a disability based on the prospective parents' genetic backgrounds.

glaucoma An eye disease characterized by abnormally high pressure inside the eyeball. If left untreated, it can cause total blindness, but if detected early, most cases can be arrested.

graphemes The smallest level of written language that corresponds to one phoneme; for example, the grapheme t represents the phoneme /t/.

group contingencies A type of behavior management and motivation procedure in which consequences (rewards, penalties, or both) are applied to the entire group or class of students contingent upon the behavior of selected students or the entire group.

guided notes Teacher-prepared handout that provides background information and standard cues with specific spaces where students can write key facts, concepts, or relationships during a lecture.

handicap Refers to the problems a person with a disability or impairment encounters in interacting with the environment. A disability may pose a handicap in one environment but not in another.

hard of hearing A level of hearing loss that makes it difficult, although not impossible, to comprehend speech through the sense of hearing alone.

hearing aid An assistive listening device that amplifies sound.

hearing impairment A hearing loss significant enough to require special education, training, or adaptations; includes deafness as well as hard-of-hearing conditions.

hearing loss As defined in the Individuals with Disabilities Education Act, "a loss in hearing, whether permanent or fluctuating, that adversely affects a child's education performance but that is not included under the definition of deafness in this section." Because it suggests a deficiency or pathology, many members of the Deaf community consider *hearing loss* an inappropriate and demeaning term.

hertz (Hz) A unit of sound frequency equal to one cycle per second; used to measure pitch.

human immunodeficiency virus (HIV) The virus that causes acquired immune deficiency syndrome (AIDS).

hydrocephalus An enlarged head caused by accumulation of cerebrospinal fluid in the cranial cavity; often causes brain damage and severe intellectual disability. A condition present at birth or developing soon afterward. Can sometimes be treated successfully with a shunt.

hyperopia Farsightedness; condition in which the image comes to a focus behind the retina instead of on it, causing difficulty in seeing near objects.

hypertonia Muscle tone that is too high; tense, contracted muscles.

hypotonia Muscle tone that is too low; weak, floppy muscles.

IEP team The group of people who create the individualized education program for a student with a disability. The team must include (a) the parents of the child with a disability; (b) at least one regular education teacher of the child; (c) at least one special education teacher; (d) a representative of the local education agency who is qualified to provide, or supervise the provision of, specially designed instruction to meet the unique needs of children with disabilities; (e) an individual who is knowledgeable about the general curriculum and the availability of resources of the local education agency; (f) an individual who can interpret the instructional implications of evaluation results, who may be a member of the team described in clauses (b) through (f); (g) at the discretion of the parent or the agency, other individuals who have knowledge or special expertise regarding the child, including related service personnel as appropriate; and (h) whenever appropriate, the child with a disability.

impairment Refers to the loss or reduced function of a particular body part or organ (e.g., a missing limb); compare with *disability* and *handicap*.

incidence The percentage of people who, at some time in their lives, will be identified as having a specific condition. Often reported as the number of cases of a given condition per 1,000 births or people of a given age.

inclusion Educating students with disabilities in regular classrooms.

Individual Growth and Development Indicators Progress monitoring assessments of developmental skills for young children.

individualized education program (IEP) The written document required by the Individuals with Disabilities Education Act for every child with a disability; includes statements of present performance, annual goals, short-term instructional objectives, specific educational services needed, extent of participation in the general education program, evaluation procedures, and relevant dates; must be signed by parents as well as educational personnel.

individualized family service plan (IFSP) A requirement of the Individuals with Disabilities Education Act for the coordination of early intervention services for infants and toddlers with disabilities from birth to age 3 years. Similar to the individualized education program, which is required for all school-age children with disabilities.

individualized health care plan (IHCP) The individualized education program component for students with special health care needs; specifies health care procedures and services administered by school personnel and a plan for emergencies.

inquiry-based learning A method of teaching science that engages students in asking research questions, planning investigations, collecting and analyzing data, deriving explanations, and communicating their findings.

intellectual disability A disability characterized by significant limitations in both intellectual functioning and adaptive behavior as expressed in conceptual, social, and practical adaptive skills; the disability originates before age 18 (American Association on Intellectual and Developmental Disabilities [AAIDD], 2020). Refers to the same population of individuals who were diagnosed previously with mental retardation.

internalizing behaviors Immature and withdrawn behaviors (e.g., social withdrawal, irrational fears, depression) characteristic of some children with emotional or behavioral disorders.

intervention assistance team A team of school personnel who help teachers devise and implement interventions for students who are experiencing academic or behavioral difficulties in the regular classroom; also called *student support team, teacher assistance team*, or *problem-solving team*.

joint attention A social communication skill in which two people interact with their shared environment in the same frame of reference. Joint attention is evident when a child looks where someone else is looking or turns head or eyes in the direction someone is pointing.

language A system used by a group of people for giving meaning to sounds, words, gestures, and other symbols to enable communication with one another. Languages can use vocal (speech sounds) or nonvocal symbols, such as American Sign Language, or use movements and physical symbols instead of sounds.

language disorder Impaired comprehension and/or use of spoken, written, or other symbol systems.

learning disabilities A general term that refers to a heterogeneous group of disorders manifested by significant difficulties in the acquisition and use of listening, speaking, reading, writing, reasoning, or mathematical abilities (NJCLD, 2016).

least restrictive environment (LRE) The educational setting that most closely resembles a regular school program and also meets the child's special educational needs. For many students with disabilities, the regular classroom is the LRE; however, the LRE is a relative concept and must be determined for each individual student with disabilities.

legal blindness Visual acuity of 20/200 or less in the better eye after the best possible correction with glasses or contact lenses, or vision restricted to a field of 20 degrees or less. Acuity of 20/200 means the eye can see clearly at 20 feet what the normal eye can see at 200 feet.

level system A behavior management system in which students access greater independence and more privileges as they demonstrate increased behavioral control; see also *token economy*.

low vision Visual impairment severe enough so that special educational services are required. A child with low vision can learn through the visual channel and generally learns to read print.

macular degeneration A deterioration of the central part of the retina, which causes difficulty in seeing details clearly.

maintenance The extent to which a learner continues to exhibit a previously learned behavior after a portion or all of the instructional intervention originally used to teach the skill has been terminated.

manifestation determination A review of the relationship between a student's misconduct and his disability conducted by the individualized education program team and other qualified personnel. Required by the Individuals with Disabilities Education Act amendments of 1997 when school officials seek to discipline a student with disabilities in a manner that would result in a change of placement, suspension, or expulsion in excess of 10 days.

meningocele A type of spina bifida in which the covering of the spinal cord protrudes through an opening in the vertebrae but the cord itself and the nerve roots are enclosed.

morphemes The smallest element of a language that carries meaning.

morphology Refers to the basic units of meaning in a language and how those units are combined into words.

multifactored evaluation (MFE) Assessment and evaluation of a child using a variety of test instruments and observation procedures. Required by the Individuals with Disabilities Education Act when assessment is for educational placement of a child who is to receive special education services. Prevents the misdiagnosis and misplacement of a student as the result of considering only one test score.

multiple disabilities Two or more disabilities in the same person; defined as a disability category in the Individuals with Disabilities Education Act as "concomitant impairments, the combination of which causes such severe educational needs that they cannot be accommodated in special education programs solely for one of the impairments."

multi-tiered system of support (MTSS) System of interventions delivered at increasing levels of intensity based on student needs; focuses on both academic and social behavior. MTSS relies on evidence-based practices at all levels, appropriate screening, ongoing progress monitoring, and team-based problem solving.

muscular dystrophy A group of diseases that gradually weakens muscle tissue; usually becomes evident by the age of 4 or 5 years.

myelomeningocele A protrusion on the back of a child with spina bifida, consisting of a sac of nerve tissue bulging through a cleft in the spine.

myopia Nearsightedness; results when light is focused on a point in front of the retina, resulting in a blurred image for distant objects.

neural hearing impairment Hearing impairment attributed to abnormality or failure of the auditory nerve pathway.

neuromotor impairment Involves the central nervous system, affecting the ability to move, use, feel, or control certain parts of the body.

norm-referenced test A test constructed so that a person's score can be compared with others of same age or grade level; contrast with *criterion-referenced test.*

normal curve A mathematically derived curve depicting the theoretical probability or distribution of a given variable (e.g., as a physical trait or test score) in the general population. Indicates that approximately 68% of the population will fall within 1 standard deviation (SD) above or below the mean, approximately 27% will fall between 1 and 2 SDs either above or below the mean, and less than 3% will achieve more extreme scores of more than 2 SDs in either direction.

normalization As a philosophy and principle, the belief that individuals with disabilities should, to the maximum extent possible, be physically and socially integrated into the mainstream of society regardless of the degree or type of disability. As an approach to intervention, the use of progressively more normal settings and procedures "to establish and/or maintain personal behaviors which are as culturally normal as possible" (Wolfensberger, 1972, p. 28).

nystagmus A rapid, involuntary, rhythmic movement of the eyes that may cause difficulty in reading or fixating on an object.

occupational therapist (OT) A professional who programs and delivers instructional activities and materials to help children and adults with disabilities learn to participate in useful activities.

ocular motility The eye's ability to move.

open head injury Result of penetration of the skull, such as caused by a bullet or a forceful blow to the head with a hard or sharp object.

operant conditioning audiometry A method of measuring hearing by teaching the individual to make an observable response to sound. For example, a child may be taught to drop a block into a box each time a light and a loud tone are presented. After this response is learned, the light is no longer presented, and the volume and pitch of the tone are gradually decreased. When the child no longer drops the block into the box, the audiologist knows the child cannot hear the tone. Sometimes used to test the hearing of nonverbal children and adults.

orientation and mobility (O&M) Two complementary sets of skills that are critical for people with visual impairments. Orientation is knowing where you are, where you are going, and how to get there by interpreting information from the environment; mobility involves moving safely and efficiently from one point to another.

orthopedic impairment Impairment of the skeletal system—bones, joints, limbs, and associated muscles.

ossicles Three small bones (hammer, anvil, and stirrup) that transmit sound energy from the middle ear to the inner ear.

other health impairment (OHI) A disability category in the Individuals with Disabilities Education Act under which a child is eligible for special education; includes diseases and special health conditions such as cancer, diabetes, and cystic fibrosis that affect a child's educational activities and performance.

otitis media An infection or inflammation of the middle ear that can cause a conductive hearing loss.

paraplegia Paralysis of the lower part of the body, including both legs; usually results from injury to or disease of the spinal cord.

partial participation A teaching approach that acknowledges that even though an individual with severe disabilities may not be able to independently perform all the steps of a given task or activity, she can often be taught to do selected components or an adapted version of the task.

partially sighted The term used for legal and governmental purposes that means visual acuity of no better than 20/70 in the better eye after correction.

perinatal Occurring at or immediately after birth.

phenylketonuria (PKU) An inherited metabolic disease that can cause severe intellectual disability; can now be detected at birth, and the detrimental effects can be prevented with a special diet.

phoneme The smallest unit of sound that can be identified in a spoken language. The English language has 42 to 46 phonemes.

phonemic awareness The ability to hear and manipulate the sounds of spoken language; critical prerequisite for learning to read. A child with phonemic awareness can orally blend sounds to make a word; isolate beginning, middle, and ending sounds in words; segment words into component sounds; and manipulate sounds within words. A component of *phonologicial awareness.*

phonological awareness The understanding and knowledge that language is made up of sounds.

phonological disorder A language disorder in which the child produces a given sound correctly in some instances but not at other times.

phonology Refers to the linguistic rules governing a language's sound system.

physical therapist (PT) A professional trained to help people with disabilities develop and maintain muscular and orthopedic capability and make correct and useful movements.

pica A form of self-injurious behavior in which the person ingests nonnutritive substances (e.g., dirt, rocks, sticks, plastic, string, feces); exhibited by some people with moderate and severe intellectual disabilities.

play audiometry A method for assessing a child's hearing ability by teaching the child to perform simple but distinct activities, such as picking up a toy or putting a ball into a cup whenever he hears the signal, either pure tones or speech.

play expansions Instructional activities in which the teacher imitates the child's play actions and then models more advanced actions for the child to imitate.

positive behavioral interventions and supports (PBIS) A three-tiered framework for preventing challenging behavior that provides universal (for all students), targeted (for some), and intensive, individualized (for few) supports and interventions so that all students learn social skills and behavioral expectations.

positive reinforcement A response is followed by the presentation of a stimulus that results in similar responses occurring more often.

postlingual hearing loss Occurring after the development of language; usually used to classify hearing losses that begin after a person has learned to speak.

postnatal Occurring after birth.

practice stage of learning After a student has learned how to perform a new skill, she should work to develop fluency with the target skill. Feedback during the practice stage of learning should emphasize the rate or speed with which the student correctly performs the skill. Compare with *acquisition stage of learning*.

pragmatics Refers to the rules that govern how language is used in a communication context.

precision teaching An instructional approach that involves (a) pinpointing the skills to be learned; (b) measuring the initial frequency or rate per minute at which the student performs those skills; (c) setting an aim, or goal, for the child's improvement; (d) monitoring progress with direct and frequent measures of response rate; (e) charting performance measures on a Standard Celeration Chart; and (f) changing the program if progress toward the performance aim is inadequate.

prelingual hearing loss Describes a hearing impairment acquired before the development of speech and language.

prenatal Occurring before birth.

prereferral intervention Individualized intervention for a student experiencing academic or behavioral difficulties in the regular classroom before referring the student for formal testing and evaluation for special education eligibility. Usually coordinated by a building-based team that helps teachers devise and implement the additional academic or behavioral supports. See *multi-tiered system of supports (MTSS)*, *positive behavioral interventions and supports (PBIS)*, and *response to intervention (RTI)*.

primary prevention Interventions designed to eliminate or counteract risk factors so that a disability is never acquired; aimed at all children.

problem-based learning An instructional strategy in which students work in groups to seek solutions to real-world problems.

profound disabilities Functioning at a level no higher than a typical 2-year-old child in all behavioral and cognitive domains and requiring intensive supports and continuous monitoring.

project-based learning An instructional activity in which students work in groups to investigate an authentic question and produce a product that answers the question.

quadriplegia Paralysis of all four limbs.

receptive language disorder A language impairment characterized by difficulty in understanding language; contrast with *expressive language disorder*.

refraction The bending or deflection of light rays from a straight path as they pass from one medium (e.g., air) into another (e.g., the eye). Used by eye specialists in assessing and correcting vision.

repeated reading A technique for increasing reading fluency in which a student orally reads the same passage, usually three to five times, during each session. With each successive reading and following systematic error correction from the teacher, the student tries to increase the number of words read correctly per minute. When the student achieves a predetermined fluency criterion on a given passage, a new passage is introduced. The difficulty level of successive passages gradually increases over time.

residual hearing The remaining hearing, however slight, of a person who is deaf.

respite care The temporary care of an individual with disabilities by nonfamily members; provides much-needed support for many families of children with severe disabilities.

response cards Cards, signs, or other items that are simultaneously held up by all students to display their response to a question or problem presented by the teacher; response cards enable every student in the class to respond to each question or item.

response to intervention (RTI) A systematic prereferral and early intervention process that consists of universal screening and several tiers of increasingly intensive trials of research-based interventions before referral for assessment for special education eligibility. The Individuals with Disabilities Education Act of 2004 stipulates that schools can use RTI to determine a child's eligibility for special education under the specific learning disabilities category.

rubella German measles; when contracted by a woman during the first trimester of pregnancy, may cause visual impairments, hearing impairments, intellectual disabilities, or other congenital impairments in the child.

SAFMEDS (Say All Fast a Minute Each Day Shuffled) A deck of cards with a question, vocabulary term, or problem printed on one side of each card and the answer on the other side. A student answers as many items in the deck as she can during 1-minute practice trials by looking at the question or problem, stating an answer, flipping the card over to reveal the correct answer, and putting each card on a "correct" or "incorrect" pile.

savant syndrome Extraordinary ability or knowledge in a particular area (e.g., memorization, mathematical calculations, drawing, music) while functioning in the intellectual disability range in all other areas.

secondary prevention Interventions directed at reducing or eliminating the effects of existing risk factors; aimed at children exposed to or displaying specific risk factors.

self-evaluation A procedure in which a person compares his performance of a target behavior with a predetermined goal or standard; often a component of self-management. Sometimes called *self-assessment*.

self-management The personal application of behavior change tactics that produces a desired change in behavior. This is an intentionally broad, functional definition in that the desired change in the target behavior must occur for self-management to be demonstrated (see Cooper et al., 2020).

self-monitoring A procedure whereby a person systematically observes his behavior and records the occurrence or nonoccurrence of a target behavior. Also called *self-recording* or *self-observation*.

semantics Refers to the meaning in language.

sensory hearing impairment Hearing impairment that entails damage to the cochlea.

severe disabilities A term used to refer to challenges faced by individuals with severe and profound intellectual disability, autism, or physical or sensory impairments combined with marked developmental delay. People with severe disabilities exhibit extreme deficits in intellectual functioning and need systematic instruction for basic skills such as self-care and communicating with others.

sheltered employment Work by people with disabilities in a segregated setting, including a work activities center, operated by a private nonprofit agency that employs people with disabilities certified under special provisions of federal minimum wage laws.

shunt A tube that diverts fluid from one part of the body to another; often implanted in people with hydrocephalus to remove extra cerebrospinal fluid from the head and send it directly into the heart or intestines.

sickle cell disease An autosomal recessive disorder that affects the red blood cells' capacity to carry oxygen and leads to several complications, including severe pain, infections, organ damage, acute chest syndrome, and stroke.

sighted-guide technique A method by which a sighted person can help a person with visual impairments travel. The person with visual impairment grasps the sighted person's arm just above the elbow and walks half a step behind in a natural manner.

simple partial seizure A type of seizure characterized by sudden jerking motions with no loss of consciousness. Partial seizures may occur weekly, monthly, or only once or twice a year.

social stories An intervention for teaching social skills that uses individualized stories usually constructed with one sentence per page accompanied by photographs or simple line drawings depicting a social situation from the viewpoint of the student. Often used with children with autism spectrum disorders to decrease anxiety about the situation, help them learn relevant social cues and the expected behaviors, explain how to behave to achieve desired outcomes from the situation, and help understand the event from the perspective of others.

specific learning disability See *learning disabilities.*

speech Using breath and muscles to create the specific sounds of spoken language.

speech impairments Speech that "deviates so far from the speech of other people that it (1) calls attention to itself, (2) interferes with communication, or (3) provokes distress in the speaker or the listener" (Van Riper & Erickson, 1996, p. 110). The three basic types of speech impairments are articulation, fluency, and voice.

speech reception threshold (SRT) The decibel (sound-volume) level at which an individual can understand half of the words during a speech audiometry test; the SRT is measured and recorded for each ear.

speechreading A process of understanding a spoken message by observing the speaker's lips in combination with information gained from facial expressions, gestures, and the context or situation.

spina bifida A congenital malformation of the spine in which the vertebrae that normally protect the spine do not develop fully; may involve loss of sensation and severe muscle weakness in the lower part of the body.

spina bifida occulta A type of spina bifida that usually does not cause serious disability. Although the vertebrae do not close, no protrusion of the spinal cord and membranes is present.

standard deviation A descriptive statistic that shows the average amount of variability among a set of scores. A small standard deviation indicates that the scores in the sample are distributed close to the mean; a larger standard deviation indicates that more scores in the sample fall further from the mean.

stereotypy Repetitive, nonfunctional movements (e.g., hand flapping, rocking).

strabismus A condition in which one eye cannot attain binocular vision with the other eye because of imbalanced muscles.

stuttering Fluency disorder of speaking marked by rapid-fire repetitions of consonant or vowel sounds, especially at the beginning of words; prolongations; hesitations; interjections; and complete verbal blocks; compare with *cluttering.*

summative assessment Any type of evaluation of student performance or learning that occurs after instruction has been completed (e.g., a test given at the end of a grading period or school year).

supported living Personalized networks of natural supports to help people with disabilities live successfully in homes of their own in the community.

syntax The system of rules governing the meaningful arrangement of words in a language.

task analysis Breaking a complex skill or chain of behaviors into smaller, teachable units.

Tay-Sachs disease A progressive nervous system disorder causing profound intellectual disability, deafness, blindness, paralysis, and seizures. Usually fatal by age 5 years. Caused by a recessive gene; blood test can identify carrier; analysis of enzymes in fetal cells provides prenatal diagnosis.

technology-dependent student A "student who needs both a medical device to compensate for the loss of a vital body function and substantial and ongoing nursing care to avoid death or further disability" (Office of Technology Assessment, 1987, p. 3).

tertiary prevention Interventions designed to minimize the impact of a specific condition or disability; aimed at children with disabilities.

theory of mind The intuitive ability to distinguish and interpret one's own and other people's thoughts, motives, and beliefs (i.e., perspective taking).

tiered lesson A lesson that includes different extensions of the same basic lesson for groups of students of differing abilities. For example, after the whole class participates in a basic lesson on a poem, three groups of students might work on follow-up activities or assignments of basic, medium, and high difficulty.

time delay A technique for transferring stimulus control from a teacher-provided prompt (e.g., teacher saying the word printed on a card) to a target stimulus (e.g., printed word). The teacher presents the prompt and target stimulus concurrently, and after the student has responded correctly to several trials, the teacher (a) presents the target stimulus alone and waits 3 or 4 seconds before providing the prompt (constant time delay) or (b) presents the target stimulus alone and waits for a gradually increasing amount of time (e.g., 1 second, 2 seconds) before providing the prompt (progressive time delay). Time delay is successful when the student begins responding to the target stimulus before the prompt.

time trials A fluency-building activity in which students correctly perform a particular skill (e.g., segmenting sounds, identifying animal species, writing answers to addition and subtraction problems) as many times as they can in a brief period, usually no longer than 1 minute.

token economy An instructional and behavior-management system in which students earn tokens (e.g., stars, points, poker chips) for performing specified behaviors. Students accumulate their tokens and exchange them at prearranged times for their choice of activities or items from a menu of backup rewards (e.g., stickers, hall monitor for a day).

total communication An approach to educating deaf students that combines oral speech, sign language, and fingerspelling.

transition IEP Specifies desired postschool outcomes in four areas (employment, postsecondary education, residential, and recreation/leisure) and instructional programming and supports to help the student attain those outcomes; required part of each student's individualized education program by age 16 years.

transition services A coordinated set of activities for a child with a disability designed to facilitate the child's movement from school to postschool activities, including postsecondary education, employment, independent living, and community participation; see *transition.*

traumatic brain injury (TBI) An acquired injury to the brain caused by an external physical force, resulting in total or partial functional disability, psychosocial impairments, or both that adversely affect a child's educational performance.

tunnel vision Visual impairment in which a person has good central vision but poor peripheral vision.

tympanic membrane (eardrum) Located in the middle ear, the eardrum moves in and out to variations in sound pressure, changing acoustical energy to sound energy.

type 1 diabetes (formerly called *juvenile diabetes* or *early-onset diabetes*) A disease characterized by inadequate secretion or use of insulin and the resulting excessive sugar in the blood and urine. Managed with diet or medication (or both) but can be difficult to control. Can cause coma and eventually death if left untreated or treated improperly. Can also lead to visual impairments and the need for limb amputation. Not curable at the present time.

type 2 diabetes The most common form of diabetes; results from insulin resistance (the body's failure to properly use insulin), combined with relative insulin deficiency. Occurs most often in adults who are overweight, but the recent increase in childhood obesity has led to a rise in the incidence of type 2 diabetes in children.

universal design for learning (UDL) An approach to developing curriculum materials and lessons that incorporates concepts from architecture and product design to make access and interaction with the materials accessible, motivating, and engaging for all learners.

universal precautions A set of safety guidelines (e.g., wearing protective gloves, handwashing) that interrupt the chain of infection spread by potential biohazards such as blood and bodily fluids.

visual acuity The ability to clearly distinguish forms or discriminate details at a specified distance.

visual cortex Interprets electrical signals from the optic nerve into visual images; located in the occipital lobe at the back of the brain.

visual efficiency A term used to describe how effectively a person uses his or her vision. Includes such factors as control of eye movements, near and distant visual acuity, and speed and quality of visual processing.

visual impairment an impairment in vision that, even with correction, adversely affects a child's educational performance. The term includes both partial sight and blindness.

vocational rehabilitation A program designed to help adults with disabilities obtain and hold employment.

voice disorder The "abnormal production and/or absences of vocal quality, pitch, loudness, resonance, and/or duration, which is inappropriate for an individual's age and/or sex" (ASHA, 1993, p. 40).

work center A structured work environment where people with disabilities receive employment training and perform work for pay; viewed as an unacceptable transition outcome by most special educators and employment services professions because of sub-minimum-wage pay and segregated placement. Formerly called *sheltered workshop*.

References

AAIDD Ad Hoc Committee on Terminology and Classification. (2010). *Intellectual disability: Definition, classification, and systems of supports* (11th ed.). American Association on Intellectual and Developmental Disabilities.

Abrams, B. J. (2005). Becoming a therapeutic teacher for students with emotional and behavioral disorders. *Teaching Exceptional Children, 38*(2), 40–45.

Achenbach, T. M. (2020). *The Achenbach System of Empirically Based Assessment (ASEBA)*. http://www.aseba.org.

Adams, C. M., & Pierce, R. L. (2014). Science. In J. A. Plucker & C. M. Callahan (Eds.), *Critical issues and practices in gifted education: What the research says*. Prufrock Press.

ADHD Parents Medication Guide. (2013). Joint publication of the American Academy of Child and Adolescent Psychiatry and the American Psychiatric Association. https://www.psychiatry.org/patients-families/adhd/what-is-adhd

Adrian, M., McCauley, E., Berk, M. S., Asarnow, J. R., Korslund, K., Avina, C., Gallop, R., & Linehan, M. M. (2019). Predictors and moderators of recurring self-harm in adolescents participating in a comparative treatment trial of psychological interventions. *Journal of Child Psychology and Psychiatry, 60*(10), 1123–1132.

Agran, M., & Krupp, M. (2011). Providing choice making in employment programs: The beginning or end of self-determinations? *Education and Training in Autism and Developmental Disabilities, 46*(4), 565–575.

Agran, M., Blanchard, C., Wehmeyer, M., & Hughes, C. (2002). Increasing problem-solving skills of students with developmental disabilities participating in general education. *Remedial and Special Education, 23*, 279–288.

Agran, M., Hong, S., & Blankenship, K. (2007). Promoting the self-determination of students with visual impairments: Reducing the gap between knowledge and practice. *Journal of Visual Impairment and Blindness, 101*, 453–464.

Agran, M., Hughes, C., Thoma, C. A., & Scott, L. A. (2016). Employment social skills: What skills are really valued? *Career Development and Transition for Exceptional Individuals, 39*(2), 111–120.

Ahearn, W. H. (2010). What every behavior analyst should know about the "MMR causes autism" hypothesis. *Behavior Analysis in Practice, 3*(1), 46–52.

Al Otaiba, S. (2001). IRA outstanding dissertation award for 2001: Children who do not respond to early literacy instruction: A longitudinal study across kindergarten and first grade [Abstract]. *Reading Research Quarterly, 36*, 344–345.

Al-Hassan, S., & Gardner, R., III. (2002). Involving immigrant parents of students with disabilities in the educational process. *Teaching Exceptional Children, 35*(2), 52–58.

Alawad, H., & Musyoka, M. (2018). Examining the effectiveness of fingerspelling in improving the vocabulary and literacy skills of deaf students. *Creative Education, 9*, 456–468.

Alber, S. R., & Heward, W. L. (1996). "GOTCHA!" Twenty-five behavior traps guaranteed to extend your students' academic and social skills. *Intervention in School and Clinic, 31*, 285–289.

Alber, S. R., Nelson, J. S., & Brennan, K. B. (2002). A comparative analysis of two homework study methods on elementary and secondary school students' acquisition and maintenance of social studies content. *Education and Treatment of Children, 26*, 172–196.

Alber-Morgan, S., & Joseph, L. M. (2013). Using self-questioning, summarizing, and self-monitoring to increase reading comprehension. In R. T. Boon & V. G. Spencer (Eds.), *Adolescent literacy strategies for content comprehension in inclusive classrooms* (pp. 125–140). Paul H. Brookes Company.

Alber-Morgan, S. R. (2010). *Using RTI to teach literacy to diverse learners, K–8*. Corwin.

Alber-Morgan, S. R., Helton, M. R., Oif, A., & Konrad, M. (2019). Adapt curriculum tasks and materials for specific learning goals. In J. McLeskey, L. Maheady, B. Billingsley, M. Brownell, & Tim Lewis (Eds.), *HLPs for inclusive classrooms*. Routledge.

Alber-Morgan, S. R., Ramp, E. M., Anderson, L. L., & Martin, C. M. (2007). The effects of repeated readings, error correction, and performance feedback on the fluency and comprehension of middle school students with behavior problems. *Journal of Special Education, 41*, 17–30.

Alberto, P. A., & Fredrick, L. D. (2000). Teaching picture reading as an enabling skill. *Teaching Exceptional Children, 33*(6), 60–64.

Aldrich, F. K., & Parkin, A. J. (1989). Listening at speed. *British Journal of Visual Impairment, 7*(1), 16–18.

Ali, Z. (2001). Pica in people with intellectual disability: A literature review of etiology, epidemiology and complications. *Journal of Intellectual and Developmental Disability, 26*, 205–215.

Allday, R. A., Hinkson-Lee, K., Hudson, T, Neilsen-Gatti, S., Kleinke, A., & Russel, C. S. (2012). Training general educators to increase behaviour-specific praise: Effects on students with EBD. *Behavioral Disorders, 37*, 87–98.

Allen, K. E., Hart, B. M., Buell, J. S., Harris, F. R., & Wolf, M. M. (1964). Effects of social reinforcement on isolate behavior of a nursery school child. *Child Development, 35*, 511–518.

Allman, C. B., & Lewis, S. (2014). *ECC Essentials: Teaching the expanded core curriculum to students with visual impairments.* American Printing House for the Blind.

Graham, S., & Harris, K. R. (2018). An examination of the design principles underlying a self-regulated strategy development study based on the writers in community model. *Journal of Writing Research, 10*, 139–187.

Kim, Y., Park, C., & Park, Y. (2015). Dimensions of discourse-level oral language skills and their relations to reading comprehension and written composition: An exploratory study. *Reading and Writing: An Interdisciplinary Journal, 28*, 633–654.

Williams, M. E., Atkins, M., & Soles (2009). Assessment of Autism in Community Settings: Discrepancies in classification. Journal of Autism and Developmental Disorders, 39, 660–669.

Alper, S., & Raharinirina, S. (2006). Assistive technology for individuals with disabilities: A review and synthesis of the literature. *Journal of Special Education Technology, 21*, 47.

Alphonso, V. C., & Flanagan, D. P. (2018). *Essentials of specific learning disability identification* (2nd ed.). Wiley.

Alsalamah, A. (2017). Use of the self-monitoring strategy among students with attention deficit hyperactivity disorder: A systematic review. *Journal of Education and Practice, 8*, 118–125.

Alves, K. D., Kennedy, M. J., Brown, T. S., & Solis, M. (2015). Story grammar instruction with third and fifth grade students with learning disabilities and other struggling readers. *Learning Disabilities: A Contemporary Journal,13*(1), 73–93.

American Academy of Pediatrics. (2011). ADHD: Clinical practice guideline for the diagnosis, evaluation, and treatment of attention-deficit/hyperactivity disorder in children and adolescents. *Pediatrics, 128*, 1007–1022.

American Academy of Pediatrics. (2018). *Vaccine safety: Examine the evidence*. https://www.healthychildren.org/English/safety-prevention/immunizations/Pages/Vaccine-Studies-Examine-the-Evidence.aspx

American Association on Intellectual and Developmental Disabilities. (2020). *Definition of intellectual disability*. Author. https://www.aaidd.org/intellectual-disability/definition

American Association on Mental Retardation. (1994). Policy on facilitated communication. *AAMR News & Notes*, *7*(5), 1.

American College of Medical Genetics. (2004). *Newborn screening: Toward a uniform screening panel and system*. Report commissioned by the Health Resources and Services Administration. Supplemental report published in 2006 available at https://www.acmg.net/PDFLibrary/NBS-Uniform-Screening-Panel.pdf

American Foundation for the Blind. (2004). *The national agenda for the education of children and youths with visual impairments, including those with multiple disabilities, Revised*. Author. https://www.afb.org/national-agenda-education

American Foundation for the Blind. (2020a). *Glossary of eye conditions*. http://www.afb.org/info/living-with-vision-loss/eye-conditions/12

American Foundation for the Blind. (2020b). *Blindness and low vision*. https://www.afb.org/blindness-and-low-vision

American Optometric Association. (2020). *Eye and vision problems*. http://www.aoa.org/patients-and-public/eye-and-vision-problems?sso=y

American Printing House for the Blind. (2016). *Book Port Plus user guide*. Author. https://tech.aph.org/bt_info.htm

American Printing House for the Blind. (2018). *Fiscal year 2019 budget request to for carrying out the Act to Promote the Education of the Blind of March 3,1879*. Author. https://www2.ed.gov/about/overview/budget/budget19/justifications/j-aphb.pdf

American Printing House for the Blind. (2020). *Mobility devices for young children*. https://familyconnect.org/multiple-disabilities/independent-living-skills/amds-precanes-and-long-canes/135/

American Psychiatric Association. (2000). *Diagnostic and statistical manual of mental disorders: DSM-IV-TR* (4th ed.). Author.

American Psychiatric Association. (2013). *Diagnostic and statistical manual of mental disorders (DSM-5)* (5th ed). Author.

American Psychological Association. (1994, August). *Resolution on facilitated communication by the American Psychological Association*. Author.

American Speech-Language-Hearing Association. (2014). *Schools survey: SLP caseload characteristics report*. Author. http://www.asha.org/uploadedFiles/2014-Schools-Survey-SLP-Caseload-Characteristics.pdf#search=%222014%22

American Speech-Language-Hearing Association. (2018). *Effects of hearing loss on development*. https://www.asha.org/public/hearing/disorders/effects.htm

American Speech-Language-Hearing Association. (2019a). *Stuttering*. Author. http://www.asha.org/public/speech/disorders/stuttering/

American Speech-Language-Hearing Association. (2019b). *Augmentative and alternative communication*. https://www.asha.org/PRPSpecificTopic.aspx?folderid=8589942773§ion=Key_Issues

American Speech-Language-Hearing Association. (2020a). *Selective mutism*. http://www.asha.org/public/speech/disorders/SelectiveMutism/

American Speech-Language-Hearing Association. (2020b). *Childhood fluency disorders*. https://www.asha.org/Practice-Portal/Clinical-Topics/Childhood-Fluency-Disorders/

American Speech-Language-Hearing Association. (1993/2020). *Definitions of communication disorders and variations*. https://www.asha.org/policy/RP1993-00208/

An, X., Curby, T. W., & Brock, L. L. (2019). Is the child really what's being rated? Sources of variance in teacher ratings of socioemotional skills. *Journal of Psychoeducational Assessment*, *37*(7), 899–910.

Anderegg, M. L., Vergason, G. A., & Smith, M. C. (1992). A visual representation of the grief cycle for use by teachers with families of children with disabilities. *Remedial and Special Education*, *13*(2), 17–23.

Anderson, B. N., & Martin, J. A. (2018). What K–12 teachers need to know about teaching gifted black girls battling perfectionism and stereotype threat. *Gifted Child Today*, *41*(3), 117–124.

Anderson, C. (2014). *Simons Simplex collection: The key to findings in three major autism genetics studies*. Interactive Autism Network. http://www.iancommunity.org/cs/simons_simplex_community/key_genetic_findings

Anderson, C. M., Smith, T., & Wilczynski, S. M. (Eds.). (2018). School-based interventions for students with autism spectrum disorder [Special Issue]. *Behavior Modification*, *42*(1), 3–8.

Anderson, D. H., Trinh, S. M., Caldarella, P., Hansen, B. D., & Richardson, M. J. (2018). Increasing positive playground interaction for kindergarten students at risk for emotional and behavioral disorders. *Early Childhood Education Journal*, *46*, 487–496.

Anderson, L. W., Krathwohl, D. R., Airasian, P. W., Cruikshank, K. A., Mayer, R. E., Pintrich, P. R., Raths, J., & Wittrock, M. C. (2001). *A taxonomy for learning, teaching, and assessing: A revision of Bloom's Taxonomy of Educational Objectives (Complete ed.)*. Longman.

Anderson, G. M. (2014). Biochemical biomarkers in autism. In Volkmar et al. (Eds.), *Handbook of autism and pervasive developmental disorders*, 4th edition, pp. 457–481. Hoboken, NJ: Wiley.

Angell, M. E., Stoner, J. B., & Fulk, B. M. (2010). Advice from adults with physical disabilities on fostering self-determination during the school years. *Teaching Exceptional Children*, *42*(3), 64–75.

Ankeny, E. M., Wilkins, J., & Spain, J. (2009). Mothers' experiences of transition planning for their children with disabilities. *Teaching Exceptional Children*, *41*(6), 28–36.

Anthony, D. (1971). *Signing essential English*. Anaheim School District.

Antle, B. J. (2004). Factors associated with self-worth in young people with physical disabilities. *Health and Social Work*, *29*, 167–175.

Anxiety Disorders Association of America. (2020). *Understanding the facts of anxiety disorders and depression is the first step*. Author. http://www.adaa.org/understanding-anxiety

APSE. (2020). *APSE statement on Employment First*. Author. https://apse.org/employment-first/employment-first-statement/

Araujo, B. E. (2009). Best practices in working with linguistically diverse families. *Intervention in School and Clinic*, *45*, 116–123.

Archer, A. L., & Hughes, C. A. (2011). *Explicit instruction: Effective and efficient teaching*. Guilford Press.

Archer, A. L., Gleason, M. M., & Isaacson, S. L. (2008). *Rewards writing: Teacher's guide*. Sopris West.

Arden, S. V., Gandhi, A. G., Zumeta Edmonds, R., & Danielson, L. (2017). Toward more effective tiered systems: Lessons from national implementation efforts. *Exceptional Children*, *83*, 269–280.

Arishi, L., & Boyle, C. (2017). Inclusive education and the politics of difference: Considering the effectiveness of labelling in special education. *Educational and Child Psychology*, *34*(4), 9–19.

Armstrong v. Kline. (1979). *Education for the Handicapped Law Report* 551:195 (E.D. Pa. 1979).

Arndt, S. A., Konrad, M., & Test, D. W. (2006). Effects of the self-directed IEP on student participation in planning meetings. *Remedial and Special Education*, *27*, 194–207.

Arter, C. (1997). Listening skills. In H. Mason & S. McCall (Eds.), *Visual impairment: Access to education for children and young people* (pp. 143–148). Fulton.

Arthur, M. (2004). Patterns amongst behavior states, socio-communicative and activity variables in educational programs for students with profound and multiple disabilities. *Journal of Developmental and Physical Disabilities*, *16*, (125–49).

Artiles, A. J., Harris-Murri, N., & Rostenberg, D. (2006). Inclusion as social justice: Critical notes on discourses, assumptions, and the road ahead. *Theory into Practice, 45*, 260–268.

Association for Science in Autism Treatment. (2020). Refrigerator mother. https://asatonline.org/?s=refrigerator+mother

Assouline, S. G., Marron, M., & Colangelo, N. (2014). Acceleration: The fair and equitable intervention for highly able students. In J. A. Plucker & C. M. Callahan (Eds.), *Critical issues and practices in gifted education: What the research says*. Prufrock Press.

Asthma and Allergy Foundation of America. (2020). *Asthma facts and figures*. https://www.aafa.org/asthma-facts/

Attwood, T. (2008). *The complete guide to Asperger's syndrome* (rev. ed.). Jessica Kingsley.

Augestad, L. B. (2017). Mental health among children and young adults with visual impairments: A systematic review. *Journal of Visual Impairment & Blindness, 111*(5), 261–425.

Autism Navigator. (2020). *For families of children at risk for autism*. Florida State University. https://autismnavigator.com/family-resources/

Autism Society. (2019). *Asperger's syndrome*. https://www.autism-society.org/what-is/aspergers-syndrome/

Avant, D. W., & Swerdlik, M. E. (2016). A collaborative endeavor: The roles and functions of school social workers and school psychologists in implementing multi-tiered system of supports/response to intervention. *School Social Work Journal, 41*(1), 56–72.

Axe, J. B., & Sainato, D. M. (2010). Matrix training of preliteracy skills with preschoolers with autism. *Journal of Applied Behavior Analysis, 43*, 635–652.

Ayers, K. M., Lowrey, K. A., Douglas, K. H., & Sievers, C. (2011). I can identify Saturn but I can't brush my teeth: What happens when curricular focus for students with severe disabilities shifts. *Education and Training in Autism and Developmental Disabilities, 46*, 11–21.

Babikian, T., & Asarnow, R. F. (2009). Neurocognitive outcomes and recovery after pediatric TBI: Meta-analytic review of the literature. *Neuropsychology, 23*, 283–296.

Baddeley, A. (2000). The episodic buffer: A new component of working memory? *Trends in Cognitive Sciences, 4*, 417–423.

Baer, D. M. (1999). *How to plan for generalization* (2nd ed.). PRO-ED.

Baer, D. M. (2005). Letters to a lawyer. In W. L. Heward, T. E. Heron, N. A. Neef, S. M. Peterson, D. M. Sainato, G. Cartledge, R. Gardner III, L. D. Peterson, S. B. Hersh, & J. C. Dardig (Eds.), *Focus on behavior analysis in education: Achievements, challenges, and opportunities* (pp. 3–30). Merrill/Pearson.

Baer, R. M., & Daviso, A. W., III. (2013). Independent living and community participation. In R. W. Flexer, T. J. Simmons, P. Luft, & R. M. Baer (Eds.), *Transition planning for secondary students with disabilities* (4th ed., pp. 306–327). Merrill/Pearson.

Bailey, D., Skinner, D., Correa, V., Arcia, E., Reyes-Blanes, M., Rodriguez, P., Vazquez, E., & Skinner, M. (1999a). Needs and supports reported by Latino families of young children with developmental disabilities. *American Journal on Mental Retardation, 104*, 437–451.

Bailey, D., Skinner, D., Correa, V., Blanes, M., Vasquez, E., & Rodriguez, P. (1999b). Awareness, use, and satisfaction with services for Latino parents of young children with disabilities. *Exceptional Children, 65*, 367–381.

Bailey, D. B., Raspa, M., & Fox, L. C. (2012). What is the future of family outcomes and family centered services? *Topics in Early Childhood Special Education, 31*, 216–223.

Bak, S. (1999). Relationships between inappropriate behaviors and other factors in young children with visual impairments. *RE:view, 31*, 84–91.

Baker, S. (2011). *Research brief 1: The importance of fingerspelling for reading*. Gallaudet University Science of Learning Center on Visual Language and Visual Learning.

Baker, S., & Baker, K. (1997). Educating children who are deaf or hard of hearing: Bilingual-bicultural education. *ERIC Digest #553*. (ERIC Document Reproduction Service No. ED 416 671).

Baldwin, L., Omdal, S. N., & Perele, D. (2015). Beyond stereotypes: Understanding, recognizing, and working with twice-exceptional learners. *Teaching Exceptional Children, 47*(4), 216–225.

Balefire Labs. (2013, August 26). *Only two of top 10 ed apps in iTunes are worth buying* [Blog post]. https://karenmahon.com/2013/08/28/only-two-of-the-top-10-edapps-in-itunes-are-worth-buying/

Ball, H. B. (2018, February). Starting a high school mentoring program for the gifted: Opportunities and challenges. *Teaching for High Potential*, 1–14.

Bambara, L. M., Burns, R., Thomas, A., & Singley, D. (2020). Building skills for home and community. In F. Brown, J. McDonnell, & M. E. Snell (Eds.), *Instruction of students with severe disabilities* (9th ed., pp. 490–523). Pearson.

Banda, D. R., & Grimmett, E. (2008). Enhancing social and transition behaviors of persons with autism through activity schedules: A review. *Education and Training in Developmental Disabilities, 43*(3), 324–333.

Bandini, L., Curin, C., Phillips, S., Anderson, S. E., Maslin, M., & Must, A. (2017). Changes in food selectivity in children with autism spectrum disorder. *Journal of Autism and Developmental Disorders, 47*(2), 439–446.

Banks, J. A., & Banks, C. A. M. (Eds.). (2016). *Multicultural education: Issues and perspectives* (9th ed.). Allyn & Bacon.

Banks, J. A., & Banks, C. A. M. (Eds.). (2020). *Multicultural education: Issues and perspectives* (10th ed.). Wiley.

Barbash, S. (2012). *Clear teaching: With Direct Instruction, Siegfried Engelmann discovered a better way of teaching*. Education Consumers Foundation. [Available at http://www.education-consumers.org/CT_111811.pdf]

Barclay, L. (2012). *Learning to listen/listening to learn: Teaching listening skills to students with visual impairments*. AFB Press.

Barczak, M. A. (2019). Simulated and community-based instruction: Teaching students with intellectual and developmental disabilities to make financial transactions. *Teaching Exceptional Children, 51*(4), 313–321.

Barkley, R. A. (2012). *Executive functions: What they are, how they work, and why they evolved*. Guilford.

Barkley, R. A. (2015). *Attention-deficit hyperactivity disorder: A handbook for diagnosis and treatment* (4th ed.). Guilford.

Barkley, R. A. (2017). What causes ADHD? http://russellbarkley.org/factsheets/WhatCausesADHD2017.pdf

Barlow, J. A. (2001). Prologue: Recent advances in phonological theory and treatment. *Language, Speech, and Hearing Services in Schools, 32*, 225–228.

Barnard-Brak, L., Brewer, A., Chestnut, S. R., Richman, D., & Schaeffer, A. M. (2016). The sensitivity and specificity of the social Communication Questionnaire for autism spectrum with respect to age. *Autism Research, 9*(8), 838–845.

Baron-Cohen, S. (2001). Theory of mind in normal development and autism. *Prisme, 34*, 174–183.

Baron-Cohen, S., Allen, J., & Gillberg, C. (1992). Can autism be detected at 18 months? The needle, the haystack, and the CHAT. *British Journal of Psychiatry, 161*, 839–843.

Baron-Cohen, S., Leslie, A. M., & Frith, U. (1985). Does the autistic child have a "theory of mind"? *Cognition, 21*, 37–46.

Barton, E. E., & Pavilanis, R. (2012). Teaching pretend play to young children with autism. *Young Exceptional Children, 15*, 5–17.

Barton, E. E., Choi, G., & Mauldin, E. (2019). Teaching sequences of pretend play to children with disabilities. *Journal of Early Intervention, 41*, 13–29.

Bayley, N. (2005). *Bayley Scales of Infant and Toddler Development* (3rd ed.). San Antonio, TX: PsychCorp.

Barton, E. E., Ledford, J. R., Zimmerman, K. N., & Pokorski, E. A. (2018). Increasing the engagement and complexity of block play in young children. *Education and Treatment of Children, 41*, 169–196.

Barton, E. E., Reichow, B., Wolery, M., & Chen, C. (2011). We can all participate! Adapting circle time for children with autism. *Young Exceptional Children, 14*, 2–21.

Bass-Ringdahl, S. M. (2010). The relationship of audibility and the development of canonical babbling in young children with hearing impairment. *Journal of Deaf Studies and Deaf Education, 14*, 287–310.

Bat-Chava, Y. (2000). Diversity of Deaf identities. *American Annals of the Deaf, 145*, 420–428.

Bateman, B. D. (2017). Individualized education programs for children who have disabilities. In J. M. Kauffman, D. P. Hallahan, & P. C. Pullen (Eds.), *Handbook of special education* (2nd ed., pp. 87–104). Routledge.

Bateman, B. D., & Herr, C. M. (2019). *Writing measurable IEP goals and objectives* (3rd ed.). Attainment Company.

Bateman, B. D., & Linden, M. L. (2012). *Better IEPs: How to develop legally correct and educationally useful programs* (5th ed.). Attainment Company.

Batshaw, M. L., Roizen, N. J., & Lotrecchiano, G. R. (Eds.). (2019). *Children with disabilities* (8th ed.). Brookes.

Batten, G., Oakes, P. M., & Alexander, T. (2014). Factors associated with social interactions between deaf children and their hearing peers: A systematic literature review. *Journal of Deaf Studies and Deaf Education, 19*(3), 285–302.

Bauer, P. E. (2008). Perspective: Prenatal screening for Down syndrome. *Intellectual and Developmental Disabilities, 46*, 247–251.

Bauman-Waengler, J. (2020). *Articulation and phonology in speech sound disorders: A clinical focus*. Pearson.

Baumgart, D., Brown, L., Pumpian, I., Nisbet, J., Ford, A., Sweet, M., Messina, R., & Schroeder, J. (1982). Principle of partial participation and individualized adaptations in educational programs for severely handicapped students. *Journal of the Association for Persons with Severe Handicaps, 7*, 17–27.

Bausch, M. E., & Ault, M. J. (2008). Assistive technology implementation plan: A tool for improving outcomes. *Teaching Exceptional Children, 41*(1), 6–14.

BBC News. (2019, April 23). *Greta Thunberg: Teen activist says UK is 'irresponsible' on climate*. https://www.bbc.com/news/uk-48017083

Bean, S. M. (2010). *Developing leadership potential in gifted students*. Prufrock Press.

Bearss, K., Johnson, C., Smith, T., Lecavalier, L., Swiezy, N., Aman, M., McAdam, D. B., Butter, E., Stillitano, C., Minshawi, N., Sukhodolsky, D. G., Mruzek, D. W., Turner, K., Neal, T., Hallett, V., Mulick, J. A., Green, B., Handen, B., Deng, Y., ... Scahill, L. (2015). Effect of parent training vs parent education on behavioral problems in children with autism spectrum disorder: A randomized clinical trial. *Journal of the American Medical Association, 313*(15), 1524–1533.

Beaulieu, L., Hanley, G. P., & Roberson, A. A. (2012). Effects of responding to a name and group call on preschoolers' compliance. *Journal of Applied Behavior Analysis, 45*, 685–707.

Beaver, B. N., Reeve, S. A., Reeve, K. F., & DeBar, R. M. (2017). Self-reinforcement compared to teacher-delivered reinforcement during activity schedules on the iPod Touch. *Education and Training in Autism and Developmental Disabilities, 52*(4), 5393–404.

Becerra-Culqui, T. A., Getahun, D., Chiu, V., Sy, L. S., & Tseng, H. U. (2018). Prenatal tetanus, diphtheria, acellular pertussis vaccination and autism spectrum disorder. *Pediatrics, 142*(3): e20180120.

Beck, J., Broers, J., Hogue, E., Shipstead, J., & Knowlton, E. (1994). Strategies for functional community-based instruction and inclusion for children with mental retardation. *Teaching Exceptional Children, 26*(2), 44–48.

Behavior Analyst Certification Board. (2020). *Board Certified Behavior Analyst*. https://www.bacb.com/bcba/

Behaviorbabe. (2020). *SAFMEDS—Say All Fast a Minute Each Day Shuffled*. https://www.behaviorbabe.com/safmeds.htm

Behr, S. K., Murphy, D. L., & Summers, J. A. (1992). *User's manual: Kansas inventory of parental perceptions* (KIPP). University of Kansas, Beach Center on Families and Disability.

Beighton, C., & Wills, J. (2017). Are parents identifying positive aspects to parenting their child with an intellectual disability or are they just coping? A qualitative exploration. *Journal of Intellectual Disabilities, 21*, 325–345.

Beirne-Smith, M., Patton, J. R., & Hill, S. (2015). *An introduction to intellectual disability* (8th ed.). Pearson.

Belanger, J., & Gagné, F. (2006). Estimating the size of the gifted/talented population from multiple identification criteria. *Journal for the Education of the Gifted, 30*(2), 131–163.

Belcastro, F. (1993). Teaching addition and subtraction of whole numbers to blind students: A comparison of two methods. *Focus on Learning Problems in Mathematics, 15*(1), 14–22.

Bell, M. C., & Fahme, T. A. (2018). Functional analysis screening for multiple topographies of problem behavior. *Journal of Applied Behavior Analysis, 51*(3), 528–537.

Belmont, J. M. (1966). Long-term memory in mental retardation. *International Review of Research in Mental Retardation*, 1, 219–255.

Belote, M., & Maier, J. (2014, Fall). Why deaf-blindness and autism can look so much alike. *reSources, 19*(2). California Deaf-Blind Services. http://files.cadbs.org/200002495-2f170310b5/Belote%20-%20Maier%20reSources%20Fall%202014.pdf

Beneke, M. R., Newton, J. R., Vinh, M., Blanchard, S. B., & Kemp, P. (2019). Practicing inclusion, doing justice: Disability, identity and belonging in early childhood. *Zero to Three, 39*(3), 26–34.

Bergeron, R., & Floyd, R. G. (2006). Broad cognitive abilities of children with mental retardation: An analysis of group and individual profiles. *American Journal on Mental Retardation, 111*, 417–432.

Berkeley, S., & Larson, A. (2018). Fostering self-regulation of students with learning disabilities: Insights from 30 years of reading comprehension intervention research. *Learning Disabilities Research & Practice, 33*(2), 75–86.

Berkeley, S., & Riccomini, P. J. (2011). Academic progress monitoring. In J. M. Kauffman & D. P. Hallahan (Eds.), *Handbook of special education* (pp. 334–347). Routledge.

Berkson, G. (2004). Intellectual and physical disabilities in prehistory and early civilization. *Mental Retardation, 42*, 195–208.

Berringer, V. W. (2019). *Reading and writing acquisition: A developmental neuropsychological perspective*. Routledge.

Besnoy, K. D., & McDaniel, S. C. (2016). Going up in dreams and esteem: Cross-age mentoring to promote leadership skills in high school–age gifted students. *Gifted Child Today, 39*(1), 18–30.

BeSpecular. (2016). *What is BeSpecular?* https://www.bespecular.com/

Best, S. J. (2010a). Physical disabilities. In S. J. Best, K. W. Heller, & J. L. Bigge (Eds.), *Teaching individuals with physical or multiple disabilities* (6th ed., pp. 32–58). Merrill/Pearson.

Best, S. J. (2010b). Health impairments and infectious diseases. In S. J. Best, K. W. Heller, & J. L. Bigge (Eds.), *Teaching individuals with physical or multiple disabilities* (6th ed., pp. 82–109). Merrill/Pearson.

Best, S. J., Heller, K. W., & Bigge, J. L. (2010). *Teaching individuals with physical or multiple disabilities* (6th ed.). Merrill/Pearson.

Bettelheim, B. (1967). *The empty fortress: Infantile autism and the birth of the self*. Collier-Macmillan.

Betz, C. L., & Nehring, W. M. (2007). *Promoting health care transitions for adolescents with special health care needs and disabilities*. Baltimore: Brookes.

Bianco, M., Harris, B., Garrison-Wade, D., & Leech, N. (2011). Gifted girls: Gender bias in gifted referrals. *Roeper Review, 33*, 170–181.

Bicard, D. F., Ervin, A., Bicard, S. C., & Baylot-Casey, L. (2012). Differential effects of seating arrangement on disruptive behavior of fifth grade students during independent work. *Journal of Applied Behavior Analysis, 45*, 407–411.

Bichay-Awadalla, K., Huaqing, C., Bulotsky-Shearer, R. J., & Carta, J. J. (2020). Bidirectional relationship between language skills and behavior problems in preschool children from low-income families. *Journal of Emotional and Behavioral Disorders, 2*, 1–15.

Bierman, K. L., Coie, J. D., Dodge, K. A., Greenberg, M. T., Lochman, J. E., McMahon, R. J., & Pinderhughes, E. E. (2020). *The fast track program for children at risk: Preventing antisocial behavior*. Guilford.

Bigge, J. L., Stump, C. S., Spagna, M. E., & Silberman, R. K. (1999). *Curriculum, assessment, and instruction for students with disabilities*. Wadsworth.

Biklen, D. (1990). Communication unbound: Autism and praxis. *Harvard Educational Review, 60*, 291–314.

Bildiren, A. (2018). Developmental characteristics of gifted children aged 0–6 years: Parental observations. *Early Child Development and Care, 188*(8), 997–1011.

Billingsley, G. M., McKenzie, J. M., & Scheuermann, B. K. (2018). The effects of a structured classroom management system in secondary resource classrooms. *Exceptionality*. https://doi.org/10.1080/09362835.2018.1522257

Bisland, A. (2004). Developing leadership skills in young gifted students. *Gifted Child Today, 27*, 24–29.

Blacher, J. (1984). A dynamic perspective on the impact of a severely handicapped child on the family. In J. Blacher (Ed.), Severely handicapped children and their families (pp. 3–50). Academic Press.

Blackburn, B. R., & Witzel, B. S. (2018). *Rigor in the RTI and MTSS classroom: Practical tools and strategies*. Routledge.

Blake, J. J., Kim, E. S., Lund, E. M., Zhou, Q., Kwok, O., & Benz, M. R. (2016). Predictors of bully victimization in students with disabilities: A longitudinal examination using a national data set. *Journal of Disability Policy Studies, 26*(4), 199–208.

Blalock, G., Kochhar-Bryant, C., Test, D. W., Kohler, P., White, W., Lehmann, J., Bassett, D., & Patton, J. (2003). The need for comprehensive personnel preparation in transition and career development: DCDT position statement. *Career Development for Exceptional Individuals, 26*, 207–226.

Blatt, B. (1976). *Revolt of the idiots: A story*. Exceptional Press.

Blau, I., & Hameiri, M. (2017). Ubiquitous mobile educational data management by teachers, students and parents: Does technology change school-family communication and parental involvement. *Education and Information Technologies, 22*, 1231–1247.

Blaxhill, M. F. (2004). What's going on? The question of time trends in autism. *Public Health Reports, 119*, 536–551.

Blesson, A., & Cohen, J. S. (2019). Genetic counseling in neurodevelopmental disorders. *Cold Spring Harbor Perspectives in Medicine*, Article a036533. https://doi.org/10.1101/cshperspect.a036533

Blissymbolics Communication International. (2019). *About Blissymbolics*. Author. http://blissymbolics.org/index.php/about-blissymbolics

Block, M. E. (2016). *A teacher's guide to including students with disabilities in general physical education* (4th ed.). Brookes.

Bloom, B. S. (1980). The new direction in educational research: Alterable variables. *Phi Delta Kappan, 61*, 382–385.

Bloom, B. S., Englehart, M., Furst, E., Hill, W., & Krathwohl, D. (1956). *Taxonomy of educational objectives: The classification of educational goals. Handbook I: Cognitive domain*. Longmans, Green.

Blue-Banning, M., Summers, J. A., Frankland, H. C., Nelson, L. L., & Beegle, G. (2004). Dimensions of family and professional partnerships: Constructive guidelines for collaboration. *Exceptional Children, 70*, 167–184.

Bluestone, C. D., & Klein, J. O. (2007). *Otitis media in infants and children* (4th ed.). Philadelphia: Saunders.

Board of Education of the Hendrick Hudson Central School District v. Rowley, 102 S.Ct. 3034 (1982).

Boavida, T., Aguiar, C., & McWilliam, R. A. (2014). A training program to improve IFSP/IEP goals and objectives through the routines-based interview. *Topics in Early Childhood Special Education, 33*, 200–211.

Bogdan, R., & Biklen, D. (1977). Handicapism. *Social Policy, 7*(5), 14–19.

Bondy, A. H., & Tincani, M. (2018). Effects of response cards on students with autism spectrum disorder or intellectual disability. *Education and Training in Autism and Developmental Disabilities, 53*(1), 59–72.

Book, D., Paul, T. L., Gwalla-Ogisi, N., & Test, D. W. (1990). No more bologna sandwiches. *Teaching Exceptional Children, 22*(2), 62–64.

Boon, R. T., Paal, M., & Cornelius-Freyre, M. (2015). A review of story mapping instruction for secondary students with LD. *Learning Disabilities: A Contemporary Journal, 13*(2), 117–140.

Boon, R. T., Urton, K., Grünke, M., & Rux, T. A. (2019). Mnemonic strategies in mathematics instruction for students with learning disabilities: A narrative review. *Learning Disabilities: A Multidisciplinary Journal, 24*(2), 49–62.

Boothe, D. (2004). Gender differences in achievement and aptitude test results: Perspectives from the recent literature. In D. Boothe & J. Stanley (Eds.), *In the eyes of the beholder: Critical issues for diversity in gifted education* (pp. 179–189). Prufrock Press.

Bornstein, H. (1974). Signed English: A manual approach to English language development. *Journal of Speech and Hearing Disorders, 3*, 330–343.

Botts, B. H., Hershfeldt, P. A., & Christensen-Sandfort, R. J. (2008). Snoezelen®: Empirical review of product representation. *Focus on Autism and Other Developmental Disabilities, 24*, 17.

Bouchard, D., & Tétreault, S. (2000). The motor development of sighted children and children with moderate low vision aged 8–13. *Journal of Visual Impairments and Blindness, 94*, 564–573.

Bouck, E. C. (2011). Functional curriculum models for secondary students with mild mental impairment. *Education and Training in Autism and Developmental Disabilities, 46*, 399–409.

Bouck, E. C., Satsangi, R., & Bartlett, W. (2017). Supporting grocery shopping for students with intellectual disability: A preliminary study. *Disability and Rehabilitation: Assistive Technology, 12*(6), 605–613.

Bouck, E. C., Satsangi, R., & Park, J. (2018). The concrete-representational-abstract approach for students with learning disabilities: An evidence-based practice synthesis. *Remedial and Special Education, 39*(4), 211–228.

Bouffard, S. (July, 2008). *Tapping into technology: The role of the internet in family–school communication*. Harvard Family Research Project. http://www.hfrp.org/publications-resources/browse-our-publications/tapping-into-technology-the-role-of-the-internet-in-family-school-communication

Boushey, A. (2001). The grief cycle—One parent's trip around. *Focus on Autism and Other Developmental Disabilities, 16*, 27–30.

Boutot, E. A., & Bryant, D. P. (2005). Social integration of students with autism. *Education and Training in Developmental Disabilities, 40*, 14–23.

Boutot, E. A., & Hume, K. (2012). Beyond time out and table time: Today's applied behavior analysis for students with autism. *Education and Training in Autism and Developmental Disabilities, 47*, 23–38.

Bowe, F. (2000). *Teaching individuals with physical and multiple disabilities* (4th ed.). Merrill/Pearson.

Bower, E. M. (1960). *Early identification of emotionally handicapped children in the schools*. Thomas.

Bower, E. M. (1982). Defining emotional disturbance: Public policy and research. *Psychology in the Schools, 19*, 55–60.

Boyd-Ball, A. (2007, June). *Native Americans with disabilities.* University of Oregon.

Boykin, A. W. (1983). The academic performance of Afro-American children. In J. Spence (Ed.), *Achievement and achievement motives* (pp. 324–371). Freeman.

Boyle, J. R. (2010). Note-taking skills of middle school students with and without learning disabilities. *Journal of Learning Disabilities, 43*(6), 530–540.

Boyle, J. R. (2013). Strategic note-taking for inclusive middle school science classrooms. *Remedial and Special Education, 34*(2), 78–90.

Boyle, J. R., Forchelli, G. A., & Chariss, K. (2015). Note-taking interventions to assist students with disabilities in content area classes. *Preventing School Failure, 59*(3), 186–195.

Braddock, D., Hemp, R., Rizzolo, M. C., Hafner, L., Tanis, E. S., & Wu, J. (2011). *The state of the states in developmental disabilities: 2011.* University of Colorado, Coleman Institute for Cognitive Disabilities.

Bradley, V. J., Knoll, J., & Agosta, J. M. (Eds.). (1992). *Emerging issues in family support.* American Association on Mental Retardation.

Brambring, M. (2007). Divergent development of manual skills in children who are blind or sighted. *Journal of Visual Impairment and Blindness, 101,* 212–225.

Brame, R., Mulvey, E. P., Schubert, C. A., & Piquero, A. R. (2018). Recidivism in a sample of serious adolescent offenders. *Journal of Quantitative Criminology, 34*(1), 167–187.

Brandon, R. R., & Brown, M. R. (2009). African American families in the special education process. *Intervention in School and Clinic, 45,* 251.

Braun, S. S., & Bierman, K. L. (2020). Emotion socialization in schools. *Child and Adolescent Development.* https://doi.org/10.1002/9781119171492.wecad185

Bredecamp, S. (2020). *Effective practices in early childhood education: Building a foundation* (4th ed.). Pearson.

Brigance Early Childhood Screens (3rd ed.). (2013). Curriculum Associates.

Brigance, A. H. (2010). *Brigance Comprehensive Inventory of Basic Skills—II.* Curriculum Associates.

Bristol, M., Cohen, D., Costello, J., Denckla, M., Eckberg, T., Kallen, R., Kraemer, H., Lord, C. Maurer, R., McIlvane, W., Minshew, N. Sigman, M., & Spence, M. (1996). State of the science in autism: Report to the National Institute of Health. *Journal of Autism and Developmental Disorders, 26,* 121–154.

Broadhead, M. T., Higbee, T. S., Pollard, J. S., Akers, J. S., & Gerencser, K. R. (2014). The use of linked activity schedules to teach children with autism to play hide-and-seek. *Journal of Applied Behavior Analysis, 47,* 645–650.

Brobst, J. B., Clopton, J. R., & Hendrick, S. S. (2009). Parenting children with autism spectrum disorders. *Focus on Autism and Other Developmental Disabilities, 24,* 38–49.

Brock, M. E. (2018). Trends in the educational placement of students with intellectual disability in the United States over the past 40 years. *American Journal on Intellectual and Developmental Disabilities, 123*(4), 305–314.

Brock, M. E., Carter, E. W., & Biggs, E. E. (2020). Supporting peer interactions, friendships, and belonging. In F. Brown, J. McDonnell, & M. E. Snell (Eds.), *Instruction of students with severe disabilities* (9th ed., pp. 384–417). Pearson.

Brocki, K. C., Eninger, L., Thorell, L. B., & Bohlin, G. (2010). Interrelations between executive function and symptoms of hyperactivity/impulsivity and inattention in preschoolers: A two year longitudinal study. *Journal of Abnormal Child Psychology, 38,* 163–171.

Brogaard, B. (2012). *Kim Peek: The real Rain Man. Psychology Today.* https://www.psychologytoday.com/us/blog/the-superhuman-mind/201212/kim-peek-the-real-rain-man

Bronicki, G. J., & Turnbull, A. P. (1987). Family–professional interactions. In M. E. Snell (Ed.), *Systematic instruction of persons with severe handicaps.* (3rd ed., pp. 9–35). Merrill/Pearson.

Broomhead, K. (2013). Blame, guilt and the need for 'labels'; insights from parents of children with special educational needs and educational practitioners. *British Journal of Special Education, 40,* 14–21.

Brosh, C. R., Fisher, L. B., Wood, C. L., & Test, D. W. (2018). High-probability request sequence: An evidence-based practice for individuals with autism spectrum disorder. *Education and Training in Autism and Developmental Disabilities, 53(3),* 381–395.

Browder, D., Ahlgrim-Delzell, L., Flowers, C., & Baker, J. (2012). An evaluation of a multicomponent early literacy program for students with severe developmental disabilities. *Remedial and Special Education, 33,* 237–246.

Browder, D. M. (2000). *Comments made as guest faculty for OSU teleconference seminar: Contemporary issues in special education.* The Ohio State University.

Browder, D. M. (2001). *Curriculum and assessment for students with moderate and severe disabilities.* Guilford.

Browder, D. M. (2013). "Eighth grade work!" Teaching general curriculum content to students with severe disabilities. In W. L. Heward, *Exceptional children: An introduction to special education* (10th ed., pp. 432–433). Pearson.

Browder, D. M., & Spooner, F. (2006). *Teaching language arts, math, and science to students with significant cognitive disabilities.* Brookes.

Browder, D. M., Ahlgrim-Delzell, L., Courtade Little, G., & Snell, M. E. (2006). General curriculum access. In M. E. Snell & F. Brown (Eds.), *Instruction of students with severe disabilities* (6th ed., pp. 489–525). Pearson.

Browder, D. M., Ahlgrim-Delzell, L., Spooner, F., Mims, P. J., & Baker, J. N. (2009). Using time delay to teach literacy to students with severe developmental disabilities. *Exceptional Children, 75,* 343–364.

Browder, D. M., Lee, A., & Mims, P. J. (2011). Using shared stories and individual response modes to promote comprehension and engagement in literacy for students with multiple, severe disabilities. *Education and Training in Autism and Developmental Disabilities, 46,* 339–351.

Browder, D. M., Spooner, F., & Courtade, G. R. (2020). *Teaching students with moderate and severe disabilities* (2nd ed.). Guilford.

Browder, D. M., Spooner, F., Lo, Y. Y., Saunders, A. F., Root, J. R., Ley Davis, L., & Brosh, C. R. (2018). Teaching students with moderate intellectual disability to solve word problems. *The Journal of Special Education, 51*(4), 222–235.

Brown v. Board of Education of Topeka, 347 U.S. 483 (1954).

Brown, F., McDonnell, J., & Snell, M. E. (Eds.). (2020). *Instruction of students with severe disabilities* (9th ed.). Pearson.

Brown, L., Farrington, K., Suomi, J., & Zeigler, M. (1999). Work-wage relationships and individuals with disabilities. *Journal of Vocational Rehabilitation, 13*(1), 5–13.

Brown, L., Ford, A., Nisbet, J., Sweet, M., Shiraga, B., & Gruenewald, L. (Eds.). (1982). *Educational programs for severely handicapped students* (Vol. XII). MMSD.

Brown, L., Long, E., Udvari-Solner, A., Davis, L., VanDeventer, P., Ahlgren, C., Johnson, F., Gruenewald, L., & Jorgensen, J. (1989). The home school: Why students with severe disabilities must attend the schools of their brothers, sisters, friends, and neighbors. *Journal of the Association for Persons with Severe Handicaps, 14,* 1–7.

Brown, L., Schwartz, P., Udvari-Solner, A., Kampschroer, E. F., Johnson, F., Jorgensen, J., & Gruenewald, L. (1991). How much time should students with severe intellectual disabilities spend in regular education classrooms and elsewhere? *Journal of the Association for Persons with Severe Handicaps, 16,* 39–47.

Brown, V. L., Cronin, M. E., & Bryant, D. P. (2012). *Test of mathematical abilities* (3rd ed.). PRO-ED.

Brown, V. L., Wiederholt, J. L., & Hammill, D. D. (2008). *Test of reading comprehension* (4th ed.). PRO-ED.

Bruce, S. M., Nelson, C., Perez, A., Stutzman, B., & Barnhill, B. A. (2016). The state of research on communication and literacy in deafblindness. *American Annals of the Deaf, 161*(4), 424–443.

Bruhn, A., & Watt, S. (2012). Improving behavior by using multicomponent self-monitoring within a targeted reading intervention. *Behavioral Disorders, 38*, 3–17.

Bruhn, A., McDaniel, S., & Kreigh, C. (2015). Self-monitoring interventions for students with behavior problems: A systematic review of current research. *Behavioral Disorders, 40*, 102–121.

Brulles, D., Peters, S. J., & Sauders, R. (2012). Schoolwide mathematics achievement within the gifted cluster grouping model. *Journal of Advanced Academics, 23*, 200–216.

Buck Institute for Education. (2020). http://bie.org

Bulgren, J. A., Deshler, D. D, & Lenz, B. K. (2007). Engaging adolescents with LD in higher order thinking about history concepts using integrated content enhancement routines. *Journal of Learning Disabilities, 40*, 121–133.

Bull, R., Marschark, M., Nordman, E., Sapere, P., & Skene, W. A. (2018). The approximate number system and domain-general abilities as predictors of math ability in children with normal hearing and hearing loss. *British Journal of Developmental Psychology, 36*, 236–254.

Bureau of Labor Statistics, U.S. Department of Labor. (2020). *Persons with a disability: Labor force characteristics—2019*. http://www.bls.gov/news.release/pdf/disabl.pdf

Burgoon, J. K., Guerrero, L. K., & Floyd, K. (2010). *Nonverbal communication*. Routledge.

Burns, D. A., & Thompson, S. D. (2014). Turning mealtimes into learning opportunities: Integrating feeding goals into IEPs. *Teaching Exceptional Children, 46*(6), 179–186.

Bursuck, W. D., & Damer, M. (2015). *Teaching reading to students who are at risk or have disabilities: A multi-tier, RTI approach* (3rd ed.). Pearson.

Bybee, J., & Zigler, E. (1998). Outerdirectedness in individuals with and without mental retardation: A review. In J. A. Burack, R. M. Hodapp, & E. Zigler (Eds.), *Handbook of mental retardation* (pp. 434–460). Cambridge University Press.

Byzek, J. (2001, February). Committed couples. *New Mobility: The Magazine for Active Wheelchair Users*. https://newmobility.com/2001/02/committed-couples/

Cagliani, R. R., Ayres, K. M., Whiteside, E., & Ringdahl, J. E. (2017). Picture exchange communication system and delay to reinforcement. *Journal of Developmental and Physical Disabilities, 29*, 925–939.

Cakiroglu, O. (2014). Effects of preprinted response cards on rates of academic response, opportunities to respond, and correct on academic responses of students with mild intellectual disability. *Journal of Intellectual & Developmental Disability*, 39(1), 73–85.

Caldarella, P., Larsen, R. A. A., Williams, L. Downs, K. R., Wills, H. P., & Wehby, J. H. (2020a). Effects of teachers' praise-to-reprimand ratios on elementary students' on-task behavior. *Educational Psychology*. https://doi.org/10.1080/01443410.2020.1711872

Caldarella, P., Larsen, R. A. A., Williams, L., Wills, H. P., & Wehby, J. H. (2020b). "Stop doing that!": Effects of teacher reprimands on student disruptive behavior and engagement. *Journal of Positive Behavior Interventions*. https://doi.org/10.1177/1098300720935101

Callahan, C. M., & Dickson, R. K. (2014). Mentors and mentorships. In J. A. Plucker & C. M. Callahan (Eds.), *Critical issues and practices in gifted education: What the research says* (pp. 413–426). Prufrock Press.

Callahan, K., Rademacher, J. A., & Hildreth, B. L. (1998). The effect of parent participation in strategies to improve the homework performance of students who are at risk. *Remedial and Special Education, 19*(3), 131–141.

Callus, A. M. (2017). 'Being friends means helping each other, making coffee for each other': Reciprocity in the friendships of people with intellectual disability. *Disability & Society, 32*(1), 1–16.

Camodeca, A., Todd, K. Q., & Croyle, J. (2020). Utility of the Asperger Syndrome Diagnostic Scale in the assessment of autism spectrum disorders. *Journal of Autism and Developmental Disorders, 50*, 513–523.

Campbell, A. R., Bowman-Perrott, L., Burke, M. D., & Sallese, M. R. (2018). Reading, writing, math, and content-area interventions for improving behavioral and academic outcomes of students with emotional and behavioral disorders. *Learning Disabilities: A Contemporary Journal, 16*(2), 119–138.

Campbell, F. A., & Ramey, C. T. (1994). Effects of early intervention on intellectual and academic achievement: A follow-up study of children from low-income families. *Child Development, 65*, 684–689.

Campbell, J. (2007). Understanding the emotional needs of children who are blind. *Journal of Visual Impairment and Blindness, 101*, 351–355.

Cannella-Malone, H. I., Brooks, D. G., & Tullis, C. A. (2013). Using self-directed video prompting to teach students with intellectual disabilities. *Journal of Behavioral Education, 22*, 169–189.

Cannella-Malone, H. I., Konrad, M., & Pennington, R. C. (2015). ACCESS! Teaching writing skills to students with intellectual disability. *Teaching Exceptional Children, 47*(5), 272–280.

Cannella-Malone, H. I., Miller, O., Schaefer, J. M., Jimenez, E. D., Page, E. J., & Sabielny, L. M. (2016). Using video prompting to teach leisure skills to students with significant disabilities. *Exceptional Children, 82*(4), 463–478.

Cannella-Malone, H. I., O'Reilly, M. F., Sigafoos, J., & Chan, J. M. (2008). Combined curricular intervention with brief hands down to decrease hand mouthing and the use of arm splints for a young boy with profound disabilities. *Education and Training in Developmental Disabilities, 43*, 360–366.

Cannella-Malone, H. I., Sabielny, L. M., Jimenez, E. D., & Miller, M. (2013). Pick one! Conducting preference assessment with students with significant disabilities. *Teaching Exceptional Children, 45*(6), 16–23.

Cantrell, R. J., Fusara, J. A., & Dougherty, E. A. (2000). Exploring the effectiveness of journal writing on learning social studies: A comparative study. *Reading Psychology, 21*, 1–11.

Cantu, C. O. (2004). Wheelchair positioning: Foundation in wheelchair selection. *Exceptional Parent, 34*(5), 33–35.

Carlin, M. T., Chrysler, C., & Sullivan, K. (2007). Conjunctive search in individuals with and without mental retardation. *American Journal on Mental Retardation, 112*, 54–65.

Carlin, M. T., Soraci, S. A., & Strawbridge, C. P. (2005). Generative learning during visual search for scene changes: Enhancing free recall of individuals with and without mental retardation. *American Journal on Mental Retardation, 110*, 13–22.

Carlson, C. L. (2013). Adolescent literacy, dropout factories, and the economy: The relationship between literacy, graduation rates, and economic development in the United States. *Journal of Education and Human Development, 2*(1), 1–8.

Carnine, D. W., Silbert, J., Kame'enui, E. J., Slocum, T. E., & Travers, P. A. (2017). *Direct instruction reading* (6th ed). Hoboken, NJ: Pearson.

Carroll, R. A., & Kodak, T. (2015). Using instructive feedback to increase response variability during intraverbal training for children with autism spectrum disorder. *The Analysis of Verbal Behavior, 31*(2), 183–199.

Carta, J., & Greenwood, C. (2010). The social IGDI: Early Social Indicator (ESI). In J. Carta, C. Greenwood, D. Walker, & J. Buzhardt (Eds.), *Individual Growth and Developmental Indicators: Tools for monitoring progress and measuring growth in young children* (pp. 91–108). Paul H. Brookes.

Carter, E. W., Asmus, J., Moss, C. K., Biggs, E. E., Bolt, D. M., Born, T. L., Brock, M. E., Cattey, G. N., Chen, R., Cooney, M., Fesperman, E., Hochman J. M., Huber, H. B., Leguia, J. L., Lyons, G., Moyseenko, K. A., Riesch, L. M., Shalev, R. A., Vincent, L. B., & Weir, K. (2016). Randomized evaluation of peer support arrangements to support the inclusion of high school students with severe disabilities. *Exceptional Children, 82*, 209–233.

Carter, E. W., Austin, D., & Trainor, A. A. (2011). Factors associated with the early work experiences of adolescents with severe disabilities. *Intellectual and Developmental Disabilities, 49*, 233–247.

Cartledge, G., & Dukes, C. (2009). Disproportionality of African American children in special education: Definition and dimensions (pp. 382–399). In L. C. Tillman (Ed.), *The SAGE handbook of African American education*. SAGE Publications.

Cartledge, G., & Kleefeld, J. (2009). *Taking part: Introducing social skills to children* (2nd ed.). Research Press.

Cartledge, G., & Kourea, L. (2008). Culturally responsive classrooms for culturally diverse students with and at risk for disabilities. *Exceptional Children, 74*, 351–371.

Cartledge, G., Kea, C. D., & Ida, D. J. (2000). Anticipating differences—celebrating strengths: Providing culturally competent services for students with serious emotional disturbance. *Teaching Exceptional Children, 32*(3), 6–12.

Cartledge, G., Kea, C. D., Watson, M., & Oif, A. (2016). Special education disproportionality: A review of response to intervention and culturally relevant pedagogy. *Multiple Voices for Ethnically Diverse Exceptional Learners, 16*(1), 29–49.

Cascella, P. W., & McNamara, K. M. (2005). Empowering students with severe disabilities to actualize communication skills. *Teaching Exceptional Children, 37*(3), 38–43.

Casner-Lotto, J., & Barrington, L. (2006). *Are they really ready to work? Employers' perspectives on the basic knowledge and applied skills of new entrants to the 21st*

Castellano, J., & Frazier, A. D. (2011). *Special populations in gifted education*. Prufrock Press.

Cavendish, W., Connor, D. J., & Rediker, E. (2017). Engaging students and parents in transition-focused individualized education programs. *Intervention in School and Clinic, 52*, 228–235.

Cavioni, V., Grazzani, I., & Ornaghi, V. (2017). Social and emotional learning for children with learning disability: Implications for inclusion. *International Journal of Emotional Education, 9*(2), 100–109.

Cavkaytar, A., & Pollard, E. (2009). Effectiveness of parent and therapist collaboration program (PTCP) for teaching self-care and domestic skills to individuals with autism. *Education and Training in Mental Retardation and Developmental Disabilities, 44*(3), 381–395.

Cawthon, S. W. (2001). Teaching strategies in inclusive classrooms with deaf students. *Journal of Deaf Studies and Deaf Education, 6*, 212–225.

Cease-Cook, J., Fowler, C., & Test, D. W. (2015). Strategies for creating work-based learning experiences in schools for secondary students with disabilities. *Teaching Exceptional Children, 47*(6), 352–358.

Cedar Rapids Community School District v. Garret F., 67 U.S. L. W. 4165 (1999).

Celeste, M. (2006). Play behaviors and social interactions of a child who is blind: In theory and practice. *Journal of Visual Impairment and Blindness, 100*, 75–90.

Celiberti, D. (2017). Interview with Sabrina Freeman. *Science in Autism Treatment, 14*(1), 3–10.

Center for Applied Special Technology. (2020). *About Universal design for learning UDL*. CAST. http://www.cast.org/our-work/about-udl.html

Center on the Developing Child. (2020). *Activities guide: Enhancing and practicing executive function skills with children from infancy to adolescence*. Harvard University. http://developingchild.harvard.edu/resources/tools_and_guides/enhancing_and_practicing_executive_function_skills_with_children/

Centers for Disease Control and Prevention. (2013). Mental health surveillance among children—United States, 2005–2011. *MMWR Suppl., 2*(2). http://www.cdc.gov/mmwr/preview/mmwrhtml/su6202a1.htm?s_cid=su6202a1_w

Centers for Disease Control and Prevention. (2014). *Key findings: Trends in the parent-report of health care provider-diagnosis and medication treatment for ADHD: United States, 2003–2011*. http://www.cdc.gov/ncbddd/adhd/features/key-findings-adhd72013.html

Centers for Disease Control and Prevention. (2019a). *What is fragile X syndrome?* Author. https://www.cdc.gov/ncbddd/fxs/facts.html

Centers for Disease Control and Prevention. (2019b). *Fetal alcohol spectrum disorders*. Author. https://www.cdc.gov/ncbddd/fasd/facts.html

Centers for Disease Control and Prevention. (2020a). *Data & statistics on autism spectrum disorder*. U.S. Department of Health & Human Services. https://www.cdc.gov/ncbddd/autism/data.html

Centers for Disease Control and Prevention. (2020b). *Autism prevalence rises in communities monitored by CDC*. U.S. Department of Health & Human Services. https://www.cdc.gov/media/releases/2020/p0326-autism-prevalence-rises.html

Centers for Disease Control and Prevention. (2020c). *Attention deficit/hyperactivity disorder*. U.S. Department of Health and Human Services. https://www.cdc.gov/ncbddd/adhd/data.html

Centers for Disease Control and Prevention. (2020d). *Attention deficit/hyperactivity disorder: Treatment*. U.S. Department of Health and Human Services. https://www.cdc.gov/ncbddd/adhd/treatment.html

Centers for Disease Control and Prevention. (2020e). *Epilepsy data and statistics*. U.S. Department of Health and Human Services. https://www.cdc.gov/epilepsy/data/index.html

Centers for Disease Control and Prevention. (2020f). *National Diabetes Statistics Report: Estimates of Diabetes and Its Burden in the United States, 2020*. U.S. Department of Health and Human Services. https://www.cdc.gov/diabetes/pdfs/data/statistics/national-diabetes-statistics-report.pdf

Centers for Disease Control and Prevention. (2020g). *Sickle cell disease: Complications and treatment*. http://www.cdc.gov/ncbddd/sicklecell/treatments.html

Centers for Disease Control and Prevention. (2020h). *HIV transmission*. U.S. Department of Health and Human Services. http://www.cdc.gov/hiv/basics/transmission.html

Centers for Disease Control and Prevention. (2020i). *Cerebral palsy*. U.S. Department of Health and Human Services. https://www.cdc.gov/ncbddd/cp/index.html

Centers for Disease Control and Prevention. (2020j). *Spina bifida*. U.S. Department of Health and Human Services. https://www.cdc.gov/ncbddd/spinabifida/

Cerney, J. (2007). *Deaf education in America*. Gallaudet University Press.

Cervantes, P., Shalev, R., & Donnelly, L. (2019). Definition and diagnosis. In J. L. Matson (Ed.), *Handbook of intellectual disabilities* (pp. 45–59). Springer.

Charania, S. M., LeBlanc, L. A., Carr, J. E., & Gunby, K. (2010). Teaching effective hand raising to children with autism during group instruction. *Journal of Applied Behavior Analysis, 43*, 493–497.

Chard, D. J., & Kame'enui, E. J. (2000). Struggling first-grade readers: The frequency and progress of their reading. *The Journal of Special Education, 34*, 28–38.

Chen, D., & Downing, J. E. (2006a). *Tactile learning strategies: Interacting with children who have visual impairments and multiple disabilities*. AFB Press.

Chen, D., & Downing, J. E. (2006b). *Tactile strategies for children who have visual impairments and multiple disabilities: Promoting communication and learning skills*. AFB Press.

Cheng, L.-R. L. (2012). Language and linguistically-culturally diverse children. In V. A. Reed (Ed.), *An introduction to children with language disorders* (4th ed., pp. 352–392). Pearson.

Cherkasova, M. V., & Hechtman, L. (2009). Neuroimaging in attention-deficit hyperactivity disorder: Beyond the frontostriatal circuitry. *Canadian Journal of Psychiatry, 54,* 651–664.

Chesley, G. M., & Calaluce, P. D. (1997). The deception of inclusion. *Mental Retardation, 35,* 488–490.

Chestnut, S. R., Wei, T., Barnard-Brak, L., & Richman, D. M. (2017). A meta-analysis of the Social Communication Questionnaire: Screening for autism spectrum disorder. *Autism, 21*(8), 920–928.

Chiarotti, F., & Venerosi, A. (2020). Epidemiology of autism spectrum disorders: A review of worldwide prevalence estimates since 2014. *Brain Sciences, 10,* 274. https://doi.org/10.3390/brainsci10050274

Child Trends. (2013). *Parental involvement in schools.* Author. https://www.childtrends.org/?indicators=parental-involvement-in-schools

Chitiyo, J., & May, M. E. (2018). Factors predicting sustainability of the schoolwide positive behavior intervention support model. *Preventing School Failure, 62*(2), 94–104.

Chou, I., Kuo, C., Huang, Y., Grainge, M. J., Valdes, A. M., See, L., Yu, K., et al. (2017). Familial aggregation and heritability of schizophrenia and co-aggregation of psychiatric illnesses in affected families. *Schizophrenia Bulletin, 43*(5), 1070–1078.

Chow, J. C., & Wehby, J. H. (2018). Associations between language and problem behavior: A systematic review and correlational meta-analysis. *Educational Psychology Review, 30*(1), 61–82.

Christensen-Sandfort, R. J., & Whinnery, S. B. (2013). Impact of milieu teaching on communication skills of young children with autism spectrum disorder. *Topics in Early Childhood Special Education, 32*(4), 211–222.

Chua, B. Y. E., & Poon, K. K. (2018). Studying the implementation of PECS in a naturalistic special education school setting. *Educational & Child Psychology, 35,* 60–75.

Cihak, D. F., Alberto, P. A., Kessler, K. B., & Taber, T. A. (2004). An investigation of instructional scheduling arrangements for community-based instruction. *Research in Developmental Disabilities, 25*(1), 67–88.

Cihak, D. F., Kessler, K., & Alberto, P. A. (2008). Use of a handheld prompting system to transition independently through vocational tasks for students with moderate and severe intellectual disabilities. *Education and Training in Developmental Disabilities, 43,* 102–110.

Cimera, R. E., Wehman, P., West, M., & Burgess, S. (2012). Do sheltered workshops enhance employment outcomes for adults with autism spectrum disorder? *Autism, 16,* 87–94.

Ciullo, S., & Reutebuch, C. (2013). Computer-based graphic organizers for students with LD: A systematic review of literature. *Learning Disabilities Research & Practice, 28*(4), 196–210.

Ciullo, S., Falcomata, T. S., Pfannenstiel, K., & Billingsley, G. (2015). Improving learning with science and social studies text using computer-based concept maps for students with disabilities. *Behavior Modification, 39*(1), 117–135.

Clark, B. A. (2009). Responding to the profoundly different brains of highly gifted. *Gifted Education Communicator, 40*(4), 12–13.

Clark, B. A. (2013). *Growing up gifted* (8th ed.). Pearson.

Clark, K. A., & Test, D. W. (2020). *The effects of UPGRADE Your Performance on employment soft skills of students with intellectual and developmental disabilities: A study of generalization.*

Clark, K. A., Konrad, M., & Test, D. W. (2018). UPGRADE your performance: Improving soft skills of students with disabilities. *Journal of Vocational Rehabilitation, 49,* 351–365.

Clark, K. A., Test, D. W., & Konrad, M. (2019). Teaching soft skills to students with disabilities using UPGRADE your performance. *Education and Training in Autism and Developmental Disabilities, 54,* 41–56.

Clarke, L. S., Haydon, T., Bauer, A., & Epperly, A. C. (2016). Inclusion of students with an intellectual disability in the general education classroom with the use of response cards. *Preventing School Failure, 60*(1), 35–42.

Clausen, J. A. (1967). Mental deficiency: Development of a concept. *American Journal of Mental Deficiency, 71,* 727–745.

Cmar, J. L., McDonnall, M. C., & Crudden, A. (2018). Transportation self-efficacy and employment among individuals with visual impairments. *Journal of Vocational Rehabilitation, 48,* 257–268.

Cobb, B., Lehmann, J., Newman-Gonchar, R., & Morgen, A. (2009). Self-determination for students with disabilities: A narrative metasynthesis. *Career Development for Exceptional Individuals, 32*(2), 108–114.

Cobb Morocco, C., Clay, K., Parker, C. E., & Zigmond, N. (2006). Walter Cronkite High School: A culture of freedom and responsibility. *Learning Disabilities Research & Practice, 21,* 146–158.

Cohen, H., Amerine-Dickens, M., & Smith, T. (2006). Early intensive behavioral treatment: Replication of the UCLA Model in a community setting. *Journal of Developmental and Behavioral Pediatrics, 27,* S145–S155.

Cohen, M. J., & Gerhardt, P. F. (2015). *Visual supports for people with autism: A guide for parents and* professionals (2nd ed.) Brookes.

Colangelo, N., Assouline, S. G., & Gross, M. U. M. (2004). *A nation deceived: How schools hold back America's brightest students.* University of Iowa Press.

Cole, C. M., Waldron, N., & Majd, M. (2004). Academic progress of students across inclusive and traditional settings. Mental Retardation, 42, 136–144.

Cole, S. M., Murphy, H. R., Frisby, M. B., Grossi, T. A., & Hannah, R. B. (2020). The relationship of special education placement and student academic outcomes. *The Journal of Special Education.* https://doi.org/10.1177/0022466920925033

Collins, B. C. (2007). *Moderate and severe disabilities: A foundational approach.* Merrill/Pearson.

Collins, B. C., Evans, A., Creech-Galloway, C., Karl, J., & Miller, A. (2010). Comparison of the acquisition and maintenance of teaching functional core content sight words in special and general education settings. *Focus on Autism and Other Developmental Disabilities, 22,* 220–233.

Collins, B. C., Hager, K. D., & Galloway, C. C. (2011). Addition of functional content during core content instruction with students with moderate disabilities. *Education and Training in Autism and Developmental Disabilities, 46,* 22–39.

Collins, B. C., Karl, J., Riggs, L., Galloway, C. C., & Hager, K. D. (2010). Teaching core content with real-life applications to secondary students with moderate and severe disabilities. *Teaching Exceptional Children, 43*(1), 52–59.

Collins, B. C., Karl, J., Riggs, L., Galloway, C. C., & Hager, K. D. (2010). Teaching core content with real-life applications to secondary students with moderate and severe disabilities. *Teaching Exceptional Children, 43*(1), 52–59.

Commission on Education of the Deaf. (1988). *Toward equality: Education of the deaf.* Washington, DC: U.S. Government Printing Office.

Common, E. A., Bross, L. A., Oakes, W. P., Cantwell, E. D., Lane, K. L., & Germer, K. A. (2019). Systematic review of high probability requests in K-12 settings: Examining the evidence base. *Behavioral Disorders, 45,* 3–21.

Conley, R. W. (2003). Supported employment in Maryland: Successes and issues. *Mental Retardation, 41,* 237–249.

Conners, C. K. (2000). Attention-deficit/hyperactivity disorder: Historical development and overview. *Journal of Attention Disorders, 3,* 173–191.

Connolly, A. J. (2007). *KeyMath—3: A diagnostic inventory of essential skills.* Pearson.

Connolly, C. M., Rose, J., & Austen, S. (2006). Identifying and assessing depression in prelingually deaf people: A literature review. *American Annals of the Deaf, 151*, 49–60.

Connolly, E. J., & Jackson, D. B. (2019). Adolescent gang membership and adverse behavioral, mental health, and physical health outcomes in young adulthood. *Criminal Justice and Behavior, 46*(11), 1566–1586.

Connor, D., Cavendish, W., Gonzalez, T., & Jean-Pierre, P. (2019). Is a bridge even possible over troubled waters? The field of special education negates the overrepresentation of minority students: A DisCrit analysis. *Race Ethnicity and Education, 22*(6), 723–745.

Connor, D. F. (2015). Stimulant and nonstimulant medications for childhood ADHD. In R. A. Barkley (Ed.), *Attention-deficit hyperactivity disorder* (4th ed., pp. 666–685). Guilford.

Conroy, M. A. (2016). Moving the dial for students with emotional and behavioral disorders: Ensuring early access to intensive supports. *Journal of Emotional and Behavioral Disorders, 24*(3), 191–193.

Conroy, M. A., & Brown, W. H. (2006). Early identification, prevention, and early intervention with young children at risk for emotional and behavioral disorders: Issues, trends, and a call for action. *Behavioral Disorders, 29*, 224–236.

Convertino, C., Borgna, G., Marschark, M., & Durkin, A. (2014). Word and world knowledge among deaf learners with and without cochlear implants. *Journal of Deaf Studies and Deaf Education, 19*(4), 471–483.

Cook, B. G. (2001). A comparison of teachers' attitudes toward their included students with mild and severe disabilities. *Journal of Special Education, 34*, 203–213.

Cook, B. G. (2004). Inclusive teachers' attitudes toward their students with disabilities: A replication and extension. *The Elementary School Journal, 104*, 307–320.

Cook, B. G., & Tankersley, M. (2013). *Research-based practices in special education*. Pearson.

Cook, B. G., Cameron, D. L., & Tankersley, M. (2007). Inclusive teachers' attitudinal ratings of their students with disabilities. *The Journal of Special Education, 40*, 230–238.

Cook, R. E., Klein, M. D., & Chen, D. (2020). *Adapting early childhood curricula for children with disabilities and special needs* (10th ed.). Pearson.

Cook, S. C., Collins, L. W., Morin, L. L., & Riccomini, P. J. (2019). Schema-based instruction for mathematical word problem solving: An evidence-based review for students with learning disabilities. *Learning Disability Quarterly, 43*(2), 75–87. https://doi.org/10.1177/0731948718823080

Cooke, N. L., Mackiewicz, S. M., Wood, C. L., & Helf, S. (2009). The use of audio prompting to assist mothers with limited English proficiency in teaching their pre-kindergarten children English vocabulary. *Education and Treatment of Children, 32*(2), 213–229.

Cooper, H. L., & Nichols, S. K. (2007). Technology and early braille literacy: Using the Mountbatten Pro Brailler in primary-grade classrooms. *Journal of Visual Impairment and Blindness, 101*, 22–31.

Cooper, J. O., Heron, T. E., & Heward, W. L. (2020). *Applied behavior analysis* (3rd ed.). Pearson.

Cooper, K. J., & Browder, D. M. (1998). Enhancing choice and participation for adults with severe disabilities in community-based instruction. *Journal of the Association for Persons with Severe Handicaps, 23*, 252–260.

Copeland, S. R., & McDonnell, J. (2020). Teaching academic skills. In F. Brown, J. McDonnell, & M. E. Snell (Eds.), *Instruction of students with severe disabilities* (9th ed., pp. 452–489). Pearson.

Copeland, S. R., Hughes, C., Carter, W. W., Guth, C., Presley, J. A., Williams, C. R., & Fowler, S. E. (2004). Increasing access to general education: Perspectives of participants in a high school peer support program. *Remedial and Special Education, 25*, 342–352.

Corn, A. L., & Erin, J. N. (Eds.). (2010). *Foundations of low vision: Clinical and functional perspectives* (2nd ed.). AFB Press.

Corn, A. L., & Lusk, K. E. (2010). Perspectives on low vision. In A. L. Corn & J. N. Erin (Eds.), *Foundations of low vision: Clinical and functional perspectives* (2nd ed., pp. 3–34). AFB Press.

Corn, A. L., Erin, J. N., Ferrenkipf, C., Huebner, K. M., McNear, D., Spungin, S. J., & Torres, I. (Eds.). (2004). *When you have a visually impaired student in your classroom: A guide for teachers*. AFB Press.

Corn, A., & Ryser, G. (1989). Access to print for students with low vision. *Journal of Visual Impairment & Blindness, 83*, 340–349.

Cornett, R., & Daisey, M. (2001). *The cued speech resource book for parents of deaf children*. National Cued Speech Association.

Correa, V. I., Bonilla, Z. E., & Reyes-MacPherson, M. E. (2011). Support networks of single Puerto Rican mothers of children with disabilities. *Journal of Children and Family Studies, 20*, 66–77.

Correa, V. I., Jones, H. A., Thomas, C. C., & Morsink, C. V. (2005). *Interactive teaming: Enhancing programs for students with special needs* (4th ed.). Merrill/Pearson.

Cortiella, C., & Horowitz, S. H. (2014). *The state of learning disabilities: Facts, trends and emerging issues*. National Center for Learning Disabilities.

Costello, E. J., Foley, D. L., & Angold, A. (2006). 10-year research update review: The epidemiology of child and adolescent psychiatric disorders: II. Developmental epidemiology. *Journal of the American Academy of Child and Adolescent Psychiatry, 45*(1), 8–25.

Coster, W. J., & Haltiwanger, J. T. (2004). Social-behavioral skills of elementary students with physical disabilities included in general education classrooms. *Remedial and Special Education, 25*, 95–103.

Council for Children with Behavioral Disorders. (1993, June). Staff position statement: Inclusion. CCBD *Newsletter*, p. 1.

Council for Children with Behavioral Disorders. (2000, October). *Draft position paper on terminology and definition of emotional or behavioral disorders*. Author, A Division of the Council for Exceptional Children.

Council for Exceptional Children. (2014). *2014 CEC policy manual*. Author.

Council for Exceptional Children. (2015). *Federal outlook for exceptional children*. Author.

Council for Exceptional Children. (2019). *Issue brief: Education appropriations*. Author. https://www.cec.sped.org/~/media/Files/Policy/2018%20Updated%20Issue%20Briefs/IB%20Appropriations%20SELS%20Final.pdf

Council for Exceptional Children. (2020). *CEC initial and advanced preparation standards*. Author. https://www.cec.sped.org/Standards/Special-Educator-Professional-Preparation-Standards/CEC-Initial-and-Advanced-Preparation-Standards

Couvillon, M. A., Yell, M. L., & Katsiyannis, A. (2018). Endrew F. v. Douglas County School District (2017) and special education law: What teachers and administrators need to know. *Preventing School Failure: Alternative Education for Children and Youth, 62*(4), 289–299.

Coyne, M. D., Kame'enui, E. J., & Carnine, D. W. (Eds.). (2011). *Effective teaching strategies that accommodate diverse learners* (4th ed.). Pearson.

Craft, M. A., Alber, S. R., & Heward, W. L. (1998). Teaching elementary students with developmental disabilities to recruit teacher attention in a general education classroom: Effects on teacher praise and academic productivity. *Journal of Applied Behavior Analysis, 31*, 399–415.

Crandell, C. C., & Smaldino, J. J. (2001). Rehabilitative technologies for individuals with hearing loss and normal hearing. In J. Katz (Ed.), *Handbook of clinical audiology* (5th ed., pp. 607–630). Lippincott, Williams, & Wilkins.

Creech-Galloway, C., Collins, B. C., Knight, V., & Bausch, M. E. (2013). Using simultaneous prompting with an iPad to teach the Pythagorean theorem to adolescents with moderate and severe disabilities. *Research and Practice in Severe Disabilities, 38*, 222–232.

Cregenzán-Royo, O., Brun-Gasca, C., & Fornieles-Deu, A. (2018). Expressed emotion and impulsiveness in mothers of children with fragile X syndrome and Down syndrome: The relation to behavioral problems in their offspring. *Research in Developmental Disabilities, 83*, 179–189.

Crocket, L. J., Wasserman, A. M., Rudasill, K. M., Hoffman, L., & Kalutskaya I. (2018). Temperamental anger and effortful control, teacher–child conflict, and externalizing behavior across the elementary school years. *Child Development, 89*(6), 2176–2195.

Crone, D. A., Hawken, L. S., & Horner, R. H. (2020). *Building positive behavior support systems in schools: Functional behavioral assessment* (2nd ed.). Guilford.

Cronin, M. E., Patton, J. R., & Wood, S. J. (2007). *Life skills instruction* (2nd ed.). PRO-ED.

Cross, T. L., & Coleman, L. J. (2014). School-based conception of giftedness. *Journal for the Education of the Gifted, 37*(1), 94–103.

Crossley, R. (1988). *Unexpected communication attainments by persons diagnosed as autistic and intellectually impaired*. Deal Communication Centre.

Crozier, S., & Tincani, M. J. (2005). Using a modified social story to decrease disruptive behavior of a child with autism. *Focus on Autism and Other Developmental Disabilities, 20*, 150–157.

Cruickshank, W. M. (1986). *Disputable decisions in special education*. University of Michigan Press.

Crum, K. I., Waschbusch, D. A., & Willoughby, M. T. (2016). Callous-unemotional traits, behavior disorders, and the student-teacher relationship in elementary school students. *Journal of Emotional and Behavioral Disorders, 24*(1) 16–29.

Cullen, J. M., & Alber-Morgan, S. R. (2015). Technology mediated self-prompting of daily living skills for adolescents and adults with disabilities: A review of the literature. *Education and Training in Autism and Developmental Disabilities, 50*, 43–55.

Cullen, J. M., Alber-Morgan, S. R., Simmons-Reed, E. A., & Izzo, M. V. (2017). Effects of self-directed video prompting using iPads on the vocational task completion of young adults with intellectual and developmental disabilities. *Journal of Vocational Rehabilitation, 46*, 361–375.

Cummins, J. (2002). Foreword. In P. Gibbons (Ed.), *Scaffolding language, scaffolding learning: Teaching second language learners in the mainstream classroom*. Heinemann.

Cunningham, W., & Villasenor, P. (2014). *Employer voices, employer demands, and implications for public skills development policy*. (World Bank Policy Research Working Paper No. 6853). World Bank. https://doi.org/10.1596/1813-9450-6853

Curwin, R. L., Mendler, A. N., & Mendler, B. D. (2018). *Discipline with dignity: How to build responsibility, relationships, and respect in your classroom*. ASCD.

Cystic Fibrosis Foundation. (2020). *About cystic fibrosis*. https://www.cff.org/What-is-CF/About-Cystic-Fibrosis/

Da Fonte, M. A., & Boesche, M. C. (2019). *Effective augmentative and alternative communication practices: A handbook for school-based practitioners*. Routledge.

Daley, D., Van Der Oord, S., Ferrin, M., Cortese, S., Danckaerts, M., Doepfner, M., Van den Hoofdakker, B. J., Coghill, D., Thompson, M., Asherson, P., Banaschewski, T., Brandeis, D., Buitelaar, J., Dittmann, R. W., Hollis, C., Holtmann, M., Konofal, E., Lecendreux, M., Rothenberger, A., ... Sonuga-Barke, E. J. (2018). Practitioner Review: Current best practice in the use of parent training and other behavioural interventions in the treatment of children and adolescents with attention deficit hyperactivity disorder. *The Journal of Child Psychology and Psychiatry, 59*, 932–947.

Daley, T. C., & Carlson, E. (2009). Predictors of change in eligibility status among preschoolers in special education. *Exceptional Children, 75*, 412–426.

Dardig, J. C. (2006). A friendship program for future special education teachers. In W. L. Heward, *Exceptional children: An introduction to special education* (8th ed., pp. 624–626). Merrill/Pearson.

Dardig, J. C. (2008). *Involving parents of students with special needs: 25 ready-to-use strategies*. Corwin.

Dart, E. H., Aurora, P. G., Collins, T. A., & Doll, B. (2019). Progress monitoring measures for internalizing symptoms: A systematic review of the peer-reviewed literature. *School Mental Health, 11*, 265–275.

Datchuk, S. M. (2017). A direct instruction and precision teaching intervention to improve the sentence construction of middle school students with writing difficulties. *The Journal of Special Education, 51*(2), 62–71.

Davenport, C., & Alber-Morgan, S. R. (2016). I have a child with a cochlear implant in my preschool classroom. Now what? *Teaching Exceptional Children, 49*, 41–48.

Davenport, L. A., & Johnston, S. S. (2015). Using most-to-least prompting and contingent consequences to teach numeracy in inclusive early childhood classrooms. *Topics in Early Childhood Special Education, 34*(4), 250–261.

Davenport, T. N., & Eidelman, S. M. (2008). Affordability of family care for an individual with intellectual and developmental disabilities. *Intellectual and Developmental Disabilities, 46*, 396–399.

Davern, L. (2004). School-to-home notebooks: What parents have to say. *Teaching Exceptional Children, 36*(5), 22–27.

Davis, M. T., & Cumming, I. K. (2019a). Planning and implementing student-led IEPs for students with EBD. *Beyond Behavior, 28*(2), 90–98.

Davis, M. T., & Cumming, I. K. (2019b). Practical strategies for improving postsecondary outcomes for students with EBD, *Preventing School Failure, 63*(4), 325–333.

Davis-Temple, J., Jung, S., & Sainato, D. M. (2014). Teaching young children with special needs and their peers to play board games: Effects of a least to most prompting procedure to increase independent performance. *Behavior Analysis in Practice, 7*, 21–30.

De Bortoli, T., Balandin, S., Foreman, P., Arthur-Kelly, M., & Mathisen, B. (2012). Mainstream teachers' experiences of communicating with students with multiple and severe disabilities. *Education and Training in Autism and Developmental Disabilities, 47*(2), 236–252.

De Valenzuela, J. S., Copeland, S. R., Huaqing Qi, C., & Park, M. (2006). Examining educational equity: Revisiting the disproportionate representation of minority students in special education. *Exceptional Children, 72*, 425–441.

DeafTEC (n.d.). Student perspectives. https://www.jhsph.edu/offices-and-services/student-affairs/disability-support-services/_documents/Deaftec_Tips.pdf

DeAvila, E. (1976). Mainstreaming ethnically and linguistically different children: An exercise in paradox or a new approach? In R. I. Jones (Ed.), *Mainstreaming and the minority child* (pp. 93–108). Council for Exceptional Children.

Debonis, D. A., & Donohue, C. L. (2008). *Survey of audiology fundamentals for audiologists and health professionals*. Allyn & Bacon.

Deer, B. (2010, January 31). "Callous, unethical and dishonest": Dr. Andrew Wakefield. https://www.thetimes.co.uk/article/callous-unethical-and-dishonest-dr-andrew-wakefield-7nccglr3vkr

Deidrick, K. K. M., & Farmer, J. E. (2005). School reentry following traumatic brain injury. *Preventing School Failure, 49*, 23–33.

DeLana, M., Gentry, M. A., & Andrews, J. (2007). The efficacy of ASL/English bilingual education: Considering public schools. *American Annals of the Deaf, 152*.

Delano, M. E., Walker, V. L., & Snell, M. E. (2020). Teaching self-care skills. In F. Brown, J. McDonnell, & M. E. Snell (Eds.), *Instruction of students with severe disabilities* (9th ed., pp. 340–383). Pearson Education.

Delgado, P., Avila, V., Fajardo, I., & Salmeron, L. (2019). Training young adults with intellectual disability to read critically on the internet. *Journal of Applied Research in Intellectual Disabilities*. *32*(3), 666–677.

Dell, A. G., Newton, D., & Petroff, J. (2016). *Assistive technology in the classroom: Enhancing the school experiences of students with disabilities* (3rd ed.). Pearson.

Deltman, S. J., Dowell, R. C., Choo, D., Arnott, W., Abrahams, Y., Davis, A., Dornan, D., Leigh, J., Constantinescu, G., Cowan, R., & Briggs, R. J. (2016). Long-term communication outcomes for children receiving cochlear implants younger than 12 months: A multicenter study. *Otology & Neurotology 37*, 82–95.

Dennis L. R., & Stockall, N. (2015). Using play to build the social competence of young children with language delays: Practical guidelines for teachers. *Early Childhood Education, 43*, 1–7.

DeQuinzio, J. A., Taylor, B. A., & Tomasi, B. J. (2018). Observational learning and children with autism: Discrimination training of known and unknown stimuli. *Journal of Applied Behavior Analysis, 51*, 802–818.

Deris, A. R., & DiCarlo, C. F. (2013). Back to basics: Working with young children with autism in inclusive classrooms. *Support for Learning, 28*, 53–56.

Deshler, D. D., & Lenz, B. K. (1989). The strategies instructional approach. *International Journal of Disability, Development, and Education, 6*(3), 203–244.

Deshler, D. D., Schumaker, J. B., Bulgren, J. A., Lenz, B. K., Jantzen, J., Adams, G., Carnine, D., Grossen, B., Davis, B., & Marquis, J. (2001). Making things easier: Connecting new knowledge to things students already know. *Teaching Exceptional Children, 33*(4), 82–85.

DeSimone, J. R., & Parmar, R. S. (2006). Middle school math teachers' beliefs about inclusion of students with learning disabilities. *Learning Disabilities Research & Practice, 21*, 98–110.

DeThorne, L. S., Hengst, J., Fisher, K., & King, A. (2014). Keep your eye on the prize: Implementing AAC within the broader context of communication competence. *Young Exceptional Children, 14*, 39–50.

DeThorne, L. S., Petrill, S. A., Schatschneider, C., & Cutting, L. (2010). Conversational language use as a predictor of early reading development: Language history as a moderating variable. *Journal of Speech, Language, Hearing Research, 53*, 209–223.

DeWalt, D. A., Berkman, N. D., Sheridan, S., Lohr, K. N., & Pignone, M. P. (2004). Literacy and health outcomes: A systematic review of the literature. *Journal of General Internal Medicine, 19*, 1228–1239.

DiCicco-Bloom, E., Lord, C., Zwaigenbaum, L. Courchesne, E., Dager, S. R., Schmitz, C., Schultz, R. T., Crawley, J., & Young, L. J. (2006). The developmental neurobiology of autism spectrum disorder. *The Journal of Neuroscience, 26*(26), 6897–6906.

Dickson, C. A., Deutsch, C. K., Wang, S. S., & Dube, W. V. (2006). Matching-to-sample assessment of stimulus overselectivity in students with intellectual disabilities. *American Journal on Mental Retardation, 111*, 447–453.

Didion, L. A., Toste, J. R., & Wehby, J. H. (2020). Response cards to increase engagement and active participation of middle school students with EBD. *Remedial and Special Education, 41*(2), 111–123.

Diegelmann, K. M., & Test, D. W. (2018). Effects of a self-monitoring checklist as a component of the self-directed IEP. *Education and Training in Autism and Developmental Disabilities, 53*(1), 73–83.

Diezman, C. M., & Watters, J. J. (2001). The collaboration of mathematically gifted students on challenging tasks. *Journal for the Education of the Gifted, 25*, 7–31.

DiGuiseppi, C., Hepburn, S., Davis, J. M., Fidler, D. J., Hartway, S., Lee, N. R., Miller, L., Ruttenber, M., & Robinson, C. (2010). Screening for autism spectrum disorders in children with Down syndrome. *Journal of Developmental and Behavioral Pediatrics, 31*, 181–191.

Dillon, M. B. M., Radley, K. C., Tingstrom, D. H., Dart, E. H., & Barry, C. T. (2019). The effects of tootling via ClassDojo on student behavior in elementary classrooms. *School Psychology Review, 48*(1), 18–30.

Dimitropoulos, A., Feurer, I. D., Butler, M. G., & Thompson, T. (2001). Emergence of compulsive behavior and tantrums in children with Prader-Willi syndrome. *American Journal of Mental Retardation, 106*, 39–51.

Division for Early Childhood. (2014). *DEC recommended practices in early intervention/early childhood special education*. Council for Exceptional Children. http://www.dec-sped.org/recommendedpractices

Dockrell, J. E., & Messer, D. (2004). Later vocabulary acquisition. In R. Berman (Ed.), *Language development across childhood and adolescence: Psycholinguistic and crosslinguistic perspectives* (pp. 35–52). Trends in Language Acquisition Research 3. John Benjamins.

Dogoe, M., & Banda, D. R. (2009). Review of research using constant time delay to teach chained tasks to persons with developmental disabilities. *Education and Training in Autism and Developmental Disabilities*, 44, 177–186.

Doherty, A., Bracken, M., & Gormley, L. (2018). Teaching children with autism to initiate and respond to peer mands using picture exchange communication system (PECS). *Behavior Analysis in Practice, 11*, 279–288.

Doll, E. A. (1941). The essentials of an inclusive concept of mental deficiency. *American Journal of Mental Deficiency, 46*, 214–219.

Donley, C. R., & Williams, G. (1997). Parents exhibit children's progress at a poster session. *Teaching Exceptional Children, 29*(4), 46–51.

Donovan, M. S., & Cross, C. T. (2002). *Minority students in special and gifted education*. National Academies Press.

Doren, B., Murray, C., & Gau, J. M. (2014). Salient predictors of school dropout among secondary students with learning disabilities. *Learning Disabilities Research and Practice, 29*, 150–159.

Dornan, D., Hickson, L., Murdoch, B., Houston, T., & Constantinescu, G. (2010). Is auditory-verbal therapy effective for children with hearing loss? *Volta Review, 110*, 361–387.

Dosen, A., & Day, K. (Eds.). (2001). *Treating mental illness and behavior disorders in children and adults with mental retardation*. American Psychiatric Press.

Douglas, K. H., Uphold, N. M., Steffen, S., & Kroesch, A. M. (2018). Promoting literacy with self-created grocery lists on mobile devices. *The Journal of Special Education, 51*, 201–210.

Douma, J. C. H., Dekker, M. C., de Ruiter, K. P., Tick, N. T., & Koot, H. M. (2007). Antisocial and delinquent behaviors in youths with mild or borderline disabilities. *American Journal on Mental Retardation, 112*, 207–220.

Downing, J. E., Hanreddy, A., & Peckham-Hardin, K. (2015). *Teaching communication skills to students with severe disabilities* (3rd ed.). Brookes.

Downing, J. E., Spencer, S., & Cavallaro, C. (2004). The development of an inclusive elementary school: Perceptions from stakeholders. *Research and Practice for People with Severe Disabilities, 29*, 11–24.

Downs, K. R., Caldarella, P., Larsen, R. A. A., Charlton, C. T., Wills, H. P., Kamps, D. M., & Wehby, J. H. (2019). Teacher praise and reprimands: The differential response of students at risk of emotional and behavioral disorders. *Journal of Positive Behavior Interventions, 21*(3), 135–147.

Downs, R. C., & Downs, A. (2010). Practice in early intervention for children with autism: A comparison with the National Research Council recommended practices. *Education and Training in Autism and Developmental Disabilities, 45*(2), 150–159.

Dowse, J. M. (2009). Jeanna Mora Dowse: Featured teacher. In W. L. Heward, *Exceptional Children: An introduction to special education* (9th ed., pp. 370–371, 374). Pearson.

Doyle, M. B., & Giangreco, M. F. (2013). Guiding principles for including secondary students with intellectual disabilities in general education classes. *American Secondary Education Journal, 42*(1), 57–72.

Drasgow, E. (1998). American Sign Language as a pathway to linguistic competence. *Exceptional Children, 64*, 329–342.

Duchaine, E. L., Jolivette, K., Frederick, L. D., & Alberto, P. A. (2018). Increase engagement and achievement with response cards: Science and mathematics inclusion classes. *Learning Disabilities: A Contemporary Journal 16*(2), 157–176.

Duffy, J. R. (2013). *Motor speech disorders: Substrates, differential diagnosis, and management* (3rd ed.). Elsevier.

Dunlap, G., Iovannone, R., Kincaid, D., Wilson, K., Christiansen, K., Strain, P. S., & English, C. (2010). *Prevent, teach, reinforce: The school-based model of individualized positive behavior support.* Brookes.

Dunlap, G., Iovannone, R., Kincaid, D., Wilson, K., Christiansen, K., & Strain, P. S. (2019). *Prevent, teach, reinforce: The school-based model of individualized positive behavior support* (2nd ed.). Brookes.

Dunn, L. M., & Dunn, D. M. (2006). *Peabody Picture Vocabulary Test—4.* Pearson.

Dunst, C. (2001). Participation of young children with disabilities in community learning activities. In M. Guralnick (Ed.), *Early childhood inclusion: Focus on change* (pp. 307–333). Brookes.

DuPaul, G. J., & Langberg, J. M. (2015). Educational impairments in children with ADHD. In R. A. Barkley (Ed.), Attention-deficit hyperactivity disorder: A handbook for diagnosis and treatment (pp. 169–190). The Guilford Press.

DuPaul, G. J., & Stoner, G. (2014). *ADHD in the schools: Assessment and intervention strategies* (3rd ed.). Guilford.

DuPaul, G. J., Belk, G. D., & Puzino, K. (2016). Evidence-based interventions for attention deficit hyperactivity disorder in children and adolescents. In L. A. Theodore (Ed.), *Handbook of evidence-based interventions for children and adolescents.* Springer.

DuPaul, G. J., Gormley, M. J., & Laracy, S. D. (2013). Comorbidity of LD and ADHD: Implications of DSM-5 for assessment and treatment. *Journal of Learning Disabilities, 46*, 43–51.

Durand, V. M., & Crimmins, D. (1992). *The Motivation Assessment Scale.* Monaco & Associates.

Dyches, T. T., Carter, N. J., & Prater, M. A. (2012). A teacher's guide to communicating with parents: Practical strategies for developing successful partnerships. Pearson.

Dykens, E. M., Hodapp, R. M., & Finucane, B. M. (2000). *Genetics and mental retardation syndromes: A new look at behavior and interventions.* Brookes.

Dyson, L. (1996). The experiences of families of children with learning disabilities: Parental stress, family functioning, and sibling self-concept. *Journal of Learning Disabilities, 29*(3), 280–286.

Edens, R. M., Murdick, N. L., & Gartin, B. C. (2003). Preventing infection in the classroom: The use of universal precautions. *Teaching Exceptional Children, 35*(4), 62–66.

Editors of *The Lancet.* (2010, February 2). Retraction—Ileal-lymphoid-nodular hyperplasia, non-specific colitis, and pervasive developmental disorder in children. *The Lancet, 375*(9713), 445.

Ehlers, S., Gillberg, C., & Wing, L. (1999). A screening questionnaire for Asperger syndrome and other high-functioning autism spectrum disorders in school age children. *Journal of Autism and Developmental Disorders, 29*, 129–141.

Ehren, B. J. (2000). Maintaining a therapeutic focus and sharing responsibility for student success: Keys to in-classroom speech-language services. *Language, Speech, and Hearing Services in Schools, 31*, 219–229.

Eikeseth, S., Smith, T., Jahr, E., & Eldevik, S. (2002). Intensive behavioral treatment at school for 4- to 7-year-old children with autism: A 1-year comparison controlled study. *Behavior Modification, 26*, 49–68.

Eldevik, S., Hastings, R. P., Hughes, J. C., Jahr, E., Eikeseth, S., & Cross, S. (2010). Using participant data to extend the evidence base for intensive behavioral intervention for children with autism. *American Journal on Intellectual and Developmental Disabilities, 115*, 364–380.

Ellis, E. S., & Howard, P. W. (2007). Graphic organizers: Power tools for teaching students with learning disabilities. *Current Practice Alerts*, Issue 13. Division for Learning Disabilities and Division for Research, Council for Exceptional Children. Retrieved September 12, 2011, from http://teachingld.org/alerts#the-alert-series.

Ellis, N. R. (1963). The stimulus trace and behavior inadequacy. In N. R. Ellis (Ed.), *Handbook of mental deficiency* (pp. 134–158). McGraw-Hill.

Emerson, R. W., Adams, C., Nishino, T., Hazlett, H. C., Wolff, J. J., Zwaigenbaum, L., Constantino, J. N., Shen, M. D., Swanson, M. R., Elison, J. T., Kandala, S., Estes, A. M., Botteron, K. N., Collins, L., Dager, S. R., Evans, A. C., Gerig, G., Gu, H., McKinstry, R. C., ... Piven, J. (2017). Functional neuroimaging of high-risk 6-month-old infants predicts a diagnosis of autism at 24 months of age. *Science Translational Medicine, 9*(393), Article eaag2882. https://doi.org/10.1126/scitranslmed.aag2882

Emmorey, K. (2002). *Language, cognition, and the brain: Insights from sign language research.* Erlbaum.

Endrew F. v. Douglas County School District, 137 S.Ct. 988 (2017).

Engelmann, S. (1977). Sequencing cognitive and academic tasks. In R. D. Kneedler & S. G. Tarver (Eds.), *Changing perspectives in special education* (pp. 46–61). Merrill/Pearson.

Engelmann, S. (2004). *Expressive writing.* McGraw-Hill/SRA.

Engelmann, S., & Bruner, E. C. (2008). *SRA reading mastery signature edition: Teacher's guide—Grade K (learning through literature).* SRA/McGraw-Hill.

Engelmann, S., & Carnine, D. W. (1982). *Theory of instruction: Principles and applications* (rev. ed.). ADI Press.

Engelmann, S., & Silbert, J. (2001). *Reasoning & writing.* McGraw-Hill.

Engelmann, S., Osborn, S., & Hanner, S. (2008). *Corrective reading: Comprehension B1 and B2.* SRA/McGraw-Hill.

Englund, L. W. (2009). Designing a Web site to share information with parents. *Intervention in School and Clinic, 45*, 45–51.

Ennis, R. P., & Losinski, M. (2019). SRSD fractions: Helping students at risk for disabilities add/subtract fractions with unlike denominators. *Journal of Learning Disabilities, 52*(5), 399–412.

Ennis, R. P., Schwab, J. R., & Jolivette, K. (2013). Using precorrection as a secondary-tier intervention for reducing problem behaviors in instructional and noninstructional settings. *Beyond Behavior, 22*(1), 40–47.

Enright, R. (2000). If life is a journey, make it a joyride: Some tips for young people. *Exceptional Parent, 31*(7), 50–51.

Epilepsy Foundation of America. (2020a). *Don't let myths and misconceptions rule your life!* Author. https://www.epilepsy.com/article/2014/3/dont-let-myths-and-misconceptions-rule-your-life

Epilepsy Foundation of America. (2020b). *Seizure and epilepsy medicines.* Author. http://www.epilepsy.com/learn/treating-seizures-and-epilepsy/seizure-and-epilepsy-medicines

Epstein, M. H. (2004). *Behavioral and Emotional Rating Scale (BERS-2): A strength-based approach to assessment.* PRO-ED.

Epstein, M. H., Hertzog, M. A., & Reid, R. (2001). The Behavioral and Emotional Rating Scale: Long term test-retest reliability. *Behavioral Disorders, 26*, 314–320.

Erber, N. P. (2011). *Auditory communication for Deaf children.* ACER Press.

Erin, J. N., & Topor, I. (2010). Instruction in visual techniques, including those with multiple disabilities. In A. L. Corn & J. N. Erin (Eds.), *Foundations of low vision: Clinical and functional perspectives* (2nd ed., pp. 398–441). AFB Press.

Erting, C. J., Thumann-Prezioso, C., & Benedict, B. (2000). Bilingualism in a deaf family: Fingerspelling in early childhood. In P. E. Spencer, C. J. Erting, & M. Marschark (Eds.), *The deaf child in the family and at school: Essays in honor of Kathryn P. Meadow-Orlans* (pp. 41–54). Erlbaum.

Espelage, D. L., Van Ryzin, M. J., & Holt, M. K., (2018). Trajectories of bully perpetration across early adolescence: Static risk factors, dynamic covariates, and longitudinal outcomes. *Psychology of Violence, 8*(2), 141–150.

Estabrooks, W., Mclver-Lux, K., & Rhodes, E. A. (2016). *Auditory-Verbal Therapy: For young children with hearing loss and their families, and the practitioners who guide them.* Plural Publishing.

Estell, D. B., Jones, M. H., Pearl, R., & Van Acker, R. (2009). Best friendships of students with and without learning disabilities across late elementary school. *Exceptional Children, 76*, 110–124.

Evans, J. C., & Smith, J. (1993). Nursing planning, intervention, and evaluation for altered neurologic function. In D. B. Jackson & R. B. Saunders (Eds.), *Child health nursing: A comprehensive approach to the care of children and their health* (pp. 1353–1430). Lippincott.

Everhart, J. M., Alber-Morgan, S. R., & Park, J. H. (2011). Effects of computer-based practice on the acquisition and maintenance of basic academic skills for children with moderate to intensive educational needs. *Education and Training in Autism and Developmental Disabilities, 46*, 556–564.

Everling, S. (2013). Tips for beginning teachers. In W. L. Heward, *Exceptional children: An introduction to special education* (10th ed., pp. 306–307). Pearson.

Fagan, A. A., Lewis, A. N., & Catalano, R. F. (2020). Prevention of adolescent mental, emotional, and behavioral health disorders: A global perspective. *The Encyclopedia of Childhood and Adolescent Development*. https://doi.org/10.1002/9781119171492.wecad340

Fahey, K. R., Hulit, L. M., & Howard, M. R. (2019). *Born to talk: An introduction to speech and language development* (7th ed.). Pearson.

Fairchild, G., Hawes, D. J., Frick, P. J., Copeland, W. E., Odgers, C. L., Franke, B., Freitag, C. M., & De Brito, S. A. (2019). Conduct disorder. *Nature Reviews, 5*, 1–25.

Falkenberg, C., & Barbetta, P. (2013). The effects of a self-monitoring package on homework completion and accuracy of students with disabilities in an inclusive general education classroom. *Journal of Behavioral Education, 22*(3), 190–210.

Fan, X., & Chen, M. (2001). Parental involvement and students' academic achievement: A meta-analysis. *Educational Psychology Review, 13*, 1–22.

Fanari, R., Maloni, C., & Massidda, D. (2019). Visual and spatial working memory abilities predict early math skills: A longitudinal study. *Frontiers in Psychology, 10*, 1–9.

Fargas-Malet, M., McSherry, D., Larkin, E., & Robinson, C. (2010). Research with children: Methodological issues and innovative techniques, *Journal of Early Childhood Research, 8*, 175–192.

Farmer, T. W., Conroy, M., Farmer, E. M. Z., & Sutherland, K. (2020). *Handbook of research on emotional and behavioral disorders.* Routledge.

Faw, G. D., Davis, P. K., & Peck, C. (1996). Increasing self-determination: Teaching people with mental retardation to evaluate residential options. *Journal of Applied Behavior Analysis, 29*, 173–188.

Feiner, S. K. (2002, April). Augmented reality: A new way of seeing. *Scientific American*, 50–55.

Feldman, D. L., Smith, A. T., & Waxton, B. L. (2017). *"Why we drop out": Understanding and disrupting student pathways to leaving school.* Teachers College Press.

Fenlon, A. G., McNabb, J., & Pidlypchak, H. (2010). "So much potential in reading!" Developing meaningful literacy routines for students with multiple disabilities. *Teaching Exceptional Children, 43*(1), 42–48.

Ferguson, D. L., & Baumgart, D. (1991). Partial participation revisited. *Journal of the Association for Persons with Severe Handicaps, 16*, 218–227.

Ferguson, D. L., Willis, C., & Meyer, G. (1996). Widening the stream: Ways to think about including "exceptions" in schools. In D. H. Lehr & F. Brown (Eds.), *People with disabilities who challenge the system* (pp. 99–112). Brookes.

Ferguson, P. M. (2003). A place in the family: An historical interpretation of research on parental reactions to having a child with a disability. *Journal of Special Education, 36*, 124–130.

Ferguson, P. M., & Ferguson, D. L. (2016). The promise of adulthood. In F. Brown, M. E. Snell, & J. McDonnell (Eds.), *Instruction of students with severe disabilities* (8th ed., pp. 556–589). Pearson.

Ferrell, K. A. (2006). Your child's development. In M. C. Holbrook (Ed.), *Children with visual impairments: A parents' guide* (2nd. ed., pp. 85–108). Woodbine House.

Ferrell, K. A., & Spungin, S. J. (Eds.). (2011). *Reach out and teach: Helping your child who is visually impaired learn and grow.* American Federation for the Blind.

Fetko, E. E., Collins, B. C., Hager, K. D., Schuster, J. W., & Spriggs, A. (2013). Using peer tutors and a simultaneous prompting procedure to teach a leisure skill to students with disabilities. *Education and Training in Autism and Developmental Disabilities, 48*(3), 400–411.

Fidler, D. J., Hepburn, S. L., Mankin, G., & Rogers, S. J. (2005). Praxis skills in young children with Down syndrome, other developmental disabilities, and typically developing children. *American Journal of Occupational Therapy, 59*(2), 129–138.

Fidler, D. J., Hepburn, S. L., Most, D. E., Philofsky, A., & Rogers, S. J. (2007). Emotional responsivity in young children with Williams syndrome. *American Journal on Mental Retardation, 110*, 312–322.

Fidler, D. J., Philofsky, A., Hepburn, S. L., & Rogers, S. J. (2005). Nonverbal requesting and problem-solving by toddlers with Down syndrome. *American Journal on Mental Retardation, 110*, 312–322.

Fiedler, C. R., Chiang, B., Van Haren, B., Jorgensen, J., Halberg, S., & Boreson, L. (2008). Culturally responsive practices in schools. A checklist to address disproportionality in special education. *Teaching Exceptional Children, 40*(5), 52–59.

Fiedler, C. R., Simpson, R. L., & Clark, D. M. (2007). *Parents and families of children with disabilities: Effective school-based support services.* Merrill/Pearson.

Finkelstein, N., Hanson, T., Huang, C. W., Hirschman, B., & Huang, M. (2010). *Effects of problem based economics on high school economics instruction* (NCEE 2010-4002). National Center for Education Evaluation and Regional Assistance, Institute of Education Sciences, U.S. Department of Education.

Finn, C. E., Rotherham, A. J., & Hokanson, C. R., Jr. (Eds.). (2001). *Rethinking special education for a new century.* Thomas B. Fordham Foundation and the Progressive Policy Institute.

Fishbein, D. H., Michael, L., Guthrie, C., Carr, C., & Raymer, J. (2019). Associations between environmental conditions and executive cognitive functioning and behavior during late childhood: A pilot study. *Frontiers in Psychology, 10*, 1–12.

Fisher, C. S., Berliner, C. D., Filby, N. N., Marliave, R., Cahen, L. S., & Dishaw, M. M. (1980). Teaching behaviors, academic learning time, and student achievement. In C. Denham & A. Lieberman (Eds.), *Time to learn* (pp. 7–22). National Institute of Education.

Fisher, M., & Meyer, L. H. (2002). Development and social competence after two years for students enrolled in inclusive and self-contained educational programs. *Research and Practice for People with Severe Disabilities, 27*, 165–174.

Fishley, K. M., Konrad, M., Hessler, T., & Keesey, S. (2012). Effects of GO FASTER on morpheme definition fluency for high school students with high-incidence disabilities. *Learning Disabilities Research & Practice, 27*, 104–115.

Fitzgerald, J. L., & Watkins, M. W. (2006). Parents' rights in special education: The readability of procedural safeguards. *Exceptional Children, 72*, 497–510.

Flaute, A. J., Peterson, S. M., Van Norman, R. K., Riffle, T., & Eakins, A. (2005). Motivate me! 20 tips for using a MotivAider® for improving your classroom. *Teaching Exceptional Children Plus, 2*(2), Article 3.

Fleischmann, A. (2004). Narratives published on the Internet by parents of children with autism: What do they reveal and why is it important? *Focus on Autism and Other Developmental Disabilities, 19*, 25–43.

Fletcher, J. M., Lyons, G. R., Fuchs, L. S., & Barnes, M. A. (2019). *Learning disabilities for identification to intervention* (2nd ed.). Guilford Press.

Flexer, R. W., Baer, R. M., Luft, P., & Simmons, T. (2013). *Transition planning for secondary students with disabilities* (4th ed.). Merrill/Pearson.

Flora, S. R. (2004). *The power of reinforcement*. State University of New York Press.

Flora, S. R. (2007). *Taking America off drugs: Why behavioral therapy is more effective for treating ADHD, OCD, depressions, and other psychological problems*. SUNY Press.

Flores, M. T., Jenkins, L. N., Reinke, W. M., & McKown, L. (2018). General education teachers' natural rates of praise: A preliminary investigation. *Behavioral Disorders, 43*(4) 411–422.

Florian, L., Hollenweger, J., Simeonsson, R. J., Wedell, K., Riddell, S., Terzi, L., & Holland, A. (2006). Cross-cultural perspectives on the classification of children with disabilities: Part I. Issues in the classification of children with disabilities. *Journal of Special Education, 40*, 36–45.

Foil, C. R., & Alber, S. R. (2002). Fun and effective ways to build your students' vocabulary. *Intervention in School and Clinic, 37*, 131–139.

Follari, L. (2019). *Foundations and best practices in early childhood education* (4th ed.). Pearson.

Fonger, A. M., & Malott, R. W. (2019). Using shaping to teach eye contact to children with autism spectrum disorder. *Behavior Analysis in Practice, 12*, 216–221.

Ford, D. Y. (1998). The underrepresentation of minority students in gifted education. *The Journal of Special Education, 32*(1), 4–14.

Ford, D. Y. (2010). Recruiting and retaining gifted students from diverse ethnic, cultural, and language groups. In J. A. Banks & C. A. M. Banks (Eds.), *Multicultural education: Issues and perspectives* (7th ed., pp. 371–391). Wiley.

Ford, D. Y. (2011). *Multicultural gifted education*. Prufrock Press.

Ford, D. Y., & Toldson, I. A. (2015, July 5). Study on Black, Hispanic children in special ed wrong, regressive. *Diverse Issues in Higher Education*. https://diverseeducation.com/article/76088/

Ford, D. Y., Wright, B. L., Washington, A., & Hensfield, M. S. (2016). Access and equity denied: Key theories for school psychologists to consider when assessing Black and Hispanic students for gifted education. *School Psychology Forum, 10*(3), 265–277.

Forness, S. R., & Kavale, K. A. (2000). Emotional or behavior disorders: Background and current status of the E/BD terminology and definition. *Behavioral Disorders, 25*, 264–269.

Forness, S. R., Freeman, S. F. N., Paparella, T., Kauffman, J. M., & Walker, H. M. (2012). *Journal of Emotional and Behavioral Disorders, 20*, 4–18.

Forness, S. R., Kavale, K. A., Crenshaw, T. M., & Sweeney, D. P. (2000). Best practice in treating children with ADHD: Does not using medication in a comprehensive intervention program verge on malpractice? *Beyond Behavior, 10*(2), 4–7.

Fowler, C. H., Konrad, M., Walker, A., Test, D. W., & Wood, W. M. (2007). Self-determination interventions' effects on the academic performance of students with developmental disabilities. *Education and Training in Developmental Disabilities, 42*(3), 270–285.

Fox, L., Vaughn, B. J., Wyatte, M. L., & Dunlap, G. (2002). "We can't expect other people to understand": Family perspectives on problem behavior. *Exceptional Children, 68*, 437–450.

Francis, G. L., Duke, J. M., Kliethermes, A., Demetro, K., & Graff, H. (2018). Apps to support a successful transition to collect for students with ASD. *Teaching Exceptional Children, 51*(2), 111–124.

Francis, G. L., Haines, S. J., & Nagro, S. A. (2017). Developing relationships with immigrant families: Learning by asking the right questions. *Teaching Exceptional Children, 50*(2), 95–105.

Frank, A. R., & Sitlington, P. L. (1993). Graduates with mental disabilities: The story three years later. *Education and Training in Mental Retardation, 28*, 30–37.

Frankenberger, W., & Cannon, C. (1999). Effects of Ritalin on academic achievement from first to fifth grade. *International Journal of Disability, Development, and Education, 46*, 199–221.

Frankenburg, W. K., & Dodds, J. B. (1990). *The Denver II training manual*. Denver Developmental Materials.

Frey, J. R., & Kaiser, A. P. (2011). The use of play expansions to increase the diversity and complexity of object play in young children with disabilities. *Topics in Early Childhood Special Education, 31*, 99–111.

Friend, M., & Bursuck, W. D. (2019). *Including students with special needs: A practical guide for classroom teachers* (8th ed.). Pearson Education.

Friend, M., & Cook, L. (2017). *Interactions: Collaboration skills for school professionals* (8th ed.). Pearson Education.

Frostig, M., & Horne, D. (1973). *The Frostig program for the development of visual perception* (rev. ed.). Chicago: Follett.

Frostig, M., Lefever, D. W., & Whittlesey, J. R. B. (1964). *The Marianne Frostig development test of visual perception*. Palo Alto, CA: Consulting Psychologists Press.

Fuchs, D., Fuchs, L. S., & Compton, D. L. (2012). Smart RTI: A next-generation approach to multilevel prevention. *Exceptional Children, 78*, 263–279.

Fuchs, D., Fuchs, L. S., & Stecker, P. M. (2010). The "blurring" of special education in a new continuum of general education placements. *Exceptional Children, 76*, 301–323.

Fuchs, L. S., & Fuchs, D. (2007a). A model for implementing responsiveness to intervention. *Teaching Exceptional Children, 39*(5), 14–20.

Fuchs, L. S., & Fuchs, D. (2007b). *What is scientifically based research on progress monitoring?* National Center on Student Progress Monitoring. Available online: https://eric.ed.gov/?id=ED502460

Fuchs, L. S., Fuchs, D., Compton, D. L., Wehby, J., Schumacher, R. F., Gersten, R., & Jordan, N. C. (2015). Inclusion versus specialized intervention for very-low-performing students: What does access mean in an era of academic challenge? *Exceptional Children, 81*(2), 134–157.

Fuchs, L. S., Fuchs, D., & Hollenbeck, K. N. (2007). Extending responsiveness to intervention to mathematics at first and third grades. *Learning Disabilities Research and Practice, 22*, 13–24.

Fujiura, G. T. (2003). Continuum of intellectual disabilities: Demographic evidence for the "forgotten generation." *Mental Retardation, 41*, 420–429.

Fujiura, G. T., & Yamaki, K. (2000). Trends in demography of childhood poverty and disability. *Exceptional Children, 66*, 187–199.

Fullerton, E. K., Conroy, M. A., & Correa, V. I. (2009). Early childhood teachers' use of specific praise statements with young children at risk for behavioral disorders. *Behavioral Disorders, 34*, 118–135.

Furlong, M. J., Morrison, G. M., & Jimerson, S. (2004). Externalizing behaviors of aggression and violence in the school context. In R. B. Rutherford, M. M. Quinn, & S. R. Mathur (Eds.), *Handbook of research in emotional and behavioral disorders* (pp. 243–261). Guilford.

Furtak, E. M., Seidel, T., Ivarson, H., & Briggs, D. C. (2012). Experimental and quasi-experimental studies of inquiry-based science teaching: A meta-analysis. *Review of Educational Research, 82*, 300–329.

Gabriels, R. L., Agnew, J. A., Miller, L. J., Gralla, J., Pan, Z., Goldson, E., Ledbetter, J. C., Dinkins, J. P., & Hooks, E. (2008). Is there a relationship between restricted, repetitive, stereotyped behaviors and interests and abnormal sensory response in children with autism spectrum disorders? *Research in Autism Spectrum Disorders, 2*, 660–670.

Gage, N. A., Lewis, T. J., & Stichter, J. P. (2012). Functional behavioral assessment-based interventions for students with or at risk for emotional and/or behavioral disorders in school: A hierarchical linear modelling meta-analysis. *Behavioral Disorders, 37*(2), 55–77.

Gage, N. A., Scott, T., Hirn, R., & MacSuga-Gage, A. S. (2018). The relationship between teachers' implementation of classroom management practices and student behavior in elementary school. *Behavioral Disorders, 43*(2), 302–315.

Gage, N. A., Whitford, D. K., & Katsiyannis, A. (2018). A review of schoolwide positive behavior interventions and supports as a framework for reducing disciplinary exclusions. *The Journal of Special Education, 52*(3), 142–151.

Gagné, F. (2003). Transforming gifts into talents: The DMGT as a developmental theory. In N. Colangelo & G. A. Davis (Eds.), *Handbook of gifted education* (3rd ed., pp. 60–74). Allyn & Bacon.

Gajria, M., & Jitendra, A. K. (2016). Effective strategies for developing reading comprehension. In R. Schiff & R. M. Joshi (Eds.), *Interventions in learning disabilities: A handbook on systematic training programs for individuals with learning disabilities* (pp. 119–137). Springer.

Gallagher, D. J., Heshusius, L., Iano, R. P., & Skrtic, T. M. (2004). *Challenging orthodoxy in special education: Dissenting voices*. Love.

Gallagher, J. J. (1984). The evolution of special education concepts. In B. Blatt & R. J. Morris (Eds.), *Perspectives in special education: Personal orientations* (pp. 210–232). Scott, Foresman.

Gallagher, P. A., Floyd, J. H., Stafford, A. M., Taber, T. A., Brozovic, S. A., & Alberto, P. A. (2000). Inclusion of students with moderate and severe disabilities in educational and community settings: Perspectives from parents and siblings. *Education and Training in Mental Retardation and Developmental Disabilities, 35*, 135–147.

Gallaudet Research Institute. (2013, November). *Regional and national summary report of data from the 2012–2013 annual survey of deaf and hard of hearing children and youth*. GRI, Gallaudet University.

Garay, S. V. (2003). Listening to the voices of deaf students: Essential transition issues. *Teaching Exceptional Children, 35*(4), 44–48.

Garber, H., & Heber, R. (1973). *The Milwaukee Project: Early intervention as a technique to prevent mental retardation* [Technical paper]. University of Connecticut.

Garber, M., & Huebner, K. M. (2017). Visual impairment: Terminology, demographics, society. In M. C. Holbrook, T. McCarthy, & C. Kamei-Hannan (Eds.), *Foundations of education: History and theory of teaching children and youths with visual impairments* (3rd ed., pp. 50–72). AFB Press.

Garberoglio, C. L., Palmer, J. L., Cawthon, S. W., & Sales, A. (2019). *Deaf people and educational attainment in the United States: 2019*. Washington, DC: U.S. Department of Education, Office of Special Education Programs, National Deaf Center on Postsecondary Outcomes.

Hougen, M. (2014). *Evidence-based reading instruction for adolescents, grades 6–12* (Document No. IC-13). Retrieved from University of Florida, Collaboration for Effective Educator, Development, Accountability, and Reform Center website: http://ceedar.education.ufl.edu/tools/innovation-configurations/

Swenson, A. M. (2013). *A second look at large print materials*. Retrieved from http://ctserc.org/s/index.php?option=com_content&view=article&id=1193

Torrance, E. P. (2018). *Torrance tests of creative thinking*. Scholastic Testing Service.

Van Timmeren, E. A., Van der Schans, C. P., Van der Putten, A. A. J., Krijnen, W. P., Steenbergen, H. A., van Schrojenstein Lantman-de Valk, H. M. J., & Waninge, A. (2017). Physical health issues in adults with severe or profound intellectual and motor disabilities: A systematic review of cross-sectional studies. *Journal of Intellectual Disability Research, 61*(1), 30–49.

Garcia-Albea, E., Reeve, S. A., & Reeve, K. F. (2014). Using audio script fading and multiple-exemplar training to increase vocal interaction in children with autism. *Journal of Applied Behavior Analysis, 47*, 325–343.

Gardner, H. (2006). *Multiple intelligences: New horizons in theory and practice*. Basic Books.

Gardner, R., III, Nobel, M. M., Hessler, T., Yawn, C. D., & Heron, T. E. (2007). Tutoring system innovations: Past practice to future prototypes. *Intervention in School and Clinic, 43*(2), 71–81.

Garrick Duhaney, L. M., & Salend, S. (2000). Parental perceptions of inclusive educational placement. *Remedial and Special Education, 21*, 121–128.

Garwood, J. D., McKenna, J. W., & Ciullo, S. (2020). Early reading instruction with embedded behavioral supports for children with emotional and behavioral disorders. *Beyond Behavior*. https://doi.org/10.1177/1074295619900380

Gauvreau, A. N., & Schwartz, I. S. (2013). Using visual supports to promote appropriate behavior in young children with autism and related disorders. *Young Exceptional Children*. Monograph Series No. 15.

Gear, S., Bobzien, J., Judge, S., & Raver, S. A. (2011). Teaching social skills to enhance work performance in a child care setting. *Education and Training in Autism and Developmental Disabilities, 46*, 40–51.

Gense, M. H., & Gense, D. J. (1994). Identifying autism in children with blindness and visual impairments. *RE:view, 26*, 55–62.

Gentry, M. (2014). Cluster grouping. In J. A. Plucker & C. M. Callahan (Eds.), *Critical issues and practices in gifted education: What the research says*. Prufrock Press.

Geruschat, D. R., & Corn, A. L. (2006). A look back: 100 years of literature on low vision. *Journal of Visual Impairment and Blindness, 100*, 646–671.

Gestwicki, C. (2016). *Developmentally appropriate practice: Curriculum and development in early education* (6th ed.). Cengage Learning.

Getch, Y., Bhukhanwala, F., & Neuharth-Pritchett, S. (2007). Strategies for helping children with diabetes in elementary and middle schools. *Teaching Exceptional Children, 39*(3), 46–51.

Giangreco, M. F. (2020). "How can a student with severe disabilities be in a fifth-grade class when he can't do fifth-grade level work?" Misapplying the least restrictive environment. *Research and Practice for Persons with Severe Disabilities, 45*(1), 23–27.

Giangreco, M. F., Cloninger, C. J., & Iverson, V. S. (2011). *Choosing options and accommodations for children: A guide to educational planning for students with disabilities* (3rd ed.). Brookes.

Giangreco, M. F., & Doyle, M. B. (2007). *Quick-guides to inclusion: Ideas for education students with disabilities* (2nd ed.). Baltimore: Brookes.

Giangreco, M. F., Shogren, K. A., & Dymond, S. K. (2020). Educating students with severe disabilities: Foundational concepts and practices. In F. Brown, J. McDonnell, & M. E. Snell (Eds.), *Instruction of students with severe disabilities* (9th ed., pp. 1–27). Pearson.

Giler, J. Z. (2011). *Socially ADDept: Teaching social skills to children with ADHD, LD, and Asperger's* (rev. ed.). Wiley.

Gillespie, A., & Graham, S. (2014). A meta-analysis of writing interventions for students with learning disabilities. *Exceptional Children, 80*, 454–473.

Gilliam, L. M. (2019). *Magical management in the classroom: Using humor to speak their language*. Rowman & Littlefield.

Gillies, R. M. (2016). Cooperative learning: Review of research and practice. *Australian Journal of Teacher Education, 41*(3), 3.

Gilmore, J. H., Knickmeyer, R. C., & Gao, W. (2018). Imaging structural and functional brain development in early childhood. *Neuroscience, 19*, 123–137.

Gilroy, S. P., Leader, G., & McCleery, J. P. (2018). A pilot community-based randomized comparison of speech generating devices and the picture exchange communication system for children diagnosed with autism spectrum disorder. *Autism Research, 11*, 1701–1711.

Gilson, C. B., Carter, E. W., & Biggs, E. E. (2017). Systematic review of instructional methods to teach employment skills to secondary students with intellectual and developmental disabilities. *Research and Practice for Persons with Severe Disabilities, 42*, 89–107.

Ginis, K. A. M., Ma, J. K., Latimer-Cheung, A. E., & Rimmer, J. H. (2016). A systematic review of review articles addressing factors related to physical activity participation among children and adults with physical disabilities. *Health Psychology Review, 10*, 478–494.

Gitlin, L. N., Mount, J., Lucas, W., Weirich, L. C., & Gramberg, L. (1997). The physical costs and psychosocial benefits of travel aids for persons who are visually impaired or blind. *Journal of Visual Impairment and Blindness, 91*, 347–359.

Glaeser, B. C., Pierson, M. R., & Fritschman, N. (2003). Comic strip conversation: A positive behavioral support strategy. *Teaching Exceptional Children, 36*(2), 14–19.

Glidden, L. M., & Switzky, H. N. (2006). *International review of research in mental retardation, Vol. 31: Mental retardations, personality, and motivational systems.* Elsevier.

Goldblatt, E., & Most, T. (2018). Cultural identity of young deaf adults with cochlear implants in comparison to deaf without cochlear implants and hard-of-hearing young adults. *Journal of Deaf Studies and Deaf Education, 23*, 228–239. https://doi.org/10.1093/deafed/eny007

Goldin-Meadow, S. (2003). *The resilience of language: What gesture creation in deaf children can tell us about how all children learn language.* Psychology Press.

Goldman, R., & Fristoe, M. (2000). *Goldman-Fristoe Test of Articulation—2.* PRO-ED.

Goldstein, A. P. (2000). *The prepare curriculum: Teaching prosocial competencies* (rev. ed.). Research Press.

Goldstein, S., & Goldstein, M. (1998). *Managing attention-deficit hyperactivity disorder in children: A guide for practitioners* (2nd ed.). Wiley.

Gollnick, D. M., & Chinn, P. C. (2013). *Multicultural education in a pluralistic society* (9th ed.). Pearson.

Gompel, M., van Bon, W. J. J., & Schreuder, R. (2004). Reading by children with low vision. *Journal of Visual Impairments and Blindness, 98*, 77–89.

Gonzalez-Mena, J. (2017). *Child, family, and community: Family-centered early care and education* (7th ed.). Pearson.

Good, R. H., Kaminski, R. A., et al. (2011). *DIBELS next assessment manual.* Eugene, OR: Dynamic Measurement Group. Retrieved from http://www.dibels.org.

Goodman, L. V. (1976). A bill of rights for the handicapped. *American Education*, 12(6), 6–8.

Goodnight, C. I., Whitley, K. G., & Brophy-Dick, A. A. (2019). Effects of response cards on fourth-grade students' participation and disruptive behavior during language arts lessons in an inclusive elementary classroom. *Journal of Behavioral Education.* https://doi.org/10.1007/s10864-019-09357-2

Goodrich, G. L., Kirby, J., Wagstaff, P., Oros, T., & McDevitt, B. (2004). A comparative study of reading performance with a head-mounted laser display and conventional low vision devices. *Journal of Visual Impairments and Blindness, 98*, 148–159.

Graham, S., Collins, A. A., & Rigby-Wills, H. (2017). Writing characteristics of students with learning disabilities and typically achieving peers: A meta-analysis. *Exceptional Children, 83*(2), 199–218.

Graham, S., & Harris, K. (1992). Cognitive strategy instruction in written language for learning disabled students. In S. Vogel (Ed.), *Educational alternatives for students with learning disabilities* (pp. 91–115). SpringerVerlag.

Graham, S., & Harris, K. R. (2018). An examination of the design principles underlying a self-regulated strategy development study. *Journal of Writing Research, 10*(2), 139–187.

Grandin, T. (1995). *Thinking in pictures and other reports of my life with autism.* Vintage Books.

Grandin, T. (2006, August 14). Seeing in beautiful, precise pictures. *Morning Edition* [Radio program]. National Public Radio. https://www.npr.org/templates/story/story.php?storyId=5628476

Grandjean, P., & Landrigan, P. J. (2014). Neurobehavioural effects of developmental toxicity. *Lancet Neural, 13*, 330–338.

Grantham, T. C., Ford, D. Y., Henfield, M. S., Trotman Scott, M., Harmon, D. A., Procher, S., & Price, C. (2011). *Gifted and advanced Black students in school.* Prufrock Press.

Gray, C. A., & Attwood, T. (2010). *The new social story book* (10th ed.). Future Horizons.

Green, K. B., Mays, N. M., & Jolivette, K. (2011). Making choices: A proactive way to improve behaviors for young children with challenging behavior. *Beyond Behavior, 20*(1), 25–31.

Green, V. A., Pituch, K. A., Itchon, J., Choi, A., O'Reilly, M., & Sigafoos, J. (2006). Internet survey of treatments used by parents of children with autism. *Research in Developmental Disabilities, 27*, 70–84.

Greene, G. (2014).Transition of culturally and linguistically diverse youth with disabilities: Challenges and opportunities. *Journal of Vocational Rehabilitation, 40*, 239–245.

Greene, G. (2018). The emperor has no clothes: Improving the quality and compliance of ITPs. *Career Development and Transition for Exceptional Individuals, 41*, 146–155.

Greene, I., McTiernan, A., & Holloway, J. (2018). Cross-age peer tutoring and fluency-based instruction to achieve fluency with mathematics computation skills: A randomized controlled trial. *Journal of Behavioral Education, 27*(2), 145–171.

Greenwood, C. R., Delquadri, J., & Carta, J. J. (1997). *Together we can: Classwide peer tutoring to improve basic academic skills.* Sopris West.

Greenwood, C. R., Delquadri, J., & Hall, R. V. (1984). Opportunity to respond and student academic achievement. In W. L. Heward, T. E. Heron, D. S. Hill, & J. Trap-Porter (Eds.), *Focus on behavior analysis in education* (pp. 58–88). Merrill/Pearson.

Gresham, F. (2002). Responsiveness to intervention: An alternative approach to the identification of learning disabilities. In R. Bradley, L. Danielson, & D. P. Hallahan (Eds.), *Identification of learning disabilities: Research to practice* (pp. 467–519). Erlbaum.

Gresham, F. M., & MacMillan, D. L. (1997a). Autistic recovery? An analysis and critique of the empirical evidence on the Early Intervention Project. *Behavioral Disorders, 22*, 185–201.

Gresham, F. M., & MacMillan, D. L. (1997b). Denial and defensiveness in the place of fact and reason: Rejoinder to Smith and Lovaas. *Behavioral Disorders, 22*, 219–230.

Gresham, R. M., & Elliot, S. N. (2014). Social skills assessment and training in emotional and behavioral disorders. In H. M. Walker & R. M. Gresham (Eds.), *Handbook of evidence-based practices for emotional and behavioral disorders: Applications in schools* (pp. 152–172). Guilford Press.

Griffin, C., Hammis, D., & Geary, T. (2007). *The job developer's handbook: Practical tactics for customized employment.* Brookes.

Griffin, H. C., Williams, S. C., Davis. M. L., & Engelman, M. (2002). Using technology to enhance cues for children with low vision. *Teaching Exceptional Children, 35*(2), 36–42.

Griffin-Shirley, N., & Trusty, S. (2017). Orientation and mobility. In M. C. Holbrook, C. Kamei-Hannan, & T. McCarthy (Eds.), *Foundations of education: Instructional strategies for teaching children and youths with visual impairments* (3rd ed., pp. 654–698). AFB Press.

Grigal, M., Hart, D., Smith, F. A., Domin, D., & Sulewski, J. (2013). *Think College National Coordinating Center: Annual report on the transition and postsecondary programs for students with intellectual disabilities.* University of Massachusetts Boston, Institute for Community Inclusion.

Grigal, M., Test, D. W., Beattie, J., & Wood, W. (1997). An evaluation of transition components of individualized education programs. *Exceptional Children, 63,* 357–372.

Grigorenko, E. L., Compton, D. L., Fuchs, L. S., Wagner, R. K., Willcutt, E. G., & Fletcher, J. M. (2019). Understanding, educating, and supporting children with specific learning disabilities: 50 years of science and practice. *American Psychologist.* Advance online publication: http://dx.doi.org/10.1037/amp0000452.

Grossi, T. (Ed.). (2013). *Teaching transition skills in inclusive schools.* Brookes.

Grossi, T. A. (1998). Using a self-operated auditory prompting system to improve the work performance of two employees with severe disabilities. *Journal of the Association for Persons with Severe Handicaps, 23,* 149–154.

Grossi, T. A., & Heward, W. L. (1998). Using self-evaluation to improve the work productivity of trainees in a community-based restaurant training program. *Education and Training in Mental Retardation and Developmental Disabilities,* 33, 248–263.

Guerette, A. R., Lewis, S., & Mattingly, C. (2011). Students with low vision describe their visual impairments and visual functioning. *Journal of Visual Impairment and Blindness, 105,* 287–298.

Guerette, H., & Zabihaylo, C. (2010). *Mastering the environment through audition, kinesthesia, and cognition: An O&M approach to training for guide dog travel.* AFB Press.

Guest, C. M., Collis, G. M., & McNicholas, J. (2006). Hearing dogs: A longitudinal study of social and psychological effects on deaf and hard-of-hearing recipients. *Journal of Deaf Studies and Deaf Education, 11,* 252–261.

Guiding Eyes for the Blind. (2019). *FAQs.* Author. https://www.guidingeyes.org/about/faqs/

Guilford, J. P. (1967). *The nature of human intelligence.* McGraw-Hill.

Guilford, J. P. (1987). Creativity research: Past, present and future. In S. Isaksen (Ed.), *Frontiers of creativity research* (pp. 33–66). Bearly.

Gül, S. O. (2016). The combined use of video modeling and social stories in teaching social skills for individuals with intellectual disability. *Educational Sciences: Theory & Practice, 16*(1), 83–107.

Guralnick, M. J. (1997). *The effectiveness of early intervention.* Brookes.

Guralnick, M. J. (2005). Early intervention for children with intellectual disabilities: Current knowledge and future prospects. *Journal of Applied Research in Intellectual Disabilities, 18,* 313–324.

Guralnick, M. J. (2019). *Effective early intervention: The developmental systems approach.* Paul H. Brookes Publishing.

Gustafson, G., Pfetzing, D., & Zawolkow, E. (1980). *Signing exact English.* Modern Signs.

Haber, M. G., Mazzotti, V. L., Mustian, A. L., Rowe, D. A., Bartholomew, A. L., Test, D. W., & Fowler, C. H. (2016). What works, when, for whom, and with whom: A meta-analytic review of predictors of postsecondary success for students with disabilities. *Review of Educational Research, 86,* 123–162.

Hadley, P. A. (1998). Language sampling protocols for eliciting text-level discourse. *Language, Speech, and Hearing Services in the Schools, 29,* 132–147.

Haegele, J. A., Brian, A., & Goodway, J. (2015). Fundamental motor skills and school-aged individuals with visual impairments: A review. *Journal of Autism and Developmental Disorders, 2,* 320–327.

Hagaman, J. L., & Casey, K. J. (2017). Paraphrasing strategy instruction in content area text. *Intervention in School and Clinic, 52*(4), 210–217.

Hage, C., & Leybaert, J. (2006). The effect of cued speech on the development of spoken language. In P. E. Spencer & M. Marschark (Eds.), *Advances in the spoken-language development of deaf and hard-of-hearing children* (pp. 193–211). Oxford University Press.

Hagiwara, H., & Shogren, K. A. (2019). Collaborate with families to support student learning and secure needed services. In J. McLeskey, L. Maheady, B. Billingsley, M. T. Brownell, & T. J. Lewis (Eds.), *High leverage practices for inclusive classrooms* (pp. 34–47). Routledge.

Haibach, P. S., Wagner, M. O., & Lieberman, L. J. (2014). Determinants of gross motor skill performance of children with visual impairments. *Research in Developmental Disabilities, 35,* 2577–2584.

Hale, J. E. (2001). *Learning while black: Creating educational excellence for African American children.* Johns Hopkins University Press.

Haliday, L., Tuomainen, O., & Rosen, S. (2017). Language development and impairment in children with mild to moderate sensorineural hearing loss. *Journal of Speech, Language, and Hearing Research, 60,* 1551–1567.

Hall, B. J., Oyer, H. J., & Haas, W. H. (2001). *Speech, language, and hearing disorders: A guide for the teacher* (3rd ed.). Allyn & Bacon.

Halle, S., Ninness, C., Ninness, S. K., & Lawson, D. (2016). Teaching social skills to students with autism: A video modeling social stories approach. *Behavior and Social Issues, 25*(1) 42–54.

Halloran, J. (2019). *Social skills for kids.* PESI Publishing & Media.

Halpern, A. S. (1985). Transition: A look at the foundations. *Exceptional Children, 51,* 479–486.

Ham, R. (1986). *Techniques of stuttering therapy.* Prentice Hall.

Hammill, D. D., & Newcomer, P. L. (2008). *Test of Language Development Intermediate—3.* PRO-ED.

Hampshire, P. K., & Hourcade, J. J. (2014). Teaching play skills to children with autism using visually structured tasks. *Teaching Exceptional Children, 46,* 26–31.

Haynes, W., & Pindzola, R. (2012). *Diagnosis and evaluation in speech pathology* (8th ed.). Upper Saddle River, NJ: Pearson.

Hanhan, S. F. (2008). Parent-teacher communication: Who's talking? In G. Olsen & M. L. Fuller (Eds.), *Home-school relations: Working successfully with parents and families* (pp. 104–126). Allyn & Bacon.

Hanley, G. P. (2012). Functional assessment of problem behavior: Dispelling myths, overcoming implementation obstacles, and developing new lore. *Behavior Analysis in Practice, 5*(1), 54–72.

Hanley, G. P., Jin, C. S., Vanselow, N. R., & Hanratty, L. A. (2014). Producing meaningful improvements in problem behavior of children with autism via synthesized analyses and treatments. *Journal of Applied Behavior Analysis, 47,* 16–36.

Hannah, M. E., & Midlarsky, E. (2005). Helping by siblings of children with mental retardation. *American Journal on Mental Retardation, 110,* 87–99.

Happé, F. (2003). Theory of mind and the self. *Annals of the New York Academy of Science, 1001,* 134–144.

Hardman, M. L., McDonnell, J., & Welch, M. (1997). Perspectives on the future of IDEA. *Journal of the Association for Persons with Severe Handicaps, 22,* 61–77.

Harjusola-Webb, S., Hubbell, S. P., & Bedsem, P. (2012). Increasing prosocial behaviors of young children with disabilities in inclusive classrooms using a combination of peer-mediated intervention and social narratives. *Beyond Behavior, 21,* 19–36.

Harlacher, J. E., Roberts, N. E., & Merrell, K. W. (2006). Classwide interventions for students with ADHD. *Teaching Exceptional Children, 39*(2), 6–12.

Harmston, K. A., Strong, C. J., & Evans, D. D. (2001). International pen-pal correspondence for students with language-learning disabilities. *Teaching Exceptional Children, 33*(3), 46–51.

Harn, W., Bradshaw, M., & Ogletree, B. (1999). The speech-language pathologist in the schools: Changing roles. *Intervention in School and Clinic, 34,* 163–169.

Harris, K. R., Graham, S., Aitken, A. A., Barkel, A., Houston, J., & Ray, A. (2016). Teaching spelling, writing, and reading for writing: Powerful evidence-based practices. *Teaching Exceptional Children, 49*(4), 262–272.

Harry, B. (2003). Trends and issues in serving culturally diverse families of children with disabilities. *Journal of Special Education, 36*, 131–138.

Harry, B. (2008). Collaboration with culturally and linguistically diverse families: Ideal versus reality. *Exceptional Children, 74*, 372–388.

Harry, B., & Klingner, J. K. (2006). *Why are so many minority students in special education? Understanding race and disability in schools.* Teachers College Press.

Harry, B., & Klingner, J. (2007). Discarding the deficit model. *Educational Leadership, 64*(5), 16–21.

Harry, B., Rueda, R., & Kalyanpur, M. (1999). Cultural reciprocity in sociocultural perspective: Adapting the normalization principle for family collaboration. *Exceptional Children, 66*, 123–136.

Hart, B., & Risley, T. R. (1995). *Meaningful differences in the everyday experience of young American children.* Brookes.

Hart, B., & Risley, T. R. (1999). *The social world of children learning to talk.* Brookes.

Hart Barnett, J. E., & Whalon, K. J. (2014). *Friendship 101: Helping students build social competence.* Council for Exceptional Children.

Harte, H. A. (2009). What teachers can learn from mothers of children with autism. *Teaching Exceptional Children, 42*(1), 24–30.

Hartman, K., Gresham, F. M., & Byrd, S. (2017). Student internalizing and externalizing behavior screeners: Evidence for reliability, validity, and usability in elementary schools. *Behavioral Disorders, 42*(3), 108–118.

Hartman, M. A. (2009). Step by step: Creating a community-based transition program for students with intellectual disabilities. *Teaching Exceptional Children, 41*(6), 6–11.

Hatlen, P. (2000). The core curriculum for blind and visually impaired students, including those with additional disabilities. In M. C. Holbrook & A. J. Koenig (Eds.), *Foundations of education, Vol. II: Instructional strategies for teaching children and youths with visual impairments* (2nd ed., pp. 779–784). AFB Press.

Hattie, J. (2012). *Visible learning for teachers: Maximizing impact on learning.* Routledge.

Hatzenbuhler, E. G., Molteni, J. D., & Axe, J. B. (2019). Increasing play skills in children with autism spectrum disorder via peer-mediated matrix training. *Education and Treatment of Children, 42*(3), 295–319.

Havey, J. M. (1999). School psychologists' involvement in special education due process hearings. *Psychology in the Schools, 36*(2), 117–121.

Hawkins, L., & Brawner, J. (1997). *Educating children who are deaf/hard of hearing: Total communication.* ERIC Clearinghouse on Disabilities and Gifted Education. (ERIC Document Reproduction Service No. ED 414 677).

Hayiou-Thomas, M. E., Carroll, J. M., Leavett, R., Hulme, C., & Snowling, M. J. (2017). When does speech sound disorder matter for literacy? The role of disordered speech errors, co-occurring language impairment and family risk of dyslexia. *Journal of Child Psychology and Psychiatry, 58*, 197–205.

Haywood, H. C. (2006). Broader perspectives on mental retardation. In H. N. Switzky & S. Greenspan (Eds.), *What is mental retardation? Ideas for an evolving disability in the 21st century* (rev. ed.). American Association on Intellectual and Developmental Disabilities.

Heaton, P., Williams, K., Cummins, O., & Happé, F. (2008). Autism and pitch processing splinter skills. *Autism, 12*(2), 203–219.

Heber, R. F. (1961). *A manual on terminology and classification in mental retardation. A monograph supplement to the American Journal of Mental Deficiency, 64* (Monograph Suppl.).

Heikua, U., Linna, S.-L., Olsén, P., Hartikaiinen, A.-L., Taanila, A., & Järvelin, M.-R. (2005). Etiological survey on intellectual disabilities in the Northern Finland birth cohort 1986. *American Journal on Mental Retardation, 110*, 171–180.

Heller, K. W., Dangel, H., & Sweatman, L. (1995). Systematic selection of adaptations for students with muscular dystrophy. *Journal of Developmental and Physical Disabilities, 7*, 253–265.

Heller, K. W., Forney, P. E., Alberto, P. A., Best, S. J., & Schwartzman, M. N. (2008). *Understanding physical, health, and multiple disabilities* (2nd ed.). Pearson.

Heller, K. W., Fredrick, L. D., Best, S., Dykes, M. K., & Cohen, E. T. (2000). Specialized health care procedures in the schools: Training and service delivery. *Exceptional Children, 66*, 173–186.

Helton, M. R., & Alber-Morgan, S. R. (2018). Helping parents understand applied behavior analysis: Creating a parent guide in 10 steps. *Behavior Analysis in Practice, 11*, 496–503.

Helton, M. R., & Alber-Morgan, S. R. (2020). Improving young children's behavior with GAMES: Group-contingency approaches for managing elementary-classroom settings. *Young Exceptional Children, 23*(1), 24–35.

Henfield, M. S., Owens, D., & Moore, J. L., III. (2008). Influences on young gifted African Americans' school success: Implications for elementary school counselors. *The Elementary School Journal, 108*, 392–406.

Henry, L. (2008). Short-term memory coding in children with intellectual disabilities. *American Journal on Mental Retardation, 113*, 187–200.

Heron, T. E., & Heward, W. L. (2000). *Total tutoring for special and general educators [instructor's manual].* The Ohio State University Special Education Program.

Herron, M. D. (1971). The nature of scientific enquiry. *School Review, 79*(2), 171–212.

Hersh, M. (2013). Deafblind people, communication, independence, and isolation. *Journal of Deaf Studies and Deaf Education, 18*(4), 446–463.

Hertz-Picciotto, I., & Delwiche, L. (2009). The rise of autism and the role of age at diagnosis. *Epidemiology, 20*, 84–90.

Hessler, T., & Konrad, M. (2008). Using curriculum-based measurement to drive IEPs and instruction in written expression. *Teaching Exceptional Children, 41*(2), 28–37.

Hester, P. P., Hendrickson, J. M., & Gable, R. A. (2009). Forty years later—The value of praise, ignoring, and rules for pre-schoolers at risk for behavior disorders. *Education and Treatment of Children, 32*, 513–535.

Hetzner, A. (2007, March 30). Disparity shows in special ed: State deems 25 districts' minority enrollment disproportionate. *Milwaukee Journal Sentinel.*

Heward, W. L. (1994). Three "low-tech" strategies for increasing the frequency of active student response during group instruction. In R. Gardner III, D. M. Sainato, J. O. Cooper, T. E. Heron, W. L. Heward, J. Eshleman, & T. A. Grossi (Eds.), *Behavior analysis in education: Focus on measurably superior instruction* (pp. 283–320). Brooks/Cole.

Heward, W. L. (2003). Ten faulty notions about teaching and learning that hinder the effectiveness of special education. *Journal of Special Education, 36*(4), 186–205.

Heward, W. L. (2005). Reasons applied behavior analysis is good for education and why those reasons have been insufficient. In W. L. Heward, T. E. Heron, N. A. Neef, S. M. Peterson, D. M. Sainato, G. Cartledge, R. Gardner III, L. D. Peterson, S. B. Hersh, & J. C. Dardig (Eds.), *Focus on behavior analysis in education: Achievements, challenges, and opportunities* (pp. 316–348). Merrill/Pearson.

Heward, W. L. (2011). *Helping school-age students with autism succeed in the regular classroom.* Invited address at the Association for Behavior Analysis International's 2011 Autism Conference, Washington, DC, United States.

Heward, W. L. (2019). Use strategies that promote active student engagement. In J. McLeskey, L. Maheady, B. Billingsley, M. T. Brownell, & T. J. Lewis (Eds.), *High-leverage practices for inclusive classrooms* (pp. 251–263). Routledge/Council for Exceptional Children.

Heward, W. L., & Twyman, J. S. (Guest Eds.). (2021). Special Issue on Direct Instruction. *Behavior Analysis in Practice*.

Heward, W. L., & Wood, C. (2015). *Improving educational outcomes in America: Can a low-tech, generic teaching practice make a difference?* Wing Institute. Online at: http://www.winginstitute.org/uploads/docs/2013WingSummitWH.pdf

Heward, W. L., Heron, T. E., & Cooke, N. L. (1982). Tutor huddle: Key element in a classwide peer tutoring system. *Elementary School Journal*, *83*, 115–123.

Heward, W. L., Heron, T. E., Gardner, R., III, & Prayzer, R. (1991). Two strategies for improving students' writing skills. In G. Stoner, M. R. Shinn, & H. M. Walker (Eds.), *A school psychologist's interventions for regular education* (pp. 379–398). National Association of School Psychologists.

Hill, J. L. (1999). *Meeting the needs of students with special physical and health care needs*. Merrill/Pearson.

Hobbs, N. (Ed.). (1976a). *Issues in the classification of children* (Vol. 1). Jossey-Bass.

Hobbs, N. (Ed.). (1976b). *Issues in the classification of children* (Vol. 2). Jossey-Bass.

Hodal, A. S. (2018). Rapid infant prefrontal cortex development and sensitivity to early environmental experience. *Developmental Review*, *48*, 113–144.

Hodapp, R. M., & DesJardin, J. L. (2002). Genetic etiologies of mental retardation: Issues for interventions and interventionists. *Journal of Developmental and Physical Disabilities*, *14*, 323–338.

Hodapp, R. M., & Dykens, E. M. (2007). Behavioral effects of genetic retardation disorders. In J. W. Jacobson, J. A. Mulick, & J. Rojahn (Eds.), *Handbook of intellectual and developmental disabilities* (pp. 115–131). Springer.

Hodgetts, S., Nicholas, D., & Zwaigenbaum, L. (2013). Home sweet home? Families' experiences with aggression in children with autism spectrum disorders. *Focus on Autism and Other Developmental Disabilities*, *28*, 166–174.

Hoff, E. (2013). Interpreting the early language trajectories of children from low SES and language minority homes: Implications for closing achievement gaps. *Developmental Psychology*, *49*, 4–14.

Holbrook, M. C., D'Andrea, F. M., & Wormsley, D. P. (2017). Literacy skills. In M. C. Holbrook, C. Kamei-Hannan, & T. McCarthy (Eds.), *Foundations of education: Instructional strategies for teaching children and youths with visual impairments* (3rd ed., pp. 374–426). AFB Press.

Holden, G. W. (2019). *Parents and the dynamics of child rearing*. Routledge.

Holehan, K. M., & Zane, T. (2020, May). Facilitated communication reincarnated: Is there science behind that? *Science in Autism Treatment*, *17*(5).

Holland, K. D. (2006). Understanding the parent of the special needs child. *Exceptional Parent*, *36*(8), 60–62.

Hollo, A., & Hirn, R. G. (2015). Teacher and student behaviors in the contexts of grade-level and instructional grouping. *Preventing School Failure*, *59*(1), 30–39.

Holm, M. (2011). Project-based instruction: A review of the literature on effectiveness in prekindergarten through 12th grade classrooms. *Rivier Academic Journal*, *7*(2), 1–13.

Holz, N. E., Zohsel, K., Laucht, M., Banaschewski, T., Hohmann, S., & Brandeis, D. (2018). Gene x environment interactions in conduct disorder: Implications for future treatments. *Neuroscience & Biobehavioral Reviews*, *91*, 239–258.

Honig v. Doe, 485 U.S. 305, 108 S.Ct. 592, 98 L.Ed. 2d 686 (1988).

Hoover, H. D., Dunbar, S. B., & Frisbie, D. A. (2007). *Iowa Tests of Basic Skills*. Riverside.

Horn, A. L., Gable, R. A., & Bobzien, J. L. (2020). Constant time delay to teach students with intellectual disability. *Preventing School Failure*, *64*(1), 89–97.

Horn, A. L., Gable, R. A., Bobzien, J. L., Tonelson, S. W., & Rock, M. L. (2019). Teaching young adults job skills using a constant time delay and ecoaching intervention package. *Career Development and Transition for Exceptional Individuals*, *43*(1), 29–39.

Horn, C. (2010). Response cards: An effective intervention for students with disabilities. *Education and Training in Autism and Developmental Disabilities*, *45*, 116–123.

Hornby, G. (2015). Inclusive special education: Development of a new theory for the education of children with special educational needs and disabilities. *British Journal of Special Education*, *42*(3), 234–256.

Horner, R. H., & Sugai, G. (2015). School-wide PBIS: An example of applied behavior analysis implemented at a scale of social importance. *Behavior Analysis in Practice*, *8*(1), 80–85.

Horner, R. H., Eberhard, J. M., & Sheehan, M. R. (1986). Teaching generalized table bussing. *Behavior Modification*, *10*(4), 457–471.

Horvath, B. (2006). Helping students step into adult life with confidence. In W. L. Heward (Ed.), *Exceptional children: An introduction to special education* (8th ed., pp. 602–603). Merrill/Pearson.

Hosp, M. K., Hosp, J. L., & Howell, K. W. (2016). *The ABCs of CBM: A practical guide to curriculum-based measurement* (2nd ed.). Guilford Press.

Hott, B. L., & Brigham, F. (2020). Effects of response options on the mathematics performance of secondary students with emotional or behavioral disorders. *Exceptionality*, *28*, 1–15.

Houtenville, A. J. (2013). *2013 annual compendium on disability statistics*. University of New Hampshire, Institute on Disability.

Houwen, S., Visscher, C., Limmink, K. A. P. M., & Hartman, E. (2009). Motor skill performance of children and adolescents with visual impairments: A review. *Exceptional Children*, *75*, 464–492.

Howard, J. S., Stanislaw, H., Green, G., Sparkman, C. R., & Cohen, H. G. (2014). Comparison of behavior analytic and eclectic early interventions for young children with autism after three years. *Research in Developmental Disabilities*, *35*(12), 3326–3344.

Howard, V. F., Williams, B. F., & Lepper, C. (2005). *Very young children with special needs: A formative approach for today's children* (3rd ed.). Upper Saddle River, NJ: Merrill/Prentice Hall.

Howard, V. F., Williams, B. F., Miller, D., & Aiken, E. (2014). *Very young children with special needs* (5th ed.). Pearson.

Hrastinki, I., & Wilbur, R. B. (2016). Academic achievement of deaf and hard-of-hearing students in an ASL/English bilingual program. *Journal of Deaf Studies and Deaf Education*, 21(2), 156–170.

Hsiao, Y. (2018). Parental stress in families of children with disabilities. *Intervention in School and Clinic*, *53*, 201–205.

Hudson, L. J. (1997). *Classroom collaboration*. Perkins School for the Blind.

Huebner, K. M., Garber, M., & Wormsley, D. P. (2006). *Student-centered educational placement decisions: The meaning, interpretation, and application of least restrictive environment for students with visual impairments*. Division of Visual Impairments (DVI) of the Council for Exceptional Children.

Hughes, C., Carter, E., Dye, M., & Byers, C. (2013). Including students in general education: The Peer Buddy program. In W. L. Heward, *Exceptional children: An introduction to special education* (10th ed., pp. 446–447). Pearson.

Hughes, C., Copeland, S., Fowler, S., & Church-Pupke, P. (2002). Quality of life. In K. Storey, P. Bates, & D. Hunter (Eds.), *The road ahead: Transition to adult life for persons with disabilities* (pp. 157–171). Training Resource Network.

Hughes, C., Golas, M., Cosgriff, J., Brigham, N., Edwards, C., & Cashen, K. (2011). Effects of a social skills intervention among high school students with intellectual disabilities and autism and their general education peers. *Research and Practice for Persons with Severe Disabilities*, *36*, 46–61.

Hughes, C., Washington, B. H., & Brown, G. L. (2008). Supporting students in the transition from school to adult life. In F. R. Rusch (Ed.), *Beyond high school: Preparing adolescents for tomorrow's challenges* (2nd ed., pp. 266–287). Merrill/Pearson.

Hughes, C. A., Morris, J. R., Therrien, W. J., & Benson, S. K. (2017). Explicit instruction: Historical and contemporary contexts. *Learning Disabilities Research & Practice*, *32*(3), 140–148.

Hughes, J. E. A., Ward, J., Gruffydd, E., Baron-Cohen, S., Smith, P., Allison, C., & Simner, J. (2018). Savant syndrome has a distinct psychological profile in autism. *Molecular Autism*, *9*, 53. https://doi.org/10.1186/s13229-018-0237-1

Huguenin, N. H. (2000). Reducing overselective attention to compound visual cues with extended training in adolescents with severe mental retardation. *American Journal on Mental Retardation*, *111*, 447–453.

Hulit, L. M., Howard, M. R., & Fahey, K. R. (2015). *Born to talk: An introduction to speech and language development* (6th ed.). Pearson.

Hunt, P., Kozleski, E., Lee, J., Mortier, K., Fleming, D., Hicks, T., Balasubramanian, L., Leu, G. Bross, L. A., Munandar, V., Dunlap, K., Stepaniuk, I., Aramburo, C., & Oh, Y. (2020). Implementing comprehensive literacy instruction for students with severe disabilities in general education classrooms. *Exceptional Children*, *86*(3), 330–347.

Hunter, W. C., Maheady, L., Jasper, A. D., Williamson, R. L., Murley, R. C., & Stratton, E. (2015). Numbered heads together as a tier 1 instructional strategy in multitiered systems of support. *Education and Treatment of Children*, *38*(3), 345–362.

Huss, J. A. (2006). Gifted education and cooperative learning: A miss or a match. *Gifted Child Today*, *29*, 19–23.

Hutchins, N. S., Burke, M. D., Bowman-Perrott, L., Tarlow, K. R., & Hatton, H. (2019). The effects of social skills interventions for students with EBD and ASD: A single-case meta-analysis. *Behavior Modification*. https://doi.org/10.1177/0145445519846817

Hutinger, P. L., Marshall, S., & McCarten, K. (1983). *Core curriculum: Macomb 0–3 regional project* (3rd ed.). Western Illinois University.

Hutton, A. M., & Caron, S. L. (2005). Experience of families with children with autism in rural New England. *Focus on Autism and Other Developmental Disabilities*, *20*, 180–189.

Hyde, M., & Power, D. (2006). Some ethical dimensions of cochlear implantation for Deaf children and their families. *Journal of Deaf Studies and Deaf Education*, *11*, 102–111.

Hyman, S. L., Levy, S. E., Myers, S. M., & AAP Council on Children with Disabilities, Section on Developmental and Behavioral Pediatrics. (2020). Identification, evaluation, and management of children with autism spectrum disorder. *Pediatrics*, *145*(1), Article e20193447.

Iadarola, S., Levato, L., Harrison, B., Smith, T., Lecavalier, L., Johnson, C., Swiezy, N., Bearss, K., & Scahill, L. (2018). Teaching parents behavioral strategies for autism spectrum disorder (ASD): Effects on stress, strain, and competence. *Journal of Autism and Developmental Disorders*, *48*, 1031–1040.

Inge, K. J., & Moon, M. S. (2006). Vocational preparation and transition. In M. E. Snell & F. Brown (Eds.), *Instruction of students with severe disabilities* (6th ed., pp. 328–374). Merrill/Pearson.

Institute for Community Inclusion. (2019). *Think College: Dual enrollment*. https://thinkcollege.net/resources/innovation-exchange/dual-enrollment

Institute on Communication and Inclusion at Syracuse University. (2020). *Research statement*. https://ici.syr.edu/resources/research-statement/

Interactive Autism Network. (2011). *IAN research findings: Treatment series*. http://www.iancommunity.org/cs/ian_treatment_reports/overview

International Dyslexia Association. (2002). *Definition of dyslexia*. Author. Retrieved July 19, 2014, at http://www.interdys.org/ewebeditpro5/upload/Definition.pdf

Irving Independent School District v. Tatro, 104 S. Ct. 3371, 82 L.Ed. 2d 664 (1984).

Ispen, C. (2006). Health, secondary conditions, and employment outcomes for adults with disabilities. *Journal of Disability Policy Studies*, *17*, 77–87.

Ita, C. M., & Friedman, H. A. (1999). The psychological development of children who are deaf or hard of hearing: A critical review. *Volta Review*, *101*, 165–181.

Itard, J. M. G. (1806/1962). *The wild boy of Aveyron* (G. Humphrey & M. Humphrey, Eds. and Trans.). Prentice Hall. (Original work published in Paris by Guoyon).

Ives, B. (2007). Graphic organizers applied to secondary algebra instruction for students with learning disorders. *Learning Disabilities Research & Practice*, *22*, 110–118.

Ivey, M. L., Heflin, L. J., & Alberto, P. (2004). The use of social stories to promote independent behaviors in novel events for children with PDD-NOS. *Focus on Autism and Other Developmental Disabilities*, *19*, 164–176.

Ivy, J. W., Meindl, J. N., Overly, E., & Robson, K. M. (2017). Token economy: A systematic review of procedural descriptions. *Behavior Modification*, *41*(5), 708–737.

Iwata, B. A., Dorsey, M., Slifer, K., Bauman, K., & Richman, G. (1994). Toward a functional analysis of self-injury. *Journal of Applied Behavior Analysis*, *27*, 197–209.

Jacobson, J. W., Foxx, R. M., & Mulick, J. (2016). Facilitated communication: The ultimate fad treatment. In R. M. Foxx & J. Mulick (Eds.), *Controversial therapies for autism and intellectual disabilities: Fads, fashion and science in professional practice* (2nd ed., pp. 283–302). Routledge.

Jacobson, W. H. (2013). The *art and science of teaching orientation and mobility to persons with visual impairments* (2nd ed.). AFB Press.

Jain, A., Marshall, J., Buikema, A., Bancroft, T., Kelly, J. P., & Newschaffer, C. J. (2015). Autism occurrence by MMR vaccine status among U.S. children with older siblings with and without autism. *Journal of the American Medical Association*, *313*(15), 1534–1540.

Jamal, L., Schupmann, W., & Berkman, B. E. (2019). An ethical framework for genetic counseling in the genomic era. *Journal of Genetic Counseling*. https://doi.org/10.1002/jgc4.1207

Janney, R. E., King-Sears, M. E., & Snell, M. E. (2015). *Collaborative teaming* (3rd ed.). Baltimore: Brookes.

Jantz, K. M. (2011). Support groups for adults with Asperger's syndrome. *Focus on Autism and Other Developmental Disabilities*, *26*, 119–118.

Jayanthi, M., Gersten, R., & Baker, S. (2008). *Mathematics instruction for students with learning disabilities or difficulty learning mathematics: A guide for teachers*. RMC Research Corporation, Center on Instruction.

Jenkins, L. N., Floress, M., & Reinke, W. (2015). Rates and types of teacher praise: A review and future directions. *Psychology in the Schools*, *52*(5), 463–476.

Jernigan, K. (1993, August). The pitfalls of political correctness: Euphemisms excoriated. *Braille Monitor*, 865–867.

Jerome, J., Frantino, E. P., & Sturmey, P. (2007). The effects of errorless learning and backward chaining on the acquisition of internet skills in adults with developmental disabilities. *Journal of Applied Behavior Analysis*, *40*, 185–189.

Jessup, G., Bundy, A. C., Broom, A., & Hancock, N. (2018). Fitting in or feeling excluded: The experiences of high school students with visual impairments. *Journal of Visual Impairment & Blindness*, *112*(3), 261–273.

Jimenez, B. A., Lo, Y., & Saunders, A. (2014). The additive effects of scripted lessons plus guided notes on science quiz scores of students with intellectual disabilities and autism. *Journal of Special Education*, *47*, 231–244.

Jitendra, A. K., Lein, A. E., Im, S., Alghamdi, A. A., Heftel, S. B., & Mouanoutoua, J. (2018). Mathematical interventions for secondary students with learning disabilities and mathematics difficulties: A meta-analysis. *Exceptional Children*, *84*(2) 177–196.

Jo, W., Hee, J., Ananda Harianoto, R., So, J. H., Lee, H., Lee, H. J., & Moon, M. (2016). Introduction of 3D printing technology in the classroom for visually impaired students. *Journal of Visual Impairment & Blindness, 110*(2), 115–121.

Johnson, D. W., & Johnson, R. T. (2017). *Joining together: Group theory and group skills* (12th ed.). Pearson Education.

Johnson, J., Rahn, N. L., & Bricker, D. (2015). *An activity-based approach to early intervention* (4th ed.). Brookes.

Johnson, J. W., Reid, R., & Mason, L. H. (2011). Improving the reading recall of high school students with ADHD. *Remedial and Special Education, 20,* 1–11.

Johnson, S. I. (2004). Using funds of knowledge to create literacy lessons. *Making Connections.* http://www.aps.edu/language-and-cultural-equity/newsletters/december2004.pdf

Johnson, T. L., Chin, E. M., & Hoon, A. H. (2019). Cerebral palsy. In M. L. Batshaw, N. J. Roizen, & G. R. Lotrecchiano (Eds.), *Children with disabilities* (8th ed.). Brookes.

Johnson, T. P. (1986). *The principal's guide to the educational rights of handicapped students.* Reston, VA.

Johnston, M. K., Kelly, C. S., Harris, F. R., & Wolf, M. M. (1966). An application of reinforcement principles to the development of motor skills of a young child. *Child Development, 37,* 370–387.

Johnston, S. S., & Blue, C. W. (2020). Teaching communication skills. In F. Brown, J. McDonnell, & M. E. Snell (Eds.), *Instruction of students with severe disabilities* (9th ed., pp. 418–451). Pearson.

Jones, D. E., Clatterbuck, C. C., Marquis, J., Turnbull, H. R., & Moberly, R. L. (1996). Educational placements for children who are ventilator assisted. *Exceptional Children, 63,* 47–57.

Jones, W., & Klin, A. (2013). Attention to eyes is present but in decline in 2–6-month-old infants later diagnosed with autism. *Nature, 504,* 427–431.

Joseph, L. M., & Konrad, M. (2009). Twenty ways to help students self-manage their academic performance. *Intervention in School and Clinic, 44,* 246–249.

Jozwik, S. L., Cuenca-Carlino, Y., Mustian, A. L., & Douglas, K. H. (2019). Evaluating a self-regulated strategy development reading-comprehension intervention for emerging bilingual students with learning disabilities. *Preventing School Failure, 63*(2), 121–132.

Juarez, A., Best, S. J., & Bigge, J. L. (2010). Adaptations in physical education, leisure education, and recreation. In S. J. Best, K. W. Heller, & J. L. Bigge (Eds.), *Teaching individuals with physical or multiple disabilities* (6th ed., pp. 311–341). Pearson.

Jung, J. Y., & Gross, M. U. M. (2014). Highly gifted students. In J. A. Plucker & C. M. Callahan (Eds.), *Critical issues and practices in gifted education: What the research says* (305–314). Prufrock Press.

Justen, J. E. (1976). Who are the severely handicapped? A problem in definition. *AAESPH Review, 1*(2), 1–12.

Justice, L. M., & Redle, E. E. (2014). *Communication sciences and disorders: A clinical evidence-based approach* (3rd ed.). Pearson.

Kagan J. (2018). Perspectives on two temperamental biases. *Philosophical Transactions, Royal Society B,* 373: 20170158. http://dx.doi.org/10.1098/rstb.2017.0158

Kagan, S., & Kagan, M. (2009). *Kagan cooperative learning.* Kagan Publishing.

Kaiser, A. P., & Grim, J. C. (2006). Teaching functional communication skills. In M. E. Snell & F. Brown (Eds.), *Instruction of students with severe disabilities* (6th ed.). Merrill/Pearson.

Kalb, L. G., Law, J. K., Landa, R., & Law, R. A. (2010). Onset patterns prior to 36 months in autism spectrum disorders. *Journal of Autism and Developmental Disorders, 40*(11), 1389–1402.

Kalbfleisch, M. L. (2013). Twice-exceptional students: Gifted students with learning disabilities. In C. M. Callahan & H. L. Hertberg-Davis (Eds.), *Fundamentals of gifted education* (pp. 358–368). Routledge.

Kame'enui, E. J. (1993). Diverse learners and the tyranny of time: Don't fix blame; fix the leaky roof. *The Reading Teacher, 46,* 376–383.

Kamps, D. M., Dugan, E. P., Leonard, B. R., & Daoust, P. M. (1994). Enhanced small group instruction using choral responding and student interactions for children with autism and developmental disabilities. *American Journal on Mental Retardation, 99,* 60–73.

Kang, J., Dunn, M., & Blank, A. (2018). *Labor force characteristics of people with a disability.* U.S. Bureau of Labor Statistics.

Kanner, A. M., & Schafer, P. O. (2006). Seizures and teens: When seizures aren't the only problem. *Exceptional Parent, 36*(11), 50, 52–55.

Kanner, L. (1943). Autistic disturbance of affective contact. *Nervous Child, 2,* 217–250.

Kaplan, S. N. (2019). Advocacy differentiating differentiation. *Gifted Child Today, 42*(1), 58–59.

Karchmer, M. A., & Mitchell, R. E. (2011). Demographic and achievement characteristics of deaf and hard-of-hearing students. In M. Marschark & P. E. Spencer (Eds.), *Oxford handbook of deaf studies, language, and education* (2nd ed., pp. 18–31). Oxford University Press.

Karl, J., Collins, B. C., Hager, K. D., Schuster, J. W., & Ault, M. J. (2013). Teaching core content embedded in a functional activity to students with moderate cognitive disabilities using a simultaneous prompting procedure. *Education and Training in Autism and Developmental Disabilities, 48*(3), 363–378.

Karten, T. (2017). *Building on the strengths of students with special needs: How to move beyond disability labels in the classroom.* ASCD.

Kasari, C., Freeman, S., & Paparella, T. (2006). Joint attention and symbolic play in young children with autism: A randomized controlled intervention study. *Journal of Child Psychology and Psychiatry, 47,* 611–620.

Kassardjian, A., Leaf, J. B., Ravid, D., Leaf, J. A., Alcalay, A., Dale, S., Tsuji, K., Taubman, M., Leaf, R., McEachin, J., & Oppenheim-Leaf, M. L. (2014). Comparing the teaching interaction procedure to social stories: A replication study. *Journal of Autism and Developmental Disorders, 44,* 2329–2340.

Katsiyannis, A., & Maag, J. W. (2001). Manifestation determination as a golden fleece. *Exceptional Children, 68,* 85–96.

Katsiyannis, A., & Yell, M. L. (2000). The Supreme Court and school health services: Cedar Rapids v. Garret F. *Exceptional Children, 66,* 317–326.

Katz, E., & Girolametto, L. (2013). Peer-mediated intervention for preschoolers with ASD implemented in early childhood education settings. *Topics in Early Childhood Education, 33,* 133–143.

Kauffman, J. M. (2011). *Toward a science of education: The battle between rogue and real science.* Full Court Press.

Kauffman, J. M., & Badar, J. (2013). How we might make special education for students with emotional or behavioral disorders less stigmatizing. *Behavioral Disorders, 39*(1), 16–27.

Kauffman, J. M., & Landrum, T. J. (2018). *Characteristics of emotional and behavioral disorders of children and youth* (11th ed.). Pearson.

Kauffman, J. M., Felder, M., Ahrbeck, B., Badar, J., & Schneiders, K. (2018). Inclusion of all students in general education? International appeal for a more temperate approach to inclusion. *Journal of International Special Needs Education, 21*(2), 1–10.

Kauffman, J. M., Hallahan, D. P., Pullen, P. C., & Badar, J. (2018). *Special education: What it is and why we need it.* Routledge.

Kauffman, J. M., Travers, J. C., & Badar, J. (2020). Why *some* students with severe disabilities are not placed in general education. *Research and Practice for Persons with Severe Disabilities, 45*(1), 28–33.

Kaufman, A. (2000). Clothing-selection habits of teenage girls who are sighted and blind. *Journal of Visual Impairments and Blindness, 94,* 527–531.

Kayfitz, A. D., Gragg, M. N., & Orr, R. R. (2010). Positive experiences of mothers and fathers of children with autism. *Journal of Applied Research in Intellectual Disabilities, 23,* 337–343.

Kazdin, A. E. (2009). *The Kazdin method for parenting the defiant child*. Mariner Books.

Kearns, D. M., & Fuchs, D. (2013). Does cognitively focused instruction improve the academic performance of low-achieving students? *Exceptional Children, 79*(3), 263–290.

Keenan, M., & Dillenberger, K. (2020). Drama in the courtroom: Defending the rights of children diagnosed with autism. *The Barrister*. http://www.barristermagazine.com/drama-in-the-courtroom-defending-the-rights-of-children-diagnosed-with-autism/

Kellems, R. O., Frandsen, K., Cardon, T. A., Knight, K., & Andersen, M. (2018). Effectiveness of static pictures vs. video prompting for teaching functional life skills to students with autism spectrum disorders. *Preventing School Failure: Alternative Education for Children and Youth, 62*, 129–139.

Kellems, R. O., Mourra, K., Morgan, R. L., Riesen, T., Glasgow, M., & Huddleston, R. (2016). Video modeling and prompting in practice: Teaching cooking skills. *Career Development and Transition for Exceptional Individuals, 39*(3), 185–190.

Keller, C. L., & Duffy, M. L. (2005). "I said that?" How to improve our instructional behavior in just 5 minutes per day through data-based self-evaluation. *Teaching Exceptional Children, 37*(4), 36–39.

Kelly, R. R. (2014). *Beyond high school*. http://www.handsandvoices.org/articles/education/ed/V13-1_beyondHS.htm

Kemmery, M. A., & Compton, M. V. (2014). Are you Deaf or hard of hearing? Which do you go by: Perceptions of identity in families of students with hearing loss. *The Volta Review, 114*(2), 157–192.

Kemp, C., Kidshida, Y., Carter, M., & Sweller, N. (2013). The effect of activity type on the engagement and interaction of young children with disabilities in inclusive childcare settings. *Early Childhood Research Quarterly, 28*, 134–143.

Kennedy, A. M., & Haydon, T. (2020). Forming and sustaining high-quality student–teacher relationships to reduce minor behavioral incidents. *Intervention in School and Clinic*. https://doi.org/10.1177/1053451220942197

Kerr, B. A., Vuyk, M. A., & Rea, C. (2012). Gendered practices in the education of gifted girls and boys. *Psychology in the Schools, 49*, 647–655.

Kerr, M. M., & Nelson, C. M. (2010). *Strategies for managing behavior problems in the classroom* (6th ed.). Pearson.

Kessler Foundation/National Organization on Disability. (2010). *The ADA, 20 years later*. Author.

Kilpatrick, D. A. (2015). *Essentials of assessing, preventing, and overcoming reading difficulties*. Wiley.

Kim, D. S., & Emerson, R. W. (2014). Effect of cane technique on obstacle detection with the long cane. *Journal of Visual Impairment and Blindness, 108*, 335–340.

Kim, J., Stangl, A., Eisenberg, A., & Yeh, T. (2014). Tactile picture books for young children with visual impairment. *Tactile Embedded Interaction*, February 16–19, 2014.

Kim, J. S., Hemphill, L., Troyer, M., Thomson, J. M., Jones, S. M., LaRusso, M. D., & Donovan, S. (2017). Engaging struggling adolescent readers to improve reading skills. *Reading Research Quarterly, 52*, 357–382.

King, E. W. (2005). Addressing the social and emotional needs of twice-exceptional learners. *Teaching Exceptional Children, 38*(1), 16–20.

King, G., Baxter, D., Rosenbaum, P., Zwaigenbaum, L., & Bates, A. (2009). Belief systems of families of children with autism spectrum disorders or Down syndrome. *Focus on Autism and Other Developmental Disabilities, 24*, 50–64.

King, S. J., DeCaro, J. J., Karchmer, M. A., & Cole, K. J. (2001). *College and career programs for deaf students* (11th ed.). Gallaudet University and National Technical Institute for the Deaf.

King-Sears, M. E., & Bowman-Kruhm, M. (2010). Attending to specialized reading instruction for adolescents with mild disabilities. *Teaching Exceptional Children, 42*(4), 30–40.

King-Sears, M. E., Janney, R., & Snell, M. E. (2015). *Collaborative teaming*. Brookes.

Kingsley, M. (1997). The effects of a visual loss. In H. Mason & S. McCall (Eds.), *Visual impairment: Access to education for children and young people* (pp. 23–29). Fulton.

Kiriakopoulos, E. (2018). *Preparing for back to school success*. Epilepsy Foundation. https://www.epilepsy.com/article/2018/8/preparing-back-school-success

Kirk, S. A., McCarthy, J. J., & Kirk, W. D. (1968). *Illinois test of psycholinguistic abilities* (rev. ed.). Urbana, IL: University of Illinois Press.

Klein, J. (1994). Supported living: Not just another "rung" on the continuum. *TASH Newsletter, 20*(7), 16–18.

Klein, R. E., McHugh, E., Harrington, S. L., Davis, T., & Lieberman, L. J. (2005). Adapted bicycles for teaching riding skills. *Teaching Exceptional Children, 37*(6), 50–56.

Kleinert, H., Towles-Reeves, E., Quenemoen, R., Thrulaow, M., Fluegge, L., Weseman, L., & Kerbel, A. (2015). Where students with the most significant disabilities are taught: Implications for general curriculum access. *Exceptional Children, 81*(3), 312–328.

Kleweno, C. P., Seibel, E. J., Viirre, E. S., Kelly, J. P., & Furness, T. A. (2001). The virtual-retinal display as a low-vision computer interface: Pilot study. *Journal of Rehabilitation Research and Development, 38*, 431–441.

Klingner, J., & Eppolito, A. M. (2014). *English language learners: Distinguishing between language acquisition and learning disabilities*. Council for Exceptional Children.

Kluth, P. (2004). Autism, autobiography, and adaptations. *Teaching Exceptional Children, 36*(4), 42–47.

Kluwin, T. N., & Moores, D. F. (1989). Mathematics achievement of hearing impaired adolescents in different placements. *Exceptional Children, 55*, 327–335.

Knackendoffel, A., Dettmer, P., & Thurston, L. P. (2018). *Collaborating, consulting, and working in teams for students with special needs* (8th ed.). Pearson.

Knight, V. F., Creech-Galloway, C. E., Karl, J. M., & Collins, B. C. (2018). Evaluating supported etext to teach science to high school students with moderate intellectual disability. *Focus on Autism and Other Developmental Disabilities, 33*, 227–236.

Knoll, J. A., & Wheeler, C. B. (2005). My home and community: Developing supports for adult living. In R. W. Flexer, T. J. Simmons, P. Luft, & R. M. Baer (Eds.), *Transition planning for secondary students with disabilities* (2nd ed., pp. 499–539). Merrill/Pearson.

Knowlton, E. (1998). Considerations in the design of personalized curricula supports for students with developmental disabilities. *Education and Training in Mental Retardation and Developmental Disabilities*, 33, 95–107.

Koball, H., & Jiang, Y. (2018). *Basic facts about low-income children: Children under 18 years, 2016*. National Center for Children in Poverty, Columbia University Mailman School of Public Health.

Kochhar-Bryant, C. A. (2008). *Collaboration and system coordination for students with special needs: From early childhood to the postsecondary years*. Merrill/Pearson.

Kochhar-Bryant, C. A., & Greene, G. (2009). *Pathways to successful transition for youth with disabilities: A developmental approach* (2nd ed.). Pearson.

Koegel, R. L., Openden, D., & Koegel, L. K. (2004). A systematic desensitization paradigm to treat hypersensitivity to auditory stimuli in children with autism in family contexts. *Research and Practice for Persons with Severe Disabilities, 29*, 122–134.

Koenig, A. J. (2006). Growing into literacy. In M. C. Holbrook (Ed.), *Children with visual impairments: A parents' guide* (2nd ed., pp. 265–295). Woodbine House.

Koestler, F. A. (2004). *The unseen minority: A social history of blindness in the United States*. AFB Press.

Kokina, A., & Kern, L. (2010). Social story interventions for students with autism spectrum disorders: A meta-analysis. *Journal of Autism and Developmental Disorders, 40*, 812–826.

Komesaroff, L. (2007). *Disabling pedagogy: Power, politics, and Deaf education*. Gallaudet Press.

Konold, T. R., Walthall, J. C., & Pianta, R. C. (2004). The behavior of child behavior ratings: Measurement structure of the Child Behavior Checklist across time, informants, and child gender. *Behavioral Disorders, 29*, 372–383.

Konrad, M. (2008). Twenty ways to involve students in the IEP process. *Intervention in School and Clinic, 43*, 236–239.

Konrad, M. (2020). NOW strategy [Manuscript in preparation].

Konrad, M., Joseph, L. M., & Eveleigh, E. (2009). A meta-analytic review of guided notes. *Education and Treatment of Children, 32*, 421–444.

Konrad M. K., & Alber-Morgan, S. R. (2020). SPLASH strategy [Manuscript in preparation].

Konrad, M. K., Joseph, L. M., & Itoi, M. (2011). Using guided notes to enhance instruction for all students. *Intervention in School and Clinic, 46*, 131–140.

Korkmaz, B. (2011). Theory of mind and neurodevelopmental disorders of childhood. *Pediatric Research, 69*, 101–108.

Korver, A. M. H., Smith, R. J. H., Van Camp, G., Schleiss, M. R., Bitner-Glindzicz, M. A. K., Lustig, L. R., Usami, S., & Boudewyns, A. N. (2018). *Nature Reviews Disease Primers, 3*, 1–37. https://doi.org/10.1038/nrdp.2016.94

Koslowski, N., Klein, K., Arnold, K., Koesters, M., Schuetzwohl, M., Salize, H. J., & Puschner, B. (2016). Effectiveness of interventions for adults with mild to moderate intellectual disabilities and mental health problems: Systematic review and meta-analysis. *The British Journal of Psychiatry, 209*(6), 469–474.

Kostelnik, M. J., Soderman, A. K., Whiren, A. P., & Rupiper, M. L. (2019). *Developmentally appropriate curriculum: Best practices in early childhood education* (7th ed.). Pearson.

Kostewicz, D. E., & Kubina, R. M. (2011). Building science reading fluency for students with disabilities with repeated readings to a fluency criterion. *Learning Disabilities: A Multidisciplinary Journal, 17*, 89–104.

Kourassanis-Velasquez, J., & Jones, E. A. (2019). Increasing joint attention in children with autism and their peers. *Behavior Analysis in Practice, 12*, 78–94.

Kourea, L., Konrad, M., & Kazolia, T. (2019). Effects of a guided-notes intervention program on the quiz and note-taking Greek history performance of high school students with learning difficulties in Cyprus. *Education and Treatment of Children, 42*(1), 47–71.

Kranak, M. C., Alber-Morgan, S. R., & Sawyer, M. R. (2017). A parametric analysis of specific praise rates on the on-task behavior of elementary students with autism. *Education and Treatment of Autism and Developmental Disabilities, 52*(4), 453–464.

Krathwohl, D. R. (2002). A revision of Bloom's Taxonomy: An overview. *Theory into Practice, 41*, 212–218.

Kreiner J., & Flexer, R. (2009). Assessment of leisure preferences for students with severe developmental disabilities and communication difficulties. *Education and Training in Developmental Disabilities, 44*, 280–288.

Kremer, K., Flower, A., Huang, J., & Vaughn, M. G. (2016). Behavior problems and children's academic achievement: A test of growth-curve models with gender and racial differences. *Children and Youth Services Review, 67*, 95–104.

Kristensen, T., & Wilberg, J. H. (2015). *Be my eyes*. http://bemyeyes.org

Kritikos, E. P., McLoughlin, J. A., & Lewis, R. B. (2018). *Assessing students with special needs* (8th ed.). Pearson.

Kroth, R. L., & Edge, D. (2007). *Communicating with parents and families of exceptional children* (4th ed.). Love.

Kryzak, L. A., & Jones, E. A. (2017). Sibling self-management: Programming for generalization to improve interactions between typically developing siblings and children with autism spectrum disorders. *Developmental Neurorehabilitation, 20*, 525–537.

Kubina, R. M., & Yurich, K. K. L. (2012). *The precision teaching book*. Greatness Achieved.

Kugel, R. B., & Wolfensberger, W. (Eds.). (1969). *Changing patterns in residential services for the mentally retarded*. Superintendent of Documents.

Kuna, J. (2001). The Human Genome Project and eugenics: Identifying the impact on individuals with mental retardation. *Mental Retardation, 39*, 158–160.

Kunesh, C. E., & Noltemeyer, A. (2019). Understanding disciplinary disproportionality: Stereotypes shape pre-service teachers' beliefs about Black boys' behavior. *Urban Education, 54*, 471–498.

Kurt, O., & Kutlu, M. (2019). Effectiveness of social stories in teaching abduction-prevention skills to children with autism. *Journal of Autism and Developmental Disorders, 49*, 3807–3818.

Lahav, O., Schloerb, D. W., & Srinivasan, M. A. (2015). Virtual environments for people who are visually impaired integrated into an orientation and mobility program. *Journal of Visual Impairment & Blindness, 109*, 5–16.

Lake, J. F., & Billingsley, B. S. (2000). An analysis of factors that contribute to parent-school conflict in special education. *Remedial and Special Education, 21*, 240–251.

Lakin, C., Larson, S., & Kim, S. (March, 2011). *The effects of community vs. institutional living on the daily living skills of persons with developmental disabilities?* Evidence-Based Policy Brief published by the National Association of State Directors of Developmental Disability Services and the Association of University Centers on Disability. http://www.aucd.org/docs/councils/core/Evidence-Based%20Policy%20Brief_1.pdf

Lalvani, P. (2008). Mothers of children with Down syndrome: Constructing the sociocultural meaning of disability. *Intellectual and Developmental Disabilities, 46*, 436–455.

Lam, E. A., & McMaster, K. L. (2014). Predictors of responsiveness to early literacy intervention: A 10-year update. *Learning Disability Quarterly*, 37(3), 134–147.

Lamb, R., Miller, D., Lamb, R., Akmal, T., & Hsiao, J. (2018). Examination of the role of training and fidelity of implementation in the use of assistive communications for children with autism spectrum disorder: A meta-analysis of the Picture Exchange Communication System. *British Journal of Special Education, 45*, 454–472.

Lambert, M. C., Cartledge, G., Lo, Y., & Heward, W. L. (2006). Effects of response cards on disruptive behavior and academic responding by fourth-grade urban students. *Journal of Positive Behavioral Interventions, 8*, 88–99.

Lancaster, J. (1806). *Improvements in education*. Collins & Perkins.

Lancioni, G. E., O'Reilly, M. F., Singh, N. N., Sigafoos, J., Didden, R., Oliva, D., & Severini, L. (2006). A microswitch-based program to enable students with multiple disabilities to choose among environmental stimuli. *Journal of Visual Impairment and Blindness, 100*, 488–493.

Landa, R. J., Holman, K. C., & Garrett-Mayer, E. (2007). Social and communication development in toddlers with early and later diagnosis of autism spectrum disorders. *Archives of General Psychiatry, 64*(7), 853–864.

Landi, N., & Purdue, M. V. (2019). Neuroimaging genetics studies of specific reading disability and developmental language disorder: A review. *Language and Linguistics Compass, 13*(9), 1–37.

Landrum, T. J., & McDuffie-Landrum, K. (2014). *Learning styles: Current practice alerts*, Issue 21. Division for Learning Disabilities and Division for Research, Council for Exceptional Children.

Lane, G., Matthews, B., Ellison, C., & Palmer, C. (2016). There's more to a dog guide than meets the eye: A preliminary exploration of potential health benefits of dog guide use. *International Journal of Orientation & Mobility, 8*(1), 27–36.

Lane, H. (2003). *Afterword*. National Center on Deaf-Blindness. https://nationaldb.org/library/page/1930

Lane, K. L., Menzies, H. M., Oakes, W. P., & Kalberg, J. R. (2019). *Developing a schoolwide framework to prevent and manage learning and behavior problems* (2nd ed.). Guilford Press.

Lane, K. L., Oakes, W. P., Menzies, H. M., & Germer, K. A. (2014). Screening and identification approaches for detecting students at risk. In H. M. Walker & R. M. Gresham (Eds.), *Handbook of evidence-based practices for emotional and behavioral disorders: Applications in schools* (pp. 129–151). Guilford Press.

Lane, K. L., Wehby, J. H., & Cooley, C. (2006). Teacher expectations of student's classroom behavior across the grade span: Which social skills are necessary for success? *Exceptional Children, 72,* 153–167.

Lanfranchi, S., Baddeley, A., Gathercole, S., & Vianello, R. (2012). Working memory in Down syndrome: Is there a dual task deficit? *Journal of Intellectual Disability Research, 56*(2), 157–166.

Lange, C. M., Lane-Outlaw, S., Lange, W. E., & Sherwood, D. L. (2013). American Sign Language/English bilingual model: A longitudinal study of academic growth. *Journal of Deaf Studies and Deaf Education, 18*(4), 532–544.

Langer, N., Benjamin, C., Becker, B. L. C., & Gaab, N. (2019). Comorbidity of reading disabilities and ADHD: Structural and functional brain characteristics. *Human Brain Mapping, 40,* 2677–2698.

Lanovaz, M. J., Sladeczek, I. E., & Rapp, J. T. (2011). Effects of music on vocal stereotypy in children with autism. *Journal of Applied Behavior Analysis, 44,* 647–651.

Larson, S. A., Lakin, K. C., Anderson, L., Kwak, N., Hak Lee, J., & Anderson, D. (2001). Prevalence of mental retardation and developmental disabilities: Estimates from the 1994/1995 National Health Interview Survey Disability Supplements. *American Journal of Mental Retardation, 105,* 231–252.

Larsson, E. V. (2013). *Is applied behavior analysis (ABA) and early intensive behavioral intervention (EIBI) an effective treatment for autism? A cumulative history of impartial independent reviews.* The Lovaas Institute for Early Intervention Midwest Headquarters. https://www.behavior.org/resources/649.pdf

Lattimore, L. P., Parsons, M. B., & Reid, D. H. (2006). Enhancing job-site training of supported workers with autism: A reemphasis on simulation. *Journal of Applied Behavior Analysis, 39,* 91–102.

Lawrence, S., Smith, S., & Banerjee, R. (2016). *Preschool inclusion: Key findings from research and implications for policy.* Child Care and Early Education Research Connections. https://files.eric.ed.gov/fulltext/ED579178.pdf

Layng, T. V. J., & Twyman, J. S. (2014). Education + technology + innovation = learning? In M. Murphy, S. Redding, & J. Twyman (Eds.), *Handbook on innovations in learning* (pp. 135–150). Center on Innovations in Learning, Temple University; Information Age Publishing.

Leaf, J. B., Oppenheim-Leaf, M. L., Dotson, W. H., Johnson, V. A., Courtemanche, A. B., Sheldon, J. B., & Sherman, J. A. (2011). Effects of no-no prompting on teaching expressive labeling of facial expressions to children with and without a pervasive developmental disorder. *Education and Training in Autism and Developmental Disabilities, 46,* 186–203.

Leaf, J. B., Oppenheim-Leaf, M. L., Leaf, R. B., Taubman, M., McEachin, J., Parker, T., Waks, A. B., & Mountjoy, T. (2015). What is the proof? A methodological review of studies that have utilized social stories. *Education and Training in Autism and Developmental Disabilities, 50,* 127–141.

Ledford, J. R., Chazin, K. T., Harbin, S. R., & Ward, S. E. (2017). Massed trials versus trials embedded into game play: Child outcomes and preference. *Topics in Early Childhood Special Education, 37*(2), 107–120.

Lee, D. L., Belifore, P. J., & Budin, S. G. (2008). Riding the wave: Creating a momentum of school success? *Teaching Exceptional Children, 40*(3), 65–70.

Lee, J., & Yoon, S. Y. (2017). The effects of repeated reading on reading fluency for students with reading disabilities: A meta-analysis. *Journal of Learning Disabilities, 50*(2), 213–224.

Lehr, D. H., & McDaid, P. (1993). Opening the door further: Integrating students with complex health care needs. *Focus on Exceptional Children, 25*(6), 1–8.

Lehr, D., & Harayama, N. (2016). Understanding and meeting the health care needs of students with severe disabilities. In F. E. Brown, J. J. McDonnell, & M. E. Snell (Eds.), *Instruction of students with severe disabilities* (8th ed., pp. 264–291). Pearson.

Leigh, S. A., & Barclay, L. A. (2000). High school braille readers: Achieving academic success. *RE:view, 32,* 123–131.

Lemay, R. (2006). Social role valorization insights into the social integration conundrum. *Mental Retardation, 44,* 1–12.

Lemons, C. J., Vaughn, S., Wexler, J., Kearns, D. M., & Sinclair, A. C. (2018). Envisioning an improved continuum of special education services for students with learning disabilities: Considering intervention intensity. *Learning Disabilities Research and Practice, 33,* 131–143.

Lemons, G. (2011). Diverse perspectives of creativity testing: Controversial issues when used for inclusion into gifted programs. *Journal for the Education of the Gifted, 34,* 742–772.

Letso, S. (2013). Social and adaptive behavior in the context of family life. In P. Gerhardt & D. Crimmins (Eds.), *Social skills and adaptive behavior in learners with autism spectrum disorders* (pp. 3–16). Brookes.

Levitt, P., & Eagleson, K. L. (2018). The ingredients of healthy brain and child development. *Bringing Science to Law and Policy, 57,* 75–88.

Levy, F., Hay, D., & Bennett, K. (2006). Genetics of attention deficit hyperactivity disorder: A current review and future prospects. *International Journal of Disability, Development and Education, 53,* 5–20.

Lewis, M. P. (Ed.). (2015). *Ethnologue: Languages of the world* (18th ed.). SIL International.

Lewis, T. J., Hudson, S., Richter, M., & Johnson, N. (2004). Scientifically supported practices in emotional and behavioral disorders: A proposed approach and brief review of current practices. *Behavioral Disorders, 29,* 247–259.

Lewis, T. J., Scott, T. M., Wehby, J. H., & Wills, H. P. (2014). Direct observation of teacher and student behavior in school settings: Trends, issues and future directions. *Behavioral Disorders, 39*(4), 190–200.

Li, A. (2004). Classroom strategies for improving and enhancing visual skills in students with disabilities. *Teaching Exceptional Children, 36*(6), 38–46.

Lifshitz, H., Irit, H., & Weisse, I. (2007). Self-concept, adjustment to blindness, and quality of friendship among adolescents with visual impairments. *Journal of Visual Impairment and Blindness, 101,* 96–107.

Lighthouse International. (2020). *Vision A–Z.* https://www.lighthouseguild.org/vision-a-z/

Lim, S.-Y. (2008). Parent involvement in education. In G. Olsen & M. L. Fuller (Eds.), *Home-school relations: Working successfully with parents and families* (pp. 127–150). Allyn & Bacon.

Lindsay, S., Cagliostro, E., Albarico, M., Mortaji, N., & Karon, L. (2018). A systematic review of the benefits of hiring people with disabilities. *Journal of Occupational Rehabilitation, 28,* 634–655.

Lindstrom L., Benz, M., & Johnson, M. (1997). From school grounds to coffee grounds: An introduction to school-based businesses. *Teaching Exceptional Children, 29*(4), 18–22.

Lindstrom, L., Doren, B., Metheny, J., Johnson, P., & Zane, C. (2007). Transition to employment: Role of the family in career development. *Exceptional Children, 73,* 348–366.

Lindstrom, L., Doren, B., & Miesch, J. (2011). Waging a living: Career development and long-term employment outcomes for young adults with disabilities. *Exceptional Children, 77,* 13.

Ling, D. (2002). *Speech and the hearing-impaired child: Theory and practice* (2nd ed.). Plural Publishing.

Lino, M., Kuczynski, K., Rodriguez, N., & Schap, T. (2017). *Expenditures on children by families, 2015. Miscellaneous Publication No. 1528–2015.* U.S. Department of Agriculture, Center for Nutrition Policy and Promotion.

Lippke, B. A., Dickey, S. E., Selmar, J. W., & Soder, A. L. (1997). *Photo Articulation Test* (3rd ed.). PRO-ED.

Lipscomb, S., Haimson, J., Liu, A. Y., Burghardt, J., Johnson, D. R., & Thurlow, M. L. (2017). *Preparing for life after high school: The characteristics and experiences of youth in special education. Findings from the National Longitudinal Transition Study 2012. Volume 2: Comparisons across disability groups: Full report* (NCEE 2017–4018). U.S. Department of Education.

Lo, L. (2014). Readability of individualized education programs. *Preventing School Failure, 58,* 96–102.

Lo, Y., & Cartledge, G. (2006). FBA and BIP: Increasing the behavior adjustment of African American boys in schools. *Behavioral Disorders, 31,* 147–161.

Lo, Y., Burk, B., & Anderson, A. L. (2014). Using progressive video prompting to teach students with moderate intellectual disability to shoot a basketball. *Education and Training in Autism and Developmental Disabilities, 49,* 354–367.

Lo, Y., Correa, V., & Anderson, A. (2014). Culturally responsive social skill instruction for Latino male students. *Journal of Positive Behavior Interventions, 17*(1), 15–27.

Lockwood, A., & Coulter, A. (2017). Rights without labels: Thirty years later. *Communique, 45*(6), 29–30.

Lohmeier, K. L. (2005). Implementing the expanded core curriculum in specialized schools for the blind. *RE:view, 37*(3), 126–133.

Lord, C., Risi, S., Lambrecht, L., Cook, E. H., Jr., Leventhal, B. L., DiLavore, P. C., Pickles, A., & Rutter, M. (2000). The Autism Diagnostic Observation Schedule-generic: A standard measure of social and communicative deficits associated with the spectrum of autism. *Journal of Autism and Developmental Disorders, 30,* 205–223.

Loughery, O. T., Betz, A. M., Majdalany, L. M., & Nicholson, K. (2014). Using instructive feedback to teach category names to children with autism. *Journal of Applied Behavior Analysis, 45,* 425–430.

Lovaas, O. I. (1987). Behavioral treatment and normal educational and intellectual functioning in young autistic children. *Journal of Consulting and Clinical Psychology, 55,* 3–9.

Lovaas, O. I. (1994, October). Comments made during Ohio State University teleconference on applied behavior analysis. The Ohio State University, Columbus.

Lovett S., & Rehfeldt, R. A. (2014). An evaluation of multiple exemplar instruction to teach perspective-taking skills to adolescents with Asperger syndrome. *Behavioral Development Bulletin, 19,* 22–36.

Lowenthal, B. (2001). *Abuse and neglect: The educator's guide to the identification and prevention of child maltreatment.* Brookes.

Lubin, J., & Polloway, E. A. (2016). Mnemonic instruction in science and social studies for students with learning problems: A review. *Learning Disabilities: A Contemporary Journal, 14*(2), 207–224.

Lubinski, D. (2016). From Terman to today: A century of findings on intellectual precocity. *Review of Educational Research, 86*(4), 900–944.

Lucas, J. W., & Benson, V. (2019). *Tables of Summary Health Statistics for the U.S. Population: 2018 National Health Interview Survey. National Center for Health Statistics.* https://www.cdc.gov/nchs/nhis/SHS/tables.htm

Luckasson, R., & Schalock, R. L. (2015). Standards to guide the use of clinical judgment in the field of intellectual disability. *Intellectual and Developmental Disabilities, 53*(3), 240–251.

Lueck, A. H. (Ed.). (2004). *Functional vision: A practitioner's guide to evaluation and intervention.* New York: AFB Press.

Lulinski, A., Tanis, E. S., & Nelis, T. (2018). *Use of state institutions for people with intellectual and developmental disabilities in the United States. Data Brief (1).* Boulder: States of the States in Intellectual and Developmental Disabilities Project, Coleman Institute for Cognitive Disabilities, University of Colorado.

Lunsford, L. G. (2011). Psychology of mentoring: The case of talented college students. *Journal of Advanced Academics, 22*(3), 474–498.

Lupkowski-Shoplik, A., Behrens, W. A., & Assouline, S. G. (2018). *Developing academic acceleration policies: Whole grade, early entrance & single subject.* National Association for Gifted Children. https://www.nagc.org/sites/default/files/key%20reports/Developing%20Academic%20%20%20Acceleration_10-23-18.pdf

Luria, S. R., O'Brien, R. L., & Kauffman, J. C. (2016). Creativity in gifted identification: Increasing accuracy and diversity. *Annals of the New York Academy of Sciences, 1377,* 44–52.

Lusk, K. E., & Corn, A. L. (2006a). An initial study of dual-media learning: Part 2. *Journal of Visual Impairment and Blindness, 100,* 653–665.

Lusk, K. E., & Corn, A. L. (2006b). Learning and using print and Braille: A study of dual-media learners Part 1. *Journal of Visual Impairment and Blindness, 100,* 606–619.

Lyall, K., Croen, L., Daniels, J., Fallin, M. D., Ladd-Acosta, C., Lee, B. K., Park, B. Y., Snyder, N. W., Schendel, D., Volk, H., Windham, G. C., & Newschaffer, C. (2017). The changing epidemiology of autism spectrum disorders. *Annual Review of Public Health, 38,* 81–102.

Lynch, E. W., & Hanson, M. J. (2011). *Developing cross-cultural competence: A guide for working with children and their families* (4th ed.). Brookes.

Maag, J. W. (2016). *Behavior management: From theoretical implications to practical applications* (3rd ed.). Cengage Learning.

Maag, J. W., & Reid, R. (1994). Attention-deficit hyperactivity disorder: A functional approach to assessment and treatment. *Behavioral Disorders, 20,* 5–23.

MacArthur, C. A., Philippakos, Z. A., & Ianetta, M. (2015). Self-regulated strategy instruction in college developmental writing. *Journal of Educational Psychology, 107*(3), 855–867.

Mackiewicz, S. M., Wood, C. L., Cooke, N. L., & Mazzotti, V. L. (2011). Effects of peer tutoring with audio prompting on vocabulary acquisition for struggling readers. *Remedial and Special Education, 32,* 345–354.

Madaus, J. W. (2006). Employment outcomes of university graduates with learning disabilities. *Learning Disability Quarterly, 29,* 19–31.

Madaus, J. W., Pivarnick, L., Patnoad, M., Scarpati, S., Richard, N., Wright Hirsch, D., Carbone, E., & Gable, R. K. (2010). Teaching food safety skills to students with disabilities. *Teaching Exceptional Children, 42*(4), 44–51.

Maggin, D. M., Wehby, J. H., Farmer, T. W., & Brooks, D. S. (2016). Intensive interventions for students with emotional and behavioral disorders: Issues, theory, and future directions. *Journal of Emotional and Behavioral Disorders, 24*(3), 127–137.

Maggin, D. M., Wehby, J. H., & Gilmour, A. F. (2016). Intensive academic interventions for students with emotional and behavioral disorders: An experimental framework. *Journal of Emotional and Behavioral Disorders, 24*(3), 138–147.

Magro, K. (2020, February 12). *Autism is one word attempting to describe millions of different stories.* Autism Speaks. https://www.autismspeaks.org/blog/autism-one-word-attempting-describe-millions-different-stories

Maheady, L., Mallette, B., & Harper, G. F. (2006). Four classwide peer tutoring models: Similarities, differences, and implications for research and practice. *Reading and Writing Quarterly, 22,* 65–89.

Mahshie, S. N. (1995). *Educating deaf children bilingually.* Gallaudet University Press.

Maker, C. J. (1993). Creativity, intelligence, and problem solving: A definition and design for cross-cultural research and measurement related to giftedness. *Gifted Education International, 9*(2), 68–77.

Maker, C. J. (1996). Identification of gifted minority students: A national problem, needed changes, and a promising solution. *Gifted Child Quarterly, 40*, 41–50.

Maker, C. J. (2001). DISCOVER: Assessing and developing problem solving. *Gifted Education International, 15*, 232–251.

Maker, C. J. (2005). *The DISCOVER project: Improving assessment and curriculum for diverse gifted learners* (RM05206). National Research Center of the Gifted and Talented.

Maki, K. E., & Adams, S. R. (2019). Specific learning disabilities identification: Do the identification methods and data matter? *Learning Disability Quarterly*. Advance online publication. https://doi.org/10.1177/0731948719826296

Maltby, L. E., Callahan, K. L., Frielander, S., & Shetgiri, R. (2019). Infant temperament and behavioral problems: Analysis of high-risk infants in child welfare. *Journal of Public Child Welfare, 13*(5), 512–528.

Mank, D., Cioffi, A., & Yovanoff, P. (1998). Employment outcomes for people with severe disabilities: Opportunities for improvement. *Mental Retardation, 36*, 205–216.

Manning, W. H., & DiLollo, A. (2017). *Clinical decision making in fluency disorders* (4th ed.). Plural Publishing.

Marchant, M., & Anderson, D. H. (2012). Improving social and academic outcomes for all learners through the use of teacher praise. *Beyond Behavior, 21*(3), 22–28.

Marder, C. (2009). *Facts from the Special Education Elementary Longitudinal Study: Perspective on students' disabilities classifications*. U.S. Department of Education.

Markelz, A. M., & Taylor, J. C. (2016). Effects of teacher praise on attending behaviors and academic achievement of students with emotional and behavioral disabilities. *The Journal of Special Education Apprenticeship, 5*(1), 1–15.

Marland, S. (1972). *Education of the gifted and talented* (Vol. 1). Report to the U.S. Congress by the U.S. Commissioner of Education. Office of Education (DHEW). (ERIC Document Reproduction Service No. ED 056 243).

Marschark, M. (2007). *Raising and educating a deaf child: A comprehensive guide to the choices, controversies, and decisions faced by parents and educators* (paperback ed.). Oxford University Press.

Marschark, M., Machmer, E., Spencer, L. J., Borgna, G., Durkin, A., Convertino, C. (2018). Language and psychosocial functioning among deaf learners with and without cochlear implants. *Journal of Deaf Education and Deaf Studies, 23*, 28–40. https://doi.org/10.1093/deafed/enx035

Marschark, M., Schick, B., & Spencer, P. (2006). Understanding sign language development of deaf children. In B. Schick, M. Marschark, & P. Spencer (Eds.), *Advances in the sign language development of deaf children* (pp. 3–18). Oxford University Press.

Marschark, M., Tang, G., & Knoors, H. (2014). *Bilingualism and bilingual deaf education*. Oxford University Press.

Marston, J. R., Loomis, J. M., Klatzky, R. L., & Golledge, R. G. (2007). Nonvisual route following with guidance from a simple haptic or auditory display. *Journal of Visual Impairment and Blindness, 101*, 203–211.

Martin, C. A., Drasgow, E., & Halle, J. W. (2015). Training teachers to enhance the play skills of young children with developmental disabilities during outdoor time by embedding instructional interactions. *Journal of Early Intervention, 37*(4), 247–269.

Martin, J. E., Hennessey, M. N., McConnell, A. E., Terry, R. A., & Willis, D. M. (2015). *Transition assessment and goal generator*. University of Oklahoma's Zarrow Center.

Martin, J. E., Huber Marshall, L., & Sale, P. (2004). A 3-year study of middle, junior high, and high school IEP meetings. *Exceptional Children, 70*, 285–297.

Martin, J. E., Van Dycke, J. L., Christensen, W. R., Greene, B. A., Gardner, J. E., & Lovett, D. L. (2006). Increasing student participation in IEP meetings: Establishing the Self-Directed IEP as evidence-based practice. *Exceptional Children, 72*, 187–200.

Martin, J. E., Woods, L. L., & Sylvester, L. (2008). Building an employment vision: Culturally attuning vocational interests, skills, and limits. In F. R. Rusch (Ed.). *Beyond high school: Preparing adolescents for tomorrow's challenges* (2nd ed., pp. 78–109). Merrill/Pearson.

Martin-Key, N., Brown, T., & Fairchild, G. (2017). Empathic accuracy in male adolescents with conduct disorder and higher versus lower levels of callous-unemotional traits. *Journal of Abnormal Child Psychology, 45*, 1385–1397.

Mastropieri, M. A., & Scruggs, T. E. (2018). *The inclusive classroom: Strategies for effective differentiated instruction* (6th ed.). Pearson Education.

Mather, N., & Goldstein, S. (2001). *Learning disabilities and challenging behaviors*. Brookes.

Mather, N., Goldstein, S., & Eklund, K. (2015). *Learning disabilities and challenging behaviors: Using the building blocks model to guide intervention and classroom management* (3rd ed.). Brookes Publishing.

Matheson, C., Olsen, R. J., & Weisner, T. (2007). A good friend is hard to find: Friendship among adolescents with disabilities. *American Journal on Mental Retardation, 112*, 319–329.

Matuszny, R. M., Banda, D. R., & Coleman, T. J. (2007). A progressive plan for building collaborative relations with parents from diverse backgrounds. *Teaching Exceptional Children, 39*(4), 24–31.

Maurice, C., & Taylor, B. A. (2005). Early intensive behavioral intervention for autism. In W. L. Heward, T. E. Heron, N. A. Neef, S. M. Peterson, D. M. Sainato, G. Cartledge, R. Gardner III, L. D. Peterson, S. B. Hersh, & J. C. Dardig (Eds.), *Focus on behavior analysis in education: Achievements, challenges, and opportunities* (pp. 31–52). Merrill/Pearson.

Mayer, C., & Akamatsu, C. T. (1999). Bilingual-bicultural models of literacy education for deaf students: Considering the claims. *Journal of Deaf Studies and Deaf Education, 4*, 1–8.

Mayer-Davis, E. J., Lawrence, J. M., Dabelea, D., Divers, J., Isom, S., Dolan, L., Imperatore, G., Linder, B. L., Marcovina, S., Pettitt, D. J., Pihoker, C., Saydah, S., & Wagenknecht, L. (2017). Incidence trends of type 1 and type 2 diabetes among youths, 2002–2012. *New England Journal of Medicine, 376*, 1419–1429.

Mayer-Johnson. (2008). *The Picture Communication Symbols*. Mayer-Johnson LLC.

Mayes, R. D., & Moore, J. L. (2016). Adversity and pitfalls of twice-exceptional urban learners. *Journal of Advanced Academics, 27*(3), 167–189.

Mayhew, M. J., Rockenbach, A. N., Bowman, N. A., Seifert, T. A., Wolniak, G. C., Pascarella, E. T., & Terenzini, P. T. (2016). *How college affects students: 21st century evidence that higher education works* (Vol. 3). Jossey-Bass.

Mazumdar, S., Winter, A., Liu, K. Y., & Bearman, P. (2013). Spatial clusters of autism births and diagnoses point to contextual drivers of increased prevalence. *Social Science Medicine, 95*, 87–96.

Mazzocco, M. M. M., Chan, J., & Prager, E. O. (2018). Working memory and specific learning disability. In T. P. Alloway (Ed.), *Working Memory and Clinical Developmental Disorders*. New York: Routledge.

Mazzotti, V. L., Kelley, K. R., & Coco, C. M. (2015). Effects of self-directed summary of performance on postsecondary education students' participation in person-centered planning meetings. *The Journal of Special Education, 48*, 243–255.

Mazzotti, V. L., Rowe, D. A., Cameto, R., Test, D. W., & Morningstar, M. E. (2013). Identifying and promoting transition evidence-based practices and predictors of success: A position paper of the Division on Career Development and Transition.

Career Development and Transition for Exceptional Individuals, 36, 140–151.

Mazzotti, V. L., Rowe, D. A., Kelley, K., Test, D. W., Fowler, C. H., Kohler, P., & Kortering, L. J. (2009). Linking transition assessment and postsecondary goals: Key elements in the secondary transition planning process. *Teaching Exceptional Children, 42*(2), 44–51.

Mazzotti, V. L., Rowe, D. A., Sinclair, J., Poppen, M., Woods, W. E., & Shearer, M. L. (2016). Predictors of post-school success: A systematic review of NLTS2 secondary analyses. *Career Development and Transition for Exceptional Individuals, 39*, 196–215.

Mazzotti, V. L., Rowe, D. A., Wall, J. C., & Bradley, K. E. (2018). Increasing self-advocacy for secondary students with disabilities: Evaluating effects of ME! *Inclusion, 6*(3), 194–207.

McAdam, D. B., O'Cleirigh, C. M., & Cuvo, A. J. (1993). Self-monitoring and verbal feedback to reduce stereotypic body rocking in a congenitally blind adult. *RE:view, 24*, 163–172.

McAfee, O., Leong, D. J., & Bodrova, E. (2016). *Assessing and guiding young children's development and learning* (6th ed.). Pearson.

McCallum, R. S., Krohn, K. R., Skinnder, C. H., Hilton-Prillhart, A., Hopkins, M., Waller, S., & Polite, F. (2011). Improving reading comprehension of at-risk high-school students: The art of reading program. *Psychology in the Schools, 48*, 78–86.

McClannahan, L. E., & Krantz, P. J. (2010). *Activity schedules for children with autism: Teaching independent behavior* (2nd ed.). Woodbine House.

McConnell, B. M., & Kubina, R. (2016). Parents using explicit reading instruction with their children at-risk for reading difficulties. *Education and Treatment of Children, 39*, 115–139.

McConnell, B. M., & Kubina, R. M. (2014). Connecting with families to improve students' school attendance: A review of the literature. *Preventing School Failure, 58*, 249–256.

McCoy, D. C., Jones, S., Roy, A., & Raver, C. C. (2018). Classifying social-emotional trajectories through elementary school: Impacts of the Chicago School Readiness Project. *Developmental Psychology, 54*, 772–787.

McDonald, K. L., & Gibson, C. E. (2018). Peer rejection and disruptive behavioral disorders. In J. E. Lochman & W. Matthys (Eds.). *The Wiley handbook of disruptive and impulse-control disorders* (pp. 323–338). Wiley.

McDonnell, J., Snell, M. E., Brown, F., Coleman, O., & Eichelberger, C. (2020). Individualized instructional strategies. In F. Brown, J. McDonnell, & M. E. Snell (Eds.), *Instruction of students with severe disabilities* (9th ed., pp. 156–206). Pearson.

McEachin, J. J., Smith, T., & Lovaas, I. O. (1993). Long-term outcome for children with autism who received early intensive behavioral treatment. *American Journal on Mental Retardation, 97*, 359–372.

McGonigel, M. J., Woodruff, G., & Roszmann-Millican, M. (1994). The transdisciplinary team: A model for family-centered early intervention. In L. J. Johnson, R. J. Gallagher, M. J. LaMontagne, J. B. Jordan, J. J. Gallagher, P. L. Hutinger, & M. B. Karnes (Eds.). *Meeting early intervention challenges: Issues from birth to three* (pp. 95–131). Brookes.

McGowan, D., Little, C. W., Coventry, W. L., Corley, R., Olson, R. K., Samuelsson, S., & Byrne, B. (2019). Differential influences of genes and environment across the distribution of reading ability. *Behavior Genetics, 49*, 425–431.

McGraw-Hill. (2004). *Corrective mathematics*. Author.

McGraw-Hill. (2013). *Connecting math concepts*. Author.

McKenna, J. W., & Flower, A. (2014). Get them back on track: Use of the Good Behavior Game to improve student behavior. *Beyond Behavior, 23*(2) 20–26.

McKenna, J., Shin, M., Solis, M., Mize, M., & Pfannenstiel, K. (2019). Effects of single-case reading interventions for students with and at-risk of emotional and behavioral disorders in grades K–12: A quantitative synthesis. *Psychology in the Schools, 56*(4), 608–629.

McKenna, J., Solis, M., Brigham, F., & Adamson, R. (2019). The responsible inclusion of students receiving special education services for emotional disturbance: Unraveling the practice to research gap. *Behavior Modification, 43*(4), 587–611.

McLamed, J. C., & Reiman, J. W. (2017). *Collaboration and conflict resolution in education*. The Center for Appropriate Dispute Resolution in Special Education. https://www.cadreworks.org/resources/collaboration-and-conflict-resolution-education

McLaughlin, J. A., & Lewis, R. B. (2008). *Assessing students with special needs* (7th ed.). Merrill/Pearson.

McLaughlin, M. J., Dyson, A., Nagle, K., Thurlow, M., Rouse, M., Hardman, M., Norwich, B., Burke, P. J., & Perlin, M. (2006). Cross-cultural perspectives on the classification of children with disabilities: Part II. Implementing classification systems in schools. *Journal of Special Education, 40*, 46–58.

McLeskey, J., & Waldron, N. L. (2011). Educational programs for elementary students with learning disabilities: Can they be both effective and inclusive? *Learning Disabilities Research & Practice, 26*(1), 46–57.

McLeskey, J., Rosenberg, M., & Westling, D. (2018). *Inclusion: Effective practices for all students* (3rd ed.). Pearson.

McLone, D. G., & Ito, J. (1998). *An introduction to spina bifida*. Children's Memorial Hospital (Chicago), Spina Bifida Team.

McMahon, E. (2014). The role of specialized schools for students with visual impairments in the continuum of placement options: The right help, at the right time, in the right place. *Journal of Visual Impairment & Blindness, 108*(6), 449–459.

McMahon, J., & Cullinan, V. (2016). Exploring eclecticism: The impact of educational theory on the development and implementation of comprehensive education programmes (CEP's) for young children with Autism Spectrum Disorder (ASD). *Research in Autism Spectrum Disorders, 32*, 1–12.

McMaster, K. L., Fuchs, D., & Fuchs, L. S. (2006). Peer-assisted learning strategies: The promise and limitations of peer-mediated instruction. *Reading and Writing Quarterly, 22*, 5–25.

McNamara, J. K., & Willoughby, T. (2010). A longitudinal study of risk taking behaviours in adolescents with learning disabilities. *Learning Disabilities Research and Practice, 25*(1), 11–24.

McNicholas, P. J., Floyd, R. G., Woods, I. L., Jr., Singh, L. J., Manguno, M. S., & Maki, K. E. (2018). State special education criteria for identifying intellectual disability: A review following revised diagnostic criteria and Rosa's Law. *School Psychology Quarterly, 33*(1), 75–82.

Meadan, H., & Halle, J. W. (2004). Social perceptions of students with learning disabilities who differ in social status. *Learning Disabilities Research and Practice, 19*, 71–82.

Meadan, H., Sheldon, D. L., Appel, K., & DeGrazia, R. L. (2010). Developing a long-term vision: A road map for students' success. *Teaching Exceptional Children, 43*(2), 8–14.

Meadows, N. B., Neel, R. S., Scott, C. M., & Parker, G. (1994). Academic performance, social competence, and mainstream accommodations: A look at mainstreamed and nonmainstreamed students with serious behavioral disorders. *Behavioral Disorders, 19*, 170–180.

Mechling, L. C. (2007). Assistive technology as a self-management tool for prompting students with intellectual disabilities to initiate and complete daily tasks: A literature review. *Education and Training in Developmental Disabilities, 42*, 253–269.

Mechling, L. C., Pridgen, L. S., & Cronin, B. A. (2005). Computer-based video instruction to teach students with intellectual disabilities to verbally respond to questions and make purchases in fast food restaurants. *Education and Training in Developmental Disabilities*, 40, 47–59.

Meindl, J. N., & Cannella-Malone, H. I. (2011). Initiating and responding to joint attention bids in children with autism: A review of the literature. *Research in Developmental Disabilities, 32*(5), 1441–1454.

Mellard, D., McKnight, M., & Jordan, J. (2011). RTI tier structures and instructional intensity. *Learning Disabilities Research & Practice, 25*, 217–225.

Menard, C. (1999, September 2). *Pica and the brain.* Message posted to St. John's University Autism and Developmental Disabilities List, archived at http://maelstrom.stjohns.edu/archives/autism.html

Menzies, H. M., Lane, K. L., Oakes, W. P., & Ennis, R. P. (2017). Increasing students' opportunities to respond: A strategy for supporting engagement. *Intervention in School and Clinic, 52*(4), 204–209.

Mercer, C. D., Mercer, A. R., & Pullen, P. C. (2011). *Teaching students with learning problems* (8th ed.). Pearson Education.

Merrells, J., Buchanan, A., & Waters, R. (2018). The experience of social inclusion for people with intellectual disability within community recreational programs. A systematic review. *Journal of Intellectual and Developmental Disability, 43*, 381–391.

Merrick, M. T., Ports, K. A., Ford, D. C., Afifi, T. O., Gershoff, E. T., & Grogan-Kaylord, A. (2017). Unpacking the impact of adverse childhood experiences on adult mental health. *Child Abuse and Neglect, 69*, 10–19.

Merrill, E. C. (2005). Preattentive orienting in adolescents with mental retardation. *American Journal on Mental Retardation, 110*, 28–35.

Metz, B., Mulick, J. A., & Butter, E. M. (2015). Autism: A 21st century fad magnet. In R. M. Foxx, & J. A. Mulick (Eds.), *Controversial therapies for autism and intellectual disabilities: Fads, fashion, and science in professional practice* (2nd ed., pp. 169–194). Taylor & Francis.

Michaels, C. A., & Ferrara, D. L. (2005). Promoting post-school success for all: The role of collaboration in person-centered transition planning. *Journal of Educational and Psychological Consultation, 16*, 287–313.

Migliore, A., Grossi, T. A., Mank, D., & Rogan, P. (2008). Why do adults with intellectual disabilities work in sheltered workshops? *Journal of Vocational Rehabilitation, 28*(1), 29–40.

Miguel, C. F., & Kobari-Wright, V. V. (2013). The effects of tact training on the emergence of categorization and listener behavior in children with autism. *Journal of Applied Behavior Analysis, 46*, 669–773.

Miles, B. (2003). *Talking the language of the hands to the hands: The importance of hands for the person who is deafblind.* The National Center on Deaf-Blindness. https://nationaldb.org/library/page/1930

Miller, B., & Taber-Doughty, T. (2014). Self-monitoring checklists for inquiry problem-solving methods for students with intellectual disability. *Education and Training in Autism and Developmental Disabilities, 49*, 555–567.

Miller, C. J., Sanchez, J., & Hynd, G. W. (2003). Neurological correlates of reading disabilities. In H. L. Swanson, K. R. Harris, & S. Graham (Eds.), *Handbook of learning disabilities* (pp. 242–255). Guilford.

Miller, M., Cooke, N. L., Test, D. W., & White, R. (2003). Effects of friendship circles on the social interactions of elementary age student with mild disabilities. *Journal of Behavioral Education, 12*, 167–184.

Miller, M. M., & Menacker, S. J. (2013). Vision and visual impairment. In M. L. Batshaw, N. J. Roizen, & G. Lotrecchiano (Eds.), *Children with disabilities* (7th ed., pp. 169–188). Brookes.

Miller, S. P., & Kaffar, B. J. (2011). Developing addition and regrouping competence among second grade students. *Investigations in Math Learning, 4*, 35–51.

Miltenberger, R. G., Valbuena, D., & Sanchez, S. (2019). Functional assessment of challenging behavior. *Current Developmental Disorders Reports, 6*, 202–208.

Milton, J. H., Flores, M. M., Moore, A. J., Taylor, J. L., & Burton, M. E. (2019). Using the concrete-representational-abstract sequence to teach conceptual understanding of basic multiplication and division. *Learning Disability Quarterly, 42*(1), 32–45.

Minor, L. B., Schessel, D. A., & Carey, J. P. (2004). Meniere's disease. *Current Opinion in Neurology, 17*(1), 9–16.

Mires, C. B., & Lee, D. L. (2017). Calvin won't sit down! The daily behavior report card: A practical technique to change student behavior and increase school–home communication. *Beyond Behavior, 26*, 89–95.

Missall, K., & McConnell, S. R. (2010). Early literacy and language IGDIs for preschool-aged children. In J. Carta, C. Greenwood, D. Walker, & J. Buzhardt (Eds.), *Individual Growth and Developmental Indicators: Tools for monitoring progress and measuring growth in young children* (pp. 181–201). Paul H. Brookes.

Missett, T. C. (2014). *The social and emotional characteristics of gifted students.* National Association for Gifted Children.

Mitchell, B., Kern, L., & Conroy, M. (2019). Supporting students with emotional or behavioral disorders: State of the field. *Behavioral Disorders, 44*, 70–84.

Mittan, R. J. (2009). How to tell friends and dates about epilepsy. *Exceptional Parent, 39*(6/7), 94–96.

Modabbernia, A., Velthorst, E., & Reichenberg, A. (2017). Environmental risk factors for autism: An evidence-based review of systematic reviews and meta-analyses. *Molecular Autism, 8*(13). https://doi.org/10.1186/s13229-017-0121-4

Moeyaert, M., Klingbeil, D. A., Rodabaugh, E., & Turan, M. (2019, July 13). Three-level meta-analysis of single-case data regarding the effects of peer tutoring on academic and social-behavioral outcomes for at-risk students and students with disabilities. *Remedial and Special Education.* https://doi.org/10.1177/0741932519855079

Mofield, E. L., & Parker Peters, M. (2015). The relationship between perfectionism and overexcitabilities in gifted adolescents. *Journal for the Education of the Gifted, 38*(4) 405–427.

Moll, L. C., Amandi, C., Neff, D., & Gonzalez, N. (1992). Funds of knowledge for teaching: Using a qualitative approach to connect homes and classrooms. *Theory Into Practice, 31*(2), 132–141.

Monikowski, C., & Winston, E. A. (2011). Interpreters and interpreter education. In M. Marschark & P. E. Spencer (Eds.), *Oxford Handbook of Deaf Studies, Language, andEeducation* (paperback ed., pp. 367–378). Oxford University Press.

Montague, M., Enders, C., Cavendish, W., & Castro, M. (2011). Academic and behavioral trajectories for at-risk adolescents in urban schools. *Behavioral Disorders, 36*, 141–156.

Montgomery, J. M., Stoesz, B. M., & McCrimmon, A. W. (2012). Emotional intelligence, theory of mind, and executive functions as predictors of social outcomes in young adults with Asperger syndrome. *Focus on Autism and Other Developmental Disabilities, 28*(1), 4–13.

Moon, S., Simonsen, M. L., & Neubert, D. A. (2011). Perceptions of supported employment providers: What students with developmental disabilities, families, and educators need to know for transition planning. *Education and Training in Autism and Developmental Disabilities, 46*, 94–105.

Moore, J. E. (2006). 100 years of trends and issues in employment, rehabilitation, and legislation. *Journal of Visual Impairment and Blindness, 100*, 453–458.

Moores, D. F. (1993). Total inclusion/zero rejection models in general education: Implications for deaf children. *American Annals of the Deaf, 138*, 251.

Morgan, C., & Wine, B. (2018). Evaluation of behavioral skills training for teaching work skills to a student with autism spectrum disorder. *Education and Treatment of Children, 41*, 223–232.

Morgan, R. L., & Riesen, T. (2016). *Promoting successful transition to adulthood for students with disabilities.* Guilford.

Morgan, R. L., Kupferman, S., Jex, E., Preece, H., & Williams, S. (2017). Promoting student transition planning by using a self-directed summary of performance. *Teaching Exceptional Children, 50*(2), 66–73.

Morocco, C. C., Brigham, N., & Aguilar, C. M. (2006). *Visionary middle schools: Signature practices and the power of local innovation*. Teachers College.

Morris, B. K. (2020). *Social stories*. http://www.pbisworld.com/tier-3/social-stories/how-to-make-a-social-story-fact-sheet/

Morris, D., Trathen, W., Perney, J., Gill, T., Schlagal, R., Ward, D., & Frye, E. M. (2017). Three DIBELS tasks vs. three informal reading/spelling Tasks: A comparison of predictive validity. *Reading Psychology, 38*(3), 289–320.

Morris, T. L., & March, J. (Eds.). (2004). *Anxiety disorders in children and adolescents* (2nd ed.). Guilford.

Morrison, G. S. (2018). *Early childhood education today* (14th ed.). Pearson.

Morse, T. E., & Schuster, J. W. (2000). Teaching elementary students with moderate intellectual disabilities how to shop for groceries. *Exceptional Children, 66*, 273–288.

Morse, W. C. (1985). *The education and treatment of socioemotionally impaired children and youth*. Syracuse University Press.

Mostert, M. P. (2010). Facilitated communication and its legitimacy: 21st century developments. *Exceptionality, 18*, 31–41.

Moyson, T., & Roeyers, H. (2011). The quality of life of siblings of children with autism spectrum disorder. *Exceptional Children, 78*, 41–55.

Mueller, T. G., & Vick, A. M. (2018). Rebuilding the family–professional partnership through facilitated individualized education program meetings: A conflict prevention and resolution practice. *Journal of Educational and Psychological Consultation, 29*(2), 99–127. Published on-line. https://doi.org/10.1080/10474412.2018.1470934

Mujezinovic, F., & Alfirevic A. (2007). Procedure-related complications of amniocentesis and chorionic villous sampling: A systematic review. *Obstetrics & Gynecology, 110*, 687–694.

Multimodal Treatment Study Group. (1999). A 14-month randomized clinical trial of treatment strategies for attention-deficit/hyperactivity disorder. *Archives of General Psychiatry, 56*, 1088–1096.

Mulvey, E. P. (2011, March). Highlights from Pathways to Desistance: A longitudinal study of serious adolescent offenders. *OJJDP Juvenile Justice Fact Sheet*. Office of Juvenile Justice and Delinquency Prevention. https://ncjrs.gov/pdffiles1/ojjdp/230971.pdf.

Munir, K. M. (2016). The co-occurrence of mental disorders in children and adolescents with intellectual disability/intellectual developmental disorder. *Current Opinion in Psychiatry, 29*(2), 95–102.

Munson, L. J., & Hunt, N. (2005). Teachers grieve! What can we do for our colleagues and ourselves when a student dies? *Teaching Exceptional Children, 37*(4), 48–51.

Murdock, L. C., Dantzler, J. A., Walker, A. N., & Wood, L. B. (2014). The effect of a platform swing on the independent work behaviors of children with autism spectrum disorders. *Focus on Autism and Other Developmental Disabilities, 29*, 50–61.

Murphy, C. M. (2003). *Using functional assessment to determine the maintaining contingencies of non-contextual speech by children with autism* [Unpublished master's thesis]. The Ohio State University, Columbus.

Murphy, J., & Zlomke, K. (2014). Positive peer reporting in the classroom: A review of intervention procedures. *Behavior Analysis in Practice, 7*, 126–137.

Muscular Dystrophy Coordinating Committee. (2020). *Muscular dystrophy information page*. https://mdcc.nih.gov/

Musetti, A., Eboli, G., Cavallini, F., & Corsano, P. (2019). Social relationships, self-esteem, and loneliness in adolescents with learning disabilities. *Clinical Neuropsychiatry, 16*(4), 133–140.

Musti-Rao, S., & Haydon, T. (2011). Strategies to increase behavior-specific teacher praise in an inclusive environment. *Intervention in School and Clinic, 47*, 91–97.

Musu-Gillette, L., Robinson, J., McFarland, J., KewalRamani, A., Zhang, A., & Wilkinson-Flicker, S. (2016). *Status and trends in the education of racial and ethnic groups* 2016 (NCES 2016–007). U.S. Department of Education, National Center for Education Statistics. https://nces.ed.gov/pubs2016/2016007.pdf

Naglieri, J. A. (2007). *Naglieri Nonverbal Ability Test* (2nd ed.). Pearson.

Naglieri, J. A., & Ford, D. Y. (2005). Increasing minority children's participation in gifted classes using the NNAT: A response to Lohman. *Gifted Child Quarterly, 49*, 29–31.

Nagro, S. A., Fraser, D. W., & Hooks, S. D. (2019). Lesson planning with engagement in mind: Proactive classroom management strategies for curriculum instruction. *Intervention in School and Clinic, 54*(3), 131–140.

National Academies of Sciences, Engineering, and Medicine; Division of Behavioral and Social Sciences and Education; Committee on National Statistics; Board on Children, Youth, and Families; Committee on Building an Agenda to Reduce the Number of Children in Poverty by Half in 10 Years. (2019). Consequences of child poverty. In S. Le Menestral & G. Duncan (Eds.), *A roadmap to reducing child poverty*. National Academies Press (US).

National Association for the Education of Young Children. (2009). *Developmentally appropriate practice in early childhood programs serving children from birth through age 8*. https://www.naeyc.org/positionstatements/dap

National Association for Gifted Children. (2009, March). *Position statement: Grouping*. Author. https://www.nagc.org/sites/default/files/Position%20Statement/Grouping%20Position%20Statement.pdf

National Association for Gifted Children. (2010, March). *Position statement: Redefining giftedness for a new century: Shifting the paradigm*. Author. https://www.nagc.org/sites/default/files/Position%20Statement/Redefining%20Giftedness%20for%20a%20New%20Century.pdf

National Association for Gifted Children. (2020a). *What is giftedness?* Author. https://www.nagc.org/resources-publications/resources/what-giftedness

National Association for Gifted Children. (2020b). *State definitions of giftedness*. Author. https://www.nagc.org/state-definitions-giftedness

National Association of the Deaf. (2002). *Position statement on inclusion*. [Approved by the NAD Board of Directors on January 26, 2002.] Author. http://www.nad .org/issues/education/k-12/inclusion

National Association of the Deaf. (2018). *Early intervention for infants and toddlers*. https://www.nad.org/resources/early-intervention-for-infants-and-toddlers/

National Association of State Directors of Developmental Disabilities Services. (2019). *Adult family survey: 2018–19 final report*. Author. https://www.nationalcoreindicators.org/upload/core-indicators/AFS_2018-19_FINALupdate_1_17.pdf

National Autism Center. (2020). *Evidence-based practice and autism in the schools*. Author. http://www.nationalautismcenter.org/090605-2/

National Center for Education Statistics. (2012). *The Nation's Report Card: Writing 2011* (NCES 2012–470). Institute of Education Sciences, U.S. Department of Education.

National Center for Education Statistics. (2018). *Characteristics of public school teachers in the United States*. U. S. Department of Education. https://nces.ed.gov/programs/coe/indicator_clr.asp

National Center for Education Statistics. (2019a). *Concentration of public school students eligible for free or reduced-price lunch*. U. S. Department of Education. https://nces.ed.gov/programs/coe/indicator_clb.asp

National Center for Education Statistics. (2019b). *Characteristics of public school teachers in the United States*. U. S. Department of Education. https://nces.ed.gov/programs/coe/indicator_clr.asp

National Center for Health Statistics. (2017). *National Health Interview Survey (NHIS)*. www.cdc.gov/nchs/nhis.htm

National Conference of State Legislatures. (2018). *Autism and insurance coverage: State laws*. Author. http://www.ncsl.org/research/health/autism-and-insurance-coverage-state-laws.aspx#2

National Council on Disability. (2018a). *Every Student Succeeds Act and students with disabilities*. National Council on Disability. https://ncd.gov/sites/default/files/NCD_ESSA-SWD_Accessible.pdf

National Council on Disability. (2018b). *Broken promises: The underfunding of IDEA*. National Council on Disability. https://ncd.gov/sites/default/files/NCD_BrokenPromises_508.pdf

National Council on Disability. (2018c). *The segregation of students with disabilities*. Washington, DC: Author. https://ncd.gov/sites/default/files/NCD_Segregation-SWD_508.pdf

National Council on Disability. (2018d). *National disability employment policy, from the New Deal to the real deal: Joining the industries of the future*. Author.

National Down Syndrome Society. (2020). *What is Down syndrome?* Author. https://www.ndss.org/about-down-syndrome/down-syndrome/

National Education Association. (2006). *The twice-exceptional dilemma*. Author.

National Human Genome Research Institute. (2019). *About autism*. National Institutes of Health. https://www.genome.gov/25522099

National Institute for Direct Instruction. (2017). *Comprehensive bibliography on Direct Instruction*. Eugene, OR: Author. [available at: https://www.nifdi.org]

National Institute of Mental Health. (2020). *Schizophrenia*. https://www.nimh.nih.gov/health/statistics/schizophrenia.shtml

National Institute of Neurological Disorders and Stroke. (2020). *Autism spectrum disorder fact sheet*. https://www.ninds.nih.gov/Disorders/Patient-Caregiver-Education/Fact-Sheets/Autism-Spectrum-Disorder-Fact-Sheet#3082_6

National Institute on Deafness and Other Communication Disorders. (2016). *Quick statistics about hearing*. https://www.nidcd.nih.gov/health/statistics/quick-statistics-hearing

National Institute on Deafness and Other Communication Disorders. (2017a). *Noise induced hearing loss*. https://www.nidcd.nih.gov/health/noise-induced-hearing-loss

National Institute on Deafness and Other Communication Disorders. (2017b). *Cochlear implants*. https://www.nidcd.nih.gov/health/cochlear-implants

National Institutes of Health. (2020). *Williams syndrome*. Author. https://ghr.nlm.nih.gov/condition/williams-syndrome

National Joint Committee on Learning Disabilities. (2016). Learning disabilities: Issues on definition. *Asha, 33*, (Suppl. 5), 18–20.

National Research Council. (2001). *Educating children with autism*. National Academy Press.

National Spinal Cord Injury Statistical Center. (2020). *Spinal cord injury facts and figures at a glance*. https://www.nscisc.uab.edu/Public/Facts%20and%20Figures%202020.pdf

Neef, N. A., Bicard, D. F., & Endo, S. (2001). Assessment of impulsivity and the development of self-control in students with attention-deficit hyperactivity disorder. *Journal of Applied Behavior Analysis, 34*, 397–407.

Nehring, W. M. (2010). Cerebral palsy. In P. Jackson Allen & J. A. Vessey (Eds.), *Primary care of the child with a chronic condition* (5th ed., pp. 326–346). Elsevier.

Nelson, J. R., Stage, S., Duppong-Hurley, K., Synhorst, L., & Epstein, M. H. (2007). Risk factors predictive of the problem behavior of children at risk for emotional and behavioral disorders. *Exceptional Children, 73*, 367–379.

Nelson, L. G. L., Summers, J. A., & Turnbull, A. P. (2004). Boundaries in family-professional relationships: Implications for special education. *Remedial and Special Education, 25*, 153–165.

Neu, T. (2003). When the gifts are camouflaged by disability: Identifying and developing the talent in gifted students with disabilities. In J. A. Castellano (Ed.), *Special populations in gifted education: Working with diverse gifted learners* (pp. 151–162). Allyn & Bacon.

Newborg, J. (2005). *Battelle Developmental Inventory* (2nd ed.). Riverside Publishing.

Newkirk-Turner, B. L., & Johnson, V. E. (2018). Curriculum-based language assessment with culturally and linguistically diverse students in the context of mathematics. *Language, Speech, and Hearing Services in Schools, 49*, 189–196.

Newman, L. (2004). *Family involvement in the educational development of youth with disabilities. A Special Topic Report from the National Longitudinal Transition Study-2 (NLTS-2)*. SRI International.

Newman, L., Wagner, M., Cameto, R., & Knokey, A. M. (2009). *The post-high school outcomes of youth with disabilities up to 4 years after high school. A report of findings from the National Longitudinal Transition Study-2 (NLTS2)* (NCSER 2009–3017). SRI International. http://www.nlts2.org/reports/2009_04/nlts2_report_2009_04_complete.pdf

Newman, L., Wagner, M., Cameto, R., Knokey, A. M., & Shaver, D. (2010). *Comparisons across time of the outcomes of youth with disabilities up to 4 years after high school. A report of findings from the National Longitudinal Transition Study-2 (NLTS2)*. SRI International. http://www.nlts2.org/reports/2010_09/nlts2_report_2010_09_complete.pdf

Newman, L., Wagner, M., Knokey, A.-M., Marder, C., Nagle, K., Shaver, D., Wei, X., with Cameto, R., Contreras, E., Ferguson, K., Greene, S., and Schwarting, M. (2011). *The post-high school outcomes of young adults with disabilities up to 8 years after high school. A report from the National Longitudinal Transition Study-2 (NLTS2)* (NCSER 2011–3005). SRI International. https://ies.ed.gov/ncser/pubs/20113005/pdf/20113005.pdf

Newman, L. A., Madaus, J. W., & Javitz, H. S. (2016). Effect of transition planning on postsecondary support receipt by students with disabilities. *Exceptional Children, 82*, 497–514.

Next Chapter Book Club. (2019). https://www.nextchapterbookclub.org/about-us#program

Niemiec, R. M., Shogren, K. A., & Wehmeyer, M. L. (2017). Character strengths and intellectual and developmental disability: A strengths-based approach from positive psychology. *Education and Training in Autism and Developmental Disabilities, 52*(1), 13–25.

Nijs, S., & Maes, B. (2014). Social peer interactions in persons with profound intellectual and multiple disabilities. *Education and Training in Autism and Developmental Disabilities, 49*(1), 153–165.

Nirje, B. (1969). The normalization principle and its human management implications. In R. Kugel & W. Wolfensberger (Eds.), *Changing patterns in residential services for the mentally retarded* (pp. 181–195). President's Committee on Mental Retardation.

Noens, I. L. J., & van Berckelaer-Onnes, I. A. (2005). Captured by details: Sense-making, language and communication in autism. *Journal of Communication Disorders, 38*, 123–141.

Nolan, J. D., & Filter, K. J. (2012). A function-based classroom behavior intervention using non-contingent reinforcement plus response cost. *Education & Treatment of Children, 35*, 419–430.

Nordness, P. D., Hagaman, J. L., Herskovitz, R., & Leader-Janssen, E. (2019). POWER UP: A persuasive writing strategy for secondary students with emotional and behavioral disorders. *Journal of Education and Learning, 8*(4), 32–42.

Northern, J. L., & Downs, M. P. (2014). *Hearing in Children* (6th ed.). Plural Publishing.

Northup, J., Galley, V., Edwards, S., & Fountain, L. (2001). The effects of methylphenidate in the classroom: What dosage, for which children, for what problems? *School Psychology Quarterly, 16*, 303–323.

O'Brien, M. (2019). Pica. In J. L. Matson (Ed.), *Handbook of intellectual disabilities* (pp. 607–625). Springer.

O'Connor, E. A., Yasik, A. E., & Horner, S. L. (2016). Teachers' knowledge of special education laws: What do they know? *Insights into Learning Disabilities, 13*(1), 7–18.

O'Connor, R. E., Bocian, K. M., Beach, K. D., Sanchez, V., & Flynn, L. J. (2013). Special education in a 4-year response to intervention (RtI) environment: Characteristics of students with learning disability and grade of identification. *Learning Disabilities Research & Practice, 28*(3), 98–112.

O'Donnell, J., & Kirkner, S. L. (2014). The impact of a collaborative family involvement program on Latino families and children's educational performance. *School Community Journal, 24*, 211–234.

O'Donovan, M., et al. (2014). Biological insights from 108 schizophrenia-associated genetic loci. *Nature, 511*, 412–413.

O'Handley, R. D., Olmi, D. J., Dufrene, B. A., Tingstrom, D. H., & Whipple H. (2020). The effects of behavior-specific praise and public posting in secondary classrooms. *Psychology in the Schools, 57*, 1097–1115.

O'Neill, M. (2006). Delinquent or disabled? Harmonizing the IDEA definition of "emotional disturbance" with the educational needs of incarcerated youth. *Hastings Law Journal, 57*(6). https://repository.uchastings.edu/hastings_law_journal/vol57/iss6/3

O'Neill, R. E., Albin, R. W., Horner, R. H., Storey, K., & Sprague, J. R. (2015). *Functional assessment and program development for problem behavior: A practical handbook* (3rd ed.). Cengage Learning.

O'Neill, S. J., McDowell, C., & Leslie, J. C. (2018). A comparison of prompt delays with trial-and-error instruction in conditional discrimination training. *Behavior Analysis in Practice, 11*(4), 370–380.

O'Reilly, M. F., Lancioni, G. E., & Kierans, I. (2000). Teaching leisure social skills to adults with moderate mental retardation: An analysis of acquisition, generalization, and maintenance. *Education and Training in Mental Retardation and Developmental Disabilities, 35*, 250–258.

Odding, E., Roebroeck, M. E., & Stam, H. J. (2006). The epidemiology of cerebral palsy: Incidence, impairments and risk factors. *Disability Rehabilitation, 28*, 183–191.

Odom, S. L., Buysse, V., & Soukakou, E. (2011). Inclusion for young children with disabilities: A quarter century of research perspectives. *Journal of Early Intervention, 33*, 344–356.

Office of Juvenile Justice and Delinquency Prevention. (2020). *Statistical briefing book*. U.S. Department of Justice. https://www.ojjdp.gov/ojstatbb/crime/qa05101.asp?qaDate=2018

Office of Special Education and Rehabilitation Services. (2006). *IDEA regulations: Identification of specific learning disabilities*. U.S. Department of Education. https://sites.ed.gov/idea/files/Identification_of_SLD_10-4-06.pdf

Office of Technology Assessment. (1987). *Technology-dependent children: Hospital v. home care—A technical memorandum*. OTA-TM-H-38. Author.

Olivos, E. M. (2009). Collaboration with Latino families: A critical perspective of home-school interactions. *Intervention in School and Clinic, 45*, 109–115.

Olmstead, J. E. (Ed.). (2005). *Itinerant teaching: Tricks of the trade for teachers of students with visual impairments* (2nd ed.). AFB Press.

Olsen, R., & Sutton, J. (1998). More hassle, more alone: Adolescents with diabetes and the role of formal and informal support. *Child: Care, Health, and Development, 24*(1), 31–39.

Olson, R. K., Keenan, J. M., Byrne, B., & Samuelson, S. (2019). Etiology of developmental dyslexia (pp. 391–412). In L. Verhoven, C. Perfetti, & K. Pugh (Eds.), *Developmental dyslexia across languages and writing systems*. Cambridge University Press.

Olson, S. L., Davis-Kean, P., Chen, M., Lansford, J. E., Bates, J. E., Pettit, G. S., & Dodge, K. A. (2018). Mapping the growth of heterogeneous forms of externalizing problem behavior between early childhood and adolescence: A comparison of parent and teacher ratings. *Journal of Abnormal Child Psychology, 46*, 935–950.

Olszewski-Kubilius, P., & Clarenbach, J. (2014). Closing the opportunity gap: Program factors contributing to academic success in culturally different youth. *Gifted Child Today, 37*, 103–110.

Onslow, M., Packman, A., & Harrison, E. (2003). *The Lidcombe Program of early stuttering intervention: A clinician's guide*. PRO-ED.

Orelove, F. P. (1984). The educability debate: A review and a look ahead. In W. L. Heward, T. E. Heron, D. S. Hill, & J. Trap-Porter (Eds.), *Focus on behavior analysis in education* (pp. 271–281). Merrill/Pearson.

Orsmond, G. I., & Seltzer, M. M. (2000). Brothers and sisters of adults with mental retardation: Gendered nature of the sibling relationship. *American Journal of Mental Retardation, 105*, 486–508.

Osborne, L. A., & Reed, P. (2009). The relationship between parenting stress and behavior problems of children with autism spectrum disorders. *Exceptional Children, 76*, 54–73.

Osterhaus, S. A. (2011). *Teaching math to visually impaired students*. Texas School for the Blind and Visually Impaired. http://www.tsbvi.edu/math/

Oswald, D. P. (1994). Facilitator influence in facilitated communication. *Journal of Behavioral Education, 4*, 191–200.

Oswald, D. P., Haworth, S. M., MacKenzie, B. K., & Willis, J. H. (2017). Parental report of the diagnostic process and outcome: ASD compared with other developmental disabilities. *Focus on Autism and Other Developmental Disabilities, 32*(2), 152–160.

Overton, T. (2016). *Assessing learners with special needs: An applied approach* (8th ed.). Pearson.

Owens, R. E., & Farinella, K. A. (2019). *Introduction to communication disorders: A lifespan evidence-based perspective* (6th ed.). Pearson.

Owens, R. E., Jr. (2016). *Language development: An introduction* (9th ed.). Pearson.

Owiny, R. L., Spriggs, A. D., Sartini, E. C., & Mills, J. R. (2018). Evaluating response cards as evidence based. *Preventing School Failure, 62*(2), 59–72.

Ozcan, N., & Cavkaytar, A. (2009). Parents as teachers: Teaching parents how to teach toilet skills to their children with autism and mental retardation. *Education and Training in Autism and Developmental Disabilities, 44*, 237–243.

Ozonoff, S., Dawson, G., & McPartland, J. C. (2015). *A parent's guide to high-functioning autism spectrum disorder* (2nd ed.). The Guilford Press.

Packman, A., Onslow, M., Webber, M., Harrison, E., Arnott, S., Bridgman, K., Carey, B., Sheedy, S., O'Brian, S., MacMillan, V., & Lloyd, W. (2014). *The Lidcombe Program treatment guide: January 2014*. https://www.lidcombeprogram.org/wp-content/uploads/2015/04/Lidcombe-Program-Treatment-Guide-March-2014.pdf

Paclawsky, T. R., Matson, J. L., Rush, K. S., Smalls, Y., & Vollmer, T. R. (2000). Questions about behavioral function (QABF): A behavioral checklist for functional assessment of aberrant behavior. *Research in Developmental Disabilities, 21*, 223–229.

Paff, M., Alexandru-Abrams, D., Muhonen, M., & Loudon, W. (2018). Ventriculoperitoneal shunt complications: A review. *Interdisciplinary Neurosurgery, 13*, 66–70.

Page, E. B. (1972). Miracle in Milwaukee: Raising the IQ. *Educational Researcher, 15*, 8–16.

Palmer, D. S., Fuller, K., Arora, T., & Nelson, M. (2001). Taking sides: Parents' views on inclusion for their children with severe disabilities. *Exceptional Children, 67*, 467–484.

Palmer, N., Beam, A., Agniel, D., Eran, A., Manrai A., et al. (2017). Association of sex with recurrence of autism spectrum disorder among siblings. *JAMA Pediatrics, 171*(11), 1107–1112.

Papageorgiou, E. A., Karagrigoriou, A., Tsaliki, E., Velissariou, V., Carter, N. P., & Patsalis, P. C. (2011). Fetal-specific DNA methylation ratio permit noninvasive prenatal diagnosis of trisomy 21. *Nature Medicine, 17*(4), 510–513.

Paradiz, V., Kelso, S., Nelson, A., & Earl, A. (2018). Essential self-advocacy and transition. *Pediatrics, 141*, 373–380.

Parent to Parent USA. (2018). *What Is Parent to Parent?* Author. http://www.p2pusa.org/parents/

Parette, H. P., & Brotherson, M. J. (1996). Family participation in assistive technology assessment for young children with mental retardation and developmental disabilities. *Education and Training in Mental Retardation and Developmental Disabilities, 31*, 29–43.

Parette, H. P., & Petch-Hogan, B. (2000). Approaching families: Facilitating culturally/linguistically diverse family involvement. *Teaching Exceptional Children, 33*(2), 4–10.

Parette, H. P., Meadon, H., Doubet, S., & Hess, J. (2010). Supporting families of young children with disabilities using technology. *Education and Training in Autism and Developmental Disabilities, 45*(4), 552–565.

Parish, S. L., Rose, R. A., Grinstein-Weiss, M., Richman, E. L., & Andrews, M. E. (2008). Material hardship in U.S. families raising children with disabilities. *Exceptional Children, 75*, 71–92.

Park, J. H., Alber-Morgan, S. R., & Cannella-Malone, H. I. (2011). Effects of mother-implemented Picture Exchange Communication System training on spontaneous communicative behaviors of young children with autism spectrum disorders. *Topics in Early Childhood Special Education, 31*(1), 37–47.

Park, J. H., Alber-Morgan, S. R., & Fleming, C. (2011). Collaborating with parents to implement behavioral interventions for children with challenging behaviors. *Teaching Exceptional Children, 43*(3), 22–30.

Park, S., & Holloway, S. D. (2017). The effects of school-based parental involvement on academic achievement at the child and elementary school level: A longitudinal study. *The Journal of Educational Research, 110*, 1–16.

Parsons, M. P., Rollyson, J. H., & Reid, D. H. (2013). Teaching practitioners to conduct behavioral skills training: A pyramidal approach for training multiple human service staff. *Behavior Analysis in Practice, 6*(2), 4–16.

Patterson, G. R. (1982). *Coercive family process*. Castalia.

Patterson, G. R., Reid, J. B., & Dishion, T. J. (1992). *Antisocial boys: Vol 4. A social interactional approach*. Castalia.

Patterson, J., & Leonard, B. (1994). Caregiving and children. In E. Kahana, D. Biegel, & M. Wykle (Eds.), *Family caregiving across the lifespan* (pp. 133–158). Sage Publications.

Patton, J. R., Jayanthi, M., & Polloway, E. A. (2001). Home-school collaboration about homework: What do we know and what should we do? *Reading and Writing Quarterly: Overcoming Learning Difficulties, 17*, 227–242.

Paul, P. V., & Whitlow, G. M. (2011). *Hearing and deafness: An introduction for health and education professionals*. Jones and Bartlett.

Payne, K. T. (2011). Multicultural differences in human communication disorders. In N. B. Anderson & G. H. Shames (Eds.), *Human communication disorders: An introduction* (8th ed., pp. 84–109). Pearson.

Payne, L., Marks, L. J., & Bogan, B. L. (2007). Using curriculum-based assessment to address the academic and behavioral deficits of students with emotional and behavioral disorders. *Beyond Behavior, 16*, 3–6.

Pearle, J. G. (2016). Teacher-provided positive attending to improve student behavior. *Teaching Exceptional Children, 48*, 250–257.

Pearson, N. A., Patton, J. R., & Mruzek, D. W. (2016). *ABDS: Adaptive behavior diagnostic scale*. PRO-ED.

Pease, L. (2000). Creating a communication environment. In S. Aitken, M. Buultjenns, C. Clark, J. T. Eyre, & L. Pease (Eds.), *Teaching children who are deafblind: Contact communication and learning* (pp. 35–82). Fulton.

Pennsylvania Association for Retarded Children (PARC) v. Commonwealth of Pennsylvania, 343 F. Supp. 279 (1972).

Pereira, L. C., & Lavoie, J. (2018). Friends, foes, and self-defense: Students with EBD navigating social conflicts and bullying. *Emotional and Behavioral Difficulties, 23*(1), 15–27.

Perla, F., & O'Donnell, B. (2004). Encouraging problem solving in orientation and mobility. *Journal of Visual Impairments and Blindness, 98*, 47–52.

Perrin, J. M., Bloom, S. R., & Gortmaker, S. L. (2007). The increase of childhood chronic conditions in the United States. *Journal of the American Medical Association, 297*, 2755–2759.

Perske, R. (2004). Nirje's eight planks. *Mental Retardation, 42*, 147–150.

Peters, L., Bulthe, J., Daniels, N., de Beeck, H. O., & Smedt, B. D. (2018). Dyscalculia and dyslexia: Different behavioral, yet similar brain activity profiles during arithmetic. *NeuroImage: Clinical, 18*, 663–674.

Peters, S. J., & Engerrand, K. G. (2016). Equity and excellence: Proactive efforts in the identification of underrepresented students for gifted and talented services. *Gifted Child Quarterly, 60*(3), 159–171.

Peters, S. J., Gentry, M., Whiting, G. W., & McBee, M. T. (2019). Who gets served in gifted education? Demographic representation and a call for action. *Gifted Child Quarterly, 63*(4), 273–287.

Peterson, D. B., Gragg, S. L., & Spencer, T. D. (2018). Predicting reading problems 6 years into the future: Dynamic assessment reduces bias and increases classification accuracy. *Language, Speech, and Hearing Services in Schools, 49*, 875–888.

Peterson, L. C., & Thompson, R. H. (2018). How teaching perspective taking to individuals with autism spectrum disorders affects social skills: Findings from research and suggestions for practitioners. *Behavior Analysis in Practice, 11*, 467–478.

Peterson, S. M., & Neef, N. A. (2020). Functional behavior assessment. In J. O. Cooper, T. E. Heron, & W. L. Heward, *Applied behavior analysis* (3rd ed., pp. 500–524). Pearson.

Pew Research Center. (2014, February). *The rising cost of not going to college*. http://www.pewsocialtrends.org/2014/02/11/the-rising-cost-of-not-going-to-college/

Phillips, B. A., Conners, F., & Curtner-Smith, M. E. (2017). Parenting children with Down syndrome: An analysis of parenting styles, parenting dimensions, and parental stress. *Research in Developmental Disabilities, 68*, 9–19.

Phillips, C. L., Hile, J. L., & Jardes, T. L. (2013). A team approach for the transition to middle school and beyond for a young man who is deafblind and gifted. *Journal of Visual Impairment and Blindness, 107(6)*, 523–524.

Phillips, C. L., Iannaccone, J. A., Rooker, G. W., & Hagopian, L. P. (2017). Noncontingent reinforcement for the treatment of severe problem behavior: An analysis of 27 consecutive applications. *Journal of Applied Behavior Analysis, 50*, 357–376.

Pierce, J. M., Spriggs, A. D., Gast, D. L., & Luscre, D. (2013). Effects of visual activity schedules on independent classroom transitions for students with autism. *International Journal of Disability Development and Education, 60*(3).

Piirto, J. (2007). *Talented children and adults: Their development and education*. Prufrock Press.

Piirto, J. (2011). *Creativity for 21st century skills: How to embed creativity into the curriculum*. Sense Publishers.

Pindzola, R. H., Plexico, L. W., & Hayes, W. O. (2016). *Diagnosis and evaluation in speech pathology* (9th ed.). Pearson.

Pinquart, M. (2017). Systematic review: Bullying involvement of children with and without chronic physical illness and/or physical/sensory disability—a meta-analytic comparison with healthy/nondisabled peers. *Journal of Pediatric Psychology, 42*, 245–259.

Piper, B. J., Ogden, C. L., Simoyan, O. M., Chung, D. Y., Caggiano, J. F., Nichols, S. D., & McCall, K. L. (2018). Trends in use of prescription stimulants in the United States and Territories, 2006 to 2016. *PLoS One, 13*(11), Article e0206100.

Pivik, J., McComas, J., & LaFlamme, M. (2002). Barriers and facilitators to inclusive education. *Exceptional Children, 67*, 97–102.

Plucker, J. A., Beghetto, R. A., & Dow, G. T. (2004). Why isn't creativity more important to educational psychologists? Potentials, pitfalls, and future directions in creativity research. *Educational Psychologist, 39*, 83–96.

Polloway, E. A., Smith, J. D., Patton, J. R., & Smith, T. E. C. (1996). Historic changes in mental retardation and developmental disabilities. *Education and Training in Mental Retardation and Developmental Disabilities*, 31, 3–12.

Ponchillia, P. E., MacKenzie, N., Long, R. G., Denton-Smith, P., Hicks, T. L., & Miley, P. (2007). Finding a target with an accessible global positioning system. *Journal of Visual Impairment and Blindness, 101*, 479–488.

Popham, M., Counts, J., Ryan, J. B., & Katsiyannis, A. (2019). A systematic review of self-regulation strategies to improve academic outcomes of students with EBD. *Journal of Research in Special Educational Needs,18*(4), 239–253.

Popkin, J., & Skinner, C. H. (2003). Enhancing academic performance in a classroom serving students with serious emotional disturbance: Interdependent group contingences with randomly selected components. *School Psychology Review, 32*, 271–284.

Poppes, P. P., van der Putten, A. J., & Vlaskamp, C. C. (2010). Frequency and severity of challenging behavior in people with profound intellectual and multiple disabilities. *Research in Developmental Disabilities, 31*, 1269–1275.

Porterfield, K. (1998). British researchers identify genetic area affecting speech. *ASHA Leader*, 3(4), 1–4.

Potts, E. A., & Howard, L. (2011). *How to co-teach: A guide for general and special educators*. Brookes.

Potvin, D., & Ratto, A. B. (2019). Autism spectrum disorders. In M. L. Batshaw, L. Pellegrino, & N. J. Roizen (Eds.), *Children with disabilities* (8th ed.). Brookes.

Povenmire-Kirk, T. C., Bethune, L. K., Alverson, C. Y., & Kahn, L. G. (2015). A journey, not a destination: Developing cultural competence in secondary transition. *Teaching Exceptional Children, 47*(6), 319–328.

Povenmire-Kirk, T. C., Test, D. W., Flowers, C. P., Diegelmann, K. M., Bunch-Crump, K., Kemp-Inman, A., & Goodnight, C. L. (2018). CIRCLES: Building an interagency network for transition planning. *Journal of Vocational Rehabilitation, 49*, 45–57.

Poyadue, F. S. (1993). Cognitive coping at Parents Helping Parents. In A. P. Turnbull, J. M. Paterson, S. K. Behr, D. L. Murphy, J. G. Marquis, & M. J. Blue-Banning (Eds.), *Cognitive coping, families, and disability* (pp. 95–110). Brookes.

Prabhala, A. (2007, February 10). Mental retardation is no more—new name is intellectual and developmental disabilities. *AAIDD News*.

Prelock, P. A. (2000a). Epilogue: An intervention focus for inclusionary practice. *Language, Speech, and Hearing Services in Schools, 31*, 296–298.

Prelock, P. A. (2000b). Prologue: Multiple perspectives for determining the roles of speech-language pathologists in inclusionary classrooms. *Language, Speech, and Hearing Services in Schools, 31*, 213–218.

Price, R., Marsh, A. J., & Fisher, M. H. (2018). Teaching young adults with intellectual and developmental disabilities community-based navigation skills to take public transportation. *Behavior Analysis in Practice, 11*(1), 46–50.

Pritchard, D., Penney, H., & Mace, R. C. (2018). The ACHIEVE! program: A point and level system for reducing severe problem behavior. *Behavioral Interventions, 33*, 41–55.

Pryce, L., Tweed, A., Hiltons, A., & Priest, H. M. (2017). Tolerating uncertainty: Perceptions of the future for ageing parent carers and their adult children with intellectual disabilities. *Journal of Applied Research in Intellectual Disabilities, 30*, 84–96.

Public Schools of North Carolina. (2019). *School-based enterprise*. Author. https://ec.ncpublicschools.gov/disability-resources/intellectual-disabilities/ocs/school-based-enterprise.pdf

Pullen, P. C., Lane, H. B., Ashworth, K. E., & Lovelace, S. P. (2017). Specific learning disabilities (pp. 286–299). In J. M. Kauffman, D. P. Hallahan, and P. C. Pullen (Eds.), *Handbook of special education* (2nd ed.). Routledge.

Puranik, C. S., & Lonagan, C. J. (2017). Early writing deficits in preschoolers with oral language difficulties. *Journal of Learning Disabilities, 45*, 179–190.

Pyle, N., Flower, A., Fall, A. M., & Williams, J. (2016). Individual-level risk factors of incarcerated youth. *Remedial and Special Education, 37*, 172–186.

Qi, S., & Mitchell, R. (2012). Large-scale academic achievement testing of deaf and hard-of-hearing students: Past, present, and future. *Journal of Deaf Studies and Deaf Education, 17*, 1–18.

Quintero, N., & McIntyre, L. L. (2010). Sibling adjustment and maternal well-being: An examination of families with and without a child with autism spectrum disorders. *Focus on Autism and Other Developmental Disabilities, 25*, 37–46.

Rafferty, L. A. (2010). Step-by-step: Teaching students to self-monitor. *Teaching Exceptional Children, 43*(2), 50–58.

Rajeh, A., Amanullah, S., Shivakumar, K., & Cole, J. (2017). Interventions in ADHD: A comparative review of stimulant medications and behavioral therapies. *Asian Journal of Psychiatry, 25*, 131–135.

Ramani, G. B., & Brownell, C. A. (2014). Preschoolers' cooperative problem solving: Integrating play and problem solving. *Journal of Early Childhood Research, 12*, 92–108.

Ramey, C. T. (2018). The Abecedarian Approach to social, educational, and health disparities. *Clinical Child and Family Psychology Review, 21*, 527–544.

Ramey, C. T., Bryant, D. M., Wasik, B. H., Sparling, J. J., Fendt, K. H., & LaVange, L. M. (1992). The Infant Health and Development Program for low birthweight, premature infants: Program elements, family participation, and child intelligence. *Pediatrics, 89*, 454–465.

Ramey, D., Lydon, S., Healy, S., McCoy, A., Holloway, J., & Mulher, T. (2016). A systematic review of the effectiveness of precision teaching for individuals with developmental disabilities. *Review Journal of Autism and Developmental Disorders, 3*, 179–195.

Ramig, P. R., & Pollard, R. (2011). Stuttering and other disorders of fluency. In N. B. Anderson & G. H. Shames (Eds.), *Human communication disorders: An introduction* (8th ed., pp. 132–163). Pearson.

Rao, S. S. (2000). Perspectives of an African American mother on parent-professional relationships in special education. *Mental Retardation, 38*, 475–488.

Rapport, M. J., Barr, A., & Jones, M. (2016). Key concepts in understanding motor disabilities. In F. E. Brown, J. J. McDonnell, & M. E. Snell (Eds.), *Instruction of students with severe disabilities* (8th ed.). Pearson.

Raskind, M. H., Margalit, M., & Higgins, E. L. (2006). "My LD": Children's voices on the Internet. *Learning Disability Quarterly, 29*, 253–268.

Raven, J. C., Court, J. H., & Raven, J. (1983). *Manual for Raven's Progressive Matrices and Vocabulary Scales: Advanced progressive matrices*. Lewis.

Ray, A. B., Graham, S., & Liu, X. (2018). Effects of SRSD college entrance essay exam instruction for high school students with disabilities or at-risk for writing difficulties. *Reading and Writing, 32*, 1507–1529.

Raz, R., Roberts, A. L., Lyall, K., Hart, J. E., Just, A. C., Laden, F., & Weisskopf, M. G. (2015). Autism spectrum disorder and particulate matter air pollution before, during, and after pregnancy: A nested case–control analysis within the Nurses' Health Study II Cohort. *Environmental Health Perspectives, 123*(3), 264–270.

Rea, P. J., McLaughlin, V. L., & Walther-Thomas, C. (2002). Outcomes for students with learning disabilities in inclusive and pullout programs. *Exceptional Children, 68*, 203–222.

Reed, F. D. D., Strouse, M. C., Jenkins, S. R., Price, J., Henely, A. J., & Hirst, J. M. (2014). Barriers to independent living for individuals with disabilities and seniors. *Behavior Analysis in Practice, 7*, 70–77.

Reed, V. A. (2017). *An introduction to children with language disorders* (5th ed.). Pearson.

Reid, R., Lienemann, T. O., & Hagaman, J. L. (2013). *Strategy instruction for students with learning disabilities*. Guilford.

Reid, R., Trout, A. L., & Schartz, M. (2005). Self-regulation interventions for children with attention deficit/hyperactivity disorder. *Exceptional Children, 71*, 361–377.

Reilly, A., Campbell, D., & Chiasson, K. (2012). Families and their children with disabilities. In G. Olsen & M. L. Fuller (Eds.), *Home-school relations: Working successfully with parents and families* (4th ed., pp. 151–174). Allyn & Bacon.

Reinert, K. S., Higbee, T. S., & Nix, L. D. (2020). Creating digital activity schedules to promote independence and engagement. *Behavior Analysis in Practice, 13*, 577–595.

Reis, S. M. (2013). Still a problem? Gifted girls and women. In C. M. Callahan & H. L. Hertberg-Davis (Eds.), *Fundamentals of gifted education* (pp. 343–357). Routledge.

Reiss, S. M., & Reiss, M. M. (2004). Curiosity and mental retardation: Beyond IQ. *Mental Retardation, 42*, 77–81.

Reis, S. M., & Renzulli, J. S. (2015). Five dimensions of differentiation. *Gifted Education Press Quarterly, 29*(3), 2–9.

Reis, S. M., Baum, S. M., & Burke, E. (2014). An operational definition of twice-exceptional learners: Implications and applications. *Gifted Child Quarterly, 58*(3), 217–230.

Reis, S. M., Renzulli, J. S., & Burns, D. E. (2016). *Curriculum compacting: A guide to differentiating instruction through enrichment and acceleration*. Prufrock Press.

Renzulli, J. S. (1978). What makes giftedness? Reexamining a definition. *Phi Delta Kappan, 60*(3), 180–184.

Renzulli, J. S., & Reis, S. M. (2013). The schoolwide enrichment model. In C. M. Callahan & H. L. Hertberg-Davis (Eds.), *Fundamentals of gifted education* (pp. 199–211). Routledge.

Reschly, D. J. (2005). Learning disabilities identification: Primary intervention, secondary intervention, and then what? *Journal of Learning Disabilities, 38*, 510–515.

Resetar, J. L., Noell, G. H., & Pellegrin, A. L. (2006). Teaching parents to use research supported systematic strategies to tutor their children in reading. *School Psychology Quarterly, 21*, 241–261.

Reuben, J. D., Shaw, D. S., Neiderhiser, J. M., Natsuaki, M. N., Reiss, D., & Leve, L. D. (2016). Warm parenting and effortful control in toddlerhood: Independent and interactive predictors of school-age externalizing behavior. *Journal of Abnormal Child Psychology, 44*(6), 1083–1096.

Reynolds, J. L., Cochrane, W. S., Furey, W. M., & Matvichuk, T. A. (2020). Working together: A process to support teachers in increasing specific praise statements. *Intervention in School and Clinic, 55*(3), 162–168.

Reynolds, M. C., Zetlin, A. G., & Heistad, D. (1996). *A manual for 20/20 analysis*. Temple University, Center for Research in Human Development and Education. (ERIC Document Reproduction Service No. ED 358 183).

Rhode, G., Jenson, W. R., & Williams, N. A. (2020). *The tough kid book: Practical classroom management strategies* (3rd ed.). Sopris West.

Rhodes, R. L., Ochoa, S. H., & Ortiz, S. O. (2005). *Assessing culturally and linguistically diverse students: A practical guide*. Council for Exceptional Children.

Ricci-Balich, J., & Behm, J. A. (1996). Pediatric rehabilitation nursing. In S. P. Hoeman (Ed.), *Rehabilitation nursing: Process and application* (pp. 660–682). Mosby.

Richards, T. L. (2001). Functional magnetic resonance imaging of the brain: Application of fMRI and fMRS to reading disabilities and education. *Learning Disability Quarterly, 24*, 189–203.

Ridgley, R., Snyder, P. A., McWilliam, R. A., & Davis, G. E. (2011). Development and initial validation of a professional development intervention to enhance the quality of individualized family service plans. *Infants & Young Children, 24*, 309–328.

Riesen, T., & Jameson, M. J. (2018). Comparison of prompting procedures to teach work tasks to transition-aged students with disabilities. *Education and Training in Autism and Developmental Disabilities, 53*, 100–110.

Riesen, T., Schultz, J., Morgan, R., & Kupferman, S. (2014). School-to-work barriers as identified by special educators, vocational rehabilitation counselors, and community rehabilitation professionals. *Journal of Rehabilitation, 80*, 33–44.

Rimm, S. B., Siegle, D., & Davis, G. A, (2018). *Education of the gifted and talented* (7th ed.). Pearson.

Risley, T. (2005). Montrose M. Wolf (1935–2004). *Journal of Applied Behavior Analysis, 38*, 279–287.

Rivera, C. J., & Baker, J. N. (2013). Teaching students with intellectual disability to solve for *x*. *Teaching Exceptional Children, 46*(2), 14–21.

Roberts, C. D., Stough, L. M., & Parrish, L. H. (2002). The role of genetic counseling in the elective termination of pregnancies involving fetuses with disabilities. *Journal of Special Education, 36*, 48–55.

Roberts, E. L., Ju, S., & Zhang, D. (2016). Review of practices that promote self-advocacy for students with disabilities. *Journal of Disability Policy Studies, 26*(4), 209–220.

Roberts, J. E., Schaaf, J. M., Skinner, M., Wheeler, A., Hooper, S., Hatton, D. D., & Bailey, D. B. (2005). Academic skills of boys with fragile X syndrome: Profiles and predictors. *American Journal on Mental Retardation, 110*, 107–120.

Roberts, K., DeQuinzio, J. A., & Taylor, B. L. (2020). Using behavioral skills training to teach interview skills to young adults with autism. *Journal of Behavioral Education*. https://doi.org/10.1007/s10864-020-09389-z

Roberts, R. E., Attkisson, C. C., & Rosenblatt, A. (1998). Prevalence of psychopathology among children and adolescents. *American Journal of Psychiatry, 155*, 715–725.

Robins, D. L., Casagrande, K., Barton M., Chen, C. A., Dumont-Mathieu, T., & Fein, D. (2015). Validation of the Modified Checklist for Autism in Toddlers, Revised with Follow-up (M-CHAT-R/F). *Pediatrics, 133*(1), 37–45.

Robins, D. L., Fein, D., & Barton M. (2009). *The Modified Checklist for Autism in Toddlers, Revised with Follow-Up (M-CHAT-R/F)*. Self-published. https://www.m-chat.org/index.php

Robinson Spohn, J., Timko, T. C., and Sainato, D. M. (1999). Increasing the social interactions of preschool children with disabilities during mealtimes: The effects of an interactive placemat game. *Education and Treatment of Children, 22*(1), 1–18.

Robles, M. M. (2012). Executive perceptions of the top 10 soft skills needed in today's workplace. *Business Communication Quarterly, 75*, 453–465.

Rodriguez, R. J., Blatz, E. T., & Elbaum, B. (2014). Strategies to involve families of Latino students with disabilities: When parent initiative is not enough. *Intervention in School and Clinic, 49*, 263–270.

Roeper, A., & Silverman, L. K. (2009). Giftedness and moral promise. In D. Ambrose & T. Cross (Eds.), *Morality, ethics, and gifted minds*. Springer Science.

Rogan, P. (1996). Natural supports in the workplace: No need for a trial. *Journal of the Association for Persons with Severe Handicaps, 21*, 178–180.

Rogan, P., Grossi, T. A., Mank, D., Haynes, D., Thomas, E., & Majd, C. (2002). What happens when people leave the workshop? Outcomes of workshop participants now in SE. *Supported Employment Infolines, 13*(4), 1, 3.

Rogan, P., Hagner, D., & Murphy, S. (1993). Natural supports: Reconceptualizing job coach roles. *Journal of the Association for Persons with Severe Handicaps, 18*, 275–281.

Rogers, K. (2006). *A menu of options for grouping gifted students*. Prufrock Press.

Roid, G. H. (2003). *Stanford-Binet Intelligence Scales* (5th ed.). Riverside.

Roitch, J., & Watson, S. (2019). An overview of dyslexia: Definition, characteristics, assessment, identification, and intervention. *Science Journal of Education, 7*(4), 81–86.

Rojewski, J. W., Lee, I. H., & Gregg, N. (2014). Intermediate work outcomes for adolescents with high-incidence disabilities. *Career Development and Transition for Exceptional Individuals, 37*, 106–118.

Rojewski, J. W., Lee, I. H., & Gregg, N. (2015). Causal effects of inclusion on postsecondary education outcomes of individuals with high-incidence disabilities. *Journal of Disability Policy Studies, 25*(4), 210–219.

Roscoe, E. M., Kindle, A. E., & Pence, S. E. (2010). Functional analysis and treatment of aggression maintained by preferred conversational topics. *Journal of Applied Behavior Analysis, 43*, 723–727.

Roseberry-McKibbin, C. (2007). *Language disorders in children: A multicultural and case perspective*. Allyn & Bacon.

Roseberry-McKibbin, C. (2018). *Multicultural students with special language needs: Practical strategies for assessment and intervention* (4th ed.). Academic Communication Associates.

Rosenbaum, S., & Simon, P. (2015). *Speech and language disorders in children: Implications for the Social Security Administration's Supplemental Security Income Program*. National Academy of Sciences.

Rosenbloom, R., Wills, H. P., Mason, R., Huffman, J. M., & Mason, B. A. (2019). The effects of a technology-based self-monitoring intervention on on-task, disruptive, and task-completion behaviors for adolescents with autism. *Journal of Autism and Developmental Disorders, 49*, 5047–5062.

Rosenblum, L. P. (2000). Perceptions of the impact of visual impairments on the lives of adolescents. *Journal of Visual Impairments and Blindness, 94*, 434–445.

Ross, D. B., & Johnson, N. (2017). Social studies. In M. C. Holbrook, C. Kamei-Hannan, & T. McCarthy (Eds.), *Foundations of education: Instructional strategies for teaching children and youths with visual impairments* (3rd ed., pp. 427–448). AFB Press.

Ross, M., & Levitt, H. (2000). Developments in research and technology: Otoacoustic emissions. *Volta Voices, 7*, 30–31.

Rous, B. S., & Hallum, R. A. (2012). Transition services for young children with disabilities: Research and future directions. *Topics in Early Childhood Special Education, 31*, 232–240.

Rouse, C. A., Alber-Morgan, S. R., Cullen, J. M., & Sawyer, M. R. (2014). Using prompt fading to teach self-questioning to fifth graders with LD: Effects on reading comprehension. *Learning Disabilities Research and Practice, 29*, 116–124.

Rouse, C. A., Everhart, J. M., & Alber-Morgan, S. R. (2014). Effects of self-monitoring and recruiting teacher attention on pre-vocational skills. *Education and Training in Autism and Developmental Disabilities, 49*, 313–327.

Rouse-Billman, C. A., & Alber-Morgan, S. R. (2019). Effects of a self-questioning prompt fading strategy on fourth graders' reading comprehension. *Preventing School Failure, 63*, 352–358.

Rowe, D. A., & Test, D. W. (2013). Effects of simulation to teach students with disabilities basic finance skills. *Remedial and Special Education, 34*(4), 237–248.

Rowe, D. A., Alverson, C. Y., Unruh, D. K., Fowler, C. H., Kellems, R., & Test, D. W. (2015). A Delphi study to operationalize evidence-based predictors in secondary transition. *Career Development and Transition for Exceptional Individuals, 38*, 113–126.

Rowland, A. S., Skipper, B. J., Umbach, D. M., Rabiner, D. L., Campbell, R. A., Naftel, A. J., & Sandler, D. P. (2015). The prevalence of ADHD in a population-based sample. *Journal of Attention Disorders, 19*, 741–754.

Royer, D. J., Lane, K. L., Dunlap, K. D., & Ennis, R. P. (2019). A systematic review of teacher-delivered behavior-specific praise on K–12 student performance. *Remedial and Special Education, 40*(2), 112–128.

Rueda, R., Monzo, L., Shapiro, J., Gomez, J., & Blacher, J. (2005). Cultural models of transition: Latina mothers of young adults with developmental disabilities. *Exceptional Children, 71*, 401–414.

Ruiz, S., & Kubina, R. M. (2017). Impact of trial-based functional analysis on challenging behavior and training: A review of the literature. *Behavior Analysis: Research and Practice, 17*(4), 347–356.

Rumrill, P. D., Cook, B. G., & Stevenson, N. A. (2020). *Research in special education: Designs, methods, and applications*. Charles C Thomas.

Rush, A. J., & Francis, A. (Eds.). (2000). Expert consensus guideline series: Treatment of psychiatric and behavioral problems in mental retardation. *American Journal of Mental Retardation, 105*, 159–228.

Russell-Minda, E., Jutai, J. W., Graham Strong, J., Campbell, K. A., Gold, D., Pretty, L., & Wilmot, L. (2007). The legibility of typefaces for readers with low vision: A research review. *Journal of Visual Impairment and Blindness, 101*, 402–415.

Rutherford, R. B., Quinn, M. M., & Sathur, R. (Eds.). (2007). *Handbook of research in emotional and behavioral disorders*. Guilford.

Rutter, M. (1976). *Helping troubled children*. Plenum.

Rutter, M. (2002). Address to the Second International Annual Meeting for Autism Research.

Rutter, M., Le Couteur, A., & Lord, C. (2003). *Autism Diagnostic Interview-Revised*. WPS.

Ryan, G., Brady, S., Holloway, J., & Lydon, H. (2019). Increasing appropriate conversation skills using a behavioral skills training package for adults with intellectual disability and autism spectrum disorder. *Journal of Intellectual Disabilities, 23*(4), 567–580.

Ryndak, D. L., & Fisher, D. (Eds.). (2007). *The foundations of inclusive education: A compendium of articles on effective strategies to achieve inclusive education* (2nd ed.). Association for Persons with Severe Handicaps.

Ryndak, D. L., Orlando, A., & Burnette, K. K. (2020). Creating and implementing inclusive education. In F. Brown, J. McDonnell, & M. E. Snell (Eds.), *Instruction of students with severe disabilities* (9th ed., pp. 207–231). Pearson.

Sacks, S. Z., Wolffe, K. E., & Tierney, D. (1998). Lifestyles of students with visual impairments—adolescents. Preliminary studies of social networks. *Exceptional Children, 64*, 463–478.

Sadeh, S., & Sullivan, A. L. (2017). Ethical and legal landmines: Causal inference in special education decisions. *Psychology in the Schools, 54*, 1134–1147.

Sadowska, D., Stemplewski, R., & Szeklicki, R. (2017). Postural control in young people with visual impairments and various risks of falls. *Journal of Visual Impairment & Blindness, 111*(3), 261–270.

Safer, D. J., Zito, J. M., & Fine, E. M. (1996). Increased methylphenidate usage for attention-deficit disorder in the 1990s. *Pediatrics, 98*, 1084–1088.

Sainato, D. M., Morrison, R. S., Jung, S., Axe, J., & Nixon, P. A. (2015). A comprehensive inclusion program for kindergarten children with autism spectrum disorder. *Journal of Early Intervention, 37*, 208–225.

Salend, S. J. (2016). *Creating inclusive classrooms: Effective, differentiated and reflective practices* (8th ed.). Pearson.

Salend, S. J., & Garrick Duhaney, L. M. (2005). Understanding and addressing the disproportionate representation of students of color in special education. *Intervention in School and Clinic, 40*, 213–221.

Salgado, T. M., Fedrigon, A., Riccio Omichinski, D., Meade, M. A., & Farris, K. B. (2018). Identifying medication management smartphone app features suitable for young adults with developmental disabilities: Delphi consensus study. *JMIR Mhealth Uhealth, 26*, e129.

Salisbury, R. (Ed.). (2008). *Teaching pupils with visual impairment: A guide to making the school curriculum accessible*. Routledge.

Salvia, J., Ysseldyke, J. E., & Witmer, S. (2017). *Assessment in special and inclusive education* (13th ed.). Cengage.

Sandin, S., Lichtenstein, P., Kuja-Halkoa, R., Larsson, H., Hultman, C. M., & Reichenbeg, A. (2014). The familial risk of autism. *Journal of the American Mediation Association, 311*(17), 1770–1777.

Sandmel, K. N., Brindle, M., Harris, K. R., Lane, K. L., Graham, S., Nackel, J., Mathias, R., & Little, A. (2009). Making it work: Differentiating tier two self-regulated strategies development in writing in tandem with school wide positive behavioral support. *Teaching Exceptional Children, 42*(2), 22–33.

Sanford, C., Newman, L., Wagner, M., Cameto, R., Knokey, A.-M., & Shaver, D. (2011). *The post-high school outcomes of young adults with disabilities up to 6 years after high school. Key findings from the National Longitudinal Transition Study-2 (NLTS2)* (NCSER 2011–3004). SRI International. https://ies.ed.gov/ncser/pubs/20113004/pdf/20113004.pdf

Sanson, A. V., Letcher P. L. C., & Havighurst, S. S. (2018). Child characteristics and their reciprocal effects on parenting. In M. Sanders & A. Morawska (Eds.), *Handbook of parenting and child development across the lifespan*. Springer.

Sansosti, F. J., & Powell-Smith, K. A. (2008). Using computer-presented social stories and video models to increase the social communication skills of children with high-functioning autism spectrum disorders. *Journal of Positive Behavior Intervention 10*(3), 162–178.

Sansosti, F. J., Lavik, K. B., & Sansosti, J. M. (2012). Family experiences through the autism diagnostic process. *Focus on Autism and Other Developmental Disabilities, 27*, 81–92.

Sapienza, C., Hicks, D. M., & Ruddy, B. H. (2011). Voice disorders. In N. B. Anderson & G. H. Shames (Eds.), *Human communication disorders: An introduction* (8th ed., pp. 202–237). Pearson.

Sartini, E. C., Knight, V. F., & Collins, B. C. (2013). Ten guidelines to facilitate social groups for students with complex special needs. *Teaching Exceptional Children, 45*(3), 54–62.

Satterstrom, F. K., Kosmicki, J. A., Wang, J., Breen, M. S., De Rubeis, S., An, J.-Y., Peng, M., Collins, R., Grove, J., Klei, L., Stevens, C., Reichert, J., Mulhern, M. S., Artomov, M., Gerges, S., Sheppard, B., Xu, X., Bhaduri, A., Norman, U., ... Buxbaum, J. D. (2020). Large-scale exome sequencing study implicates both developmental and functional changes in the neurobiology of autism. *Cell, 180*(3), 568–584.

Savage, J., Ferguson, C. J., & Flores, L. (2017). The effect of academic achievement on aggression and violent behavior: A meta-analysis. *Aggression and Violent Behavior, 37*, 91–101.

Savage, M. N. (2014). Self-operated auditory prompting systems: Creating and using them to support students with disabilities. *Teaching Exceptional Children, 47*(1), 46–55.

Scarlett, W. G. (Ed.). (2015). *The Sage encyclopedia of classroom management: An A-to-Z guide*. Sage.

Schafer, P. O., & DiLorio, C. (2006). Self-management in epilepsy care: Putting teen and families in the center. *Exceptional Parent, 36*(6), 46–48.

Scheetz, N. A. (2012). *Deaf education in the 21st century: Topics and trends*. Allyn & Bacon.

Schick, B., Williams, K., & Kupermintz, H. (2006). Look who's being left behind: Educational interpreters and access to education for deaf and hard-of-hearing students. *Journal of Deaf Studies and Deaf Education, 11*, 3–20.

Schilling, E. J., & Getch, Y. Q. (2012). Getting my bearings: Issues facing adolescents with traumatic brain injury. *Teaching Exceptional Children, 45*(1), 54–63.

Schizophrenia Working Group of the Psychiatric Genomics Consortium, Ripke, S., Neale, B. M., Corvin, A., Walters, J. T. R., Farh, K.-H., Holmans, P. A., Lee, P., Bulik-Sullivan, B., Collier, D. A., Huang, H., Pers, T. H., Agartz, I., Agerbo, E., Albus, M., Alexander, M., Amin, F., Bacanu, S. A., Begemann, M., ... O'Donovan, M., et al. (2014). Biological insights from 108 schizophrenia-associated genetic loci. *Nature, 511*, 412–413.

Schlosser, R. W., Hemsley, B., Shane, H., Todd, J., Lang, R., Lilienfeld, S. O., Trembath, D., Mostert, M., Fond, S., & Odom, S. (2019). Rapid prompting method and autism spectrum disorder: Systematic review exposes lack of evidence. *Review Journal of Autism and Developmental Disorders, 6*, 403–412.

Schnoes, C., Reid, R., Wagner, M., & Marder, C. (2006). ADHD among students receiving special education services: A national survey. *Exceptional Children, 72*, 483–496.

Schnoor, C. I., Freeman-Green, S., & Test, D. W. (2016). Response cards as a strategy for increasing opportunities to respond: An examination of the evidence. *Remedial and Special Education, 37*(1), 41–51.

Schonert-Reichl, K. A. (1993). Empathy and social relationships in adolescents with behavioral disorders. *Behavioral Disorders, 18*, 189–204.

Schopler, E., Van Bourgondien, M. E., Wellman, G. J., & Love, S. R. (2010). *The childhood autism rating scale (CARS2)* (2nd ed.). Western Psychological Services.

Schorr, E. A., Roth, F. P., & Fox, N. A. (2008). A comparison of the speech and language skills of children with cochlear implants and children with typical hearing. *Communicative Disorders Quarterly, 29*(4), 195–210.

Schorr, E. A., Roth, F. P., & Fox, N. A. (2009). Quality of life for children with cochlear implants: Perceived benefits and problems and the perception of single words and emotional sounds. *Journal of Speech, Language and Hearing Research, 52*, 141–152.

Schrank, F. A., McGrew, K. S., & Mather, N. (*2014*). *Woodcock-Johnson IV Tests of Cognitive Abilities*. Riverside.

Schreibman, L. (2005). *The science and fiction of autism*. Harvard University Press.

Schuiringa, H., Van Nieuwenhuijzen, M., De Castro, B. O., Lochman, J. E., & Matthys, W. (2017). Effectiveness of an intervention for children with externalizing behavior and mild to borderline intellectual disabilities: A randomized trial. *Cognitive Therapy and Research, 41*(2), 237–251.

Schultz, R. T., Chawarska, K., & Volkmar, F. R. (2006). The social brain in autism: Perspectives from neuropsychology and neuroimaging. In S. Moldin & J. L. R. Rubenstein (Eds.), *Understanding autism: From basic neuroscience to treatment* (pp. 323–348). Taylor & Francis.

Schultz, T. R., Schmidt, C. T., & Stichter, J. P. (2011). A review of parent education programs for parents of children with autism spectrum disorders. *Focus on Autism and Other Developmental Disabilities, 26*, 96–104.

Schulz, J. B. (1985). The parent–professional conflict. In H. R. Turnbull & A. P. Turnbull (Eds.), *Parents speak out: Then and now* (pp. 3–11). Merrill/Pearson.

Schumm, J. S., Moody, S. W., & Vaughn, S. (2000). Grouping for reading instruction: Does one size fit all? *Journal of Learning Disabilities, 33*, 477–488.

Schick, B., Williams, K., & Kupermintz, H. (2006). Look who's being left behind: Educational interpreters and access to education for deaf and hard-of-hearing students. *Journal of Deaf Studies and Deaf Education, 11*, 3–20.

Schwartz, C. E., Snidman, N., & Kagan, J. (1999). Adolescent social anxiety and outcome of inhibited temperament in childhood. *Journal of the American Academy of Child and Adolescent Psychiatry, 38*, 1008–1015.

Schwartz, R. G., & Marton, K. (2011). Articulatory and phonological disorders. In N. B. Anderson & G. H. Shames (Eds.), *Human communication disorders: An introduction* (8th ed., pp. 132–163). Pearson.

Scorgie, K., & Sobsey, D. (2000). Transformational outcomes associated with parenting children who have disabilities. *Mental Retardation, 38*, 195–206.

Scott, T. M., Alter, P. J., & Hirn, R. (2011). An examination of typical classroom context and instruction for students with and without behavioral disorders. *Education and Treatment of Children, 34*, 619–642.

Scruggs, T. E., & Mastropieri, M. A. (2017). Making inclusion work with co-teaching. *Teaching Exceptional Children, 49*(4), 284–293.

Scullin, M. H. (2006). Large state-level fluctuations in mental retardation classifications related to introduction of renormed intelligence test. *American Journal on Mental Retardation, 111*, 322–335.

Sehyr, Z. S., Petrich, J., & Emmorey, K. (2017). Fingerspelled and printed words are recoded into a speech-based code in short-term memory. *Journal of Deaf Studies and Deaf Education, 22*, 72–87. https://doi.org/10.1093/deafed/enw068

Semel, E., Wiig, E. H., & Secord, W. (2003). *Clinical evaluation of language fundamentals* (4th ed.). Psychological Corporation.

Seward, J., Schuster, J. W., Ault, M. J., Collins, B. C., & Hall, M. (2014). Comparing simultaneous prompting and constant time delay to teach leisure skills to students with moderate intellectual disability. *Education and Training in Autism and Developmental Disabilities, 49*, 381–395.

Sexson, S. B., & Dingle, A. D. (2001). Medical disorders. In F. M. Kline, L. B. Silver, & S. C. Russell (Eds.), *The educator's guide to medical issues in the classroom* (pp. 29–48). Brookes.

Shapiro, E. S., DuPaul, G. J., & Bradley-King, K. L. (1998). Self-management as a strategy to improve the classroom behavior of adolescents with ADHD. *Journal of Learning Disabilities, 31*, 545–555.

Shaver, D., Newman, L., Huang, T., Yu, J., & Knokey, A. (2011). *Facts from NLTS2: The secondary school experiences and academic performance of students with hearing impairments*. U.S. Department of Education.

Shaver, D. M., Marshark, M., Newman, L., & Marder, C. (2014). Who is where? Characteristics of deaf and hard-of-hearing students in regular and special schools. *Journal of Deaf Studies and Deaf Education, 19*, 203–219.

Shaw, R., & Trief, E. (2009). *Everyday activities to promote visual efficiency: A handbook for working with young children with visual impairments*. AFB Press.

Shaywitz, B. A., Shaywitz, S. E., Blachman, B. A., Pugh, K. R., Fulbright, R. K., Skudlarski, P., Menci, W. E., Constable, R. T., Holahan, J. M., Marchione, K. E., Fletcher, J. M., Lyon, G. R., & Gore, J. C. (2004). Development of left occipitotemporal systems for skilled reading in children after a phonologically-based intervention. *Biological Psychiatry, 55*, 926–933.

Shaywitz, S. E. (2003). *Overcoming dyslexia: A new and complete science-based program for reading problems at any level*. Alfred A. Knopf.

Sheldrick, R. C., Maye, M. P., & Carter, A. S. (2017). Age at first identification of autism spectrum disorder: An analysis of two US surveys. *Journal of the American Academy of Child & Adolescent Psychiatry, 56*(4), 313–320.

Sheridan, S. M. (2010). *The Tough Kid social skills book*. Ancora Publishing.

Shogren, K. A., Garnier Villarreal, M., Lang, K., & Seo, H. (2017). Mediating role of self-determination constructs in explaining the relationship between school factors and postschool outcomes. *Exceptional Children, 83*(2), 165–180.

Shogren, K. A., Toste, J., Mahal, S., & Wehmeyer, M. L. (2017). Intrinsic motivation. In K. A. Shogren, M. L. Wehmeyer, & N. N. Singh (Eds.), *Handbook of positive psychology in intellectual and developmental disabilities: Translating research into practice* (pp. 285–295). Springer Nature.

Shogren, K. A., Wehmeyer, M. L., Palmer, S. B., Rifenbark, G. G., & Little, T. D. (2015). Relationships between self-determination and postschool outcomes for youth with disabilities. *The Journal of Special Education, 48*(4), 256–267.

Shogren, K. A., Wehmeyer, M. L., & Thompson, J. R. (2017). Person-centered and student-directed planning. In M. L. Wehmeyer & K. A. Shogren (Eds.), *Handbook of research-based practices for educating students with intellectual disability* (pp. 167–182). Routledge.

Shonkoff, J. P., & Meisels, S. J. (Eds.). (2000). *Handbook of early childhood intervention* (2nd ed.). Cambridge University Press.

Silbaugh, B. C., & Facomata, T. S. (2019). Effects of a lag schedule with progressive time delay on sign mand variability in a boy with autism. *Behavior Analysis in Practice, 12*, 124–132.

Silberman, S. (2019, September 24). *Greta Thunberg became a climate activist not in spite of her autism, but because of it.* https://www.vox.com/first-person/2019/5/6/18531551/greta-thunberg-autism-aspergers

Sileo, N. M. (2005). Design HIV/AIDS prevention education: What are the roles and responsibilities of classroom teachers? *Intervention in School and Clinic, 40*, 177–181.

Silverman, L. K. (1995). Highly gifted children. In J. L. Genshaft, M. Bireley, & C. L. Hollinger (Eds.), *Serving gifted and talented students: A resource for school personnel* (pp. 124–160). PRO-ED.

Silvestri, S. M., & Heward, W. L. (2016). The neutralization of special education, revisited. In R. M. Foxx & J. A. Mulick (Eds.), *Controversial therapies in developmental disabilities: Fads, fashion, and science in professional practice* (2nd ed.). Lawrence Erlbaum Associates.

Silvia, P. J. (2015). Intelligence and creativity. *Educational Psychology Review, 27*, 599–606.

Simmons, D. C., Kame'enui, E. J., Coyne, M. D., Chard, D. J., & Hairrell, A. (2011). Effective strategies for teaching beginning reading. In M. D. Coyne, E. J. Kame'enui, & D. W. Carnine (Eds.), *Effective teaching strategies that accommodate diverse learners* (4th ed., pp. 51–84). Pearson.

Simmons, J. (2019). RAPID skills training. https://cbacares.com/rst/

Simmons, T. J., & Flexer, R. W. (2013). Transition to employment. In R. W. Flexer, T. J. Simmons, P. Luft, & R. M. Baer (Eds.), *Transition planning for secondary students with disabilities* (4th ed., pp. 279–305). Pearson.

Simonsen, B., & Sugai, G. (2019). School-wide positive behavioral interventions and supports: A systems-level application of behavioral principles. In S. G. Little & A. Akin-Little (Eds.), *Applying psychology in the schools book series. Behavioral interventions in schools: Evidence-based positive strategies* (pp. 35–60). American Psychological Association. https://doi.org/10.1037/0000126-003

Simpson, K., Adams, D., Alston-Knox, C., Heussler, H. S., & Keen, D. (2019). Exploring the sensory profiles of children on the autism spectrum using the Short Sensory Profile-2 (SSP-2). *Journal of Autism and Developmental Disorders, 49*, 2069–2079.

Simpson, R. L. (2004a). Inclusion of students with behavior disorders in general education settings. *Behavioral Disorders, 30*, 19–31.

Simpson, R. L. (2004b). Finding effective intervention and personnel preparation practices for students with autism spectrum disorders. *Exceptional Children, 70*, 135–144.

Simpson, R. L., & Myles, B. S. (1995). Effectiveness of facilitated communication with children and youth with autism. *Journal of Special Education, 28*, 424–439.

Sims, D. G., & Gottermeier, L. (1995). Computer-assisted, interactive video methods for speechreading instruction: A review. In K. Erik-Spens & G. Plant (Eds.), *Speech, communication and profound deafness* (pp. 220–241). Whurr.

Singh, R. K. J., Sng, J., Yeong, M. M. Y., Nadeson, V., & Ong, C. C. P. (2018). Getting everyone in the same room: The combined therapist approach to teaching independence in clean intermittent catheterization. *Journal of Pediatric Surgical Nursing, 7*, 126–131.

Singleton, J. L., & Tittle, M. D. (2000). Deaf parents and their hearing children. *Journal of Deaf Studies and Deaf Education, 5*(3), 221–235.

Siperstein, G. N., Parker, R. C., Norins Bardon, J., & Widaman, K. F. (2007). A national study of youth attitudes toward the inclusion of students with intellectual disabilities. *Exceptional Children, 73*, 435–455.

Siperstein, G. N., Wiley, A. L., & Forness, S. R. (2011). School context and the academic and behavioral progress of students with emotional disturbance. *Behavioral Disorders, 36*(3), 172–184.

Sirois, M. S., Bernier, A., & Lemelin, J. P. (2019). Child temperamental anger, mother–child interactions, and socio-emotional functioning at school entry. *Early Childhood Research Quarterly, 47*(1), 30–38.

Sitlington, P. L., Neubert, D. A., & Clark, G. M. (2010). *Comprehensive transition education and services for students with disabilities* (5th ed.). Pearson.

Skau, L., & Cascella, P. W. (2006). Using assistive technology to foster speech and language skills at home and in preschool. *Teaching Exceptional Children, 38*(6), 12–17.

Skeels, H. M., & Dye, H. B. (1939). A study of the effects of differential stimulation on mentally retarded children. *Convention Proceedings, American Association on Mental Deficiency, 44*, 114–136.

Skibo, H., Mims, P., & Spooner, F. (2011). Teaching number identification to students with severe disabilities using response cards. *Education and Training in Developmental Disabilities, 46*, 124–133.

Skinner, B. F. (1957). *Verbal behavior*. Appleton-Century-Crofts.

Slade, N., Eisenhower, A., Carter, A. S., & Blacher, J. (2018). Satisfaction with individualized education programs among parents of young children with ASD. *Exceptional Children, 84*, 242–260.

Slaton, J. D., Hanley, G. P., & Raftery, K. J. (2017). Interview-informed functional analyses: A comparison of synthesized and isolated components. *Journal of Applied Behavior Analysis, 50*, 252–277.

Slavin, R. E. (1995). *Cooperative learning: Theory, research and practice* (2nd ed.). Allyn & Bacon.

Slayton, J. D., & Hanley, G. P. (2018). Nature and scope of synthesis in functional analysis and treatment for problem behavior. *Journal of Applied Behavior Analysis, 51*(4), 943–973.

Small, L. H. (2016). *Fundamental of phonetics: A practical guide for students* (4th ed.). Pearson.

Smith, J. D. (2004). The historical contexts of special education: Framing our understanding of contemporary issues. In A. McCray Sorrells, H. J. Rieth, & P. T. Sindelar (Eds.), *Critical issues in special education: Access, diversity, and accountability* (pp. 1–15). Allyn & Bacon.

Smith, J. D., & Hilton, A. (1997). The preparation and training of the educational community for the inclusion of students with developmental disabilities: The MRDD position. *Education and Training of Mental Retardation and Developmental Disabilities, 32*, 3–10.

Smith, J. D., & Mitchell, A. L. (2001a). Disney's Tarzan, Edgar Rice Burroughs' eugenics, and visions of utopian perfection. *Mental Retardation, 39*, 221–225.

Smith, J. D., & Mitchell, A. L. (2001b). "Me? I'm not a drooler. I'm the assistant": Is it time to abandon mental retardation as a classification? *Mental Retardation, 39*, 144–146.

Smith, J. D., & Prior, M. (1995). Temperament and stress resilience in school-age children: A within-families study. *Journal of the American Academy of Children and Adolescent Psychiatry, 34*, 168–179.

Smith, P. D., Gast, D. L., Logan, K. R., & Jacobs, H. A. (2001). Customizing instruction to maximize functional outcomes for students with profound multiple disabilities. *Exceptionality, 9*(3), 135–145.

Smith, S. W., & Brownell, M. T. (1995). Individualized education programs: From intent to acquiescence. *Focus on Exceptional Children, 28*(1), 1–12.

Smith, T., & Lovaas, O. I. (1998). Intensive and early behavioral intervention with autism: The UCLA Young Autism Project. *Infants and Young Children, 10*(3), 67–78.

Smith, T., Eikeseth, S., Klevstrand, M., & Lovaas, O. I. (1997). Intensive behavioral treatment for preschoolers with severe mental retardation and pervasive developmental disorders. *American Journal on Mental Retardation, 102*, 238–249.

Smith, T., Groen, A. D., & Wynn, J. W. (2000). Randomized trial of intensive early intervention for children with pervasive developmental disorder. *American Journal on Mental Retardation, 105*, 269–285.

Smith Myles, B., Coffin, A. B., Owens, D. J., & Yantes, C. (2014). Characteristics of adults with high-functioning autism spectrum disorders. In M. Tincani & A. Bondy (Eds.), *Autism spectrum disorders in adolescents and adults: Evidence-based and promising interventions* (pp. 3–23). Guilford Press.

Smith Myles, B. S., Jones-Bock, S., & Simpson, R. L. (2000). *Asperger syndrome diagnostic scale*. PRO-ED.

Snider, V. E., Busch, T., & Arrowood, L. (2003). Teacher knowledge of stimulant medication and ADHD. *Remedial and Special Education, 24*, 46–56.

Sniezyk, C. J., & Zane, T. L. (2015). Investigating the effects of sensory integration theory in decreasing stereotypy. *Focus on Autism and Other Developmental Disabilities, 30*, 13–22.

Snyder, T. D., de Brey, C., & Dillow, S. A. (2016). *Digest of education statistics 2015 (NCES 2016–014)*. National Center for Education Statistics, Institute of Education Sciences, U.S. Department of Education.

Social Security Administration. (2019). *Disability evaluation under Social Security*. https://www.ssa.gov/disability/professionals/bluebook/2.00-SpecialSensesandSpeech-Adult.htm#2_02

Solis, M., Miciak, J., Vaughn, S., & Fletcher, J. M. (2014). Why intensive interventions matter: Longitudinal studies of adolescents with reading disabilities and poor reading comprehension. *Learning Disability Quarterly, 37*, 218–229.

Solomon, B. (2007). When all you need is rest. *Exceptional Parent, 37*(4), 38–39.

Song, Y., & Ferretti, R. P. (2013). Teaching critical questions about argumentation through the revising process: Effects of strategy instruction on college students' argumentative essays. *Reading and Writing, 26*, 67–90.

Sonnenschein, S. (1981). Parents and professionals: An uneasy relationship. *Teaching Exceptional Children, 14*, 62–65.

Sontag, E., Sailor, W., & Smith, J. (1977). The severely/profoundly handicapped: Who are they? Where are we? *Journal of Special Education, 11*(1), 5–11.

Soukup, J. H., Wehmeyer, M. L., Bashinski, S. M., & Bovaird, J. A. (2007). Classroom variables and access to the general curriculum for students with disabilities. *Exceptional Children, 74*, 101–120.

Southall, C., & Campbell, J. M. (2015). What does the research say about social perspective-taking interventions for students with HFASD. *Exceptional Children, 81*, 194–208.

Southall, C. M., & Gast, D. L. (2011). Self-management procedures: A comparison across the autism spectrum. *Education and Training in Autism and Developmental Disabilities*, *46*(2), 155–177.

Sowell, E. R., Thompson, P. M., Welcome, S. E., Henkenius, A. L., Toga, A. W., & Peterson, B. S. (2003). Cortical abnormalities in children and adolescents with attention-deficit hyperactivity disorder. *The Lancet*, *362*, 1699–1707.

Sparrow, S. S., Cicchetti, D. V., & Saulnier, C. A. (2016). *Vineland Adaptive Behavior Scales* (3rd ed.). Pearson Assessments.

Spencer, M., & Wagner, R. K. (2018). The comprehension problems of children with poor reading comprehension despite adequate decoding: A meta-analysis. *Review of Educational Research*, *88*(3), 366–400.

Spencer, M., Quinn, J. M., & Wagner, R. K. (2014). Specific reading comprehension disability: Major problem, myth, or misnomer? *Learning Disabilities Research & Practice*, *29*(1), 3–9.

Sperry, L., Neitzel, J., & Engelhardt-Wells, K. (2010). Peer-mediated instruction and intervention strategies for students with autism spectrum disorders. *Preventing School Failure*, *54*, 256–264.

Spina Bifida Association. (2020a). *What is spina bifida?* https://www.spinabifidaassociation.org/what-is-spina-bifida/

Spina Bifida Association. (2020b). *Hydrocephalus and shunts.* https://www.spinabifidaassociation.org/what-is-spina-bifida/

Spinelli, C. G. (2012). *Classroom assessment for students in special and general education* (3rd ed.). Pearson.

Spirito, A., & Overholser, J. C. (Eds.). (2003). *Evaluating and treating adolescent suicide attempters: From research to practice*. Academic Press.

Splett, J. W., Garzona, M., Gibson, N., Wojtalewicz, D., Raborn, A., & Reinke, W. M. (2019). Teacher recognition, concern, and referral of children's internalizing and externalizing behavior problems. *School Mental Health*, *11*, 228–239.

Spooner, F., & Browder, D. M. (2015). Raising the bar: Significant advances and future needs for promoting learning for students with severe disabilities. *Remedial and Special Education*, *36*, 28–32.

Spooner, F., Knight, V., Browder, D., Jimenez, B. A., & DiBiase, W. (2011). Evaluating evidence-based practices in teaching science content to students with severe developmental disabilities. *Research and Practice for Persons with Severe Disabilities*, *36*, 62–75.

Spriggs, A. D., Mimms, P. J., van Dijk, W., & Knight, V. F. (2017). Examination of the evidence base for using visual activity schedules with students with intellectual disability. *The Journal of Special Education*, *51*, 14–26.

Squires, J., & Bricker, D. (2009). *Ages and Stages Questionnaires (ASQ-3)* (3rd ed.). Brookes.

SRI International. (2005). *Declassification—students who leave special education: A special topic report from the special education elementary longitudinal study*. Author.

Srick, R. (2009). *CHAMPS: A proactive & positive approach to classroom management*. Ancora Publishing.

Stahl, K. A. D., Flannagan, K., & McKenna, M. C. (2020). *Assessment for reading instruction* (4th ed.). Guilford.

Stainback, S., & Stainback, W. (1996a). *Controversial issues confronting special education: Divergent perspectives* (2nd ed.). Allyn & Bacon.

Stainback, S., & Stainback, W. (Eds.). (1996b). *Inclusion: A guide for educators* (2nd ed.). Brookes.

Stainback, S., Stainback, W., & Ayres, B. (1996). Schools as inclusive communities. In S. Stainback & W. Stainback (Eds.), *Controversial issues confronting special education: Divergent perspectives* (2nd ed., pp. 31–43). Allyn & Bacon.

Stanfa, K., & Johnson, N. (2015). Improving braille reading fluency: The bridge to comprehension. *The Journal of Blindness Innovation and Research*, *5*(2). https://nfb.org/images/nfb/publications/jbir/jbir15/jbir050204abs.html

Stanton-Chapman, T. L., & Brown, T. S. (2015). A strategy to increase the social interactions of 3-year-old children with disabilities in an inclusive classroom. *Topics in Early Childhood Special Education*, 35(1), 4–14.

State, T. M., Simonsen, B., Hirn, R. G., & Wills, H. (2019). Bridging the research-to-practice gap through effective professional development for teachers working with students with emotional and behavioral disorders. *Behavioral Disorders*, *44*(2), 107–116.

States, J., Detrich, R., & Keyworth, R. (2019). *Active student responding (ASR) overview*. The Wing Institute. https://www.winginstitute.org/instructional-delivery-student-respond

Steege, M. W., Pratt, J. L., Wickerd, G., Guare, R., & Watson, T. S. (2019). *Conducting school-based functional behavioral assessments: A practitioner's guide* (3rd ed.). Guilford.

Steere, D. E., & DiPipi-Hoy, C. (2012). When you can't get out: Strategies for supporting community-based instruction. *Teaching Exceptional Children*, *45*(2), 60–67.

Stein, M., Kinder, D., Silbert, J., Carnine, D. W., & Rolf, K. (2018). *Direct instruction mathematics* (5th ed.). Pearson.

Stephens, T. M., & Wolf, J. S. (1989). *Effective skills in parent/teacher conferencing* (2nd ed.). Ohio State University, College of Education, School Study Council of Ohio.

Stephenson, J., & Carter, M. (2011). Use of multisensory environments in school for students with severe disabilities: Perceptions from schools. *Education and Training in Autism and Other Developmental Disabilities*, *46*, 276–290.

Sternberg, R. J. (2007). Who are the bright children? *Educational Researcher*, *36*(3), 148–155.

Sternberg, R. J. (2017). ACCEL: A new model for identifying the gifted. *Roeper Review*, *39*, 152–169.

Sternberg, R. J. (2018). Creative giftedness is not just what creativity tests test: Implications of a triangular theory of creativity for understanding creative giftedness. *Roeper Review*, *40*, 158–165.

Stetser, M., & Stillwell, R. (2014). *Public high school four-year on-time graduation rates and event dropout rates: School years 2010–11 and 2011–12. First look* (NCES 2014–391). U.S. Department of Education. National Center for Education Statistics. http://nces.ed.gov/pubsearch

Stevens, E. A., Walker, M. A., & Vaughn, S. (2017). The effects of reading fluency interventions on the reading fluency and reading comprehension performance of elementary students with learning disabilities: A synthesis of the research from 2001 to 2014. *Journal of Learning Disabilities*, *50*(5), 576–590.

Stevenson, J., Kreppner, J., Pimperton, H., Worsfold, S., & Kennedy, C. (2015). Emotional and behavioural difficulties in children and adolescents with hearing impairment: A systematic review and meta-analysis. *European Child and Adolescent Psychiatry*, *24*, 477–496. https://doi.org/10.1007/s00787-015-0697-1

Sticken, J., & Kapperman, G. (2010). Integration of visual skills for independent living. In A. L. Corn & J. N. Erin (Eds.), *Foundations of low vision: Clinical and functional perspectives* (2nd ed., pp. 97–110). AFB Press.

Stiegler, L. N. (2005). Understanding pica behavior: A review for clinical and education professionals. *Focus on Autism and Other Developmental Disabilities*, *20*, 27–38.

Stiegler, L. N., & Davis, R. (2010). Understanding sound sensitivity in individuals with autism spectrum disorder. *Focus on Autism and Other Developmental Disabilities*, *25*, 65–75.

Stinson, M. S., Elliot, L. B., & Easton, D. (2014). Deaf/Hard-of-hearing and other postsecondary learners' retention of STEM content with tablet computer-based notes. *Journal of Deaf Studies and Deaf Education*, *19*, 251–261.

Stith, J. L., & Drasgow, E. (2005). Including children with cochlear implants in general education elementary classrooms. *Teaching Exceptional Children Plus*, 2(1) Article 2. https://eric.ed.gov/?id=EJ966529

Stocco, C., Thompson, R., Hart, J., & Soriano, H. (2017). Improving the interview skills of college students using behavioral skills training. *Journal of Applied Behavior Analysis*, *50*, 495–510.

Stockard, J., Wood, T. W., Coughlin, C., & Rasplica Khoury, C. (2018). The effectiveness of Direct Instruction curricula: A meta-analysis of a half century of research. *Review of Educational Research, 88*(4), 479–507.

Stocker, J. D., Schwartz, R., Kubina, R. M., Kostewicz, D., & Kozloff, M. (2019). Behavioral fluency and mathematics intervention research: A review of the last 20 years. *Behavioral Interventions, 34*, 102–117.

Stokoe, W. (1960). *The calculus of structure.* Gallaudet University Press.

Stokoe, W., Armstrong, D. F., & Wilcox, S. (1995). *Gesture and the nature of language.* Cambridge University Press.

Stoner, J. B., Jones Bock, S., Thompson, J. R., Angell, M. E., Heyl, B. S., & Crowley, E. P. (2005). Welcome to our world: Parent perceptions of interactions between parents of young children with ASD and education professionals. *Focus on Autism and Other Developmental Disabilities, 20*, 39–51.

Storey, K. (2007). Review of research on self-management interventions in supported employment settings for employees with disabilities. *Career Development for Exceptional Individuals, 30*, 24–34.

Storey, K. (2019). *Case studies in transition and employment for students and adults with disabilities.* Charles C Thomas.

Storey, K. (2020). *Case studies for inclusion in education: Strategies and guidelines for educating students with disabilities in the general education environment.* Charles C Thomas.

Storey, K., & Miner, C. (2017). *Systematic instruction of functional skills for students and adults with disabilities* (2nd ed.). Charles C Thomas.

Strand, J., & Kreiner, J. (2005). Recreation and leisure in the community. In R. W. Flexer, T. J. Simmons, P. Luft, & R. M. Baer (Eds.), *Transition planning for secondary students with disabilities* (2nd ed., pp. 460–482). Merrill/Pearson.

Stremel, K. (2008). *Communication interactions: It takes two.* National Center on Deaf-Blindness. http://documents.nationaldb.org/products/Communication.pdf

Stremel, K., Molden, V., Leister, C., Matthews, J., Wilson, R., Goodall, D. V., & Hoston, J. (1990). *Communication systems and routines: A decision making process.* U.S. Office of Special Education.

Strickland, B. B., & Turnbull, A. P. (1993). *Developing and implementing Individualized Education Programs* (3rd ed.). Merrill/Pearson.

Stromer, R., Kimball, J., Kinney, E., & Taylor, B. (2006). Activity schedules, computer technology, and teaching children with autism spectrum disorders. *Focus on Autism and Other Developmental Disabilities, 21*, 14–24.

Strunk, J. A. (2010). Respite care for families of special needs children: A systematic review. *Journal of Developmental and Physical Disabilities, 22*, 615–630.

Stuart v. Nappi, 443 F. Supp. 1235 (D. Conn. 1978).

Stuart, M. E., Lieberman, L., & Hand, K. E. (2006). Beliefs about physical activity among children who are visually impaired and their parents. *Journal of Visual Impairment and Blindness, 100*, 223–234.

Stuart, S. K., Flis, L. D., & Rinaldi, C. (2006). Connecting with families: Parents speak up about preschool services for their children with autism spectrum disorders. *Teaching Exceptional Children, 39*(1), 46–51.

Stuttering Foundation (2019a). *FAQ.* Author. http://www.stutteringhelp.org/faq

Stuttering Foundation (2019b). *Notes to the teacher: The child who stutters at school.* Author. https://www.stutteringhelp.org/notes-teacher-child-who-stutters-school

Sugai, G., & Horner, R. H. (2020). Sustaining and scaling positive behavioral interventions and supports: Implementation drivers, outcomes, and considerations. *Exceptional Children, 86*(2), 120–136.

Suk, A. L., Sinclair, T. E., Osmani, K. J., & Williams-Diehm, K. (2020). Transition planning: Keeping cultural competence in mind. *Career Development and Transition for Exceptional Individuals, 43*(2), 122–127.

Sun, C. K., Tseng, P. T., Wu, C. K., Li, D. J., Chen, T. Y., Stubbs, B., Carvalho, A. F., Chen, Y. W., Lin, P. Y., Cheng, Y. S., & Wu, M. K. (2019). Therapeutic effects of methylphenidate for attention-deficit/hyperactivity disorder in children with borderline intellectual functioning or intellectual disability: A systematic review and meta-analysis. *Scientific Reports, 9*, Article 15908. https://doi.org/10.1038/s41598-019-52205-6

Sun, R. (2017). Intergenerational age gaps and a family member's well-being. A family systems approach. *Journal of Intergenerational Relationships, 14*, 320–337.

Sundberg, M. L. (2008). *Verbal Behavior Milestones Assessment and Placement Program: The VB-MAPP.* AVB Press.

Sundberg, M. L. (2020). Verbal behavior. In J. O. Cooper, T. E. Heron, & W. L. Heward, *Applied behavior analysis* (3rd ed., pp. 412–449). Pearson.

Sunderland, L. C. (2004). Speech, language, and audiology services in public schools. *Intervention in School and Clinic, 39*, 209–217.

Swanson, H. L. (2000). Issues facing the field of learning disabilities. *Learning Disability Quarterly, 23*, 37–50.

Swanson, H. L., & Hoskyn, M. (1998). Experimental intervention research on students with learning disabilities: A meta-analysis of treatment outcomes. *Review of Educational Research, 68*(3), 277–321.

Swedeen, B. L., Carter, E. W., & Molfenter, N. (2010). Getting everyone involved: Identifying transition opportunities for youth with severe disabilities. *Teaching Exceptional Children, 43*(2), 38–49.

Szabo, J. L. (2000). Maddie's story: Inclusion through physical and occupational therapy. *Teaching Exceptional Children, 33*(2), 26–32.

Szidon, K., Ruppar, A., & Smith, L. (2015). Five steps for developing effective transition plans for high school students with autism spectrum disorder. *Teaching Exceptional Children, 47*(3), 147–152.

Szumski, G., Smogorzewska, J., & Karwowski, M. (2017). Academic achievement of students without special educational needs in inclusive classrooms: A meta-analysis. *Educational Research Review, 21*, 33–54.

Szymanski, L., & King, B. H. (1999). Practice parameters for the assessment and treatment of children, adolescents, and adults with mental retardation and co-morbid mental disorders. *Journal of the American Academy of Children and Adolescent Psychiatry, 38*(12 Suppl.), 5S–31S.

Talbott, E., & Thiede, K. (1999). Pathways to antisocial behavior among adolescent girls. *Journal of Emotional and Behavioral Disorders, 7*, 31–39.

Tam, K. Y. B., Heward, W. L., & Heng, M. A. (2006). Effects of vocabulary instruction, error correction, and fluency-building on oral reading rate and comprehension of English-language learners who are struggling readers. *Journal of Special Education, 40*, 79–93.

Targett, P. S., & Wehman, P. (2011). Employment: Community-based choices. In. P. Wehman, *Essentials of transition planning* (pp. 127–143). Brookes.

TASH. (2000, March). *TASH resolution on deinstitutionalization.* Author. http://tash.org/about/resolutions/tash-resolution-deinstitutionalization/

Tassé, M. J., Perkins, E. A., Jorgensen Smith, T., & Chapman, R. (2019). Behavioral health services for persons with intellectual and developmental disabilities. In B. Levin & A. Hanson (Eds.), *Foundations of behavioral health* (pp. 253–272). Springer.

Tassé, M. J., Schalock, R. L., Balboni, G., et al. (2012). The construct of adaptive behavior: Its conceptualization, measurement, and use in the field of intellectual disability. *American Journal of Intellectual and Developmental Disability, 117*, 291–303.

Tassé, M. J., Schalock, R. L., Thissen, D., Balboni, G., Bersani, H. A., Borthwick-Duffy, S. A., Spreat, S., Widaman, K. F., & Zhang, D. (2017). *Diagnostic Adaptive Behavior Scale: User's manual*. American Association on Intellectual and Developmental Disabilities.

Taylor, L. E., Swerdfeger, A. L., & Eslick, G. D. (2014). Vaccines are not associated with autism: An evidence-based meta-analysis of case-control and cohort studies. *Vaccine, 32*, 3623–3629.

Taylor, S. J. (2005). Caught in the continuum: A critical analysis of the principle of the least restrictive environment. *Research and Practice for Persons with Severe Disabilities, 30*, 218–230.

Tekin-Iftar, E., & Birkan, B. (2010). Small group instruction for students with autism: General case training and observational learning. *The Journal of Special Education, 44*(1), 50–63.

Terman, L. (Ed.). (1925). *Genetic studies of genius* (Vol. 1). Stanford University Press.

Terzi, L. (2005). Beyond the dilemma of difference: The capability approach to disability and special education needs. *Journal of Philosophy of Education, 39*, 443–459.

Test, D. W. (2012). *Evidence-based instructional practices for transition*. Brookes.

Test, D. W., Bartholomew, A., & Bethune, L. (2015). What high school administrators need to know about secondary transition evidence-based practices and predictors for students with disabilities. *NASSP Bulletin, 99*, 254–273.

Test, D. W., Fowler, C. H., Wood, W. M., Brewer, D. M., & Eddy, S. (2005). A conceptual framework of self-advocacy for students with disabilities. *Remedial and Special Education, 26*, 43–54.

Test, D. W., Mason, C., Hughes, C., Konrad, M., Neale, M., & Wood, W. M. (2004). Student involvement in Individualized Education Program meetings. *Exceptional Children, 70*, 391–412.

Test, D. W., Mazzotti, V., Mustian, A., Fowler, C., Kortering, L., & Kohler, P. (2009). Evidence-based secondary transition predictors for improving postschool outcomes for students with disabilities. *Career Development and Transition for Exceptional Individuals*, 32, 160–181.

Test, D. W., Richter, S., Knight, V., & Spooner, F. (2011). A comprehensive review and meta-analysis of the social stories literature. *Focus on Autism and Other Developmental Disabilities, 26*, 49–62.

The Conference Board, Corporate Voices for Working Families, the Partnership for 21st Century Skills, and the Society for Human Resource Management (2006). *Are they really ready to work? Employers' perspectives on the basic knowledge and applied skills of new entrants to the 21st century US workforce.* Partnership for 21st Century Skills http://eric.ed.gov/fulltext/ED519465.pdf

Thistle, J. J., McNaughton, D., Nippold, M., & Reichle, J. (2015). Teaching active listing skills to pre-service speech-language pathologists: A first step in supporting collaboration with parents of young children who require AAC. *Language, Speech & Hearing Services in Schools, 46*, 44–55.

Thompson, J. R., Doepke, K., Homes, A., Pratt, C., Smith Byles, B., Shogren, K. A., & Wehmeyer, M. L. (2017). *Person-centered planning with the Supports Intensity Scale-A version: A guide for planning teams*. American Association on Intellectual and Developmental Disabilities.

Thompson, T. (2009). *Freedom from meltdowns*. Brookes.

Thornton, L. C., & Frick, P. J. (2018). Aggression and conduct disorders. In Johnny L. Matson (Ed.), *Handbook of childhood psychopathology and developmental disabilities assessment*. Springer.

Tiger, J. H., Hanley, G. P., & Bruzek, J. (2008). Functional communication training: A review and practical guide. *Behavior Analysis in Practice, 1*(1), 16–23.

Timothy W. v. Rochester, N. H., School District, 875 F.2d 954 (1st Cir. 1989), *cert. denied* 493 U.S. 983, 110 S.Ct. 519 (1989).

Tincani, M., & De Mers, M. (2016). Meta-analysis of single-case research design studies on instructional pacing. *Behavior Modification, 40*(6), 799–824.

Tincani, M., & Twyman, J. S. (2016). *Enhancing engagement through active student response*. Center on Innovations in Learning.

Tindal, G., Nese, J. F. T., Stevens, J. J., & Alonzo, J. (2016). Growth on oral reading fluency measures as a function of special education and measurement sufficiency. *Remedial and Special Education, 37*, 28–40.

Todd, A. W., Horner, R. H., & Sugai, G. (1999). Self-monitoring and self-recruited praise: Effects on problem behavior, academic engagement, and work completion in a typical classroom. *Journal of Positive Behavior Interventions, 1*, 66–76.

Todd, N. W. (2015). The etiologies of childhood hearing impairment. In *NCHAM eBook: A resource guide for early detection and intervention*. National Center for Hearing Assessment and Management.

Tomaseone, J. R., Flood, S. M., Ma, J. K., Scime, N. V., Burke, S. M., Sleeth, L., Marrocco, S., & The SCRIRE Research Team. (2018). Physical activity self-management interventions for adults with spinal cord injury: Part 1—A systematic review of the use and effectiveness of behavior change techniques. *Psychology of Sport & Exercise, 37*, 274–285.

Tomblin, J. B. (2017). Genetics of childhood language disorders. In R. G. Schwartz (Ed.), *Handbook of child language disorders* (2nd ed., pp. 254–273). Taylor & Francis.

Tomblin, J. B., Harrison, H., Ambrose, S. E., Walker, E. A., Oleson, J. J., & Moeller, M. P. (2015). Language outcomes in young children with mild to severe hearing loss. *Ear and Hearing, 36*, 76–91.

Tomlin, M., & Reed, P. (2012). Effects of fixed-time reinforcement delivered by teachers for reducing problem behavior in special education classrooms. *Journal of Behavioral Education, 21*(2), 150–162.

Tomlinson, C. A. (2017). *How to differentiate instruction in academically diverse classrooms* (3rd ed.). ASCD.

Tomlinson, C. A., Kaplan, S. N., Renzulli, J. S., Purcell, J. H., Leppien, J. H., Burns, D. E., Strickland, C. A., & Imbeau, M. B. (2009). *The parallel curriculum: A design to develop learner potential and challenge advanced learners* (2nd ed.). Corwin.

Toms, O., Campbell-Whatley, G., Stuart, S., & Schultz, T. (2018). The effects of check-in check-out on the academic planning and behavior of African American males. *Journal of Multicultural Education, 12*, 278–293.

Torgesen, J. K. (2009). The response to intervention instructional model: Some outcomes from a large-scale implementation in Reading First schools. *Child Development Perspectives, 3*, 38–40.

Torgesen, J. K., & Bryant, B. (2004). *Test of Phonological Awareness—Second edition: PLUS*. PRO–ED.

Torres, C., & Black, R. S. (2018). Culturally responsive self-regulated strategy development in writing for college students with disabilities. *Multiple Voices for Ethnically Diverse Exceptional Learners, 18*(1), 42–59.

Tourette Syndrome Association. (2020). *What Is Tourette?* http://www.tsa-usa.org/Medical/whatists_cov.html

Trach, J. S. (2008). Natural supports in the workplace and beyond. In F. R. Rusch (Ed.). *Beyond high school: Preparing adolescents for tomorrow's challenges* (2nd ed., pp. 250–265). Merrill/Pearson.

Trask-Tyler, S. A., Grossi, T. A., & Heward, W. L. (1994). Teaching young adults with developmental disabilities and visual impairments to use tape-recorded recipes: Acquisition, generalization, and maintenance of cooking skills. *Journal of Behavioral Education, 4*, 283–311.

Travers, J., Tincani, M., Whitby, P., & Boutot, A. (2014). Alignment of sexuality education and self-determination for people with significant disabilities: A review of research and future directions. *Education and Training in Autism and Developmental Disabilities, 49*, 232–247.

Travers, J. C., Krezmien, M. P., Mulcahy, C., & Tincani, M. (2014). Racial disparity in administrative autism identification across the United States during 2000 and 2007. *The Journal of Special Education, 48*(3), 155–166.

Treffert, D. A. (2014). Savant syndrome: Realities, myths and misconceptions. *Journal of Autism and Developmental Disorders, 44*(3), 564–571.

Tremblay, P. (2013). Comparative outcomes of two instructional models for students with learning disabilities: Inclusion with co-teaching and solo-taught special education. *Journal of Research in Special Education Needs, 13*(4), 251–258.

Tucci, S. T., & Easterbrooks, S. R. (2015). A syllable segmentation, letter-sound, and initial-sound intervention with students who are deaf or hard of hearing and use sign language. *The Journal of Special Education, 48*, 279–289. https://doi.org/10.1177/0022466913504462

Tullis, C. A., Cannella-Malone, H. I., Basbigill, A. R., Yeager, A., Fleming, C. V., Payne, D., & Wu, P. F. (2011). Review of the choice and preference assessment literature for individuals with severe to profound disabilities. *Education and Training in Autism and Developmental Disabilities, 46*(4), 576–595.

Turnbull, A. P., & Ruef, M. (1996). Family perspectives on problem behavior. *Mental Retardation, 34*, 280–293.

Turnbull, A., Turnbull, H. R., Erwin, E. J., Soodak, L. C., & Shogren, K. A. (2015). *Families, professionals, and exceptionality: Positive outcomes through partnerships and trust* (7th ed.). Pearson.

Turnbull, H., Turnbull, P., Wehmeyer, M., & Park, J. (2003). A quality of life framework for special education outcomes. *Remedial and Special Education, 24*, 67–74.

Turnbull, H. R., Huerta, N. E., & Stowe, M. J. (2009). *What every teacher should know about the Individuals with Disabilities Act as amended in 2004* (2nd ed.). Pearson.

Turner-Henson, A., Holaday, B., Corser, N., Ogletree, G., & Swan, J. H. (1994). The experiences of discrimination: Challenges for chronically ill children. *Pediatric Nursing, 20*, 571–577.

Twyman, J. S. (2014). Envisioning education 3.0: The fusion of behavior analysis, learning science and technology. *Mexican Journal of Behavior Analysis, 40*, 20–38.

Twyman, J. S., & Heward, W. L. (2018). How to improve student learning in every classroom now. *International Journal of Educational Research, 87*, 78–90.

U.S. Department of Education. (2014). *Thirty-sixth Annual Report to Congress on the implementation of the Individuals with Disabilities Education Act, 2014*. Author.

U.S. Department of Education. (2018). Fortieth annual report to Congress on the implementation of the Individuals with Disabilities Education Act, 2014. Office of Special Education and Rehabilitative Services.

U.S. Department of Education. (2019a). *Forty-first annual report to Congress on the implementation of the Individuals with Disabilities Education Act*. Office of Special Education and Rehabilitative Services.

U.S. Department of Education. (2019b). National Center for Education Statistics, Schools and Staffing Survey (SASS). See *Digest of Education Statistics 2019*, table 209.22.

U.S. Department of Education. (2020a). *IDEA Section 618 Data Products*. Office of Special Education and Rehabilitative Services. https://www2.ed.gov/programs/osepidea/618-data/static-tables/index.html

U.S. Department of Education, National Center for Education Statistics, Common. (2020b). *English language learners in public schools*. https://nces.ed.gov/programs/coe/indicator_cgf.asp

U.S. Department of Education, National Center for Education Statistics. (2020c). *Trends in high school dropout and completion rates in the United States: 2019*. https://nces.ed.gov/pubs2020/2020117.pdf

U.S. Department of Health and Human Services. (2018). *Newborn screening: Toward a uniform screening panel and system*. Health Resources and Services Administration. https://www.hrsa.gov/sites/default/files/hrsa/advisory-committees/heritable-disorders/newborn-uniform-screening-panel.pdf

U.S. Department of Health and Human Services. (2020). *Recommended newborn screening panel*. Health Resources and Services Administration. http://www.hrsa.gov/advisorycommittees/mchbadvisory/heritabledisorders/recommendedpanel/index.html

U. S. National Library of Medicine. (2020a). *What are the different ways in which a genetic condition can be inherited?* https://ghr.nlm.nih.gov/primer/inheritance/inheritancepatterns

U.S. National Library of Medicine. (2020b). *Tay-Sachs disease*. http://ghr.nlm.nih.gov/condition/tay-sachs-disease

U.S. Office of Education. (1977). *Procedures for evaluating specific learning disabilities. Federal Register, 42*, 65082–65085.

Uchida, M., Spencer, T. J., Faraone, S. V., & Biederman, J. (2018). Adult outcomes of ADHD: An overview of results from the MGH longitudinal family studies of pediatrically and psychiatrically referred youth with and without ADHD of both sexes. *Journal of Attention Disorders, 22*, 523–535.

Uffen, E. (1997). Speech and language disorders: Nature or nurture? *ASHA Leader, 2*(14), 8.

United States Association of Blind Athletes. (2020). *COVID-19: Risks and challenges for the visually impaired*. https://www.usaba.org/covid-19-risks-and-challenges-for-the-visually-impaired/

University of Oregon (2018–2019). *Dynamic Indicators of Basic Early Literacy Skills (DIBELS®)* (8th ed.). University of Oregon. https://dibels.uoregon.edu

Uphold, N. M., Walker, A. R., & Test, D. W. (2007). Resources for involving students in their IEP process. *Teaching Exceptional Children Plus, 3*(4) Article 1.

Utley, C. A., & Obiakor, F. E. (2001). Learning problems or learning disabilities of multicultural learners: Contemporary perspectives. In C. Utley & F. Obiakor (Eds.), *Special education, multicultural education, and school reform: Components of quality education for learners with mild disabilities* (pp. 90–117). Thomas.

Valle, J. W., & Connor, D. J. (2019). *Rethinking disability: A disability studies approach to inclusive practices* (2nd ed.). Routledge.

Valli, C., Lucas, C., Mulrooney K. J., & Rankin, M. N. P. (2011). *The linguistics of American Sign Language: An introduction* (5th ed.). Gallaudet University Press.

Van Cleve, J. V. (Ed.). (2007). *The Deaf history reader*. Gallaudet Press.

van den Pol, R. A., Iwata, B. A., Ivancic, M. T., Page, T. J., Neef, N. A., & Whitley, F. P. (1981). Teaching the handicapped to eat in public places: Acquisition, generalization and maintenance of restaurant skills. *Journal of Applied Behavior Analysis, 14*, 61–69.

van der Lee, J. H., Mokkink, L. B., Grootenhuis, M. A., Heymans, H. S., & Offringa, M. (2007). Definitions and measurement of chronic health conditions in childhood: A systematic review. *Journal of the American Medical Association, 297*, 2741–2751.

Van Dycke, J. L., Martin, J. E., & Lovett, D. L. (2006). Why is this cake on fire? Inviting students into the IEP process. *Teaching Exceptional Children, 38*(3), 42–47.

Van Heijst, B. F. C., & Geurts, H. M. (2015). Quality of life in autism across the lifespan: A meta-analysis. *Autism, 19*, 158–167.

van Karnebeek, C. D. M., Scheper, F. Y., Abeling, N. G., Alders, M. K., Barth, P. G., Hoovers, J. M. N., Koevoets, C., Wanders, R. J. A., & Hennekam, R. C. M. (2005). Etiology of mental retardation in children referred to a tertiary care center: A prospective study. *American Journal on Mental Retardation, 110*, 253–267.

Van Riper, C., & Erickson, R. L. (1996). *Speech correction: An introduction to speech pathology and audiology* (9th ed.). Allyn & Bacon.

Van Riper, M. (2007). Families of children with Down syndrome: Responding to "a change in plans" with resilience. *Journal of Pediatric Nursing, 22*, 116–128.

Van Tassel-Baska, J. (2013). The integrated curriculum model. In C. M. Callahan & H. L. Hertberg-Davis (Eds.), *Fundamentals of gifted education* (pp. 315–326). Routledge.

Vanegas, S. B., & Abdelrahim, R. (2016). Characterizing the systems of support for families of children with disabilities: A review of the literature. *Journal of Family Social Work, 19*, 286–327.

Vannest, K. J., Burke, M. D., Payne, T. E., Davis, C. R., & Soares, D. A. (2011). Electronic progress monitoring of IEP goals and objectives. *Teaching Exceptional Children, 43*(5), 40–51.

Vannest, K. J., Davis, J. L., Davis, C. R., Mason, B. A., & Burke, M. D. (2010). Effective intervention and measurement with a daily behavior report card: A meta-analysis. *School Psychology Review*, 39(4), 654–672.

Vaughn, S., & Wanzek, J. (2014). Intensive interventions in reading for students with reading disabilities: Meaningful impacts. *Learning Disabilities Research & Practice,29*(2), 46–53.

Vaughn, S., Zumeta, R., Wanzek, J., Cook, B., & Klinger, J. (2014). *Intensive interventions for students with learning disabilities in the RTI era*. Position Statement #1.

Vissers, L. E., Gilissen, C., & Veltman, J. A. (2016). Genetic studies in intellectual disability and related disorders. *Nature Reviews Genetics*, *17*(1), 9–18.

Vogelgesang, K. L., Bruhn, A. L., Coghill-Behrends, W. L., Kern, A. M., & Troughton, L. C. W. (2016). A single-subject study of a technology-based self-monitoring intervention. *Journal of Behavioral Education*, *25*, 478–497.

Volk, H. E., Lurmann, F., Penfold, B., Hertz-Picciotto, I., & McConnell, R. (2013). Traffic-related air pollution, particulate matter, and autism. *JAMA Psychiatry*, *70*(1), 71–77.

Voltz, D. L. (1994). Developing collaborative parent-teacher relationships with culturally diverse parents. *Intervention in School and Clinic*, *29*, 288–291.

Vu, J. A., Babikian, T., & Asarnow, R. F. (2011). Academic and language outcomes in children after traumatic brain injury: A meta-analysis. *Exceptional Children*, *77*, 263–281.

Wagner, L. (2009, June). *Juvenile re-offense report*. Lane County Department of Youth Services.

Wagner, M., & Newman, L. (2012). Longitudinal transition outcomes of youth with emotional disturbances. *Psychiatric Rehabilitation Journal*, *35*(3), 199–208.

Wagner, M., Kutash, K., Duchnowski, A. J., Epstein, M. H., & Sumi, C. (2005). The children and youth we serve: A national picture of the characteristics of students with emotional disturbances receiving special education. *Journal of Emotional and Behavioral Disorders*, *11*, 194–197.

Wagner, M., Newman, L., Cameto, R., & Levine, P. (2005). *Changes over time in the early postschool outcomes of youth with disabilities: A report of findings from the National Longitudinal Transition Study (NLTS) and the National Longitudinal Transitional Study-2*. SRI International.

Wagner, M., Newman, L., Cameto, R., & Levine, P. (2006). *The academic achievement and functional performance of youth with disabilities. A report from the National Longitudinal Transition Study-2 (NLTS2)* (NCSER 2006–300o). SRI International.

Wagner, M., Newman, L., Cameto, R., Levine, P., & Marder, C. (2007). *Perceptions and expectations of youth with disabilities. A special topic report of findings from the National Longitudinal Transition Study-2 (NLTS2)* (NCSER 2007–3006). SRI International.

Wagner, R. K., Torgeson, J. K., & Rahsotte, C. A. (1999). *Comprehensive Test of Phonological Processing*. PRO-ED.

Wahl, H., Kämmerer, A., Holz, F., Miller, D., Becker, S., Kaspar, R., & Himmelsbach, I. (2006). Psychosocial intervention for age-related macular degeneration: A pilot project. *Journal of Visual Impairment and Blindness*, *101*, 533–544.

Wakefield, A. J., Murch, S. H., Anthony, A., Linnell, J., Casson, D. M., Malik, M., Berelowitz, M., Dhillon, A. P., Thomson, M. A., Harvey, P., Valentine, A., Davies, S. E., & Walker-Smith, J. A. (1998). Ileal-lymphoid-nodular hyperplasia, non-specific colitis, and pervasive developmental disorder in children. *The Lancet*, *351*, 637–641.

Waldron, N., McLeskey, J., & Redd, L. (2011). Setting the direction: The role of the principal in developing an effective, inclusive school. *Journal of Special Education Leadership*, *24*, 51–60.

Walker, A. R., Richter, S., Uphold, N. M., & Test, D. W. (2010). Review of the literature on community-based instruction across grade levels. *Education and Training in Autism and Developmental Disabilities*, 456(3), 242–267.

Walker, B., Shippen, M. E., Alberto, P., Houchins, D. E., & Cihak, D. F. (2005). Using the expressive writing program to improve the writing skills of high school students with learning disabilities. *Learning Disabilities Research & Practice*, *20*(3), 175–183.

Walker, D., & Carta, J. J. (2010). The communication IGDI: Early Communication Indicator. In J. J. Carta, C. R. Greenwood, D. Walker, & J. Buzhardt (Eds.), *Using IGDIs: Monitoring progress and improving intervention results for infants and young children* (pp. 39–56). Brookes.

Walker, H. M. (1997). *The acting out child: Coping with classroom disruption* (2nd ed.). Sopris West.

Walker, H. M., & Gresham, R. M. (Eds.). (2014). *Handbook of evidence-based practices for emotional and behavioral disorders: Applications in schools*. Guilford.

Walker, H. M., McConnell, S., Holmes, D., Todis, B., Walker, J., & Golden, N. (1988). *The ACCEPTS program: A curriculum for children's effective peer and teacher skills*. PRO-ED.

Walker, H. M., Severson, H. H., & Feil, E. G. (2014). *Systematic screening for behavior disorders (SSBD)* (2nd ed. for pre-K–Grade 9). Pacific Northwest.

Walker, H. M., & Sprague, J. R. (1999). The path to school failure, delinquency, and violence: Causal factors and some potential solutions *Intervention in School and Clinic*, *35*, 67–73.

Walker, H. M., Todis, B., Holmes, D., & Horton, G. (1988). *ACCESS: Adolescent curriculum for communication and effective social skills*. PRO-ED.

Walker, L. A. (1986). *A loss for words: The story of deafness in a family*. Harper & Row.

Wallace, G., & Hammill, D. (2002). *Comprehensive Receptive and Expressive Vocabulary Test* (2nd ed.). PRO-ED.

Wandry, D., Wehmeyer, M., & Glor-Scheib, S. (2013). *Life centered education: The teacher's guide*. Council for Exceptional Children.

Wang, J., Bettini, E., & Cheyney, K. (2013). Students with emotional and behavioral disorders as peer tutors. *Beyond Behavior*, 23(1), 12–22.

Washburn, J., & Billingsley, B. (2019). Leading effective meetings with professionals and families. In J. McLeskey, L. Maheady, B. Billingsley, M. T. Brownell, & T. J. Lewis (Eds.), *High leverage practices for inclusive classrooms* (pp. 15–33). Routledge.

Watkins, C. L. (1997). *Project Follow Through: A case study of contingencies influencing instructional practices of the educational establishment*. Cambridge Center for Behavioral Studies. https://www.behavior.org/resources/901.pdf

Watkins, C. L., & Slocum, T. A. (2003). The components of Direct Instruction. *Journal of Direct Instruction*, *3*(2), 75–110.

Watkins, L., O'Reilly, M., Kuhn, M., Gevarter, C., Lancioni, G. E., Sigafoos, J., & Lang, R. (2015). A review of peer-mediated social interaction interventions for students with autism in inclusive settings. *Journal of Autism and Developmental Disorders*, *45*, 1070–1083.

Watt, M. (2020). *Aspiring to a more inclusive world: Molly Watt*. https://www.mollywatt.com/blog

Webb-Johnson, G. C. (2003). Behaving while black: A hazardous reality for African American learners. *Beyond Behavior*, *12*(2), 3–7.

Webber, J., & Plotts, C. A. (2008). *Emotional and behavioral disorders: Theory and practice* (5th ed.). Allyn & Bacon.

Wechsler, D. (2009). *Wechsler Memory Scale—Fourth Edition (WMS–IV) technical and interpretive manual*. Pearson.

Wechsler, D. (2014). *Wechsler Intelligence Scale for Children* (5th ed.). Psychological Corporation.

Wehby, J. H., & Lane, K. L. (2019). Classroom management. In S. G. Little & A. Akin-Little (Eds.), *Behavioral interventions in schools: Evidence-based positive strategies* (pp. 61–76). American Psychological Association.

Wehman, P. (2011). *Essentials of transition planning*. Brookes.

Wehman, P., & Kregel, J. (Eds.). (2020). *Functional curriculum for elementary and secondary students with special needs* (3rd ed.). PRO-ED.

Wehman, P., Kregel, J., Shafer, M., & West, M. (1989). *Emerging trends in supported employment: A preliminary analysis of 27 states.* Virginia Commonwealth University, Rehabilitation Research and Training Center.

Wehman, P., Taylor, J., Brooke, V., Avellone, L., Whittenbury, H., Ham, W., Brooke, A. M., & Carr, S. (2018). Toward competitive employment for persons with intellectual and developmental disabilities: What progress have we made and where do we need to go. *Research and Practice for Persons with Severe Disabilities, 43,* 131–144.

Wehmeyer, M. L. (2006). Self-determination and individuals with severe disabilities: Reexamining meanings and misinterpretations. *Research and Practice in Severe Disabilities,* 30, 113–120.

Wehmeyer, M. L., Shogren, K., Palmer, S., Williams-Diehm, K., Little, T., & Boulton, A. (2012). Impact of the *Self-Determined Learning Model of Instruction* on student self-determination: A randomized-trial placebo control group study. *Exceptional Children, 78,* 135–153.

Wei, X., Yu, J. W., & Shaver, D. (2014). Longitudinal effects of ADHD in children with learning disabilities or emotional disturbances. *Exceptional Children, 80,* 205–219.

Weiner, M. T., Day, S. J., & Galvan, D. (2013). Deaf and hard of hearing students' perspectives on bullying and school climate. *American Annals of the Deaf, 158,* 334–343.

Weintraub, F. J., & Abeson, A. (1974). New education policies for the handicapped: The quiet revolution. *Phi Delta Kappan, 55,* 526–529, 569.

Wenzel, C., & Rowley, L. (2010). Teaching social skills and academic strategies to college students with Asperger's syndrome. *Teaching Exceptional Children, 42*(5), 44–50.

Werfel, K. L. (2017). Emergent literacy skills in preschool children with hearing loss who use spoken language: Initial findings from the Early Language and Literacy Acquisition (ELLA) study. *Language, Speech, and Hearing Services in Schools,48,* 249–259.

Werts, M. G., Hoffman, E. M., & Darcy, C. (2011). Acquisition of instructive feedback: Relation to target stimulus. *Education and Training in Autism and Developmental Disabilities,* 46, 134–149.

Werts, M. G., Wolery, M., Gast, D. L., & Holcomb, A. (1996). Sneak in some extra learning by using instructive feedback. *Teaching Exceptional Children, 28*(3), 70–71.

Wesson, C., Wilson, R., & Higbee Mandlebaum, L. (1988). Learning games for active student responding. *Teaching Exceptional Children, 20*(2), 12–14.

West, E., Leon-Guerrero, R., & Stevens, D. (2007). Establishing codes of acceptable schoolwide behavior in a multicultural society. *Beyond Behavior, 16*(2), 32–38.

Westling, D. L., Carter, E. W., DeFonte, M. A., & Kurth, J. A. (2021). *Teaching students with severe disabilities* (6th ed.). Pearson.

Wetherby, A., Woods, J., Allen, L., Cleary, J., Dickinson, H., & Lord, C. (2004). Early indicators of autism spectrum disorders in the second year of life. *Journal of Autism and Developmental Disorders, 34,* 473–493.

Wheeler, D. L., Jacobson, J. W., Paglieri, R. A., & Schwartz, A. A. (1993). An experimental assessment of facilitated communication. *Mental Retardation, 31,* 49–60.

Whitaker, S. (2008). The stability of IQ in people with low intellectual ability: An analysis of the literature. *Intellectual and Developmental Disabilities, 45,* 120–128.

Whitaker, S., & Gordon, S. (2012). Floor effects on the WISC-IV. *International Journal of Developmental Disabilities, 58*(2), 111–119.

Whitford, D. K., Liaupsin, C. J., Umbreit, J., & Ferro, J. B. (2013). Implementation of a single comprehensive function-based intervention across multiple classrooms for a high school student. *Education & Treatment of Children, 36,* 147–167.

Wieland, N., & Baker, B. L. (2010). The role of marital quality and spousal support in behaviour problems of children with and without intellectual disability. *Journal of Intellectual Disability Research, 54,* 620–633.

Wild, T. A., & Koehler, K. E. (2017). Science. In M. C. Holbrook, C. Kamei-Hannan, & T. McCarthy (Eds.), *Foundations of education: Instructional strategies for teaching children and youths with visual impairments* (3rd ed., pp. 449–478). AFB Press.

Wilens, T. E., Biederman, J., & Spencer, T. J. (2002). Attention deficit/hyperactivity disorder across the lifespan. *Annual Review of Medicine, 53,* 113–131.

Will, M. C. (1986). Educating children with learning problems: A shared responsibility. *Exceptional Children, 52,* 411–415.

Willard-Holt, C. (1998). Academic and personality characteristics of gifted students with cerebral palsy: A multiple case study. *Exceptional Children, 65,* 37–50.

Willcutt, E. G., Pennington, B. F., & DeFries, J. C. (2000). Etiology of inattention and hyperactivity/impulsivity in a community sample of twins. *Journal of Abnormal Child Psychiatry, 28,* 149–159.

Willey, L. H. (Ed.). (2003). *Asperger syndrome in adolescence: Living with the ups, the downs, and things in between.* Jessica Kingsley.

Williams, C. B., & Finnegan, M. (2003). From myth to reality: Sound information for teachers about students who are deaf. *Teaching Exceptional Children, 35*(3), 40–45.

Williams, K. J., Wray, J. J., & Wheeler, D. M. (2005). Intravenous secretin for autism spectrum disorder. *Cochrane Database of Systematic Reviews* 3:CD003495.

Williams, V. L., & Cartledge, G. (1997). Passing notes to parents. *Teaching Exceptional Children, 30*(1), 30–34.

Williamson, G. G. (1978). The individualized education program: An interdisciplinary endeavor. In B. Sirvis, J. W. Baken, & G. G. Williamson (Eds.), *Unique aspects of the IEP for the physically handicapped, homebound, and hospitalized.* Council for Exceptional Children.

Willings, C. (2020). *Adjust lighting & reduce glare.* https://www.teachingvisuallyimpaired.com/adjust-lighting.html

Wills, H., & Mason, B. (2014). Implementation of a self-monitoring application to improve on-task behavior: A high-school pilot study. *Journal of Behavioral Education, 23,* 421–434.

Wilson, C. L. (1995). Parents and teachers: "Can we talk?" *LD Forum, 20*(2), 31–33.

Wing, L. (1998). The history of Asperger syndrome. In E. Schopler, G. B. Mesibov, & L. J. Kunce (Eds.), *Asperger syndrome or high-functioning autism?* (pp. 11–28). Plenum.

Winter-Messiers, M. A. (2007). From tarantulas to toilet brushes: Understanding the special interest areas of children and youth with Asperger syndrome. *Journal of Remedial and Special Education, 28,* 140–152.

Winzer, M. (2009). *From integration to inclusion: A history of special education in the 20th century.* Gallaudet University Press.

Witty, P. A. (Ed.). (1951). *The gifted child.* Heath.

Wolery, M., & Ledford, J. R. (2014). Monitoring child progress. In M. E. McLean, M. L. Hemmeter, & P. Snyder (Eds.), *Essential elements for assessing infants and preschoolers with special needs.* Pearson.

Wolfe, L. H., Heron, T. E., & Goddard, Y. I. (2000). Effects of self-monitoring on the on-task behavior and written language performance of elementary students with learning disabilities. *Journal of Behavioral Education, 10,* 49–73.

Wolfensberger, W. (1972). *Normalization: The principle of normalization in human services.* National Institute on Mental Retardation.

Wolfensberger, W. (1983). Social role valorization: A proposed new term for the principle of normalization. *Mental Retardation, 21,* 234–239.

Wolfensberger, W. (2000). A brief overview of social role valorization. *Mental Retardation, 38*, 105–123.

Wolffe, K., & Kelly, S. M. (2011). Instruction in areas of the expanded core curriculum linked to transition outcomes for students with visual impairments. *Journal of Visual Impairment and Blindness, 105*, 340–349.

Wolford, P. L., Alber, S. R., & Heward, W. L. (2001). Teaching middle school students with learning disabilities to recruit peer assistance during cooperative learning group activities. *Learning Disabilities and Research and Practice, 16*, 161–173.

Wolfram, W., & Schilling, N. (2015). *American English: Dialects and variation* (3rd ed.). Wiley-Blackwell.

Wolters, N., Knoors, H., Cillessen, A. H. N., & Verhoven, L. (2014). Social adjustment of deaf early adolescents at the start of secondary school: The divergent role of withdrawn behavior in peer status. *Exceptional Children, 80*, 438–453.

Wong, C., Odom, S. L., Hume, K. A., Cox, C. W., Fettig, A., Kurcharczyk, S., et al. (2015). Evidence-based practices for children, youth, and young adults with autism spectrum disorder: A comprehensive review. *Journal of Autism and Developmental Disorders, 45*(7), 1951–1966.

Wong, C., Odom, S. L., Hume, K. Cox, A. W., Fettig, A., Kucharczyk, S., & Schultz, T. R. (2014). *Evidence-based practices for children, youth, and young adults with autism spectrum disorder*. The University of North Carolina, Frank Porter Graham Child Development Institute, Autism Evidence-Based Practice Review Group. http://autismpdc.fpg.unc.edu/sites/autismpdc.fpg.unc.edu/files/2014-EBP-Report.pdf

Wood, C. L., Kisinger, K. W., Brosh, C. R., Fisher, L. B., & Muharib, R. (2018). Stopping behavior before it starts: Antecedent interventions for challenging behavior. *Teaching Exceptional Children, 50*(6), 356–363.

Woodcock, R. W. (2011). *Woodcock Reading Mastery Tests—3rd Edition*. American Guidance Services.

Woodman, A. C., Demers, L., Crossman, M. K., Warfield, M. E., & Hauser-Cram, P. (2018). Part C Early Intervention dosage and growth in adaptive skills from early childhood through adolescence. *Early Childhood Research Quarterly, 43*, 73–82.

Worcester, N. A., Nesman, T. M., Mendez, L. M., R. & Keller, H. R. (2008). Giving voice to parents of young children with challenging behavior. *Exceptional Children, 74*, 509–525.

Workforce Innovation and Opportunity Act of 2014, PL 113–128, STAT. 1634.

Wormsley, D. P. (2004). *Braille literacy: A functional approach*. AFB Press.

Worrell, F. C., Subotnik, R. F., Olszewski-Kubilius, P., & Dixson, D. D. (2019). Gifted students. *Annual Review of Psychology, 70*, 551–576.

Wortham, S. C., & Hardin, B. J. (2020). *Assessment in early childhood education* (8th ed.). Pearson.

Wright, C. F., & Burton, H. (2009). The use of cell-free fetal nucleic acids in maternal blood for non-invasive prenatal diagnosis. *Human Reproduction Update, 15*(1), 139–151.

Wright, P. W. D., & Wright, P. D. (2006). *Wrightslaw: Special education law* (2nd ed.). Harbor House Law Press.

Xin, J. F., & Sutman, F. X. (2011). Using the smart board in teaching social stories to students with autism. *Teaching Exceptional Children, 33*, 18–24.

Xin, W., Yu, J. W., & Shaver, D. (2014). Longitudinal effects of ADHD in children with learning disabilities or emotional disturbances. *Exceptional Children, 80*, 205–219.

Yairi, E. (1998). Is the basis for stuttering genetic? *American Speech-Language-Hearing Association, 70*(1), 29–32.

Yairi, E., & Ambrose, N. (2013). Epidemiology of stuttering: 21st century advances. *Journal of Fluency Disorders, 38*(2), 66–87.

Yairi, E., & Seery, C. H. (2014). *Stuttering: Foundations and clinical applications* (2nd ed.). Pearson.

Yell, M. L. (2019a). *The law and special education* (5th ed.). Pearson.

Yell, M. L. (2019b). Endrew F. v. Douglas County School District (2017): Implications for educating students with emotional and behavioral disorders. *Behavioral Disorders, 45*(1), 53–62.

Yell, M. L., & Bateman, D. F. (2017). Endrew F. v. Douglas Country School District (2017): FAPE and the Supreme Court. *Teaching Exceptional Children, 50*, 1–9.

Ylvisaker, M. (2005). Children with cognitive, behavioral, communication, and academic difficulties. In W. M. High, A. M. Sander, M. A. Struchen, & K. A. Hart (Eds.), *Rehabilitation for traumatic brain injury* (pp. 205–234). Oxford University Press.

Yoshinaga-Itano, C. (2006). Early identification, communication modality, and the development of speech and spoken language skills: Patterns and considerations. In P. E. Spencer & M. Marschark (Eds.), *Advances in the spoken language development of deaf and hard-of-hearing children* (pp. 298–327). Oxford University Press.

Young, N. D., & Johnson, K. (2019). The potency of the response to intervention framework (pp. 11–22). In N. D. Young, A. Fain, & T. A. Citro (Eds.), *Creating compassionate classrooms*. Vernon Press.

Young, N. D., Michael, C. N., & Citro, T. A. (2018). *From floundering to fluent: Reaching and teaching struggling readers*. Rowman and Littlefield.

Yuan, T., & Jiang, H. (2019). Culturally responsive teaching for children from low-income, immigrant families. *Young Exceptional Children, 22*(3), 150–161.

Yurick, A. L., Robinson, P. D., Cartledge, G., Lo, Y., & Evans, T. L. (2006). Using peer-mediated repeated readings as a fluency-building activity for urban learners. *Education & Treatment of Children, 29*, 469–506.

Zafeiriou, D. I., Ververi, A., Dafoulis, V., Kalyva, E., & Vargiami, E. (2013). Autism spectrum disorders: The quest for genetic syndromes. *American Journal of Medical Genetics, 162*(4), 327–366.

Zambo, D. M. (2010). Strategies to enhance the social identities and social networks of adolescent students with disabilities. *Teaching Exceptional Children, 43*(2), 28–35.

Zane, T. (2011, Summer). Apophenia: One explanation for the adoption of fad treatments in autism. Clinical corner: Educating for inclusion. *Science in Autism Treatment, 8*(2), 12–14.

Zane, T., Davis, C., & Rosswurm, M. (2008). The cost of fad treatments in autism. *Journal of Early and Intensive Behavior Intervention, 5*(2), 44–51.

Zebehazy, K. T., & Smith, T. J. (2011). An examination of characteristics related to the social skills of youths with visual impairments. *Journal of Visual Impairment and Blindness, 105*, 84–95.

Zechella, A. N., & Raval, V. V. (2018). Parenting children with intellectual and developmental disabilities in Asian Indian families in the United States. *Journal of Child & Family Studies, 25*, 1295–1309.

Zelinsky, N. A., & Shadish, W. (2018). A demonstration of how to do a meta-analysis that combines single-case designs with between-groups experiments: The effects of choice making on challenging behaviors performed by people with disabilities. *Developmental Neurorehabilitation, 21*(4), 266–278.

Zelleke, T. G., Depositario-Cabacar, D. F. T., & Gaillard, W. D. (2019). Epilepsy. In M. L. Batshaw, N. J. Roizen, & L. Pellegrino (Eds.), *Children with disabilities* (8th ed.). Brookes.

Zhang, J., & Wheeler, J. J. (2011). A meta-analysis of peer-mediated interventions for young children with autism spectrum disorders. *Education and Training in Autism and Developmental Disabilities, 46*, 62–77.

Zigmond, N. (2003). Where should students with disabilities receive special education services? Is one place better than another? *The Journal of Special Education, 37*, 193–199.

Zigmond, N. (2007). Delivering special education is a two-person job: A call for unconventional thinking. In J. B. Crockett, M. M. Gerber, & T. J. Landrum (Eds.), *Radical reform of special education: Essays in honor of James M. Kauffman*. Erlbaum.

Zigmond, N., & Kloo, A. (2011). General and special education are (and should be) different. In J. M. Kauffman & D. P. Hallahan (Eds.), *Handbook of special education* (pp. 160–172). Taylor & Francis.

Zigmond, N., Kloo, A., & Lemons, C. J. (2011). IEP Team decision-making for more inclusive assessments: Policies, percentages, and personal decisions. In S. Elliott, R. Kettler, P. Beddow, & A. Kirz (Eds.), *Handbook of accessible achievement tests for all students* (pp. 69–82). Springer.

Zigmond, N., Kloo, A., & Volonino, V. (2009). What, where, and how? Special education in the climate of full inclusion. *Exceptionality, 17*, 189–204.

Zijlstra, H. P., & Vlaskamp, C. (2005). The impact of medical conditions on the support of children with profound intellectual and multiple disabilities. *Journal of Applied Research in Intellectual Disabilities, 18*, 151–161.

Zimmerman, K. N., Ledford, J. R., & Severini, K. E. (2019). Brief report: The effects of a weighted blanket on engagement for a student with ASD. *Focus on Autism and Other Developmental Disabilities, 34*, 15–19.

Zirkus, K. J., & Morgan, J. J. (2020). Enhancing self-determination skills for students with emotional and behavioral disorders. *Intervention in School and Clinic, 55*(4), 238–244.

Zubal-Ruggieri, R. (2007). Making links, making connections: Internet resources for self-advocates and people with developmental disabilities. *Intellectual and Developmental Disabilities, 45*, 209–215.

Name Index

A

AAIDD Ad Hoc Committee on Terminology and Classification, 99, 100, 102, 108, 109, 110
AAP Council on Children with Disabilities, 208
Abdelrahim, R., 73, 74
Abeling, N.G., 109
Abeson, A., 60
Abrahams, Y., 272
Abrams, B.J., 187
Achenbach, T.M., 174
Adams, C.M., 208, 398
Adams, D., 199
Adams, G., 135
Adams, S.R., 146
Adamson, R., 188
ADHD Parents Magazine, 323
Adrian, M., 166
Afifi, T.O., 173
Agnew, J.A., 199
Agniel, D., 205
Agosta, J.M., 71, 72
Agran, M., 106, 114, 312, 364
Aguilar, C.M., 153, 427
Ahearn, W.H., 207
Ahlgren, C., 374
Ahlgrim-Delzell, L., 114, 362, 369
Aiken, E., 80
Airasian, P.W., 397
Aitken, A.A., 133
Akamatsu, C.T., 279
Akers, J.S., 215
Akmal, T., 252
Al Otaiba, S., 241
Al-Hassan, S., 85–87
Alawad, H., 277
Albarico, M., 451
Alber-Morgan, S.R., 25, 113, 114, 133, 144, 148, 151, 155, 168, 171, 180, 186, 212, 213, 215, 272, 309, 456, 459
Alber, S.R., 105, 153, 168, 169, 180, 200, 222, 249
Alberto, P.A., 55, 119, 151, 181, 217, 249, 341, 342, 456
Albin, R.W., 176
Alcalay, A., 217
Alders, M.K., 109
Aldrich, F.K., 308
Alexander, T., 265
Alexandru-Abrams, D., 332
Alfirevic, A., 111
Alghamdi, A.A., 133
Ali, Z., 106
Allday, R.A., 180
Allen, K.E., 180
Allen, L., 208
Allison, C., 199
Allman, C.B., 304
Alonzo, J., 42
Alper, S., 341
Alphonso, V.C., 130, 138
Alsalamah, A., 320, 321
Alston-Knox, C., 199
Alter, P.J., 180, 181
Alverson, C.Y., 79, 448, 452
Alves, K.D., 153
Aman, M., 91, 212
Amandi, C., 75
Amanullah, S., 323
Ambrose, N., 238, 249
Ambrose, S.E., 271
American Academy of Pediatrics, 207, 323
American Association on Mental Retardation, 220
American College of Medical Genetics, 421
American Federation for the Blind, 8
American Foundation for the Blind, 296, 311
American Optometric Association, 296
American Printing House for the Blind, 293, 305, 308
American Speech-Language-Hearing Association, 166, 231, 235, 239
Amerine-Dickens, M., 211
An, J.-Y., 206
An, X., 162
Anderegg, M.L., 70
Andersen, M., 460
Anderson, 179, 222
Anderson, B.N., 387
Anderson, C., 206
Anderson, D., 109, 184
Anderson, L., 109
Anderson, L.L., 25, 133
Anderson, L.W., 397
Anderson, S.E., 202
Andrews, J., 279
Andrews, M.E., 74
Angell, M.E., 78, 343
Angold, A., 170
Ankeny, E.M., 445
Anthony, A., 207
Anthony, D., 277
Antle, B.J., 333
Anxiety Disorders Association of America, 166
APA (American Psychiatric Association), 100, 166, 196, 197, 318, 319, 320
APA (American Psychological Association), 220
Appel, K., 73
APSE, 456
Aramburo, C., 372
Araujo, B.E., 74, 77
Archer, A.L., 147, 151
Arcia, E., 74, 75, 77
Arden, S.V., 61
Arishi, L., 8
Armstrong v. Kline, 18
Armstrong, D.F., 278
Arndt, S.A., 51
Arnold, K., 106
Arnott, S., 248
Arnott, W., 272
Arora, T., 55
Arrowood, L, 323, 324
Arter, C., 306, 308
Arthur-Kelly, M., 375
Arthur, M., 355
Artiles, A.J., 57
Artomoy, M., 206
Asarnow, J.R., 166
Asarnow, R.F., 354, 355, 359, 373
ASHA (American Speech-Language-Hearing Association), 236, 238, 251, 253, 264, 265
Asherson, P., 320
Ashworth, K.E., 134
Asmus, J., 56, 120
Asperger, H., 195
Association for Science in Autism Treatment (ASAT), 205
Assouline, S.G., 395
Asthma and Allergy Foundation of America, 328
Attkisson, C.C., 170
Attwood, T., 202, 217
Augestad, L.B., 292
Ault, M.J., 29, 341, 364, 461
Aurora, P.G., 164

Austen, S., 265
Austin, D., 452
Autism Navigator, 208
Autism Society, 202
Autism Speaks, 8
Avant, D.W., 39
Avellone, L., 454
Avila, V., 451
Avina, C., 166
Axe, J., 56
Axe, J.B., 186, 213
Ayres, B., 57
Ayres, K.M., 252, 364

B

Babikian, T., 354, 355, 359, 373
Badar, J., 8, 364, 374
Baddeley, A., 104, 134
Baer, D.M., 119, 211, 213, 222, 357
Baer, R.M., 446, 453, 461
Bailey, D., 74, 75, 77
Bailey, D.B., 110, 423
Bak, S., 293
Baker, B.L., 73
Baker, J., 362
Baker, J.N., 113, 369
Baker, K., 279
Baker, S., 152, 279
Balandin, S., 375
Balasubramanian, L., 372
Balboni, G., 102
Baldwin, L., 393
Balefire Labs, 219
Bambara, L.M., 114, 361, 363, 461
Banaschewski, T., 171, 320
Bancroft, T., 207
Banda, D.R., 92, 116, 215
Bandini, L., 202
Banerjee, R., 56
Banks, C.A.M., 10, 44, 74
Banks, J.A., 10, 44, 74
Barbash, S., 150
Barbetta, P., 321
Barclay, L., 308
Barclay, L.A., 295
Barczak, M.A., 113, 369
Barkel, A., 133
Barkley, R.A., 318, 319, 320
Barlow, J.A., 248
Barnard-Brak, L., 209
Barnes, M.A., 130, 132, 133, 134
Barnhill, B.A., 372
Baron-Cohen, S., 197, 199, 208
Barr, A., 342
Barrington, L., 107
Barry, C.T., 186
Barth, P.G., 109
Bartholomew, A., 447, 460
Bartholomew, A.L., 447
Bartlett, W., 113
Barton, E.E., 428
Barton, M., 208, 209
Basbigill, A.R., 364
Bashinski, S.M., 113
Bass-Ringdahl, 267
Bassett, D., 453
Bat-Chava, Y., 281
Bateman, B.D., 46, 48, 50, 51
Bates, A., 70
Bates, J.E., 162
Batshaw, M.L., 326, 359
Batten, G., 265
Bauer, P.E., 73, 103, 111
Baum, S.M., 393
Bauman-Waengler, J., 237
Baumgart, D., 370, 371
Bausch, M.E., 341, 364
Baxter, D., 70
Bayley, 422
Baylot-Casey, L., 184
BBC News, 204
Beach, K.D., 141
Beam, A., 205
Bean, S.M., 400
Bearman, P., 204
Bearss, K., 91, 212
Beattie, J., 51
Beaulieu, L., 371
Beaver, B.N., 213
Becerra-Culqui, T.A., 207
Beck, J., 113
Becker, B.L.C., 137
Becker, S., 290
Becker, Wesley, 150
Bedsem, P., 429
Beegle, G., 76, 78
Beghetto, R.A., 388
Behavior Analyst Certification Board, 371
Behm, J.A., 342
Behr, S.K., 70
Behrens, W.A., 395
Beighton, C., 70
Beime-Smith, M., 108
Beirne-Smith, M., 111
Belanger, J., 389
Belcastro, F., 299
Belifore, P.J., 184
Belk, G.D., 320
Bell, M.C., 177
Belmont, J.M., 104
Belote, M., 357
Benedict, B., 277
Beneke, M.R., 57
Benjamin, C., 137
Bennett, K., 320
Benson, S.K., 147
Benson, V., 325
Benz, M., 452, 457
Benz, M.R., 345
Berelowitz, M., 207
Bergeron, R., 104
Berk, M.S., 166
Berkeley, S., 42, 133
Berkman, B.E., 111
Berkman, N.D., 450
Berliner, C.D., 115
Bernier, A., 171
Berringer, V.W., 137
Bersani, H.A., 102
Besnoy, K.D., 400
Best, S.J., 325, 330, 332, 336, 339, 340, 341, 342, 460
Bethune, L., 447, 460
Bethune, L.K., 79
Bettelheim, B., 205
Bettini, E., 186
Betz, 341
Betz, A.M., 116
Bhaduri, A., 206
Bhukhanwala, F., 327, 341
Bianco, M., 393
Bicard, D.F., 184, 320
Bicard, S.C., 184
Bichay-Awadalla, K., 166
Biederman, J., 319, 337
Bierman, K.L., 186, 189
Bigge, J.L., 45, 325, 330, 339, 340, 342, 460
Biggs, E.E., 56, 120, 376, 456
Biklen, D., 220, 462
Bildiren, A., 387
Billingsley, B.S., 82, 84, 85
Billingsley, G., 153

Birkan, B., 197
Bisland, A., 400
Bitner-Glindzicz, M.A.K., 267
Blacher, J., 70, 74, 77
Blachman, B.A., 137
Black, R.S., 147
Blackburn, B.R., 131, 144
Blake, J.J., 345
Blalock, G., 453
Blanchard, C., 114
Blanchard, S.B., 57
Blanes, M., 75
Blank, A., 440, 441
Blankenship, K., 312
Blatt, B., 458
Blatz, E.T., 77
Blau, I., 87
Blaxhill, M.F., 204
Blesson, A., 111
Blissymbolics Communication International, 252
Block, M.E., 363
Bloom, B.S., 187, 397
Bloom, S.R., 325
Blue-Banning, M., 76, 78
Blue, C.W., 362
Bluestone, 267
Boavida, T., 427
Bobzien, J., 450, 452
Bobzien, J.L., 29, 452
Bocain, K.M., 141
Bodrova, E., 422
Boesche, M.C., 251, 252
Bogan, B.L., 166
Bogdan, R., 462
Bohlin, G., 319
Bolt, D.M., 56, 120
Bondy, A.H., 213
Bonilla, Z.E., 74
Book, D., 308
Boon, R.T., 152, 153
Boreson, L., 44
Borgna, G., 272
Born, T.L., 56, 120
Bornstein, H., 277
Borthwick-Duffy, S.A., 102
Botteron, K.N., 208
Botts B.H., 29
Bouchard, D., 292
Bouck, E.C., 113, 121, 152
Boudewyns, A.N., 267
Bouffard, S., 87
Boulton, A., 105, 114
Boushey, A., 70
Boutot, E.A., 212
Bovaird, J.A., 113
Bowe, F., 336
Bower, E.M., 163
Bowman-Kruhm, M., 148
Bowman-Perrott, L., 178
Bowman, N.A., 441
Boyd-Ball, A., 75
Boykin, A.W., 44
Boyle, C., 8
Boyle, J.R., 147, 154
Bracken, M., 213
Braddock, D., 454, 458
Bradley-King, K.L., 321
Bradley, K.E., 52
Bradley, V.J., 71, 72
Bradshaw, M., 253
Brady, S., 214
Brain Injury Association of America, 359
Brambring, M., 292
Brame, R., 170
Brandeis, D., 171, 320
Brandon, R.R., 74, 77
Braun, S.S., 186
Brawner, J., 277
Bredecamp, S., 413, 428
Breen, M.S., 206
Brennan, K.B., 153
Brewer, A., 209
Brian, A., 292
Bricker, D., 421, 432
Bridgman, K., 248
Brigance Early Childhood Screens, 421
Brigance, A.H., 139
Briggs, D.C., 398
Briggs, R.J., 272
Brigham, F., 181, 188
Brigham, N., 153, 375
Brindle, M., 152
Bristol, 195
Broadhead, M.T., 215
Brobst, J.B., 73
Brock, L.L., 162
Brock, M.E., 56, 120, 376
Brocki, K.C., 319
Broers, J., 113
Brogaard, B., 199
Bronicki, G.J., 82–83
Brooke, A.M., 454
Brooke, V., 454
Brooks, D.G., 368, 456
Brooks, D.S., 188, 189
Broom, A., 292
Brophy-Dick, A.A., 181
Brosh, C.R., 103, 213, 371
Bross, L.A., 371, 372
Brotherson, M.J., 341
Browder, D., 362
Browder, D.M., 50, 103, 113, 114, 362, 364, 367, 369, 450
Brown, F., 60, 250, 343, 367, 369, 370, 372
Brown, G.L., 452
Brown, L., 361, 370, 374, 375, 376, 452
Brown, M.R., 74, 77
Brown, T., 169
Brown, T.S., 153, 424, 429
Brown, V.L., 138
Brown, W.H., 174
Brownell, C.A., 429
Brownell, M.T., 51
Brozovic, S.A., 55
Bruce, S.M., 372
Bruhn, A., 184, 321
Bruhn, A.L., 322
Brulles, D., 404
Brun-Gasca, C., 110
Bruner, E.C., 148, 150
Bruzek, J., 213
Bryant, B., 244
Bryant, D.M., 414
Bryant, D.P., 138
Buchanan, A., 460
Buck Institute, 400
Budin, S.G., 184
Buell, J.S., 180
Buikema, A., 207
Buitelaar, J., 320
Bulgren, J.A., 135, 153
Bull, R., 264
Bulotsky-Shearer, R.J., 166
Bulthe, J., 137
Bunch-Crump, K., 446
Bundy, A.C., 292
Bureau of Labor Statistics, 441
Burgess, S., 456
Burghardt, J., 169
Burgoon, J.K., 230
Burke, E., 393
Burke, M.D., 86, 178
Burke, P.J., 8

Burke, S.M., 337
Burnette, K.K., 376
Burns, D.A., 361
Burns, D.E., 394, 395
Burns, R., 114, 361, 363, 461
Bursuck, W.D., 56, 148
Burton, H., 111
Burton, M.E., 152
Busch, T., 323, 324
Butler, M.G., 108
Butter, E., 91, 212, 219
Buxbaum, J.D., 206
Buysse, V., 424
Bybee, J., 104
Byrd, S., 189
Byrne, B., 137
Byzek, J., 333

C

Caggiano, J.F., 323
Cagliani, R.R., 252
Cagliostro, E., 451
Cahen, L.S., 115
Cakiroglu, 181
Calaluce, P.D., 82–83
Caldarella, P., 180
Callahan, C.M., 401
Callahan, K., 93, 171
Callus, A.M., 106
Cambell, K.A., 303
Cameron, D.L., 55
Cameto, R., 79, 357, 440, 441, 442, 452
Camodeca, A., 209
Campbell-Whatley, G., 183
Campbell, A.R., 178
Campbell, D., 70
Campbell, F.A., 414
Campbell, J., 292
Campbell, J.M., 197
Campbell, P.H., 343
Campbell, R.A., 319, 320
Cannella-Malone, H.I., 113, 197, 364, 368, 371, 456, 459
Cannon, C., 323
Cantrell, R.J., 151
Cantu, C.O., 342
Cantwell, E.D., 371
Carbone, E., 113
Cardon, T.A., 460
Carey, B., 248
Carey, J.P., 267
Carlin, M.T., 104
Carlson, C.L., 450
Carlson, E., 42
Carnine, D.W., 135, 146, 150, 152, 154
Caron, S.L., 70, 73, 207
Carr, C., 171
Carr, J.E., 222
Carr, S., 454
Carroll, J.M., 237
Carroll, R.A., 116
Carta, J., 423
Carta, J.J., 58, 166, 423
Carter, A.S., 77, 208
Carter, E.W., 56, 120, 355, 367, 369, 376, 452, 456
Carter, M., 220, 424
Carter, N.J., 83
Carter, N.P., 111
Carter, W.W., 376
Cartledge, G., 25, 43, 44, 74, 86, 168, 179, 181, 321
Carvalho, A.F., 104
Casagrande, K., 209
Cascalla, P.W., 362
Cascella, P.W., 249
Casey, K.J., 147
Cashen, K., 375
Casner-Lotto, J., 107
Casson, D., 207
Castellano, J., 391, 392
Catalano, R.F., 174
Cattey, G.N., 56, 120
Causton-Theoharis, J., 370
Cavallaro, C., 374
Cavallini, F., 135
Cavendish, W., 43, 445, 446
Cavioni, V., 135
Cavkaytar, A., 72, 92
Cawthon, S.W., 281
CCBD (Council for Children with Behavorial Disorders), 188
CDC (Centers for Disease Control and Prevention), 108, 170, 199, 204, 319, 320, 323, 326, 327, 329, 330, 331, 359
Cease-Cook, J., 453
CEC (Council for Exceptional Children), 19, 30, 59
Celeste, M., 292
Center for Applied Special Technology, 17
Center for Change in Transition Services, 444
Center on the Developing Child, 319
Cerney, J., 281
Cervantes, P., 109
Chan, J.M., 371
Chapman, R., 106
Charania, S.M., 222
Chard, D.J., 29, 155
CHARGE Syndrome Foundation, 360
Charlton, C.T., 180
Chawarska, K., 205
Chazin, K.T., 430
Chen, C., 428
Chen, C.A., 209
Chen, D., 428, 431, 432
Chen, D.C., 295, 299, 362, 372
Chen, Deborah, 419
Chen, M., 69, 162
Chen, R., 56, 120
Chen, T.Y., 104
Chen, Y.W., 104
Cheng, L.-R.L., 245, 246
Cheng, Y.S., 104
Cherkasova, M.V., 320
Chesley, G.M., 82–83
Chestnut, S.R., 209
Cheyney, K., 186
Chiang, B., 44
Chiarotti, F., 204
Chiasson, K., 70
Chin, E.M., 331
Chinn, P.C., 74
Chitiyo, J., 181
Chiu, V., 207
Choi, A., 219
Choi, G., 428
Choo, D., 272
Chou, I, 171
Chow, J.C., 166
Christensen-Sandfort, R.J., 29, 251
Christensen, W.R., 51
Christiansen, K., 222
Chrysler, C., 104
Chua, B.Y.E., 252
Chung, D.Y., 323
Church-Pupke, P., 461
Cicchetti, D.V., 102
Cihak, D.F., 119, 151, 456
Cillessen, A.H.N., 265
Cimera, R.E., 456
Cioffi, A., 454
Citro, T.A., 132
Ciullo, S., 153, 178
Clarenbach, J., 400
Clark, B.A., 387, 390, 391, 392, 393, 397
Clark, D.M., 85
Clark, G.M., 446, 453

Clark, K.A., 107, 114, 184, 450, 456
Clatterbuck, C.C., 344
Clausen, J.A., 99
Clay, K., 56
Cleary, J., 208
Cloninger, C.J., 51, 69, 366
Clopton, J.R., 73
Cmar, J.L., 306, 307
Cobb Morocco, C., 56
Cobb, B., 114
Coco, C.M., 445
Coffin, A.B., 202
Coghill-Behrends, W.L., 322
Coghill, D., 320
Cohen, H., 211
Cohen, J.S., 111
Cohen, M.J., 215, 216
Coie, J.D., 189
Colangelo, N., 395
Cole, C.M., 55
Cole, J., 323
Cole, S.M., 55
Coleman, L.J., 388
Coleman, O., 370
Coleman, T.J., 92
Collins, A.A., 133
Collins, B., 367, 369
Collins, B.C., 29, 114, 341, 363, 364, 365, 369, 376, 461
Collins, L., 208
Collins, L.W., 152
Collins, R., 206
Collins, T.A., 164
Collis, G.M., 274
Commission on Education of the Deaf, 281
Common, E.A., 371
Compton, D.L., 29, 134, 135
Compton, M.V., 261
Conley, R.W., 454
Conners, C.K., 318
Connolly, A.J., 138
Connolly, C.M., 265
Connor, D., 43
Connor, D.F., 323
Connor, D.J., 8, 445, 446
Conroy, M., 164, 166, 172, 189
Conroy, M.A., 174
Constable, R.T., 137
Constantinescu, G., 272, 276
Constantino, J.N., 208
Contreras, E., 79, 440, 442
Convertino, C., 272
Cook, B.G., 28, 55, 56, 155
Cook, E.H., Jr., 209
Cook, L., 46
Cook, R., 419
Cook, R.E., 428, 431, 432
Cook, S.C., 152
Cooke, N.L., 57, 92, 426
Cooley, C., 168, 178
Cooney, M., 56, 120
Cooper, H.L., 299
Cooper, J.O., 176, 178, 184, 212
Cooper, K.J., 364
Cooper, S.R., 369
Copeland, S.R., 43, 113, 376, 461
Copeland, W.E., 171
Corley, R., 137
Corn, 300, 301
Corn, 303
Corn, A.L., 295, 300, 303, 309
Cornelius-Freyer, M., 153
Cornett, O., 277
Cornett, R., 277
Correa, V.I., 45, 74, 75, 77
Corsano, P., 135
Corser, N., 345
Cortese, S., 320
Cortiella, C., 136
Cosgriff, J., 375
Costello, E.J., 170
Coster, W.J., 333
Coughlin, C., 151
Coulter, A., 8
Council for Exceptional Children, 61, 371
Counts, J., 166
Courchesne, E., 205
Court, J.H., 392
Courtade Little, G., 114
Courtade, G.R., 367
Courtemanche, A.B., 368
Couvillon, M.A., 48
Coventry, W.L., 137
Cowan, R., 272
Cox, A.W., 212
Cox, C.W., 212, 221, 222
Coyne, M.D., 29, 146, 154
Craft, M.A., 105, 168
Craig, M., 439, 463
Crandell, C.C., 276
Crawley, J., 205
Creech-Galloway, C., 114, 351, 363, 364, 378–379
Cregenzán-Royo, O., 110
Crenshaw, T.M., 323
Crimmins, D., 176
Crocket, L.J., 172
Croen, L., 206
Cronin, B.A., 113
Cronin, M.E., 114, 138
Cross, C.T., 43
Cross, S., 212
Cross, T.L., 388
Crossley, R., 220
Crossman, M.K., 415
Crowley, E.P., 78
Croyle, J., 209
Crozier, S., 217, 218
Crudden, A., 306, 307
Cruickshank, W.M., 128, 309
Cruikshank, K.A., 397
Crum, K.I., 169
Cuenca-Carlino, Y., 147
Cullen, J.M., 114, 151, 168, 215, 309, 456, 459
Cullinan, V., 212
Cumming, I.K, 51, 167
Cummins, J., 246
Cummins, O., 199
Cunningham, W., 107
Curby, T.W., 162
Curin, C., 202
Cutting, L., 241
Cuvo, A.J., 293
Cystic Fibrosis Foundation, 329

D

D'Andrea, F.M., 299
Da Fonte, M.A., 251, 252
Dabelea, D., 327
Dafoulis, V., 206
Dager, S.R., 205, 208
Daisey, M., 277
Dale, S., 217
Daley, D., 320
Daley, T.C., 42
Damer, M., 148
Danckaerts, M., 320
Dangel, H., 339
Daniels, J., 206
Daniels, N., 137

Danielson, L., 61
Dantzler, J.A., 219
Daoust, P.M., 222
Darcy, D., 116
Dardig, J.C., 84, 85, 88–89, 461
Dart, E.H., 164, 186
Datchuk, S.M., 151
Davenport, C., 272
Davenport, L.A., 430
Davenport, T.N., 72
Davern, L., 86
Davies, S.E., 207
Davis-Kean, P., 162
Davis-Temple, J., 428
Davis, A., 272
Davis, B., 135
Davis, C., 220
Davis, C.R., 86
Davis, G.A., 387, 390, 391, 393, 394, 395, 396, 400
Davis, G.E., 427
Davis, J.L., 86
Davis, J.M., 206
Davis, L., 374
Davis, M.L., 303
Davis, M.T., 51, 167
Davis, P.K., 364
Davis, R., 199
Davis, T., 340
Daviso, A.W., III, 461
Dawson, G., 202
Day, S.J., 265
de Beeck, H.O., 137
De Bortoli, T., 375
De Brito, S.A., 171
De Castro, B.O., 106
De Mers, M., 371
De Rubeis, S., 206
de Ruiter, K.P., 106
De Valenzuela, J.S., 43
DeafTEC, 282
DeAvila, E., 247
DeBar, R.M., 213
Debonis, D.A., 266
Deer, B., 207
DeFonte, M.A., 355, 367, 369
DeFries, J.C., 320
DeGrazia, R.L., 73
Deidrick, K.K.M., 373
Dekker, M.C., 106
DeLana, M., 279
Delano, M.E., 46
Delgado, P., 451
Dell, A.G., 340
Delquadri, J., 58, 115
Deltman, S.J., 272
Delwiche, L., 204
Demers, L., 415
Demetro, K., 77, 451
Deng, Y., 91, 212
Dennis, L.R., 428
Denton-Smith, P., 306
Depositario-Cabacar, D.F.T., 326
DeQuinzo, J.A., 197, 214
Deris, A.R., 428
Deshler, D.D., 135, 147, 153
DeSimone, J.R., 55, 155
DesJardin, J.L., 110
DeThorne, L.S., 241, 252
Detrich, R., 115
Dettmer, P., 376
Deutsch, C.K., 104
DeWalt, D.A., 450
Dhillon, A.P., 207
DiCarlo, C.F., 428
DiCicco-Bloom, E., 205
Dickey, S.E., 244
Dickinson, H., 208
Dickson, C.A., 104
Dickson, R.K., 401
Didden, R., 364
Didion, L.A., 181
Diegelmann, K.M., 51, 446
Diezman, C.M., 405
DiGuiseppi, C., 206
DiLavore, P.C., 209
Dillenberger, K., 212
Dillon, M.B.M., 186
Dilollo, A., 248
DiLorio, C., 327
Dimitropoulos, A., 108
Dingle, A.D., 325, 333
Dinkins, J.P., 199
DiPipi-Hoy, C., 369
Dishaw, M.M., 115
Dishion, T.J., 173
Dittman, R.W., 320
Divers, J., 327
Division for Early Childhood, 420, 426, 434
Dixson, D.D., 390, 391
Dockrell, J.E., 249
Dodds, J.B., 421
Dodge, K.A., 162, 189
Doepfner, M., 320
Doepke, K., 100
Dogoe, M., 116
Doherty, A., 213
Dolan, L., 327
Doll, B., 164
Doll, E.A., 99, 128
Domin, D., 441
Donley, C.R., 91
Donnelly, L., 109
Donohue, C.L., 266
Donovan, M.S., 43
Donovan, S., 450
Doren, B., 74, 440, 446
Dorman, D., 272
Dornan, D., 276
Dotson, W.H., 368
Doubet, S., 72
Dougherty, E.A., 151
Douglas, K.H., 147, 364, 451
Douma, J.C.H., 106
Dow, G.T., 388
Dowell, R.C., 272
Downing, J., 362
Downing, J.E., 236, 295, 299, 374
Downs, A., 220
Downs, K.R., 180
Downs, M.P., 263, 266
Downs, R.C., 220
Dowse, J.M., 291, 311
Doyle, M.B., 56, 120
Drasgow, E., 272, 279
Dube, W.V., 104
Duchaine, E.L., 181
Duchnowski, A.J., 170, 174
Duffy, J.R., 242
Duffy, M.L., 180
Dufrene, B.A., 180
Dugan, E.P., 222
Duke, J.M., 77, 451
Dukes, C., 43
Dumont-Mathieu, T., 209
Dunbar, S.B., 138
Dunlap, G., 73, 222
Dunlap, K., 372
Dunlap, K.D., 180
Dunn, D.M., 244
Dunn, L.M., 244

Dunn, M., 440, 441
Dunst, C., 69
DuPaul, G.J., 134, 320, 321, 323
Duppong-Hurley, K., 171
Durand, V.M., 176
Durkin, A., 272
Dyches, T.T., 83
Dyck, N.J., 376
Dye, H.B., 413
Dykens, E.M., 109
Dymond, S.K., 59, 60, 370, 374
Dyson, A., 8
Dyson, L., 81

E

Eagleson, K.L., 413
Eakins, A., 322
Earl, A., 254
Easterbrooks, S.R., 264
Easton, D., 273
Eboli, G., 135
Edens, R.M., 329
Edge, D., 85, 91, 93, 94
Edwards, C., 375
Edwards, S., 323
Ehlers, S., 209
Ehren, B.J., 254
Eichelberger, C., 370
Eidelman, S.M., 72
Eikeseth, S., 211, 212
Eisenberg, A., 299
Eisenhower, A., 77
Eklund, K., 134
Elbaum, B., 77
Eldevik, S., 212
Elison, J.T., 208
Elliot, L.B., 273
Elliot, S.N., 179
Ellis, E.S., 153
Ellis, N.R., 104
Ellison, C., 305
Emerson, R.W., 208, 305
Emmorey, K., 277, 279
Endo, S., 320
Engelhardt-Wells, K., 213
Engelman, M., 303
Engelmann, S., 138, 148, 150, 151
Engerrand, K.G., 391
Englehart, M., 397
Englund, L.W., 87
Eninger, L., 319
Ennis, R.P., 116, 147, 180, 184
Enright, R., 343
Epilepsy Foundation of America, 326, 327
Eppolito, A.M., 247
Epstein, M.H., 170, 171, 174, 175
Eran, A., 205
Erber, N.P., 276
ERIC/OSEP Special Project, 78
Erickson, R.L., 236
Erin, J.N., 300, 301, 309
Erting, C.J., 277
Ervin, A., 184
Erwin, E.J., 51, 75, 76, 77, 80, 91, 93, 433
Eslick, G.D., 207
Espelage, D.L., 164
Estabrooks, W., 275, 276
Estell, 134
Estes, A.M., 208
Evans, A., 114, 364
Evans, A.C., 208
Evans, D.D., 249
Evans, J.C., 340
Evans, T.L., 25
Eveleigh, E., 153
Everhart, J.M., 113
Everling, S., 239

F

Facomata, T.S., 213
Fagan, A.A., 174
Fahey, K.R., 232, 233, 235, 241
Fahme, T.A., 177
Fairchild, G., 169, 171
Fajardo, I., 451
Falcomata, T.S., 153
Falk, B.M., 343
Falkenberg, C., 321
Fall, A.M., 450
Fallin, M.D., 206
Fan, X., 69
Fanari, R., 134
Faraone, S.V., 337
Fargus-Malet, M., 415
Farinella, K.A., 233, 238, 241, 243
Farmer, E.M.Z., 189
Farmer, J.E., 373
Farmer, T.W., 188, 189
Farrington, K., 452
Farris, K.B., 337
Faw, G.D., 364
Fedrigon, A., 337
Feil, E.G., 175
Fein, D., 208, 209
Feiner, S.K., 302
Feldman, D.L., 166
Fendt, K.H., 414
Fenlon, A.G., 368
Ferguson, C.J., 166
Ferguson, D.L., 353, 371, 442, 462
Ferguson, K., 79, 440, 442
Ferguson, P.M., 70, 166, 442, 462
Ferrara, D.L., 445
Ferrell, K.A., 291, 301, 306
Ferrenkipf, C., 300
Ferretti, R.P., 147
Ferrin, M., 320
Ferro, J.B., 320
Fesperman, E., 56, 120
Fetko, E.E., 363
Fettig, A., 212, 221, 222
Feurer, I.D., 108
Fidler, D.J., 104, 108, 206
Fiedler, C.R., 44, 85
Filby, N.N., 115
Filter, K.J., 320
Fine, E.M., 323
Finkelstein, N., 400
Finn, C.E., 42, 61
Finnegan, M., 264
Finucane, B.M., 109
Fishbein, D.H., 171
Fisher, C.S., 115
Fisher, D., 56, 375
Fisher, K., 252
Fisher, L.B., 213, 371
Fisher, M., 374
Fisher, M.H., 113
Fishley, K.M., 25
Fitzgerald, J.L., 85
Flanagan, D.P., 130, 138
Flannagan, K., 29
Flaute, A.J., 322
Fleischmann, A., 207
Fleming, C.V., 364
Fleming, D., 372
Fletcher, J.M., 130, 132, 133, 134, 137, 450
Flexer, R., 364
Flexer, R.W., 446, 453, 454
Flexor, R.W., 29

Flood, S.M., 337
Flora, S.R., 180, 323
Flores, L., 166
Flores, M.M., 152
Flores, M.T., 180
Floress, M., 180
Florian, L., 8
Flower, A., 166, 186, 450
Flowers, C., 362
Flowers, C.P., 446
Floyd, J.H., 55
Floyd, K., 230
Floyd, R.G., 104, 109
Fluegge, L., 358, 374
Flynn, L.J., 141
Foil, C.R., 249
Foley, D.L., 170
Follari, L., 413
Fond, S., 220
Fonger, A.M., 213
Ford, A., 361, 370
Ford, D.C., 173
Ford, D.Y., 43, 44, 388, 391, 392, 397
Foreman, P., 375
Forness, S.R., 163, 166, 170, 323
Forney, P.E., 341, 342
Fornieles-Deu, A., 110
Fountain, L., 323
Fowler, C., 69, 79, 453
Fowler, C.H., 105, 443, 444, 446, 447, 448, 452
Fowler, S.E., 376, 461
Fox, L., 73
Fox, L.C., 423
Fox, N.A., 272
Foxx, R.M., 220
Fraley, M., 412, 430, 435
Francis, A., 106
Francis, G.L., 77, 451
Frandsen, K., 460
Frank, A.R., 456
Franke, B., 171
Frankenberger, W., 323
Frankenburg, W.K., 421
Frankland, H.C., 76, 78
Frantino, E.P., 213
Fraser, D.W., 184
Frazier, A.D., 391, 392
Frederick, L.D., 181, 249
Freeman-Green, S., 116, 181
Freeman, S., 212
Freeman, S.F.N., 170
Freitag, C.M., 171
Frey, J.R., 428
Frick, P.J., 171
Friedman, H.A., 265
Frielander, S., 171
Friend, M., 46, 56
Frisbie, D.A., 138
Frisby, M.B., 55
Fristoe, M., 244
Frith, U., 197, 208
Fritschman, N., 217
Frostig & Horne, 128
Frostig, Lefever & Whittlesey, 128
Frostig, M., 64, 73, 128
Fuchs, D., 29, 38, 58, 59, 60, 61, 62, 135, 142, 146
Fuchs, L.S., 29, 38, 58, 59, 60, 61, 62, 130, 132, 133, 134, 135, 142
Fujiura, G.T., 74, 109
Fulbright, R.K., 137
Fuller, K., 55
Fullerton, 180
Furlong, M.J., 170
Furness, T.A., 302
Furst, E., 397
Furtak, E.M., 398
Fusara, J.A., 151

G

Gaab, N., 137
Gable, R.A., 29, 180, 452
Gable, R.K., 113
Gabriels, R.L., 199
Gage, N.A., 172, 176, 181
Gagné, F., 386, 389
Gaillard, W.D., 326
Gajria, M., 147, 151
Gallagher, D.J., 61
Gallagher, P.A., 55
Gallaudet Research Institute, 265, 266, 272, 275, 277, 279, 281
Galley, V., 323
Gallop R., 166
Galloway, C.C., 364, 365, 369
Galvan, D., 265
Gandhi, A.G., 61
Gao, W., 413
Garay, S.V., 273
Garber, H., 413
Garber, M., 293, 311
Garberoglio, 282
Garcia-Albea, E., 213
Gardner, H., 386
Gardner, J.E., 51
Gardner, R., III, 57, 58, 85–87, 88
Garrett-Mayer, E., 207, 208
Garrick Duhaney, L.M., 44, 55
Garrison-Wade, D., 393
Gartin, B.C., 329
Garwood, J.D., 178
Garzona, M., 164, 174
Gast, D.L., 116, 215, 222, 368
Gathercole, S., 104
Gau, J.M., 440
Gauvreau, A.N., 215
Gear, S., 450, 452
Geary, T., 454
Gense, D.J., 293
Gense, M.H., 293
Gentry, M., 43, 404
Gentry, M.A., 279
Gerencser, K.R., 215
Gerges, S., 206
Gerhardt, P.F., 215, 216
Gerig, G., 208
Germer, K.A., 174, 371
Gershoff, E.T., 173
Gersten, R., 29, 135, 152
Geruschat, D.R., 295
Gestwicki, C., 424
Getahun, D., 207
Getch, Y., 327, 341
Getch, Y.Q., 373
Geurts, H.M., 462
Gevarter, C., 213, 429
Giangreco, M.F., 51, 56, 59, 60, 69, 120, 366, 370, 374
Gibson, C.E., 168
Gibson, N., 164, 174
Giler, J. Z., 134
Gilissen, C., 109
Gillberg, C., 209
Gillespie, A., 152
Gilliam, L.M., 187
Gillies, R.M., 57, 120, 121
Gilmore, J.H., 413
Gilmour, A.F., 178
Gilroy, S.P., 252
Gilson, C.B., 456

Ginis, K.A.M., 460
Girolametto, L., 429
Gitlin, L.N., 305
Glaeser, B.C., 217
Glasgow, M., 113
Gleason, M.M., 151
Glidden, L.M., 104
Glor-Scheib, S., 453
Goddard, Y.I., 321
Golas, M., 375
Gold, D., 303
Goldblatt, E., 261
Golden, N., 179
Goldin-Meadow, S., 279
Goldman, R., 244
Goldson, E., 199
Goldstein, A.P., 179
Goldstein, M., 323
Goldstein, S., 134, 318, 323
Golledge, R.G., 306
Gollnick, D.M., 74
Gomez, J., 74
Gompel, M., 303
Gonzalez-Mena, J., 80, 82, 83
Gonzalez, N., 75
Gonzalez, T., 43
Good, R. H., 140
Goodall, D.V., 342
Goodman, L.V., 60
Goodnight, C.L., 181, 446
Goodway, J., 292
Gordon, S., 101
Gore, J.C., 137
Gormley, L., 213
Gormley, M.J., 134
Gortmaker, S.L., 325
Gottermeier, L., 277
Graff, H., 77, 451
Gragg, M.N., 70
Graham Strong, J., 303
Graham, S., 133, 147, 148, 152
Grainge, M.J., 171
Gralla, J., 199
Gramberg, L., 305
Grandin, T., 203
Grandjean, P., 206
Grantham, T.C., 388
Gray, C.A., 217
Grazzani, I., 135
Green, B., 91, 212
Green, K.B., 184
Green, V.A., 219
Greenberg, M.T., 189
Greene, B.A., 51
Greene, G., 79, 444, 453
Greene, I., 25
Greene, S., 79, 440, 442
Greenwood, C., 166, 423
Greenwood, C.R., 58, 115
Gregg, N., 56, 155, 442
Gresham, F.M., 189, 211, 320
Gresham, R.M., 162, 164, 179
Griffin-Shirley, N., 304
Griffin, C., 454
Griffin, H.C., 303
Grigal, M., 51, 441
Grigorenko, E.L., 134
Grim, J.C., 250, 251
Grimmett, E., 215
Grinstien-Weiss, M., 74
Groen, A.D., 211
Grogan-Kaylord, A., 173
Grootenhuis, M.A., 325
Gross, M.U.M., 395
Grossen, B., 135, 149, 154
Grossi, T.A., 55, 106, 309, 446, 456
Grove, J., 206
Gruenewald, L., 361, 374, 376
Gruffydd, E., 199
Grünke, M., 152
Gu, H., 208
Guare, R., 177
Guerette, A.R., 300
Guerette, H., 305
Guerrero, L.K., 230
Guest, C.M., 274
Guiding Eyes for the Blind, 305
Guilford, J.P., 384, 388
Gül, S.O., 217
Gunby, K., 222
Guralnick, M.J., 415
Gustafson, G., 277
Guth, C., 376
Guthrie, C., 171
Gwalla-Ogisi, N., 308

H

Haas, W.H., 241, 242
Haber, M.G., 447
Hadley, P.A., 245
Haegele, J.A., 292
Hafner, L., 454, 458
Hagaman, J.L., 147, 148
Hage, C., 277
Hager, K.D., 363, 364, 365, 369
Hagiwara, H., 86
Hagner, D., 455
Hagopian, L.P., 71, 371
Haibach, P.S., 292
Haimson, J., 169
Hairrell, A., 29
Hak Lee, J., 109
Halberg, S., 44
Hale, J.E., 44
Haliday, L., 264
Hall, B.J., 241, 242
Hall, M., 29, 461
Hall, R.V., 115
Halle, J.W., 134
Halle, S., 217
Hallett, V., 91, 212
Halloran, J., 134
Hallum, R.A., 424
Halpern, A.S., 442
Haltiwanger, J.T., 333
Ham, R., 248
Ham, W., 454
Hameiri, M., 87
Hammill, D.D., 138, 244
Hammis, D., 454
Hampshire, P.K., 428
Hancock, N., 292
Handen, B., 91, 212
Hanhan, S.F., 81, 85
Hanley, G.P., 177, 213, 371
Hannah, M.E., 73
Hannah, R.B., 55
Hanner, S., 148
Hanratty, L.A., 213
Hanreddy, A., 236
Hanson, M.J., 80
Hanson, T., 400
Happé, F., 197, 199
Harayama, N., 332, 333, 341
Harbin, S.R., 430
Hardin, B.J., 420, 422, 423
Hardman, M.L., 8, 9
Harjusola-Webb, S., 429
Harlacher, J.E., 320
Harmon, D.A., 388
Harmston, K.A., 249

Harn, W., 253
Harper, G.F., 58, 116
Harrington, S.L., 340
Harris-Murri, N., 57
Harris, B., 393
Harris, F.R., 180
Harris, K.R., 133, 148, 152
Harrison, B., 212
Harrison, E., 248
Harrison, H., 271
Harry, B, 44, 77
Harry, B., 43, 44, 77, 78
Hart Barnett, J.E., 120
Hart Bennett, J.E., 106
Hart, B., 138, 233, 235
Hart, B.M., 180
Hart, D., 441
Hart, J., 214
Hart, J.E., 206
Harte, H.A., 69
Hartikaiinen, A.-L., 109
Hartman, E., 291
Hartman, K., 189
Hartman, M.A., 121
Hartway, S., 206
Harvey, P., 207
Hastings, R.P., 212
Hatlen, P., 312
Hattie, J., 115, 120
Hatton, D.D., 110
Hatton, H., 178
Hatzenbuhler, E.G., 186
Hauser-Cram, P., 415
Havey, J.M., 55
Havighurst, S.S., 171
Hawes, D.J., 171
Hawkins, L., 277
Haworth, S.M., 208
Hay, D., 320
Haydon, T., 180, 187
Hayes, W.O, 237
Hayiou-Thomas, M.E., 237
Haynes, W., 238
Haynes, D., 456
Haywood, H.C., 103
Hazlett, H.C., 208
Healy, S., 25
Heaton, P., 199
Heber, R., 413
Heber, R.F., 99
Hechtman, L., 320
Heflin, L.J., 217
Heftel, S.B., 133
Heikua, U., 109
Heistad, D., 9
Helf, S., 92, 426
Heller, K.W., 325, 339, 340, 341, 342
Helton, M.R., 155, 171, 186, 212
Hemp, R., 454, 458
Hemphill, L., 450
Hemsley, B., 220
Hendrick, S.S., 73
Hendrickson, J.M., 180
Henely, A.J., 458
Henfield, M.S., 388, 392
Hengst, J., 252
Henkenius, A.L., 320
Hennekam, R.C.M., 109
Henry, L., 104
Hensfield, M.S., 391, 392
Hepburn, S.L., 104, 108, 206
Heron, T.E., 57, 58, 88, 176, 178, 184, 212, 321
Herr, C.M., 50
Herron, M.D., 398
Hersh, M., 372
Hershfeldt, P.A., 29
Herskovitz, R., 147
Hertz-Picciotto, I., 204, 206
Hertzog, M.A., 175
Heshusius, L., 61
Hess, J., 72
Hessler, T., 25, 57, 140
Hester, P.P., 180
Hetzner, A., 109
Heussler, H.S., 199
Heward, W.L., 29, 39, 58, 61, 88, 105, 106, 115, 119, 140, 149, 168, 169, 176, 178, 180, 181, 182, 184, 200, 212, 221, 222, 309, 357
Heyl, B.S., 78
Heymans, H.S., 325
Hicks, D.M., 240, 249
Hicks, T., 372
Hicks, T.L., 306
Hickson, L., 276
Higbee Mandlebaum, L., 92
Higbee, T.S., 215, 216
Higgens, E.L., 134
Hildreth, B.L., 93
Hile, J.L., 357
Hill, J.L., 326, 333, 358
Hill, S., 108, 111
Hill, W., 397
Hilton-Prillhart, A., 151
Hilton, A., 59
Himmelsbach, I., 290
Hinkson-Lee, K., 180
Hirn, R., 172, 180, 181, 188
Hirn, R.G., 181
Hirschman, B., 400
Hirst, J.M., 458
Hobbs, N., 9
Hochman, J.M., 56, 120
Hodal, A.S., 413
Hodapp, R.M., 109, 110
Hodgetts, S., 202
Hoff, E., 245
Hoffman, E.M., 116
Hoffman, L., 172
Hogue, E., 113
Hohmann, S., 171
Hokanson, C.R., Jr., 42, 61
Holaday, B., 345
Holahan, J.M., 137
Holbrook, M.C., 299
Holcomb, A., 116
Holden, G.W., 171
Holehan, K.M., 220
Holland, A., 8
Holland, K.D., 70
Hollenbeck, K.N., 38
Hollenweger, J., 8
Hollis, C., 320
Hollo, A., 181
Holloway, J., 25, 214
Holloway, S.D., 69
Holm, M., 400
Holman, K.C., 207, 208
Holmes, D., 179
Holt, M.K., 164
Holtmann, M., 320
Holz, F., 290
Holz, N.E., 171
Homes, A., 100
Hong, S., 312
Hooks, E., 199
Hooks, S.D., 184
Hoon, A.H., 331
Hooper, S., 110
Hoover, H.D., 138
Hoovers, J.M.N., 109
Hopkins, M., 151
Hoppe, J., 67, 83

Horn, A.L., 29, 452
Horn, C., 181
Hornby, G., 155
Horner, R.H., 176, 181, 182, 322
Horner, S.L., 20
Horowitz, S.H., 136
Horvath, B., 443
Hoskyn, M., 147
Hoston, J., 342
Hott, B.L., 181
Houchins, D.E., 151
Hougen, M., 450
Hourcade, J.J., 428
Houston, J., 133
Houston, T., 276
Houtenville, A.J., 441
Houwen, S., 291
Howard, J.S., 80, 90
Howard, V. F., 212
Howard, L., 56
Howard, M.R., 232, 233, 235, 241
Howard, P.W., 153
Howard, V.F., 80
Hratinski, I., 264
Hsiao, J., 252
Huang, C.W., 400
Huang, J., 166
Huang, M., 400
Huang, T., 264, 281
Huang, Y., 171
Huaqing, C., 43, 166
Hubbell, S.P., 429
Huber, H.B., 120
Huddleston, R., 113
Hudson, S., 179
Hudson, T., 180
Huebner, K.M., 293, 300, 311
Huerta, N.E., 54
Huffman, J.M., 213
Hughes, C., 106, 114, 375, 376, 452, 461
Hughes, C.A., 147
Hughes, J.C., 212
Hughes, J.E.A., 199
Huguenin, N.H., 104
Hulit, L.M., 232, 233, 235, 241
Hulme, C., 237
Hultman, C.M., 205
Hume, K., 212
Hume, K.A., 212, 221, 222
Hunt, N., 333
Hunt, P., 372
Hunter, W.C., 121
Huss, J.A., 405
Hutchins, N.S., 178, 179
Hutinger, P.L., 434
Hutton, A.M., 70, 73, 207
Hyde, M., 272
Hyman, S.L., 208

I

Iadarola, S., 212
Ianetta, M., 147
Iannaccone, J.A., 71, 371
Iano, R.P., 61
Ida, D.J., 74
IDEA Regulations, 16
Im, S., 133
Imbeau, M.B., 394
Imperatore, G., 327
Inge, K.J., 456
Institute for Community Inclusion, 441
Institute on Communication and Inclusion at Syracuse University, 220
Iovannone, R., 222
IRIS Center, 304
Irit, H., 292
Isaacson, S.L., 151
Isom, S., 327
Ispen, C., 461
Ita, C.M., 265
Itard, J.M.G., 111
Itchon, J., 219
Ito, J., 332
Itoi, M., 153
Ivancic, M.T., 119
Ivarson, H., 398
Iverson, V.S., 51, 69, 366
Ives, B., 153
Ivey, M.L., 217
Ivy J.W., 185
Iwata, B.A., 119
Izzo, M.V., 456

J

Jacobs, H.A., 368
Jacobson, J.W., 220
Jacobson, W.H., 304
Jahr, E., 212
Jain, A., 207
Jamal, L., 111
Jameson, M.J., 452
Janney, R.E., 45, 120
Jantz, K.M., 450
Jantzen, J., 135
Jardes, T.L., 357
Järvelin, M.-R., 109
Jasper, A.D., 121
Javitz, H.S., 442
Jayanthi, M., 92, 152
Jean-Pierre, P., 43
Jenkins, L.N., 180
Jenkins, S.R., 458
Jenson, W.R., 164, 168, 172, 174, 184
Jernigan, K., 10
Jerome, J., 213
Jessup, G., 292
Jex, E., 447
Jiang, H., 44
Jiang, Y., 74
Jimenez, B.A., 153
Jimenez, E., 459
Jimenez, E.D., 113
Jimerson, S., 170
Jin, C.S., 213
Jitendra, A.K., 133, 147, 151
Johnson, A., 127, 156–157
Johnson, C., 91, 212
Johnson, D.R., 169
Johnson, D.W., 57
Johnson, F., 374, 376
Johnson, J., 432
Johnson, J.W., 151
Johnson, K., 131, 194, 223
Johnson, M., 452, 457
Johnson, N., 179, 298, 299
Johnson, P., 74
Johnson, R.T., 57
Johnson, S.I., 75
Johnson, T.L., 331
Johnson, T.P., 20
Johnson, V.A., 368
Johnson, V.E., 44
Johnston, M.K., 180
Johnston, S.S., 362, 430
Joint Committee on Infant Hearing, 267
Jolivette, K., 181, 184
Jones, Bock, S., 78
Jones, D.E., 344
Jones, E.A., 73, 197
Jones, H.A., 45
Jones, M., 342

Jones, S., 164
Jones, S.M., 450
Jones, W., 207
Jordan, J., 44
Jordan, N.C., 29, 135
Jorgensen Smith, T., 106
Jorgensen, J., 44, 374, 376
Joseph, L.M., 151, 153, 184, 321
Jozwik, S.L., 147
Ju, S., 254
Juarez, A., 460
Judge, S., 450, 452
Jung, S., 56, 428
Just, A.C., 206
Justen, J.E., 352
Justice, L.M., 243
Jutai, J.W., 303

K

Kaffar, B.J., 152
Kagan, J., 171
Kagan, M., 120, 121
Kagan, S., 120, 121
Kahn, L.G., 79
Kaiser, A.P, 250, 251
Kaiser, A.P., 428
Kalb, L.G., 208
Kalberg, J.R., 168
Kalbfleisch, M.L., 393
Kalutskaya, I., 172
Kalyanpur, M., 77
Kalyva, E., 206
Kambs, D.M., 222
Kame'enui, E.J., 29, 115, 146, 150, 154, 155
Kämmerer, A., 290
Kamps, D.M., 180
Kampschroer, E.F., 376
Kandala, S., 208
Kang, J., 440, 441
Kanner, A.M., 326, 333
Kanner, L., 195, 205
Kansas Dept. of Education, 356
Kaplan, S.N., 394, 395
Kapperman, G., 303
Karagrigoriou, A., 111
Karchmer, M.A., 263, 264
Karl, J., 114, 364
Karl, J.M., 363
Karon, L., 451
Karten, T., 8
Karwowski, M., 56
Kasari, C., 212
Kaspar, R., 290
Kassardjian, A., 217
Katsiyannis, A., 19, 48, 166, 181, 344, 345
Katz, E., 429
Kauffman, J.C., 388
Kauffman, J.M., 8, 29, 59, 60,166, 170, 220, 364, 374
Kaufman, A., 309
Kavale, K.A., 163, 323
Kayfitz, A.D., 70
Kazdin, A.E., 91
Kazolia, T., 153
Kea, C.D., 43, 74
Kearns, D.M., 56, 146
Keen, D., 199
Keenan, J.M., 137
Keenan, M., 212
Keesey, S., 25
Kellems, R., 448, 452
Kellems, R.O., 113, 460
Keller, C.L., 180
Keller, H.R., 72
Kelley, K., 443, 444, 446
Kelley, K.R., 445
Kelly, C.S., 180
Kelly, J.P., 207, 302
Kelly, S.M., 306
Kelso, S., 254
Kemmery, M.A., 261
Kemp-Inman, A., 446
Kemp, C., 424
Kemp, P., 57
Kennedy, A.M., 187
Kennedy, C., 265
Kennedy, M.J., 153
Kephart, 128
Kerbel, A., 358, 374
Kern, A.M., 322
Kern, L., 164, 166, 172, 217
Kerr, M.M., 87, 184, 393
Kessler Foundation/National Organization on Disability, 462
Kessler, K.B., 119, 456
Kewal Ramani, A., 79
Keyworth, R., 115
Kidshida, Y., 424
Kierans, I., 461
Kilpatrick, D.A., 132
Kim, D.S., 305
Kim, E.S., 345
Kim, J., 299
Kim, J.S., 450
Kim, Y., 241
Kincaid, D., 222
Kinder, D., 152
Kindle, A.E., 371
King-Sears, M.E., 45, 120, 148
King, A., 252
King, B.H., 109
King, E.W., 393
King, G., 70
Kingsley, M., 291, 293
Kiriakopoulos, E., 334
Kirk, S.A., 128
Kirk, S., 128
Kirkner, S.L., 69
Kisinger, K.W., 371
Klatsky, R.L., 306
Kleefeld, J., 179
Klei, L., 206
Klein, J., 458
Klein, D.M., 419, 431
Klein, J. O., 267
Klein, K., 106
Klein, M.D., 428, 432
Klein, R.E., 340
Kleinert, H., 358, 374
Kleinke, A., 180
Kleithermes, A., 451
Klevstrand, M., 211
Kleweno, C.P, 302
Kliethermes, A., 77
Klin, A., 207
Klingbeil, D.A., 57
Klingner, J., 247
Klingner, J.K., 43, 44
Kloo, A., 29, 46, 60
Kluth, P., 203
Kluwin, T.N., 281
Knickmeyer, R.C., 413
Knight K., 460
Knight, V.F., 181, 217, 363, 364, 376, 450, 461
Knokey, A., 264, 281
Knokey, A.-M., 79
Knokey, A.M., 440, 441, 442
Knoll, J.A., 442
Knoors, H., 265, 279
Knowlton, E., 113, 114
Koball, H., 74
Kobari-Wright, V.V., 213

Kochhar-Bryant, C.A., 55, 70, 71, 453
Kodak, T., 116
Koegel, L.K., 199
Koegel, R.L., 199
Koehler, K.E., 299
Koenig, A.J., 298, 306
Koesters, M., 106
Koestler, F.A., 312
Koevoets, C., 109
Koger, F., 361, 363
Kohler, P., 69, 79, 443, 444, 446, 453
Kokina, A., 217
Komesaroff, L., 272
Konofal, E., 320
Konold, T.R., 174
Konrad, M., 25, 51, 52, 105, 107, 113, 114, 140, 143, 147, 148, 153, 155, 184, 321, 450, 456
Koot, H.M., 106
Korkmaz, B., 197
Korslund, K., 166
Kortering, L., 69, 79
Kortering, L.J., 443, 444, 446
Korver, A.M.H., 267
Koslowski, N., 106
Kosmicki, J.A., 206
Kostelnik, M.J., 424
Kostewicz, D.E., 25
Kourassanis-Velasquez, J., 197
Kourea, L., 44, 153
Kovach, D., 25, 30–31
Kozleski, E., 372
Kozloff, M., 25
Kranak, M.C., 180, 213
Krantz, P.J., 216
Krathwohl, D.R., 397
Kregel, J., 446, 453, 454
Kreigh, C., 184
Kreiner, J., 364, 460
Kremer, K., 166
Kreppner, J., 265
Krezmien, M.P., 43, 461
Kristensen, T., 307
Kritikos, E.P., 101
Kroesch, A.M., 451
Krohn, K.R., 151
Kroth, R.L., 85, 91, 93, 94
Krupp, M., 364
Kryzak, L.A., 73
Kubina, R.M., 25, 69, 72, 92, 176
Kubina, Rick, 141
Kucharczyk, S., 212
Kuczynski, K., 71
Kugel, R.B., 458
Kuhn, M., 213, 429
Kuja-Halkoa, R., 205
Kuna, J., 111
Kunesh, C.E., 44
Kuo, C., 171
Kupermintz, H., 281
Kupferman, S., 107, 447
Kurcharczyk, S., 212, 221, 222
Kurt, O., 217
Kurth, J.A., 355, 367, 369
Kutash, K., 170, 174
Kutlu, M., 217
Kwak, N., 109
Kwok, O., 345

L

Ladd-Acosta, C., 206
Laden, F., 206
LaFlamme, M., 345
Lahav, O., 302
Lake, J.F., 82
Lakin, C., 458
Lakin, K.C., 109
Lalvani, P., 70
Lam, E.A., 132
Lamb, R., 252
Lambert, M.C., 181
Lambrecht, L., 209
Lancaster, J., 58
Lancioni, G.E., 213, 364, 429, 461
Landa, R., 208
Landa, R.J., 207, 208
Landi, N., 137
Landrigan, P.J., 206
Landrum, T.J., 146, 166, 170
Lane, G., 305
Lane, H., 373
Lane, H.B., 134
Lane, K.L., 116, 152, 168, 174, 178, 180, 184, 371
Lanfranchi, S., 104
Lang, R., 213, 220, 429
Langberg, J.M., 320
Lange, C.M., 279
Langer, N., 137
Lanovaz, M.J., 198
Lansford, J.E., 162
Laracy, S.D., 134
Larkin, E., 415
Larsen, R.A.A., 180
Larson, A., 133
Larson, S.A., 109
Larsson, E.V., 212
Larsson, H., 205
LaRusso, M.D., 450
Latimer-Cheung, A.E., 460
Lattimore, L.P., 452
Laucht, M., 171
LaVange, L.M., 414
Lavoie, J., 168
Law, J.K., 208
Law, R.A., 208
Lawrence, J.M., 327
Lawrence, S., 56
Lawson, D., 217
Layng, T.V.J., 218
Le Couteur, A., 209
Le Menestrel, Duncan & National Academies of Sciences, Engineering, and Medicine, 110
Leader-Janssen, E., 147
Leader, G., 252
Leaf, J.A., 217
Leaf, J.B., 217, 368
Leaf, R., 217
Leaf, R.B., 217
Leavett, R., 237
LeBlanc, L.A., 222
Lecavalier, L., 91, 212
Lecendreux, M., 320
Ledbetter, J.C., 199
Ledford, J.R., 219, 423, 428, 430
Lee, A., 362
Lee, B.K., 206
Lee, D.L., 86, 184
Lee, I.H., 56, 155, 442
Lee, J., 25, 372
Lee, N.R., 206
Leech, N., 393
Leguia, J.L., 56, 120
Lehman, J., 114
Lehmann, J., 453
Lehr, D., 332, 333, 341
Lehr, D.H., 344
Lehtinen, L., 128
Leigh, J., 272
Leigh, S.A., 295
Lein, A.E., 133
Leister, C., 342
Lemay, R., 122

Lemelin, J.P., 171
Lemons, C.J., 46, 56
Lemons, G., 388
Lenz, B.K., 135, 147, 153
Leon-Guerrero, R., 44
Leonard, B., 70, 222
Leong, D.J., 422
Lepper, C., 80
Leppien, J.H., 394
Leslie, A.M., 197, 208
Leslie, J.C., 371
Letcher, P.L.C., 171
Letso, S., 223
Leu, G., 372
Levato, L., 212
Leve, L.D., 171
Leventhal, B.L., 209
Levine, P., 357, 442
Levitt, H., 268
Levitt, P., 413
Levy, F., 320
Levy, S.E., 208
Lewis, A.N., 174
Lewis, M.P., 230
Lewis, P., 361
Lewis, R.B., 101, 246
Lewis, S., 300
Lewis, T.J., 29, 175, 176, 179
Ley Davis, L., 103
Leybaert, J., 277
Li, A., 301, 302
Li, D.J., 104
Liaupsin, C.J., 320
Lichtenstein, P., 205
Lieberman, L.J., 292, 340
Lienemann, T.O., 148
Lifshitz, H., 292
Lilienfeld, S.O., 220
Limmink, K.A.P.M., 291
Lin, P.Y., 104
Linden, M.L., 48, 51
Linder, B.L., 327
Lindsay, S., 451
Lindstrom, L., 74, 446, 452, 457
Linehan, M.M., 166
Ling, D., 276
Linna, S.-L., 109
Linnell, J., 207
Lino, M., 71
Lippke, B.A., 244
Lipscomb, S., 169
Little, A., 152
Little, C.W., 137
Little, T., 105, 114
Little, T.D., 114
Liu, A.Y., 169
Liu, K.Y., 204
Liu, X., 147
Lloyd, W., 248
Lo, L., 44, 113
Lo, Y., 25, 103, 153, 168, 181, 321
Lochman, J.E., 106, 189
Lockwood, A., 8
Logan, K.R., 368
Lohmeier, K.L., 308
Lohr, K.N., 450
Lonagan, C.J., 237
Long, E., 374
Long, R.G., 306
Loomis, J.M., 306
Lord, C., 205, 208, 209
Losinski, M., 147
Lotrecchiano, G.R., 326
Loudon, W., 332
Loughery, O.T., 116
Lovaas, O.I., 211, 378
Love, S.R., 209
Lovelace, S.P., 134
Lovett, D., 51
Lovett, D.L., 51
Lovett, S., 197
Lovitt, T.C., 10, 136
Lowenthal, B., 326
Lowrey, K.A., 364
Lubin, J., 153
Lubinski, D., 388
Lucas, C., 278
Lucas, J.W., 325
Lucas, W., 305
Luckasson, R., 100
Lueck, A.H., 301
Luft, P., 446, 453
Lulinski, A., 458
Lund, E.M., 345
Lupkowski-Shoplik, A., 395
Luria, S.R., 388
Lurmann, F., 206
Luscre, D., 215
Lusk, K.E., 300, 303
Lustig, L.R., 267
Lyall, K., 206
Lydon, H., 214
Lydon, S., 25
Lynch, E.W., 80
Lyon, G.R., 137
Lyons, G., 56, 120
Lyons, G.R., 130, 132, 133, 134

M

Ma, J.K., 337, 460
Maag, J.W., 19, 162, 320
MacArthur, C.A., 147
Mace, R.C., 185
Machmer, E., 272
MacKenzie, B.K., 208
MacKenzie, N., 306
Mackiewicz, S.M., 57, 92, 426
MacMillan, D.L., 211
MacMillan, V., 248
MacSuga-Gage, A.S., 172
Madaus, J.W., 113, 441, 442
Maes, B., 356
Maggin, D.M., 178, 188, 189
Magro, K., 197
Maheady, L., 57, 58, 116, 121
Mahshie, S.N., 280
Maid, C., 456
Maier, J., 357
Majd, M., 55
Majdalany, L.M., 116
Maker, J., 385, 386, 392
Maki, K.E., 109, 146
Malik, M., 207
Mallette, B., 57, 58, 116
Maloni, C., 134
Malott, R.W., 213
Maltby, L.E., 171
Manguno, M.S., 109
Mank, D., 454, 456
Mankin, G., 104
Manning, W.H., 248
Manrai, A., 205
March, J., 166
Marchant, M., 184
Marchione, K.E., 137
Marcovina, S., 327
Marder, C., 7, 79, 281, 320, 440, 442
Margalit, M., 134
Markelz, A.M., 180
Marks, L.J., 166
Marland, S., 384–385

Marliave, R., 115
Marquis, J., 135, 344
Marrocco, S., 337
Marron, M., 395
Marschark, M., 264, 272, 279, 280
Marsh, A.J., 113
Marshall, J., 207
Marshall, S., 434
Marshark, M., 281
Marston, J.R., 306
Martin-Key, N., 169
Martin, C.M., 25, 133
Martin, J.A., 387
Martin, J.E., 51, 429, 444, 452, 453
Martinez, D., 317
Marton, K., 237, 238
Maslin, M., 202
Mason, B., 321
Mason, B.A., 86, 213
Mason, L.H., 151
Mason, R., 213
Massidda, D., 134
Mastropieri, M.A., 56
Mastroppieri, M.A., 56
Mather, N., 134, 138, 318, 323
Matheson, C., 106, 460
Mathias, R., 152
Mathisen, B., 375
Matson, J.L., 176
Matthews, B., 305
Matthews, J., 342
Matthys, W., 106
Mattingly, C., 300
Matuszny, R.M., 92
Mauldin, E., 428
Maurice, C., 220
May, M.E., 181
Maye, M.P., 208
Mayer-Davis, E.J., 327
Mayer-Johnson, 376
Mayer, C., 279
Mayer, R.E., 397
Mayes, R.D., 393
Mayhew, M.J., 441
Mays, N.M., 184
Mazumdar, S., 204
Mazzotti, V.L., 52, 57, 69, 79, 443, 444, 445, 446, 447, 452, 458
McAdam, D.B., 91, 212, 293
McAfee, O., 422
McBee, M.T., 43
McCall, K.L., 323
McCallum, R.S., 151
McCarten, K., 434
McCauley, E., 166
McClannahan, L.E., 216
McCleery, J.P., 252
McComas, J., 345
McConnell, B.M., 69, 72, 92
McConnell, R., 206
McConnell, S., 179, 426
McConnell, S.R., 423
McCoy, A., 25
McCoy, D.C., 164
McCrimmon, A.W., 199
McDaid, P., 344
McDaniel, S., 184
McDaniel, S.C., 400
McDonald, K.L., 168
McDonnall, M.C., 306, 307
McDonnell, J., 9, 60, 113, 367, 369, 370, 372
McDowell, C., 371
McDuffy-Landrum, K., 146
McEachin, J., 217
McEachin, J.J., 211
McFarland, J., 79
McGonigel, M.J., 46
McGowan, D., 137
McGrew, K.S., 138
McHugh, E., 340
McIntyre, L.L., 71, 73
McIver-Lux, K., 275, 276
McKenna, J., 178, 188
McKenna, J.W., 178, 186
McKenna, M.C., 29
McKinstry, R.C., 208
McKnight, M., 44
McKown, L., 180
McLamed, J.C., 83
McLaughlin, J.A., 246
McLaughlin, M.J., 8
McLaughlin, V.L., 155
McLeskey, J., 29, 55, 56, 59, 60
McLone, D.G., 332
McLoughlin, J.A., 101
McMahon, E., 219, 312
McMahon, J., 212
McMahon, R.J., 189
McMaster, K.L., 58, 132
McNabb, J., 368
McNamara, J.K., 135
McNamara, K.M., 362
McNaughton, D., 80
McNear, D., 300
McNicholas, J., 274
McNicholas, P.J., 109
McPartland, J.C., 202
McSherry, D., 415
McTiernan, A., 25
McWilliam, R.A., 427
Meadan, H., 69, 73, 134
Meade, M.A., 337
Meadon, H., 72
Meadows, N.B., 188
Mechling, L.C., 113, 456
Meindl, J.N., 185, 197
Meisels, S.J., 415
Mellard, D., 44
Menacker, S.J., 296
Menard, C., 202
Menci, W.E., 137
Mendez, L.M.R., 72
Menzies, H.M., 116, 168, 174
Mercer, A.R., 54, 152
Mercer, C.D., 54, 152
Merrell, K.W., 320
Merrells, J., 460
Merrick, M.T., 173
Merrill, E.C., 104
Messer, D., 249
Messina, R., 370
Metheny, J., 74
Metz, B., 219
Meyer, G., 353
Meyer, L.H., 374
Michael, C.N., 132
Michael, L., 171
Michaels, C.A., 445
Miciak, J., 450
Midlarsky, E., 73
Miesch, J., 446
Migliore, A., 456
Miguel, C.F., 213
Miles, B., 373
Miley, P., 306
Miller, A., 114, 364
Miller, B., 114
Miller, C.J., 137
Miller, D., 80, 252, 290
Miller, L., 206
Miller, L.J., 199
Miller, M., 120

Miller, M.M., 296
Miller, O., 113
Miller, S.P., 152
Mills, J.R., 181
Miltenberger, R.G., 176
Milton, J.H., 152
Mimms, P.J., 181, 461
Mims, P.J., 362, 368, 369
Miner, C., 451
Minor, L.B., 267
Minshawi, N., 91, 212
Mires, C.B., 86
Missal, K., 423
Missett, T.C., 387
Mitchell, A.L., 9, 103
Mitchell, B., 164, 166, 172
Mitchell, R., 264
Mitchell, R.E., 263, 264
Mittan, R.J., 327
Mize, M., 178
Moberly, R.L., 344
Modabbernia, A., 206
Moeller, M.P., 271
Moeyaert, M., 57
Mofield, E.L., 387
Mokkink, L.B., 325
Molden, V., 342
Molfenter, N., 452
Moll, L.C., 75
Molteni, J.D., 186
Monikowski, C., 273
Montague, M., 174
Montgomery, J.M., 199
Monzo, L., 74
Moody, S.W., 155
Moon, M.S., 456
Moon, S., 452
Moore, A.J., 152
Moore, J.E., 295
Moore, J.L., 393
Moore, J.L., III, 392
Moores, D.F., 281
Morgan, C., 214
Morgan, J.J., 164
Morgan, R., 107
Morgan, R.L., 29, 113, 447
Morgen, A., 114
Morin, L.L., 152
Morningstar, M.E., 452
Morocco, C.C., 153
Morris, B.K., 217
Morris, J.R., 147
Morris, T.L., 166
Morrison, G.M., 170
Morrison, G.S., 424, 426, 432
Morrison, R., 426
Morrison, R.S., 56
Morse, T.E., 119
Morse, W., 186
Morsink, C.V., 45
Mortaji, N., 451
Mortier, K., 372
Moss, C.K., 56, 120
Most, D.E., 108
Most, T., 261
Mostert, M.P., 220
Mouanoutoua, J., 133
Mount, J., 305
Mountjoy, T., 217
Mourra, K., 113
Moyseenko, K.A., 56, 120
Moyson, T., 73
Mruzek, D.W., 91, 102, 212
Mueller, T.G., 103
Muharib, R., 371
Muhonen, M., 332
Mujezinovic, F., 111
Mulcahy, C., 43, 461
Mulher, T., 25
Mulhern, M.S., 206
Mulick, J.A., 91, 212, 219, 220
Mulrooney, K.J., 278
Multimodal Treatment Study Group, 323
Mulvey, E.P., 170
Munandar, V., 372
Munir, K.M., 106
Munson, L.J., 333
Murch, S.H., 207
Murdick, N.L., 329
Murdoch, B., 276
Murdock, L.C., 219
Murley, R.C., 121
Murphy, C.M., 198
Murphy, D.L., 70
Murphy, H.R., 55
Murphy, J., 186
Murphy, S., 455
Murray, C., 440
Musetti, A., 135
Must, A., 202
Musti-Rao, S., 180
Mustian, A., 69, 79
Mustian, A.L., 147, 447
Musu-Gillette, L., 79
Musyoka, M., 277
Myers, S.M., 208
Myles, B.S., 220

N

Nackel, J., 152
Nadeson, V., 332
NAEYC (National Association for the Education of Young Children), 424, 426
Naftel, A.J., 319, 320
NAGC (National Association for Gifted Children), 385, 387, 403
Nagle, K., 8, 79, 440, 442
Naglieri, J.A., 392
Nagro, S.A., 184
National Association for the Gifted, 7
National Association of State Directors of Developmental Disabilities Services, 106
National Association of the Deaf, 272, 279, 281
National Autism Center, 8
National Center for Education Statistics, 44, 147
National Center for Health Statistics, 293
National Center on Deaf-Blindness, 357, 359, 360
National Conference State Legislatures, 72
National Council on Disability, 21, 30, 43
National Down Syndrome Society, 108
National Education Association, 393
National Human Genome Research Institute, 205
National Institute for Direct Instruction, 151
National Institute of Mental Health, 171
National Institutes of Health, 108
National Library Service for the Blind and Physically Handicapped, 298
National Professional Development Center on Autism Spectrum Disorders, 212
National Research Council, 197, 205
National Spinal Cord Injury Statistical Center, 333
Natsuaki, M.N., 171
NCD (National Council on Disability), 456
Neal, T., 91, 212
Neef, N.A., 119, 176, 177, 178, 320
Neel, R.S., 188
Neff, D., 75
Nehring, W.M., 330, 341
Neiderhiser, J.M., 171
Neilsen-Gatti, S., 180
Neitzel, J., 213
Nelis, T., 458

Nelson, A., 254
Nelson, C., 372
Nelson, C.M., 87, 184
Nelson, J.R., 171
Nelson, J.S., 153
Nelson, L.L., 76, 78
Nelson, M., 55
Nese, J.F.T., 42
Nesman, T.M., 72
Neu, T., 394
Neubert, D.A., 446, 452, 453
Neuharth-Pritchett, S., 327, 341
Newborg, J., 422
Newcomer, P.L., 244
Newkirk-Turner, B.L., 44
Newman-Gonchar, R., 114
Newman, L., 69, 79, 169, 264, 281, 357, 440, 441, 442
Newman, L.A., 442
Newschaffer, C.J., 206, 207
Newton, D., 340
Newton, J.R., 57
Next Chapter Book Club, 451
Nicholas, D., 202
Nichols, S.D., 323
Nichols, S.K., 299
Nicholson, K., 116
NIDCD (National Institute on Deafness and Other Communication Disorders), 265, 267, 272
Nielson-Pugmire, M., 161, 185, 189–190
Niemiec, R.M., 103
Nijs, S., 356
NINDS (National Institution of Neurological Disorders and Stroke), 206
Ninness, C., 217
Ninness, S.K., 217
Nippold, M., 80
Nirje, B., 122
Nisbet, J., 361, 370
Nishino, T., 208
Nix, L.D., 216
Nixon, P.A., 56
NJCLD (National Joint Committee on Learning Disabilities), 131
Nobel, M.M., 57
Noell, G.H., 69, 92
Noens, I.L.J., 201
Nolan, J.D., 320
Noltemeyer, A., 44
Nordman, E., 264
Nordness, P.D., 147
Norins Bardon, J., 56
Norman, U., 206
Northern, J.L., 263, 266
Northup, J., 323
Norwich, B., 8
NSTTAC, 443
NTID (National Technical Institute for the Deaf), 273

O

O'Brian, S., 248
O'Brien, M., 106
O'Brien, R.L., 388
O'Cleirigh, C.M., 293
O'Connor, E.A., 20
O'Connor, R.E., 141
O'Donnell, B., 305
O'Donnell, J., 69
O'Donovan, M., 171
O'Handley, R.D., 180
O'Neill, M., 163
O'Neill, R.E., 176
O'Neill, S.J., 371
O'Reilly, M., 213, 219, 429
O'Reilly, M.F., 364, 371, 461
Oakes, P.M., 265
Oakes, W.P., 116, 168, 174, 371
Obiaker, F.E., 44
Ochoa, S.H., 246
Odding, E., 330
Odgers, C.L., 171
Odom, S., 212, 220
Odom, S.L., 212, 221, 222, 424
Office of Special Education and Rehabilitation Services, 131
Offringa, M., 325
Ogden, C.L., 323
Ogletree, B., 253
Ogletree, G., 345
Oh, Y., 372
Ohtake, Y., 363
Oif, A., 43, 155
Oleson, J.J., 271
Oliva, D., 364
Olivos, E.M., 74
Olmi, D.J., 180
Olmstead, J.E., 309
Olsén, P., 109
Olsen, R.J., 106, 460
Olson, R.K., 137, 333
Olson, S.L., 162
Olszewski-Kubilius, P., 390, 391, 400
Omdal, S.N., 393
Ong, C.C.P., 332
Onslow, M., 248
Openden, D., 199
Oppenheim-Leaf, M.L., 217, 368
Orelove 84, 377
Orlando, A., 376
Ornaghi, V., 135
Orr, R.R., 70
Orsmond, G.I., 73
Ortiz, S.O., 246
Osborn, S., 148
Osborne, L.A., 202
Osmani, K.J., 79
Osterhaus, S.A., 299
Oswald, D.P., 208, 220
Overholser, J.C., 166
Overly, E., 185
Overton, T., 101
Owens, D., 392
Owens, D.J., 202
Owens, R.E., 233, 238, 241, 243
Owens, R.E., Jr., 235, 236, 243
Owiny, R.L., 181
Oyer, H.J., 241, 242
Ozcan, N., 72
Ozonoff, S., 202

P

Paal, M., 153
Packman, A., 248
Paclawsky, T.R., 176
Paff, M., 332
Page, E.B., 414
Page, E.J., 113
Page, T.J., 119
Paglieri, R.A., 220
Palmer, C., 305
Palmer, D.S., 55
Palmer, N., 205
Palmer, S., 105, 114
Palmer, S.B., 114
Pan, Z., 199
Papageorgiou, E.A., 111
Paparella, T., 170, 212
Paradiz, V., 254
Parette, H.P., 72, 91, 341
Parish, S.L., 74
Park, B.Y., 206
Park, J.H., 69, 73, 92, 113, 171, 252
Park, M., 43
Park, S., 69

Parker Peters, M., 387
Parker, C.E., 56
Parker, G., 188
Parker, R.C., 56
Parker, T., 217
Parkin, A.J., 308
Parmar, R.S., 55, 155
Parrish, L.H., 111
Parsons, M.B., 452
Parsons, M.P., 214
Pascarella, E.T., 441
Patnoad, M., 113
Patsalis, P.C., 111
Patterson, G.R., 173
Patterson, J., 70
Patton, J.R., 92, 102, 108, 111, 114, 121, 453
Paul, P.V., 276, 277
Paul, T.L., 308
Pavilanis, R., 428
Payne, D., 364
Payne, K.T., 246
Payne, L., 166
Payne, T.E., 86
Pearson, N.A., 102
Pease, L., 357
Peck, C., 364
Peckham-Hardin, K., 236
Peek, K., 199
Peirano, C., 287, 307, 313
Pellegrin, A.L., 69, 92
Pence, S.E., 371
Penfold, B., 206
Peng, M., 206
Penney, H., 185
Pennington, B.F., 320
Pennington, R.C., 113
Pereira, L.C., 168
Perele, D., 393
Perez, A., 372
Perkins, E.A., 106
Perla, F., 305
Perlin, M., 8
Perrin, J.M., 325
Perske, R., 122
Petch-Hogan, B., 91
Peters, L., 137
Peters, S.J., 43, 390, 391, 404
Peterson, B.S., 320
Peterson, L.C., 197
Peterson, S.M., 176, 177, 178, 322
Petrich, J., 277
Petrill, S.A., 241
Petroff, J., 340
Pettit, G.S., 162
Pettitt, D.J., 327
Pew Research Center, 441
Pfannenstiel, K., 153, 178
Pfetzing, D., 277
Philippakos, Z.A., 147
Phillips, C.L., 71, 357, 371
Phillips, S., 202
Philofsky, A., 104, 108
Pianta, R.C., 174
Pickard, E., 228–229, 256–257
Pickles, A., 209
Pidlypchak, H., 368
Pierce, J.M., 215
Pierce, R.L., 398
Pierson, M.R., 217
Pignone, M.P., 450
Pihoker, C., 327
Piirto, J., 385, 386, 388, 394, 398
Pimperton, H., 265
Pinderhughes, E.E., 189
Pindzola, R.H., 238
Pinquart, M., 345
Pintrich, P.R., 397
Piper, B.J., 323
Piquero, A.R., 170
Pituch, K.A., 219
Pivarnick, L., 113
Piven, J., 208
Pivik, J., 345
Plexico, L.W., 237
Plotts, C.A., 170
Plucker, J.A., 388
Pokorski, E.A., 428
Polite, F., 151
Pollard, E., 92
Pollard, J.S., 215
Pollard, R., 248
Polloway, E.A., 92, 121, 153
Ponchillia, P.E., 306
Poon, K.K., 252
Popham, M., 166
Popkin, J., 186
Poppen, M., 447, 458
Poppes, P.P., 356
Porterfield, K., 242
Ports, K.A., 173
Potts, E.A., 56
Potvin, D., 205
Povenmire-Kirk, T.C., 79, 446
Powell-Smith, K.A., 217
Power, D., 272
Poyadue, F.S., 70
Prabhala, A., 10
Prater, M.A., 83
Pratt, C., 100
Pratt, J.L., 177
Prayzer, R., 58, 88
Preece, H., 447
Prelock, P.A., 254
Presley, J.A., 376
Pretty, L., 303
Price, C., 388
Price, J., 458
Price, R., 113
Pridgen, L.S., 113
Prior, M., 171
Pritchard, D., 185
Procher, S., 388
Public Schools of North Carolina, 457
Pugh, K.R., 137
Pullen, P.C., 54, 134, 152
Pumpian, I., 370
Puranik, C.S., 237
Purcell, J.H., 394
Purdue, M.V., 137
Puschner, B., 106
Puzino, K., 320
Pyle, N., 450

Q

Qi, S., 264
Quenemoen, R., 358, 374
Quinn, J.M., 133
Quinn, M.M., 166
Quintero, N., 71, 73

R

Rabiner, D.L., 319, 320
Raborn, A., 164, 174
Rademacher, J.A., 93
Radley, K.C., 186
Rafferty, L.A., 321
Raftery, K.J., 371
Raharinirina, S., 341
Rahn, N.L., 432
Rahsotte, C.A., 244
Rajeh, A., 323

Ramani, G.B., 429
Ramey, C.T., 414
Ramey, D., 25
Ramig, P.R., 248
Ramp, E.M., 25, 133
Rankin, M.N.P., 278
Rao, S.S., 82
Rapp, J.T., 198
Rapport, M.J., 342
Raskind, M.H., 134
Raspa, M., 423
Rasplica Khoury, C., 151
Raths, J., 397
Ratto, A.B., 205
Raval, V.V., 70, 75
Raven, J., 392
Raven, J.C., 392
Raver, C.C., 164
Raver, S.A., 450, 452
Ravid, D., 217
Ray, A., 133
Ray, A.B., 147
Raymer, J., 171
Raz, R., 206
Rea, C., 393
Rea, P.J., 155
Redd, L., 55
Rediker, E., 445, 446
Redle, E.E., 243
Reed, V.A., 241
Reed, F.D.D., 458
Reed, P., 202, 235
Reeve, K.F., 213
Reeve, S.A., 213
Rehfeldt, R.A., 197
Reichenberg, A., 205, 206
Reichert, J., 206
Reichle, J., 80
Reichow, B., 428
Reid, D.H., 214, 452
Reid, J.B., 173
Reid, R., 148, 151, 175, 320
Reilly, A., 70
Reiman, J.W., 83
Reinert, K.S., 216
Reinke, W.M., 164, 174, 180
Reis, S.M., 393, 395, 397
Reiss, D., 171
Reiss, M.M., 103
Reiss, S.M., 103
Renzulli & Reis 13, 396
Renzulli, J., 385, 386
Renzulli, J.S., 394, 395, 397
Reschly, D.J., 142
Resetar, J.L., 69, 92
Reuben, J.D., 171
Reutebuch, C., 153
Reyes-Blanes, M., 74, 75, 77
Reyes-MacPherson, M.E., 74
Reynolds, M.C., 9
Rhode, G., 164, 168, 172, 174, 184
Rhodes, E.A., 275, 276
Rhodes,R.L., 246
Ricci-Balich, J., 342
Riccio Omichinski, D., 337
Riccomini, P.J., 42, 152
Richard, N., 113
Richards, T.L., 137
Richman, D., 209
Richman, E.L., 74
Richter, A., 461
Richter, M., 179
Richter, S., 119, 217
Riddell, S., 8
Ridgley, R., 427
Riesch, L.M., 56, 120
Riesen, T., 29, 107, 113, 452
Rifenbark, G.G., 114
Riffle, T., 322
Rigby-Wills, H., 133
Rimm, S.B., 387, 390, 391, 393, 394, 395, 396, 400
Rimmer, J.H., 460
Ringdahl, J.E., 252
Risi, S., 209
Risley, T., 180
Risley, T.R., 138, 233, 235
Rivera, C.J., 113
Rizzolo, M.C., 454, 458
Roberson, A.A., 371
Roberts, A.L., 206
Roberts, C.D., 111
Roberts, E.L., 254
Roberts, J.E., 110
Roberts, K., 214
Roberts, N.E., 320
Roberts, R.E., 170
Robins, D.L., 208, 209
Robinson Spohn, J., 430
Robinson, C., 206, 415
Robinson, J., 79
Robinson, P.D., 25
Robles, M.M., 107
Robson, K.M., 185
Rock, M.L., 29, 452
Rockenbach, A.N., 441
Rodabaugh, E., 57
Rodriguez, N., 71
Rodriguez, P., 74, 75, 77
Rodriguez, R.J., 77
Roebroeck, M.E., 330
Roeyers, H., 73
Rogan, P., 455, 456
Rogers, K., 404, 406
Rogers, S.J., 104, 108
Roid, G.H., 101
Roitch, J., 132
Roizen, N.J., 326
Rojewski, J.W., 56, 155, 442
Rolf, K., 152
Rollyson, J.H., 214
Rooker, G.W., 71, 371
Root, J.R., 103
Roscoe, E.M., 371
Rose, J., 265
Rose, R.A., 74
Roseberry-McKibbin, C., 245
Rosen, S., 264
Rosenbaum, P., 70
Rosenbaum, S., 242
Rosenberg, M., 56
Rosenblatt, A., 170
Rosenbloom, R., 213
Rosenblum, L.P., 292, 309, 310
Ross, M., 268
Ross, D.B., 299
Rosswurm, M., 220
Rostenberg, D., 57
Roszmann-Millican, M., 46
Roth, F.P., 272
Rothenberger, A., 320
Rotherham, A.J., 42, 61
Rous, B.S., 424
Rouse-Billman, C.A., 151
Rouse, C.A., 114, 151, 168, 215
Rouse, M., 8
Rowe, D.A., 52, 119, 443, 444, 446, 447, 448, 452
Rowland, A.S., 319, 320
Rowley, L., 450
Roy, A., 164
Royer, D.J., 180
Rudasill, K.M., 172
Ruddy, B.H., 240, 249

Rueda, R., 74, 77
Ruipiper, M.L., 424
Ruiz, S., 176
Rumrill, P.D., 28
Ruppar, A., 443
Rusch, F.R., 455
Rush, A.J., 106
Rush, K.S., 176
Russel, C.S., 180
Russell-Minda, E., 303
Rutherford, R.B., 166
Ruttenber, M., 206
Rutter, M., 164, 205, 209
Rux, T.A., 152
Ryan, G., 214
Ryan, J.B., 166
Ryndak, D.L., 56, 375, 376
Ryser, G., 303

S

Sabielny, L.M., 113
Sacks, S.Z., 308
Sadeh, S., 163
Sadowska, D., 291
Safer, D.J., 323
Sailor, W., 9
Sainato, D.M., 56, 213, 426, 428, 430, 431
Salend, S., 55
Salend, S.J., 44, 56, 120
Salgado, T.M., 337
Salisbury, R., 295
Salize, H.J., 106
Sallese, M.R., 178
Salmeron, L., 451
Salmon, D., 426
Salvia, J., 101
Samuelson, S., 137
Samuelsson, S., 137
Sanchez, S., 176
Sanchez, V., 141
Sandin, S., 205
Sandler, D.P., 319, 320
Sandmel, K.N., 152
Sanford, C., 440
Sanson, A.V., 171
Sansosti, F.J., 217
Sapere, P., 264
Sapienza, C., 240, 249
Sartini, E.C., 181, 376
Sathur, R., 166
Satsangi, R., 113, 152
Satterstrom, F.K., 206
Sauders, R., 404
Saulnier, C.A., 102
Saunders, A.F., 103, 153
Savage, J., 166
Savage, M.N., 309
Sawyer, M.R., 114, 151, 168, 180, 213, 215
Saydah, S., 327
Scahill, L., 91, 212
Scarlett, W.G., 184
Scarpati, S., 113
Schaaf, J.M., 110
Schaefer, J.M., 113
Schaeffer, A.M., 209
Schafer, P.O., 326, 327, 333
Schalock, R.L., 100, 102
Schap, T., 71
Schartz, M., 320
Schatschneider, C., 241
Scheetz, N.A., 275, 277, 279
Schendel, D., 206
Scheper, F.Y., 109
Schessel, D.A., 267
Schick, B., 281
Schick, B., 279
Schilling, E.J., 373
Schilling, N., 231
Schleiss, M.R., 267
Schloerb, D.W., 302
Schlosser, R.W., 220
Schmidt, C.T., 91
Schmitz, C., 205
Schnoes, C., 320
Schnoor, C.I., 181
Schnorr, C.I., 116
Schonert-Reichl, K.A., 169
Schopler, E., 209
Schorr, E.A., 272
Schrank, F.A., 138
Schreibman, L., 205
Schreuder, R., 303
Schroeder, J., 370
Schubert, C.A., 170
Schuetzwohl, M., 106
Schuiringa, H., 106
Schultz, J., 107
Schultz, R.T., 205
Schultz, T., 183
Schultz, T.R., 91, 212
Schulz, J.B., 73
Schumacher, R.F., 29, 135
Schumaker, J.B., 135
Schumm, J.S., 155
Schupmann, W., 111
Schuster, J.W., 29, 119, 363, 364, 461
Schwab, J.R., 184
Schwarting, M., 79, 440, 442
Schwartz, A.A., 220
Schwartz, C.E., 171
Schwartz, I.S., 215
Schwartz, P., 376
Schwartz, R., 25
Schwartz, R.G., 237, 238
Schwartzman, M.N., 341, 342
Scime, N.V., 337
Scorgie, K., 73
Scott, C.M., 188
Scott, L.A., 106
Scott, T., 172
Scott, T.M., 175, 180, 181
Scruggs, T.E., 56
Scullin, M.H., 109
Secord, W., 244
See, L., 171
Seery, C.H., 238, 240
Sehyr, Z.S., 277
Seibel, E.J., 302
Seidel, T., 398
Seifert, T.A., 441
Selmar, J.W., 244
Seltzer, M.M., 73
Semel, E., 244
Severini, K.E., 219
Severini, L., 364
Severson, H.H., 175
Seward, J., 29, 461
Sexson, S.B., 325, 333
Shadish, W., 371
Shafer, M., 454
Shalev, R.A., 56, 109, 120
Shane, H., 220
Shapiro, B., 359
Shapiro, E.S., 321
Shapiro, J., 74
Shaver, D., 79, 134, 264, 281, 319, 440, 442
Shaver, D.M., 281
Shaw, D.S., 171
Shaw, R., 301
Shaywitz, B.A., 137
Shaywitz, S.E., 137

Shearer, M.L., 447, 458
Sheedy, S., 248
Sheffield, J., 383–384, 407–408
Sheldon, D.L., 73
Sheldon, J.B., 368
Sheldrick, R.C., 208
Shen, M.D., 208
Sheppard, B., 206
Sheridan, S.M., 179, 450
Sherman, J.A., 368
Shetgiri, R., 171
Shin, M., 178
Shippen, M.E., 151
Shipstead, J., 113
Shiraga, B., 361
Shivakumar, K., 323
Shogren, K.A., 51, 59, 60, 75, 76, 77, 80, 86, 91, 93, 100, 103, 105, 114, 366, 370, 374, 433
Shonkoff, J.P., 415
Siegle, D., 387, 390, 391, 393, 394, 395, 396, 400
Sievers, C., 364
Sigafoos, J., 213, 219, 364, 371, 429
Silbaugh, B.C., 213
Silberman, R.K., 45
Silberman, S., 204
Silbert, J., 150, 151, 152
Sileo, N.M., 218, 329
Silverman, L.K., 387
Silvestri, S.M., 29, 61
Silvia, P.J., 388
Simeonsson, R.J., 8
Simmons-Reed, E.A., 456
Simmons, D.C., 29
Simmons, J., 91
Simmons, T., 446, 453
Simmons, T.J., 29, 454
Simner, J., 199
Simon, P., 242
Simonsen, B., 188
Simonsen, M.L., 452
Simoyan, O.M., 323
Simpson, K., 199
Simpson, R.L., 60, 85, 195, 220
Sims, D.G., 277
Sinclair, A.C., 56
Sinclair, J., 447, 458
Sinclair, T.E., 79
Singh, L.J., 109
Singh, N.N., 364
Singh, R.K.J., 332
Singleton, J.L., 263
Singley, D., 114, 361, 363, 461
Siperstein, G.N., 56, 166
Sirois, M.S., 171
Sitlington, P.L., 446, 453, 456
Skau, L., 249
Skeels, H.M., 413
Skene, W.A., 264
Skibo, H., 368
Skinnder, C.H., 151
Skinner, B.F., 244
Skinner, C.H., 186
Skinner, D., 74, 75, 77
Skinner, M., 74, 75, 77, 110
Skipper, B.J., 319, 320
Skrtic, T.M., 61
Skudlarski, P., 137
Slade, N., 77
Sladeczek, I.E., 198
Slaton, J.D., 371
Slavin, R.E., 57
Slayton, J.D., 177
Sleeth, L., 337
Slocum, T.A., 150
Slocum, T.E., 150
Smaldino, J.J., 276
Smalls, Y., 176
Smedt, B.D., 137
Smith Byles, B., 100
Smith Myles, B., 202
Smith, A.T., 166
Smith, F.A., 441
Smith, J., 9, 340
Smith, J.D., 9, 11, 59, 103, 121, 171
Smith, L., 443
Smith, M.C., 70
Smith, P., 199
Smith, P.D., 368
Smith, R.J.H., 267
Smith, S., 56
Smith, S.W., 51
Smith, T., 91, 211, 212
Smith, T.E.C., 121
Smith, T.J., 292
Smogorzewska, J., 56
Sneizyk, C.J., 219
Snell, M.E., 45, 46, 60, 114, 120, 250, 343, 367, 369, 370, 372
Sng, J., 332
Snider, V.E., 323, 324
Snidman, N., 171
Snowling, M.J., 237
Snyder, N.W., 206
Snyder, P.A., 427
Soares, D.A., 86
Sobsey, D., 73
Soder, A.L., 244
Soderman, A.K., 424
Solis, M., 153, 178, 188, 450
Solomon, B., 72
Song, Y., 147
Sonnenschein, S., 82
Sontag, E., 9
Sonuga-Barke, E.J., 320
Soodak, L.C., 51, 75, 76, 77, 80, 91, 93, 433
Soraci, S.A., 104
Soriano, H., 214
Soukakou, E., 424
Soukup, J.H., 113
Southall, C., 197
Southall, C.M., 222
Sowell, E.R., 320
Spagna, M.E., 45
Spain, J., 445
Sparling, J.J., 414
Sparrow, S.S., 102
Spencer, L.J., 272
Spencer, M., 133
Spencer, P., 279
Spencer, S., 374
Spencer, T.J., 319, 337
Sperry, L., 213
Spina Bifida Association, 332
Spinelli, C.G., 36
Spirito, A., 166
Splett, J.W., 164, 174
Spooner, F., 103, 113, 217, 367, 368, 369, 450
Sprague, J.R., 173, 176
Spreat, S., 102
Sprick, R., 184
Spriggs, A., 363
Spriggs, A.D., 181, 215, 461
Spungin, S.J., 291, 300, 301, 306
Squires, J., 421
SRI International, 42
Srinivasan, M.A., 302
SSA (Social Security Administration), 288
Stafford, A.M., 55
Stage, S., 171
Stahl, K.A.D., 29
Stainback, S., 59, 120
Stainback, W., 59, 120
Stainbeck, S., 57

Stainbeck, W., 57
Stam, H.J., 330
Stanfa, K., 298
Stangl, A., 299
Stanton-Chapman, T.L., 424, 429
State, T.M., 188
States, J., 115
Stecker, P.M., 59, 60, 61, 62
Steege, M.W., 177
Steere, D.E., 369
Steffen, S., 451
Stein, M., 152
Stemplewski, R., 291
Stepaniuk, I., 372
Stephens, T.M., 85
Stephenson, J., 220
Sternberg, R.J., 386, 390
Stetser, M., 440
Stevens, C., 206
Stevens, D., 44
Stevens, J.J., 42
Stevenson, J., 265
Stevenson, N.A., 28
Stichter, J.P., 91, 176
Sticken, J., 303
Stiegler, L.N., 199, 202
Stillitano, C., 91, 212
Stillwell, R., 440
Stinson, M.S., 273
Stith, J.L., 272
Stocco, C., 214
Stockall, N., 428
Stockard, J., 151
Stocker, J.D., 25
Stoesz, B.M., 199
Stokoe, W., 278
Stoner, G., 323
Stoner, J.B., 78, 343
Storey, K., 56, 176, 451, 452, 456
Stormount and Reinke 2009, 180
Stough, L.M., 111
Stowe, M.J., 54
Strain, P.S., 222
Strand, J., 460
Stratton, E., 121
Strauss, A., 128
Strawbridge, C.P., 104
Stremel, K., 342, 362
Strickland, B.B., 50
Strickland, C.A., 394
Stromer, R., 216
Strong, C.J., 249
Strouse, M.C., 458
Strunk, J.A., 71
Stuart, M.E., 292
Stuart, S.K., 83
Stubbs, B., 104
Stultz, J., 260–261, 272, 279, 283
Stump, C.S., 45
Sturmey, P., 213
Stuttering Foundation, 238, 240
Stutzman, B., 372
Subotnik, R.F., 390, 391
Sugai, G., 181, 182, 322
Suk, A.L., 79
Sukhodolsky, D.G., 91, 212
Sulewski, J., 441
Sullivan, A.L., 163
Sullivan, K., 104
Sumi, C., 170, 174
Summers, J.A., 70, 76, 78
Sun, C.K., 104
Sun, R., 69
Sundberg, M.L., 213, 244, 245
Sunderland, L.C., 238
Suomi, J., 452
Sutherland, K., 189
Sutman, F.X., 217
Sutton, J., 333
Swan, J.H., 345
Swanson, H.L., 136, 147
Swanson, M.R., 208
Sweatman, L., 339
Swedeen, B.L., 452
Sweeney, D.P., 323
Sweet, M., 361, 370
Sweller, N., 424
Swenson, A.M., 303
Swerdfeger, A.L., 207
Swerdlik, M.E., 39
Swiezy, N., 91, 212
Switzky, H.N., 104
Sy, L.S., 207
Sylvester, L., 452, 453
Synhorst, L., 171
Szabo, J.L., 338
Szeklicki, R., 291
Szidon, K., 443
Szumski, G., 56
Szymanski, L., 109

T

Taanila, A., 109
Taber-Doughty, T., 114
Taber, T.A., 55, 119
TAGG (Transition Assessment and Goal Generator), 444
Talbott, E., 170
Tang, G., 279
Tanis, E.S., 454, 458
Tankersley, M., 28, 55
Targett, P.S., 456
Tarlow, K.R., 178
TASH, 352, 458
Tassé, M.J., 102, 106
Taubman, M., 217
Taylor, B.A., 197, 220
Taylor, B.L., 214
Taylor, J., 454
Taylor, J.C., 180
Taylor, J.L., 152
Taylor, L.E., 207
Taylor, S.J., 57, 120, 204
Tekin-Iftar, E., 197
Terenzini, P.T., 441
Terman, L., 384
Terzi, L., 8, 9
Test, D.W., 51, 52, 69, 79, 105, 107, 114, 116, 119, 181, 184, 213, 217, 308, 443, 444, 446, 447, 448, 450, 452, 453, 456, 460, 461
Tétreault, S., 292
The Stuttering Foundation, 239, 240
Therrien, W.J., 147
Thiede, K., 170
Thissen, D., 102
Thistle, J.J., 80
Thoma, C.A., 106
Thomas, A., 114, 461
Thomas, C.C., 45
Thomas, E., 456
Thompson, J.R., 78, 100
Thompson, M., 320
Thompson, P.M., 320
Thompson, R., 214
Thompson, R.H., 197
Thompson, S.D., 361
Thompson, T., 108, 202
Thomson, J.M., 450
Thomson, M.A., 207
Thorell, L.B., 319

Thornton, L.C., 171
Thrulaow, M., 358, 374
Thumann-Prezioso, C., 277
Thunberg, G., 204
Thurlow, M., 8
Thurlow, M.L., 169
Thurston, L.P., 376
Tick, N.T., 106
Tierney, D, 308
Tiger, J.H., 213
Timko, T.C., 430
Tincani, M., 43, 213, 217, 371, 461
Tindal, G., 42
Tingstrom, D.H., 180, 186
Tittle, M.D., 263
Todd, A.W., 322
Todd, J., 220
Todd, K.Q., 209
Todd, N.W., 266
Todis, B., 179
Toga, A.W., 320
Toldson, I.A., 43
Tomaseone, J.R., 337
Tomasi, B.J., 197
Tomblin, J.B., 242, 271
Tomlinson, C.A., 394, 395
Toms, O., 183
Tonelson, S.W., 29, 452
Topor, I., 301
Torgesen, J.K., 142
Torgeson, J.K., 244
Torrance, E.P., 388
Torres, C., 147
Torres, I., 300
Toste, J.R., 181
Tourette Syndrome Association, 166
Towles-Reeves, E., 358, 374
Trach, J.S., 454, 455
Trainor, A.A., 452
Trask-Tyler, S., 115, 309
Travers, J.C., 43, 364, 374, 461
Travers, P.A., 150
Treffert, D.A., 199
Trembath, D., 220
Tremblay, P., 155
Trief, E., 301
Trotman Scott, M., 388
Troughton, L.C.W., 322
Trout, A.L., 320
Troyer, M., 450
Trusty, S., 304
Tsaliki, E., 111
Tseng, H.U., 207
Tseng, P.T., 104
Tsuji, K., 217
Tucci, S.T., 264
Tullis, C.A., 364, 368, 456
Tuomainen, O., 264
Turan, M., 57
Turnbull, A.P., 50, 51, 75, 76, 77, 80, 82–83, 91, 93, 433
Turnbull, H.R., 51, 54, 75, 76, 77, 80, 91, 93, 344, 433, 441
Turnbull, P., 441
Turner-Henson, A., 345
Turner, K., 91, 212
Twyman, J.S., 39, 182, 218, 219

U

U.S. Dept. of Education, 7, 26, 27, 43, 74, 109, 120, 136, 155, 156, 167, 170, 188, 204, 221, 241, 253, 254, 265, 281, 293, 308, 309, 312, 325, 344, 358, 359, 374, 390, 416, 440
U.S. Dept. of Health and Human Services, 111, 421
U.S. National Library of Medicine, 328, 329
U.S. Office of Education, 130
Uchida, M., 337
Udvari-Solner, A., 370, 374, 376
Uffen, E., 242
Umbach, D.M., 319, 320
Umbreit, J., 320
United States Association of Blind Athletes, 309
University of Orgeon, 140
Unruh, D.K., 448, 452
Uphold, N.M., 52, 119, 451, 461
Urton, K., 152
Usami, S., 267
Utley, C.A., 44

V

Valbuena, D., 176
Valdes, A.M., 171
Valentine, A., 207
Valle, J.W., 8
Valli, C., 278
van Berckelaer-Onnes, I.A., 201
van Bon, W.J.J., 303
Van Bourgondien, M.E., 209
Van Camp, G., 267
Van Cleve, J.V., 275
Van den Hoofdakker, B.J., 320
van den Pol, R.A., 119
van der Lee, J.H., 325
Van Der Oord, S., 320
van der Putten, A.J., 356
van Dijk, W., 181, 461
Van Dycke, J.L., 51
Van Haren B., 44
van Heijst, B.F.C., 462
van Karnebeek, C.D.M., 109
Van Nieuwenhuijzen, M., 106
Van Norman, R.K., 322
Van Riper, C., 236
Van Riper, M., 70
Van Ryzin, M.J., 164
Van Tassel-Baska, J., 394
van Timmeren, 356
VanDeventer, P., 374
Vanegas, S.B., 73, 74
Vannest, K.J., 86
Vanselow, N.R., 213
Vargiami, E., 206
Vasquez, E., 74, 75, 77
Vaughn, S., 133, 146
Vaughn, B.J., 73
Vaughn, M.G., 166
Vaughn, S., 56, 148, 155, 450
Velissariou, V., 111
Velthorst, E., 206
Veltman, J.A., 109
Venerosi, A., 204
Vergason, G.A., 70
Verhoven, L., 265
Ververi, A., 206
Vianello, R., 104
Vick, A.M., 103
Viirre, E.S., 302
Villaseñor, P., 107
Vincent, L.B., 56, 120
Vinh, M., 57
Visscher, C., 291
Vissers, L.E., 109
Vlaskamp, C.C., 356
Vogelgesang, K.L., 322
Volk, H., 206
Volk, H.E., 206
Volkmar, F.R., 205
Vollmer, T.R., 176
Volonino, V., 60

Voltz, D.L., 81
Vu, J.A., 354, 355, 359, 373
Vuyk, M.A., 393

W

Wagenknecht, L., 327
Wagner, L., 170
Wagner, M., 79, 169, 170, 174, 320, 357, 440, 441, 442
Wagner, M.O., 292
Wagner, R.K., 133, 134, 244
Wahl, H., 290
Wakefield, A.J., 206, 207
Waks, A.B., 217
Waldron, N., 55
Waldron, N.L., 29, 56, 59, 60
Walker-Smith, J.A., 207
Walker, A., 105
Walker, A.N., 219
Walker, A.R., 52, 119, 461
Walker, B., 151
Walker, D., 423
Walker, E.A., 271
Walker, H.M., 162, 164, 170, 173, 174, 175, 179, 189
Walker, J., 179
Walker, L.A., 277
Walker, V.L., 46
Wall, J.C., 52
Wallace, G., 244
Waller, S., 151
Walthall, J.C., 174
Walther-Thomas, C., 155
Wanders, R.J.A., 109
Wandry, D., 453
Wang, J., 186, 206
Wang, S.S., 104
Wanzek, J., 148
Ward, J., 199
Ward, S.E., 430
Warfield, M.E., 415
Waschbusch, D.A., 169
Washburn, J., 84, 85
Washington, A., 391, 392
Washington, B.H., 452
Wasik, B.H., 414
Wasserman, A.M., 172
Waters, R., 460
Watkins, C.L., 150
Watkins, L., 213, 429
Watkins, M.W., 85
Watson, M., 43
Watson, S., 132
Watson, T.S., 177
Watt, M., 357
Watt, S., 321
Watters, J.J., 405
Waxton, B.L., 166
Webb-Johnson, G.C., 44
Webber, J., 170
Webber, M., 248
Wechsler, D., 101, 138
Wedell, K., 8
Wehby, J.H., 29, 135, 166, 168, 175, 178, 180, 181, 184, 188, 189
Wehman, P., 446, 453, 454, 456
Wehmeyer, M.L., 100, 103, 105, 113, 114, 441, 453
Wei, T., 209
Wei, X., 79, 134, 440, 442
Weiner, M.T., 265
Weintraub, F.J., 60
Weir, K., 56, 120
Weirich, L.C., 305
Weisner, T., 106, 460
Weisse, I., 292
Weisskopf, M.G., 206
Welch, M., 9
Welcome, S.E., 320
Wellman, G.J., 209
Wenzel, C., 450
Werfel, K.L., 264
Werner, 128
Werts, M.G., 116
Weseman, L., 358, 374
Wesson, C., 92
West, E., 44
West, M., 454, 456
Westling, D., 56
Westling, D.L., 355, 367, 369
Wetherby, A., 208
Wexler, J., 56
Whalon, K.J., 106, 120
Wheeler, A., 110
Wheeler, C.B., 442
Wheeler, D.L., 220
Wheeler, J.J., 73
Whinnery, S.B., 251
Whipple H., 180
Whiren, A.P., 424
Whitaker, S., 101
White, W., 453
Whiteside, E., 252
Whitfield, K., 35, 56, 62–63
Whitford, D.K., 181, 320
Whiting, G.W., 43
Whitley, F.P., 119
Whitley, K.G., 181
Whitlow, G.M., 276, 277
Whittenbury, H., 454
Wickerd, G., 177
Widaman, K.F., 56, 102
Wiederholt, J.L., 138
Wieland, N., 73
Wiig, E.H., 244
Wilberg, J.H., 307
Wilbur, R.B., 264
Wilburn, M., 98, 121, 122–123
Wilcox, S., 278
Wild, T.A., 299
Wilens, T.E., 319
Wiley, A.L., 166
Wilkins, J., 445
Wilkinson-Flicker, S., 79
Will, M., 442
Will, M.C., 442
Willard-Holt, C., 330
Willcutt, E.G., 134, 320
Willey, L.H., 203
Williams, M.E., 216
Williams-Diehm, K., 79, 105, 114
Williams, B.F., 80
Williams, C.B., 264
Williams, C.R., 376
Williams, G., 91
Williams, J., 450
Williams, K., 199, 281
Williams, L., 180
Williams, N.A., 164, 168, 172, 174, 184
Williams, S., 447
Williams, S.C., 303
Williams, V.L., 86
Williamson, G.G., 46
Williamson, R.L., 121
Willings, C., 303
Willis, C., 353
Willis, J.H., 208
Willoughby, M.T., 169
Willoughby, T., 135
Wills, H., 321
Wills, H.P., 175, 180, 188, 213
Wills, J., 70
Wilmot, L., 303
Wilson, C.L., 78
Wilson, K., 222

Wilson, R., 92, 342
Wiltshire, S., 199
Windham, G.C., 206
Wine, B., 214
Wing, L., 195, 209
Winston, E.A., 273
Winter-Messiers, M.A., 199
Winter, A., 204
Winzer, M., 275
WIOA (Workforce Innvation and Opportunity), 456
Witmer, S., 101
Wittrock, M.C., 397
Witty, P.A., 384
Witzel, B.S., 131, 144
Wojtalewicz, D., 164, 174
Wolery, M., 116, 423, 428
Wolf, J.S., 85
Wolf, M.M., 180
Wolfe, L.H., 321
Wolfensberger, W., 122, 458
Wolff, J.J., 208
Wolffe, K., 306
Wolffe, K.E., 308
Wolford, P.L., 168
Wolfram, W., 231
Wolniak, G.C., 441
Wolters, N., 265
Wong, C., 212, 221, 222
Wood, C.L., 39, 57, 92, 213, 371, 426
Wood, L.B., 219
Wood, S.J., 114
Wood, T.W., 151
Wood, W., 51
Wood, W.M., 105
Woodcock, R.W., 138
Woodman, A.C., 415
Woodruff, G., 46
Woods, I.L., Jr., 109
Woods, J., 208
Woods, L.L., 452, 453
Woods, W.E., 447, 458
Worcester, N.A., 72
Workforce Innovation and Opportunity Act, 454
Wormsley, D.P., 298, 299, 311
Worrell, F.C., 390, 391
Worsfold, S., 265
Wortham, S.C., 420, 422, 423
Wright Hirsch, D., 113
Wright, B.L., 391, 392
Wright, C.F., 111
Wright, P.D., 62, 74, 345
Wright, P.W.D., 62, 74, 345
Wu, C.K., 104
Wu, J., 454, 458
Wu, M.K., 104
Wu, P.F., 364
Wyatte, M.L., 73
Wynn, J.W., 211

X

Xin, J.F., 217
Xin, W., 319
Xu, X., 206

Y

Yairi, E., 238, 240, 242, 249
Yamaki, K., 74
Yantes, C., 202
Yasik, A.E., 20
Yawn, C.D., 57
Yeager, A., 364
Yeh, T., 299
Yell, M.L., 12, 19, 48, 344, 345
Yeong, M.M.Y., 332
Ylvisaker, M., 373
Yoon, S.Y., 25
York-Barr, J., 370
Yoshinaga-Itano, C., 279
Young, L.J., 205
Young, N.D., 131, 132
Yovanoff, P., 454
Ysseldyke, J.E., 101
Yu, J., 264, 281
Yu, J.W., 134, 319
Yu, K., 171
Yuan, T., 44
Yurick, A.L., 25

Z

Zabihaylo, C., 305
Zafeiriou, D.I., 206
Zambo, D.M., 375
Zane, C., 74
Zane, T., 220
Zane, T.L., 219
Zawolkow, E., 277
Zebehazy, K.T., 292
Zechella, A.N., 70, 75
Zeigler, M., 452
Zelinsky, N.A., 371
Zelleke, T.G., 326
Zetlin, A.G., 9
Zhang, A., 79
Zhang, D., 102, 254
Zhang, J., 73
Zhou, Q., 345
Zigler, E., 104
Zigmond, N., 29, 46, 56, 60
Zimmerman, K.N., 219, 428
Zirkus, K.J., 164
Zito, J.M., 323
Zlomke, K., 186
Zohsel, K., 171
Zubal-Ruggieri, R., 463
Zumeta Edmonds, R., 61
Zwaigenbaum, L., 70, 202, 205, 208

Subject Index

A

AAC (*see* augmentative and alternative communication)
AAIDD (American Association on Intellectual and Development Disabilities), 10, 99
  intellectual disability definition, 99–100
ABA (*see* applied behavior analysis)
ABC recording, 176
ABDS (Adaptive Behavior Diagnostic Scale), 102
Abecedarian Project, 414
Ability-achievement discrepancy, learning disabilities and, 130
Academic curriculum, students with intellectual disabilities, 113
Academic learning time, 115
Achievement tests, 138. *See also* standardized tests
  Iowa Test of Basic Skills, 138
  KeyMath-3, 138
  Test of Mathematical Abilities, 138
  Test of Reading Comprehension, 138
  Wechsler Individual Achievement Test III, 138
  Woodcock Reading Mastery Tests, 138
  Woodcock-Johnson IV Tests of Achievement, 138
Acquired hearing loss, 266–267
Acquired immune deficiency syndrome (AIDS), 329
Acquisition stage of learning, feedback, 116, 118
Active listening, 79–80
  versus passive, 80
Active student response (ASR), 115, 116
ADA (Americans with Disabilities Act), 20–21, 22
Adapted physical education, 339
Adaptive behavior, 102–103
  ABDS (Adaptive Behavior Diagnostic Scale), 102
  conceptual skills, 102
  DABS (Diagnostic Adaptive Behavior Scale), 102
  daily living skills, 106
  early service eligibility, 422
  practical skills, 102
  self-care, 106
  social relationships, 106
  social skills, 102
  Vineland Adaptive Behavior Scales, 102
ADHD (*see* attention-deficit/hyperactivity disorder)
ADOS-2 (Autism Diagnostic Observation Schedule), 209
Adulthood, 77
  college attendance, 440–441
  community involvement, 442, 457–460
  employment, 441, 451–457
  high school completion, 440
  independent living, 457–460
  postsecondary education, 440–441
  recreation/leisure, 460–461
  self-directed video prompting, 459–460
  social engagement, 461
  supported living, 458
  transition IEP, 443–447
  transition services, 442–443
  transition success, 447–461
AIDS (*see* acquired immune deficiency syndrome)
Alphabetic principle, 37
Alternative teaching, co-teaching, 56
Amendment to Title I of the Elementary and Secondary Education Act, 21
Amendments to the Education of the Handicapped Act, 22
Amendments to the Elementary and Secondary Education Act, 21
American Psychiatric Association, intellectual disabilities, 100, learning disorders definition, 132; autism spectrum disorder, 196
American Sign Language (ASL), 260–261, 274
  bi-bi (bilingual-bicultural) approach, 278–279
  as language of instruction, 279
Amniocentesis, 110
Animal assistance, 341
Annual review, 38, 42
Anorexia nervosa, 165
Anxiety disorders, 165
Applied behavior analysis (ABA), 212–214
Apgar scale, 420
  evaluation scale, 421
The Arc, 68
ARCH National Respite Network and Resource Center, 72
Armstrong v Kline, 18
ARND (alcohol-related neurodevelopmental disorder), 108
ASD (*see* autism spectrum disorder)
ASDS (Asperger Syndrome Diagnostic Scale), 209
ASEBA (Achenbach System of Empirically Based Assessment), 174
ASI-R (Autism Diagnostic Interview-Revised), 209
ASL (*see* American Sign Language)
Asperger syndrome, 202–203. *See also* autism spectrum disorder
  characteristics, 202–203
ASR (active student response), 115, 116
Assistive technology, 17, 340–341, vi
Association for Children with Learning Disabilities (ACLD), 128
Association for Science in Autism Treatment (ASAT), 68
ASSQ (Autism Spectrum Screening Questionnaire), 209
Asthma, 348
At risk, definition, 6, 31
Attention-deficit/hyperactivity disorder (ADHD)
  academic achievement, 320
  behaviorally based interventions, 320–321
  brain damage system, 318
  causes, 320
  comorbidity, 320
  definition, 318–319
  diagnosis, 318–319
  eligibility for special education, 319
  hyperactivity and impulsivity, 318
  hyperkinetic impulse disorder of children, 318
  inattention, 318
  learning disabilities and, 134
  medication, 321, 323, 324
  minimal brain dysfunction, 318
  postencephalitic disorder, 318
  prevalence, 319
  self-monitoring, 321–322
  subtypes, 319
  treatment, 320–324
Audiology, 15
Audition, 262
Auditory learning
  auditory training, 276
  auditory-verbal therapy, 276
  cued speech, 277
  fingerspelling, 277
  manually coded English, 277
  speechreading, 276–277
  total communication, 277
Augmentative and alternative communication (AAC), 228
  aided AAC techniques, 251
  PECS (Picture Exchange Communication System), 252
  symbol sets, 251–252
  symbol systems, 251–252
  unaided AAC techniques, 251

Augmented reality, low vision and, 302
Autism spectrum disorder. *See also* Asperger syndrome
ABA (applied behavior analysis), 212–214
ADOS-2 (Autism Diagnostic Observation Schedule), 209
ASDS (Asperger Syndrome Diagnostic Scale), 209
ASI-R (Autism Diagnostic Interview-Revised), 209
ASSQ (Autism Spectrum Screening Questionnaire), 209
autistic psychopathology, 195
behavior skills training (BST), 214
behavior traps, 200–201
CARS-2 (Childhood Autism Rating Scale), 209
causes, 205
challenging behavior, 202
cognitive functioning, 199, 201–202
communication and, 198
definition, 195–196
diagnosis, 209
diagnostic criteria, 196–197
DSM and, 196–197
DTT (discrete trial training), 212–213
early infantile autism, 195
echolalia, 198
educational approaches, 210–221
EIBI (early intensive behavioral intervention), 211–212
environmental factors, 206–207
epigenetics and, 206
evidence-based practices, 219–221
executive functioning and, 199
false-belief tests, 197
facilitated communication, 220
genetic factors, 205–206
high-functioning, 199, 202
historical events in education, 210–211
hypersensitivity, 199
hyposensitivity, 199
IDEA definition, 196
identifying, 207–209
instructional technology, 218–219
IQ scores, 201–202
joint attention, 197
language and, 198
low-functioning, 199
M-CHAT-R/F, 208–209
MMR (mumps-measles-rubella) vaccine, 206–207
neuropathology, 205
overselectivity, 201
PDD-NOS, 196
PECS (Picture Exchange Communication System), 213
pica, 202
positive attributes, 203–204
prevalence, 204–205
racial disparity in representation, 43
regular classroom, 221–222
resource classroom, 222–223
Sallie-Anne task and, 197
sameness, 198–199
savant syndrome, 199
SCQ (Social Communication Questionnaire), 209
screening, 208–209
sensory stimuli, responses, 199
social interactions, 197
social stories, 217–218
special classroom, 222–223
stereotypy, 198
strengths, 203–204
theory of mind and, 197
twins, 205–206
uneven skill development, 199
unproven treatments, 220–221
visual activity schedules, 215–216
Autosomal recessive disorders, 328–329

B

Battelle Developmental Inventory, 422
Behavior intervention plan (BIP), 176, 184
Behavior traps, 200–201
Behavioral excesses, intellectual disabilities, 106–107
Bell-shaped curve, IQ scores, 101
BERS (Behavioral and Emotional Rating Scale), 175
Best Buddies, 461
BICS (basic interpersonal communication skills), 245–246
Biological risk, early intervention, 416
Bipolar disorder, 165
Blindness. *See also* deaf-blindness; low vision
braille and, 297–298
cognition, 291
computer access, 299–300
definitions, 288–289
field of vision, 288–289
functionally blind, 290
language, 291
legal blindness, 288
mobile devices, 299–300
mobility and, 291–292
motor development, 291–292
Nemeth code, 298
partially sighted, 288
print reading aids, 299
social adjustment and, 292–293
specialized instruction, 295–300
tactile aids, 299
totally blind, 290
Bloom's taxonomy, 397–398
Board Certified Behavior Analyst (BCBA), 127, 177
Board of Education of the Hendrick Hudson Central School District v. Rowley (1982), 18
Braille, 297–298
Brain damage, 359
learning disabilities and, 137
Brain disorders, EBD and, 170–171
Brain dysfunction
dyslexia and, 137
learning disabilities and, 137
Brain dysgenesis, EBD and, 170
Brain function, 354
Brain injury, EBD and, 170. *See also* traumatic brain injury
Bridging the Word Gap National Research Network, 235
Brigance Comprehensive Inventory of Basic Skills, 139
Brown v. Board of Education of Topeka, 11
BST (behavior skills training), ASD and, 214
Bulimia nervosa, 165
BuzzMob, 87

C

CALP (cognitive academic language proficiency), 245–246
Cataracts, 295, 296
CBM (*see* curriculum-based measurement)
CCBD (Council for Children with Behavioral Disorders), emotional or behavioral disorder, 163
CEC (*see* Council for Exceptional Children)
CEEDAR (Collaboration for Effective Educator Development, Accountability, and Reform), v
Cerebral palsy, 330–331
Challenging behavior
ASD and, 202
intellectual disabilities, 106–107
learning disabilities and, 134–135
CHARGE Syndrome, 360
Child behavior checklist (CBCL), 174–175
Childhood Autism Rating Scale (CARS-2), 209
Childhood stage of child with disabilities, 76
Children with Learning Disabilities Act, 129
Choral responding, 39
Chorionic villi sampling (CVS), 111
ClassDojo, 87
Classwide Peer Tutoring, 57, 58–59
Classwide Student Tutoring Teams, 58
Juniper Gardens Children's Project model, 58
Ohio State University model, 58
Peer-Assisted Learning Strategies, 58

Closed head injury, 354
Closed needs assessment, 91–92
Cochlear implants, 271–273
Coercive pain control, EBD and, 172
Cognitive functioning
  ASD and, 201–202
  blindness, 291
  early service eligibility, 422
  intellectual disabilities, 103–105
  low vision, 291
Collaboration, 45
College attendance, 440–441
Coma, 355
Commercial facilities, ADA and, 20–21
Communication
  accepting parent statements, 78–79
  active listening, 79–80
  ASD and, 198
  BuzzMob, 87
  ClassDojo, 87
  definition, 229
  early service eligibility, 422
  encouragement, 80
  explaining, 230
  expression, 230
  face-to-face, 83–85
  family-professional partnership, 78–80
  focus, 80
  guidelines, 90
  home-school, 83–90
  HomeworkNOW, 87
  informing, 230
  language, 230–232
  low-incidence disabilities, 355
  low-incidence disabilities, curriculum, 362
  narrating, 229
  nonlinguistic cues, 230
  paralinguistic behaviors, 230
  questioning effectively, 80
  Remind, 87
  requesting, 230
  RERUN (reflect, explain, reason, understand, negotiate), 82–83
  speech, 232–233
  speech and language development, 233–235
  telephone communication, 87–90
  written, 85–87
Communication disorders
  AAC (augmentative and alternative communications), 228, 251–252
  BICS (basic interpersonal communication skills), 245–246
  CALP (cognitive academic language proficiency), 245–246
  causes, 242
  classroom, 253–254
  collaborative consultation, 253
  community, 254
  curriculum, 253–254
  definition, 235
  difference *versus* disability, 246
  ELL (English Language Learner), 245–246
  evaluation, 244–245
  fluency disorders, 238–240, 248–249
  functional, 242
  IDEA, 236
  language delay, 241
  language disorders, 236, 241, 249–251
  monitoring, 253
  placement, 253–257
  prevalence, 241–242
  pull-out, 253
  screening, 243
  self-advocacy, 254–255
  separate classroom, 254
  speech impairments, 236
  speech-sound errors, 237–238, 247–248
  teacher observation, 243
  voice disorder treatment, 249
  voice disorders, 240–241
Community involvement as adult, 442, 457–460
Community-based instruction, 119
Compensatory intervention, 24
Conceptual skills, 102
Concussion, 354
Conductive hearing impairment, 265
Conflict resolution, 82–83
Consultation, 45
Content areas, 152–154
Content enhancement, 152
Continuum of alternative placements, 53–54
  homebound, 54
  hospital, 54
  regular classroom, 54
  residential school, 54
  resource classroom, 53, 54
  self-contained classroom, 53
  separate classroom, 53, 54
  separate school, 54
Cooperative learning, 120–121
  classwide peer tutoring, 57
  inclusion and, 57
  intellectual disabilities and, 120
Coordination, 45
Cortical visual impairment (CVI), 295, 296
Co-teaching
  inclusion and, 56
  one teaching/one helping, 56
  parallel teaching, 56
  station teaching, 56
  team teaching, 56
Council for Exceptional Children (CEC), v, 5
Counseling services, 15
C-Print, 15
Cranmer abacus, 299
Criterion-referenced tests, 138–139
CUES learning strategy, 147
Cultural bias in referral procedures, 44
Cultural differences, families and, 74–76
Cultural mismatch, 79
Cultural reciprocity, 77–78
Culturally responsive services, 77–78
Culturally responsive transition planning, 79
Curriculum-based measurement (CBM), 138, 139–141, 144
Cystic fibrosis, 328

D

Daily living skills, 106
Deaf community, 263
  ASL as language of instruction, 279
  language, 261
Deaf culture, 261
Deaf-blindness
  causes, 360
  characteristics, 356–357
  CHARGE syndrome, 360
  definition, 353
  educational programs, 372–373
  prevalence, 359
  tactile teaching techniques, 372
Deafness. *See also* hearing loss
  academic achievement and, 264
  alerting devices, 274
  ASL (American Sign Language), 273–274, 278–279
  assessment, infants, 267–268
  audiogram, 269
  auditory brain stem response, 268
  auditory learning, 276–277
  behavior observation audiometry, 269
  captioning, 274
  cochlear implants, 271–272
  culture, 263
  definition, 261
  ear, anatomy of, 262
  education, 274–281

English literacy and, 263–264
fingerspelling, 278
group assistive listening devices, 271
hearing aids, 270–271
historical events in education, 275
infants, auditory behaviors, 267–268
operant conditioning audiometry, 269
oral/aural approaches to education, 275–277
otoacoustic emission screening, 268
play audiometry, 269
postsecondary education, 282–283
prevalence, 265
pure-tone audiometry, 268–269
residual hearing, 261
Registry of Interpreters for the Deaf, 273
social functioning and, 265
speech and, 264
speech reception test, 269
speech-to-text translation, 273–274
SRT (speech reception threshold), 269
student placement, 281–282
student tips, 282
TDD (telecommunication devices for the deaf), 274
TT (text telephones), 274
TTYs (teletypes), 274
visual phonics, 263–264
Denasality, 240
Depression, 165
Developmental delay, 8
early intervention and, 416
Developmental Disabilities Assistance and Bill of Rights Act, 22
Developmentally appropriate practice (DAP), 424, 426
Diabetes, 327–328
Diabetic retinopathy, 296
Diagnostic Adaptive Behavior Scale (DABS), 102
Diagnostic and Statistical Manual of Mental Disorders, 5th Edition (DSM-5), 132
Dialects, 231
DIBELS (Dynamic Indicators of Basic Early Literacy Skills), 140
Differential acceptance, EBD and, 187
Differentiated model of giftedness and talent, 386
Differential reinforcement of other behavior (DRO), 351
Direct daily measurement, 140–141
Disability
definition, 6, 31
family responses, 70
Discrete trial training (DTT), 212–213
Division for Children with Learning Disabilities (DCLD), 128, 129
Down syndrome, 110
intellectual disabilities and, 108
ASD (autism spectrum disorder), 196–197
Due process, 12
Dysarthria, 242
Dyslexia, 132, 137

E

Ear anatomy, 262
Early childhood special education, 413
Apgar scale, 420, 421
Battelle Developmental Inventory, 422
center-based programs, 433–434
combined home-center programs, 434
curriculum, 423–424
developmentally appropriate practice, 424, 426
direct systematic observation, 423
eligibility for services, 422
embedded learning, 430
families and, 434
home-based programs, 432–433
hospital-based programs, 432
IEP goals, 427–428
IFSP goals, 427–428
Individual Growth and Development Indicators, 423
newborn blood test screening, 420–421
peer-mediated interventions, 429–430
physical environment, 432
preschool activity schedule, 430–432
preschoolers, 417–419
program planning, 423
progress monitoring, 423
puppets in classroom, 426–427
screening, 420–422
teaching play, 428–429
Early identification and assessment, 15
Early intervention, 16–17, 413
Abecedarian Project, 414
Apgar scale, 420, 421
biological risk conditions, 416
developmental delays, 416
direct systematic observation, 423
eligibility for services, 422
environmental risk conditions, 416
established risk conditions, 416
IDEA and, 415–417
IFSP (individualized family service plan), 416–417, 418–419
Individual Growth and Development Indicators, 423
Infant and Health Development Program, 414–415
infants and toddlers, 416–417
Milwaukee Project, 413–414
newborn blood test screening, 420–421
screening, 420–422
Skeels and Dye study, 413
Educate America Act, 22
Education Amendments of 1970, 21
Education environments, percent of school-age students, 27
Education for All Handicapped Children Act (PL 94-142), 22, 68
Education for the Handicapped Act Amendments of 1986, 22
Educational environments, 26
EHA (Education for all Handicapped Children Act), 19
EIBI (early intensive behavioral intervention), ASD and, 211
Electronic Daily Report Card, 86
Elementary, Secondary, and Other Educational Amendments, 21
Elementary and Secondary Education Act, 21, 385
Eligibility determination, 37
ELLs (English Language Learners), 74, 245–246
Embedded learning
early childhood special education, 430
preschool activity schedule, 430–432
Emotional development, early service eligibility, 422
Emotional disturbance, 162 *see also* emotional or behavioral disorders
Emotional or behavioral disorders (EBD), 161
academic achievement, 166–167
adulthood, 164
alterable variables, 187
anorexia nervosa, 165
anxiety disorders, 165
attention function interventions, 178
biological factors, 170–171
bipolar disorder, 165
brain disorders and, 170–171
bulimia nervosa, 165
CCBD definition, 164
coercive pain control, 172
community and, 173
contingency contracting, 184
choral responding and, 167
cumulative effects, 173–174
curriculum goals, 177–179
depression, 165
differential acceptance, 187
differential reinforcement of alternative or incompatible behavior, 184
direct observation and measurement, 175–176
emotional disturbance, 162
environmental factors, 171–173
escape function interventions, 178
externalizing behaviors, 163–164
extinction, 184

Emotional or behavioral disorders (EBD) (*Continued*)
FBA (functional behavior assessment), 176–177
federal definition, 162–163
gender and, 170
generalized anxiety disorder, 165
genetics and, 171
home and, 171
intelligence and, 168
internalizing behaviors, 164–166
interpersonal relationships, 168–169
interventions, 178
juvenile justice system involvement, 169–170
measurable dimensions of behavior, 175
mood disorders, 165
noncompliance, 164
OCD (obsessive/compulsive disorder), 165
overcorrection, 184
parent-child relationship, 171
phobias, 165
placement options, 187–189
point prevalence, 170
prevalence, 170
PTSD (posttraumatic stress disorder), 165
recruiting reinforcement, 169
response cost, 184
schizophrenia, 166
school and, 172–173
screening tests, 174–175
selective mutism, 165
shaping, 184
social maladjustment, 162
social skills, 168–169, 178–179
staying in school, 167
student responding, 180–181
SWPBIS, 181–184
teacher attention, recruiting, 168–169
teacher praise, 179–180
teacher-student relationship, 186–187
teaching practices, 179–186
temperament and, 171
Tourette syndrome, 166
Empathetic relationships, EBD and, 187
Employment, 441
ADA and, 20
competitive, 453–456
natural supports, 455
sheltered, 456
transition success, 451–457
Endrew F. v. Douglas County School District, 18
English language learner (ELL), 74
Environmental risk, early intervention, 416
Epigentics, ASD and, 206
Epilepsy, 326–327
Equal protection, 12
ESSA (Every Student Succeeds Act), 21
ESY (extended school year), 17–18
Etiology of intellectual disabilities, 109–110
Every Student Succeeds Act, 22
Exceptional children
classification, 8–9
description, 6–7
labeling, 8
percentages of, 7
Executive functioning
ADHD and, 319
ASD and, 199
Expressive language disorder, 236
Externalizing behaviors, EBD, 163–164
Eye anatomy, 293–294

F

Face-to-face communication, 83–85
Facilitated communication, 220
False-belief tests, 197
Families, 69–70
child's changing needs, 75–76
cultural differences, 74–76
culturally responsive services, 77–78
early childhood special education, 434
education system views, 75
English language learner (ELL), 74
experiences with disability, 75
family orientation, 74
funds of knowledge, 75
Hispanic, 75
immigrants, undocumented, 74
kinship system, 74
Native American, 75
negative education experiences, 75
poverty, 74
Puerto Rican, 75
resilience model, 71, 72
respite care, 71
stages, 71
tasks, 71
views on disability, 75
Family involvement, 94–95. *See also* parent involvement
effectiveness, 69
IEP teams and, 69
legislation, 68
level of, 93–94
parents as change advocates, 68
Family-professional partnership, 76–83
barriers to, 81–83
communication, 78–80
conflict resolution, 82–83
cultural reciprocity, 77–78
culturally responsive services, 77–78
dialoguing, 82
life-cycle stages of individuals with disabilities, 76–77
FAPE (*see* free appropriate public education)
FASDs (fetal alcohol spectrum disorders), intellectual disabilities and, 108
FBA (*see* functional behavior assessment)
Feedback, 116, 118
FLASH learning strategy, 148
Fluency, 25–26
Fluency disorders, communication
cluttering, 240
stuttering, 238, 240
treatment, 248–249
fMRI (functional magnetic resonance imaging), 137
Formative assessment methods, 139
Fragile X syndrome, 110
intellectual disabilities and, 108
Free appropriate public education (FAPE), 11, 18,
educational benefit and, 18
Friendship training, intellectual disabilities and, 120
Full inclusion, 59–60
Functional behavior assessment (FBA), 176–177
ABC recording, 176
descriptive, 176–177
functional analysis, 177
indirect, 176
Functional curriculum, 24
students with intellectual disabilities, 113–114
Functional skills, low-incidence disabilities, 361

G

General education teachers, IEPs and, 51
Generalization
fluency and, 25
intellectual disabilities, 104
Generalized anxiety disorder, 165
Genetic counseling, 111
Genetics
autism and, 205–206
emotional or behavioral disorders and, 171
epigenetics, 206

hearing loss and, 266
intellectual disabilities and, 110
Gifted and talented
ability grouping, 403–404
acceleration, 395
African American, 391–392
assessment, 390–394
Bloom's taxonomy, 397–398
boys, 393
consulting teacher model, 406–407
cooperative learning groups, 405–406
creativity in, 388
curriculum compacting, 395–396
curriculum differentiation, 395
differentiated model, 386
with disabilities, 393–394
DISCOVER model, 392
educational approaches, 394–403
enrichment, 396
federal definitions, 384–385
girls, 393
Hispanic/Latino, 391–392
identifying, 390–394
individual differences, 389
inquiry-based learning, 398–399
international experiences, 403
internship programs, 400–401
Junior Great Books, 401
leadership skills, 400
mentor programs, 400–401, 403
multicultural assessment/identification, 390–392
multiple intelligences theory, 386
NAGC definition, 385
Native American, 391–392
neuromotor development, 387
neurosensory development, 387
performance grouping, 406
precociousness in, 388
prevalence, 389–390
problem-based learning, 399–400, 401
problem-solving perspective (Maker), 386
progressive filtering, 390
project-based learning, 400, 401
pull-out programs, 404
resource room, 404
special classrooms, 404
special schools, 404
specialized courses, 401
states' definitions, 386–387
summer programs, 403
talent development definition (Piirto), 386
three-trait definition (Renzulli), 385
tiered lessons, 397–398
triarchic theory of intelligence, 386
underrepresented, 392
Gifted and Talented Children's Education Act of 1978, 22
Glaucoma, 295, 296
Graphic organizers, content areas, 153
Group contingencies, EBD and, 186
Guided notes, 143–144

H

Handicap, definition, 6, 31
Handicapped Children's Early Assistance Act (1968), 21
Handicapped Children's Protection Act, 22
Hard of hearing, 261
Health impairments
acute conditions, 325
age of onset, 335–336
AIDS (acquired immune deficiency syndrome), 329
animal assistance, 341
assistive technology, 340–341
asthma, 348
autosomal recessive disorders, 328–329
chronic conditions, 325
definitions, 324
diabetes, 327–328
educational performance, factors, 334–336
environmental modifications, 339–340
epilepsy, 326–327
historical events in education, 335–336
HIV (human immunodeficiency virus), 329
IHCP (individualized health care plan), 341
inclusiveness, 345–346
independence, 342–344
neuromotor impairment, 324–325
OTs (occupational therapists), 338
PE (physical education), 339
placement, 344–346
prevalence, 325
PTs (physical therapists), 338
related services, 344–345
self-esteem, 342–344
specialists, 338
teaming and, 338
visibility and, 335–336
Hearing
audiometric zero, 262
audition, 262
decibels (dB), 262
HTL (hearing-threshold level), 262
sound, nature of, 262–263
Hearing aids, 270–271
Hearing loss, 263–264. *See also* deafness
acquired, 266, 267
bilateral, 266
classification, 269–270
CMV (congenital cytomegalovirus) and, 267
conductive hearing impairment, 265
definition, 261
ear, anatomy of, 262
genetic factors, 266
hard of hearing, 261
maternal rubella and, 266
mixed hearing impairment, 266
postlingual hearing loss, 266
prelingual hearing loss, 266
prematurity and, 267
prevalence, 265
residual hearing, 261
sensorineural hearing impairment, 265–266
sensory hearing impairment, 265–266
unilateral, 266
vocabulary, 264
Hematoma, brain, 354
Heredity, learning disabilities and, 137
High school completion, 440
Historical events in special education
autism spectrum disorders, 210–211
court cases, 11-12, 18-19
deafness, 275
health impairments, 335–336
intellectual disabilities, 112
learning disabilities, 128–129
legislation, 12-17, 19-22
physical disabilities, 335–336
visual impairment, 297
HIV (human immunodeficiency virus), 329
HLPs (High-Leverage Practices), v, viii
Homebound students, alternative placement and, 54
Home-school communication, 83–90
HomeworkNOW, 87
Honig v. Doe, 19
Hospital, alternative placement and, 54

Hypernasality, 240
Hyperopia (farsightedness), 296
Hypersensitivity, ASD and, 199
Hyponasality, 240
Hyposensitivity, ASD and, 199

I

IDEA (*see* Individuals with Disabilities Education Act)
IEP (*see* individualized education program)
IEP team, 46–47
  family involvement, 69
IFSP (*see* individualized family service plan)
IHCP (individualized health care plan), 341
IHDP (Infant and Health Development Program), 414–415
Illinois Test of Psycholinguistic Abilities (ITPA), 128
Immigrant families, 74
Impairment, definition, 6, 31
Inclusive education, 55–56
  cochlear implants and, 272–273
  cooperative learning and, 57, 120–121
  co-teaching and, 56
  elements, 60
  full inclusion, 57, 59–60
  versus LRE, 55
  visual impairment, 309–312
Incredible Years, 91
Independent living in adulthood, 457–460
Individual Growth and Development Indicators, 423
Individualized education program (IEP), 13, 37
  annual review, 38, 42
  components, 47–48
  countable behaviors, 14, 50
  developing, 48
  example, 49
  formats, 48–51
  functions, 48–51
  general education teachers and, 51
  goals, 50
  not countable behaviors, 14, 50
  not observable behaviors, 14, 50
  observable behaviors, 14, 50
  placement, 38, 41
  problems and solutions, 51–52
  program planning, 41
  progress monitoring, 38, 42
  reevaluation, 38, 42
  student involvement, 51–52
  transition IEP, 443–447
Individualized family service plan (IFSP), 17, 416–417, 418–419, 427–428
Individuals with Disabilities Education Act (IDEA), 12, 22, 68
  1997 amendments, 19
  ADHD and, 319
  assistive technology, 17
  autism definition, 196
  classifications and, 8
  deafness, 261
  discipline, 19
  early intervention, 16–17, 415–417
  eligibility, 8
  FAPE, 18
  free appropriate public education, 13
  hearing loss, 261
  IFSP (individualized family service plan), 17
  infant and toddler early intervention, 16–17
  intellectual disability definition, 99
  legal challenges, 17–19
  LRE (least restrictive environment), 15
  nondiscriminatory evaluation, 13
  parent participation, 16
  preschoolers and, 16
  procedural safeguards, 16
  purposes, 12–13
  regulations, 16
  shared decision making, 16
  special education for preschoolers, 417–419
  speech or language impairment, 236
  transition services, 442–443
  universal design for learning, 17
  visual impairment, 290
  zero reject, 13
Infants and toddlers, early intervention, 16–17, 416–417
Instruction, special education as, 24–27
Instructional design, 146
Instructional technology, ASD and, 218–219
Instructionally based intervention, 23.
  See also intervention
Instructive feedback, 116
Intellectual disabilities, 10
  adaptive behavior, 102–103, 106
  amniocentesis, 110
  attention, 104
  behavioral excesses, 106–107
  challenging behavior, 106–107
  characteristics of students, 103–106
  classification, 100
  cognitive functioning, 103–105
  of cultural-family origin, 110
  curriculum, 111–114
  chorionic villi sampling (CVS), 111
  definitions, 98–99
  educational approaches, 111–119
  etiology, 109–111
  generalization, 104
  genetics and, 110
  historical events in education, 112
  instructional methods, 114–119
  IQ score, 100
  learning rate, 103
  maintenance, 104
  memory, 104
  motivation, 104–105
  normalization, 122
  phenylketonuria (PKU) and, 108, 111
  positive attributes, 103
  prenatal conditions associated, 108
  prevalence, 108–109
  prevention, 110–111
  psychosocial disadvantages, 110
  rubella, 110
  screening, 111
  self-determination, 105
  social role valorization, 122
  student placement, 119–121
Intellectual functioning, 101
Intellectual functioning assessments, 100–102
Intelligence as hypothetical construct, 101
Intelligence tests, 138
Interdisciplinary teams, 46
International Dyslexia Association, 132
Interpreting services, 15
Intervention
  compensatory, 24
  preventative, 23
  remedial, 23
Intervention assistance team, prereferral intervention, 36
Iowa Tests of Basic Skills, 138
IQ tests, 100–101
  ASD and, 201–202
  cutoff score, 101
  score distribution, 101
  scores, severe disabilities, 352
Itinerant teacher model, 309–312

J

Jacob K. Javits Gifted and Talented Students Education Act, 22, 385
Joint attention, 197
juvenile justice system, EBD (emotional or behavioral disorders) and, 169–170

K

Kazdin Method, 91
KeyMath-3, 138
KidSkills, 184
KidTools, 184
Kinship system, 74

L

Labeling and classification, 8–10, 31
Language, 230–232
ASD and, 198
ASL (American Sign Language), 278–279
barriers, 74
blindness, 291
Deaf community, 261
delay, 241
dialects, 231–232
early service eligibility, 422
low vision, 291
morphology, 231
onomatopoeic words, 231
pragmatics, 231
semantics, 231
syntax, 231
Language disorders, 236
aphasia, 242
causes, 242
expressive language disorder, 236
language learning disability (LLD), 241
naturalistic strategies, 250–251
receptive language disorder, 236
treatment, 249–251
vocabulary building, 249–250
Laws and regulations, 10–12, 17–19
Learned helplessness, 104
Learning disabilities. *See also* learning disorders
ability-achievement discrepancy and, 130
achievement tests, 138
ADHD and, 134
APA definition, 132
assessment, 138–146
brain damage and, 137
brain dysfunction and, 137
CBM (curriculum-based measurement), 139–141
challenging behavior and, 134–135
criterion-referenced tests, 138–139
educational approaches, 146–155
experiential factors, 138
federal definition, 129–130
formative assessment methods, 139
GT (gifted and talented) students, 393
heredity and, 137
historical events in the field, 128
identification, 138–146
intelligence tests, 138
interpersonal problems, 134
low achievement, 135–136
low self-esteem and, 135
math and, 133–134
NJCLD definition, 131–132
positive focus benefits, 136
precision teaching, 140
prevalence, 136
reading and, 132–133
regular classroom, 155
resource room, 156
RTI (response to intervention), 131, 141–142, 144–146
self-efficacy and, 135
separate classrooms, 156
signature characteristic, 135–136
social skills and, 134
specific learning disability, 129–130
written language and, 133
Learning Disabilities Association of America, 68, 128
Learning disorders. *See* learning disabilities
Learning objectives, 14
Learning rate, 103
Learning strategies, 147–148
Least restrictive environment (LRE), 11, 38, 53–55, 57
Legal blindness, 288
Legislation, 21–22
Life-cycle stages of individuals with disabilities, 76–77
Literacy, low-incidence disabilities, 362–363
Long-term memory, 104
Low self-esteem, learning disabilities and, 135
Low vision, 290
classrooms and, 303–304
cognition, 291
functional visual skills, 302
language, 291
large-print materials, 303
optical devices, 301–302, 303
print reading, 302–303
social adjustment and, 292–293
specialized instruction, 300–304
visual efficiency, 301
Low-incidence disabilities, 352. *See also* profound disabilities; severe disabilities
causes, 359–360
community-based instruction, 369–370
CHARGE Syndrome, 360
choice making, 363–364
communication curriculum, 362
curriculum, 360–366
deaf-blindness, 353
functional skills, 361
general education curriculum, 364
instructional methods, 366–372
instructional targets, 364
literacy, 362–363
mental age, 360
multiple and severe disabilities, 355–356
multiple disabilities, 353
neighborhood schools, 374–376
placement, 374–377
prevalence, 358–359
recreation and leisure curriculum, 363
regular classrooms, 376–377
self-care, 361
social relationships and, 375
TBI (traumatic brain injury), 353
LRE (*see* least restrictive environment)

M

Maintenance, intellectual disabilities, 104
Manifestation determination, 19
Marianne Frostig Developmental Test of Visual Perception, 128
Math skills, 133–134, 152
Measurable dimensions of behavior, 175
Medical services, 15
Memory, 104, 134
Mènière's disease, 267
Mental deficiency, 99
Mental retardation, 99
Mental Retardation Facility and Community Center Construction Act (1963), 21
Mentoring programs, vi
MFE (multifactored evaluation), 37, 40–41
Milwaukee Project, 413–414
Mirror model of parent involvement, 93–94
MMR (mumps-measles-rubella) vaccine, 206–207
Mood disorders, 165
Morphology, 231
Motivation, intellectual disabilities, 104–105
Motor development
blindness and low vision, 291–292
early service eligibility, 422
low-incidence disabilities, 355

MRI (magnetic resonance imaging), 137
MTSS (multi-tiered system of support) framework, 38, v
  SWPBIS and, 181
Multidisciplinary evaluation team, 41
Multidisciplinary teams, 46
Multifactored evaluation (MFE), 37, 40–41
Multiple disabilities
  causes, 359–360
  characteristics, 355–356
  definition, 353
  instructional methods, 366–372
  partial participation and, 370–371
  positive behavioral support, 371
  prevalence, 358
  small-group instruction, 371–372
  teacher challenges and rewards, 377–378
Muscular dystrophy, 332–333
Myopia (nearsightedness), 296

N

NAEYC (National Association for the Education of Young Children), 426, 428
National Defense Education Act (1958), 21
National Joint Committee on Learning Disabilities (NJCLD), 129
National Longitudinal Transition Studies, 440
National Parent Teacher Association, 69
National Parental Information and Resource Coordination Center, 69
National Society for Crippled Children, 68
Neighborhood schools, low-incidence disabilities and, 374–376
Neuromotor impairment, 324–325
  definition, 131–132
No Child Left Behind Act of 2001, 22
Nonacademic needs, educational approaches, 154
Nonlinguistic cues, 230
Normal curve, IQ scores, 101
Normalization, 122
Norm-referenced tests, 100–101
NOW! learning strategy, 147

O

Obsessive-compulsive behavior, 106
Occupational therapy, 15
Occupational therapist (OT), 15
OCD (obsessive/compulsive disorder), 165
Onomatopoeic words, 231
Open needs assessment, 91
Opportunities to respond, 115; *see also* active student response
Oral language skills, 133
Oral reading fluency, 144
Orientation and mobility (O&M), 304–306
Orientation and mobility services, 15
Orthopedic impairment, 324
OT (*see* occupational therapist), 338
Outer-directedness, 104

P

PACER Center, 69
Paralinguistic behaviors, 230
Parallel teaching, co-teaching, 56
Paraplegia, 333
PARC (Pennsylvania Association for Retarded Children) v. Commonwealth of Pennsylvania (1972), 12
Parent appreciation letters, 88–89
Parent counseling and training, 15
Parent education and training programs, 91
Parent involvement, 16, 68–69, 79, 90–95. *See also* family involvement
Parent to Parent, 91
Parents of children with learning/behavior problems, 72
Parents of children with disabilities, 70–77
Parent-teacher conferences, 84–85
Partial participation, 370
  misapplication, 371
PBIS (*see* positive behavioral interventions and supports)
PDD-NOS (pervasive developmental disorder not otherwise specified), 196
PECS (*see* Picture Exchange Communication System)
Peer buddy programs
  intellectual disabilities and, 120
  severe disabilities, 376–377
Peer monitoring, EBD and, 186
Peer reporting, positive, EBD and, 186
Peer support and confrontation, EBD and, 186
Peer tutoring. *See also* CWPT (Classwide Peer Tutoring)
  EBD and, 186
  intellectual disabilities and, 120
Peer-Assisted Learning Strategies, 58
Peer-mediated interventions, vi
  early childhood special education, 429–430
Phenylketonuria (PKU), 111, 420
Phobias, 165
Phonemic awareness, reading and, 132
Phonological awareness, reading and, 132
Physical disabilities
  age of onset, 335–336
  animal assistance, 341
  assistive technology, 340–341
  cerebral palsy, 330–331
  education performance, factors, 334–336
  environmental modifications, 339–340
  historical events in education, 335–336
  IHCP (individualized health care plan), 341
  inclusiveness, 345–346
  independence, 342–344
  lifting, 342, 343
  muscular dystrophy, 332–333
  neural tube defects, 331
  orthopedic impairment, 324
  OTs (occupational therapists), 338
  paraplegia, 333
  PE (physical education), 339
  placement, 344–346
  positioning/seating/movement, 342
  prevalence, 325
  PTs (physical therapists), 338
  quadriplegia, 333
  related services, 344–345
  self-esteem, 342–344
  specialists, 338
  spina bifida, 331–332
  spina bifida occulta, 332
  spinal chord injuries, 333
  teaming and, 338
  transferring, 342, 343
  visibility and, 335–336
  intellectual disabilities and, 108
Physical therapist (PT), 338
Physical therapy, 338
physical disabilities, Picture Exchange Communication System (PECS), 213
Play expansions, early childhood special education, 428–429
Positive behavioral interventions and supports (PBIS), 38, 127
Positive behavioral support, low-incidence disabilities, 371
Positive peer reporting, EBD and, 186
Positive reinforcement, 116
Postencephalitic disorder, 318
Postlingual hearing loss, 266
Postschool outcomes, 439–441
Postsecondary education, 440–441, 447–451
Poverty, 74
Practical skills, 102
Practice stage of learning, feedback, 116, 118
Prader-Willi syndrome, 106, 108
Pragmatics, 231
Precision teaching, 140
Prelingual hearing loss, 266
Prenatal conditions intellectual disabilities and, 108
Prereferral intervention process, 36–40
Preschoolers, 16
  activity schedule, early childhood special education, 430–432
  early childhood special education, 417–419
Preventative intervention, 23

Problem-solving perspective on GT students, 386
Problem-solving team, 36
Procedural safeguards, 16
Profound disabilities
 definition, 352–353
 educability, 357
Program planning, 41
Progress monitoring, 38, 42, 139
Psychological services, 15
Psychosocial disadvantages, intellectual disabilities, 110
PTSD (posttraumatic stress disorder), 165
Public accommodations, ADA and, 20
Public entities, ADA and, 20

Q

Quadriplegia, 333
Quiz-Quiz-Trade, 121

R

Racial bias in referral procedures, 44
RAPID Skills Training, 91
RCs (response cards), 181–182
Reading
 alphabetic principle, 137
 ART reading strategy, 151
 CWPM (correct words per minute), 144
 Direct Instruction programs, 148, 150–151
 dyslexia, 132
 early reading instruction, 149
 educational approaches, 148–151
 KWL reading strategy, 151
 language comprehension, 149
 learning disabilities and, 132–133
 letter-phoneme relationship, 149
 letter-sound relationships, 149
 mnemonic learning strategies, 151
 oral language skills and, 133
 ORF (oral reading fluency), 144
 phenomes, 137
 phonemic awareness, 132, 149
 phonological awareness, 132
 secondary students, 450–451
 sounding out words, 149
 TWA reading strategy, 151
Receptive language disorder, 236
Referrals
 cultural bias, 44
 inappropriate, bias and, 44
 prereferral, 36–40
 racial bias, 44
Rehabilitation Act Amendments, 22
Rehabilitative counseling services, 15
Related services, 15–16, 18, 45–46, 338, 344–345
Remedial intervention, 23
Repeated reading, fluency and, 25
Research-to-practice gap, 28–31
Residential school, alternative placement and, 54
Residual hearing, 261
Resonance disorder, 240
Resource classroom, 53
Respite care, 71, 72
Response requirements, 118
Response to intervention (RTI), v, 38, 131
 guidelines, 146
 learning disability identification, 144–146
 progress monitoring, 145
 tiers, 142–143
Risk ratio, representation, 43
ROP (retinopathy of prematurity), 296
Rosa's Law, 10
Rowley/Endrew test, 19
RP (retinitis pigmentosa), 296

S

SAFMEDS (Say All Fast a Minute Each Day Shuffled), 25–26
Sallie-Anne task, 197
Scaffolding, 146
Savant syndrome, 199
Schizophrenia, 166
Schoolwide positive behavioral interventions and supports (SWPBIS), 181–182
 BIP (behavior intervention plan), 184
 check-in/check-out recording form, 185
 classroom management, 184
 continuum, 183
 group contingencies, 186
 MTSS and, 181
 peer mediation and support, 186
 self-evaluation, 184
 self-management, 184
 self-monitoring and, 184
Section 504 of the Rehabilitation Act of 1973, 20, 21
Selective mutism, 165
Self-advocacy
 adulthood, 462–463
 communication disorders and, 254–255
Self-care
 intellectual disabilities, 106
 low-incidence disabilities, 361
Self-contained classroom, 53
Self-determination, 105
 adulthood, 462–463
 social role valorization and, 122
 students with intellectual disabilities, 114
Self-efficacy, learning disabilities and, 135
Self-esteem, health impairments/physical disabilities, 342–344
Self-evaluation, SWPBIS and, 184
Self-help skills, low-incidence disabilities, 356
Self-injury, 106
Self-management, SWPBIS and, 184
Self-monitoring
 ADHD and, 321–322
 SWPBIS, 184
SEM (Schoolwide Enrichment Model), 396
Sensorineural hearing impairment, 265–266
Sensory hearing impairment, 265–266
Sensory stimuli, ASD and, 199
Services, 15–16
Severe disabilities
 causes, 359–360
 characteristics, 355–356
 definition, 352
 ecological assessment, 367
 educability, 357
 instructional methods, 366–372
 partial participation and, 370–371
 peer helpers, 376–377
 positive behavioral support, 371
 small-group instruction, 371–372
 teacher challenges and rewards, 377–378
Shaken-baby syndrome, 360
Shared decision making, 16
Sheltered employment, 456
Siblings without disabilities, 73
Sickle cell disease, 329
Skeels and Dye study, 413
Skills, low-incidence disabilities and, 355
Small-group instruction, low-incidence disabilities, 371–372

SMART (Specific, Measurable, Actionable, Relevant, Time), 62
Social adjustment/maladjustment, 162
  blindness and low vision, 292–293
  early service eligibility, 422
Social Communication Questionnaire (SCQ), 209
Social role valorization, 122
Social skills, 102
  learning disabilities and, 134
Social stories, 217–218
Social work services in schools, 15
Special education
  defining features, 28
  definition, 27–28
  dimensions, 28
  future, 60–62
  history, 11–12
  as instruction, 24–27
  as intervention, 23–24
Special Education Act (1961), 21
Specific learning disabilities, 129–130
  ability-achievement discrepancy, 130–131
  definition, federal, 129–130
  exclusion, 131
  IQ, achievement and, 130
  RTI (response to intervention), 131
  special education need, 131
Speech
  articulation, 232
  deafness and, 264
  hearing loss and, 264
  phonation, 232
  resonation, 232
  respiration, 232
Speech and language development, 233–235
Speech impairments, 236
  causes, 242
  dysarthria, 242
Speech organs, 232
Speech-language pathology services, 16
Speech-sound errors, 237–238, 247–248
Spina bifida, 331–332
Spina bifida occulta, 332
Spinal cord injuries, 333
SPLASH learning strategy, 148
Standard celeration chart, 141
standardized tests, 100. *See also* achievement tests
Stanford-Binet Intelligence Scales, 101
Station teaching, co-teaching, 56
Still's disease, 318
Stimulus conditions, 118
Strabismus, 295, 296
Stuart v. Nappi (1978), 19
Student study team, 41
Student support team, 36
Stuttering, 238, 240
SWPBIS (*see* schoolwide positive behavioral interventions and supports)
Systematic Screening for Behavioral Disorders (SSBD), 175

T

Talent development concept, GT students, 386
Talented students. *See* GT (gifted and talented) students
TASH (formerly The Association for Persons with Severe Handicaps), 68, 352
Tay-Sachs disease, 329
TBI (*see* traumatic brain injury)
Teacher assistance team, 36
Teacher attention, 168–169
Teachers, transition teachers, 29
Teacher-student relationships, EBD and, 186–187
Teaching play, early childhood special education, 428–429
Team teaching, co-teaching, 56
Teaming, 45–47
Technology-Related Assistance for Individuals with Disabilities Act of 1988, 22
Telecommunications, ADA and, 21
Test of Mathematical Abilities, 138
Test of Reading Comprehension, 138
Theory of mind, autism and, 197
Timothy W. v. Rochester School District (1989), 19
Tourette syndrome, 166
Transdisciplinary teams, 46
Transfer of stimulus control, 116
Transition teachers, 29
Transition to adulthood, v
  activities, 445–446
  age-appropriate assessment, 443–444
  collaboration, 446
  course work, 445
  curriculum activities, 453
  goals, 444–445, 461–463
  services, 442–443, 445–446
Transportation services, 16
TRAP learning strategy, 147
Traumatic brain injury (TBI)
  anoxia, 355
  causes, 360
  characteristics, 357–358
  closed brain injury, 354
  definition, 353
  educational considerations, 373–374
  prevalence, 359
  shaken-baby syndrome, 360
Trials to criterion, 103
Triarchic theory of intelligence, 386
Twice exceptional, 393-394
TypeWell, 15

U

UDL (*see* universal design for learning)
United Cerebral Palsy Association, 68
Universal design (UDL) (universal design for learning), 17
  IDEA and, 17
UPGRADE, 107, 456

V

Vineland Adaptive Behavior Scales, 102
Vision specialists, 310
Visual activity schedules, 215–216
Visual impairment
  age at onset, 290
  cataracts, 295
  causes, 296
  classrooms, 304–305, 310–311
  cortical visual impairments, 295
  definitions, 290
  equal opportunities, 312–313
  expanded core curriculum, 304–309
  eye and, 293–294
  functional life skills, 308–309
  functional visual skills, 302
  glaucoma, 295
  historical events in education, 297
  inclusive classroom, 309–312
  independence, 307
  itinerant teacher model, 309–312
  nystagmus, 295
  orientation and mobility instruction, 304–306
  placement, 309–313
  refractive errors, 294
  residential schools, 312
  self-operated auditory prompts, 308–309
  strabismus, 295
  structural impairment, 295
  types, 296
Visual maps, 154

Visual phonics, 263–264
Voice disorders
denasality, 240
dysphonia, 240
hypernasality, 240
hyponasality, 240
nodes, 240
phonation disorder, 240
polyps, 240
resonance disorder, 240
treatment, 249
vocal nodules, 240

W–Z

Wechsler Individual Achievement Test III, 138
Wechsler Intelligence Scale for Children (WISC-V), 101
Williams syndrome, intellectual disabilities and, 108
Woodcock Reading Mastery Tests, 138
Woodcock-Johnson IV Tests of Achievement, 138
Working memory, math skills and, 134
Writing, 151–152
Written communication, 85–89
Written language, learning disabilities and, 133